Adolescence and Emerging Adulthood

fourth edition

A CULTURAL APPROACH

JEFFREY JENSEN ARNETT

Clark University

WITHDRAWN

PEARSON

Boston Columbus Indianapolis New York San Francisco Upper Saddle River
Amsterdam Cape Town Dubai London Madrid Milan Munich Paris Montreal Toronto
Delhi Mexico City Sao Paulo Sydney Hong Kong Seoul Singapore Taipei Tokyo

VP/Editorial Director: Leah Jewell
Executive Editor: Jeff Marshall
Associate Editor: LeeAnn Doherty
Editorial Assistant: Amy Trudell
Director of Marketing: Brandy Dawson
Marketing Manager: Nicole Kunzmann
Marketing Assistant: Jen Lang
Managing Editor: Maureen Richardson
Project Manager: Annemarie Franklin
Operations Specialist: Sherry Lewis

Senior Art Director: Leslie Osher
Art Director: Suzanne Duda
Text and Cover Designer: Kathy Mrozek
Manager, Visual Research: Beth Brenzel
Photo Researcher: Rachel Lucas
Manager, Rights and Permissions: Zina Arabia
Image Permission Coordinator: Jan Marc Quisumbing
Full-Service Project Management: Assunta Petrone
Composition: Preparé Inc.
Printer/Binder: Courier/Kendallville

This book was set in 10/12 New Baskerville.

Credits and acknowledgments borrowed from other sources and reproduced, with permission, in this textbook appear on page 458.

10 9 8 7 6 5 4 3 2 1
ISBN 13: 978-0-13-507479-4
ISBN 10: 0-13-507479-7

To
Robin, Kelly, Nathan,
Raina, Paris,
and Miles—
so much to look forward to!

Brief Contents

Contents

Special Focus Boxes

CULTURAL FOCUS

HISTORICAL FOCUS

RESEARCH FOCUS

Preface

New to the Fourth Edition

I am delighted that with this edition of *Adolescence and Emerging Adulthood* we have added an online component called *MyDevelopmentLab* (visit www.pearsonhighered.com or ask your Pearson publishing representative for access information). This website contains terrific video material to illustrate topics such as ethnic identity and eating disorders. In addition, the website contains the following pedagogical materials:

- **chapter learning objectives** to help students focus on key concepts.
- **online quizzes** that include instant scoring and coaching responses.
- **web links** specific to each chapter that provide a valuable source of supplemental materials for learning and research.
- **built-in gradebook** that gives students the ability to forward essay responses and graded quizzes to their instructors.
- **an extensive faculty module** that includes PowerPoint slides, presentation graphics, and lecture ideas and activities.

This is the first edition of the book to include *My Development Lab*, and we will be continuing to develop it in future editions.

Another major change in this edition was that I eliminated Chapter 14. In the first three editions of the book, there was a brief Chapter 14 entitled "Adolescence and Emerging Adulthood in the 21st Century" that provided a summary of the cultural background and experiences of adolescents in different regions of the world. In this edition I decided this material would be better placed in Chapter 1 as a way of giving students a broad cultural perspective for the chapters that follow.

In reviews and responses to the first three editions of this book, instructors and reviewers have consistently mentioned three key strengths: (1) the cultural approach; (2) the inclusion of emerging adulthood along with adolescence; and (3) the quality of the writing. I have sought to enhance those strengths in the fourth edition. Research on adolescence around the world is growing, so there is even more cultural information than before. Recently I served as Editor-in-Chief of the two-volume *International Encyclopedia of Adolescence*, which appeared in 2007 and contained chapters from nearly 100 countries around the world. This position made it possible for me to enhance the cultural content of the text-

book as never before, with new material from Africa, Asia, Europe, and the Americas. Every chapter in the fourth edition includes new material, from the encyclopedia and other sources, that will enhance students' understanding of cultural similarities and differences and how the development of adolescents and emerging adults is influenced by the culture they live in.

Encouraged by the response to the material on emerging adulthood in the first three editions, I have continued to expand it in the fourth edition. Exciting developments in theory and research are taking place in this area, as more and more scholars recognize its importance and turn their attention to it, and I have sought to reflect those developments in this edition. Every chapter includes the latest, most up-to-date theory and research related to emerging adulthood. It has been gratifying to me to see how other textbooks have now incorporated theory and research on emerging adulthood, but as the originator of the idea I think it is not unreasonable for me to state that if you would like to have the most comprehensive and recent material on emerging adulthood in a textbook you will find it here.

As for the writing style, I have continued to strive to make the book not only highly informative but also lively and fun to read. The best textbooks achieve both these goals.

In addition to enhancing the aspects of the book that were so favorably received in the first three editions, I have made numerous changes, large and small, to each chapter. Hundreds of new citations from 2006–2009 have been added to this edition, incorporating the most recent findings in the field. Other changes have been made in response to comments and suggestions by instructors who reviewed the third edition. Still other changes were made on my own initiative, as I read the chapters before embarking on the fourth edition and made judgments about what should be added, changed, or deleted. For example, I added a section on bullying to the chapter on Friends and Peers, including information on "cyberbullying" through the Internet.

I have added new material to the fourth edition, but also deleted material that was in the third edition. There is an unfortunate tendency for textbooks to add additional material with each edition, so that eventually they become about as thick as the phone book (and just about as interesting to read). I have tried to head off that tendency early on by resolving with each edition to make judicious cuts for each addition I make. I hope this approach will continue to make the textbook both up-to-date and enjoyable to read.

Distinctive Features of This Book

Adolescence is a fascinating time of life, and for most instructors it is an enjoyable topic to teach. For many students taking the course, it is the time of life they have just completed or are now passing through. Learning about development during this period is for them a journey of self-discovery, in part. Students who are beyond this period often enjoy reflecting back on who they were then, and they come away with a new understanding of their past and present selves. What students learn from a course on adolescence sometimes confirms their own intuitions and experiences, and sometimes contradicts or expands what they thought they knew. When it works well, a course on adolescence can change not only how students understand themselves, but how they understand others and how they think about the world around them. For instructors, the possibility the course offers for students' growth of understanding is often stimulating. My goal in writing this textbook has been to make it a book that will assist instructors and students in making illuminating connections as they pursue an understanding of this dynamic and complex age period.

I wrote this book with the intention of presenting a fresh conception of adolescence, a conception reflecting what I believe to be the most promising and exciting new currents in the field. There are four essential features of the conception that guided this book: (1) a focus on the cultural basis of development; (2) an extension of the age period covered to include "emerging adulthood" (roughly ages 18 to 25) as well as adolescence; (3) an emphasis on historical context; and (4) an interdisciplinary approach to theories and research. All of these features distinguish this textbook from other textbooks on adolescence.

The Cultural Approach

In teaching courses on adolescence, from large lecture classes to small seminars, I have always brought into the classroom a considerable amount of research from other cultures. I am trained mainly as a developmental psychologist, a field that has traditionally emphasized universal patterns of development rather than cultural context. However, my education also included three years as a postdoctoral student at the Committee on Human Development at the University of Chicago, and the program there emphasized anthropology, which places culture first and foremost. Learning to take a cultural approach to development greatly expanded and deepened my own understanding of adolescence, and I have seen the cultural approach work this way for my students as well. Through an awareness of the diversity of cultural practices, customs, and beliefs about adolescence, we expand our conception of the range of developmental possibilities. We also gain a greater understanding of adolescent development in our own culture, by learning to see it as only one of many possible paths.

Taking a cultural approach to development means infusing discussion of every aspect of development with a cultural perspective. I present the essentials of the cultural approach in the first chapter, and it then serves as a theme that runs through every chapter. Each chapter also includes a *Cultural Focus* box in which an aspect of development in a specific culture is explored in-depth—for example, male and female circumcision in north Africa, adolescents' family relationships in India, and young people's sexuality in the Netherlands.

My hope is that students will learn not only that adolescent development can be different depending on the culture, but how to *think culturally*—that is, how to analyze all aspects of adolescent development for their cultural basis. This includes learning how to critique research for the extent to which it does or does not take the cultural basis of development into account. I provide this kind of critique at numerous points throughout the book, with the intent that students will learn how to do it themselves by the time they reach the end.

Emerging Adulthood

Not only is adolescence an inherently fascinating period of life, but we are currently in an especially interesting historical moment with respect to this period. Adolescence in our time begins far earlier than it did a century ago, because puberty begins for most people in industrialized countries at a much earlier age, due to advances in nutrition and health care. Yet, if we measure the end of adolescence in terms of taking on adult roles such as marriage, parenthood, and stable full-time work, adolescence also ends much later than it has in the past, because these transitions are now postponed for many people into at least the mid-20s.

My own research over the past decade has focused on development among young people from their late teens through their mid-20s in the United States and Europe. I have concluded, on the basis of this research, that this period is not really adolescence, but it is not really adulthood either, not even "young adulthood." In my view, the transition to adulthood has become so prolonged that it constitutes a separate period of the life course in industrialized societies, lasting about as long as adolescence. This view is now widely held by other scholars as well.

Thus, a second distinguishing feature of the conception guiding this textbook is that the age period covered includes not only adolescence (ages 10–18) but also "emerging adulthood," extending from (roughly) ages 18 to 25. In theoretical papers, research papers, and two books, I have presented a theory of emerging adulthood, conceptualizing it as the age of identity explorations, the age of instability, the self-focused age, the age of feeling in-between, and the age of possibilities. I describe this theory in some detail in the first chapter, and use it as the framework for discussing emerging adulthood in the chapters that follow. This is mainly a textbook on adolescence, and in any case there is not as much research on emerging adulthood as there is on adolescence, so the balance of material in each chapter is tilted quite strongly toward adolescence. However, each chapter contains material that pertains to emerging adulthood.

The Historical Context

Given the differences between adolescence now and adolescence in the past, knowledge of the historical context of development is crucial to a complete understanding of this age period. Students will have a richer understanding of adolescent development if they are able to contrast the lives of young people in the present with the lives of young people in other times. Toward this end, I provide historical material in each chapter. Furthermore, each chapter contains a *Historical Focus* box that describes some aspect of young people's development during a specific historical period—for example, adolescents' family lives during the Great Depression, the "Roaring Twenties" and the rise of youth culture, and work among British adolescents in the 19th century.

An emphasis on the historical context of development is perhaps especially important now, with the accelerating pace of cultural change that has taken place around the world in recent decades due to the influence of globalization. Especially in economically developing countries, the pace of change in recent decades has been dramatic, and young people often find themselves growing up in a culture that is much different than the one their parents grew up in. Globalization is a pervasive influence on the lives of young people today, in ways both promising and troubling, and for this reason I have made it one of the unifying themes of the book.

An Interdisciplinary Approach

The cultural approach and the emphasis on historical context are related to a fourth distinguishing feature of the conception offered in this book, the interdisciplinary approach to theories and research. Psychology is of course represented abundantly, because this is the discipline in which most research on adolescent development takes place. However, I also integrate materials from a wide range of other fields. Much of the theory and research that is the basis for a cultural understanding of adolescence comes from anthropology, so anthropological studies are strongly represented. Students often find this material fascinating, because it challenges effectively their assumptions about what they expect adolescence to be like. Interesting and important cultural material on adolescence also comes from sociology, especially with respect to European and Asian societies, and these studies find a place here. The field of history is notably represented, for providing the historical perspective discussed above. Other disciplines used for material include education, psychiatry, medicine, and family studies.

The integration of materials across disciplines means drawing on a variety of research methods. The reader will find many different research methods represented here, from questionnaires and interviews to ethnographic research to biological measurements. Each chapter contains a *Research Focus* box, in which the methods used in a specific study are described.

Chapter Topics

My goal of presenting a fresh conception of young people's development has resulted in chapters on topics not as strongly represented in most other textbooks. Most textbooks have a discussion of moral development, but this textbook has a chapter on cultural beliefs, including moral development, religious beliefs, political beliefs, and a discussion of individualistic and collectivistic beliefs in various cultures. The chapter on cultural beliefs provides a good basis for a cultural understanding of adolescent development, because it emphasizes how cultural beliefs shape the socialization that takes place in every other context of development, from family to schools to media.

Most textbooks include a discussion of gender issues at various points, and some include a separate chapter on gender, but in this textbook there is a chapter on gender that focuses on cultural variations and historical changes in gender roles, in addition to discussions of gender issues in other chapters. Gender is a fundamental aspect of social life in every culture, and the vivid examples of gender roles and expectations in non-Western cultures should help students to become more aware of how gender acts as a defining framework for young people's development in their own culture as well.

This textbook also has an entire chapter on work, which is central to the lives of adolescents in developing countries because a high proportion of them are not in school. The work chapter includes extensive discussion of the dangerous and unhealthy work conditions often experienced by adolescents in developing countries as their economies enter the global economy. In industrialized societies, the transition from school to work is an important part of emerging adulthood for most people, and that transition receives special attention in this chapter.

An entire chapter on media is included, with sections on television, music, movies, cigarette advertising, computer games and the Internet, and a new section in the fourth edition on social-networking websites such as Facebook and MySpace. Media are a prominent part of young people's lives in most societies today, but this is a topic that receives surprisingly little attention in most other textbooks. In fact, my textbook is the only major textbook on adolescence to include an entire chapter on media. This neglect is puzzling, given that adolescents in industrialized societies spend more time daily using media than they spend in school, with family, or with friends. I find young people's media uses to be not only an essential topic but a perpetually fascinating one, and students today almost invariably share this fascination, since they have grown up immersed in a media environment.

One chapter found in most other textbooks but not this one is a chapter on theories. In my view, having a separate chapter on theories gives students a misleading impression of the purpose and function of theories in the scientific enterprise. Theories and research are intrinsically related, with good theories inspiring research and good research leading to changes and innovations in theories. Presenting theories separately turns theory chapters into a kind of Theory Museum, separate and sealed off from research. Instead, I present theoretical material throughout the book, in relation to the research the theory has been based on and has inspired.

Each chapter contains a number of *Thinking Critically* questions. Critical thinking has become a popular term in academic circles and it has been subject to a variety of definitions, so I should explain how I used the term here. The purpose of the critical thinking questions is to inspire students to attain a higher level of analysis and reflection about the ideas and information in the chapters than they would be likely to reach simply by reading the chapter. With the critical thinking questions I seek to encourage students to connect ideas across chapters, to consider hypothetical questions, and to apply the chapter materials to their own lives. Often, the questions have no "right answer." Although they are mainly intended to assist students in attaining a high level of thinking as they read, instructors have told me that the questions also serve as lively material for class discussions or writing assignments.

Acknowledgments

Preparing a textbook is an enormous enterprise that involves a wide network of people, and I have many people to thank for their contributions. Becky Pascal, my original editor at Addison–Wesley, was the one who recruited me to write the book, and her excitement over my new ideas for a textbook helped persuade me to take on the project. Jeff Marshall, the current Pearson editor of the book, and Susan Hartman, Editor-in-Chief of Psychology, have provided welcome support for the book in this edition with the addition of *My Development Lab*.

The reviewers of the first three editions of the book were indispensable for the many comments and suggestions for improvement they provided. I would like to thank:

Denise M. Arehart, *University of Colorado–Denver;*
Belinda Blevins-Knabe, *University of Arkansas–Little Rock;*
Tanecia Blue, *Texas Tech University;*
Curtis W. Branch, *Columbia University;*
Melissa M. Branch; *SUNY College of Brookport;*
Christy Buchanan, *Wake Forest University;*
Jane Brown, *University of North Carolina–Chapel Hill;*
Stephen Burgess, *Southwestern Oklahoma State University;*
Laurie Chapin, *Colorado State University;*
Gabriela Chavira, *CSUN;*
Gary Creasey, *Illinois State University;*
Elizabeth Daniels, *University of California–Los Angeles;*
Gypsy M. Denzine, *Northern Arizona University;*
Shavari Dixit, *San Jose State University;*
Bonnie B. Dowdy, *Dickinson College;*
Elaine Eshbaugh, *University of Northern Iowa;*
Shirley Feldman, *Stanford University;*
Diane Fiebel, *Raymond Walters College;*
Paul Florsheim, *University of Utah;*
Suzanne Freedman, *University of Northern Iowa;*
Andrew Fuligni, *New York University;*
Nancy Galambos, *University of Victoria;*
Albert Gardner, *University of Maryland;*
Sheryl Ginn, *Wingate University;*
Rebecca Griffith, *College of the Sequoias;*
Jessica Gomel, *California University–Fullerton;*
Julia A. Graber, *Columbia University;*
Malinda Hendricks Green, *University of Central Oklahoma;*
William R. Holt, *University of Massachusetts–Dartmouth;*
Virginia Gregg, *North Adams State College;*
Susan Harter, *University of Denver;*
Joyce A. Hemphill, *University of Wisconsin;*
Daniel Houlihan, *Minnesota State University;*
Sharon Page Howard, *University of Arkansas–Little Rock;*
Karen G. Howe, *The College of New York;*
Janis Jacobs, *Pennsylvania State University;*
Patricia Jarvis, *Illinois State University;*
Marianne Jones, *CSU–Fresno;*
Joline N. Jones, *Worcester State College;*
David Kinney, *Central Michigan University;*
Steven Kirsh, *SUNY–Geneseo;*
Martin Kokol, *Utah Valley State College;*
Reed Larson, *University of Illinois;*
Dawn Lewis, *Price George's Community College;*
Jennifer Maggs, *Pennsylvania State University;*
Joseph G. Marrone, *Siena College;*
Terry Maul, *San Bernardino Valley College;*
Jeylan Mortimer, *University of Minnesota;*
Christian Mueller, *University of Memphis;*
Gail Overbey, *Southeast Missouri State;*
Merryl Patterson, *Austin Community College;*
Daniel Perkins, *University of Florida;*
Daniel Repinski, *SUNY–Geneseo;*
Julio Rique, *Northern Illinois University;*
Vicki Ritts, *St. Louis Community College–Meramec;*
Richard Rodgerson, *University of Minnesota;*
Kathleen M. Shanahan, *University of Massachusetts–Amherst;*
Merry Sleigh-Ritzer, *George Mason University;*
Andrew Smiller, *SUNY Oswego;*
Maureen Smith, *San Jose State University;*
Susan M. Sobel, *Middle Tennessee State University;*
Shirley Theriot, *University of Texas Arlington;*
Julie Thompson, *Duke University;*
Lisa Turner, *University of South Alabama;*

Randy Vinzant, *Hinds Community College;*
Naomi Wagner, *San Jose State University;*
Niobe Way, *New York University;*
Belinda Wholeben, *Rockford College;*
Missi Wilkenfeld, *Texas A&M University;*
Sandy Wurtele, *University of Colorado–Colorado Springs;*
James Youniss, *Catholic University of America;*
Joan Zook, *SUNY–Geneseo.*

I am grateful for the time and care expended by these reviewers to give me detailed, well-informed reviews.

Finally, I wish to thank the many students and instructors who have contacted me since the publication of the first edition to tell me how they have responded to the textbook and how it has shaped their thinking about human development. One of the reasons I wrote the textbook was that I love to teach, and it was attractive to think that instead of teaching a few dozen students a year I could assist instructors in teaching thousands of students a year. I hope students and instructors will continue to let me know their thoughts, not just about what I have done well but about how it can be done even better next time.

JEFFREY JENSEN ARNETT
Department of Psychology
Clark University

About the Author

Jeffrey Jensen Arnett

The author with his wife Lene Jensen and soon-to-be adolescents Miles and Paris, age 9.

is a Research Professor in the Department of Psychology at Clark University in Worcester, Massachusetts. During 2005 he was a Fulbright Scholar at the University of Copenhagen, Denmark. He has also taught at Oglethorpe University and the University of Missouri. He was educated at Michigan State University (undergraduate), the University of Virginia (graduate school), and the University of Chicago (post-doctoral studies). His research interests are in risk behavior (especially cigarette smoking), media use in adolescence (especially music), and a wide range of topics in emerging adulthood. He is editor of the *Journal of Adolescent Research* and of two encyclopedias, the *International Encyclopedia of Adolescence* (2007) and the *Encyclopedia of Children, Adolescents, and the Media* (2006). His book *Emerging Adulthood: The Winding Road from the Late Teens through the Twenties,* was published in 2004 by Oxford University Press. His edited book (with Jennifer Tanner), *Emerging Adults in America: Coming of Age in the 21st Century,* was published by APA Books in 2006. He lives in Worcester, Massachusetts with his wife Lene Jensen and their nine-year-old twins, Miles and Paris. For more information on Dr. Arnett and his research, see **www.jeffreyarnett.com.**

1 Introduction

OUTLINE

In the dim dawn light of a simple reed house in Tehuantepec, Mexico, 16-year-old Conchita leans over an open, barrel-shaped oven. Although it is just dawn, she has already been working for 2 hours making tortillas. It is difficult work, kneeling beside the hot oven, and hazardous, too; she has several scars on her arm from the times she has inadvertently touched the hot steel. She thinks with some resentment of her younger brother, who is still sleeping and who will soon be rising and going off to school. Like most girls in her village, Conchita can neither read nor write because it is only the boys who go to school.

But she finds consolation in looking ahead to the afternoon, when she will be allowed to go to the center of town to sell the tortillas she has made beyond those that her family will need that day. There she will see her girlfriends, who will be selling tortillas and other things for their families. And there she hopes to see the boy who spoke to her, just a few words, in the town square two Sunday evenings ago. The following Sunday evening she saw him waiting in the street across from her home, a sure sign that he is courting her. But her parents would not allow her out, so she hopes to get a glimpse of him in town (based on Chinas 1991).

In a suburban home in Highland Park, Illinois, USA, 14-year-old Jodie is standing before the mirror in her bedroom with a dismayed look, trying to decide whether to change her clothes again before she goes to school. She has already changed once, from the blue sweater and white skirt to the yellow-and-white blouse and blue jeans, but now she is having second thoughts. "I look awful," she thinks to herself. "I'm getting so fat!" For the past 3 years her body has been changing rapidly, and now she is alarmed to find it becoming rounder and larger seemingly with each day. Vaguely she hears her mother calling her from downstairs, probably urging her to hurry up and leave for school, but the stereo in her room is playing a Pink CD so loud it drowns out what her mother is saying. "I'm not here for your entertainment," Pink sings. "You don't really wanna mess with me tonight."

In Amakiri, Nigeria, 18-year-old Omiebi is walking to school. He is walking quickly, because the time for school to begin is near, and he does not want to be one of the students who arrive after morning assembly has started and are grouped together and made to kneel throughout the assembly. Up ahead he sees several of his fellow students, easily identifiable by the gray uniforms they are all required to wear, and he breaks into a trot to join them. They greet him, and together they continue walking. They joke nervously about the exam coming up for the West African School Certificate. Performance on that exam will determine who is allowed to go on to university.

Omiebi is feeling a great deal of pressure to do well on the exam. He is the oldest child of his family, and his parents have high expectations that he will go to university and become a lawyer, then help his three younger brothers go to university or find good jobs in Lagos, the nearest big city. Omiebi is not really sure he wants to be a lawyer, and he would find it difficult to leave the girl he has recently begun seeing. However, he likes the idea of moving away from tiny Amakiri to the university in Lagos, where, he has heard, all the homes have electricity and all the latest American movies are showing in the theaters. He and his friends break into a run over the last stretch, barely making it to school and joining their classes before the assembly starts (based on Hallos & Leis, 1989).

THREE ADOLESCENTS, IN THREE DIFFERENT CULTURES, with three very different lives. Yet all are adolescents: All have left childhood but have not yet reached adulthood; all are developing into physical and sexual maturity and learning the skills that will enable them to take part in the adult world.

Although all of them are adolescents, what makes these three adolescents so different is that they are growing up in three distinct cultures. Throughout this book we will take a cultural approach to understanding development in adolescence by examining the ways that cultures differ in what they allow adolescents to do and what they require them to do, the different things that cultures teach adolescents to believe, and the different patterns that cultures provide for adolescents' daily lives. Adolescence is a cultural construction, not simply a biological phenomenon. Puberty—the set of biological changes involved in reaching physical and sexual maturity—is universal, and the same biological changes take place in puberty for young people everywhere, although with differences in timing and in cultural meanings. But adolescence is more than the events and processes of puberty. **Adolescence** is a period of the life course between the time puberty begins and the time adult status is approached, when young people are preparing to take on the roles and responsibilities of adulthood in their culture. To say that adolescence is culturally constructed means that cultures vary in how they define adult status and in the content of the adult roles and responsibilities adolescents are learning to fulfill. Almost all cultures have some kind of adolescence, but the length and content and daily experiences of adolescence vary greatly among cultures (Larson, Wilson, & Rickman, 2010; Schlegel & Barry, 1991).

In this chapter, we will lay a foundation for understanding the cultural basis of adolescence by beginning with a look at how adolescence has changed throughout the history of Western cultures. Historical change is also cultural change; for example, the United States of the early 21st century is different culturally from the United States of 1900 or 1800. Seeing how adolescence changes as a culture changes will emphasize the cultural basis of adolescence.

Another way this chapter will lay the foundation for the rest of the book is by introducing the concept of emerging adulthood. This textbook covers not only adolescence

"The adolescent stage has long seemed to me one of the most fascinating of all themes. These years are the best decade of life…. It is a state from which some of the bad, but far more of the good qualities of life and mind arise."

—G. Stanley Hall, *Adolescence* (1904), pp. XVIII, 351.

(roughly ages 10 to 18) but emerging adulthood (roughly ages 18 to 25). Emerging adulthood is a new idea, a new way of thinking about this age period. In this chapter I describe what it means. Each chapter that follows will contain information about emerging adulthood as well as adolescence.

This chapter also sets the stage for what follows by discussing the scientific study of adolescence and emerging adulthood. I will present some of the basic features of the scientific method as it is applied in research on these age periods. It is important to understand adolescence and emerging adulthood not just as periods of the life course but as areas of scientific inquiry, with certain standard methods and certain conventions for determining what is valid and what is not.

Finally, this chapter will provide the foundation for the chapters to come by previewing the major themes and the framework of the book. This will introduce you to themes that will be repeated often in subsequent chapters, and will let you know where we are headed through the course of the book. Special attention will be given to the cultural approach that is central to this book, by presenting an overview of adolescence in various regions of the world.

Adolescence in Western Cultures: A Brief History

Seeing how people in other times have viewed adolescence provides a useful perspective for understanding how adolescence is viewed in our own time. In this brief historical survey, we begin with ancient times 2,500 years ago and proceed through the early 20th century.

Adolescence in Ancient Times

Ideas about adolescence as a stage of the life course go back a long way in the history of Western cultures. In ancient Greece (4th and 5th centuries B.C.), the source of so many ideas that influenced Western history, both Plato and Aristotle viewed adolescence as the third distinct stage of life, after infancy (birth to age 7) and childhood (ages 7 to 14). In their framework, adolescence extended from age 14 to 21. Both of them viewed adolescence as the stage of life in which the capacity for reason first developed. Writing (in 4 B.C.) in *The Republic*, Plato argued that serious education should begin only at adolescence. Before age 7, according to Plato, there is no point in beginning education because the infant's mind is too undeveloped to learn much, and during childhood (ages 7 to 14) education should focus on sports and music, which children can grasp. Education in science and math should be delayed until adolescence, when the mind is finally ready to apply reason in learning these subjects.

---

adolescence A period of the life course between the time puberty begins and the time adult status is approached, when young people are in the process of preparing to take on the roles and responsibilities of adulthood in their culture.

life-cycle service A period in their late teens and 20s in which young people from the 16th to the 19th century engaged in domestic service, farm service, or apprenticeships in various trades and crafts.

During the Children's Crusade, European adolescents attempted to travel to Jerusalem, with disastrous results.

The Children crossing the Alps

Aristotle, who was a student of Plato's during his own adolescence, had a view of adolescence that was in some ways similar to Plato's. Aristotle viewed children as similar to animals, in that both are ruled by the impulsive pursuit of pleasure. It is only in adolescence that we become capable of exercising reason and making rational choices. However, Aristotle argued that it takes the entire course of adolescence for reason to become fully established. At the beginning of adolescence, in his view, the impulses remain in charge and even become more problematic now that sexual desires have developed. It is only toward the end of adolescence—about age 21, according to Aristotle—that reason establishes firm control over the impulses.

THINKING CRITICALLY •••

Plato and Aristotle argued that young people are not capable of reason until at least age 14. Give an example of how the question of when young people are capable of reason is still an issue in our time.

Adolescence From Early Christian Times Through the Middle Ages

A similar focus on the struggle between reason and passion in adolescence can be found in early Christianity. One of the most famous and influential books of early Christianity was Saint Augustine's autobiographical *Confessions*, which he wrote in about A.D. 400. In his *Confessions*, Augustine described his life from early childhood until his conversion to Christianity at age 33. A considerable portion of the autobiography focused on his teens and early 20s, when he was a reckless young man living an impulsive, pleasure-seeking life. He drank large quantities of alcohol, spent money extravagantly, had sex with many young women, and fathered a child outside of marriage. In the autobiography, he repents his reckless youth and argues that conversion to Christianity is the key not

"The young are in character prone to desire and ready to carry any desire they may have formed into action. Of bodily desires it is the sexual to which they are most disposed to give way, and in regard to sexual desire they exercise no self-restraint."
—Aristotle, *Rhetoric*, Ca. 330 B.C.

only to eternal salvation but to the establishment of the rule of reason over passion here on earth, within the individual.

Over the following millennium, from Augustine's time through the Middle Ages, the historical record on adolescence is sparse, as it is on most topics. However, one well-documented event that sheds some light on the history of adolescence is the "Children's Crusade," which took place in 1212. Despite its name, it was composed mostly of young people in their teens, including many university students (Sommerville, 1982). In those days, university students were younger than today, usually entering between ages 13 and 15.

The young crusaders set out from Germany for the Mediterranean coast, believing that when they arrived there the waters would part for them as the Red Sea had for Moses. They would then walk over to the Holy Land (Jerusalem and the areas where Jesus had lived), where they would appeal to the Muslims to allow Christian pilgrims to visit the holy sites. Adults, attempting to take the Holy Land by military force, had already conducted several Crusades. The Children's Crusade was an attempt to appeal to the Muslims in peace, inspired by the belief that Jesus had decreed that the Holy Land could be gained only through the innocence of youth.

Unfortunately, the "innocence" of the young people—their lack of knowledge and experience—made them a ripe target for the unscrupulous. Many of them were robbed, raped, or kidnapped along the way. When the remainder arrived at the Mediterranean Sea, the sea did not open after all, and the shipowners who promised to take them across instead sold them to the Muslims as slaves. The Children's Crusade was a total disaster, but the fact that it was undertaken at all suggests that many people of that era viewed adolescence as a time of innocence and saw that innocence as possessing a special value and power.

Adolescence From 1500 to 1890

Beginning in about 1500, young people in some European societies typically took part in what historians term **life-cycle service**, a period in their late teens and 20s in which young people would engage in domestic service, farm service, or apprenticeships in various trades and crafts (Ben-Amos, 1994). Life-cycle service involved moving out of the family

"For this space then (from my nineteenth year, to my eight and twentieth), we lived seduced and seducing, deceived and deceiving, in diverse lusts."
—Augustine, *Confessions*, A.D. 400

household and into the household of a "master" to whom the young person was in service for a period lasting (typically) 7 years. Young women were somewhat less likely than young men to engage in life-cycle service, but even among women a majority left home during adolescence, most often to take part in life-cycle service as a servant in a family. Life-cycle service also was common in the United States in the early colonial period in New England (beginning in the 17th century), but in colonial New England such service usually took place in the home of a relative or family friend (Rotundo, 1993).

In the young United States, the nature of adolescence soon began to change. Life-cycle service faded during the 18th and 19th centuries. As the American population grew and the national economy became less based in farming and more industrialized, young people increasingly left their small towns in their late teens for the growing cities. In the cities, without ties to a family or community, young people soon became regarded as a social problem in many respects. Rates of crime, premarital sex, and alcohol use among young people all increased in the late 18th and early 19th centuries (Wilson & Herrnstein, 1985). In response, new institutions of social control developed—religious associations, literary

During the 19th century, adolescents often worked under difficult and unhealthy conditions, such as in this coal mine/factory. Why did laws in early 20th century begin to exclude them from adult work?

societies, YMCAs, and YWCAs—where young people were monitored by adults (Kett, 1977). This approach worked remarkably well: In the second half of the 19th century, rates of crime, premarital pregnancies, alcohol use, and other problems among young people all dropped sharply (Wilson & Herrnstein, 1985).

The Age of Adolescence, 1890–1920

Although I have been using the term *adolescence* in this brief history for the sake of clarity and consistency, it was only toward the end of the 19th century and the beginning of the 20th century that *adolescence* became a widely used term (Kett, 1977). Before this time, young people in their teens and early 20s were more often referred to as **youth** or simply as young men and young women (Modell & Goodman, 1990). However, toward the end of the 19th century important changes took place in this age period in Western countries that made a change of terms appropriate.

In the United States and other Western countries, the years 1890–1920 were crucial in establishing the characteristics of modern adolescence. Key changes during these years included the enactment of laws restricting child labor, new requirements for children to attend secondary school, and the development of the field of adolescence as an area of scholarly study. For these reasons, historians call the years 1890–1920 the "Age of Adolescence" (Tyack, 1990).

Toward the end of the 19th century, the industrial revolution was proceeding at full throttle in the United States and other Western countries. There was a tremendous demand for labor to staff the mines, shops, and factories. Adolescents and even preadolescent children were especially in demand, because they could be hired cheaply. The 1900 U.S. census reported that three quarters of a million children aged 10 to 13 were employed in factories, mines, and other industrial work settings. Few states had laws restricting the ages of children in the workplace, even for work such as coal mining

Life-cycle service was common in Western countries from about 1500 to about 1800. This woodcut shows a printer's apprentice.

youth Prior to the late 19th century, the term used to refer to persons in their teens and early twenties.

TABLE 1.1 Key Terms to Know

Here are some terms used throughout the book that you should be sure to know.

Culture.	*Culture* is the total pattern of a group's customs, beliefs, art, and technology. Thus, a culture is a group's common way of life, passed on from one generation to the next.
The West.	The United States, Canada, Europe, Australia, and New Zealand make up the West. They are all industrialized countries, they are all representative democracies with similar kinds of governments, and they share to some extent a common cultural history. In the present, they are all characterized by secularism, consumerism, and capitalism, to one degree or another. *The West* usually refers to the majority culture in each of the countries, but each country also has cultural groups that do not share the characteristics of the majority culture and may even be in opposition to it.
Industrialized countries.	The term *industrialized countries* includes the countries of the West along with Eastern countries such as Japan and South Korea. All of them have highly developed economies that have passed through a period of industrialization and are now based mainly on services (such as law, banking, sales, and accounting) and information (such as computer-related companies).
Majority culture.	The majority culture in any given society is the culture that sets most of the norms and standards and holds most of the positions of political, economic, intellectual, and media power. The term *American majority culture* will be used often in this book to refer to the mostly White middle-class majority in American society.
Society.	A *society* is a group of people who interact in the course of sharing a common geographical area. A single society may include a variety of cultures with different customs, religions, family traditions, and economic practices. Thus, a society is different from a culture: Members of a culture share a common way of life, whereas members of a society may not. For example, American society includes a variety of different cultures, such as the American majority culture, African American culture, Latino culture, and Asian American culture. They share certain characteristics by virtue of being Americans—for example, they are all subject to the same laws, and they go to similar schools—but there are differences among them that make them culturally distinct.
Traditional cultures.	The term *traditional culture* refers to a culture that has maintained a way of life based on stable traditions passed from one generation to the next. These cultures do not generally value change but rather place a higher value on remaining true to cultural traditions. Often traditional cultures are "preindustrial," which means that the technology and economic practices typical in industrialized countries are not widely used. However, this is not always true; Japan, for example, is still in many ways traditional, even though it is also one of the most highly industrialized countries in the world. When we use the term *traditional cultures*, naturally this does not imply that all such cultures are alike. They differ in a variety of ways, but they have in common that they are firmly grounded in a relatively stable cultural tradition, and for that reason they provide a distinct contrast to the cultures of the West.
Developing countries.	Most previously traditional, preindustrial cultures are becoming industrialized today as a consequence of globalization. The term *developing countries* is used to refer to countries where this process is taking place. Examples include most of the countries of Africa and South America, as well as Asian countries such as Thailand and Vietnam.
Socioeconomic status.	The term *socioeconomic status (SES)* is often used to refer to social class, which includes educational level, income level, and occupational status. For adolescents and emerging adults, because they have not yet reached the social class level they will have as adults, *SES* is usually used in reference to their parents' levels of education, income, and occupation.
Young people.	In this book the term *young people* is used as shorthand to refer to adolescents and emerging adults together.

(Tyack, 1990). Nor did many states restrict the number of hours children or adults could work, so children often worked 12-hour days for as little as 35¢ a day.

As more and more young people entered the workplace, however, concern for them also increased among urban reformers, youth workers, and educators. In the view of these adults the young people were being exploited and harmed (physically and morally) by their involvement in adult work. These activists successfully fought for legislation that prohibited companies from hiring preteen children and severely limited the number of hours that could be worked by young people in their early teens (Kett, 1977).

Along with laws restricting child labor came laws requiring a longer period of schooling. Up until the late 19th century, many states did not have any laws requiring children to attend school, and those that did required attendance only through primary school (Tyack, 1990). However, between 1890 and 1920 states began to pass laws requiring attendance not only in primary school but in secondary school as well. As a consequence, the proportion of adolescents in school increased dramatically; in 1890, only 5% of young people age 14 to 17 were in school, but by 1920 this figure had risen to 30% (Arnett & Taber, 1994). This change contributed to making this time the Age of Adolescence, because it marked a more distinct separation between adolescence as a period of continued schooling and adulthood as a period that begins after schooling is finished.

The third major contributor to making the years 1890–1920 the Age of Adolescence was the work of G. Stanley Hall

"At no time of life is the love of excitement so strong as during the season of accelerated development of adolescence, which craves strong feelings and new sensations."

—G. Stanley Hall, *Adolescence*, 1904, Vol. 1, p. 368

G. Stanley Hall, the founder of the scholarly study of adolescence.

2006). To a large extent, he based his ideas on the now-discredited theory of **recapitulation**, which held that the development of each individual recapitulates or reenacts the evolutionary development of the human species as a whole. He believed the stage of adolescence reflected a stage in the human evolutionary past when there was a great deal of upheaval and disorder, with the result that adolescents experience a great deal of **storm and stress** as a standard part of their development. (For more on the "storm and stress" debate, see the Historical Focus box on pages 10–11.) No reputable scholar today adheres to the theory of recapitulation. Nevertheless, Hall did a great deal to focus attention and concern on adolescents, not only among scholars but among the public at large. Thus, he was perhaps the most important figure in making the years 1890–1920 the Age of Adolescence.

This brief history of adolescence provides only a taste of what adolescence has been like in various eras of history. However, because the history of adolescence is one of the themes of this book, historical information will appear in every chapter.

THINKING CRITICALLY •••

Do you agree or disagree with the view that adolescence is inevitably a time of storm and stress? Specify what you mean by storm and stress, and explain the basis for your view.

Laws requiring children to attend school were passed in the early 20th century.

and the beginning of the study of adolescence as a distinct field of scholarship (Modell & Goodman, 1990). Hall was a remarkable person whose achievements included obtaining the first Ph.D. in psychology in the United States, becoming the founder of the American Psychological Association, and serving as the first president of Clark University. In addition, Hall was one of the initiators of the **child study movement** in the United States, which advocated scientific research on child and adolescent development and the improvement of conditions for children and adolescents in the family, school, and workplace.

Among his accomplishments, Hall wrote the first textbook on adolescence, published in 1904 as a two-volume set ambitiously titled *Adolescence: Its Psychology and Its Relations to Physiology, Anthropology, Sociology, Sex, Crime, Religion, and Education.* Hall's textbook covered a wide range of topics, such as physical health and development, adolescence cross-culturally and historically, and adolescent love. A surprising number of Hall's observations have been verified by recent research, such as his description of biological development during puberty, his assertion that depressed mood tends to peak in the mid-teens, and his claim that adolescence is a time of heightened responsiveness to peers (Arnett, 2006a). However, much of what he wrote is dated and obsolete (Youniss,

child study movement Late 19th century group, led by G. Stanley Hall, that advocated research on child and adolescent development and the improvement of conditions for children and adolescents in the family, school, and workplace.

recapitulation Now-discredited theory that held that the development of each individual recapitulates the evolutionary development of the human species as a whole.

storm and stress Theory promoted by G. Stanley Hall asserting that adolescence is inevitably a time of mood disruptions, conflict with parents, and antisocial behavior.

national survey Questionnaire study that involves asking a sample of persons in a country to respond to questions about their opinions, beliefs, or behavior.

One of the best known and most enduring studies of adolescents in the United States is the Monitoring the Future (MTF) study conducted by the University of Michigan. Beginning in 1975, every year the MTF study has surveyed thousands of American adolescents on a wide range of topics, including substance use, political and social attitudes, and gender roles. The survey involves about 50,000 adolescents annually in the 8th, 10th, and 12th grades in 420 schools. (For detailed information on the study, see www.monitoringthefuture.org).

This kind of study is called a **national survey**. A **survey** is a study that involves asking people questions about their opinions, beliefs, or behavior (Salkind, 2003; Thio, 1997). Usually, closed questions are used, meaning that participants are asked to select from a predetermined set of responses, so that their responses can be easily added and compared.

If it is a national survey, that does not mean, of course, that every person in the country is asked the survey questions! Instead, as this chapter describes, researchers seek a sample—that is, a relatively small number of people whose responses are taken to represent the larger population from which they are drawn. Usually, national surveys such as the one described here use a procedure called **stratified sampling**, in which they select participants so that various categories of people are represented in proportions equal to their presence in the population (Goodwin, 1995). For example, if we know that 52% of the

13- to 17-year-olds in the United States are female, we want the sample to be 52% female; if we know that 13% of 13- to 17-year-olds are African American, the sample should be 13% African American; and so on. The categories used to select a stratified sample often include age, gender, ethnic group, education, and socioeconomic status (SES).

The other characteristic of a national survey is usually that the stratified sample is also a **random sample**, meaning that the people selected for participation in the study are chosen randomly—no one in the population has a better or worse chance of being selected than anyone else (Salkind, 2003; Shaughnessy & Zechmeister, 1985). You could do this by putting all possible participants' names in a hat and pulling out as many participants as you needed or by paging through a phone book and putting your finger down in random places, but these days the selection of a random sample for national surveys is usually done by a computer program. Selecting a random sample enhances the likelihood that the sample will be genuinely representative of the larger population. The MTF study selects a random sample of 350 students within each school. In addition, a random sample of MTF participants is followed biennially beyond high school, extending (so far) into the early 30s.

Although the MTF study includes many topics, it is best known for its findings regarding substance use. We will examine these findings in detail in Chapter 13.

Adolescence and Emerging Adulthood

"When our mothers were our age, they were engaged. . . . They at least had some idea what they were going to do with their lives. . . . I, on the other hand, will have a dual degree in majors that are ambiguous at best and impractical at worst (English and political science), no ring on my finger and no idea who I am, much less what I want to do. . . . Under duress, I will admit that this is a pretty exciting time. Sometimes, when I look out across the wide expanse that is my future, I can see beyond the void. I realize that having nothing ahead to count on means I now have to count on myself; that having no direction means forging one of my own."

—Kristen, age 22 (Page, 1999, pp. 18, 20)

In the various eras of history described in the previous section, when people referred to adolescents (or youth or whatever term a particular era or society used), they usually indicated that they meant not just the early teen years but the late teens and into the 20s as well. When G. Stanley Hall (1904) initiated the scientific study of adolescence early in the 20th century, he defined the age range of adolescence as beginning at 14 and ending at 24 (Hall, 1904, vol. 1, p. xix). In contrast, today's scholars generally consider adolescence to begin at about age 10 and end by about age 18. Studies published in the major journals on adolescence rarely include samples with ages higher than 18 (Arnett, 2000a). What happened between Hall's time and our own to move scholars' conceptions of adolescence forward chronologically in the life course?

Two changes stand out as explanations. One is the decline that took place during the 20th century in the typical

survey A questionnaire study that involves asking a large number of people questions about their opinions, beliefs, or behavior.

stratified sampling Sampling technique in which researchers select participants so that various categories of people are represented in proportions equal to their presence in the population.

random sample Sampling technique in which the people selected for participation in a study are chosen randomly, meaning that no one in the population has a better or worse chance of being selected than anyone else.

age of the initiation of puberty. At the beginning of the 20th century, the median age of **menarche** (a girl's first menstruation) in Western countries was about 15 (Eveleth & Tanner, 1976). Because menarche takes place relatively late in the typical sequence of pubertal changes, this means that the initial changes of puberty would have begun at ages 13 to 15 for most boys and girls (usually earlier for girls than for boys), which is just where Hall designated the beginning of adolescence. However, the median age of menarche (and, by implication, other pubertal changes) declined steadily between 1900 and 1970 before leveling out, so that by now the typical age of menarche in the United States is 12.5 (Vigil, Geary, & Byrd-Craven, 2005). The initial changes of puberty begin about 2 years earlier, thus the designation of adolescence as beginning at about age 10.

As for when adolescence ends, the change in this age may have been inspired not by a biological change but by a social change: the growth of secondary school attendance to a normative experience for adolescents in the United States and other Western countries. As noted earlier, in 1890 only 5% of Americans aged 14 to 17 were enrolled in high school. However, this proportion rose steeply and steadily throughout the 20th century, reaching 95% by 1985 (Arnett & Taber, 1994). Because attending high school is now nearly universal among American adolescents and because high school graduation usually takes place at age 18, it makes sense for scholars studying American adolescents to place the end of adolescence at age 18. Hall did not choose 18 as the end of adolescence because for most adolescents of his time no significant transition took place at that age. Education ended earlier, work began earlier, and leaving home took place later. Marriage and parenthood did not take place for most people until their early to mid-20s (Arnett & Taber, 1994), which may have been why Hall designated age 24 as the end of adolescence.

Hall viewed the late teens and early 20s as an especially interesting time of life. I agree, and I think it would be a mistake to cut off our study of adolescence in this book at age 18. A great deal happens in the late teens and early 20s that is related to development earlier in adolescence and that has important implications for the path that development takes in adulthood. I have termed this period **emerging adulthood**, and I consider it to include roughly the ages 18 to 25 (Arnett, 1998a, 2000a, 2004a, 2006b; 2007a; 2010; Arnett & Taber, 1994).

Five characteristics distinguish emerging adulthood from other age periods (Arnett, 2004a, 2006a; Reifman et al., 2006). Emerging adulthood is:

1. the age of identity explorations;

2. the age of instability;

3. the self-focused age;

4. the age of feeling in-between; and

5. the age of possibilities.

Perhaps the most distinctive characteristic of emerging adulthood is that it is the *age of identity explorations*. That is, it is an age when people explore various possibilities in love and work as they move toward making enduring choices. Through trying out these different possibilities they develop a more definite identity, including an understanding of who they are, what their capabilities and limitations are, what their beliefs and values are, and how they fit into the society around them. Erik Erikson (1950), who was the first to develop the idea of identity, asserted that it is mainly an issue in adolescence; but that was over 50 years ago, and today it is mainly in emerging adulthood that identity explorations take place (Arnett, 2000a, 2004a, 2005b; Côté, 2005; Schwartz et al., 2005).

The explorations of emerging adulthood also make it the *age of instability*. As emerging adults explore different possibilities in love and work, their lives are often unstable. A good illustration of this instability is their frequent moves from one residence to another. As Figure 1.1 shows, rates of residential change in American society are much higher at ages 18–29 than at any other period of life. This reflects the explorations going on in emerging adults' lives. Some move out of their parents' household for the first time in their late teens to attend a residential college, whereas others move out simply to be independent (Goldscheider & Goldscheider, 1999). They may move again when they drop out of college or when they graduate. They may move to cohabit with a ro-

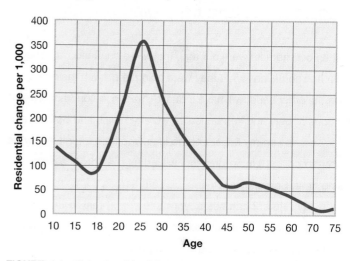

FIGURE 1.1 Rate of residential change by age. Why does the rate peak in emerging adulthood?

Source: U.S. Bureau of the Census (2003).

---

menarche A girl's first menstrual period.

emerging adulthood Period from roughly ages 18 to 25 in industrialized countries during which young people become more independent from parents and explore various life possibilities before making enduring commitments.

mantic partner and then move out when the relationship ends. Some move to another part of the country or the world to study or work. For nearly half of American emerging adults, residential change includes moving back in with their parents at least once (Goldscheider & Goldscheider, 1999). In some countries, such as in southern Europe, emerging adults remain home rather than moving out; nevertheless, they may still experience instability in education, work, and love relationships (Douglass, 2005, 2007).

Emerging adulthood is also a *self-focused age*. Most American emerging adults move out of their parents' home at age 18 or 19 and do not marry and have their first child until at least their late 20s (Arnett, 2000a). Even in countries where emerging adults remain home through their early 20s, such as in southern Europe and Asian countries, including Japan, they establish a more independent lifestyle than they had as adolescents (Douglass, 2005). Emerging adulthood is a time in between adolescents' reliance on parents and adults' long-term commitments in love and work, and during these years emerging adults focus on themselves as they develop the knowledge, skills, and self-understanding they will need for adult life. In the course of emerging adulthood, they learn to make independent decisions about everything from what to have for dinner to whether or not to go to graduate school.

To say that emerging adulthood is a self-focused time is not meant pejoratively. There is nothing wrong with being self-focused during emerging adulthood. It is normal, healthy, and temporary. The goal of their self-focusing is learning to stand alone as self-sufficient persons, but emerging adults do not see self-sufficiency as a permanent state. Rather, they view it as a necessary step before committing themselves to lasting relationships with others, in love and work.

Another distinctive feature of emerging adulthood is that it is an *age of feeling in-between*, not adolescent but not fully adult either. When asked, "Do you feel that you have reached adulthood?" the majority of emerging adults respond neither yes nor no but with the ambiguous "in some ways yes, in some ways no" (Arnett, 1994a, 1997, 1998a, 2000a, 2001a, 2003a, 2004a). As Figure 1.2 shows, it is only when people reach their late 20s and early 30s that a clear majority feel they have reached adulthood. Most emerging adults have the subjective feeling of being in a transitional period of life, on the way to adulthood but not there yet. This "in-between" feeling in emerging adulthood has been found in a wide range of countries, including Argentina (Facio & Micocci, 2003), Israel (Mayseless & Scharf, 2003), the Czech Republic (Macek et al., 2007), China (Nelson et al., 2004), and Denmark (Arnett et al., 2009).

Finally, emerging adulthood is the age of possibilities, when many different futures remain possible, when little about a person's direction in life has been decided for certain. It tends to be an age of high hopes and great expectations, in part because few of their dreams have been tested in the fires of real life. In one national survey of 18- to 24-year-olds in the United States, nearly all—96%—agreed with the statement "I am very sure that someday I will get to where I want to be in life" (Hornblower, 1997). The dreary, dead-end jobs, the bitter divorces, the disappointing and disrespectful children that some of them

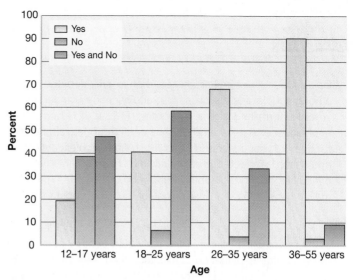

FIGURE 1.2 Age differences in response to the question "Do you feel that you have reached adulthood?"
Source: Arnett (2000a).

will find themselves experiencing in the years to come—few of them imagine in emerging adulthood that this is what the future holds. This optimism in emerging adulthood has been found in other countries as well (Arnett et al., 2009; Nelson & Chen, 2007).

One feature of emerging adulthood that makes it the age of possibilities is that emerging adults typically have left their family of origin but are not yet committed to a new network of relationships and obligations. For those who have come from a troubled family, this is their chance to try to straighten the parts of themselves that have become twisted. No longer dependent on their parents, and no longer subject to their parents' problems on a daily basis, they may be able to make independent decisions—perhaps to move to a different area or go to college—that turn their lives in a dramatically different direction (Arnett, 2004a; Masten et al., 2006). Even for those who have come from families that are relatively happy and healthy, emerging adulthood is an opportunity to transform themselves so that they are not merely made in their parents' images but have made independent decisions about what kind of person they wish to be and how they wish to live. For this limited window of time—7, perhaps 10 years—the fulfillment of all their hopes seems possible, because for most people the range of their choices for how to live is greater than it has ever been before and greater than it will ever be again.

Emerging adulthood does not exist in all cultures. Cultures vary widely in the ages that young people are expected to enter full adulthood and take on adult responsibilities

"But when, by what test, by what indication does manhood commence? Physically, by one criterion, legally by another. Morally by a third, intellectually by a fourth—and all indefinite."
—Thomas De Quincey, *Autobiography*, 1821

HISTORICAL FOCUS • The "Storm and Stress" Debate

One of G. Stanley Hall's ideas that is still debated today among scholars is his claim that adolescence is inherently a time of storm and stress. According to Hall, it is normal for adolescence to be a time of considerable upheaval and disruption. As Hall described it (Arnett, 1999a), adolescent storm and stress is reflected in especially high rates of three types of difficulties during the adolescent period: conflict with parents, mood disruptions, and risk behavior (such as substance use and crime).

Hall (1904) favored the **Lamarckian** evolutionary ideas that many prominent thinkers in the early 20th century considered to be a better explanation of evolution than Darwin's theory of natural selection. In Lamarck's now-discredited theory, evolution takes place as a result of accumulated experience. Organisms pass on their characteristics from one generation to the next not in the form of genes (which were unknown at the time Lamarck and Darwin devised their theories) but in the form of memories and acquired characteristics. These memories and acquired characteristics would then be reenacted or *recapitulated* in the development of each individual in future generations. Thus Hall, considering development during adolescence, judged it to be "suggestive of some ancient period of storm and stress" (1904, vol. 1, p. xiii). In his view, there must have been a period of human evolution that was extremely difficult and tumultuous; ever since, the memory of that period had been passed from one generation to the next and was recapitulated in the development of each individual as the storm and stress of adolescent development.

In the century since Hall's work established adolescence as an area of scientific study, the debate over adolescent storm and stress has simmered steadily and boiled to the surface periodically. Anthropologists, led by Margaret Mead (1928), countered Hall's claim that a tendency toward storm and stress in adolescence is universal and biological by describing non-Western cultures in which adolescence was neither stormy nor stressful. In contrast, psychoanalytic theorists, particularly Anna Freud (1946, 1958, 1968, 1969), have been the most outspoken proponents of the storm and stress view.

Anna Freud viewed adolescents who did not experience storm and stress with great suspicion, claiming that their outward calm concealed the inward reality that they must have "built up excessive defenses against their drive activities and are now crippled by the results" (1968, p. 15). She viewed storm and stress as universal and inevitable, to the extent that its absence signified a serious psychological problem: "To be normal during the adolescent period is by itself abnormal" (1958, p. 267).

What does more recent scholarship indicate about the validity of the storm and stress view? A clear consensus exists among current scholars that the storm and stress view proposed by Hall and made more extreme by Anna Freud and other psychoanalysts is not valid for most adolescents (Arnett, 1999a; Steinberg, 2001; Susman et al., 2003). The claim that storm and stress is characteristic of all adolescents, and that the source of it is purely biological, is clearly false. Scholars today tend to emphasize that most adolescents like and respect their parents, that for

---

(Arnett & Galambos, 2003; Schlegel & Barry, 1991). Emerging adulthood exists only in cultures in which young people are allowed to postpone entering adult roles such as marriage and parenthood until at least their mid-20s (Arnett, 2000a; Arnett, 2010). Thus, emerging adulthood exists mainly in industrialized societies such as the United States, Canada, most of Europe, Australia, New Zealand, and Japan (Arnett, 2000a; Bynner, 2005; Douglass, 2005, 2007). However, in many other areas of the world, emerging adulthood is becoming more prevalent as cultures become more industrialized and more integrated into a global economy (Galambos & Martinez, 2007; Macek et al., 2007; Nelson & Chen, 2007). This topic will be addressed often in the chapters to come.

Emerging adulthood is a recent phenomenon historically. In the United States, the median age of marriage is at a record high—about 26 for women and 28 for men—and has risen steeply over the past 40 years (Arnett, 2006b). Also, a higher proportion of young Americans than ever before attend at least some college—currently, over 60% (National Center for Education Statistics, 2009). Similar changes have taken place in recent decades in other industrialized countries (Arnett, 2007a; Bynner, 2005; Douglass, 2005, 2007; see Table 1.2). This postponement of adult responsibilities into the mid- to late 20s makes possible the explorations of emerging adulthood. With growing industrialization and economic integration worldwide, emerging adulthood is likely to become increasingly common around the world in the 21st century (Arnett, 2000a, 2002a).

In this book, then, we will cover three periods: **early adolescence**, from age 10 to 14; **late adolescence**, from age 15 to

---

Lamarckian Reference to Lamarck's ideas, popular in the late 19th and early 20th centuries, that evolution takes place as a result of accumulated experience such that organisms pass on their characteristics from one generation to the next in the form of memories and acquired characteristics.

early adolescence Period of human development lasting from about age 10 to about age 14.

late adolescence Period of human development lasting from about age 15 to about age 18.

most adolescents their mood disruptions are not so extreme that they need psychological treatment, and that most of them do not engage in risk behavior on a regular basis.

On the other hand, studies in recent decades have also indicated some support for what might be called a "modified" storm and stress view (Arnett, 1999a). Research evidence supports the existence of some degree of storm and stress with respect to conflict with parents, mood disruptions, and risk behavior. Not all adolescents experience storm and stress in these areas, but adolescence is the period when storm and stress is more likely to occur than at other ages. Conflict with parents tends to be higher in adolescence than before or after adolescence (Paikoff & Brooks-Gunn, 1991; Smetana, 2005). Adolescents report greater extremes of mood and more frequent changes of mood, compared with preadolescents or adults (Larson & Richards, 1994), and depressed mood is more common in adolescence than it is in childhood or adulthood (Bond et al., 2005; Petersen et al., 1993). Rates of most types of risk behavior rise sharply during adolescence and peak during late adolescence or emerging adulthood. The different aspects of storm and stress have different peak ages: conflict with parents in early to midadolescence, mood disruptions in midadolescence, and risk behavior in late adolescence and emerging adulthood (Arnett, 1999a).

We will explore each aspect of storm and stress in more detail in later chapters. For now, however, it should be emphasized that even though evidence supports a modified storm and stress view, this does not mean that storm and stress is typical of all adolescents in all places and times. Cultures vary

Risk behavior peaks in late adolescence and emerging adulthood.

in the degree of storm and stress experienced by their adolescents, with storm and stress relatively low in traditional cultures and relatively high in Western cultures (Arnett, 1999a). Also, within every culture individuals vary in the amount of adolescent storm and stress they experience.

18; and emerging adulthood, from age 18 to about 25. Including all three of these periods will provide a broad age range for our examination of the various aspects of young people's development—the biological, psychological, and social changes they experience over time. Because studies on early and late adolescence are more abundant than studies on emerging adulthood, most of the information in the book will refer to adolescence, but each chapter will contain some information on emerging adulthood.

THINKING CRITICALLY •••

Is 25 a good upper age boundary for the end of emerging adulthood? Where would you put the upper age boundary, and why?

The Transition to Adulthood

Adolescence is generally viewed as beginning with the first noticeable changes of puberty (Feldman & Elliott, 1990). The end of adolescence, as we have defined it here, is also quite clear: age 18, when most people in industrialized societies have reached the end of their secondary school education. Age 18 also marks the beginning of emerging adulthood, as that is when most young people begin the exploratory activities that characterize emerging adulthood. But what marks the end of emerging adulthood? If emerging adulthood is in many ways a period of transition from adolescence to full adulthood, how does a person know when the

TABLE 1.2	Median Marriage Age (Females) in Selected Countries		
Industrialized Countries	Age	Developing Countries	Age
United States	26	Egypt	19
Canada	28	Morocco	20
Germany	30	Ghana	19
France	29	Nigeria	17
Italy	29	India	20
Japan	29	Indonesia	19
Australia	28	Brazil	21

Sources: Douglass, 2007; Population Reference Bureau (2000); United Nations Economic Commission for Europe (2005).

A young person in three periods: early adolescence (ages 10–14), late adolescence (ages 15–18), and emerging adulthood (ages 18–25).

transition to adulthood is complete? The answer to this question is complex and varies notably among cultures. First, we examine cultural similarities in views of adulthood, then cultural variations.

THINKING CRITICALLY •••

In your view, what marks the attainment of adulthood for yourself? For others, generally?

The Transition to Adulthood: Cross-Cultural Themes

"Sometimes I feel like I've reached adulthood, and then I'll sit down and eat ice cream directly from the box, and I keep thinking, 'I'll know I'm an adult when I don't eat ice cream right out of the box anymore.' . . . But I guess in some ways I feel like I'm an adult. I'm a pretty responsible person. I mean, if I say I'm going to do something, I do it. Financially, I'm fairly responsible with my money. But there are still times where I think, 'I can't believe I'm 25.' A lot of times I don't really feel like an adult."

—Lisa, age 25 (Arnett, 2004a, p. 14)

In industrialized societies, there are a variety of possible ways one could define the transition to adulthood. Legally, the transition to adulthood takes place in most respects at age 18. This is the age at which a person becomes an adult for various legal purposes, such as signing legally binding documents and being eligible to vote. One could also define the transition to adulthood as entering the roles that are typically considered to be part of adulthood: full-time work, marriage, and parenthood (Hogan & Astone, 1986).

But what about young people themselves? How do young people today conceptualize the transition to adulthood? In the past decade, many studies have examined what young people in industrialized societies view as the key markers of the transition to adulthood. The results of the studies have been remarkably similar, in countries including the United States (Arnett, 1998a, 2003b; Nelson, 2003), Argentina (Facio & Micocci, 2003), the Czech Republic (Macek, 2007), Romania (Nelson et al., 2008), the United Kingdom (Horowitz and Bromnick, 2008), Israel (Mayseless & Scharf, 2003), South Korea (Arnett, 2001b), and China (Nelson, Badger, & Wu, 2004). In these studies young people from their early teens to their late 20s agreed that the most important markers of the transition from adolescence to adulthood are *accepting responsibility for oneself, making independent decisions,* and *becoming financially independent,* in that order. These three criteria rank highest not just across cultures and nations but across ethnic groups and social classes.

Note the similarity among the top criteria: All three are characterized by **individualism**; that is, all three emphasize the importance of learning to stand alone as a self-sufficient person without relying on anyone else. The values of individualism, such as independence and self-expression, are often contrasted with the values of **collectivism**, such as duties and obligations to others. The criteria for adulthood favored by emerging adults in industrialized societies reflect the individualistic values of those societies (Bellah et al., 1985; Douglass et al., 2005; Harkness, Super, & van Tijen, 2000; Triandis, 1995).

individualism Cultural belief system that emphasizes the desirability of independence, self-sufficiency, and self-expression.

collectivism A set of beliefs asserting that it is important for persons to mute their individual desires in order to contribute to the well-being and success of the group.

interdependence The web of commitments, attachments, and obligations that exist in some human groups.

The Transition to Adulthood: Cultural Variations

In addition to the top three criteria for adulthood that have been found across cultures—accepting responsibility for oneself, making independent decisions, and becoming financially independent—studies have found distinctive cultural criteria as well. Young Israelis viewed completing military service as important for becoming an adult, reflecting Israel's requirement of mandatory military service (Mayseless & Scharf, 2003). Young Argentines especially valued being able to support a family financially, perhaps reflecting the economic upheavals Argentina has experienced for many years (Facio & Miccoci, 2003). Emerging adults in Korea and China viewed *being able to support their parents financially* as necessary for adulthood, reflecting the collectivistic value of obligation to parents found in Asian societies (Naito & Gielen, 2003; Nelson et al., 2004).

What about traditional cultures? Do they have different ideas about what marks the beginning of adulthood, compared to industrialized societies? The answer appears to be yes. Anthropologists have found that in virtually all traditional, non-Western cultures, the transition to adulthood is clearly and explicitly marked by *marriage* (Schlegel & Barry, 1991). It is only after marriage that a person is considered to have attained adult status and is given adult privileges and responsibilities. In contrast, very few of the young people in the studies mentioned above indicated that they considered marriage to be an important marker of the transition to adulthood. In fact, in industrialized societies marriage ranks near the bottom in surveys of possible criteria for adult status.

What should we make of that contrast? One possible interpretation would be that traditional cultures elevate marriage as the key transition to adulthood because they prize the collectivistic value of **interdependence** more highly than the individualistic value of independence, and marriage signifies that a person is taking on new interdependent relationships outside the family of origin (Arnett, 1995a, 1998a; Markus & Kitiyama, 1991; Shweder et al., 2006). Marriage is a social event rather than an individual, psychological process, and it represents the establishment of a new network of relationships with all the kin of one's marriage partner. This is especially true in traditional cultures, where family members are more likely than in the West to be close-knit and to have extensive daily contact with one another. Thus, cultures that value interdependence view marriage as the most important marker of entering adulthood because of the ways marriage confirms and strengthens interdependence.

Still, these conclusions about traditional cultures are based mainly on the observations of the anthropologists who have studied them. If you asked young people in these cultures directly about their own conceptions of what marks the beginning of adulthood, perhaps you would get a variety of answers other than marriage. For example, Susan Davis and Douglas Davis (1989) asked young Moroccans (aged 9 to 20), "How do you know you're grown up?" They found that the two most common types of responses were (1) those that em-

Marriage is of great significance as a marker of adulthood in traditional cultures. Here, a Burmese bride and groom (center) and their attendants.

phasized chronological age or physical development, such as the beginning of facial hair among boys; and (2) those that emphasized character qualities, such as developing self-control (see the Cultural Focus box on page 15). Few of the young people mentioned marriage, even though Davis and Davis (1989) stated that in Moroccan culture generally, "after marriage, one is considered an adult" (p. 59). This suggests that further investigation of young people's conceptions of the transition to adulthood in traditional cultures may prove enlightening and that their views may not match the conceptions of adulthood held by adults.

The Scientific Study of Adolescence and Emerging Adulthood

Insights into development during adolescence and emerging adulthood can be gained in many ways. There are some excellent autobiographies of these periods such as *This Boy's Life* by Tobias Wolff (1987) and the autobiography of Anne Frank (1942/1997). Journalists have written accounts of various aspects of these periods, often focusing on a particular young person or a small group (for one example, see Bamberger [2004]). Some terrific novels have been written that focus on adolescence and emerging adulthood, such as J. D. Salinger's *Catcher in the Rye* (1951/1964), Anchee Min's *Katherine* (1995), and Russell Banks's *The Rule of the Bone* (1995).

I will draw on sources in all these areas for illustrations and examples. However, the main focus in this book will be on the scientific study of adolescence and emerging adulthood. You will be learning about development during adolescence and emerging adulthood as an area of the social sciences. You will read about the most important and influential studies that have contributed to this field. In every chapter of the book you will find a Research Focus box that explores a specific study in depth and discusses in detail the methods used in the study.

What does it mean for scholars to engage in the scientific study of adolescence and emerging adulthood? It means to apply the standards of the **scientific method** to the questions we investigate (Cozby, Worden, & Kee, 1989; Goodwin, 1995; Salkind, 2003; Shaughnessy & Zechmeister, 1985). The scientific method includes standards of **hypotheses**, **sampling**, **procedure**, **method**, analysis, and interpretation.

Every scientific study begins with an idea: A scholar wants to find an answer to a question, and on the basis of a theory or previous research, the scholar proposes one or more hypotheses. A hypothesis is the scholar's idea about one possible answer to the question of interest. For example, a scholar may be interested in the question "Why are girls more likely than boys to become depressed in adolescence?" and propose the hypothesis "Girls are more likely to become depressed because they tend to blame themselves when they experience conflict with others." The scholar would then design a study to test that hypothesis. The hypotheses of a study are crucial, because they influence the sampling, measures, analysis, and interpretation that follow.

With respect to sampling, scholars who study adolescents and emerging adults seek to obtain a **sample** that represents the **population** they are interested in. Suppose, for example, a scholar wants to study adolescents' attitudes toward contraception. The waiting room of a clinic offering contraceptive services would probably not be a good place to look for a sample, because the adolescents coming to such a clinic are quite likely to have more favorable attitudes toward contraception than adolescents in general; otherwise, why would they be coming to a place that offers contraceptive services? Instead, if the population of interest is adolescents in general, it would be better to sample them through schools or through a telephone survey that selected households randomly from the community.

On the other hand, if a scholar is particularly interested in attitudes toward contraception among the population of adolescents who are already using or planning to use contraception, then a clinic offering contraceptive services would be a good place to find a sample. It all depends on the population the scholar wishes to study and on the questions the scholar wishes to address. The goal is to seek out a sample that will be **representative** of the population of interest (Goodwin, 1995; Shaughnessy & Zechmeister, 1985). If the

sample is representative of the population, then the findings from the sample will be **generalizable** to the population. In other words, the findings from the sample will make it possible to draw conclusions about not just the sample itself but also the larger population of adolescents that the sample is intended to represent.

The third consideration of the scientific method, *procedure*, refers to the way the study is conducted and the data are collected. One standard aspect of the procedure in scientific studies of human beings is **informed consent** (Goodwin, 1995). Human subjects in any scientific study are supposed to be presented with a **consent form** before they participate (Shaughnessy & Zechmeister, 1985). Consent forms typically include information about who is conducting the study, what the purposes of the study are, what participation in the study involves (e.g., filling out a questionnaire on contraceptive use), what risks (if any) are involved in participating, and what the person can expect to receive in return for participation. Consent forms also usually include a statement indicating that participation in the study is voluntary and that persons may withdraw from participation in the study at any time.

The use of consent forms is not always possible (for example, in telephone surveys), but whenever possible they are included in the procedure for scholars studying adolescents and emerging adults. For adolescents under age 18, the consent of one of their parents is also usually required as part of a study's procedures.

Another aspect of the procedure is the circumstances of the data collection. Scholars try to collect data in a way that will not be biased. For example, scholars must be careful not to phrase questions in an interview or a questionnaire in a way that seems to lead people toward a desired response. They must also assure participants that their responses will be confidential, especially if the study concerns a sensitive topic such as sexual behavior or drug use.

The scientific method also includes a variety of specific methods for data collection. A method is a strategy for collecting data. In the next section, we will consider a variety of methods used in research on adolescence and emerging adulthood. This will also be a way of introducing some of the major studies on adolescence and emerging adulthood that I will be referring to often in the course of the book.

THINKING CRITICALLY •••

You have probably read about topics concerning adolescence and emerging adulthood in newspapers and magazines. Find a recent article and analyze whether or not it meets the criteria for scientific research.

---

scientific method A systematic way of finding the answers to questions or problems that includes standards of sampling, procedure, and measures.

hypotheses Ideas, based on theory or previous research, that a scholar wishes to test in a scientific study.

sampling Collecting data on a subset of the members of a group.

procedure Standards for the way a study is conducted. Includes informed consent and certain rules for avoiding biases in the data collection.

method A scientific strategy for collecting data.

sample The people included in a given study, who are intended to represent the population of interest.

population The entire group of people of interest in a study.

representative Characteristic of a sample that refers to the degree to which it accurately represents the population of interest.

CULTURAL FOCUS • Moroccan Conceptions of Adolescence

The anthropologists Susan Davis and Douglas Davis (1989, 1995, 2007) have been studying adolescents in Morocco for nearly three decades, originally as part of the Harvard Adolescence Project described in this chapter. One of the questions that has interested them in their research concerns the qualities Moroccans associate with adolescence.

The most important concept in Moroccan views of adolescence is 'aql, an Arabic word that has connotations of reasonableness, understanding, and rationality. Self-control and self-restraint are also part of 'aql: To possess 'aql means to have control over your needs and passions and to be able and willing to restrain them out of respect for those around you. Moroccans see 'aql as a quality expected of adults and often lacking in adolescents.

'Aql is expected to develop in both males and females during adolescence, but males are believed to take a decade longer to develop it fully! This appears to be due to sharp differences in gender roles and expectations. Unlike males, females are given a variety of responsibilities from an early age, such as household work and taking care of younger siblings, so it is more important for them to develop 'aql earlier to meet the demands of these responsibilities. It is quite common, not just in Morocco but worldwide in traditional cultures, that much more work is required of females in adolescence than of males (Schlegel & Barry, 1991; Whiting & Edwards, 1988).

Another term Moroccans use in reference to adolescence is taysh, which means reckless, rash, and frivolous. This quality is especially associated with awakening sexuality and the possible violations of social norms this awakening may inspire (female virginity before marriage is very important to Moroccans). Taysh is a quality associated with adolescence in the views of many Moroccans, as illustrated in this exchange between Susan Davis and Naima, a mother of two adolescents:

SUSAN: What does this word taysh mean?
NAIMA: It starts at the age of 15, 16, 17, 18, 19 until 20. [It lasts] until she develops her 'aql. She is frivolous [taysha] for about 4 years.
SUSAN: How do you know they have reached that age? How would you know when Najet [her daughter, age 13] gets there?
NAIMA: You can recognize it. The girl becomes frivolous. She starts caring about her appearance, dressing well, wearing fancy clothes and showy things, you

Moroccan adolescents.

understand. . . . She also messes up her school schedule. She either leaves too early or comes too late [i.e., she may be changing her schedule to meet boys]. You have to be watchful with her at that juncture. If you see she is on the right path, you leave her alone. If you notice that she is too late or far off the timing, then you have to set the record straight with her until the age of adolescence is over. When she is 20 years of age, she recovers her ability to reason and be rational.

SUSAN: When your son Saleh [age 14] reaches the age of adolescence, how would you know it?
NAIMA: I will notice that he doesn't come home on time, he will start skipping school . . . He will start following girls. . . . Girls will start complaining, 'Your son is following me.' This is the first consequence.
SUSAN: So it's similar to the girl—the girl will dress in a fancy way, while the boy will start getting interested in her.
NAIMA: That's it.

Moroccans explicitly state that marriage marks the end of adolescence and the entry into adulthood. However, from their use of the terms 'aql and taysh, we can see that the transition to adulthood also involves intangible qualities similar to the ones important in other cultures. Can you see the similarities between 'aql and taysh and the qualities important in conceptions of the transition to adulthood discussed in this chapter?

---

generalizable Characteristic of a sample that refers to the degree to which findings based on the sample can be used to make accurate statements about the population of interest.

informed consent Standard procedure in social scientific studies that entails informing potential participants of what their participation would involve, including any possible risks.

consent form Written statement provided by a researcher to potential participants in a study, informing them of who is conducting the study, the purposes of the study, and what their participation would involve, including potential risks.

THINKING CRITICALLY •••

How is the Moroccan conception of adolescence similar to and different from the view of Plato and Aristotle described earlier in this chapter?

Methods Used in Research

Scholars conduct research on adolescence and emerging adulthood in a variety of academic disciplines, including psychology, sociology, anthropology, education, and medicine. They use a variety of different methods in their investigations.

Two key issues with many methods are **reliability** and **validity**. There are a variety of types of reliability, but in general, a method has high reliability if it obtains similar results on different occasions (Shaughnessy & Zechmeister, 1985). For example, if a questionnaire asked girls in their senior year of high school to recall when their first menstrual period occurred, the questionnaire would be considered reliable if most of the girls answered the same on one occasion as they did when asked the question again 6 months later. Or, if adolescents were interviewed about the quality of their relationships with their parents, the measure would be reliable if the adolescents' answers were the same for two different interviewers (Goodwin, 1995).

Validity refers to the truthfulness of a method (Shaughnessy & Zechmeister, 1985). A method is valid if it measures what it claims to measure. For example, IQ tests are purported to measure intellectual abilities, but as we shall see in Chapter 3, this claim is controversial. Critics claim that IQ tests are not valid (i.e., that they do not measure what they are supposed to measure). Notice that a measure is not necessarily valid even if it is reliable. It is widely agreed that IQ tests are reliable—people generally score about the same on one occasion as they do on another—but the validity of the tests is disputed. In general, it is more difficult to establish validity than reliability.

We will examine questions of reliability and validity throughout the book. For now, we turn to the methods.

Questionnaires The most commonly used method in social science research is the questionnaire (Salkind, 2003; Sudman & Bradburn, 1989). Usually, questionnaires have a **closed question** format, which means that participants are provided with specific responses to choose from (Sudman & Bradburn, 1989). Sometimes the questions have an **open-ended question** format, which means that participants are allowed to state their response following the question. One advantage of closed questions is that they make it possible to collect and an-

alyze responses from a large number of people in a relatively short time (Shaughnessy & Zechmeister, 1985). Everyone responds to the same questions with the same response options.

For this reason, closed questions have often been used in large-scale surveys conducted on adolescents and emerging adults. One of the most valuable of these surveys is the Monitoring the Future survey conducted annually by the Institute for Social Research at the University of Michigan (see the Research Focus box in this chapter for more information about this survey).

Interviews Although questionnaires are the dominant type of method used in the study of adolescence and emerging adulthood, the use of questionnaires has certain limitations (Arnett, 2005c; Sudman & Bradburn, 1989). When a closed question format questionnaire is used, the range of possible responses is already specified, and the participant must choose from the responses provided. The researcher tries to cover the responses that seem most plausible and most likely, but it is impossible in a few brief response options to do justice to the depth and diversity of human experience. For example, if a questionnaire contains an item such as "How close are you to your mother? A. very close; B. somewhat close; C. not very close; D. not at all close," it is probably true that an adolescent who chooses "very close" really is closer to his or her mother than the adolescent who chooses "not at all close." But this alone does not begin to capture the complexity of the relationship between an adolescent and a parent.

Interviews are intended to provide the kind of individuality and complexity that questionnaires usually lack (Arnett, 2005c; Briggs, 1989). An interview allows a scholar to hear adolescents and emerging adults describe their lives in their own words, with all the uniqueness and richness that such descriptions make possible. An interview also allows a scholar to know the whole person and see how the various parts of the person's life are intertwined. For example, an interview on an adolescent's family relationships might reveal how the adolescent's relationship with her mother is affected by her relationship with her father, and how the whole family has been affected by certain events—perhaps a family member's loss of a job, psychological problems, medical problems, or substance abuse.

Interviews provide **qualitative** data, as contrasted with the **quantitative** data of questionnaires, and qualitative data can be interesting and informative. However, like questionnaires, interviews have limitations (Salkind, 2003; Shaughnessy & Zechmeister, 1985; Sudman & Bradburn, 1989). Because interviews do not typically provide preclassified responses the way questionnaires do, interview responses have

---

reliability Characteristic of a measure that refers to the extent to which results of the measure on one occasion are similar to results of the measure on a separate occasion.

validity The truthfulness of a measure, that is, the extent to which it measures what it claims to measure.

closed question Questionnaire format that entails choosing from specific responses provided for each question.

open-ended question Questionnaire format that involves writing in responses to each question.

interview Research method that involves asking people questions in a conversational format, such that people's answers are in their own words.

Margaret Mead and a Samoan adolescent.

to be coded according to some plan of classification. For example, if you asked the interview question "What occupation do you plan to have by age 30?" you might get a fascinating range of responses from a sample of adolescents or emerging adults. Those responses would help to inform you about the entire range of occupations young people imagine themselves having as adults. However, to make sense of the data and present them in a scientific format, at some point you would have to code the responses into categories—business, arts, professional/technical, trades, and so on. Only in this way would you be able to say something about the pattern of responses among your sample.

Coding interview data takes time, effort, and money. This is one of the reasons far more studies are conducted using questionnaires than using interviews. However, some excellent studies have been conducted using interview data. For example, William Julius Wilson, a sociologist, has conducted

studies of hundreds of African American emerging adults in poor neighborhoods in Chicago (Tienda & Wilson, 2002; Wilson, 1987, 1996). His research focuses on the difficulties many young urban African Americans face in pursuing educational and occupational opportunities. He analyzes the connections between high unemployment among young urban African Americans and the schools they attend, the neighborhoods they live in, their beliefs about work and education, their family circumstances, and employers' views of them as potential employees. In his books, he combines quantitative and qualitative data to portray the lives of young African Americans in a way that is extremely lively, insightful, and enlightening. Wilson's quantitative data provide the reader with a clear understanding of the overall pattern of young people's lives in urban areas, but at the same time his qualitative examples bring to life the individual perspectives and circumstances of the people he studies. We will learn more about Wilson's studies, especially in Chapter 11 on work.

Ethnographic Research Another way scholars have learned about adolescence and emerging adulthood is through **ethnographic research** (Jessor, Colby, & Shweder, 1996). In ethnographic research, scholars spend a considerable amount of time among the people they wish to study, often by actually living among them. Information gained in ethnographic research typically comes from scholars' observations, experiences, and conversations with the people they are studying. Ethnographic research is commonly used by anthropologists, usually in studying non-Western cultures. Anthropologists usually report the results of their research in an **ethnography**, a book that presents an anthropologist's observations of what life is like in a particular culture.

The first ethnography on adolescence was written by Margaret Mead (1928). Mead studied the people of Samoa, a group of islands in the South Pacific. One of the inspirations of her study was to see whether the "storm and stress" said by G. Stanley Hall to be typical of American adolescents would also be present in a non-Western culture where life was much different than in American society. She reported that, contrary to Hall's claim that adolescent storm and stress is biologically based and therefore universal, most adolescents in Samoa passed through adolescence smoothly, with little sign of turmoil or upheaval.

After Mead's ethnography of Samoan adolescence, several decades passed before anthropologists gave much attention to adolescence. However, in the 1980s, two eminent anthropologists at Harvard University, Beatrice and John Whiting, set out to remedy this neglect. They initiated the **Harvard Adolescence Project**, in which they sent young

qualitative Data that is collected in verbal rather than numerical form, usually in interviews.

quantitative Data that is collected in numerical form, usually on questionnaires.

ethnographic research Research in which scholars spend a considerable amount of time among the people they wish to study, usually living among them.

ethnography A book that presents an anthropologist's observations of what life is like in a particular culture.

Harvard Adolescence Project Project initiated by Beatrice and John Whiting of Harvard University in the 1980s, in which they sent young scholars to do ethnographic research in seven different cultures in various parts of the world.

scholars to do ethnographic research in seven different cultures in various parts of the world: the Inuit (Eskimos) of the Canadian Arctic; Aborigines in northern Australia; Muslims in Thailand; the Kikuyu of Kenya; the Ijo of Nigeria; rural Romania; and Morocco.

The project produced a series of extremely interesting and enlightening ethnographies (Burbank, 1988; Condon, 1987; Davis & Davis, 1989; Hollos & Leis, 1989). These ethnographies show the enormous variation that exists in the nature of adolescence in cultures around the world. I will be drawing from these ethnographies often in the course of the book.

Biological Measurement The biological changes of puberty are a central part of adolescent development, so research on adolescence includes measurement of biological functioning. One area of this research has focused on the timing and pace of different aspects of physical development during puberty, such as genital changes and the growth of pubic hair. Several decades ago a British physician, J. M. Tanner, conducted a series of studies that carefully monitored adolescents' physical changes and established valid information about the timing and sequence of these changes (Eveleth & Tanner, 1976; Tanner, 1962). More recently, scholars have conducted research measuring hormonal levels at various points during adolescence and looking at the ways hormonal levels are related to adolescents' moods and behavior (e.g., McBurnett et al., 2005; Susman, 1997; Susman, Dorn, & Schiefelbein, 2003). There has also been a recent surge of interest in research on adolescent brain functioning (Paus, 2008). We will examine biological research on adolescence in various chapters of the book, especially Chapter 2 (Biological Foundations).

Experimental Research An approach used in many kinds of scientific research is the **experimental research method** (Salkind, 2003). In the simplest form of this design, two groups of participants are randomly selected from a population, with one group (the **experimental group**) receiving a treatment of some kind and the other group (the **control group**) receiving no treatment. Because participants were randomly assigned to either the experimental group or the control group, it can be reasonably assumed that the two groups did not differ prior to the experiment. Following the treatment of the experimental group, the two groups are given a posttest, and any differences between the two groups are attributed to the treatment.

The experimental research method is frequently used in media research. For example, in one study African American adolescents aged 11–16 were randomly assigned to an exper-

imental group that viewed rap videos or a control group that did not (Johnson, Adams, Ashburn, & Reed, 1995). Following the experimental group's treatment—their exposure to the rap videos—both groups responded to a story about teen dating violence. It was found that in the posttest, girls (but not boys) in the experimental group showed greater acceptance of dating violence than girls in the control group.

Another area of adolescent research for which the experimental research method is commonly used is **interventions**. Interventions are programs intended to change the attitudes or behavior of the participants. For example, a variety of programs have been developed to prevent adolescents from starting to smoke cigarettes, by promoting critical thinking about cigarette advertising or by attempting to change attitudes associating smoking with peer acceptance (e.g., Horn, Dino, Kalsekar, & Mody, 2005). The adolescents participating in such a study are randomly assigned to either the experimental group receiving the intervention or the control group that does not receive the intervention. After the intervention, the two groups are assessed for their attitudes and behavior regarding smoking. If the intervention worked, the attitudes or behavior of the experimental group should be less favorable toward smoking than those of the control group.

Natural Experiments Experiments are in many ways the scientific ideal, because they allow scientists to identify cause and effect with some precision. In the experiment just described, by assigning adolescents randomly to the experimental group or the control group and then exposing only the experimental group to the antismoking intervention, the results provide definite evidence of whether or not the intervention caused changes to occur in attitudes and behavior related to smoking. However, many of the most important questions scholars seek to answer regarding adolescence and emerging adulthood cannot be answered through these kinds of experiments. For example, although many scholars are interested in how school quality influences adolescents' learning, they cannot assign adolescents randomly to high-quality or low-quality schools, for obvious ethical reasons.

Because scholars usually cannot control the environments adolescents and emerging adults experience, they sometimes take advantage of **natural experiments**. A natural experiment is a situation that exists naturally—in other words, the researcher does not control the situation—but that provides interesting scientific information to the perceptive observer. For example, although scholars cannot assign adolescents randomly to schools of high or low quality, they can assess adolescents' learning before and after they experience schools that are of high or low quality, thus taking advantage of a natural experiment to learn more about

experimental research method A research method that entails assigning participants randomly to an experimental group that received a treatment and a control group that does not receive the treatment, then comparing the two groups in a posttest.

experimental group In experimental research, the group that receives the treatment.

control group In experimental research, the group that does not receive the treatment.

interventions Programs intended to change the attitudes and/or behavior of the participants.

natural experiment A situation that occurs naturally but that provides interesting scientific information to the perceptive observer.

Monozygotic (MZ) twins can be used in research as participants in a natural experiment, because they have exactly the same genotype.

the influence of school quality (e.g., Brand et al., 2003; Rutter, 1983).

One important natural experiment used in the study of adolescents and emerging adults is adoption. The question of how genes and environment interact in development is of great interest to scholars who study adolescent and emerging adults, and adoption provides important insights into this question. Unlike in most families, children in adoptive families are raised by adults with whom they have no biological relationship. Because one set of parents provides the child's genes and a different set of parents provides the environment, it is possible to examine the relative contributions of genes and environment to the child's development. Similarities between adoptive parents and adopted children are likely to be due to the environment provided by the parents, because the parents and children are biologically unrelated. Similarities between adopted children and their biological parents are likely to be due to genetics, because the environment the children grew up in was not provided by the biological parents. One surprising result of adoption studies on intelligence is that adoptees are actually *less* similar to their adoptive parents in adolescence than they were in childhood, even though they have lived with them longer (McGue, 2008). Chapter 3, on cognitive development, presents more on this intriguing research.

Twin studies are another type of natural experiment. Identical or **monozygotic (MZ) twins** have exactly the same genotype, whereas fraternal or **dizygotic (DZ) twins** have about half their genotype in common, the same as other siblings. By comparing the degree of similarity in MZ compared to DZ twins, we gain information about the extent to which a characteristic is genetically based. If MZ twins are more similar on a characteristic than DZ twins are, this may be due to genetics, since MZ twins are more genetically similar.

Throughout the book, I will present studies using a wide variety of methods. For now, the methods just described provide you with an introduction to the approaches used most often.

Analysis and Interpretation

Once the data for a study have been collected using methods of one kind or another, statistical analyses are usually conducted to examine relationships between different parts of the data. Often, the analyses are determined by the hypotheses that generated the study. For example, a researcher studying adolescents' relationships with parents may hypothesize, based on a theory or on past research, that adolescents are closer to their mothers than to their fathers, then test that hypothesis with a statistical analysis comparing the quality of adolescents' relationships with mothers and with fathers.

Once the data are analyzed, they must be interpreted. When scientists write up the results of their study for publication in a scientific journal, they interpret the results of the study in light of relevant theories and previous research. One of the key issues in interpreting research is the issue of **correlation versus causation**. A correlation is a predictable relationship between two variables: Knowing one of the variables allows you to predict the other with some degree of accuracy. But just because two variables are correlated does not mean that one causes the other.

Consider an example. In studies of adolescent work, a negative correlation is typically found between hours worked and commitment to school (Barling & Kelloway, 1999). That is, the more adolescents work, the less committed to school they tend to be. But whether this correlation also means causation requires interpretation. One possible interpretation is that working many hours causes adolescents to be less committed to school. Another possible interpretation is that being less committed to school causes adolescents to work more hours. It is also possible that both high work hours and low commitment to school are caused by a third variable: a relatively low IQ, or a personality high in sensation seeking, or growing up in a low-income family. Although the issue of correlation versus causation can be unraveled to some extent by using a **longitudinal study** design that follows adolescents over time, and by considering the results of other studies that have asked similar questions in different ways, the conclusions drawn also depend on the judgment of the scholars who are interpreting the data. Misinterpreting correlation as causation is a mistake made frequently, even by scientists, as we will see in the course of this book.

monozygotic (MZ) twins Twins with exactly the same genotype. Also known as identical twins.

dizygotic (DZ) twins Twins with about half their genotype in common, the same as for other siblings. Also known as fraternal twins.

correlation versus causation A correlation is a predictable relationship between two variables, such that knowing one of the variables makes it possible to predict the other. However, just because two variables are correlated does not mean that one causes the other.

longitudinal study A study in which data is collected from the participants on more than one occasion.

THINKING CRITICALLY •••

From your daily life, think of an example of how you or people you know may have mistaken correlation for causation. Then think of how you would design a study to show whether or not causation is truly involved.

Once a scholar writes a manuscript describing the methods used, the results of the statistical analyses, and the interpretation of the results, the scholar typically submits the manuscript to a professional journal. The editor of the journal then sends the manuscript out for review by other scholars. In other words, the manuscript is **peer-reviewed** for its scientific accuracy and credibility and for the importance of its contribution to the field. The editor relies on the reviews by the scholars' peers in deciding whether or not to accept the manuscript for publication. If the editor determines that the manuscript has passed the peer-review process successfully, the article is published in the journal. Some of the journals that publish peer-reviewed articles on adolescence and emerging adulthood are *Journal of Adolescent Research, Youth & Society, Journal of Adolescence, Journal of Youth Studies, Journal of Youth & Adolescence,* and *Journal of Research on Adolescence.* In addition to research articles, most journals publish occasional theoretical articles and review articles that integrate findings from numerous other studies. Scholars studying adolescence and emerging adulthood also publish the results of their research in books, and often these books go through the peer-review process.

THINKING CRITICALLY •••

Choose a topic on adolescence and emerging adulthood that you would be interested in studying. Which methodological approach would you use, and why?

Theories and Research

A crucial part of the scientific process in any field is the development of theories. A good theory presents a set of interconnected ideas in an original and insightful way and points the way to further research. Theories and research are intrinsically connected: A theory generates hypotheses that can be tested in research, and research leads to modifications of the theory, which generate further hypotheses and further research. A good example of this is G. Stanley Hall's storm and stress theory. His theory has generated a great deal of re-

search in the past century; in turn, this research has resulted in modifications of his theory because it showed that storm and stress was not as extreme and was not universal in adolescence as he had proposed. Research still continues on the questions his theory provoked, such as the extent to which conflict with parents is common in adolescence (Arnett, 1999a; Laursen, Coy, & Collins, 1998).

This book includes no separate chapter on theories, not because I do not think theories are important but because I think theories and research are intrinsically connected and should be presented together. Theories are presented in every chapter in relation to the research they have generated and the questions they have raised for future research. However, in the next section I present an outline of a cultural theory of development that applies to a wide range of topics.

Bronfenbrenner's Ecological Theory

One important cultural theory is Urie Bronfenbrenner's **ecological theory** of human development (Bronfenbrenner, 1980, 1998, 2000, 2005). Bronfenbrenner presented his theory as a reaction to what he viewed as an overemphasis in developmental psychology on the immediate environment, especially the mother-child relationship. The immediate environment is important, Bronfenbrenner argued, but much more than this is involved in children's development. Bronfenbrenner's theory was intended to draw attention to the broader cultural environment that people experience as they develop, and to the ways the different levels of a person's environment interact. In recent writings (Bronfenbrenner, 2000, 2005; Bronfenbrenner & Morris, 1998), Bronfenbrenner added a biological dimension to his framework and termed it a "bioecological theory," but the distinctive contribution of the theory remains in its portrayal of the cultural environment.

According to Bronfenbrenner, five key levels or *systems* play a part in human development (see Figure 1.3):

- The **microsystem** is Bronfenbrenner's term for the immediate environment, the settings where people experience their daily lives. This is where the person's direct interactions and relationships take place. Microsystems in most cultures include relationships with each parent, with siblings, and perhaps with extended family (if any live in close proximity and are seen on a regular basis); with peers/friends; with teachers; and with other adults (such

---

peer-reviewed When a scholarly article or book is evaluated by a scholar's peers (i.e., other scholars) for scientific credibility and importance.

ecological theory Urie Bronfenbrenner's sociocultural theory of human development, with five interrelated systems: the microsystem (the immediate environment), the mesosystem (connections between microsystems), the exosystem (institutions such as schools and community organizations), the macrosystem (the overarching system of cultural beliefs and values), and the chronosystem (the changes in the individual and the cultural environment over time).

microsystem Bronfenbrenner's term for the settings where people experience their daily lives, including relationships with parents, siblings, peers/friends, teachers, and employers.

context The environmental settings in which development takes place.

as coaches, religious leaders, and employers). Bronfenbrenner emphasizes that the child is an *active* agent in the microsystems; for example, children are affected by their parents but children's behavior affects their parents as well; children are affected by their friends but they also make choices about whom to have as friends. The microsystem is where most research in developmental psychology has focused; today, however, most developmental psychologists use the term **context** rather than microsystem to refer to immediate environmental settings.

- The **mesosystem** is the network of interconnections between the various microsystems. For example, a child who is experiencing abusive treatment from parents may become difficult to handle in relationships with teachers; or, if a parent's employer demands longer hours in the workplace, the parent's relationship with the child may be affected.

- The **exosystem** refers to the societal institutions that have indirect but potentially important influences on development. In Bronfenbrenner's theory, these institutions include schools, religious institutions, and media. For example, in Asian countries such as South Korea, competition to get into college is intense and depends chiefly on adolescents' performance on a national exam at the end of high school; consequently, the high school years are a period of extreme academic stress.

- The **macrosystem** is the broad system of cultural beliefs and values, and the economic and governmental systems that are built on those beliefs and values. For example, in countries such as Iran and Saudi Arabia, cultural beliefs and values are based in the religion of Islam, and the economic and governmental systems of those countries are also based on the teachings of Islam. In contrast, in the West, beliefs in the value of individual freedom are reflected in a free market economic system and in governmental systems of representative democracy.

- Finally, the **chronosystem** refers to changes that occur in developmental circumstances over time, both with respect to individual development and to historical changes. For example, with respect to individual development, losing your job is a much different experience at 15 than it would be at 45; with respect to historical changes, the occupational opportunities open to young women in many countries are much broader than they were half a century ago.

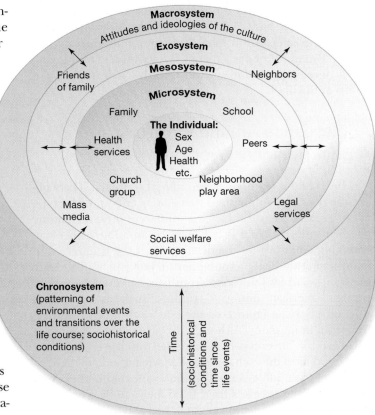

FIGURE 1.3 Bronfenbrenner's ecological theory.
Source: Feldman (2006).

There are many characteristics of Bronfenbrenner's ecological theory that make it important and useful for the cultural approach that will be taken in this book. Many developmental theories make no mention of culture, but culture is an important component of Bronfenbrenner's theory. He recognizes that cultural beliefs and values are the basis for many of the other conditions of children's development. Furthermore, his theory recognizes the importance of historical changes as influences on development, as we will here. Also, Bronfenbrenner emphasized that children and adolescents are active participants in their development, not merely the passive recipients of external influences, and that view will be stressed throughout this book as well.

Some parts of the theory will be addressed differently in this book. I think media play a more central and direct role in development than they do in Bronfenbrenner's theory,

mesosystem In Bronfenbrenner's ecological theory, the network of interconnections between the microsystems.

exosystem In Bronfenbrenner's ecological theory, societal institutions such as schools, religious institutions, systems of government, and media.

macrosystem In Bronfenbrenner's ecological theory, the broad system of cultural beliefs and values, and the economic and governmental systems that are built on those beliefs and values.

chronosystem In Bronfenbrenner's ecological theory, changes that occur in developmental circumstances over time, both with respect to individual development and to historical changes.

and I would emphasize the macrosystem of cultural beliefs and values as the basis of the rest of the socialization environment to a greater extent than Bronfenbrenner does. Nevertheless, Bronfenbrenner's theory is a useful way of thinking about development, and we will refer back to it at various points in the book.

Adolescence Around the World: A Brief Regional Overview

The heart of this textbook is the cultural approach. Throughout the book it is emphasized that adolescents and emerging adults around the world have very different lives, depending on their culture. What it is like to be an adolescent or an emerging adult in the American middle class is different in many ways from being a young person in Egypt, or Thailand, or Brazil—and also different from being a young person in certain American minority cultures, such as the urban African American culture or the culture of recent Mexican American immigrants. Although the physical changes of puberty are similar everywhere, cultures differ greatly in how they respond to these changes and in what they allow and expect from their adolescents. Cultural context underlies every aspect of young people's lives, from their family relations to their school participation to their sexuality to their media use. As background for understanding the cultural material presented in the chapters to come, here is a brief overview of the cultural context of adolescence in the major regions of the world.

Sub-Saharan Africa

Africa has been described as "a rich continent whose people are poor" (Nsamenang, 1998). The countries of Africa are extremely rich in natural resources such as oil, gold, and diamonds. Unfortunately, due to exploitation by the West in the 19th century followed by corruption, waste, and war in the 20th century, this natural wealth has not yet translated into economic prosperity for the people of Africa. On the contrary, sub-Saharan Africa has the worst performance of any region of the world on virtually every measure of living standards, including income per person, access to clean water, life expectancy, and prevalence of disease (United Nations Development Programme, 2009). Consequently, adolescents in Africa face challenges to their physical health and survival that are more formidable than in any other region of the world.

Although the problems facing young people in Africa are daunting, there are some bright spots, too. In the past decade, the civil wars that flared in many countries in the 1990s died down. Several African governments, most notably South Africa, moved toward more open, stable, and democratic gov-

African adolescents often care for younger siblings.

ernments. Recent economic growth in Africa has been among the strongest of any world region (Zakaria, 2008). There is hope that these positive changes will endure and provide Africa's adolescents with a more promising future.

African cultures also have strengths in their tradition of large families and strong, supportive family relationships (Nsamenang, 2010). In nearly all other regions of the world, birth rates have fallen steadily in recent decades and most women have only one or two children. However, in Africa the current birth rate is five children per woman (Population Reference Bureau, 2009). Consequently, African adolescents typically have many siblings, and they often have responsibilities for caring for their younger siblings. In adolescence and beyond, African siblings have close ties of mutual obligation and support (Nsamenang, 2007).

North Africa and the Middle East

In North Africa and the Middle East, the Muslim religion is the predominant influence on all aspects of cultural life. The strength of Islam varies from countries in which all government policies are based on Islamic principles and texts (e.g., Kuwait and Saudi Arabia) to countries in which the influence of Islam is strong but a semblance of democracy and diversity of opinion also exist (e.g., Jordan and Morocco).

Patriarchal authority—in which the father's authority in the family is to be obeyed unquestioningly—has a long tradi-

---

patriarchal authority Cultural belief in the absolute authority of the father over his wife and children.

chador or **burka** A garment that covers the hair and most of the face, worn by many girls and women in Muslim societies.

filial piety Confucian belief, common in many Asian societies, that children are obligated to respect, obey, and revere their parents, especially the father.

Adolescents in North Africa and the Middle East blend Islamic traditions with modern ways.

Asian cultures such as Japan strongly emphasize education.

tion in the cultures of North Africa and the Middle East and is supported by Islam (Booth, 2002). Discussion of family rules in Muslim families is uncommon. Even to suggest such a thing would be considered an unacceptable affront to the authority of the parents, especially the father.

Part of the tradition of patriarchal authority is the dominance of men over women. Islamic societies have a long tradition of keeping tight control over women's appearance and behavior. In many Islamic societies girls and women are required to wear a **chador** or **burka**, which are garments that cover the hair and part or all of the face and body. Muslim girls and women are often expected to wear these garments in public as a way of being modest, beginning at puberty. In some Islamic societies, women are not allowed to go out of the house unless accompanied by a male (Booth, 2002). Virginity before marriage is highly prized, and violation of this taboo can result in the most severe punishments, even death (Constable, 2000). Although in many Muslim countries young women exceed young men in educational attainment (UNDP, 2009), in adulthood women are generally discouraged from working outside the home. Consequently, adolescent girls in many countries in North Africa and the Middle East face sharply limited opportunities in adulthood.

Although the cultures of North Africa and the Middle East are deeply rooted in Islamic traditions, they are changing in response to globalization. Many young people in this region today are highly attracted to the popular culture and information technologies of the West (e.g., Booth, 2002; Davis & Davis, 1989, 2007). Nevertheless, Islam currently remains strong, even among the young, and the strength of fundamentalist Islam is growing.

Asia

Asia comprises a vast and diverse area, ranging from countries that are highly industrialized (e.g., Japan) to countries that have recently industrialized (e.g., South Korea) to countries that are rapidly industrializing (e.g., China). Nevertheless, these countries share certain common characteristics and challenges.

The cultures of Asia have been profoundly influenced by Confucianism, a set of beliefs and precepts attributed to the philosopher Confucius, who lived around 550 to 480 B.C. One of the tenets of Confucianism is **filial piety**, which holds that children should respect, obey, and revere their parents, especially the father. Part of filial piety is the expectation that the children, in particular the oldest son, have the responsibility of caring for their parents when the parents become elderly (Nelson et al., 2004). Consequently, Asian adolescents are more likely than adolescents in other parts of the world to have a grandparent living in their household (Stevenson & Zusho, 2002).

The Confucian tradition places a strong emphasis on education, which is one of the reasons for the intense focus on education in the lives of young people in Asian cultures today. As we will see in Chapter 10, high school tends to present strong pressures for young people in Asian societies, because performance on college entrance exams largely determines their path through adult life. This system is facing increasing criticism within Asian societies by those who argue that young people should not be subjected to such pressure at a young age and should be allowed more time for fun (Lee & Larson, 2000; Nelson & Chen, 2007).

India

Geographically, India is part of Asia, but it is has such a large population (over a billion people) and a distinctive cultural tradition that it merits separate attention here. Unlike the rest of Asia, India's cultural tradition is based not in Confucianism but in the Hindu religion. However, India also has the second largest Muslim population in the world (after Indonesia), nearly 300 million.

India is one of the few countries in the world that does not have compulsory education for children or adolescents (Chaudhary & Sharma, 2007; Verma & Saraswathi, 2002). Consequently, many young people are illiterate, especially girls in rural areas. Many parents do not believe girls should be educated beyond a minimal ability to write letters and keep household accounts. Rural areas in India have relatively few schools, and those that exist tend to be poorly funded and staffed by teachers who are poorly trained. Access to education is much higher in urban areas, for girls as well as boys. In its urban areas India also has a large number of highly educated emerging adults, especially in fields such as medicine and information technologies, and they have made

Many Indian adolescents work in manufacturing jobs such as carpet weaving.

Educational attainment is increasing among adolescents in Latin America.

India a world economic leader in these areas (Chaudhary & Sharma, 2007).

Also contributing to high illiteracy in India is widespread child and adolescent labor, with jobs ranging from carpet weaving to mines, cigarette manufacturing, and gem polishing, often in extremely unsafe and unhealthy conditions (Burra, 1997; ILO, 2002). Parents often prefer to have their children and adolescents working, and thus contributing to the family income, rather than attending school. Consequently, the government has taken few steps to restrict child and adolescent labor.

A distinctive feature of Indian culture is the **caste system**. According to this tradition, people are believed to be born into a particular caste based on their moral and spiritual conduct in their previous life (reincarnation is central to the Hindu beliefs held by most Indians). A person's caste then determines his or her status in Indian society. Only persons of elite castes are considered to be eligible for positions of wealth and power. Persons of lower castes are considered worthy only of the lowest paying, dirtiest, lowest status jobs. Also, marrying outside one's caste is strongly discouraged. Adolescents from lower castes are less likely to attend school than adolescents from higher castes, which restricts the jobs available to them as adults (Verma & Saraswathi, 2000).

Family relations are notably strong and warm in Indian families. Adolescents in India spend most of their leisure time with their families rather than with their friends, and

they are happiest when with their families (Larson et al., 2000). Even highly educated emerging adults in India often prefer to have their parents arrange their marriage, which shows how deeply they trust and rely on their parents (Reddy & Gibbons, 2002). Indian families are discussed in further detail in Chapter 5.

Latin America

Latin America comprises a vast land area of diverse cultures but they share a common history of colonization by southern European powers, particularly Spain, and a common allegiance to the Roman Catholic religion. For young people in Latin America, two of the key issues for the 21st century are political stability and economic growth (Galambos & Martinez, 2007). For many decades, the countries of Latin America have experienced repeated episodes of political and economic instability, but today prospects look somewhat brighter. Although political instability continues in some countries, for the most part Latin American countries have now established stable democracies. Economically, too, the situation has improved in recent years in most of Latin America. However unemployment among adults is high throughout Latin America, and unemployment among young people is even higher, often exceeding 25% (Galambos & Martinez, 2007; Welti, 2002).

If the recent trend of political stability can be sustained, economic growth in Latin America is likely to improve. Young people in Latin America are obtaining increased education, which should help prepare them for the increasingly information-based global economy. Also, the birth rate in this region has declined sharply in the past two decades, and consequently the children who are now growing up should face less competition in the job market as they enter adolescence and emerging adulthood (Galambos & Martinez, 2007).

The West

"The West" is less a regional grouping than a cultural grouping that refers to the countries of Europe, the United States, Canada, Australia, and New Zealand. Western countries are notably stable, democratic, and affluent. Young people in the

caste system Hindu belief that people are born into a particular caste based on their moral and spiritual conduct in their previous life. A person's caste then determines their status in Indian society.

In the West, adolescents' leisure is often media-based.

"Hungarians, Czechoslovaks and Bulgarians try to imitate everything that is American—and I mean *EVERYTHING*.... If we keep going like this, our small countries will gradually lose their national cultures."

—Miklos Vamos, Hungarian Journalist, 1994

West generally have access to opportunities for secondary and higher education, and they can choose from a wide range of occupations (Arnett, 2002b). Most young people in the West have a wide range of leisure opportunities. In contrast to adolescents in other regions of the world, adolescents in the West spend most of their time (outside school) in leisure with their friends, rather than studying or working for their families. A substantial proportion of their leisure is media-based, including television, computer games, text messaging, listening to portable music, and using social networking websites such as MySpace and Facebook.

Although young people in Western countries are obtaining increased education, with many of them remaining in school through their early 20s, educational opportunities are not evenly distributed in most Western countries (Arnett, 2002b). Emerging adults in minority groups often obtain higher education at rates considerably lower than emerging adults in the majority cultures (National Center for Education Statistics [NCES], 2009). Unemployment is also high among emerging adults in Western countries, especially among minorities (Sneeding & Phillips, 2002). Throughout Western countries, young minorities are disadvantaged in the workplace in part because of lower levels of education and training and in part because of prejudice and discrimination from the majority (Kracke et al., 1998; Liebkind & Kosonen, 1998).

Implications of Cultural Context

The overview I have just presented gives a brief look at the cultural contexts of adolescence and emerging adulthood, and you will be learning a lot more about young people's lives in different parts of the world in the course of the book. However, even this general overview shows you how different it is to be an adolescent or emerging adult depending on where in the world you live. Adolescents in some cultures are likely to be in school for most of a typical day through their teens and even into emerging adulthood; adolescents in other cultures begin working early in life and have little chance of obtaining education beyond grade school. Adolescents in some cultures grow up as part of a large extended family; adolescents in other cultures grow up in a small nuclear family and may not even have

a sibling. Emerging adults in some cultures have a wide range of occupational possibilities; for emerging adults in other cultures the range is narrow or nonexistent, as lack of education leaves them unprepared for any but the most unskilled labor, or, for young women, as cultural beliefs about women's roles exclude them from the workplace.

This is why cultural context is essential to a full understanding of the adolescent and emerging adult experience. Throughout the book, I will present examples from many different cultures for each topic we address. In each chapter I also present a box called Cultural Focus, which looks in more detail at one particular culture with respect to the topic of the chapter. In addition, I often critique research from a cultural perspective. By the time you finish this book I would like you to be able to *think culturally*, so that you can analyze and critique research for whether it does or does not take culture into account.

Other Themes of the Book

In additon to the cultural approach, a number of other themes will be part of every chapter: historical contrasts, the interdisciplinary approach, gender issues, and globalization.

Historical Contrasts

In the same way that we can learn a lot about adolescence and emerging adulthood from comparing different cultures, we can also learn a great deal by comparing the lives of adolescents and emerging adults today to the lives of their counterparts in other times. Throughout the book, I provide historical information on each of the topics we discuss. Also, each chapter has a box entitled Historical Focus that provides more detailed information on a specific issue in a specific historical period.

Interdisciplinary Approach

Most scholars studying adolescence and emerging adulthood are psychologists. They have been trained in psychology, and they work as professors in the psychology departments of colleges and universities. However, many scholars in other disciplines also study adolescence and emerging adulthood. Anthropology's recent studies we have already discussed. Sociology has a long tradition of scholarship on adolescence and emerging adulthood, including some of the most important studies in such areas as peer relations, delinquency, and the transition to adulthood. Physicians, especially psychiatrists and pediatricians, have also made important contributions, most notably concerning the biology of adolescence and emerging adulthood and the treatment of psychological disorders that may occur during these age periods, such as depression. Scholars in education have contributed insightful work on adolescents' and emerging adults' development in relation to school, as well as other topics. In recent decades historians have published a number of excellent studies on adolescence and emerging adulthood.

The boundaries we set up between different disciplines are useful in some ways, but they are essentially artificial. If you want to understand development in adolescence and emerging adulthood, you should seek insights wherever you can find them. I want you to have as full an understanding of adolescence and emerging adulthood as possible by the time you finish this book, and toward that goal I will use material from psychology, anthropology, sociology, education, history, and other disciplines.

Gender Issues

In every culture, gender is a key issue in development throughout the life span (Carroll & Wolpe, 2005; Hatfield & Rapson, 2006). The expectations cultures have for males and females are different from the time they are born. Children become aware of their own gender by the time they are about 2 years old, and with this awareness they grow sensitive to the differences in what is considered appropriate behavior for each gender. Differences in cultural expectations related to gender typically become more pronounced at puberty. Adolescence and emerging adulthood are, among other things, periods of preparation for taking on adult roles in the family and in work. In most cultures, these roles differ considerably depending on whether you are male or female, so the expectations for male and female adolescents and emerging adults differ accordingly. Expected behaviors in the courtship and sexual behavior that are typically part of adolescence and emerging adulthood also differ considerably between males and females in most cultures.

Although all cultures have different expectations for males and females, the degree of the differences varies greatly among cultures. In the majority cultures of the West these days, the differences are relatively blurred: Men and women hold many of the same jobs, wear many of the same clothes (e.g., blue jeans, T-shirts), and enjoy many of the same entertainments. If you have grown up in the West, you may be surprised to learn how deep gender differences go in many other cultures. For example, in Morocco, boys are more or less expected to become sexually experienced before marriage (Davis & Davis, 1989, 2007). Girls, on the other hand, are expected to be virgins on their wedding night. Thus, the boys' first sexual experience is typically with a prostitute. The morning after a wedding, bride and groom are obliged to hang the sheet from their bed out the window, complete with a bloody stain on it to prove that the girl's hymen was broken on the wedding night, confirming that she had been a virgin until that time.

Although nothing comparable to this exists in the West, there are gender-specific expectations in the West, too. Even now, there are few male nurses or secretaries or full-time fathers, and there are few female truck drivers or engineers or U.S. senators. The differences in expectations for males and females may be more subtle in the West than in some other cultures, but they remain powerful, and they are a key part of adolescence and emerging adulthood. Throughout the book, I bring up gender differences for each of the topics we address, and Chapter 5 is devoted specifically to gender issues. By the end of the book, I want you to have a broader sense of how males and females are treated differently in cultures around the world, and of how your own culture has shaped your development in gender-specific ways you may not have realized before now.

Globalization

Researchers on adolescence have recently begun giving more attention to cultural influences on development in adolescence and emerging adulthood. However, this attention to culture comes at a time in world history when the boundaries that give cultures their distinctiveness are becoming steadily fainter (Arnett, 2002a; Fukuyama, 1993; Zakaria, 2008), and the world is becoming increasingly integrated into a global culture—a "global village," as the social philosopher Marshall McLuhan put it some years ago. No traditional culture has remained exempt from these changes. You can go to the remotest rain forest culture in Venezuela, the northernmost Arctic village in Canada, or the smallest mountain village of New Guinea, and you will find that every one of them is being drawn inexorably into a common world culture. Our exploration of development in adolescence and emerging adulthood would not be complete without an account of these changes, which reflect the **globalization** of adolescence and emerging adulthood (Arnett, 2002a; Larson et al., 2010).

Globalization means that increasing worldwide technological and economic integration is making the world "smaller," more homogeneous. As a consequence of the globalization of adolescence and emerging adulthood, young people around the world experience increasingly similar environments. Adolescents and emerging adults in many parts of the world are growing up listening to much of the same music, watching many of the same movies, going to school for an increasing number of years, learning how to use personal computers, drinking the same soft drinks, and wearing the same brands of blue jeans. The appeal of being connected to a global culture appears to be especially high among adolescents and emerging adults (Arnett, 2002a; Schlegel,

---

globalization Increasing worldwide technological and economic integration, which is making different parts of the world increasingly connected and increasingly similar culturally.

bicultural Having an identity that includes aspects of two different cultures.

resilience Overcoming adverse environmental circumstances to achieve healthy development.

The globalization of adolescence: A Venezuelan adolescent's T-shirt depicts characters from the American TV show *The Simpsons*.

1998, 2000). Perhaps this is because they are more capable than children of seeking out information beyond the borders of their own culture—through travel and the Internet, for example—and are less committed to established roles and a set way of life than adults are.

THINKING CRITICALLY •••

Have you traveled to another country in recent years? If so, can you think of examples you have witnessed that reflect the globalization of adolescence? If not, can you think of examples you have read about or heard about? What positive and negative consequences do you anticipate from the globalization of adolescence?

Globalization does not mean that young people everywhere are growing up in exactly the same way or becoming exactly alike in their cultural identity. The more typical pattern worldwide is that young people are becoming increasingly **bicultural** in their identities, with one identity for participation in their local culture and one identity for participation in the global culture (Arnett, 2002a), for example through e-mail or in interactions with foreign visitors. It

should also be noted that although many young people participate eagerly in the global culture, other adolescents and emerging adults are at the forefront of growing resistance to globalization, for example in protests against the actions of the World Bank and the International Monetary Fund (Arnett, 2002a; Welti, 2002).

Throughout the book, I present examples of how globalization is affecting the lives of adolescents and emerging adults. We will consider how this trend is likely to affect their futures in both positive and negative ways.

Framework of the Book

Following this introductory chapter, the book is divided into three sections. The first section, Foundations, includes chapters on five different areas of development: Biological Foundations, Cognitive Foundations, Cultural Beliefs, Gender, and The Self. These chapters describe the areas that form the foundation for young people's development across a variety of aspects of their lives. Together, these chapters form the basis for understanding development as it takes place in various contexts.

Thus, the first section sets the stage for the second section, called Contexts. Context is the term scholars use to refer to the environmental settings in which development takes place. This section has chapters on six different contexts: Family Relationships; Friends and Peers; Love and Sexuality; School; Work; and Media.

The third section is entitled Problems and Resilience. The sole chapter in this section addresses problems ranging from risky automobile driving to drug use to depression. It also examines **resilience**, which is the ability of children and adolescents who are at-risk for problems to avoid falling prey to those risks.

SUMMING UP

This chapter has introduced you to the central ideas and concepts that we will be considering throughout the rest of the book. The following summarizes the key points we have discussed:

- The cultural approach taken in this book means that adolescence and emerging adulthood will be portrayed as being culturally constructed; cultures determine what the experience of these age periods is like. It will be emphasized that what it is like to be an adolescent or an emerging adult varies widely among cultures.

- Adolescence has a long history in Western societies as a specific period of life between childhood and adulthood. However, it was only during the years 1890–1920 that adolescence developed into its modern form, as a period of life when young people are largely excluded from adult work and spend their time mostly among their peers.

- *Emerging adulthood* is the term for the period from ages 18 to 25. The distinctive characteristics of this age period are that it is the age of identity explorations, the age of instability, the self-focused age, the age of feeling in-between, and the age of possibilities.

- The scientific method includes standards of hypotheses, sampling, procedure, method, analysis, and interpretation. A variety of specific methods for data collection are used in the study of adolescence and emerging adulthood, ranging from questionnaires and interviews to ethnographic research to experimental research.

- Bronfenbrenner's ecological theory emphasizes the cultural environment that people experience as they develop and the ways the different levels of a person's environment interact. There are five levels or *systems* in the theory: microsystem, mesosystem, exosystem, macrosystem, and chronosystem.

- The cultural context of adolescence and emerging adulthood varies widely by world regions. These cultural differences influence a variety of aspects of development in adolescence and emerging adulthood, from physical health to education and work to family relationships.

- The book is divided into three major sections: Foundations, Contexts, and Problems and Resilience.

In each chapter, this Summing Up section briefly restates the main points of the chapter and then offers some reflections on what we know at this point and what we have yet to learn.

The study of adolescence and emerging adulthood is relatively new. Adolescence has been established as a distinct field only since G. Stanley Hall's work was published a century ago; emerging adulthood is only just now becoming a distinct area of study. As you will see in the chapters to come, a remarkable amount has already been learned about these age periods. However, so far most research has focused on young people in the American majority culture. That focus is now broadening to include other groups in American society as well as young people in other cultures around the world. One goal of this book is to make you familiar with research on adolescence and emerging adulthood in many different cultures, so that you will be able to take a cultural approach in your own understanding of how young people develop during these years.

KEY TERMS

adolescence 2
life-cycle service 3
youth 4
culture 5
the West 5
industrialized countries 5
American majority culture 5
society 5
traditional culture 5
developing countries 5
socioeconomic status (SES) 5
young people 5
child study movement 6
recapitulation 6
storm and stress 6
national survey 7
survey 7
stratified sampling 7
random sample 7
menarche 8
emerging adulthood 8
Lamarckian 10
early adolescence 10
late adolescence 10

individualism 12
collectivism 12
interdependence 13
scientific method 14
hypotheses 14
sampling 14
procedure 14
method 14
sample 14
population 14
representative 14
generalizable 14
informed consent 14
consent form 14
reliability 16
validity 16
closed question 16
open-ended question 16
interview 16
qualitative 16
quantitative 16
ethnographic research 17
ethnography 17
Harvard Adolescence Project 17

experimental research method 18
experimental group 18
control group 18
intervention 18
natural experiment 18
monozygotic (MZ) twins 19
dizygotic (DZ) twins 19
correlation versus causation 19
longitudinal study 19
peer-reviewed 20
ecological theory 20
microsystem 20
context 21
mesosystem 21
exosystem 21
macrosystem 21
chronosystem 21
patriarchal authority 22
chador or burka 23
filial piety 23
caste system 24
globalization 26
bicultural 27
resilience 27

INTERNET RESOURCES

http://www.earaonline.org

The web site for the European Association for Research on Adolescence. Information on membership, conferences, and recent news pertaining to the organization.

http://www.s-r-a.org

The official web site of the Society for Research on Adolescence (SRA), which is the main organization for scholars on adolescence. Contains information about conferences and publications related to adolescence.

http://www.ssea.org

The web site of the Society for the Study of Emerging Adulthood. Contains information about conferences on emerging adulthood, resources for teaching courses on emerging adulthood, and a bibliography of useful articles and books on the topic.

FOR FURTHER READING

Arnett, J. J. (2007). *International encyclopedia of adolescence.* New York: Routledge. Two volumes with chapter-length entries on adolescence in nearly 100 countries in every part of the world.

Arnett, J. J. (2004). *Emerging adulthood: The winding road from the late teens through the twenties.* New York: Oxford University Press. An overview of my theory and research on emerging adulthood, with chapters on topics ranging from love and sex to work to beliefs and values.

Arnett, J. J., & Tanner, J. L. (Eds.) (2006). *Emerging adults in America: Coming of age in the 21st century.* A recent edited book containing a summary of the existing scholarship on emerging adulthood in the United States. Contains chapters on a wide variety of topics, such as identity development, family relationships, mental health, sexuality, and media use.

Hall, G. S. (1904). *Adolescence: Its psychology and its relation to physiology, anthropology, sociology, sex, crime, religion, and education* (Vols. I & II). Englewood Cliffs, NJ: Prentice Hall. These are two thick volumes, each over 500 pages, but you may find it enjoyable to browse through them to get a sense of Hall's ideas. This will also give you a sense of how the scientific approach to the study of adolescence has changed since Hall's time.

2 CHAPTER

Biological Foundations

OUTLINE

"I had my first period at twelve, knew about it before and wasn't scared. I thought I was feeling pretty good, because then I would know I was growing up to be a lady, you know. And I really had a nice feeling." *African American adolescent girl (Konopka, 1976, p. 48)*

"I didn't know about [menstruation]. [My mother] never told me anything like that. I was scared, I just started washing all my underclothing hoping that my mother won't find out but she came in and caught me washing it, and she started laughing at me. But she never did tell me what it was. . . . I mean she told me it wasn't anything to worry about, it's something that happens, you know, but she didn't tell me what it meant and stuff like that." *Latina adolescent girl (Konopka, 1976, pp. 47–48)*

"Since I've gotten more physically mature I get a lot of stares when I go out. Sometimes it feels nice or funny when I'm with my friends, especially when it's someone nice. But when it's some weirdo or when some older man says something like "Oooooooh," then it's scary and I want to say, 'I'm only twelve, leave me alone.'" *Denise, age 12 (Bell, 1998, p. 24)*

"I can't stand what I look like right now! Sometimes I just want to put a bag over my head to hide my face. It's all broken out with zits and oily places. I can wash it ten times a day and it's still the same." *Pablo, age 15 (Bell, 1998, p. 10)*

"Pubic hair scared the shit out of me. I saw all these little bumps and I didn't know what they were. I thought maybe I had [a sexually transmitted disease] but I hadn't even had sex." *Juan (Bell, 1998, p. 20)*

"[The first time I ejaculated] I'm almost positive that it was a wet dream. The problem was that I didn't know what it was. I was surprised that I had wet my bed—what did I do? I only found out a year later what it was." *White American adolescent boy (Stein & Reiser, 1993, p. 377)*

THESE EXAMPLES ILLUSTRATE THE WIDE RANGE OF reactions that adolescents have to some of the events that indicate the development of physical and sexual maturity. They also suggest the ways that cultures influence young people's interpretations of the biological events of puberty, in part by informing them—or neglecting to inform them—about the changes that will be taking place in their bodies.

Although adolescence is a culturally constructed period of life, the biological changes of puberty are a central part of development during adolescence in all cultures. Many changes take place, and they are often dramatic. There you are, growing at a more or less steady rate through childhood, and then suddenly the metamorphosis begins—growth spurt, pubic hair, underarm hair, acne, changes in body shape, breast development and menarche in girls, first ejaculation and facial hair in boys, and much more. The changes are often exciting and joyful, but adolescents experience them with other emotions as well—fear, surprise, annoyance, and anxiety. Reaching the key changes earlier or later than most peers is especially a source of anxiety.

The biological changes of puberty are similar across cultures, but in this chapter we will see that biological events interact with cultural influences. Culture influences the timing of biological events, and cultures respond in a variety of ways to the biological changes that signify adolescents' attainment of physical—and sexual—maturity. Adolescents, in turn, rely on information provided by their cultures for interpreting the changes taking place within their bodies and in their physical appearance.

In this chapter we will begin with a description of the hormonal changes that lead to the biological changes of puberty. This will be followed by a description of the physical changes of puberty, including changes in height, weight, muscle-to-fat ratio, and strength. Next will be a description of primary sex characteristics (sperm and egg production) and secondary sex characteristics (such as the growth of pubic hair and the development of breasts). Then we will examine cultural, social, and psychological responses to puberty, including the different experiences of adolescents who mature relatively early or relatively late. The chapter closes with an examination of the interactions between genetic and environmental influences.

The Biological Revolution of Puberty

The word **puberty** is derived from the Latin word *pubescere*, which means "to grow hairy." But adolescents do a lot more in puberty than grow hairy. After developing gradually and steadily during childhood, at puberty the body undergoes a biological revolution that dramatically changes the adolescent's anatomy, physiology, and physical appearance. By the time adolescents enter emerging adulthood, they look much different than before puberty, their bodies function much differently, and they are biologically prepared for sexual reproduction. These changes result from events that occur in the endocrine system during puberty.

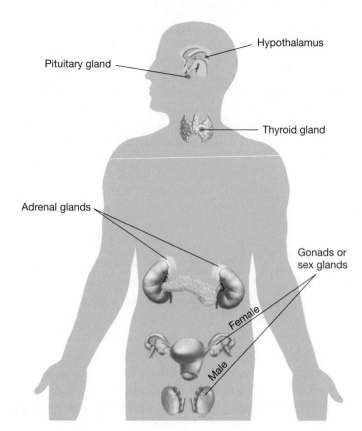

FIGURE 2.1 The major glands involved in pubertal change.

The Endocrine System

The **endocrine system** consists of glands in various parts of the body. These glands release chemicals called **hormones** into the bloodstream, and the hormones affect the development and functioning of the body. Let us take a look at each of the glands that are part of the endocrine system and at the hormones they secrete during puberty (see Figure 2.1).

The Initiation of Puberty in the Hypothalamus The hormonal changes of puberty begin in the **hypothalamus**, a bean-sized structure located in the lower part of the brain, beneath the cortex. The hypothalamus has profound and diverse effects on physiological and psychological motivation and functioning in areas such as eating, drinking, and sexuality. In addition to these functions, the hypothalamus stimulates and

---

puberty The changes in physiology, anatomy, and physical functioning that develop a person into a mature adult biologically and prepare the body for sexual reproduction.

endocrine system A network of glands in the body. Through hormones, the glands coordinate their functioning and affect the development and functioning of the body.

hormones Chemicals, released by the glands of the endocrine system, that affect the development and functioning of the body, including development during puberty.

hypothalamus The "master gland," located in the lower part of the brain beneath the cortex, that affects a wide range of physiological and psychological functioning and stimulates and regulates the production of hormones by other glands, including the ones involved in the initiation of puberty.

gonadotropin-releasing hormone (GnRH) Hormone released by the hypothalamus that causes gonadotropins to be released by the pituitary.

leptin A protein, produced by fat cells, that signals the hypothalamus to initiate the hormonal changes of puberty.

pituitary gland A gland about half an inch long located at the base of the brain that releases gonadotropins as part of the body's preparation for reproduction.

regulates the production of hormones by other glands. To initiate puberty, the hypothalamus begins gradually to increase its production of **gonadotropin-releasing hormone (GnRH)**, releasing GnRH in pulses at intervals of about 2 hours (DeRose & Brooks-Gunn, 2006). The increase in GnRH begins in middle childhood, at least a year or two before even the earliest bodily changes of puberty.

But what causes the hypothalamus to increase GnRH production? Recent evidence indicates that this increase occurs once a threshold level of body fat is reached (Alsaker & Flammer, 2006). During middle childhood the proportion of fat in the body gradually increases, and once the threshold level is reached the increase in GnRH is triggered in the hypothalamus. Fat cells produce a protein, **leptin**, that provides the signal to the hypothalamus (Mantzoros, 2000; Shalatin & Philip, 2003; Spear, 2000). Consequently, for adolescents who are excessively thin due to illness, extreme exercise, or malnutrition, puberty is delayed. Other factors known to influence the timing of puberty include genetics, stress, socioeconomic status (SES), and environmental toxins (Belsky et al., 2007; DeRose & Brooks-Gunn, 2006; Finkelstein, 2001a; Kipke, 1999).

The Pituitary Gland and the Gonadotropins The increase in GnRH affects the **pituitary gland**, a gland about half an inch long located at the base of the brain. GnRH is appropriately named gonadotropin-releasing hormone because that is what it does when it reaches the pituitary gland—it causes hormones called **gonadotropins** to be released from the pituitary. The two gonadotropins are **follicle-stimulating hormone (FSH)** and **luteinizing hormone (LH)**. FSH and LH stimulate the development of **gametes**—egg cells in the ovaries of the female and sperm in the testes of the male. FSH and LH also influence the production of sex hormones by the ovaries and testes, which will be described in more detail below.

The Gonads and the Sex Hormones The ovaries and testes are also known as the **gonads**, or sex glands. In response to stimulation from the FSH and LH released by the pituitary gland, the gonads increase their production of the **sex hormones**. There are two classes of sex hormones, the **estrogens** and the **androgens**. With respect to pubertal development,

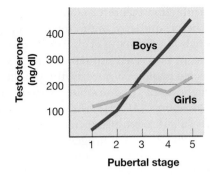

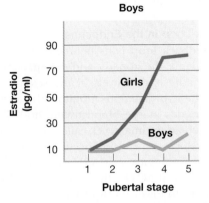

FIGURE 2.2 Sex differences in hormonal changes during puberty.
Source: Nottelmann et al. (1987).

the most important estrogen is **estradiol** and the most important androgen is **testosterone**. Increases in these hormones are responsible for most of the observable bodily changes of puberty, such as breast growth in females and facial hair in males.

Estradiol and testosterone are produced in both males and females, and throughout childhood the levels of these hormones are about the same in boys and girls (DeRose & Brooks-Gunn, 2006). However, once puberty begins the balance changes dramatically, with females producing more estradiol than males and males producing more testosterone than females (Figure 2.2). By the mid-teens, estradiol production is about eight times as high in females as it was before puberty, but only about twice as high for males (Nottelmann et al., 1987; Susman, 1997). Similarly, in males

gonadotropins Hormones (FSH and LH) that stimulate the development of gametes.

follicle-stimulating hormone (FSH) Along with LH, stimulates the development of gametes and sex hormones in the ovaries and testicles.

luteinizing hormone (LH) Along with FSH, stimulates the development of gametes and sex hormones in the ovaries and testicles.

gametes Cells, distinctive to each sex, that are involved in reproduction (egg cells in the ovaries of the female and sperm in the testes of the male).

gonads The ovaries and testicles. Also known as the sex glands.

sex hormones Androgens and estrogens that cause the development of primary and secondary sex characteristics.

estrogens The sex hormones that have especially high levels in females from puberty onward and are mostly responsible for female primary and secondary sex characteristics.

androgens The sex hormones that have especially high levels in males from puberty onward and are mostly responsible for male primary and secondary sex characteristics.

estradiol The estrogen most important in pubertal development among girls.

testosterone The androgen most important in pubertal development among boys.

testosterone production is about 20 times as high by the mid-teens as it was before puberty, but in females it is only about four times as high (Nottelmann et al., 1987; Susman, 1997).

Androgens are produced not only by the sex glands but also by the adrenal glands. At puberty, the pituitary gland increases production of a hormone known as **adrenocorticotropic hormone (ACTH)**, which causes the adrenal glands to increase androgen production (Archibald, Graber, & Brooks-Gunn, 2003). The androgens released by the adrenal gland have the same effects as the androgens released by the testes, contributing to changes such as the development of increased body hair.

The Feedback Loop in the Endocrine System From infancy onward, a **feedback loop** runs between the hypothalamus, the pituitary gland, the gonads, and the adrenal glands that monitors and adjusts the levels of the sex hormones (see Figure 2.3). The hypothalamus monitors the levels of androgens and estrogens in the bloodstream, and when the sex hormones reach an optimal level, called the **set point**, the hypothalamus reduces its production of GnRH. The pituitary responds to the reduction in GnRH by reducing its production of FSH, LH, and ACTH; the gonads and adrenal glands, in turn, respond to lower levels of FSH and LH by reducing the amount of sex hormones they produce.

A commonly used metaphor for the set point is a thermostat. If you set the thermostat at 70 degrees, when the temperature falls below that level the furnace comes on. As the furnace heats the rooms, the temperature rises, and when it reaches 70 degrees again the furnace turns off. In your body, when the levels of the sex hormones fall below their set points, their production by the gonads increases. Once the levels rise again to the set points, their production decreases.

When puberty begins, the set points for androgens and estrogens rise in the hypothalamus, with the set point for androgens rising higher in males than in females and the set point for estrogens rising higher in females than in males. In other words, during childhood the gonads produce only a relatively small amount of sex hormones before the set point of the hypothalamus is reached and the hypothalamus signals the gonads to decrease production of the sex hormones. As puberty begins, however, and the set points for the sex hormones rise in the hypothalamus, the gonads can produce an increasing amount of the sex hormones before the hypothalamus instructs them to decrease production. To return to the thermostat metaphor, it is as if the thermostat were set at 40 degrees during childhood, so that the "heat" of sex hormone production is triggered only occasionally. In the course

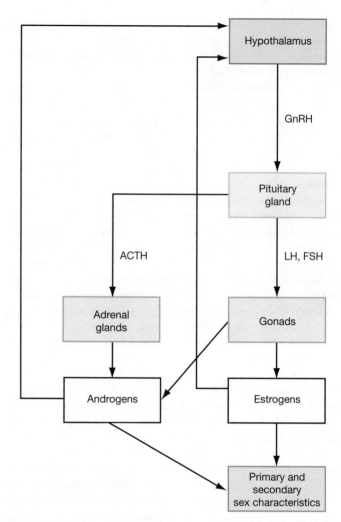

FIGURE 2.3 The feedback loop.
Source: Adapted from Grumbach et al. (1974).

of puberty, it is as if the thermostat rises to 80, and the "heat" of sex hormone production rises accordingly.

Physical Growth During Puberty

The increases in the levels of the sex hormones discussed in the previous section result in a variety of dramatic changes in the bodies of adolescents. One of these changes is the rate of physical growth. After proceeding at an even pace since early childhood, growth suddenly surges when puberty arrives. In fact, one of the earliest signs of puberty for both girls and boys is the **adolescent growth spurt**. Figure 2.4 shows the typical rate of growth in height from birth through age 19, in-

adrenocorticotropic hormone (ACTH) The hormone that causes the adrenal glands to increase androgen production.

feedback loop System of hormones involving the hypothalamus, the pituitary gland, and the gonads, which monitors and adjusts the levels of the sex hormones.

set point Optimal level of sex hormones in the body. When this point is reached, responses in the glands of the feedback loop cause the production of sex hormones to be reduced.

adolescent growth spurt The rapid increase in height that takes place at the beginning of puberty.

peak height velocity The point at which the adolescent growth spurt is at its maximum rate.

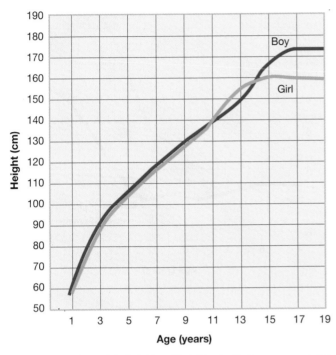

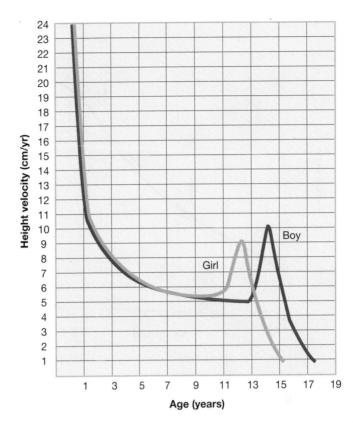

FIGURE 2.4 Growth in height and height velocity for average males and females.

Source: Adapted from Marshall (1978).

cluding the adolescent growth spurt. At **peak height velocity**, when the adolescent growth spurt is at its maximum, girls grow at about 3.5 inches (9.0 cm) per year, and boys grow at about 4.1 inches (10.5 cm) per year (Tanner, 1971). For both girls and boys, the rate of growth at peak height velocity is the highest it has been since they were 2 years old.

As Figure 2.4 shows, girls typically reach the beginning of their growth spurt as well as their peak height velocity about 2 years earlier than boys. This is true of other aspects of physical development in puberty as well: Girls mature about 2 years ahead of boys. Until the growth spurt begins, throughout childhood boys are slightly taller on average than girls of the same age (DeRose & Brooks-Gunn, 2006). Girls become taller on average for about 2 years in early adolescence, from age 11 to 13, the 2 years when they have hit their growth spurt but boys have not. However, the earlier maturation of girls contributes to their smaller adult height, because the adolescent growth spurt also marks the beginning of the end of growth in height. Because girls begin their growth spurt earlier, they also reach their final height earlier—about age 16, on average, compared with about age 18 for boys (Archibald et al., 2003). Higher levels of testosterone also contribute to a higher average final height in boys (Underwood & Van Wyk, 1981).

THINKING CRITICALLY •••

What are some of the social and psychological consequences of the fact that girls mature about 2 years earlier than boys during puberty?

Girls typically reach their growth spurt 2 years earlier than boys.

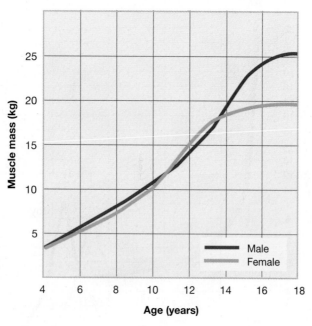

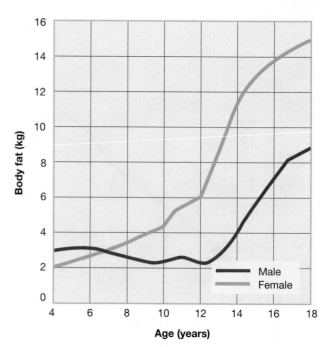

FIGURE 2.5 Sex differences in muscle mass and body fat during puberty.

Source: Adapted from Grumbach et al. (1974).

During the adolescent growth spurt, not all parts of the body grow at the same pace. A certain amount of **asynchronicity** in growth during this time explains why some adolescents have a "gangly" look early in puberty, as some parts of the body grow faster than others. The **extremities**—feet, hands, and head—are the first to hit the growth spurt, followed by the arms and legs (Archibald et al., 2003). Some parts of the head grow more than others. The forehead becomes higher and wider, the mouth widens, the lips become fuller, and the chin, ears, and nose become more prominent (Mussen et al., 1990). The torso, chest, and shoulders are the last parts of the body to reach the growth spurt and therefore the last to reach the end of their growth.

In addition to the growth spurt, a spurt in muscle growth occurs during puberty, primarily because of the increase in testosterone (Tanner, 1971). Because boys experience greater increases in testosterone than girls do, they also experience greater increases in muscle growth. As Figure 2.5 shows, before puberty girls and boys are very similar in their muscle mass.

Levels of body fat also surge during puberty, but body fat increases more for girls than for boys, as Figure 2.5 shows. As a consequence of these sex differences in muscle and fat growth, by the end of puberty boys have a muscle-to-fat ratio of about 3:1, whereas the muscle-to-fat ratio for girls is 5:4 (Grumbach et al., 1974). Other sex differences in body shape also develop during puberty. Hips and shoulders widen among both girls and boys, but hips widen more than shoulders in girls and shoulders widen more than hips in boys.

THINKING CRITICALLY •••

Given that girls naturally gain substantially more body fat than boys during puberty, why do some cultures create physical ideals that demand thinness in females once they reach puberty?

In both boys and girls, the heart becomes larger during puberty—on average, its weight almost doubles (Litt & Vaughan, 1987)—and the heart rate falls, but boys' hearts grow more than girls' hearts do and their heart rates fall to a lower level (Tanner, 1971). By age 17, the average girl's heart rate is about five beats per minute faster than the average boy's (Eichorn, 1970; Neinstein, 1984). A similar change takes place in the growth of the lungs. A measure of lung size called **vital capacity**, which means the amount of air that can be exhaled after a deep breath, increases rapidly for both boys and girls during puberty, but increases more for boys than for girls (Litt & Vaughan, 1987).

These sex differences in physical growth and functioning result in sex differences in strength and athletic ability during adolescence and beyond. Before puberty boys and girls are about equal in strength and athletic performance, but during puberty boys overtake girls, and the difference remains throughout adulthood (DeRose & Brooks-Gunn, 2006).

---

asynchronicity Uneven growth of different parts of the body during puberty.

extremities The feet, hands, and head.

vital capacity The amount of air that can be exhaled after a deep breath, which increases rapidly during puberty, especially for boys.

Gender differences also exist in cultural expectations for physical activity in many cultures, with adolescent girls sometimes being discouraged from participating in sports in order to conform to cultural ideas of what it means to be "feminine." Boys are more likely to exercise in adolescence, and this gender difference contributes to the difference in athletic performance between adolescent boys and girls (Smoll & Schutz, 1990). This has remained true even in recent years, despite an increase in organized athletic activities for girls from childhood onward. A World Health Organization survey of 15-year-olds in 26 Western countries found that in every country, boys were more likely than girls to say they exercised vigorously at least twice a week outside of school (Smith, 2000). Across countries, about three fourths of boys exercised at least twice a week, compared with about one half of girls. In studies that take amount of exercise into account, the muscle-to-fat ratio is still higher for boys than for girls, but the difference is not as large as in studies that do not take exercise into account (DeRose & Brooks-Gunn, 2006).

Obesity Although it is normal and healthy for young people to gain some weight during puberty, for many young people their weight gain goes well beyond what is healthy. Obesity has become a major health problem in industrialized countries and is becoming a problem in developing countries as well (Hong et al., 2007; Werner & Bodin, 2007). Obesity is defined by medical authorities as weighing 20% or more above the maximum healthy weight for height, for males, and 25% or more for females (Davies & Fitzgerald, 2008). Rates of obesity are especially high in the United States. As Figure 2.6 shows, the proportion of 15-year-olds who are obese is far greater in the United States than in other industrialized countries (Lissau et al., 2004; Wang, Monteiro, & Popkin, 2002). About 14% of American adolescents aged 12–17 are classified as obese, a sharp rise from 5% during the period 1966 to 1980 (Fleming & Towey, 2003; National Center for Health Statistics, 2000). The problem is especially severe among African Americans and Latinos, whose obesity rates in adolescence are about 50% higher than the rate for Whites (Fleming & Towey, 2003). Obese adolescents have higher leptin levels, so it may be that increased obesity has contributed to the earlier onset of puberty among African American and Latino girls in recent decades (Shalitin, 2003; Sun et al., 2005).

What is responsible for the disturbing trends in obesity among American adolescents? Not surprisingly, diet and exercise are implicated. Nearly one third of American adolescents eat at least one fast-food meal per day (e.g., McDonald's, Wendy's, KFC), and fast-food meals tend to be extremely high in calories, loaded with fat and sugar (Bowman et al., 2004). Furthermore, fast-food portions have increased dramatically in recent years (Fleming & Towey, 2003), as the burgers and drinks and French fry portions have become "supersized." The American lifestyle is more automobile-oriented than in most other industrialized coun-

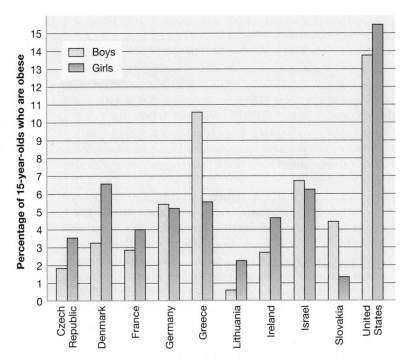

FIGURE 2.6 Rates of obesity among adolescents in selected countries. Why are rates of obesity so high among adolescents in the United States?

Source: Bowman et al. (2004).

tries, so American adolescents ride in cars more and walk or bike-ride less (Arnett & Balle-Jensen, 1993). American adolescents exercise less than medical experts recommend (Fleming & Towey, 2003), and African American females have especially low rates of exercise.

One recent study found a steep decline in physical activity from age 9 to 15 (Nader et al., 2008). Rather than using reports of physical activity from the participants or their parents, the researchers had the participants wear an "accelerometer," a device that measures movement, for one week. At age 9, children engaged in about 3 hours of physical activity a day on both weekdays and weekends. However, from age 9 to 15 the rate of physical activity declined steadily, and at age 15 physical activity was down to less than an hour on weekdays and just a half-hour on weekends. The study did not investigate the reasons for the decline.

Time watching television has been found to be related to obesity (Dowda et al., 2001), but American adolescents watch about the same amount of television as adolescents in other industrialized countries (Flammer, Alsaker, & Noack, 1999), so television-watching cannot explain the cross-national difference in obesity. Computer games have also been blamed (Davies & Fitzgerald, 2008), but again, computer games are popular in countries with widely different rates of adolescent obesity. Similarly, obesity has been found to run in families—when parents are obese, adolescents are at higher risk for obesity (Corrado et al., 2004; Davies & Fitzgerald, 2008; Dowda et al., 2001)—which suggests that heredity may be involved, but this cannot explain the steep increase in obesity in recent decades.

One trend that does shed light on the recent increase in obesity in the United States is the increased presence of soft-drink and junk food machines in schools. Only one fourth of American elementary schools allow vending machines, but this proportion rises to two thirds in middle school and nearly 100% in high schools (Fleming & Towey, 2003). Often, soft-drink companies pay schools money in return for being allowed to place their vending machines there, and cash-hungry schools are usually easy to persuade (Wechsler et al., 2001). Soft-drink companies have also begun to offer money to after-school youth organizations such as the Boys and Girls Clubs of America and the YMCA in return for being able to market to the adolescents who attend their programs (Boyle, 2004). Some have begun to criticize this practice, but like the schools, few youth organizations have been able to resist the money.

Obesity in adolescence is a source of concern not just because it is unhealthy in adolescence but because it predicts long-term health problems (Davies & Fitzgerald, 2008; Fleming & Towey, 2003). About 80% of obese adolescents remain obese in adulthood (Engeland et al., 2004). A variety of health risks result from obesity in adulthood, including diabetes, stroke, and heart disease (Boyle, 2004; Corrado et al., 2004). To address the problem, medical professionals have developed interventions intended to reduce obesity during childhood and adolescence, usually through the schools. Successful programs have a variety of components, including nutrition education, dietary assessment, modifications of meals offered in the school, and efforts to increase physical activity (Stice, Shaw, & Marti, 2006). However, such programs also face barriers, especially resistance from adolescents who see no need to change and parents who are disinclined to become more involved.

Physical Functioning in Emerging Adulthood Although most people reach their maximum height by the end of adolescence, in other ways emerging adulthood rather than adolescence is the period of peak physical functioning. Even after maximum height is attained, the bones continue to grow in density, and peak bone mass is reached in the 20s (Zumwalt, 2008). A measure of physical stamina called **maximum oxygen uptake**, or **VO₂ max**, which reflects the ability of the body to take in oxygen and transport it to various organs, also peaks in the early 20s (Plowman, Drinkwater, & Horvath, 1979). Similarly, **cardiac output**, the quantity of blood flow from the heart, peaks at age 25 (Lakatta, 1990). Reaction time is also faster in the early 20s than at any other time of life. Studies of grip strength among men show the same pattern, with a peak in the 20s followed by a steady decline (Kallman, Plato, & Tobin, 1990).

For most people, the peak of their physical functioning comes during emerging adulthood.

Of course, like the sex differences in adolescence discussed earlier, most aspects of optimal physical functioning in emerging adulthood could be due in part to greater physical activity and exercise among emerging adults compared with adolescents or older adults (Goldberg, Dengel, & Hagberg, 1996). However, taking physical activity and exercise into account explains only a small portion of peak physical functioning in emerging adulthood. All together, for most people emerging adulthood is the time of life when they are at the zenith of their health and strength.

One way to demonstrate this is at the extreme, in terms of peak performances in athletic activity. Several studies have been conducted on the ages of athletes' best performances (Ericsson, 1990; Schultz & Curnow, 1988; Stones & Kozma, 1996). The peak ages have been found to vary depending on the sport, with swimmers youngest (the late teens) and golfers oldest (about age 31). However, for most sports the peak age of performance comes during the 20s.

Emerging adulthood is also the period of the life span with the least susceptibility to physical illnesses (Gans, 1990). This is especially true in modern times, when vaccines and medical treatments have dramatically lowered the risk of diseases such as polio that used to strike mainly during these years (Hein, 1988). Emerging adults are no longer vulnerable to the illnesses and diseases of childhood, and with rare exceptions they are not yet vulnerable to diseases such as cancer and heart disease that rise in prevalence later in adulthood. The immune system is at its most effective during the emerging adult years. Consequently, the late teens and early

---

maximum oxygen uptake (VO₂ max) A measure of the ability of the body to take in oxygen and transport it to various organs; peaks in the early 20s.

cardiac output A measure of the quantity of blood pumped by the heart.

health promotion Efforts to reduce health problems in young people through encouraging changes in the behaviors that put young people at risk.

primary sex characteristics The production of eggs and sperm and the development of the sex organs.

secondary sex characteristics Bodily changes of puberty not directly related to reproduction.

ovum Mature egg that develops from follicle in ovaries about every 28 days.

spermarche Beginning of development of sperm in boys' testicles at puberty.

20s are the years of fewest hospital stays and fewest days spent sick in bed at home (Gans, 1990). In many ways, then, emerging adulthood is an exceptionally healthy time of life (Millstein, Petersen, & Nightingale, 1993).

This is not the whole story, however. The lifestyles of many emerging adults often include a variety of factors that undermine health, such as poor nutrition, lack of sleep, and the high stress of trying to juggle school and work or multiple jobs (Ma et al., 2002; Steptoe & Wardle, 2001). Furthermore, in the United States and other industrialized countries the late teens and early 20s are the years of highest incidence of a variety of types of disease, injury, and death due to behavior. Automobile accidents are the leading cause of death among emerging adults in industrialized countries, and injuries and deaths from automobile accidents are higher in the late teens and early 20s than at any other period of the life course (Heuveline, 2002; National Highway Traffic Safety Administration, 2008). Homicide is another common cause of death in industrialized countries during emerging adulthood (Heuveline, 2002; National Center for Health Statistics, 1999). Rates of contracting sexually transmitted diseases, including HIV, are highest in the early 20s (Teitler, 2002; Wenstock et al., 2004). Most kinds of substance use and abuse also peak in the early 20s (Arnett, 2005d; Eisner, 2002).

We will discuss the causes of these problems in Chapter 13. For now, it is worth noting that in recent decades health experts have reached a consensus that the source of most physical health problems in the teens and early 20s is in young people's behavior (e.g., Gans, 1990; Heuveline, 2002; Irwin, 1993). As a result, programs emphasizing **health promotion** during these years have become more common. Programs in health promotion tend to emphasize prevention of problems through encouraging changes in the behaviors that put young people at risk (e.g., driving at high speeds, having unprotected sex, binge drinking). Many of these programs focus on the early adolescent years, in the belief that these are years when patterns of behavior are being established that may endure into late adolescence, emerging adulthood, and beyond.

The success of such programs has been mixed so far, as we will see in more detail in Chapter 13. However, some programs work better than others. Child Trends, a nonprofit research center on children and families, has published an extensive review of programs intended to encourage healthy behavior and lifestyles among adolescents (Hatcher & Scarpa, 2001). After reviewing 230 studies, it was concluded that the most successful programs take a multifaceted approach (taking into consideration the adolescent, family members, peers, and the community); focus on changing behavior rather than on distributing information; and include follow-up sessions to reinforce the effects of the intervention.

Primary Sex Characteristics

In addition to the changes in physical growth and functioning described so far, two other kinds of changes take place in the adolescent's body in response to increased sex hormones during puberty. **Primary sex characteristics** involve the production of eggs and sperm and the development of the sex organs. **Secondary sex characteristics** are other bodily changes of puberty, not including the ones related directly to reproduction.

Egg and Sperm Production As noted, increases in the sex hormones at puberty cause eggs to develop in the ovaries of females and sperm to be produced in the testes of males. The development of the gametes is quite different for the two sexes. Females are born with about 400,000 immature eggs in each ovary. By puberty, this number has declined to about 80,000 in each ovary. Once a girl reaches menarche (her first menstrual period) and begins having menstrual cycles, one egg develops into a mature egg, or **ovum** (plural: ova), every 28 days or so. Females release about 400 eggs over the course of their reproductive lives.

In contrast, males have no sperm in their testes when they are born, and they do not produce any until they reach puberty. The first production of sperm in boys is called **spermarche** (Laron et al., 1980), and it takes place on average at age 12 (Finkelstein, 2001c). Once spermarche arrives, boys produce sperm in astonishing quantities. There are between 30 and 500 million sperm in the typical male ejaculation, which means that the average male produces

> "I was about six months younger than everyone else in my class, and so for about six months after my friends had begun to develop (that was the word we used, develop), I was not particularly worried. I would sit in the bathtub and look down at my breasts and know that any day now, any second now, they would start growing like everyone else's. They didn't... . 'Don't worry about it,' said my friend Libby some months later, when things had not improved. 'You'll get them after you're married.' 'What are you talking about?' I said. 'When you get married,' Libby explained, 'Your husband will touch your breasts and rub them and kiss them and they'll grow.'"
>
> —Nora Ephron 2000, *Crazy Salad*, pp. 2–4

millions of sperm every day. If you are a man, you will probably produce over a million sperm during the time you read this chapter—even if you are a fast reader!

Why so many? One reason is that the environment of the female body is not very hospitable to sperm. The female's immune system registers sperm as foreign bodies and begins attacking them immediately. A second reason is that sperm have, in relation to their size, a long way to go to reach the ovum. They have to make their way along and through the various structures of the female reproductive anatomy. So it helps to have a lot of sperm wiggling their way toward the ovum, because this increases the likelihood that some of them may make it to the ovum at the right time for fertilization to take place.

The Male and Female Reproductive Anatomy The changes of puberty prepare the body for sexual reproduction, and during puberty the sex organs undergo a number of important changes as part of that preparation. In males, both the penis and the testes grow substantially in puberty (King, 2005). The penis doubles in length and diameter. In its mature form, the flaccid (limp) penis averages 3 to 4 inches in length and about 1 inch in diameter. The tumescent (erect) penis averages $5\frac{1}{2}$ to 6 inches in length and $1\frac{1}{2}$ inches in diameter. The growth of the testes during puberty is even more pronounced—they increase $2\frac{1}{2}$ times in length and $8\frac{1}{2}$ times in weight, on average. The dramatic growth of the testes reflects the production of the many millions of sperm.

In females, the external sex organs are known as the **vulva**, which includes the **labia majora** (Latin for "large lips"), the **labia minora** (Latin for "small lips"), and the **clitoris**. The vulva grows substantially in puberty (King,

2005). The ovaries also increase greatly in size and weight. Just as the testes grow as a consequence of sperm production, the growth of the ovaries reflects the growth of maturing ova. Furthermore, the uterus doubles in length during puberty, growing to a mature length of about 3 inches, about the size of a closed fist. The vagina also increases in length, and its color deepens.

As noted earlier, an ovum is released in each monthly cycle. The two ovaries typically alternate months, with one releasing an ovum and then the other. The ovum moves along the fallopian tube and travels to the uterus. During this time, a lining of blood builds up in the uterus in preparation for the possibility of receiving and providing nutrients for the fertilized egg. If the ovum becomes fertilized by a sperm during its journey to the uterus, the fertilized egg begins dividing immediately. When it reaches the uterus it implants in the wall of the uterus and continues developing. If the ovum is not fertilized, it is evacuated during menstruation along with the blood lining of the uterus.

Although menarche is a girl's first menstruation, it is not the same as the first ovulation. On the contrary, the *majority* of a girl's menstrual cycles in the first 2 years after menarche do not include ovulation, and in the third and fourth years only about one third to one half of cycles include ovulation (Finkelstein, 2001d). It is only after 4 years of menstruation that girls consistently ovulate with each menstrual cycle. This early inconsistency leads some sexually active adolescent girls to believe they are infertile, but this is an unfortunate misunderstanding. Fertility may be inconsistent and unpredictable during the first 4 years after menarche, but it is certainly possible for most girls. Whether boys experience a similar lag between spermarche and the production of sperm capable of fertilizing an egg is not known.

Secondary Sex Characteristics

All the primary sex characteristics are directly related to reproduction. In addition to these changes, numerous other bodily changes take place as part of puberty but are not directly related to reproduction. These changes are known as secondary sex characteristics.

Some secondary sex characteristics develop for only males or only females, but for the most part the changes that happen to one sex also happen to the other, to some degree. Both males and females grow hair in their pubic areas and underneath their arms. Both also grow facial hair—you knew that males do, but you may not have realized that females also grow hair, just a slight amount, on their faces during puberty. Similarly, increased hairiness on the arms and legs is more pronounced in males, but females also grow more hair on their limbs at puberty. Boys also begin to grow hair on

---

vulva External female sex organs, including the labia majora, the labia minora, and the clitoris.

labia majora Part of vulva; Latin for "large lips."

labia minora Part of vulva; Latin for "small lips."

clitoris Part of vulva in which females' sexual sensations are concentrated.

breast buds The first slight enlargement of the breast in girls at puberty.

areola Area surrounding the nipple on the breast; enlarges at puberty.

their chests, and sometimes on their shoulders and backs as well, whereas girls typically do not.

Both males and females experience various changes in their skin and bones (Eveleth & Tanner, 1990; Tanner, 1971). The skin becomes rougher, especially around the thighs and upper arms. The sweat glands in the skin increase production, making the skin oilier and more prone to acne, and resulting in a stronger body odor. Also, bones become harder and thicker throughout the body (Zumwalt, 2008). Males and females both experience a deepening of the voice as the vocal cords lengthen, with males experiencing a steeper drop in pitch.

Even breast development, though obviously a secondary sex characteristic that occurs in females, also occurs in a substantial proportion of males. About one fourth of boys experience enlargement of the breasts about midway through puberty (Bell, 1998; Tanner, 1970). This can be a source of alarm and anxiety for adolescent boys, but for the majority of them the enlargement recedes within a year.

For girls, the breasts go through a series of predictable stages of development (Figure 2.7). The earliest indication of breast development, a slight enlargement of the breasts known as **breast buds**, is also one of the first outward signs of puberty in most girls (Tanner, 1971). During this early stage, there is also an enlargement of the area surrounding the nipple, called the **areola**. In the later stages of breast development, the breasts continue to enlarge, and the areola first rises with the nipple to form a mound above the breast, then recedes to the level of the breast while the nipple remains projected (Archibald et al., 2003).

Table 2.1 provides a summary of the physical changes in males and females during puberty.

THINKING CRITICALLY •••

Puberty involves the development of sexual maturation. Among the secondary sex characteristics described here, which are viewed in your culture as enhancing sexual interest and attractiveness between males and females? Which are not?

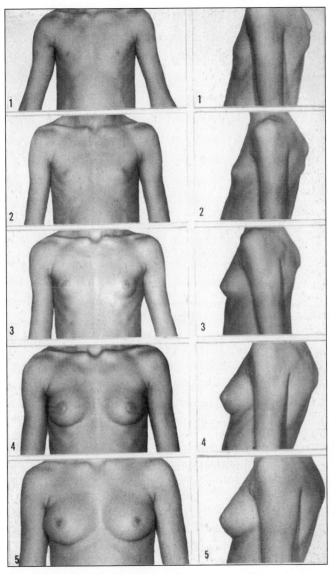

FIGURE 2.7 Stages of breast development.

Source: Marshall and Tanner (1970).

TABLE 2.1	Physical Changes During Adolescence	
Both Sexes	**Males Only**	**Females Only**
Pubic hair	Sperm production	Ovulation/menstruation
Underarm hair	Wider shoulders and chest	Breast development
Facial hair	Increased proportion of muscle to fat	Broader hips/pelvis
Arm and leg hair	Chest hair	Increased proportion of fat to muscle
Rougher skin (especially thighs, upper arms)	Shoulder and back hair	
Oilier skin, stronger body odor		
Harder bones		
Lower voice		
Growth spurt		
Larger forehead		
Wider mouth		
Fuller lips		
More prominent chin, ears, nose		

TABLE 2.2 The Sequence of Physical Changes at Puberty

Boys		Girls	
Characteristic	**Age of first appearance (years)**	**Characteristic**	**Age of first appearance (years)**
1. Growth of testes, scrotal sac	$9\frac{1}{2}$–$13\frac{1}{2}$	1. Growth of pubic hair	8–14
2. Growth of pubic hair	10–15	2. Growth of breasts	8–13
3. Growth spurt	$10\frac{1}{2}$–16	3. Growth spurt	$9\frac{1}{2}$–$14\frac{1}{2}$
4. Growth of penis	$10\frac{1}{2}$–$14\frac{1}{2}$	4. Menarche	10–$16\frac{1}{2}$
5. Change in voice	11–15	5. Underarm hair	10–16
6. Spermarche	12–14	6. Oil and sweat production, acne	10–16
7. Facial and underarm hair	12–17		
8. Oil and sweat production, acne	12–17		

Source: Adapted from Goldstein (1976).

The Order of Pubertal Events

Puberty is composed of many events and processes, typically stretching out over several years (Table 2.2). A great deal of variability exists among individuals in the timing of pubertal events. Among young people in industrialized countries the first pubertal events may occur as early as age 8 in girls and age 9 or 10 in boys, or as late as age 13 (Ge et al., 2007; Herman-Giddens et al., 1997; Herman-Giddens, Wang, & Koch, 2001; Sun et al., 2005). The duration between the initiation of the first pubertal event and full pubertal maturation can be as short as a year and a half or as long as 6 years (Tanner, 1962). Consequently, in the early teens some adolescents may have nearly finished their pubertal development while others have barely begun. Because adolescents experience the first events of puberty at different ages and proceed through puberty at different rates, age alone is a very poor predictor of an adolescent's pubertal development (Archibald et al., 2003).

More consistency can be seen in the order of pubertal events than in the ages they begin or the amount of time it takes to complete them (Archibald et al., 2003; Finkelstein, 2001c). For girls, downy pubic hair is often the first sign of the beginning of puberty, followed closely by the appearance of breast buds (for about 20% of girls, breast buds precede the first sign of pubic hair). The next event for girls is usually the growth spurt, along with the growth of the sexual and reproductive organs (vulva, uterus, and vagina). Menarche, the development of underarm hair, and the secretion of increased skin oil and sweat occur relatively late in puberty for most girls.

For boys, the first outward sign of puberty is usually the growth of the testes, along with or closely followed by the beginning of pubic hair (Archibald et al., 2003). These events are followed (usually about a year later) by the initiation of the growth spurt and the increased growth of the penis, along with the beginning of the deepening of the voice. Spermarche takes place at age 12 to 14 for most boys. In boys as in girls, the growth of underarm hair and the secretion of in-

creased skin oil and sweat take place relatively late in puberty. For boys, facial hair is also one of the later developments of puberty, usually beginning about 2 years after the first outward events of puberty.

Virtually all the studies we have been considering in this section have been conducted with White adolescents in the West. In fact, the main source of our information about physical growth and functioning in adolescence remains the studies by Tanner and his colleagues (see the Research Focus box), which were mostly conducted 30 to 40 years ago on British adolescents who were in foster homes. Tanner's findings have been verified in numerous studies of White adolescents in the United States (Archibald et al., 2003; Susman et al., 2003), but we do not have similarly detailed information on other ethnic and cultural groups around the world.

Three studies demonstrate the variations that may exist in other groups. Among the Kikuyu, a culture in Kenya, boys show the first physical changes of puberty *before* their female peers (Worthman, 1987), a reversal of the Western pattern. In a study of Chinese girls, Lee, Chang, and Chan (1963) found that pubic hair began to develop in most girls about 2 years after the development of breast buds, and only a few months before menarche. This is a sharp contrast to the pattern for the girls in Tanner's studies, who typically began to develop pubic hair at about the same time they developed breast buds, usually 2 years before menarche (Tanner, 1971). Also, in an American study (Herman-Giddens et al., 1997; Herman-Giddens et al., 2001), many African American girls were found to begin developing breast buds and pubic hair considerably earlier than White girls. At age 8, nearly 50% of the African American girls had begun to develop breasts or pubic hair or both, compared with just 15% of the White girls. This was true even though Black and White girls were similar in their ages of menarche. Similarly, pubic hair and genital development began earlier for African American boys than White boys. Studies such as these indicate that it is important to investigate further cultural differences in the rates, timing, and order of pubertal events.

Given a similar environment, variation in the order and timing of pubertal events among adolescents appears to be due to genetics. The more similar two people are genetically, the more similar they tend to be in the timing of their pubertal events, with identical twins the most similar of all (Ge et al., 2007; van den Berg, 2007). However, the key phrase here is "given a similar environment." In reality, the environments adolescents experience differ greatly, both within and between countries. These differences have profound effects on the timing of puberty, as we will see in detail in the following section.

Cultural, Social, and Psychological Responses to Puberty

Whatever their culture, all humans go through the physical and biological changes of puberty. However, even here culture's effects are profound. Cultural diets and levels of health and nutrition influence the timing of the initiation of puberty. Perhaps more importantly, cultures define the meaning and significance of pubertal change in different ways. These cultural definitions in turn influence the ways that adolescents interpret and experience their passage through puberty. We will look at culture and pubertal timing first and next at culture and the meaning of puberty. Then we will examine social and personal responses to puberty, with a focus on differences between adolescents who mature relatively early and adolescents who mature relatively late.

Culture and the Timing of Puberty

How do cultures influence the timing of the initiation of puberty? The definition of culture includes a group's technologies. Technologies include food production and medical

Menarche is often marked by a ritual in traditional cultures. Here, girls of the N'Jembe tribe of West Africa prepare for their initiation.

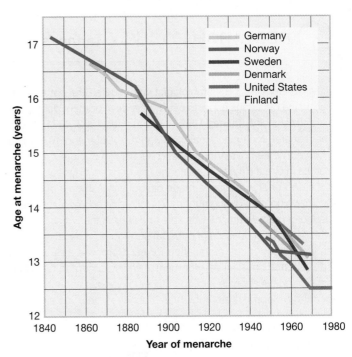

FIGURE 2.8 The decline in the age of menarche in Western countries.
Source: Adapted from Eveleth & Tanner (1990).

care, and the age at which puberty begins is strongly influenced by the extent to which food production provides for adequate nutrition and medical care provides for good health throughout childhood. In general, puberty begins earlier in cultures where good nutrition and medical care are widely available (Eveleth & Tanner, 1990).

Persuasive evidence for the influence of technologies on pubertal timing comes from historical records showing a steady decrease in the average age of menarche in Western countries over the past 150 years. This kind of change in a population over time is called a **secular trend** (Bullough, 1981). As you can see from Figure 2.8, a secular trend downward in the age of menarche has occurred in every Western country for which records exist. Menarche is not a perfect indicator of the initiation of puberty—as we have discussed, the first outward signs of puberty appear much earlier for most girls, and of course menarche does not apply to boys. However, menarche is a reasonably good indicator of when other events have begun, and it is a reasonable assumption that if the downward secular trend in the age of puberty has occurred for females, it has occurred for males as well. Menarche is also the only aspect of pubertal development for which we have records going back so many decades. Scholars believe that the secular trend in the age of menarche is due to improvements in nutrition and medical care that have taken place during the past 150 years (Archibald et al., 2003; Bullough, 1981). As medical advances have reduced illnesses

secular trend A change in the characteristics of a population over time.

RESEARCH FOCUS • Tanner's Longitudinal Research on Pubertal Development

J. M. Tanner was a British biologist who studied the pattern and sequence of various aspects of physical development during puberty (Marshall & Tanner, 1969, 1970; Tanner, 1962, 1971, 1991). His research took place mainly during the 1960s and 1970s and involved White boys and girls who were living in state-run foster homes in Great Britain. Through the use of direct physical evaluations and photographs, he made careful assessments of growth and development during puberty. By following adolescents over a period of many years, he was able to establish the typical ages at which various processes of pubertal development begin and end, as well as the range of variation for each process. His work on adolescents' physical development is widely accepted by scholars on adolescence; in fact, the stages of various aspects of pubertal development are known as "Tanner stages," as shown in the examples for breast development in females (see Figure 2.7) and genital development in males (see accompanying photo).

Tanner and his colleagues focused on specific aspects of physical development during puberty: the growth spurt, the development of pubic hair, genital maturity in boys, the development of breasts in girls, and menarche in girls (Figure 2.9). For breast development (girls), genital maturity (boys), and pubic hair, Tanner described a sequence of five stages. Stage 1 is the prepubertal stage, when no physical changes have appeared. Stage 5 is the stage when maturity has been reached and growth is completed. Stages 2, 3, and 4 describe levels of development in between. In addition to the stages, Tanner described other bodily changes such as muscle growth and the composition of the blood (Tanner, 1971).

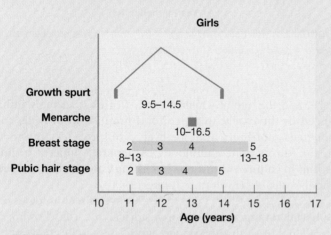

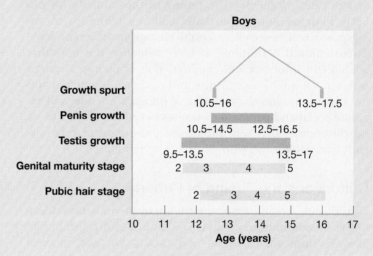

FIGURE 2.9   Typical age ranges for pubertal development.
Source: Adapted from Marshall & Tanner (1970), p. 22.

and advances in food production have enhanced nutrition, puberty has come sooner.

Further evidence of the role of nutrition and medical care in pubertal timing comes from cultural comparisons in the present. When we look around the world, we find that the average age of menarche is lowest in industrialized countries, where adequacy of nutrition and medical care is highest (Eveleth & Tanner, 1990). For girls in the United States, the average age of menarche is currently 12.5 (Brooks-Gunn & Paikoff, 1997; McDowell et al., 2007; Susman et al., 2003). In contrast, the average is higher in developing countries, where nutrition may be limited and medical care is often rare or non-existent (Eveleth & Tanner, 1990). In countries that have un-dergone rapid economic development in recent decades, such as China and South Korea, a corresponding decline in the average age of menarche has been recorded (Graham, Larsen, & Xu, 1999; Park, Shim, Kim, & Eun, 1999).

One illuminating contrast is between African girls in Africa and African American girls in the United States. In African countries the average age of menarche varies widely, but in none of them is it as low as for girls in the United States, and in some African countries the average age of menarche is as high as 15, 16, or even 17 years old (Eveleth & Tanner, 1990). In contrast, the average age of menarche for African American girls is just 12.2 (Herman-Giddens et al., 1997). The lower age of menarche for African American

cross-sectional study Study that examines individuals at one point in time.

reaction range Term meaning that genes establish a range of possible development and environment determines where development takes place within that range.

The adolescents Tanner studied were mainly from low SES families, and many of them probably did not receive optimal physical care during childhood (Marshall & Tanner, 1970). They were living in foster homes, which indicates that there had been problems of some kind in their families. Thus, the adolescents in Tanner's studies were not selected randomly and were in many ways not truly representative of the larger population of adolescents, even the larger population of White British adolescents. Nevertheless, Tanner's description of development in puberty has held up very well. Studies of normal White American adolescents have found patterns very similar to the ones Tanner described (Brooks-Gunn & Reiter, 1990; Susman et al., 2003). Since his original studies, Tanner and his colleagues have also researched development during puberty in other countries in various parts of the world and have found that the timing and pace of development during puberty vary widely depending on the levels of nutrition and medical care available to adolescents (Eveleth & Tanner, 1990).

Tanner's research was longitudinal. A longitudinal study is a study in which the same individuals are followed across time and data on them are collected on more than one occasion. The range of time involved can vary from a few weeks to an entire lifetime. This kind of study is different from a **cross-sectional study**, which examines individuals at one point in time. Both kinds of studies are valuable, but there are certain kinds of information that can be gained only with a longitudinal study. For example, in Tanner's research, the only way to find out how long it typically takes for females to develop from Stage 1 to Stage 5 of breast development is through a longitudinal study. If breast development were assessed with a cross-sectional study, it would be difficult to tell for each girl how long it had taken for her to develop

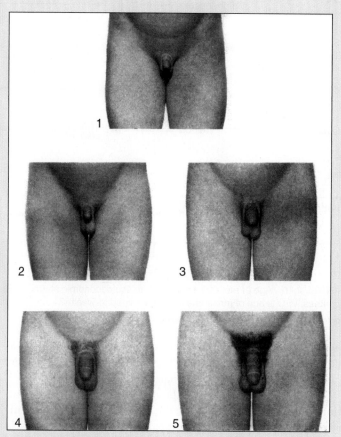

Photos of boys' genital maturity from Tanner's studies.

to that stage and how long it would take for her to develop to the next stage. With a longitudinal study, this can be assessed quite precisely.

girls compared with African girls is very likely due to African American girls' considerably better nutrition and medical care.

Studies also show that within countries, as you can see in Figure 2.10, adolescent girls from affluent families tend to menstruate earlier than girls from poorer families, in places as diverse as Hong Kong, Tunisia, Iraq, South Africa, and the United States (Eveleth & Tanner, 1990). Again, we can infer that economic differences result in differences in the nutrition and medical care these girls receive, which in turn influence the timing of menarche.

With respect to nutrition in particular, substantial evidence shows that girls who are involved in activities in which there is a great deal of pressure to keep down their weight, such as ballet and gymnastics, experience later menarche and have inconsistent periods once they begin to menstruate (Picard, 1999). The body responds to their low weight as a nutritional deficiency and delays menarche.

THINKING CRITICALLY •••

In your view, what potential social and psychological problems may develop as a consequence of girls showing signs of reaching puberty (such as initial breast development) as early as 8 or 9 years old?

Given that the secular trend in the age of menarche was steadily downward for over a century in industrialized countries, will girls someday begin menstruating in middle childhood or even earlier? Apparently not. In most industrialized countries, the median age of menarche has been more or less stable since about 1970 (Herman-Giddens et al., 1997; McDowell et al., 2007; Susman et al., 2003). Although there is some evidence that a downward secular trend for breast development and pubic hair may have continued since that time (Herman-Giddens et al., 2001), human females appear to have a genetically established **reaction range** for the age of

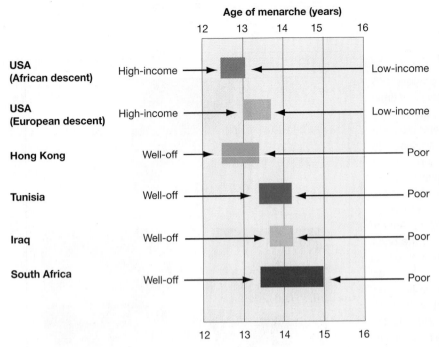

Age of menarche (years)

USA (African descent) — High-income / Low-income

USA (European descent) — High-income / Low-income

Hong Kong — Well-off / Poor

Tunisia — Well-off / Poor

Iraq — Well-off / Poor

South Africa — Well-off / Poor

FIGURE 2.10 Age of menarche in relation to socioeconomic status (SES) in various countries. Why is age of menarche inversely related to wealth?

Source: Adapted from Eveleth & Tanner (1990).

menarche. This means that genes establish a range of possible times when menarche may begin and environment determines the actual timing of menarche within that range.

In general, the healthier the environment, the lower the timing of menarche. However, the reaction range has boundaries: Even under relatively unhealthy conditions, most girls will eventually reach menarche, and even in conditions of optimal health there is a lower boundary age that menarche is unlikely to fall below. Because the timing of menarche in industrialized countries has changed little in recent decades, it appears that girls in these countries have reached the lower boundary age of their reaction range for menarche.

Cultural Responses to Puberty: Puberty Rituals

Puberty has been marked with rituals in many cultures through history as the departure from childhood and the entrance into adolescence, particularly in traditional cultures. Not all traditional cultures have such rituals, but they are quite common, especially for girls. Schlegel and Barry (1991) analyzed information on adolescent development across 186 traditional cultures and reported that the majority of them had some kind of ritual initiation into adolescence at the beginning of puberty: 68% had a puberty ritual for boys, 79% for girls (Schlegel & Barry, 1991).

For girls, menarche is the pubertal event that is most often marked by ritual (Schlegel & Barry, 1991). In many cultures, menarche initiates a monthly ritual related to menstruation that lasts throughout a woman's reproductive life. It is remarkably common for cultures to have strong beliefs concerning the power of menstrual blood. Such beliefs are not universal, but they have been common in all parts of the world, in a wide variety of cultures. Menstrual blood is often believed to present a danger to the growth and life of crops, to the health of livestock, to the success of hunters, and to the health and well-being of other people, particularly the menstruating woman's husband (Buckley & Gottlieb, 1988; Herdt & Leavitt, 1998; Howie & Shail, 2005). Consequently, the behavior and movement of menstruating women are often restricted in many domains, including food preparation and consumption, social activities, religious practices, bathing, school attendance, and sexual activities (Mensch, Bruce, & Greene, 1998).

The views of cultures toward menstrual blood are not uniformly negative, however (Buckley & Gottlieb, 1988; Howie & Shail, 2005). Often, menstrual blood is viewed as having positive powers as well. For example, it is sometimes seen as promoting fertility and is used in fertility rituals. Some cultures use menstrual blood in the treatment of medical conditions, and some use it to make love potions (Ladurie, 1979). Sometimes both positive and negative beliefs about menstruation exist within the same culture.

An example of cultural ambivalence toward menstruation can be found among the Asante, a culture in the African nation of Ghana (Buckley & Gottlieb, 1988). Among the Asante, menstruating women are subject to numerous stringent

Puberty rituals for boys often require them to endure physical pain. Here, the traditional stick fight between adolescents in the Xhosa tribe of southern Africa.

One interesting example of a puberty ritual for both males and females comes from the islands known as Samoa, in the Pacific Ocean near New Zealand. Samoa became known to many Americans early in the 20th century when the anthropologist Margaret Mead wrote a book about Samoan adolescence, *Coming of Age in Samoa* (1928), that was widely read in the United States (and, in fact, all over the world). Many people were fascinated by the stark contrast between adolescence in Samoa and adolescence in the West.

One of the ways Samoa differed from the West was in having a ritual to mark the beginning of adolescence. The traditional rite of passage into adolescence involved an elaborate process of tattooing sometime between ages 14 and 16 (Coté, 1994). The tattoos were made in elaborate geometric patterns and extended from the waist to the knees (see accompanying photo). Having the tattoos put on was painful, especially for males, whose tattoos were more elaborate than the ones for females and usually took 2 to 3 months to complete, whereas the tattoos for females took only 5 to 6 days. But the young men experienced it together and took satisfaction in sharing the ordeal of it and supporting one another. In spite of the pain, few young men or young women declined to take part in it because being tattooed was considered essential to sexual attractiveness and to being accepted as a legitimate candidate for full adult status.

This tattooing ritual has been profoundly affected by the globalization of adolescence. In the past 100 years, Samoan culture has changed a great deal (Coté, 1994; McDade & Worthman, 2004). Christian missionaries arrived and sought to stamp out a variety of native practices they considered immoral, including the ritual of tattooing. The rise of secondary education and the widening of economic opportunities for Samoans who immigrated to nearby New Zealand undermined the traditional economy and caused the tattooing ritual to be viewed as irrelevant or even shamefully "primitive" by some Samoans. By now, most Samoans have abandoned their cooperative, traditional ways for participation in the wage labor of the global economy.

Recently, however, tattooing for young men has undergone a revival. Currently, the majority of young men get tattoos in their teens to demonstrate their pride in the traditional ways of their culture, as part of an explicit attempt to resist the total absorption of their indigenous culture into the global culture (Coté, 1994).

Tattooing is a traditional rite of passage for Samoan adolescents.

regulations concerning where they may go and what they may do, and the penalty for violating these taboos can be death. However, the Asante also celebrate girls' menarche with an elaborate ritual celebration. The menarcheal girl sits in public view under a canopy (a symbol of honor usually reserved for royalty), while others come before her to congratulate her, present her with gifts, and perform songs and dances in her honor. Thus, on this occasion menstruation is celebrated, even though the rest of the time it is viewed with a great deal of dread and fear.

Practices among Orthodox Jews show a similar ambivalence, with a shift toward a more positive balance in recent decades. Traditionally, when girls told their mothers they had reached menarche, mothers responded with a sudden ritualistic slap on the face (Brumberg, 1997). This gesture was intended to inform the daughter of the future difficulties awaiting her in her life as a woman. Following menarche, each time they menstruated Orthodox women were obliged to have a ritual bath called **mikveh** a week after their period

mikveh Among Orthodox Jews, the traditional ritual bath taken by a woman 7 days after her menstrual period was finished, as a way of ridding herself of the uncleanness believed to be associated with menstruation.

was finished, as a way of cleansing themselves of the impurity believed to be associated with menstruation. Today, the slap has been retired. The mikveh still exists, but today the bath has more positive connotations. Orthodox Jewish women report that it makes them feel connected to other Jewish women—their current Jewish friends as well as Jewish women of history (Kaufman, 1991). Also, because sexual intercourse is prohibited among Orthodox Jewish couples from the time a woman begins her period until the time she completes mikveh, mikveh also marks the woman's readiness for resuming lovemaking with her husband, and consequently it has connotations of sexual anticipation (Kaufman, 1991).

Puberty rituals for males do not focus on a particular biological event comparable to menarche for females, but the rites for males nevertheless share some common characteristics. In particular, they typically require the young man to display courage, strength, and endurance (Gilmore, 1990). Daily life in traditional cultures often requires these capacities from young men in warfare, hunting, fishing, and other tasks, so the rituals could be interpreted as letting them know what will be required of them as adult men and testing whether they will be up to adulthood's challenges.

The rituals for boys have often been violent, requiring boys to submit to and sometimes engage in bloodletting of various kinds. Among the Sambia of New Guinea, for example, a boy climbs onto the back of a "sponsor," who runs through a gauntlet of older men who beat the boy on his back until it is bloody (Herdt, 1987). The Samburu of West Africa have a public circumcision ritual for boys on the threshold of adolescence (Gilmore, 1990). Among the Amhara of Ethiopia, boys were forced to take part in whipping contests in which they faced off and lacerated each other's faces and bodies (LeVine, 1966). Some boys went further in proving their fortitude by scarring their arms with red-hot embers. Among the Tewa people of New Mexico (also known as the Pueblo Indians), at some point between the ages of 12 and 15 boys were taken away from their homes, purified in ritual ceremonies, and then stripped naked and lashed on the back with a whip that drew blood and left permanent scars.

Although these rituals may sound cruel if you have grown up in the West, adults of these cultures have believed that the rituals are necessary for boys to make the passage out of childhood toward manhood and be ready to face life's challenges. In all these cultures, however, with globalization the rituals have become less frequent or have disappeared altogether in recent decades (see the Cultural Focus box). Because traditional cultures are changing rapidly in response to globalization, the traditional puberty rituals no longer seem relevant to young people's futures (Burbank, 1988; Herdt & Leavitt, 1998).

THINKING CRITICALLY •••

Are there any rituals in Western cultures that are comparable to the puberty rituals in traditional cultures? Should people in Western cultures recognize and mark the attainment of puberty more than they do now? If so, why, and how?

Social and Personal Responses to Puberty

"I first menstruated when I was 13 and a half. The first thing I did was go to my mom. I wasn't sure exactly if I had begun to menstruate or not, but my mom knew. She had explained to me in great detail what would happen. She gave me a hug and I remember her saying, 'Now my little girl is a woman.' I remember thinking at the time how corny it was that she said that, but it made me feel a little better. My mother promised not to tell my dad, since I made her swear, although she told my grandmother, who sympathized with my plight by calling it 'the curse.' My grandmother told me how ignorant she was when she got hers and how she had asked my great grandmother if her brother Ed would get it, too."

—Erin, age 20 (Arnett, unpublished data)

The West does not have puberty rituals like those of traditional cultures. Nevertheless, in the West as in traditional cultures, the people in adolescents' social environment respond to the changes in adolescents' bodies that signify puberty and the development of sexual maturity. Adolescents in turn form their personal responses to puberty based in part on the information provided by the people in their social environment. First, let's look at the adjustments that take place in parent-adolescent relations when puberty begins, then at adolescents' personal responses to puberty.

Parent-Adolescent Relations and Puberty When young people reach puberty, the metamorphosis that takes place affects not only them personally but their relations with those closest to them, especially their parents. Just as adolescents have to adjust to the changes taking place in their bodies, parents have to adjust to the new person their child is becoming.

How do parent-adolescent relations change at puberty? For the most part, studies of adolescents and their parents in the American majority culture find that relations tend to become cooler when pubertal changes become evident (Holmbeck & Hill, 1991; Larson & Richards, 1994; Paikoff & Brooks-Gunn, 1991; Sarigiani & Petersen, 2000). Conflict increases and closeness decreases. Parents and adolescents seem to be less comfortable in each other's presence when puberty is reached, especially in their physical closeness. In one especially creative study demonstrating this change, researchers went to a shopping mall and an amusement park and observed 122 pairs of mothers and children aged 6 to 18 (Montemayor & Flannery, 1989). For each pair, the researchers observed them for 30 seconds and recorded whether they were talking, smiling, looking at, or touching each other. The most notable result of the study is shown in Figure 2.11. Early adolescents (ages 11–14) and their mothers were much less likely than younger children and their mothers to touch each other, and late adolescents (ages 15–18) and their mothers touched even less. Mothers and early adolescents talked more than mothers and younger children, sug-

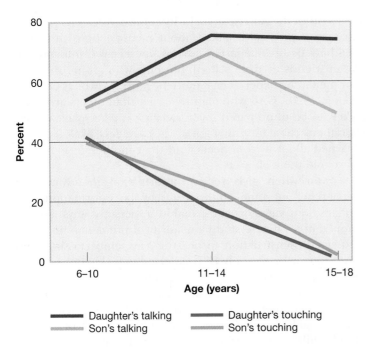

FIGURE 2.11 Frequency of adolescent-mother touching and talking.

Source: Montemayor & Flannery (1989).

gesting that parent-child communication styles shift toward talking and away from touching as puberty is reached.

Other studies have found that the physical changes of puberty, not age alone, lead to the change in parent-adolescent relations (Paikoff & Brooks-Gunn, 1991). If a child reaches puberty relatively early, relations with parents change relatively early; if a child reaches puberty relatively late, relations with parents change relatively late. For example, one study of 10- to 15-year-olds found that regardless of age, those who had reached puberty felt less close to their mothers and less accepted by their fathers (Steinberg, 1987a, 1988). Studies have also found that conflict with parents tends to be especially high for adolescents who mature early (Laursen & Collins, 1994; Sagestrano et al., 1999).

What is it about reaching puberty that causes parent-child relations to change? At this point, the answer is uncertain. Various explanations have been proposed, centering mostly on how the biologically based **incest taboo** between parents and children becomes activated once children reach sexual maturity, resulting in more distant relations (Belsky et al., 2007). If this explanation were true, however, one would expect to find distancing between adolescents and their parents in nearly all cultures, but this is not the case. In fact, the studies that have found distancing to take place at puberty have been mainly studies of two-parent White American families and one study of African American families (Sagestrano

et al., 1999). Distancing is not as common in Latino families or in divorced mother-headed families (Anderson, Hetherington, & Clingempeel, 1989; Molina & Chassin, 1996).

Distancing is also not typical in traditional cultures. Schlegel and Barry's (1991) survey of traditional cultures found that girls in traditional cultures often grow closer to their mothers during adolescence because they often spend much of their days side by side in shared labor. Furthermore, in traditional cultures as in the American majority culture, adolescents of both sexes tend to be closer to their mothers than to their fathers (Claes, 1998; Larson & Richards, 1994). If increased distance in adolescence were due to the incest taboo, one would expect adolescent sons to be closer to fathers, not mothers. Thus, the unanswered question appears to be, what is it about the American majority culture that leads to greater distancing between parents and children when children reach puberty?

Another finding with regard to parents and puberty is that puberty tends to begin earlier for girls in families with a stepfather or other adult male not biologically related to the girl (Belsky et al., 2007; Ellis & Garber, 2000). This has been found to occur in other mammals as well: Exposure to unrelated adult males causes females to reach puberty earlier, evidently because of exposure to the males' **pheromones**, which are airborne chemicals produced by the sweat glands (Miracle, Miracle, & Baumeister, 2003). Why the pheromones of unrelated males would stimulate puberty in girls is not well understood. It has also been found that family stress and conflict are related to early puberty in girls (Ellis & Garber, 2000; Moffitt et al., 1992; Steinberg, 1988). Again, the reason for this is not known.

Personal Responses to Menarche and Semenarche Although menarche occurs relatively late in pubertal development for most girls, their responses to it have received a great deal of attention from researchers. This may be because menarche is a more momentous event than other female pubertal changes. The growth of pubic hair, the development of breasts, and most other pubertal changes occur gradually, almost imperceptibly from one day to the next, whereas menarche is suddenly there one day, when there was nothing to herald it the day before. Similarly, menarche is easier for scientists to measure—it is easier to identify when menarche begins than to pinpoint the beginning of other more gradual changes. Menarche also holds a special significance in that it signifies that ovulation is beginning and reproductive maturity is arriving. Of course, boys' first ejaculation holds a similar significance, but it has received far less research, perhaps because of its relation to masturbation, a taboo topic in the West as it is in most cultures (Laquer, 2004).

---

incest taboo The prohibition on sexual relations between family members. Believed to be biologically based, as children born to closely related parents are at higher risk for genetic disorders.

pheromones Airborne chemicals, secreted by the sweat glands, that have effects on other mammals of the same species.

> "Each time I have a period ... I have the feeling that in spite of all the pain, unpleasantness, and nastiness, I have a sweet secret and that is why, although it is nothing but a nuisance to me in a way, I always long for the time that I shall feel that secret within me again."
>
> —Anne Frank (1942/1997), *Diary of a Young Girl*, p. 117

How do girls respond to menarche? Almost all the research on this topic has been conducted on girls in the American majority culture, and for them the short answer would be: positively for the most part but with shades of ambivalence. In a study of over 600 girls, Brooks-Gunn and Ruble (1982) found that girls often reported that menarche made them feel more "grown up." Many girls also indicated that they welcomed menarche because it allowed them to catch up to peers who had already begun menstruating and signified their capacity to bear children. Studies that follow girls over time find that menarche is followed by increases in social maturity, prestige with peers, and self-esteem (Archibald et al., 2003).

Not all reactions to menarche are positive, however. Both culture and biology may shade girls' reactions. Cultures may provide girls with no information to help them anticipate it, or with a view that leads them to anticipate it in a negative way. During the 19th century in American society, many girls received no information about menarche before it occurred, and they often responded with shock and fear when they were one day surprised by it (Brumberg, 1997; see the Historical Focus box). Across cultures, evidence from anthropological studies in cultures as diverse as rural Turkey, Malaysia, and Wales suggests that even today girls often are provided with no information at all to prepare them for menarche, with the result that it is experienced with fear and dismay (Howie & Shail, 2005). The following is an example from an Egyptian woman's memoir:

> It would be difficult for anyone to imagine the panic that seized hold of me one morning when I woke to find blood trickling down beneath my thighs . . . I was obliged to overcome the fear and shame which possessed me and speak to my mother. I asked her to take me to a doctor for treatment. To my utter surprise she was calm and cool and did not seem to be affected by her daughter's serious condition. She explained that this was something that happened to all girls and that it recurs every month for a few days. On the last day when the flow ceased, I was to cleanse myself of this 'impure blood' by having a hot bath... . I was therefore to understand that in me there was something degrading which appeared regularly in the form of this impure blood, and that it was something to be ashamed of, to hide from others. (Saadawi, 1980, p. 45)

premenstrual syndrome (PMS) The combination of behavioral, emotional, and physical symptoms that occur in some females the week before menstruation.

Within the American majority culture, research indicates that most girls have talked about menstruation with their mothers before menarche arrives, or received information from friends or from school, but girls who are unprepared for menarche experience it more negatively (Brooks-Gunn & Reiter, 1990). Girls who mature earlier than others are more likely to be unprepared for it. Because it takes place earlier for them than for other girls, they are less likely to have learned about it from peers, and their mothers may not yet have told them about it.

Even when girls receive information in advance of menarche, in some cultures it may be information that shapes their views of menstruation in negative ways. For example, in a Chinese study, a majority of premenarcheal girls expected menstruation to be annoying, embarrassing, and confusing, whereas only 10% expected to feel happy or excited (Yeung, 2005). Negative expectations of menarche were especially high among girls who accepted traditional Chinese beliefs about menstruation, such as beliefs that menstruation brings bad luck, that women should not wash hair or eat cold food while menstruating, and that it is easier to get sick during or after menstruation. A study of Mexican premenarcheal girls found similarly negative expectations for menarche, based in similarly negative cultural views of menstruation (Marván et al., 2007). Research also indicates that girls whose mothers, peers, or other sources have led them to expect menstruation to be unpleasant report greater discomfort once menarche occurs (Brooks-Gunn & Ruble, 1982; Tang, Yeung, & Lee, 2004; Teitelman, 2004).

The results of studies of girls' responses to menarche indicate vividly that the degree to which cultures provide knowledge and shape expectations for menarche can have important effects on how girls experience it. However, studies also indicate that most girls and women experience a certain amount of biologically based discomfort associated with menstruation. Among adolescent girls, most report some degree of **premenstrual syndrome (PMS)**, the combination of behavioral, emotional, and physical symptoms that occur in the week before menstruation (Dean et al., 2006). Various studies have found that from one half to three fourths of adolescent girls experience discomfort related to their menstrual cycles, with symptoms including cramps, backaches, headaches, fatigue, and depression, as well as general discomfort (Brooks-Gunn & Ruble, 1982; Fisher, Trieller, & Napolitano, 1989; Klein & Litt, 1983; Meaden, Hartlage, & Cook-Karr, 2005; Yonkers et al., 2006). The most common source of discomfort is cramps, experienced by 30–50% of girls and women (Finkelstein, 2001d). Even among girls whose experience of menarche is mostly positive, many dislike the messiness of dealing with menstrual blood and the obligation of carrying around supplies to deal with it every month (Brooks-Gunn & Ruble, 1982; Tang, Yeung, & Lee, 2003). Also, some girls report disliking the limits menstruation places on their activities.

Seen in this light, it is easier to understand the ambivalence girls often experience when they begin menstruating. They like the confirmation that they are developing normally toward reproductive maturity, but they may not like the dis-

Some traditional cultures have harbored false beliefs about menstruation, such as the belief that menstrual blood has magical power that can cause crops to fail. However, false beliefs about menstruation are not exclusive to traditional cultures. In the United States, erroneous and even bizarre beliefs about menstruation were widespread until relatively recent times. Furthermore, menarche has been shrouded in shame and secrecy, leaving many girls entirely ignorant of it until they suddenly found themselves bleeding incomprehensibly. The history of American beliefs about menstruation and menarche is described in *The Body Project: An Intimate History of American Girls* by Joan Jacobs Brumberg (1997).

Throughout the 19th century, menstruation and menarche were regarded as taboo topics in most middle-class American families. An 1895 study of Boston high school girls indicated that 60% had no knowledge of menarche before it occurred. A popular 1882 advice book for mothers railed against the "criminal reserve" and "pseudo-delicacy" that led mothers to fail to prepare their girls for menarche. Another 19th-century advice writer reported that "numbers of women" had written to tell her that they were totally unprepared for menarche, including one who wrote, "It has taken me nearly a lifetime to forgive my mother for sending me away to boarding school without telling me about it." A Cornell professor and author of books for young people reported that many college girls believed they were internally wounded when menarche arrived. At the time, menarche occurred later than it does now (typically age 15 or 16) and college entrance was earlier (16 or 17), so many girls experienced menarche at college.

Why such secrecy? Because middle-class Americans of that era believed they had a duty to protect girls' "innocence" for as long as they could. Children who grew up on farms learned a lot about the facts of life by observing and caring for farm animals, but parents in the middle class sought to protect

Mothers in the 19th century rarely discussed menarche with their daughters.

their children from such raw realities. They associated menarche with budding sexuality, and they were zealous about protecting girls' virginity until marriage. As part of this effort, they often attempted to delay menarche by having girls avoid sexually "stimulating" foods such as pickles! Menarche came anyway, pickles or not, but they believed it was best to keep girls in ignorance of menarche—and sexuality—for as long as possible.

In the course of the 20th century, as the sexual restrictiveness of the 19th century faded, menarche and menstruation gradually became more openly discussed. The Girl Scouts were among the first organizations to discuss menstruation openly. Beginning in the 1920s, attaining the Health Winner merit badge required young Girl Scouts to read about menarche and talk to their troop leader about it. A substantial amount of information was communicated through the media. In the 1920s, as mass-produced "sanitary napkins" became popular (previously, cotton rags or cheesecloth had been typically used to stanch menstrual blood), ads for sanitary napkins helped to open up discussion of menstruation. Companies making sanitary napkins distributed pamphlets on menstruation to girls through mothers, teachers, and the Girl Scouts during the 1930s and 1940s. In the 1940s a cartoon produced by the Disney Company, "The Story of Menstruation," was seen by 93 million American school girls. Magazines for girls, such as *Seventeen*, provided advice on how to handle menstruation while remaining active.

Today, it is rare for an American girl to experience menarche in total ignorance of what is happening to her body. Perhaps because menarche now takes place at around age 12, cultural beliefs in American society no longer associate menarche with sexuality but rather with health and hygiene. It may be that dissociating menarche from sex has been important in allowing it to be discussed more openly. As we will see in later chapters, however, open discussions of adolescent sexuality remain rare in American society.

comfort and practical requirements that accompany menstruation each month. However, adolescent girls and adult women experience a great range of physical responses to menstruation. At the extreme, a very small proportion of girls and women experience premenstrual symptoms that are

severe enough to interfere with their daily functioning; on the other hand, some experience no symptoms at all, and there is a great deal of variability in between these two extremes (Dean et al., 2006; Yonkers et al., 2008). Poor diet, high stress, alcohol use, insufficient sleep, and lack of exercise all make PMS symptoms more severe, but orgasms relieve menstrual cramps for many women (Carroll & Wolpe, 1996). Ibuprofen and other medications are also effective treatments for cramps (Finkelstein, 2001d).

For boys, perhaps the closest analogue to menarche is first ejaculation, sometimes known as **semenarche** (not to be confused with spermarche, which was described earlier in this chapter). Very little research has taken place on this topic. Two small studies (Gaddis & Brooks-Gunn, 1985; Stein & Reiser, 1993) found that boys' reactions to semenarche were mostly positive. They enjoyed the pleasurable sensations of it, and, like girls' experience of menarche, it made them feel more grown up. However, ambivalence existed for boys as well. Many reported that surprise or fear was part of the experience. Most girls in Western countries now receive some information about menarche before it happens, but parents rarely talk to their boys about semenarche (Frankel, 2002).

Culture certainly influences boys' interpretation of semenarche. It may occur through "wet dreams" or masturbation, and there is a long history of shame and censure associated with masturbation in the West (Frankel, 2002; Laquer, 2004). Perhaps for this reason, American boys tend to tell no one after they experience semenarche (Gaddis & Brooks-Gunn, 1985). In contrast, a study of boys in Nigeria found that boys tended to tell their friends about semenarche soon after it took place (Adegoke, 1993), perhaps reflecting less of a stigma associated with masturbation in Nigerian culture.

THINKING CRITICALLY •••

What kind of preparation for menarche/semenarche would you recommend be provided for today's adolescents? At what age? If schools provide information on menarche/semenarche, should that information include a discussion of the relation between these events and sexuality?

Early and Late Pubertal Timing

"Everybody thought there was something wrong with me because I still looked like a ten-year-old until I was fifteen or sixteen. That has been really a bad experience for me, because everybody was changing around me and I was standing still. I was changing in my head but not my body. My parents were even going to take me to the doctor to see if I was deformed or something like that, but they didn't, and finally last year I started to grow. My voice started changing and everything, so I guess I'm normal after all, but I think it's going to be awhile before I stop feeling like I'm different from everybody else."

—Steven, age 17 (quoted in Bell, 1998, p. 14)

In some respects, social and personal responses to puberty are intertwined. That is, one factor that determines how ado-

lescents respond to reaching puberty is how others respond. In industrialized societies, one aspect of others' responses that adolescents seem to be acutely aware of concerns perceptions of whether they have reached puberty relatively early or relatively late compared with their peers.

Within cultures, the timing of puberty appears to be based mainly on genetic factors (Anderson et al., 2007). Mothers' age of menarche strongly predicts their daughters' (Belsky et al., 2007). Sisters' ages of menarche are highly correlated, and correlations are especially high between identical twin sisters (Ge et al., 2007; van den Berg, 2007). However, as noted earlier in the chapter, there is some evidence that environmental factors such as stress may trigger earlier puberty (DeRose & Brooks-Gunn, 2006).

The timing of puberty is especially important in industrialized countries. One interesting feature of puberty rites in traditional cultures is that eligibility for the rites is not typically based on age but on pubertal maturation. This is obvious with regard to rites related to menarche; a girl participates the first time she menstruates. However, boys' participation in puberty rites is also based on maturation rather than age. Typically, the adults of the community decide when a boy is ready, based on his level of physical maturation and on their perceptions of his psychological and social readiness (Schlegel & Barry, 1991). Consequently, the precise age of reaching puberty matters little; everyone gets there eventually.

In contrast, chronological age has much more significance in industrialized countries, as reflected in the fact that the school systems in industrialized countries are **age-graded**—that is, children are grouped on the basis of age rather than developmental maturity. As a result, the 7th grade, for example, includes children who are all 12 or 13 years old, but their pubertal development is likely to vary widely, from those who have not experienced any pubertal changes to those who are well on the way to full maturity. Grouping them together in the same classrooms for many hours each day adds to the intensity of comparisons between them and makes them highly aware of whether they are early, late, or "on time," compared with others.

A great deal of research has been conducted on early versus late maturation among adolescents in the West, extending back over a half century. The results are complex. They differ depending on gender, and the short-term effects of maturing early or late appear to differ from the long-term effects. The effects also differ depending on the area of development considered: body image, popularity, school performance, or behavior problems. To help clarify these differences, we will look at the results of these studies separately for girls and boys.

Early and Late Maturation Among Girls The effects of early maturation are especially negative for girls. Findings from a variety of Western countries concur that early-maturing girls are at risk for numerous problems, including depressed mood,

---

semenarche A male's first ejaculation.

age-graded Organized by age, for example in schools.

negative body image, eating disorders, substance use, delinquency, aggressive behavior, school problems, and conflict with parents (Lanza & Collins, 2002; Lynne et al., 2007; Mendle et al., 2007; Obeidallah, Brennan, Brooks-Gunn, & Earls, 2004; Sagestrano et al., 1999; Weichold, Silbereisen, & Schmitt-Rodermund, 2003; Westling et al., 2008; Wichstrom, 2001).

Why is early maturation such a problem for girls in the West? One reason involves cultural values about physical appearance. Because early maturation typically leads to a shorter and heavier appearance, it is a disadvantage in Western cultures that value thinness in females' appearance. This helps explain why early-maturing girls have higher rates of depressed mood, negative body image, and eating disorders (Lien et al., 2007; Mendle et al., 2007). Notably, African American and Latina girls do not show these effects of early maturation, perhaps because these cultures are less likely to have a tall and thin physique as the female ideal (Ge, Elder, Regnerus, & Cox, 2001; Hayward, Gotlib, Schraedley, & Litt, 1999).

A second reason for the problems of early-maturing girls is that their early physical development draws the attention of older boys, who then introduce them to an older group of friends and to substance use, delinquency, and early sexual activity (Lynne et al., 2007; Petersen, 1993; Weichold et al., 2003; Westling et al.,. 2008). So when early-maturing girls have higher rates of these behaviors than other girls their age, it may be because they are behaving more like their friends who are older than they are.

Late-maturing girls share few of early-maturing girls' problems, although they suffer from teasing and negative body image during the years when other girls have begun to develop and they have not (Weichold et al., 2003). By their late teens, however, they tend to have a more favorable body image than other girls (Simmons & Blyth, 1987), probably because they are more likely to end up with the lean body build that tends to be regarded as attractive in Western majority cultures.

Studies on the long-term effects of early maturation for girls are mixed. Some studies find that most of the negative effects diminish by the late teens (Posner, 2006; Weichold et al., 2003). However, one British study (Sandler, Wilcox, & Horney, 1984) and one Swedish study (Stattin & Magnusson, 1990) found that early-maturing girls entered marriage and parenthood earlier. Also, an American study reported that at age 24, women who had been early maturers had more psychological and social problems than women who had reached puberty "on time" (Graber, Seeley, Brooks-Gunn, & Lewinsohn, 2004). So, more research into the long-term consequences of early maturation seems warranted.

THINKING CRITICALLY •••

In the light of the difficulties often experienced by early-maturing girls, can you think of anything families, communities, or schools could do to assist them?

Early and Late Maturation Among Boys In contrast to girls, for whom early maturation has overwhelmingly negative effects, the effects of early maturation for boys are positive in

> "A girl could claim to have her period for months and nobody would ever know the difference. Which is exactly what I did. All you had to do was make a big fuss over having enough nickels for the Kotex machine and walk around clutching your stomach and moaning for three to five days a month about the Curse and you could convince anybody… . 'I can't go. I have cramps.' 'I can't do that. I have cramps.' And most of all, gigglingly, blushingly: 'I can't swim. I have cramps.' Nobody ever used the hard-core word. Menstruation. God, what an awful word. Never that. 'I have cramps.'"
>
> —Nora Ephron 2000, *Crazy Salad*, pp. 2–3

some ways and negative in others. Early-maturing boys tend to have more favorable body images and to be more popular than other boys (Graber, Lewinsohn, Seeley, & Brooks-Gunn, 1997; Weichold et al., 2003). This may be because early-maturing boys get their burst of growth and muscular development before other boys do, which gives them a distinct advantage in the sports activities that are so important to male prestige in middle school and high school. Also, the earlier development of facial hair, lowered voice, and other secondary sex characteristics may make early-maturing boys more attractive to girls. Early-maturing boys may also have a long-term advantage. One study that followed early-maturing adolescent boys 40 years later found that they had achieved greater success in their careers and had higher marital satisfaction than later-maturing boys (Taga et al., 2006).

However, not everything about being an early-maturing boy is favorable. Like their female counterparts, early-maturing boys tend to become involved earlier in delinquency, sex, and substance use (Silbereisen & Kracke, 1997; Westling et al., 2008; Wichstrom, 2001; Williams & Dunlop, 1999). Some studies report that early-maturing boys have higher rates of emotional distress (Ge, Conger, & Elder,

Adolescents of the same age have many different levels of physical maturity. How does age-grading of schools accentuate these differences?

"I think it's disgusting that you all pick on me because I'm big!" Laura said, sniffling . . .

"Don't you think I know all about you and your friends? Do you think it's any fun to be the biggest kid in the class?"

"I don't know," I said. "I never thought about it."

"Well, try thinking about it. Think about how you'd feel if you had to wear a bra in fourth grade and how everybody laughed and how you always had to cross your arms in front of you. And about how the boys called you dirty names just because of how you looked."

I thought about it. "I'm sorry, Laura," I said.

"I'll bet!"

"I really am. If you want to know the truth . . . well, I wish I looked more like you than like me."

"I'd gladly trade places with you."

—From *Are You There, God? It's Me, Margaret* by Judy Blume (1970)

2001), despite their more positive body images. Late-maturing boys also show evidence of problems. Compared to boys who mature "on time," late-maturing boys have higher rates of alcohol use and delinquency (Andersson & Magnusson, 1990; Williams & Dunlop, 1999). They also have lower grades in school (Weichold et al., 2003). There is some evidence that late-maturing boys have elevated levels of substance use and deviant behavior well into emerging adulthood (Biehl et al., 2007; Graber et al., 2004).

In sum, the effects of early and late maturation differ considerably between girls and boys. For girls, early maturation puts them at risk for a host of problems, but late maturation does not. For boys, both early and late maturation make them at risk for problems, but early maturation also includes some benefits. The problems of early-maturing girls appear to be due in part to their associations with older boys, but the sources of the problems of early- and late-maturing boys are not clear.

As you read about these studies of early- and late-maturing boys and girls, keep in mind that each of these groups displays a great deal of variance. Although early and late maturation are related to certain kinds of general outcomes on a group level, the effects for individuals will naturally depend on their particular experiences and relationships.

Also keep in mind that, so far, nearly all the studies conducted on pubertal timing have involved adolescents in the majority cultures of Western countries (Güre et al., 2006; Lien et al., 2006). I suggested earlier that the effects of maturing early or late may be due to the age-grading that exists in these countries, but right now we do not know how adolescents respond to pubertal timing in cultures where no age-graded schooling exists.

Biological Development and the Environment: The Theory of Genotype–Environment Interactions

For many decades in the social sciences, scholars have debated the relative importance of biology and the environment in human development. In this **nature–nurture debate**, some scholars have claimed that human behavior can be explained by biological factors (nature) and that environment matters little, whereas others have claimed that biology is irrelevant and that human behavior can be explained by environmental factors (nurture). In recent years, most scholars have reached a consensus that both biology and environment play key roles in human development, although they continue to debate the relative strength of nature and nurture (Lerner, 2006).

Given the profound biological changes that take place in adolescence and emerging adulthood, nature–nurture issues are perhaps especially relevant to these periods of life. One influential theory on this topic that I will be relying on occasionally in this book is the **theory of genotype–environment interactions** (Scarr, 1993; Scarr & McCartney, 1983). According to this theory, both genotype (a person's inherited genes) and environment make essential contributions to human development. However, the relative strengths of genetics and the environment are difficult to unravel because our genes actually influence the kind of environment we experience. Based on our genotypes, we *create our own environments*, to a considerable extent. These genotype–environment interactions take three forms: passive, evocative, and active.

Passive genotype–environment interactions occur in biological families because *parents provide both genes and environment for their children*. This may seem obvious, but it has profound implications for how we think about development. Take this father–daughter example. Dad has been good at

nature–nurture debate Debate over the relative importance of biology and the environment in human development.

theory of genotype–environment interactions Theory that both genetics and environment make essential contributions to human development but are difficult to unravel because our genes actually influence the kind of environment we experience.

passive genotype–environment interactions Situation in biological families that parents provide both genes and environment for their children, making genes and environment difficult to separate in their effects on children's development.

evocative genotype–environment interactions Occur when a person's inherited characteristics evoke responses from others in their environment.

active genotype–environment interactions Occur when people seek out environments that correspond to their genotypic characteristics.

drawing things ever since he was a boy, and now he makes a living as a commercial illustrator. One of the first birthday presents he gives to his little girl is a set of crayons and colored pencils for drawing. She seems to like it, and he provides her with increasingly sophisticated materials as she grows up. He also teaches her a number of drawing skills as she seems ready to learn them. By the time she reaches adolescence, she's quite a proficient artist herself and draws a lot of the art for school clubs and social events. She goes to college and majors in architecture, and then goes on to become an architect. It is easy to see how she became so good at drawing, given an environment that stimulated her drawing abilities so much—right?

Not so fast. It is true that Dad provided her with a stimulating environment, but he also provided her with half her genes. If there are any genes that contribute to drawing ability—such as genes that promote spatial reasoning and fine motor coordination—she may well have received those from Dad, too. The point is that in a biological family, it is very difficult to separate genetic influences from environmental influences because *parents provide both*, and they are likely to provide an environment that reinforces the tendencies they have provided to their children through their genes.

So you should be skeptical when you read studies about parents and adolescents in biological families claiming that the behavior of parents is the cause of the characteristics of adolescents. Remember from Chapter 1: Correlation is not necessarily causation! Just because a *correlation* exists between the behavior of parents and the characteristics of adolescents does not mean the parents *caused* the adolescents to have those characteristics. Maybe causation was involved, but in biological families it is difficult to tell. The correlation could be due to the similarity in genes between the biological parents and their adolescents rather than to the environment the biological parents provided.

One good way to unravel this tangle is through adoption studies. These studies avoid the problem of passive genotype–environment interactions because one set of parents provided the adolescents' genes but a different set of parents provided the environment. So when adolescents are more similar to their adoptive parents than to their biological parents, it is possible to make a strong case that this similarity is due to the environment provided by the adoptive parents, and when adolescents are more similar to their biological parents than to their adoptive parents it is likely that genes played a strong role. We will examine specific adoption studies in future chapters.

Evocative genotype–environment interactions occur when a person's inherited characteristics evoke responses from others in their environment. If you had a son who started reading at age 3 and seemed to love it, you might buy him more books; if you had a daughter who could sink 20-foot jump shots at age 12, you might arrange to send her to basketball camp. Did you ever baby-sit or work in a setting where there were many children? If so, you probably found that children differ in how sociable, cooperative, and obedient they are. In turn, you may have found that you reacted

differently to them, depending on their characteristics. That is what is meant by evocative genotype–environment interactions—with the crucial addition of the assumption that characteristics such as reading ability, athletic ability, and sociability are at least partly based on genetics.

Active genotype–environment interactions occur when people seek out environments that correspond to their genotypic characteristics. The child who reads easily may ask for books as birthday gifts; the adolescent with an ear for music may ask for piano lessons; the emerging adult for whom reading has always been slow and difficult may choose to begin working full time after high school rather than going to college. The idea here is that people are drawn to environments that match their inherited abilities.

Genotype–Environment Interactions Over Time

The three types of genotype–environment interactions operate throughout childhood, adolescence, and emerging adulthood, but their relative balance changes over time (Scarr, 1993). In childhood, passive genotype–environment interactions are especially pronounced, and active genotype–environment interactions are relatively weak. This is because the younger a child is, the more parents control the daily environment the child experiences and the less autonomy the child has to seek out environmental influences outside the family. However, with age, especially as children move through adolescence and emerging adulthood, the balance changes. Parental control diminishes, so passive genotype–environment interactions also diminish. Autonomy increases, so active genotype–environment interactions also increase. Evocative genotype–environment interactions remain relatively stable from childhood through emerging adulthood.

The theory of genotype–environment interactions is by no means universally accepted by scholars on human development. In fact, it has been the source of vigorous debate in the field (Baumind, 1993; Scarr, 1993). Some scholars question the theory's claim that characteristics such as sociability,

When adolescents have skills or interests similar to their parents, is the similarity due to environment or genetics?

reading ability, and athletic ability are substantially inherited. However, it is currently one of the most important new theories of human development, and you should be familiar with it as part of your understanding of development during adolescence and emerging adulthood. I find the theory provocative and illuminating, and I will be referring to it in the chapters to come.

THINKING CRITICALLY •••

Think of one of your abilities in relation to the genes and environment your parents have provided to you, and describe how the various types of genotype–environment interactions may have been involved in your development of that ability.

SUMMING UP

This chapter has presented the biological changes that take place during puberty as well as the cultural, social, and personal responses that result from these changes. Here are the main points we have covered in this chapter:

- During puberty, a set of remarkable transformations takes place in young people's bodies. Hormonal changes lead to changes in physical functioning and to the development of primary and secondary sex characteristics.

- The hormonal changes of puberty begin in the hypothalamus, initiated when a threshold level of leptin is reached. The chain of events in the endocrine system runs from the hypothalamus to the pituitary gland to the gonads and adrenal glands to the hypothalamus again, in a feedback loop that monitors the levels of the sex hormones (androgens and estrogens). The set points for the sex hormones rise in the course of puberty.

- Physical growth during puberty includes the growth spurt as well as increases in muscle mass (especially in boys) and body fat (especially in girls). The heart and lungs also grow dramatically, especially for boys.

- Obesity has become a serious public health problem in industrialized countries, especially the United States, and the prevalence of this problem increases sharply during adolescence. The increase in obesity in recent years is due mainly to increases in consumption of foods high in fat and sugar (especially fast food) and a decrease in rates of exercise.

- In many respects, emerging adulthood is a time of peak physical functioning for most people, when athletic performance peaks and susceptibility to illness and disease is at its nadir. However, emerging adults are at higher risk than people of other ages for certain problems due to lifestyle and behavior, including automobile fatalities, homicide, and sexually transmitted diseases.

- Primary sex characteristics are related directly to reproduction. Females are born with all their eggs already in their ovaries, but males produce sperm only once they reach puberty.

- Secondary sex characteristics develop at puberty but are not directly related to reproduction. Girls show the first development of secondary sex characteristics about

2 years earlier than boys. The order of pubertal events is quite predictable, but adolescents vary greatly in the ages the events begin and how long it takes to complete them.

- Cultures influence the timing of puberty through cultural technologies in nutrition and medical care. The initiation of puberty is earlier when nutrition and medical care are good, and consequently the age of beginning puberty decreased steadily in industrialized countries during the 20th century and is now decreasing in developing countries.

- Many traditional cultures have rituals that give meaning to pubertal changes, usually focused on menarche for girls and on tests of courage, strength, and endurance for boys.

- Cultures influence adolescents' experiences of puberty by providing or failing to provide young people with information about what is happening to their bodies. Menarche can be traumatic when girls are unprepared for it, but girls today typically know about it long before it arrives.

- In industrialized countries, the cultural practice of age-graded schooling means that the timing of puberty has important consequences for adolescents who begin puberty relatively early or relatively late. Early maturation is especially problematic for girls.

- According to the theory of genotype–environment interactions, the influences of genetics and the environment are difficult to separate because in some ways genes shape the kind of environment we experience. During adolescence and emerging adulthood, passive genotype–environment interactions decrease and active genotype-environment interactions increase.

Perhaps the most notable single fact in this chapter is that the typical age of reaching puberty has declined steeply in industrialized countries over the past 150 years, so that now the first evident changes of puberty take place between ages 10 and 12 for most adolescents in these countries, sometimes even earlier. Reaching puberty means reaching sexual maturity, and in many ways the cultural beliefs and practices of industrialized countries still have not adjusted to the fact that young people now reach the threshold of sexual maturity at such an early age. Parents are often unsure of when or how to talk to children about their changing bodies and their sexual feelings. School officials are often equally unsure about what to communicate to children. Adolescent peers exchange information among themselves, but what they tell each other is not always accurate or healthy. Consequently, adolescents often experience their biological changes with limited information about the psychological and social implications of what is happening to their bodies.

In this area even more than in most of the areas we will discuss in this book, we know little about the experiences of young people outside of the middle-class majority cultures of Western countries. How do young people in traditional cultures respond to the biological changes of puberty? And what about adolescents in minority cultures in Western societies? In the decades to come, research on these questions may provide us with better information about the different ways that cultures may enhance young people's passage through the dramatic transformations of puberty.

KEY TERMS

INTERNET RESOURCES

http://www.ama-assn.org/ama/pub/category/1947.html

The American Medical Association's Program on Child and Adolescent Health provides this web site as a source of health-related information. It includes information on injury prevention, nutrition, and physical fitness, among other topics. The information is intended to be understandable to the general public, not just physicians and other health care providers.

http://www.cdc.gov/HealthyYouth/index.htm

This Centers for Disease Control and Prevention web site focuses on adolescent health. It provides statistics as well as information on medical treatments and health promotion programs.

FOR FURTHER READING

Bell, R. (1998). *Changing bodies, changing lives: A book for teens on sex and relationships* (3rd ed.). New York: Random House. A lively account of the changes of puberty, including bodily changes as well as sexuality and relationships. Written to help adolescents understand their changing bodies, it includes many illuminating quotes.

Brumberg, J. J. (1997). *The body project: An intimate history of American girls.* New York: Random House. A highly readable history of changes in American beliefs and attitudes regarding the physical development of adolescent girls. Includes fascinating information about menarche and menstruation, skin care, standards of body shape and size, and sexuality. For each topic, changes from the early 19th century to the present are discussed.

Haywood, C. (Ed.). (2003). *Puberty and psychopathology.* New York: Cambridge University Press. A collection of chapters on the physical, social, and psychological changes of puberty, with a focus on how those changes place some adolescents at risk for psychological problems.

Markstrom, C.A. (2008). *Empowerment of North American Indian girls: Ritual expressions at puberty.* Lincoln, Nebraska: University of Nebraska Press. A fascinating examination of puberty rituals for adolescent girls in four Native American cultures: Apache, Navajo, Lakota, and Ojibwa. Of particular interest is the distinctive Apache Sunrise Dance, which is described and analyzed in detail. Also includes information on Native American beliefs concerning menarche and menstruation.

3 Cognitive Foundations

Namo has a problem. It is early morning, and he is standing with some friends on the shore of Truk Island in the South Pacific. The friends (all in their late teens) have planned a spearfishing trip for today, but as Namo looks out over the ocean he notices signs that disturb him. The movement and color of the clouds, the height and activity of the waves, all suggest a storm on the way. He looks over their equipment—spears, a small outboard motorboat with a single motor (no oars or sails), some liquid refreshments. If they were planning with safety in mind they would at least take oars, but he knows that a large part of the appeal of the trip is the risk involved, with the opportunity it presents to demonstrate their courage. The small boat, the dubious weather, and the large sharks common in the area where they will be swimming as they spearfish will present them with ample opportunity today to test their bravery. As he matches the anticipated challenges with their capacities, he is confident they will measure up to them. Quelling his doubts, he jumps in the boat and they set off (based on Marshall, 1979).

Elke has a problem. She is sitting in the staff room of a hospital in Bremen, Germany, and analyzing the medical charts of a patient being treated for ovarian cysts. Something is not quite right—the diagnosis is ovarian cysts, but the levels of some of the patient's hormones are much higher than normal and suggest that something else besides the cysts is problematic. At age 22, Elke has been studying medicine for 3 years and has learned a great deal, but she is well aware that she has not yet accumulated the knowledge and experience the doctors have. She wonders, should she tell them what she thinks?

Mike has a problem. He is sitting in his 8th-grade classroom in San Francisco, California, and puzzling over the problems on the math quiz in front of him. "Amy received 70% of the votes in the election for class president," reads the first one. "If her opponent received the remaining 21 votes, how many people voted in the election?" Mike stares at the question and tries to remember how to solve such a problem. He was working on one last night that was just like this; how did it go? He has difficulty recalling it, and his attention begins to drift off to other topics—the basketball game coming up this Friday, the Fifty Cent song he was listening to on his iPod on the way to school, the legs of the girl in the white skirt two rows in front of him—wow! "Ten minutes," intones the teacher from the front of the room. "You have ten more minutes." Seized with panic, he focuses again on the problem in front of him.

ADOLESCENTS AND EMERGING ADULTS ALL OVER the world confront intellectual challenges as part of their daily lives. Often, as in the cases of Namo and Elke, their challenges are similar in type and magnitude to the challenges faced by adults, although usually they have less authority and responsibility than adults have. In industrialized countries, many of the intellectual challenges adolescents face take place in the school setting, as in Mike's case. As we shall see, however, the changes that occur in cognitive development during adolescence and emerging adulthood affect all aspects of their lives, not just their school performance.

In this chapter we will look at changes in how adolescents and emerging adults think, how they solve problems, and how their capacities for memory and attention change. These changes entail what scholars call **cognitive development**. We will begin by talking about Jean Piaget's theory of cognitive development and some of the research based on it. Piaget's theory describes general changes in mental structures and problem-solving abilities that take place during childhood and adolescence. Next we will discuss some of the cognitive changes that occur during emerging adulthood. Then we will consider theory and research on information processing. In contrast to the Piagetian approach, which describes general changes in cognitive development, the information-processing approach focuses on a detailed examination of specific cognitive abilities such as attention and memory.

Later in the chapter we will look at the practical use of cognitive abilities in critical thinking and decision making, and the ways that ideas about cognitive development can be applied to social topics. Following this discussion, we will examine the major intelligence tests and studies that have used these tests to investigate the cognitive development of adolescents and emerging adults. Next we will present exciting new findings on brain development in adolescence and emerging adulthood. Finally, we will discuss the role of culture in cognitive development.

Piaget's Theory of Cognitive Development

Unquestionably, the most influential theory of cognitive development from infancy through adolescence is the one developed by the Swiss psychologist **Jean Piaget** (pronounced pee-ah-*jay*), who lived from 1896 to 1980. Piaget was quite the adolescent prodigy. He developed an early fascination with the workings of the natural world, and he published articles on mollusks while still in his early teens.

After receiving his Ph.D. at age 21 for his studies of mollusks, Piaget shifted his interests to human development. He took a job that involved intelligence testing with children, and he was intrigued by the kinds of wrong answers children would give. It seemed to him that children of the same age not only answered the questions in similar ways when they gave the correct answer, but also gave similar kinds of wrong answers. He concluded that age differences in patterns of wrong answers reflected differences in how children of various ages thought about the questions. Older children not only know more than younger children, he decided, they also think differently.

This insight became the basis of much of Piaget's work over the next 60 years. Piaget's observations convinced him that children of different ages think differently and that changes in cognitive development proceed in distinct stages (Piaget, 1972). Each stage involves a different way of thinking about the world. The idea of **stages** means that each person's

Jean Piaget.

cognitive abilities are organized into a coherent **mental structure**; a person who thinks within a particular stage in one aspect of life should think within that stage in all other aspects of life as well because all thinking is part of the same mental structure (Keating, 1991, 2004). Because Piaget focused on how cognition changes with age, his approach (and the approach of those who have followed in his tradition) is known as the **cognitive-developmental approach**.

According to Piaget, the driving force behind development from one stage to the next is **maturation** (Inhelder & Piaget, 1958). All of us have within our genotypes a prescription for cognitive development that prepares us for certain changes at certain ages. A reasonably normal environment is necessary for cognitive development to occur, but the effect of the environment on cognitive development is limited. You cannot teach an 8-year-old something that only a 13-year-old can learn, no matter how sophisticated your teaching techniques. In the same way, by the time the 8-year-old reaches age 13, the biological processes of maturation will make it easy for him or her to understand the world as a typical child of 13 understands it, and no special teaching will be required.

---

cognitive development Changes over time in how people think, how they solve problems, and how their capacities for memory and attention change.

Jean Piaget Influential Swiss developmental psychologist, best known for his theories of cognitive and moral development.

stage A period in which abilities are organized in a coherent, interrelated way.

mental structure The organization of cognitive abilities into a single pattern, such that thinking in all aspects of life is a reflection of that structure.

cognitive-developmental approach Approach to understanding cognition that emphasizes the changes that take place at different ages.

maturation Process by which abilities develop through genetically based development with limited influence from the environment.

TABLE 3.1 Piaget's Stages of Cognitive Development

Ages	Stage	Characteristics
0–2	Sensorimotor	Learn to coordinate the activities of the senses with motor activities.
2–7	Preoperational	Capable of symbolic representation, such as in language, but limited ability to use mental operations.
7–11	Concrete operations	Capable of using mental operations, but only in concrete, immediate experience; difficulty thinking hypothetically.
11–15/20	Formal operations	Capable of thinking logically and abstractly, capable of formulating hypotheses and testing them systematically; thinking is more complex, and can think about thinking (metacognition).

Piaget's emphasis on the importance of maturation contrasted with the views of other theorists, who believed that there were no inherent limits to development or that environmental stimulation could override them (Flavell, Miller, & Miller, 2002). The emphasis on maturation also separated Piaget from other theorists in that Piaget portrayed maturation as an active process in which children seek out information and stimulation in the environment that matches the maturity of their thinking. This contrasted with the view of other theorists such as the behaviorists, who saw the environment as acting on the child through rewards and punishments rather than seeing the child as an active agent.

Piaget proposed that the active construction of reality takes place through the use of **schemes**, which are structures for organizing and interpreting information. For infants, schemes are based on sensory and motor processes such as sucking and grasping, but after infancy schemes become symbolic and representational, as words, ideas, and concepts.

The two processes involved in the use of schemes are **assimilation** and **accommodation**. Assimilation occurs when *new information is altered to fit an existing scheme*, whereas accommodation entails *changing the scheme to adapt to the new information*. Assimilation and accommodation usually take place together in varying degrees; they are "two sides of the same cognitive coin" (Flavell et al., 2002, p. 5). For example, an infant who has been breast-feeding may use mostly assimilation and a slight degree of accommodation when learning to suck from the nipple on a bottle, but if sucking on a ball or the dog's bone the infant would be able to use assimilation less and need to use accommodation more.

People of other ages, too, use both assimilation and accommodation whenever they are processing cognitive information. One example is right in front of you. In the course of reading this textbook, you will read things that sound familiar to you from your own experience or previous reading, so that you can easily assimilate them to what you already know.

Other information, especially the information about cultures other than your own, will be contrary to the schemes you have developed and will require you to use accommodation in order to expand your knowledge and understanding of development in adolescence and emerging adulthood.

Stages of Cognitive Development in Childhood and Adolescence

Based on his own research and his collaborations with his colleague Barbel Inhelder, Piaget devised a theory of cognitive development to describe the stages that children's thinking passes through as they grow up (Inhelder & Piaget, 1958; Piaget, 1972; see Table 3.1). Piaget termed the first 2 years of life the **sensorimotor stage**. Cognitive development in this stage involves learning how to coordinate the activities of the senses (such as watching an object as it moves across your field of vision) with motor activities (such as reaching out to grab the object). Next, from about age 2 to about age 7, is the **preoperational stage**. Here the child becomes capable of representing the world symbolically, such as through the use of language and in play such as using a broom to represent a horse. However, children in this stage are still very limited in their ability to use mental operations—that is, in their ability to manipulate objects mentally and reason about them in a way that accurately represents how the world works. For example, children of this age are easily enchanted by stories about how a pumpkin changed into a stagecoach or a frog into a prince, because with their limited understanding of the world these are not just fanciful tales but real possibilities.

Concrete operations is the next stage, lasting from about age 7 to about age 11. During this stage, children become more adept at using **mental operations**, and this skill leads to a more advanced understanding of the world. For example, they understand that if you take water from one glass and pour it into a taller, thinner glass, the amount of water

scheme A mental structure for organizing and interpreting information.

assimilation The cognitive process that occurs when new information is altered to fit an existing scheme.

accommodation The cognitive process that occurs when a scheme is changed to adapt to new information.

sensorimotor stage Cognitive stage in first 2 years of life that involves learning how to coordinate the activities of the senses with motor activities.

preoperational stage Cognitive stage from age 2 to 7 during which the child becomes capable of representing the world symbolically—for example, through the use of language—but is still very limited in ability to use mental operations.

concrete operations Cognitive stage from age 7 to 11 in which children learn to use mental operations but are limited to applying them to concrete, observable situations rather than hypothetical situations.

mental operations Cognitive activity involving manipulating and reasoning about objects.

remains the same. Mentally, they can reverse this action and conclude that the amount of water could not have changed just because it was poured into a different container. However, children in this stage focus on what can be experienced and manipulated in the physical environment (Flavell et al., 1993; Gray, 1990). They have difficulty transferring their reasoning to situations and problems that require them to think systematically about possibilities and hypotheses. That is where the next stage, formal operations, comes in.

Formal Operations in Adolescence

The stage of **formal operations** begins at about age 11 and reaches completion somewhere between ages 15 and 20, according to Piaget (1972), so this is the stage most relevant to cognitive development in adolescence. Children in concrete operations can perform simple tasks that require logical and systematic thinking, but formal operations allows adolescents to reason about complex tasks and problems involving multiple variables. Essentially, formal operations involves the development of the ability to think scientifically and apply the rigor of the scientific method to cognitive tasks.

To demonstrate how this works, let us look at one of the tasks Piaget used to test whether a child has progressed from concrete to formal operations. This task is known as the **pendulum problem** (Inhelder & Piaget, 1958). Children and adolescents are shown a pendulum (consisting of a weight hanging from a string and then set in motion) and asked to try to figure out what determines the speed at which the pendulum sways from side to side. Is it the heaviness of the weight? the length of the string? the height from which the weight is dropped? the force with which it is dropped? They are given various weights and various lengths of string to use in their deliberations.

Children in concrete operations tend to approach the problem with random attempts, often changing more than one variable at a time. They may try the heaviest weight on the longest string dropped from medium height with medium force, then a medium weight on the smallest string dropped from medium height with lesser force. When the speed of the pendulum changes, it remains difficult for them to say what caused the change because they altered more than one variable. If they happen to arrive at the right answer—it's the length of the string—they find it difficult to explain why. This is crucial, for Piaget; cognitive advances at each stage are reflected not just in the solutions children devise for problems but in their explanations for how they arrived at the solution.

It is only with formal operations that we can find the right answer to a problem like this and explain why it is the right answer. The formal operational thinker approaches

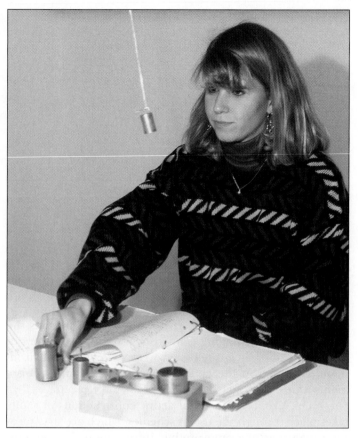

The pendulum problem. What are the strengths and weaknesses of this task as a measure of adolescents' cognitive development?

the pendulum problem by utilizing the kind of hypothetical thinking involved in a scientific experiment. "Let's see, it could be weight; let me try changing the weight while keeping everything else the same. No, that's not it; same speed. Maybe it's length; if I change the length while keeping everything else the same, that seems to make a difference; it goes faster with a shorter string. But let me try height, too; no change; then force; no change there, either. So it's length, and only length, that makes the difference." Thus, the formal operational thinker changes one variable while holding the others constant and tests the different possibilities systematically. Through this process, the formal operational thinker arrives at an answer that not only is correct but can be defended and explained. The capacity for this kind of thinking, which Piaget (1972) termed **hypothetical-deductive reasoning**, is at the heart of Piaget's concept of formal operations.

THINKING CRITICALLY •••

Think of a real-life example of how you have used hypothetical-deductive reasoning.

---

formal operations Cognitive stage from age 11 on up in which people learn to think systematically about possibilities and hypotheses.

pendulum problem Piaget's classic test of formal operations, in which persons are asked to figure out what determines the speed at which a pendulum sways from side to side.

hypothetical-deductive reasoning Piaget's term for the process by which the formal operational thinker systematically tests possible solutions to a problem and arrives at an answer that can be defended and explained.

In Piaget's research, as well as the research of many others, adolescents perform the pendulum problem and similar tasks significantly better than preadolescent children (Elkind, 2001; Lee & Freire, 2003). The transitional period from concrete operations to formal operations on these tasks usually takes place from age 11 to 14 (Keating, 2004).

The problems Piaget used to assess the attainment of formal operations were essentially scientific problems, involving the capacity to formulate hypotheses, test them systematically, and then make deductions (that is, draw conclusions) on the basis of the results (Inhelder & Piaget, 1958; Piaget & Inhelder, 1969). However, a number of other aspects of formal operations focus less on scientific thinking and more on logical or applied reasoning (Ginsberg & Opper, 1988; Keating, 2004). These include the development of capacities for **abstract thinking**, **complex thinking**, and thinking about thinking (called **metacognition**). Piaget discussed all of these capacities, but since then other scholars have done considerable research on them as well.

Abstract Thinking

Something that is abstract is something that is strictly a mental concept or process; it cannot be experienced directly, through the senses. Examples of abstract concepts include time, friendship, and faith. You were introduced to several abstract concepts in Chapters 1 and 2, including culture, the West, and adolescence itself. You cannot actually see, hear, taste, or touch these things; they exist only as ideas. *Abstract* is often contrasted with *concrete*, which refers to things you can experience through the senses. The contrast is especially appropriate here because the stage preceding formal operations is termed "concrete operations." Children in concrete operations can apply logic only to things they can experience directly, concretely, whereas the capacity for formal operations includes the ability to think abstractly and apply logic to mental operations as well (Fischer & Pruyne, 2003; Piaget, 1972; Schmidt & Thompson, 2008).

Suppose I tell you that $A = B$ and $B = C$, and then ask you, does $A = C$? It is easy for you, as a college student, to see that the answer is yes, even though you have no idea what A, B, and C represent. However, children thinking in terms of concrete operations tend to be mystified by this problem. They need to know what A, B, and C represent. In contrast, you realize that it does not matter what they are. The same logic applies to A, B, and C no matter what they represent.

But abstract thinking involves more than just the capacity to solve this kind of logical puzzle. It also involves the capacity to think about abstract concepts such as justice, freedom, goodness, evil, and time. Adolescents become capable of engaging in discussions about politics, morality, and religion

in ways they could not when they were younger be[cause] adolescence they gain the capacity to understand an[d] abstract ideas involved in such discussions (Adelson, Kohlberg, 1976). Recent research on brain development [sug]gests that the capacity for abstract thinking is based o[n] growth spurt in the brain in late adolescence and emerging adulthood that strengthens the connections between the frontal cortex and the other parts of the brain (Fischer & Pruyne, 2003). We will discuss brain development further later in the chapter.

Complex Thinking

Formal operational thinking is more complex than the kind of thinking that occurs in concrete operations. Concrete operational thinkers tend to focus on one aspect of things, usually the most obvious, but formal operational thinkers are more likely to see things in greater complexity and perceive multiple aspects of a situation or an idea. This greater complexity can be seen in the use of metaphor and sarcasm.

Metaphor With formal operations, adolescents become capable of understanding metaphors that are more subtle than metaphors they may have understood earlier (Sternberg & Nigro, 1980; Winner, 1988). Metaphors are complex because they have more than one meaning, the literal, concrete meaning as well as less obvious, more subtle meanings. Poems and novels are full of metaphors. Consider, for example, this passage in a poem by T. S. Eliot entitled "A Dedication to My Wife":

> No peevish winter wind shall chill
> No sullen tropic sun shall wither
> The roses in the rose-garden which is ours and ours only.

On one level, the meaning of the passage is about the hardiness of the roses in a garden, but there is a second meaning as well. The roses are a metaphor of the author's optimism for the enduring vitality of the love between him and his wife. Adolescents can grasp multiple meanings such as this to a degree that children usually cannot (Gibbs, Leggitt, & Turner, 2002; Sternberg & Nigro, 1980).

One recent study examined understandings of metaphors in adolescents and emerging adults ages 11–29 (Duthie et al., 2008). As the metaphors, the study used sayings such as "One bad apple spoils the whole barrel." Early adolescents tended to describe the meanings of the metaphors in concrete terms (e.g., age 11, "There's a big barrel of apples and a woman picks up one that is rotten and there are worms in it and the worms go to all the other apples"). In later adolescence and emerging adulthood,

---

abstract thinking Thinking in terms of symbols, ideas, and concepts.

complex thinking Thinking that takes into account multiple connections and interpretations, such as in the use of metaphor, satire, and sarcasm.

metacognition The capacity for "thinking about thinking" that allows adolescents and adults to monitor and reason about their thought processes.

Increased enjoyment of sarcasm reflects adolescents' growing cognitive abilities.

understanding of the metaphors became more abstract and more focused on their social meanings (e.g., age 21, "One bad comment can spoil the entire conversation").

Sarcasm Sarcasm is another example of complex communication. As with metaphors, more than one interpretation is possible. "Nice pants," someone says to you as they greet you. That has a literal meaning, as a compliment for your fine taste in fashion. But depending on who says it, and how they say it, it could have another, quite different meaning: "What an ugly pair of pants! You sure look like a fool." Adolescents become capable of understanding (and using) sarcasm in a way children cannot, and as a result sarcasm is more often part of adolescents' conversations (Eder, 1995). Media that employ sarcasm, such as *Mad* magazine and *The Simpsons* television show, are more popular among adolescents than other age groups, perhaps because adolescents enjoy using their newly developed abilities for understanding sarcasm (Katz, Blasko, & Kazmerski, 2004).

One study examined how understanding of sarcasm changes from middle childhood through adolescence (Demorest et al., 1984). Participants of various ages were presented with stories in which they were asked to judge whether a particular remark was sincere, deceptive, or sarcastic (for example, "That new haircut you got looks terrific"). Children aged 9 or younger had difficulty identifying sarcastic remarks, but 13-year-olds were better at it than 9-year-olds, and college students were better than 13-year-olds.

Metacognition: Thinking About Thinking

One of the abstractions adolescents develop the capacity to think about with formal operations is their own thoughts. They become aware of their thinking processes in a way that children are not, and this ability enables them to monitor and reason about those processes. This capacity for "thinking about thinking," known as metacognition, enables adolescents to learn and solve problems more efficiently (Klaczynski, 2005, 2006; Kuhn, 1999; Roeschl-Heils, Schneider, & van Kraayenoord, 2003; Rozencwajg, 2003). In fact, one study indicates that instructing adolescents in metacognitive strategies improves their academic performance (Kramarski, 2004).

Metacognition first develops in adolescence, but it continues to develop in emerging adulthood and beyond. One study compared adolescents and adults of various ages (Vukman, 2005). They were given various problems and asked to "think out loud" so that the researchers could record their metacognitive processes. Self-awareness of thinking processes rose from adolescence to emerging adulthood and again from emerging adulthood to midlife, then declined in later adulthood.

You probably use metacognition to some degree as you read; almost certainly you use it when studying for an exam. As you move along from sentence to sentence, you may monitor your comprehension and ask yourself, "What did that sentence mean? How is it connected to the sentence that preceded it? How can I make sure I remember what that means?" As you study for an exam, you look over the material you are required to know, asking yourself if you know what the concepts mean and determining which are most important for you to know.

Metacognition applies not only to learning and problem solving but also to social topics—thinking about what you think of others and what they think of you. We will explore these topics in the section on social cognition later in the chapter.

Limitations of Piaget's Theory

Piaget's theory of cognitive development has endured remarkably well. Decades after he first presented it, Piaget's theory remains the dominant theory of cognitive development from birth through adolescence (Elkind, 2001). However, that does not mean that the theory has been verified in every respect. On the contrary, Piaget's theory of formal operations is the part of his theory that has been critiqued the most and that has been found to require the most modifications, more than his ideas about development at younger ages (Keating, 2004; Lee & Freire, 2003). The limitations of Piaget's theory of formal operations fall into two related categories: individual differences in the attainment of formal operations and the cultural basis of adolescent cognitive development.

Individual Differences in Formal Operations Recall from earlier in the chapter that Piaget's theory of cognitive development puts a strong emphasis on maturation. Although he acknowledged some degree of **individual differences**, especially in the timing of transitions from one stage to the next, Piaget asserted that most people proceed through the same stages at about the same ages because they experience the same maturational processes (Inhelder & Piaget, 1958). Every 8-year-old is in the stage of concrete operations; every 15-year-old should be a formal operational thinker. Furthermore, Piaget's idea of stages means that 15-year-olds should reason in formal operations in all aspects of their lives because the same mental structure should be applied no matter what the nature of the problem (Keating, 2004).

Abundant research indicates decisively that these claims were inaccurate, especially for formal operations (Lee & Freire, 2003; Overton & Byrnes, 1991). In adolescence and even in adulthood, a great range of individual differences exists in the extent to which people use formal operations. Some adolescents and adults use formal operations over a wide range of situations; others use it selectively; still others appear to use it rarely or not at all. One review indicated that by 8th grade, only about one third of adolescents can be said to have reached formal operations (Strahan, 1983). Other reviews find that, on any particular Piagetian task of formal operations, the success rate among late adolescents and adults is only 40% to 60%, depending on the task and on individual factors such as educational background (Keating, 2004; Lawson & Wollman, 2003). Thus even in emerging adulthood and beyond, a large proportion of people use formal operations either inconsistently or not at all.

Even people who demonstrate the capacity for formal operations tend to use it selectively, for problems and situations in which they have the most experience and knowledge (Flavell, Miller, & Miller, 1993). For example, adolescents who are experienced chess players may apply formal operational thinking to chess strategies, even though they may not have performed well on standard Piagetian tasks such as the pendulum problem (Chi, Glaser, & Rees, 1982). An adolescent with experience working on cars may find it easy to apply principles of formal operations in that area but have difficulty performing classroom tasks that require formal operations.

A specific kind of experience, in the form of science and math education, is also important for the development of formal operations. Adolescents who have had courses in math and science are more likely than other adolescents to exhibit formal operational thought (Keating, 2004; Lawson & Wollman, 2003), especially when the courses involve hands-on experience. This makes sense, if you think about the kinds of reasoning required for formal operations. The hypothetical-deductive reasoning that is so important to formal opera-

tions is taught as part of science classes; it is the kind of thinking that is the basis of the scientific method. Not surprisingly, it is easier for adolescents to develop this kind of thinking if they have systematic instruction in it, and the more they have applied hypothetical-deductive thinking to problems in science classes, the more likely they are to perform well on tasks (such as the pendulum problem) used to assess formal operations.

Gray (1990) suggests that Piaget underestimated how much effort, energy, and knowledge it takes to use formal operations. According to Gray (1990), concrete operations are sufficient for most daily tasks and problems, and because formal operations are so much more difficult and taxing, people often will not use formal operations even if they have the capacity to do so. Formal operations might be useful for scientific thinking, but most people will not go to the time and trouble to apply it to every aspect of their daily lives. When people have a problem, they generally do not feel the need to understand the true nature of the problem, they just want it resolved. Thus, the concept of formal operations is inadequate for describing how most people—adolescents as well as adults—solve practical problems and draw causal inferences in their everyday lives (Keating, 2004; Kuhn, 1992; Lave, 1988).

Culture and Formal Operations Questions have been raised about the extent to which cultures differ in whether their members reach formal operations at all. By the early 1970s, numerous studies indicated that cultures varied widely in the prevalence with which their members displayed an understanding of formal operations on the kinds of tasks that Piaget and others had used to measure it. A consensus had formed among scholars that in many cultures formal operational thought (as measured with Piagetian tasks) does not develop and that this was particularly true in cultures that did not have formal schooling (Cole, 1996).

Piaget responded to these criticisms by suggesting that even though all persons reach the potential for formal operational thinking, they apply it first (and perhaps only) to areas in which their culture has provided them with the most experience and expertise (Piaget, 1972). In other words, it may not make sense to give such tasks as the pendulum problem to people in all cultures because the materials and the task may be unfamiliar to them. However, if you use materials and tasks familiar to them and relevant to their daily lives, you may find that they display formal operational thinking under those conditions.

Studies like the ones described in the Cultural Focus box indicate that Piaget's ideas about cognitive development in adolescence can be applied to non-Western cultures as long as they are adapted to the ways of life of each culture. There is widespread support among scholars for the proposition that the stage of formal operations constitutes a universal

individual differences Approach to research that focuses on how individuals differ within a group, for example, in performance on IQ tests.

In traditional cultures, practical activities sometimes require formal operations. Here, adolescents in Samoa help build the roof of a shelter.

human potential, but the forms it takes in each culture are derived from the kinds of cognitive requirements people in the culture face (Cole, 1996). However, in every culture there is likely to be considerable variation in the extent to which adolescents and adults display formal operational thought, from persons who display it in a wide variety of circumstances to persons who display it little or not at all.

THINKING CRITICALLY •••

If abstract thinking is required for the formation of ideas about politics, morality, and religion, how can you explain why such ideas exist even in cultures in which math and science education is rare?

Cognitive Development in Emerging Adulthood: Postformal Thinking

In Piaget's theory, formal operations is the end point of cognitive development. Once formal operations is fully attained, by age 20 at the latest, cognitive maturation is complete.

However, like many aspects of Piaget's theory of formal operations, this view has been altered by research. In fact, research indicates that cognitive development often continues in important ways during emerging adulthood. This research has inspired theories of cognitive development beyond formal operations, known as **postformal thinking** (Sinnott, 1998; 2003). Two of the most notable aspects of postformal thinking in emerging adulthood concern advances in pragmatism and reflective judgment.

Pragmatism

Pragmatism involves adapting logical thinking to the practical constraints of real-life situations. Theories of postformal thought emphasizing pragmatism have been developed by several scholars (Basseches, 1984, 1989; Labouvie-Vief, 1998, 2006; Labouvie-Vief & Diehl, 2002; Sinnott, 2003). All these theories propose that the problems faced in normal adult life often contain complexities and inconsistencies that cannot be addressed with the logic of formal operations.

According to Labouvie-Vief (1982, 1990, 1998, 2006), cognitive development in emerging adulthood is distinguished from adolescent thinking by a greater recognition and incorporation of practical limitations to logical thinking. In this view, adolescents exaggerate the extent to which logical thinking will be effective in real life. In contrast, emerging adulthood brings a growing awareness of how social factors and factors specific to a given situation must be taken into account in approaching most of life's problems.

For example, in one study Labouvie-Vief (1990) presented adolescents and emerging adults with stories and asked them to predict what they thought would happen. One story described a man who was a heavy drinker, especially at parties. His wife had warned him that if he came home drunk one more time, she would leave him and take the children. Some time later he went to an office party and came home drunk. What would she do?

Labouvie-Vief found that adolescents tended to respond strictly in terms of the logic of formal operations: The wife said she would leave if her husband came home drunk once more, he came home drunk, therefore she will leave. In contrast, emerging adults considered many possible dimensions of the situation. Did he apologize and beg her not to leave? Did she really mean it when she said she would leave him? Does she have some place to go? Has she considered the possible effects on the children? Rather than relying strictly on logic, with a belief in definite wrong and right answers, the emerging adults tended to be postformal thinkers in the sense that they realized that the problems of real life often involve a great deal of complexity and ambiguity. However, Labouvie-Vief (2006) emphasizes that with postformal

---

postformal thinking Type of thinking beyond formal operations, involving greater awareness of the complexity of real-life situations, such as in the use of pragmatism and reflective judgment.

pragmatism Type of thinking that involves adapting logical thinking to the practical constraints of real-life situations.

Until recent decades, Inuit (formerly known as Eskimo) children and adolescents of the Canadian Arctic had never attended school (Balikci, 1970; Condon, 1987; Stern, 2003). If Inuit adolescents had tried to perform the tasks of formal operations, they probably would have done poorly (Cole, 1996).

But did they, nevertheless, possess and use formal operational thinking? Consider the kind of work adolescent boys and girls performed by the age of 12 or 13 (Balikci, 1970; Condon, 1987).

Boys
Harnessing dog team for sledge
Pushing and pulling sledge when stuck in snow
Preparing bows and arrows, harpoons, and spears for hunting
Helping to build snowhouses
Helping to erect skin tents
Hunting polar bears, seals, etc.
Fishing

Girls
Cutting fresh ice
Fetching water
Gathering moss for fire
Caring for infants and small children
Sewing
Tanning animal skins
Cooking

Not all these tasks would require formal operations. Assigning them to adolescents (rather than children) may have been appropriate simply because adolescents' larger physical size meant they could perform many tasks better than children, such as fetching water and helping to move a sledge that was stuck in the snow. Other tasks, however, would be likely to demand the kind of thinking involved in formal operations.

Take the hunting trips that adolescent boys would participate in with their fathers, or sometimes undertake by themselves. To become successful, a boy would have to think through the components involved in a hunt and test his knowledge of hunting through experience. If he were unsuccessful on a particular outing, he would have to ask himself why. Was it because of the location he chose? the equipment he took along? the tracking method he used? Or were there other causes? On the next hunt he might alter one or more of these factors to see if his success improved. This would be hypothetical-deductive reasoning, altering and testing different variables to arrive at the solution to a problem.

Or take the example of an adolescent girl learning to tan animal hides. Tanning is an elaborate process, involving several complicated steps. Girls were given responsibility for this task on their own beginning at about age 14. If a girl failed to do it properly, as would sometimes happen, the hide would be ruined, and her family would be disappointed and angry with her. She would have to ask herself, where did the process go wrong? Mentally, she would work her way back through the

Many of the daily tasks of Inuit life require formal operations.

various steps in the process, trying to identify her error. This, too, is formal operational thinking, mentally considering various hypotheses in order to identify a promising one to test.

In recent decades, globalization has come to the Inuit, and adolescents spend most of their day in school rather than working alongside their parents (Condon, 1987, 1995; Kral, Burkhardt, & Kidd, 2002; Stern, 2003). As a result, they have a greater range of opportunities than they had before. Some of them go to larger nearby cities after high school to receive professional training of various kinds. By now, they face many of the same cognitive demands as adolescents in the Canadian majority culture.

As has so often happened in the course of globalization, however, there have been negative repercussions as well (Kassam, 2006; Kral et al., 2002; Leineweber & Arensman, 2003). Many adolescents find school boring and irrelevant to their lives, and some of them turn to alcohol, glue sniffing, and shoplifting to add excitement. Inuit young people are not only in transition between childhood and adulthood but also in transition between two incompatible ways of life, and the transition has not been easy to make.

thinking as with formal thinking, not everyone continues to move to higher levels of cognitive complexity, and many people continue to apply earlier, more concrete thinking in emerging adulthood and beyond.

A similar theory of cognitive development in emerging adulthood has been presented by Michael Basseches (1984, 1989). Like Labouvie-Vief, Basseches (1984) views cognitive development in emerging adulthood as involving a recognition that formal logic can rarely be applied to the problems most people face in their daily lives. **Dialectical thought** is Basseches's term for the kind of thinking that develops in emerging adulthood, involving a growing awareness that problems often have no clear solution and that two opposing strategies or points of view may each have some merit (Basseches, 1984). For example, people may have to decide whether to quit a job they dislike without knowing whether their next job will be more satisfying.

Some cultures may promote dialectical thinking more than others. Peng and Nisbett (1999) have proposed that Chinese culture traditionally promotes dialectical thought by advocating an approach to knowledge that strives to reconcile contradictions and combine opposing perspectives by seeking a middle ground. In contrast, they argue, the European American approach tends to apply logic in a way that polarizes contradictory perspectives in an effort to determine which is correct.

To support this theory, Peng and Nisbett (1999) conducted studies comparing Chinese and American college students. They found that the Chinese students were more likely than the Americans to prefer dialectical proverbs containing contradictions. The Chinese students were also more likely to prefer dialectical arguments, involving argument and counter-argument, over arguments that used classical Western logic. In addition, when two apparently contradictory propositions were presented, the Americans tended to embrace one and reject the other, whereas the Chinese students were moderately accepting of both propositions, seeking to reconcile them.

What is it about the college environment that promotes reflective judgment?

THINKING CRITICALLY •••

Think of a problem you have had in your life lately. Can you apply the insights of Labouvie-Vief and Basseches to the problem?

Reflective Judgment

Reflective judgment, another cognitive quality that has been found to develop in emerging adulthood, is the capacity to evaluate the accuracy and logical coherence of evidence and arguments. An influential theory of the development of reflective judgment in emerging adulthood has been proposed by William Perry (1970/1999), who based his theory on his studies of college students in their late teens and early 20s. According to Perry (1970/1999), adolescents and first-year college students tend to engage in **dualistic thinking**, which means they often see situations and issues in polarized terms—an act is either right or wrong, with no in-between; a statement is either true or false, regardless of the nuances or the situation to which it is being applied. In this sense, they lack reflective judgment. However, reflective judgment begins to develop for most people in their late teens. First a stage of **multiple thinking** takes place, in which emerging adults believe there are two or more sides to every story, two or more legitimate views of every issue, and that it can be difficult to justify one position as the only true or accurate one. In this stage, people tend to value all points of view equally, even to the extent of asserting that it is impossible to make any judgments about whether one point of view is more valid than another.

By the early 20s, according to Perry, multiple thinking develops into **relativism**. Like people in the stage of multiple thinking, relativists are able to recognize the legitimacy of competing points of view. However, rather than denying that one view could be more persuasive than another, relativists attempt to compare the merits of competing views. Finally, by the end of their college years, many emerging adults reach a stage of **commitment** in which they commit themselves to certain points of view they believe to be the most valid, while being open to reevaluating their views if new evidence is presented to them.

dialectical thought Type of thinking that develops in emerging adulthood, involving a growing awareness that most problems do not have a single solution and that problems must often be addressed with crucial pieces of information missing.

reflective judgment The capacity to evaluate the accuracy and logical coherence of evidence and arguments.

dualistic thinking Cognitive tendency to see situations and issues in polarized, absolute, black-and-white terms.

multiple thinking Cognitive approach entailing recognition that there is more than one legitimate view of things and that it can be difficult to justify one position as the true or accurate one.

relativism Cognitive ability to recognize the legitimacy of competing points of view but also compare the relative merits of competing views.

commitment Cognitive status in which persons commit themselves to certain points of view they believe to be the most valid while at the same time being open to reevaluating their views if new evidence is presented to them.

Research on reflective judgment indicates that significant gains may take place in emerging adulthood (King & Kitchener, 2002, 2004; Kitchener & King, 2006; Kitchener et al., 1993; Pascarella & Terenzini, 1991). However, the gains that take place in emerging adulthood appear to be due more to education than to maturation (King & Kitchener, 2002, 2004; Labouvie-Vief, 2006; Pirttilae-Backman & Kajanne, 2001)—that is, people who pursue a college education during emerging adulthood show greater advances in reflective judgment than people who do not. Also, Perry and his colleagues acknowledged that the development of reflective judgment is likely to be more common in a culture that values pluralism and whose educational system promotes tolerance of diverse points of view (Perry, 1970/1999). However, thus far little cross-cultural research has taken place on reflective judgment.

THINKING CRITICALLY •••

The Constitution of the United States specifies a minimum age of 35 before a person can be elected president. Why do you suppose this is so? What cognitive qualities might be insufficiently developed before that age for a person to be capable of exercising the duties of the office?

The Information-Processing Approach

The approach of Piaget and the scholars who have continued his line of theory and research describes how adolescents and emerging adults develop capacities such as hypothetical-deductive reasoning, abstract thinking, and reflective judgment. The focus is on how the development of these general cognitive capacities is reflected in young people's performance on specific tasks such as the pendulum problem. Piaget also emphasized the way cognitive abilities change with age, from preadolescence to adolescence, from concrete operations to formal operations.

The **information-processing approach** to understanding cognitive development in adolescence is quite different. Rather than viewing cognitive development as **discontinuous**, that is, as separated into distinct stages, the way Piaget did, the information-processing approach views cognitive change as **continuous**, meaning gradual and steady. However, the information-processing approach usually does not have a developmental focus (Rebok, 1987). The focus is not on how mental structures and ways of thinking change with age but on the thinking processes that exist at all ages. Nevertheless, some studies of information processing do compare adolescents or emerging adults to people of other ages.

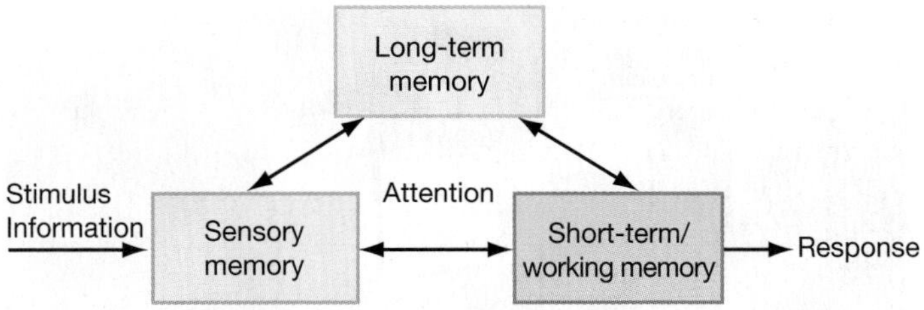

FIGURE 3.1 A model of information processing. Attention and memory are the key components.

The original model for the information-processing approach was the computer (Hunt, 1989). Information-processing researchers and theorists have tried to break down human thinking into separate parts in the same way that the functions of a computer are separated into capacities for *attention*, *processing*, and *memory*. In the pendulum problem, someone taking the information-processing approach would examine how adolescents draw their attention to the most relevant aspects of the problem, process the results of each trial, remember the results, and retrieve the results from previous trials to compare to the most recent trial. In this way the information-processing approach is a **componential approach** (Sternberg, 1983) because it involves breaking down the thinking process into its various components.

Recent models of information processing have moved away from a simple computer analogy and recognized that the brain is more complex than any computer (Ashcraft, 2002). Rather than occurring in a step-by-step fashion as in a computer, in human thinking the different components operate simultaneously, as Figure 3.1 illustrates. Nevertheless, the focus of information processing remains on the components of the thinking process, especially attention and memory.

Let us look at each of the components of information processing and how they change during adolescence and emerging adulthood. For all of the components, adolescents perform better than younger children, and for some, emerging adults perform better than adolescents.

Attention

Information processing begins with stimulus information that enters the senses (see Figure 3.1), but much of what you see, hear, and touch is processed no further. For example, as you are reading this, there may be sounds in the environment, other sights in your visual field, and the feeling of your body in the seat where you are reading, but if you are focusing on what you are reading most of this information goes no

information-processing approach An approach to understanding cognition that seeks to delineate the steps involved in the thinking process and how each step is connected to the next.

discontinuous A view of development as taking place in stages that are distinct from one another rather than as one gradual, continuous process.

continuous A view of development as a gradual, steady process rather than as taking place in distinct stages.

componential approach Description of the information-processing approach to cognition, indicating that it involves breaking down the thinking process into its various components.

Capacities for selective attention and divided attention improve during adolescence. Does divided attention impede learning?

monitor, the connections, or the computer itself. Adolescents are better than children at focusing on the most relevant aspects of a problem (Casteel, 1993; Miller & Weiss, 1981).

THINKING CRITICALLY •••

Design a simple study to assess the abilities of adolescents or emerging adults for selective attention, and a separate study on their learning abilities under conditions of divided attention.

Storing and Retrieving Information: Short-Term and Long-Term Memory

Memory is a key part of information processing, perhaps even the most important part. Drawing your attention to something and processing information about it would not do you much good if you could not store the results in your memory and call them back into your mind when you needed them. Because memory is so important to learning, a great deal of research has taken place on it. One important distinction scholars have made is between short-term and long-term memory. **Short-term memory** is memory for information that is currently the focus of your attention. It has a limited capacity and retains information for only a short time, usually about 30 seconds or less. **Long-term memory** is memory for information that is committed to longer-term storage, so that you can draw on it again after a period when your attention has not been focused on it. The capacity of long-term memory is unlimited, and information is retained indefinitely. You can probably think of things you experienced 10 or more years ago that you can still call up from your long-term memory. Both short-term and long-term memory improve substantially between childhood and adolescence (Dempster, 1984; Fry & Hale, 1996).

further than sensory memory. The only information you process is the information on which you focus your attention. Are you able to read a textbook while someone else in the same room is watching television? Are you able to have a conversation at a party where music and other conversations are blaring loudly all around you? These are tasks that require **selective attention**—the ability to focus on relevant information while screening out information that is irrelevant (Casteel, 1993). Adolescents tend to be better than preadolescent children at tasks that require selective attention, and emerging adults are generally better than adolescents (Huang-Pollock, Carr, & Nigg, 2002; Manis, Keating, & Morrison, 1980). Adolescents are also more adept than preadolescents at tasks that require **divided attention**—reading a book and listening to music at the same time, for example—but even for adolescents divided attention may result in less efficient learning than if attention were focused entirely on one thing. One study found that watching TV interfered with adolescents' homework performance but listening to music did not (Pool, Koolstra, & van der Voort, 2003).

One aspect of selective attention is the ability to analyze a set of information and select the most important parts of it for further attention. When you listen to a lecture in class, for example, your attention may fluctuate. You may monitor the information being presented and increase or decrease your level of attention according to your judgment of the information's importance. This aspect of selective attention is also a key part of problem solving; one of the initial steps of solving any problem is to decide where to direct your attention. For example, if your computer fails to boot up, the first thing you try to do is to decide where the source of the problem is—the

There are two types of short-term memory (Ashcraft, 2002). One type is involved in the input and storage of new information. This type of short-term memory has a limited capacity. The most common test of short-term memory capacity is to recite lists of numbers or words, gradually increasing the length, and see how many the person can remember without making a mistake. So if I give you the list "1, 6, 2, 9," you can probably remember that pretty easily. Now try this: "8, 7, 1, 5, 3, 9, 2, 4, 1." Not so easy, is it? But you are certainly better at this kind of test now than when you were 8 or 10. Short-term memory capacity increases throughout childhood and early adolescence until the mid-teens, and remains stable after about age 16 at an average of seven units of information (Dempster, 1984).

---

selective attention The ability to focus on relevant information while screening out information that is irrelevant.

divided attention The ability to focus on more than one task at a time.

short-term memory Memory for information that is the current focus of attention.

long-term memory Memory for information that is committed to longer-term storage, so that it can be drawn upon after a period when attention has not been focused on it.

The other type of short-term memory is known as **working memory** (Baddeley, 2000; Cowan, Saults, & Elliott, 2002; Kail & Hall, 2001). Working memory is a "mental workbench" where you keep information as you are working on it (Ashcraft, 2002). It is where you analyze and reason about information in the course of making decisions, solving problems, and comprehending written and spoken language. The information may be new, or it may be called up from long-term memory, or some combination of the two. The size of a person's working memory is highly correlated with overall intelligence (Colom, Flores-Mendoza, & Rebollo, 2003). Like short-term memory capacity for new information, the capacity of working memory increases from childhood through the mid-teens and then stabilizes (Conklin et al., 2007; Keage et al., 2008; Luciana et al., 2005).

An experiment by Robert Sternberg and his colleagues demonstrates how increases in working memory take place between childhood and adolescence (Sternberg & Nigro, 1980). They presented analogies to 3rd-grade, 6th-grade, 9th-grade, and college students. For example, "Sun is to moon as asleep is to . . .?"

1. Star
2. Bed
3. Awake
4. Night

There was improvement with age, especially between the younger (3rd- and 6th-grade) and older (9th-grade and college) students. Sternberg attributed the differences to short-term working memory capacities. Analogies take a considerable amount of short-term memory space. You have to keep the first set of words ("sun is to moon") and the nature of their relationship in your working memory continuously as you consider the other possible pairings ("asleep is to star . . . asleep is to bed . . .") and analyze their relationships as well. Before adolescence, children do not have enough working memory capacity to perform tasks like this very effectively. (The correct answer is "awake," in case you are wondering.)

Long-term memory also improves in adolescence. Adolescents are more likely than preadolescent children to use **mnemonic devices** (memory strategies), such as organizing information into coherent patterns (Siegler, 1988). Think of what you do, for example, when you sit down to read a textbook chapter. You probably have various organizational strategies you have developed over the years (if you do not, you would be wise to develop some), such as writing a chapter outline, making notes in the margins, organizing information into categories, underlining key passages, and so on. By planning your reading in these ways, you remember (and learn) more effectively.

Another way long-term memory improves in adolescence is that adolescents have more experience and more knowledge than children do, and these advantages enhance the effectiveness of long-term memory (Keating, 1990, 2004). Having more knowledge helps you learn new information and store it in long-term memory. This is a key difference between short-term and long-term memory. Because the capacity of short-term memory is limited, the more information you have in there already, the less effectively you can add new information to it. With long-term memory, however, the capacity is essentially unlimited, and the more you know the easier it is to learn new information.

What makes it easier is that you already have information in your memory that you can use to form associations with the new information, which makes it more likely that the new information will be remembered (Pressley & Schneider, 1997). For example, if you have already had a course in child development or human development, some of the concepts (such as concrete operations) and big names (such as Piaget) presented here may be familiar to you. If so, the new information you come across here will be easier for you to remember than for someone who has never had a related course before, because you can make associations between the new information and the knowledge you already have. Notice the relation to Piaget's concepts of assimilation and accommodation: The more information you have in your long-term memory, the more you can assimilate new information and the less accommodation is required.

THINKING CRITICALLY •••

Among the courses you have taken in your college education, for which have you found information easiest to remember, and for which hardest? In what ways do the memory concepts presented here help explain why some courses are easier than others for retaining information?

Processing Information: Speed and Automaticity

Two other aspects of information processing also advance in adolescence. Adolescents generally process information with greater speed and **automaticity** than children (Case, 1985, 1997). With regard to speed, think of the example of a computer or video game. Adolescents are generally better at such games than children because the games typically require the player to respond to changing circumstances, and adolescents are faster at processing information as those changes occur. In experimental situations involving tasks such as matching letters, there is an increase in speed of processing from age 10 through the late teens (Fry & Hale, 1996; Hale,

---

working memory An aspect of short-term memory that refers to where information is stored as it is comprehended and analyzed.

mnemonic devices Memory strategies.

automaticity Degree of cognitive effort a person needs to devote to processing a given set of information.

In most cultures throughout history, opportunities for enhancing cognitive development through education have been much more limited for females than for males. In the United States and other Western countries, this issue pertains particularly to emerging adulthood. Historically, there has been much more debate over and resistance to the idea that females should receive higher education. Many people in the 18th and 19th centuries were vehemently opposed to the idea that females should be allowed to attend colleges and universities.

Historian Linda Kerber (1997) distinguishes three periods in the history of higher education for women. The first extended from 1700 to 1775. During this time, female literacy grew (as it did for males), but no colleges or universities accepted female students. Of course, it was also rare for males to receive higher education at that time, but at least the more privileged males had this opportunity. Females were barred entirely.

The second period extended from 1776 to 1833, and Kerber calls it the "Era of the Great Debate over the Capacities of Women's Minds." The question of whether women were cognitively capable of benefiting from higher education was hotly debated during this time. The final year of this period, 1833, was the year that the first women entered higher education, at Oberlin College, which was founded as a women's college. The third period, from 1833 to 1875, was marked by a steady expansion in opportunities for women to pursue higher education. By 1875, dozens of institutions accepted female students, and the debate over whether women should be allowed to pursue higher education had turned in favor of the proponents.

Arguments against allowing young women the opportunity for higher education had two main features. One was the claim that "too much" education for young women would be hazardous to them, because it would spoil their feminine qualities and because it might exhaust them and even make them ill. A second was the claim that women were inherently inferior to men intellectually, and therefore higher education would be wasted on them.

The first claim, that intellectual stimulation was hazardous to young women, was especially prevalent in the 18th century. A popular verse during that century read:

> Why should girls be learn'd and wise?
> Books only serve to spoil their eyes.
> The studious eye but faintly twinkles
> And reading paves the way to wrinkles.

About the same time, an influential Boston minister declared, "Women of masculine minds have generally masculine manners, and a robustness of person ill-calculated to inspire tender passion."

This argument continued to be stated during the 19th century, but as women began to break through the barriers to higher education, some men claimed that women were "scientifically" shown to be cognitively inferior. A lot of scientific activity took place in the 19th century, and a lot of pseudoscience, too. Some of the worst pseudoscience attempted to establish biologically based group differences in intelligence (Gould, 1981). Even scientists who were otherwise respectable were infected by pseudoscientific reasoning when it came to issues of intelligence. Paul Broca, perhaps the most important figure in neurology in the 19th century, claimed that the smaller brains of women demonstrated their intellectual inferiority. He knew very well that brain size is related to body size and that women's smaller brain size simply reflected their smaller

1990; Kail, 1991a, 1991b; Luna et al., 2004), with the largest gains coming in the early part of this age period.

Another aspect of processing is automaticity, that is, how much cognitive effort the person needs to devote to processing the information (Case, 1997). For example, if I give you a few computational problems—100 divided by 20, 60 minus 18, 7 times 9—you can probably do them without writing them down and without straining yourself too much. This is partly because you have done problems like this so much in the course of your life that they are almost automatic—much more than they would be for a preadolescent child.

Adolescents show greater automaticity of processing in a variety of respects, compared with preadolescent children. However, automaticity depends more on experience than on age alone. This has been shown in studies of chess players. Expert chess players have been found to process the configu-

Video games require speed of information processing.

body size rather than inferior intelligence, but his prejudice against the cognitive capacities of women allowed him to talk himself out of it:

> We might ask if the small size of the female brain depends exclusively on the small size of her body. . . . But we must not forget that women are, on average, a little less intelligent than men. . . . We are therefore permitted to suppose that the relatively small size of the female brain depends in part upon her physical inferiority and in part upon her intellectual inferiority. (1861, quoted in Gould, 1981, p. 104)

The pseudoscientific claims got even worse than that. Gustave Le Bon, the French scholar who was one of the founders of social psychology, commented:

> In the most intelligent races, as among the Parisians, there are a large number of women whose brains are closer in size to those of gorillas than to the most developed male brains. This inferiority is so obvious that no one can contest it even for a moment; only its degree is worth discussion. All psychologists who have studied the intelligence of women . . . recognize today that they represent the most inferior forms of human evolution and that they are closer to children and savages than to an adult, civilized man. They excel in fickleness, inconstancy, absence of thought and logic, and incapacity to reason. Without doubt there exist some distinguished women, very superior to the average man, but they are as exceptional as the birth of any monstrosity, as, for example, of a gorilla with two heads; consequently we may neglect them entirely. (1879, quoted in Gould, 1981)

In the 19th century, there were strong prejudices against women with regard to their intellectual abilities.

Keep in mind that Broca and Le Bon were not regarded as cranks or fools, but were two of the most important scholars of their time. They both reflected and affected attitudes toward the cognitive capacities of females that many people held in those days.

Things have changed now in the West. In all Western countries, females exceed males' performance on nearly every measure of educational achievement (Arnett, 2000d; UNDP, 2008). However, it remains true in most of the world that females receive less education than males (Mensch, Bruce, & Greene, 1998; UNDP, 2008). It is also true that certain prejudices against females' cognitive abilities continue to exist in the West, as we will discuss in the chapters on gender and school.

rations on chessboards with a high degree of automaticity, which enables them to remember the configurations better and analyze them faster and more effectively than novices do (Bruer, 1993; Chase & Simon, 1973; Chi, Glaser, & Rees, 1982). Furthermore, expert chess players who are children or adolescents demonstrate greater automaticity in processing chess configurations than novice adults do, even though the adults outperform them on other cognitive tests (Chi et al., 1982).

Automaticity is closely related to speed and to working memory capacity (Barsalou, 1992). The more automatic a cognitive task is, the faster you are able to do it. Also, the more automatic a task is, the less working memory capacity it takes, leaving more room for other tasks. For example, you may be able to read a magazine while you watch TV, but you would probably find it harder to fill out your tax forms while watching TV. This is because reading the language on tax forms, filled as it is with terms you are likely to see only on tax forms, is much less automatic to you than reading the language of a magazine.

THINKING CRITICALLY •••

Think of an example of a task you performed today in which you used automaticity.

Limitations of the Information-Processing Approach

Like Piaget's theory of cognitive development, the information-processing approach has not been without its critics. According to the critics, information-processing theorists and researchers are guilty of **reductionism**, which means breaking up a phenomenon into separate parts to such an extent that the meaning and coherence of the phenomenon as a whole become lost. From this perspective, what information-processing scholars see as a strength—the focus on the separate components of cognitive processes—is actually a weakness. In the words of one critic, this approach leads scholars to the false conclusion that "the performance is *nothing but* the serial execution of a specified set of individual processes" (Kuhn, 1992, p. 236, emphasis in original).

According to the critics, by taking a reductionist approach, information-processing scholars have lost the holistic perspective that characterized Piaget's work. That is, they fail to consider how human cognition works as a whole rather than as a set of isolated parts. The analogy of a computer once favored by information-processing scholars is misguided because human beings are not computers. Computers have no capacity for self-reflection, and no awareness of how their cognitive processes are integrated, organized, and monitored. Because self-reflection and self-awareness are central to human cognition, critics argue, overlooking them leaves the information-processing approach insufficient and inadequate.

Computers also lack emotions, and according to some scholars, emotions must be taken into account when considering cognitive functioning. Evidence suggests that adolescents' emotions tend to be more intense and more variable than either preadolescent children's or adults' emotions (Larson & Richards, 1994), so this would seem to be an especially important consideration with regard to adolescent cognition. In one study, researchers presented three dilemmas to high school students, college students, and adults (Blanchard-Fields, 1986). The dilemmas were intended to vary in the degree of emotional involvement they elicited from the participants. The low-involvement dilemma concerned conflicting accounts of a war between two fictitious nations, whereas the high-involvement dilemmas concerned a conflict between parents and their adolescent son over whether he should join them on a visit to his grandparents, and a man and a woman disagreeing over whether their unintended pregnancy should end in abortion. The researchers found that the high school and college students showed less advanced reasoning about the high-involvement dilemmas than about the low-involvement dilemmas, whereas the adults showed similar reasoning levels for all three dilemmas. This study indicates both that emotions can affect cognition and that the

effect may be greater for adolescents and emerging adults than for adults. Recent brain research seems to support this conclusion (Sercombe, 2009).

Practical Cognition: Critical Thinking and Decision Making

Some research on cognitive development in adolescence and emerging adulthood has been especially concerned with how cognition operates in real life, applied to practical situations. Two areas of research on practical cognition in adolescence and emerging adulthood are critical thinking and decision making.

The Development of Critical Thinking

In combination, the changes in cognitive development during adolescence described thus far have the potential to provide adolescents with a greater capacity for **critical thinking**, which is thinking that involves not merely memorizing information but analyzing it, making judgments about what it means, relating it to other information, and considering how it might be valid or invalid.

According to the cognitive psychologist Daniel Keating (2004; Keating & Sasse, 1996), cognitive development in adolescence provides the potential for critical thinking in several ways. First, a wider range of knowledge is available in long-term memory, across a variety of domains; thus, the ability to analyze and make judgments about new information is enhanced because more previous knowledge is available for comparison. Second, the ability to consider different kinds of knowledge simultaneously is increased, which makes it possible to think of new combinations of knowledge. Third, more metacognitive strategies are available for applying or gaining knowledge, such as planning and monitoring one's own comprehension; these strategies make it possible to think more critically about what one is learning.

However, Keating and others stress that critical-thinking skills do not develop automatically or inevitably in adolescence. On the contrary, critical thinking in adolescence requires a foundation of skills and knowledge obtained in childhood, along with an educational environment in adolescence that promotes and values critical thinking. According to Keating (2004), gaining specific knowledge and learning critical-thinking skills are complementary goals. Critical thinking promotes gaining knowledge of a topic be-

---

reductionism Breaking up a phenomenon into separate parts to such an extent that the meaning and coherence of the phenomenon as a whole becomes lost.

critical thinking Thinking that involves not merely memorizing information but analyzing it, making judgments about what it means, relating it to other information, and considering ways in which it might be valid or invalid.

behavioral decision theory Theory of decision making that describes the decision-making process as including (1) identifying the range of possible choices; (2) identifying the consequences that would result from each choice; (3) evaluating the desirability of each consequence; (4) assessing the likelihood of each consequence; and (5) integrating this information.

cause it leads to a desire for underlying explanations, and gaining knowledge of a topic makes critical thinking possible because it makes relevant knowledge available for analysis and critique.

Given the potential usefulness of critical thinking in the learning process, one might expect that critical-thinking skills would be a primary goal of teaching in schools. However, observers of the American educational system generally agree that American schools do a poor job of promoting critical thinking (Gruber & Boreen, 2003; Keating, 2004; Linn & Songer, 1991; Steinberg, 1996). Assessments of adolescents' critical-thinking skills generally find that few adolescents develop such skills and use them capably, in part because such skills are so rarely promoted in the classroom. Instead of promoting the complementary development of knowledge and critical thinking, a great deal of secondary school teaching is limited to promoting the rote memorization of concrete facts, with the limited goal that students will be able to remember those facts until a test is taken (Gruber & Boreen, 2003; Linn & Songer, 1991).

The promotion of critical thinking would require small classes and a classroom environment in which focused discourse between teachers and students was the norm (Keating, 1990; Keating & Sasse, 1996). These characteristics are not typical of American secondary schools (Linn & Songer, 1991, 1993). Asian secondary schools have been observed to have an especially strong emphasis on rote learning and to discourage critical thinking (Stevenson & Zusho, 2002). Some scholars argue that European secondary schools are better at providing a classroom environment that promotes critical thinking (Hamilton, 1990; Hamilton & Hamilton, 2006). American colleges also tend to have more success than American secondary schools in promoting critical thinking, especially in relatively small classes (Magolda, 1997). In this textbook, the Thinking Critically questions in each chapter are intended to promote critical thinking on adolescence and emerging adulthood. They also provide you with examples of what critical thinking means.

THINKING CRITICALLY •••

Did your high school successfully promote critical thinking? If not, why do you think it did not? What practical barriers exist to the promotion of critical thinking?

Can Adolescents Make Competent Decisions?

We saw in Chapter 1 that making independent decisions is one of the qualities that most adolescents and emerging adults in a variety of cultures consider to be a crucial part of becoming an adult (Arnett, 1998a; 2004a). What do studies tell us about whether adolescents possess the cognitive abilities to make decisions competently? The answer to this question has important implications, given that adolescents

in many societies are confronted with decisions about whether to use drugs (including alcohol and cigarettes), when to become sexually active, and which educational path to pursue.

This area also has political and legal implications in debates over whether adolescents should have the right to make independent decisions about using contraception, obtaining an abortion, or pursuing various medical treatments. In many American states, adolescents (under age 18) are prohibited from making independent decisions about medical treatments (Cauffman & Woolard, 2005; Steinberg & Cauffman, 1996). Also, legal contracts entered into by adolescents under age 18 do not have the same binding power as contracts signed by persons age 18 or over. Adolescents may disavow a contract any time they wish, whereas adults may not (Nurcombe & Parlett, 1994). Furthermore, crimes committed by adolescents are treated under a different legal system than crimes committed by adults, and usually more leniently, which reflects a perception that adolescents should not be held responsible for bad decisions in the same way adults are. Increasingly in the United States, states are narrowing this distinction and trying juveniles under the same rules as adults for many crimes, but most states have maintained at least some distinction in the legal system that recognizes differences in decision-making capabilities between adolescents and adults (Cauffman & Woolard, 2005; Zimring, 2000).

One prominent current perspective on adolescent decision making is **behavioral decision theory** (Beyth-Marom &

Are adolescents competent to make major decisions, such as about legal or medical issues?

Fischoff, 1997; Byrnes, Miller, & Reynolds, 1999; Fischoff, 2005; Furby & Beyth-Marom, 1992; Jacobs & Klaczynski, 2005). According to this perspective, the decision-making process includes (1) identifying the range of possible choices; (2) identifying the consequences that would result from each choice; (3) evaluating the desirability of each consequence; (4) assessing the likelihood of each consequence; and (5) integrating this information into a decision.

Studies indicate that competence in this process varies substantially with age. Compared with preadolescent children, early adolescents generally identify a wider range of possible choices, are better at anticipating the consequences of the possible choices, and are better at evaluating and integrating information (Keating, 2004). In each of these respects, however, early adolescents are less skilled than late adolescents or emerging adults (Byrnes et al., 1999).

For example, Lewis (1981) presented adolescents in grades 8, 10, and 12 with hypothetical situations regarding decisions about medical procedures. The 12th graders were more likely than the 10th or 8th graders to mention risks to be considered (83%, 50%, and 40%, from oldest to youngest), to recommend consultation with an outside specialist (62%, 46%, and 21%), and to anticipate possible consequences (42%, 25%, and 11%).

Most studies comparing late adolescents and adults have found few differences between them in the decision-making processes they use (Beyth-Marom et al., 1993; Beyth-Marom & Fischoff, 1997; Fischoff, 2005; Furby & Beyth-Marom, 1992). Why is it, then, that adolescents are so much more likely than adults to take risks such as driving while intoxicated or trying illegal drugs? One possible explanation is that adolescents and adults make different evaluations about the desirability of the possible consequences (Maggs, 1999). For example, in deciding whether to try an illegal drug that is being handed around at a party, both adolescents and adults may identify the same range of choices and the same possible consequences from these choices (Quadrel, Fischoff, & Davis, 1993), such as the possible pleasurable feelings from the drug and the possibility of being considered daring or timid by others for trying or not trying it. However, adolescents and adults may evaluate these consequences differently. Adolescents may be more attracted to the possible sensation-seeking pleasure of the drug, more eager to be considered daring by others, and more worried about being considered timid by others (Reyna & Farley, 2006). They may also evaluate the potential consequences of taking the drug as less negative than adults would. As a consequence, adolescents would be more likely than adults to try illegal drugs even though both adolescents and adults would be going through the same decision-making process (Gibbons, Gerrard, & Lane, 2003; Quadrel et al., 1993).

A recent "dual processing" theory by Paul Klaczynski (2001, 2004, 2005) has proposed that adolescent decision making is based on two different cognitive systems, one that is *analytic* and uses the reasoning of formal operations, and another that is *heuristic*, that is, based on intuitive factors such as past experience, emotions, and unconscious motivations. Klaczynski finds that even as analytic reasoning advances in the course of adolescence, heuristic factors continue to affect decision making and do not necessarily improve. His research indicates that adolescents tend to accept an argument based on questionable analytic reasoning if they have intuitive reasons for accepting the argument (Klaczynski, 1997; Klaczynski & Narasimham, 1998). This distortion in decision making declines from preadolescence to adolescence, but even adolescents and emerging adults are affected by it (Klaczynski & Gordon, 1996).

A similar view of adolescents' decision making has been proposed by Steinberg and Cauffman (1996, 2001; Cauffman & Woolard, 2005; Grisso, Steinberg, Cauffman et al., 2003; Steinberg, 2008). They argue that differences in decision-making abilities between adolescents and adults should be divided into two broad categories: those attributed to cognitive factors and those attributed to psychosocial factors (i.e., social and emotional maturity). According to Steinberg and Cauffman, most studies of decision-making abilities among adolescents and adults have explored only cognitive factors. However, they view this approach as too narrow and as likely to underestimate the differences between adolescents and adults. Instead, they propose that mature decision making should be viewed as the product of the interaction between cognitive and psychosocial factors, with competent decision making potentially undermined by a deficiency in either area. The implication of their theory is that even though adolescents may be able to show the same level of cognitive ability as adults in making a decision, adolescents may make different decisions because they are more likely than adults to be affected by psychosocial factors, such as the emotions of the moment and the desire to be accepted by peers. Research using this model indicates that it is especially adolescents aged 15 and younger whose decision-making competence is impaired by psychosocial immaturity (Grisso et al., 2003).

It should be emphasized that scholars on decision making agree that even in adulthood, the process of making decisions is rarely based purely on reason and is often inaccurate because of reasoning errors or the influence of social and emotional factors (Byrnes et al., 1999; Jacobs & Klaczynski, 2002, 2005; Klaczynski, 1997, 2001; Quadrel et al., 1993). Decision-making abilities may improve from childhood through adolescence and into emerging adulthood and beyond, but at all ages the process of decision making is often subject to errors and distortions.

Adolescents' decision making is strongly influenced by psychosocial factors.

By what age, if at all, should adolescents be allowed to decide whether to get a tattoo, whether to use birth control, and whether to live on their own? Justify your answer in terms of the decision-making concepts presented here.

Social Cognition

Cognitive development is discussed in an early chapter of this book because it is an area of development that provides a foundation for a wide range of other aspects of development, from family relations and friendships to school performance and risk behavior. Cognitive development in adolescence functions as an **organizational core** that affects all areas of thinking, no matter what the topic (Tomlinson-Keasey & Eisert, 1981).

This means that the cognitive concepts we have discussed in relation to the physical world can be applied to social topics as well. **Social cognition** is the term for the way we think about other people, social relationships, and social institutions (Evans, 2008; Flavell, 1985). Because social cognition (like cognitive development generally) is reflected in so many other areas of adolescent development, we will be discussing social cognition throughout the book. Here, as an introduction, we examine two aspects of social cognition: perspective taking and adolescent egocentrism.

Perspective Taking

Have you had a conversation lately with a young child? If you have, you may have found that such conversations tend to go most smoothly when the focus of the conversation is on them rather than you. Young children tend to assume that topics that focus on themselves are of great interest not only to themselves but to others, and it rarely occurs to them to ask themselves how your interests might differ from theirs. As children grow into adolescence, they become better at **perspective taking**, the ability to understand the thoughts and feelings of others. Of course, understanding the thoughts and feelings of others remains a challenge even for most adults. But most people improve at this as they grow up, and adolescence is an especially important period in the development of perspective taking.

Robert Selman (1976, 1980; Selman & Byrne, 1974) has been one of the most influential scholars on the development of perspective taking (De Lisi, 2005). On the basis of his research, he proposed a theory describing how perspective taking develops through a series of stages, from early childhood through adolescence. In the course of these stages, according to Selman, the egocentrism of childhood gradually develops into the mature perspective-taking ability of adolescence.

Selman has used mainly interviews as the method of his research. In the interviews, children and adolescents are provided with hypothetical situations and asked to comment on them. For example: "Dr. Miller has just finished his training to be a doctor. He was setting up an office in a new town and wanted to get a lot of patients. He didn't have much money to start out with. He found an office and was trying to decide if he should spend a lot of money to make it fancy, by putting down a fancy rug, buying fancy furniture, and expensive lighting, or if he should keep it plain, with no rug, plain furniture, and a plain lamp" (Selman, 1980, p. 42).

Responses indicating perspective-taking abilities are then elicited by asking questions concerning the doctor's thinking about attracting new patients, and asking about the point of view of patients and of society in general on the doctor's behavior (e.g., "What do you think society thinks about doctors spending money to make their offices fancy to attract people?").

Selman's research indicates that until adolescence, children's capacity for perspective taking is limited in various ways. Young children have difficulty separating their own perspective from those of others. When they reach ages 6 to 8, children begin to develop perspective-taking skills but have difficulty comparing perspectives. By preadolescence (ages 8 to 10), most children can understand that others may have a point of view that is different from their own. They also realize that taking another's perspective can assist them in understanding others' intentions and actions.

According to Selman, in early adolescence, about ages 10 to 12, children become capable for the first time of **mutual perspective taking**. That is, early adolescents understand that their perspective-taking interactions with others are mutual—just as you understand that another person has a perspective that is different from your own, you also realize that other persons understand that you have a perspective that is different from theirs. Also, unlike preadolescents, early adolescents have begun to be able to imagine how their view and the view of another person might appear to a third person. In the Dr. Miller example just presented, this stage would be reflected in the ability to explain the doctor's perceptions of how others might view both him and his patients.

> "It is the case that reality, like landscape, has infinite perspectives, all of them equally true and authentic. The only false perspective is the one that claims to be the only one."
>
> —Jose Ortega y Gasset, *The Theme of Our Time*

---

organizational core Term applied especially to cognitive development, meaning that cognitive development affects all areas of thinking, no matter what the topic.

social cognition How people think about other people, social relationships, and social institutions.

perspective taking The ability to understand the thoughts and feelings of others.

mutual perspective taking Stage of perspective taking, often found in early adolescence, in which persons understand that their perspective-taking interactions with others are mutual, in the sense that each side realizes that the other can take their perspective.

According to Selman's theory, social cognition develops further in late adolescence. After mutual perspective taking comes **social and conventional system perspective taking**, meaning that adolescents come to realize that their social perspectives and those of others are influenced not just by their interactions with each other but also by their roles in the larger society. In the Dr. Miller example, this stage would be reflected in an understanding of how the role of doctor is perceived by society and how that would influence the perspective of the doctor and his patients.

In general, Selman's research has demonstrated that perspective-taking abilities improve from childhood through adolescence. However, his research also shows that there is only a loose connection between age and perspective-taking abilities. Adolescents may reach the stage of mutual perspective taking as early as age 11 or as late as age 20 (Selman, 1980). Notice that this is similar to the findings we discussed earlier on formal operations. In both areas there is a wide range of individual differences, and people of any given age vary a great deal in their cognitive skills.

Other studies of perspective taking have found it plays an important role in adolescents' peer relationships. For example, studies have found that adolescents' perspective-taking abilities are related to their popularity among peers (Kurdek & Krile, 1982) and to their success at making new friends (Vernberg et al., 1994). Being able to take the perspective of others helps adolescents to be aware of how the things they say and do might please or displease others. Perspective taking is also related to how adolescents treat others. In a study of Brazilian adolescents (Eisenberg, Zhou, & Koller, 2001), perspective-taking abilities were found to predict sympathy and **prosocial** behavior, meaning behavior that is kind and considerate. Since perspective taking promotes these qualities, it makes sense that adolescents who are good at perspective taking would also be good at making friends.

A recent concept related to perspective taking is the concept of **theory of mind**. Theory of mind is the ability to attribute mental states to one's self and others, including beliefs, thoughts, and feelings (Kuhn, 2000). So far, most research using the theory of mind idea has been on young children, looking at how they first develop an understanding that others have a mental life independent from their own (Lillard, 2007). However, some research is turning toward adolescence. For example, a recent study using techniques for measuring brain activity found that increased understanding of theory of mind from childhood to adolescence was related to increased activation of the frontal cortex when performing theory of mind tasks (Moriguchi et al., 2007). Another recent study looked at adolescents' theory of mind in relation to their family lives and found that adolescents were quite advanced in describing their parents' thoughts and feelings

concerning the marital relationship (Artar, 2007). This will be an area to watch in the years to come.

Adolescent Egocentrism

"I remember a time in high school when everybody who was anybody wore Guess jeans. I was pretty poor back then and couldn't afford to pay $50 or $75 for a pair of jeans, so I went without. Every time I was walking down the hall with my non-Guess jeans on and heard anyone whispering or giggling behind me, I was convinced they were laughing at me because I wasn't wearing Guess jeans. It's pretty sad—now I own two pairs of Guess jeans and nobody (including myself) cares."

—Dawn, Age 20 (Arnett, Unpublished Data)

"During early adolescence I believed/pretended that a movie crew was following me around and taping everything I did. They personally picked me because I was the most popular girl in school and had the most interesting life. Or so I thought!"

—Denise, Age 21 (Arnett, Unpublished Data)

"When I was in high school a group of us would go to the cliffs at the lake and 'blind jump' at night. Usually everyone had been drinking. To add an element of danger, about 60 feet or so down the cliff there was a shelf that stuck out about 6 feet that you had to avoid. There was one guy we knew, 18 years old, who tripped when he was jumping, landed on the shelf, broke his neck and died. We all thought he must have done something stupid and that it couldn't happen to us."

—Ryan, Age 22 (Arnett, Unpublished Data)

We have seen that adolescents become less egocentric than younger children as they learn to take the perspectives of others. However, cognitive development in adolescence also leads to new kinds of egocentrism that are distinctly adolescent.

It was noted earlier in the chapter that cognitive development in adolescence includes the development of metacognition, which is the capacity to think about thinking. This development includes the ability to think about not only your own thoughts but also the thoughts of others. When these abilities first develop, adolescents may have difficulty distinguishing their thinking about their own thoughts from their thinking about the thoughts of others, resulting in a distinctive kind of **adolescent egocentrism**. Ideas about adolescent egocentrism were first put forward by Piaget (1967) and were de-

---

social and conventional system perspective taking Realizing that the social perspectives of self and others are influenced not just by their interaction with each other but by their roles in the larger society.

prosocial Promoting the well-being of others.
theory of mind The ability to attribute mental states to one's self and others, including beliefs, thoughts, and feelings.

adolescent egocentrism Type of egocentrism in which adolescents have difficulty distinguishing their thinking about their own thoughts from their thinking about the thoughts of others.

Adolescents often feel that an imaginary audience is acutely conscious of how they look and behave.

veloped further by David Elkind (1967, 1985; Alberts, Elkind, & Ginsberg, 2007). According to Elkind, adolescent egocentrism has two aspects, the imaginary audience and the personal fable.

The Imaginary Audience The **imaginary audience** results from adolescents' limited capacity to distinguish between their thinking about themselves and their thinking about the thoughts of others. Because they think about themselves so much and are so acutely aware of how they might appear to others, they conclude that others must also be thinking about them a great deal. Because they exaggerate the extent to which others think about them, they imagine a rapt audience for their appearance and behavior.

The imaginary audience makes adolescents much more self-conscious than they were before formal operations. Do you remember waking up in 7th or 8th grade with a pimple on your forehead, or discovering a mustard stain on your pants and wondering how long it had been there, or saying something in class that made everybody laugh (even though you didn't intend it to be funny)? Of course, experiences like that are not much fun as an adult either. But they tend to be worse in adolescence because the imaginary audience makes it seem as though "everybody" knows about your humiliation and will remember it for a long, long time.

The imaginary audience is not something that simply disappears when adolescence ends. Adults are also egocentric to some extent. Adults, too, imagine (and sometimes exaggerate) an audience for their behavior. It is just that this tendency is stronger in adolescence, when formal operations are first developing and the capacity for distinguishing between our own perspective and the perspective of others is less developed.

The Personal Fable The **personal fable** is built on the imaginary audience, according to Elkind (1967, 1985; Alberts et al., 2007). The belief in an imaginary audience that is highly conscious of how you look and act leads to the belief that

there must be something special, something unique, about you—otherwise, why would others be so preoccupied with you? Adolescents' belief in the uniqueness of their personal experiences and their personal destiny is the personal fable.

The personal fable can be the source of adolescent anguish, when it makes them feel that "no one understands me" because no one can share their unique experience (Elkind, 1978). It can be the source of high hopes, too, as adolescents imagine their unique personal destiny leading to the fulfillment of their dreams to be a rock musician, or a professional athlete, or a Hollywood star, or simply successful in the field of their choice. It can also contribute to risky behavior by adolescents whose sense of uniqueness leads them to believe that adverse consequences from behavior such as unprotected sex and drunk driving "won't happen to me" (Alberts et al., 2007; Arnett, 1992a).

Like the imaginary audience, the personal fable diminishes with age, but it never disappears entirely for most of us. Even most adults like to think there is something special, if not unique, about their personal experiences and their personal destiny. But the personal fable tends to be stronger in adolescence than at later ages because with age our experiences and conversations with others lead us to an awareness that our thoughts and feelings are not as exceptional as we thought (Elkind, 1978).

THINKING CRITICALLY •••

Do you think most emerging adults have outgrown adolescent egocentrism? Give examples of the imaginary audience and the personal fable that you have witnessed among your peers or experienced yourself.

The personal fable is difficult to measure because few adolescents are likely to admit—and they may not even be aware—that they believe they have a unique personal destiny

imaginary audience Belief that others are acutely aware of and attentive to one's appearance and behavior.

personal fable A belief in one's personal uniqueness, often including a sense of invulnerability to the consequences of taking risks.

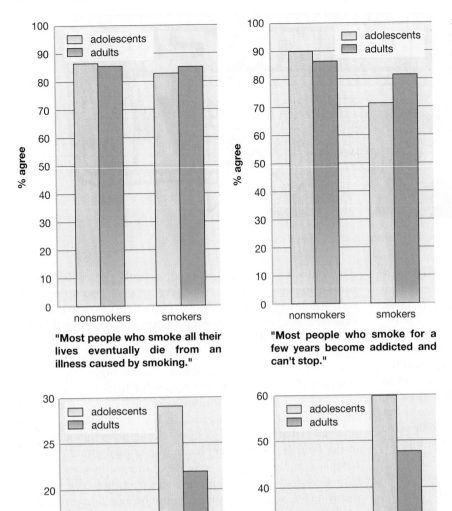

"Most people who smoke all their lives eventually die from an illness caused by smoking."

"Most people who smoke for a few years become addicted and can't stop."

"I doubt that I would die from smoking even if I smoked for 30 or 40 years."

"I could smoke for a few years and then quit if I wanted to."

FIGURE 3.2 Adolescent and adult smokers' perceptions of the risks of smoking. Does this study show evidence of the optimistic bias in adolescence?

and that misfortunes that happen to others will not happen to them. Recently, however, Elkind and his colleagues have presented a new measure of the personal fable that shows promise (Alberts, Elkind, & Ginsburg, 2007). As predicted by the theory, personal fable scores increased from early to midadolescence and were correlated with participation in risk behaviors such as substance use. Boys were higher than girls on both personal fable scores and reports of risk behavior.

A concept related to the personal fable, known as the **optimistic bias**, has been researched more extensively than the personal fable itself. The idea of the optimistic bias comes out of health psychology, and it concerns a specific aspect of the personal fable: the tendency to assume that accidents, diseases, and other misfortunes are more likely to happen to others than to ourselves (Fife-Schaw & Barnett, 2004; Weinstein, 1989). Research in this area has found that both adolescents and adults have an optimistic bias with regard to health risk behaviors such as driving while intoxicated or smoking cigarettes, but adolescents tend to have a stronger optimistic bias than adults (Arnett, 1992a; Klein & Helweg-Larsen, 2002; Weinstein, 1998).

For example, in one study adolescent and adult smokers and nonsmokers were asked about the risks of smoking for others and for themselves (Arnett, 2000b). As you can see from Figure 3.2, strong majorities of both adolescents and adults, both smokers and nonsmokers, believed that smoking is addictive and deadly for "most people." However, when they applied the risk to themselves, there was evidence of an optimistic bias. Smokers were more likely than nonsmokers to believe that they would not die as a consequence of smoking for 30 to 40 years.

Still, even most of the smokers believed that smoking would eventually be fatal for them personally, if they smoked long enough. The real heart of the optimistic bias for smoking seems to be in relation to addiction. Although the great majority of both adolescents and adults believed that "Most people who smoke for a few years become addicted and can't stop," 48% of the adult smokers and 60% of the adolescent

---

optimistic bias The tendency to assume that accidents, diseases, and other misfortunes are more likely to happen to other people than to one's self.

psychometric approach Attempt to understand human cognition by evaluating cognitive abilities using intelligence tests.

Alfred Binet French psychologist who developed the first intelligence test in the early 20th century, which later became known as the Stanford-Binet.

Stanford-Binet Widely used IQ test developed by Alfred Binet and revised by scholars at Stanford University.

intelligence quotient A measure of a person's intellectual abilities based on a standardized test.

Wechsler Intelligence Scale for Children (WISC-IV) Intelligence test for children aged 6 to 16, with six Verbal and five Performance subtests.

smokers believed that "I could smoke for a few years and then quit if I wanted to." These findings indicate that one of the reasons adolescents take up smoking in spite of the well-known health risks is that they hold an optimistic bias with regard to addiction. They do not believe they will ultimately die from smoking, not because they do not believe smoking is deadly but because they believe they will quit smoking long before it kills them. The findings also show that many adults, too, have an optimistic bias about their smoking behavior, but it may not be as strong among adults as it is among adolescents.

The Psychometric Approach: Intelligence Testing

Thus far, we have looked mostly at group patterns in cognitive functioning, describing the cognitive functioning of adolescents and emerging adults in general. Another way to look at cognitive development is to focus on individual differences, that is, on how various individuals within a group (all 16-year-olds, for example) might differ in their cognitive abilities. This is the goal of intelligence tests. Attempting to understand human cognition by evaluating cognitive abilities with intelligence tests is known as the **psychometric approach**.

Let us begin by looking at the characteristics of the most widely used intelligence tests and then examine some of the research on intelligence tests that pertains most directly to adolescence. Following that we will consider an alternative way of conceptualizing and measuring intelligence.

The Stanford-Binet and Wechsler Intelligence Tests

The first intelligence test was developed in 1905 by a French psychologist named **Alfred Binet** (pronounced bee-*nay*). Binet's test was brief, consisting of just 30 items, and assessed performance in areas such as memory and abstract thinking (Gould, 1981). In the years since its original development, it has been revised and expanded several times. Some of the most important revisions were conducted by Louis Terman of Stanford University in the 1920s, and the test is now known as the **Stanford-Binet**. The most recent revision of the test includes four content areas: verbal reasoning, quantitative reasoning, abstract/visual reasoning, and short-term memory (Bain & Allin, 2005). It can be given to people from age 2

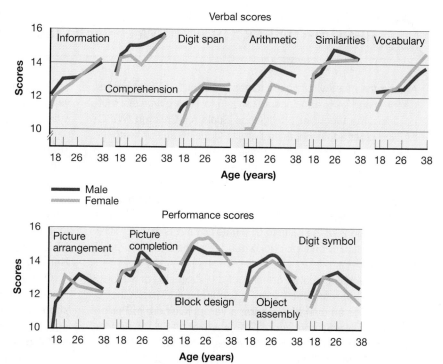

FIGURE 3.3 Changes in scores on IQ subtests, ages 16 to 38.
Source: Bayley (1968).

through adulthood. The test results in an overall score called the IQ (for **intelligence quotient**). It can be used to assess abilities within the normal range of intelligence as well as problems such as cognitive delays, mental retardation, and learning disabilities.

The other widely used IQ tests are the Wechsler scales, including the **Wechsler Intelligence Scale for Children (WISC-IV)** for children aged 6 to 16 and the **Wechsler Adult Intelligence Scale (WAIS-IV)** for persons aged 16 and up. The Wechsler tests contain two kinds of subtests, **Verbal subtests** and **Performance subtests**. The results of the Wechsler tests provide a Verbal IQ and a Performance IQ as well as an overall IQ. More detail on the WISC-IV and the WAIS-IV are provided in the Research Focus box.

As the Research Focus box indicates, **relative performance** on IQ tests is very stable—people who score higher than average in childhood tend to score higher than average as adolescents and adults, and people who score lower than average in childhood tend to score lower than average as adolescents and adults. However, some interesting patterns of change occur in **absolute performance** from midadolescence through young adulthood (Moffitt et al., 1993). Figure 3.3 shows how scores on the WAIS subtests changed from age 16 to age 38 in one

---

Wechsler Adult Intelligence Scale (WAIS-IV) Intelligence test for persons aged 16 and up, with six Verbal and five Performance subtests.

Verbal subtests In the Wechsler IQ tests, subtests that examine verbal abilities.

Performance subtests In the Wechsler IQ tests, subtests that examine abilities for attention, spatial perception, and speed of processing.

relative performance In IQ tests, performance results compared to other persons of the same age.

absolute performance In IQ tests, performance results compared to other persons, regardless of age.

Among the most widely used IQ tests are the Wechsler scales. Children and early adolescents (ages 6 to 16) are typically tested using the Wechsler Intelligence Scale for Children (WISC-IV), and older adolescents and adults (ages 16 and up) with the Wechsler Adult Intelligence Scale (WAIS-IV). The "IV" in the names indicates that this is the fourth version of the tests that has been developed. Because early versions of the tests were criticized for being culturally biased against American minority cultures (Miller-Jones, 1989), special efforts were made in more recent versions of the tests to eliminate any items that might require a particular cultural background (Psychological Corporation, 2000).

The Wechsler scales consist of 11 subtests, of which 6 are Verbal subtests and 5 are Performance subtests. The results provide an overall IQ score, a Verbal IQ score, a Performance IQ score, and scores for each of the 11 subtests. More detail on each of the subscales of the WAIS-IV is provided in Table 3.2, so you can get an idea of what IQ tests really measure.

A great deal of research has gone into the development of the Wechsler scales (Kaufman & Lichtenberger, 2006; Ryan & Lopez, 2001). One goal of this research was to establish **age norms**. Age norming means that a typical score for each age is established by testing a large random sample of people from a variety of geographical areas and social class backgrounds. An individual's IQ score is determined by comparing the individual's performance on the test to the "norm," or typical score, for people his or her age. The **median**—the point at which half of the sample scores above and half below—is assigned the score of 100, and other scores are determined according to how high or low they are in relation to the median.

Two other important considerations in the research to develop the Wechsler tests were reliability and validity. As discussed in Chapter 1, reliability is a measurement of the extent to which responses on a measure are consistent. There are a number of kinds of reliability, but one of the most important is **test-retest reliability**, which examines whether persons' scores on one occasion are similar to their scores on another occasion. The Wechsler IQ tests have high test-retest reliability, which improves as people get older (Psychological Corporation, 2000). For most people, little change in IQ scores takes place after about age 10 (Gold et al., 1995; Hertzog & Schaie, 1986).

Of course, that does not mean that your mental abilities never advance after age 10! Keep in mind that IQ is a relative score. It indicates how you compare with other people your age. So, people who score higher than their peers at age 10 are also likely to score above average at age 20, 30, 40, and so on; people whose IQs are below average at age 10 are also likely to score below average as they become older, relative to other people of the same age. There are exceptions to this general pattern. Some people change dramatically in IQ during childhood or adolescence, for better or worse (Moffitt et al., 1993), but the more typical pattern is one of great stability in IQ scores.

The validity of an instrument is the extent to which it measures what it claims to measure. For IQ tests, the validity question would be, do IQ tests really measure intelligence? Some evidence regarding this question is presented in this chapter. However, questions about validity are much harder to answer than questions about reliability, and the validity of IQ tests remains hotly debated among scholars and in the general public. In general, it can be concluded at this

longitudinal study (Bayley, 1968). Notice how absolute scores on the Verbal subtests generally improved from age 16 to 38, whereas absolute scores on the Performance subtests tended to peak in the mid-20s and then decline.

These patterns reflect a distinction that some scholars have made between fluid and crystallized intelligence (Horn, 1982; Sligh et al., 2005). **Fluid intelligence** refers to mental abilities that involve speed of analyzing, processing, and reacting to information, which is the kind of ability tapped by the Performance subtests (Performance tests reward speed of response, whereas Verbal tests do not). IQ tests indicate that this kind of intelligence peaks in emerging adulthood. **Crystallized intelligence**, in contrast, refers to accumulated knowledge and enhanced judgment based on experience. Subtests like Information, Comprehension, and Vocabulary assess this kind of intelligence, and absolute scores on these subtests tend to improve through the 20s and 30s.

THINKING CRITICALLY •••

What aspects of "intelligence" does the WAIS-IV *not* include, in your view?

---

age norms Technique for developing a psychological test, in which a typical score for each age is established by testing a large random sample of people from a variety of geographical areas and social class backgrounds.

median In a distribution of scores, the point at which half of the population scores above and half below.

test-retest reliability Type of reliability that examines whether or not persons' scores on one occasion are similar to their scores on another occasion.

point that IQ tests have reasonably good **predictive validity**; that is, high IQ scores in adolescence predict relatively high educational attainment in emerging adulthood and occupational success in young adulthood and beyond (Subotnik & Arnold, 1994). High IQs in adolescence are also predictive of positive outcomes in adulthood unrelated to education and occupation, for example, lower likelihood of divorce or alcoholism (Holahan et al., 1995).

TABLE 3.2 The WAIS-IV: Sample Items

Verbal Subtests

Information: General knowledge questions, for example, "Who wrote *Huckleberry Finn*'?"

Vocabulary: Give definitions, for example, "What does 'formulate' mean?"

Similarities: Describe relationship between two things, for example, "In what ways are an apple and an orange alike?" and "In what ways are a book and a movie alike?"

Arithmetic: Verbal arithmetic problems, for example, "How many hours does it take to drive 140 miles at a rate of 30 miles an hour?"

Comprehension: Practical knowledge, for example, "Why is it important to use zip codes when you mail letters?"

Digit Span: Short-term memory test. Sequences of numbers of increasing length are recited, and person is required to repeat them.

Performance Subtests

For all the Performance tests, scores are based on speed as well as accuracy of response.

Picture Arrangement: Cards depicting various activities are provided, and the person is required to place them in an order that tells a coherent story.

Picture Completion: Cards are provided depicting an object or scene with something missing, and the person is required to point out what is missing (for example, a dog is shown with only three legs).

Matrix Reasoning: Patterns are shown with one piece missing. The person chooses from five options the one that will fill in the missing piece accurately.

Block Design: Blocks are provided having two sides all white, two sides all red, and two sides half red and half white. A card is shown with a geometrical pattern, and the person must arrange the blocks so that they match the pattern on the card.

Digit Symbol: At the top of the sheet, numbers are shown with matching symbols. Below, sequences of symbols are given with an empty box below each symbol. The person must place the matching number in the box below each symbol..

Intelligence Tests and Adolescent Development

An enormous amount of research using IQ tests has been conducted since they were first developed. With respect to adolescence, the most notable results concern adoption studies.

As described in Chapter 1, adoption studies take advantage of a natural experiment. A natural experiment is a situation that exists naturally—in other words, the researcher does not control the situation—but that provides interesting scientific information to the perceptive observer. Adoption is a natural experiment in the sense that, unlike in most families, children in adoptive families are raised by adults with whom they have no biological relationship. This eliminates the problem of passive genotype–environment interactions we discussed in Chapter 2, in which it is difficult to know the extent to which similarities between parents and children in biological families are due to genes or environment because the parents provide both. Similarities between adoptive parents and adopted children are likely to be due to the environment provided by the parents because the parents and children are biologically unrelated. Similarities between adopted children and their biological parents are likely to be due to genetics because the environment the children grew up in was not provided by the biological parents.

---

fluid intelligence Mental abilities that involve speed of analyzing, processing, and reacting to information.

crystallized intelligence Accumulated knowledge and enhanced judgment based on experience.

predictive validity In longitudinal research, the ability of a variable at Time 1 to predict the outcome of a variable at Time 2.

An interesting pattern occurs in adoption studies that follow children from birth through adolescence (Rowe, 1995). In early and middle childhood, a substantial correlation in IQ exists between adopted children and their adoptive parents. However, by the time adopted children reach adolescence, the correlation between their IQs and the IQs of their adoptive parents has declined, even though the number of years they have all been in the same family has increased. How could this be?

What may explain it is a gradual decline with age in the influence of the immediate family environment on intellectual development, and a gradual increase in active genotype–environment interactions—that is, in the degree to which children choose their own environmental influences (Scarr & McCartney, 1983). In early and middle childhood, parents have a great deal of control over the kind of environment their children experience. Parents control decisions about how much time their children spend on homework, how much television they watch, what they do for fun on the weekends, whom they play with, and so on. However, adolescents make many of these decisions for themselves (Rowe, 1995). Parents still have important influences on adolescents, but adolescents have much more autonomy than younger children. Adolescents have a greater say in how much time they spend on homework, how much of their free time they spend reading or watching television, and who their friends will be. All these decisions contribute to intellectual development, and as a consequence adolescents bear less resemblance in IQ to their adoptive parents than younger adopted children do.

A particularly interesting line of adoption research concerns **transracial adoption**, specifically involving Black children who have been adopted by White parents (Burrow & Finley, 2004). One of the most bitter controversies surrounding intelligence tests concerns racial differences in IQ (Fraser, 1995; Gould, 1981). African Americans and Latinos generally score lower than Whites on the most widely used IQ tests (Anastasi, 1988), from childhood through adulthood. However, scholars disagree vehemently over the source of these group differences. Some assert that the differences are due to genetic ethnic/racial differences in intelligence (e.g., Herrnstein & Murray, 1995). Others assert that the differences simply reflect the fact that IQ tests concern knowledge obtained in the majority culture, which Whites are more likely than minorities to have grown up in (e.g., Brody, 1992; Fraser, 1995; Gould, 1981). Transracial adoption represents an extraordinary natural experiment, in that it involves raising African American children in the White-dominated majority culture.

And what do these studies find? In general, they indicate that when Black children are raised in adoptive White families, their IQs are as high or higher than the average IQ for Whites (Weinberg, Scarr, & Waldman, 1992). Their IQ scores decline somewhat in adolescence but nevertheless remain relatively high (Burrow & Finley, 2004). This indicates that overall differences in IQ between Whites and African Americans are due to cultural and social class differences rather than to genetics.

Black children raised by White parents tend to have higher than average IQs.

Other Conceptions of Intelligence: The Theory of Multiple Intelligences

For many centuries of Western history, intelligence has been viewed as the degree of a person's knowledge and reasoning abilities (Kail & Pellegrino, 1985). This conception of intelligence underlies the construction of intelligence tests, and it is the one that most people hold. In one study, scholars and nonscholars indicated the abilities they believed to be characteristic of an intelligent person (Sternberg et al., 1981). The scholars (psychologists studying intelligence) and nonscholars (from a variety of backgrounds) provided similar responses. Both groups viewed intelligence as being comprised mainly of verbal abilities (e.g., "good vocabulary," "high reading comprehension") and problem-solving skills (e.g., "reasons logically," "can apply knowledge to the situation at hand").

In recent years, however, alternative theories of intelligence have been proposed. These theories have sought to present a conception of intelligence that is much broader than the traditional one. One of the most influential alternative theories of intelligence has been presented by Howard Gardner. Gardner's (1983, 1989, 1999) **theory of multiple intelligences** includes eight types of intelligence. In Gardner's view only two of them, linguistic and logical-mathematical intelligences, are evaluated by intelligence tests. The other in-

According to Howard Gardner's theory, outstanding gymnasts such as Nastia Liukin could be described as being high in bodily-kinesthetic intelligence.

(Kornhaber, 2004). Gardner has also been criticized for extending the boundaries of intelligence too widely. When an adolescent learns to play piano more quickly than her peers, is this an indication of musical "intelligence" or simply of musical talent? Gardner himself has been critical of the concept of "emotional intelligence" proposed by Daniel Goleman and others (Goleman, 1997), arguing persuasively that the capacity to empathize and cooperate with others is better viewed as "emotional sensitivity" rather than intelligence (Gardner, 1999). However, Gardner is vulnerable to a similar criticism for proposing "interpersonal" and "intrapersonal" intelligences.

THINKING CRITICALLY •••

Do you agree that all the mental abilities described by Gardner are different types of intelligence? If not, which types would you remove? Are there other types you would add?

The underlying issue in alternative theories of intelligence is the question of how intelligence should be defined. If intelligence is defined simply as the mental abilities required to succeed in school, the traditional approach to conceptualizing and measuring intelligence is generally successful. However, if one wishes to define intelligence more broadly, as the entire range of human mental abilities, the traditional approach may be seen as too narrow, and an approach such as Gardner's may be preferred.

telligences are spatial (the ability to think three-dimensionally); musical; bodily kinesthetic (the kind that athletes and dancers excel in); naturalist (ability for understanding natural phenomena); interpersonal (ability for understanding and interacting with others); and intrapersonal (self-understanding). As evidence for the existence of these different types of intelligence, Gardner argues that each involves different cognitive skills, that each can be destroyed by damage to a particular part of the brain, and that each appears in extremes in geniuses as well as in *idiots savants* (the French term for people who are low in general intelligence but possess an extraordinary ability in one specialized area).

Gardner argues that schools should give more attention to the development of all eight kinds of intelligence and develop programs tailored to each child's individual profile of intelligences. He has proposed methods for assessing different intelligences, such as measuring musical intelligence by having people attempt to sing a song, play an instrument, or orchestrate a melody (Gardner, 1999). However, thus far neither Gardner nor others have developed reliable and valid methods for analyzing the intelligences he proposes

Brain Development in Adolescence

In recent years, there has been a surge of research on neurological development in adolescence and emerging adulthood that casts new light on cognitive development during these years (Casey, Getz, & Galvan, 2008; Giedd, 2008; Keating, 2004). Research technologies, especially **PET scans** (Positron Emission Tomography) and **fMRI** (functional Magnetic Resonance Imaging), have made possible a more advanced understanding of how the brain develops, because these technologies show how different parts of the brain function when performing a cognitive task (e.g., solving a math problem). This research unveils the underlying neurological basis for the kinds of changes we have discussed in this chapter in areas such as decision making and reflective judgment.

It has long been known that by age 6 the brain is already 95% of its adult size. However, when it comes to brain development, size is not everything. Equally if not more important are the connections or **synapses** between the

transracial adoption The adoption of children of one race by parents of a different race.

theory of multiple intelligences Howard Gardner's theory that there are eight separate types of intelligence.

PET scans A technique for assessing ongoing brain functioning, in which a chemical that emits positrons is injected into the body and detectors measure their activity levels in various parts of the brain.

fMRI A technique for measuring brain functioning during an ongoing activity.

synapse The point of transmission between two nerve cells.

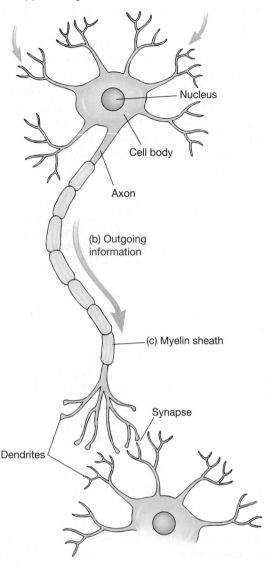

(a) Incoming information

Nucleus

Cell body

Axon

(b) Outgoing information

(c) Myelin sheath

Synapse

Dendrites

FIGURE 3.4 Two neurons and the synapse between them.

brain's **gray matter**, its outer layer, but is especially concentrated in the **frontal lobes**, the part of the brain that is right behind your forehead (Keating, 2004). The frontal lobes are involved in most of the higher functions of the brain, such as planning ahead, solving problems, and making moral judgments.

The findings about overproduction in early adolescence are surprising and fascinating, but equally fascinating is what follows it. Overproduction peaks at about age 11 or 12, but obviously that is not when our cognitive abilities peak. In the years that follow a massive amount of **synaptic pruning** takes place, in which the overproduction of synapses is whittled down considerably. In fact, between the ages of 12 and 20 the average brain loses 7% to 10% of its gray matter through synaptic pruning (Sowell et al., 1999). "Use it or lose it" seems to be the operating principle; synapses that are used remain, whereas those that are not used whither away. Recent research using fMRI methods shows that synaptic pruning is especially rapid among adolescents with high intelligence (Shaw et al., 2006).

Synaptic pruning allows the brain to work more efficiently, as brain pathways become more specialized. Imagine if you had to drive somewhere, and there were either many different back roads to get to your destination or one smooth highway. You would get there a lot faster if you took the highway. Synaptic pruning is like scrapping the many back roads in favor of one smooth highway. However, as the brain specializes in this way, it also becomes less flexible and less amenable to change.

Myelination is another important process of neurological growth in adolescence. Myelin is a blanket of fat wrapped around the main part of the neuron (Figure 3.4). It serves the function of keeping the brain's electrical signals on one path and increasing their speed. Like overproduction, myelination was previously thought to be over prior to puberty but has now been found to continue through the teens (Giedd, 2008; Paus, 1999; Sowell et al., 2002). This is another indication of how brain functioning is becoming faster and more efficient during adolescence. However, like synaptic pruning, myelination also makes brain functioning less flexible and changeable.

Finally, one last recent surprise for researchers studying brain development in adolescence has been in the growth of the **cerebellum** (see Figure 3.5). This is perhaps the biggest surprise of all because the cerebellum is part of the lower brain, well beneath the cortex, and has been long thought to be involved only in basic functions such as movement. Now, however, it turns out that the cerebellum is important for many higher functions as well, such as mathematics, music, decision making, and even social skills and understanding humor. It also turns out that the cerebellum continues to

neurons (brain cells) (Figure 3.4). Now scientists have learned that a considerable thickening of synaptic connections occurs around the time puberty begins, ages 10–12, a process neuroscientists call **overproduction** or **exuberance**. It had been known for decades that overproduction occurs during prenatal development and through the first 18 months of life, but now it turns out that a new period of overproduction occurs in early adolescence as well (Giedd, 2008; Giedd, Blumenthal, & Jeffries, 1999). Overproduction of synaptic connections occurs in many parts of the

neurons Cells of the nervous system, including the brain.

overproduction or **exuberance** A rapid increase in the production of synaptic connections in the brain.

exuberance See **overproduction**.

gray matter The outer layer of the brain, where most of the growth in brain cells occurs.

frontal lobes The part of the brain immediately behind the forehead. Known to be involved in higher brain functions such as planning ahead and analyzing complex problems.

synaptic pruning Following **overproduction**, the process by which the number of synapses in the brain are reduced, making brain functioning faster and more efficient but less flexible.

myelination Process by which myelin, a blanket of fat wrapped around the main part of the neuron, grows. Myelin serves the function of keeping the brain's electrical signals on one path and increasing their speed.

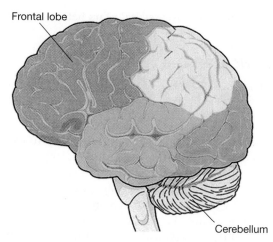

Frontal lobe

Cerebellum

FIGURE 3.5 The most important recent findings on adolescent brain development involve the frontal lobes and the cerebellum.

grow through adolescence and well into emerging adulthood (Strauch, 2003). In fact, it is the last structure of the brain to stop growing, not completing its phase of overproduction and pruning until the mid-20s, even after the frontal lobes.

So what can we conclude about brain development in adolescence and emerging adulthood on the basis of this new research? First, it is clear that the brain grows a lot more, and a lot differently, than we had known in the past. Second, the new findings confirm in many ways what we had known from studies using other methods, that adolescents are different and more advanced in their thinking than children are, but their cognitive development is not yet mature. Their abilities in areas such as making decisions, anticipating the consequences of their actions, and solving complex problems are not as advanced as they will be once they have reached adulthood and their basic brain development is more or less complete. Third, there are both gains and losses in the course of brain development in adolescence and emerging adulthood. The same neurological changes that make thinking faster and more efficient also make it more rigid and less flexible. After adolescence it is easier for people to make mature judgments about complicated issues, but not as many neurological options remain open for learning new things. However, for the most part the neurological changes of adolescence and emerging adulthood increase cognitive abilities substantially.

Culture and Cognitive Development

Although they differ in many ways, the three major perspectives on cognitive development discussed in this chapter—cognitive-developmental, information-processing, and psychometric—all underemphasize the role of culture in cognitive development. The goal of theories and research from these perspectives has been to discover principles of cognitive development that apply to all people in all times and all cultures—in other words, to strip away the effect of culture on cognition in an effort to identify universal human cognitive characteristics (Cole, 1996; Rogoff, 2003). Research on brain development also deemphasizes the role of culture.

However, in recent years a cultural approach to cognition has gained increased attention from scholars on childhood and adolescence. This approach is founded on the ideas of the Russian psychologist Lev **Vygotsky** (1896–1934). Vygotsky died of tuberculosis when he was just 37, and it took decades before his ideas about cognitive development were translated and recognized by scholars outside Russia. It is only in the past two decades that his work has been widely influential among Western scholars, but his influence is increasing as interest in understanding the cultural basis of development continues to grow (Daniels, Cole, & Wertsch, 2007; Gardiner, 2001; Maynard & Martini, 2005).

Vygotsky's theory is often referred to as a *sociocultural* theory because in his view cognitive development is inherently both a social and a cultural process (Mahn, 2003; Saxe, 1994; Tudge & Scrimsher, 2002). It is social because children learn through interactions with others and require assistance from others in order to learn what they need to know. It is cultural because what children need to know is determined by the culture they live in. As we have seen in this chapter, there are distinct cultural differences in the knowledge adolescents must acquire, from spearfishing skills in the South Pacific to the skills needed for surviving in the harsh Arctic environment of the Inuit to the verbal and scientific reasoning skills taught in schools.

Two of Vygotsky's most influential ideas are the **zone of proximal development** and **scaffolding**. The zone of proximal development is the gap between what adolescents can accomplish alone and what they are capable of doing if guided by an adult or a more competent peer. According to Vygotsky, children and adolescents learn best if the instruction they are provided is near the top of the zone of proximal development, so that they need assistance at first but gradually become capable of performing the task on their own.

Scaffolding refers to the degree of assistance provided to the adolescent in the zone of proximal development. According to Vygotsky, scaffolding should gradually decrease as children become more competent at a task. When

---

cerebellum A structure in the lower brain, well beneath the cortex long thought to be involved only in basic functions such as movement, now known to be important for many higher functions as well, such as mathematics, music, decision making, and social skills.

Vygotsky Russian psychologist who emphasized the cultural basis of cognitive development.

zone of proximal development The gap between how competently a person performs a task alone and when guided by an adult or more competent peer.

scaffolding The degree of assistance provided to the learner in the zone of proximal development, gradually decreasing as the learner's skills develop.

According to Vygotsky, cognitive development is always a social and cultural process. Here, a father in Haiti teaches his daughter how to weave baskets.

adolescents begin learning a task, they require substantial instruction and involvement from the teacher, but as they gain knowledge and skill the teacher should gradually scale back the amount of direct instruction provided. These ideas underscore the social nature of learning in Vygotsky's theory. In his view learning always takes place via a social process, through the interactions between someone who possesses knowledge and someone who is in the process of obtaining it.

An example of scaffolding and the zone of proximal development can be found in research by Tanon (1994), who studied weaving skills among male adolescents in the Dioula culture in Ivory Coast, on the western coast of Africa. An important part of the Dioula economy is making and selling large handmade cloths with elaborate designs. The training of weavers begins when they are age 10–12 and continues for several years. Boys grow up watching their fathers weave, but it is in early adolescence that they begin learning weaving skills themselves. Teaching takes place through scaffolding: The boy attempts a simple weaving pattern, the father corrects his mistakes, the boy tries again. When the boy gets it right, the father gives him a more complex pattern, thus raising the upper boundary of the zone of proximal development so that the boy continues to be challenged and his skills continue to improve. As the boy becomes more competent at weaving, the scaffolding provided by the father diminishes. Eventually the boy gets his own loom, but he continues to

consult with his father for several years before he can weave entirely by himself.

THINKING CRITICALLY •••

Think of an example of learning in your own culture that involves scaffolding and the zone of proximal development.

One scholar who has been important in extending Vygotsky's theory is Barbara Rogoff (1990, 1995, 1998, 2003, 2007). Her idea of **guided participation** refers to the teaching interaction between two people (often an adult and a child or adolescent) as they participate in a culturally valued activity. The guidance is "the direction offered by cultural and social values, as well as social partners" (Rogoff, 1995, p. 142) as learning takes place. This is like Vygotsky's idea of scaffolding, except that Rogoff is even more explicit than Vygotsky in emphasizing the importance of cultural values in determining what children and adolescents learn and how they learn it.

For example, in one study Rogoff and her colleagues observed a troop of early adolescent Girl Scouts in the United States as they sold and delivered Girl Scout cookies as a fund-raising project (Rogoff, Baker-Senett, Lacasa, & Goldsmith, 1995). The girls' involvement in the project reflected scaffolding and guided participation, as they began by taking a small observational role but gradually moved toward active participation and finally toward taking greater responsibilities in managing the sales (e.g., making calculations of how much money was due from each customer and keeping track of which customers had or had not paid). The project demonstrated the sociocultural basis of cognitive development. The girls' learning was social, because they were taught through participation in cookie selling with older girls, mothers, troop leaders, and even customers (who sometimes helped with the calculations). Their learning was also cultural, because it involved participation in a culturally valued activity and the implicit expression of cultural values such as efficiency, competition, cooperation, and responsibility.

The growing interest in a cultural approach to cognitive development is part of a broader perspective that has come to be known as **cultural psychology** (Cole, 1996; Shweder et al., 2006; Stigler, Shweder, & Herdt, 1990). In this perspective, cognition is inseparable from culture. Rather than trying to strip away the effect of culture on cognition, cultural psychologists seek to examine the ways that culture and cognition are interrelated and the profound effects that culture has on cognitive development. Rather than seeking to develop tests of cognitive abilities to examine underlying structures that apply to all aspects of thinking, cultural psy-

guided participation The teaching interaction between two people (often an adult and a child or adolescent) as they participate in a culturally valued activity.

cultural psychology Approach to human psychology emphasizing that psychological functioning cannot be separated from the culture in which it takes place.

chologists seek to analyze how people use cognitive skills in the activities of their daily lives (Segall et al., 1999). Cultural psychology is being applied to an increasing range of topics, but thus far the main focus has been on culture and cognition (Cole, 1996; Shweder et al., 2006).

Despite the rise of cultural psychology, far more research is still being conducted using the cognitive-developmental, information-processing, and psychometric approaches than is conducted using a cultural approach (Segall et al., 1999). Nevertheless, the cultural approach to adolescent cognition promises to grow in importance in the years to come.

SUMMING UP

In this chapter we have examined a variety of aspects of cognitive development in adolescence and emerging adulthood. The following summarizes the key points we have discussed:

- Piaget's theory of formal operations explains many of the changes that take place cognitively between preadolescence and adolescence, in areas including abstract thinking, complex thinking, and metacognition. However, research has shown that not all persons in all cultures reach formal operations, and most people do not use formal operations in all aspects of their lives.

- Cognitive development in emerging adulthood is distinguished by the development of certain aspects of postformal thinking, especially pragmatism and reflective judgment.

- The information-processing approach focuses on separating cognitive functioning into different components, including attention, various aspects of processing information, and various aspects of memory. However, the information-processing approach has been criticized for losing a sense of the overall thinking process in the course of breaking it down into components.

- Two aspects of practical cognition are critical thinking and decision making. Adolescents reach the potential for critical thinking, but teaching techniques in many secondary schools rarely bring this potential out; colleges and universities have more success with emerging adults. Adolescents appear to be capable of making some decisions using the same processes as adults, although psychosocial factors such as the emotions of the moment may be more likely to influence their decisions.

- Social cognition also changes during adolescence, in areas including perspective taking and adolescent egocentrism.

- Absolute scores on intelligence tests improve from the teens through the 30s for Verbal tests, but scores on Performance tests peak in the mid-20s. Howard Gardner has proposed a theory of multiple intelligences as an alternative to traditional conceptions of intelligence.

- Recent research on brain development shows that a process of overproduction and synaptic pruning takes place in the course of adolescence, which leads to more efficient but less flexible cognitive functioning. Furthermore, the cerebellum shows a surprising amount of growth in adolescence and emerging adulthood, leading to enhanced cognitive abilities in areas such as mathematics and social skills.

- Most research on cognitive development in adolescence and emerging adulthood has ignored culture in favor of seeking universal principles of cognition. However, in recent years there has been growing attention to the ideas of Vygotsky that emphasize the sociocultural basis of cognitive development, especially scaffolding and the zone of proximal development. The new field of cultural psychology emphasizes the cultural context of cognition.

The three major approaches discussed in this chapter—cognitive-developmental, information-processing, and psychometric—should be thought of as complementary rather than competing. The cognitive-developmental approach provides an overall view of cognitive changes in adolescence and emerging adulthood. From this approach we gain insights into how mental structures change with age and how changes in mental structures result in a wide range of other cognitive changes, from hypothetical-deductive reasoning to the use of sarcasm to reflective judgment. The information-processing approach focuses on the components of cognitive functioning, in areas such as attention and memory. From this approach we learn how the components of cognition work at their most basic level. We also learn how abilities for performing these functions change with age from childhood through adolescence and emerging adulthood. The psychometric approach focuses on measuring individuals' cognitive abilities. From this approach we learn about the range of individual differences in various cognitive abilities at any given age and also how the typical level of these cognitive abilities changes with age.

Together, these three approaches provide a broad understanding of cognitive changes in adolescence and emerging adulthood, especially when combined with other areas of study that are derived from these approaches, such as practical cognition and social cognition. However, the glaring omission in our understanding is the cultural basis of cognitive development. Because all three of the major approaches have neglected cultural factors in the course of seeking universal principles of cognitive development, at this point we know relatively little about the role of culture in cognitive development during adolescence and emerging adulthood. This neglect is now being rectified in the new field of cultural psychology, which has already begun to change our understanding of cognitive development in childhood and which is likely to do the same for adolescence and emerging adulthood in the years to come.

KEY TERMS

INTERNET RESOURCES

www.piaget.org
This is the official web site for the Jean Piaget Society. The Society is not solely about Piaget; instead, it is a society of scholars interested in cognitive development. It was named after Piaget to honor his contributions in this area. This web site contains information about conferences and publications (books, articles, a newsletter) on topics related to cognitive development.

FOR FURTHER READING

Gould, S. J. (1981). *The mismeasure of man.* New York: Norton. In this book, Gould describes the history of intelligence testing and how the tests have often been used to discriminate against women and minority groups in American society. Gould is a superb writer, highly readable and insightful.

Jacobs, J. E., & Klaczynsky, P. A. (2005). *The development of judgement and decision making in children and adolescents.* Mahwah, NJ: Erlbaum. An excellent summary of research on decision making, along with new theoretical ideas, by two of the top scholars in this area.

Piaget, J. (1972). Intellectual evolution from adolescence to adulthood. *Human Development, 15,* 1–12. I recommend that you read something Piaget has written, instead of simply reading how others describe his ideas. He has an insightful and original style of expression. This article would be a good choice because it focuses on issues related to adolescence and emerging adulthood.

Shweder, R. A., Goodnow, J., Hatano, G., Levine, R. A., Markus, H., & Miller, P. (2006). The cultural psychology of development: One mind, many mentalities. In W. Damon (Ed.), *Handbook of Child Development,* (6th ed. Vol. 1, pp. 865–937) New York: Wiley. An excellent overview of cultural psychology. This chapter defines cultural psychology and applies it to moral development, language development, cognitive development, and the development of the self.

4 CHAPTER Cultural Beliefs

- Should young people accept their parents' authority without question? Or do parents have an obligation to treat their children as equals or near-equals by the time the children reach adolescence and emerging adulthood?

- When making decisions about the future, which should come first, young people's individual desires and ambitions or the well-being of their families?

- Should young people spend their leisure time—Friday and Saturday evenings, for example—with their parents at home or with their friends in unsupervised activities?

- Is it best for young people to date a variety of persons before marriage in order to become experienced at intimate relationships? Or is it better if young people do not date before marriage and instead allow their parents to arrange a partner for them when it comes time for them to marry?

- Is it acceptable for young people to become sexually active prior to marriage? Is the acceptability of premarital sexual activity any different for girls than for boys?

MOST LIKELY, YOU HAVE OPINIONS ABOUT EACH OF these issues. And your particular view on these issues is probably typical of the people in your culture. However, whatever view your culture holds on these issues, it is certain that there are other cultures whose beliefs are considerably different. Cultures vary greatly in their views about the proper standards of behavior for adolescents and emerging adults. Each culture is characterized by **cultural beliefs** that provide the basis for opinions about issues such as the ones presented above (Arnett, 1995a, 2006d, 2008a).

Throughout this book, I emphasize the cultural approach to understanding development in adolescence and emerging adulthood. Adolescence and emerging adulthood are culturally constructed periods of life. As we have seen in Chapters 2 and 3, even biological and cognitive development in adolescence and emerging adulthood are shaped profoundly by cultural influences. Every chapter of this book emphasizes the cultural basis of development and presents a variety of examples of differences and similarities among adolescents and emerging adults in various cultures.

In this chapter we will focus on cultural beliefs. Why is it important to examine cultural beliefs as part of gaining a full understanding of development in adolescence and emerging adulthood? One reason is that cultural beliefs form the foundation for every aspect of socialization that takes place in a culture (Arnett, 1995a, 2006d). The kinds of rules and responsibilities parents have for adolescents, the materials schools teach and the way schools are run, the kinds of laws cultures make to restrict young people's behavior—all these practices and more are founded on cultural beliefs about

what is morally right and what is morally wrong, which behaviors should be rewarded and which punished, and what it means to be a good person (Shweder et al., 2006).

A second reason for focusing on cultural beliefs is that in many cultures adolescence and emerging adulthood are times when knowledge of these beliefs is communicated with special intensity (King & Boyatzis, 2004). As we saw in the previous chapter, adolescence brings changes in cognitive development that allow people to grasp abstract ideas and concepts in a way they could not when they were younger. Cultural beliefs are abstract; they typically include ideas about good and evil, right and wrong, vice and virtue, and so on. The fact that cultures often choose adolescence as a time for teaching these beliefs reflects a widespread intuitive awareness that this period is ripe for learning and embracing cultural beliefs.

What Are Cultural Beliefs?

Before proceeding further, let me specify what I mean when I refer to cultural beliefs. Cultural beliefs are the commonly held norms and moral standards of a culture, the standards of right and wrong that set expectations for behavior. These beliefs are usually rooted in the culture's **symbolic inheritance**, which is a set of "ideas and understandings, both implicit and explicit, about persons, society, nature and divinity" (Shweder et al., 2006, p. 868). So, cultural beliefs include both the beliefs that constitute a culture's symbolic inheritance and the norms and moral standards that arise from these beliefs.

CULTURAL FOCUS • The Bar and Bat Mitzvah

In Jewish tradition, an important event at age 13 signifies the adolescent's new responsibilities with respect to Jewish beliefs. The event is a ceremony called the **Bar Mitzvah**, and it has existed in some form for over 2,000 years. The details have changed over the centuries, and today the ceremony differs in some respects from one synagogue to another. Until recently, for example, only boys participated in the Bar Mitzvah. However, today many girls participate as well (although it is still more common for boys). For girls, the ceremony is called the **Bat Mitzvah**. According to the National Survey of Youth and Religion (described later in this chapter), 73% of Jewish adolescents in the United States have participated in a Bar or Bat Mitzvah (Smith & Denton, 2005).

Although they vary among synagogues, Bar and Bat Mitzvahs share some common elements (Davis, 1988):

- Prayers are recited stating belief in the one and only God and promising allegiance to God's commandments. Further prayers praise God and reaffirm the sacredness of the Sabbath.

- The Torah is passed from one generation to the next, literally and figuratively. (The Torah consists of the first five books of the Hebrew Bible. These are also the first five books of what Christians call the Old Testament.) The initiate and the

parents and grandparents come to the front of the synagogue. The Torah is taken from the ark (where it is normally kept) and passed from the grandparents to the parents to the initiate.

- The initiate carries the Torah around the room so that people may touch it with their hands or with a prayer book or prayer shawl, which they then kiss. The congregation remains standing as it is taken around the room.

- The Torah is returned to the front and unwrapped. Often younger children perform the unwrapping.

- The initiate recites a portion of the Torah, then reads from the Haftorah, which consists of the teachings of Jewish prophets.

- The initiate receives the blessings of the parents and rabbi.

- The initiate gives a brief talk on some aspect of Jewish teachings. Often, the talk focuses on some of the implications that might be drawn from the portions of the Torah and the Haftorah the initiate has just recited.

- The initiation is celebrated with a festive meal.

In Jewish tradition, completing the Bar/Bat Mitzvah means that the young person can now participate fully in the religious activities of the community. After their Bar/Bat Mitzvah, young

Cultural belief systems include the **roles** that are appropriate for particular persons. All cultures have **gender roles**, that is, beliefs about the kinds of work, appearance, and other aspects of behavior that distinguish women from men. Cultures may also have age-related roles—a man may be expected to be a warrior in his youth, for example, but to give up that role by middle adulthood and become part of a council of elders. Cultures may also have roles related to social status or social class. For example, in England working-class young men have a distinctive kind of dress (lots of leather and denim), language (lots of slang and profanity), and behavior (lots of fighting and drinking) (Brake, 1985). Young people everywhere become more aware of their culture's beliefs about such roles in the course of adolescence. This is partly because of increasing cognitive capacities for abstract thinking and self-reflection, and partly because reaching adolescence means that the threshold of adulthood is approaching

and young people will soon be expected to adapt themselves to the role requirements for adults in their culture.

A culture's symbolic inheritance is the basis for its norms and standards (Shweder et al., 2006). The symbolic inheritance usually includes beliefs about the ultimate meaning of human life and the place of an individual's life in the vast scheme of things. Sometimes these beliefs are religious and include ideas about where the soul of the individual came from and where it goes after death. (The idea of the soul—an intangible, individual human identity that is distinct from our bodily natures—is nearly universal in cultures' religious beliefs.) Sometimes these beliefs are political, with ideas about how the individual is part of a great historical movement heading toward an inevitable conclusion. The communist beliefs that were so influential in the 20th century are an example of this. Sometimes these beliefs are familial and communal, with the significance of an individual life being

cultural beliefs The predominant beliefs in a culture about right and wrong, what is most important in life, and how life should be lived. May also include beliefs about where and how life originated and what happens after death.

symbolic inheritance The set of ideas and understandings, both implicit and explicit, about persons, society, nature, and divinity that serve as a guide to life in a particular culture. Expressed symbolically through stories, songs, rituals, sacred objects, and sacred places.

Bar Mitzvah Jewish religious ritual for boys at age 13 that signifies the adolescents' new responsibilities with respect to Jewish beliefs.

Bat Mitzvah Jewish religious ritual for girls at age 13 that signifies the adolescents' new responsibilities with respect to Jewish beliefs.

people can be counted toward the minimum of 10 persons required for holding religious services. Also, they are now obliged to carry out the same religious rituals as adults, and their word is valid in sessions determining violations of Jewish law.

Furthermore, they are now "subject to the commandments." That is, they are now responsible for their own actions, as children are not. (Recall from Chapter 1 the importance of "responsibility for one's actions" in contemporary views of the transition to adulthood.) In fact, the Bar Mitzvah sometimes includes a part where the parents declare, "Blessed is He who has freed me from responsibility for this child's conduct." Perhaps this declaration reflects an intuitive awareness in Jewish tradition of the cognitive advances of adolescence, which make young people capable of a new level of self-reflection and decision making.

Notice how the ceremony works to inculcate cultural beliefs. The beliefs are passed, quite literally, from one generation to the next during the ceremony, as the grandparents and parents pass the Torah to the initiate. The initiate's new responsibility for carrying on those beliefs is signified by taking the Torah around the room to be blessed. The initiate also reads from the holy books, and this act—declaring aloud before the community a portion of their shared beliefs—is crucial to attaining full status as a member of the community.

Why do the Bar and Bat Mitzvah take place in adolescence?

derived from its place in a larger organization that existed before the individual was born and will continue to exist after the individual has passed on. Adolescence is a time of particular importance for cultures to communicate these beliefs about the ultimate meaning of things and to encourage young people to embrace them wholeheartedly.

In this chapter, we will first discuss the role that cultural beliefs play in the socialization of adolescents. Following this we will consider specific aspects of cultural beliefs, including religious beliefs, moral beliefs, and political beliefs.

Cultural Beliefs and Socialization

An important aspect of cultural beliefs is the set of beliefs that specifically concerns standards of right and wrong for raising children, adolescents, and emerging adults. Should young people be taught that individuals should be independent and self-sufficient, following their own desires rather than complying with the norms of the group; or should they be taught that the group comes first, that the needs and requirements of the family and community should have higher priority than the needs and desires of the individual? Should young people be allowed and encouraged to express themselves, even when what they say or do may offend other people; or should each person be pressed—and, if necessary, forced—to conform to the accepted standards of the culture?

All cultures have answers to these questions as part of their cultural beliefs, and the kinds of answers cultures devise vary widely. At the heart of these answers are cultural beliefs about **socialization**, the process by which people acquire the behaviors and beliefs of the culture they live in (Bugental & Grusec, 2006). Three outcomes are central to this process (Arnett, 1995a, 2006d; Grusec, 2002). **Self-regulation** is the capacity for exercising self-control in order to restrain one's impulses and

---

roles Defined social positions in a culture, containing specifications of behavior, status, and relations with others. Examples include gender, age, and social class.

gender roles Cultural beliefs about the kinds of work, appearance, and other aspects of behavior that distinguish women from men.

socialization The process by which people acquire the behaviors and beliefs of the culture in which they live.

self-regulation The capacity for exercising self-control in order to restrain one's impulses and comply with social norms.

comply with social norms. This includes the development of a conscience, which is the internal monitor of whether you are complying adequately with social norms; when your conscience determines that you are not, you experience guilt. **Role preparation** is a second outcome of socialization. This includes preparation for occupational roles, gender roles, and roles in institutions such as marriage and parenthood. The third outcome of socialization is the cultivation of **sources of meaning**, which indicate what is important, what is to be valued, and what is to be lived for. Human beings are uniquely existential creatures. Unlike other animals, we are capable of reflecting on our mortality and on what our lives mean in light of the hard fact that we will all die some day (Becker, 1973). Sources of meaning provide consolation, guidance, and hope to people in confronting existential questions.

These three outcomes of socialization are shared by all cultures. To survive and thrive and perpetuate themselves from one generation to the next, cultures must teach these things to their members. However, this does not mean that cultures express these goals explicitly, or that cultural members are even consciously aware of them as outcomes of socialization. Much of what cultures teach about what people should believe and value is taught implicitly, through the practices and behaviors young people are taught (Shweder et al., 2006). For example, requiring students to wear uniforms in schools teaches that conformity to group standards is more important than individual expression.

Adolescence and emerging adulthood are important periods of development with respect to each of these socialization outcomes. Self-regulation begins to be learned in infancy, but a new dimension is added to it in adolescence as regulation of sexual impulses rises in importance with puberty and the development of sexual maturity. Also, as puberty progresses and young people reach their full size and strength, it becomes more important for cultures to ensure that they have learned self-regulation so that they will not disrupt or endanger the lives of others. Role preparation also becomes more urgent in adolescence and emerging adulthood. These years are crucial for young people to prepare themselves for the occupational and social roles they will soon be expected to take on as adults. Adolescence and emerging adulthood are also

key times for the development of sources of meaning because adolescents are newly capable of grasping and understanding the abstract ideas about values and beliefs that are part of the meanings of life that cultures teach.

THINKING CRITICALLY •••

Do you think that the beliefs of all cultures are equally good and true, or do you think that the beliefs of some cultures are better and truer than the beliefs of others? Give an example of an issue that illustrates your view. If you believe that some cultural beliefs are better and truer than others, on what standard would you base your evaluation, and why?

Cultural Values: Individualism and Collectivism

Although all cultures share similar socialization *outcomes*, cultures differ widely in their socialization *values*. A central issue with respect to cultural values about socialization concerns whether cultures place more value on independence and self-expression or, alternately, on obedience and conformity as the characteristics they wish to promote in their children. This issue is sometimes portrayed as a contrast between individualism and collectivism, with individualistic cultures giving priority to independence and self-expression and collectivist cultures placing a higher value on obedience and conformity (Triandis, 1995).

A great deal of research has taken place on individualism and collectivism in the past 30 years (Brewer & Chen, 2007; Oyserman & Lee, 2008), especially focusing on cultural contrasts between the majority cultures of the West and Eastern cultures such as those in China, Japan, and Korea. Scholars have examined differences in values and beliefs among people in a wide range of cultures and have consistently found people in the West to be more individualistic and people in Eastern cultures to be more collectivistic (Hofstede, 1980; Kim & Markus, 1999; Marshall, 2008; Triandis, 1995). Scholars have also discussed the development of the self in individualistic and collectivistic cultures (Markus & Kitiyama, 1991, 2003; Shweder et al., 2006). Collectivistic cultures promote the development of an **interdependent self**, such that people place a strong value on cooperation, mutual support, harmonious social relations, and contributions to the group. In contrast, individualistic cultures promote the development of an **independent self**, such that people place a strong value on independence, individual freedoms, and individual achievements.

Several points should be kept in mind regarding individualism and collectivism. First, the belief systems of most cultures are not "pure types" of one or the other but a combination of the two in various proportions. Although the contrast between the individualistic West and the collectivistic East holds up quite well in research, some scholars have pointed out that

---

role preparation An outcome of socialization that includes preparation for occupational roles, gender roles, and roles in institutions such as marriage and parenthood.

sources of meaning The ideas and beliefs that people learn as part of socialization, indicating what is important, what is to be valued, what is to be lived for, and how to explain and offer consolation for the individual's mortality.

interdependent self A conception of the self typically found in collectivistic cultures, in which the self is seen as defined by roles and relationships within the group.

The Three Goals of Socialization. (A) Self-regulation. (B) Role preparation. (C) Sources of meaning.

most Western cultures, too, have elements of collectivism, and most Eastern cultures have elements of individualism (Killen & Wainryb, 2000; Matsumoto, 2002; Tamis-Lemonda et al., 2008). In Eastern cultures, this blend is increasingly complex as they are influenced by the West through globalization (Chang, 2008; Matsumoto, 2002; Naito & Gielen, 2003).

A second point is that individualism and collectivism describe overall tendencies for the values of cultures as a whole, but individual differences exist in every culture (Killen & Wainryb, 1998; Tamis-Lemonda et al., 2008). A culture that is individualistic overall is likely to have some people who are more collectivistic than individualistic, and a culture that is collectivistic overall is likely to have some people who are more individualistic than collectivistic.

A third point is that diversity also exists within individuals. Most people are probably not purely individualistic or purely collectivistic in their beliefs and behavior but have some combination of the two tendencies, which they may use in different settings (Killen & Wainryb, 2000; Smetana, 1993). For example, a person may be relatively individualistic at work or in school, striving for individual achievement and recognition, but relatively collectivistic at home, seeking to cooperate and maintain harmony with family members. Individualism and collectivism are not necessarily mutually exclusive but may coexist within individuals.

Keep these qualifiers in mind as we discuss individualism and collectivism in this chapter and throughout the book. As long as you remember these limitations, the concepts of individualism and collectivism remain highly useful and valid as a "shorthand" way of describing the general patterns and contrasts in beliefs among various cultures.

Broad and Narrow Socialization

In this book, we will discuss the contrast in socialization patterns between individualistic and collectivistic cultures in terms of broad and narrow socialization (Arnett, 1995a,

"The nail that stands out gets pounded down."

—Japanese proverb

2006d). Cultures characterized by **broad socialization** favor individualism. They encourage individual uniqueness, independence, and self-expression. Cultures characterized by **narrow socialization** favor collectivism. They hold obedience and conformity to be the highest values and discourage deviation from cultural expectations. *Individualism* and *collectivism* describe the general differences in values and

Collectivism is especially strong in Asian cultures. Here, a Korean family takes a walk together.

---

independent self A conception of the self typically found in individualistic cultures, in which the self is seen as existing independently of relations with others, with an emphasis on independence, individual freedoms, and individual achievements.

broad socialization The process by which persons in an individualistic culture come to learn individualism, including values of individual uniqueness, independence, and self-expression.

narrow socialization The process by which persons in a collectivistic culture come to learn collectivism, including values of obedience and conformity.

beliefs among cultures; *broad* and *narrow socialization* describe the *process* by which cultural members come to adopt the values and beliefs of an individualistic (broad) or collectivistic (narrow) culture.

The terms *broad* and *narrow* refer to the range of individual differences cultures allow or encourage—relatively broad in broad socialization, relatively narrow in narrow socialization. All socialization involves some degree of restrictiveness on individual preferences and inclinations. As Scarr (1993) noted, "cultures set a range of opportunities for development; they define the limits of what is desirable, 'normal' individual variation. . . . Cultures define the *range* and *focus* of personal variation that is acceptable and rewarded" (pp. 1335, 1337; emphasis in the original). Socialization inevitably means the establishment of limits, but cultures differ in the *degree* of restrictiveness they impose, and the degree of cultures' restrictiveness is the central contrast between broad and narrow socialization.

Because Western cultural beliefs emphasize individualism, Western cultures tend toward broad socialization. The West has a long history of emphasizing individualism in a variety of aspects of life (Bellah et al., 1985), and this includes cultural beliefs about socialization. In contrast, socialization in non-Western cultures tends to be narrower, with a greater emphasis on promoting the well-being of the family and community rather than the individual, and often including hierarchies of authority based on gender, age, and other characteristics (Kim & Markus, 1999; Markus & Kitiyama, 1991; Whiting & Edwards, 1988).

Most cultures with narrow socialization are less economically developed than those in the West. Narrow socialization is emphasized in these cultures partly because young people's work is necessary for families' survival; conformity and obedience are demanded to ensure that young people will make their necessary contributions (Schlegel & Barry, 1991). However, narrow socialization is also characteristic of some highly industrialized Asian cultures, such as Japan, although socialization in these societies may be becoming broader in response to globalization (Naito & Gielen, 2003; Noguchi, 2007; Stevenson & Zusho, 2002).

The same qualifiers that apply to individualism and collectivism also apply to broad and narrow socialization. All cultures have a considerable amount of variability, based on individuals' personalities and preferences. If we say socialization in a particular culture is broad, that does not mean that everyone in the culture has the same beliefs about the desirability of individualism. It simply means that the culture as a whole can be described as tending toward broad socialization, although individuals within the culture may vary in their beliefs. Think of the concepts of broad and narrow socialization as a simple, shorthand way of referring to an essential contrast in socialization, not as absolute categories that every culture in the world fits into cleanly.

It is important, too, to state explicitly that the concepts of individualism–collectivism and broad–narrow socialization are not meant to imply moral evaluations. With each general type of socialization there are trade-offs. Under broad socialization, because individualism is encouraged there is likely to be more

creativity and more innovation, but also a higher degree of loneliness, social problems, and disorder (Arnett, 1995a, 2006d; Bellah et al., 1985). Under narrow socialization, there may be a stronger sense of collective identity and greater social order, but at the cost of greater suppression of individual uniqueness (Arnett, 1995a, 2002a; Ho & Chiu, 1994). Each form of socialization has its costs as well as its benefits.

THINKING CRITICALLY •••

Do you agree or disagree with the view that there are pros and cons to both broad and narrow socialization? Explain your view.

Sources of Socialization

Socialization involves many aspects of a culture. You may think most readily of parents when you think of socialization, and parents usually are central to the socialization process (Bugental & Grusec, 2008). However, socialization involves other sources as well. The sources of socialization include *family* (not just parents but siblings and extended family, too), *peers and friends, school, community, the workplace, media, the legal system,* and *the cultural belief system* (Arnett, 1995a, 2006d). In general, the family's influence on socialization diminishes in adolescence (Aquilino, 2005; Scarr & McCartney, 1983), whereas the influences of peers/friends, school, community, media, and the legal system increase. Family influence in Western majority cultures diminishes further in emerging adulthood, when most emerging adults move out of their family household (Aquilino, 2005; Arnett, 2004a). Nevertheless, the family remains a powerful influence on socialization in adolescence and emerging adulthood, even if its influence is not as powerful as earlier in development.

In this book, a specific chapter will be devoted to several socialization sources, including family, peers and friends, school, the workplace, and media. Information on socialization in the community and the legal system will be presented in a variety of chapters. Table 4.1 provides a summary description of broad and narrow socialization.

Cultures can vary in their socialization from these different sources—a culture may be relatively broad in family socialization, for example, and relatively narrow in socialization through the school. However, usually a culture's sources are consistent in their socialization, because the cultural belief system is the foundation for the socialization that takes place through the other sources. Parents, teachers, community leaders, and other socialization agents in a culture carry out common socialization practices because of their shared beliefs about what is best for children and adolescents (Arnett, 1995a, 2006d; Harkness & Super, 1995; Tamis-Lemonda et al., 2008).

An Example of Socialization for Cultural Beliefs

So far, our discussion of cultural beliefs and the different forms of socialization has been abstract, describing the nature of cultural beliefs and distinguishing two general cultural approaches to socialization. Now let us look at a specific example of socialization for cultural beliefs, as an illustration of the ideas I have introduced.

An ethnography on adolescence among the indigenous people of Australia, known as the Aborigines (a-bor-*ih*-jen-eez), was written by Victoria Burbank (1988, 1994) as part of the Harvard Adolescence Project. Until about 70 years ago, the Aborigines were nomadic hunters and gatherers. They had no settled residence but moved their small communities from one place to another according to the seasons and the availability of food such as fish and sea turtles. They had few possessions; shelters and tools were manufactured easily from materials that were widely available.

A key part of traditional adolescent socialization among the Aborigines involves the ritual teaching of a set of cultural beliefs known as the Law. The Law includes an explanation of how the world began and instructions for how various ritual ceremonies should be performed, such as the circumcision ritual that is one of the rites of passage initiating adolescent boys into manhood. The Law also includes moral precepts for how interpersonal relations should be conducted. For example, there are complex rules about who may have sex with whom and who may marry whom, depending on the family and clan to which persons belong. Also, it is viewed as best if marriages are arranged by the parents rather than by the young people themselves.

The Law is presented in a series of three public ceremonies, with each ceremony representing a stage in the initiation of adolescent boys into manhood. (Although both boys and girls learn the Law, only boys participate in the rituals of

TABLE 4.1 Broad and Narrow Socialization

Broad Socialization

Source	Description
Family	Few restrictions on adolescents' behavior; adolescents spend considerable time away from family in unsupervised leisure. Parents encourage independence and self-sufficiency in adolescents.
Peers/Friends	Adolescents are allowed to choose their own friends. Adolescents make friends of different ethnic groups and social classes, based on their similar interests and attractions as individuals.
School	Teachers promote students' individuality and attempt to adapt the curriculum to each student's individual needs and preferences. Low emphasis is placed on order and obedience to teachers and school authorities. No uniforms or dress code are required.
Community	Community members do not know each other well, and adult community members exercise little or no social control over adolescents. Independence and self-expression of the individual are valued more highly than conformity to the expectations and standards of the community.
Workplace	Young people are allowed to choose for themselves among a wide range of possible occupations. Workplaces generally promote creativity and individual achievement.
Media	Media are diverse, and media content is mostly unregulated by governmental authorities. Media promote gratification of individual desires and impulses.
Legal System	Legal restrictions on behavior are minimal. The rights of the individual to a wide range of self-expression are highly valued. Punishments for most offenses are light.
Cultural Beliefs	Individualism, independence, self-expression.

Narrow Socialization

Source	Description
Family	Duty and obligation to family are valued highly. Adult family members command respect and deference. Responsibility to family is considered more important than the individual's autonomy or achievements.
Peers/Friends	Adults exercise control over adolescents' friendship choices, in part by disapproving of friendships between adolescents of different ethnic groups and social classes.
School	Emphasis is on learning the standard curriculum rather than on independent or critical thinking. Firm discipline is used in the classroom. Uniforms or conformity to strict dress code may be required.
Community	Community members know each other well and share common cultural beliefs. Adherence to the standards and expectations of the community is highly valued. Nonconformity is viewed with suspicion and treated with ostracism.
Workplace	Young people's job choices are constrained by the decisions of adults (e.g., parents, governmental authorities). Workplaces promote conformity and discourage innovative thinking that might challenge the status quo.
Media	Media are tightly controlled by governmental authorities. Media content is generally restricted to socially acceptable themes that do not threaten common moral standards.
Legal System	Legal restrictions are placed on a wide range of behavior, including sexuality and political views, and are backed by swift and severe punishment.
Cultural Beliefs	Collectivism, obedience, conformity.

In this dance ceremony, young Australian Aborigines act out tenets of the Law. Why is the meaning of the ceremony now fading for adolescents?

initiation.) In the ceremonies, various aspects of the Law are taught. Songs, dances, and the painted bodies of the performers present stories that illustrate the Law. The whole community attends. Following the ceremonies, the adolescent boys experience an extended period of seclusion in which they are given little to eat and have almost no contact with others. After learning the Law and experiencing this period of seclusion, they have a new, higher status in the community.

In the traditional teaching of the Law, we can see illustrations of the principles of socialization and cultural beliefs we have discussed. The Law is at the center of the symbolic inheritance of the Aborigines; it contains ideas about relations between the individual, society, and divine forces. The Law stresses self-regulation, especially with regard to sexual desire, by specifying rules for sexual contact. Information about roles is taught as part of the Law; adolescent boys learn the expectations for behavior that they must follow in their role as adult men. The Law also provides a source of meaning by explaining the origin of the world and by providing adolescents with a clear and secure place in their communities.

The cultural beliefs expressed in the Law are collectivistic. Adolescents are taught that they have obligations to others as part of the Law and that they must allow others to make important decisions that affect them, such as whom they shall marry. Because their beliefs are collectivistic, socialization among the Aborigines is narrow; conformity and obedience to the Law and to elders are emphasized. Adolescent boys do not decide for themselves whether to take part in the ceremonies of the Law; they *must* take part, or be ostracized.

However, like so many of the practices of traditional cultures, the relationship between adolescents and the Law has been dramatically affected by globalization (Robinson, 1997). The ceremonies still exist, and adolescents still take part. But the period of boys' seclusion that follows, which used to last about 2 months, now lasts only a week. Furthermore, adolescents are showing increasing resistance to learning and practicing the beliefs and rules of the Law at all. To many of them, the Law seems irrelevant to the world they live in, which is no longer a world of nomadic hunting and gathering but of schools, a complex economy, and modern

media. Adolescents now develop beliefs based not just on the Law but on their other experiences as well, and these experiences have made their beliefs more individualistic. Learning about the rest of the world through school and the media has led many of them to question their native cultural practices, such as arranged marriages. As Burbank (1988) observes, "Today the Law must compete with the lessons of school, church, movies, and Western music. Initiation may no longer be viewed by the initiate himself as a means to a desired end—the achievement of adult male status. Rather, it may be seen as a nonsensical ordeal of pain and privation. Under these circumstances, its ability to affect subsequent behavior may be minimized" (pp. 37–38).

In recent years, young Aborigines have also begun to display many of the modern problems of adolescence and emerging adulthood, such as unmarried pregnancy in their teens, substance use, and crime (Burbank, 1995). The power of the Law has diminished as a source of self-regulation, roles, and meaning, and for young Aborigines their new problems signify that nothing has yet arisen to take its place.

Socialization for Cultural Beliefs in the West

Can you think of anything in your own community comparable to the Aborigines' teaching of cultural beliefs for adolescents? If you grew up in the West, it may be difficult. The West has no formal, ritual teaching of individualism. In a way, that would be contrary to the whole spirit of individualism because ritual implies a standard way of doing things and individualism stresses independence from standard ways. You could find evidence of implicit teaching of individualism in adults' practices with regard to adolescence, such as the kinds of freedoms parents allow adolescents, or the range of choices adolescents are allowed for the courses they take at school. We will discuss these and other practices reflecting individualism in future chapters. But what about *beliefs*? What evidence do we have of cultural beliefs that reflect individualism?

One interesting piece of evidence comes from a famous study conducted by Helen and Robert Lynd in the 1920s (Lynd & Lynd, 1929), describing life in a typical American community they called "Middletown" (actually Muncie, Indiana). The Lynds studied many aspects of life in Middletown, including women's beliefs about the qualities they considered most important to promote in their children. Fifty years later, another group of researchers (Caplow et al., 1982) returned to Middletown and asked the residents many of the same questions, including the ones about child-rearing beliefs.

As you can see from Table 4.2, the results indicate that the child-rearing beliefs of the American majority culture changed dramatically over the 20th century (Alwin, 1988). Narrow socialization values such as obedience and loyalty to church declined in importance, whereas broad socialization values such as independence and tolerance became central to their child-rearing beliefs. This change was reflected in behavioral differences in Middletown adolescents, particularly girls. In more recent times, adolescent girls had become substantially more independent from their parents, spending more of their time away from home and depending less on

TABLE 4.2	Child-Rearing Values of Women in Middletown, 1928–1978	
	1928	1978
Loyalty to church	50	22
Strict obedience	45	17
Good manners	31	23
Independence	25	76
Tolerance	6	47

The table indicates the percentage of women in 1928 and 1978 who listed each of the indicated values as one of the three most important for their children to learn, out of a list of 15 values.

Source: Alwin (1988).

their parents for money and for information about sex. Other studies have confirmed this trend in the cultural beliefs of the American majority culture during the 20th century, away from obedience and conformity and toward individualism (Alwin, Xu, & Carson, 1994; Cohn, 1999). Even though the United States has a long tradition of valuing individualism (Bellah et al., 1985), individualistic beliefs have evidently grown stronger during the past century, and adolescents in the American majority culture today are growing up at a time when individualism is more highly valued than in the past.

THINKING CRITICALLY •••

Have you experienced any direct teaching of cultural beliefs, such as Boy/Girl Scouts, Bar or Bat Mitzvah, Sunday School, or Confirmation? If so, did these experiences form the basis for your current beliefs? If not, how do you think you developed your current beliefs?

Cultural Beliefs and the Custom Complex

The examples of the Aborigines and Middletown portray the cultural beliefs that adults hold explicitly and teach intentionally to their young people. However, cultural beliefs are also reflected in people's everyday practices, even when they are not conscious of it. Every aspect of development is influenced by the cultural context in which it takes place, and every pattern of behavior reflects something about cultural beliefs.

This means that every aspect of development and behavior in adolescence and emerging adulthood can be analyzed as a **custom complex** (Shweder et al., 2006). This term was

coined a half century ago by Whiting and Child (1953), who stated that a custom complex "consists of a customary practice and of the beliefs, values, sanctions, rules, motives and satisfactions associated with it" (1953, p. 27). More recently, scholars have placed the custom complex at the center of the growing field of cultural psychology (Shweder, 1999; Shweder et al., 2006), which examines human development from a perspective that combines psychology and anthropology.

To put it simply, a custom complex consists of typical practice in a culture and the cultural beliefs that provide the basis for that practice. I will use this term at various points in the book, but for illustration here let us briefly consider dating as an example of a custom complex.

THINKING CRITICALLY •••

Give an example of a custom complex you have experienced in your own culture. Describe how the behavior or practice reflects cultural beliefs.

Dating is something you may be used to thinking about as something that is **ontogenetic**; when adolescents reach the ages of 13, 14, or 15, it is "natural" for them to begin dating. However, analyzing dating as a custom complex shows that dating is not simply a natural part of development but a custom complex that reflects certain cultural beliefs. We can begin by noting that dating is by no means a universal practice. It is more common in the United States than in Europe (Alsaker & Flammer, 1999b), and it is discouraged in most non-Western cultures—although the practice is growing in non-Western cultures in response to globalization (Schlegel, 2000). Furthermore, even in the United States it is a recent practice. Before the 20th century, young people in the United States typically engaged not in dating but in courtship, which was structured and monitored by adults (Bailey, 1989).

How does dating represent a custom complex?

---

custom complex A customary practice and the beliefs, values, sanctions, rules, motives, and satisfactions associated with it; that is, a normative practice in a culture and the cultural beliefs that provide the basis for that practice.

ontogenetic Something that occurs naturally in the course of development as part of normal maturation; that is, it is driven by innate processes rather than by environmental stimulation or a specific cultural practice.

One of the points discussed in this chapter is that, for the most part, Western cultures do little in the way of formal teaching of cultural beliefs. Many adolescents in the United States receive some formal instruction in religious beliefs, but in other Western cultures religion is much less a part of the lives of adolescents. Even in the United States, only about half of adolescents take part regularly in religious activities (Smith & Denton, 2005).

The absence of formal moral training was discussed with particular intensity in public forums in the early 20th century in the United States as well as in Europe. Adults worried greatly that, with the decline of religion, young people would grow up without a moral orientation strong enough to guide them through an increasingly complex and dangerous world (Kett, 1977).

In Great Britain, a man named Robert Baden-Powell had an idea for how to address this perceived danger of moral decline among young people. In 1908, he started an organization called the Boy Scouts that would be dedicated to teaching moral precepts to adolescent boys aged 11 to 17 (Pryke, 2001). Boy Scouts would learn how to do woodcrafts, swim, set up a camp, cook outdoors, and perform various other outdoor survival skills. However, Baden-Powell made it clear that these activities were all intended to have a moral purpose: to socialize boys so that they would become good citizens with a high moral character (Rosenthal, 1986).

This purpose is reflected explicitly in two key parts of the Boy Scout program: the Scout Oath and the Scout Law, which all boys are required to learn (by memory) to become Scouts. The Scout Oath is as follows:

On my honor I will do my best
To do my duty to God and my country

And to obey the Scout Law:
To help other people at all times;
To keep myself physically strong,
Mentally awake, and morally straight.

The Scout Law is as follows:

A Scout is:
Trustworthy
Loyal
Helpful
Friendly
Courteous
Kind
Obedient
Cheerful
Thrifty
Brave
Clean
and Reverent.

Notice that these are mostly collectivistic rather than individualistic values. Nothing here about self-esteem or individual achievement. Instead, values such as being trustworthy, loyal, helpful, courteous, kind, and obedient are all oriented toward consideration for and service to others. In a sense, the creation of the Boy Scouts can be seen as an attempt to create an organization that would maintain some elements of collectivism in Western cultures that were becoming increasingly individualistic.

Baden-Powell's idea was instantly and phenomenally successful. Within a few years after the origin of the Boy Scouts in 1908, the organization had spread all over the world and in-

A custom complex involves both a typical practice and the cultural beliefs that underlie that practice. What cultural beliefs underlie the Western practice of dating? First, dating reflects a cultural belief that adolescents and emerging adults should be allowed to have a substantial degree of independent leisure time. This is in contrast to cultures that believe young people should spend their leisure time with their families. Second, dating reflects a cultural belief that young people should have a right to choose for themselves the persons with whom they wish to have intimate relationships. This is in contrast to cultures whose beliefs specify that young people should allow their parents to make those decisions for them. Third, dating reflects a cultural belief that some degree of sexual experience before marriage is acceptable and healthy for young people. This is in contrast to cultures that believe young people's sexual experiences should begin only after they are married.

All aspects of development in adolescence and emerging adulthood can be analyzed in this way. Family relationships, peer relations, school experiences, and more—all of them consist of a variety of custom complexes that reflect the be-

liefs of the cultures in which young people live. Thus, in the chapters to come we will use the idea of the custom complex as a way of revealing and exploring the cultural beliefs that underlie socialization.

Cultural Beliefs in Multicultural Societies

In describing cultural beliefs, cultures should not be confused with countries. Many countries contain a variety of cultures with a variety of different cultural beliefs. For this reason, in this book I speak not of an "American" cultural belief system but of the cultural beliefs of the American majority culture, as well as the cultural beliefs of minority cultures within American society.

Many studies have shown that the cultural beliefs of American minority cultures tend to be less individualistic and more collectivistic than the cultural beliefs of the American majority culture. Among Latinos, obedience to parents and obligations volved millions of adolescent boys. In 1912 the Girl Scouts was created on the basis of similar principles and quickly spread around the world to include millions of adolescent girls. Parallel organizations were created for preadolescent boys (Cub Scouts) and preadolescent girls (Brownies/Junior Girl Scouts) as well as for older adolescents (Venturing for boys and girls, Senior Girl Scouts for girls only).

The Scouting movement continues to thrive today. Membership in the Boy Scouts has remained more or less steady for the past 2 decades at about 1 million adolescents (ages 11–17) in the United States and a total of over 28 million boys in virtually every country in the world (Boy Scouts of America, 2008; World Organization of the Scout Movement, 2008). The country with the largest number of Boy Scouts is Indonesia, which has nearly 10 million. Membership in the Girl Scouts is about half the size of the Boy Scouts. Boy Scouts and Girls Scouts are the largest voluntary organizations of adolescent boys and girls in the world.

Of course, Scouting has changed considerably from its early days when, as one scholar described it, the organization stressed "glorification of discipline" and had an "obsession . . . with inculcating obedience" (Rosenthal, 1986, pp. 8, 112). The Scouting movement has adapted to the broadening of socialization in the 20th century in Western cultures by becoming less strict and focusing more on each Scout's individual development. The goals of the Girl Scout program now include helping each girl "Develop to her full potential" in addition to more collectivistic values (Girl Scouts USA, 2008). Nevertheless, the focus of Scouting remains on relatively narrow socialization.

Note that Scouting was created for young people reaching adolescence, the same period that cultures such as the

Scouting was begun with the explicit purpose of teaching values to young people.

Australian Aborigines choose for their own socialization rituals communicating cultural beliefs. As suggested earlier, this may be because people in many cultures have intuitively realized that adolescence is the period of life when the time is ripe for such socialization, because the young person's cognitive capacities have matured to a point capable of grasping abstract ideas such as duty and obligation. The initiation practices of many cultures seem to reflect a view that when young people reach adolescence, it is imperative to ensure that they have understood and embraced the beliefs of their culture before they take on the responsibilities of adult life.

Latino families tend to be more collectivistic than families in the American majority culture. Here, a Latino extended family in San Antonio, Texas.

to family are strongly emphasized. Adolescents in Latino families generally accept the authority of the parents and express a strong sense of obligation and attachment to their families (Harwood, Leyendecker, Carlson, Ascencio, & Miller, 2002; Suarez-Orozco & Suarez-Orozco, 1996). Asian American adolescents are also considerably more collectivistic and less individualistic than adolescents in the American majority culture. They spend considerably more time carrying out family chores, and they express a strong sense of duty and obligation to their families (Fuligni, Tseng, & Lam, 1999). In their conceptions of what it means to be an adult, nearly all Asian American emerging adults believe that becoming capable of supporting their parents financially is essential (Arnett, 2003a); this belief is one aspect of their collectivism. With respect to African Americans, little research has been conducted on the individualism–collectivism dimension. However, there is some evidence that African American young people are more individualistic than young people in other American minority groups but less individualistic than young people in the majority White culture (Phinney, Ong, & Madden, 2000).

Most other Western countries also have substantial minority populations whose cultural beliefs tend to be considerably more collectivistic and less individualistic than the Western majority culture. Canada has a substantial Inuit (or "First Nations") population; Australia has a Chinese immigrant population; New Zealand has a substantial number of Maoris. There is a Turkish minority culture in Germany, an Algerian minority culture in France, and a Pakistani minority culture in England—many other examples could be given. In every case, the cultural beliefs of the minority culture tend to be more collectivistic and less individualistic than those in the Western majority culture.

As noted earlier, because cultural beliefs typically provide the foundation for socialization from all other sources, usually there is a great deal of consistency of socialization across sources. But what happens when the socialization young people experience is not consistent across sources? What happens when young people are part of a minority culture whose beliefs differ from those of the majority culture? When this is the case, they may find themselves being exposed to a kind of socialization within the family that is different from the socialization they experience from sources such as school, the media, and the legal system because the majority culture tends to control sources of socialization outside the family (Arnett, 1995a, 2006d).

Because the United States has been a multicultural society from its beginnings, many adolescents throughout American history have experienced this kind of contrasting socialization environment. In recent decades, a new surge of immigration has steeply increased the proportion of people from minority cultures living in the United States, especially Latinos and Asian Americans. Projections indicate that White Americans of European background will cease to be a majority in American society by the year 2050 (Pollard & O'Hare, 1999). In other Western countries as well, immigration from non-Western countries has increased in recent decades and is expected to increase further in the decades to come. Canada has been especially open to immigrants and has received many people from Asian nations in the past decade (Sears et al., 2007). All over the West, the status and well-being of people in minority cultures is likely to be an important issue of the 21st century.

To explore how the beliefs of young people in minority cultures may be influenced by their own culture as well as the majority culture, in the next section we examine in detail a study of Chinese adolescents in Hong Kong, the United States, and Australia.

When East Meets West: Chinese Adolescents in Australia and the United States

"I've really had a bad experience with having friends that are not Chinese or not Asian, just in terms of them not understanding how I think of my family and how important they are to me, and my family obligations. . . . 'Cause my family comes first with me always, and I'll drop everything to help them out. So sometimes I've canceled on my White friends and said, 'I can't come to this because I have to do something with my family.' And they would never understand that. Or if I wanted to go somewhere and my parents said no, and I would not go, they would say, 'Well, just go. Why do you have to listen to them?' You know, 'What do you mean, they said no?' And I'm trying to explain this to them and they don't understand. But if I said that to one of my friends who was Chinese, she'd be like, 'Oh, okay. You can't go.'"

—Lin, 22-year-old Asian American (Arnett, unpublished data)

The contrast between Eastern and Western cultural beliefs makes for an especially interesting and complex socialization environment when adolescents are exposed to both. Shirley Feldman and her colleagues studied this situation among Chinese adolescents whose families had immigrated to Australia or the United States (Feldman et al., 1992). The sample included adolescents from both **first-generation families** (the adolescents and their parents were born in China before immigrating) and **second-generation families** (the adolescents were born in the West, but their parents and grandparents were born in China). For comparison, Feldman and her colleagues also included White adolescents in Australia and the United States and Chinese adolescents in Hong Kong. The adolescents were ages 15 to 18, in the 10th and 11th grades. They completed questionnaires on various aspects of their values and beliefs, including a questionnaire on individualism–collectivism.

The results indicated that even for first-generation Chinese adolescents in the United States and Australia, their values and beliefs were closer to those of White Western adolescents than to those of Chinese adolescents in Hong Kong. In a number of respects, Chinese adolescents in the West were more individualistic and less collectivistic than Chinese adolescents in Hong Kong. First-generation Chinese adolescents liv-

first-generation families The status of persons who were born in one country and then immigrated to another.

second-generation families The status of persons who were born in the country they currently reside in but whose parents were born in a different country.

ing in the West differed from Hong Kong Chinese adolescents in that they placed less value on tradition (e.g., taking part in traditional rituals) and more value on outward success (e.g., attaining wealth and social recognition). There were few differences between first-generation and second-generation Chinese adolescents, and few differences between either of these groups and the White Western adolescents.

The one collectivistic value that endured for Chinese adolescents living in Western countries concerned the variable Feldman and her colleagues called "family as residential unit," which included the belief that aging parents should live with their adult children and the belief that unmarried children should live with their parents until they marry. Chinese adolescents were more likely than White adolescents to hold these beliefs, not only Chinese adolescents in Hong Kong but also first- and second-generation Chinese adolescents in Australia and the United States. However, as you can see in Figure 4.1, the strength of this value steadily declined with acculturation into the majority culture in both the United States and Australia. Hong Kong Chinese adolescents were more likely to subscribe to these beliefs than first- or second-generation Chinese adolescents. Furthermore, first-generation Chinese adolescents were more likely to hold these beliefs than second-generation Chinese adolescents. Nevertheless, even second-generation Chinese adolescents were more likely to hold these beliefs than White Western adolescents.

THINKING CRITICALLY •••

It was stated in this section that in Chinese culture, aging parents often live with their adult children. How is this an example of a custom complex?

Overall, the results of this study show that many first- and second-generation Chinese adolescents embrace the individualistic beliefs of the Western culture they live in rather than the culture from which they and their families have come. Other studies also demonstrate this and show that the differences in beliefs between immigrant parents and their adolescent children can be a source of parent-adolescent conflict, as adolescents resist their parents' beliefs and parents feel frustrated and threatened when their adolescents adopt beliefs different from their own (Cashmore & Goodnow, 1987; Farver, Narang, & Bhadha, 2002; Rosenthal, 1984; Zhou, 1997). More generally, these studies provide good examples of the importance of conceptualizing socialization as a cultural process that has a variety of sources—not only the family but also peers, school, community, and media—with all of these sources ultimately rooted in cultural beliefs. Even though Chinese adolescents continue to live with their families in their new country, their beliefs and values change because they are exposed daily to contrary socialization influences outside the family.

Religious Beliefs

"God's a father. Like, I learned, even though you may not have a dad, he's still a father, he disciplines like a father, he's a good friend, he's a provider, he cares. It's kind of, you know he's there, you know he's watching over you, it's great but you also know that there are going to be hard times and that he's still there then."

—Kristen, age 16 (from Smith & Denton, 2005, p. 19)

"I don't think going to Mass really does anything. Sometimes I agree with what they're saying in church, but other times I'm like, 'What time is it? I wanna go home.' It doesn't really feel interesting."

—Heather, age 15 (from Smith & Denton, 2005, p. 197)

"My parents put me through Sunday School, and I was baptized and stuff. But I like the theory that all these religions, Mohammed and Buddha and Jesus, all the patterns there are very similar. And I believe that there's a spirit, an energy. Not necessarily a guy or something like that, but maybe just a power force. Like in Star Wars—the Force. The thing that makes it possible to live."

—Jared, age 24 (from Arnett, 2004, p. 171)

In most cultures throughout human history, cultural beliefs have mainly taken the form of religious beliefs. Although the content of cultures' religious beliefs is extremely diverse, virtually all cultures have religious beliefs of some kind. These beliefs typically include explanations for how the world began and what happens to us when we die.

Religious belief systems also typically contain prescriptions for socialization related to the three main outcomes: self-regulation, role preparation, and sources of meaning. Religions typically specify a code for behavior, and these codes usually contain various rules for self-regulation. For

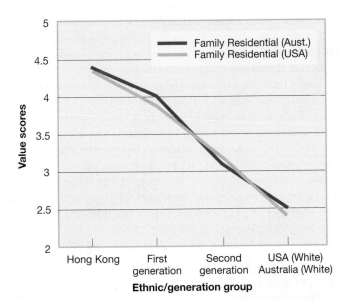

FIGURE 4.1 Cultural differences in valuing family as a residential unit.
Source: Feldman, Mont-Reynaud, & Rosenthal (1992).

example, the Ten Commandments that are part of the Jewish and Christian religions state explicit rules for self-regulation—thou shalt not kill, steal, covet thy neighbor's wife, and so on. For role preparation, gender roles in particular are emphasized in religious belief systems. Most religious belief systems contain ideas about distinct roles for males and females. For example, the Catholic Church allows men but not women to become priests. Finally, with respect to sources of meaning, most religious belief systems contain ideas about the significance of each individual's life in relation to an eternal supernatural world containing gods, supernatural forces, or the souls of one's ancestors.

In general, adolescents and emerging adults in industrialized societies are less religious than their counterparts in traditional cultures. Industrialized societies such as Japan and Western countries tend to be highly **secular**; that is, they are based on nonreligious beliefs and values. In every industrialized country, the influence of religion has gradually faded over the past two centuries (Bellah et al., 1985). Adherence to religious beliefs and practices is especially low among adolescents in Europe. For example, in Belgium only 8% of 18-year-olds attend religious services at least once a month (Goossens & Luyckx, 2007). In Spain, traditionally a highly Catholic country, only 18% of adolescents attend church regularly (Gibbons & Stiles, 2004).

Americans are more religious than people in virtually any other industrialized country, and this is reflected in the lives of American adolescents and emerging adults. Recently, the largest and most extensive study ever conducted on American adolescents' religious beliefs was completed (Smith & Denton, 2005). This study, called the National Survey of Youth and Religion (NSYR), involved over 3,000 adolescents ages 13–17 in every part of the United States, from all major ethnic groups, and included qualitative interviews with 267 of the adolescents. The results of the NSYR show that for a substantial proportion of American adolescents, religion plays an important part in their lives.

According to the NSYR, 84% of American adolescents aged 13 to 17 believe in God (or a universal spirit), 65% pray at least once a week, and 51% say religious faith is important in shaping their daily lives. Seventy-one percent feel at least somewhat close to God, 63% believe in the existence of angels, and 71% believe in a judgment day when God will reward some and punish others.

THINKING CRITICALLY •••

Why do you think Americans generally are more religious than people in other industrialized countries?

The proportion of American adolescents who take part in religious practices is lower than the proportion who report religious beliefs, but a substantial percentage do report regular religious practices. Fifty-two percent of them report attending religious services at least twice a month. Fifty-one percent say they attend Sunday school at least once a month, and 38% report being involved with a church youth group. Even if their actual participation may not be quite as high as the participation they report (see the Research Focus box), these figures indicate a strikingly positive view of religion among American adolescents.

Although religion clearly is important to many American adolescents, the directors of the NSYR concluded that it has a lower priority for most of them than many other parts of their lives, including school, friendships, media, and work. As Smith and Denton (2005) put it, "For most U.S. teenagers, [religion has] quite a small place at the end of the table for a short period of time each week (if that)" (p. 161). Furthermore, the religious beliefs of American adolescents do not tend not to follow traditional doctrines, and they often know little about the doctrine of the religion they claim to follow. Instead, they tend to embrace a general set of beliefs that Smith and Denton (2005) call "Moralistic Therapeutic Deism," with the following features:

1. A God exists who created and orders the world and watches over human life on earth.
2. God wants people to be good, nice, and fair to each other, as taught in the Bible and by most world religions.
3. The central goal of life is to be happy and to feel good about oneself.
4. God does not need to be particularly involved in one's life except when God is needed to resolve a problem.
5. Good people go to heaven when they die.

Thus, for most American adolescents today, religion is not so much about traditional ideas of sin, grace, and redemption as it is about how to be a good person and feel happy.

Many American adolescents are religious, but many others are not. What explains differences among adolescents in their religiosity? The NSYR and other studies provide similar information on this question. Family characteristics are one important influence (Smith & Denton, 2005). Adolescents are more likely to embrace religion when their parents talk about religious issues and participate in religious activities (King, Furrow, & Roth, 2002; Ream & Savin-Williams, 2003). Adolescents are less likely to be religious when their parents disagree with each other about religious beliefs (Clark & Worthington, 1987) and when their parents are divorced (Gallup & Castelli, 1989). Ethnicity is another factor. In American society, religious faith and religious practices tend to be stronger among African Americans than among Whites (Arnett, 2004a; Wallace & Williams, 1997).

---

secular Based on nonreligious beliefs and values.

social desirability The tendency for people participating in social science studies to report their behavior as they believe it would be approved by others rather than as it actually occurred.

RESEARCH FOCUS • Religious Practices and Social Desirability

According to the surveys presented in this chapter, a substantial proportion of American adolescents are actively involved in religious practices. The numbers are strikingly high, if valid. But are they valid? There is some debate among scholars on religion over the accuracy of people's self-reported religious behavior. Polls conducted by the Gallup organization over the past half century have indicated that the proportion of American adults reporting weekly attendance at religious services has remained remarkably stable during that time, at about 40% (Gallup & Castelli, 1989; Gallup & Lindsay, 1999). However, other scholars have questioned the accuracy of those self-reports. In a 1993 study, a team of sociologists measured religious participation by counting people at services and concluded that the actual rate of weekly attendance was 20% rather than 40% (Hardaway, Marler, & Chaves, 1993).

One study took the approach of investigating people's religious behavior through examining their time-use diaries (Presser & Stinson, 1998). The diaries were not kept for the purposes of recording religious practices, but the daily record of activities over several months revealed, among other things, the extent of people's attendance at religious services. Thousands of diaries were available from 1965 to 1994. Analysis of the diaries showed that the rate of weekly attendance dropped from 42% in 1965 to 26% in 1994. Although similar analyses have yet to be conducted for adolescents, the results of these studies suggest that current self-reports of religious participation among adolescents may also be inflated.

Why would people report their behavior inaccurately? Because they respond to what scholars call **social desirability** (Salkind, 2003). Socially desirable behavior is behavior that you believe others would approve. Adolescents and adults may exaggerate the extent to which they attend religious services because they believe that other people would approve of them if they did attend religious services. As the sociologist Mark Chaves observes, "Most people believe going to church is a good thing to do and, when surveyed, often say they did go to church even when they didn't" (Woodward, 1993).

Social desirability is a research issue not just for religious practices but for many other types of behavior we will examine in this book. Drug use is generally stigmatized; for this reason, young people may not always report the full extent of their drug use. Having numerous sexual partners tends to be more socially desirable for boys than for girls; perhaps for this reason, boys often report more sexual partners than girls in surveys of young people's sexual behavior. Each time you read about a study, ask yourself: Is there any reason why the young people in this study may have reported their behavior inaccurately to make it appear more socially desirable?

The relatively high rate of religiosity among African American adolescents helps explain why they have such low rates of alcohol and drug use (Wallace & Williams, 1997). However, it is not only among minority groups that religiosity is associated with favorable adolescent outcomes. In the American majority culture, adolescents who are more religious report less depression and lower rates of premarital sex, drug use, and delinquent behavior (Kerestes, Youniss, & Metz, 2004; Mason & Windle, 2002; Smith & Denton, 2005). The protective value of religious involvement is especially strong for adolescents living in the worst neighborhoods (Bridges & Moore, 2002). Religious adolescents tend to have better relationships with their parents, both with mothers and fathers (Smith & Denton, 2005; Wilcox, 2008). Also, adolescents who value religion are more likely than other adolescents to perform volunteer service to their community (Hart & Atkins, 2004; Kerestes et al., 2004; Youniss et al., 1999). In other cultures, too, religious involvement has been found to be related to a variety of positive outcomes, for example, among Indonesian Muslim adolescents (French et al., 2008).

Religiosity declines from adolescence through emerging adulthood. Both religious participation and religious beliefs decline throughout the teens, and are lower in the late teens and early 20s than at any other period of the life span (Hoge, Johnson, & Luidens, 1993; Roof, 1993; Wallace & Williams,

1997). This finding may reflect the importance of individualistic criteria to young people making the transition to adulthood, as we saw in Chapter 1. Emerging adults may feel they need to make a break with their parents' religious beliefs and

Why is religious faith especially strong among African American adolescents?

practices to establish that they are making their own decisions about their beliefs and values (Arnett & Jensen, 2002). By emerging adulthood, the beliefs of emerging adults bear little relationship to the beliefs of their parents (Arnett, 2004a). One longitudinal study found that parents' frequency of church attendance when their children were in early adolescence was unrelated to their children's religiosity 11 years later, as emerging adults (Willits & Crider, 1989). Another reason religiosity declines in emerging adulthood may be that by the time they reach their late teens young people are no longer pressured by their parents to attend church, and they resume attendance (if at all) only when they have young children of their own (Arnett & Jensen, 2004a; Hoge et al., 1993; Putnam, 2000).

Despite the decline in religiosity from adolescence to emerging adulthood, a majority of American emerging adults remain religious in some respects. As Table 4.3 shows, a strong majority of them believe in God or a higher power and about half state that their religious beliefs play an important part in their daily lives. Just as among adolescents, religious beliefs are more important to them than attending religious services.

Religious Beliefs and Cognitive Development

"As a Muslim you've got to pray five times a day, you've got to fast during Ramadan and all that. So I do all the things that I'm supposed to do as a Muslim now [that I have reached puberty]. It keeps you away from troubles."

—Majid, Pakistani emerging adult living in Great Britain
(Jacobson, 1998)

Cognitive development from childhood and adolescence leads to changes in how young people think about religion. Specifically, adolescents' ideas about religious faith tend to be more abstract and less concrete, compared with younger children. In one study, Elkind (1978) interviewed several hundred Jewish, Catholic, and Protestant children from ages 5 to 14. They were asked various questions about religion, such as "What is a Catholic?" and "Are all boys and girls in the world Christians?" They were also asked various questions about their own and their families' religious beliefs. By the time they reached their early teens and the beginning of formal operations, children's responses were more abstract and complex

TABLE 4.3 Religiosity of Emerging Adults Ages 21–28

	Percent
How often do you attend religious services?	
About 3–4 X/mo.	19
About 1–2 X/mo.	10
Once every few months	20
About 1–2 X/yr. or less	50
How important is religious faith in your daily life?	
Very important	27
Quite important	20
Somewhat important	21
Not at all important	32
To what extent do you believe that God or some higher power watches over you and guides your life?	
Strongly believe this	52
Somewhat believe this	22
Somewhat skeptical of this	16
Definitely do not believe this	10

Source: Arnett & Jensen (2002).

than at younger ages. Younger children tended to emphasize external behavior in explaining what it means to be a member of a particular faith—persons are Catholic if they go to Mass regularly, for example. In contrast, the adolescents emphasized internal and abstract criteria, such as what people believe and their relationship with God.

James Fowler has proposed a theory of stages of religious development from birth through adulthood that is linked to cognitive development (Fowler, 1981, 1991, 2006; Fowler & Dell, 2004). According to Fowler, early adolescence is a stage of **poetic-conventional faith**, in which people become more aware of the symbolism used in their faith. In this stage, according to Fowler, religious understanding becomes more complex in the sense that early adolescents increasingly believe there is more than one way of knowing the truth. Late adolescence and emerging adulthood are a stage of **individuating-reflective faith**, in which people rely less on what their parents believed and develop a more individualized faith based on questioning their beliefs and incorporating their personal experience into their beliefs. Of course, movement into this stage could also re-

---

poetic-conventional faith Fowler's term for the stage of faith development most typical of early adolescence, in which people become more aware of the symbolism used in their faith and religious understanding becomes more complex in the sense that early adolescents increasingly believe that there is more than one way of knowing the truth.

individuating-reflective faith Fowler's term for the stage of faith most typical of late adolescence and emerging adulthood, in which people rely less on what their parents believed and develop a more individualized faith based on questioning their beliefs and incorporating their personal experience into their beliefs.

Ramadan A month in the Muslim year that commemorates the revelation of the Koran from God to the prophet Muhammad, requiring fasting from sunrise to sunset each day and refraining from all sensual indulgences.

Koran The holy book of the religion of Islam, believed by Muslims to have been communicated to Muhammad from God through the angel Gabriel.

When they reach adolescence, Muslims are expected to participate in the month-long fast of Ramadan.

day or a few days, especially around the time they are nearing puberty. They are commended for doing so by older children and adults, but they are not obligated. However, once they have reached puberty young people are expected to fast during Ramadan (Jacobson, 1998). In fact, it is considered shameful for a person who has clearly reached physical maturity not to fast. Thus, in adolescence, religious practices among Muslims become less open to individual choice and more guided by social pressures. Socialization for their religious behavior becomes narrower; less individual variability is tolerated in whether they observe the fast.

In some urban areas, there have been recent reports that some adolescents are rebelling by refusing to observe the fast, but in the smaller rural communities the narrow socialization pressures of family and community can be intense, and few adolescents resist (Davis & Davis, 1989; Ghuman, 1998; Nanji, 1993). Or, more accurately, because they have been raised in a culture that values fasting at Ramadan, by the time young people reach adolescence nearly all of them eagerly take part in the fast. They have accepted the beliefs of their culture as their own beliefs, and they usually do not have to be coerced or pressured into participating.

THINKING CRITICALLY •••

Is it possible to apply Fowler's theory of changes in religious beliefs in adolescence to the beliefs and practices of Muslim adolescents with respect to Ramadan, or not?

Cultural Beliefs and Moral Development

Religious beliefs are usually learned from one's culture, although the development of adolescents' religious thinking is based in part on their cognitive development. What about moral development? To what extent are adolescents' moral beliefs dependent on their culture's beliefs, and to what extent are adolescents' moral beliefs a result of cognitive processes common to adolescents everywhere?

Scholars who have studied and theorized about adolescents' moral development have largely viewed it as rooted in universal cognitive processes. This is true of the theories of the two most influential scholars on adolescent moral development, Jean Piaget and Lawrence Kohlberg. However, their views have recently begun to be challenged by scholars who emphasize the role of cultural beliefs in moral development. We will consider Piaget's and Kohlberg's ideas first, then other points of view, including the cultural approach.

Piaget's Theory

Piaget (1932) developed his ideas about moral development using several different methods. He watched children play games (such as marbles) to see how they discussed the

flect an integration of religious faith with the individualistic values of the American majority culture. Fowler's theory is based on studies of people in the American majority culture, and people in less individualistic cultures may not go through the "individuating" process Fowler describes.

One contrast to the individuating process of religious development in the American majority culture can be found in cultures where Islam is the dominant religion. In Islam, the most important change that occurs at adolescence involves the holy month that Muslims call **Ramadan** (Al-Mateen & Afzal, 2004; Nanji, 1993). Ramadan commemorates the revelation of the Muslim holy book, the **Koran**, from God to the prophet Muhammad. During this month each year, Muslims are forbidden from taking part in any indulgences, and they are required to fast (that is, refrain from eating, drinking, and sexual activity) from sunrise to sunset every day. The final day of Ramadan is celebrated with a great feast. There are a billion Muslims in the world's population, and Muslims all over the world observe Ramadan. (Most of the world's Islamic population is not in the Middle East but in Asia—Indonesia has the largest Muslim population of any country in the world, with India and Pakistan second and third.)

Before puberty, young Muslims have no obligation to participate in fasting. Girls are supposed to fast for the first time after they reach menarche. The judgment of whether a boy is old enough to be expected to fast is based on signs such as beard growth and changes in body shape (Davis & Davis, 1989). Preadolescent children sometimes fast for a rules. He played games with them himself and asked them questions during the games (e.g., Can the rules be changed? How did the rules begin?) in order to investigate how they would explain the origin of rules and how they would react to violations of the rules. Also, he presented children with hypothetical situations involving lying, stealing, and punishment to see what kinds of judgments they would make about how to determine whether an action was right or wrong.

On the basis of his research, Piaget concluded that children have two distinct approaches to reasoning about moral issues, based on the level of their cognitive development. **Heteronomous morality**, which corresponds to the preoperational stage, from about age 4 to about age 7. Moral rules are viewed as having a sacred, fixed quality. They are believed to be handed down from figures of authority (especially parents) and can be altered only by them. **Autonomous morality** is reached at the beginning of adolescence with the onset of formal operations at about age 10–12 and involves a growing realization that moral rules are social conventions that can be changed if people decide they should be changed. (From age 7 to age 10 there is a transitional stage between heteronomous and autonomous moral thinking, with some properties of each.)

The stage of autonomous morality also involves growing complexity in moral thinking in the sense that autonomous moral thinkers take into account people's motivations for behavior rather than focusing only on the consequences. For example, a child who breaks several dishes by accident is seen as less guilty than a child who breaks a single dish while doing something wrong such as stealing.

Piaget's interest in the rules of children's games reflected his belief that moral development is promoted by interactions with peers. In Piaget's view, peers' equal status requires them to discuss their disagreements, negotiate with one another, and come to a consensus. This process gradually leads to an awareness of the rules of games and from there to a more general awareness of moral rules. According to Piaget, parents are much less effective than peers in promoting children's moral development because parents' greater power and authority make it difficult for children to argue and negotiate with them as equals.

Kohlberg's Theory

Lawrence Kohlberg (1958) was inspired by Piaget's work and sought to extend it by examining moral development through adolescence and into adulthood. Like Piaget, he viewed moral development as based on cognitive development, such that moral thinking changes in predictable ways as cognitive abilities develop, regardless of culture. Also like Piaget, he presented people with hypothetical moral situations and had them indicate what behavior they believed was right or wrong in those situations, and why.

Kohlberg began his research by studying the moral judgments of 72 boys aged 10, 13, and 16 from middle-class and working-class families in the Chicago area (Kohlberg, 1958). He presented the boys with a series of fictional dilemmas, each of which was constructed to elicit their moral reasoning. Here is one of the dilemmas:

> During [World War II], a city was often being bombed by the enemy. So each man was given a post he was to go to right after the bombing, to help put out the fires the bombs started and to rescue people in the burning buildings. A man named Diesing was made the chief in charge of one fire engine post. The post was near where he worked so he could get there quickly during the day but it was a long way from his home. One day there was a very heavy bombing and Diesing left the shelter in the place he worked and went toward his fire station. But when he saw how much of the city was burning, he got worried about his family. So he decided he had to go home first to see if his family was safe, even though his home was a long way off and the station was nearby, and there was somebody assigned to protect the area where his family was. Was it right or wrong for him to leave his station to protect his family? Why? (Kohlberg, 1958, pp. 372–373)

In each interview, the participant would be asked to respond to three stories such as this one. To Kohlberg, what was crucial for understanding the level of people's moral development was not whether they concluded that the actions of the persons in the dilemma were right or wrong but how they explained their conclusions. Kohlberg (1976) developed a system for classifying their explanations into three levels of moral development, with each level containing two stages, as follows:

Level 1: **Preconventional reasoning**. At this level, moral reasoning is based on perceptions of the likelihood of external rewards and punishments. What is right is what avoids punishment or results in rewards.

- Stage 1: *Punishment and obedience orientation.* Rules should be obeyed to avoid punishment from those in authority.
- Stage 2: *Individualism and purpose orientation.* What is right is what satisfies one's own needs and occasionally the needs of others, and what leads to rewards for oneself.

---

heteronomous morality Piaget's term for the period of moral development from about age 4 to about age 7, in which moral rules are viewed as having a sacred, fixed quality, handed down from figures of authority and alterable only by them.

autonomous morality Piaget's term for the period of moral development from about age 10 to age 12, involving a growing realization that moral rules are social conventions that can be changed if people decide they should be changed.

preconventional reasoning In Kohlberg's theory of moral development, the level in which moral reasoning is based on perceptions of the likelihood of external rewards and punishments.

Level 2: **Conventional reasoning**. At this level, moral reasoning is less egocentric and the person advocates the value of conforming to the moral expectations of others. What is right is whatever agrees with the rules established by tradition and by authorities.

- Stage 3: *Interpersonal concordance orientation*. Care of and loyalty to others is emphasized in this stage, and it is seen as good to conform to what others expect in a certain role, such as being a "good husband" or a "good girl."

- Stage 4: *Social systems orientation*. Moral judgments are explained by reference to concepts such as social order, law, and justice. It is argued that social rules and laws must be respected for social order to be maintained.

Level 3: **Postconventional reasoning**. Moral reasoning at this level is based on the individual's own independent judgments rather than on what others view as wrong or right. What is right is derived from the individual's perception of objective, universal principles rather than the subjective perception of either the individual (as in Level 1) or the group (as in Level 2).

- Stage 5: *Community rights and individual rights orientation*. The person reasoning at this stage views society's laws and rules as important, but also sees it as important to question them and change them if they become obstacles to the fulfillment of ideals such as freedom and justice.

- Stage 6: *Universal ethical principles orientation*. The person has developed an independent moral code based on universal principles. When laws or social conventions conflict with these principles, it is seen as better to violate the laws or conventions than the universal principles.

Kohlberg followed his initial group of adolescent boys over the next 20 years (Colby et al., 1983), interviewing them every 3 or 4 years, and he and his colleagues also conducted numerous other studies on moral reasoning in adolescence and adulthood. The results verified Kohlberg's theory of moral development in a number of important ways:

- Stage of moral reasoning tended to increase with age. At age 10, most of the participants were in Stage 2 or in transition between Stage 1 and Stage 2; at age 13, the majority were in transition from Stage 2 to Stage 3; by ages 16 to 18, the majority were in Stage 3 or in transition to Stage 4; and by ages 20 to 22, 90% of the participants were in Stage 3, in transition to Stage 4, or in Stage 4. However,

even after 20 years, when all of the original participants were in their 30s, few of them had proceeded to Stage 5, and none had reached Stage 6 (Colby et al., 1983). Kohlberg eventually dropped Stage 6 from his coding system (Kohlberg, 1986).

- Moral development proceeded in the predicted way, in the sense that the participants did not skip stages but proceeded from one stage to the next highest.

- Moral development was found to be cumulative, in the sense that the participants were rarely found to slip to a lower stage over time. With few exceptions, they either remained in the same stage or proceeded to the next highest stage.

The research of Kohlberg and his colleagues also indicated that moral development was correlated with socioeconomic status (SES), intelligence, and educational level. Middle-class boys tended to be in higher stages than working-class boys of the same age, boys with higher IQs tended to be in higher stages than boys with lower IQs, and boys who received a college education tended to reach higher stages than boys who did not (Mason & Gibbs, 1993; Weinreich, 1974).

Research based on Kohlberg's theory has also included cross-cultural studies in countries all over the world such as Turkey, Japan, Taiwan, Kenya, Israel, and India (Gibbs et al., 2007; Snarey, 1985). Many of these studies have focused on moral development in adolescence and emerging adulthood. In general, the studies confirm Kohlberg's hypothesis that moral development as classified by his coding system progresses with age. Also, as in the American studies, participants in longitudinal studies in other cultures have rarely been found to regress to an earlier stage or to skip a stage of moral reasoning. However, Stage 5 postconventional thinking has been found to be even more rare in non-Western cultures than in the United States (De Mey et al., 1999; Kohlberg, 1981; Snarey, 1985).

Does this mean that people in non-Western cultures tend to engage in lower levels of moral reasoning than people in the West, perhaps because of lower educational levels (Kohlberg, 1986)? Or does the absence of Stage 5 reasoning in non-Western cultures reflect a cultural bias built into Kohlberg's classification system, a bias in favor of Western secularism and individualism (Shweder, Mahapatra, & Miller, 1990)? These questions have been the source of some controversy, as we will see in more detail when the cultural approach is described shortly.

conventional reasoning In Kohlberg's theory of moral development, the level of moral reasoning in which the person advocates the value of conforming to the moral expectations of others. What is right is whatever agrees with the rules established by tradition and by authorities.

postconventional reasoning In Kohlberg's theory of moral development, the level in which moral reasoning is based on the individual's own independent judgments rather than on egocentric considerations or considerations of what others view as wrong or right.

Critiques of Kohlberg

It would be difficult to overstate the magnitude of Kohlberg's influence on the study of moral development in adolescence. Not only was he highly productive himself and in his collaborations with colleagues, but he also inspired many other scholars to investigate moral development according to the stage theory he proposed (e.g., Gibbs et al., 2007; Rest, 1986; Walker, 1984, 1989). However, his theory has also been subject to diverse criticisms. The critiques can be divided into two main types: the gender critique and the cultural critique.

The Gender Critique Did you notice that Kohlberg's original research sample included only males? Later, when he began to study females as well, he initially found that in adolescence females tended to reason at a lower moral level than males of the same age. This finding inspired a former student of his, Carol Gilligan, to develop a critique that claimed his theory was biased toward males, undervaluing the perspective of females, whom she viewed as having a different moral "voice" than males.

According to Gilligan (1982), Kohlberg's theory of moral development is biased in favor of a **justice orientation**. This orientation places a premium on abstract principles of justice, equality, and fairness when judgments are made about moral issues. The primary consideration is whether these principles have been followed. For example, in the sample dilemma described earlier, a person reasoning with the justice orientation would focus on whether the fire chief was being fair in checking on his family first, and on whether justice would be better served if he went to his post instead. Gilligan argued that males are more likely than females to approach moral issues with a justice orientation, with the result that males tend to be rated as more "advanced" morally in Kohlberg's system.

However, according to Gilligan, the justice orientation is not the only legitimate basis for moral reasoning. She contrasted the justice orientation with what she termed the **care orientation**, which involves focusing on relationships with others as the basis for moral reasoning. For example, in the sample dilemma above, someone reasoning from the care orientation would focus on the relationships between the fire chief and his family and community, viewing the dilemma in terms of the relationships involved and the needs of each person rather than in terms of abstract principles. Gilligan claimed that the care orientation is more likely to be favored by females and that Kohlberg's system would rate moral reasoning from this perspective as lower than moral reasoning from the justice orientation.

Gilligan particularly focused on early adolescence as a period when girls come to realize that their concerns with intimacy and relationships are not valued by a male-dominated

Carol Gilligan has proposed that the moral reasoning of adolescent girls is based on a care orientation.

society, with the result that girls often "lose their voice"; that is, they become increasingly insecure about the legitimacy of their ideas and opinions (Gilligan, 2008; Gilligan, Lyons, & Hanmer, 1990). Gilligan criticized Kohlberg's theory of moral development, as well as other prominent theories of human development by Freud, Piaget, and Erikson, for being too male-oriented in presenting the independent, isolated individual as the paragon of mental health, thus undervaluing females' tendencies toward interdependence and relational thinking.

Gilligan's gender critique has inspired a great deal of attention and research since she first articulated it in 1982. What does the research say about her claims? For the most part, studies support Gilligan's contention that males and females tend to emphasize somewhat different moral concerns (Galotti, 1989; Galotti, Kozberg, & Farmer, 1991; Skoe & Gooden, 1993). For example, when adolescents are asked to recall their personal moral dilemmas, girls are more likely than boys to report dilemmas that involve interpersonal relationships (Galotti, 1989; Skoe & Gooden, 1993). However, when reasoning about hypothetical moral issues, there are no differences between adolescent boys and girls in their use of "care" reasoning (Pratt, Skoe, & Arnold, 2004).

Furthermore, evidence does not support Gilligan's claim that Kohlberg's system is biased in favor of males. In the most comprehensive test of this claim, Lawrence Walker (1984, 1989) analyzed the results from 108 studies that had used Kohlberg's system to rate stages of moral development. Walker combined the results from the various studies statistically to see whether any overall differences existed in how males and females were rated. The results indicated that no significant differences existed between males and females as rated by Kohlberg's system.

---

justice orientation A type of moral orientation that places a premium on abstract principles of justice, equality, and fairness.

care orientation Gilligan's term for the type of moral orientation that involves focusing on relationships with others as the basis for moral reasoning.

The Cultural Critique Although Kohlberg did not deny that culture has some influence on moral development, in his view the influence of culture is limited to how well cultures provide opportunities for individuals to reach the highest level of moral development (Jensen, 1997b, 2003). To Kohlberg, cognitive development is the basis for moral development. Just as cognitive development proceeds on only one path (given adequate environmental conditions), so moral development has only one natural path of maturation (Kohlberg, 1976, 1986). As development proceeds and individuals' thinking becomes progressively more developed, they rise inevitably along that one and only path. Thus, the highest level of moral reasoning is also the most rational. With an adequate education that allows for the development of formal operations, the individual will realize the inadequacies and irrationality of the lower levels of moral reasoning and embrace the highest, most rational way of thinking about moral issues. By becoming able to take the perspective of each party involved in a moral situation, a person can learn to make postconventional moral judgments that are objectively and universally valid.

Recently, these assumptions have been called into question by scholars taking a cultural approach to moral development. The most cogent and penetrating critique has been presented by cultural psychologist Richard Shweder (2003; Shweder et al., 1990; Shweder et al., 2006). According to Shweder, the postconventional level of moral reasoning described by Kohlberg is not the only rational moral code and is not higher or more developed than other kinds of moral thinking. In Shweder's view, Kohlberg's system is biased in favor of the individualistic thinking of "Western elites" of the highest social classes and highest levels of Western education. Like Gilligan, Shweder objects to Kohlberg's classification of detached, abstract individualism as the highest form of moral reasoning.

Shweder notes that in research using Kohlberg's system, very few people are classified as postconventional thinkers. As we saw earlier, in studies examining moral thinking across cultures very few people outside the West are classified as reaching the postconventional level, and even in the West postconventional thinking is rare. However, in Shweder's view this is not because most people in the world have not fully developed their capacities for rational thinking. On the contrary, the fault is in Kohlberg's system and in what the system classifies as the highest level of rational moral thought.

Although Kohlberg claims that postconventional thinking is supposed to rely on objective, universal moral principles that form the basis of right and wrong regardless of the perspectives of either individuals or groups, in fact only a particular kind of objective principles are classified as postconventional under Kohlberg's system: those that reflect a secular, individualistic, Western way of thinking about moral issues. Shweder argues that people in many cultures in fact routinely make reference to objective, universal principles in their moral reasoning. However, because they view these principles as being established by tradition or religion, Kohlberg's system classifies their reasoning as conventional. Shweder sees this as a secular bias in the system.

This bias makes it difficult for people in most cultures to be classified as reaching the highest level of rationality, Level 3, because people in most cultures outside the West invoke principles of tradition or a religious authority. However, Shweder argues, it is no less rational to believe in objective principles established by a religiously based divine authority and handed down through tradition than to believe in objective principles that have a secular, individualistic basis. To argue otherwise would be to assume that all rational thinkers must be atheists or that it is irrational to accept an account of truth from beings believed to have superior powers of moral understanding, and to Shweder neither of these assertions is defensible.

Shweder supports his argument with data from a study comparing American children, adolescents, and adults with persons of similar ages in India (Shweder et al., 1990). Here, I will focus on the results specific to adolescents (aged 11 to 13), but the results were similar across all age groups. Shweder and his colleagues took a different approach to the study of moral reasoning from the one taken by Kohlberg. Rather than ask people about hypothetical situations, they asked people about specific real-life practices known to be typical in one or both countries (a sample of these practices is shown in Table 4.4). Because they believed Kohlberg was wrong to assume that it is only *how* a person explains a moral judgment that matters in moral reasoning, they recorded whether the participants viewed each practice as right or wrong. Because they believed that Kohlberg's system erred by classifying any reference to tradition or divine authority as conventional, they classified responses as postconventional if the participant made reference to universal moral principles, even if those principles were based on tradition or religious beliefs.

As you can see from Table 4.4, Indian and American adolescents often disagreed about the kinds of behavior that are right or wrong. Similar patterns were found for younger children and adults. To Shweder, these sharp divergences call into question Kohlberg's notion that moral development proceeds through similar age-related stages in all cultures. On the contrary, children learn the moral beliefs specific to their culture by an early age, and these beliefs are well ingrained by adolescence and remain stable through adulthood. Within each culture, beliefs about right and wrong were highly correlated regardless of age, but across cultures there was little agreement between Indians and Americans in any age group.

Although the Indians and Americans often disagreed about whether various practices were right or wrong, there were strong similarities between them in the kinds of moral reasoning they used. However, contrary to findings using

TABLE 4.4 View of Moral Issues by American and Indian Adolescents

Disagreement: Indians view it as right, Americans as wrong

A father's inheritance goes more to his son than to his daughter.

A husband beats his wife for disobeying his commands.

A father beats his son for skipping school.

Disagreement: Indians view it as wrong, Americans as right

A woman sleeps in the same bed as her husband during her menstrual period.

A 25-year-old son addresses his father using his father's first name.

A person eats beef regularly.

Agreement: Indians and Americans think it is wrong

Incest between brother and sister.

A man kicks a dog sleeping on the side of the road.

A father asks his son to steal flowers from a neighbor's garden, and the boy does it.

Source: Schweder et al. (1990).

Kohlberg's system that postconventional reasoning is rare in any culture, Shweder and his colleagues found postconventional reasoning to be characteristic of the majority of moral reasoning statements of children, adolescents, and adults in both countries. This is because Shweder classified moral reasoning as postconventional when people based their reasoning on any type of universal moral obligation, including those based on tradition or religious beliefs. Kohlberg's system would have classified most of those statements as conventional or left them uncoded. Shweder concluded that Kohlberg's coding system is biased toward Western values. Moral reasoning, according to Shweder, is not simply a reflection of a person's level of cognitive development but is invariably rooted in cultural beliefs.

THINKING CRITICALLY •••

Having read about Kohlberg's theory and Shweder's cultural critique of it, which do you find more persuasive, and why?

The Worldviews Approach to Moral Development Recently, Shweder and his colleagues have presented an alternative to Kohlberg's theory of moral development (Shweder et al., 1997). The new theory has been developed mostly by a former student of Shweder's, Lene Jensen (1997a, 1997b, 2000, 2003, 2009). According to Jensen, the ultimate basis of

worldview A set of cultural beliefs that explain what it means to be human, how human relations should be conducted, and how human problems should be addressed.

morality is a person's **worldview**. A worldview is a set of cultural beliefs that explain what it means to be human, how human relations should be conducted, and how human problems should be addressed. Worldviews provide the basis for *moral reasoning* (explanations for *why* a behavior is right or wrong). The outcome of moral reasoning is *moral evaluations* (judgments as to *whether* a behavior is right or wrong), which in turn prescribe *moral behaviors*. Moral behaviors reinforce worldviews. An illustration of the worldviews theory is shown in Figure 4.2.

In her research, Jensen codes people's responses to moral issues according to three types of "ethics" based on different worldviews:

The *Ethic of Autonomy* defines the individual as the primary moral authority. Individuals are viewed as having the right to do as they wish as long as their behavior does no direct harm to others.

The *Ethic of Community* defines individuals as members of social groups to which they have commitments and obligations. In this ethic, the responsibilities of roles in the family, community, and other groups are the basis of one's moral judgments.

The *Ethic of Divinity* defines the individual as a spiritual entity, subject to the prescriptions of a divine authority. This ethic includes moral views based on traditional religious authorities and religious texts (e.g., the Bible, the Koran).

Research conducted thus far has shown that emerging adults in the United States rely especially on the ethic of autonomy. Jensen (1995) found that American emerging adults relied more than midlife or older adults on the ethic of autonomy when explaining their views about moral issues such as divorce and suicide. Also, Haidt, Koller, and Dias (1993) found that college students in both the United States and Brazil used autonomy more than community on a variety of moral issues. However, one study found that emerging adults used autonomy and community in roughly equal proportions (and divinity rarely) in response to questions about the values that guide their lives and the beliefs and values

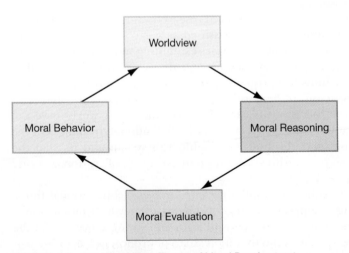

FIGURE 4.2 The Worldviews Theory of Moral Development.

they would like to pass on to the next generation (Arnett, Ramos, & Jensen, 2001). Research using the three ethics has only begun in recent years, and it remains to be seen how use of the three ethics changes in different cultures from childhood through emerging adulthood.

Morality in Everyday Life In his research on moral development, Kohlberg used only hypothetical dilemmas like the fire chief dilemma described earlier. The hypothetical dilemmas concern unusual, life-and-death issues that most people would be unlikely to experience in their own lives, such as stealing in order to save a life, the mercy killing of a terminally ill person, and a soldier's sacrifice of his life for his fellow soldiers. Kohlberg believed that this lack of connection to everyday experience was a strength of his dilemmas because people would reason about them without preconceptions or preexisting tendencies based on experience, so that only their moral reasoning competence would be tested (Walker, Pitts, Hennig, & Matsuba, 1999). As Kohlberg put it, what matters is the *structure* of moral reasoning—the underlying cognitive basis of how a person reasons about moral issues—and not the *content*, that is, the actual topic or issue they are reasoning about (Kohlberg, 1981). By responding to the dilemmas, people would reveal the structure of their moral reasoning without being distracted by the content. Using hypothetical dilemmas also makes it easier to compare people in their moral development.

The fact that the dilemmas are hypothetical does not mean they are unrelated to how people reason about morality in real life. The stage of moral reasoning people apply to Kohlberg's hypothetical dilemmas tends to be similar to the moral reasoning they apply to moral dilemmas they describe from their own lives (Walker et al., 1987; Walker et al., 1999). Also, stage of moral reasoning on Kohlbergian dilemmas is related to moral behavior. Adolescents and emerging adults who rate relatively high in Kohlberg's coding system are also less likely to engage in antisocial behavior, less likely to engage in cheating, and more likely to assist others who are in need of help (Hart, Burock, & Bonita, 2003; Rest, 1983).

However, like other aspects of Kohlberg's approach to studying moral development, the use of hypothetical dilemmas has been increasingly criticized, even by scholars who have used Kohlberg's approach. Lawrence Walker, a top scholar on moral development who has frequently used Kohlberg's dilemmas in his research, argues that "Kohlberg's cognitive-developmental paradigm [has] led to a somewhat restricted view of morality and moral functioning" (Walker et al., 1999, p. 371). By using only hypothetical dilemmas, according to Walker, "we may be ignoring some, or perhaps even much, of what is important in people's moral functioning—in particular, how they understand the moral domain and handle everyday moral issues" (Walker et al., 1999, p. 373).

In response to this concern, Walker and others have begun expanding research on morality to include the moral issues of everyday life (e.g., Jensen & Williams, 2001; Killen & Hart, 1999; Trevethan & Walker, 1989; Walker, 2004). In one study, Walker and his colleagues (1999) studied real-life moral dilemmas among Canadians in adolescence (16–19), emerging adulthood (18–25), middle adulthood (35–48), and late adulthood (65–84). The participants discussed a recent real-life moral dilemma and their most difficult moral dilemma. In contrast to the life-and-death hypothetical dilemmas, the kinds of dilemmas people reported from everyday life most often had to do with personal relationships—with parents and friends for adolescents and emerging adults, and with spouse, children, and colleagues for older participants.

Another striking difference from studies of hypothetical dilemmas was that in reasoning about real-life moral issues people of all ages often relied on practical costs (e.g., losing one's job) and benefits (e.g., having a pleasurable experience). In Kohlberg's system such considerations are rated at the lowest level, "preconventional" moral reasoning, but as one emerging adult in the study observed, "It's a lot easier to be moral when you have nothing to lose" (Walker et al., 1999, pp. 381–382)—that is, when the consequences are only hypothetical.

Also notable was that people of all ages frequently invoked religious justifications for their moral judgments. According to Walker, this calls into question Kohlberg's attempts to separate morality from religion. The pervasiveness of religious justifications was especially striking because in the area of Canada where the study took place (Vancouver, British Columbia) formal religious participation was very low (5% regular religious attendance). Thus, in many ways, Walker's study demonstrated that studying morality in everyday life greatly expands our understanding of how people reason about moral issues.

THINKING CRITICALLY •••

Think of a recent moral dilemma from your own life. What did you decide, and why did you decide it that way? How would your moral reasoning on that dilemma be scored according to Kohlberg's system? How would it be classified according to Jensen's three ethics?

Studying real-life moral issues allows for the expression of culturally distinct moral views. In a study of Chinese adults, Walker and Moran (1991) found that asking about real-life moral dilemmas revealed moral concepts based on Chinese culture, such as the importance of maintaining "face" (respect) and the belief in the traditional Confucian idea that a hierarchy of authority is valuable for social order. The studies by Shweder (Shweder et al., 1990; Shweder et al., 1998) and Jensen (1998) in India also demonstrate the cultural basis of moral reasoning. However, there is a need for more research that explores moral judgments in cultural context.

Political Beliefs

Cultural beliefs include political beliefs about desirable and undesirable features of political institutions, about what kind of political arrangements are fair or unfair, and about the extent to which human rights such as free speech and freedom of the press should be allowed. Because political thinking often involves a consideration of abstract ideas such as justice, human rights, and the distribution of wealth, it seems reasonable to expect that political thinking develops in adolescence toward greater abstraction and complexity, in a manner similar to religious thinking and moral thinking. Research on the development of political thinking seems to support this expectation. However, research in this area is limited, and it provides few insights into the cultural basis of political thinking.

One scholar who did extensive work on political development in adolescence was Joseph Adelson (1971, 1991). Adelson's research was in the tradition of Piaget and Kohlberg. He used hypothetical situations to elicit adolescents' thinking about political arrangements and ideas, and he explained political development in terms of the cognitive changes of adolescence.

Adelson's main hypothetical situation was as follows: "Imagine that a thousand men and women, dissatisfied with the way things are going in this country, decide to purchase and move to an island in the Pacific where they must devise laws and modes of government." Based on this hypothetical situation, the researchers asked adolescents numerous questions about their political views. Each adolescent was asked about the merits of different possible forms of government for the island (democracy, monarchy, etc.), and about the purpose and enforcement of laws. Adolescents were asked to consider what should be done if the government wanted to build a road across the island and a person who owned part of the land where the road was to be built refused to sell; if a law was passed to forbid smoking and people continued to smoke; and what to do about the rights of minority citizens on the island.

Adelson and his colleagues examined political development in relation to age, gender, social class, and IQ, but the only variable found to be related to political thinking was age. Studying adolescents aged 11 to 18, they found a profound shift in political thinking beginning at ages 12 to 13 and completed by ages 15 to 16. The shift involved three key changes: a change in what Adelson called "cognitive mode," a sharp decline in support for authoritarian political systems, and the development of the capacity for ideology.

The change in cognitive mode included several changes related to the development of formal operations, such as increased use of abstract ideas and increased tendency to see laws as human constructions rather than as absolute and unchangeable. Older adolescents were more likely than younger adolescents to use abstract ideas instead of concrete examples. For example, when asked about the purpose of laws, a typical older adolescent responded, "to ensure safety and enforce the government," whereas a typical younger adolescent said laws are necessary "so people don't steal or kill." Similarly, when asked questions about the nature of government, older adolescents were more likely to refer to abstract ideas such as community or society, whereas younger adolescents' statements were more concrete and specific, referring, for example, to the president or the mayor.

Changes in cognitive mode also led to changes in adolescents' views of laws. The youngest adolescents viewed laws as eternal and unchangeable. However, by about age 15 adolescents were more likely to see laws as social constructions that could be changed if the people governed by them wished to change them. In Adelson's view, this reflected the development of formal operations and a growing tendency to see laws less as concrete objects and more as social arrangements subject to change. This is similar to what Kohlberg described in moral development as the development from Level 1 thinking, emphasizing a fixed moral code, to Level 2 thinking, emphasizing the changeable, socially created quality of moral and legal rules. Kohlberg and Adelson found a similar change at a similar time, from age 10 to 15.

The second key change observed by Adelson and his colleagues between early and late adolescence was a sharp decline in authoritarian political views. Younger adolescents tended to be remarkably authoritarian. For example, to enforce a law prohibiting cigarette smoking, they approved of procedures such as hiring police informers and hiding spies in the closets of people's homes! "To a large and various set of questions on crime and punishment," noted Adelson, "they consistently propose one form of solution: punish, and if that does not suffice, punish harder" (Adelson, 1971, p. 1023). Older adolescents' thinking was, again, more complex. They tried to balance the goal of the law with considerations such as individual rights and long-term versus short-term costs and benefits. On an index of authoritarianism used in the study, 85% of the youngest participants were rated in the highest category, compared with only 17% of the 17- and 18-year-olds.

The third key change involved the capacity to develop an ideology. This means that the older adolescents had developed a set of beliefs that served as the basis for their political attitudes. In addressing Adelson's questions, they spoke of principles reflecting a belief in some combination of individual and community rights, rather than being limited to a focus on immediate and concrete solutions as the younger adolescents were.

More recent studies of the development of political thinking in adolescence have confirmed many of Adelson's findings (Flanagan & Botcheva, 1999). For example, Judith Torney-Purta (1990, 1992, 2004) has described how political thinking becomes increasingly abstract and complex during adolescence, progressing from the concrete, simple views of preadolescence to the more coherent, abstract ideology of late adolescence. Several scholars have confirmed Adelson's finding that authoritarianism declines in adolescence (Flanagan & Botcheva, 1999). For example, tolerance of opposing or offensive political views increases from childhood to adolescence and peaks in late adolescence (Sigelman & Toebben, 1992). Recent studies on political development have also touted the promise of the Internet as a source of international knowledge, which, under a teacher's guidance, could promote tolerance and perspective taking in adolescents' political views (Flanagan & Botcheva, 1999; Lupia & Philpot, 2005; Torney-Purta, 1990, 1992).

Political Ideas as Cultural Beliefs

Like Piaget and Kohlberg, Adelson was seeking to establish a path of development through stages that would apply to young people everywhere. However, neither Adelson nor others have attempted to apply his ideas to cultures other than the American majority culture, so it is difficult to say how similar the developmental path of political thinking he described would be to the path followed by adolescents in a much different culture. However, if we borrow a little from the research and critiques on moral development, we can state two likely hypotheses. One hypothesis is that there would be some common changes in political thinking with age from early adolescence to late adolescence across cultures because the abstract ideas invoked by the older adolescents in Adelson's studies reflect their more advanced cognitive abilities. The second hypothesis is that it is also likely that the pattern observed by Adelson reflects adolescents' socialization into the political ideas that are part of the beliefs of a particular culture.

Adelson and his colleagues studied adolescents in three different countries, but they were similar countries—the United States, Great Britain, and Germany, countries with similar laws and political institutions. What would they find if they asked similar questions of adolescents in China, in Saudi Arabia, or among the Australian Aborigines? It seems likely that the political ideas of adolescents in those cultures would reflect the dominant political ideas of their societies and would differ accordingly from American adolescents. Aristotle, the ancient Greek philosopher, was one of the most brilliant persons who ever lived, yet he believed that dictatorship was superior to democracy, that some men were born to be slaves, and that women were inferior to men in virtually every respect. Was he less developed or less logical than the typical 16-year-old of our time? Not likely. What is more likely is that he, like us, reflected the cultural beliefs of his time and place.

Emerging Adults' Political Involvement

Little research has been done on political thinking in emerging adulthood, but in Western Europe as well as in Canada and the United States, the political participation of emerging adults is strikingly low by conventional measures such as voting rates and involvement in political parties (e.g., Barrio, Moreza & Linaza, 2007; Botcheva, Kalcher, & Leiderman, 2007; Meeus, 2007; Sears, Simmering, & MacNeil, 2007). Emerging adults tend to have lower conventional political participation in comparison not only to adults but also to previous generations of young people. They tend to be skeptical of the motivations of politicians and to see the activities of political parties as irrelevant to their lives. One recent study of young people in eight European countries found that low levels of trust in political authorities and political systems were consistent from adolescence through emerging adulthood (Hooghe & Wilkenfeld, 2008).

However, the rejection of conventional politics should not be construed as a lack of interest in improving the state of their communities, their societies, and the world (Arnett, 2002b). On the contrary, emerging adults in the West are more likely than older adults to be involved in organizations devoted to particular issues, such as environmental protection and efforts against war and racism (e.g., Goossens & Luyckx, 2007; Meeus, 2007). In one nationwide survey of college freshmen in the United States, only 28% said they were interested in politics, but 81% had done volunteer work and 45% had participated in a political demonstration (Kellogg, 2001). Often frustrated by and alienated from conventional political processes, emerging adults choose instead to direct their energies toward specific areas of importance to them, where they believe they are more likely to see genuine progress.

Furthermore, emerging adults have often been involved in movements at the political extremes, including protests, revolutionary movements, and terrorism. The leaders of politically extreme groups are usually in midlife or later, but many of their most zealous followers are often emerging adults. There are many recent historical examples. The "Cultural Revolution" that took place in China from 1966 to 1975 and involved massive destruction and violence toward anyone deemed to be a threat to the "purity" of Chinese communism was instigated by Chairman Mao and his wife Jiang Ching but carried out almost entirely by fervent Chinese emerging adults (MacFarquhar & Schoenhals, 2006). Terrorist attacks by Muslim extremists against Western (especially American) targets—most notably the attacks of September 11, 2001—have been planned by older men but executed almost entirely by young men in the 18–29 age range (Sen & Samad, 2007).

These examples involve destruction and violence, but emerging adults have been prominent in peaceful political movements as well. For example, when the collapse of communism began in Eastern Europe in 1989, it was initiated by emerging adults (Garza, 2006). The "Velvet Revolution" in Czechoslovakia began with a massive but nonviolent student-led strike and demonstration (Macek, 2006). When some of the students were beaten, shot, and killed, the rest of Czechoslovakian society rose up in outrage. The communist government soon resigned in the face of the massive protests, and from there the dominoes fell all across Eastern Europe as communist governments resigned or were thrown out. Young people played a prominent role in the revolutions that led to the fall of communism in many of these countries (Flanagan & Botcheva, 1999). In Hungary, young people organized demonstrations agitating for independence, and the first new political party after the fall of communism was an explicitly youth-centered party with membership restricted to persons under age 35. In Bulgaria, young people were active in the strikes and demonstrations that led to the fall of the communist government, and representatives of student movements took a prominent role in the new parliament (Botcheva et al., 2007).

Emerging adults are more likely than older adults to participate in political demonstrations.

Why are emerging adults especially likely to be involved in extreme political movements? One reason is that they have fewer social ties and obligations than people in other age groups (Arnett, 2005b). Children and adolescents can be restrained from involvement by their parents. Young, middle, and older adults can be deterred from involvement by their commitments to others who depend on them, especially a spouse and children. However, emerging adulthood is a time when social commitments and social control are at their nadir. Emerging adults have more freedom than people at other age periods, and this freedom allows some of them to become involved in extreme political movements.

Another possibility is that their involvement is identity related. Recall that one of the key developmental features of emerging adulthood is that it is a time of identity explorations. One aspect of identity explorations is ideology or worldview (Erikson, 1968; Arnett, 2004). Emerging adulthood is a time when people are looking for an ideological framework for explaining the world, and some emerging adults may be attracted to the definite answers provided by extreme political movements. Embracing an extreme political ideology may relieve the discomfort that can accompany the uncertainty and doubt of ideological explorations. Still, these explanations beg the question: Since only a small minority of emerging adults are involved in these extreme movements, why them and not the others?

SUMMING UP

In this chapter, we have examined various aspects of the cultural beliefs underlying the socialization of adolescents and emerging adults, and you have been introduced to many of the ideas that are part of the cultural approach that will be taken in the chapters to come. The key points of the chapter are as follows:

- Socialization is the process by which people acquire the behaviors and beliefs of the culture they live in. Three outcomes central to this process are self-regulation, role preparation, and the cultivation of sources of meaning.

- Cultural beliefs usually tend toward either individualism or collectivism, with individualistic cultures giving priority to independence and self-expression and collectivist cultures placing a higher value on obedience and conformity. *Broad socialization* and *narrow socialization* are the terms for the process by which cultural members come to adopt the values and beliefs of an individualistic or a collectivistic culture. Sources of socialization include family, peers and friends, school, community, media, the workplace, the legal system, and cultural beliefs.

- A custom complex consists of a distinctive cultural practice and the cultural beliefs that are the basis for that practice. Many aspects of development and behavior in adolescence and emerging adulthood can be understood as custom complexes.

- Cultural beliefs are often based on religious beliefs. Most industrialized countries today tend to be secular rather than religious, but religiosity is stronger in the United States than in European countries. Ideas about religious faith tend to become more abstract and less concrete in adolescence, compared with preadolescence.

- Kohlberg's theory of moral development proposed that moral development occurs in a universal sequence regardless of culture. However, Shweder has disputed this assumption in research comparing Indian and American adolescents, and Jensen has proposed a worldviews theory as a culturally based alternative to Kohlberg's theory.

- Like religious and moral beliefs, political beliefs become more abstract and complex in the course of adolescence. Emerging adults are often disengaged from conventional politics, but many of them are involved in organizations working toward change in a specific area, and some are attracted to extreme political movements.

The ideas about cultural beliefs presented in this chapter form a foundation for understanding development in adolescence and emerging adulthood using a cultural approach. Individualism and collectivism provide a useful way of distinguishing between two general types of cultural beliefs, although these are rough categories and cultures do not necessarily fit neatly into one or the other. *Broad socialization* and *narrow socialization* describe the process through which individualism and collectivism become beliefs that are held by adolescents and emerging adults. The idea of the custom complex is useful for directing our attention to the cultural beliefs that lie behind everything that people in a culture do as a customary practice. Religious, moral, and political beliefs are different kinds of cultural beliefs that people use for guiding their behavior and making sense of the world around them.

The development of ideas about cultural beliefs has mostly proceeded separately from research on adolescence and emerging adulthood. Only in recent years have scholars on adolescence and emerging adulthood begun to recognize cultural beliefs as an essential part of understanding these age periods. This new melding of the cultural approach with research on adolescence and emerging adulthood is producing a great deal of illuminating and exciting research, which we will be examining in the chapters to come.

KEY TERMS

cultural beliefs 93
symbolic inheritance 93
Bar Mitzvah 94
Bat Mitzvah 94
roles 94
gender roles 94
socialization 95
self-regulation 95
role preparation 96
sources of meaning 96
interdependent self 96

independent self 96
broad socialization 97
narrow socialization 97
custom complex 101
ontogenetic 101
first-generation families 104
second-generation families 104
secular 106
social desirability 107
poetic-conventional faith 108
individuating-reflexive faith 108

Ramadan 109
Koran 109
heteronomous morality 110
autonomous morality 110
preconventional reasoning 110
conventional reasoning 111
postconventional reasoning 111
justice orientation 112
care orientation 112
worldview 114

INTERNET RESOURCES

http://www.youthandreligion.org
This is the web site for the National Study of Youth and Religion, the largest and most comprehensive study of American adolescents' and emerging adults' religious beliefs ever conducted. The site contains information about the study as well as ongoing reports of the results as the study follows the original sample of adolescents through emerging adulthood.

FOR FURTHER READING

Gilligan, C. (1982). *In a different voice: Psychological theory and women's development.* Cambridge, MA: Harvard University Press. Even though Gilligan's predictions of male-female differences in moral reasoning have not been borne out by research, this book is worth reading for its thought-provoking critique of the male model that has often been used in theories of human development, including development in adolescence and emerging adulthood.

Trommsdorff, G. (1994). Parent–adolescent relations in changing societies: A cross-cultural study. In P. Noack, M. Hofer, & J. Youniss (Eds.), *Psychological responses to social change* (pp. 189–218). New York: Walter de Gruyter. The introduction to this chapter presents a useful overview of the literature on individualism and collectivism in relation to adolescence. Then Trommsdorff presents a study comparing adolescents in Germany, Scotland, Japan, and Indonesia with respect to the relation between the individualism or collectivism of their culture and their relationships with their parents.

Smith, C., & Denton, M. L. (2005). *Soul searching: The religious and spiritual lives of American teenagers.* New York: Oxford University Press. A fascinating account of American adolescents' religious beliefs, based on data from the National Study of Youth and Religion. This book provides a shining example of the value of combining quantitative and qualitative methods.

For more review plus practice tests, videos, flashcards, and more, log on to MyDevelopmentLab.

5 Gender

Terry undresses, feeling nervous and apprehensive, and then feels silly. After all, the photographer is a professional and has probably seen a thousand naked bodies, so what is one more. All that work in the weight room, the aerobics—why not show off, after all the work it took to get such an attractive body? "I should be proud," Terry thinks, slipping into the robe thoughtfully provided by the photographer. Once exposed to the lights of the studio, Terry gets another pang of doubt but dismisses it and drops the robe. The photographer suggests a seated pose, and Terry sits down, but he drops his hands to cover his genitals. "Move your hands to your knees, please," the photographer says gently. After all, she is a professional and knows how to put her models at ease (adapted from Carroll & Wolpe, 1996, p. 162).

THE PURPOSE OF THIS STORY, AS YOU HAVE PROBABLY guessed, is to show how readily our minds slip into assumptions about male and female roles and how surprised we are when our gender stereotypes turn out to be wrong. Thinking about the world in terms of gender comes so easily to most of us that we do not even realize how deeply our assumptions about gender shape our perceptions. The first thing most people ask when they hear someone they know has had a baby is, "Is it a boy or a girl?" From birth onward—and these days, with prenatal testing, even before birth—gender organizes the way we think about people's traits and abilities and how people behave. And at adolescence, when sexual maturity arrives, consciousness of gender and socialization pressures related to gender become especially acute.

In every chapter of this book, gender is an important topic. From family relationships to school performance to sexuality, gender similarities and differences merit our attention. Because gender is so important for so many aspects of development, we also focus in this chapter directly on gender as one of the foundations of development during adolescence and emerging adulthood. Many issues need to be addressed: What sorts of gender-specific requirements do different cultures have for young people when they reach adolescence? In what ways does gender become especially important to socialization in adolescence, and how is gender socialization expressed in the family and other settings? What are the consequences for adolescents of conforming or refusing to conform to cultural expectations for gender role behavior? These are the sorts of questions we address in this chapter.

Because information on gender is relevant to all the chapters of this book, in this chapter I present especially extensive sections on cultural and historical patterns of gender socialization in adolescence, as a foundation for the chapters to come. These sections will be followed by an examination of gender socialization in modern Western societies. Then we will consider gender stereotypes in emerging adulthood and reasons for the persistence of gender stereotypes even when the evidence supporting them is weak. Finally, we will consider the ways globalization is changing gender expectations for adolescents and emerging adults in traditional cultures.

Before we proceed, however, let's clarify the difference between gender and sex. In general, social scientists use the term **sex** to refer to the *biological status of being male or female*. **Gender**, in contrast, refers to the *social categories of male and female* (Helgeson, 2002; Tobach, 2004; Unger & Crawford, 1996). Use of the term *sex* implies that the characteristics of males and females have a biological basis. Use of the term *gender* implies that characteristics of males and females may be due to cultural and social beliefs, influences, and perceptions. For example, the fact that males grow more muscular at puberty and females develop breasts is a sex difference. However, the fact that girls tend to have a more negative body image than males in adolescence is a gender difference. In this chapter, our focus will be on gender.

Adolescents and Gender in Traditional Cultures

For adolescents in traditional cultures, gender roles and expectations infuse virtually every aspect of life, even more so than in the West. Adolescent boys and girls in traditional cultures often have very different lives and spend little time in each other's presence. The expectations for their behavior as adolescents and for the kinds of work they will do as adults are sharply divided, and as a result their daily lives do not often overlap (Howard, 1998; Schlegel & Barry, 1991). Furthermore, for both males and females the gender requirements tend to intensify at adolescence and to allow for very little deviation from the norm. In cultures where socialization is narrow, it tends to be narrowest of all with regard to gender expectations.

Let's look first at the gender expectations for girls in traditional cultures, then at the gender expectations for boys.

From Girl to Woman

Girls in traditional cultures typically work alongside their mothers from an early age. Usually by age 6 or 7, they help take care of younger siblings and cousins (DeLoache & Gottlieb, 2000; Whiting & Edwards, 1988). By 6 or 7 or even earlier, they also help their mothers obtain food, cook, make clothes, gather firewood, and perform all of the other activities that are part of running a household. By adolescence, girls typically work alongside their mothers as near-equal partners (Schlegel & Barry, 1991). The authority of mothers over their daughters is clear, but by adolescence daughters have learned the skills involved in child care and running a household so well that they can contribute an amount of work that is more or less equal to their mothers' work.

One important gender difference that occurs at adolescence in traditional cultures is that boys typically have less contact with their families and considerably more contact with their peers than they did before adolescence, whereas girls typically maintain a close relationship with their mothers and spend a great deal of time with them on a daily basis (Schlegel & Barry, 1991). This difference exists partly because girls are more likely to work alongside their mothers than boys are to work alongside their fathers, but even when adolescent boys work with their fathers they have less contact and intimacy with them than adolescent girls typically have with their mothers. This interdependence between mothers and daughters does not imply that girls remain suppressed in a dependent, childlike way. For example, Schlegel (1973) described how among the Hopi, a Native American tribe, mother-daughter relationships are extremely close throughout life, yet adolescent girls are exceptionally confident and assertive.

Nevertheless, in traditional cultures socialization becomes broader for boys in adolescence and stays narrow or becomes even narrower for girls. In the words of one team of scholars, "During adolescence, the world expands for boys and contracts for girls. Boys enjoy new privileges reserved for men; girls endure new restrictions observed for

By adolescence, girls in traditional cultures often work alongside their mothers as near equals. Here, a mother and daughter in a Mexican village make tortillas.

women" (Mensch et al., 1998, p. 2). In the company of their mothers and often with other adult women as well, adolescent girls' daily lives remain within a hierarchy of authority. Girls are subject to the authority of all adult women because of the women's status as adults and because of their older age (e.g., Chinas, 1991; Davis & Davis, 1989).

Another reason for the narrower socialization of girls at adolescence is that the budding sexuality of girls is more likely to be tightly restricted than is the budding sexuality of boys (Howard, 1998; Mensch et al., 1998; Whiting, Burbank, & Ratner, 1986). Typically, adolescent boys in traditional cultures are allowed and even expected to gain some sexual experience before marriage. Sometimes this is true of girls as well (e.g., Burbank, 1988; Coté, 1994), but for girls more variability exists across cultures, from cultures that allow or encourage them to become sexually active before marriage to cultures that punish girls' loss of virginity before marriage with death, and every variation in between (Whiting et al., 1986). When adolescent girls are expected to be virgins and adolescent boys are expected not to be, boys sometimes gain their first sexual experience with prostitutes or with older women who are known to be friendly to the sexual interests of adolescent boys (e.g., Davis & Davis, 1989; Howard, 1998). However, this double standard also sets up a great deal of sexual and personal tension between adolescent girls and boys, with boys pressing for girls to relax their sexual resistance and girls fearful of the shame and disgrace that will fall on them (and not on the boy) if they should give in.

---

sex The biological status of being male or female.

gender The social categories of male and female, established according to cultural beliefs and practices rather than being due to biology.

provide In the manhood requirements of traditional cultures, the requirement of being able to provide economically for one's self as well as a wife and children.

An excellent example of gender-specific expectations for adolescent girls in traditional cultures comes from the work of Chinas (1991), who studied adolescent girls and women in a Mexican village. As Chinas describes it, socialization becomes narrower for girls once they reach puberty. Before puberty, girls are often sent to the town plaza to shop for food at the outdoor market. In the course of performing this task they become shrewd shoppers, adept at making change and performing mental addition and subtraction. However, in Mexican culture virginity is demanded for girls before marriage. Consequently, once they reach puberty girls are no longer allowed to go to the town plaza alone and are generally kept under close surveillance to reduce the likelihood of premarital sexual adventures.

During adolescence, girls' activities in the village mainly involve learning how to run a household. Middle childhood is a time of learning how to care for children (usually the girls' younger siblings), but by adolescence other girls in middle childhood take over some of the child care, and adolescent girls spend their time learning household skills such as making and cooking tortillas, sewing, and embroidery. School is not a part of the adolescent girl's experience. If she has had the opportunity to go to school at all, it would have been only for a year or so at age 6 or 7, just long enough to become literate. Boys, in contrast, are much more likely to be allowed to attend school until age 12 or older.

From about age 10 to about age 16 girls are provided few opportunities to interact with boys. Talking to boys at these ages is strongly discouraged, and in small villages a girl's behavior can be monitored almost constantly, if not by her parents or her brothers than by other adults who know her. However, around age 16 girls are considered to be reaching marriageable age, and they are allowed to attend public fiestas under the watchful eye of an older female relative—mother, aunt, or grandmother. A girl of this age will also be allowed to attend the Sunday evening *paseo*, in which the people of the village gather in the public square and stroll around the plaza, those on the outer edge in one direction and those on the inner edge in the other direction. This provides a rare chance for young people to look each other over and maybe even exchange a few words.

If a boy is interested in a girl, he will begin to wait outside her home on Sunday evenings in the hopes of being allowed to escort her to the *paseo*. This is a critical point, and although the boy is always the initiator of the courtship, here the girl has the power to make or break it. If she discourages him, he is obliged to give up the courtship. If she allows him to escort her, they are considered more or less engaged. Thereafter, he will spend most of his free evenings waiting concealed outside her home in hopes that she will emerge on some errand and he will be able to talk to her briefly. After several months, representatives of the boy approach the girl's parents on his behalf and request their consent for him to marry her. Although the girl is not asked about her own feelings, she has already indicated her consent indirectly by allowing the boy to court her.

Chinas's description of the girls in this Mexican village illustrates several themes often found in the socialization of adolescent girls in traditional cultures: early work responsibilities, close relationships with monitoring female adults, and a focus in adolescence on preparing for marriage and gender-specific adult work. The gender socialization of boys in traditional cultures is similar in some ways and different in others, as we will see in the next section.

THINKING CRITICALLY •••

Compare the gender expectations for adolescent girls in the Mexican village described by Chinas with the gender expectations for adolescent girls in your own culture. What are the similarities and differences?

From Boy to Man

One striking difference between gender expectations for girls and gender expectations for boys in traditional cultures is that for boys manhood is something that has to be *achieved*, whereas girls reach womanhood inevitably, mainly through their biological changes (Leavitt, 1998). It is true that girls are required to demonstrate various skills and character qualities before they can be said to have reached womanhood. However, in most traditional cultures womanhood is seen as something that girls attain naturally during adolescence, and their readiness for womanhood is viewed as indisputably marked when they reach menarche. Adolescent boys have no comparable biological marker of readiness for manhood. For them, the attainment of manhood is often fraught with peril and carries a definite and formidable possibility of failure.

It is striking to observe how many cultures have a term for a male who is a failed man. In Spanish, for example, a failed man is *flojo* (a word that also means flabby, lazy, useless). Similar words exist in a wide variety of other languages (Gilmore, 1990). (You can probably think of more than one example in your own language.) In contrast, although there are certainly many derogatory terms applied to women, none of them have connotations of *failure at being a woman* the way *flojo* and other terms mean *failure at being a man*.

So, what must an adolescent boy in traditional cultures do to achieve manhood and escape the stigma of being viewed as a failed man? The anthropologist David Gilmore (1990) analyzes this question across traditional cultures around the world in his book *Manhood in the Making: Cultural Concepts of Masculinity*. He concludes that in most cultures an adolescent boy must demonstrate three capacities before he can be considered a man: *provide*, *protect*, and *procreate*. He must **provide** in the sense that he must demonstrate that he has developed skills that are economically useful and that will enable him to support the wife and children he is likely to have as an adult man. For example, if adult men mainly fish,

Circumcision, which involves cutting some portion of the genitals so that they are permanently altered, is an ancient practice. We know that male circumcision goes back at least 2,500 years among the ancient Jews and other cultures in what is now known as the Middle East (Henerey, 2004). For many Jews then and now, circumcision has had great religious and communal significance, serving as a visible sign of the covenant between God and the Jewish people and as a permanent marker of a male's membership in the Jewish community. Among Jews, circumcision takes place in infancy, eight days after birth.

In most of the West today, circumcision may be performed shortly after birth for hygienic reasons, as a way of preventing certain diseases that are more likely to develop in uncircumcised males. However, in several parts of the world, circumcision takes place not in infancy but in adolescence, and not just among boys but among girls as well. Cultures with adolescent circumcision exist in the Middle East and Asia but are most prevalent in Africa (Hatfield & Rapson, 2006). In most cultures that have circumcision in adolescence, it takes place for both boys and girls. However, the nature of it and the consequences of it are quite different for males and females.

Male circumcision in adolescence typically involves cutting away the foreskin of the penis. This procedure is intensely painful, and no anesthetic of any kind is used. Boys are supposed to demonstrate their courage and fortitude by enduring the circumcision without resisting, crying, or flinching (Gilmore, 1990). There is a great deal of social pressure to be stoic. Circumcision usually occurs as a public ritual, observed by the community, and if a boy displays resistance or emotion he will be disgraced permanently before his community, and his family will be disgraced as well.

Although male circumcision is painful and traumatic, and the emotional and social effects of failure can be great, the physical effects of male circumcision are not harmful in the long run. Once the cut heals, the boy will be capable of experiencing the same pleasurable sensations in his penis as he did before the circumcision. Also, if a boy endures the circumcision without visible emotion, his status in the community will rise, for he will now be considered to have left childhood and entered adolescence.

For adolescent girls, the procedure and consequences of circumcision are considerably different. Female circumcision takes a variety of forms, but nearly always it involves the clitoris, where female sexual sensations are concentrated. In some cultures the hood of the clitoris is cut off, in some the entire clitoris is cut off, and in yet others the clitoris is cut off along with parts of the labia minora and the labia majora (Hatfield & Rapson, 2006). Figure 5.1 shows the rates of female circumcision in various African countries.

Although the circumcision of adolescent girls is not performed publicly as it usually is for boys, and although girls are not expected to remain silent and stoic during the procedure, the physical consequences of circumcision are much more severe for them (Sedgh et al., 2005). Typically, a great deal of bleeding occurs, and the possibility of infection is high. Afterward many girls have chronic pain whenever they menstruate or urinate, and their risks of urinary infections and childbirth complications are heightened. Furthermore, the operation makes sexual intercourse less pleasurable.

Why would cultures sustain a tradition like this? One reason lies in the inertia surrounding cultural practices. In general, people grow up believing that the practices and be-

the adolescent boy must demonstrate that he has learned the skills involved in fishing adequately enough to provide for a family.

Second, the adolescent boy must **protect**, in the sense that he must show that he can contribute to the protection of his family, kinship group, tribe, and other groups to which he belongs, from attacks by human enemies or animal predators. He learns this by acquiring the skills of warfare and the capacity to use weapons. Conflict between human groups has been a fact of life for most cultures throughout human history, so this is a pervasive requirement. Finally, he must learn to **procreate**, in the sense that he must gain some degree of sexual experience before marriage. He gains this experience not in order to demonstrate his sexual attractiveness but so

that he can prove that in marriage he will be able to perform well enough sexually to produce children.

Manhood requirements in traditional cultures typically involve not just the acquisition of specific skills in these three areas but also the development of certain *character qualities* that must accompany these skills to make them useful and effective (Arnett, 1998a). Learning to provide involves developing not just economic skills but also the character qualities of diligence and stamina. Learning to protect involves not just learning the skills of warfare and weapons but also cultivating the character qualities of courage and fortitude. Learning to procreate involves not just sexual performance but also the character qualities of confidence and boldness that lead to sexual opportunities.

---

protect In the manhood requirements of traditional cultures, the requirement of being able to assist in protecting one's family and community from human and animal attackers.

procreate In the manhood requirements of traditional cultures, the requirement of being able to function sexually well enough to produce children.

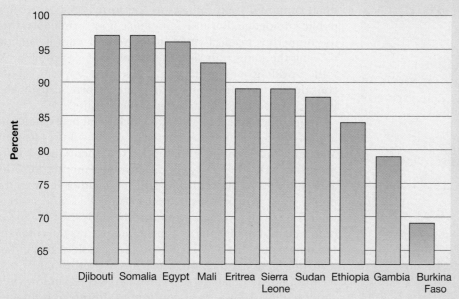

FIGURE 5.1 Rate of female circumcision in various countries.
Source: The Economist (1999).

reason is that girls in these cultures grow up knowing that a man will not marry a girl who is uncircumcised, and they also know that they must marry to have an accepted social place in their culture (French, 1992; Hayford, 2005). So, the girls usually submit voluntarily, and many even value the practice as a way of gaining higher status in their community and becoming acceptable to men as a potential marriage partner (Shweder, 2002).

In recent years, female circumcision has become an extremely controversial issue of global concern. Critics have termed it female genital mutilation (FGM) and have waged an international campaign against it (Kalev, 2005; Sedgh et al., 2005). International organizations such as the United Nations have issued reports condemning it (UNDESA, 2005). Some defenders have argued that the evidence of physical and sexual consequences is exaggerated and that the West should not impose its values on the cultures that practice female circumcision (Shweder, 2002). The critics respond that respect for cultural differences can go only so far and that practices that cause suffering to large numbers of people should be condemned and abolished in whatever culture they take place (Hatfield & Rapson, 2006; Nussbaum, 1992). Nevertheless, as of this writing, female circumcision continues to be the norm for adolescent girls in many African cultures.

liefs of their culture are good and right, and do not often question the ultimate ethical foundation for them. Another motivation for males may be that if it lowers females' enjoyment of sex, their wives may be less likely to have sex with other men (Hatfield & Rapson, 2006). Female circumcision is one way for men to exercise control over women's sexuality (Kalev, 2005).

Why would women submit to circumcision? One reason is that they have no choice. If they do not submit willingly, they may be held or tied down (Hatfield & Rapson, 2006). Another

Gilmore (1990) gives many fine examples of the manhood requirements of different cultures in his book. For example, the *Mehinaku* live in the remotest part of the world's largest rain forest in central Brazil. Their location is so remote that they are one of the few remaining cultures that have been little affected by globalization. Other than the occasional visit from a missionary or an anthropologist, they have been (so far) left alone.

For an adolescent male among the Mehinaku, learning to provide means learning to fish and hunt, which are the two main male economic activities (the females tend vegetable gardens, care for children, and run the household). Depending on the local food supply, fishing and hunting might involve going on long expeditions to promising territory, sometimes for days or weeks at a time. Thus, learning to provide means not only learning the skills involved in fishing and hunting but also developing the character qualities of diligence, stamina, and courage (because the expeditions are sometimes dangerous). Adolescent boys who fail to accompany their fathers on these trips out of laziness or weakness or fear

are ridiculed as "little girls" and told that women will find them undesirable.

THINKING CRITICALLY •••

Do you think the manhood requirements common in traditional cultures—provide, protect, and procreate—also exist in a modified form for adolescent boys in your society? Are there other qualities that are part of the requirements for manhood—not just adulthood, but manhood specifically—in your society?

Learning to protect means learning to fight and wield weapons against men of neighboring tribes. The Mehinaku themselves prefer peace and are not aggressive toward their neighbors, but their neighbors attack them on a regular basis and the men are required to defend themselves and their women and children. The men must also learn to defend themselves on their food-finding trips, which often require traveling through the territory of more aggressive tribes.

In traditional cultures, adolescent boys must learn to provide, protect, and procreate. Here, Mbuti boys in central Africa learn to hunt.

As part of their preparation for protecting, Mehinaku boys and men engage in almost daily wrestling matches. These matches are fiercely competitive, and each time a male wins he elevates his status in the community, whereas repeatedly losing is deeply humiliating and a threat to his manhood status. This puts considerable pressure on adolescent boys, because boys who cannot compete well at these matches find their progress toward legitimate manhood called into question, and they find themselves considerably less attractive to adolescent girls as potential husbands.

"When we see guys acting in certain guy ways, we must not judge them too harshly. We must view them the same way we view any other creatures of nature, such as snakes. They do things that seem inappropriate in a civilized world, but they are only following behavioral patterns that were embedded eons ago. If we are patient and understanding with them, if we seek to understand what 'makes them tick,' we can succeed in modifying their behavior and bringing them more 'in tune' with modern society. I'm talking about snakes here. Guys are hopeless."

—Dave Barry (1995), p. 41

With regard to learning to procreate, sex is the most popular topic of conversation among Mehinaku adolescent boys and men. They joke and brag about it, but they are also deeply concerned about potential failures because in their small community any failures to "perform" quickly become public knowledge. Because impotence is so formidable, they use numerous magical rituals to prevent or cure it, such as rubbing the penis with various animal or plant products. As with providing and protecting, adolescent boys are under considerable pressure to show they can perform sexually, and they are ridiculed and ostracized if they cannot.

One other aspect of Mehinaku manhood bears mentioning, because it is quite common in other cultures as well. Men and adolescent boys are supposed to spend their leisure time with each other, not at home with their mothers or wives and children. Adolescent boys and men gather daily in the public plaza to talk, wrestle, and make collective decisions, whereas girls and women are generally supposed to keep out of this central public place. A male who prefers the company of women, even his wife, is ridiculed as a "trash yard man"—a man who is not truly a man. (This is a good example of a term for a failed man, as described earlier.) Again, the pressure on adolescent boys to conform to this norm is intense. Whatever his own inclinations may be, this narrow socialization for the male role demands his conformity.

The themes of providing, protecting, and procreating can be seen clearly in adolescent boys' gender socialization among the Mehinaku. This example also illustrates the intense gender socialization pressure that often exists for adolescent boys in traditional cultures and the dire social consequences for boys who fail to measure up to culturally prescribed norms for manhood. For both boys and girls in traditional cultures, adolescence is a time when gender roles are clarified and emphasized. As we will see in the next section, increased emphasis on gender roles in adolescence has long been practiced in American society as well.

Adolescents and Gender in American History

In the same way that looking at adolescence in traditional cultures reveals sharp disparities in the socialization of males and females, looking at adolescence in American history reveals a similar pattern. As in traditional cultures, in the history of American society what it means to grow from girl to woman has been very different from what it means to grow from boy to man.

From Girl to Woman

"I'm so tired of being fat! I'm going back to school weighing 119 pounds—I swear it. Three months in which to lose thirty pounds—but I'll do it, or die in the attempt."

—Excerpt from the diary of a 15-year-old American girl in 1926 (in Brumberg, 1997, pp. 102–103)

Adolescent girls growing up in the American middle class in the 18th and 19th centuries faced expectations that both constricted and supported them more than American adolescent girls experience today. They were narrowly constricted in terms of the occupational roles they were allowed to study or enter. Few professions other than teacher, nurse, or seamstress were considered appropriate for a woman. In fact, no profession at all was considered best, so that a young woman could focus on her future roles of wife and mother.

Adolescent girls were also constricted by cultural perceptions of females, especially young females, as fragile and innocent. One key reason they were discouraged from pursuing a profession was that intellectual work was considered "unhealthy" for women. This view was connected to beliefs about menstruation, specifically the belief that intellectual work would draw a woman's energy toward her brain and away from her ovaries, thus disrupting her menstrual cycle and endangering her health (Brumberg, 1997). This is a good example of something that was claimed to be a sex difference—women were viewed as biologically less capable of intellectual work—but that turned out to be a gender difference instead (rooted in cultural beliefs). Girls were also viewed as too weak to do any important physical work.

The view of adolescent females as incapable of strenuous work is in sharp contrast to the expectations we have seen in traditional cultures, where adolescent girls work alongside their mothers with near-adult responsibilities. However, this exclusion from work applied mainly to American adolescent girls in the growing middle class. Until the mid-19th century the majority of American families were small-scale farmers (Hernandez, 1994), and in those families the lives of adolescent girls were very much like the lives of their counterparts in traditional cultures, working alongside their mothers doing useful and necessary work every day. Also, throughout the 19th and early 20th centuries many American adolescent girls worked in the factories that were springing up in the course of industrialization (Kett, 1977).

Sexuality is a third area where the lives of middle-class girls were narrowly constricted historically in American society. In American history until about the 1920s, virginity until marriage was considered essential for adolescent girls. The word **hymen** was rarely used, but adolescent girls were taught that they possessed a "jewel" or "treasure" that they should surrender only on the night of their wedding (Brumberg, 1997). Until marriage, young women were kept as innocent as possible in body and in mind.

The goal of keeping girls innocent was taken so far that many adolescent girls were not even told about menarche. Historians estimate that before the mid-20th century up to 65% of American adolescent girls were entirely unprepared for menarche (Brumberg, 1997)—and we have seen, in Chapter 2, how shocking it can be to girls who do not know it is coming. Mothers believed that by saying nothing about it they were shielding their girls for as long as possible from the dark mysteries of sex. It was only in the 1920s, sometimes called the decade of the first American sexual revolution, that virginity began to lose its near-sacred status. And it was only in the late 1940s that a majority of American girls learned about men-

Until the 1920s, middle-class American girls wore corsets once they reached puberty.

struation from school, their mothers, or other sources before menarche actually arrived (Brumberg, 1997).

A fourth area of constriction for adolescent females historically was physical appearance. We discussed in Chapter 2 how the current slim ideal of female appearance can be difficult for girls when their bodies reach puberty, but irrational ideals of female appearance are not new. Until the early 20th century, most middle-class adolescent girls and women in the West wore some version of the corset, which was designed to support the breasts and pinch the waist tightly to make it look as small as possible. By the 1920s, corsets were rarely used, replaced by bras, but the 1920s also witnessed new requirements for female appearance—shaving the legs and underarms became the convention for American women, and dieting became a common practice in an effort to attain a slim, boyish figure.

By the 1950s, boyishness was out and big breasts were in. Adolescent girls' diaries from the 1950s show a preoccupation with bras and breasts and a variety of dubious techniques for increasing breast size, from exercise programs to creams to exposing them to moonlight (Brumberg, 1997). In each era, adolescent girls have striven for the female ideal they have been socialized to desire, and have often experienced the normal course of their biological development during puberty as a great source of frustration.

Yet developing from girl to woman also had some advantages historically as compared to the present, according to

hymen The thin membrane inside a girl's vagina that is usually broken during her first experience of sexual intercourse. Tested in some cultures before marriage to verify the girl's virginity.

Joan Jacobs Brumberg (1997), a historian and the author of a thoughtful book called *The Body Project: An Intimate History of American Girls*. Brumberg acknowledges, and describes in detail, how girls in the 18th and 19th centuries in American society were constricted and sheltered and left largely ignorant of the workings of their own bodies. However, she argues that girls of those times also benefited from the existence of a wide range of voluntary organizations, such as the Young Women's Christian Association (YWCA), the Girl Scouts, and the Camp Fire Girls, in which adult women provided a "protective umbrella" for the nurturing of adolescent girls. In these organizations, the focus was not on girls' physical appearance but on service projects in the community, building relationships between adolescent girls and adult women, and developing character qualities, including self-control, service to others, and belief in God. Brumberg (1997) observes:

> Whether Christian or Jew, black or white, volunteer or professional, most women in this era shared the ethic that older women had a special responsibility to the young of their sex. This kind of mentoring was based on the need to protect all girls, not just one's own daughters, from premature sexuality and manipulation at the hands of men. Although the ethic generated all kinds of censorious directives about sexual behavior and its consequences . . . it also gave a cooperative and expansive tone to American community life. In towns and cities across the United States, middle-class matrons and young adult women performed countless mundane acts of guidance and supervision, such as showing girls how to sew, embroider, or arrange flowers, or helping them to organize collections of food and clothing for impoverished families. In all of these settings, there were chattering girls along with concerned adults, bound together by both gender and common projects. (pp. 19–20)

Today, in Brumberg's view, adolescent girls are less constricted but also more vulnerable and less integrated into the lives of adult women outside their families.

THINKING CRITICALLY •••

Would it be possible today to reconstruct the "protective umbrella" provided for adolescent girls by adult women in previous times, or would today's adolescent girls find such protection patronizing and overly restrictive?

From Boy to Man

Like gender expectations for adolescent girls, gender expectations for adolescent boys have changed markedly in the past two centuries but have also retained some consistent features. In his book *American Manhood*, historian Anthony Rotundo (1993) describes the transformations that have taken place between the American Revolution and the present in how Americans view the passage from boyhood to manhood.

In Rotundo's account, the 17th and 18th centuries in colonial America were characterized by communities that were small, tightly knit, and strongly based in religion. In this phase of what Rotundo terms **communal manhood**, the focus of gender expectations for adolescent boys was on preparing to assume adult role responsibilities in work and marriage. Rotundo calls this "communal manhood" because preparing for community and family responsibilities was considered more important than striving for individual achievement and economic success. Preparing to become "head of the household" was seen as especially important for adolescent boys because as adult men they would be expected to act as provider and protector of wife and children. Note the striking resemblance to the requirements of manhood in traditional cultures, with the common emphasis on learning to provide and protect.

During the 19th century, as American society became more urbanized, young men became more likely to leave home in their late teens for the growing American cities to make it on their own without much in the way of family ties. Rotundo calls the 19th century the era of **self-made manhood**. This was a time in American history when individualism was growing in strength and males were increasingly expected to become independent from their families in adolescence and emerging adulthood as part of becoming a man, rather than remaining closely interdependent with other family members. Although becoming a provider and protector remained important, an explicit emphasis also developed on the importance of developing the individualistic character qualities necessary for becoming a man. *Decision of character* became a popular term to describe a young man's passage from high-spirited but undisciplined youth to a manhood characterized by self-control and a strong will for carrying out independent decisions (see Kett, 1977).

One interesting historical similarity between gender expectations for young males and females was the creation during the 19th century of a wide range of voluntary organizations that brought young people of the same sex together. The organizations for girls were described above. For males, the organizations included literary societies (where young men would meet to discuss books they had read), debating societies, religious groups, informal military companies, fraternal lodges, and the Young Men's Christian Association (YMCA). Like the organizations for girls, the boys' organizations stressed the importance of developing self-control, service to others, and belief in God. However, the male organizations were less likely to be run by adults and more likely to be run by the adolescents and emerging adults

---

communal manhood Anthony Rotundo's term for the norm of manhood in 17th- and 18th-century colonial America, in which the focus of gender expectations for adolescent boys was on preparing to assume adult male role responsibilities in work and marriage.

self-made manhood Anthony Rotundo's term for the norm of manhood in 19th-century America, in which males were increasingly expected to become independent from their families in adolescence and emerging adulthood as part of becoming a man.

passionate manhood Anthony Rotundo's term for the norm of manhood in the 20th-century United States, in which self-expression and self-enjoyment replaced self-control and self-denial as the paramount virtues young males should learn in the course of becoming a man.

For both boys and girls, voluntary organizations were popular in the 19th century. Shown here are young men at a YMCA.

themselves. Perhaps for this reason, the male organizations tended to involve not just sober camaraderie but occasional boisterous play, rowdy competition, and (in some organizations) fighting and drinking alcohol, in spite of the professed commitment to self-control (Kett, 1977).

Organizations for young males also emphasized strenuous physical activity. Populations in the big cities were growing rapidly, but many men voiced concerns that growing up in a city made boys soft and weak. They advocated activities such as military training, competitive sports, and nature trips for young males because they believed that becoming a man meant becoming tough and strong. As discussed in Chapter 4, the creation of the Boy Scouts arose from this belief.

Rotundo calls the 20th century the era of **passionate manhood**, during which individualism increased still further. Although individualism grew more important in 19th-century American society, adolescent boys were nevertheless expected to learn self-control and self-denial as part of becoming a man, so that they would maintain control over their impulses. In contrast, during the 20th century passionate emotions such as anger and sexual desire became regarded more favorably as part of the manhood ideal. Self-expression and self-enjoyment replaced self-control and self-denial as the paramount virtues young males should learn in the course of becoming a man.

THINKING CRITICALLY •••

Now that you know something about the history of gender expectations for adolescents, how do you think they are likely to change (if at all) in the course of the 21st century, and why?

gender intensification hypothesis Hypothesis that psychological and behavioral differences between males and females become more pronounced at adolescence because of intensified socialization pressures to conform to culturally prescribed gender roles.

Socialization and Gender in the West

So far we have looked at gender socialization in traditional cultures and in American history. What about today's American majority culture and similar cultures in the West? What sort of socialization for gender goes on in these cultures during adolescence? We address this question by looking first at how gender socialization changes from childhood to adolescence. Then we examine American cultural beliefs about gender and gender socialization with respect to family, peers, school, and the media.

The Gender Intensification Hypothesis

Psychologists John Hill and Mary Ellen Lynch (1983; Lynch 1991) proposed that adolescence is a particularly important time in gender socialization, especially for girls. According to their **gender intensification hypothesis**, psychological and behavioral differences between males and females become more pronounced in the transition from childhood to adolescence because of intensified socialization pressures to conform to culturally prescribed gender roles. Hill and Lynch (1983) believe that it is this intensified socialization pressure, rather than the biological changes of puberty, that results in increased differences between males and females as adolescence progresses. Furthermore, they argue that the intensity of gender socialization in adolescence is greater for females than for males and that this is reflected in a variety of ways in adolescent girls' development.

In support of their hypothesis, Hill and Lynch (1983) offered several arguments and sources of evidence. During adolescence, girls become notably more self-conscious than boys about their physical appearance because looking physically attractive becomes an especially important part of the female gender role. Girls also become more interested and adept than boys in forming intimate friendships. To Hill and Lynch this is because adolescents have been socialized to believe that having intimate friendships is part of the female gender role but is inconsistent with the male gender role.

Since Hill and Lynch (1983) proposed this hypothesis, several supporting studies have been presented (Galambos, 2004; Shanahan et al., 2007; Wichstrom, 1999). In one study, boys and girls filled out a questionnaire on gender identity each year in 6th, 7th, and 8th grades (Galambos, Almeida, & Petersen, 1990). Over this two-year period, girls' self-descriptions became more "feminine" (e.g., gentle, affectionate) and boys' self-descriptions became more "masculine" (e.g., tough, aggressive). However, in contrast to Hill and Lynch's (1983) claim that gender intensification is strongest for girls, the pattern in this study was especially strong for boys and masculinity. A more recent study found that among both boys and girls, adolescents embraced gender stereotypes more than younger children did (Rowley et al., 2007). Another study found that increased conformity to gender roles during early adolescence took place primarily for adolescents whose parents influenced them toward gender conformity (Crouter, Manke, & McHale, 1995). This study indicates that gender intensification does not occur equally for all adolescents, but is especially strong among adolescents exposed to family socialization pressures to conform to traditional gender roles.

Cultural Beliefs About Gender

What sort of cultural beliefs about gender exist for adolescents and emerging adults currently growing up in American society? The results of the General Social Survey (GSS), an annual national survey of American adults, show a clear trend toward more egalitarian gender attitudes in recent decades, as Figure 5.2 shows (Cotter et al., 2009). Compared to 1977, American adults today are less likely to believe men are better politicians, less likely to see women as the ones who should take care of the home, more likely to believe working mothers can have warm relationships with their children, and less likely to believe preschoolers would suffer if mothers work.

However, the results of the GSS also show that a considerable proportion of Americans—from about one-fourth to over one-third, depending on the question—continue to harbor beliefs about gender roles not unlike those we have seen in traditional cultures: Men should hold the power and be out in the world doing things, and women should focus on caring for children and running the household. The persistence of traditional gender role beliefs in American society is also indicated in studies of gender socialization and gender stereotypes, as we shall see in the following sections.

Gender Socialization: Family, Peers, and School

The previous chapter described cultural differences in socialization. However, differences in socialization also occur within cultures, especially in the socialization of boys and girls. **Differential gender socialization** is the term for socializing males and females according to different expectations about the attitudes and behavior appropriate to each gender (Burn, 1996; Bussey & Bandura, 2004). We have seen in this chapter how intense differential socialization can be in traditional cultures and how intense it has been in American history. It also continues to exist in the West in more subtle but nevertheless effective forms. We will consider differential gender socialization with respect to family, peers, and school in detail in future chapters, but this section will serve as an introduction.

Differential gender socialization begins early, in virtually every culture. Parents dress their boys and girls differently, give them different toys, and decorate their bedrooms differently. One study found that 90% of the infants observed at an American shopping mall were wearing clothing that was gender-specific in color and/or style (Shakin, Shakin, & Sternglanz, 1985). In a classic experimental study (Sidorowicz & Lunney,

differential gender socialization The term for socializing males and females according to different expectations about what attitudes and behavior are appropriate to each gender.

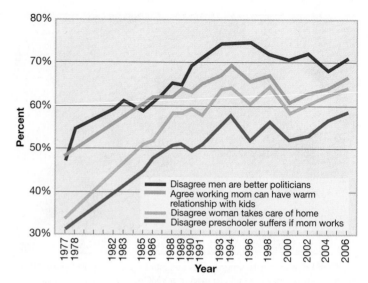

FIGURE 5.2 Changes in American Gender Attitudes, 1977–2006.
Source: General Social Survey (GSS), 1977–2006.

1980), adults were asked to play with a 10-month-old infant they did not know. All adults played with the same infant, but some were told it was a girl, some were told it was a boy, and some were given no information about its gender. There were three toys to play with: a rubber football, a doll, and a teething ring. When the adults thought the child was male, 50% of the men and 80% of the women played with the child using the football. When they thought the child was female, 89% of the men and 73% of the women used the doll in play.

In the course of growing up, children get encouragement from parents, peers, and teachers to conform to gender roles. Numerous studies attest that parents encourage gender-specific activities in their children and discourage activities they see as inconsistent with their child's gender (Bronstein, 2006; Bussey & Bandura, 2004; Lytton & Romney, 1991). In early childhood, most children play almost exclusively with same-sex peers (Maccoby, 2002). Children (especially boys) who deviate from gender norms in play suffer peer ridicule and are less popular than children who conform to gender roles (Maccoby, 2002).

During middle childhood, gender rules often become temporarily more flexible (Basow & Rubin, 1999). However, with the gender intensification of adolescence, differential socialization becomes more pronounced. Parents tend to monitor and restrict adolescent girls more tightly than adolescent boys with respect to where they are allowed to go and with whom (McHale et al., 2003). Peers punish with ridicule and unpopularity the adolescents who deviate from gender role expectations (Eder, 1995; Pascoe, 2007)—the boy who decides to take up the flute, the girl who wears unstylish clothes and no makeup.

With regard to school, research has found that teachers—both males and females—generally reinforce the traditional cultural messages regarding gender (Basow, 2004; Spencer, Porche, & Tolman, 2003). Specifically, teachers often assume that boys and girls are inherently different, with different interests and abilities; that boys are more aggressive and domi-

Why do pressures to conform to traditional gender roles intensify in adolescence?

nant; and that girls are more silent and compliant. Girls have made remarkable gains in academic achievement in recent decades and now exceed boys in nearly every area of school performance (National Center for Education Statistics, 2009; Sommers, 2000). However, the educational and occupational interests and choices of adolescent and emerging adult males and females remain different in some gender-specific ways, with girls more likely to go into traditionally female professions such as nursing and child care and boys more likely to pursue traditionally male professions such as engineering and scientific research (Basow, 2004).

These differences are at least partly a result of gender socialization in the school. For example, Matyas (1987) found that in college classes, professors of math, science, and engineering paid more attention to male students and were more likely to encourage them to become involved in research and to pursue graduate studies. Girls also tend to have less peer support for their science interests than boys do (Stake & Nickens, 2005), which may partly explain why girls are less likely to pursue science education in high school and college. One study found that the gender difference in self-perceptions of possible future occupations became wider from high school through college (Lips, 2004). We will discuss school and gender in more detail in Chapter 10.

The findings about differential socialization at home and at school do not mean that parents and teachers consciously and intentionally treat adolescent girls and boys differently. Sometimes they do, but often differential socialization simply results from the different expectations that parents and teachers have for males and females as a consequence of their own gender socialization (Bronstein, 2006). In their differential gender socialization of adolescent girls and boys, parents and teachers reflect their culture's beliefs about gender, often without even thinking consciously about what they are doing.

THINKING CRITICALLY •••

Based on your experience, give examples of differential gender socialization in childhood, adolescence, and emerging adulthood.

Media and Gender

"I read *Seventeen* magazine and like that's mostly how I got to do all my make-up, just from looking at magazines, looking at models, and seeing how they're doing it. Like I'd sit for two hours doing my make-up for something to do. It was fun."

—Margaret, age 17 (in Currie, 1999, p. 3)

The television shows, movies, and music most popular with adolescents promote many stereotypes about gender, as we will see in Chapter 12 on media. However, magazines are worth discussing here because they are the media form with the most obvious focus on gender socialization, especially the magazines read by adolescent girls. Boys read magazines, too, but their favorite magazines—*Sport*, *Gamepro*, *Hot Rod*, *Popular Science*—are not as clearly gender-focused. For girls, every issue of their favorite magazines is packed with gender-specific messages about how to be an adolescent girl (Massoni, 2004).

What sort of gender messages do adolescent girls get when they read these magazines? Several analyses of the content of girls' magazines have reported highly similar findings (Ballentine & Ogle, 2005; Currie, 1999; Duffy & Gotcher, 1996; Durham, 1998; Evans et al., 1991; Massoni, 2004; Pierce, 1993). One study (Evans et al., 1991) analyzed the content in 10 issues of three magazines for adolescent girls: *Seventeen* (the most popular), *Young Miss*, and *Sassy*. The analysis showed that the magazines relentlessly promote the

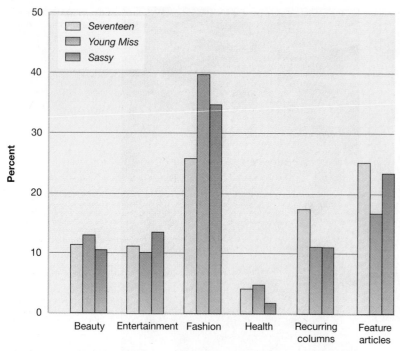

FIGURE 5.3 Content distribution of three teen magazines. The content of girls' magazines strongly emphasizes physical appearance.

Source: Evans et al. (1991).

gender socialization of adolescent girls toward the traditional female gender role. Physical appearance is of ultimate importance, and there is an intense focus on how to be appealing to boys. Figure 5.3 shows the proportion of articles devoted to each of six topics. Fashion was the most common topic in all three magazines, occupying 27% to 41% of the articles. Another 10% to 13% of the articles were devoted to beauty, and most of the articles on "health" (3% to 6%) were about weight reduction and control. Altogether for each of the magazines, from 44% to 60% of the content focused directly on physical appearance.

This percentage actually understates the focus on physical appearance because it does not include the advertisements. In the three magazines taken together, 46% of the space was devoted to advertisements (with a high of 57% in the most popular magazine, *Seventeen*). The ads were almost exclusively for clothes, cosmetics, and weight-loss programs.

In contrast to the plethora of articles and advertisements on physical appearance, there were few articles on political or social issues (although *Sassy* had more than the other two magazines). The main topic of "career" articles was modeling. There were virtually no articles on possible careers in business, the sciences, law, medicine, or any other high-status profession in which the mind would be valued more than the body. Of course, no doubt the magazine publishers would carry an abundance of articles on social issues and professional careers if they found they could sell more magazines that way. They pack the magazines with articles and ads on how to enhance physical attractiveness because that is the content to which adolescent girls respond most strongly.

Why? Perhaps adolescent girls in the West no longer get much direct instruction from older females about becoming

a woman (Brumberg, 1997). With the gender intensification of adolescence, girls become acutely aware that others expect them to look like a girl is supposed to look and act like a girl is supposed to act—but how is a girl supposed to look and act? These magazines promise to provide the answers. The message to adolescent girls is that if you buy the right products and strive to make your appearance conform to the ideal presented in the magazines, you will look and act like a girl is supposed to look and act and you will attract all the boys you want (Ballentine & Ogle, 2005; Durham, 1998; Evans et al., 1991). But you will not necessarily be happy. One recent summary of 47 studies found that the more girls were exposed to appearance magazines, the more they were dissatisfied with their own appearance (Murnen & Levine, 2007).

Analyses of a popular magazine for British girls called *Jackie* show that the content changed substantially beginning in the 1990s, from a previous focus on appearance similar to American magazines to a much different portrayal of girls as strong, responsible, independent thinkers (McRobbie, 1994). But even recent analyses of the most popular magazines for American and Canadian girls show little change in content, with physical appearance and boy-catching still predominant (Ballentine & Ogle, 2005; Currie, 1999; Durham, 1998; Massoni, 2004; Olson, 2007).

Gender Socialization as a Source of Problems

For both girls and boys, the intensified gender socialization they experience in adolescence can be a source of problems. For girls, the focus on physical appearance that is the heart of the female gender role can produce many kinds of distress (Wichstrom, 1999). Girls are more likely than boys to develop a negative body image in adolescence (Grabe et al., 2008; Rosenblum & Lewis, 1999; Siegel, 2002) hardly surprising, given the magazine ideals to which they compare themselves. The emphasis on thinness that is part of the female ideal of physical appearance leads the majority of girls to diet in adolescence (French et al., 1995), and at the extreme, some girls develop serious eating disorders that threaten their health and even their lives (Striegel-Moore & Cachelin, 1999). Adolescent girls who are overweight or regarded by their peers as physically unattractive suffer merciless ridicule (Burns & Farina, 1992; Cash, 1995). This ridicule comes not only from boys but from other girls (Eder, 1995). Even long after adolescence, close to half of adult women are dissatisfied with their physical appearance (Cash & Henry, 1995; Grabe et al., 2008).

For boys, the problem at the core of their gender role in adolescence is aggressiveness (Pollack, 1998). Boys are more aggressive than girls from infancy onward, partly for biological reasons but also because of their gender socialization (Baillergeon et al., 2007; Maccoby, 2002). During adolescence, boys are expected by their peers to be verbally aggressive, directing half-joking insults at other boys on a regular basis (Eder, 1995; Pascoe, 2007). Often these insults involve

Why does aggressiveness become more of a problem for boys in adolescence?

manhood itself; adolescent boys commonly use insults such as "wimp," "weenie," "pussy," and "faggot," calling the manhood of other boys into question. From this we can see that it is not just in traditional cultures that adolescent boys face the intimidating prospect of being regarded as a failed man. They defend themselves by using verbal aggressiveness in return and by being physically aggressive when necessary. Boys who demonstrate physical aggressiveness successfully in sports frequently have the highest status among their peers (Brown, 1990; Brown & Lohr, 1987; Pascoe, 2003, 2007).

A variety of problems stem from this emphasis on aggressiveness in the male role. Aggressiveness is used as a way of establishing social hierarchies among adolescent boys, and low-status boys suffer frequent insults and humiliations from other boys (Eder, 1995; Pascoe, 2007). Furthermore, aggressiveness contributes to problem behaviors in adolescence and emerging adulthood such as vandalism, risky driving, fighting, and crime (Arnett, 1992a; Wilson & Herrnstein, 1985). Joseph Pleck (1983; Pleck, Sonnenstein, & Ku, 1998) has shown that adolescents who value aggressiveness as part of the male gender role are especially likely to engage in problem behavior. In Pleck's analysis of data from a national American study of 15- to 19-year-old boys (Pleck et al., 1998), boys who agreed with statements such as "A young man should be tough, even if he is not big" were more likely than other boys to report school difficulties, alcohol and drug use, and risky sexual behavior. Similar results were found in a recent study of Chinese adolescents (Ma, 2005).

Cognition and Gender

Socialization interacts with cognitive development to produce adolescents' ideas about gender (Bussey & Bandura, 2004). Lawrence Kohlberg, whose ideas about moral development were discussed in Chapter 4, also proposed an influential theory of gender development known as the **cognitive-developmental theory of gender**. Kohlberg (1966) based this theory on Piaget's ideas about cognitive development, applied specifically to gender. According to Kohlberg's theory, gender is a fundamental way of organizing ideas about the world.

By the time children are about 3 years old, they understand **gender identity**; that is, they understand themselves as being either male or female (Renk et al., 2006). Once children possess gender identity, they use gender as a way of organizing information obtained from the world around them. Certain toys become "toys that girls play with," whereas others are "toys that boys play with." Certain clothes become "clothes that boys wear" and others become "clothes that girls wear." By age 4 or 5, children identify a wide range of things as appropriate for either males or females, including toys, clothing, activities, objects, and occupations (Bussey & Bandura, 2004; Serbin, Powlishta, & Gulko, 1993). Furthermore, according to cognitive-developmental theory, children seek to maintain consistency between their categories and their behavior. Kohlberg (1966) called this process **self-socialization**. Boys become quite insistent about doing things they regard as boy things and avoiding things that girls do; girls become equally intent on avoiding boy things and doing things they regard as appropriate for girls (Bussey & Bandura, 2004).

During middle childhood, from about age 6 to 10, children's perceptions of gender roles become more flexible (Basow & Rubin, 1999). Boys and girls alike enjoy sports, music, toys, and games with less concern about whether the activity is appropriate for their gender. Why this change takes place is not clear, but it appears to be due in part to the way adults and peers also become less concerned with enforcing gender norms during this period (Helgeson, 2002). It may be, too, that once gender identity is well-established children no longer find violations of gender norms so unsettling.

However, expectations become more rigid again in early adolescence, as part of the gender intensification process (Basow & Rubin, 1999). In one study, views of gender roles

---

cognitive-developmental theory of gender Kohlberg's theory, based on Piaget's ideas about cognitive development, asserting that gender is a fundamental way of organizing ideas about the world and that children develop through a predictable series of stages in their understanding of gender.

gender identity Children's understanding of themselves as being either male or female, reached at about age 3.

self-socialization In gender socialization, refers to the way that children seek to maintain consistency between the norms they have learned about gender and their behavior.

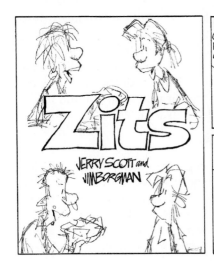

were examined among children and adolescents in grades 4–11 (Alfieri, Ruble, & Higgins, 1996). Students were presented with 12 gender-related terms, 6 "masculine" and 6 "feminine," and asked to indicate whether they thought the items described males, females, or both. The "both" response was defined as indicating greater gender role flexibility. The results indicated that gender role flexibility increased in the younger years and peaked when the participants were in 7th–8th grades, but then became steadily more rigid from that point on, through the end of high school. Boys had especially rigid views of gender roles, especially for masculine traits.

How can cognitive-developmental theory explain these changes? The hallmark of cognitive development in adolescence is formal operations, which includes the development of self-reflection and idealization. As a consequence, reaching adolescence leads to asking oneself questions about what it means to be a woman or a man, and to making judgments about how one measures up to cultural gender expectations. As adolescents become more capable of reflecting on these issues they become more concerned with compliance to gender norms, for themselves and others. Also contributing to greater gender role rigidity in adolescence is the development of sexual maturity, which makes adolescents more conscious of the gender of themselves and others in social interactions. Furthermore, parents and peers exert increased pressure to conform to gender norms (Johnson et al., 1999).

Another cognitive theory of gender that uses Piaget's ideas is **gender schema theory**. Like Kohlberg's cognitive-developmental theory, gender schema theory views gender as one of the fundamental ways that people organize information about the world. (Recall from Chapter 3 that *scheme* is Piaget's term for a structure for organizing and processing information. *Scheme* and **schema** are used interchangeably.)

According to gender schema theory, gender is one of our most important schemas from early childhood onward.

By the time we reach adolescence, on the basis of our socialization we have learned to categorize an enormous range of activities, objects, and personality characteristics as "female" or "male." This includes not just the obvious—vaginas are female, penises are male—but many things that have no inherent "femaleness" or "maleness" and are nevertheless taught as possessing gender—the moon as "female" and the sun as "male" in traditional Chinese culture, or long hair as "female" and short hair as "male" in many cultures, for example.

Gender schemas influence how we interpret the behavior of others and what we expect from them. This well-known story provides an example: "A little boy and his father were in a terrible automobile accident. The father died, but the boy was rushed to the hospital. As the boy was rushed into surgery, the doctor looked down at him and said, 'I cannot operate on this boy—he is my son!'"

How could the boy be the doctor's son, if the father died in the accident? The answer, of course, is that the doctor is the boy's *mother*. But people reading this story are often puzzled by it because their gender schemas have led them to assume the doctor was male. (This story is less effective than it used to be because so many women today are physicians. Try it on someone.) The story that began this chapter is another example. People typically assume the model is female and the photographer is male because their gender schemas lead them to this assumption, then they are surprised when they are wrong. We tend to notice information that fits within our gender schemas and ignore or dismiss information that is inconsistent with them (Helgeson, 2002).

Sandra Bem (1981a, 1993), one of the foremost proponents of gender schema theory, stresses that people apply gender schemas not just to the world around them but to themselves. Once they have learned gender schemas from their culture, they monitor their own behavior and attitudes and shape them so that they conform to cultural definitions

---

gender schema theory Theory in which gender is viewed as one of the fundamental ways that people organize information about the world.

schema A mental structure for organizing and interpreting information.

expressive traits Personality characteristics such as gentle and yielding, more often ascribed to females, emphasizing emotions and relationships.

instrumental traits Personality characteristics such as self-reliant and forceful, more often ascribed to males, emphasizing action and accomplishment.

of what it means to be male or female. In this way, according to Bem, "cultural myths become self-fulfilling prophecies" (1981a, p. 355). Thus, Bem, like Kohlberg, sees gender development as taking place in part through self-socialization, as people strive to conform to the gender expectations they perceive in the culture around them.

THINKING CRITICALLY •••

Give an example of a custom complex for gender—a cultural practice that reflects cultural beliefs related to gender roles in your culture.

Masculinity, Femininity, and Androgyny

"In our health class, the guys and the girls had to switch roles for a day. We were supposed to try to imagine what it's like to be the other one and act that way. The guy I switched with said he thought it would be so much easier to be a girl, because you wouldn't have to worry about knowing what to do or have to be smooth and cool and all that crap. . . . I just couldn't believe he was saying those things, because I always thought how much easier it would be to be a guy. You wouldn't have to worry about how you looked or how you acted. You could do whatever you felt like doing without worrying about your reputation. But he said, of course guys worry about their reputation, but it's the opposite kind of reputation. He said they have to put on this big act about how experienced they are. . . . He worries that he won't do the right thing or say the right thing."

—Penny, 11th grade, New York
(in Bell, 1998, p. 106)

The gender intensification of adolescence means that adolescents increasingly think of themselves and others in terms of what is masculine and what is feminine. But what sort of characteristics and behavior do adolescent boys and girls see as being feminine or masculine? And how is their evaluation of their own femininity and masculinity related to their overall sense of self?

Traits regarded by most members of the American majority culture as masculine or feminine are shown in Table 5.1. These traits are taken from the Bem Sex Role Inventory (BSRI; Bem, 1974), the most widely used measure of gender role perceptions. The BSRI was originally developed on the basis of college students' ratings of the traits most desirable for an American man or woman (Lips, 1993), but since it was developed similar responses have been obtained in studies of other age groups, including adolescents. A cross-national study of young people in 30 countries found similar gender role perceptions across the countries, with remarkable consistency (Williams & Best, 1990).

The items in the scale show a clear pattern. In general terms, femininity is associated with being nurturing (sympa-

TABLE 5.1 Masculine and Feminine Traits (From the Bem Sex Role Inventory)

Masculine	Feminine
Self-reliant	Yielding
Defends own beliefs	Cheerful
Independent	Shy
Athletic	Affectionate
Assertive	Flatterable
Strong personality	Loyal
Forceful	Feminine
Analytical	Sympathetic
Has leadership abilities	Sensitive to others
Willing to take risks	Understanding
Makes decisions easily	Compassionate
Self-sufficient	Eager to soothe hurt feelings
Dominant	Soft-spoken
Masculine	Warm
Willing to take a stand	Tender
Aggressive	Gullible
Acts as a leader	Childlike
Individualistic	Does not use harsh language
Competitive	Loves children
Ambitious	Gentle

Source: Bem (1974).

thetic, compassionate, gentle, etc.) and compliant (yielding, soft-spoken, childlike, etc.). In contrast, masculinity is associated with being independent (self-reliant, self-sufficient, individualistic, etc.) and aggressive (assertive, forceful, dominant, etc.). The difference in traits associated with each gender role has been described by scholars as a contrast between the **expressive traits** ascribed to females and the **instrumental traits** ascribed to males (Lips, 1993; Yaremko & Lawson, 2007).

What adolescents view as masculine or feminine is also reflected in their gender ideals, that is, their views of what their ideal man or woman would be like. Psychologist Judith Gibbons has done cross-cultural studies of adolescents' gender ideals, indicating that adolescents in many different parts of the world have similar views. Gibbons and her colleagues (Gibbons & Stiles, 2004; Stiles, Gibbons, & Schnellman, 1990) have surveyed over 12,000 adolescents aged 11 to 19 in 20 countries around the world, including countries in Europe, Central America, Asia, and Africa. In their survey, adolescents rate the importance of 10 qualities as characteristics of the ideal man or woman.

In nearly all the countries, the most important and least important qualities for the ideal man and the ideal woman were not gender specific after all. The most important quality was being "kind and honest." In contrast, having a lot of money and being popular were rated low as ideal qualities, for both the ideal man and the ideal woman. However, some differences were seen in male and female gender ideals. In all countries it was considered more important for the ideal man to have a good job than for the ideal woman to have one. Also, in nearly all countries being good-looking was viewed as more important for the ideal woman than for the ideal man.

Generally, adolescent boys and girls had similar views of the ideal man and the ideal woman, but there were some differences. Girls were more likely than boys to think it was important for the ideal man to like children. Girls were also more likely to think it was important for the ideal woman to have a good job. In contrast, boys were more likely than girls to think it was important for the ideal woman to be good-looking. Both the similarities and differences in adolescent girls' and boys' views of gender ideals are paralleled in cross-cultural findings of adults' gender ideals (Buss, 1989, 1995, 2001).

But must we think of people as being either masculine or feminine? If an adolescent girl possesses "feminine" traits, does that mean that she must be low on "masculine" traits, and vice versa for boys? Some scholars have argued that the healthiest human personalities contain both masculine and feminine traits. **Androgyny** is the term for the combination of masculine and feminine traits in one person.

The idea of androgyny first became popular in the 1970s (e.g., Bem, 1977; Spence & Helmreich, 1978). The **women's movement** of the 1960s (see Historical Focus box) had led many people in the West to reconsider ideas about male and female roles, and one outcome of this thinking was that it might be best to transcend the traditional opposition of masculine and feminine traits and instead promote the development of the best of each. In this view, there is no reason why a man could not be both independent ("masculine") and nurturing ("feminine"), or why a woman could not be both compassionate ("feminine") and ambitious ("masculine"). Androgynous persons would rate themselves highly on traits from both the "feminine" column and the "masculine" column in Table 5.1.

Advocates of androgyny have argued that being androgynous is better than being either masculine or feminine because androgynous persons have a greater repertoire of traits to draw on in their daily lives (Bem, 1977; Leszczynski & Strough, 2008). In a given situation, it might be better on some occasions to be gentle ("feminine") and on other occasions to be assertive ("masculine"). More generally, it might be best to be ambitious ("masculine") at work and affectionate ("feminine") at home. Advocates of androgyny point to research evidence that androgynous children are more flexible and creative than other children (Hemmer & Klieber, 1981), and that androgynous women are better at saying "no" to unreasonable requests (Kelly et al., 1981). In contrast, highly feminine women have been found to be higher in anxiety and lower in self-esteem (Bem, 1975). One recent study found that androgynous men and women tend to have higher "emotional intelligence" than men and women who are more stereotypically masculine or feminine (Guastello & Guastello, 2003).

But what about adolescents? Is androgyny best for them? Here the answer is more complex. In general, research evidence indicates that in adolescence, androgyny is more likely to be related to a positive self-image for girls than for boys. Androgynous girls generally have a more favorable self-image than girls who are either highly feminine or highly masculine, but highly masculine boys have more favorable self-images than boys who are feminine or androgynous (Markstrom-Adams, 1989; Orr & Ben-Eliahu, 1993).

Why would this be the case? Probably because adolescents' views of themselves are a reflection of how they measure up to cultural expectations. Due in large part to the women's movement, people in the West have become more

PLATONIC FORMS IN THE LATE 20TH CENTURY

LESSON 6: The Wonderful Man, IDEAL VS REAL

IDEAL (WHAT YOU WANT)

REAL (WHAT YOU'RE LUCKY TO GET)

♥ INTELLECTUAL — READS "INTERESTING ARTICLES" IN PLAYBOY
♥ ARTISTIC — OFTEN WEARS MATCHING SOCKS
♥ CONSIDERATE — SPATTERS JUST A BIT; ONLY LEAVES SEAT UP 50% OF THE TIME
♥ INTERESTED IN YOUR MIND — SOMETIMES LOOKS UP FROM YOUR CHEST
♥ FAITHFUL — ONLY LOOKS AT OTHER BABES IN YOUR ABSENCE
♥ HOPELESSLY ROMANTIC — ABLE TO DISTINGUISH BETWEEN CACTUS & ROSE
♥ CLASSY — KEEPS PLAYBOYS HIDDEN
♥ SENSITIVE — NOTICES WHEN YOU CRY
♥ COMMUNICATES WELL — ANSWERS PHONE SOMETIMES
♥ CROSS-CULTURAL — SWEARS IN SPANISH
♥ PROGRESSIVE — KNOWS DIFFERENCE BETWEEN "WOMAN" & "GIRL"
♥ GREAT LOVER — SEX LASTS LONGER THAN CIGARETTE
♥ CLEAN — ONLY HAS HERPES AND IT'S "UNDER CONTROL"
♥ ATHLETIC — GETS HIS OWN SECONDS
♥ LOVES KIDS & PETS — HAD SNAKE HE FED LIVE THINGS TO
♥ GOOD TASTE IN MUSIC — HAS ONE GOOD DYLAN TAPE THAT A FRIEND GAVE HIM

Jennifer Berman ©1989

androgyny A combination of "male" and "female" personality traits.

women's movement Organized effort in the 20th century to obtain greater rights and opportunities for women.

The women's movement, seeking equality of rights and opportunities for women, has a long history in the United States, dating back over a century to the time when women first organized in an effort to gain the right to vote. One especially important period in the history of the women's movement was the 1960s. The 1960s were a time of dramatic social changes in many ways—the civil rights movement, the War on Poverty, and the sexual revolution are examples—and the women's movement was one of these changes. The greatly expanded range of opportunities in education and employment that exist for adolescent girls and emerging adult women today in American society are rooted in the changes in gender role attitudes that were inspired by the women's movement in the 1960s.

Here are some of the key events of the women's movement during this period (Linden-Ward & Green, 1993; Weatherford, 1997):

- 1963: After more than 300 years in existence, Harvard University grants its first degrees to women.

- 1964: The passage of the 1964 Civil Rights Act includes a provision banning discrimination on the basis of sex. First inserted by the bill's opponents in the hopes it would kill the entire legislation, this provision becomes the basis of substantial gains in women's legal rights over the following decades.

- 1966: The National Organization for Women (NOW) is founded. NOW remains the leading organization in the women's movement to this day.

- 1968: Feminists picket the Miss America contest in Atlantic City, New Jersey, carrying signs such as "Cattle Parades Are Degrading to Human Beings." Outside the auditorium, women dump symbols of their treatment as sexual objects into a "freedom trash can"—bras, high-heeled shoes, curlers, makeup, and magazines such as *Cosmopolitan* and *Playboy*. As the winner is crowned, feminists in the balcony unfurl a large banner declaring "Women's Liberation." Because the contest was televised, the protests received enormous attention and greatly expanded public attention— positive and negative—to the women's movement.

- 1970: To commemorate the 50th anniversary of the ratification of the 19th Amendment, which allowed women to vote, NOW sponsors a nationwide strike for women's rights. Thousands of women in cities across the country march for equal rights for women.

Why were emerging adults at the forefront of the women's movement of the 1960s?

Issues related to women in emerging adulthood were part of the women's movement in the 1960s, as the example of the protest at the Miss America contest indicates. Also, many of the movement's most energetic and prominent members were young women. One of the most important books of the period was *Sexual Politics*, by Kate Millett (1970/2000), who was a graduate student at the time she wrote it. A critique of the sexism of American society, the book became a widely discussed best-seller and an inspiration to an entire generation of feminists.

However, the importance of the women's movement of the 1960s for adolescence and emerging adulthood is not only that young people played a part in it but that young women growing up today have far more opportunities and are far less restricted by gender roles than any generation of Americans before them, due substantially to the changes that began during the 1960s. Sexism is still strong in many ways in American society, but young women growing up today have many opportunities in education, occupations, and leisure that their predecessors could only imagine.

favorable toward females who are androgynous. It is regarded more favorably now than it was 40 years ago for females to be ambitious, independent, and athletic, and to possess other "masculine" traits (Brown, 2007). However, males are still expected to avoid being soft-spoken and tender, or to exhibit other "feminine" traits. Adolescents view themselves, and others, in terms of how they fit these cultural gender expectations. It is revealing that not only self-image but also peer acceptance is highest in adolescence among androgynous girls and masculine boys (Massad, 1981; Leszczynski & Strough, 2008). Among emerging adults, too, androgynous females and masculine males are viewed favorably by peers, whereas males who violate gender norms are viewed negatively (Sirin, McCreary, & Mahalik, 2004). For both adolescents and emerging adults, their evaluations of gender-related behavior reflect the expectations and values of their culture.

These patterns also may indicate that for American boys, as for their counterparts in traditional cultures, manhood is a status that is more insecure and fraught with potential failure than womanhood is for girls, so that any mixing of masculine and feminine traits in their personalities is viewed as undesirable and threatening, by themselves and others. Some scholars have also argued that, despite the changes inspired by the women's movement, males continue to have higher status in American society than females. Consequently, for a girl to act more "like a boy" means that her self-image and status among peers improves because she associates herself with the higher-status group—males—whereas for a boy to act more "like a girl" means that his self-image and peer status decline because he is associating himself with the lower-status group—females (Brown, 2007; Unger & Crawford, 1996).

Gender Roles in American Minority Groups

"In terms of the guys, one of the hardest things I see is they need to become tough. You have to save face, you have to argue it out. The lack of tolerance is much more pronounced [than among girls]. The readiness to fight has a lot to do with the environment of our schools and cities."

—Teacher, predominantly African American and Latino high school, Boston (Suarez-Orozco & Qin-Hilliard, 2004)

Gender roles in American minority cultures differ in important ways from gender roles in the majority culture. What kinds of gender role socialization takes place for young people in these cultures?

For African Americans, some scholars have argued that the female role contains a variety of characteristics that reflect the difficult challenges that Black women have faced historically, from the era of slavery to the present. These characteristics include self-reliance, assertiveness, and perseverance (Hooks, 1981; Terrelonge, 1989). Similar strengths are found in Black adolescent girls, who tend to have higher self-esteem and less concern with physical appearance than White girls do (Basow & Rubin, 1999; Vasquez & Fuentes, 1999). One study found that Black adolescent girls often critique and reject the ideals of female attractiveness presented in teen magazines (Duke, 2002).

The gender role of Black men also reflects African American history, but in a different way. Over the centuries, Black men in America have been frequently subjected to insults to their manhood, from their status as property during slavery to their denigration as "boys" (no matter what their age) in some parts of the United States, until recently. Even today, economic conditions in many American cities make it difficult for Black men to fill the male's traditional "provider" role (Wilson, 1987, 1996).

Young black males sometimes adopt the "Cool Pose" as a way of guarding against threats to their manhood.

As a consequence of these humiliations, according to some scholars, many young Black men adopt extreme characteristics of the male role in order to declare their masculinity in spite of the discrimination they experience (Stevenson, 2004). These characteristics include physical toughness, risk taking, and aggressiveness. Richard Majors (1989; Majors & Billson, 1992) describes the "Cool Pose" common to young Black men in urban areas of the United States. The "Cool Pose" is a set of language and behavior intended to display strength, toughness, and detachment. This style is demonstrated in creative, sometimes flamboyant performances in a variety of settings, from the street to the basketball court to the classroom. These performances are meant to convey pride and confidence. According to Majors (1989), although this aggressive assertion of masculinity helps young Black men guard their self-esteem and their dignity, it can be damaging to their relationships because it requires a refusal to express emotions or needs that they fear would make them vulnerable.

In recent years, adult African American men in some urban areas have attempted to provide an alternative ideal of manhood for young men, an ideal that emphasizes responsibility and diligence rather than aggressiveness. In one major project, the United States' oldest African American college fraternity, Alpha Phi Alpha, pairs volunteer alumni in its chapters nationwide with African American boys in high-risk neighborhoods (Alpha Phi Alpha, 2009; Ferrier, 1996). Boys in these neighborhoods typically have no fathers present—overall, nearly 70% of African American children are born to single mothers (U.S. Bureau of the Census, 2009)—and the mentors seek to provide boys with male guidance and positive male role models, as well as assistance and encouragement in their school work. The project features a solemn ceremony in which the boys make the following "Manhood Pledge":

We were born males, not men.

We will become men when we learn the art and science of manhood.

We vow to work to become men, to leave childhood, boyhood behind us.

We vow to seek knowledge of the best way to relate to our-selves, to our Almighty,

To our families, and to the community . . .

We vow to be the positive example of manhood, and Brotherhood,

To be a Brother to Brother,

Brother to Sisters,

And Brother to the community and institutions to which we belong . . .

We vow to live the seven "R's" of Righteousness, Respect, Responsibility, Restraint, Reciprocity, Rhythm, and Redemption.

We know that life is hard work, but we accept that challenge for ourselves, for you, for life, for the future.

Note the religious tone of the pledge, with words such as "Righteousness" and "Redemption." This religious emphasis pervades the program—the boys are required to attend church and to be involved in three church activities—and reflects the strong religiosity of African American culture we discussed in Chapter 4. The program can be seen as an effort to establish an explicit code for manhood, similar to the traditional cultures we discussed earlier in this chapter. Research has not yet been conducted on the outcomes of this project, but studies on other mentoring projects show that they vary greatly in their effectiveness, depending on the characteristics of the program (Rhodes, 2002).

Among Latinos, gender roles have been highly traditional until recently, much along the lines of the traditional cultures described earlier in this chapter (Abreu, Goodyear, Campos, & Newcomb, 2000; Howard et al., 2002; Rivadeneyra & Ward, 2005; Vasquez & Fuentes, 1999). The role of women was concentrated on caring for children, taking care of the home, and providing emotional support for the husband. The Catholic Church has been very strong among Latinos historically, and women have been taught to emulate the Virgin Mary by being submissive and self-denying. The role of men, in contrast, has been guided by the ideology of **machismo**, which emphasizes males' dominance over females. Men have been expected to be the undisputed head of the household and to demand respect and obedience from their wives and children. The traditional aspects of manhood have been strong among Latinos—providing for a family, protecting the family from harm, and procreating a large family (Arciniega et al., 2008).

However, in recent years evidence has emerged that gender expectations among Latinos have begun to change, at least with respect to women's roles. Latina women are now employed at rates similar to Whites, and a Latina feminist movement has emerged (Denner & Guzmán, 2006; Taylor et al., 2007). This movement does not reject the traditional emphasis on the importance of the role of wife and mother, but

seeks to value these roles while also expanding the roles available to Latinas. A recent study found that although Latina adolescent girls are aware of the traditional gender expectations of their culture, they often strive to negotiate a less traditional and more complex and personal form of the female gender role in their relationships with family, peers, and teachers (Denner & Dunbar, 2004).

Like Latinos, Asian American adolescents have often received traditional gender role socialization that their parents brought along to the United States from their culture of origin (Chao, 1994). In addition, Asian Americans are subjected to media stereotypes of Asian American women as submissive and "exotic" (Lee & Vaught, 2003), and of Asian American men as high in intelligence but poor at sports and less masculine than other men. As a result of these stereotypes, Asian American adolescent boys often experience a sense of gender role inferiority (Qin, 2009; Sue, 2005).

Adolescents and emerging adults who are members of American minority cultures are exposed not only to the gender roles of their own culture but also to the gender roles of the majority culture, through school, media, and friends and peers who may be part of the majority culture. This may make it possible for young people in American minority cultures to form a variety of possible gender concepts based on different blends of the gender roles in their minority culture and the gender roles of the larger society. However, moving toward the gender roles of the majority culture often results in conflict with parents who have more traditional views, especially for girls and especially concerning issues of independence, dating, and sexuality (Fuentes & Vasquez, 1999; Qin, 2009). We will discuss this issue further in the chapter on dating and sexuality (Chapter 9).

Gender Stereotypes in Emerging Adulthood

Given the differential gender socialization that people in American society experience in childhood and adolescence, it should not be surprising to find that by the time they reach emerging adulthood they have different expectations for males and females. Most research on gender expectations in adulthood has been conducted by social psychologists, and because social psychologists often use college undergraduates as their research participants much of this research pertains to emerging adults' views of gender. Social psychologists have especially focused on gender stereotypes. A **stereotype** occurs when people believe others possess certain characteristics simply as a result of being a member of a particular group. Gender stereotypes, then, attribute certain characteristics to others simply on the basis of whether they are male or female (Kite et al., 2008). Gender stereotypes can be viewed as one aspect of gender schemas. Gender schemas

---

machismo Ideology of manhood, common in Latino cultures, which emphasizes males' dominance over females.

stereotype A belief that others possess certain characteristics simply as a result of being a member of a particular group.

include beliefs about objects (dresses are "female") and activities (football is "male") as well as people, but gender stereotypes are beliefs specifically about people.

One area of particular interest with regard to emerging adulthood is research on college students' gender stereotypes involving work. Generally, this research indicates that college students often evaluate women's work performance less favorably than men's. In one classic study, Goldberg (1968) asked college women to evaluate the quality of several articles supposedly written by professionals in a variety of fields. Some of the articles were in stereotypically female fields such as dietetics, some were in stereotypically male fields such as city planning, and some were in gender-neutral fields. There were two identical versions of each article, one supposedly written by, for example, "John McKay" and the other written by "Joan McKay." The results indicated that the women rated the articles more highly when they thought the author was a man. Even articles on the "female" fields were judged as better when written by a man. Other studies have found similar results with samples of both male and female college students (Cejka & Eagly, 1999; Paludi & Strayer, 1985). Although not all studies have shown a tendency for men's work to be evaluated more favorably, when differences are found they tend to favor men (Lips, 1993; Top, 1991). Recent studies have continued to find strong gender stereotypes related to work (Johnson et al., 2008; White & White, 2006).

THINKING CRITICALLY •••

Do you think your professors evaluate your work without regard to your gender? Does it depend on the subject area?

However, some studies have also found that when a person's behavior violates stereotypical gender expectations, the result may be a "boomerang effect" that works in their favor (Weber & Crocker, 1983). In one study, college students were presented with photographs supposedly taken by finalists in two photography contests, one for football and one for tennis (Heilman, Martell, & Simon, 1988). Some students were told the photographs were taken by a female finalist, and some were told they were taken by a male finalist; actually, both groups of students were shown the same photographs. In the football photography contest, photos supposedly taken by females were evaluated more highly than photos supposedly taken by males, whereas in the tennis photography contest no gender-related difference in evaluations was found. Because football (unlike tennis) is strongly associated with the male gender role, the researchers concluded that the females in the football contest were **overevaluated** because they had violated gender role expectations.

Similarly, in a study in which students evaluated two female and two male speakers on a strongly female-specific topic, "sex bias in the counseling of women," the male speakers were evaluated more highly (Gilbert, Lee, & Chiddix, 1981). Again, this indicates that an overevaluation of performance resulted from defying gender role expectations. These findings show that gender-related evaluations of performance can be complicated, and often depend on the specific characteristics of the person and on the specific area in which the person is being evaluated.

Gender-related evaluations may also depend on the age of the evaluator. As noted, most studies in this area have been done exclusively on college students, but one recent study compared males who were early adolescents, late adolescents, or college students (Lobel, Nov-Krispin, Schiller, & Feldman, 2004). Participants were given a description of either an average or outstanding male election candidate behaving gender-stereotypically or counter-stereotypically and were asked to indicate their personal election choice, the likelihood that others would choose each candidate, and how successful the candidate would be if he were elected. Adolescents were more likely than the emerging adult college students to favor the gender-stereotypical candidate. No differences were found between the two stages of adolescence. This suggests that gender stereotypes may wane from adolescence to emerging adulthood.

The Persistence of Beliefs About Gender Differences

Although some gender differences exist in adolescence and emerging adulthood with respect to various aspects of development, for the most part the differences are not large. Even when a statistically significant difference exists between males and females, for most characteristics there is nevertheless more similarity than difference between the genders. For example, even if it is true overall that adolescent girls are emotionally closer to their parents than adolescent boys are, there are nevertheless many adolescent boys who are closer to their parents than the typical adolescent girl.

Most human characteristics fall into something resembling what is called a **normal distribution** or a **bell curve**; that is, a small proportion of people rate much higher than most other people, a small proportion rate much lower than most people, but most people fall somewhere in the middle, somewhere around average. Think of height as an example. You may have a friend who is 4 foot 10 inches and another friend who is 6 feet 10 inches, but most of the people you know are probably between 5 and 6 feet tall.

---

overevaluation Evaluating persons favorably because they violate gender norms.

normal distribution or **bell curve** The bell-shaped curve that represents many human characteristics, with most people around the average and a gradually decreasing proportion toward the extremes.

social roles theory Theory that social roles for males and females enhance or suppress different capabilities, so that males and females tend to develop different skills and attitudes, which leads to gender-specific behaviors.

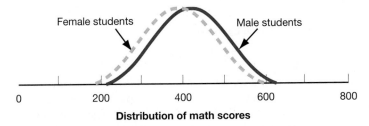

Female students   Male students

| | | | | | | | |
0   200   400   600   800

Distribution of math scores

FIGURE 5.4 Overlap of bell curves. Although the difference in math performance between males and females in this study was statistically significant, there was a great deal of overlap in performance between the two groups.

Source: Benbow & Stanley (1980).

The point, with regard to gender, is that even when gender differences exist between males and females, for most characteristics the portion of the two bell curves that overlaps is much greater than the portion that is distinctive to either gender. (The same is true for children and adults as well as adolescents.) For example, Figure 5.4 shows the distribution of male and female adolescents from a famous study that found a significant gender difference in math performance (Benbow & Stanley, 1980). As you can see, the two distributions overlap far more than they differ. When people hear that "adolescent boys do better at math than adolescent girls," they tend to think of the two distributions as mostly or entirely separate, without realizing that the similarity between the genders is actually greater than the difference between them. Indeed, whenever you read about studies reporting gender differences (including in this textbook), keep in mind that the distributions of males and females usually overlap a great deal (Tavris, 1992).

Why, then, do so many stereotypes about gender persist? Why do so many people continue to think of the genders as radically different in many ways, as "opposite" sexes? Two reasons can be offered. One reason stems from the development of gender schemas. Gender schemas tend to shape the way we notice, interpret, and remember information according to our expectations about the genders. Once we have formed ideas about how males and females are different, we tend to notice events and information that confirm our expectations and disregard or dismiss anything that does not. In several studies of children and adolescents, for example, boys and girls recalled gender-stereotyped people and activities better than those that were nonstereotyped, and this tendency was strongest for the boys and girls who already possessed the strongest gender stereotypes (Furnham & Singh, 1986; Stangor & Ruble, 1987, 1989). Also, studies of college students have found that when they are shown males and females performing an equal number of gender-stereotyped and non–gender-stereotyped behaviors, they consistently overestimate the number of gender-stereotyped behaviors performed (Martin, 1987). These studies illustrate how our gender schemas draw our attention to examples that confirm our expectations, so that we per-

ceive the behavior of others to be more gender consistent than it actually is.

A second reason for the persistence of our beliefs about gender differences in capabilities is that the social roles of men and women seem to confirm those beliefs. According to **social roles theory**, social roles for males and females enhance or suppress different capabilities (Eagly, 1987; Eagly, Wood, & Johannesen-Schmidt, 2004). Differential gender socialization leads males and females to develop different skills and attitudes, which leads to different behaviors. The differences in behavior seem to confirm the appropriateness of the different roles (Davies-Netzley, 2002).

For example, caring for children is part of the female gender role in most cultures, including the American majority culture. In the American majority culture most girls are given dolls as children, and many are given some responsibility for caring for younger siblings. When they reach early adolescence, girls learn that baby-sitting is one of the options available to them as a way to earn money; boys, in contrast, learn that baby-sitting is something girls do but not boys. When they reach emerging adulthood, women are more likely than men to enter child care as a profession, perhaps including majoring in early childhood education in college. When they have children of their own, young women are also more likely than young men to devote themselves to full-time care of their own children.

Thus, as a consequence of differential gender socialization, and because girls grow up seeing child care as a possible future role but boys do not, girls are more likely to develop skills and attitudes that involve caring for children. As a consequence of developing these skills and attitudes, they are more capable of and more interested in devoting themselves to child care in their personal and professional lives as adolescents and emerging adults. The different behavior of women and men regarding child care confirms cultural beliefs that women are "naturally" more loving and nurturant than men. So, we see males and females doing different things, and we conclude that it must be because they are inherently different, overlooking the way their behavior has been shaped by differential gender socialization and by the social roles offered by their culture.

THINKING CRITICALLY •••

Consider the overlapping bell curves of math abilities in adolescence. Then use social roles theory to explain why so few women are in fields such as engineering and architecture.

Gender and Globalization

As today's adolescents grow into adulthood, what kind of world will they face in terms of gender roles? In the West, adolescent girls today have opportunities that were unknown to women in previous eras of Western history. Formal prohibitions no longer exist to women becoming

RESEARCH FOCUS • Meta-Analyses of Gender Differences

Doing research on adolescence and emerging adulthood usually means collecting data through methods such as questionnaires or interviews. However, sometimes a scholar will approach a research question by taking data that other scholars have collected in a variety of studies and combining it into one analysis to obtain an overview of studies in an area. **Meta-analysis** is the term for the statistical technique that integrates the data from many studies into one comprehensive statistical analysis. This technique has been used frequently in research on gender differences (e.g., Friedman, 1989; Grabe et al., 2008; Maccoby & Jacklin, 1974), including gender differences in adolescence (e.g., Baker & Perkins-Jones, 1993). Meta-analysis is used more often in research on gender than in most other areas, partly because so many studies have been published on gender differences. However, it can be used on any topic for which numerous studies exist.

A meta-analysis indicates whether a difference exists between groups (e.g., males and females) and also indicates the size of the difference. The difference between the groups is called the **effect size**, and it is usually represented by the letter d. In a meta-analysis, the effect size is computed for each study by subtracting the mean of one group (e.g., females) from the mean of the other group (e.g., males) and then dividing the result by the within-group standard deviation for the two groups combined (Hyde, 1992). The within-group standard deviation is a measure of how much variability exists within each group. The convention in these analyses is that a d of .20 indicates a small effect size, .50 a medium effect size, and .80 a large effect size (Cohen, 1969). First, d is calculated for each study, and then the ds are averaged across all the studies included in the meta-analysis.

Table 5.2 shows the results of a meta-analysis of gender differences on mathematics achievement tests for 8th-grade adolescents in 19 countries. As you can see, for the most part the effect sizes are very small—only three of the studies found an effect size above .20 in favor of males, and only one found an effect size above .20 in favor of females. Overall, the average effect size for the seven countries where boys' performance was significantly better than girls was .18, and the average effect size for the four countries where girls' performance was significantly better than boys was .16. Thus, the meta-analysis provides a useful overview of cross-national gender differences on math performance and shows that, overall, the differences between boys' and girls' math performance in eighth grade is neither large nor consistent.

TABLE 5.2 National Sex Differences on Eighth-Grade Mathematics Test

Country	Mean for Boys	Mean for Girls	$X_M–X_F$ Difference	Effect Size
Superior Performance of Boys				
France	17.02	14.18	2.84*	.37
Israel	18.79	17.74	1.05*	.11
Luxembourg	13.34	11.74	1.60*	.25
Netherlands	22.00	20.23	1.77*	.17
New Zealand	14.60	13.51	1.09*	.10
Ontario, Canada	17.72	16.94	.78*	.08
Swaziland	9.29	7.89	1.40*	.21
Equal Performance				
British Columbia	19.55	19.27	.28	.03
England-Wales	15.38	14.92	.46	.04
Hong Kong	16.59	16.09	.50	.05
Japan	23.84	23.80	.04	.004
Nigeria	9.50	9.05	.45	.07
Scotland	16.83	16.68	.15	.01
Sweden	10.70	11.18	−.48	−.06
United States	14.98	15.12	−.14	−.01
Superior Performance of Girls				
Belgium-French	19.44	20.54	−1.10*	−.12
Finland	13.24	14.87	−1.63*	−.17
Hungary	22.36	23.62	−1.26*	−.13
Thailand	12.09	14.16	−2.07*	−.22

*Indicates female and male scores were significantly different according to an F test, $p < .01$. Note effect sizes, which are all in the small range.

Source: Baker & Perkins-Jones (1993).

doctors, lawyers, professors, engineers, accountants, athletes, or anything else they wish. As we have seen in this chapter, it is not quite that simple. Direct and indirect gender role socialization often steers adolescent girls away from math- and science-oriented careers. Nevertheless, statistics show definite signs of change. The proportion of females in fields such as medicine, business, and law is considerably higher than 20 years ago (Bianchi & Spain, 1996; Dey & Hurtado, 1999; U.S. Bureau of the Census, 2009) and is remarkable compared with 50 or 100 years ago. Whether similar changes will occur in male-dominated fields such as engineering and architecture is difficult to predict. However, women tend to earn less money than men even when they are doing similar work, which shows that gender equality has a ways to go.

In countries outside the West, for the most part adolescent girls have much less in the way of educational and occupational opportunities, not only compared with boys in their own countries but compared with girls in the West. In most developing countries, adolescent girls are considerably less likely than adolescent boys to go to secondary school (Mensch, Bruce, & Greene, 1998; United Nations, 2009) because adolescents' education requires families to sacrifice the labor of an otherwise potentially productive adolescent (and sometimes families must also pay for the schooling). Families tend to be less willing to make this sacrifice for adolescent girls than for adolescent boys, in part because girls tend to leave the household after marriage, whereas boys often remain within the household or nearby as part of a close extended family.

However, discrimination against girls may change as globalization proceeds and traditional cultures become increasingly industrialized and connected to the global economy. Traditional gender roles are often rooted partly in biological differences that determine the kind of work that men and women can perform in a preindustrial economy. Men's greater size and strength give them advantages in work such as hunting and fishing. Women's biological capacity for childbearing restricts their roles mainly to childbearing and childrearing. When they are unable to control their reproductive lives through contraception, they spend most of their late teens, 20s, and 30s either pregnant or nursing.

As economies become more developed and complex, brain matters more than brawn and men's physical advantage does not apply to work that involves analyzing and processing information. Economic development also usually includes increased access to contraception; in turn, access to contraception makes women's adult roles less focused on childbearing and childrearing alone. Because traditional cultures are likely to continue to move further in the direction of economic development, their gender roles are likely to become more egalitarian as well. There

In traditional cultures, boys are more likely than girls to be able to attend secondary school. Here is a school in Pakistan.

is some evidence that this change is taking place internationally, although it is happening slowly (United Nations, 2009). And there is evidence that adolescents may lead the way, in studies that find adolescents in developing countries have less conservative perceptions of gender roles than adults do (Mensch et al., 1998; United Nations, 2009; Yang, 1986).

SUMMING UP

In this chapter we have examined theories and research concerning the significance of gender in development during adolescence and emerging adulthood. The information in this chapter provides an introduction to many issues concerning gender that will be explored in more detail in the chapters to come. The main points of the chapter are as follows:

- In traditional cultures gender roles tend to be sharply divided, and during adolescence boys' and girls' daily lives are often separate. Girls spend their time with adult women learning skills important for child care and running a household, whereas boys learn the skills necessary for the requirements of the male role: provide, protect, and procreate.

- In earlier periods of American history, adolescent girls were constricted in many ways, but they also benefited

meta-analysis A statistical technique that integrates the data from many studies into one comprehensive statistical analysis.

effect size The difference between two groups in a meta-analysis, represented by the letter d.

from a "protective umbrella" of involvement and concern by adult women. Ideals of manhood have also changed in the course of American history, from "communal manhood" to "self-made manhood" to the "passionate manhood" that is the current ideal.

- In American society today, boys and girls receive differential gender socialization from birth, and gender-related socialization pressures intensify at adolescence. Research shows that pressures to conform to gender expectations come from the family, peers, and teachers. For girls, the magazines they like best relentlessly emphasize physical appearance.

- The cognitive-developmental theory of gender and gender schema theory state that we tend to organize our perceptions of the world according to schemas of male and female, and we categorize a wide range of behavior and objects on this basis.

- Research indicates that there is a widespread tendency across cultures to classify some traits as "feminine" and others as "masculine." Androgyny is the term for combining "feminine" and "masculine" traits within one person. Among adolescents, androgyny tends to be acceptable for girls but not for boys.

- Among emerging adults, gender stereotypes sometimes lead them to evaluate women's work less favorably than men's. However, gender stereotypes appear to be weaker in emerging adulthood than in adolescence.

- Although research generally finds few substantial differences between males and females in most respects, perceptions of gender differences persist, partly because gender schemas are resistant to change once established and partly because males' and females' social roles seem to confirm stereotypes about gender differences in some respects.

- Views of gender have changed substantially in the West in the past century and are likely to change in developing countries in the future as a result of economic development and globalization.

Theories and research have established quite well how gender socialization takes place and have identified the specific influences in adolescence that promote conformity to gender expectations. The evidence also portrays quite vividly the costs that gender expectations exact from adolescents and emerging adults. For girls, the emphasis on physical appearance in adolescence is a frequent source of anxiety and distress. Also, girls are sometimes dissuaded from pursuing certain high-status, high-paying educational and occupational paths because they learn to regard these paths as incompatible with being female; as emerging adults, their work may be regarded less favorably simply because they are female. In traditional cultures, girls are often excluded even from opportunities to attend secondary school.

Adolescent boys face different sorts of gender-based restrictions and obstacles, no less daunting. Boys in traditional cultures have to achieve manhood by developing the required skills for providing, protecting, and procreating. The price of failing to meet these requirements is humiliation and rejection. In the West, gender socialization pressures on boys are less formal but nevertheless formidable. Whatever their personal inclinations, adolescent boys must learn to use verbal and physical aggressiveness to defend themselves against insults to their manhood from other boys. Adolescent boys who cross the gender divide and display "feminine" traits such as sensitivity to the feelings of others risk ridicule and rejection, like their counterparts in traditional cultures.

You might wonder, given the negatives associated with gender socialization in adolescence and emerging adulthood, and given the limitations that gender roles place on the development of young people's potentials, why gender socialization is so highly emphasized and why conformity to gender roles is so highly valued across virtually all cultures and across history as well. Perhaps the answer lies in the ways that gender roles provide us with schemas, with frameworks for understanding how the world works. Because they are just reaching sexual maturity, adolescents and emerging adults are especially eager for information about what their potential mates may find attractive. Gender schemas and gender roles provide them with that information.

Although beliefs about gender may be useful in some ways for making sense of the world, they can also be misleading because they oversimplify the complexity of real life. Remember that any statement about gender differences involves comparing three billion of the world's people to the other three billion. Although overall differences exist between males and females, there is also a tremendous amount of variability within each group on nearly every characteristic. As you think about gender issues in your own life, as you read social science research, and as you read this book, any time you find broad statements about gender characteristics—males are more [fill in the blank] than females, females are more [fill in the blank] than males—it would be wise to keep this in mind and approach such statements with a critical eye.

At this point, we know relatively little about how young people themselves perceive the gender socialization process. Future studies may investigate this question. It may be especially interesting to investigate this question with emerging adults. We have discussed emerging adulthood as a period when explorations of worldviews are common and when critical-thinking skills are more developed than in adolescence. Does this mean that some emerging adults may begin to question the gender expectations of their culture? Do emerging adults feel less constricted by gender roles and more comfortable with androgyny? Or is this true of only some emerging adults, in some peer groups, in some cultures?

KEY TERMS

INTERNET RESOURCES

www.unece.org

Contains the Gender Statistics Database for the United Nations Economic Commission for Europe. Provides gender-related statistics on topics such as education and family.

http://www.un.org/esa/socdev/unyin/wyr07.htm

Contains the 2009 World Youth Report published by the United Nations Department of Economic and Social Affairs, which includes abundant information on gender issues concerning adolescents in developing countries.

FOR FURTHER READING

Brumberg, J. J. (1997). *The body project: An intimate history of American girls.* New York: Random House. A fascinating examination of gender role expectations for girls in the United States over the past 200 years.

Gibbons, J. L., & Stiles, D. A. (2004). *The thoughts of youth: An international perspective on adolescents' ideal persons.* Green-wich, CT: IAP Information Age Publishing. Presents results of the author's 21-country study of adolescents' view of the ideal man and woman. The authors' methods included the creative approach of having the adolescents draw pictures of their ideal man and woman, and they present many of those drawings in the book.

Gilmore, D. (1990). *Manhood in the making: Cultural concepts of masculinity.* New Haven, CT: Yale University Press. Gilmore's superb account of the gender expectations for adolescent boys in a variety of traditional, nonindustrialized cultures.

PEARSON
mydevelopmentlab™

For more review plus practice tests, videos, flashcards, and more, log on to MyDevelopmentLab.

6 The Self

The Catcher in the Rye, by J. D. Salinger (1951/1964), is probably the best-known novel of adolescence. It consists entirely of one long self-reflective monologue by the main character, Holden Caulfield. Holden is talking to someone, but we never learn who the person is—a psychologist, perhaps? He gives a long narrative about a dramatic 24-hour period of his life. It begins when he abruptly leaves the prep school where he had been enrolled, feeling alienated from his schoolmates, sick to death at what he perceives as their hypocrisy and shallowness. Afraid to go home—this is not the first time he has had trouble at school—he instead goes into New York City, where he has a series of misadventures, culminating in a physical and psychological collapse.

Holden tells the whole complicated (and often hilarious) story to the reader through the course of the book. However, it is not really the events that are the focus of Holden's tale but Holden himself. It is about his attempts to understand who he is and how he fits into the world around him, a world he finds confusing, bruising, and sad. He is reluctant to move toward entering the adult world, because nearly all adults seem to him to be pathetic or corrupt. He much prefers the world of children. Throughout the book he expresses his tender and perhaps romanticized view of their innocence and sweetness. His growing self-awareness has come as an unpleasant shock, because in his view it has jarred him out of the Eden of his childhood innocence.

HOLDEN IS NOT A TYPICAL ADOLESCENT. IT IS HIS atypical sensitivity and wit that make him such a compelling character in *The Catcher in the Rye*. Nevertheless, he provides a good example of how issues of the self come to the forefront of development in adolescence. He engages in self-reflection about his maturity, or lack of it ("I act quite young for my age . . ."). He evaluates himself, sometimes negatively ("I'm a terrific liar . . ."). He has moments of elation, but more moments of loneliness and sadness, in which he broods about death and the cruelties of life. He tries to work out issues of identity, of who he is and what he wants out of life, concluding—at least for now—that the only future that appeals to him is the imaginary one of being the "catcher in the rye," the guardian of playing children.

The issues Holden confronts in his monologue are the kinds of issues we will address in this chapter on the self. As we saw in Chapter 3 on cognitive development, moving into adolescence results in new capacities for self-reflection. Adolescents can think about themselves in a way that younger children cannot. The ability for abstract thinking that develops in adolescence includes asking abstract questions about one's self, such as "What kind of person am I? What characteristics make me who I am? What am I good at, and not-so-good at? How do other people perceive me? What kind of life am I likely to have in the future?" Younger children can ask these questions, too, but only in a rudimentary way. With

adolescents' growing cognitive capacities, they can now ask these questions of themselves more clearly, and they can come up with answers that are more complex and insightful.

This enhanced cognitive capacity for self-reflection has a variety of consequences. It means that adolescents change in their *self-conceptions*, that is, in their answers to the question "What kind of person am I?" It means that adolescents change in their *self-esteem*, that is, in their capacity for evaluating their fundamental worth as a person. It means that adolescents change in their *emotional understanding*, as they become more aware of their own emotions and as their enhanced understanding of themselves and others affects their daily emotional lives. It also means that adolescents change in their *identities*, that is, in their perceptions of their capacities and characteristics and how these fit into the opportunities available to them in their society. All of these changes continue through emerging adulthood, but identity issues are especially central to emerging adulthood, even more than in adolescence in many respects.

We will discuss each of these aspects of the self in this chapter, and end with a look at young people's experiences and states of mind when they are alone. First, however, we consider the cultural approach to concepts of the self. Although self-reflection increases in adolescence as a part of normal cognitive development, the culture young people live in has profound effects on how they experience this change.

"All of us, at some moment, have had a vision of our existence as something unique, untransferable, and very precious. This revelation almost always takes place during adolescence. Self-discovery is above all the realization that we are alone: it is the opening of an impalpable, transparent wall—that of our consciousness—between the world and ourselves. It is true that we sense our aloneness almost as soon as we are born, but children and adults can transcend their solitude and forget themselves in games or work. The adolescent, however, vacillates between infancy and youth, halting for a moment before the infinite richness of the world. He is astonished at the fact of his being, and this astonishment leads to reflection: as he leans over the river of his consciousness, he asks himself if the face that appears there, disfigured by the water, is his own. The singularity of his being, which is pure sensation in children, becomes a problem and a question."

—Octavio Paz (1985, p. 9)

Culture and the Self

The general distinction introduced in Chapter 4, between individualistic and collectivistic cultures, and between broad socialization values and narrow socialization values, comes into play in considerations of the self, and perhaps especially on this topic. As noted in Chapter 4, in discussing cultural differences in conceptions of the self, scholars typically distinguish between the *independent self* promoted by individualistic cultures and the *interdependent self* promoted by collectivistic cultures (Cross & Gore, 2003; Markus & Kitayama, 1991; Shweder et al., 2006).

Cultures that promote an independent, individualistic self also promote and encourage reflection about the self. In such cultures it is seen as a good thing to think about yourself, to consider who you are as an independent person, and to think highly of yourself (within certain limits, of course—no culture values selfishness or egocentrism). Americans are especially known for their individualism and their focus on self-oriented issues. It was an American who first invented the term *self-esteem* (William James, in the late 19th century), and the United States continues to be known to the rest of the world as a place where the independent self is valued and promoted (Green, Deschamps, & Páez, 2005; Triandis, 1995).

However, not all cultures look at the self in this way and value the self to the same extent. In collectivistic cultures, characterized by narrow socialization, an interdependent conception of the self prevails. In these cultures, the interests of the group—the family, the kinship group, the ethnic group, the nation, the religious institution—are supposed to come first, before the needs of the individual. This means that it is not necessarily a good thing, in these cultures, to think highly of yourself. People who think highly of themselves, who possess a high level of self-esteem, threaten the harmony of the group because they may be inclined to pursue their personal interests regardless of the interests of the groups to which they belong.

Thus, children and adolescents in these cultures are socialized to mute their self-esteem and to learn to consider the interests and needs of others to be at least as important as the interests and needs of themselves (Lalonde & Chandler, 2004; Whiting & Edwards, 1988). By adolescence, this means that the "self" is thought of not so much as a separate, independent being, essentially apart from others, but as *defined by* relationships with others, to a large extent (Kundu & Adams, 2005). This is what it means for the self to be interdependent rather than independent (Markus & Kitayama, 1991; Nishikawa et al., 2007). In the perspective of these cultures, the self cannot be understood apart from social roles and obligations.

We will learn in more detail about different ways of thinking about the self as we move along in this chapter. Throughout the chapter, keep in mind that cultures vary in the way their members are socialized to think about the self.

THINKING CRITICALLY •••

Based on what you have learned so far in this book, what would you say are the economic reasons traditional cultures would promote an interdependent self?

Self-Conceptions

Adolescents think about themselves differently than younger children do, in a variety of respects. The changes in self-understanding that occur in adolescence have their foundation in the more general changes in cognitive functioning discussed in Chapter 3. Specifically, adolescent self-conceptions, like adolescent cognitive development overall, become more *abstract* and more *complex*.

More Abstract

"The hardest thing is coming to grips with who you are, accepting the fact that you're not perfect—but then doing things anyway. Even if you are really good at something or a really fine person, you also know that there's so much you aren't. You always know all the things you don't know and all the things you can't do. And however much you can fool the rest of the world, you always know how much bullshit a lot of it is."

—Nan, age 17 (in Bell, 1998, p. 78)

According to Susan Harter (1999, 2006a, 2006b), a scholar who has done extensive work on the development of self-conceptions from childhood through adolescence, with increasing age children describe themselves less in concrete terms ("I have a dog named Buster and a sister named Carrie") and more in terms of their traits ("I'm pretty smart, but I'm kind of shy"). For adolescents, self-conceptions become still more trait-focused, and the traits become more abstract, as they describe themselves in terms of intangible personality characteristics. For example, one 15-year-old girl in a study on self-conceptions described herself as follows:

> What am I like as a person? Complicated! I'm sensitive, friendly, outgoing, popular, and tolerant, though I can also be shy, self-conscious, even obnoxious. . . . I'm a pretty cheerful person, especially with my friends. . . . At home I'm more likely to be anxious around my parents. (Harter, 1990b, p. 352)

Notice the use of all the abstractions. "Sensitive." "Outgoing." "Cheerful." "Anxious." Adolescents' capacity for abstraction makes these kinds of descriptions possible.

One aspect of this capacity for abstraction in adolescents' self-conceptions is that they can distinguish between an **actual self** and **possible selves** (Markus & Nurius, 1986; Oyserman & Fryberg, 2006; Whitty, 2002). Scholars distinguish two kinds of possible selves, an ideal self and a feared self (Martin, 1997). The **ideal self** is the person the adolescent would like to be (for example, an adolescent may have an ideal of becoming highly popular with peers or highly successful in athletics or music). The **feared self** is the person the adolescent imagines it is possible to become but dreads becoming (for example, an adolescent might fear becoming an alcoholic, or fear becoming like a disgraced relative or friend). Both kinds of possible selves require adolescents to think abstractly. That is, possible selves exist only as abstractions, as *ideas* in the adolescent's mind.

The capacity for thinking about an actual, an ideal, and a feared self is a cognitive achievement, but this capacity may be troubling in some respects. If you can imagine an ideal self, you can also become aware of the discrepancy between your actual self and your ideal self, between what you are and what you wish you were. If the discrepancy is large enough, it can result in feelings of failure, inadequacy, and depression. Studies have found that the size of the discrepancy between the actual and ideal self is related to depressed mood in both adolescents and emerging adults (Choi & Lee, 1998; Moretti & Wiebe, 1999). Furthermore, the discrepancy between the actual and the ideal self is greater in midadolescence than in either early or late adolescence (Strachen & Jones, 1982). This helps explain why depression is very rare before adolescence, but rates of depressed mood rise in early adolescence and peak in midadolescence (Petersen et al., 1993).

However, awareness of actual and possible selves provides some adolescents with a motivation to strive toward their ideal self and avoid becoming the feared self (Cota-Robles, Neiss, & Hunt, 2000; Markus & Nurius, 1986; Oyserman & Fryberg, 2006). One study of an intervention designed to encourage adolescents to develop an academic possible self found that among the adolescents in the intervention, academic initiative and grades improved while depression and school misbehavior declined, compared to the control group (Oyserman, Bybee, & Terry, 2006).

Emerging adults, too, are often inspired by the vision of a possible self. In fact, one of the distinctive features of emerging adulthood mentioned in Chapter 1 is that it is the "age of possibilities" (Arnett, 2004a). In one Australian study (Whitty, 2002), early emerging adulthood (ages 17–22) was found to be a time of "grand dreams" of being wealthy and having a glamorous occupation, but beyond emerging adulthood (ages 28–33) the visions of a possible self became more realistic, if still optimistic.

Most scholars who have studied this topic see it as healthiest for adolescents to possess both an ideal self and a feared self. One study that compared delinquent adolescents to other adolescents found that the nondelinquent adolescents tended to have this balance between an ideal self and a feared self. In contrast, the delinquent adolescents possessed a feared self but were less likely than other adolescents to have a clear conception of an ideal self to strive for (Oyserman & Markus, 1990).

More Complex

A second aspect of adolescents' self-understanding is that it becomes more complex. Again, this is based on a more general cognitive attainment, the formal operational ability to perceive multiple aspects of a situation or idea. Scholars have found that adolescents' self-conceptions become more complex especially from early adolescence to middle adolescence. Harter (1986) conducted a study in which she asked adolescents in 7th, 9th, and 11th grades to describe themselves. The results showed that the extent to which adolescents described themselves in contradictory ways (e.g., shy and fun-loving) increased sharply from 7th to 9th grade and then declined slightly in 11th grade.

Harter and her colleagues have found that recognizing these contradictions in their personalities and behavior can be confusing to adolescents, as they try to sort out "the real me" from the different aspects of themselves that appear in different situations (Harter, 1999; Harter, Bresnick, Bouchey, & Whitesell, 1997). However, adolescents' contradictory descriptions do not necessarily mean that they are confused

---

actual self A person's perception of the self as it is, contrasted with the possible self.

possible selves A person's conception of the self as it potentially may be. May include both an ideal self and a feared self.

ideal self The person an adolescent would like to be.

feared self The self a person imagines it is possible to become but dreads becoming.

about which of the two contradictory descriptions apply to their actual selves. To some extent, the contradictions indicate that adolescents, more than younger children, recognize that their feelings and their behavior can vary from day to day and from situation to situation (Harter, 1990a). Rather than simply saying "I'm shy" as a younger child might, an adolescent might say "I'm shy when I'm around people I don't really know, but when I'm around my friends I can be kind of wild and crazy."

A related aspect of the increasing complexity of self-conceptions is that adolescents become aware of times when they are exhibiting a **false self**, a self that they present to others while realizing that it does not represent what they are actually thinking and feeling (Harter, 1990a, 2002; Harter, Marold, Whitesell, & Cobbs, 1996; Harter et al., 1997). With whom would you think adolescents would be most likely to exhibit their false selves—friends, parents, or dates? Harter's research indicates that adolescents are most likely to put on their false selves with dating partners, and least likely with their close friends, with parents in between. Most adolescents in Harter's research indicate that they sometimes dislike putting on a false self, but many also say that some degree of false self behavior is acceptable and even desirable, to impress someone or to conceal aspects of the self they do not want others to see.

THINKING CRITICALLY •••

Why do you think a false self is most likely to be shown to dating partners? Would the false self be gradually discarded as the dating partner becomes a boyfriend or girlfriend, or not?

Self-Esteem

Self-esteem is a person's overall sense of worth and well-being. **Self-image, self-concept**, and **self-perception** are closely related terms, referring to the way people view and evaluate themselves. A great deal has been written and discussed about self-esteem in the past 50 years in American society, especially concerning adolescents. In the 1960s and 1970s, self-esteem enhancement programs for young people became popular, based on the idea that making children and adolescents "feel better about themselves" would have a variety of positive effects on other aspects of functioning, such as school achievement and relationships with peers (DuBois, 2003; DuBois & Tevendale, 1999; Harter, 1990b). In the 1980s and 1990s, particular concern developed about self-esteem among girls and about evidence showing that girls

Adolescents are most likely to show a false self to dating partners.

often experience a drop in self-esteem as they enter adolescence (American Association of University Women, 1993; Gilligan, Lyons, & Hanmer, 1990).

All this concern about self-esteem is a distinctly American phenomenon. Americans value high self-esteem to a greater extent than people in other countries (Triandis, 1995), even compared to people in other Western countries, and the gap between Americans and non-Western countries in this respect is especially great (Whiting & Edwards, 1988). For example, in traditional Japanese culture, self-criticism is a virtue and high self-esteem is a character problem (Heine, Lehman, Markus, & Kitayama, 1999). The American concern with self-esteem is part of American individualism (Bellah et al., 1985).

The cultural focus on self-esteem in American society has led to a considerable amount of research on adolescent self-esteem by American scholars in recent decades. This research has shed light on a number of issues, including changes in self-esteem from preadolescence through adolescence, different aspects of self-esteem, self-esteem and physical appearance, and influences on self-esteem.

false self The self a person may present to others while realizing that it does not represent what he or she is actually thinking and feeling.

self-esteem A person's overall sense of worth and well-being.

self-image A person's evaluation of his or her qualities and relations with others. Closely related to self-esteem.

self-concept Persons' views of themselves, usually including concrete characteristics (such as height and age) as well as roles, relationships, and personality characteristics.

self-perception A person's view of his or her characteristics and abilities. Closely related to self-esteem.

baseline self-esteem A person's stable, enduring sense of worth and well-being.

Self-Esteem From Preadolescence Through Adolescence

Several longitudinal studies of self-esteem have followed samples from preadolescence through adolescence or from adolescence through emerging adulthood, and these studies generally find that self-esteem declines in early adolescence, then rises through late adolescence and emerging adulthood (Block & Robins, 1993; Harter, 2006b; O'Malley & Bachman, 1983; Robins et al., 2002). A number of developmental reasons explain why self-esteem might follow the pattern of a decline in early adolescence followed by a rise in late adolescence and emerging adulthood. The "imaginary audience" that we have discussed as part of adolescents' cognitive development can make them self-conscious in a way that decreases their self-esteem when they first experience it in early adolescence (Elkind, 1967, 1985). That is, as adolescents develop the capacity to imagine that others are especially conscious of how they look and what they say and how they act, they may suspect or fear that others are judging them harshly.

And they may be right. Adolescents in Western cultures tend to be strongly peer-oriented and to value the opinion of their peers highly, especially on day-to-day issues such as how they are dressed and what they say in social situations (Berndt, 1996). But as discussed in Chapter 3, their peers have developed new cognitive capacities for sarcasm and ridicule, which tend to be dispensed freely toward any peer who seems odd or awkward or uncool (Eder, 1995; Rosenblum & Way, 2004). So, the combination of greater peer-orientation, greater self-consciousness about evaluations by peers, and peers' potentially harsh evaluations contributes to declines in self-esteem in early adolescence. Self-esteem rises in late adolescence and emerging adulthood as peers' evaluations become less important (Berndt, 1986; Galambos et al., 2006).

On the other hand, the degree of decline in early adolescents' self-esteem should not be exaggerated. Although a substantial proportion of adolescents experience a decline in self-esteem during early adolescence, many others do not. One study followed a sample from 6th grade through 10th grade, and showed that different children have different patterns of change in self-esteem as they move through adolescence (Zimmerman et al., 1997). Figure 6.1 shows the patterns. Self-esteem across the total sample declined only slightly, and only about one third of adolescents (the "high to low" and "low and decreasing" groups) followed a pattern of decline. The majority of adolescents were either consistently high or increased slightly in self-esteem during the period of the study. Other studies have reported similar patterns (Deihl, Vicary, & Deike, 1997; Hirsch & DuBois, 1991; Pahl, Greene, & Way, 2000, 2005).

Diversity in self-esteem also exists among different American ethnic groups. Despite being subject to centuries of slavery, discrimination, and racism, African Americans tend to have higher self-esteem than other ethnic groups, and the difference increases with age from childhood through adolescence and emerging adulthood (Bracly, Bámaca, &

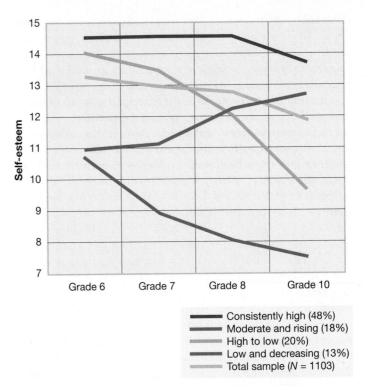

FIGURE 6.1 Trajectories of self-esteem through adolescence.
Source: Zimmerman et al. (1997).

Umaña-Taylor, 2004; Gaylord-Harden et al., 2007; Twenge & Crocker, 2002). White adolescents tend to have higher self-esteem than Latinos, Asian Americans, or Native Americans (Twenge & Crocker, 2002). Asian Americans are often lowest in studies that compare adolescents of different ethnic groups (Rosenblum and Way, 2004). The reasons for these ethnic differences are rooted in cultural differences, with self-esteem promoted most in African American culture and least in Asian American cultures (Greene & Way, 2005). The interdependent self favored in Asian cultures tends to discourage high self-evaluations and encourage a focus on the needs and concerns of others (Heine et al., 1999; Nishikawa et al., 2007).

THINKING CRITICALLY •••

What hypothesis would you propose to explain the ethnic differences in adolescent self-esteem described above? How would you test your hypothesis?

Different Aspects of Self-Esteem

As scholars have studied self-esteem, they have concluded that it has different aspects in addition to overall self-esteem. Morris Rosenberg, the scholar who developed the widely used Rosenberg Self-Esteem Scale, distinguished between baseline self-esteem and barometric self-esteem (Rosenberg, 1986). **Baseline self-esteem** is a person's stable, enduring sense of worth and well-being. People with high baseline self-esteem might have an occasional bad day in which they feel incompetent or self-critical, but still have high baseline self-esteem because most days they evaluate themselves positively. In contrast, people with low baseline self-esteem might continue to have a poor opinion of themselves even though they have some days when things go well and they have positive feelings about themselves.

Barometric self-esteem is the fluctuating sense of worth and well-being people have as they respond to different thoughts, experiences, and interactions in the course of a day. According to Rosenberg, early adolescence is a time when variations in barometric self-esteem are especially intense (Rosenberg, 1986). An adolescent might have a disagreement with a parent over breakfast and feel miserable, then go to school and have some fun with friends before class and feel good, then get back a test in biology with a poor grade and feel miserable again, then get a smile from an attractive potential love interest and feel great—all in just a few hours.

The Experience Sampling Method (ESM) studies, in which adolescents wear beeper watches and record their moods and activities when beeped at random times, confirm Rosenberg's insights by showing just this kind of rapid fluctuation of moods among adolescents in a typical day (Larson & Richards, 1994). ESM studies find that adults and preadolescents experience changes in their moods as well, but not with the same frequency or intensity as adolescents. Other studies confirm that adolescents' self-esteem varies depending on who they are with (Harter, Waters, & Whitesell, 1998). Furthermore, adolescents vary in how much their barometric self-esteem fluctuates, with some relatively stable across time and contexts and some highly variable (Harter & Whitesell, 2003). The more enjoyable and secure their social relationships, the more stable their self-esteem is.

Other aspects of adolescent self-esteem have been investigated by Susan Harter (1989, 1990a, 1990b, 1997, 1999, 2001, 2003, 2006a). Her *Self-Perception Profile for Adolescents* distinguishes the following eight domains of adolescent self-image:

- Scholastic competence
- Social acceptance
- Athletic competence
- Physical appearance
- Job competence
- Romantic appeal
- Behavioral conduct
- Close friendship.

Examples of items from each subscale are provided in the Research Focus box, along with more information about the scale. In addition to the eight subscales on specific domains of self-esteem, Harter's scale also contains a subscale for global (overall) self-esteem.

Harter's research indicates that adolescents do not need to have a positive self-image in all domains to have high global self-esteem. Each domain of self-image influences global self-esteem only to the extent that the adolescent views that domain as important. For example, some adolescents may view themselves as having low athletic competence, but that would influence their global self-esteem only if it was important to them to be good at athletics. Nevertheless, some domains of self-esteem are more important than others to most adolescents, as we will see in the next section.

Self-Esteem and Physical Appearance

Which of Harter's eight aspects of self-image would you expect to be most important in adolescence? Research by Harter and others has found that physical appearance is most strongly related to global self-esteem, followed by social acceptance from peers (DuBois et al., 1996; Harter, 1989, 1990b, 1999, 2001, 2003, 2006a, 2006b; Shapka & Keating, 2005). A similar link between physical appearance and self-esteem has been found for emerging adults (Mendelson, Mendelson, & Andrews, 2000).

Adolescent girls are more likely than boys to emphasize physical appearance as a basis for self-esteem. This gender difference largely explains the gender difference in self-esteem that occurs at adolescence in most Western cultures. Girls have a more negative body image than boys in adolescence and are more critical of their physical appearance. They are less satisfied with the shape of their bodies than boys are, and the majority of them believe they weigh too much and have attempted to diet (Irwin, Igra, Eyre, & Millstein, 1997; Simmons & Blyth, 1987). Because girls tend to evaluate their physical appearance negatively, and because physical appearance is at the heart of their global self-esteem, girls' self-esteem tends to be lower than boys' during adolescence (DuBois et al., 1996; Frost & McKelvie, 2004; Klomsten, Skaalvik, & Espnes, 2004; Shapka & Keating, 2005).

The prominence of physical appearance as a source of self-esteem also helps explain why girls' self-esteem is especially likely to decline as they enter early adolescence. As we have seen in Chapter 2, girls are often highly ambivalent about the changes that take place in their physical appearance when they reach puberty. Reaching puberty means becoming more womanly, which is good, but becoming more womanly means gaining weight in certain places, which is not good in some cultures. Because the physical ideal for American females is so thin, reaching an age where nature promotes rounder body development makes it difficult for adolescent girls to feel good about themselves (Frost &

---

barometric self-esteem The fluctuating sense of worth and well-being people have as they respond to different thoughts, experiences, and interactions in the course of a day.

response bias On a questionnaire, the tendency to choose the same response for all items.

internal consistency A statistical calculation that indicates the extent to which the different items in a scale or subscale are answered in a similar way.

RESEARCH FOCUS • Harter's Self-Perception Profile for Adolescents

The most widely used measure of the self in adolescence is Susan Harter's (1988, 1999, 2003, 2006a, 2006b) Self-Perception Profile for Adolescents. The scale consists of nine sub-scales of five items each, for a total of 45 items. Eight of the subscales assess specific domains of self-image, and the ninth subscale assesses overall ("global") self-worth. The format of the items is to present two statements about "teenagers." The adolescent then selects which of the statements most applies to him or her, and whether the statement is "sort of true for me" or "really true for me." Examples of items from each subscale are shown in Table 6.1.

Notice that for some items, the response that signifies high self-esteem comes first (before the "BUT"), whereas for other items the high self-esteem response comes second (after the "BUT"). The reason for this variation is to avoid a **response bias**, which is the tendency to choose the same response for all items. If the high self-esteem response came first for all items, after a few items an adolescent might start simply checking the first box without reading the item closely. Altering the arrangement of the items helps to avoid a response bias.

Reliability and validity are two qualities sought in any questionnaire. To establish the reliability of the subscales, Harter calculated the **internal consistency** of each one. Internal consistency is

a statistic that indicates the extent to which the different items in a scale or subscale are answered in a similar way. Harter's sub-scales showed high internal consistency, which means that adolescents who reported a positive self-perception on one item of a subscale also tended to report a positive self-perception on the other items of the subscale, and adolescents who reported a negative self-perception on one item of a subscale also tended to report a negative self-perception on the other items.

What about the validity of the scale? Recall from Chapter 1 that the validity of a scale is the extent to which it really measures what it claims to measure. One way to establish validity is to see whether findings using the scale are consistent with findings using other methods. Research using the Harter scale has found that girls rate themselves lower than boys on physical appearance and global self-worth, but higher than boys on close friendships (Harter, 1988, 1999, 2006b). Because these findings are consistent with findings from other studies, the findings appear to support the validity of the Harter scale. However, Harter's research has taken place mostly on adolescents in the American middle class. The measure may not be as valid for adolescents in other cultures, especially in Eastern cultures such as Japan and China, in which it is socially disapproved to evaluate yourself positively (Nishikawa et al., 2007).

TABLE 6.1   Sample Items From the *Self-Perception Profile for Adolescents*

Scholastic Competence

Some teenagers have trouble figuring out the answers in school BUT Other teenagers almost always can figure out the answers.

Social Acceptance

Some teenagers are popular with others their age BUT Other teenagers are not very popular.

Athletic Competence

Some teenagers do not feel that they are very athletic BUT Other teenagers feel that they are very athletic.

Physical Appearance

Some teenagers think that they are good looking BUT Other teenagers think that they are not very good looking.

Job Competence

Some teenagers feel that they are ready to do well at a part-time job BUT Other teenagers feel that they are not quite ready to handle a part-time job.

Romantic Appeal

Some teenagers feel that other people their age will be romantically attracted to them BUT Other teenagers worry about whether people their age will be attracted to them.

Behavioral Conduct

Some teenagers often get in trouble for the things they do BUT Other teenagers usually don't do things that get them in trouble.

Close Friendship

Some teenagers are able to make really close friends BUT Other teenagers find it hard to make really close friends.

Global Self-Worth

Some teenagers are happy with themselves most of the time BUT Other teenagers are often not happy with themselves.

Source: Harter (1988).

> "Girls compare their own bodies to our cultural ideals and find them wanting. Dieting and dissatisfaction with bodies have become normal reactions to puberty. . . . Girls are terrified of being fat, as well they should be. Girls hear the remarks made about heavy girls in the halls of their schools. No one feels thin enough. Because of guilt and shame about their bodies, young women are constantly on the defensive. . . . Almost all adolescent girls feel fat, worry about their weight, diet and feel guilty when they eat."
>
> —Mary Pipher (1994), *Reviving Ophelia: Saving the Selves of Adolescent Girls*, pp. 184–185

McKelvie, 2004; Graber et al., 1994; Keel et al., 1997; Rosenblum & Lewis, 1999). The focus on physical attractiveness as a source of self-esteem is further promoted by the fact that reaching adolescence also means facing evaluations from others as a potential romantic/sexual partner, and for girls especially, physical attractiveness is the primary criterion for this evaluation (Galambos, Almeida, & Petersen, 1990; Hill & Lynch, 1983).

It should be emphasized that the research that has found a decline in girls' self-esteem in adolescence and a gender difference in perceived physical appearance has been mainly on White adolescents. Evidence indicates that African American girls evaluate their physical appearance quite differently than White girls do. In one study of junior high and high school students, 70% of the African American girls were satisfied with their bodies, compared with just 10% of the White girls (Parker et al., 1995). Furthermore, a majority of the African American girls (64%) and very few of the White girls agreed that "it is better to be somewhat overweight than somewhat underweight." This ethnic difference in perceived physical appearance helps explain why White American girls tend to have lower self-esteem than boys in adolescence, whereas in American minority groups the reverse is true (DuBois et al., 1996; Greene & Way, 2005; Mendelson et al., 2000). However, some evidence suggests that Black and Asian young women evaluate themselves according to skin color, with those having relatively dark skin also having negative perceptions of their attractiveness (Bond & Cash, 1992; Sahay & Piran, 1997).

Causes and Effects of Self-Esteem

What leads some adolescents to have high self-esteem and others to have low self-esteem? Feeling accepted and approved by others—especially parents and peers—is the influence identified by theorists and researchers as the most important (DuBois, 2003; Greene & Way, 2005; Farruggia et al., 2004; Harter, 1990b, 1999, 2006a, 2006b). As noted earlier, because peers become especially prominent in the social world of adolescents they gain considerable power over self-

esteem in adolescence compared with earlier ages, but parents are important as well. Although adolescents often spend less time with their parents and have more conflict with them than before adolescence, adolescents' relationships with parents remain crucial (Allen & Land, 1999; Larson & Richards, 1994). If parents provide love and encouragement, adolescent self-esteem is enhanced; if parents are denigrating or indifferent, adolescents respond with lower self-esteem (Berenson, Crawford, Cohen, & Brook, 2005). Approval from adults outside the family, especially teachers, contributes to self-esteem as well (Hill & Holmbeck, 1986).

School success has also been found to be related to self-esteem in adolescence (Bachman & O'Malley, 1986; DuBois & Tevendale, 1999), especially for Asian American adolescents (Szezulski, Martinez, & Reyes, 1994). But which comes first? Do adolescents gain in self-esteem when they do well in school, or does self-esteem directly influence adolescents' performance in school? In the 1960s and 1970s, the predominant belief in American education was that self-esteem is more of a cause of school success than a consequence.

Numerous programs were instituted to try to enhance students' self-esteem, by praising them and trying to teach them to praise themselves, in the hopes that this would raise their school performance. However, scholars eventually concluded that these programs did not work (DuBois, 2003; Harter, 1990b). More recent studies have shown that school success tends to be a cause rather than a consequence of self-esteem (DuBois & Tevendale, 1999; Liu, Kaplan, & Risser, 1992; Rosenberg, Schooler, & Schoenbach, 1989). In fact, adolescents who have inflated self-esteem—that is, they rate themselves more favorably than parents, teachers, and peers rate them—tend to have greater conduct problems in the classroom, compared with their peers (DuBois, 2003; DuBois et al., 1998). The best way to improve adolescents' school-related self-esteem is to teach them knowledge and skills that can be the basis of real achievements in the classroom (Bednar, Wells, & Peterson, 1995; DuBois, 2003).

In other areas of functioning, the question of the effects of self-esteem is controversial, with some scholars claiming that self-esteem has a wide range of effects whereas others argue that, like the findings regarding school performance, functioning in other areas is a cause of self-esteem rather than an effect (see Donnellan et al. [2005] for a discussion of this issue). One study indicates that the effects of self-esteem may depend on which domains are high and which are low (Wild, Flisher, Bhana, & Lombard, 2004). *Low* self-esteem in the family and school domains and *high* self-esteem in the peer domain were associated with multiple risk behaviors in adolescents of both sexes. In a longitudinal study of early adolescents (DuBois & Silverthorn, 2004), low self-esteem at Time 1 predicted associations with deviant peers at Time 2, which was in turn related to risk behavior, but there was no direct association between low self-esteem and risk behavior. These studies reflect the complexity of the relations between self-esteem and adolescents' behavior.

THINKING CRITICALLY •••

Americans generally consider it healthy to have high self-esteem. Is it possible for self-esteem to be too high? If so, how would you be able to tell when that point is reached? Is it subjective, based simply on each person's opinion, or could you define that point objectively?

Self-Esteem in Emerging Adulthood

Although self-esteem tends to decline from preadolescence to adolescence, for most people it rises during emerging adulthood (Galambos, Barker, & Krahn, 2006; Harter, 1999; O'Malley & Bachman, 1983; Roberts, Caspi, & Moffitt, 2001; Schulenberg & Zarrett, 2006). Figure 6.2 shows this pattern. There are a number of reasons why self-esteem increases over this period. Physical appearance is important to adolescents' self-esteem, and by emerging adulthood most people have passed through the awkward changes of puberty and may be more comfortable with how they look. Also, feeling accepted and approved by parents contributes to self-esteem, and from adolescence to emerging adulthood relationships with parents generally improve while conflict diminishes (Arnett, 2003a; Galambos et al., 2006; O'Connor, Allen, Bell, & Hauser, 1996). Peers and friends are also important to self-esteem, and entering emerging adulthood means leaving the social pressure cooker of secondary school, where peer evaluations are a part of daily life and can be harsh (Gavin & Furman, 1989; Pascoe, 2007).

Also, reaching emerging adulthood usually means having more control over the social contexts of everyday life, which makes it possible for emerging adults to emphasize the contexts they prefer and avoid the contexts they find disagreeable, in a way that adolescents cannot. For example,

adolescents who dislike school and do poorly have little choice but to attend school, where poor grades may repeatedly undermine their self-esteem. However, in emerging adulthood they can leave school and instead engage in full-time work that they may find more gratifying and enjoyable, thus enhancing their self-esteem.

The Emotional Self

Among the issues of the self that adolescents confront is how to understand and manage their emotions. One of the most ancient and enduring observations of adolescence is that it is a time of heightened emotions. Over 2,000 years ago, the Greek philosopher Aristotle observed that youth "are heated by Nature as drunken men by wine." About 250 years ago, the French philosopher Jean-Jacques Rousseau made a similar observation: "As the roaring of the waves precedes the tempest, so the murmur of rising passions announces the tumultuous change" of puberty and adolescence. Around the same time that Rousseau was writing, a type of German literature was developing that became known as "*sturm und drang*" literature—German for "storm and stress." In these stories, young people in their teens and early 20s experienced extreme emotions of angst, sadness, and romantic passion. Today, too, most American parents see adolescence as a time of heightened emotional fluctuations (Buchanan et al., 1990; Buchanan & Holmbeck, 1998).

What does contemporary research tell us about the validity of these historical and popular ideas about adolescent emotionality? Probably the best sources of data on this question are the ESM studies (Csikszentmihalyi & Larson, 1984; Larson & Ham, 1993; Larson & Richards, 1994) in which people record their emotions and experiences when they are "beeped" at random times during the day. What makes the ESM method especially valuable for addressing the question

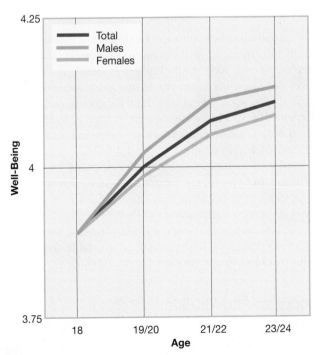

FIGURE 6.2 Self-esteem rises during emerging adulthood.

Source: Monitoring the Future (2003).

Negative moods become more common in adolescence.

of adolescent emotionality is that it assesses emotions at numerous specific moments, rather than having adolescents make an overall judgment of their emotional fluctuations. Furthermore, ESM studies have also been conducted on preadolescents and adults. Thus, if we compare the patterns of emotions reported by the different groups, we can get a good sense of whether adolescents report more extremes of emotions than preadolescents or adults.

The results indicate that they do (Larson, Csikszentmihalyi, & Graef, 1980; Larson & Richards, 1994). Adolescents report feeling "self-conscious" and "embarrassed" two to three times more often than their parents and are also more likely than their parents to feel awkward, lonely, nervous, and ignored. Adolescents are also moodier when compared to preadolescents. Comparing preadolescent 5th graders to adolescent 8th graders, Larson and Richards (1994) describe the emotional "fall from grace" that occurs during that time, as the proportion of time experienced as "very happy" declines by 50%, and similar declines take place in reports of feeling "great," "proud," and "in control." The result is an overall "deflation of childhood happiness" (p. 85) as childhood ends and adolescence begins. This finding is consistent with the decline in self-esteem described previously.

Recent research indicates that brain development may contribute to adolescents' emotionality (Giedd, 2002). In one study comparing adolescents (ages 10–18) to emerging adults and young adults (ages 20–40), participants were shown pictures of faces displaying strong emotions (Baird et al., 1999). When adolescents processed the emotional information from the photos, brain activity was especially high in the amygdala, a primitive part of the brain involved in emotions, and relatively low in the frontal lobes, the part of the brain involved in higher functions such as reasoning and planning. The reverse was true for adults. This seems to indicate that adolescents often respond to emotional stimuli more with the heart than with the head, whereas adults tend to respond in a more controlled and rational way. Studies also indicate that the hormonal changes of puberty contribute to increased emotionality in early adolescence (Susman & Rogol, 2004).

However, most scholars see these emotional changes as due to cognitive and environmental factors more than to biological changes (Buchanan et al., 1992; Susman & Rogol, 2004). According to Larson and Richards (1994), adolescents' newly developed capacities for abstract reasoning "allow them to see beneath the surface of situations and envision hidden and more long-lasting threats to their well-being" (p. 86). Larson and Richards (1994) also argue that experiencing multiple life changes and personal transitions during adolescence (such as the onset of puberty, changing schools, and the first romantic and sexual experiences) contributes to adolescents' emotional volatility. Nevertheless, Larson and Richards (1994) emphasize that it is not just that adolescents experience potentially stressful events but *how* they experience and interpret them that underlies their emotional volatility. Even in response to the same or similar events, adolescents report more extreme and negative moods than preadolescents or adults.

How does emotionality change during the course of adolescence? Larson and Richards assessed their original ESM

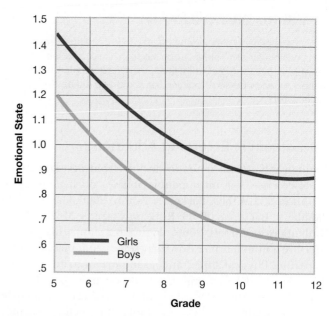

FIGURE 6.3 Decline in average emotional state from grades 5–12. Source: Larson et al., (2002).

sample of 5th–8th graders four years later, in 9th–12th grades (Larson et al., 2002). As Figure 6.3 shows, they found that the decline in positive emotional states continued through 9th and 10th grades and then leveled out. Also, the older adolescents were less volatile in their emotions; that is, the changes in their emotions from one time to the next were less extreme.

THINKING CRITICALLY •••

Adolescent girls have lower overall self-esteem than adolescent boys, yet boys have lower average emotional states than girls do. Is this a contradiction, or is it possible that both these findings could be true?

What about other cultures? Is adolescent emotionality especially an American phenomenon, or does it take place in other cultures as well? Only limited evidence is available to answer this question. However, in one study the ESM method was used with adolescents and their parents in India (Verma & Larson, 1999). The results indicated that, in India as in the United States, adolescents reported more extremes of emotion than their parents did.

Few studies have examined emotionality in emerging adulthood, but one recent longitudinal study found that from age 18 to 25, negative emotions (such as feeling depressed or angry) decrease (Galambos et al., 2006). This finding fits well with the research on self-esteem in showing that for most people the self becomes happier and more stable from adolescence to emerging adulthood (Arnett, 2004a).

Gender and the Emotional Self: Do Adolescent Girls Lose Their "Voice"?

One of the most influential theorists on the self-development of girls in adolescence has been Carol Gilligan. In Chapter 4, we discussed how Gilligan and her colleagues have proposed that adolescent girls and boys tend to think differently about moral issues, with girls emphasizing care and boys emphasizing justice. Gilligan and her colleagues have also argued that there are gender differences in the self in adolescence. They claim that early adolescence is a crucial turning point in self-development, in which boys learn to assert their opinions, whereas girls lose their "voice" and become reticent and insecure (Brown & Gilligan, 1992; Gilligan, 2008; Gilligan, Lyons, & Hanmer, 1990).

In Gilligan's view, from early childhood onward girls and boys differ in their emotional responses to social relationships. She sees girls as more sensitive to the nuances of human relationships from an early age, more observant of the subtleties of social interactions, and more interested in cultivating emotional intimacy in their relationships with others. Girls have a "different voice" than boys, not just in their views of moral issues but in their views of human relationships more generally.

Early adolescence is crucial, according to Gilligan, because it is at this point that girls become aware of an irreconcilable conflict in the gender expectations that the American majority culture has for females. On the one hand, girls perceive that independence and assertiveness are valued in their culture, and that people who are ambitious and competitive are most likely to be rewarded in their education and in their careers. On the other hand, they perceive that their culture values females mainly for their physical appearance and for feminine traits such as nurturance and care for others, and rejects girls and women as selfish when they show the traits the culture rewards most, such as independence and competitiveness. As a result, girls in early adolescence typically succumb to the gender social-

ization of their culture and become more insecure and tentative about their abilities, more likely to mute their voices in an effort to be socially accepted. At the extreme, according to Gilligan, the muting of girls' voices is reflected in an escalation in such problems as depression and eating disorders when girls reach adolescence.

In her views of adolescent girls' emotional development, Gilligan's influence has been profound. Her writings have received a wide audience, not just in the social sciences but also among the general public. A clinical psychologist, Mary Pipher (1994), wrote a book called *Reviving Ophelia* drawing heavily on Gilligan's ideas about the emotional selves of adolescent girls, and it became a best-seller. One of the schools in which Gilligan has conducted her research, a private girls' school in upstate New York, was so impressed by Gilligan's findings that school authorities revised the entire school curriculum in an effort to preserve girls' voices in adolescence by emphasizing cooperation over competition and making special efforts to encourage girls to express themselves.

However, here as in her research in moral development, Gilligan has attracted as many critics as admirers. These critics have argued that Gilligan exaggerates the differences between boys and girls in adolescence (Greene & Maccoby, 1986; Sommers, 2000; Tavris, 1992). For example, it is true that girls' self-esteem declines in early adolescence, but boys' self-esteem declines as well, something Gilligan rarely acknowledges (e.g., DuBois et al., 1996). A related criticism is of Gilligan's research methods. As in her studies of moral development, her studies of gender differences in the self in adolescence have rarely included boys. She studies girls and then makes assumptions about how they differ from the patterns that might be found among boys (e.g., Brown & Gilligan, 1992; Gilligan et al., 1990). Also, she typically presents the results of her research only in the form of excerpts from the interviews she and her colleagues have conducted, and commentaries on those excerpts. Critics find this approach weak methodologically and difficult to judge for reliability and validity (Sommers, 2000).

Although Gilligan's research methods may have certain flaws, other researchers have begun to explore the issues she has raised, using more rigorous methods. In one study, Susan Harter and her colleagues examined Gilligan's idea of losing one's voice in adolescence, but they included boys as well as girls (Harter et al., 1997; Harter, Waters, Whitesell, & Kastelic, 1998). Harter and colleagues gave the adolescents a questionnaire to measure the degree of their "voice" (expressing an opinion, disagreeing, etc.), and another questionnaire to measure the degree of their self-reported masculinity and femininity. The results indicated some support for Gilligan's theory, in that "feminine" girls reported lower levels of "voice" than boys did. In contrast, androgynous girls—those who reported having both masculine and feminine traits—were equal to boys in "voice." However, Harter's research does not support Gilligan's claim that girls' "voice" declines as they enter adolescence (Harter, 1999). Only the more "feminine" girls were lower than boys in "voice," not girls in general.

According to Carol Gilligan, girls risk losing confidence in themselves when they reach adolescence.

Among Erik Erikson's many innovative contributions to the field of human development were his studies in **psychohistory**, which is the psychological analysis of important historical figures. His most extensive works of psychohistory were his analyses of the development of Mohandas K. Gandhi, the leader of the independence movement in India in the mid-20th century, and Martin Luther, the theologian and leader of the Protestant Reformation in the 16th century. His study of Luther is of particular interest for our purposes because he focused on Luther's development during adolescence and emerging adulthood. In fact, the title of his book on Luther is *Young Man Luther* (1958).

According to Erikson, two events were especially important in Luther's identity formation. The first event took place in 1505, when Luther was 21. He was about to begin studying law. Since his childhood, his father had decreed that he would become a lawyer, and he was on the verge of fulfilling his father's dream. However, shortly before beginning his first semester of law school, as he was traveling to the college where he was to be enrolled, he was caught in a severe thunderstorm. A bolt of lightning struck the ground close to where he was taking shelter from the storm and may even have thrown him to the ground. In his terror, he cried out to St. Anne for protection from the storm

Martin Luther as a young man.

and promised that he would become a monk if he survived. The storm abated, and a few days later Luther entered a monastery in accordance with his promise to St. Anne—without informing his father, who was enraged when he learned what Luther had done.

The second event took place 2 years later, when Luther was 23. He was with his fellow monks in the choir of the monastery, listening to a reading from the Bible that described Jesus' cure of a man who was possessed by a demon (Mark 9:17). Suddenly, Luther threw himself to the ground, raving and roaring "It isn't me! It isn't me!" Erikson (and others) interpreted this event as indicating the depth of Luther's fear that he could never eradicate his sense of moral and spiritual inadequacy, no matter what he did, no matter how good a monk he was. By shouting "It isn't me!" Luther "showed himself possessed even as he tried most loudly to deny it" (Erikson, 1958, p. 23). Erikson and others have seen this event as pivotal in Luther's identity development. His sense that nothing he could do would be good enough to make him holy in the eyes of God eventually led him to reject the Catholic Church's emphasis on doing good works to earn entry into heaven and to create a new religious doctrine based on the idea that faith

---

THINKING CRITICALLY •••

Based on your experience and observation, do you agree or disagree with Gilligan's view that girls lose their "voice" in adolescence? Do boys?

Identity

"For me, I'm exploring who I am—trying to find out more who I am, because I'm not really sure any more. Because up till about seventh grade, I was just a kid. I was me and I never really thought

about it. But now I've thought about it a lot more and I'm starting to have to make decisions about who I want to be."

—Conrad, age 13 (in Bell, 1998, p. 72)

One of the most distinctive features of adolescence is that it is a time of thinking about who you are, where your life is going, what you believe in, and how your life fits into the world around you. These are all issues of **identity**. It is the adolescent's nascent capacity for self-reflection that makes consideration of identity issues possible. Adolescents are able to consider themselves in the abstract, in the "third

---

psychohistory The psychological analysis of important historical figures.

identity Individuals' perceptions of their characteristics and abilities, their beliefs and values, their relations with others, and how their lives fit into the world around them.

identity versus identity confusion Erikson's term for the crisis typical of the adolescent stage of life, in which individuals may follow the healthy path of establishing a clear and definite sense of who they are and how they fit into the world around them, or follow the unhealthy alternative of failing to form a stable and secure identity.

and faith alone was enough to make a person worthy and saved before God.

Erikson's study of Luther illustrates several aspects of his theory of identity formation. First, Erikson viewed identity formation as centering on an identity crisis. More recent theorists and researchers tend to use the term *exploration* rather than *crisis* to describe the process of identity formation, but Erikson used the term *crisis* deliberately. As he wrote in *Young Man Luther*:

> Only in ill health does one realize the intricacy of the body; and only in a crisis, individual or historical, does it become obvious what a sensitive combination of interrelated factors the human personality is—a combination of capacities created in the distant past and of opportunities divined in the present; a combination of totally unconscious preconditions developed in individual growth and of social conditions created and recreated in the precarious interplay of generations. In some young people, in some classes, at some periods in history, this crisis will be minimal; in other people, classes, and periods, the crisis will be clearly marked off as a critical period, a kind of "second birth," apt to be aggravated either by widespread neuroticisms or by pervasive ideological unrest. . . . Luther, so it seems, was a rather endangered young man, beset with a syndrome of conflicts. (pp. 14–15)

Thus, Erikson viewed Luther's youth, including the two crisis events described above, as an extreme example of the identity crisis that all adolescents go through in one form or another.

Second, Erikson's study of Luther shows his sensitivity to the cultural and historical context of identity development. Throughout the book, Erikson emphasizes the match between Luther's unusual personality and the historical and cultural circumstances in which he lived. Had Luther grown up in a different time and place, he would have developed a much different identity. In analyzing Luther, Erikson shows the importance in identity development of the person looking inward and assessing his or her individual abilities and inclinations, then looking outward to possibilities available in the social and cultural environment. Successful identity development lies in reconciling the individual's abilities and desires with the possibilities and opportunities offered in the environment.

Third, in describing Luther's development Erikson shows that identity formation reaches a critical point during the identity crisis, but it begins before that time and continues well after. In explaining Luther, Erikson describes not only his adolescence and emerging adulthood but also his childhood, particularly his relationship with his loving but domineering father. Also, Erikson describes how Luther's identity continued to develop through his adulthood. The two key crises took place in his early 20s, but it was not until his early 30s that he broke away from the Catholic Church and established a new religious denomination. In the decades that followed, his identity developed further as he married, had children, and continued to develop his religious ideas.

person," in a way that younger children cannot. During adolescence and continuing through emerging adulthood, explorations are made into various aspects of identity, culminating in commitments that set the foundation for adult life.

Because adolescence and emerging adulthood are crucial periods for identity development, theorists and researchers have devoted a considerable amount of attention to this topic. In this section, we will look first at Erikson's theory of the adolescent identity crisis, then at the research that has been conducted to explore Erikson's theory. After that, we will consider the roles of gender and culture in adolescent identity development, with a special focus on ethnic identity.

Erikson's Theory

Erik Erikson (1902–1994) is one of the most influential scholars in the history of the study of adolescent development. Indeed, he has had a substantial influence on the study of human development from infancy to old age. Drawing on his diverse experience as a teacher, psychoanalyst, ethnographer among Native Americans, and therapist of World War II veterans, he developed a comprehensive theory of human development across the life span. However, the primary focus of Erikson's work was on adolescence, and adolescent development is where he has had his greatest influence.

In Erikson's theory of human development, each period of life is characterized by a distinctive developmental issue or "crisis," as he described in his classic book *Childhood and Society* (Erikson, 1950). Each of these crises holds the potential for a healthy path of development and an unhealthy path. For example, Erikson views infancy as a period of *trust versus mistrust*. Infant development follows a healthy path, in Erikson's theory, when the infant establishes a secure sense of trust with at least one person who can be counted on to provide protection and loving care. The unhealthy path is mistrust, which results from a failure to establish that secure sense of trust.

Each stage of life has a central crisis of this kind, according to Erikson (1950). In adolescence, the crisis is **identity versus identity confusion**. The healthy path in adolescence involves establishing a clear and definite sense of who you are and how you fit into the world around you. The unhealthy alternative is identity confusion, which is a failure to form a stable and secure identity. Identity formation involves reflecting on what your traits, abilities, and interests are, and then sifting through the range of life choices available in your culture, trying out various possibilities, and ultimately making commitments. The key areas in which identity is formed are love, work, and ideology (beliefs and values) (Erikson, 1968). In Erikson's view, a failure to establish commitments in these areas by the end of adolescence reflects identity confusion.

Erikson did not assert that adolescence is the only time when identity issues arise and that once adolescence is over identity issues have been resolved, never to return. Identity issues exist early in life, from the time children first realize they have an existence separate from others, and continue far beyond adolescence as adults continue to ask themselves questions about who they are and how they fit into the world around them. As Erikson observed, "A sense of identity is never gained nor maintained once and for all. . . . It is constantly lost and regained" (1959, p. 118).

Nevertheless, Erikson saw adolescence as the time when identity issues are most prominent and most crucial to development. Furthermore, Erikson argued that it is important to establish a clear identity in adolescence as a basis for initial commitments in adult life and as a foundation for later stages of development. Erikson viewed this as true of all his stages; developing via the healthy path provides a stable foundation for the next stage of development, whereas developing via the unhealthy path is problematic not only in that stage but as an unreliable foundation for the stages to come.

How does an adolescent develop a healthy identity? In Erikson's view, identity formation is founded partly in the **identifications** the adolescent has accumulated in childhood (Erikson, 1968). Children *identify* with their parents and other loved ones as they grow up—that is, children love and admire them and want to be like them. When adolescence comes, adolescents reflect on their identifications, rejecting some and embracing others. The ones that remain are integrated into the adolescent self, combined of course with the adolescent's own individual characteristics. Thus, adolescents create an identity in part by modeling themselves after parents, friends, and others they have loved in childhood, not simply imitating them but integrating parts of their loved ones' behavior and attitudes into their own personality.

Erik Erikson proposed that the central developmental issue of adolescence is identity versus identity confusion.

The other key process that contributes to identity formation, according to Erikson, is exploring various possible life options. Erikson described adolescence as often including a **psychosocial moratorium**, a period when adult responsibilities are postponed as young people try on various possible selves. Thus, falling in love is part of identity formation because during this process you get a clearer sense of yourself through intimate interactions with other persons. Trying out various possible jobs—and, for college students, various possible majors—is part of identity formation, too, because these explorations give you a clearer sense of what you are good at and what you truly enjoy. Erikson saw ideological exploration as part of identity formation as well. "Trying out" a set of religious or political beliefs by learning about them and participating in organizations centered around a particular set of beliefs serves to clarify for adolescents what they believe and how they wish to live. In Erikson's view, the psychosocial moratorium is not characteristic of all societies but only those with individualistic values, in which individual choice is supported (Erikson, 1968).

Most young people in Western societies go through the explorations of the psychosocial moratorium and then settle

---

identifications Relationships formed with others, especially in childhood, in which love for another person leads one to want to be like that person.

psychosocial moratorium Erikson's term for a period during adolescence when adult responsibilities are postponed as young people try on various possible selves.

negative identity Erikson's term for an identity based on what a person has seen portrayed as most undesirable or dangerous.

on more enduring choices in love, work, and ideology as they enter adulthood. However, some young people find it difficult to sort out the possibilities that life presents to them, and they remain in a state of identity confusion after their peers have gone on to establish a secure identity. For many of these adolescents, according to Erikson, this may be a result of unsuccessful adaptation in previous stages of development. Just as identity formation provides the foundation for further development in adulthood, development in childhood provides the basis for development in adolescence. If development in any of the earlier stages has been unusually problematic, then identity confusion is more likely to be the outcome of adolescent development. For other adolescents, identity confusion may be the result of an inability to sort through all the choices available to them and decide among them.

At the extreme, according to Erikson, such adolescents may develop a **negative identity**, "an identity perversely based on all those identifications and roles which, at critical stages of development, had been presented to them as most undesirable or dangerous" (Erikson, 1968, p. 174). Such adolescents reject the range of acceptable possibilities for love, work, and ideology offered by their society, and instead deliberately embrace what their society considers unacceptable, strange, contemptible, and offensive. Youth subcultures such as skinheads and "metalheads" (fans of heavy metal music) have been formed by adolescents who share a negative identity (Arnett, 1996; Roe, 1992).

Research on Identity

Erikson was primarily a theoretical writer and a therapist rather than a researcher, but his ideas have inspired a wealth of research over the past 30 years. One of Erikson's most influential interpreters has been James Marcia (1966, 1980, 1989, 1993, 1994, 1999; Marcia & Carpendale, 2004). Marcia constructed a measure called the Identity Status Interview that classified adolescents into one of four identity statuses: *diffusion, moratorium, foreclosure,* or *achievement*. This system of four categories, known as the **identity status model**, has also been used by scholars who have constructed questionnaires to investigate identity development in adolescence rather than using Marcia's interview (e.g., Adams, 1999; Benson, Harris, & Rogers, 1992; Grotevant & Adams, 1984; Kroger, 2007).

As shown in Table 6.2, each of these classifications involves a different combination of *exploration* and commit-

"Is the sense of identity conscious? At times, of course, it seems only too conscious. For between the double prongs of inner need and inexorable outer demand, the as yet experimenting individual may become the victim of a transitory extreme identity consciousness, which is the common core of the many forms of 'self-consciousness' typical for youth. Where the processes of identity formation are prolonged (a factor which can bring creative gain), such preoccupation with the 'self-image' also prevails. We are thus most aware of our identity when we are just about to gain it and when we (with that startle which motion pictures call a 'double take') are somewhat surprised to make its acquaintance; or, again, when we are just about to enter a crisis and feel the encroachment of identity confusion."

—Erik Erikson (1968), p. 165

ment. Erikson (1968) used the term **identity crisis** to describe the process through which young people construct their identity, but Marcia and other current scholars prefer the term *exploration* (Adams et al., 1992; Grotevant, 1987; Kroger, 2007; Marcia & Carpendale, 2004; Waterman, 1992, 2007). Crisis implies that the process inherently involves anguish and struggle, whereas exploration implies a more positive investigation of possibilities.

Identity diffusion is a status that combines no exploration with no commitment. For adolescents in identity diffusion, no commitments have been made among the choices available to them. Furthermore, no exploration is taking place. The adolescent at this stage is not seriously attempting to sort through potential choices and make enduring commitments.

TABLE 6.2   The Four Identity Statuses

		Commitment	
		Yes	No
Exploration	Yes	Achievement	Moratorium
	No	Foreclosure	Diffusion

---

identity status model An approach to conceptualizing and researching identity development that classifies people into one of four identity categories: foreclosure, diffusion, moratorium, or achievement.

identity crisis Erikson's term for the intense period of struggle that adolescents may experience in the course of forming an identity.

identity diffusion An identity status that combines no exploration with no commitment. No commitments have been made among the available paths of identity formation, and the person is not seriously attempting to sort through potential choices and make enduring commitments.

Identity moratorium involves exploration but no commitment. This is a stage of actively trying out different personal, occupational, and ideological possibilities. This classification is based on Erikson's (1968) idea of the psychosocial moratorium, discussed earlier. Different possibilities are being tried on, sifted through, some discarded and some selected, in order for adolescents to be able to determine which of the available possibilities are best suited to them.

Adolescents who are in the **identity foreclosure** classification have not experimented with a range of possibilities but have nevertheless committed themselves to certain choices—commitment, but no exploration. This is often a result of their parents' strong influence. Marcia and most other scholars tend to see exploration as a necessary part of forming a healthy identity, and therefore see foreclosure as unhealthy. We will discuss this issue further shortly.

Finally, the classification that combines exploration and commitment is **identity achievement**. Identity achievement is the classification for young people who have made definite personal, occupational, and ideological choices. By definition, identity achievement is preceded by a period of identity moratorium in which exploration takes place. If commitment takes place without exploration, it is considered identity foreclosure rather than identity achievement.

Two findings stand out from the many studies that have been conducted using the identity status model. One is that adolescents' identity status tends to be related to other aspects of their development (Berzonsky, 1992; Kroger, 2003, 2007; Swanson, Spencer, & Petersen, 1998). The identity achievement and moratorium statuses are notably related to a variety of favorable aspects of development. Adolescents in these categories of identity development are more likely than adolescents in the foreclosure or diffusion categories to be self-directed, cooperative, and good at problem solving. Adolescents in the achievement category are rated more favorably in some respects than adolescents in the moratorium category. As you might expect, moratorium adolescents are more likely than achievement adolescents to be indecisive and unsure of their opinions (Marcia, 1980).

In contrast, adolescents in the diffusion and foreclosure categories of identity development tend to have less favorable development in other areas as well (Abu-Rayya, 2006; Adams, 1999; Josselson, 1989; Kroger, 2003; Waterman, 2007). Diffusion is considered to be the least favorable of the identity statuses and is viewed as predictive of later psychological problems (Marcia, 1980; Meeus, Iedema, Helsen, & Vollebergh, 1999). Compared with adolescents in the achievement or moratorium statuses, adolescents in the diffusion status are lower in self-esteem and self-control. Diffusion status is also related to high anxiety, apathy, and disconnected relationships with parents.

The foreclosure status is more complex in its relation to other aspects of development (Papini et al., 1989; Phinney, 2000). Adolescents in the foreclosure status tend to be higher on conformity, conventionality, and obedience to authority than adolescents in the other statuses (Kroger, 2003). These are generally considered negative outcomes by researchers from Western majority cultures, although they are virtues in many non-Western cultures (Heine et al., 1999; Shweder et al., 2006). Also, adolescents with the foreclosure status tend to have especially close relationships with their parents, which may lead them to accept their parents' values and guidance without going through a period of exploration as adolescents with the achievement status have done (Phinney, 2000). Again, this is sometimes portrayed as negative by psychologists who believe it is necessary to go through a period of exploration in order to develop a mature identity, but this view rests partly on values that favor individualism and independent thinking.

The other prominent finding in research on identity formation is that it takes longer to reach identity achievement than scholars had expected. In fact, for most young people this status is reached—if at all—in emerging adulthood or beyond rather than in adolescence. Studies that have compared adolescents from ages 12 through 18 have found that, although the proportion of adolescents in the diffusion category decreases with age and the proportion of adolescents in the identity achievement category increases with age, even by early emerging adulthood less than half are classified as having reached identity achievement (Christopherson, Jones, & Sales, 1988; Kroger, 2003; Meeus et al., 1999; van Hoof, 1999; Waterman, 1999). An example of this pattern, reported in an American study (Waterman, 1999), is shown in Figure 6.4. Similar findings were reported in a study of 12- to 27-year olds in the Netherlands (Meeus et al., 1999).

Studies of college students find that progress toward identity achievement also takes place during the college years, but mainly in the specific area of occupational identity rather than for identity more generally (Waterman, 1992). Some studies indicate that identity achievement may come faster for emerging adults who do not attend college, perhaps because in the college environment young people's ideas about themselves are challenged and they are encouraged to question previously held ideas (Arehart & Smith, 1990; Lytle, Bakken, & Romig, 1997; Munro & Adams, 1997). However, even for noncollege emerging adults, the majority have not reached identity achievement by age 21 (Kroger, 1999, 2003; Waterman, 1999).

---

identity moratorium An identity status that involves exploration but no commitment, in which young people are trying out different personal, occupational, and ideological possibilities.

identity foreclosure An identity status in which young people have not experimented with a range of possibilities but have nevertheless committed themselves to certain choices—commitment, but no exploration.

identity achievement The identity status of young people who have made definite personal, occupational, and ideological choices following a period of exploring possible alternatives.

postmodern identity A conception of identity as complex and as highly variable across contexts and across time.

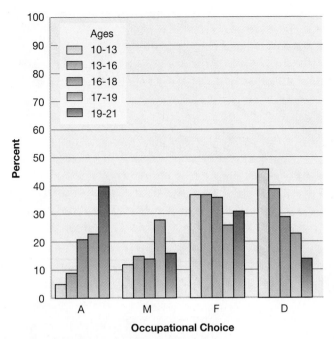

FIGURE 6.4 Changes in identity status with age.

The numbers indicate the percentage of people in each identity status category at each age. A = Achievement, M = Moratorium, F = Foreclosure, D = Diffusion.

Source: Waterman (1999).

Emerging adulthood is now regarded by many identity researchers as an especially important time for identity development (Coté, 2006). Even 40 years ago, Erikson observed that it was taking longer and longer for young people in industrialized societies to achieve identity formation. He commented on the "prolonged adolescence" that was becoming increasingly common in such societies and how this was leading to a prolonged period of identity formation, "during which the young adult through free role experimentation may find a niche in some section of his society" (1968, p. 156). Considering the changes that have taken place since Erikson made this observation in the 1960s, including much higher ages of marriage and parenthood and longer education, Erikson's observation applies to far more young people today than it did then (Coté, 2000, 2006). Indeed, the conception of emerging adulthood as a distinct period of life is based to a considerable extent on the fact that, over recent decades, the late teens and early 20s have become a period of "free role experimentation" for an increasing proportion of young people (Arnett, 2000a, 2004a, 2007a). The achievement of an adult identity comes later, compared with earlier generations, as many emerging adults use the years of their late teens and early 20s for identity explorations in love, work, and ideology.

Critiques and Elaborations of Identity Theory and Research

Erikson's theory has dominated identity theory and research for over half a century, and like any long-standing theory it has been critiqued and modified over time. Three of the most prominent critiques have been a critique of the identity status model, a gender critique, and a cultural critique. Two important elaborations of identity theory and research have been the study of ethnic identity among minority groups and the analysis of how globalization influences identity development. The following sections explore each of these topics.

The Identity Status Model: A Postmodern Perspective In recent years, the identity status model has come under increasing criticism from scholars who view it as a narrow and outdated model of identity formation (Coté, 2000; Schacter, 2005a, 2005b; Schwartz, 2005; van Hoof, 1999; van Hoof & Raaijmakers, 2003). According to these critics, identity is not nearly as stable and unitary as the identity status model portrays it, nor does identity development proceed through a predictable set of stages that culminate in identity achievement some time in late adolescence or emerging adulthood. On the contrary, in this view, the most common form of identity today is the **postmodern identity**, which is composed of diverse elements that do not always form a unified, consistent self.

The postmodern identity changes across contexts, so that people may show a different identity to friends, family, coworkers, and others. It also changes continuously, not just in adolescence and emerging adulthood but throughout the life course, as people add new elements to their identities and discard others. As noted in Chapter 1, a similar theme has been sounded by globalization theorists, who have argued that young people around the world increasingly develop a complex identity that combines elements from their culture and the global media culture and that changes as these cultures change (Arnett, 2002a; Giddens, 2000; Hermans & Kempen, 1998). The identity status model continues to dominate research on identity development in adolescence and emerging adulthood, but the postmodern critique may lead to new methods that will expand our understanding of identity issues.

THINKING CRITICALLY •••

Which better fits your own sense of identity, the identity status model or the postmodern identity theory? How would you devise a study to test the claims of the postmodern identity theorists?

Gender and Identity Another critique of identity theory and research concerns the role of gender. Erikson has been the subject of theoretical critiques for being biased toward male development (Gilligan, 1982; Miller, 1976; Sorell & Montgomery, 2001). Erikson believed that to some extent "anatomy is destiny," meaning that there are sex differences in psychological development, including identity development, that are based on biological sex differences (Erikson, 1950, 1968). Specifically, he believed that women's biology, represented by the "inner space" of the uterus and the capacity for bearing children, makes them oriented toward relationships with others, whereas men's biology, represented by the penis, makes them oriented toward independent, instrumental activity. With regard to adolescence, in Erikson's theory forming an identity means becoming separate and independent from others. Consequently, according to Carol Gilligan (1982) and others, Erikson presents the male goal of striving for an independent identity in adolescence as the healthy standard for normal development. In contrast, females' simultaneous emphasis on relationships with others is a less desirable deviation from normal development (Archer, 1992; Sorell & Montgomery, 2001).

However, defenders of Erikson, and even many of his feminist critics, argue that in his descriptions of females as relational and males as active and instrumental he was simply reflecting the social conditions of the time when he first developed his ideas, the mid-20th century (Archer, 2002; Kroger, 2002; Sorell & Montgomery, 2001, 2002). Also, scholars now agree that independence and connectedness are often balanced differently in males' and females' sense of identity—that is, more toward independence for males, more toward connectedness for females—not because of biological sex differences, as Erikson believed, but because of culturally based differences in gender role socialization, beginning at birth and continuing throughout life (Gilligan, 1982; Josselson, 1992; Sorell & Montgomery, 2001, 2002).

What does the research say? Some studies have found gender differences in identity formation, especially in relation to occupational exploration (Kroger, 2007; Waterman, 1992). That is, some evidence suggests that females are more willing than males to constrain their occupational exploration to maintain their relationships (Archer, 1989; Cooper & Grotevant, 1987; Marcia, 1993; Patterson et al., 1992). For example, females might be less willing than males to take advantage of an educational or occupational opportunity that would require them to move a great distance because that would mean leaving their parents, their friends, and perhaps their romantic partner.

In Erikson's theory, this means that intimacy is often a higher priority than identity for females, whereas for males identity tends to come before intimacy (Gilligan, 1982; Lytle et al., 1997; Miller, 1991; Scheidel & Marcia, 1985; Surrey, 1991). According to Erikson, **intimacy versus isolation** is the central issue of young adulthood. Establishing intimacy means uniting your newly formed identity with another person in an intimate relationship. The alternative is isolation, characterized by an inability to form an enduring intimate relationship. Research on the relation between identity and intimacy has often focused on gender differences. Most studies indicate that developmental processes of forming an identity and establishing intimacy take place simultaneously for females, whereas males tend to achieve identity before intimacy (Lytle et al., 1997; Miller, 1991; Surrey, 1991).

intimacy versus isolation Erikson's term for the central issue of young adulthood, in which persons face alternatives between committing themselves to another person in an intimate relationship or becoming isolated as a consequence of an inability to form an enduring intimate relationship.

Intimacy issues may arise alongside identity issues for some young women.

Culture and Identity Erik Erikson's cultural background was diverse—he was the son of Danish parents, raised in Germany, and spent most of his adult life in the United States—and he was acutely aware of the relation between culture and identity formation. He spent time as an ethnographer among the Sioux and Yurok tribes of Native Americans, and he devoted a chapter in *Childhood and Society* (1950) to adolescent identity development in these tribes. Nevertheless, virtually all of the research inspired by Erikson's theory has taken place among White middle-class adolescents in the United States. What can we say about identity development among adolescents in other cultures?

One observation that can be made is that, although Erikson sought to ground his theory in historical and cultural context (Erikson, 1950, 1968; Kroger, 2002), his discussion of identity development nevertheless assumes an independent self that is allowed to make free choices in love, work, and ideology. The focus of Erikson's identity theory is on how young people develop an understanding of themselves as unique individuals. However, as we have discussed, this conception of the self is distinctively Western and is historically recent (Baumeister, 1987; Markus & Kitiyama, 1991; Shweder et al., 2006; Sorell & Montgomery, 2001). In most cultures until recently, the self has been understood as interdependent, defined in relation to others, rather than as independent. Even today, Erikson's assertions of the prominence of identity issues in adolescence may apply more to modern Western adolescents than to adolescents in other cultures.

A related cultural observation is that the psychosocial moratorium, the period of exploration that Erikson viewed as a standard part of identity formation, is considerably more

Identity explorations are often limited in traditional cultures, especially for girls. Here, girls in Zambia cultivate a field.

possible in some cultures than others (Arnett, 2006a; Sorell & Montgomery, 2001). In today's industrialized societies, there are few pressures on young people to become economic contributors in childhood or adolescence. Young people in these societies are generally allowed a long psychological moratorium in adolescence and emerging adulthood to try out various possible life choices in love, work, and ideology. However, the experience of adolescence is often much different in traditional cultures. Explorations in love are clearly limited or even nonexistent in cultures where dating is not allowed and marriages are either arranged by parents or strongly influenced by them. Explorations in work are limited in cultures where the economy is simple and offers only a limited range of choices.

Limitations on exploration in both love and work are narrower for girls in traditional cultures than for boys. With regard to love, as noted in Chapter 4, some degree of sexual experimentation is encouraged for adolescent boys in most cultures, but for girls sexual experimentation is more likely to be restricted or forbidden (Whiting et al., 1986). With regard to work, in most traditional cultures today and for most of human history in every culture, adolescent girls have been designated by their cultures for the roles of wife and mother, and these were essentially the only choices open to them (Mensch et al., 1998).

In terms of ideology, too, a psychosocial moratorium has been the exception in human cultures rather than the standard. In most cultures, young people have been expected to grow up to believe what adults teach them to believe, without questioning it. It is only in recent history, and mainly in industrialized Western countries, that these expectations have changed and that it has come to be seen as desirable for adolescents and emerging adults to think for themselves, decide on their own beliefs, and make their life choices independently (Arnett, 1998a; Bellah et al., 1985).

For modern young people in the West, then, identity development is a longer and more complex process than in the past and compared with traditional cultures. As we will see later in this chapter, this is increasingly true for the rest of the world as well, as industrialization increases worldwide and as

Western values of individualism influence traditional cultures through globalization (Arnett, 2002a; Schlegel, 2000; Suárez-Orozco, 2004).

Ethnic Identity

In discussing identity, we have noted that in Erikson's theory the three key areas of identity formation are love, work, and ideology. For a large and growing proportion of adolescents in industrialized societies, one aspect of ideology is beliefs about what it means to be a member of an ethnic minority within a society dominated by the majority culture. Scholarly attention to this topic has increased in recent years as immigration from developing countries to industrialized societies has grown and as scholars have begun to devote greater attention to cultural issues in development (Berry et al., 2006; Phinney, 1990, 2000, 2006).

Like other identity issues, issues of ethnic identity come to the forefront in adolescence because of the cognitive capacities that adolescents develop (Pahl & Way, 2006; Portes, Dunham, & Castillo, 2000; Wong, 1997). One aspect of the growing capacity for self-reflection among adolescents who belong to ethnic minorities is likely to be a sharpened awareness of what it means for them to be a member of their minority group. Group terms such as *African American, Chinese Canadian,* and *Turkish Dutch* take on a new meaning as adolescents can now think about what these terms mean and how the term for their ethnic group applies to themselves. Also, as a consequence of their growing capacity to think about what others think about them, adolescents become more acutely aware of the prejudices and stereotypes that others may hold about their ethnic group.

Because adolescents and emerging adults who are members of ethnic minorities have to confront such issues, identity development is likely to be more complex for them than for those who belong to the majority culture (Phinney, 2000, 2006; Phinney & Alipuria, 1987). Consider, for example, identity development in the area of love. Love—along with dating and sex—is an area where cultural conflicts are especially likely to arise for adolescents who are members of

TABLE 6.3 Four Possible Ethnic Identity Statuses

		Identification With Ethnic Group	
		High	**Low**
Identification with Majority Culture	**High**	Bicultural	Assimilated
	Low	Separated	Marginal

Examples

Assimilation: "I don't really think of myself as Asian American, just as American."

Separation: "I am not part of two cultures. I am just Black."

Marginality: "When I'm with my Indian friends, I feel White, and when I'm with my White friends, I feel Indian. I don't really feel like I belong with either of them."

Biculturalism: "Being both Mexican and American means having the best of both worlds. You have different strengths you can draw from in different situations."

Source: Based on Phinney & Devich-Navarro (1997).

ethnic minorities. Part of identity development in Western majority cultures means trying out different possibilities in love by forming emotionally intimate relationships with different people and gaining sexual experience. However, this model is in sharp conflict with the values of many ethnic minority groups. In most Asian American groups, for example, recreational dating is disapproved and sexual experimentation before marriage is considered disgraceful—especially for females (Miller, 1995; Qin, 2009; Talbani & Hasanali, 2000; Wong, 1997). Similarly, among Latinos, gaining sexual experience in adolescence is considered wrong for girls, and they are often highly restricted by their parents and their brothers to prevent any violation of this norm (Inclan & Herron, 1990). Young people in these ethnic groups face a challenge in reconciling the values of their ethnic group on such issues with the values of the majority culture, to which they are inevitably exposed through school, the media, and peers (Markstrom-Adams, 1992; Miller, 1995; Qin, 2009; Phinney & Rosenthal, 1992).

How, then, does identity development take place for young people who are members of minority groups within Western societies? To what extent do they develop an identity that reflects the values of the majority culture, and to what extent do they retain the values of their minority group? One scholar who has done extensive work on these questions among American minorities is Jean Phinney (1990, 2000, 2006; Phinney & Alipuria, 1987; Phinney & Devich-Navarro, 1997; Phinney & Rosenthal, 1992). On the basis of her research, Phinney has concluded that adolescents who are members of minority groups have four different ways of responding to their awareness of their ethnicity (Table 6.3).

Assimilation is the option that involves leaving behind the ways of one's ethnic group and adopting the values and way of life of the majority culture. This is the path that is reflected in the idea of American society as a "melting pot" that blends people of diverse origins into one national culture. **Marginality** involves rejecting one's culture of origin but also feeling rejected by the majority culture. Some adolescents feel little identification with the culture of their parents and grandparents, nor do they feel accepted and integrated into American society. **Separation** is the approach that involves associating only with members of one's own ethnic group and rejecting the ways of the majority culture. **Biculturalism** involves developing a dual identity, one based in the ethnic group of origin and one based in the majority culture. Being bicultural means moving back and forth between the ethnic culture and the majority culture, and alternating identities as appropriate.

Which of these ethnic identity statuses is most common among minority adolescents? The bicultural status is the most common status among Mexican Americans and Asian Americans, as well as among some European minority groups such as Turkish adolescents in the Netherlands (Neto, 2002; Phinney, Dupont, et al., 1994; Rotheram-Borus, 1990; Verkuyten, 2002). However, separation is the most common ethnic identity status among African American adolescents, and marginality is pervasive among Native American adolescents (see the Cultural Focus box). Of course, each ethnic group is diverse and contains adolescents with a variety of different ethnic identity statuses.

Adolescents tend to be more aware of their ethnic identity when they are in the minority. For example, in one study,

assimilation In the formation of an ethnic identity, the approach that involves leaving the ethnic culture behind and adopting the ways of the majority culture.

marginality In the formation of ethnic identity, the option that involves rejecting one's culture of origin but also feeling rejected by the majority culture.

separation In the formation of ethnic identity, the approach that involves associating only with members of one's own ethnic group and rejecting the ways of the majority culture.

biculturalism In the formation of ethnic identity, the approach that involves developing a dual identity, one based in the ethnic group of origin and one based in the majority culture.

hybrid identity An identity that integrates elements of various cultures.

Adolescents with a bicultural ethnic identity are able to alternate their identities depending on the group they are with.

Latino adolescents attending a predominately non-Latino school reported significantly higher levels of ethnic identity than adolescents in a predominately Latino or a balanced Latino/non-Latino school (Umaña-Taylor, 2005). Recently, Phinney (2006, 2008) has proposed that emerging adulthood may be an especially important time for developing ethnic identity because emerging adults often enter new contexts (new schools, new jobs, perhaps new living situations) that may involve greater contact with people outside their ethnic group and thus sharpen their awareness of their ethnic identity.

Is a strong ethnic identity related to other aspects of development in adolescence and emerging adulthood? The answer to this question is complex. Some studies have found that ethnic identity status is unrelated to characteristics such as self-esteem, grades in school, and social competence (Rotheram-Borus, 1990). However, some recent studies have found that adolescents who are bicultural or assimilated have higher self-esteem (e.g., Farver, Bhadha, & Narang, 2002). Furthermore, recent research has found that having a strong ethnic identity is related to a variety of other favorable aspects of development, such as overall well-being, academic achievement, and lower rates of risk behavior (Giang & Wittig, 2006; McMahon & Watts, 2002; St. Louis & Liem, 2005; Yasui et al., 2005; Yip & Fuligni, 2002).

Some scholars have argued that, for African American adolescents in particular, cultivating pride in their ethnic identity is an important part of their identity formation, especially in a society where they are likely to experience discrimination because of the color of their skin (Spencer & Markstrom-Adams, 1990; Ward, 1990). However, other scholars have argued that promoting ethnic identity may lead adolescents to adopt a separation identity that cuts them off from the majority culture in a way that inhibits their personal growth (Phinney & Rosenthal, 1992). These scholars express concern that some minority adolescents may come to define themselves in opposition to the majority culture—developing a negative identity, in Erikson's (1968) terms—in a way that may interfere with developing a positive identity of their own.

The separation response is, at least in part, a result of the discrimination and prejudice that minorities often face in American society and that young people become more fully aware of as they reach adolescence. Their awareness of discrimination may also increase with the length of time their family has been in the United States. An interesting finding in this research is that foreign-born adolescents tend to believe in the American ideal of equal opportunity more than minority adolescents whose families have been in the United States for a generation or more (Phinney, DuPont et al., 1994; Suarez-Orosco & Suarez-Orozco, 1996). This suggests that recent immigrants may expect that they or their children will become assimilated into the great American melting pot, but after a generation or two many of them come up against the realities of ethnic prejudice in American society, leading to more of a separation identity. African American adolescents tend to be more in favor of separation than adolescents from other ethnic groups (Phinney, Devich-Navarro et al., 1994), perhaps because most of them are from families who have been in the United States for many generations and who have experienced a long history of slavery, racism, and discrimination (Hemmings, 1998).

Identity and Globalization

One identity issue that has risen in prominence in recent years is how globalization influences identity, especially for adolescents and emerging adults. Two aspects of identity stand out as issues related to globalization (Arnett, 2002a). First, as noted in Chapter 1, because of globalization more young people around the world now develop a bicultural identity, with one part of their identity rooted in their local culture while another part stems from an awareness of their relation to the global culture. For example, India has a growing, vigorous high-tech economic sector, led largely by young people. However, even the better-educated young people, who have become full-fledged members of the global economy, still mostly prefer to have an arranged marriage, in accordance with Indian tradition (Verma & Saraswathi, 2002). They also generally expect to care for their parents in old age, again in accordance with Indian tradition. Thus they have one identity for participating in the global economy and succeeding in the fast-paced world of high technology, and another identity, rooted in Indian tradition, that they maintain with respect to their families and their personal lives.

Although developing a bicultural identity means retaining a local identity alongside a global identity, there is no doubt that many cultures are being modified by globalization, specifically by the introduction of global media, free market economics, democratic institutions, increased length of formal schooling, and delayed entry into marriage and parenthood (Jensen, 2008; Larson et al., 2010). These changes often alter traditional cultural practices and beliefs, and may lead less to a bicultural identity than to a **hybrid identity**, integrating local culture with elements of the global culture (Hermans & Dimaggio, 2007; Hermans & Kempen, 1998).

Increasing immigration is one of the forces promoting globalization (Hermans & Dimaggio, 2007; Jensen, 2008),

Native American young people exhibit greater difficulties in many respects than any other American minority group (Goldston et al., 2008; Markstrom, 2008). They have the highest prevalence rates for use of alcohol, cigarettes, and illicit drugs (O'Connell et al., 2007; Wallace et al., 2003). They have the highest school dropout rate and the highest teenage pregnancy rate (Garwick et al., 2008). Especially alarming is the suicide rate among Native American young people aged 15 to 24, which is three times as high as the rate for Whites (Goldston et al., 2008). Suicide is the leading cause of death among young Native Americans. Native Canadians (also known as First Nations peoples) are similar to Native Americans in their levels of substance use, school dropout, teenage pregnancy, and suicide (Chandler et al., 2004).

To a large extent, scholars view the difficulties of Native American young people as rooted in problems of the self (Katz, 1995; Lefley, 1976; Markstrom, 2008). The self-esteem of Native American adolescents tends to be substantially lower than that of other ethnic groups (Dinges, Trimble, & Hollenbeck, 1979; Dodd, Nelson, & Hofland, 1994; Liu et al., 1994). Young Native Americans have also been found to have problems forming an identity in adolescence and emerging adulthood, as they attempt to reconcile the socialization of their Native American cultures with the influences and demands of the dominant White majority culture (Dodd et al., 1994; Lefley, 1976; Liu et al., 1994).

The explanation for problems of the self among young Native Americans is partly historical and partly contemporary. In historical terms, during the 19th century Native American cultures were decimated and finally overcome by the spread of European American settlement into the vast areas of the United States that Native American tribes once dominated (Tveskov, 2008). The devastation of their cultures was deep and thorough, as they were betrayed repeatedly by the U.S. government, killed in large numbers, forced to leave their homelands, and ultimately herded onto reservations in the most desolate parts of the country. This alone would be enough to explain substantial disruption to their cultural life to the present day, with consequent effects on the socialization and development of their young people.

In the 20th century, additional government practices added to and prolonged the cultural destruction suffered by Native Americans. For most of the century, Native American children were forced to attend schools run not by the adults of their community but by the Bureau of Indian Affairs (BIA), a federal agency. The goal of these schools was complete assimilation of Native American children and adolescents into the ways of the majority culture—and, correspondingly, the annihilation of their attachment to their own culture's beliefs, values, knowledge, and customs (Unger, 1977). Often, these schools were boarding schools where the children lived during the school year, completely isolated from their families and communities.

Given these conditions, and given that constructing the self requires a cultural foundation (Shweder et al., 2006), many Native American young people found it difficult to construct a stable and coherent self. These educational practices finally changed in the 1970s, when federal legislation was passed giving Native Americans substantial control over their schools (John, 1998). Still, like the effects of losing their lands and being forced to enter reservations a century ago, the damage from

and identities become even more complicated for young people who are immigrants. They may develop identities that combine their native culture, the local culture to which they have immigrated, and the global culture, along with various hybrids, leading to a multicultural identity or a complex hybrid identity. Furthermore, people living in a culture to which immigrants have come may incorporate aspects of the immigrants' culture into their own identities. Thus for an increasing number of the world's young people, as Hermans and Kempen (1998) observe, "Different and contrasting cultures can be part of a repertoire of collective voices playing their part in a multivoiced self" (p. 1118).

A second identity-related consequence of globalization is that it seems to be leading to an increase in identity confusion—a marginalized identity, in Phinney's scheme—among young people in traditional cultures. As local cultures change in response to globalization, most young people manage to adapt to the changes and develop a bicultural or hybrid identity that provides the basis for living in their local culture and also participating in the global culture. For some young people, however, adapting to the rapid changes taking place in their cultures is more difficult. The images, values, and opportunities they perceive as being part of the global culture undermine their belief in the value of local cultural practices. At the same time, the ways of the global culture seem out of reach to them, too foreign to everything they know from their direct experience. Rather than becoming bicultural, they may experience themselves as marginalized, excluded from both their local culture and the global culture, truly belonging to neither.

Identity confusion among young people may be reflected in problems such as depression, suicide, and substance use. A variety of cultures have experienced a sharp increase in suicide and substance use among their young people since their rapid move toward joining the global culture (Arnett, 2002a; Burbank, 1988; Condon, 1987; Leichty, 1995; Rubinstein, 1995). This increase in these problems seems to indicate the difficulty that some young people in traditional cultures experience in forming a stable identity in the context of the rapid social changes caused by globalization.

the cultural annihilation practices of the schools has endured in Native American cultures.

Today, threats to the selves of Native American young people remain from the historical legacy of cultural destruction and from the bleak conditions they face as they look ahead to adulthood. The legacy of cultural destruction makes it difficult for them to form a bicultural identity; Native American cultures and the American majority culture are not easily combined because for many young Native Americans accepting White society even as part of a bicultural identity would amount to betraying their own people in light of the suffering they have endured at the hands of Whites (Deyhle, 1995). At the same time, government practices undermining Native American cultural socialization over the 20th century were effective, so that many young people no longer share their culture's traditional beliefs or know much about their culture's traditional way of life. As Deyhle (1998) observes, "On the one hand, due to the racism against [Native Americans] in the Anglo community and youth's insistence on cultural integrity, the Anglo world is not available to them. On the other hand, the traditional lives of their ancestors no longer exist" (p. 6).

Thus, many young Native Americans find themselves with a marginal ethnic identity status, alienated from both the majority culture and their own culture, living between two worlds and at home in neither. Conditions in their communities are grim—rates of poverty and unemployment among Native Americans are exceptionally high (John, 1998)—but the predominantly White majority culture does not accept them and is not accepted by them. Their high rates of substance use, school leaving, teenage pregnancy, and suicide reflect their difficulties in con-

The self-development of young Native Americans is often fraught with difficulties.

structing a self under these conditions. Although some recent hopeful signs have been seen—for example, in rising rates of college enrollment—overall, young Native Americans' prospects remain formidably bleak.

Young people in traditional cultures may develop a bicultural or hybrid identity in response to globalization. Here, a young man in India reads Harry Potter.

Whether this means that young people in traditional cultures are more likely than young people in the West to experience identity confusion remains to be studied.

The Self, Alone

One of the reasons that adolescents are able to engage in the frequent self-reflection that allows them to consider their self-conceptions, self-esteem, emotional states, and identity is that they are often by themselves. Studies of time use among American adolescents indicate that they spend about one fourth of their time alone, which is more time than they spend with either their families or their friends (Larson, Csikszentmihalyi, & Graef, 1982; Larson & Richards, 1994).

The ESM studies provide some interesting data on adolescents' experiences of being alone (Larson et al., 1982; Larson & Richards, 1994). These studies find that a substantial proportion of adolescents' time alone is spent in their bedrooms, with the door closed. Is this a lonely time for them? Yes, but it also has benefits. During their time alone their moods tend to be low—they are more likely than at other times to report feeling weak, lonely, and sad. However, after a period alone their mood tends to rise. Larson and Richards (1994) conclude that adolescents use their time alone for self-reflection and mood management. They listen to music, they lie on their beds, they groom themselves in the mirror, they brood, they fantasize. When their time alone is done, they tend to feel restored, ready to face the slings and arrows of daily life again.

Larson and Richards (1994) provide a revealing example of one adolescent girl's experience of being alone. She was alone about one fourth of the times she was beeped, the typical rate. Often, she reported feeling lonely during her times alone. She brooded over her looks, she brooded over how all the girls except herself seemed to have a boyfriend. Yet, she wrote, "I like to be by myself. I don't have to be worried or aggravated by my parents. I have noticed that when I'm alone I feel better sometimes." Then she added, in large print, "*!NOT ALWAYS!*," reflecting her ambivalence (Larson & Richards, 1994, p. 102).

Being alone can be constructive, then, as long as an adolescent does not have too much of it. Studies have found that adolescents who spend an unusually high proportion of their time alone tend to have higher rates of school problems, depression, and other psychological difficulties (Achenbach & Edelbrock, 1986; Larson & Richards, 1994). However, the same studies have found that adolescents who are rarely alone also have higher rates of school problems and depression. A moderate amount of time alone can be healthy for adolescents because, as Larson and Richards (1994) observe,

Adolescents spend more time by themselves than with family or friends.

"After a long day in which their emotions are played upon by peers, teachers, and family members, a measured period of time by themselves, to reflect, regroup, and explore, may be just what they need" (p. 103).

Just as being alone does not necessarily mean being lonely, a person can be lonely even when among others. Robert Weiss (1973) made an important and influential distinction between two types of loneliness, social loneliness and emotional loneliness. **Social loneliness** occurs when people feel that they lack a sufficient number of social contacts and relationships. In contrast, **emotional loneliness** occurs when people feel that the relationships they have lack sufficient closeness and intimacy. Thus, social loneliness reflects a deficit in the *quantity* of social contacts and relationships, whereas emotional loneliness reflects a deficit in the emotional *quality* of a person's relationships (Adams et al., 1988; Asher et al., 1990; DiTommaso & Spinner, 1997; Larson, 1990). Young people may experience either or both of these types of loneliness in their teens and early 20s.

Emerging adulthood is a period when time alone is especially high (Incavou, 2002). According to time use studies across the life span, young people aged 19 to 29 spend more of their leisure time alone than any persons except the elderly, and more of their time in productive activities (school and work) alone than any other age group under 40 (Larson, 1990). Emerging adults have also been found

social loneliness Condition that occurs when people feel that they lack a sufficient number of social contacts and relationships.

emotional loneliness Condition that occurs when people feel that the relationships they have lack sufficient closeness and intimacy.

Emotional loneliness is common in the first year of college, even though college students are often around other people.

to report greater feelings of loneliness than either adolescents or adults (Rokach, 2000), and there are good reasons why these years would be lonelier. Most emerging adults move out of the home by age 18 or 19 (Goldscheider & Goldscheider, 1999) to go to college or just to live independently. This move may have many advantages, such as giving emerging adults more independence and requiring them to take on more responsibility for their daily lives, but it also means that they are no longer wrapped in the relative security of the family environment. They may be glad to be on their own in many ways, but nevertheless they may find themselves to be lonely more often than when they had lived at home (DiTommaso & Spinner, 1997). Most young people in industrialized societies do not enter marriage—and the emotional support and companionship that usually go along with it—until their mid- to late 20s (Arnett, 2006a; Douglass, 2007). For many young people, emerging adulthood is a period between the companionship of living with family and the companionship of marriage or some other long-term partnership (Arnett, 2000a, 2005b).

In the college environment, emerging adults rarely experience social loneliness but emotional loneliness is common (Wiseman, 1995). The first year of college has been found to be an especially lonely period for emerging adults (Cutrona, 1982; Larose & Boivin, 1998), even though they are meeting many new people. A college freshman living in a dormitory may have people around virtually every moment of the day—while sleeping, eating, studying, working, and going to class—but still feel lonely if those social contacts are not emotionally rewarding.

THINKING CRITICALLY •••

Compared with young people in Western cultures, do you think young people in traditional cultures would be more or less likely to experience loneliness?

SUMMING UP

In this chapter we have addressed a variety of aspects of the self in adolescence and emerging adulthood, including self-conceptions, self-esteem, the emotional self, identity, and being alone. The main points of the chapter are as follows:

- Cultures differ greatly in their views of the self, with some promoting an independent self that is high in self-esteem and others promoting an interdependent self that is defined by relations with others.

- Self-conceptions become more abstract in adolescence. This includes the development of the capacity to distinguish between an actual self and two types of possible selves, an ideal self and a feared self. Self-conceptions in adolescence also become more complex, with an increased awareness that different aspects of the self might be shown to different people and in different situations. This includes an awareness that one may show a false self to others at times.

- Research indicates that self-esteem tends to decline in early adolescence and rise through late adolescence and emerging adulthood. Self-esteem does not decline among all adolescents, but is more likely to decline for girls than for boys and more likely to decline among Whites than among African Americans. The most influential aspects of self-esteem in adolescence are physical appearance and peer acceptance.

- The ESM studies show that adolescents tend to experience more extremes of emotions, especially negative ones such as feeling embarrassed or awkward, compared with preadolescents or adults. Carol Gilligan has argued that gender differences exist in emotional self-development during adolescence, as girls "lose their voice" in the course of conforming to cultural pressures for the female role, rather than asserting their authentic selves. However, research has provided limited support for this claim.

- According to Erik Erikson, the key issue in adolescent development is identity versus identity confusion, and the three principal areas of identity formation are love, work, and ideology. The identity status model has guided most research in this area by classifying adolescents into one of four statuses: foreclosure, diffusion, moratorium, and achievement. For young people in Western societies, identity formation usually involves a psychosocial moratorium (a period of exploration of various life possibilities) that continues through emerging adulthood.

- Adolescents who are members of ethnic minorities face the challenge of developing an ethnic identity in addition to an identity in the areas of love, work, and ideology. Four possible alternatives of ethnic identity formation are assimilation, marginality, separation, and biculturalism.

- Globalization is influencing identity issues in adolescence and emerging adulthood. Specifically, it is leading to the development of more bicultural and hybrid identities that combine elements of the local culture with elements of the global culture, and it appears to be leading to greater identity confusion among young people in some traditional cultures.

- The ESM studies find that adolescents are alone about one fourth of the time. Although their moods tend to be low during these times, they often use these times for reflection and regeneration. Emotional loneliness tends to be high among college freshmen.

Studies of the self in adolescence and emerging adulthood are especially common in American society. Because of the American tradition of individualism, issues of the self have been of more interest and concern to Americans than to people in other societies, and this is reflected in the interests of American scholars. The distinction between the independent self and the interdependent self is an important one, but so far this idea has not been applied much to research on adolescence and emerging adulthood.

KEY TERMS

actual self 149

possible selves 149

ideal self 149

feared self 149

false self 150

self-esteem 150

self-image 150

self-concept 150

self-perception 150

baseline self-esteem 151

barometric self-esteem 152

response bias 153

internal consistency 153

psychohistory 158

identity 158

identity versus identity confusion 159

identifications 160

psychosocial moratorium 160

negative identity 161

identity status model 161

identity crisis 161

identity diffusion 161

identity moratorium 162

identity foreclosure 162

identity achievement 162

postmodern identity 163

intimacy versus isolation 164

assimilation 166

marginality 166

separation 166

biculturalism 166

hybrid identity 167

social loneliness 170

emotional loneliness 170

INTERNET RESOURCES

http://www.ssc.uwo.ca/sociology/identity/links.htm

The web site for the journal *Identity*. Many of the articles in the journal pertain to adolescence or emerging adulthood. The site also contains information on conferences and membership in the Society for Research on Identity Formation.

http://www.psych.neu.edu/ISSI/

The web site for the International Society for Self and Identity. The site contains information about publications and conferences related to the self.

FOR FURTHER READING

Erikson, E. (1968). *Identity: Youth and crisis*. New York: Norton. Erikson's classic book on the development of identity during adolescence and emerging adulthood.

Giddens, A. (2000). *Runaway world: How globalization is reshaping our lives*. New York: Routledge. A major theorist on globalization ponders its effects on the self and relationships.

Markus, H. R., & Kitayama, S. (1991). Culture and the self: Implications for cognition, emotion, and motivation. *Psychological Review*, 98, 224–253. Presents the authors' now widely used cultural distinction between independent and interdependent selves.

For more review plus practice tests, videos, flashcards, and more, log on to MyDevelopmentLab.

7
CHAPTER

Family Relationships

"When my first boyfriend broke up with me last year, I was really depressed and he kept saying I should talk to my mom. So I did. And she made me feel a lot better. . . . My mom and I are really close now. I feel like she's a friend, not just my mother."

—Gretchen, age 17 (Bell, 1998, p. 70)

"[My mother] says, 'I just don't want to hear anymore; go back to your room.' And I think, as a human being, she shouldn't be able to say that to me without getting my response back; I just don't feel that's right."

—14-year-old girl (Konopka, 1985, p. 67)

"Everything was going along like usual and then all of a sudden my dad started doing crazy things—like staying out real late, not telling my mom where he was, showing up late for work or not showing up at all. My parents were arguing a lot and he would get real defensive, so it just kept building up and up. . . . And pretty soon my dad came to me and said, 'Well, you know, me and your mom are having problems and I think I'm going to have to leave.' And we both started crying. . . . I didn't want to cry, I was trying not to cry, but I couldn't help it."

—Gordon, age 17 (Bell, 1998, p. 67)

FAMILY LIFE! IT CAN BE THE SOURCE OF OUR DEEPEST attachments as well as our most bitter and painful conflicts. For young people and their parents, frequent adjustments are required in their relationships as adolescents and emerging adults gain more autonomy, inexorably moving away from their families toward the larger world and new attachments outside the family. These adjustments do not always proceed smoothly, and conflicts can result when young people and their parents have different perceptions of the most desirable pace and scope of this growing autonomy. For many adolescents and emerging adults in Western societies, family life is further complicated by their parents' divorce and perhaps remarriage, which require adjustments that many young people find difficult.

Despite these complications, for most young people the family remains a crucial source of love, support, protection, and comfort (Blum & Rinehart, 2000). Family members, especially parents, are the people admired most by the majority of adolescents and emerging adults and are among the people to whom they have the closest attachments (Allen & Land, 1999; Claes, 1998; Halvor, Hanne-Trine, & Bjorkheim, 2000). For example, in one national (American) study, over 80% of adolescents aged 12–14 reported that they think highly of their parents, nearly 60% stated that their parents are people they want to be like, and about 75% reported that their parents are always there to help them with what is important to them (Moore, Chalk, Scarpa, & Vandivere, 2002). Adolescents and emerging adults also typically attribute their core moral values to the influence of their parents (Offer & Schonert-Reichl, 1992; Wyatt & Carlo, 2002).

In this chapter, we will explore many aspects of the family lives of adolescents and emerging adults. We will begin with a look at various aspects of the family system in which adolescents develop, including parents' development at midlife, sibling relationships, and relationships with extended family members. Then we will focus on the central relationships in adolescents' family systems, their relationships with their parents. This will include a discussion of the effects of various parenting styles on adolescents' development and an examination of adolescents' attachments to parents. Emerging adults' relationships to parents will be examined as well.

In the second half of the chapter we will turn to challenges and difficulties in young people's relationships with parents. We will examine the basis for conflict with parents in adolescence. We will also look at the historical context of adolescents' family lives, including changes in family life over the past 200 years as well as more recent family changes—rising rates of divorce, remarriage, single-parent households, and dual-earner families—and how these changes have influenced adolescents' development. The chapter will close with a look at the causes and effects of physical and sexual abuse in the family and the problems faced by adolescents who live on the streets, in the United States and around the world.

The Adolescent in the Family System

One useful framework for making sense of the complex ways family members interact with each other is the **family systems approach**. According to this approach, to understand family functioning one must understand how each relationship within the family influences the family as a whole (Goldenberg & Goldenberg, 2005; Minuchin, 1974, 2002; Steinberg & Silk, 2002). The family system is composed of a variety of subsystems. For example, in a family consisting of two parents and an adolescent, the subsystems would be mother and adolescent, father and adolescent, and mother and father. In families with more than one child, or with extended family members who are closely involved in the family, the family system becomes a more complex network of subsystems, consisting of each **dyadic relationship** (a relationship of two persons) as well as every possible combination of three or more persons.

The family systems approach is based on two key principles. One is that each subsystem influences every other subsystem in the family. For example, a high level of conflict between the parents affects not only the relationship between the two of them but also the relationship that each of them has with the adolescent (Bradford et al., 2004; Emery & Tuer, 1993; Wilson & Gottman, 1995).

A second, related principle of the family systems approach is that a change in any family member or family subsystem results in a period of **disequilibrium** (or imbalance) until the family system adjusts to the change. When a child reaches adolescence, the changes that accompany adolescent development make a certain amount of disequilibrium normal and inevitable. A key change is the advent of puberty and sexual maturity, which typically results in disequilibrium in relationships with each parent, as we saw in Chapter 2. Changes also take place as a result of adolescents' cognitive development, which may lead to disequilibrium because of the way cognitive changes affect adolescents' perceptions of their parents. When emerging adults leave home, the disequilibrium caused by leaving often changes their relationships with their parents for the better (Aquilino, 2006; Arnett, 2003a, 2004a; Graber & Dubas, 1996). Parents change, too, and the changes they experience may result in disequilibrium in their relationships with their children (Steinberg & Silk, 2002; Steinberg & Steinberg, 1994). Other, less normative changes that may take place in adolescence or emerging adulthood can also be a source of disequilibrium—the parents' divorce, for example, or psychological problems in the adolescent or in one or both parents. For both normative and nonnormative changes, adjustments in the family system are required to restore a new equilibrium.

In the following sections, we will examine three aspects of the family system that have implications for adolescents' development: changes in parents at midlife, sibling relationships, and extended family relationships.

Parents' Development During Midlife

"I'm ready for a giant change, because a little change just won't do it for me. My kids are getting ready to leave home soon, and I want to sell the house and do something crazy, like go around the world for a year, or move back into the city and get a job or go back to school. I'm not willing to wait till I get cancer or until somebody dies, or until Peter and I divorce to make a change. At least now we can still enjoy ourselves."

—Ellie, 39-year-old mother of three adolescents
(Bell, 1998, p. 67)

For most parents, their children's development during adolescence and emerging adulthood overlaps with their own development during midlife. As noted in Chapter 1, the median age of marriage and first childbirth in industrialized societies today is quite high, usually in the mid- to late 20s. If adolescence begins at about age 10, this means that most parents in industrialized societies are nearing age 40 when their first child enters adolescence, and age 40 is usually considered the beginning of midlife (Brim, Ryff, & Kessler, 2004; Levinson, 1978; Shweder, 1998). Of course, a great deal of

---

family systems approach An approach to understanding family functioning that emphasizes how each relationship within the family influences the family as a whole.

dyadic relationship A relationship between two persons.

disequilibrium In the family systems approach, this term is used in reference to a change that requires adjustments from family members.

midlife crisis The popular belief, largely unfounded according to research, that most people experience a crisis when they reach about age 40, involving intensive reexamination of their lives and perhaps sudden and dramatic changes if they are dissatisfied.

At midlife, most parents of adolescents are reaching the prime of life in many respects.

People's personalities also tend to become more flexible and adaptive when they reach midlife. For example, in one large study of German adults at midlife, during their 40s and 50s most people reported a steady rise in what the researchers called "flexible goal adjustment," as defined by affirmative responses to items such as "I can adapt quite easily to changes in a situation" (Brandtstadter, 2006; Brandtstadter & Baltes-Götz, 1990; Brandtstadter & Greve, 1994). It appears, then, that as their children reach adolescence, most parents are likely to be flexible enough to adapt their parenting to adolescents' changing development and growing autonomy. The results of studies on midlife adults also suggest that adolescents' growing autonomy may be welcomed by most parents, because it gives parents more time to enjoy their own lives.

One change that has been much discussed in popular culture is the "empty-nest syndrome," referring to the adjustments that parents must make in midlife when their youngest child leaves home. Although popular stereotypes suggest that this is a difficult time for parents, in fact most parents handle it easily. For example, in one study of women's responses to the "empty nest," only one third reported that a significant adjustment was required when their last child left home, and of this one third, more of them reported it as a positive adjustment than as a negative adjustment (Harris, Ellicott, & Holmes, 1986). In general, parents' marital satisfaction and overall life satisfaction improve when their adolescent children enter emerging adulthood and leave the nest (Campbell et al., 2007; Noller, Feeney, & Ward, 1997; Whitbourne & Willis, 2006). Disequilibrium is not necessarily negative, and for most parents the disequilibrium in the family system that results from children's leaving home is experienced as positive.

THINKING CRITICALLY •••

Why do you think parents respond favorably when their children leave home?

variability exists in most industrialized societies, and a substantial proportion of people have their first child in their teens or in their 30s or 40s. But even for people who have their children relatively early or relatively late, their children's development in adolescence and emerging adulthood is likely to overlap at least in part with their own development during midlife, if it can be said that midlife lasts roughly from age 40 to 60.

What kinds of developmental changes take place during midlife that may have an impact on the family system? Studies have consistently found that, for most people in most respects, midlife is an especially satisfying and enjoyable time of life (Brim et al., 2004; Lachman, 2004; Shweder, 1998). Although most people do perceive a decline in energy, physical health, creativity, and physical attractiveness when they reach midlife, they perceive increases in wisdom, competence, psychological health, and respect from others. Despite popular beliefs that midlife is typically a time of "**midlife crisis**," for most people midlife is in many ways the prime of life.

This is true in a variety of ways. Job satisfaction peaks in middle adulthood, as does the sense of having job status and power (Feldman, 2003; Gallagher, 1993). Earning power tends to increase, so that many couples who struggled financially when their children were younger find themselves financially secure for the first time during midlife (Noller, Feeney, & Ward, 1997; Whitbourne & Willis, 2006). Gender roles become less restrictive and more flexible for both men and women, not only in the West but in non-Western cultures as well (Etaugh & Bridges, 2006; Shweder, 1998).

Although reaching midlife is positive for most adults, there is variability at midlife as there is at other ages (Lachman, 2004). For men in blue-collar professions that require physical strength and stamina, such as construction or factory work, job performance becomes more difficult to sustain in middle adulthood and job satisfaction declines (Sparrow & Davies, 1988). Only about one fourth of divorces take place after age 40, but midlife divorces tend to be even more emotionally and financially difficult than divorces at younger ages, especially for women (Etaugh & Bridges, 2006; McDaniel & Coleman, 2003). Also, although most adults do not experience a midlife crisis, for the minority of adults who undergo an unusually intense period of reevaluation and reappraisal at midlife, their relationships with their adolescents tend to be negatively affected by it (Hauser et al., 1991; Steinberg & Steinberg, 1994). In short, evaluating the influence of parents' midlife development on the family systems that adolescents and emerging adults experience requires taking into account the specific characteristics of the parents' lives.

In nearly every chapter of this book I refer to research using the Experience Sampling Method (ESM), which involves having people carry wristwatch beepers and then beeping them randomly during the day so that they can record their thoughts, feelings, and behavior. This method is an exceptionally creative and unusual approach to studying adolescents' lives. Some of the most interesting and important findings so far using this method concern the interactions and relationships between adolescents and their families. Here, let's look at ESM research in greater detail.

Reed Larson and Maryse Richards are the two scholars who have done the most to apply the ESM to adolescents and their families. In their classic book *Divergent Realities: The Emotional Lives of Mothers, Fathers, and Adolescents* (Larson & Richards, 1994), they described the results of a study that included a sample of 483 American adolescents in 5th through 9th grades, and another sample of 55 5th through 8th graders and their parents. All were two-parent, White families. All three family members (adolescent, mother, and father) were beeped at the same times, about 30 times per day between 7:30 in the morning and 9:30 at night, during the week of the study. (More recently, Larson and Richards have published articles that follow up this sample through 12th grade; see Larson et al., 2002; Richards, Crowe, Larson, & Swarr, 2002. They have also begun to publish results of ESM research with African American families; see Bohnert, Richards, Kolmodin, & Lakin, 2008.)

When beeped, the family members paused from whatever they were doing and recorded a variety of information in the notebooks that the researchers had given them for the study. The notebooks contained items about their objective situation when beeped: where they were, whom they were with, and what they were doing. There were also items about their subjective situation. They rated the degree to which they felt happy to unhappy, cheerful to irritable, and friendly to angry, as well as how hurried, tired, and competitive they were feeling. The results provide "an emotional photo album . . . a set of snap-

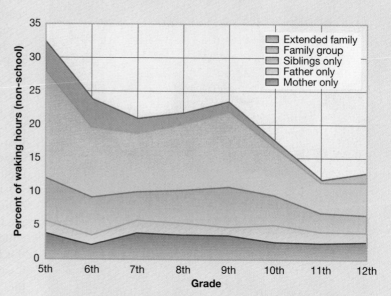

FIGURE 7.1 Changes in time spent with family members during adolescence.

Source: Larson et al. (1996).

shots of what [adolescents] and [their] parents go through in an average week" (Larson & Richards, 1994, p. 9).

What do the results tell us about the daily rhythms of American adolescents' family lives? One striking finding of the study was how little time adolescents and their parents actually spent together on a typical day. Mothers and fathers each averaged about an hour a day spent in shared activities with their adolescents, and their most common shared activity was watching television. The amount of time adolescents spent with their families dropped by 50% between 5th and 9th grades and declined even more sharply between 9th and 12th grades, as you can see in Figure 7.1. In turn, there was an increase from 5th to 9th grade in the amount of time adolescents spent alone in their bedrooms.

Sibling Relationships

For about 80% of American adolescents, and similar proportions in other industrialized societies, the family system also includes relationships with at least one sibling (U.S. Bureau of the Census, 2009). The proportion of families with siblings is even higher in developing countries, where birth rates tend to be higher and families with only one child are rare (Population Reference Bureau, 2009).

Five common patterns can be identified in adolescents' relationships with their siblings (Stewart, Beilfuss, & Verbrugge, 1998). In the **caregiver relationship**, one sibling serves parental functions for the other. This kind of

caregiver relationship Between siblings, a relationship in which one sibling serves parental functions for the other.

buddy relationship Between siblings, a relationship in which they treat each other as friends.

critical relationship Between siblings, a relationship characterized by a high level of conflict and teasing.

rival relationship Between siblings, a relationship in which they compete against each other and measure their success against one another.

casual relationship Between siblings, a relationship that is not emotionally intense, in which they have little to do with one another.

The study also revealed some interesting gender differences in parent-adolescent relationships. Mothers were more deeply involved than fathers with their adolescents, both for better and for worse. The majority of mother-adolescent interactions were rated positively by both of them, especially experiences such as talking together, going out together, and sharing a meal. Adolescents, especially girls, tended to be closer to their mothers than to their fathers and had more conversations with them about relationships and other personal issues. However, adolescents' negative feelings toward their mothers increased sharply from 5th to 9th grade, and certain positive emotions decreased. For example, the proportion of interactions with the mother in which adolescents reported feeling "very close" to her fell from 68% in 5th grade to just 28% by 9th grade. Also, adolescents reported more conflicts with their mothers than with their fathers—although fathers were often called in if Mom's authority failed to achieve the results she desired—and the number of conflicts between mothers and adolescents increased from 5th to 9th grades.

As for fathers, they tended to be only tenuously involved in their adolescents' lives, a "shadowy presence," as Larson and Richards put it. For most of the time they spent with their adolescents, the mother was there as well, and the mother tended to be more directly involved with the adolescent when the three of them were together. Moms were usually on the "front lines" of parenting, whereas for fathers parenting was more of a voluntary, leisure-time activity. Fathers averaged only 12 minutes per day alone with their adolescents, and 40% of this time was spent watching TV together. Fathers and their adolescents did not talk much, and when they did, sports was the most common topic.

THINKING CRITICALLY •••

Why do you think fathers tend to be less involved than mothers in the lives of their adolescents? Do you think this will remain true when the current generation of adolescents grows up and becomes parents?

Fathers usually reported being in a good mood during the rare times they and their adolescents were doing something together. In contrast, adolescents' enjoyment of their time with their fathers decreased between 5th and 9th grades, especially for girls. Fathers tended to dominate when they were with their adolescents, and adolescents often resented it. Dad may have been enjoying their time together, but by 9th grade the adolescent usually was not. The "divergent realities" experienced in adolescents' families seem to be especially sharp between fathers and adolescents.

Larson and Richards used the term *the Six O'Clock Crash* to describe what happens when Mom and Dad come home from work in the early evening and face a barrage of demands—greeting each other, fixing dinner, taking care of household chores, and dealing with the emotions each has piled up during the day. The burden of household tasks fell mostly on mothers rather than fathers, even when both parents worked an equal number of hours. Adolescents were even less help than fathers. They did only half as much household work as fathers, who already did a lot less than mothers. And even when they helped out, they often did so grudgingly and resentfully; they interpreted requests for help as harassment. As the authors put it, "Many of these adolescents, especially boys, felt little responsibility for their family's needs, and were therefore annoyed when asked to do their part" (Larson & Richards, 1994, p. 100).

At the same time, however, the study showed that parents are often important sources of comfort and security for adolescents. Adolescents brought home to the family their emotions from the rest of the day. If their parents were responsive and caring, adolescents' moods improved and their negative emotions were relieved. In contrast, if adolescents felt their parents were unavailable or unresponsive, their negative feelings deepened.

In sum, the study demonstrates the enduring importance of parents in the lives of adolescents. Also, because the study included the perspectives of fathers and mothers as well as adolescents, interacting in pairs as well as all together, the results provide a vivid sense of the interconnected emotions and perspectives within the family system.

---

relationship is most common between an older sister and younger siblings, in both Western and non-Western cultures (Whiting & Edwards, 1988). In the **buddy relationship**, siblings treat each other as friends. They try to be like one another, and they enjoy being together. A **critical relationship** between siblings is characterized by a high level of conflict and teasing. In a **rival relationship**, siblings compete against each other and measure their success against one another. Finally, in a **casual relationship** between siblings, the relationship between them is not emotionally intense, and they may have little to do with one another.

Adolescents' relationships with their siblings can take any one of these forms, or any combination of them

(Noller, 2005; Zukow-Goldring, 2002). A critical relationship between siblings is common. In fact, in studies that compare adolescents' relationships with siblings to relationships with parents, grandparents, teachers, and friends, adolescents report more frequent conflicts with their siblings than with anyone else. Common sources of conflict include teasing, possessions (e.g., borrowing a sibling's clothes without permission), responsibility for chores, name-calling, invasions of privacy, and perceived unequal treatment by parents (Goodwin & Roscoe, 1990; Noller, 2005; Updegraff et al., 2005).

However, even though adolescents tend to have more conflicts with siblings than in their other relationships, conflict with siblings is lower in adolescence than at younger ages

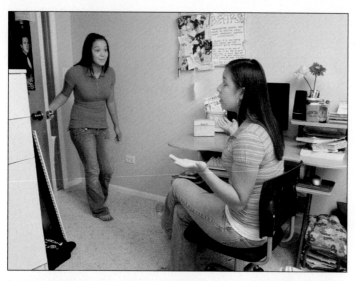
Adolescents tend to have more conflict with siblings than with anyone else.

(Brody, 2004; Buhrmester & Furman, 1990; Noller, 2005). From childhood to adolescence, relationships with siblings become more casual and less emotionally intense, partly because adolescents gradually spend less time with their siblings (Hetherington, Henderson, & Reiss, 1999). Adolescents' involvement in friendships and employment takes them outside the family environment for an increasing amount of time (Larson & Richards, 1994), resulting in less time and less conflict with siblings.

THINKING CRITICALLY •••

Thus far, little research has taken place on sibling relationships in emerging adulthood. Based on your own observations and experience, what would you expect research to indicate about how sibling relationships change from adolescence to emerging adulthood?

Nevertheless, many adolescents have a buddy relationship with their siblings and feel close to them. When asked to list the most important people in their lives, most adolescents include their siblings (Blyth, Hill, & Thiel, 1982), and siblings are often an important source of emotional support (Noller, 2005; Seginer, 1998). Adolescents who have two or more siblings may be closer to one sibling than to the others. With respect to their "favorite" brother or sister, adolescents rate the level of closeness as similar to their relationship with their best friend (Greenberger et al., 1980). However, for sibling relationships in general, adolescents rate the level of closeness as lower than in their relationships with parents or friends (Buhrmester & Furman, 1987; Updegraff, McHale, & Crouter, 2002).

Adolescent siblings in divorcing families often experience a heightened intensity in both hostility and warmth in their relationship (Noller, 2005; Sheehan, Darlington, & Feeney, 2004). They report greater conflict than adolescents in nondivorced families during the period when the divorce is occurring, but they also report greater closeness because of the support they provide each other during that stressful time, and the closeness tends to endure after the conflict sub-

sides (Bush & Ehrenberg, 2003). This is a good example of how one subsystem in the family, the relationship between the parents, affects another subsystem in the family, the relationship between siblings.

Little research has been done on sibling relationships in emerging adulthood (Aquilino, 2005). However, one study of adolescents and emerging adults in Israel found that emerging adults spent less time with their siblings than adolescents did but also felt more emotional closeness and warmth toward their siblings (Scharf, Shulman, & Avigad-Spitz, 2005). Conflict and rivalry were also reported to be less intense by emerging adults than by adolescents. Qualitative analyses showed that emerging adults had a more mature perception of their relationship with their siblings than adolescents did, in the sense that they were better able to understand their siblings' needs and perspectives.

In traditional cultures, the caregiver relationship between siblings is the most common form. Adolescents in traditional cultures often have child-care responsibilities. In Schlegel and Barry's (1991) analysis of adolescence in traditional cultures, over 80% of adolescent boys and girls had frequent responsibility for caring for younger siblings. This responsibility promotes close attachments between siblings. Time together and closeness are especially high between siblings of the same gender mainly because in traditional cultures daily activities are often separated by gender. Caregiver relationships between siblings are also common in African American families, in part because many African American families are headed by single mothers who rely on older siblings to help with child care (Brody et al., 2003).

Adolescents in traditional cultures often take care of younger siblings. Here, an adolescent girl and her younger sibling in Kenya.

Conflict tends to be low between adolescent siblings in traditional cultures, because age serves as a powerful determinant of status (Whiting & Edwards, 1988). Older siblings are understood to have authority over younger ones, simply by virtue of being older. This lessens conflict because it is accepted that the older sibling has the right to exercise authority—although of course sometimes younger siblings resist their older siblings' authority (Schlegel & Barry, 1991). Also, siblings in traditional cultures often rely on one another economically throughout life, which means that they all have an interest in maintaining harmony in the relationship (Schlegel & Barry, 1991). For example, Hollos and Leis's (1989) ethnography of Nigerian adolescents described how they frequently rely on older siblings to provide them with connections that will lead to employment.

Extended Family Relationships

In traditional cultures, young men generally remain in their family home after marriage, and young women move into their new husband's home (Schlegel & Barry, 1991). This practice has been remarkably resistant to the influence of globalization so far. It remains the typical pattern, for example, in the majority cultures of India and China, the two most populous countries in the world, as well as in most other traditional cultures in Asia and Africa. Consequently, children in these cultures typically grow up in a household that includes not only their parents and siblings but also their grandparents, and often their uncles, aunts, and cousins as well (Whiting & Edwards, 1988).

These living arrangements promote closeness between adolescents and their extended family. In Schlegel and Barry's (1991) cross-cultural analysis, daily contact was as high with grandparents as with parents for adolescents in traditional cultures, and adolescents were usually even closer to their grandparents than to their parents. Perhaps this is because parents typically exercise authority over adolescents, which may add ambivalence to adolescents' relationships

with their parents, whereas grandparents are less likely to exercise authority and may focus more on nurturing and supporting adolescents.

Similar patterns of closeness to grandparents have been found among adolescents in American minority cultures. Asian American adolescents typically grow up with grandparents either in the home or living nearby, and they report high levels of nurturing and support from their grandparents (Fuligni, Tseng, & Lam, 1999; Sung, 1979). Many Mexican American adolescents have grandparents living in their household, and closeness in extended family relationships is highly valued in Mexican culture (Harwood et al., 2002; Suarez-Orozco & Suarez-Orozco, 1996).

African American families also have a tradition of extended family households (Wilson, 1989). Several studies have described how African American extended families provide mutual support, sharing financial resources and parenting responsibilities (McAdoo, 1996; Oberlander et al., 2007). About 70% of African American adolescents are in single-parent families, and extended family support has been found to be especially important in reducing the emotional and economic stresses of single parenthood (Ruiz & Silverstein, 2007; Wilson, 1989). The effects of this support are evident in the lives of adolescents. For example, extended family support in African American families is negatively related to adolescents' involvement in problem behavior and positively related to their grades in school (Hamilton, 2005; Taylor, 1994, 1996, 1997).

Extended family members are also important figures in the lives of adolescents in Western majority cultures. About 80% of American adolescents list at least one member of their extended family among the people most important to them, and closeness to grandparents is positively related to adolescents' well-being (Blyth et al., 1982; Ruiz & Silverstein, 2007). However, in the American majority culture, adolescents' contact with extended family members is relatively infrequent, in part because extended family members often live many miles away. American adolescents have significantly less contact with their extended family members compared with adolescents in European countries because members of European extended families are more likely to live in close proximity (Alsaker & Flammer, 1999b; Arnett & Balle-Jensen, 1993). Also, for Americans closeness to extended family members declines substantially between childhood and adolescence (Buhrmester & Furman, 1987; Levitt, Guacci-Franco, & Levitt, 1993).

An exception to this pattern occurs among adolescents in divorced families, who tend to have increased rather than decreased contact with their grandparents during adolescence, especially with their maternal grandfather (Clingempeel et al., 1992). This suggests that the maternal grandfather fills the father's role in these families, to some extent, by spending more time with his grandchildren than he would if the father were present. Mothers and adolescents in divorced families may have greater need for the grandfather's support and assistance, given the economic and emotional strains that often occur in divorced families (Hetherington et al., 1998).

Grandparents tend to be important figures in the lives of African American adolescents.

Parenting Styles

"My parents are never home. They're either off on a trip or away at work or something. Like, I get home from school and there's a note on the table about what I can make myself for supper and not to expect them. They don't show up at my games or band concerts. I mean, am I an orphan or what?"

—Julian, age 14 (Bell, 1998, p. 57)

"My father's so strict, if I look at him funny he knocks me under the table. That's how he was raised; that's how he treats me."

—Patrick, age 16 (Bell, 1998, p. 64)

"My mother told me I couldn't go with a guy in a car until I was in my senior year of high school. I argued with her about that, but in a nice way. We ended up compromising, and she said I could ride with someone as long as she knew who the person was."

—Dorene, age 15 (Bell, 1998, p. 56)

Because parents are so important in the development of children, social scientists have devoted a great deal of research to the quality of parent-child relationships and to the effects of parenting. One branch of this research has involved the study of **parenting styles**—that is, the kinds of practices that parents exhibit in relation to their children and the effects of these practices. For over 50 years, scholars have engaged in research on this topic, and the results have been quite consistent (Collins & Laursen, 2004; Maccoby & Martin, 1983; Steinberg, 2001). Virtually all of the prominent scholars who have studied parenting have described it in terms of two dimensions: demandingness and responsiveness (also known by other terms such as *control* and *warmth*). Parental **demandingness** is the degree to which parents set down rules and expectations for behavior and require their children to comply with them. Parental **responsiveness** is the degree to which parents are sensitive to their children's needs and express love, warmth, and concern.

Many scholars have combined these two dimensions to describe different kinds of parenting styles. For many years, the best-known and most widely used conception of parenting styles was the one articulated by Diana Baumrind (1968, 1971, 1991a, 1991b). Her research on middle-class American families, along with the research of other scholars inspired by

TABLE 7.1 Parenting Styles and the Two Dimensions of Parenting

		Demandingness	
		High	Low
Responsiveness	High	Authoritative	Permissive
	Low	Authoritarian	Disengaged

her ideas, has identified four distinct parenting styles (Collins & Laursen, 2004; Maccoby & Martin, 1983; Steinberg, 2000; see Table 7.1).

Authoritative parents are high in demandingness and high in responsiveness. They set clear rules and expectations for their children. Furthermore, they make clear what the consequences will be if their children do not comply, and they make those consequences stick if necessary. However, authoritative parents do not simply "lay down the law" and then enforce it rigidly. A distinctive feature of authoritative parents is that they *explain* the reasons for their rules and expectations to their children, and they willingly engage in discussion with their children over issues of discipline, sometimes leading to negotiation and compromise. Authoritative parents are also loving and warm toward their children, and they respond to what their children need and desire.

Authoritarian parents are high in demandingness but low in responsiveness. They require obedience from their children, and they punish disobedience without compromise. None of the verbal give-and-take common with authoritative parents is allowed by authoritarian parents. They expect their commands to be followed without dispute or dissent. Also, they show little in the way of love or warmth toward their children. Their demandingness takes place without responsiveness, in a way that shows little emotional attachment and may even be hostile.

Permissive parents are low in demandingness and high in responsiveness. They have few clear expectations for their children's behavior, and they rarely discipline them. Instead, their emphasis is on responsiveness. They believe that children need love that is truly "unconditional." They may see discipline and control as having the potential to damage their children's healthy tendencies for developing creativity and expressing themselves however they wish. They provide their children with love and warmth and give them a great deal of freedom to do as they please.

Disengaged parents are low in both demandingness and responsiveness. Their goal may be to minimize the amount of

parenting styles The patterns of practices that parents exhibit in relation to their children.

demandingness The degree to which parents set down rules and expectations for behavior and require their children to comply with them.

responsiveness The degree to which parents are sensitive to their children's needs and express love, warmth, and concern for them.

authoritative parents A parenting style in which parents are high in demandingness and high in responsiveness, i.e., they love their children but also set clear standards for behavior and explain to their children the reasons for those standards.

authoritarian parents Parenting style in which parents are high in demandingness but low in responsiveness, i.e., they require obedience from their children and punish disobedience without compromise, but show little warmth or affection toward them.

time and emotion they devote to parenting. Thus, they require little of their children and rarely bother to correct their behavior or place clear limits on what they are allowed to do. They also express little in the way of love or concern for their children. They may seem to have little emotional attachment to them.

Parenting Styles as Custom Complexes

These four parenting styles can be understood as custom complexes. As described in Chapter 4, a custom complex consists of a typical cultural practice and the beliefs underlying it. What beliefs are reflected in the parenting styles described above? Research on parents' child-rearing goals shows that American parents tend to value independence highly as a quality they wish to promote in their children (Alwin, 1988; Hoffman, 1988). Authoritarian parenting clearly discourages independence, but the other three parenting styles—authoritative, permissive, and disengaged—reflect parents' beliefs that it is good for adolescents to learn **autonomy**—that is, to learn to be independent and self-sufficient, to learn to think for themselves and be responsible for their own behavior (Zimmer-Gembeck & Collins, 2003).

Authoritative parents promote autonomy in positive ways through encouraging discussion and give-and-take that teaches adolescents to think independently and make mature decisions. Permissive and disengaged parents promote this outcome in a negative way—that is, through the absence of restraint that allows adolescents a great deal of autonomy without parental guidance. As we will see in the next section, the differences in how these parenting styles promote autonomy result in different effects on adolescents' development. Nevertheless, in combination the prominence of these parenting styles in the families of American adolescents reflects the prominence of individualism in American cultural beliefs (Alwin, 1988). This is an example of how cultural beliefs form the basis for the socialization that occurs in the family and elsewhere, as discussed in Chapter 4.

The Effects of Parenting Styles on Adolescents

A great deal of research has been conducted on how parenting styles influence adolescents' development. A summary of the results is shown in Table 7.2. In general, authoritative parenting is associated with the most favorable outcomes, at least by American standards. Adolescents who have authoritative parents tend to be independent, self-assured, creative, and socially skilled (Baumrind, 1991a, 1991b; Collins &

TABLE 7.2 Adolescent Outcomes Associated With Parenting Styles

Authoritative	Authoritarian	Permissive	Disengaged
Independent	Dependent	Irresponsible	Impulsive
Creative	Passive	Conforming	Delinquent
Self-assured	Conforming	Immature	Early sex, drugs
Socially skilled			

Larsen, 2004; Steinberg et al., 1994; Steinberg, 2000). They also tend to do well in school and to get along well with their peers and with adults (Spera, 2005; Steinberg, 1996, 2000). Authoritative parenting helps adolescents develop characteristics such as optimism and self-regulation that in turn have positive effects on a wide range of behaviors (Jackson et al., 2005; Purdie, Carroll, & Roche, 2004).

All the other parenting styles are associated with some negative outcomes, although the type of negative outcome varies depending on the specific parenting style (Baumrind, 1991a, 1991b; Goldstein, Davis-Kean, & Eccles, 2005; Lamborn et al., 1991; Steinberg et al., 1994; Steinberg, 1996, 2000). Adolescents with authoritarian parents tend to be dependent, passive, and conforming. They are often less self-assured, less creative, and less socially adept than other adolescents. Adolescents with permissive parents tend to be immature and irresponsible. They are more likely than other adolescents to conform to their peers. Adolescents with disengaged parents tend to be impulsive. Partly as a consequence of their impulsiveness, and partly because disengaged parents do little to monitor their activities, adolescents with disengaged parents tend to have higher rates of problem behaviors such as delinquency, early sexual involvement, and use of drugs and alcohol.

Authoritative parenting tends to be better for adolescents for a number of reasons (Steinberg, 2000). Adolescents are at a point in their lives when they have become capable of exercising more autonomy and self-regulation than when they were younger (Steinberg, 1990, 1996; Zimmer-Gembeck & Collins, 2003). In order to be able to move into adult roles after adolescence, they need to be given a greater amount of autonomy and required to exercise a greater amount of responsibility (Steinberg & Levine, 1997). At the same time, they lack the experience with the world and with their own impulses and abilities that adults have; consequently, an excess of autonomy may leave them aimless or even lead them into harm (Dornbusch et al., 1990). Authoritative parenting

---

permissive parents Parenting style in which parents are low in demandingness and high in responsiveness. They show love and affection toward their children but are permissive with regard to standards for behavior.

disengaged parents Parenting style in which parents are low in both demandingness and responsiveness and relatively uninvolved in their children's development.

autonomy The quality of being independent and self-sufficient, capable of thinking for one's self.

achieves a balance between allowing enough autonomy for adolescents to develop their capacities and at the same time requiring them to exercise their increased autonomy in a responsible way. All the other parenting styles either fail to allow as much autonomy or allow it without requiring the kind of responsibility that is associated with healthy development.

Authoritative parenting combines demandingness with responsiveness, which includes affection, emotional attachment, love, and concern for the adolescent's needs and well-being. Parents' responsiveness helps adolescents to learn to believe in their own worthiness as people. It also leads adolescents to identify with their parents and seek to please them by embracing the values their parents hold and by behaving in ways the parents will approve (Baumrind, 1991a, 1991b). The other parenting styles either lack responsiveness or provide it without requiring an adequate level of demandingness.

Inconsistency between parents also tends to be related to negative outcomes for adolescents. Most studies of parenting in adolescence assess one parent or combine ratings for the two parents into one rating, but studies that examine differences have produced interesting results. For example, Johnson, Shulman, and Collins (1991) had 5th, 8th, and 11th graders rate their parents on various items. Parents were categorized into one of two general types, authoritative or permissive. Fifth graders generally viewed their parents as similar—only 9% rated them in different categories—but the proportion perceiving a discrepancy rose with age, to 23% of 8th graders and 31% of 11th graders.

Adolescents who perceived inconsistency between their parents were lower on self-esteem and school performance compared not only with those who perceived both parents as authoritative but also with those who perceived both parents as permissive. A study by Wentzel and Feldman (1993) pro-

duced similar results: Adolescents who perceived inconsistency in the parenting styles of their parents were lower than other adolescents on self-control and academic motivation.

THINKING CRITICALLY •••

How would you categorize the parenting style of your parents when you were in adolescence? Was it the same for you as for your siblings (if you have any)? To what extent did their parenting influence you, and to what extent did you evoke certain parenting behaviors from them?

A More Complex Picture of Parenting Effects

Although parents undoubtedly affect their adolescents profoundly by their parenting, the process is not nearly as simple as the cause-and-effect model just described. Sometimes discussions of parenting make it sound as though parenting style A automatically and inevitably produces adolescent type X. However, enough research has taken place by now to indicate that the relationship between parenting styles and adolescent development is considerably more complex than that (Collins, Maccoby, Steinberg, Hetherington, & Bornstein, 2000). Adolescents not only are affected by their parents but also affect their parents in return. Scholars refer to this principle as **reciprocal** or **bidirectional effects** between parents and children (Collins & Laursen, 2004; Crouter & Booth, 2003; Patterson & Fisher, 2002).

Recall our discussion of evocative genotype–environment interactions in Chapter 2. Adolescents are not like billiard balls that head predictably in the direction they are propelled. They have personalities and desires of their own that they bring to the parent-adolescent relationship. Thus, ado-

reciprocal effects In relations between parents and children, the concept that children not only are affected by their parents but affect their parents in return. Also called bidirectional effects.

bidirectional effects In relations between parents and children, the concept that children not only are affected by their parents but affect their parents in return. Also called reciprocal effects.

differential parenting When parents' behavior differs toward siblings within the same family.

nonshared environmental influences Influences experienced differently among siblings within the same family, e.g., when parents behave differently with their different children.

Adolescent siblings within the same family often report different experiences with their parents.

lescents may evoke certain behaviors from their parents. An especially aggressive adolescent may evoke authoritarian parenting, perhaps because the parents find that authoritative explanations of the rules are simply ignored, and their responsiveness diminishes as a result of the adolescent's repeated violations of their trust. An especially mild-tempered adolescent may evoke indulgent parenting because parents may see no point in laying down specific rules for an adolescent who has no inclination to do anything outrageous anyway.

Research involving siblings indicates that reciprocal effects occur in parent-adolescent relationships. The interesting finding of these studies is that adolescent siblings *within the same family* often give very different accounts of what their parents are like toward them (Daniels et al., 1985; Hoffman, 1991; Kowal & Krull, 2004; Plomin & Daniels, 1987). For example, one study investigated families with two adolescents aged 11 to 17 and found that siblings perceived significant differences in their parents' love for them, their parents' closeness to them, their parents' use of discipline, and the degree to which their parents involved them in family decisions (Daniels et al., 1985).

Thus, one adolescent may see her parents as admirably demanding and responsive, the epitome of the authoritative parent, whereas her brother describes the same parents as dictatorial, unresponsive, authoritarian parents. These differences in how adolescents perceive their parents' behavior are in turn related to differences in the adolescents: The ones who perceive their parents as authoritative tend to be happier and to be functioning better in a variety of ways (Daniels et al., 1985). Overall, little similarity in personality exists between adolescent siblings (Neiderhiser et al., 2007; Wright et al., 2008), which suggests that whatever effect parents have, it is different for different adolescents within the same family.

Does this research discredit the claim that parenting styles influence adolescents? No, but it modifies this claim (Collins & Laursen, 2004; Collins et al., 2000; Kerr & Stattin, 2003). Parents do have beliefs about what is best for their adolescents, and they try to express those beliefs through their behavior toward their adolescents (Alwin, 1988). However, parents' actual behavior is affected not only by what they

believe is best but also by how their adolescents behave toward them and how their adolescents seem to respond to their parenting. Being an authoritative parent is easier if your adolescent responds to the demandingness and responsiveness you provide, and not so easy if your love is rejected and your rules and the reasons you provide for them are ignored. Parents whose efforts to persuade their adolescents through reasoning and discussion fall on deaf ears may be tempted either to demand compliance (and become more authoritarian) or to give up trying (and become permissive or disengaged).

Recently, an ambitious research project has gone deeper than previous research into the complexities of adolescents' family lives (Neiderhiser et al., 2007; Reiss, Neiderhiser, Hetherington, & Plomin, 2000). This project studied 720 families from various areas of the United States, and two same-sex siblings within each family, including identical twins, fraternal twins, full siblings, half siblings, and biologically unrelated stepsiblings. The research design enabled the researchers to examine questions of genetic and environmental family influences on adolescents, as well as the different experiences of siblings within the same family. The research methods used in the study included not only questionnaires but interviews, videotaped family interactions, and information on the adolescents' social world outside the family. The average ages of the siblings when the study began were 12 and 15, and the families were followed over a 3-year period.

In terms of dimensions of *warmth* and *negativity*, there was evidence for **differential parenting**, meaning that parents' behavior often differed toward siblings within the same family (Feinberg & Hetherington, 2001). Differential parenting resulted in **nonshared environmental influences**, meaning that the siblings experienced quite different family environments, and the consequences of these differences were evident in adolescents' behavior and psychological functioning. Also, the influence of genetics seemed to be especially strong for parental negativity, in the sense that the more alike two siblings were genetically, the more alike parents' behavior was toward them with respect to negativity (Feinberg, Neiderhiser, Howe, & Hetherington, 2001). This seems to indicate evocative genotype–environment interactions because it suggests that the parents' negativity was evoked by the adolescents' genetically based behavior.

Furthermore, parents and adolescents often differed in their reports of parenting behavior (Feinberg et al., 2001), with parents reporting more warmth and less negativity for themselves than their adolescents reported for them. For younger adolescents, the more different their reports were from their parents' reports, the more likely they were to be functioning poorly (Feinberg, Howe, Reiss, & Hetherington, 2000). This suggests that it is important to include multiple reports of parenting behavior rather than only the adolescents' reports, as most studies do.

Parenting in Other Cultures

Almost all the research on parenting styles has taken place in American society, and most of it has centered on families in the American majority culture. What do parent-adolescent

India is currently the second most populous country in the world, with a population of over 1 billion people. By the middle of the 21st century, it will pass China and reach a population of 1.5 billion, about four times the projected population of the United States. India is an astonishingly diverse country, with a wide variety of religions, languages, and regional cultures. Nevertheless, scholars generally believe that a common Indian culture can be identified (Segal, 1998), including with regard to young people and their families. The features of the Indian family provide a good illustration of young people's family lives in a traditional culture.

Indian families have many features in common with other traditional cultures discussed in this book. Collectivistic values are strong, and the well-being and success of the family are considered more important than the well-being and success of the individual (Saraswathi, 1999, 2007). There is a strong emphasis on sacrifice, and children are taught from an early age to relinquish their own desires for the sake of the family as a whole. Interdependence among family members is stressed throughout life, emotionally, socially, and financially (Gupta, 1987; Chaudhary & Sharma, 2007).

As in most traditional cultures, the Indian family has a clear hierarchy based on age (Kakar, 1998; Reddy & Gibbons, 1999; Saraswathi, 2006; Segal, 1998). Respect for elders is strongly emphasized. Even in childhood, older children are understood to have definite authority over anyone younger than they are; even in adulthood, older adults merit respect and deference from younger adults simply on the basis of being older. Because it is common for young married couples to live with the husband's parents rather than establishing a separate residence, many households with children contain grandparents and often uncles, aunts, and cousins as well.

This pattern is changing because Indian society is becoming increasingly urbanized, and extended family households are less common in urban areas than in rural areas. Nevertheless, even now 80% of India's population is rural and tends to live according to traditional family arrangements (Carson et al., 1999; Chaudhary & Sharma, 2007).

One feature that is distinctive to the traditional Indian family is the idea that the parents, especially the father, are to be regarded by their children as a god would be regarded by a devotee. The Hindu religion, which most Indians believe, has many gods of varying degrees of power, so this is not like stating that the father is like "God" in a Western sense. Nevertheless, the analogy of a father being like a god to his children effectively symbolizes and conveys the absolute nature of his authority within the family.

These features of the Indian family have important implications for the development of adolescents and emerging adults. The inherent authority of parents and the emphasis on respect for elders mean that parents expect obedience even from adolescents and emerging adults. Traditional Indian families include little of the explanation of rules and discussion of decisions that characterize the relationships between adolescents and parents in authoritative Western families. For parents to explain the reasons for their rules, or for young people to demand to take part in family decisions, would be considered an offense to the parents' inherent authority. This does not mean the parents are "authoritarian," in the scheme of parenting styles described by Western social scientists. On the contrary, warmth, love, and affection are known to be especially strong in Indian families (Chaudhary & Sharma, 2007; Kakar, 1998; Larson et al., 2000). Indian parenting is better described by the "traditional" parenting style discussed in this chapter.

---

relationships look like if we step outside of the American experience and look around the world, especially toward non-Western cultures?

Probably the most striking difference is how rare the authoritative parenting style is in non-Western cultures. Remember, a distinctive feature of authoritative parents is that they do not rely on the authority of the parental role to ensure that adolescents comply with their commands and instructions. They do not simply lay down the law and expect to be obeyed. On the contrary, authoritative parents *explain the reasons* for what they want adolescents to do and *engage in discussion* over the guidelines for their adolescents' behavior (Baumrind, 1971, 1991a; Steinberg & Levine, 1997).

Outside of the West, however, this is an extremely rare approach to adolescent socialization. In traditional cultures, parents expect that their authority will be obeyed, without question and without requiring an explanation (Schlegel & Barry, 1991; Whiting & Edwards, 1988). This is true not only

Most traditional cultures emphasize respect and obedience toward parents. Here, a Latino adolescent and his father.

Adolescents in India benefit from close family relationships.

The authority of parents in Indian families also means that there are not the same expectations of autonomy for adolescents and emerging adults as there are in Western families (Gupta, 1987; Larson et al., 2000; Reddy & Gibbons, 1999; Segal, 1998; Shukla, 1994). Indian adolescents spend most of their leisure time with their families, not with their friends. Dating and sexual relationships before marriage are almost nonexistent (Chaudhary & Sharma, 2007). Most marriages are arranged by the parents, not chosen independently by the young people themselves. Emerging adults usually remain in their parents' homes until marriage.

What are the consequences of these family practices for the development of Indian adolescents and emerging adults? A Western reader may be tempted to regard the practices of Indian families as "unhealthy" because of their hierarchical, patriarchal quality and because of the way that the autonomy of young people is suppressed. However, it is probably more accurate to view Indian family socialization as having both costs and benefits, like other cultural forms of socialization (Arnett, 1995a, 2006b). For young people in India, there are clearly costs in terms of individual autonomy. To be expected to be obedient to your parents even in your teens and 20s (and beyond), to be discouraged from ever questioning your parents' authority and judgment, and to have your parents control crucial life decisions in love and work clearly means that young people's autonomy is restricted in Indian families.

However, Indian family practices have clear benefits as well. Young people who grow up in a close, interdependent Indian family have the benefit of family support and guidance as they enter adult roles. Because they respect their parents' age and experience, they value the advice their parents provide about what occupation to pursue and whom to marry (Kakar, 1998; Saraswathi, 2007). Having a strong sense of family interdependence also provides Indian young people with a strong family identity, which may make them less lonely and vulnerable as they form an individual identity. Indian adolescents have low rates of delinquency, depression, and suicide compared with Western adolescents (Chaudhary & Sharma, 2007; Kakar, 1998).

The influence of globalization can be seen in Indian culture as in other traditional cultures. Western styles of dress, language, and music are popular among young Indians. In urban middle-class families, the traditional Indian pattern of parental authority is changing, and parents' relationships with their adolescents increasingly involve discussion and negotiation (Larson et al., 2000; Patel-Amin & Power, 2002; Reddy & Gibbons, 1999). Nevertheless, young Indians remain proud of the Indian tradition of close families, and they express the desire to see that tradition endure (Mullatti, 1995).

of nonindustrial traditional cultures but also of industrialized traditional cultures outside the West, most notably Asian cultures such as China, Japan, Vietnam, and South Korea (Fuligni et al., 1999; Tseng, 2004; Zhang & Fuligni, 2006; Zhou, 1997). As noted in Chapter 1, Asian cultures have a tradition of filial piety, meaning that children are expected to respect, obey, and revere their parents throughout life (Lieber, Nihira, & Mink, 2004). In other traditional cultures as well, the *role of parent* carries greater inherent authority than it does in the West. Parents are not supposed to provide reasons why they should be respected and obeyed. The simple fact that they are parents and their children are children is viewed as sufficient justification for their authority (see the Cultural Focus box for an example).

Does this mean that the typical parenting style in traditional cultures is authoritarian? No, although sometimes scholars have come to this erroneous conclusion. Keep in mind that authoritarian parenting combines high demandingness with *low responsiveness*. Parents in traditional cultures are indeed high in demandingness, and their demandingness is often of a more uncompromising quality than is typical in the West. However, it is not true that parents in traditional cultures are typically low in responsiveness. On the contrary, parents and adolescents in nonindustrialized traditional cultures often develop a closeness that is nearly impossible in Western families because they spend virtually all of their days together, working side by side (boys with their fathers, girls with their mothers), in a way that the economic structure of industrialized societies prevents (Schlegel & Barry, 1991). Parents and adolescents in industrialized traditional cultures such as Asian cultures also maintain a strong degree of closeness that is reflected in a sense of interdependence and in shared activities and mutual obligations (Fuligni et al., 1999; Hardaway & Fuligni, 2006; Lim & Lim, 2004).

However, parental responsiveness may be expressed quite differently in non-Western cultures. For example, parents in non-Western cultures rarely use praise with their children (Whiting & Edwards, 1988), and in many Asian cultures open expressions of affection and warmth between parents and adolescents are uncommon (Jeffries, 2004). But are typical parents of adolescents in non-Western cultures responsive—do they have deep emotional attachments to their adolescents, do they love them, are they deeply concerned with their well-being? Unquestionably, the answer is yes.

If parents in non-Western cultures cannot be called authoritarian, what *are* they? The fact is, they do not fit very well into the parenting scheme presented earlier. They are generally closest to authoritative parents because, like them, they tend to be high in demandingness and high in responsiveness. However, as noted, their demandingness is very different from the demandingness of the authoritative American or Western parent.

Diana Baumrind (1987), the scholar who originally invented the terminology for the parenting styles we have been discussing, has recognized the problem of fitting traditional cultures into her scheme. Accordingly, she has proposed the term **traditional parenting style** to describe the kind of parenting typical in traditional cultures—high in responsiveness and high in a kind of demandingness that does not encourage discussion and debate but rather expects compliance by virtue of cultural beliefs supporting the inherent authority of the parental role (Baumrind, 1987).

The difficulty of fitting other cultures into Baumrind's scheme applies not only to non-Western traditional cultures but also to ethnic minority cultures that are part of American society. Studies indicate that African American, Latino, and Asian American parents are less likely than White parents to be classified as authoritative and more likely to be classified as authoritarian (e.g., Dornbusch et al., 1987; Feldman et al., 1991; Steinberg et al., 1994; Steinberg, Dornbusch, & Brown, 1992). However, because none of these studies used Baumrind's "traditional" category as one of the classifications, it is somewhat difficult to say what this means. If parents in these studies were high in responsiveness and also high in an uncompromising demandingness that rejects discussion and explanation, they would not have fit well into either the authoritative or the authoritarian categories used by the researchers.

In recent years, Asian American psychologists have argued that designations of authoritative and authoritarian cannot be easily applied to Asian American parents (Chao, 2001; Chao & Tseng, 2002; Lim & Lim, 2004). They suggest that researchers may misunderstand Asian American parenting and mislabel it as authoritarian because it involves a degree and type of demandingness that is typical of Asian families but that may be perceived as wrong by a White researcher unfamiliar with Asian cultural beliefs. Asian American adolescents show none of the negative effects typically associated with authoritarian parenting. On the contrary, they have higher educational achievement, lower rates of behavioral problems, and lower rates of psychological problems, compared with White adolescents (Chao & Tseng, 2002; Huynh & Fuligni, 2008; Steinberg, 1996). Furthermore, family attitudes of interdependence among Asian American adolescents and emerging adults are related to their high rates of academic achievement and their low rates of problems (Tseng, 2004). This suggests that cultural context is crucial to predicting the effects parenting will have on adolescents.

Latino parents in American society have also typically been classified as authoritarian (Busch-Rossnagel & Zayas, 1991). The Latino cultural belief system places a premium on the idea of *respeto*, which emphasizes respect for and obedience to parents and elders, especially the father (Halgunseth et al., 2006; Harwood et al. 2002). The role of the parent is considered to be enough to command authority, without requiring that the parents explain their rules to their children. Again, however, this does not mean that their parenting is authoritarian. Another pillar of Latino cultural beliefs is **familismo**, which emphasizes the love, closeness, and mutual obligations of Latino family life (Halgunseth et al., 2006; Harwood et al., 2002). This hardly sounds like the aloofness and hostility characteristic of the authoritarian parent, and in fact studies confirm the positive effects of *familismo* on Latino adolescents (Fuligni et al., 1999; Suarez-Orozco & Suarez-Orozco, 1996).

Attachments to Parents

"[My parents are] always there and I feel I can always go to them and they always say something that will make me feel better."

—17-year-old girl (Konopka, 1985, p. 71)

"It's like if I get in some really, really bad trouble then my friends might get afraid, you know, and go away. But my parents will always be there."

—Devon, African American adolescent (Jeffries, 2004, p. 120)

---

traditional parenting style The kind of parenting typical in traditional cultures, high in responsiveness and high in a kind of demandingness that does not encourage discussion and debate but rather expects compliance by virtue of cultural beliefs supporting the inherent authority of the parental role.

familismo Concept of family life characteristic of Latino cultures that emphasizes the love, closeness, and mutual obligations of family life.

attachment theory Theory originally developed by British psychiatrist John Bowlby, asserting that among humans as among other primates, attachments between parents and children have an evolutionary basis in the need for vulnerable young members of the species to stay in close proximity to adults who will care for and protect them.

We have noted that adolescents consistently state that their parents are among the most important figures in their lives, and that most young people maintain a sense of emotional closeness to their parents throughout adolescence and emerging adulthood. An influential theory describing emotional relationships between parents and children is **attachment theory**. This theory was originally developed by British psychiatrist John Bowlby (1969, 1973, 1980), who argued that among humans as among other primates, attachments between parents and children have an evolutionary basis in the need for vulnerable young members of the species to stay in close proximity to adults who will care for and protect them. Bowlby's colleague, American psychologist Mary Ainsworth (1967, 1982), observed interactions between mothers and infants and described two general types of attachment: **secure attachment**, in which infants use the mother as a "secure base from which to explore" when all is well, but seek physical comfort and consolation from her if frightened or threatened; and **insecure attachment**, in which infants are wary of exploring the environment and resist or avoid the mother when she attempts to offer comfort or consolation.

Although most of the early research and theory on attachment focused on infancy, both Bowlby and Ainsworth believed that the attachment formed with the **primary caregiver** (usually but not necessarily the mother) in infancy forms the foundation for attachments to others throughout a person's life. Bowlby quoted a phrase from Sigmund Freud to describe this concept, in which Freud stated that the relationship with the mother is "the prototype of all [future] love relations" (Freud, 1940/1964, p. 188). According to Bowlby (1969), in the course of interactions with the primary caregiver, the infant develops an **internal working model** that shapes expectations and interactions in relationships with others throughout life. This implies that in adolescence and emerging adulthood, the quality of relationships with others—from friends to teachers to romantic partners to the parents themselves—will all be shaped, for better or worse, by the quality of the attachments to parents experienced in infancy.

This is a provocative and intriguing claim. How well does it hold up in research? First, abundant research indicates that a secure attachment to parents *in adolescence* is related to favorable outcomes. Secure attachments to parents are related to a variety of aspects of adolescents' well-being, including self-esteem and psychological and physical health (Allen & Kuperminc, 1995; Allen & Land, 1999; Juang & Nguyen, 1997). Adolescents who have secure attachments to parents tend to have closer relationships with friends and romantic

Secure attachments to parents are related to adolescents' well-being in a variety of respects.

partners (Allen & Bell, 1995; Laible, Carlo, & Rafaelli, 2000; Roisman et al., 2001). Security of attachment to parents in adolescence also has been found to predict a variety of outcomes in emerging adulthood, including educational and occupational attainment, psychological problems, quality of romantic relationships, and drug use (Allen et al., 2007; Cooper et al., 2004; Mayseless & Scharf, 2007; O'Connor et al., 1996).

Another prediction of attachment theory involves the compatibility between autonomy and **relatedness** in adolescence. According to attachment theory, autonomy (being capable of self-direction) and relatedness (feeling close to parents emotionally) should be compatible rather than opposing dynamics in relations with parents. That is, in infancy as well as in adolescence, if children feel close to their parents and confident of their parents' love and concern, they are likely to be able to develop a healthy sense of autonomy from parents as they grow up (Allen & Bell, 1995). Rather than promoting prolonged dependence on parents, a secure attachment gives children the confidence to go out into the world, using the comfort of that attachment as a "secure base from which to explore."

This prediction from attachment theory is supported by research. Adolescents who are the most autonomous and self-reliant also tend to report close, affectionate relationships with their parents (Allen et al., 1994; Ryan & Lynch, 1989; Zimmer-Gembeck & Collins, 2003). Adolescents who have trouble establishing autonomy in adolescence also tend to have more difficulty maintaining a healthy level of relatedness to parents.

---

secure attachment Type of attachment to caregiver in which infants use the caregiver as a "secure base from which to explore" when all is well, but seek physical comfort and consolation from her if frightened or threatened.

insecure attachment Type of attachment to caregiver in which infants are timid about exploring the environment and resist or avoid the caregiver when she attempts to offer comfort or consolation.

primary caregiver The person mainly responsible for caring for an infant or young child.

internal working model In attachment theory, the term for the cognitive framework, based on interactions in infancy with the primary caregiver, that shapes expectations and interactions in relationships to others throughout life.

relatedness The quality of being emotionally close to another person.

An imbalance between autonomy and relatedness (i.e., too little of one or both) tends to be related to a variety of negative outcomes, such as psychological problems and drug use (Allen et al., 1994; Zimmer-Gembeck & Collins, 2003).

However, these studies do not really test the heart of attachment theory, which is the claim that attachments *in infancy* form the basis for all later relationships, including those in adolescence and emerging adulthood. What do studies indicate on this crucial issue? Several longitudinal studies on attachment have by now followed samples from infancy to adolescence, and they provide mixed support for the predictions of attachment theory (Grossman, Grossman, & Waters, 2005). Waters and colleagues (2000) reported that 72% of the children in their sample received the same attachment classification at age 21 as they did at 1 year of age. One study found that a prolonged separation from parents during infancy or early childhood predicted a less secure attachment to parents in adolescence, in accord with attachment theory, which asserts that early separation from parents can result in long-term difficulties in emotional development (Woodward, Fergusson, & Belsky, 2000).

Another study found that attachment classification in infancy predicted the quality of interactions with others at ages 10 and 15 (Sroufe, Carlson, & Schulman, 1993). When the children in the original infancy study reached age 10, the researchers invited them to attend a summer camp where their relations with peers could be observed. At age 10, the children who had been securely attached in infancy were judged to be more skilled socially, more self-confident, and less dependent on other campers. Five years later, the researchers arranged a camp reunion where the children could again be evaluated. At age 15, adolescents who had been securely attached in infancy were more open in expressing their feelings and were more likely to form close relationships with peers. However, in a more recent follow-up, these researchers found no continuity between security of attachment to parents in infancy and at age 19 (Sroufe et al., 2005; Weinfield, Sroufe, & Egeland, 2000). Similar results were reported in a longitudinal study by Lewis and colleagues (2000).

In recent years, most attachment researchers have modified the claim that infant attachment is the foundation of all later relationships (Egeland & Carlson, 2004; Grossman et al., 2005). Instead, they view infant attachment as establishing tendencies and expectations that may then be modified by later experiences in childhood, adolescence, and beyond. This view of attachment is also more bidirectional, viewing the quality of attachment as due not only to the behavior of the parent but to the temperament and behavior of the child as well.

Parent-Adolescent Conflict

"This is a dangerous world, what with all the drugs and drunk drivers and violent crime and kids disappearing and you name it. I know my kids are pretty responsible, but can I trust all their friends? Are they going to end up in some situation they can't get out of? Are they going to get in over their heads? You can never be sure, so I worry and set curfews and make rules about where they can go and who they can go with. Not because I want to be a tough dad, but because I want them to be safe."

—John, father of a 16-year-old son and a 13-year-old daughter (Bell, 1998, p. 54)

"My father is very strict and had a great deal of rules when I was in high school, which usually could not be bent for anything. My father was very worried about the fact that I was getting older and interested in boys so much. This worrying led him to lay down strict rules which led to many arguments between us. He wouldn't let me date until I was 16—by this he meant 'don't even speak to a boy until you're 16!' He would hardly let me go anywhere."

—Danielle, age 19 (Arnett, unpublished data)

Although children and adolescents typically develop attachments to their parents, the course of family life does not always run smoothly, and this seems to be especially true for families with adolescents. For a variety of reasons, adolescence can be a difficult time for relationships with parents.

The degree of parent-adolescent conflict should not be exaggerated. Early theories of adolescence, such as those of G. Stanley Hall (1904) and Anna Freud (1946), claimed that it was universal and inevitable that adolescents rebel against their parents and that parents and adolescents experience intense conflict for many years. Anna Freud (1946) even asserted that adolescents would not develop normally without this kind of turmoil in their relationships with their parents.

Few scholars on adolescence believe this anymore. Over the past few decades, numerous studies have shown that it is simply not true. In fact, adolescents and their parents agree on many of the most important aspects of their views of life and typically have a great deal of love and respect for one another (Moore et al., 2002; Offer & Schonert-Reichl, 1992; Smetana, 2005). Two studies in the 1960s were among the first and most important in dispelling the stereotype of pervasive and fierce conflict in parent-adolescent relationships (Douvan & Adelson, 1966; Offer, 1969). Both studies found that the great majority of adolescents like their parents, trust them, and admire them. Both studies also found that adolescents and their parents frequently disagreed, but the arguments were usually over seemingly minor issues such as curfews, clothes, grooming, and use of the family car. These arguments usually did not seriously threaten the attachments between parents and their adolescents.

More recent studies confirm this pattern (e.g., Moore et al., 2002; Steinberg, 1990, 2000). These studies report that adolescents typically love and care about their parents and are confident that their parents feel the same about them. Like the earlier studies, recent studies find that arguments

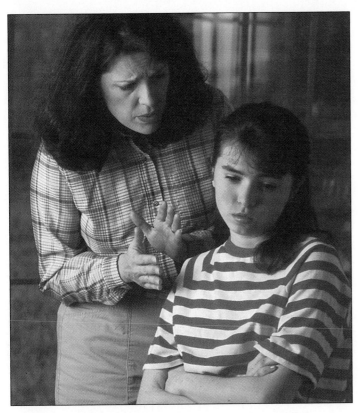
Conflict in adolescence is especially frequent and intense between mothers and daughters.

However, let's not get carried away with the rosy portrait of family harmony, either. Studies also indicate that conflict with parents increases sharply in early adolescence, compared with preadolescence, and remains high for several years before declining in late adolescence (Arnett, 1999a; Dworkin & Larson, 2001; Larson & Richards, 1994; Laursen, Coy, & Collins, 1998). Figure 7.2 shows the pattern of conflict across adolescence, from a longitudinal study that observed mothers and sons in videotaped interactions on five occasions over 8 years (Granic, Dishion, & Hollenstein, 2003). A Canadian study found that 40% of adolescents reported arguments with their parents at least once a week (Sears et al., 2006). Frequency of conflict between *typical* adolescents and their parents is higher than between *distressed* marital couples (Buchanan, Maccoby, & Dornbusch, 1991). Conflict in adolescence is especially frequent and intense between mothers and daughters (Collins & Laursen, 2004). Both parents and adolescents report more frequent conflict in early adolescence than prior to adolescence; by midadolescence, conflict with parents tends to become somewhat less frequent but more intense (Laursen et al., 1998). It is only in late adolescence and emerging adulthood that conflict with parents diminishes substantially (Arnett, 2003a; 2004a).

Perhaps as a consequence of these conflicts, parents tend to perceive adolescence as the most difficult stage of their children's development (Buchanan et al., 1990). In a recent study in the Netherlands, 56% of Dutch parents viewed adolescence as the most difficult time to be a parent, compared to 5% for infancy and 14% for the toddler period (Meeus, 2006). Although midlife tends to be an especially fruitful and satisfying time for adults, for many of them their satisfaction with their relationships with their children diminishes when their children reach adolescence (Gecas & Seff, 1990; Gladding, 2002). As conflict rises between parents and adolescents, closeness declines (Larson & Richards, 1994; Laursen & Collins, 2004).

between parents and adolescents generally concern seemingly minor issues such as curfews, clothing, musical preferences, and the like (Smetana, 1988, 2005; Steinberg & Levine, 1997). Parents and adolescents may disagree and argue about these issues, but they usually agree on key values such as the importance of education, the value of hard work, and the desirability of being honest and trustworthy (Gecas & Seff, 1990).

Chores are a common source of conflict between parents and adolescents.

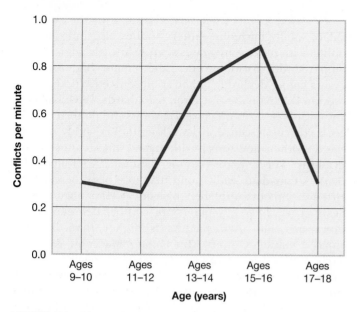

FIGURE 7.2 Observed conflicts per minute between mother and son in 30-minute videotaped interactions over an 8-year period.

Source: Granic, Dishion, and Hollenstein (2003).

Sources of Conflict With Parents

"One minute my mother treats me like I'm old enough to do this or this—like help her out at home by doing the marketing or making dinner or babysitting my little brother. And she's always telling me, 'You're thirteen years old now, you should know better than that!' But then the next minute, when there's something I really want to do, like there's a party that everyone's going to, she'll say, 'You're too young to do that.'"

—Elizabeth, age 13 (Bell, 1998, p. 55)

THINKING CRITICALLY •••

Apply the idea of the custom complex to parent-child conflict in the American majority culture. How do the typical topics of conflict reflect certain cultural beliefs?

But why do parents and adolescents argue more than they did earlier? Why would early adolescence be a time when conflict with parents is especially high? Part of the explanation may lie in the biological and cognitive changes of adolescence. Biologically, adolescents become bigger and stronger during puberty, making it more difficult for parents to impose their authority by virtue of their greater physical presence. Also, puberty means sexual maturity, which means that sexual issues may be a source of conflict—at least indirectly—in a way they would not have been in childhood (Arnett, 1999a; Steinberg, 1990). Early-maturing adolescents tend to

have more conflict with parents than adolescents who mature "on time," perhaps because sexual issues arise earlier (Collins & Laursen, 2004).

Cognitively, increased abilities for thinking abstractly and with more complexity make adolescents better arguers than preadolescents and make it more difficult for parents to prevail quickly in arguments with their children. According to psychologist Judith Smetana, conflict may also reflect the different ways adolescents and their parents perceive and define the range of adolescents' autonomy (Smetana, 1989; 2005). Parents frequently view issues of conflict as matters of desirable social convention, whereas adolescents regard these issues as matters of personal choice. Smetana's research indicates that, especially in early adolescence, parents and adolescents often disagree about who should have the authority over issues such as dress and hairstyles, choice of friends, and the state of order (or disorder) in the adolescent's bedroom (Smetana, 1989, 2005; Smetana & Asquith, 1994; Smetana & Gaines, 1999). Parents tend to see these as issues they should decide, or at least influence and set boundaries for; adolescents, however, tend to see the issues as matters of personal choice that should be theirs to decide by now. Perhaps the peak of conflict occurs in early adolescence because that is the time when adolescents are first pressing for a new degree of autonomy, and parents are adjusting to their adolescents' new maturity and struggling over how much autonomy they should allow. In the view of Smetana and other scholars on adolescents and families, conflict can be constructive and useful because it promotes the development of a new equilibrium in the family system that allows adolescents greater autonomy (Collins, 1997; Laursen & Collins, 2004; Steinberg, 2004).

Although most parent-adolescent conflict is over apparently minor issues, some issues that seem trivial on the surface may in fact be substitutes for more serious underlying issues (Arnett, 1999a). For example, most American parents and adolescents have limited communication about sexual issues. Especially in the era of AIDS and other sexually transmitted diseases, it would be surprising indeed if most parents did not have some concerns about their adolescents' sexual behavior, yet they find it difficult to speak to their adolescents directly about sexual issues. As a result, they may say "You can't wear that to school" when they mean "That's too sexually provocative." They may say "I don't know if it's a good idea for you to date him" when they really mean "He has that lean and hungry look—I worry that he will want you to have sex, and I worry that you'll like the idea." And "You have to be home by 11:00" may mean "The movie ends at ten, and I don't want you to have time to have sex between the time the movie ends and the time you come home."

Sexual issues are not the only issues that may be argued about in this indirect way. "I don't like that crowd you're hanging around with lately" could mean "They look like the type who might use drugs, and I worry that they might persuade you to use them, too." Arguments about curfews may reflect parents' attempts to communicate that "The sooner you come in, the less likely it is that you and your friends will have drunk enough beer to put yourselves at risk for a terrible automobile accident."

Seen in this light, these arguments are not necessarily over trivial issues but may be proxies for arguments over serious issues of life and death (Arnett, 1999a). Parents have legitimate concerns about the safety and well-being of their adolescents, given the high rates of adolescents' risky behavior (as we will see in Chapter 13), but they also know that in the American majority culture they are expected to loosen the reins substantially when their children reach adolescence. The result may be that they express their concerns indirectly, through what seem to be less serious issues.

Culture and Conflict With Parents

Although the biological and cognitive changes of adolescence may provide a basis for parent-adolescent conflict, this does not mean that such conflict is universal and "natural." Biological and cognitive changes take place among adolescents in all cultures, yet parent-adolescent conflict is not typical in all cultures (Arnett, 1999a). Cultures can take the raw material of nature and shape it in highly diverse ways. This is no less true for parent-adolescent conflict than for the other topics addressed in this book.

In traditional cultures, it is rare for parents and adolescents to engage in the kind of frequent, petty conflicts typical of parent-adolescent relationships in the American majority culture (Schlegel & Barry, 1991; Whiting & Edwards, 1988). Part of the reason is economic. In traditional cultures, family members tend to rely on each other economically. In many of these cultures, family members spend a great deal of time together each day, working on family economic enterprises. Children and adolescents depend on their parents for the necessities of life, parents depend on children and adolescents for the contribution of their labor, and all family members are expected to assist one another routinely and help one another in times of need. Under such conditions, the pressure to maintain family harmony is intense because the economic interdependence of the family is so strong (Schlegel & Barry, 1991).

However, more than economics and the structure of daily life are involved in the lower levels of parent-adolescent conflict in traditional cultures. Levels of conflict are low in parent-adolescent relationships not only in nonindustrialized traditional cultures but also in highly industrialized traditional cultures, such as Japan and Taiwan (Zhou, 1997), as well as in the Asian American and Latino cultures that are part of American society (Chao, 1994; Harwood et al., 2002; Suarez-Orozco & Suarez-Orozco, 1996). This indicates that even more important than economics are cultural beliefs about parental authority and the appropriate degree of adolescent independence. As discussed earlier, the role of parent carries greater authority in traditional cultures than in the West, and this makes it less likely that adolescents in such cultures will express disagreements and resentments toward their parents (Arnett, 1999a; Phinney et al., 2005).

THINKING CRITICALLY •••

How would you predict parent-adolescent conflict in traditional cultures will be affected by globalization?

This does not mean that adolescents in traditional cultures do not sometimes feel an inclination to resist or defy the authority of their parents (Phinney et al., 2005; Phinney & Ong, 2002). Like Western adolescents, they undergo biological and cognitive changes at puberty that may incline them toward such resistance. But socialization shapes not only the way people behave but their cultural beliefs, their whole way of looking at the world (Arnett, 1995a, 2006b; Shweder et al., 1998). Someone who has been raised in a culture where the status and authority of parents and other elders are taught to them and emphasized constantly in direct and indirect ways is unlikely at adolescence to question their parents' authority, regardless of their new biological and cognitive maturity. Such questioning is simply not part of their cultural beliefs about the way the world is and the way it should be. Even when they disagree with their parents, they are unlikely to mention it because of their feelings of duty and respect (Phinney & Ong, 2002).

A key point in understanding parent-adolescent relationships in traditional cultures is that the independence that is so important to Western adolescents is not nearly as prized in non-Western cultures. In the West, as we have seen, regulating the pace of adolescents' autonomy is often a source of parent-adolescent conflict. However, parents and adolescents in the West agree that independence is the ultimate goal for adolescents as they move into adulthood (Aquilino, 2006). Individuals in the West are supposed to reach the point, during emerging adulthood, where they no longer live in their parents' household, no longer rely on their parents financially, and have learned to stand alone as self-sufficient individuals (Arnett, 1998a; 2004a). The pace of the adolescent's growing autonomy is a source of contention between parents and adolescents not because parents do not want their adolescents to become independent, but because the ultimate goal of self-sufficiency that both of them value requires continual adaptations and adjustments in their relationship as they move toward that goal. Increasing autonomy prepares adolescents for life in a culture where they will be expected to be capable of independence and self-sufficiency. The discussion, negotiation, and arguments typical of parent-adolescent relationships in the West may also help prepare adolescents for participation in a politically diverse, democratic society.

Outside of the West, independence is not highly valued as an outcome of adolescent development (Schlegel & Barry, 1991). Financially, socially, and even psychologically, interdependence is a higher value than independence, not only during adolescence but throughout adulthood (Markus & Kitayama, 1991, 2003; Phinney, Kim-Jo, Osorio, & Vilhalmsdottir, 2005). According to Schlegel and Barry (1991), in traditional cultures "independence as we know it would be regarded as not only egocentric but also foolhardy beyond reason" (p. 45) because of the ways that family members rely on each other economically. Just as a dramatic increase in

In non-Western cultures, adolescents and their parents often depend economically on each other, which minimizes conflict. Here, a boy and his father in Bangladesh plow rice paddies together.

autonomy during adolescence prepares Western adolescents for adult life in an individualistic culture, learning to suppress disagreements and submit to the authority of one's parents prepares adolescents in traditional cultures for an adult life in which interdependence is among the highest values and throughout life each person has a clearly designated role and position in a family hierarchy.

Emerging Adults' Relationships With Parents

"In high school, I went out of my way to avoid conversations with my parents because I felt that a lot of things they wanted to know about didn't concern them. I find now that my parents know less about my life because I'm not at home. They don't ask me as many questions, so I enjoy having conversations with them."

—Tara, age 23 (Arnett, 2003a)

"In high school I was rude, inconsiderate, and got into many fights with my mom. Since coming to college I realize how much she means to me and how much she goes out of her way for me. I've grown to have a true appreciation for her."

—Matt, age 21 (Arnett, 2004a, p. 57)

"They're still my parents, but there's more—I don't know if friendship is the right word, but like I go out with them and just really enjoy spending time with them, and they're not in a parental role as much. It's not a disciplining role, it's just more of a real comfortable friendship thing."

—Nancy, age 28 (Arnett, 2004a, p. 58)

"Over the past year I have become very close with my dad. Before college there was a definite parent-child relationship with my father. Now he is more like a mentor or friend. Overall, the relationship between my parents and I has been a growing mutual respect."

—Luke, age 20 (Arnett, 2004a, p. 58)

In most Western majority cultures, most young people move out of their parents' home sometime during emerging adulthood. In the United States, leaving home typically takes place around ages 18 to 19 (Goldscheider & Goldscheider, 1999). The most common reasons for leaving home stated by emerging adults are going to college, cohabiting with a partner, or simply the desire for independence (Goldscheider & Goldscheider, 1999; Juang et al., 1999; Silbereisen et al., 1996).

When a young person leaves home, a disruption in the family system takes place that requires family members to adjust. As we have seen, parents generally adjust very well, and in fact report improved marital satisfaction and life satisfaction once their children leave (Campbell et al., 2007; Whitbourne & Willis, 2006). What about the relationship between parents and emerging adults? How is it influenced by the young person's departure?

Typically, relationships between parents and emerging adults improve once the young person leaves home. In this case, at least, absence makes the heart grow fonder. Numerous studies have confirmed that emerging adults report greater closeness and fewer negative feelings toward their parents after moving out (e.g., Aquilino, 2006; Arnett, 2003a; O'Connor et al., 1996; Shaver, Furman, & Buhrmester, 1985; Smetana et al., 2004). Furthermore, emerging adults who move out tend to get along better with their parents than those who remain at home. For example, Dubas and Petersen (1996) followed a sample of 246 young people from age 13 through age 21. At age 21, the emerging adults who had moved at least an hour away (by car) from their parents reported the highest levels of closeness to their parents and valued their parents' opinions most highly. Emerging adults who remained home had the poorest relations with their parents in these respects, and those who had moved out but remained within an hour's drive were in between the other two groups.

What explains these patterns? Some scholars have suggested that leaving home leads young people to appreciate their parents more (Arnett, 2004a; Katchadourian & Boli, 1985). Another factor may be that it is easier to be fond of

Relationships with parents tend to improve when emerging adults leave home.

someone you no longer live with. Once emerging adults move out, they no longer experience the day-to-day friction with their parents that inevitably results from living with others. They can now control the frequency and timing of their interactions with their parents in a way they could not when they were living with them. They can visit their parents for the weekend, for a holiday, or for dinner, enjoy the time together, and still maintain full control over their daily lives. As a 24-year-old woman in my research put it, "I don't have to talk to them when I don't want to, and when I want to, I can" (Arnett, 2004a, p. 49).

In the United States, although most emerging adults move out of their parents' home in their late teens, a substantial proportion (about one fourth) stay home through their early 20s (Goldscheider & Goldscheider, 1999). Staying at home is more common among Latinos, Blacks, and Asian Americans than among White Americans (Fuligni & Witkow, 2004). The reason for this appears to be their greater emphasis on family closeness and interdependence, and less emphasis on being independent as a value in itself. For example, one emerging adult in my research (Arnett, 2004a) lived with her Chinese American mother and Mexican American father throughout her college years at the University of California-Berkeley. She enjoyed the way staying home allowed her to remain in close contact with them. "I loved living at home. I respect my parents a lot, so being home with one of them was actually one of the things I liked to do most," she said. "Plus, it was free!" (Arnett, 2004a, p. 54). For Latinos and Asian Americans, an additional reason for staying home is specific to young women, and concerns the high value placed on virginity before marriage.

About 40% of American emerging adults "return to the nest" at least once after they leave (Goldscheider & Goldscheider, 1999; Aquilino, 2006). There are many reasons why emerging adults sometimes move home again (Arnett, 2004a; Goldscheider & Goldscheider, 1999). For those who left home for college, moving back home may be a way of

bridging their transition to postcollege life after th[ey] ate or drop out. It gives them a chance to decide w[hat] next, be it graduate school, a job near home, or a jo[b] away. For those who left home for independence, so[me] feel that the glow of independence dims after a while [the] freedom of doing what they want when they want becomes outweighed by the burden of taking care of a household and paying all their own bills. An early divorce or a period of military service are other reasons emerging adults give for returning home (Goldscheider & Goldscheider, 1999). Under these circumstances, too, coming home may be attractive to young people as a transition period, a chance to get back on their feet before they venture again into the world.

Emerging adults and their parents react in a range of ways when emerging adults move back home (Arnett, 2004a). For some, the return home is welcome and the transition is managed easily. A successful transition home is more likely if parents recognize the change in their children's maturity and treat them as adults rather than adolescents. For others, however, the return home is a bumpy transition. Parents may have come to enjoy having the nest all to themselves, without children to provide for and feel responsible for. Emerging adults may find it difficult to have parents monitoring them daily again, after a period when they had grown used to managing their own lives. In my research (Arnett, 2004a), after Mary moved home she was dismayed to find that her mother would wait up for her when she went out with her boyfriend, just like it was high school all over again. They did not argue openly about it, but it made Mary feel "like she was sort of 'in my territory' or something" (p. 53). For many emerging adults, moving back home results in ambivalence. They are grateful for the support their parents provide, even as they resent returning to the subordinate role of a dependent child (White, 2002). Perhaps because of this ambivalence, the return home tends to be brief, with two thirds of emerging adults moving out again within one year (Aquilino, 2006).

In European countries, emerging adults tend to live with their parents longer than in the United States, especially in southern and eastern Europe (Douglass, 2005, 2007). Figure 7.3 shows the patterns in various European countries, as compared to the United States (Iacovov, 2002). A number of practical reasons explain why European emerging adults stay home longer. European university students are more likely than American students to continue to live at home while they attend university. European emerging adults who do not attend university may have difficulty finding or affording an apartment of their own. Also important are European cultural values that emphasize mutual support within the family while also allowing young people substantial autonomy. Young Europeans find that they can enjoy a higher standard of living by staying at home rather than living independently, and at the same time enjoy substantial autonomy. Italy provides a good case in point (Chisholm & Hurrelman, 1995; Krause, 2005). Ninety-four percent of Italians aged 15 to 24 live with their parents, the highest percentage in the European Union (EU). However, only 8% of them view their living arrangements as a problem—the lowest percentage

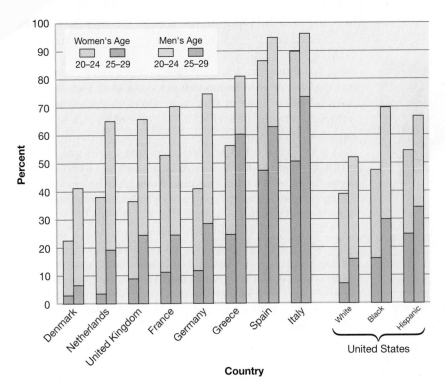

FIGURE 7.3 Percent of emerging adults living at home in Europe and the United States. Source: Iacovov, M. (2002).

among EU countries. Many European emerging adults remain at home contentedly through their early 20s, by choice rather than necessity.

There is more to the changes in relationships with parents from adolescence to emerging adulthood than simply the effects of moving out, staying home, or moving back in. Emerging adults also grow in their ability to understand their parents (Arnett, 2004a). As we have seen, adolescence is in some ways an egocentric period, and adolescents often have difficulty taking their parents' perspectives. They sometimes cast a pitiless gaze on their parents, magnifying their deficiencies and becoming easily irritated by their imperfections. As emerging adults mature and begin to feel more adult themselves, they become more capable of understanding how their parents look at things. They come to see their parents as persons and begin to realize that their parents, like themselves, have a mix of qualities, merits as well as faults.

Parents change, too, in how they view their children and how they relate to them. Their role as monitor of their children's behavior and enforcer of household rules diminishes, giving way to a more relaxed and amiable relationship with their children. The changes in parents and their emerging adult children allow them to establish a new intimacy, more open than before, with a new sense of mutual respect. They begin to relate to each other as adults, as friends, as equals, or at least as near-equals. There are exceptions, of course: some parents find it difficult to let their "baby" grow up, and some emerging adults are reluctant to accept the responsibilities of becoming self-sufficient adults. For the most part,

however, both parents and emerging adults are able and willing to adjust to a new relationship as near-equals (Arnett, 2004a).

In summary, studies in both the United States and Europe show that emerging adults can maintain or enhance the closeness they feel to their parents even as they become more autonomous. This is similar to the pattern we have already seen for adolescents. For both adolescents and emerging adults, autonomy and relatedness are complementary rather than opposing dimensions of their relationships with their parents (O'Connor et al., 1996).

Historical Change and the Family

To gain a complete understanding of adolescents' and emerging adults' family relationships today, it is necessary to understand the historical changes that are the basis for current patterns of family life. Many of the changes that have taken place in Western societies over the past two centuries have had important effects on families. Let's take a look briefly at these changes, considering how each has affected adolescents' and emerging adults' family lives. We will focus on the American example, but similar changes have taken place in other industrialized countries in the past two centuries and are taking place today in economically developing countries. We will first examine changes over the past two centuries, then focus on changes during the past 50 years.

Patterns Over Two Centuries

Three of the changes that have influenced family life over the past two centuries are a lower birth rate, longer life expectancy, and a movement from predominantly rural residence to predominantly urban residence. In contrast to young people today, young people of 200 years ago tended to grow up in large families; in 1800, women in the United States gave birth to an average of *eight* children (Harevan, 1984)! It was much more common then for children to die in infancy or early childhood, but nevertheless, adolescents who were among the eldest children were much more likely to have responsibility for younger children than they are today, when the average number of births per mother is just two (U.S. Bureau of the Census, 2009). In this respect, adolescents' family lives 200 years ago in the West were like the lives of adolescents in many traditional cultures today (Schlegel & Barry, 1991; Lloyd, 2005).

Longer life expectancy is another change that has affected the way young people experience family life. Up until about 1900, the average human life expectancy was about 45 (Kett, 1977); now it is over 70 and still rising (U.S. Bureau of the Census, 2009). Because of the lower life expectancy in

Between 1830 and the present, the proportion of farm families fell from about 70% to less than 2%.

TABLE 7.3	The Changing Functions of the Family	
Function	Performing Institution, 1800	Performing Institution, 2000
Educational	Family	School
Religious	Family	Church/Synagogue
Medical	Family	Medical profession
Economic Support	Family	Employer
Recreational	Family	Entertainment industry
Affective	Family	Family

Each of these changes has had effects on young people's family lives. Overall, we can say that the range of functions the family serves has been greatly reduced, many of them taken over by other social institutions (Coleman, 1961). The family in our time has mainly emotional or **affective functions**—the family is supposed to provide its members with love, nurturance, and affection above all else.

Table 7.3 shows some of the functions the family once served and the institutions that now serve those functions. As you can see, the only one of those functions that still remains within the family is the affective function. Although the family also contributes in the other areas, the main context of those functions has moved out of the family. Most young people living in industrialized countries do not rely on their parents to educate them, treat their medical problems, make a place for them in the family business, or provide recreation. Rather, young people look to their parents mainly for love, emotional support, and some degree of moral guidance (Allen & Land, 1999; Offer & Schonert-Reichl, 1992).

The Past 50 Years

Family life today not only is much different than it was 200 years ago, but it also has changed dramatically in the past 50 years. During this time, the most dramatic changes have been the rise in the divorce rate, the rise in the proportion of children in single-parent households, and the rise in the prevalence of dual-earner families. Once again, let's look at each of these changes with an eye to their implications for development in adolescence and emerging adulthood.

earlier times, marriages frequently ended in the death of a spouse in young or middle adulthood (Hetherington, Arnett, & Hollier, 1986). Thus, adolescents frequently experienced the death of a parent and the remarriage of their widowed parent.

Increased urbanization has also resulted in changes in family life. Up until about 200 years ago, most people lived and worked on a family farm. As recently as 1830, nearly 70% of American children lived in farm families (Hernandez, 1997). By 1930, this figure had dropped to 30%, and today it is less than 2%. This means that the majority of adolescents 200 years ago would have grown up in a rural area in a farm family, with their daily lives structured around farmwork and spent almost entirely with their families. As people moved off the farms, they migrated increasingly to the cities. Emerging adults often led the way, leaving their farm families to head for the bright lights of the big city (Kett, 1977). This meant new opportunities for education and employment, as well as greater opportunities for premarital sex, alcohol use, and other temptations of urban life (Wilson & Herrnstein, 1985).

Rise in the Divorce Rate Fifty years ago divorce was relatively rare in American society, compared with the present. The rate of divorce actually declined between 1950 and 1960 (Figure 7.4). However, between 1960 and 1975 the divorce rate more than doubled, before

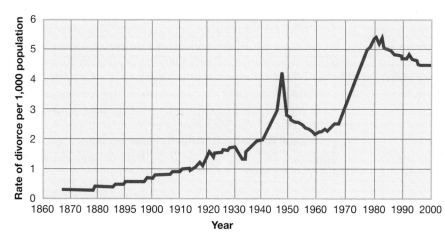

FIGURE 7.4 Changes in divorce rate, United States.

affective functions Emotional functions of the family, pertaining to love, nurturance, and attachment.

The Great Depression was the most severe economic cataclysm of the 20th century. It began with a plunge in the American stock market in 1929 and soon spread around the world. In the United States by 1932, at the depth of the Depression, stocks had dropped to just 11% of their 1929 value, thousands of companies had collapsed, thousands of banks had failed, and hundreds of thousands of families had been evicted from their homes (Manchester, 1973). One-third of adult men were unemployed, and homelessness and malnutrition were rampant. The average family suffered a decline in income of 40% (Elder, 1974/1999).

What sort of effects did these historical events have on adolescents' development? Sociologist Glen Elder and his colleagues have analyzed longitudinal data from a study that followed families beginning in the early 1930s (Elder, 1974/1999; Elder, Caspi, & Van Nguyen, 1986; Elder, Van Nguyen, & Caspi, 1985). Known as the Oakland Growth Study, the project followed the families of 167 adolescents born in 1920–1921, from 1932 when the adolescents were 11 to 12 years old until 1939 when they were 18 to 19 years old. Later follow-ups took place in the 1950s and again in the 1960s. All the families were White, and slightly more than half were middle-class prior to the Depression.

The families varied greatly in how much they suffered economically during the Depression, and many of the scholars' comparisons concerned "deprived" versus "nondeprived" families. Most deprived families suffered income declines of half or more of their 1929 income. The nondeprived families suffered a loss averaging about 20% of their 1929 income—certainly substantial, but not as devastating as in the deprived families.

Economic difficulties affected adolescents' family lives in a variety of ways. The economic upheaval of the Depression put a considerable strain on family relationships, especially in deprived families. Many of the fathers in the deprived families were frustrated and ashamed because of their inability to find work and support their families, and their relationships with their wives and children often deteriorated as a result. Fathers often became more punitive toward their children and more prone to anger and irritability toward their wives as well as their children. The more angry and punitive the fathers became, the more their children were likely to suffer declines in social and psychological well-being.

For other family members, the effects of economic deprivation were more complex and were surprisingly positive in many ways. As the father's status in deprived families declined, the mother's often rose. On average the mother in deprived families was viewed by her adolescent children as more powerful, supportive, and attractive than the father.

Economic deprivation tended to bring adult responsibilities into the lives of adolescents at an early age. By age 14 or 15, adolescents in deprived families were more likely than those in nondeprived families to be employed in part-time jobs—about two-thirds of boys in deprived families and nearly half of girls

declining slightly between 1975 and the present. Americans have one of the highest divorce rates in the world (Kelly, 2003; McKenry & Price, 1995). The current rate is so high that nearly half of the current generation of young people are projected to experience their parents' divorce by the time they reach their late teens (Hetherington & Kelly, 2002). Furthermore, over three fourths of those who divorce eventually remarry, with the result that over one fourth of young people spend some time in a stepfamily by the time they reach age 18 (Hernandez, 1997). Within American society, the divorce rate is especially high among African Americans. Also, people with a high school education or less have a much higher rate of divorce than people with a college degree or more (Popenoe, 2007).

Rise in the Rate of Single-Parent Households The rise in the divorce rate has contributed to a simultaneous rise in the rate of single-parent households. Although most divorced parents remarry, they have a period between marriages as single parents. In about 90% of divorces, it is the mother who is the **custodial parent**—that is, the parent who lives in the same household as the children following the divorce (Emery, 1999).

In addition to the rise in single-parent households through divorce, there has been an increase in the proportion of children born outside of marriage. This increase has occurred for both White and Black families in American society, but especially for Black families. Currently, about one third of White children and two thirds of Black children are born to single mothers (U.S. Bureau of the Census, 2009). Combining the rates of divorced single-parent households and the rates of single-parent, never-married households, only 20% of Blacks and 40% to 45% of Whites grow up through age 18 living with both of their biological parents (Hernandez, 1997).

---

custodial parent The parent who lives in the same household as the children following a divorce.

dual-earner family A family in which both parents are employed.

were employed by that age. For example, one boy in Elder's study washed dishes in the school cafeteria after school, then supervised the work of six newspaper delivery boys. Adolescent girls often worked as baby-sitters or in local stores. Adolescents' earnings were usually contributed to the family's needs. Deprived families also required more household work from adolescents, especially girls, in part because mothers in these families were more likely to be employed. Adolescents from deprived families tended to marry earlier than adolescents from nondeprived families.

The effects of early family responsibilities were generally positive. Adolescents who were employed displayed more responsible use of money and more energetic and industrious behavior compared with those who were not. In general, adolescents in deprived families felt that they played an important role in the lives of their families. Although they were required to take on responsibilities at an early age, those responsibilities were clearly important and meaningful to their families.

However, some negative effects were seen as well, especially for adolescent girls in deprived families. Girls in deprived families showed greater moodiness, lower social competence, and greater feelings of inadequacy compared with girls in nondeprived families. These effects were especially strong for girls who felt rejected by their fathers. Girls in deprived families were also less likely than other girls to take part in social activities such as dating, in part because of their greater household responsibilities.

During the Great Depression, adolescents often took part-time jobs to help their families. Here, a Connecticut girl in 1933.

Taken together, the results of Elder's study show the complex interactions that take place between historical events and adolescents' family lives. The study also shows that even under conditions of extreme adversity, many adolescents are highly resilient and will thrive in spite of—or even because of—the adversity.

Rise in the Rate of Dual-Earner Families In the 19th and early 20th centuries, the rise of industrialization took most employment outside of the home and farm into factories, larger businesses, and government organizations. It was almost exclusively men who obtained this employment; women were rarely employed in the economic enterprises of industrialization. During the 19th century, their designated sphere became the home, and their designated role was the cultivation of a family life that their husband and children would experience as a refuge from the complex and sometimes bruising world of industrialized societies (Lasch, 1979).

This trend changed about 50 years ago with the rise of **dual-earner families**, as mothers followed fathers out of the home and into the workplace. Over the past 50 years, employment among women with school-aged children has increased steadily, as shown in Figure 7.5. Mothers of adolescents are more likely than mothers of younger children to be employed outside of the home (U.S. Bureau of the Census,

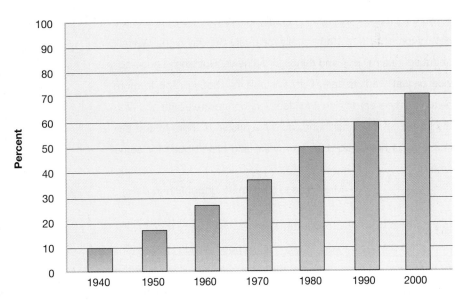

FIGURE 7.5 Proportion of children with mothers in the labor force, 1940–2000.

Source: Hernandez, 1997; U.S. Bureau of the Census, 2002.

2009). Part of the increase is related to the increase in rates of divorce and single parenthood discussed earlier, which have often left the mother as the only source of the family's income. Mothers in nondivorced families may also work to help the family maintain an adequate income (Schneider & Waite, 2005).

Of course, noneconomic reasons are often involved as well. Many educational and occupational opportunities have opened up to women in the past 50 years that had been denied to them before. Research indicates that most employed mothers would continue to work even if they had enough money (Hochschild, 2001; Schneider & Waite, 2005). Women in professional careers as well as restaurant servers and factory workers generally report that they are committed to their jobs, enjoy having a work role as well as family roles, and desire to continue to work.

Effects of Divorce, Remarriage, Single Parenthood, and Dual-Earner Families

Now that we have reviewed the historical background of the current American family, let's take a look at how divorce, remarriage, single parenthood, and dual-earner families are related to young people's behavior and to their perceptions of their family lives.

Divorce

"When I was 15 my parents separated. I continued to live with my mother but would visit my father on Sunday. During that time we would do something 'entertaining,' like go to a movie, which relieved the pressure from us to actually interact. . . . My parents are now divorced and my father calls me every Sunday night. We talk about school, my job, and things in the news. But when I need advice or just want to talk, I always call my mother. She is more aware of my everyday life and I feel very comfortable with her. With my father, on the other hand, our relationship is more forced because he is not up-to-date on my life and hasn't been for some time."

—Marilyn, age 21 (Arnett, unpublished data)

"My parents were divorced, so the money was pretty thin. My father was a psycho and didn't pay child support. When I was in junior high I wanted everything that the other kids had—Liz Claiborne purses, designer clothes, etc. I would pester my mother for money constantly, sometimes to the point where she would be in tears because she wanted to give me things but couldn't afford to do so."

—Dawn, age 20 (Arnett, unpublished data)

Because the rate of divorce is so high and has risen so dramatically in the past 50 years in many countries, scholars have devoted a great deal of attention to investigating the effects of divorce. Across a wide range of countries, studies consistently find that young people whose parents have divorced are at higher risk for a wide variety of negative outcomes compared with young people in nondivorced families, in areas including behavior problems, psychological distress, and academic achievement (Breivik & Olweus, 2006; Hetherington & Kelly, 2002). With regard to behavior problems, adolescents whose parents have divorced have higher rates of drug and alcohol use and tend to initiate sexual intercourse at an earlier age, compared with adolescents in nondivorced families (Buchanan, 2000). With regard to psychological distress, adolescents with divorced parents are more likely to be depressed and withdrawn (Meeus, 2006). Those who feel caught in a loyalty conflict between their parents are especially likely to be anxious and depressed following the divorce (Buchanan et al., 1991; Buchanan, Maccoby, & Dornbusch, 1996). Adolescents in divorced families also are more likely to report having psychological problems and more likely to receive mental health treatment (Buchanan, 2000; Chase-Lansdale, Cherlin, & Kiernan, 1995; Cherlin, 1999). With regard to academic achievement, young people from divorced families tend not to do as well in school as their peers (Amato, 1993; Jeynes, 2002), and they are less likely to attend college than young people from nondivorced families (Aquilino, 2006; Astone & McLanahan, 1995).

In general, adolescents show fewer negative effects of parental divorce than younger children do (Buchanan, 2000; Klaff, 2007), perhaps because adolescents are less dependent on their parents, spend more time with their peers outside of the family household, and have greater cognitive capacities

Exposure to conflict between parents leads to a variety of problems in children and adolescents.

to understand and adapt to what is happening. However, even many years after the divorce, the painful memories and feelings linger for many adolescents and emerging adults (Cartwright, 2006; Laumann-Billings & Emery, 2000). In emerging adulthood, the effects of parental divorce are evident in greater problems in forming close romantic relationships (Aquilino, 2005; Herzog & Cooney, 2002; Wallerstein, Lewis, & Blakeslee, 2000). As they anticipate a possible marriage of their own, emerging adults from divorced families tend to be somewhat wary of entering marriage, but especially determined to avoid having a divorce of their own (Arnett, 2004a; Darlington, 2001). Nevertheless, the risk of divorce is higher for young people from divorced families (Amato, 2001).

Although the findings on the effects of divorce are consistent, a great deal of variability exists in how adolescents and emerging adults respond to and recover from their parents' divorce (Cherlin, 1999). As one prominent research team observed, "the fact that a young person comes from a divorced family does not, in itself, tell us a great deal about how he or she is faring on embarking into adulthood" (Zill, Morrison, & Coiro, 1993, p. 100). To say that a young person's parents are divorced tells us only about **family structure**. *Family structure* is the term scholars use to refer to the outward characteristics of the family—whether or not the parents are married, how many adults and children live in the household, whether or not there is a biological relationship between the family members (e.g., in stepfamilies), and so on. However, in recent years scholars studying divorce have focused primarily on **family process** (Klaff, 2007)—that is, the quality of family members' relationships, the degree of warmth or hostility between them, and so on. So it is important to go beyond the simple question—Why does divorce have negative effects on children and adolescents?—to the more complex and enlightening question—How does divorce influence family process in ways that, in turn, influence children and adolescents?

Perhaps the most important aspect of family process with regard to the effects of divorce on children and adolescents is exposure to conflict between parents (Emery, 1999; Sbarra & Emery, 2008). Divorce involves the dissolution of a relationship that is, for most adults, at the heart of their emotional lives and their personal identities (Wallerstein & Blakeslee, 1996). Because the marriage relationship carries such a large freight of hopes and desires, it rarely sinks without numerous explosions occurring along the way. Living in the household where the divorce is taking place, children and adolescents will likely be exposed to their parents' hostility and recriminations before, during, and after the divorce, which is often painful, stressful, and damaging (Hetherington & Kelly, 2002; Kelly, 2000).

In nondivorced families, too, parents' conflict has damaging effects on children's development (Bradford, 2004; Emery, 1999; Kelly, 2000). In fact, numerous studies have found that adolescents and emerging adults in high-conflict nondivorced households have poorer adjustment than adolescents and adults in low-conflict divorced households (Amato, 2000; Emery, 1999). Longitudinal studies that include data before and after divorce indicate that adolescents' problems after divorce often began long before the divorce, as a consequence of high conflict between their parents (Buchanan, 2000; Cherlin, Chase-Lansdale, & McCrae, 1998; Kelly, 2000; Peris & Emery, 2005). Thus, it is exposure to parents' conflicts, not simply the specific event of divorce, that is especially damaging to children and adolescents.

A second important aspect of family process to consider with regard to the effects of divorce is that divorce affects parenting practices. Divorce is highly stressful and painful to most of the adults who experience it (Wallerstein & Blakeslee, 1996), and not surprisingly it affects many aspects of their lives, including how they carry out their role as parents. The burdens fall especially on mothers. As the sole parent in the household, the mother has to take on all the parenting that was previously shared with the father, and often has increased employment responsibilities now that the father's income no longer comes directly into the family—not to mention handling by themselves the leaky roof, the sick pet, the disabled car, and all the other typical stresses of daily life.

So it is understandable that mothers' parenting tends to change following divorce, usually for the worse. Especially in the first year following divorce, mothers tend to be less affectionate, more permissive, and less consistent in their parenting than they were before the divorce took place or than they will be after a few years have passed (Buchanan, 2000; Hetherington & Kelly, 2002). Adolescents in divorced families have greater freedom than adolescents in nondivorced families in matters such as how to spend their money and how late to stay out, but younger adolescents especially may find it to be more freedom than they can handle wisely.

Another way parenting may change after divorce is that the mother may rely on the adolescent as a confidant (Afifi et al., 2007; Silverberg-Koerner, Wallace, et al., 2004). This is a mixed blessing for adolescents. They may enjoy becoming closer to their mothers while at the same time finding it difficult to hear about their parents' marital troubles and their mothers' difficulties in the aftermath of the divorce (Buchanan, Eccles, & Becker, 1992). Emerging adults may be able to handle this role better. Some studies find that emerging adults who experience their parents' divorce become closer to their mothers after the divorce (White, Brinkerhoff, & Booth, 1985) and are closer to their mothers than emerging adults in nondivorced families (Cooney, 1994).

As for relations with fathers, in most families children's contact with their father declines steadily in the years following divorce. By age 15, American adolescents in divorced families live an average of 400 miles away from their fathers,

---

family structure The outward characteristics of a family, such as whether or not the parents are married.

family process The quality of relationships among family members.

and almost half have not seen their father in over a year (Hetherington & Kelly, 2002). Even when divorced fathers and adolescents remain in close proximity, fathers complain that it often becomes difficult to arrange meetings as adolescents become increasingly involved in activities of their own (Dudley, 1991). Also, divorced fathers are frequently the target of young people's resentment and blame following divorce (Cooney, 1994; Cooney et al., 1986). Children often feel pressured to take sides when their parents divorce, and because mothers are usually closer to their children before the divorce, children's sympathies and loyalties are more often with the mother than with the father (Furstenberg & Cherlin, 1991). Thus, young people in divorced households tend to have more negative feelings and fewer positive feelings toward their fathers compared with young people in nondivorced families (Cooney, 1994; Wells & Johnson, 2001; Zill et al., 1993).

A third factor in considering the effects of divorce on young people is the increase in economic stress that typically results from divorce (Jeynes, 2002; Klaff, 2007). With the father's income no longer coming directly into the household, money is often tight in mother-headed households following divorce. In the aftermath of divorce, the income in mother-headed families decreases by an average of 40% to 50% (Smock, 1993). Some studies claim that the problems children and adolescents exhibit following divorce are due largely to these economic problems (Blum, Boyle, & Offord, 1988).

THINKING CRITICALLY •••

In addition to the factors mentioned here, can you think of other things that might influence adolescents' responses to divorce, for better or worse?

Several factors help to ameliorate the negative effects of divorce on adolescents. Adolescents who maintain a good relationship with their mothers tend to function well in the aftermath of divorce (Emery, 1999). Also, when divorced parents are able to maintain a civil relationship and communicate without hostility, their children and adolescents are less likely to exhibit the negative effects of divorce (Buchanan et al., 1996; Sbarra & Emery, 2008). A related factor of importance is consistency of parenting between the separate households of the mother and the father. If parents maintain consistency with each other in parenting—which they are more likely to do if they are communicating well—their adolescents benefit (Buchanan et al., 1992, 1996).

Of course, maintaining communication and consistency is not easy between two parents who have experienced a di-

divorce and often harbor hostile feelings toward one another (Hetherington & Kelly, 2002). In recent decades, **divorce mediation** has grown as a way of minimizing the damage to children and adolescents that may result from heightened parental conflict during and after divorce (Emery, Sbarra, & Grover, 2005; Sbarra & Emery, 2008). In divorce mediation, a professional mediator meets with divorcing parents to help them negotiate an agreement that both will find acceptable. Research has shown that mediation can settle a large percentage of cases otherwise headed for court and lead to remarkably improved relationships between divorced parents and their children, as well as between divorced parents, even 12 years after divorce (Emery et al., 2005).

Remarriage

"For a while [my stepfather] tried, I always call it 'tried to be my dad,' you know, but it wasn't in a good way, it was in a bad way. I felt like he was trying to boss me around or something, and I didn't feel he had any right to. It had just been me and mom all that time and I didn't like somebody else coming in. So I guess right from the beginning we just never really got along. We kind of avoided each other as much as possible."

—Leanne, age 23 (Arnett, 2004a, p. 69)

"[My stepfather] is a very wonderful man. He always has been, but we just didn't appreciate him. But I think that would be the same for any kid. Really, I don't know that you appreciate your parents until you're older and can look back and think 'Wow. They were pretty incredible.'"

—Lillian, age 24 (Arnett, 2004a, p. 70)

In the light of the factors that seem to be most strongly related to adolescents' problems following divorce—parental conflict, disruptions in parenting, and economic stress—you might think that the mother's remarriage would greatly improve the well-being of adolescents in divorced families. (I focus here on mothers' remarriage because it is usually the mother who has custody of the children.) The mother and her new husband have just chosen to get married, so presumably they are getting along well. The mother's parenting could be expected to become more consistent now that she is happier in her personal life. She is not on her own as a parent anymore now that she has her new husband to help her with parenting and daily household tasks. As for economic stress, presumably it eases now that the stepfather's income comes into the family.

Despite these favorable prospects, studies find that adolescents typically take a turn for the worse when their mothers remarry. In general, adolescents in stepfamilies have a greater likelihood of a variety of problems compared with

divorce mediation An arrangement in which a professional mediator helps divorcing parents negotiate an agreement that both will find acceptable.

their peers in nondivorced families, including depression, anxiety, and conduct disorders (Hetherington & Stanley-Hagan, 2002; Jeynes, 2007). The academic achievement of adolescents in stepfamilies tends to be lower than in nondivorced families, and in some studies lower than in divorced families, too (Jeynes, 1999, 2007). Adolescents in stepfamilies are also more likely to be involved in delinquent activities, not only compared with adolescents in nondivorced families but also compared with adolescents in divorced families (Dornbusch et al., 1985).

Furthermore, although following divorce adolescents tend to have fewer problems than younger children, following remarriage the reverse is true—adolescents have more problems adjusting to remarriage compared with younger children (Hetherington & Stanley-Hagan, 2000, 2002; Zill & Nord, 1994). Adolescent girls tend to have an especially negative reaction to their mothers' remarriage (Hetherington, 1993). The reasons for this are not clear, but one possibility is that the girls develop a closer relationship with their mothers following divorce, and this closeness is disrupted by the mother's remarriage (Hetherington & Kelly, 2002; Stoll et al., 2005).

Why do adolescents often respond unfavorably to their mother's remarriage? Scholars who have studied remarriage emphasize that, although remarriage may seem as though it should be positive for children and adolescents, it also represents another disruption of the family system, another stressful change that requires adjustment (Capaldi & Patterson, 1991; Hetherington & Stanley-Hagan, 2002). The toughest time for families after divorce tends to be 1 year following the divorce (Hetherington & Kelly, 2002). After that, family members usually begin to adjust, and their functioning typically improves substantially after 2 years have passed. Remarriage disrupts this new equilibrium.

With remarriage, family members have to adapt to a new family structure and integrate a new person into a family system that has already been stressed and strained by divorce. The precarious quality of this integration is illustrated by the finding in one study that many stepfathers and adolescents do not mention each other when listing their family members, even 2 years following the remarriage (Hetherington, 1991)! Adolescents and their mothers often experience "divergent realities" when the stepfather enters the family, with the mother happier because of her new husband's love and support but the adolescent regarding him as an unwelcome intruder (Silverberg-Koerner, et al., 2004; Stoll et al., 2005).

With remarriage as with divorce, adolescents' responses are diverse, and the influence of family process as well as family structure must be recognized. A key family process issue is the extent to which the stepfather attempts to exercise authority over the adolescent (Bray & Kelly, 1998; Hetherington, 1993; Moore & Cartwright, 2005). A stepfather who attempts to remind an adolescent that the curfew hour is 11:00 P.M. or that it is the adolescent's turn to do the laundry may well receive the withering retort, "You're *not* my father!" Younger children are more likely to accept a stepfather's authority, but adolescents tend to resist or reject it.

Relationships between stepparents and adolescents must overcome a number of other hazards in addition to the issue of the stepfather's authority (Ganong & Coleman, 2004; Visher & Visher, 1988). Establishing an attachment to a stepparent can be difficult at an age when adolescents are spending less time at home and becoming more peer oriented. Adolescents (and younger children as well) may also have divided loyalties and may fear that establishing an attachment to the stepfather amounts to a betrayal of their father. Also, because adolescents are reaching sexual maturity, they may find it difficult to welcome their mother's new marriage partner into the household. They are more likely than younger children to be aware of the sexual relationship between mother and stepfather, and they may be uncomfortable with this awareness.

All of these considerations present a formidable challenge for stepfathers and adolescents as they attempt to establish a good relationship. However, many stepfathers and adolescents do meet these challenges successfully and establish a relationship of warmth and mutual respect (Ganong & Coleman, 2004; Hetherington & Stanley-Hagan, 2000). Also, in emerging adulthood relationships with stepparents often improve substantially (Arnett, 2004a). Just as with parents, emerging adults come to see their stepparents more as persons than simply as stepparents. Emerging adults and stepparents get along much better once they do not live in the same household and can control (and limit) the amount of contact they have.

Single Parenthood

Just as in divorced families, adolescents in never-married, single-parent households are at greater risk for a variety of problems, including low school achievement, psychological problems such as depression and anxiety, and behavioral problems such as substance use and early initiation of sexual activity (McLanahan & Sandefur, 1994). However, just as in divorced families, family process is at least as important as family structure. Many never-married single parents have relationships with their adolescent children that are characterized by love, mutual respect, and mutual support, and adolescents in these families tend to do as well as or better than adolescents in two-parent families.

Also, looking at family structure only in terms of the parents can be misleading. As noted earlier in the chapter, African Americans have a long tradition of extended family households, in which one or more grandparents, uncles, aunts, or cousins also live in the household (Oberlander et al., 2007). An extended family structure has been found to provide important assistance to single-parent African American families, through the sharing of emotional and financial support and parenting responsibilities. Extended family members not only provide direct support to adolescents, but also help adolescents indirectly by supporting the single parent, which enhances her parenting effectiveness (Taylor, Casten, & Flickinger, 1993).

Dual-Earner Families

With both parents gone from the household for at least part of a typical day in most Western families, and with parents so important in the socialization of their children and adolescents, scholars have turned their attention to the questions: What happens when both parents are employed? What are the consequences for adolescents' development?

For the most part, few substantial effects have been found on adolescents from living in a dual-earner family as compared with a family where only one parent is employed (Crouter & McHale, 2005; Galambos, 2004). For example, the ESM studies indicate that no differences exist between dual-earner families and families in which the mother is not employed, in terms of both the quantity and the quality of time that mothers spend with their adolescents (Richards & Duckett, 1994).

However, other studies have found that the effects of dual-earner families depend on the gender of the adolescent and on whether both parents are working full-time. The effects of being in a dual-earner family are often quite positive for adolescent girls. These girls tend to be more confident and have higher career aspirations than girls whose mothers are not employed (Crouter & McHale, 2005), perhaps because of the model the mother provides through her participation in the workplace.

THINKING CRITICALLY •••

Describe how living in a dual-earner family influences adolescents, in terms of the concept of the mesosystem in Bronfenbrenner's ecological theory (introduced in Chapter 1).

In contrast, several studies have found that adolescent boys in dual-earner families do not function as well as boys in families with only one employed parent. Adolescent boys (but not girls) in dual-earner families have more arguments

Most American adolescents today live in a dual-earner family.

with their mothers and siblings compared with boys whose mothers are not employed (Crouter & McHale, 2005; Montemayor, 1984). Apparently, these conflicts result from the greater household responsibilities required of adolescents when the mother is employed, and from the fact that boys resist these responsibilities more than girls do. Having two full-time working parents is also associated with poorer school performance for boys in middle-class and upper-middle-class families, although not for boys in lower social classes (Bogenschneider & Steinberg, 1994). However, boys' school performance is not affected if one parent works part-time.

The number of hours worked by the parents is an important variable in other studies as well. Adolescents, both boys and girls, are at higher risk for various problems if both parents work full-time than if one parent works just part-time. The risks are especially high for adolescents who are unsupervised by parents or other adults on a daily basis for several hours between the time school ends and the time a parent arrives home from work. These adolescents tend to have higher rates of social isolation, depression, and drug and alcohol use (Carnegie Council on Adolescent Development, 1992; Galambos & Maggs, 1991; Jacobson & Crockett, 2000; Richardson et al., 1993; Voydanoff, 2004). In one study of nearly 5,000 8th graders, those who were on their own at least 11 hours a week were twice as likely to be using alcohol and other drugs (Richardson et al., 1989).

Another key variable in considering the effects of dual-earner families is the quality of the relationships between the parents and the adolescent (Galambos & Ehrenberg, 1997). Adolescents in dual-earner families are more likely to function well if parents maintain monitoring from a distance, for example, by having their children check in with them by phone (Galambos & Maggs, 1991; Pettit et al., 1999; Waizenhofer et al., 2004). If parents can manage to maintain adequate levels of demandingness and responsiveness even when both of them are working, their adolescents generally function well.

Physical and Sexual Abuse in the Family

Although most adolescents and emerging adults generally have good relationships with their parents, some young people are subject to physical or sexual abuse. Rates of abuse in American society are difficult to establish because this is an area in which social desirability is especially strong—physical and sexual abuse involves behaviors that most families would not readily disclose to others. However, numerous studies indicate that physical abuse is more likely to be inflicted on adolescents than on younger children (Kaplan, 1991; Kilpatrick et al., 2000; Williamson, Borduin, & Howe, 1991). Sexual abuse typically begins just before adolescence and then continues into adolescence. About 10% of American college students state that they have been sexually abused by a family member (Haugaard, 1992; Nevid, Rathus, & Greene, 2003). Similar figures were reported in a national survey of Canadian adolescents aged 13 to 16 (Holmes & Silverman,

1992). In the following sections we look first at physical abuse, then at sexual abuse.

Physical Abuse

What leads parents to inflict physical abuse on their adolescent children? One well-established finding is that abusive parents are more likely than other parents to have been abused themselves as children (Kashani et al., 1992; Nevid et al., 2003; Simons, Whitback et al., 1991). They are also more likely to have experienced parental conflict, harsh discipline, or the loss of a parent as they were growing up (Nevid et al., 2003).

This does not mean that children who are abused are destined to grow up to abuse their own children; in fact, the majority of them will not (Zigler & Hall, 1989). It does mean, however, that being abused is a strong risk factor for becoming an abusive parent, perhaps because some children who are abused learn the wrong lessons about how to parent their own children (Cappell & Heiner, 1990; Kashani et al., 1992; Nevid et al., 2003).

Other factors that are related to parents' physical abuse of their children and adolescents tend to involve family stresses or problems in the parents' lives. Abuse is more likely to occur in poor than in middle-class families, in large than in small families, and in families in which parents have problems such as depression, poor health, or alcohol abuse (Hansen, Conaway, & Christopher, 1990; Nevid et al., 2003; Whipple & Webster-Stratton, 1991). Abusive parents also tend to be poorly skilled at parenting and at coping with life stresses (Hansen & Warner, 1992).

Physical abuse is related to a variety of difficulties in the lives of adolescents. Abused adolescents tend to be more aggressive in interactions with peers and adults (Wolfe et al., 2001). This may occur as a result of modeling their behavior after the aggressive behavior displayed by their parents, although it is also possible that passive genotype–environment interactions are involved (i.e., that abusing parents may pass down genes to their children that contribute to aggressiveness). Abused adolescents are more likely than other adolescents to engage in antisocial behavior and substance use (Bensley, Van Eeenwyk, Spieker, & Schoder, 1999; Kilpatrick et al., 2000). They are also more likely than other adolescents to be depressed and anxious, to perform poorly in school, and to have difficulty in their peer relationships (Naar-King, Silvern, Ryan, & Sebring, 2002; Shonk & Cicchetti, 2001; Weiss et al., 1992). However, these consequences are not inevitable; many abused adolescents are surprisingly resilient and grow up to be normal adults and nonabusive parents (Corby, 1993).

Sexual Abuse

The causes of sexual abuse by parents are quite different from the causes of physical abuse. Physical abuse is more commonly inflicted on boys than on girls, whereas sexual abuse is usually inflicted on girls by their brothers, fathers, or stepfathers (Cyr, Wright, McDuff, & Perron, 2002; Haugaard, 1992; Holmes & Silverman, 1992; Watkins & Bentovim, 1992). Unlike physically abusive parents, sexually abusive fathers are usually not aggressive, but rather tend to be insecure and socially awkward around adults (Briere, 1992; Finkelhor, 1990; Nevid et al., 2003). Because they feel inadequate in their relationships with adults—including, usually, their wives—they prefer to seek sexual satisfaction from children, who are easier for them to control (Haugaard, 1992). Sexual abuse usually results from motives such as these, rather than being an expression of affection that got out of control. On the contrary, fathers who abuse their adolescent daughters tend to have been detached and distant from them when they were younger (Parker & Parker, 1986). Sexual abuse is more likely to be committed by stepfathers than by fathers, perhaps because there is no biological incest taboo between stepfathers and their stepdaughters (Briere, 1992; Cyr et al., 2002; Watkins & Bentovim, 1992).

The effects of sexual abuse tend to be even more profound and pervasive than the effects of physical abuse. Parental sexual abuse constitutes an ultimate breach of trust—rather than providing care and protection, the parent has exploited the child's need for nurturance and protection for the sake of his own needs. Consequently, many of the effects of parental sexual abuse are evident in the victim's social relationships. Adolescents who have been sexually abused tend to have difficulty trusting others and forming stable intimate relationships (Cherlin et al., 2004). During the period of sexual abuse and for many years afterward, many victims of sexual abuse experience depression, high anxiety, and social withdrawal (Berget et al., 2003; Kendall-Tackett, Williams, & Finkelhor, 2001). Adolescent victims may react with one extreme or the other in their sexual behavior, becoming either highly avoidant of sexual contacts or highly promiscuous (Kendall-Tackett et al., 2001). Other consequences of sexual abuse include substance abuse, higher risk for a variety of psychological disorders, and suicidal thoughts and behavior (Bensley et al., 1999; Bergen et al., 2003; Yoder, Hoyt, & Whitbeck, 1998).

THINKING CRITICALLY •••

Explain the effects of sexual abuse in terms of attachment theory.

Although sexual abuse is among the most harmful things a parent can do to a child, one third of sexually abused children demonstrate few or no symptoms as a result (Kendall-Tackett et al., 2001). Support from the mother after a father's or stepfather's sexual abuse has been disclosed is especially important to girls' recovery from sexual abuse; daughters cope far better if their mothers believe their account of the abuse and comfort and reassure them, rather than rejecting or blaming them (Briere, 1992; Haugaard & Reppucci, 1988). Psychotherapy can also contribute to the girl's recovery (Rust & Troupe, 1991).

Leaving Early: Runaways and "Street Children"

Running Away From Home

"I skipped out of school two days and my dad found out and he just gave it to me with his belt. I had bruises all over my hands and all over my legs. And my mother couldn't do anything about it and she was upset with me at the time, so that Friday I ran away."

—15-year-old girl (Konopka, 1985, p. 78)

For some adolescents, family life becomes unbearable to them for one reason or another, and they run away from home. It is estimated that about 1 million adolescents run away from home each year in the United States (Whitbeck & Hoyt, 1999). About one fourth of these adolescents are not so much runaways as "throwaways"—their parents have forced them to leave home (Gullotta, 2003). In any case, about 80% to 90% of adolescents who leave home remain within 50 miles of home, often staying with a friend or relative, and return within a week (Tomb, 1991). Adolescents who stay away from home for weeks or months, or who never return at all, are at high risk for a wide variety of problems (Rosenthal & Rotheram-Borus, 2005; Whitbeck & Hoyt, 1999).

Not surprisingly, adolescents who run away from home have often experienced high conflict with their parents, and many have experienced physical or sexual abuse from their parents (Chen et al., 2004). For example, in one study of runaway adolescents in Toronto, 73% had experienced physical abuse and 51% had experienced sexual abuse (McCarthy, 1994). Boys are more likely to have experienced physical abuse, and girls are more likely to have experienced sexual abuse (Cauce et al., 2000). Other family factors related to running away from home include low family income, parental alcoholism, high conflict between parents, and parental neglect of the adolescent (McCarthy, 1994; Whitbeck & Hoyt, 1999). Characteristics of the adolescent also matter. Adolescents who run away are more likely than other adolescents to have been involved in criminal activity, to use illegal drugs, and to have had problems at school (Mallet et al., 2005). They are also more likely to have had psychological difficulties such as depression and emotional isolation (Rohde, Noell, Ochs, & Seeley, 2001; Whitbeck & Hoyt, 1999), and they are more likely to be gay or lesbian (Noell & Ochs, 2001).

Although leaving home often represents an escape from a difficult family life, running away is likely to lead to other problems. Adolescents who run away from home tend be highly vulnerable to exploitation. Many of them report being robbed, physically assaulted, sexually assaulted, and malnourished (Tyler, Hoyt, & Whitbeck, 2000; Tyler et al., 2004; Whitbeck & Hoyt, 1999). In their desperation they may seek money through "survival sex," including trading sex for food or drugs, or becoming involved in prostitution or pornography (Tyler et al., 2004). A study of 390 runaway adolescent boys and girls demonstrated the many problems they may have (McCarthy & Hagan, 1992). Nearly half had stolen food and over 40% had stolen items worth over $50. Forty-six percent had been jailed at least once, and 30% had provided sex in exchange for money. Fifty-five percent had used hallucinogenic drugs, and 43% had used cocaine or crack. Other studies have found that depression and suicidal behavior are common among runaway adolescents (Votta & Manion, 2004; Whitbeck et al., 2004; Yoder et al., 1998). In one study that compared homeless adolescents to other adolescents, the homeless adolescents were 13 times as likely to report feeling depressed, and 38% of them had attempted suicide at least once (Rohde et al., 2001).

Many urban areas have shelters for adolescent runaways. Typically, these shelters provide adolescents with food, protection, and counseling (Dekel et al., 2003; McCarthy & Hagan, 1992). They may also assist adolescents in contacting their families, if the adolescents wish to do so and if it would be safe for them to go home. However, many of these shelters lack adequate funding and have difficulty providing services for all the runaway adolescents who come to them.

"Street Children" Around the World

The United States is far from being the only country where adolescents can be found living on the streets of urban areas. "Street children," many of them adolescents, can be found in virtually every country in the world (Raffaelli & Larson, 1999). It is estimated that the total number of street children worldwide may be as high as 100 million (UNICEF, 2003). Many street children are homeless, but others roam the streets during the day and return to their families to sleep most nights. The main forces leading adolescents to the street vary in world regions, from family dysfunction in the West, to poverty in Asia and Latin America, to poverty, war, and family breakdown (due to AIDS) in Africa. In this section, we examine the lives of street children in three countries: India, Brazil, and Kenya.

In India (Verma, 1999), it is estimated that there are 11 million street children. In addition to poverty, reasons for

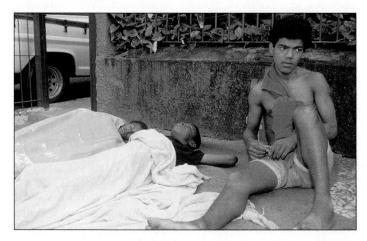

Daily life is a struggle for adolescents who live on the street. Here, boys in Rio de Janeiro, Brazil.

living on the street include overcrowded homes, physical abuse, and parental substance abuse. About half of Indian street children are homeless; of those who are homeless, four out of five have families who are homeless as well. Most street children work, as beggars, vendors, shoe shiners, or car cleaners. Street children have high rates of a variety of diseases such as cholera and typhoid, and they are vulnerable to physical and sexual abuse. They are sought as prostitutes by men who believe they are less likely than older prostitutes to have AIDS. They report frequent conflicts with their parents over low earnings, disobedience, and watching movies (a very popular form of recreation in India). However, the majority of Indian street children also report feeling loved and supported by their families. Furthermore, they typically form gangs with other street children, and gang affiliation provides a sense of identity, belonging, and mutual support. Far from being discouraged and despondent, most street children in India show remarkable resilience and report enjoying "the thrill of street life and freedom of action and movement" (Verma, 1999, p. 11).

In Brazil (Diversi, Moraes filho, & Morelli, 1999), estimates of the number of street children range from 7 million to 30 million. Many are driven to the streets by poverty, and they go there seeking food, money, or clothes. Some return home in the evening, bringing to their families what they have collected on the streets. Others return home rarely, if at all. Many experience a gradual transition from home to street, going to the streets for a few hours at a time at first, then for longer periods as they make friends with other street children, returning home for shorter and shorter periods. Their daily lives are a struggle for survival, as they are constantly trying to find food, a place to bathe, and a place to sleep, while being harassed by drug dealers and police. They are viewed by their society as "little criminals" and "future thieves," and many of them do engage in crime, drug use, and prostitution in response to their desperate condition. As Diversi et al. (1999) observe, "the need for money or clothes may seem more real in the decision to have sex with strangers than the hypothetical possibility that they might get pregnant or contract a venereal disease; stealing a watch that will give them $5 in exchange, especially when their stomachs are growling or they are craving a drug that will temporarily free them from the depressive consciousness of their condition, will likely outweigh the hypothetical notion of a cold cell in the event that they get caught" (p. 31).

In their study of street children in Kenya, Aptekar and Ciano-Federoff (1999) draw a distinction between street boys and street girls. In Kenya as in most non-Western countries, street boys far outnumber street girls. Aptekar and Ciano-Federoff (1999) found that street boys typically maintain contact with their families, often continuing to live with them and bringing most of their money home, especially in single-mother families. The boys demonstrate impressive resourcefulness, forming friendships, taking advantage of aid programs, and developing cognitive skills (for example, buying cheap items in one place and selling them in another for a slight profit). In contrast, street girls have often left home to avoid sexual abuse, and once on the street they typically have no contact with their families, nor do they form friendships with other girls. On the street, they are evaluated mainly in sexual terms: If they are considered unattractive they are shunned, and if they are viewed as attractive they are forced into prostitution. Often, the leaders of street boy gangs take several street girls as "wives," providing them with food and protection from other boys in return for sex.

Overall, street children across the world often exhibit remarkable resilience and manage to develop cognitive skills, make friends, and maintain supportive family relationships in the face of extremely difficult conditions. However, they are at high risk for serious problems ranging from diseases to substance abuse to prostitution, especially girls, and their prospects for adult life are grim indeed.

SUMMING UP

In this chapter, we have explored a wide range of topics related to the family lives of adolescents and emerging adults. Following are the main points of the chapter:

- The family systems approach is based on two key principles: that each subsystem influences the other subsystems in the family and that a change in any family member or subsystem—such as when parents reach midlife, adolescents reach puberty, or emerging adults leave home—results in a period of disequilibrium that requires adjustments.

- Adolescents in industrialized countries generally have higher conflict with siblings than in their other relationships, but most adolescents have a casual relationship with siblings in which their contact is limited. In traditional cultures, a caregiver relationship between siblings is the most common form. Because grandparents in traditional cultures often live in the same household as their children and grandchildren, adolescents tend to be as close to their grandparents as to their parents.

- The two key dimensions of parenting styles focused on by scholars are demandingness and responsiveness. Authoritative parenting, which combines high demandingness with high responsiveness, has generally been found to be related to positive outcomes for adolescents in the American majority culture. Studies of non-Western cultures indicate that the "traditional" parenting style that combines responsiveness with a stricter form of demandingness is most common in those cultures.

- According to attachment theory, attachments formed in infancy are the basis for relationships throughout life. Although sufficient evidence is not yet available to test this claim, studies of attachment involving adolescents and emerging adults indicate that attachments to parents are related to young people's functioning in numerous ways and that autonomy and relatedness in relationships with parents are compatible rather than competing qualities.

- Research shows that conflict between parents and children tends to be highest during early adolescence, and many American parents experience their children's adolescence as a difficult time. Parent-adolescent conflict tends to be lower in traditional cultures because of the greater economic interdependence of family members and because the role of parent in those cultures holds greater authority.

- Emerging adults who move away from home tend to be closer emotionally to their parents and experience less conflict with them than those who remain at home. Most emerging adults get along better with their parents than they did as adolescents.

- Profound social changes in the past two centuries have influenced the nature of adolescents' family lives, including decreasing family size, lengthening life expectancy, and increasing urbanization. Changes over the past 50 years include increases in the prevalence of divorce, single-parent households, and dual-earner families.

- Parents' divorce tends to be related to negative outcomes for adolescents, including behavioral problems, psychological distress, problems in intimate relationships, and lower academic performance. However, there is considerable variation in the effects of divorce, and the outcomes for adolescents depend not just on family structure but on family process.

- Adolescents tend to respond negatively to their parents' remarriage, but again a great deal depends on family process, not just family structure.

- Dual-earner families have become much more common since World War II. For today's adolescents, having two parents who work tends to be unrelated to most aspects of their functioning. However, some studies have found some negative effects for boys and for adolescents in families where both parents work full-time.

- Adolescents who are physically abused tend to be more aggressive than other adolescents, more likely to engage in criminal behavior, and more likely to do poorly in school, among other problems.

- Sexual abuse in families takes place most commonly between daughters and their fathers or stepfathers, who are often incompetent in their relationships with adults. Sexual abuse has a variety of negative consequences, especially in girls' abilities to form intimate emotional and sexual relationships.

- Running away from home is most common among adolescents who have experienced family problems such as physical or sexual abuse, high conflict, or parents' alcoholism. Adolescents who stay away from home for more than a week or two are at high risk for problems such as physical assault, substance use, and suicide attempts. Street children around the world exhibit high rates of these and other problems, but many of them are strikingly resilient.

Even though adolescents spend considerably less time with their families than they did when younger and even though emerging adults typically move out of the family household, family relationships play a key role in development during adolescence and emerging adulthood, both for better and for worse. Home is where the heart is, and where a part of it remains; adolescents and emerging adults continue to be attached to their parents and to rely on them for emotional support, even as they gain more autonomy and move away from their families literally and figuratively.

The power of the family on development is considerable, but family life is not always a source of happiness. Conflict with parents is higher in adolescence than prior to adolescence. Adolescents and emerging adults often experience pain and difficulties when their parents divorce or remarry, although the effects vary widely. The family is sometimes the setting for physical or sexual abuse, and some adolescents find their family lives so unbearable that they run away from home.

The many cultural changes of the past two centuries have resulted in profound changes in the kinds of family lives young people experience. Rates of divorce, single-parent households, and dual-earner families all rose dramatically in Western societies during the second half of the 20th century. In many ways, the family's functions in the lives of adolescents and emerging adults have been reduced in the past century, as new institutions have taken over functions that used to be part of family life. Still, the family endures as the emotional touchstone of young people's lives all over the world.

KEY TERMS

INTERNET RESOURCES

www.ncfr.org
Web site for the National Council on Family Relations (NCFR). Contains information about their journals and annual conferences. The group does not focus on adolescence alone, but many of the members conduct research on adolescence and families.

FOR FURTHER READING

Grossman, K. E., Grossman, K., and Waters, E. (Eds.) (2005). *Attachment from infancy to adulthood: The major longitudinal studies.* New York: Guilford. Presents the results of several attachment studies beginning in infancy and extending into adolescence and emerging adulthood.

Larson, R., & Richards, M. H. (1994). *Divergent realities: The emotional lives of mothers, fathers, and adolescents.* New York: Basic Books. Describes the results of Larson and Richards's research using the ESM. It provides an excellent, insightful, and vivid portrayal of adolescents' family lives in the American majority culture.

8 CHAPTER Friends and Peers

"A best friend to me is someone you can have fun with and you can also be serious with about personal things—about girls, or what you're going to do with your life or whatever. My best friend Jeff and I can talk about things. His parents are divorced too, and he understands when I feel bummed out about the fights between my mom and dad. A best friend is someone who's not going to make fun of you just because you do something stupid or put you down if you make a mistake. If you're afraid of something or someone, they'll give you confidence." (Bell, 1998, p. 80)

THIS STATEMENT, MADE BY A 13-YEAR-OLD BOY, IS AN eloquent expression of the value of friendship in adolescence—or at any age, for that matter. At all ages, we value friends as people we can both have fun with and be serious with. We look for friends who understand us, in part based on common interests and experiences. We rely on friends to be gentle with us when we make mistakes and to support us and prop up our confidence when we are in doubt or afraid.

Friendship is of special value and importance during adolescence and emerging adulthood. These are periods of life in which the emotional center of young people's lives is shifting from their immediate families to persons outside the family (Youniss & Smollar, 1985). This does not mean that parents cease to be important. As described in the previous chapter, the influence of parents remains prominent in many ways throughout adolescence, and attachments to parents remain strong for most emerging adults as well. Nevertheless, in most cultures the influence of parents diminishes as young people become more independent and spend less and less of their time at home. Eventually, most young people in Western societies move away from home and, at some point, form an enduring romantic partnership. However, during their teens and early 20s few adolescents or emerging adults have yet formed a romantic partnership that will endure into adulthood. Friends provide a bridge between the close attachments young people have to their family members and the close attachment they will eventually have to a romantic partner.

During adolescence, it is not only close friends who become important but also the larger world of peers. In industrialized societies, adolescents typically attend large middle schools and high schools with a complex peer culture. These schools are usually much larger than the primary schools they attended as children. In their schools, group hierarchies are established, with some adolescents clearly understood to be high in status and others clearly viewed as having low status. Being an adolescent in Western societies means, in part, learning to navigate through this school-based peer culture.

In this chapter we will consider both close relationships with friends and social relationships in the larger peer culture. We will begin by examining friendships. First, adolescents' relationships with friends and family will be compared and contrasted. Then we will explore various developmental changes that take place in friendships from middle childhood through adolescence, with a special focus on intimacy as a key quality of adolescent friendships. We will also examine the factors involved in choosing friends, particularly the similarities that draw adolescent friends to one another. This will be followed by a discussion of "peer pressure," or "friends' influence" as it will be discussed here. There will also be a section on friends and leisure activities in emerging adulthood.

In the second half of the chapter, we will examine larger peer social groups, including cliques and crowds. This section will feature a discussion of popularity and unpopularity in adolescence, including bullying. Finally, we will explore the idea of a common "youth culture" with values and styles that set it apart from the ways of adults.

Peers and Friends

Before we proceed, we need to distinguish *peers* from *friends* because the two terms are sometimes erroneously believed to be the same. **Peers** are simply people who have certain aspects of their status in common. For example, Louis Armstrong and Dizzy Gillespie are peers because they are generally considered to be two of the greatest trumpet

Friendships are especially important during adolescence and emerging adulthood.

players who ever lived. When social scientists use the term *peers*, they usually are referring to the more concrete aspects of status, especially age. So, for our purposes, peers are people who are about the same age. For adolescents, peers consist of the large network of their same-age classmates, community members, and coworkers.

Friends, of course, are something quite different. For adolescents, their friends tend to be peers—people who are about their age. However, not all their peers are friends. **Friends** are people with whom you develop a valued, mutual relationship. This is clearly different from simply being in the same age group.

Family and Friends

In the previous chapter we talked about how, in the American majority culture, the amount of time spent with family decreases from childhood to adolescence, while the amount of conflict with parents increases (Larson & Richards, 1994; Youniss & Smollar, 1985). Parents remain important figures in the lives of adolescents, but the level of warmth and closeness between parents and their children typically declines (Collins & Laursen, 2004). As they move through their teens, American adolescents move steadily away from the social world of their families.

As they move away from their parents, adolescents become increasingly involved with their friends. We have noted

"A faithful friend is the medicine of life."

—Ecclesiastes 6:16

that from the age of 6 or 7, all children in industrialized societies spend the better part of a typical day in school with their peers. However, during adolescence, young people increasingly spend time with other young people their age not only at school but in their leisure time after school, in the evenings, on weekends, and during the summer and other breaks from school.

The Experience Sampling Method (ESM) studies testify to the change in proportion of time spent with friends and parents that occurs during adolescence (Larson et al., 1996). As noted in Chapter 7, the amount of time spent with family decreases by about half from 5th to 9th grade, then declines even more steeply from 9th through 12th grade (Larson et al., 2002). In contrast, time spent with same-sex friends remains stable, and time with other-sex friends increases (Richards et al., 2000). Another study found similar results, using a slightly different method (Buhrmester & Carbery, 1992). Adolescents aged 13 to 16 were interviewed daily over a 5-day period about how much time they spent in interactions with parents and friends. The average with parents was 28 minutes per day, whereas the average with friends was 103 minutes per day—almost four times as great.

Relationships with family and friends during adolescence change not only in quantity but also in quality. Adolescents indicate that they depend more on friends than on their parents or siblings for companionship and intimacy (French, Rianasari, Pidada, Nelwan, & Buhrmester, 2001; Furman & Buhrmester, 1992; Nickerson & Nagle, 2005; Updegraff, McHale, & Crouter, 2002). Friends become increasingly important during adolescence—the source of adolescents' happiest experiences, the people with whom they feel most comfortable, the ones they feel they can talk to most openly (Richards et al., 2002). A Dutch study found that 82% of adolescents named spending free time with friends as their favorite activity (Meeus, 2006).

One classic study comparing the quality of adolescents' relationships with friends and parents was carried out by Youniss and Smollar (1985), who surveyed over a thousand adolescents aged 12 to 19. Over 90% of these adolescents indicated that they had at least one close friend "who means a lot to me." In addition, the majority (about 70%) agreed with each of these statements:

My close friend understands me better than my parents do.

I feel right now in my life that I learn more from my close friends than I do from my parents.

I'm more myself with my close friends than with my parents.

Youniss and Smollar (1985) also asked adolescents to indicate whether they would prefer parents or friends as the ones they would go to for discussion of various issues. The results are shown in Figure 8.1. Parents were preferred for issues related to education and future occupation, but for more personal issues friends were preferred by large margins.

---

peers People who share some aspect of their status, such as being the same age.

friends Persons with whom an individual has a valued, mutual relationship.

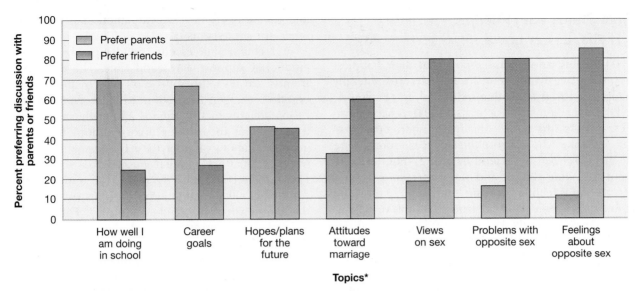

FIGURE 8.1 Percentage of adolescents preferring to discuss topics with friends or parents.
Source: Youniss & Smollar (1985), p. 294.

Why do you think many adolescents find it more difficult to be close to their parents than to their friends? Is this phenomenon cultural or developmental, or both?

In another study comparing orientations to parents and friends, young people in 4th grade, 7th grade, 10th grade, and college were asked to indicate which relationships provided them with the most emotional support (Furman & Buhrmester, 1992). For the 4th graders, parents were their main sources of support. However, for the 7th graders—moving into adolescence—same-gender friends were equal to parents as sources of support, and for the 10th graders same-gender friends had surpassed parents. For the college students—now in emerging adulthood—the pattern changed again. By that time, romantic partners were the main sources of support.

European studies comparing relationships with parents and friends show a pattern similar to American studies (Zeijl, te Poel, Bois-Reymond, Ravesloot, & Meulman, 2000). For example, a study of Dutch adolescents (aged 15 to 19) asked them with whom they "communicate about themselves, about their personal feelings, and about sorrows and secrets" (Bois-Reymond & Ravesloot, 1996). Nearly half of the adolescents named their best friend or their romantic partner, whereas only 20% named one or both parents (only 3% their fathers). Studies in other European countries confirm that adolescents tend to be happiest when with their friends and that they tend to turn to their friends for advice and information on social relationships and leisure, although they tend to come to parents for advice about education and career plans (Hurrelmann, 1996).

The results of the studies comparing relationships with parents and friends suggest that not only are friends highly important in young people's lives, but in many ways they are even more important than parents (Harris, 1999). However, this does not necessarily mean that close relationships with parents are incompatible with having close friendships (Youniss & Smollar, 1985). On the contrary, studies indicate that adolescents who have secure attachments to their parents are also more likely to develop secure attachments to friends (Ducharme, Doyle, & Markiewicz, 2002; Furman, Simon, Shaffer, & Bouchey, 2002; Liu, 2008). The more adolescents are able to trust and confide in their parents, the more likely they are to describe the same qualities in their relationships with their friends.

Although the direct influence of parents diminishes during adolescence, parents shape their adolescents' peer relationships in a variety of indirect ways. Through parents' choices of where to live, where to send their adolescents to school (e.g., public versus private school), and where to attend religious services (or whether to attend at all), parents influence the peer networks their adolescents are likely to experience and the pool of peers from which adolescents are likely to select their friends (Cooper & Ayers-Lopez, 1985; Ladd & LeSieur, 1995). Also, parents often engage in active management of their adolescents' friendships by encouraging the friendship or communicating disapproval (Mounts, 2004; Tilton-Weaver & Galambos, 2004). In addition, parents influence adolescents' personalities and behavior through their parenting practices, which in turn affect adolescents' friendship choices (Laird et al., 2008). For example, in one study of 3,700 adolescents (Brown et al., 1993), adolescents with parents who encouraged academic achievement and who monitored their adolescents' activities were found to have higher grades and lower levels of illicit drug use; grades and illicit drug use were in turn related to adolescents' choices of friends.

Emotional States With Friends: Higher Highs, Lower Lows

In the ESM studies, adolescents report that their happiest moments take place with friends, and they are generally much happier with friends than with family (Larson & Crouter, 2002). Larson and Richards (1994) describe two principal reasons for this. One is that in a close friend adolescents find someone who mirrors their own emotions. One 7th-grade girl described her friend by saying, "She feels the same about the same things, and she understands what I mean. Mostly, she is feeling the same things. . . . And if she doesn't, she'll say 'Yeah, I understand what you're talking about'" (Larson & Richards, 1994, p. 92). This girl and her friend both took part in an ESM study, and when they were "beeped" while together their moods were usually the same, usually highly positive. This is in sharp contrast to adolescents' moods with parents, as we saw in the previous chapter. Adolescents often experience negative moods when with parents, and there is often a deep split in moods between the parent who is enjoying their time together and the adolescent who feels low and would like to be somewhere else.

A second reason that adolescents enjoy their time with friends so much more than their time with parents, according to Larson and Richards (1994), is that adolescents feel free and open with friends in a way they rarely do with parents. Perhaps this is the essence of friendship—friends accept and value you for who you really are. For adolescents, sometimes this means being able to talk about their deepest feelings, especially about their budding romantic relationships. Sometimes it means getting a little crazy, goofing around, letting loose with adolescent exuberance. Larson and Richards (1994) described an escalating dynamic of manic joy they sometimes captured in "beeped" moments, when adolescents would be feeding on each other's antics to their increasing delight. In one episode, a group of boys were hanging around in one of their backyards when they started spraying each other with a hose, taunting each other and laughing. In another episode, adolescent girls at a sleepover were found dancing on the pool table, laughing and hugging each other. As Figure 8.2 shows, shared enjoyment among adolescent friends is especially high on weekend nights, which Larson

and Richards (1998) call "the emotional high point of the week" for adolescents (p. 37).

Of course, adolescent friendships are not only about emotional support and good times. In the ESM studies, friends are also the source of adolescents' most negative emotions—anger, frustration, sadness, and anxiety. Adolescents' attachments to friends and their strong reliance on friends leave them vulnerable emotionally. They worry a great deal about whether their friends like them and about whether they are popular enough. Larson and Richards (1994) observed that "Triangles, misunderstandings, and conflicting alliances were a regular part of the social lives of the [adolescents] we studied" (p. 94). For example, when one boy showed up an hour and a half late to meet his friend, the friend angrily rejected him and avoided him for days. During this time the boy spent much of his time alone, feeling guilty—"I'll just think about it and I'll get upset" (p. 95)—until they reconciled. Overall, however, positive feelings are much more common with friends than with family during adolescence, and enjoyment of friends increases steadily through the adolescent years (Richards et al., 2002).

Family and Friends in Traditional Cultures

As in the West, adolescence in traditional cultures entails less involvement with family and greater involvement with peers. Schlegel and Barry (1991), in their cross-cultural analysis, reported that this pattern is typical in cultures worldwide:

> At all stages of life beyond infancy, from the rough-and-tumble play group of childhood to the poignant, ever-diminishing cluster of aged cronies, persons of similar ages congregate. Such groups take on special meaning in adolescence, when young people are temporarily released from intense identification with a family. In childhood, people depend for their very life on the natal family; in adolescence, they are neither so dependent as they were nor so responsible as they will be. It is then that peer relations can take on an intensity of attachment that they lack at other stages of the life cycle. (p. 68)

Although this pattern applies widely around the world, an important difference between Western cultures and the traditional cultures described by Schlegel and Barry (1991) is that traditional cultures are more likely to have substantial gender differences in adolescents' relationships with peers and family. Specifically, in traditional cultures, involvement with peers and friends tends to be much greater for boys than for girls. Adolescent girls spend more time with same-sex adults than boys do; they have more contact and more intimacy with their mothers than boys do with either parent, and they also have more contact with their grandmothers, aunts, and other adult females than boys do with adult males. Among the Zapotecs of Mexico, for example, adolescent girls spend their days in the household among adult women, learning cooking, sewing, and embroidery, whereas boys work alone or in groups in the fields during the day and congregate with each other in the village in

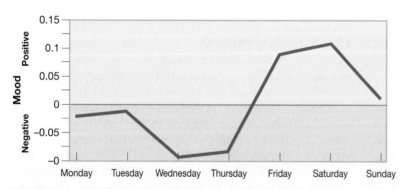

FIGURE 8.2 This graph of mood changes among 9th–12th grade American adolescents shows that their moods are most positive on the weekends, when they are most likely to be spending leisure time with friends.

Source: Larson & Richards (1998).

In traditional cultures, adolescent boys spend more time with friends than adolescent girls do. Here, boys on the island of Mauritania play together.

the evening (Chinas, 1991). However, Schlegel and Barry stress that for both male and female adolescents in traditional cultures more of their time is spent with their families than in the West, where schooling takes adolescents away from their families and into a peer society for the better part of each day.

Even in traditional cultures where most adolescents attend school, the social and emotional balance between friends and family remains tilted more toward family than it does for adolescents in the West. For example, in India adolescents tend to spend their leisure time with family rather than friends, not because they are required to do so but because of collectivistic Indian cultural values and because they enjoy their time with family (Larson et al., 2000; Saraswathi, 1999). Among Brazilian adolescents, emotional support is higher from parents than friends (Van Horn & Cunegatto Marques, 2000). In a study comparing adolescents in Indonesia and the United States, Indonesian adolescents rated their family members higher and their friends lower on companionship and enjoyment, compared to American adolescents (French et al., 2001). Nevertheless, friends were the primary source of intimacy in both countries. Thus, it may be that adolescents in non-Western countries remain close to their families even as they also develop greater closeness to their friends during adolescence, whereas in the West closeness to family diminishes as closeness to friends grows.

Developmental Changes in Friendships

We have seen that friends become more important in adolescence than they have been prior to adolescence. But what is it about development from late childhood to adolescence that makes friends increasingly important? And how is friendship quality different in adolescence than in late childhood?

Intimacy in Adolescent and Emerging Adult Friendships

"When I was younger [my friends and I] just played. Now we talk over things and discuss problems. Then it was just a good time. Now you have to be open and able to talk."
—15-year-old boy (Youniss & Smollar, 1985, p. 105)

"I feel close to my friends when I've had troubles and stuff. I've been able to go to them and they'll help me. Last spring I let my friend know all about me, how my family was having trouble and stuff. I felt close to her and like she would keep this and not tell anyone else about it."
—13 year-old girl (Radmacher & Azmitia, 2006, p. 428)

"A time I felt really close to a friend was my senior trip to Mexico. There was one night, my friend and I were in our hotel room just hanging out and smoking a Cuban cigar. And we ended up talking about a lot of stuff, our lives, our plans, what we hoped for the future. I felt especially close to him because I don't usually open up. Sharing is difficult for me."
—Young man, age 19 (Radmacher & Azmitia, 2006, p. 440)

Probably the most distinctive feature of adolescent friendships, compared with friendships in late childhood, is intimacy. **Intimacy** is the degree to which two people share personal knowledge, thoughts, and feelings. Adolescent friends talk about their thoughts and feelings, confide hopes and fears, and help each other understand what is going on with their parents, their teachers, and peers to a far greater degree than younger children do.

Harry Stack Sullivan (1953) was the first theorist to develop ideas on the importance of intimacy in adolescent friendships. In Sullivan's view, the need for intimacy with friends intensifies in early adolescence. Around age 10, according to Sullivan, most children develop a special friendship with "a *particular* member of the same sex who becomes a chum or close friend" (Sullivan, 1953, p. 245, emphasis in original). Children at this age become cognitively capable of a degree of perspective taking and empathy they did not have earlier in childhood, and this new capacity enables them to form friendships in which they truly care about their chums as individuals rather than simply as play partners.

Over the next few years, during early adolescence, a relationship with a chum enhances development in a variety of ways. Chums promote further development of perspective taking, as they share their thoughts. Their mutual attachment gives them the motivation to try to see things from one

intimacy The degree to which two people share personal knowledge, thoughts, and feelings.

another's point of view. Also, chums provide honest evaluations of each others' merits and faults. This contributes to identity formation, as adolescents develop a more accurate self-evaluation of their abilities and personalities.

Since Sullivan described his theory, numerous scholars have presented research supporting his assertion of the importance of intimacy in adolescent friendships (Berndt, 2004). We have already noted how adolescents tend to rely more on their friends than on their parents for confiding important personal information, especially as it pertains to romantic and sexual issues. Also, adolescents are more likely than younger children to disclose personal information to their friends (Berndt, 1996; Radmacher & Azmitia, 2006). When adolescents are asked what they would want a friend to be like or how they can tell that someone is their friend, they tend to mention intimate features of the relationship. They state, for example, that a friend is someone who understands you, someone you can share your problems with, someone who will listen when you have something important to say (Berndt & Perry, 1990; Bukowski, Newcomb, & Hoza, 1987). Younger children are less likely to mention these kinds of features and more likely to stress shared activities—we both like to play basketball, we ride bikes together, we play computer games, and so on. Adolescents also describe their friends as the ones who help them work through personal problems (such as conflicts with parents or the end of a romance) by providing emotional support and advice (Savin-Williams & Berndt, 1990).

Adolescents rate trust and loyalty as more important to friendship than younger children do (Berndt & Perry, 1990; Hartup & Overhauser, 1991). Adolescents describe their friends as the ones who won't talk behind their backs or say nasty things to others about them. This is related to the emphasis on intimacy. If you are going to open up your heart to someone and reveal things you would not reveal to anyone else, you want to be especially sure that they would not use that knowledge against you. In fact, when adolescents explain why a close friendship has ended, they most often mention some form of breaking trust as the reason—failing to keep a secret, breaking promises, lying, or competing over a romantic partner (Youniss & Smollar, 1985).

Let's take a closer look at two studies that show the development of intimacy in adolescent friendships, one that looks at differences between late childhood and early adolescence and another that examines differences from early adolescence to emerging adulthood. In one study (Diaz & Berndt, 1982), pairs of best friends in 4th grade (late childhood) and 8th grade (early adolescence) were asked to provide information about each other's background characteristics (birth date, telephone number, etc.), preferences (favorite sport, favorite subject in school, etc.), and thoughts and feelings (what the friend worries about, gets mad about, etc.). Late childhood best friends knew as much as the early adolescent best friends about each other's background characteristics, but early adolescent friends knew more about each other's preferences, thoughts, and feelings.

In another study (Radmacher & Azmitia, 2006), early adolescents (ages 12–13) and emerging adults (ages 18–20) described a time when they felt especially close to a friend. Emerging adults' accounts contained more self-disclosure

Friendships in late childhood tend to be based on shared activities, whereas adolescents are more likely to rely on friends for intimacy and support.

and fewer shared activities, compared to early adolescents. Among the emerging adults (but not the early adolescents) there was a gender difference. Self-disclosure promoted emotional closeness for young women, whereas for young men shared activities were usually the basis of feeling emotional closeness. We explore gender differences in more detail in the next section.

Intimacy and Adolescent Development

One way of explaining the increased importance of intimacy in adolescents' friendships is in terms of cognitive changes. Recall from Chapter 3 that thinking becomes more *abstract* and *complex* during adolescence. As we discussed, these advances influence not only how adolescents solve problems but also how they understand their social relationships, that is, their social cognition. Greater ability for abstract thinking makes it possible for adolescents to think about and talk about more abstract qualities in their relationships—affection, loyalty, and trust, for example (Berndt, 1992; Hartup & Overhauser, 1991; Youniss & Smollar, 1985). Greater ability for complex thinking can be applied to adolescents' social relationships. Adolescents are newly aware of all the complex webs and alliances and rivalries that exist in human relationships, and friends are the ones they can talk to about it all—who just broke up with whom, who had a really embarrassing moment in math class, how to get a good grade out of the new English teacher, and so on (Adler & Adler, 1998; Eder, 1995). Talking about these social cognitive topics promotes the kind of exchange of personal knowledge and perspectives that constitutes intimacy.

Also consider that many events are taking place as part of puberty and sexual maturity that lend themselves to the development of intimacy between friends. We have seen how much difficulty adolescents have talking to their parents about sexual issues. Friends are much preferred. Momentous things are happening—changes in the body, first romances, first kisses, and so on. Sharing personal thoughts and feelings about these topics promotes intimacy between friends.

Gender is also important in the development of intimacy in adolescent friendships. Although both boys and girls go through the cognitive changes of adolescence to a similar degree, and both go through puberty and sexual maturity, there are consistent gender differences in the intimacy of adolescent friendships, with girls tending to have more intimate friendships than boys (Bauminger et al., 2008; DuBois & Hirsch, 1993; McNelles & Connolly, 1999; Roy, Benenson, & Lilly, 2000). Girls spend more time than boys talking to their friends (Raffaelli & Duckett, 1989), and they place a higher value on talking together as a component of their friendships (Apter, 1990; Youniss & Smollar, 1985). Girls also rate their friendships as higher in affection, helpfulness, and nurturance, compared with boys' ratings of their friendships (Lempers & Clark-Lempers, 1993). And girls are more likely than boys to say they trust and feel close to their friends (Raja, McGee, & Stanton, 1992; Shulman et al., 1997). In contrast, boys are more likely to emphasize shared activities as the basis of friendship, such as sports or hobbies (Connolly & Konarski, 1994; DuBois & Hirsch, 1993; Radmacher & Azmitia, 2006).

What explains these gender differences? Thus far, not many studies have looked for the reasons behind gender differences in the intimacy of adolescent friendships. However, there is ample research on gender differences in socialization that has implications here. From early in life, girls are more likely than boys to be encouraged to express their feelings openly (Bussey & Bandura, 2004; Maccoby, 1990). Boys who talk openly about how they feel risk being called a "wimp," a "wuss," or some other unflattering term. This is even more true in adolescence than earlier because with puberty and sexual maturity both males and females become more conscious of what it means to be a male and what it means to be a female. Engaging in intimate conversation is usually associated with being female, so adolescent girls may cultivate their abilities for it whereas adolescent boys may be wary of moving too much in that direction.

Nevertheless, intimacy does become more important to boys' friendships in adolescence, even if not to the same extent

Intimacy tends to be higher in girls' friendships than in boys' friendships.

as for girls. In one recent study of African American, Latino, and Asian American boys from poor and working-class families, Niobe Way (2004) reported themes of intimacy that involved sharing secrets, protecting one another physically and emotionally, and disclosing feelings about family and friends.

Choosing Friends

Why do people become friends? For adolescents, as for children and adults, one of the key reasons identified in many studies is *similarity*. People of all ages tend to make friends with people who are similar to them in age, gender, and other characteristics (Rose, 2002; Rubin et al., 2008). Similarities important in adolescent friendships include educational orientation, media and leisure preferences, participation in risk behavior, and ethnicity.

Adolescent friends tend to be similar in their educational orientations, including their attitudes toward school, their levels of educational achievement, and their educational plans (Berndt, 1996; Brown, 2004; Crosnoe, Cavanaugh, & Elder, 2003). During emerging adulthood, too, in the college setting there are often groups of friends who study a lot together and seem very serious about getting a good education, and other groups of friends who party a lot together and seem very intent on having a good time. You may have friends who expect you to study with them the night before the big biology exam, or you may have friends who expect you to join them at the local nightspot and to heck with the biology exam. Adolescents and emerging adults tend to prefer as friends people who would make the same choice as they would in this kind of situation (Osgood et al., 1996; Popp et al., 2008).

Another common similarity in adolescent friendships is in preferences for media and leisure activity. Adolescent friends tend to like the same kinds of music, wear the same styles of dress, and prefer to do the same things with their leisure time (e.g., Arnett, 1996; Mathur & Berndt, 2006). These similarities make relations between friends smoother and help them avoid conflict. An adolescent who is a devoted fan of hip-hop is likely to be more interested in becoming friends with another adolescent who also loves hip-hop than with an adolescent who considers hip-hop to be obnoxious noise. If one adolescent likes to play computer games during leisure time and another prefers to play sports, the two are unlikely to become friends.

A third common similarity among adolescent friends is in risky activities. Adolescent friends tend to resemble each other in the extent to which they drink alcohol, smoke cigarettes, try drugs, drive dangerously, get in fights, shoplift, vandalize, and so on (Berndt, 1996; Hoffman et al., 2007; Osgood et al., 1996; Stone et al., 2000). Adolescents engage in

In adolescence and emerging adulthood, friends tend to be similar in educational goals.

these risk behaviors to varying degrees—some on a regular basis, some now and then, some not at all. Because adolescents usually take part in risk behavior with friends, they tend to choose friends who resemble themselves in willingness to participate. We will talk in more detail about this aspect of adolescent friendships in the next section.

Although ethnic similarity between friends is typical at all ages, adolescence is a time when ethnic boundaries in friendships often become sharper. During childhood ethnicity is related to friendship, but not strongly. However, as children enter adolescence friendships become less interethnic, and by late adolescence they are generally ethnically segregated (Kao & Joyner, 2004). This has been found to be true in Europe and Israel as well as the United States (Titzmann et al., 2007).

Why would this be so? One factor may be that as they grow into adolescence, young people become increasingly aware of interethnic tensions and conflict in their societies, and this awareness fosters mutual suspicion and mistrust. Similarly, as adolescents begin to form an ethnic identity, they may begin to see the divisions between ethnic groups as sharper than they had perceived them before. As noted in Chapter 6, for some adolescents part of forming an ethnic identity is rejecting associations with people of other ethnicities (Phinney, 2000; Phinney & Devich-Navarro, 1997).

Ethnic similarity in adolescent friendships also reflects ethnic segregation in schools and neighborhoods. The peers adolescents meet in their schools and neighborhoods tend to be from their own ethnic group, so this is the group from which they draw their friends (Mouw & Entwistle, 2008).

Because ethnic segregation tends to exist throughout societies, ethnic segregation in friendships does not end when adolescence ends. In college and throughout adulthood, interethnic friendships are fairly uncommon (Oliver & Ha, 2008). So, the ethnic segregation in adolescents' friendships reflects the patterns of the society they live in. Nevertheless, as shown in the Cultural Focus box, some young people do form interethnic friendships.

"To like and dislike the same things, that is indeed true friendship."

—Sallust, ca. 50 B.C.

CULTURAL FOCUS • Interethnic Friendships Among British Girls

In Europe a considerable proportion of young people's interactions with peers takes place through youth clubs (Alsaker & Flammer, 1999a). Time in school is focused solely on education. Extracurricular activities such as sports teams, dances, and parties are sponsored by youth clubs rather than schools. In most Western European countries, a majority of young people belong to at least one youth club (Alsaker & Flammer, 1999a).

Helena Wulff (1995a) studied interracial friendships among adolescent girls in a youth club in a working-class section of London, England. Wulff, a Swedish anthropologist, used interviews as the main method of her research, along with observations of the girls in the youth club. She focused especially on the friendships among 20 Black and White girls aged 13 to 16. The Black girls were the English-born daughters of immigrants from former British colonies such as Jamaica and Nigeria. Wulff was especially interested in exploring the interethnic friendships among the girls, which she noticed were very common at the club.

In many ways, the friendships among the girls had little to do with ethnicity and were similar to the friendships described among adolescent girls in the United States and other countries. Their most common activity together was talking, mostly about boys and about male celebrities they admired (e.g., singers, actors). They also talked a great deal about aspects of appearance—the latest hairstyles, clothes, cosmetics, and jewelry. Other favorite shared activities were listening to recorded music and dancing in their bedrooms and at parties and teen nightclubs. They occasionally took part in risky activities together such as shoplifting or smoking marijuana.

Although they spent a great deal of time together enjoying shared activities, when they spoke to Wulff about their friendships the girls emphasized not shared activities but the importance of intangible qualities, especially trust. A friend, they told Wulff, is "someone you can share things with, like problems, and also someone you can trust," as well as "someone you can

Interethnic friendships are common among British girls.

talk to, tell secrets and all that and you know they won't . . . tell anybody else" (Wulff, 1995a, p. 68). Again, this is highly similar to the perspective reported in studies of American adolescent friends (Berndt, 1996; Youniss & Smollar, 1985).

However, the girls were also conscious of ethnic issues and explicitly addressed those issues in their friendships. They were well aware that racism and ethnic inequality are pervasive in British society. In reaction to this, and in resistance to it, they deliberately emphasized Black elements in their youth styles, taking "an interesting revenge against the low-class position of most Blacks" (Wulff, 1995a, p. 71). Thus, they listened especially to predominantly Black forms of music such as reggae, ska, and "jazzfunk." Some—Whites as well as Blacks—wore their hair in a mass of thin plaits most often worn by Blacks. They mixed Black and White components in their clothing and their jewelry. In the various aspects of their common style, according to Wulff (1995a), "the concern with and the search for ethnic equality run through them all. . . . they cultivated their own aesthetic of ethnic equality through their youth styles" (pp. 72–73).

Friends' Influence and Peer Pressure

"Friends can push you into doing stuff you know you shouldn't be doing. You try and say no and they'll probably end up beating you up or something. My friends tell me to do something and I do it. They're a lot older than me. Like they'll tell me we're going to play basketball, so they come by and pick me up and we end up going to the liquor store. And I say, 'Hey, man, what's in the bag?' and they say, 'Gin. Now shut up and take a drink.'"

—Lionel, age 14 (Bell, 1998, p. 74)

"If the kids in my group are smoking marijuana they say, 'You want to try it?' If you say no, they say 'Fine.' That's all there is to it. No one forces you. And no one puts you down."

—Aaron, age 14 (Bell, 1998, p. 76)

One of the topics involving adolescents' peer relationships that has received the most attention is "peer pressure." Scholars on adolescence have devoted considerable theoretical and research attention to it, and the general public (at least in the United States) believes that peer pressure is a central part of adolescence, something all adolescents have to learn to deal with in the course of growing up (Berndt, 1996; Brown et al., 2008).

Friends and Peers   **219**

Friends' influence is a more accurate term than *peer pressure* for the social effects adolescents experience. Remember the difference between friends and peers: Peers are simply the more or less anonymous group of other people who happen to be the same age as you are; friends are emotionally and socially important in a way that peers are not. When people talk about peer pressure, what they really mean is friends' influence. When we think of an adolescent girl standing around with a group of other adolescents as they pass around a joint, and we imagine them handing it to her expecting her to take a puff, we assume that the people she is hanging around with are her friends, not merely her peers. If we overhear an argument between an adolescent boy who wants to get his navel pierced and his parents who regard that as a bizarre notion, and he says "everybody else is doing it!" we can probably guess he means every one of his friends, not everybody else in his entire school. Friends can have a substantial influence on adolescents, but the effects of the entire peer group are weak (Berndt, 1996).

What do you think of first when you think of how adolescents are influenced by their friends? Often, the assumption is that the influences of adolescent friends are negative. The influence of friends is often blamed for adolescents' involvement in a wide range of risk behaviors, including alcohol and other drug use, cigarette smoking, and delinquent behavior (Brown et al., 2008; Dishion et al., 2008).

Actually, however, evidence suggests that the influence of friends is important not only in encouraging adolescents to participate in risk behavior but also in *discouraging* risk behavior, as well as in supporting them emotionally and helping them cope with stressful life events (Berndt & Savin-Williams, 1993; Brown, 2004; Hartup, 1993). Both types of friends' influence—the type that pertains to risk behavior and the type that pertains to support—appear to follow a similar developmental pattern, rising in strength in early adolescence and peaking in the mid-teens, then declining in late adolescence (Allen et al., 2006; Berndt, 1996). Let's take a look at the research on each of these aspects of friends' influence.

THINKING CRITICALLY •••

What has been your experience with friends' influence? Has it ever led you to do something you wish you had not done? To what extent has it been positive or negative?

Friends' Influence: Risk Behavior

A correlation exists between the rates of risk behaviors that adolescents report for themselves and the rates they report for their friends. This is true for alcohol use, cigarette use, use of illegal drugs, sexual behavior, risky driving practices, and criminal activity (Dishion et al., 2008; Gaughan, 2006; Prinstein, Boergers, & Spirito, 2001; Sieving, Perry, & Williams, 2000; Unger, 2003).

But what does this mean exactly? Because a correlation exists between the behavior adolescents report and the behavior they report for their friends, can we conclude that adolescents' participation in these behaviors is *influenced* by their friends? Not on the basis of a correlation alone. As we discussed in Chapter 1, one of the simplest and most important principles of statistics is that *correlation is not the same as causation.* Just because two events happen together does not mean that one causes the other. Unfortunately, this principle is often overlooked in the conclusions drawn from studies of similarities among adolescent friends.

There are two good reasons to question whether the correlations in these studies reflect causation (Arnett, 2007). One is that, in most studies, reports of both the adolescents' behavior and the behavior of their friends come from the adolescents themselves. However, numerous studies that have obtained separate reports of behavior from adolescents and their friends indicate that adolescents generally perceive their friends as more similar to themselves than they actually are (according to the friends' reports) in their alcohol use, cigarette use, use of illegal drugs, and sexual attitudes (Bauman & Fisher, 1986; Graham, Marks, & Hansen, 1991; Iannotti & Bush, 1992; Prinstein & Wang, 2005). Perhaps

Adolescent friends tend to have similar levels of substance use. Is this similarity due to peer pressure or selective association?

because of egocentrism, adolescents perceive more similarity between themselves and their friends than is actually the case, which inflates the correlations in the risk behavior they report for themselves and their friends.

The second and perhaps even more important reason for doubting that correlation can be interpreted as causation in studies of risk behavior among adolescents and their friends is **selective association**, the principle that most people (including adolescents) tend to choose friends who are similar to themselves (Berndt, 1996; Rose, 2002; Popp et al., 2008). As we discussed earlier, friends tend to be similar to one another in a variety of ways, and this is in part because people *seek out* friends who are similar to themselves. Thus, the correlation between adolescents' risk behavior and their friends' risk behavior might exist partly or even entirely because they have selected each other as friends on the basis of the similarities they have in common, including risk behavior, not because they have influenced each other in their risk behavior. In friendships, the old cliché is true—birds of a feather flock together (Hamm, 2000; Urberg, Degirmencioglu, & Tolson, 1998).

Fortunately, several longitudinal studies have been conducted on risk behavior that help to unravel this issue. These studies indicate that both selection and influence contribute to similarities in risk behavior among adolescent friends. That is, adolescents are similar in risk behavior before they become friends, but if they stay friends they tend to become even more similar, increasing or decreasing their rates of participation in risk behavior so that they more closely match one another. This pattern has been found to be true for cigarette use (Hoffman et al., 2007), alcohol use (Popp et al., 2008), other drug use (Farrell & Danish, 1993), delinquency (Dobkin et al., 1995), and aggressive behavior (Botvin & Vitaro, 1995).

As noted, evidence also suggests that friends can influence each other not only toward participation in risk behavior but also *against* it (Maxwell, 2002). It depends on who your friends are, and some adolescents are adamantly against risk behavior. In one study, adolescents who did not smoke indicated that they believed their friends would disapprove if they started smoking (Urberg, Shyu, & Liang, 1990), and in another, adolescents were more likely to report that their friends pressured them *not* to use alcohol than to use it (Keefe, 1994). In a study that compared various areas of friends' influence, adolescents rated pressure to participate in risk behavior as the *weakest* of five areas of possible influence, well below pressure to participate in school activities and to conform to styles of dress and grooming (Clasen & Brown, 1985). This study also found that pressure against participation in risk behavior was more common than pressure in favor of it.

This is not meant to dismiss entirely the role of friends' influence in encouraging risk behavior in adolescence. No doubt, friends' influence does occur for some adolescents for some types of risk behavior on some occasions. But we must not exaggerate this influence, and we should interpret the research on this topic carefully. Friends' influence is one part of the story of some adolescents' participation in risk behavior, but it is only one part, and the closer you look at it the smaller it seems (Arnett, 2007).

Friends' Influence: Support and Nurturance

"Julie was on the swimming team with me, and she was scared to compete because she thought she wouldn't beat the other person. I was trying to tell her, 'Come on, you can do it.' But she always thought she wasn't good enough. And that was the way she felt about everything, not just swimming. Since I was her best friend, I really talked to her. 'You can do it. You're great. Do it for our team.' I kept boosting her confidence, and you know, after awhile she did do it. We all cheered for her and she was terrific."

—Marlianne, age 18 (Bell, 1998, p. 81)

Harry Stack Sullivan (1953) tended to emphasize the positive over the negative aspects of adolescents' friendships. In Sullivan's view, intimate friendships in adolescence are important for building self-esteem. These friendships also help adolescents develop their social understanding, according to Sullivan, as they compare their own perspective with their friends' perspective. More recently, Thomas Berndt (1996; 2004) has specified four types of support that friends may provide to each other in adolescence:

- **Informational support** is advice and guidance in solving personal problems, such as those involving friends, romantic relationships, parents, or school. Because of their similar ages, adolescents are often going through similar experiences. This is particularly true of friends because they tend to choose one another partly on the basis of their similarities. Intimate friendships give adolescents a source of support because they can talk about their most personal thoughts and feelings with someone they believe will accept and understand them.

- **Instrumental support** is help with tasks of various kinds. Adolescent friends support each other by helping with homework, assisting with household chores, lending money, and so on.

---

selective association The principle that most people tend to choose friends who are similar to themselves.

informational support Between friends, advice and guidance in solving personal problems.

instrumental support Between friends, help with tasks of various kind.

- **Companionship support** is being able to rely on each other as companions in social activities. Did you ever experience the anxiety, in your teens, of having no friend to go with to the school dance, or the big basketball game, or a much-discussed party? Adolescent friends support each other by being reliable companions for these kinds of events, as well as for more routine daily events—having someone to eat with at lunch or someone to sit with on the bus, and so on.
- **Esteem support** is the support adolescent friends provide by congratulating their friends when they succeed and encouraging them or consoling them when they fail. Adolescents support their friends by being "on their side" whether things go well or badly.

THINKING CRITICALLY •••

Give an example of each of the four types of friendship support described in this section, from your own experience.

What sort of effects do these kinds of support have on adolescents' development? Cross-sectional studies have found that support and nurturance in adolescents' friendships are positively associated with psychological health (Keefe & Berndt, 1996; Urberg et al., 2004) and negatively associated with depression and psychological disturbance (Licitra-Kleckler & Waas, 1993; Way & Chen, 2000). However, because these studies are cross-sectional, it could be that adolescents with more favorable characteristics attract support and nurturance from friends, rather than that friends' support and nurturance cause the favorable characteristics. Recent longitudinal studies in this area have found supportive friendships to lead to higher self-esteem and lower depressive symptoms as well as improvements in academic performance (Altermatt & Pomerantz, 2005; Crosnoe et al., 2003). However, longitudinal studies have also found that supportive friendships have a mixed relation to risk behavior, sometimes decreasing risk behavior (Laird et al., 2005) and sometimes increasing it (Miller-Johnson et al., 2003; Wills et al., 2004) when friends participate in risk behavior as one of the activities they enjoy together.

Although adolescent friendships are usually with members of their own gender, platonic (nonromantic) friendships among adolescent boys and girls may be of special importance as sources of support in some cultures. One recent study examined adolescent friendships among Mexican-origin immigrants in the United States (Stanton-Salazar & Spina, 2005). Using a combination of qualitative and quantitative methods, the study found that the adolescents often relied on their friends to cope with emotionally challenging situations. Adolescent boys especially benefited from having a girl as a source of emotional support, perhaps because the boys could express their feelings more openly in a friendship with a girl. Platonic friendships are becoming more common in many cultures as gender roles become less rigid, so this is an area that may draw more research attention in years to come (Grover et al., 2007).

Friends and Leisure Activities in Emerging Adulthood

In general, far more research has been done on relationships with friends and peers in adolescence than in emerging adulthood. Nevertheless, friendships may be especially important in emerging adulthood for a number of reasons. Emerging adults typically leave home, and we might expect that attachments and activities with friends would rise in importance once young people no longer experience family relations as part of their daily environment. Similarly, because most emerging adults are unmarried, having no marriage partner as a source of support might be expected to give them a greater incentive than married persons to seek contacts with friends (Helgeson, 2002).

The best data on activities with friends in emerging adulthood come from a study by Osgood and Lee (1993), who investigated leisure activities in a telephone survey of 827 Nebraska residents aged 18 and older. Their data provide insights into activities with friends in emerging adulthood and also allow us to make comparisons between emerging adulthood and older ages.

Osgood and Lee (1993) inquired about participation in a variety of types of leisure activities (such as going to parties or music concerts), most of which we can assume would take place with friends. The average emerging adult in the study spent a considerable amount of time in leisure activities with friends. Most emerging adults (aged 18 to 28 in their study) said they get together with friends at least once a week, for no specific purpose. The typical emerging adult went to a party at least once a month and went to bars nearly that often. Emerging adults also went to movies once or twice a month, on average, and to music concerts at least a few times a year.

In all of these respects, average rates of participation in leisure activities with friends were considerably higher among emerging adults than among older adults. However, even within emerging adulthood these activities steadily declined. Eighteen-year-olds had a more active leisure life with friends than 23-year-olds, and 23-year-olds were more active than 28-year-olds.

---

companionship support Between friends, reliance on each other as companions in social activities.

esteem support The support friends provide each other by providing congratulations for success and encouragement or consolation for failure.

cliques Small groups of friends who know each other well, do things together, and form a regular social group.

crowds Large, reputation-based groups of adolescents.

Friends spend a large amount of their leisure time together in emerging adulthood.

Osgood and Lee (1993) found that little of this decline during emerging adulthood could be explained by entering marriage, but that having a child reduced participation in every aspect of leisure with friends. Even for those who did not become parents from age 18 to 28, however, leisure with friends declined substantially over this period. It may be that some kinds of leisure that emerging adult friends often engage in—parties, bars, and so on—simply lose their charm by the late 20s.

THINKING CRITICALLY •••

How would you explain the decline in leisure activities with friends that Osgood and Lee (1993) found between age 18 and age 28? Keep in mind that they found that marriage does not explain the decline; also keep in mind that for most people their first child is not born until their late 20s, and most of the decline takes place before then.

Cliques and Crowds

So far we have focused on close friendships. Now we turn to larger groups of friends and peers. Scholars generally make a distinction between two types of adolescent social groups, cliques and crowds. **Cliques** are small groups of friends who know each other well, do things together, and form a regular social group (Brown & Klute, 2003; Dunphy, 1969). Cliques have no precise size—3 to 12 is a rough range—but they are small enough so that all the members of the clique feel they know each other well, and they think of themselves as a cohesive group (Brown & Klute, 2003). Sometimes cliques are defined by distinctive shared activities—for example, working on cars, playing music, playing basketball, surfing the Internet—and sometimes simply by shared friendship (a group of friends who eat lunch together every school day, for example).

Crowds, in contrast, are larger, reputation-based groups of adolescents who are not necessarily friends and do not necessarily spend much time together (Brown et al., 2008; Brown & Klute, 2003; Horn, 2003). A recent review of 44 studies on adolescent crowds concluded that five major types of crowds are found in many schools (Sussman et al., 2007):

- *Elites* (a.k.a. populars, preppies). The crowd recognized as having the highest social status in the school.
- *Athletes* (a.k.a. jocks). Sports-oriented students, usually members of at least one sports team.
- *Academics* (a.k.a. brains, nerds, geeks). Known for striving for good grades and for being socially inept.
- *Deviants* (a.k.a. druggies, burnouts). Alienated from the school social environment, suspected by other students of using illicit drugs and engaging in other risky activities.
- *Others* (a.k.a. normals, nobodies). Students who do not stand out in any particular way, neither positively nor negatively; mostly ignored by other students.

Within each of these crowds, of course, there are cliques and close friends (Urberg et al., 2000). However, the main function of crowds is not to provide a setting for adolescents' social interactions and friendships. Crowds mainly serve the function of helping adolescents to locate themselves and others within the secondary school social structure. In other words, crowds help adolescents to define their own identities and the identities of others. Knowing that others think of you as a brain has implications for your identity—it means you are the kind of person who likes school, does well in school, and perhaps has more success in school than in social situations. Thinking of someone else as a druggie tells you something about that person (whether or not it is accurate)—he or she uses drugs, of course, probably dresses unconventionally, and does not seem to care much about school.

Members of both cliques and crowds tend to be similar to each other in the same way that friends are—age, gender, and ethnicity, as well as educational attitudes, media and leisure preferences, and participation in risky activities (Brown et al., 2008; Brown & Klute, 2003; Kinney, 1993, 1999; Meeus, 2006; Miller-Johnson & Costanzo, 2004). Crowds, however, are not so much groups of friends as social categories, so their characteristics differ in important ways from friendships and cliques, as we will explore later. First, we examine one of the distinctive characteristics of adolescent cliques.

Sarcasm and Ridicule in Cliques

Recall from Chapter 3 that the cognitive changes of adolescence, particularly the increased capacity for complex thinking, make adolescents capable of appreciating and using sarcasm more than they did prior to adolescence. Sarcasm—and a sharper form of sarcasm, ridicule—plays a part in adolescent friendships and clique interactions. In one study, Gavin and Furman (1989) studied young people in 5th through 12th grades and found that critical evaluations of one another were a typical part of the social interactions in adolescent cliques. Sarcasm and ridicule were included in what they called "antagonistic interactions." Such interactions were common among the adolescents they studied. Antagonistic interactions were directed both at members within the group and at those outside the group and were more common in early and middle adolescence than in late adolescence.

The authors of the study suggested a number of possible reasons for these kinds of interactions. One function of antagonistic interactions is that they promote the establishment of a dominance hierarchy—higher-status members dish out more sarcasm and ridicule than they take. Also, antagonistic interactions serve to bring nonconformist group members into line and reinforce clique conformity, which helps to buttress the cohesiveness of the group. If an adolescent boy comes to school wearing a shirt with monkeys on it (as a friend of mine once did), and all his clique friends laugh at him all day (as we did), he will know better than to wear that shirt again (he didn't) if he wants to remain part of their clique.

Sarcasm and ridicule of people outside the clique also serve to strengthen clique identity by clarifying the boundaries between "us" and "them." Erik Erikson remarked on this tendency among adolescents:

> They become remarkably clannish, intolerant, and cruel in their exclusion of others who are "different," in skin color or cultural background, in tastes and gifts, and often in entirely petty aspects of dress and gesture arbitrarily selected as the signs of an in-grouper or an out-grouper. (Erikson, 1959, p. 97)

To Erikson, the motive was mainly psychological—sarcasm and ridicule are used by adolescents at a time when they are unsure of their identities, as part of the process of sorting through who they are and who they are not. Antagonistic interactions are a way of easing their anxiety about these issues by drawing attention to others who are implied to be both inferior to and very different from themselves.

Schlegel and Barry (1991) describe an interesting variation on the use of sarcasm and ridicule in traditional cultures. They provide several examples of cultures where groups of adolescent boys use sarcasm and ridicule to enforce conformity to cultural standards of behavior and punish those who violate them. Their uses of sarcasm and ridicule are directed not just toward other adolescents but toward adults.

The Mbuti Pygmies of Africa, for example, consider it improper to be argumentative. Persons who violate this prohibition are likely to find themselves awakened very early the next morning by a group of adolescent boys making loud noises, climbing on their hut and pounding on the roof, tearing off leaves and sticks. Among the Hopi in the American Southwest, when a man is known to be visiting a woman at night while her husband is away, the adolescent boys of the village publicize and punish his adultery by leaving a trail of ashes during the night between his house and hers for everyone to see the next morning.

In a historical example, Gillis (1974) describes how in various parts of Europe in the 16th and 17th centuries, groups of unmarried males in their teens and early 20s had an unwritten responsibility for enforcing social norms. Using profane songs and mocking pantomimes, they would publicly mock violators of social norms—the adulterer, the old man who had married a young bride, the widow or widower who had remarried a bit hastily following the death of a spouse. In Gillis's description, "a recently remarried widower might find himself awakened by the clamor of the crowd, an effigy of his dead wife thrust up to his window and a likeness of himself, placed backward on an ass, drawn through the streets for his neighbors to see" (Gillis, 1974, p. 30).

Thus, in some culturally approved circumstances, young people are given permission to do what under other circum-

Humorous ridicule is common in adolescent cliques.

stances would be seen by adults as intolerable, even criminal behavior (Schlegel & Barry, 1991). Allowing young people to use sarcasm and ridicule in a socially constructive way enforces community standards and saves the adults the trouble of doing so.

Relational Aggression

"At a gathering one day, I happened to kiss a boy that one of my friends had a crush on. By the next day it was all over school and Emily, my friend who had the crush, had ordered all of the other girls not to talk to me. They made a Web page about me that said mean, untrue things, such as that I was a lesbian, that I had had sex with at least 20 guys, and that I was pregnant. As I walked down the halls at school, the girls would scream "SLUT!," "WHORE!", and many other hurtful words. . . . I went home every day and cried, begging my mom to let me switch schools. My mother dismissed the problem as 'girls being girls' and figured that as we neared high school the girls would grow out of this 'phase' and become more mature. They didn't. The name-calling and slandering and spreading of rumors went on as my eating disorder grew progressively worse. At last my mother realized the seriousness of the situation and allowed me to transfer to a Catholic school my junior year."

—Simmons, 2004, pp. 24–25

Among cliques of adolescent girls, a phenomenon related to sarcasm and ridicule has been identified in recent years. **Relational aggression** is the term for behavior that includes not only sarcasm and ridicule but gossiping, spreading rumors, snubbing, and excluding others from the clique (Underwood, 2003). In short, relational aggression is nonphysical aggression that harms others by damaging relationships. We have discussed, in Chapter 5, how physical aggression often becomes a problem for adolescent boys as they learn the gender role requirements of being a man. However, some scholars assert that if the definition of aggression includes relational aggression as well, then adolescent boys and girls are about equal in their aggressive behavior (Crick & Rose, 2000). Boys engage in relational aggression, too, but it has been found to be more common among girls (Coyne et al., 2006). For example, in one study of 11- and 14-year-old adolescents in the United States and Indonesia, relational aggression behaviors such as relationship manipulation, social ostracism, and spreading malicious rumors were more common among girls than boys in both countries (French, Jansen, & Pidada, 2002).

Why do girls exhibit more relational aggression than boys? According to scholars in this area, girls resort to relational aggression because their gender role prohibits more direct expressions of disagreement and conflict (Crick & Rose, 2000; Simmons, 2002; Underwood, 2003). They *experience*

anger, but they are not allowed to *express* it openly, even in a verbal form. Consequently, for girls aggression often takes the more covert and indirect form of relational aggression. Relational aggression can also be a way of asserting dominance. Studies have shown that high-status adolescent girls are more likely than other girls to be high in relational aggression (Cillessen & Rose, 2005; Rose et al., 2004).

Being the target of relational aggression is associated with feelings of depression and loneliness (Prinstein, Boergers, & Vernberg, 2001; Underwood, 2003). Relational aggression is also associated with negative outcomes for the aggressors. Adolescents and emerging adults who use relational aggression are prone to problems such as depression and eating disorders (Simmons, 1999, 2002; Storch et al., 2004; Werner & Crick, 1999).

Developmental Changes in Crowds

"Like it's really easy to go, 'He's a jock, or he's a punk, or she's alternative' or whatever. There's lots of different groups, but once you start hanging out with one group, you pretty much get labeled, which kind of sucks, since I think, if anything, you find your group because of who you are, not because they influenced you to be like them. It's like you seek out people who you like, and you go hang out with them."

—Maria, high school student (Bell, 1998, p. 71)

If you think back, you can probably remember the different crowds that existed in your high school. Now think of your elementary school, say, 5th grade. Most likely you find it harder to name any crowds from elementary school. Crowd definition and membership seem to become important in adolescence, and not before. This may be partly because of the cognitive changes of adolescence (Brown & Klute, 2003; O'Brien & Bierman, 1988; Sussman et al., 2007). Crowd labels are abstract categories, each with some abstract defining characteristics—degree of popularity, attitudes toward school, and so on—and the capacity for abstract thinking is one of the cognitive advances of adolescence. As noted earlier, crowds may also become more important in adolescence because identity issues become important in adolescence. Adolescents are more concerned than younger children with asking questions about who they are—and who others are. Crowds help adolescents ascribe definite characteristics to themselves and to others as they grow through the process of identity formation in adolescence.

Although the focus on crowds in adolescence reflects developmental characteristics such as cognitive changes and identity formation, the cultural basis of crowds is also important.

relational aggression A form of nonphysical aggression that harms others by damaging their relationships, for example by excluding them socially or spreading rumors about them.

In industrialized societies, the fact that most adolescents remain in school at least until their late teens and the fact that these schools are almost always strictly age-graded makes crowd definition especially important. Spending so much time around peers on a daily basis elevates the importance of peers as social reference groups—that is, as groups that influence how adolescents think about how they compare to others (Brown et al., 2008). Also, crowds are especially likely to exist in large secondary schools where a crowd structure is useful in helping adolescents make sense of a complex social context (Brown & Klute, 2003). In the many cultures around the world where adolescents spend most of their time with family members or with groups of mixed ages, crowds have no relevance to their lives.

For adolescents in American society, however, crowds are an important part of their social lives, especially in early to midadolescence. Bradford Brown and David Kinney and their colleagues (Brown & Klute, 2003; Brown, Mory, & Kinney, 1994; Kinney, 1993, 1999; Sussman et al., 2007) have described how crowd structure changes during adolescence, becoming more differentiated and more influential from early to midadolescence, then less hierarchical and less influential from mid- to late adolescence (see Figure 8.3). In Kinney's (1993, 1999) longitudinal research on adolescent crowds in a small Midwestern city, he found that early adolescents (grades 6 to 8) perceived only two distinct crowds—a small group of popular, high-status adolescents (the trendies), and a larger group composed of everybody else (the dweebs). By midadolescence (grades 9 to 10), however, the adolescents identified five crowds in their high school. Trendies were still on top as the high-status crowd, followed in status by normals and headbangers (heavy metal music fans), with *grits* (known for their rural attire, e.g., overalls) and punkers (known for liking punk music) on the bottom of the status hierarchy. Among late adolescents

(grades 11 to 12), the same crowds were identified, but two others, skaters (skateboard enthusiasts) and hippies, had been added to the mix, along with a hybrid crowd of grits-headbangers.

Kinney (1993, 1999) and Brown (Brown and Klute, 2003) have also noted changes in the role and importance of crowds through adolescence. As crowds become more differentiated in midadolescence, they also become more central to adolescents' thinking about their social world. Among Kinney's 9th graders, nearly all agreed about their school's crowd structure, and their perceptions of the influence of these crowds was very high. By 11th grade, however, the significance of crowds had begun to diminish, and the adolescents saw them as less important in defining social status and social perceptions. This finding parallels studies of friends' influence, which report friends' influence to be most intense during midadolescence, diminishing in the later high school years (Brown et al., 2008).

Scholars on adolescence generally see this pattern as reflecting the course of identity development (Brown & Klute, 2003; Varenne, 1982). During early to midadolescence, identity issues are especially prominent, and crowd structures help adolescents define themselves. The distinctive features of the crowd they belong to—the clothes they wear, the music they like best, the way they spend their leisure time, and so on—are ways for adolescents to define and declare their identities. By late adolescence, when their identities are better established, they no longer feel as great a need to rely on crowds for self-definition, and the importance of crowds diminishes. By that time, they may even see crowds as an impediment to their development as individuals. As they grow to adopt the individualism of the American majority culture, membership in any group—even a high-status one—may be seen as an infringement on their independence and uniqueness.

One reflection of this resistance to crowd identification is that adolescents do not always accept the crowd label attributed to them by their peers. According to one study (Brown, 1989), only 25% of the students classified by other students as jocks or druggies classified themselves that way, and only 15% of those classified as nobodies and loners by their peers also picked this classification for themselves. Thus, adolescents may readily sort their fellow students into distinct crowds, but they may be more likely to see themselves as the

**Middle School
(Grades 6–8)**

**Early High School
(Grades 9–10)**

FIGURE 8.3 Changes in crowd structure during adolescence.

Source: Brown, Mory, & Kinney (1994).

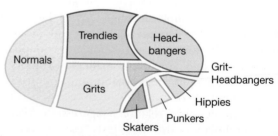

**Later High School
(Grades 11–12)**

kind of person who is too distinctively individual to fit neatly into a crowd classification.

THINKING CRITICALLY •••

Why do you think adolescents resist identifying themselves as part of a particular crowd, even though they routinely apply crowd labels to others?

Nevertheless, both self-reported and other-reported crowd membership are related to a variety of other characteristics in the United States and Europe (Delsing et al., 2007; La Greca et al., 2001; Prinstein & La Greca, 2002; Sussman et al., 2007; Verkooijen et al., 2007). Deviants tend to be highest in risk behaviors (such as substance use and delinquency) and lowest in school performance and social acceptance; Academics tend to be lowest in risk behavior and (of course) highest in school performance; and Elites tend to be highest in social acceptance and in between the other groups on risk behaviors and school performance.

There is also evidence that adolescents use their beliefs about the characteristics of specific crowds to make judgments about the adolescents in that crowd. In one study (Horn, Killen, & Stangor, 1999), 9th-grade American adolescents were asked whether it was acceptable to punish a group of students (e.g., "jocks," "brains") for a transgression (e.g., damaging school property at a dance). The results showed that, even when there was no evidence of who had actually committed the transgression, students were more likely to believe it was acceptable to punish the entire group if the transgression was consistent with stereotypical perceptions of the group being blamed. For example, it was more acceptable to punish the jocks for damaging school property than to punish them for breaking into the school computer system. This indicates that adolescents' crowd beliefs influence their social and moral judgments regarding the people they perceive to be part of these groups.

Crowds in American Minority Cultures Research on crowds in American minority cultures has revealed some interesting similarities and differences compared with the patterns in the American majority culture (Brown et al., 2008; Brown & Mounts, 1989; Fordham & Ogbu, 1986). With respect to similarities, scholars have found that in high schools with mostly non-White students, the same kinds of crowds exist as among White adolescents—Elites, Athletes, Academics, and so on. This makes sense because students in these schools would experience the same age-grading, the same cognitive changes, and the same identity issues that contribute to the formation of crowds among White adolescents. For minority adolescents, too, crowds serve as reference groups and as a way to establish a status hierarchy.

An interesting difference applies, however, to high schools that have multiethnic populations. In these high schools, adolescents tend to see fewer crowd distinctions in other ethnic groups than they do in their own. To non-Asians, for example, all Asian American students are part of

In multiethnic high schools, adolescents who belong to the same ethnic group are often seen by others as being part of one crowd. Here, Latino adolescents pose while a friend takes a picture.

the Asian crowd, whereas the Asian students themselves distinguish among Asian Elites, Asian Athletes, and so on. Also of interest is that in multiethnic high schools there tends to be little crossing of ethnic boundaries in crowd membership, just as with clique membership and friendships. However, one exception to this rule is that adolescent boys with a common interest in sports—the Athletes—are more likely than other adolescents in high school to form a multiethnic crowd (Damico & Sparks, 1986).

Crowds Across Cultures Although crowds as found in American schools do not really exist in traditional cultures, many traditional cultures do have a distinct social group of young people.

Traditional cultures often have one adolescent peer crowd in the community, rather than diverse crowds with different attributes and statuses as in American schools. The adolescent peer crowd in traditional cultures is also less strictly age-graded—adolescents of a variety of ages may be part of the adolescent peer crowd. Still, it could be called a peer crowd in the sense that it is a group of adolescents who spend time together on a daily basis and have a sense of themselves as being a distinct group with a distinct group identity.

In some traditional cultures, the center of adolescent social life is a separate dwelling, a **dormitory** where the community's adolescents sleep and spend their leisure time (Schlegel & Barry, 1991). In most cases, they do not spend all their time there—adolescents typically work alongside their parents and have their meals with their families. The dormitory is a place for relaxing and having fun with other adolescents.

Often, this fun includes sexual experimentation. The adolescents sleep in the dormitory, and this setting provides the

---

dormitory In some traditional cultures, a dwelling in which the community's adolescents sleep and spend their leisure time.

One fruitful way that adolescent crowds have been studied is through **participant observation** (Hodkinson, 2005). This research method involves taking part in various activities with the people you are interested in studying. As the scholar, you participate in the activities, but you also use that participation as an opportunity to observe and record the behavior of others.

Participant observation is related to the ethnographic method we discussed in Chapter 1, which is typically used by anthropologists. However, anthropologists using ethnographic methods usually live among the people they are studying. Participant observation does not go quite that far—the scholar takes part in many activities with the group of interest, but without actually living among them on a daily basis. Nevertheless, participant observation shares many of the strengths of the ethnographic method. Both methods allow the scholar to observe the behavior of people in action, as it actually occurs, rather than relying on later memories of behavior as questionnaires and interviews do.

One of the scholars who has done participant observation of adolescent crowds is the sociologist David Kinney of Central Michigan University. For several years, Kinney's research has involved blending in with adolescent crowds in high schools and observing their behavior. He also conducts interviews with adolescents to supplement his observations.

Kinney's participant observation research has provided some of the best information we have on the composition of adolescent crowds and how they change from middle school through high school (e.g., Kinney, 1993, 1999). For example, he has observed how crowds in middle school tend to be divided simply into the popular crowd (trendies) and the unpopular crowd (dweebs), whereas in high school the crowds tend to be more diverse and defined by common interests and styles (e.g., skaters, headbangers). Kinney's interviews, too, provide valuable data on adolescent peer groups, for example, on the sometimes brutal process of establishing social hierarchies among peers through sarcasm and ridicule, as exemplified in this quotation:

> [In middle school] you were afraid of getting laughed at about anything you did because if you did one thing that was out of the ordinary, and you weren't expected to do anything out of the ordinary, then you were laughed at and made fun of, and you wouldn't fit the group at all, and then, of course, you were excluded and then you didn't even exist. (Kinney, 1993, p. 27)

Kinney obtains permission from school officials first, of course. For the most part, the adolescents know he is not "one of them," and he does not attempt to hide that fact. However, effective participation does require blending into the social setting as thoroughly as possible, and Kinney takes steps to achieve that goal:

> I attempted to carve out a neutral identity for myself at the school by making and maintaining connections with students in a wide variety of peer groups and by being open to their different viewpoints. . . . I also distanced myself from adult authority figures by dressing in jeans and casual shirts and by emphasizing my status as a college student writing a paper about teenagers' high school experiences. (Kinney, 1993, p. 25)

Of course, participant observation of adolescents is easier for someone who looks young, as Kinney did when he began his research as a graduate student. An older scholar, gray-haired and clearly a long way from adolescence, would be more conspicuous and would have a more difficult time being accepted by adolescents as a participant in their activities (Wulff, 1995a). As a young scholar, Kinney was able to "hang out" with various adolescent crowds, not just in school but at sports events, dances, and parties, and have them accept and even enjoy his presence.

---

opportunity for their first sexual experiences. Even if there are separate dormitories for boys and girls, they may visit one another for sexual adventures. As Schlegel and Barry (1991) put it, the dorm is like an "extended slumber party as American teenagers know it, but often with the addition of sexual play" (p. 70). Adolescent dormitories are common in cultures in Africa, southern Asia, and the Pacific islands.

Another arrangement found in some traditional cultures is a **men's house**, a dormitory where adolescent boys sleep along with adult men who are widowed or divorced. Married men may also spend time there during the day. The men's house serves a function similar to that of the adolescent dormitory—as a place to sleep and enjoy leisure—but it is not limited to adolescents. Rather than being a setting for an adolescent peer crowd, it is a setting mainly for male pursuits and for adult men to socialize adolescent boys into the male gender role, teaching them the kinds of things that men do with their spare time.

---

participant observation A research method that involves taking part in various activities with the people being studied, and learning about them through participating in the activities with them.

men's house In some traditional cultures, a dormitory where adolescent boys sleep and hang out along with adult men who are widowed or divorced.

THINKING CRITICALLY •••

Compare and contrast the peer relations of young people in the "dormitory" of traditional cultures with the peer relations of emerging adults in American college dormitories.

Changes in Clique and Crowd Composition During Adolescence and Emerging Adulthood

In industrialized societies, the end of formal education marks a key transition in friendships and peer relationships, usually at some point in the late teens or early 20s. The school is the main arena for adolescents' relationships, and the end of educational training removes young people from a setting where most of their daily social interactions are with people their own age. In the workplaces most young people enter following the end of their education, age-grading either does not exist or is much less intense. Also, a hierarchy of social authority already exists in workplaces, so the anxiety adolescents experience about finding a place in a highly ambiguous and unstructured social hierarchy is no longer as much of an issue.

In a classic study now over 40 years old, Australian sociologist Dexter Dunphy (1963) described developmental changes in the structure of adolescent cliques and crowds. In the first stage, during early adolescence, according to Dunphy, adolescents' social lives mostly take place within same-sex cliques. Boys hang around other boys and girls hang around other girls, each of them enjoying their separate activities apart from the other sex. In the second stage, a year or two later, boys and girls become more interested in one another, and boys' and girls' cliques begin to spend some of their leisure time near each other, if not actually doing much interacting across the gender gap. Picture the setting of a party, or a school dance, or the food court of a local mall, with small groups of adolescent boys and adolescent girls watching each other, checking each other out, but rarely actually speaking to members of the other clique.

In the third stage, the gender divisions of cliques begin to break down as the clique leaders begin to form romantic relationships. The other clique members soon follow, in the fourth stage (around the mid-teens), and soon all cliques and crowds are mixed-gender groups. In the fifth and final stage, during the late teens, males and females begin to pair off in more serious relationships, and the structure of cliques and crowds begins to break down and finally disintegrates.

Does Dunphy's model still work 40 years later? Probably more at the early stages than at the later stages. Current research does confirm that early adolescents spend most of their time with same-sex friends and that gradually these cliques of same-sex friends begin to spend time together in larger mixed-sex cliques and crowds (Berndt, 1996; Connolly, Furman, & Konarski, 2000). However, whether the model holds beyond these early stages is questionable. As we have noted, the median age of marriage has risen dramatically since 1960. At that time, the median marriage age in the United States was only about 20 for women and 22 for men (Arnett & Taber, 1994), meaning that most females were married or engaged just two years beyond high school. Now the median marriage age is 26 for women and over 27 for men (U.S. Bureau of the Census, 2009), meaning that for most people marriage is far off during the high school years. In other industrialized countries, the median marriage age was also in the very early twenties 40 years ago, and is now even later than in the United States (Arnett, 2006b; Douglass, 2007).

Thus, Dunphy's model of ending up in committed intimate pairings by the end of high school probably applies more to his time, when marriage took place relatively early, than to our time, when most people marry much later. Most young people in the West have a series of romantic relationships, not just in high school but for many years after. Although many of them will have had at least one romantic relationship by the end of high school, they are likely to maintain membership in a variety of same-sex and mixed-sex groups not just through high school but well into emerging adulthood. As Figure 8.4 illustrates, ESM studies have found that the amount of time adolescents spend in other-sex groups or pairs increases from grade 9 through grade 12, but even in grade 12 more time is spent with same-sex friends than with other-sex friends (Csikszentmihalyi & Larson, 1984).

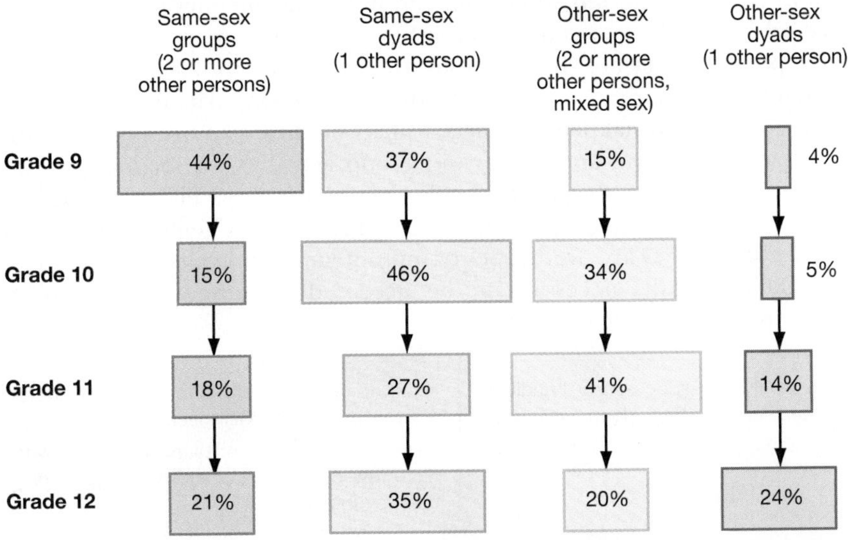

Same-sex groups (2 or more other persons)
Same-sex dyads (1 other person)
Other-sex groups (2 or more other persons, mixed sex)
Other-sex dyads (1 other person)
Grade 9
44%
37%
15%
4%
Grade 10
15%
46%
34%
5%
Grade 11
18%
27%
41%
14%
Grade 12
21%
35%
20%
24%

FIGURE 8.4 Amount of time adolescents spend in same-sex and other-sex groups or pairs.

Source: Csikszentmihalyi & Larson (1984).

Popularity and Unpopularity

"When I got to school the first day, everyone looked at me like I was from outer space or something. It was like, 'Who's that? Look at her hair. Look at what she's wearing'. That's all anybody cares about around here: what you look like and what you wear. I felt like a total outcast. As soon as I got home, I locked myself in my room and cried for about an hour."

—Tina, age 14 (Bell, 1998, p. 78)

A consistent finding in studies on peer crowds is that adolescents agree that certain of their peers are popular and certain others are unpopular. The popular, high-status crowds go by various names, including jocks, trendies, and (naturally) populars. The unpopular, low-status crowds have their characteristic names, too: nerds, geeks, dirties, and druggies (Brown & Klute, 2003; Horn, 2003; Kinney, 1993; Sussman et al., 2007).

In addition to this research on crowd popularity, a great deal of research has been done at the individual level, investigating what makes some adolescents popular and others unpopular. Typically, this research has used a method known as **sociometry**, which involves having students rate the social status of other students (McElhaney et al., 2008). Students in a classroom or a school are shown the names or photographs of other students and asked about their attitudes toward them. They may be asked directly who is popular and who is unpopular, or whom they like best and whom they like least. Another approach is more indirect, asking students whom they would most like and least like to be paired with on a class project or to have as a companion for social activities. In addition to the popularity ratings, students may rate the other students on characteristics hypothesized to be related to popularity and unpopularity, such as physical attractiveness, intelligence, friendliness, and aggressiveness.

Sociometric research has revealed some aspects of adolescent popularity that are consistent with popularity at other ages and some aspects that are especially prominent in adolescence. Physical attractiveness and social skills are factors related to popularity at all ages (Becker & Luthar, 2007). High intelligence also tends to be related to popularity, not to unpopularity, in spite of the negative crowd labels applied to nerds and geeks. What stigmatizes the nerds and geeks and makes them unpopular is not high intelligence but the perception that they lack social skills and focus on academics to the exclusion of a social life (Hartup, 1996; Kinney, 1993). Overall, however, social intelligence and general intelligence are correlated—being intelligent usually goes along with being better at figuring out what people want and how to make them like you.

The Importance of Social Skills

At all ages, including adolescence, the qualities most often associated with popularity and unpopularity can be grouped under the general term **social skills** (Nangle, Erdley, Carpenter, & Newman, 2002). People who are well liked by others tend to be friendly, cheerful, good-natured, and humorous (Becker & Luthar, 2007; Hartup, 1996). They treat others with kindness and are sensitive to others' needs. They listen well to others (that is, they are not simply wrapped up in their own concerns) and communicate their own point of view clearly (Jarvinen & Nicholls, 1996; Kennedy, 1990). They participate eagerly in the activities of their group and often take the lead in suggesting group activities and drawing others in to participate (Bryant, 1992). They manage to be confident without appearing conceited or arrogant (Hartup, 1996). In all of these ways, they demonstrate the skills that contribute to social success.

Unpopular adolescents, by contrast, tend to lack social skills. Scholars who have studied popularity and unpopularity in childhood and adolescence tend to distinguish between two types of unpopularity, reflecting different types of deficiencies in social skills (Coie et al., 1995; Inderbitzen et al., 1997; Parker & Asher, 1987). **Rejected adolescents** are actively disliked by their peers, usually because others find them to be excessively aggressive, disruptive, and quarrelsome. They tend to ignore what others want and respond to disagreements with selfishness and belligerence (Prinstein & LaGreca, 2004). These are the adolescents mentioned in sociometric ratings as peers who are disliked and whom other adolescents do *not* want as team members or companions. **Neglected adolescents** do not make enemies the way rejected adolescents do, but they do not have many friends either. They are the nobodies, the ones who are barely noticed by their peers. They have difficulty making friendships or even normal peer contacts, usually because they are shy and withdrawn, and they avoid group activities. In sociometric ratings, they are rarely mentioned as either liked or disliked—other adolescents have trouble remembering who they are. Both types of unpopular adolescents lack the social skills necessary to be accepted by others and establish durable relationships.

---

sociometry A method for assessing popularity and unpopularity that involves having students rate the social status of other students.

social skills Skills for successfully handling social relations and getting along well with others.

rejected adolescents Adolescents who are actively disliked by their peers.

neglected adolescents Adolescents who have few or no friends and are largely unnoticed by their peers.

Neglected adolescents lack the social skills necessary for making friends.

Social Skills and Social Cognition

One interesting line of research indicates that rejected adolescents' deficits in social skills are based on a deficit of social cognition, at least for males. According to the findings of this research, aggressive boys have a tendency to interpret other boys' actions as hostile even when the intention is ambiguous. Kenneth Dodge and his colleagues came to this conclusion after showing videotapes to children and adolescents depicting ambiguous situations (Dodge, 1983, 1993; Dodge & Feldman, 1990; Dodge et al., 2003; Lansford et al., 2006; Prinstein & Dodge, 2008). For example, one boy would be shown bumping into another boy who was holding a drink, causing the boy to drop the drink. Boys who had been named as aggressive by their teachers and peers were more likely to see the bump as a hostile act intended to spill the drink, whereas other boys were more likely to see it as an accident. According to Dodge, this is a problem of **social information processing**. Part of lacking social skills, for rejected boys, is seeing the world as filled with potential enemies and being too quick to retaliate aggressively when events take place that could be interpreted as hostile. To put it another way, having social skills means, in part, giving others the benefit of the doubt and avoiding the tendency to interpret their actions as hostile when they may not be hostile after all.

Aggressiveness is not always a source of unpopularity in adolescence, however. Researchers have noted that some adolescents are high in aggressiveness but also high in social skills (de Bruyn & Cillesen, 2006; Demir & Tarhan, 2001; Pakaslahti, Karjalainen, & Keitikangas-Jaervinen, 2002). They are classified as **controversial adolescents**, because they tend to generate mixed responses among their peers. Rather than being consistently popular or unpopular, they may be strongly liked as well as strongly disliked, by different people

and by the same people on different occasions. One recent study found that friendships with controversial adolescents were high in intimacy and fun but also in physical and relational aggression (Hawley et al., 2007). Another study reported that controversial adolescents were more likely than popular adolescents to be the leader of a deviant peer group (Miller-Johnson et al., 2003).

The Continuity of Popularity and Unpopularity

Popularity and unpopularity tend to be consistent from childhood through adolescence. Exceptions do exist, of course, but in general popular children become popular adolescents and unpopular children remain unpopular as adolescents. This may be partly because of stability in the qualities that contribute to popularity and unpopularity, such as intelligence and aggressiveness. We have seen, in Chapter 3, that intelligence in childhood is highly correlated with intelligence in adolescence. Aggressiveness, which is such a distinguishing quality of rejected children, also tends to be consistent from childhood to adolescence (Moffitt, 1993). The quality of the family environment influences the development of social skills, and this is true in adolescence as well as childhood (Engels, Dekovic, & Meeus, 2002; Engels, Finkenauer, Meeus, & Dekovic, 2001).

THINKING CRITICALLY •••

Would you expect popularity and unpopularity to be more important or less important among adolescents in traditional cultures compared with adolescents in industrialized societies? Why?

In addition, scholars in this area emphasize that both popularity and unpopularity in adolescence have a certain self-perpetuating quality (Dodge et al., 2003). Children who are popular are reinforced every day in their popularity. Other kids like them, are glad to see them, and want to include them in what they are doing. This kind of reinforcement strengthens their confidence in their popularity and also gives them daily opportunities to continue to develop the kinds of social skills that made them popular in the first place. Thus, it makes sense that popular children tend to become popular adolescents.

Unfortunately, unpopularity is also self-perpetuating (Brendgen et al., 1998; Dodge & Feldman, 1990; Prinstein & LaGreca, 2004). Children and adolescents who are unpopular develop a reputation with their peers as unpleasant and hard to get along with (in the case of rejected children) or submissive and weak (in the case of neglected children). These reputations, once developed, can be hard to break.

---

social information processing The interpretation of others' behavior and intentions in a social interaction.

controversial adolescents Adolescents who are aggressive but who also possess social skills, so that they evoke strong emotions both positive and negative from their peers.

Children and adolescents who have learned to see certain peers as unpopular may continue to view them negatively even if their behavior changes because they are used to thinking of them that way (Coie & Dodge, 1997). For both rejected and neglected children, being unpopular makes it less likely that they will be included in the kinds of positive social exchanges that would help them develop better social skills.

THINKING CRITICALLY •••

Would you expect popularity and unpopularity to be more important or less important in emerging adulthood compared with adolescence? Why?

Interventions for Unpopularity

Although unpopularity is often self-perpetuating, this is not always the case. Many of us can remember a period in childhood or adolescence when we felt unpopular—rejected or neglected or both. If we are lucky, we grow out of it. We develop social skills, or we develop new interests and abilities that lead to new social contacts with others who have similar interests, or we move to a new classroom or a new school where we can start fresh. Whatever the reasons, many of the young people who are unpopular during late childhood and early adolescence go on to have more satisfying friendships in adolescence and beyond (Kinney, 1993).

Adolescents who remain unpopular, however, suffer a number of negative consequences. Overall, a correlation exists between unpopularity and such consequences as depression, behavior problems, and academic problems (Hecht et al., 1998; Nolan, Flynn, & Garber, 2003; Parker & Asher, 1987; Patterson & Stoolmiller, 1991). Rejected children and adolescents are at greater risk for problems than neglected children and adolescents (Dishion & Spracklen, 1996; Wentzel & Asher, 1998). For rejected children, the aggressiveness that is often the basis of their rejection is also the basis of their other problems (Prinstein & LaGreca, 2004). They tend to end up becoming friends with other aggressive adolescents, and they have higher rates of aggression-related problems such as conflicts with peers, teachers, and parents (Feldman et al., 1995; French, Conrad, & Turner, 1995; Underwood, Kupersmidt, & Coie, 1996). They are also more likely than their peers to drop out of school (Zettergren, 2003). Neglected children tend to have a different set of problems in adolescence, such as low self-esteem, loneliness, depression, and alcohol abuse (Hecht et al., 1998; Hops et al., 1997; Kupersmidt & Coie, 1990).

Responding to the problems associated with unpopularity, educators and psychologists have devised a variety of intervention programs intended to ameliorate unpopularity and

its effects. Because social skills are the primary basis of both popularity and unpopularity, interventions for unpopularity tend to focus on learning social skills (Bierman and Montminy, 1993; Ladd et al., 2002; Nangle et al., 2002). For rejected children and adolescents, this means learning how to control and manage anger and aggressiveness. In one program (Weissberg, Caplan, & Harwood, 1991), adolescents were taught to follow a sequence of six steps when they felt themselves losing control:

1. Stop, calm down, think before you act.
2. Go over the problem and say or write down your feelings.
3. Set a positive goal for the outcome of the situation.
4. Think of possible solutions that will lead toward that goal.
5. Try to anticipate the consequences of the possible solutions.
6. Choose the best solution and try it out.

In this intervention, the adolescents who took part improved their abilities to generate constructive solutions to problem situations, and their teachers reported improvement in their social relations in the classroom following the intervention.

For neglected adolescents, interventions are designed to teach the social skills involved in making friends. Typically, adolescents are taught (through instruction, modeling, and role playing) how to enter a group, how to listen in an attentive and friendly way, and how to attract positive attention from their peers (Bierman & Montminy, 1993; Murphy & Schneider, 1994; Repinski & Leffert, 1994). These programs generally report some degree of success in improving adolescents' relations with their peers.

Interventions of this kind have also been developed for college students, with "neglected" status based on self-reports of loneliness rather than on sociometric ratings. In one effort, Gerald Adams and his colleagues (Adams et al., 1988) developed an intervention designed to improve the social skills of lonely college students. Their research had indicated that lonely college students are less perceptive than other students about nonverbal communication, less effective in their efforts to influence people, less likely to take risks in interpersonal relations, and less likely to have good listening skills. The intervention, designed to address these deficits in social skills, was found to have positive effects on social skills and feelings of being included in social situations, both immediately following the program and 3 months later.

However, most of these interventions with rejected and neglected adolescents and college students have not included long-term follow-up studies to see if the effects last. A variety of programs have demonstrated success in improving social skills during and immediately following the program, but whether such interventions result in long-term changes in unpopularity is currently unknown.

"To whom can I speak today? I am heavy-laden with trouble through lack of an intimate friend."

—Anonymous, ca. 1990 B.C.

Bullying

An extreme form of peer rejection in adolescence is **bullying**. There are three components to bullying (Olweus, 2000; Wolak et al., 2007): *aggression* (physical or verbal); *repetition* (not just one incident but a pattern over time); and *power imbalance* (the bully has higher peer status than the victim). The prevalence of bullying rises through middle childhood and peaks in early adolescence, then declines substantially by late adolescence (Pepler et al., 2006). Bullying is an international phenomenon, observed in many countries in Europe (Dijkstra et al., 2008; Gini et al., 2008), Asia (Ando et al., 2005; Hokoda et al., 2006), and North America (Pepler et al., 2008; Volk et al., 2006). In a landmark study of bullying among over 100,000 adolescents aged 11–15 in 28 countries around the world, self-reported prevalence rates of being a victim of bullying ranged from 6% among girls in Sweden to 41% among boys in Lithuania, with rates in most countries in the 10–20% range (Due et al., 2005). Across countries, in this study and many others, boys are consistently more likely than girls to be bullies as well as victims.

Bullying has a variety of negative effects on adolescents' development. In the 28-country study of adolescent bullying, victims of bullying reported higher rates of a wide range of problems, including physical symptoms such as headaches, backaches, and difficulty sleeping, as well as psychological symptoms such as loneliness, helplessness, anxiety, and unhappiness (Due et al., 2005). Many other studies have reported similar results (Olweus, 2000). Not only victims but bullies are at high risk for problems (Klomek et al., 2007). A Canadian study of bullying that surveyed adolescents for 7 years beginning at ages 10–14 found that bullies reported more psychological problems and more problems in their relationships with parents and peers than nonbullies did (Pepler et al., 2008).

Who bullies, and who is bullied? Victims tend to be low-status adolescents who are rejected by their peers (Perren & Hornung, 2005; Sentse et al., 2007; Veenstra et al., 2007). Other adolescents are reluctant to come to their defense because of their low status. The social status of bullies is more complex. Sometimes they are high-status adolescents who bully as a way of asserting and maintaining their high status—the "controversial" adolescents described earlier in the chapter (Dijkstra et al., 2008); sometimes they are middle-status adolescents who go along with bullying by high-status adolescents to avoid being targeted as a victim (Oltoff & Goossens, 2008); and sometimes they are low-status adolescents who look for a victim so there will be someone who is even lower in status than they are (Juvonen & Galvan, 2006). About one fourth of bullies are also victims (Solberg, Olweus, & Endresen, 2007).

A recent variation on bullying is **cyberbullying** (also called electronic bullying), which involves bullying behavior via e-mail, the Internet, or mobile phones (Kowalski, 2008). A Swedish study of 12- to 20-year-olds found an age pattern of cyberbullying similar to what has been found in studies of "traditional" bullying, with the highest rates in early adoles-

Bullying in adolescence is common in many countries.

cence and a decline through late adolescence and emerging adulthood (Slonje & Smith, 2008). In a recent study of nearly 4,000 adolescents in grades 6–8 in the United States, 11% reported being victims of a cyberbullying incident at least once in the past 2 months; 7% indicated that they had been cyberbullies as well as victims during this time period; and 4% reported committing a cyberbullying act (Kowalski & Limber, 2007). Notably, half of the victims did not know the bully's identity, a key difference between cyberbullying and other bullying. However, Wolak and colleagues (2007) note that cyberbullying usually involves only a single incident, so it does not meet the criterion of repetition required in the standard definition of traditional bullying and might be better termed *on-line harassment*. This is an area that has just begun to be researched, so it will be worth watching for further developments.

Youth Culture

So far in this chapter we have looked at various aspects of friendship and at peer groups such as cliques and crowds, including issues of popularity and unpopularity. In addition to research in these areas, scholars have written extensively on **youth culture**. This is the idea that, along with their smaller social groups—friendships, cliques, and crowds—young people also constitute a group as a whole, separate from children and separate from adult society, with their own distinct culture (Steinberg et al., 2006). The analysis of youth culture has a long history in the field of sociology. Sociologists generally agree that a distinctive youth culture first arose in the West during the 1920s (Frith, 1983). (More detail on the rise of youth culture is provided in the Historical Focus box.)

---

bullying In peer relations, the aggressive assertion of power by one person over another.

cyberbullying Bullying via electronic means, mainly through the Internet.

youth culture The culture of young people as a whole, separate from children and separate from adult society, characterized by values of hedonism and irresponsibility.

Youth culture arose in the United States and other Western countries during the 1920s (Brake, 1985; Parsons, 1964; Wulff, 1995a). Previous historical periods may have had some small-scale youth cultures, but the 1920s were the first time that youth culture became a widespread social phenomenon. Then as now, the participants in youth culture were mainly emerging adults in their late teens and 20s.

The youth culture values of hedonism, leisure, and the pursuit of adventure and excitement were vividly displayed in the youth culture of the 1920s. This was especially evident in sexual behavior (Allen, 1964). The sexual code of previous eras was highly restrictive, especially for girls. Adolescent girls were taught to keep themselves pure and virginal until the right man came along to lead them to the altar. This meant not only no sexual intercourse but no petting, no kissing even, until the right man appeared. There was no such thing as dating (Bailey, 1989); instead, there was courtship, in which a young man would visit a young woman in her home—only if he had serious marriage intentions, of course.

This standard changed dramatically in the 1920s. "Petting parties" became popular, at which boys and girls would meet and pair up for kissing, petting, and possibly more. In the Middletown study of high school boys and girls in a typical midwestern town in the 1920s, half of them marked as true the statement "Nine out of every ten boys and girls of high school age have petting parties" (Lynd & Lynd, 1929/1957). In *This Side of Paradise* (1920), one of F. Scott Fitzgerald's novels depicting the lives of young people during the 1920s, the narrator observed that "None of the Victorian mothers—and most of the mothers were Victorian—had any idea how casually their daughters were accustomed to being kissed." One of the heroines brazenly confessed, "I've kissed dozens of men. I suppose I'll kiss dozens more."

Jazz was also part of the hedonism and leisure of 1920s youth culture. The 1920s are sometimes referred to as the "Jazz Age" because jazz was so popular then and because that was when jazz first became recognized as a distinct musical form. Jazz music was regarded by many as stimulating sexual desire, a quality the participants in youth culture found exciting but many adults considered dangerous. Jazz dancing, too, was regarded as sexually provocative. One Cincinnati newspaper of the time observed, "The music is sensuous, the embracing of partners—the female only half dressed—is absolutely indecent; and the motions—they are such as may not be described, with any respect for propriety, in a family newspaper" (Allen, 1964, p. 5).

Numerous aspects of the style of youth culture in the 1920s reflected the changes in sexual norms. The hems of women's dresses, previously considered improper if they rose any higher than 7 inches off the ground, now rose steadily until they reached the knee, a height many adults considered scandalous. Flesh-colored stockings became popular to enhance the now-exposed knee and calf. Short, bobbed hair became the most popular hairstyle for young women. Cosmetics became widely used for the first time—rouge and lipstick, wrinkle creams, and methods for plucking, trimming, and coloring the eyebrows.

The argot of 1920s youth culture was also distinctive. There was "23-skiddoo" and "the bee's knees" to describe something young people today would call "cool"; "rumble seat" for the back seat of an automobile, where sexual encounters frequently took place; and "spooning" for what today would be called "making out" or "hooking up."

What historical influences led to the rise of youth culture in the 1920s? One important influence was the end of World War I, which had just preceded the 1920s (Allen, 1964; John-

---

What are the distinctive features of youth culture? What qualifies it as a culture? Recall from Chapter 1 that a culture is a group's distinctive way of life, including its beliefs and values, its customs, and its art and technologies. According to Talcott Parsons (1964), the sociologist who first used the term *youth culture*, the values that distinguish youth culture are *hedonism* (which means the seeking of pleasure) and *irresponsibility* (that is, the postponement of adult responsibilities). He argued that the values of youth culture are the inverse of the values of adult society. Adult society emphasizes a regular routine, delay of gratification, and acceptance of responsibilities; youth culture turns these values upside down and prizes hedonism and irresponsibility instead. Similarly, Matza and Sykes (1961) wrote that youth culture is based in **subterranean values** such as hedonism, excitement, and adventure. Adults hold these values as well but are allowed to express them only in restricted forms of leisure, whereas the youth culture of adolescents and emerging adults expresses

---

subterranean values Values such as hedonism, excitement, and adventure, asserted by sociologists to be the basis of youth culture.

style The distinguishing features of youth culture, including image, demeanor, and argot.

image In Brake's description of the characteristics of youth culture, refers to dress, hair style, jewelry, and other aspects of appearance.

demeanor In Brake's description of youth cultures, refers to distinctive forms of gesture, gait, and posture.

argot (pronounced *ar-go'*) In youth culture, a certain vocabulary and a certain way of speaking.

son, 1992). Over 2 million American young people in their late teens and 20s had gone to Europe as part of the war effort. Participation in the war removed many young people from the narrow strictures of socialization in the families and communities from which they had come, and when they returned home they resisted returning to the old restraints and taboos.

Another influence was the ideas of Sigmund Freud, which became popularized after the war (Allen, 1964). In the popularized version of Freud's theories, an uninhibited sex life was viewed as promoting psychological health. To many, this made self-control seem not just prudish but harmful. Terms that had formerly been regarded as compliments became terms of reproach and even ridicule: *Victorian, puritan, wholesome, ladylike*. The values reflected in these terms became regarded by many young people as old-fashioned and incompatible with a healthy sex life.

A third factor in the rise of youth culture was the changing status of women (Johnson, 1992). The Nineteenth Amendment, giving women the right to vote, was made law in 1920, and this law both reflected and promoted a new status for women as more equal—if not entirely equal—to men. During the 1920s, women also became substantially more likely to enter the workplace as emerging adults, although most of them quit working after marriage or after their first child was born. Having their own income gave young women independence and social opportunities that had been unavailable to them in the past.

Finally, one other factor that contributed to the rise of youth culture was the increased availability of automobiles, particularly automobiles with tops. In 1919 only 10% of American cars had tops, but by 1927 this figure had climbed to 83% (Allen, 1964). Automobiles gave middle-class young people a means of escaping from the watchful eyes of parents and neighbors to attend parties, dances, or clubs miles away. Cars also provid-

According to scholars, a distinct youth culture first developed during the 1920s.

ed, then as now, a roomy enough setting for sexual escapades in the "rumble seat" (Lynd & Lynd, 1927/1957).

Not all young people take part in youth culture, and this was no less true in the 1920s than today. Many (perhaps even most) adolescents and emerging adults continued to abide by the traditional rules of morality and behavior with regard to sexuality as well as other aspects of life (Allen, 1964; Johnson, 1992). Youth culture then and now appeals most to young people who have sensation-seeking personalities (Arnett, 1994b, 1996) and who live in conditions affluent enough to allow them to pursue the allurements of hedonism and adventure that youth culture offers.

them more openly. More recent sociologists have also emphasized the central values of hedonism and the pursuit of adventure in youth culture (Brake, 1985; Osgood & Lee, 1993).

This inversion of values is, of course, temporary. According to Parsons (1964), participation in youth culture is a "rite of passage" in Western societies. Young people enjoy a brief period in which they live by hedonism and irresponsibility before entering the adult world and accepting its responsibilities. This period lasts only from the time young people become relatively independent of their parents—especially after they leave home—until they marry. Marriage represented, for Parsons, the formal entry into adulthood and thus the departure from youth culture. At the time Parsons was writing, the typical age of marriage was much lower than it is now (Arnett, 2006a). This means that the years available for participation in youth culture have expanded dramatically and

are mainly experienced in emerging adulthood rather than adolescence.

It is not only values that distinguish youth culture. British sociologist Michael Brake (1985) has proposed that there are three essential components to the **style** of youth culture:

1. **Image** refers to dress, hairstyle, jewelry, and other aspects of appearance. An example would be rings worn in the nose, navel, or eyebrow, which are worn by some young people but rarely by adults.

2. **Demeanor** refers to distinctive forms of gesture, gait, and posture. For example, certain ways of shaking hands (e.g., a "high five") have sometimes distinguished youth cultures.

3. **Argot** (pronounced *ar-go*) is a certain vocabulary and a certain way of speaking. Examples include "cool" to refer to something desirable, and "chill out" to mean relax or calm down.

One useful way to look at these aspects of style is that each of them constitutes a custom complex (Shweder et al., 1998), as discussed in Chapter 4. That is, each distinctive form of image, demeanor, and argot in youth culture symbolizes certain values and beliefs that distinguish youth culture from adult society. For example, dressing in tattered jeans and T-shirts signifies the emphasis on leisure and hedonism in youth culture and resistance to the more formal dress requirements of adult society. Using a youthful argot considered obscene and objectionable by adults signifies resistance to the manners and expectations of adults in favor of something more down-to-earth and authentic (Arnett, 1996; Brake, 1985). More generally, all aspects of style in youth culture serve to mark the boundaries between young people and adults.

Why do youth cultures develop? Sociologists have offered a variety of explanations. One condition necessary for the development of a youth culture is a pluralistic society (Brake, 1985), in other words, a society that is broad enough in its socialization that it condones a high degree of variability among individuals and groups, including many forms of behavior and belief that depart from the norms of society as a whole. A related view has been proposed by sociologists who see youth culture as arising in modern societies as a result of increasing individualism and the weakening of personal ties (Côté & Allahar, 1996). In this view, youth culture is a way of constructing a coherent and meaningful worldview in a society that fails to provide one.

There is also Parsons's (1964) view, as we have noted, that youth cultures arise in societies that allow young people an extended period between the time they gain substantial independence from parents and the time they take on adult responsibilities. Similarly, Michael Brake (1985) proposes that youth culture provides opportunities for young people to experiment with different possible identities. According to Brake,

1920s

1950s

1960s

1990s

The changing styles of youth cultures.

> Young people need a space in which to explore an identity which is separate from the roles and expectations imposed by family, work and school. Youth culture offers a collective identity, a reference group from which youth can develop an individual identity. It provides cognitive material from which to develop an *alternative script*. . . . It represents a free area to relax with one's peers outside the scrutiny and demands of the adult world. (p. 195)

Youth culture does not necessarily exist in opposition or rebellion to adult society. As mentioned in Chapter 7, adolescents and their parents generally share many common values, such as the value of education, honesty, and hard work. This is not inconsistent with believing that the teens and early 20s represent a unique opportunity to pursue pleasure

and leisure. Both young people and their parents know that this period is temporary and that the responsibilities of adult life will eventually be assumed (Brake, 1985).

Of course, one could argue that there is not just one youth culture but many youth subcultures (Brown & Klute, 2003). The crowds we discussed earlier in this chapter represent different youth subcultures—jocks, geeks, and dirties all have their distinctive styles. And not all of these crowds are part of the larger youth culture just described. Crowds such as geeks and normals are conventional in style and do not participate in the pursuit of pleasure and leisure that defines youth culture. In contrast, crowds such as gothics and dirties clearly have a style that represents resistance to the routine and conventions of adult life. Youth subcultures have also developed around certain distinctive musical forms such as heavy metal (Arnett, 1996) and hip-hop (Clay, 2003) that are loved by some adolescents and hated by others.

Thus, adolescents participate in youth culture to different degrees—some not at all, some moderately, some intensely. Adolescence and emerging adulthood are years when some young people take part in youth culture (or a youth subculture), but most young people do so only to a limited degree and some do not at all.

Some scholars have observed that youth culture is increasing worldwide (Arnett, 2002a; Griffin, 2001; Maira, 2004). Driven by worldwide media, new youth styles make their way quickly around the world. Of course, in all countries, young people vary in how much they take part in youth culture. Nevertheless, the image, argot, and media popular among adolescents in Western youth cultures have been influential among many adolescents in non-Western countries (Schlegel, 2000). Western countries also influence one another, and although the youth culture of the United States is dominant in the West, youth cultures in other Western countries also influence some American adolescents.

THINKING CRITICALLY •••

Nearly all the scholarly work on youth culture has been theoretical rather than empirical (research based). How would you design a study to examine the validity of the theoretical ideas about youth culture presented here?

Technological Change and the Power of Youth Culture

Youth culture is largely created and spread by young people themselves (Brake, 1985). To learn the latest styles of dress, hair, and argot, and the hot new forms of music and other media, young people look mainly to each other for cues. Adults may try to control or monitor this process—to make youth culture less disruptive or to profit from selling the items popular in youth culture—but young people learn the ways of youth culture from one another, not from adults (Frith, 1983). According to anthropologist Margaret Mead (1928), in times of rapid technological change young people tend to look to one another for instruction in a variety of aspects of life.

Writing during the time youth culture was first forming, Mead (1928) described how the rate of technological change in a culture influences the degree to which adolescents receive teachings from adults or from each other. In cultures where the rate of technological change is very slow, which Mead called **postfigurative cultures**, what children and adolescents need to learn to function as adults changes little from one generation to the next. As a result, children and adolescents can learn all they need to know from their elders. For example, if a culture's economy has been based on the same

In a cofigurative culture, adolescents learn a great deal from one another, not just from adults.

methods of farming for many generations, the elders will be the authorities young people will want to look to for instruction in how to plant, cultivate, and harvest their crops.

Most cultures through most of human history have been postfigurative cultures. However, since the industrial revolution began about 500 years ago, the pace of technological change has increased with each century. Particularly in the past 100 years in industrialized countries, technological change has occurred with such speed that the skills most important in the economy change with each generation. The result is what Mead called **cofigurative cultures**, where young people learn what they need to know not only from adults but also from other young people. Learning about the styles and media of youth culture would be one example of this kind of learning. Another example would be the use of computers. An adolescent who wanted to learn how to make charts and graphs on her computer might be more likely to ask a computer-savvy friend for advice than to ask her grandparents, who may have reached retirement age before personal computers became popular.

Traditional cultures are likely to move from postfigurative to cofigurative status as globalization proceeds. We have seen an example of this in Chapter 4, where we discussed changing views among adolescent Aborigines in Australia. In the present generation of adolescents, the traditional Law describing relations between adults and children and between

postfigurative cultures Cultures in which what children and adolescents need to learn to function as adults changes little from one generation to the next, and therefore children and adolescents can learn all they need to know from their elders.

cofigurative cultures Cultures in which young people learn what they need to know not only from adults but also from other young people.

prefigurative cultures Cultures in which young people teach knowledge to adults.

men and women has become viewed by many adolescents as obsolete (Burbank, 1988). The world they are growing up in has changed too much in recent decades for the traditions of their elders to be relevant to their lives. Consequently, they are rejecting these traditions in favor of the global media of youth culture that they share with their friends and peers. These media seem to them to show where their futures lie, and with their peers they share a desire to look forward to the world shaped by globalization rather than backward to their cultural traditions.

Postfigurative and *cofigurative* describe levels of technological change and orientations to peers and adults in two kinds of cultures. Mead believed that in the future, as the pace of technological change continues to accelerate, a third type may emerge. In **prefigurative cultures**, the direction of learning would come full circle—young people would teach adults how to use the latest technology. Mead proposed this theory in 1928, long before the computer age, and in many ways her prediction has come to pass in our time. Children and adolescents in industrialized societies now grow up with computers and the Internet, and many of them soon achieve a level of skill far beyond that of their elders. A *New York Times* article contained profiles of several adolescents in their teens who have thriving and lucrative businesses creating web sites and developing computer software—with all of their business coming from adults much older than themselves (Morris, 1999).

THINKING CRITICALLY •••

Margaret Mead wrote her prediction of the arrival of prefigurative cultures in 1928. Would you say the culture you live in has reached a prefigurative state by now, at least in some respects? What examples could you give of the prefigurative pattern?

The history of the personal computer provides many other examples of revolutionary developments led by adolescents and emerging adults. Bill Gates, founder of Microsoft, developed the DOS operating system that is now the basis of most personal computer operations when he was still in his 20s. Steve Jobs started the Apple Computer Corporation by making a personal computer in his garage when he was still in his teens. Many of the older, more experienced executives and inventors at more established companies such as IBM have borrowed many of their ideas from Gates, Jobs, and other young people—one sign that the prefigurative culture predicted by Mead may have begun to arrive.

Still, it is difficult to believe that the day will ever come when *most* knowledge will be conveyed from adolescents to adults. Inevitably, adults have more experience than adolescents and have had more years to accumulate knowledge. Even now, the computer examples described above are the exception, not the rule. Most knowledge remains communicated from adults to young people rather than the other way around; the schools that adolescents and emerging adults attend are created for this purpose. And although young people learn a great deal about youth culture from their peers during adolescence and emerging adulthood, for nearly all young people youth culture is largely left behind after emerging adulthood ends and the responsibilities of adult life begin.

SUMMING UP

In this chapter we have covered diverse topics related to friends and peers, including developmental changes in friendships, how adolescents choose friends, friends' influence or "peer pressure," cliques and crowds, and youth culture. The following are the key points of this chapter:

- Friends become increasingly important during adolescence. The amount of time spent with friends increases (and time spent with family decreases), and friends become increasingly significant as confidants and as sources of personal advice and emotional support.

- A key change in friendships from preadolescence to adolescence is the increased importance of intimacy, with a focus on qualities such as trust and loyalty and an increased amount of time together spent in conversation about significant issues rather than on shared activities.

- The most important basis for friendships in adolescence is similarity, particularly in ethnicity, educational orientation, media and leisure preferences, and participation in risk behavior.

- Although *peer pressure* is often used as a negative term to describe how adolescent friends encourage each other to participate in risk behavior, studies indicate that the extent of this influence may be exaggerated because of selective association and that adolescent friends may influence each other against risk behavior as well as toward it. Friends also have a variety of positive influences on one another.

- Emerging adults take part frequently in leisure activities with friends, such as attending parties, going to movies, and getting together for no particular purpose. However, participation in leisure activities with friends declines during emerging adulthood.

- Cliques are small groups of close friends. Sarcasm and ridicule are common in adolescent cliques, to establish a dominance hierarchy and to enforce conformity to clique norms.

- Relational aggression includes sarcasm and ridicule as well as gossip and exclusion. It is especially common among adolescent girls, evidently because more direct forms of disagreement and conflict are prohibited in the female gender role.

- The age-graded school setting of Western societies lends itself to the development of reputation-based crowds as a way of defining and organizing a social structure. Traditional cultures sometimes have a version of a peer crowd, with a separate dormitory where adolescents hang out, relax, and engage in sexual play.

- The most important determinant of popularity and unpopularity in adolescence is social skills. Other qualities related to popularity are intelligence and physical attractiveness. Interventions for unpopular adolescents have shown some short-term success, but their long-term effectiveness is unknown.

- Bullying has three components: aggression, repetition, and power imbalance. Studies show that bullying in adolescence is a worldwide phenomenon. An electronic form of bullying, cyberbullying, has arisen in recent years.

- A distinctive youth culture first appeared in the West during the 1920s. According to sociologists, youth cultures are characterized by subterranean values of hedonism and irresponsibility and by a distinctive style consisting of image, demeanor, and argot. Late adolescents and emerging adults are the main participants in youth culture, but the degree of their participation varies from highly intense to not at all.

A common thread running through all the topics we have considered in this chapter is that the influence of peers on development during adolescence and emerging adulthood is substantial and has grown in the past century. Because of economic and social changes during the 20th century, adolescents now spend considerably more time with their peers on a typical day, in school and in play, and considerably less time with parents. Although peers are also important to young people in traditional cultures, the influence of peers is enhanced in industrialized societies because school brings peers together for many hours each day, away from their parents. Also, by adolescence many young people become part of a media-driven youth culture in which what is viewed as most valued, most desirable, most "cool" is based on the preferences of peers and friends, not adults.

Although we have examined a wide range of issues on peers and friends in this chapter, one crucial area we have not discussed is romantic partnerships. We will examine this in detail in the following chapter on love and sex.

KEY TERMS

peers 211
friends 212
intimacy 215
selective association 221
informational support 221
instrumental support 221
companionship support 222
esteem support 222
cliques 223
crowds 223
relational aggression 225

dormitory 227
participant observation 228
men's house 228
sociometry 230
social skills 230
rejected adolescents 230
neglected adolescents 230
social information processing 231
controversial adolescents 231
bullying 232
cyberbullying 233

youth culture 233
subterranean values 234
style 235
image 235
demeanor 235
argot 235
postfigurative cultures 237
cofigurative cultures 237
prefigurative cultures 238

INTERNET RESOURCES

www.mcps.k12.md.us/curriculum/socialstd/NSL/Unit8.pdf
Melanie Killen, whose research on group exclusion addresses discrimination between peer cliques and crowds based on gender or ethnic group membership, has helped to develop a curriculum to promote tolerance and inclusion among high school students. The curriculum can be found at this web site.

FOR FURTHER READING

Dodge, K. A. (Ed). (2008). *Understanding peer influence in children and adolescents. Duke series in child development and public policy.* New York: Guilford Press. A recent summary of research on peers and friends in childhood and adolescence, edited by a top scholar in this area.

Youniss, J., & Smollar, J. (1985). *Adolescents' relations with mothers, fathers, and friends.* Chicago: University of Chicago Press. A classic study of how changes in relationships to family and friends are intertwined during adolescence.

For more review plus practice tests, videos, flashcards, and more, log on to MyDevelopmentLab.

9 CHAPTER

Love and Sexuality

Do you remember your first kiss? I know I'll never forget mine. It took place at a junior high school dance, when I was in 9th grade (I was a late-maturing adolescent). I had taken my sort-of girlfriend there, and I think that may well have been my first real "date." So far, we had progressed only as far as me going over to visit her at her home now and then. She never slammed the door in my face—always seemed glad to see me, in fact—so I asked her to go to the dance with me.

I spent most of the evening trying to gather up sufficient courage to kiss her. We didn't dance much—we were both too timid—so I had a lot of opportunities, with both of us sitting alongside the gymnasium watching as our bolder peers danced together. It took me a long time to get up the guts to try it, but as the evening waned I knew it was getting to be now or never. At last she smiled at me sweetly—probably thinking, "Will this fool ever get around to it?"—and I leaned over to place my lips against hers, and . . .

The vice principal grabbed me by the hair, snapped my head back, and yelled, "What do you think you're doing?! That's not allowed in here!" He dragged us down to his office, and it was only after repeated assurances that we were not sex maniacs that he was persuaded not to call our parents and add to our already substantial humiliation.

I HOPE YOUR FIRST KISS WAS MORE FUN THAN THAT! As we will see in this chapter, the beginnings of love and sexuality can be a source of many emotions for adolescents— pleasure, delight, and wonder, but also fear, anxiety, and confusion. The chapter is divided into two sections: love and sexuality. In all cultures, developing into sexual maturity in adolescence and emerging adulthood involves forming close relationships with persons outside the family. Most young people eventually form a relationship in which they experience love. We begin the section on love by discussing love in its cultural context, as well as the developmental progression that adolescent love tends to follow in Western cultures and the different love scripts that adolescent boys and girls learn.

We will also consider Sternberg's theory of love and how it applies to adolescents and emerging adults. The emphasis on the cultural context of love continues with an examination of how various cultures allow or discourage adolescent passion. This is followed by a discussion about the reasons young people select a specific partner and a section on breaking up a love relationship.

Love in adolescence and emerging adulthood often includes sexuality, but sexual activity among young people may also take the form of sexual play or experimentation, not necessarily including love. In the second section of this chapter, we look at the rates of various kinds of sexual activity among adolescents and emerging adults. Then we examine the wide variety in cultural standards with regard to sex before marriage, as well as the different sexual scripts for adolescent boys and girls in American society. Next to be considered is the development of sexuality among gay, lesbian, and bisexual adolescents, and the difficulties they face in a society that mostly disapproves of their sexual orientation. In many societies, sexuality in adolescence and emerging adulthood is considered problematic in a number of ways. Toward the close of the chapter we address those problems, including contraceptive use and nonuse; pregnancy, abortion, and parenthood in adolescence; and sexually transmitted diseases. The chapter ends with an examination of sex education programs.

Love

The Changing Forms of Adolescent Love

In recent decades, the forms of early romantic relations among adolescents have changed. Before the 1970s, adolescent love in Western cultures was structured by "dating," which usually followed more or less formal rules (Furman & Hand, 2006). Boy asked girl to accompany him to some well-defined event—for example, a movie, a sports event, or a school dance. Boy picked up girl at her house, where he would meet her parents and tell them what time he would bring her home. Boy and girl would go to the event, and he would bring her home by the appointed time, perhaps after a stop somewhere for a bite to eat or some kissing and perhaps more.

Today, adolescent romantic relations tend to be much less formal. Even the terms "date" and "dating" have fallen

The Developmental Course of Adolescent Love

The prevalence of involvement in romantic relationships increases gradually over the course of adolescence. According to a national (American) study called the National Study of Adolescent Health (also known as Add Health), the percentage of adolescents reporting a current love relationship rises from 17% in 7th grade to 32% in 9th grade to 44% in 11th grade (Furman & Hand, 2006). By 11th grade, 80% of adolescents have had a romantic relationship at some point, even if they do not have one currently. Adolescents with an Asian cultural background tend to have their first romantic relationship later than adolescents with a European, African American, or Latino cultural background because Asian cultural beliefs discourage early involvement in romantic relationships and encourage minimal or no sexual involvement before marriage (Carver et al., 2003; Connolly et al., 2004; Feldman & Rosenthal, 1991; Regan et al., 2004).

Love relationships among American adolescents tend to follow a developmental sequence of four steps (Connolly et al., 2004; Padgham & Blyth, 1991). In the first step, adolescents in same-gender groups go to places where they hope to find other-gender groups (malls and fast-food restaurants are popular spots for today's American adolescents). In the second step, adolescents take part in social gatherings arranged by adults, such as parties and school dances, that include interactions between boys and girls. In the third step, mixed-gender groups arrange to go to some particular event together, such as a movie. In the final step, adolescent couples begin to date as pairs in activities such as movies, dinners, concerts, or just hanging out. This pattern of couple dating continues through emerging adulthood.

Although studies agree that heterosexual love relationships rarely begin before adolescence, actual biological maturity has little to do with when love relationships among adolescents begin. One especially interesting analysis exploring this question was carried out by Dornbusch and his colleagues (Dornbusch et al., 1981). They used data from a large national study of adolescents (aged 12 to 17) that included physicians' ratings of the adolescents' physical maturity, using the Tanner stages described in Chapter 2. They used the term "dating" to refer to love relationships because at the time of the study this term was still widely used.

In two ways they demonstrated that physical maturation did not predict whether adolescents had begun dating. First, they looked at adolescents who were of different ages (12 to 15) but who were all at Tanner's Stage 3 of physical maturity and found that the older adolescents were more likely to have begun dating even though all the adolescents were at the same level of physical maturity (see Figure 9.1). Second, they showed that adolescents of a particular age were more or less equally likely to have begun dating regardless of their level of physical maturity. For example, few of the 12-year-olds had begun dating, even though they varied widely in their level of physical maturation.

Dating today tends to be less formal than in the past. Here, an American high school dance during the 1950s.

out of fashion, replaced by "going with" or "hanging out with" or "seeing" someone (Furman & Hand, 2006). Adolescent boys and girls still go together to movies, sports events, and school dances, of course, but they are much more likely than before to spend time together informally. As we saw in Chapter 5, before the women's movement of the 1960s gender roles were much more sharply drawn in the West, and adolescent boys and girls were less likely simply to hang out together as friends. Now they often know each other as friends before they become involved romantically (Kuttler, La Greca, & Prinstein, 1999).

Adolescent love also tends to be informal today in European cultures. European scholars on adolescence indicate that the concept of a formal date hardly exists anymore in European countries (Alsaker & Flammer, 1999). Adolescents and emerging adults do pair up and become boyfriend and girlfriend. However, they rarely date in a formal way, by designating a specific event at a specific time and going out in order to explore what they would be like as a couple. More typically, they go out in mixed-gender groups, without any specific pairing up. Or a boy and a girl may go out simply as friends, without thinking of themselves as potential boyfriend and girlfriend, without the boy having the responsibility to pay the expenses, and without the implication of possible sexual activity as the evening progresses. In non-Western cultures, dating is also rare (Schlegel & Barry, 1991), as we will see in more detail later in the chapter. Dating and even informal male-female social contact in adolescence are forbidden in many cultures because of cultural values emphasizing female chastity before marriage and because adults wish to control whom their adolescents end up marrying.

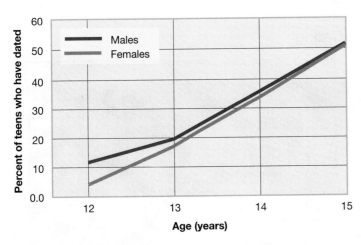

FIGURE 9.1 Proportion of adolescents at Tanner's Stage 3 of maturity who have ever had a date.

Source: Dornbusch et al. (1981).

Adolescents' reports of the reasons they form love relationships include the following (Paul & White, 1990):

- *Recreation* (fun and enjoyment)
- *Learning* (becoming more skilled at dating interactions)
- *Status* (impressing others by how often one dates and whom one dates)
- *Companionship* (sharing pleasurable activities with another person)
- *Intimacy* (establishing a close emotional relationship with another person)
- *Courtship* (seeking someone to have as a steady partner)

THINKING CRITICALLY •••

Given that sexual contact in some form is often part of adolescent love relationships, why do you suppose sex was not mentioned among adolescents' and emerging adults' reasons for forming love relationships in the studies described here?

Adolescents' reasons for forming love relationships tend to change as they enter emerging adulthood. One study investigated views of the functions of love relationships among early adolescents (6th grade), late adolescents (11th grade), and college students (Roscoe, Dian, & Brooks, 1987). The early and late adolescents expressed similar views. Both considered recreation to be the most important function, followed by intimacy and then status. In contrast, among college students intimacy ranked highest, followed by companionship, with recreation a bit lower, and status much lower. A more recent study reported similar results (Montgomery, 2005).

What adolescents look for in a romantic partner also changes with age, at least for boys. During middle adolescence, boys mention physical attractiveness prominently as a quality they prefer, whereas girls emphasize interpersonal qualities such as support and intimacy. By late adolescence, however, both males and females emphasize interpersonal qualities, and what they seek is highly similar: support, intimacy, communication, commitment, and passion (Feiring, 1996; Levesque, 1993; Montgomery, 2005; Shulman & Scharf, 2000).

Although adolescent girls have become a lot more assertive over the past 25 years in their relationships with boys, this does not mean that the old standards have expired entirely. Evidence indicates that **dating scripts**, the cognitive models that guide interactions in adolescents' love relationships, are still highly influenced by gender, with the power mostly on the side of the boys (Connolly et al., 2004; Furman & Hand, 2006). In general, males still follow a **proactive script**, and females a **reactive script**. The male script includes initiating the love relationship—calling the girl on the phone, suggesting they do something together, deciding where they will go, controlling the public domain (driving the car), and initiating sexual contact. The female script focuses on the private domain (spending considerable time on dress and grooming), responding to the male's gestures in the public domain (being picked up at her home), and responding to his sexual initiatives. Most adolescent girls are reluctant to be the initiator, although they are more likely to do so than in past generations. (Furman & Hand, 2006).

If adolescent romantic relationships often begin as friendships today, what distinguishes a friendship from a romantic relationship? Adolescents see romantic relationships as different from friendships in positive as well as negative ways (Furman & Hand, 2006; Giordano, Manning, & Longmore, 2006). Romantic relationships tend to involve more intense emotions, including positive feelings of love and happiness as well as feelings of anxiety and discomfort.

dating scripts The cognitive models that guide dating interactions.

proactive script A dating script, more common for males than for females, that includes initiating the date, deciding where they will go, controlling the public domain (e.g., driving the car and opening the doors), and initiating sexual contact.

reactive script A dating script, more common for females than males, that focuses on the private domain (e.g., spending considerable time on dress and grooming prior to the date), responding to the date's gestures in the public domain (e.g., being picked up, waiting for him to open the doors), and responding to his sexual initiatives.

"Dating" is a relatively recent cultural invention, originating in Western societies in the early 20th century. The birth of dating in the United States is described in a book by historian Beth Bailey (1989) called *From Front Porch to Back Seat: Courtship in Twentieth-Century America*. Bailey describes how, at the beginning of the 20th century, the primary system of courtship in the American middle class was not dating but "calling." A young man would "call" on a young woman, at her invitation, by visiting her at home. There he would meet her family, and then the two young people would be allowed some time together, probably in the family parlor. They would talk, perhaps have some refreshments she had prepared, and she might play piano for him.

Dating became increasingly popular in the first two decades of the 20th century, and by the early 1920s dating had essentially replaced calling as the accepted mode of courtship for young people in the American middle class. This change amounted to a revolution in American courtship. Dating meant going out to take part in a shared activity. This moved the location of courtship out of the home and into the public world—restaurants, theaters, and dance halls. It also removed the young couple from the watchful eye of the girl's family to the anonymity of the public world.

Why did calling decline and dating arise? A number of changes in American society contributed. One was that Americans were becoming increasingly concentrated into large urban areas. Families living in urban areas tended to have less space in their homes, and so the parlor and the piano that had been the focus of calling were not as likely to be available. The cities also offered more excitement, more things for young people to go out and do than small towns did. The invention and mass production of the automobile also contributed because it gave young people greater mobility and offered a greater range of places they could go.

The birth of dating greatly diminished the amount of control that could be exercised by parents and gave young people new opportunities for sexual exploration. When calling was the norm, not much was likely to go on between young lovers in the parlor that the rest of the family would not overhear. It is no coincidence that a sexual revolution took place at the same time as the change from calling to dating, with sexual experimentation before marriage—not including intercourse—becoming more accepted. Dating made the sexual revolution of the 1920s possible by providing more sexual opportunities. Nevertheless, parents maintained a degree of control in part by setting curfews (as many still do).

A second important consequence of the birth of dating was that it transferred the balance of power in courtship from

By the 1920s, dating had become common among American young people.

the female to the male. In the calling system, it was the girl who took the initiative. She could ask a young man to call on her, or not ask him. He could not ask her if it would be okay for him to call—not without being regarded as rude and unmannerly. But in the dating system, the male became the initiator. He could ask her on a date, but she could not ask him. And of course going on a date almost always meant spending money, his money, which further increased his power in the relationship. This promoted a view that she owed him sexual favors of some kind, in return for what he spent on the date. As one boy of the 1920s wrote, "When a boy takes a girl out and spends $1.20 on her (like I did the other night), he expects a little petting in return (which I didn't get)" (Bailey, 1989, p. 81).

One other point that should be mentioned is that both calling and the early decades of dating took place mostly among emerging adults rather than adolescents. Calling was considered a serious step, a prelude to a possible marriage proposal rather than simply a form of youthful recreation. Because early in the 20th century marriage did not take place for most young people until they were in their early to mid-20s, they rarely took part in calling until they were about age 20. When dating replaced calling, at first dating, too, was an activity mainly of young people in their 20s. Young people in their teens were rarely allowed to go out as unchaperoned couples. It was only toward the middle of the century, as the marriage age declined and as enrollments in high school grew, that dating began to be acceptable for young people in their teens.

Intimacy becomes more important in dating by late adolescence and emerging adulthood.

Romantic relationships are also more likely to involve sexual activity, although sex sometimes spills into adolescent friendships, as we will see later in the chapter. Having a romantic relationship is also valued for the feeling of being cared for by the romantic partner and for having a social companion in leisure activities. On the other hand, adolescents see romantic relationships as constraining their social freedom, as making them emotionally vulnerable, and as more likely than friendships to involve conflict. Frequently, the boundary between friendship and romantic relationship is not clear, with one adolescent seeing it as a friendship and the other as a romantic relationship, with misunderstandings and hurt feelings as a result (Furman & Hand, 2006).

Romantic experiences are associated with both positive and negative outcomes in adolescence (Furman, Ho, & Low, 2007). Adolescents who have a romantic relationship tend to be more popular and have a more positive self-image (Franzoni, Davis, & Vasquez-Suson, 1994; La Greca & Harrison, 2005). However, this association with positive qualities depends partly on the age of the adolescents. In particular, for early adolescent girls, participating in mixed-gender group activities such as parties and dances may be positive, but a serious love relationship tends to be related to negative outcomes such as depressed mood (Graber et al., 1997; Hayward et al., 1997; Kaltiala-Heino et al., 2003). An important reason for their depression appears to be that early adolescent girls in a serious relationship often find themselves under their boyfriends' pressure to participate in sexual activity before they feel ready (Simmons & Blyth, 1987).

A recent longitudinal study suggests that having romantic experiences may have mixed effects for other adolescents, too, not just early adolescent girls (Furman, Low, & Ho, 2009). The study surveyed 14- to 16-year-old Americans on the degree of their romantic experience, ranging from romantic interest to a serious relationship, then followed them up 1 year later. The amount of adolescents' romantic experience was associated with higher reports of social acceptance, friendship competence, and romantic competence. However, romantic experience also was associated with greater substance use and more delinquent behavior. The amount of romantic experience predicted increased substance use 1 year later.

Sternberg's Theory of Love

After two adolescents share romantic experiences, the relationship sometimes develops into love. The best-known theory of love has been developed by Robert Sternberg (1986, 1987, 1988). Sternberg proposed that different types of love involve combining three fundamental qualities of love in different ways (Figure 9.2). These three qualities are passion, intimacy, and commitment. *Passion* involves physical attraction and sexual desire. It is emotional as well as physical and may involve intense emotions such as anxiety, delight, anger, and jealousy. *Intimacy* involves feelings of closeness and emotional attachment. It includes mutual understanding, mutual support, and open communication about issues not discussed with anyone else. *Commitment* is the pledge to love someone over the long run, through the ups and downs that are often part of love. Commitment is what sustains a long-term relationship through fluctuations in passion and intimacy.

These three qualities of love are combined into seven different forms of love in Sternberg's theory, as follows:

- **Liking** is intimacy alone, without passion or commitment. This is the type of love that characterizes most friendships. Friendships often involve some level of intimacy, but without passion and without an enduring commitment. Most people have many friendships that come and go in the course of their lives.

- **Infatuation** is passion alone, without intimacy or commitment. Infatuation involves a great deal of physiological and emotional arousal, and a heightened level of sexual desire, but without emotional closeness to the person or an enduring commitment.

liking In Sternberg's theory of love, the type of love that is based on intimacy alone, without passion or commitment.

infatuation In Sternberg's theory of love, the type of love that is based on passion alone, without intimacy or commitment.

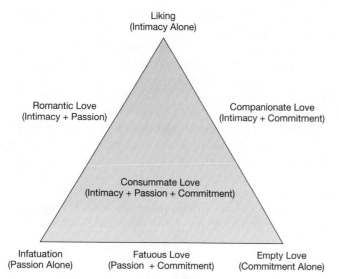

FIGURE 9.2 Sternberg's Triangular Model of Love.
Source: Sternberg (1988), p. 122.

- **Empty love** is commitment alone, without passion or intimacy. This might apply to a couple who have been married for many years and who have lost the passion and intimacy in their relationship but nevertheless remain together. It also could apply to the early stage of marriage in cultures where marriages are arranged by the parents rather than chosen by the young people themselves (Hatfield & Rapson, 2005; Schlegel & Barry, 1991). However, arranged marriages that begin as empty love may eventually develop passion and intimacy.

- **Romantic love** combines passion and intimacy, but without commitment. This is the kind of love people mean when they talk about being "in love." It is often experienced as intense and joyful, but it rarely lasts long.

- **Companionate love** combines intimacy and commitment, but without passion. It may be applied to married or long-term couples whose passion for each other has gradually waned but who have maintained the other qualities of their love. It could also be applied to unusually close friendships as well as to close family relationships.

- **Fatuous** (which means "silly" or "foolish") **love** involves passion and commitment without intimacy. This kind of love would apply to a "whirlwind" courtship where two people meet, fall passionately in love, and get married, all within a few weeks, before they even have time to know each other well.

- **Consummate love** integrates all three aspects of love into the ultimate love relationship. Of course, even if consummate love is reached in a relationship, over time passion may fade, intimacy may falter, or commitment may be betrayed. But this is the kind of love that represents the ideal for many people.

Most adolescent relationships do not last long.

empty love In Sternberg's theory of love, the type of love that is based on commitment alone, without passion or intimacy.

romantic love In Sternberg's theory of love, the type of love that combines passion and intimacy, but without commitment.

companionate love In Sternberg's theory of love, the type of love that combines intimacy and commitment, but without passion.

fatuous love In Sternberg's theory of love, the type of love that involves passion and commitment without intimacy.

consummate love In Sternberg's theory of love, the form of love that integrates passion, intimacy, and commitment.

How does Sternberg's theory of love apply to adolescence? Certainly in most adolescent love relationships, commitment is either missing or highly tentative (Feldman & Cauffman, 1999). Most adolescent relationships last only a few weeks or months; few of their relationships last a year or longer, although their relationships tend to get longer as they get older (Carver et al., 2003; Feiring, 1996; Furman & Simon, 1999). This does not mean that adolescents are incapable of commitment; it simply reflects the fact that in industrialized countries today most people are not likely to get married until they are at least in their mid- to late 20s. Under these circumstances, it is understandable that adolescents' love relationships would involve commitment much less than passion or intimacy. Commitment tends to develop in emerging adulthood, when young people begin looking more seriously for someone with whom they may have a lifelong love relationship.

One study indicated the relative strength of passion, intimacy, and commitment in adolescent love (Feiring, 1996). In this study, although the majority of the 15-year-old adolescents had been in a relationship that lasted a few months, only 10% had been in a relationship that lasted a year or longer (indicating weak commitment). However, during the relationship, contact was frequent (perhaps reflecting passion). Adolescents reported seeing their loved ones and talking to them on the phone on an almost daily basis during the relationship. Furthermore, the adolescents rated companionship, intimacy, and support as the most valued dimensions of their relationships (showing the importance of intimacy), whereas security—an aspect of commitment—ranked low.

The absence of long-term commitment in adolescence means that there are two principal types of adolescent love: infatuation and romantic love. (I do not include liking because it applies mainly to friends, not lovers.) Infatuation is common among adolescents, partly because they are new to love and the first few times they "fall in love" they may take passion alone, with its intensity of feeling and sexual desire, as enough evidence of love. For example, imagine two adolescents who sit next to one another in math class, exchange occasional smiles, maybe flirt a little before and after class. She finds herself daydreaming of him as she lies in her bedroom and listens to love songs; he starts writing her name surreptitiously in the margins of his notebook when his mind drifts during class. It feels like love to both of them, and it is a certain kind of love, but it lacks the element of intimacy that people come to desire and expect from love once they become more experienced with it.

Adolescents can experience intimacy in their relationships, too, and combine passion and intimacy to create romantic love (Collins & Sroufe, 1999). The passion is there, with its heightened emotions and sexual desire, but now it is combined with intimacy, as two adolescents spend time to-

Infatuation and romantic love are the most common types of love in adolescence.

gether and come to know each other, and they begin to share thoughts and feelings that they share with no one else. The prominence of intimacy in romantic relationships tends to grow through adolescence and into emerging adulthood (Brown, 1999; Levesque, 1993; Montgomery, 2005).

Adolescents could even experience consummate love, combining passion, intimacy, and commitment. Some "high school sweethearts" continue their relationship long after high school, and even marry and stay together their whole lives. However, this is rare among adolescents, especially in the current generation. With the typical marriage age so high, only in emerging adulthood do most young people begin thinking about committing themselves to someone for years to come (Brown, 1999; Greene et al., 1992). For this reason, adolescent love relationships rarely progress past infatuation and romantic love to consummate love.

Adolescent Passion in Non-Western Cultures

It is not only in the West, and not only in industrialized countries, that adolescents experience infatuation and romantic love. On the contrary, feelings of passion appear to be a virtually universal characteristic of young people. Jankowiak and Fischer (1992) investigated this issue systematically by analyzing the *Standard Cross-Cultural Sample*, a collection of data provided by anthropologists on 186 traditional cultures representing six distinct geographical regions around the world. They concluded that there was evidence that young people fell passionately in love in *all but one* of the 186 cultures studied. Although the other 185 cultures differed widely in geographical region, economic characteristics, and many other ways, in all of them young lovers experienced the delight and despair of passionate love, told stories about famous lovers, and sang love songs.

However, this does not mean that young people in all cultures are allowed to act on their feelings of love. On the contrary, romantic love as the basis for marriage is a fairly new cultural idea (Hatfield & Rapson, 2005). As we will see in more detail later in this chapter, in most cultures throughout most of history marriages have been arranged by parents, with little regard for the passionate desires of their adolescent children. Consequently, many cultures also have some version of the Romeo and Juliet story, about a tragic young couple whose love was thwarted by adults forbidding them to marry, and who defied this prohibition by committing suicide together (Hatfield & Rapson, 2005). These stories are commemorated and passed down through poems, songs, plays, and legends. Although these tales of dual suicide for love have a powerful appeal to adolescents all over the world, in real life eloping is a more popular strategy for evading the obstacles to love erected by adults and by cultural customs (Jankowiak & Fischer, 1992).

Falling in Love

"[The person I marry] would have to be someone who was of the same religion that I was and also the same ethnicity as me. And sometimes when I say that people take it that I'm prejudiced or something. But it's not necessarily that, because I have a lot of traditions and customs that I grew up with and I want someone who understands the same traditions and everything. So I've always looked for someone who was Latino. And I've always looked for someone who was Catholic because I'm Catholic."

—Gloria, 22-year-old Latina (Arnett, 2004a, p. 99)

How do adolescents and emerging adults choose romantic partners? Do "opposites attract," or do "birds of a feather flock together"? The bird metaphor prevails for adolescents and emerging adults and throughout adulthood (Furman & Simon, 2008; Laursen & Jensen-Campbell, 1999). Just as we have seen with friendships, people of all ages tend to be most likely to have romantic relationships with people who are similar to them in characteristics such as intelligence, social class, ethnic background, religious beliefs, personality, and physical attractiveness (Furman & Simon, 2008; Luo &

> "Fall in love, fall into disgrace."
>
> —Chinese proverb

Klohnen, 2005). Of course, sometimes opposites *do* attract, and partners fall in love even though (and perhaps because) they may differ widely in their characteristics. For the most part, however, people are attracted to others who are like themselves. Social scientists attribute this to **consensual validation**, meaning that people like to find in others an agreement, or *consensus*, with their own characteristics. Finding this consensus supports, or *validates*, their own way of looking at the world.

For example, if you have a partner who shares your religious beliefs, the two of you will validate each other in the beliefs that you possess and in the prescriptions for behavior that follow from those beliefs. However, if one of you is devout and the other is an atheist, you are likely to find that your different ways of looking at the world lead to conflicts of beliefs and behavior. One of you wants to go to religious services, the other scoffs that it is a waste of time. Most people find this kind of regular collision of preferences disagreeable, so they seek people who are like themselves to minimize the frequency of collisions (Laursen & Jensen-Campbell, 1999).

After the initial attraction, how does love develop? One promising line of theory and research has explored similarities between attachments to romantic partners and attachments to parents (Furman, 2002; Furman & Simon, 1999; Shaver & Hazan, 1993). Romantic partners try to maintain regular proximity to each other, the way children try to maintain proximity to parents. Romantic partners seek each other out for comfort and protection in times of crisis, as children do their parents. Romantic partners also use one another as a "secure base," a source of psychological security, as they go out to face the challenges in the world, the way children use their parents as a secure base. Furthermore, whether the attachment is to a lover or a parent, extended separation is experienced as a source of distress and the loss of the person is deeply painful. Of course, there are differences as well between attachments to lovers and attachments to parents, most notably that attachments between lovers include a sexual element that attachments to parents do not.

Attachment styles between lovers have been found to resemble the secure and insecure parent-child attachment styles we have already discussed (Shaver & Hazan, 1993). Secure attachments in romantic relationships are characterized by emotional support and concern for the partner's well-being. Insecure attachments take the form of either an excess of dependence on the partner or an excess of distance. It

---

consensual validation In social science studies of interpersonal attraction, the principle that people like to find in others an agreement or consensus with their own characteristics and view of life.

initiation phase In Brown's developmental model of adolescent love, the first phase, usually in early adolescence, when the first tentative explorations of romantic interests begin, usually superficial and brief, often fraught with anxiety, fear, and excitement.

status phase In Brown's developmental model of adolescent love, the second phase, in which adolescents begin to gain confidence in their skills at interacting with potential romantic partners and begin to form their first romantic relationships, assessing not just how much they like and are attracted to the person, but also how their status with friends and peers would be influenced.

has been suggested that these attachment styles to romantic partners may be based on earlier attachments to parents (Collins & Sroufe, 1999; Creasey & Hesson-McInnis, 2001; Gray & Steinberg, 1999). However, as noted in Chapter 7, this hypothesis has not yet been truly tested in long-term longitudinal studies.

One way that romantic relationships tend to be different in adolescence than in emerging adulthood or adulthood is that in adolescence the peer context of romantic relationships tends to be especially important (Brown, 1999). We have noted, especially in the previous chapter, that adolescence is a time when responsiveness to the opinions of friends and peers reaches its peak. Adolescents tend to be highly aware of and concerned about the social worlds of friendships, cliques, and crowds, and consequently friends and peers exercise considerable power over their love lives. A substantial amount of the conversation among friends, especially in early adolescence, involves questions of who likes whom and who is "going with" or "hooking up with" whom, questions often explored with much joking and teasing (Brown, 1999; Eder, 1993). Adolescent friends often monitor each other's romantic interests and are quick to offer inspiration, guidance, support, or scorn (Perlstein, 2003; Thompson, 1994).

Bradford Brown (1999) has proposed a developmental model of adolescent love that recognizes the important role played by peers and friends. Brown's model contains four phases: the **initiation phase**, the **status phase**, the **affection phase**, and the **bonding phase**. The initiation phase usually takes place in early adolescence, when the first tentative explorations of romantic interests begin. These explorations are usually superficial and brief, and are often fraught with anxiety and fear, in addition to excitement. The anxiety and fear result in part from the novelty of romantic feelings and behaviors, but also from adolescents' awareness that these new feelings and behaviors are subject to scrutiny and potential ridicule from their friends and peers.

In the status phase, adolescents begin to gain confidence in their skills at interacting with potential romantic partners, and they begin to form their first romantic relationships. In forming these relationships, they remain acutely aware of the evaluations of their friends and peers. In considering a potential romantic partner, they assess not just how much they like and are attracted to the person but how their status with friends and peers would be influenced. Peer crowds represent

Adolescents usually choose love partners whose peer crowd status is similar to their own.

a clear status hierarchy, and adolescents usually date others who have similar crowd status, but lower-status adolescents often fantasize about and may attempt a romantic relationship with someone of higher status—"nerd loves popular girl/boy" is a popular premise for many a movie and television show involving adolescents. Friends may act as messengers in the status phase, inquiring on behalf of a friend to see if a potential love partner might be interested. This is a way of gaining information without risking the direct humiliation—and loss of status—that may result from inquiring oneself.

In the affection phase, adolescents come to know each other better and express deeper feelings for each other, as

affection phase In Brown's developmental model of adolescent love, the third phase, in which adolescents come to know each other better and express deeper feelings for each other, as well as engaging in more extensive sexual activity.

bonding phase In Brown's developmental model of adolescent love, the final phase, in which the romantic relationship becomes more enduring and serious and partners begin to discuss the possibility of a lifelong commitment to each other.

well as engaging in more extensive sexual activity. Relationships in this phase tend to last several months rather than weeks or days as in the previous two phases. Because intimacy is greater in this phase, romantic relationships become more emotionally charged, and adolescents face greater challenges in managing these strong emotions. The role of peers and friends changes, too. Peers become less important as the relationship grows and the importance of status diminishes, but friends become even more important as *private eyes* who keep an eye on the friend's romantic partner to monitor faithfulness, as *arbitrators* between romantic partners when conflicts occur, and as *support systems* who provide a sympathetic ear when romantic difficulties or complexities arise. Issues of jealousy may also arise, if friends begin to resent the amount of time and closeness the adolescent devotes to the romantic partner at the expense of the friendship.

In the bonding phase, the romantic relationship becomes more enduring and serious, and partners begin to discuss the possibility of a lifelong commitment to each other. This phase usually occurs in emerging adulthood rather than adolescence. The role of friends and peers recedes in this phase, as the question of others' opinions becomes less important than issues of compatibility and commitment between the romantic partners. Nevertheless, friends may continue to provide guidance and advice, as someone to talk with about whether the romantic partner is the right person with whom to form a lifelong commitment. A recent study in Germany found support for Brown's four-stage model (Seiffge-Krenke, 2003).

When Love Goes Bad: Breaking Up

Love in adolescence and emerging adulthood is not only about affection and bonding. On the contrary, love is often the source of anxiety and distress as well. Because most young people have a series of love relationships, most of them experience "breaking up," the dissolution of a relationship, at least once (Battaglia et al., 1998).

What is breaking up like for adolescents and emerging adults? For adolescents, egocentrism may contribute to the intensity of the unhappiness following a breakup. Egocentrism's personal fable can contribute to adolescents' feelings that their suffering in the aftermath of a breakup is something that no one has ever experienced as deeply as they are experiencing it and that the pain of it will never end. "I just feel like my life's over, like there's never going to be anything to smile about again," one 17-year-old girl lamented after breaking up (Bell, 1998, p. 71). However, few systematic studies of breaking up in adolescence have been done (Brown et al., 1999).

In contrast, quite a few studies have been conducted on college students' experiences with breaking up. One of the best of these studies was conducted in the late 1970s (Hill, Rubin, & Peplau, 1979). The authors followed over 200 college couples for 2 years. By the end of the 2 year period, 45% of the couples had broken up. A variety of factors were related to likelihood of breaking up. Couples who had broken up

reported lower levels of intimacy and love in their relationship at the beginning of the study and were also less likely to be similar on characteristics such as age, SAT scores, and physical attractiveness. The broken-up couples were also less balanced at the beginning of the study, in the sense that one partner indicated substantially more commitment to the relationship than the other partner did.

Reasons the students stated for breaking up included boredom and differences in interests. However, couples rarely agreed on what had caused the breakup. Also, the two were rarely equal in how the breakup affected them. Contrary to stereotypes that portray females as more susceptible to love than males, the study found (as other studies have found) that the woman was more likely to end the relationship and that rejected men tended to be lonelier, unhappier, and more depressed than rejected women. Rejected men also found it harder than rejected women to accept the end of the relationship and to stay friends with their former partner.

In another study, Sprecher (1994) interviewed 101 college couples who had broken up, and compiled a list of the 10 most common reasons the couples gave for breaking up (Table 9.1). In contrast to Hill and colleagues (1979), Sprecher (1994) found that couples generally agreed about why they had broken up. However, like Hill and colleagues, the couples studied by Sprecher gave boredom and lack of common interests as prominent reasons for breaking up, along with factors such as different backgrounds and different attitudes regarding sex and marriage. Broken-up couples appear to lack the consensual validation that most people find attractive in an intimate relationship (Felmlee, 2001).

The emotions involved in love are intense, and breaking up often provokes sadness and a sense of loss. In one study of

TABLE 9.1 Reasons for Breaking Up

Reasons Referring to the Self

I desired to be independent.

I became bored with the relationship.

Reasons Referring to the Partner

My partner desired to be independent.

My partner became bored with the relationship.

My partner became interested in someone else.

Reasons Referring to the Couple's Interaction

We had different interests.

We had communication problems.

We had conflicting sexual attitudes and/or problems.

We had conflicting marriage ideas.

We had different backgrounds.

Source: Sprecher (1994), p. 217.

college students, *over half* of those who had broken up were at least moderately depressed two months later (Means, 1991). Increased alcohol and drug use is also common following a breakup (Davis, Shaver, & Vernon, 2003). Furthermore, breaking up can inspire "romantic harassment" that involves unwanted pursuit of the ex-partner (Langhinrichsen-Rohling et al., 2002). In one recent study of female American college students (Roberts, 2005), two thirds reported romantic harassment following the breakup of a relationship. Of these, half were classified as mild harassment (such as persistent unwanted telephone calls) and half as "stalking" (being followed and threatened by the ex-partner). The young women who experienced romantic harassment also recalled more controlling behavior by their ex-partner during the relationship.

In an earlier but more extensive study (Jason, Reichler, Easton, Neal, & Wilson 1984), romantic harassment was defined as "the persistent use of psychological or physical abuse in an attempt to continue dating someone after they have clearly indicated a desire to terminate a relationship" (p. 261). Using this definition, the researchers found that over half of female college students had been romantically harassed at some time. Romantic harassment included behavior such as telephoning late at night, repeatedly telephoning the woman at home or at work, systematically watching or following her in public, sending repeated love letters, insulting her, physically attacking her, and even threatening to kill her.

The women in the study indicated that when they confronted their harassers, the men rarely conceded that what they were doing was harassment. According to the men, they were merely trying to break through the woman's resistance and reestablish the love relationship.

The experience was highly stressful for the women. They reported feeling acute fear, anxiety, and depression during the harassment and experienced nervous physical symptoms such as stomachaches and nervous tics. The women tried a variety of strategies to deter their harassers, from ignoring them to trying to reason with them to being rude to threatening them. Some changed their phone number or moved; some had a parent or boyfriend talk to or threaten them. None of these strategies worked very well in the short term. The best defense was simply time—eventually the harassers gave up.

Choosing a Marriage Partner

Although love has its dark side, for most people love is a source of joy and contentment, and the positive emotions experienced with love become steadily stronger and more stable from early adolescence through emerging adulthood (Fehr, 1993; Fitness & Fletcher, 1993; Larson, Clore, & Woods, 1999). Eventually about 90% of people in most societies marry (King, 2005). How do young people choose a marriage partner?

In Chapter 5 on gender, we discussed the characteristics adolescents use to describe the ideal man and the ideal woman. The most important qualities considered ideal for both genders were personal qualities such as being kind and honest, whereas qualities such as having a lot of money and being popular ranked quite low (Gibbons & Stiles, 1997, 2004).

The same kinds of results have been found in studies that ask young people about the qualities they consider most important in the person they marry. Psychologist David Buss (1989) carried out a massive study of over 10,000 young people in 37 countries on this question. The countries were from all over the world, including Africa, Asia, Eastern and Western Europe, and North and South America. The questionnaire had to be translated into 37 languages, with great care taken to make the meanings of words such as "love" as similar as possible in every country. In many of the countries, a high proportion of the young people were illiterate, so the questions had to be read aloud to them.

Despite all of these challenges, the results showed impressive consistencies across countries and across genders

TABLE 9.2	The Importance of Various Traits in Mate Selection Throughout the World

Men's Ranking of Various Traits[a]	Women's Ranking of Various Traits[a]
1. Mutual attraction—love	1. Mutual attraction—love
2. Dependable character	2. Dependable character
3. Emotional stability and maturity	3. Emotional stability and maturity
4. Pleasing disposition	4. Pleasing disposition
5. Good health	5. Education and intelligence
6. Education and intelligence	6. Sociability
7. Sociability	7. Good health
8. Desire for home and children	8. Desire for home and children
9. Refinement, neatness	9. Ambitious and industrious
10. Good looks	10. Refinement, neatness
11. Ambitious and industrious	11. Similar education
12. Good cook and housekeeper	12. Good financial prospect
13. Good financial prospect	13. Good looks
14. Similar education	14. Favorable social status or rating
15. Favorable social status or rating	15. Good cook and housekeeper
16. Chastity (no previous experience in sexual intercourse)	16. Similar religious background
17. Similar religious background	17. Similar political background
18. Similar political background	18. Chastity (no previous experience in sexual intercourse)

[a]The lower the number, the more important men and women throughout the world consider this trait to be (on the average).

Source: Based on Hatfield & Rapson (2005).

(see Table 9.2). "Mutual attraction—love" ranked first among marriage criteria across countries, followed by "dependable character," "emotional stability and maturity," and "pleasing disposition." Similarity in religious and political background ranked very low, which is surprising given that (as noted earlier) people tend to marry others who are similar to them in these ways. "Good financial prospects" also ranked fairly low, as "having a lot of money" did in the studies of adolescents' views of the ideal man and the ideal woman.

Although the cross-cultural similarities were strong and striking, some cross-cultural differences were also notable.

The sharpest cross-cultural division was on the issue of chastity (marrying someone who has never had sex before). In Eastern cultures (e.g., China, India, Indonesia) and Middle Eastern cultures (Iran, Palestinian Arabs in Israel), chastity was rated as highly important. However, in the West (e.g., Finland, France, Norway, Germany), chastity was generally considered unimportant.

Arranged Marriages

As noted earlier, although romantic love is found in all cultures, it is not considered the proper basis of marriage in all cultures. In fact, the idea that romantic love should be the basis of marriage is only about 300 years old in the West and is even newer in most of the rest of the world (Hatfield & Rapson, 2005). Marriage has more often been seen by cultures as an alliance between two *families* rather than as the uniting of two individuals (Buunk, Park, & Dubbs, 2008). Parents and other adult kin have often held the power to arrange the marriages of their young people, sometimes with the young person's consent, sometimes without it. The most important considerations in an **arranged marriage** did not usually include the prospective bride and groom's love for one another—often they did not even know each other—or even their personal compatibility. Instead, the desirability of marriage between them was decided by each family on the basis of the other family's status, religion, and wealth. Economic considerations have often been of primary importance.

A cultural tradition of arranged marriage implies different expectations for the marriage relationship. Hsu (1985) has observed that Eastern and Western cultural traditions have distinct differences in expectations of intimacy in marriage. In the West, young people expect marriage to provide intimacy as well as passion and commitment. They leave their homes and families well before marriage, and they expect their closest attachment in adulthood to be with their marriage partner. For example, in one national survey in the United States, 94% of single Americans in their 20s agreed that "when you marry you want your spouse to be your soul mate, first and foremost" (Popenoe & Whitehead, 2001).

However, in the East, where many cultures have a tradition of arranged marriage, much less has been demanded of marriage. Commitment comes first, and passion is welcomed if it exists initially or develops eventually, but expectations of intimacy in marriage are modest. On the contrary, people expect to find intimacy mainly with their family of origin—their parents and their siblings—and eventually with their own children.

Currently, even cultures with a tradition of arranged marriage are beginning to change in their marriage expectations through the influence of globalization. India, for example, has a history of arranged marriage that has exist-

arranged marriage A marriage in which the marriage partners are determined not by the partners themselves but by others, usually the parents or other family elders.

cohabitation Living with a romantic partner outside of marriage.

Arranged marriages are still common in countries such as India.

ed for 6,000 years (Prakasa & Rao, 1979). Today, however, nearly 40% of adolescent Indians say they intend to choose their own mates (Saraswathi, 1999). This still leaves the majority (60%) who expect an arranged marriage, but for 40% to prefer choosing their own spouse is high compared with any time in the past, when the percentage would have been close to zero. A similar pattern is taking place in many other cultures with a tradition of arranged marriage (Stevenson & Zusho, 2002). Increasingly, young people in these cultures believe that they should be free to choose their mate or at least to have a significant role in whom their parents choose for them. Globalization has increased the extent to which young people value individual choice and the individual's pursuit of happiness, and these values are difficult to reconcile with the tradition of arranged marriage.

Consequently, in many cultures the tradition of arranged marriage has become modified. Today in most Eastern cultures, the "semiarranged marriage" is the most common practice (Naito & Gielen, 2002). This means that parents influence the mate selection of their children but do not simply decide it without the children's consent. Parents may introduce a potential mate to their child. If the young person has a favorable impression of the potential mate, they date a few times. If they agree that they are compatible, they marry. In another variation of semiarranged marriage, young people meet a potential mate on their own but seek their parents' approval before proceeding to date the person or consider marriage.

It is difficult to say if semiarranged marriage will be an enduring form or if it is a transitional stage on the way to the end of the tradition of arranged marriage. Although semiarranged marriages are now common in Eastern cultures, it is also increasingly common for young people to choose their own marriage partner without any involvement from their parents (Saraswathi, 1999; Stevenson & Zusho, 2002). Matchmaking services, including some through the Internet, have also become increasingly popular. Recreational dating remains rare in Asian cultures, but it is more common than in the past, and it may grow in the future.

Cohabitation

"I don't see how people can get married without living together. I wanted to make sure that she doesn't throw her socks on top of the sink and if she puts the top back on the toothpaste and stuff. All those little things."

—Pete, age 25 (in Arnett, 2004a, p. 108)

Increasingly in industrialized countries, marriage no longer marks the beginning of living with a romantic partner. In the United States as well as in northern European countries, **cohabitation** before marriage is now experienced by at least two thirds of emerging adults (Kiernan, 2004; Michael et al., 1995; Wu, 1999). The percentage is highest in Sweden, where nearly all young people cohabit before marriage (Duvander, 1999; Hoem, 1992). Cohabitation tends to be brief and unstable for young Americans. One study found that half of cohabiting relationships lasted less than a year, and only 1 in 10 couples were together 5 years later (Bumpass & Liu, 2000). In contrast, cohabiting couples in European countries tend to stay together as long as married couples (Hacker, 2002).

However, in Europe there are distinct differences in cohabitation between north and south (Kiernan, 2002, 2004). Emerging adults in southern Europe are considerably less likely than their counterparts in the north to cohabit; most emerging adults in southern Europe live at home until marriage (Chisholm & Hurrelmann, 1995; Douglass, 2005), especially females. Perhaps because of the Catholic religious tradition in the south, cohabitation carries a moral stigma in the south that it does not have in the north.

Young people choose to cohabit in part because they wish to enhance the likelihood that when they marry, it will last. Indeed, in a national (American) survey of 20- to 29-year-olds, 62% agreed that "living together with someone before marriage is a good way to avoid eventual divorce" (Popenoe & Whitehead, 2001). Emerging adults from divorced families are especially likely to cohabit because they are especially determined to avoid their parents' fate (Arnett, 2004; Cunningham & Thornton, 2007). However, cohabitation before marriage is related to higher rather than lower likelihood of later divorce (Cohan & Kleinbaum, 2002; Kiernan, 2002, 2004).

This may be because cohabiting couples become used to living together while maintaining separate lives in many ways, especially financially, so that they are unprepared for the compromises required by marriage. Also, even before cohabitation begins, emerging adults who cohabit tend to be different from emerging adults who do not, in ways that are related to higher risk of divorce: less religious, more skeptical of the institution of marriage, and more accepting of divorce (Cohan & Kleinbaum, 2002; Stanley et al., 2004; Wu, 1999). However, one recent analysis concluded that cohabitation itself increases the risk of divorce because it leads some couples who are not compatible to marry anyway, out of "the inertia of cohabitation" (Stanley, Rhoades, & Markman, 2006).

Why do you think cohabitation before marriage is related to higher likelihood of divorce?

Sexuality

As we have discussed throughout this book, puberty and the development of sexual maturation are central to adolescence. We have seen how reaching sexual maturity has multiple effects on young people's development, from relationships with parents to gender intensification. However, like other aspects of development in adolescence and emerging adulthood, sex cannot be understood apart from its cultural context. Because human beings are shaped so much by their cultural and social environment, when considering sexual issues we have to think not just of sex but of **sexuality**, that is, not just biological sexual development but also sexual values, beliefs, thoughts, feelings, relationships, and behavior. Thus, our focus in this section will be not just on sex but on sexuality.

Rates of Adolescent Sexual Activity

Most of the research on adolescent sexuality focuses on sexual intercourse, perhaps because of concerns about problems such as adolescent pregnancy and sexually transmitted diseases. However, intercourse is only one part of adolescent sexuality, and it is not the most widespread or the most frequent part of adolescent sexual activity. Most Western adolescents have a considerable amount of other kinds of sexual experience before they have intercourse for the first time, and for most, intercourse is reached through a progression of stages lasting many years (Carver et al., 2003). The progression often begins with masturbation, followed by necking and petting, sexual intercourse, and oral sex.

Masturbation

"Even if you know [masturbation] is normal and all that, you still lock the door! You don't go around advertising that you're doing it. There are all these jokes like, 'What are you doing after school today?' 'Oh, I'm going home to beat off.' You know, 'Ha-ha-ha-ha.' That kind of thing. But even if everybody does it and everybody knows everybody does it, you still pretend you don't."

—Johnny, age 15 (in Bell, 1998, p. 97)

For many adolescents, especially boys, their first sexual experiences take place alone. Consistently for over a half century, American studies have found that the majority of boys

sexuality Biological sexual development as well as sexual values, beliefs, thoughts, feelings, relationships, and behavior.

begin masturbating by age 13 and that about 90% of boys masturbate by age 19 (Halpern, Udry, Suchindran, & Campbell, 2000; King, 2005; Masters, Johnson, & Kolodny, 1994). Masturbation among adolescent boys tends to occur frequently, about five times a week on average (Bockting & Coleman, 2003).

For girls, the picture is quite different. In studies a half century ago, only about 15% of females reported masturbating by age 13 and only about 30% by age 20 (Kinsey et al., 1953). In more recent studies, these percentages have increased, but it remains true that girls report considerably lower rates of masturbation than boys. About 33% of girls report masturbating by age 13, and 60% to 75% by age 20 (Chilman, 1983; Masters et al., 1994). Girls who masturbate do so less frequently than boys, although with considerable individual variability (Leitenberg et al., 1993). For both boys and girls, masturbation is not just a sexual release for adolescents who are not having intercourse. On the contrary, adolescents who have had sexual intercourse are more likely to masturbate than adolescents who have not (Bockting & Coleman, 2003).

The recent increase in adolescent girls' reports of masturbation is related to changes in cultural attitudes toward more acceptance of female sexuality and more acceptance of masturbation. By the late 1970s, over 70% of adolescents in their mid-teens agreed that "it's okay for a boy/girl my age to masturbate" (Hass, 1979). However, this is one of those areas where it is useful to ask about the validity of people's self-reports of their behavior. It could be that part of the increase in reported rates of girls' masturbation is due to girls' greater willingness to report it. For reasons of social desirability, they may have been less willing to report it 50 years ago than they are today. Even today, masturbation may be a particularly problematic topic in terms of self-report. Sex researchers find that both adolescents and adults are more reluctant to discuss masturbation than any other topic (Halpern et al., 2000). Although masturbation is both normal and harmless, many young people still feel guilty and frightened by it (Bell, 1998; Stein & Reiser, 1994). There is a long and bizarre cultural history of masturbation in the West, including claims that it causes a wide variety of ills, from pimples to epilepsy to insanity to death (Laqueur, 2004). Part of that anxious legacy endures today despite the sexual revolutions of the 20th century.

Do you think you would answer honestly if you were involved in a study on sexual behavior? Why or why not?

Necking and Petting

"When I was with my boyfriend and we were all alone for the first time, we were making out. . . . We were French-kissing real long kisses, so sometimes I had to pull away to catch my breath. He was rubbing my back and I was rubbing his."

—Jennifer, age 14 (in Bell, 1998, p. 115)

TABLE 9.3 Average Age at First Experience of Various Sexual Behaviors, American Adolescents

	Average Age at First Experience	
	Males	Females
Kissing	13.9	15.0
Touch breast	14.9	16.2
Touch penis	15.7	16.6
Touch vagina	15.4	16.4
Sexual intercourse	16.3	17.3
Oral sex	16.9	17.8

Source: Feldman et al., 1999.

After masturbation, sexual experience for White American adolescents tends to follow a sequence from kissing through intercourse and oral sex (Feldman, Turner, & Aranjo, 1999). Kissing and necking (mutual touching and stroking above the waist) are the first sexual experiences most White adolescents have with a sexual partner. Very little research has been done on this early stage of adolescent sexual experience, but one study found that 73% of 13-year-old girls and 60% of 13-year-old boys had kissed at least once (Coles & Stokes, 1985). The same study found that 35% of the girls reported having their breasts touched by a boy, and 20% of the boys reported touching a girl's breast. By age 16, a majority of boys and girls have engaged in this breast-touching aspect of necking. The next step in the sequence is usually petting (mutual touching and stroking below the waist). By age 18, 60% of adolescent boys report vaginal touching and 77% of adolescent girls report penile touching. A more recent study that asked emerging adults to recall their earlier sexual behavior reported a similar sequence at similar ages, as shown in Table 9.3 (Feldman et al., 1999).

Sexual Intercourse and Oral Sex

"When I had intercourse for the first time it was because I really wanted to do it. We talked about it and sort of planned when we would do it. . . . The actual intercourse wasn't as great for me as I thought it would be, but the part leading up to it and the part being together afterwards was really nice."

—Serena, age 19 (in Bell, 1998, p. 124)

The most researched topic on adolescent sexuality is the timing of adolescents' first episode of sexual intercourse. Research on this topic in the United States goes back almost to the beginning of the 20th century. These studies indicate that between 1925 and 1965 the proportion of high school students who reported having had intercourse at least once changed little. The reported rate was consistently 10% for females and 25% for males (Chilman, 1983). However, rates have changed dramatically since 1965. The proportion of high school students who reported having sexual intercourse at least once rose through the 1970s and 1980s and reached 54% in the early 1990s before declining slightly in the past decade (48% in the most recent national survey; CDC, 2008). The proportion rises steadily from 33% in 9th grade to 65% in 12th grade (CDC, 2008). The average age of first intercourse is similar in the United States and most European countries—around age 17 (Avery & Lazdane, 2008; CDC, 2008).

Prevalence rates of intercourse increased for American college students in the 1960s and 1970s but have changed little in recent decades. For several decades prior to the 1960s, about 40% of college students reported having had intercourse at least once. A steep increase took place in the late 1960s and early 1970s, and by the mid-1970s 75% of college students reported having had intercourse (Dreyer, 1982). This proportion increased slightly to about 80% in the 1980s and has remained stable over the past 20 years (Hatfield & Rapson, 2005).

Patterns of first sexual intercourse in American society show distinct ethnic differences. According to national surveys by the Centers for Disease Control and Prevention (2008), the proportion of high school students in grades 9–12 who have had intercourse is lowest for White adolescents (44%), with Latino adolescents somewhat higher (52%) and African American adolescents (67%) highest. African American adolescents also report earlier ages of first intercourse. Sixteen percent of African American adolescents report having intercourse by age 13, compared with just 8% of Latino adolescents and 4% of White adolescents.

The earlier timing of intercourse among Black adolescents appears to be related in part to a different progression of stages in their sexual behavior. Rather than moving gradually from kissing through various stages of necking and petting and then to intercourse, African American adolescents are more likely to skip stages and move quickly to intercourse. This may help explain the high rates of adolescent pregnancy among African Americans, which we will discuss later in the chapter. The quick progression from kissing to intercourse may leave African American adolescents with less time to consider the potential consequences of intercourse and to prepare themselves for it by obtaining contraception somewhere during the earlier steps of sexual contact.

Research has indicated that Asian Americans are considerably less likely to engage in sexual activity in adolescence, compared with any of the other major American ethnic groups (Connolly et al., 2004; Feldman et al., 1999). Asian American adolescents tend to have an especially strong sense of duty and respect toward their parents, and many of them view sexual relations in adolescence as something that would disappoint and shame their parents. Asian American adolescents' social interactions with the other sex tend to take place in groups through the late teens, and physical contact between adolescent boys and girls tends to be limited to holding hands and kissing. Boys as well as girls tend to view sexual intercourse as something that should wait until marriage or at least until they are "very seriously involved" (Feldman et al., 1999). Adolescents in Asian countries experience similarly conservative sexual norms (Naito & Guillen, 2002).

RESEARCH FOCUS • Sex, Lies, and Methodology

For obvious reasons, studies of adolescent sexuality are based almost entirely on self-report. This raises the question of how truthful people are about what they report. Sex involves many sensitive and private issues, and people may be unwilling to disclose information on these issues accurately even if they are promised that their responses will be anonymous.

One way around this problem involves having adolescents respond on a computer to prerecorded questions given through headphones. In a national study of sexual behavior among 1,600 adolescent males aged 15 to 19 (Harmon, 1998), adolescents who listened to questions on the headphones and answered them on a computer screen were far more likely to report high-risk sexual behavior than adolescents who answered the questions in the traditional questionnaire format. The computer group was 4 times as likely to report having had sex with another male (5.5% to 1.5%), 14 times as likely to report sex with an intravenous drug user (2.8% to 0.2%), and 5 times as likely to report that they were "always" or "often" drunk or high when they had sex (10.8%

to 2.2%). These differences remained after the researchers controlled statistically for ethnic background and school performance. The gap between computer answers and questionnaire answers was greatest among adolescents who did well in school, indicating that these adolescents felt they had more of an image to maintain and so were more influenced by social desirability.

Other studies of sensitive topics such as illegal drug use also have found that use of a computer results in higher reports of the behavior (Harmon, 1998; Supple, Aquilino, & Wright, 1999). Scholars suggest that people generally experience a decrease in their inhibitions when a computer mediates their communication. One scholar, Sherry Turkle of the Massachusetts Institute of Technology, observed: "We know our computers are networked, but we still experience them as a blank screen for our own self-reflection" (Harmon, 1998, p. A-14). This may make it easier for adolescents (and others) to disclose their participation in behavior they perceive to be disapproved by their society.

Having sexual intercourse once does not necessarily initiate a pattern of frequent intercourse from that point onward. The average length of a sexual relationship among American adolescents is 6 months, and only one-third last more than 7 months (Manlove et al., 2006). In between relationships, adolescents may have periods when they are not sexually active. A recent national study found that one fourth of the high school students who had ever had sexual intercourse had not had sex in the previous 3 months (CDC, 2008).

Most adolescent sexual activity, especially sexual intercourse, takes place within the context of a romantic relationship (Furman et al., 2009). According to a national study, of American adolescents who had had sex, 77% indicated that their most recent sexual partner was also their romantic partner (Manlove et al., 2006). However, many adolescents also have occasional episodes of recreational sex, popularly known today as "hooking up" (a one-time sexual experience between uncommitted partners, which may or may not include intercourse). In one national study, over 60% of sexually active adolescents reported having at least one episode of sexual intercourse with an uncommitted partner (Giordano et al., 2006). However, partners in hooking up were not usually strangers. In fact, in 70% of hooking up episodes, the partner was a friend, acquaintance, or ex-boyfriend/girlfriend, and only 6% were with a partner the adolescent had just met. Sexual activity between friends sometimes serves as a bridge toward building a romantic relationship (Furman & Hand, 2006).

One other area for which rates of sexual behavior should be mentioned is oral sex. Most studies find that, for most young people, their first episode of oral sex comes at a later age than their first episode of sexual intercourse. Ac-

cording to one recent national American study of 15- to 19-year-olds, 54% of girls and 55% of boys reported ever having oral sex (Lindberg, Jones, & Santelli, 2008). Sexual intercourse experiences predicted oral sex; within 6 months of their first episode of sexual intercourse, 82% of the participants had engaged in oral sex. A national Canadian study found similar rates of oral sex—30% in Grade 9 and 50% in Grade 11 (Sears et al., 2006). Among college students, the reported rates are considerably higher. In one study, 86% of college males and 80% of college females reported at least one experience with oral sex in the past year (Gladue, 1990).

For many adolescents, necking is their first sexual experience with a partner.

Pornography

"I'm not going to say I've never watched porn. I mean, what can you do? It's part of life. If you're going to look at it and you're going to watch it, that's your decision, I guess. I don't watch it on a regular basis. Every now and then, of course, but . . . it doesn't affect me."

—Luke, age 16 (in Regnerus, 2007, p. 177)

Because adolescence is a time of reaching sexual maturity, interest in sexual topics and sexual issues is high. Yet, as we have seen, actual participation in sexual activity during adolescence is mixed, and in many cases low or nonexistent. Many adolescents are not sexually active, and even those who are sexually active have long periods when they have no regular partner. Even in emerging adulthood, when sexual activity is more common than in adolescence, it is substantially lower than among typical married adults. Some cultures strongly prohibit sexual activity of all kinds before marriage, as we shall see in the next section.

Perhaps for these reasons, pornography has long been appealing to many adolescents and emerging adults, especially males. For many decades, pornographic magazines have shown naked women in sexual poses, and pornographic movies have depicted various sex acts. In recent years, with the invention of the Internet, pornographic material has suddenly become much easier to obtain. In fact, of all the many uses of the Internet, the number one use above all is accessing pornography (Carroll et al., 2008).

What do we know about the viewing of pornographic materials among adolescents specifically? A national survey of 10- to 17-year-olds in the United States found that 8% of 10- to 13-year-olds and 20% of 14- to 17-year-olds had viewed pornography, with about half of this exposure taking place on the Internet (Ybarra & Mitchell, 2005). Viewing pornography was far more common among boys; only 5% of pornography viewers were girls. Pornography viewers were more likely than nonviewers to report delinquency and substance use, but of course this is a correlation, not causation. It does not mean that viewing pornography causes delinquency and substance use in adolescence.

A study of Internet pornography use among Chinese adolescents showed much higher rates of use, despite (or because of?) the more restrictive and conservative sexual attitudes of Chinese culture (Lo & Wei, 2005). In this study, 38% of high school students had ever viewed Internet pornography. Viewing pornography was related to more favorable attitudes toward premarital sex and greater likelihood of reported sexual activity. Once again, however, this is a correlation and does not show causation.

In the United States, pornography use appears to be far higher among emerging adults than among adolescents. In a study of college students at six sites around the country, 87% of the young men and 31% of the young women reported viewing Internet pornography (Carroll et al., 2008). Notably, 67% of the young men and 49% of the young women agreed that viewing pornography is acceptable, which means that many of the young men who reported viewing pornography did not view this behavior as acceptable, whereas many young women who did not view pornography believed it was acceptable to do so. Here as in the other studies, viewing pornography was related to risk behaviors, specifically sexual risk behaviors and substance use, but here again this is a correlation rather than causation. As we will see in more detail in Chapter 12 on media use, it is often difficult to establish causality in media research because people make choices about media consumption that reflect their preexisting personal qualities and behavior patterns.

A study of emerging adults in Sweden found high rates of viewing Internet pornography among both men and women (Häggström-Nordin & Hanson, 2005). Ninety-eight percent of young men and 72% percent of young women in this study had ever viewed pornography. Viewing pornography was related to reported experiences of having sexual intercourse with a friend and to earlier timing of first episode of sexual intercourse. In a qualitative study by this research team (Häggström-Nordin et al., 2006), Swedish emerging adults expressed mixed feelings about pornography viewing. They described it as interesting and pleasurable to view, but also expressed concerns about the submissive and degrading ways women are depicted in pornography and the separation of sex from intimacy.

Cultural Beliefs and Adolescent Sexuality

Even though adolescents in all cultures experience similar biological processes in reaching sexual maturity, cultures vary enormously in how they view adolescent sexuality. The best description of this variation remains a book that is now over 50 years old, *Patterns of Sexual Behavior* by Ford and Beach (1951). These two anthropologists compiled information about sexuality from over 200 cultures. On the basis of their analysis, they described three types of cultural approaches to adolescent sexuality: restrictive, semirestrictive, and permissive.

Restrictive cultures place strong prohibitions on adolescent sexual activity before marriage. One way of enforcing this prohibition is to require strict separation of boys and girls from early childhood through adolescence. In several parts of the world, from East Africa to the rain forests of Brazil, from about age 7 until marriage boys and girls live mostly separate lives, boys with fathers and other men or with each other, girls with their mothers and other women. In other restrictive cultures, the prohibition on premarital sex is enforced through strong social norms. Young people in Asia and South America tend to disapprove strongly of premarital sex (Buss, 1989), reflecting the view they have been taught by their cultures.

restrictive cultures Cultures that place strong prohibitions on adolescent sexual activity before marriage.

Female virginity before marriage is highly valued in Arab countries. Here, adolescent girls in Saudi Arabia.

Finally, **permissive cultures** encourage and expect adolescent sexuality. In fact, in some permissive cultures sexual behavior is encouraged even in childhood, and the sexuality of adolescence is simply a continuation of the sex play of childhood. One example of this type of culture is the people of the Trobriand Islands in the South Pacific. In Ford and Beach's (1951) description:

> Sexual life begins in earnest among the Trobrianders at six to eight years for girls, ten to twelve for boys. Both sexes receive explicit instruction from older companions whom they imitate in sex activities. . . . At any time an [adolescent] couple may retire to the bush, the bachelor's hut, an isolated yam house, or any other convenient place and there engage in prolonged sexual play with full approval of their parents. (pp. 188–191)

It should be noted that these descriptions are from the past. In recent decades, the Trobrianders as well as many other permissive cultures have become less permissive in response to globalization and the censure of Christian missionaries (Hatfield & Rapson, 2005).

Which of these categories best applies to the current norms in the American majority culture? When Ford and Beach published *Patterns of Sexual Behavior* in 1951, they classified American society as restrictive. However, a great deal has changed in adolescent sexuality in American society over the past 50 years. Adolescent sexual activity has become far more prevalent during this time, and the attitudes of both adults and adolescents toward adolescent sexuality have become much less restrictive (Michael et al., 1995). Semirestrictive is probably a better classification of the American majority culture today. For the most part, American parents look the other way with respect to their adolescents' sexuality, especially by the time their adolescents reach the late teens. Even though they may not approve of their adolescents' having sexual intercourse, they allow dating and romantic relationships to flourish during adolescence, knowing that at least some expression of adolescent sexuality is likely under these circumstances.

However, the semirestrictive approach to adolescent sexuality in the American majority culture is tinged with ambivalence (Crockett, Raffaelli, & Moilanen, 2002). In the best study conducted so far of American adults' sexual attitudes and behavior, 60% of a national sample of adults aged 18 to 59 agreed with the statement that "Premarital sex among teenagers is always wrong" (Michael et al., 1995). These results indicate that although Americans may agree that sex in early adolescence is unwise and should be discouraged, there is little consensus in American society about the moral stand-

In some countries, the sanctions against premarital sex even include the threat of physical punishment and public shaming. A number of Arab countries take this approach, including Algeria, Syria, and Saudi Arabia. Premarital female virginity is a matter of not only her honor but the honor of her family, and if she is known to lose her virginity before marriage, the males of her family may punish her, beat her, or even kill her (Shaaban, 1991). Although many cultures also value male premarital chastity, no culture punishes violations of male premarital chastity with such severity. Thus, restrictive cultures are usually more restrictive for girls than for boys. A **double standard** in cultural views of adolescent sexuality is common worldwide (Crawford & Popp, 2003; Hatfield & Rapson, 2005).

THINKING CRITICALLY •••

What do you think explains the gender double standard regarding young people's sexuality that exists in so many cultures?

Semirestrictive cultures also have prohibitions on premarital adolescent sex. However, in these cultures the formal prohibitions are not strongly enforced and are easily evaded. Adults in these cultures tend to ignore evidence of premarital sexual behavior as long as young people are fairly discreet. However, if pregnancy results from premarital sex, the adolescents are often forced to marry. The Samoans studied by Margaret Mead (1928) are an example of this kind of culture. Adolescent love affairs were common among the Samoans when Mead studied them, but pregnant girls were expected to marry.

---

double standard Two different sets of rules for sexual behavior, one applying to males and the other females, with rules for females usually being more restrictive.

semirestrictive cultures Cultures that have prohibitions on premarital adolescent sex, but the prohibitions are not strongly enforced and are easily evaded.

permissive cultures Cultures that encourage and expect sexual activity from their adolescents.

Young people's sexuality is viewed quite differently in northern Europe than in the United States. Northern Europeans tend to be considerably more liberal about sexuality than Americans and much more tolerant of sexual involvements by late adolescents and emerging adults (Arnett & Balle-Jensen, 1993). However, this does not mean that young people's sexuality in these countries is uncomplicated. Research by Manuela du Bois-Reymond and Janita Ravesloot (1996) provides interesting insights into young people's sexuality in northern Europe.

Bois-Reymond and Ravesloot (1996) interviewed 60 young people (aged 15 to 22) and their parents in a city in the Netherlands, a country that has long had liberal attitudes toward sexuality. The data collected in the study were mostly qualitative, based on interviews that were coded in various ways. The interviews focused on communication about sexual issues with peers and parents.

With regard to peers, most young people reported little pressure from peers to engage in sex. However, there was social pressure on girls—but not boys—to avoid changing sexual partners frequently. It was socially approved among peers for both boys and girls to be sexually active and to have intercourse with a steady partner, but girls experienced peer disapproval for having numerous partners. As one 18-year-old girl remarked, "My best friends do not allow me to date every boy . . . each week another one is not done . . . we think that's stupid" (p. 181). Thus, liberal attitudes toward sexuality among peers had limits, and a double standard was applied to the sexual behavior of boys and girls.

As for parents, most of them accepted sexual involvements by their adolescents and emerging adults. The authors noted that in the Netherlands as in most other northern European countries, "parents are prepared to either permit or tolerate premarital sexual behavior in their children, under one main condition: sexual relationships must be monogamous and serious, based on feelings of true love" (p. 182). However, this attitude did not mean that communication about sexuality was easy for young people and their parents. On the contrary, the authors observed "a certain embarrassment about communicating about sexuality among the parents. Their children feel this embarrassment and therefore refrain from confidential communication about their sexual lives" (p. 193). Fathers were particularly unlikely to be involved in communication about sexual issues with their children.

Because of their mutual discomfort in discussing sexuality, Dutch young people and their parents often seemed to misunderstand each other. In particular, parents often perceived themselves as more permissive about sexual behavior and more open about sexual communication than their children perceived them to be. For example, one father described himself as lenient: "I do not interfere with anything. . . . I am not able to do that . . . it's not my business" (p. 191); however, his 19-year-old daughter saw him much differently: "I am not allowed to go upstairs for a few hours [with my boyfriend]. . . . I'm using the pill in secret and that's annoying. . . . He badgers the life out of me to come home early . . . always restrictions" (p. 191).

The authors interpreted this conflict in perspectives as stemming from the fact that the parents had grown up in a much more sexually restrictive time. They viewed themselves as liberal and as tolerant of their children's sexual behavior—and by the standards of the previous generation they were, but not by the standards of their children, who had become still more liberal about sexuality. Parents worried about their children having sex too early, about STDs, and about premarital pregnancy. They liked to see themselves as allowing their children a great deal of freedom and autonomy, but given these concerns, many of them attempted to manage their children's sex lives in ways the parents viewed as subtle and indirect but the children saw as overbearing.

In sum, although Dutch society is more permissive about young people's sexuality than American society, Bois-Reymond and Ravesloot's (1996) research indicates that in Dutch society, too, communication about sexuality is fraught with ambiguity. Young people must deal with the double standard that exists among their peers regarding males' and females' sexual behavior. In their families, young people and their parents have difficulty discussing sexuality openly and often differ in how they perceive the parents' attitudes and behavior. The "divergent realities" that have been found to be common in relationships between young people and their parents in the United States (Larson & Richards, 1994) appear to exist in the Netherlands as well.

---

ing of adolescent sexuality in the late teens. Many Americans think that it is acceptable for adolescents in their late teens to have sexual intercourse, but many others do not.

Ford and Beach's (1951) framework was based on anthropologists' ethnographies. In recent years, other social scientists have conducted surveys in numerous countries that demonstrate the wide variability in cultural approaches to adolescent sexuality around the world. Table 9.4 shows some examples. Premarital sex is common in Western European countries, and African countries such as Nigeria and Kenya report rates of premarital sex similar to the West. Premarital sex is somewhat less common in South America, although the large differences in reported premarital sex by male and female adolescents in countries such as Brazil and Chile suggest that males exaggerate their sexual activity or females underreport theirs (or both). Finally, premarital

TABLE 9.4	Percentage of Young Men and Women Who Have Engaged in Premarital Sexual Relations		
Country	Age	Men (percent)	Women (percent)
United States	20	84	61
Norway	20	78	86
United Kingdom	19–20	84	85
Germany	20	78	83
Mexico	15–19	44	13
Brazil	15–19	73	28
Chile	15–19	48	19
Colombia	20	89	65
Liberia	18–21	93	82
Nigeria	19	86	63
Hong Kong	27	38	24
Japan	16–21	15	7
Republic of Korea	12–21	17	4

Source: Hatfield & Rapson (2005).

sex is least common in Asian countries such as Japan and South Korea, where the emphasis on female virginity before marriage is still very strong. Missing from the table are figures from the Arab countries (no Arab country allows social scientists to ask adolescents about their sexual behavior), but ethnographic studies indicate that rates of premarital sex in those countries are even lower than in Asia because of the severe penalties for girls who violate the prohibition (Davis & Davis, 1989).

Gender and the Meanings of Sex

"In our school, if you don't go around bragging about how far you got and what you did with the girl you were out with, well, then they start calling you fag or queer or something like that. . . . I think most guys lie about how far they go and what they do just to keep their image up."

—Henry, age 15 (in Bell, 1998, p. 105)

"You know how it's okay for a guy to go around telling everybody about how horny he is and bragging about how he's going to get some this weekend? Well if a girl ever said those things, everybody would call her a slut."

—Diana, age 16 (in Bell, 1998, p. 105)

sexual scripts Cognitive frameworks, often different for males and females, for understanding how a sexual experience is supposed to proceed and how sexual experiences are to be interpreted.

Although no one in the West advocates death for adolescent girls who engage in premarital sex, even in the West some degree of gender double standard exists in cultural attitudes toward adolescent sexuality (Crawford & Popp, 2003; Moore & Rosenthal, 2006). Just as in dating, adolescent girls and boys in the West learn different **sexual scripts** (Frith & Kitzinger, 2001; Gagnon, 1973)—that is, different cognitive frameworks for understanding how a sexual experience is supposed to proceed and how sexual experiences are to be interpreted. In general, both girls and boys expect the boy to "make the moves" (i.e., to be the sexual initiator), whereas the girl is expected to set the limits on how far the sexual episode is allowed to progress. Studies have also found that girls are more likely than boys to have sexual scripts that include romance, friendship, and emotional intimacy, whereas for boys sexual attraction tends to outweigh emotional factors (Eyre & Millstein, 1999; Hatfield & Rapson, 2005).

Evidence of differing sexual scripts for adolescent girls and boys can also be found in studies of adolescents' responses to their first sexual intercourse (Moore & Rosenthal, 2006). Boys' responses to first intercourse are generally highly positive. They most commonly report feeling excitement, satisfaction, and happiness (Oswald, Bahne, & Feder, 1994), and they take pride in telling their friends about it. In contrast, girls tend to be considerably more ambivalent. Almost half of them indicate that the main reason for having first intercourse was affection/love for their partner, compared with only one

Males and females tend to interpret their sexual experiences differently.

fourth of males (Michael et al., 1995; Sears et al., 2006). However, they are less likely than boys to find the experience either physically or emotionally satisfying. Although many report feeling happy and excited about it, they are much more likely than boys to report feeling afraid, worried, guilty, and concerned about pregnancy (Oswald et al., 1994), and they are much less likely than boys to tell their friends (Sprecher et al., 1995). This seems to indicate that the sexual script for girls is more fraught with ambivalence than the script for boys, as a result of cultural attitudes that view girls (but not boys) who engage in premarital sex as morally wrong.

Gender differences in sexual scripts are reflected in sexual fantasies as well as in interpretations of sexual experience. One study (Miller & Simon, 1980) found that although a majority of both male and female college students reported feeling sexual arousal when fantasizing about necking or intercourse with "someone you love or are fond of," fantasies of sexual episodes with strangers with whom they had no emotional attachment were much more common among males (79%) than among females (22%). Furthermore, females were more likely than males to be sexually aroused by thoughts of "doing nonsexual things with someone you are fond of or in love with." The authors of the study concluded that "For males, the explicitly sexual is endowed with erotic meaning regardless of the emotional context. For females, the emotional context is endowed with erotic meaning without regard for the presence or absence of explicitly sexual symbols" (1980, p. 403).

The fact that girls can get pregnant and boys cannot may partly explain why girls are more ambivalent about premarital sex, especially premarital sex in the absence of a committed relationship. If pregnancy results, the consequences are likely to be much more serious for her than for him—physically, socially, and emotionally. However, cultural attitudes also reinforce the tendencies that arise from biological differences in consequences, and may in fact be more important than the biological differences. Many investigators of sexual attitudes in Western countries have observed that adolescent sex is more disapproved for girls than for boys (Brooks-Gunn & Paikoff, 1997; Durham, 1998; Hird & Jackson, 2001; Michael et al., 1995; Moore & Rosenthal, 2006). Because of this double standard, adolescent girls who are engaging in sexual intercourse are more likely than boys to be seen as bad or unlovable, by themselves as well as by others (Crawford & Popp, 2003; Graber, Brooks-Gunn, & Galen, 1999; Jackson & Cram, 2003). Under these circumstances, adolescent girls may find it difficult to experience their sexuality as a source of pleasure and joy (Fine, 1988).

Characteristics of Sexually Active Adolescents

Even by grades 9 to 12, about half of American adolescents have never had sexual intercourse, and others may have had sex once or twice but are not currently in a sexual relationship. As noted earlier, different ethnic groups in American society have quite different rates of sexual intercourse in ado-

lescence. What other characteristics distinguish adolescents who are having sex from adolescents who are not, and what factors are related to the timing of adolescents' first episodes of sexual intercourse?

At high school age, adolescents who remain virgins and adolescents who are nonvirgins are similar in some ways and different in others. The two groups have similar levels of self-esteem and overall life satisfaction (Billy et al., 1988; Jessor et al., 1983). However, adolescents who remain virgins through high school are more likely than nonvirgins to be late maturing in the timing of their pubertal development (Caspi & Moffitt, 1991; Magnusson, Stattin, & Allen, 1986), and they tend to have higher levels of academic performance and academic aspirations (Wyatt, 1990). They are also more likely to be politically conservative and to participate in religious activities (Smith & Denton, 2005).

Sharper differences exist between adolescents who have their first episode of sexual intercourse relatively early in adolescence (age 15 or younger) and other adolescents (Crockett & Rafaelli, 2003). Adolescents who have early sexual intercourse are more likely than other adolescents to be early users of drugs and alcohol as well. They are also more likely than other adolescents to be from single-parent families and to have grown up in poverty. The early involvement of African American adolescents in sexual activity can be explained to a large extent by the higher rates of single-parent families and poverty among African Americans. Numerous scholars who have studied early sexual intercourse among African American adolescents in poor families have concluded that poverty gives these adolescents less to hope and plan for, so that they have less of an incentive to refrain from becoming sexually active in order to avoid pregnancy and preserve their future prospects (Crump et al., 1999; Lauritsen, 1994; Wilson, 1996).

Perhaps surprisingly, few differences exist in family relationships between early sexually active adolescents and other adolescents. Most studies find no differences between adolescents in these groups in *parental monitoring*—the extent to which parents know where their adolescents are and what they are doing (Blum, 2002; Casper, 1990; Newcomer & Udry, 1985). However, one study that focused on African American and Latino adolescents found that parental monitoring was associated with lower likelihood of having sexual intercourse in adolescence and fewer partners for adolescents who did have intercourse (Miller, Forehand, & Kotchick 1999). This suggests that the effect of parental monitoring on adolescents' sexual behavior may depend on the cultural context.

Research is also mixed regarding the role that communication between parents and adolescents about sexual issues plays in the timing of adolescents' first intercourse. According to one national (American) study, girls whose mothers talk to them frequently about sex have their first sexual intercourse at a *younger* age than their peers do ("Mum's Not the Word," 1999). However, another national study reported that adolescents' perceptions of parents' disapproval of sexual intercourse in the teen years was associated with later age of first intercourse (Blum, 2002). Also, adolescents who have closer relationships with their mothers are less likely to report having sex, more likely to use contraception if they do have sex, and less likely to become pregnant (Claes et al., 2005; Dittus & Jaccard, 2000; Miller, 1998).

With respect to the influence of peers, when most of the adolescents in a clique are sexually active, they establish a norm within the clique that having sex is acceptable. The remaining virgins in the clique may be influenced toward sexual involvement through their exposure to that norm and to experienced potential sex partners (Miller & Moore, 1990; Rodgers & Rowe, 1993). Of course, selective association may be involved here. Adolescent virgins who are hanging around a group of nonvirgins are likely to have characteristics in common with the nonvirgins that also contribute to decisions of whether to become sexually active, such as lower academic goals and lower religiosity.

Also, girls who mature early tend to attract attention from older boys, which tends to result in the girls' becoming sexually active earlier than other girls (Petersen, 1993). More generally, girls with older boyfriends (3 or more years older) are more likely to be sexually active and more likely to be subject to sexual coercion (Darroch, Landry, & Oslak, 1999; Gowen, et al., 2002, 2004; Young & d'Arcy, 2005). Older boys are more likely to expect sex as part of a romantic relationship, and they have more power and status in relationships with younger girls. Consequently, girls with older boyfriends are more likely to accept their sexual demands, in an effort to maintain a relationship that gives them status. However, girls with older boyfriends also tend to be more interested in sex than other girls their age are (Gowen et al., 2004).

Sexual Harassment and Date Rape

Like love, sex has its dark side. Sexual interactions among adolescents and emerging adults are not always enjoyable or even voluntary. Two of the problems that arise in sexual interactions are sexual harassment and date rape.

Sexual Harassment During adolescence, **sexual harassment** is a pervasive part of peer interactions. Sexual harassment is usually defined as including a wide range of behaviors, from mild harassment such as name-calling, jokes, and leering looks to severe harassment involving unwanted touching or sexual contact (Connolly & Goldberg, 1999; Uggen & Blackstone, 2004). Rates of sexual harassment in adolescence are strikingly high. Among early adolescents, research by Connolly and colleagues indicates that the incidence of sexual harassment increases from grades 5 through 8, with over 40% of 8th graders reporting that they have been victims of sexual harassment from their peers (Connolly & Goldberg, 1999; Connolly, McMaster, Craig, & Pepler, 1998; McMaster, Connolly, Pepler, & Craig, 1997). Rates of sexual harassment for adolescents in high school are even higher—around 80% for girls and 60% to 75% for boys (AAUW, 1993; Lee et al., 1996; see Figure 9.3). Early-maturing girls are especially likely to be targeted for sexual harassment—from both boys and girls (Craig, Pepler, Connolly, & Henderson, 2001; Goldstein et al., 2007).

Sexual and romantic joking and teasing are a common part of adolescents' peer interactions, making it difficult to tell where the border is between harmless joking and harmful ha-

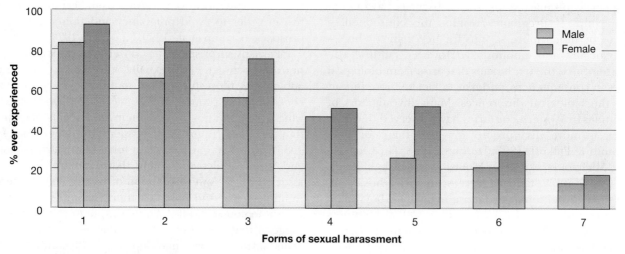

1. Made sexual comments, jokes, gestures, or looks
2. Touched, grabbed, or pinched you in sexual way
3. Intentionally brushed up against you in a sexual way
4. Pulled at your clothing in a sexual way
5. Blocked your way or cornered you in a sexual way
6. Forced you to kiss him/her
7. Forced you to do something sexual, other than kissing

FIGURE 9.3 Percentage of male and female high school students who have ever experienced various forms of sexual harassment.
Source: Lee et al. (1996).

sexual harassment A wide range of threatening or aggressive behaviors related to sexuality, from mild harassment such as name-calling, jokes, and leering looks to severe harassment involving unwanted touching or sexual contact.

date rape An act of sexual aggression in which a person, usually a woman, is forced by a romantic partner, date, or acquaintance to have sexual relations against her will.

coming out For homosexuals, the process of acknowledging their homosexuality and then disclosing the truth to their friends, family, and others.

rassment. Indeed, the majority of adolescents who report being sexually harassed also report sexually harassing others (Lee et al., 1996). Teachers and other school personnel who witness adolescents' interactions may be reluctant to intervene, unsure of what should qualify as harassment (Lee et al., 1996; Stein, 1995). However, being the victim of persistent harassment can be extremely unpleasant for adolescents, and can result in anxiety and depression as well as declining school performance (Connolly & Goldberg, 1999; Gruber & Fineran, 2008).

Sexual harassment continues into emerging adulthood and beyond. It has been estimated that over half of American women will experience sexual harassment at some time during their professional lives (Uggen & Blackstone, 2004). From early adolescence through adulthood, females are more likely than males to be the victims of sexual harassment, and males are more likely than females to be the harassers (Connolly et al., 1998; Uggan & Blackstone, 2004).

Date Rape **Date rape** takes place when a person, usually a woman, is forced by a romantic partner, date, or acquaintance to have sexual relations against her will. Studies indicate that 15% of adolescent girls and 25% of emerging adult women (aged 18 to 24) in the United States have experienced date rape (Michael et al., 1995; Vicary, Klingaman, & Harkness, 1995). Rates are highest of all for girls who have sex at an early age: nearly three fourths of girls who have intercourse before age 14 report having had intercourse against their will (Alan Guttmacher Institute, 2002).

Alcohol plays a big part in date rape on college campuses (King, 2005). Being intoxicated makes women less effective in communicating reluctance to have sex and makes men more likely to ignore or overpower a woman's resistance. When intoxicated, men are more likely to interpret women's behavior, such as talking to them or dancing with them, as indicating sexual interest (Fisher, Cullen, & Turner, 2000). However, even when sober, young men and women often interpret date rape incidents differently (Miller & Benson, 1999). In their accounts of such incidents, young men often deny they forced sex on the woman and say they interpreted the way the young woman dressed or offered affection as cues that she wanted sex. In contrast, young women describing the same incident deny that their dress or behavior was intended to be sexually alluring and say that the men were coercive and ignored their verbal or nonverbal resistance to sex.

Gay, Lesbian, and Bisexual Adolescents

"After people at school found out I was gay, a lot of them kind of kept a distance from me. I think they were scared that I was going to do something to them. . . . I guess that was one of the reasons I didn't come out sooner, because I was afraid that they would be scared of me. It's stupid and crazy, but a lot of people feel that way."

—Jamie, age 17 (in Bell, 1998, p. 141)

So far we have discussed adolescent dating, love, and sexuality in terms of the attractions and relationships between males and

TABLE 9.5 Same-sex Romantic Attractions, Sexual Behavior, and Sexual Identity

Sexual domain	Females			Males		
	Age 16	Age 17	Age 22	Age 16	Age 17	Age 22
Same-sex romantic attractions	5%	4%	13%	7%	5%	5%
Same-sex sexual behavior	1%	1%	4%	1%	1%	3%
Sexual identity: Gay/Lesbial			1%			2%
Bisexual			3%			1%

Source: Savin-Williams and Ream (2007). The question about sexual identity was asked only at age 22.

females. But what about young people who are sexually attracted to other persons of the same sex? What is it like for them to reach the age where issues of dating, love, and sex become more prominent? First, important distinctions between same-sex attractions, same-sex sexual behavior, and homosexual identity should be noted. A recent national longitudinal study in the United States included several questions about same-sex and other-sex attractions and sexual behavior (Savin-Williams, 2007). Questionnaire data were collected at ages 16, 17, and 22. As shown in Table 9.5, at each age considerably more adolescents and emerging adults experienced same-sex romantic attractions than engaged in same-sex sexual behavior. At age 22, more emerging adults reported same-sex romantic attractions than reported same-sex sexual behavior or a gay, lesbian, or bisexual (GLB) identity, especially among women. Other studies have reported slightly higher levels of GLB attractions, sexual behavior, and sexual identity, but there is a consistent pattern across studies that prevalence of same-sex attractions is higher than same-sex behavior, which is in turn higher than prevalence of GLB identity (Savin-Williams, 2005).

Here is an example of the complex relations between sexual attraction, behavior, and identity. At age 15, Stephanie and Lolita were best friends. Stephanie recalled,

"Lolita would sleep over a lot and one night she was talking about her boyfriend Juan and talking about sex . . . We had been very affectionate, like most girlfriends. I asked her how he kissed her, and so she kissed me like her Juan did. This was quite a shocker. From then on we kissed a lot when we got together, and began touching and caressing. To make it 'okay,' one of us would be the boy . . . She's straight as far as I know . . . I was the only girl she did anything with. We never said we were lesbians." (Savin-Williams, 2005, p. 212)

Adolescence is an especially important period with respect to establishing a GLB identity. In the past in Western cultures, and still today in many of the world's cultures, many people would keep this knowledge to themselves all their lives because of the certainty that they would be stigmatized and ostracized if they disclosed the truth. Today in most Western cultures, however, GLBs commonly engage in a process of **coming out**, which involves a person's recognizing

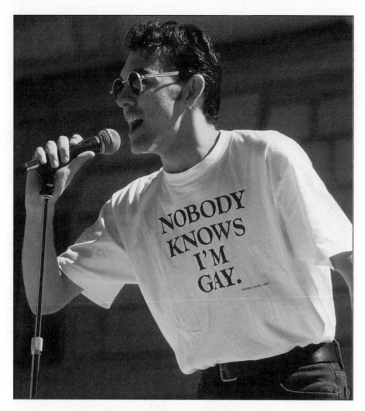

Adolescence is usually the time when homosexuals become fully aware of their orientation.

his or her own sexual identity and then disclosing the truth to friends, family, and others (Flowers & Buston, 2001; Savin-Williams, 2001). Awareness of a GLB sexual identity usually begins in early adolescence, with disclosure to others coming in late adolescence or emerging adulthood (Floyd & Bakeman, 2006). The average of coming out has declined in recent decades, from 21 in the 1970s to 16 in the present, perhaps because of growing acceptance of homosexuality (Savin-Williams, 2005).

GLBs usually disclose their sexual identity first to a friend; fewer than 10% tell a parent first (Savin-Williams, 1998; 2001). Coming out is often a long process, as information is disclosed gradually to others. For many GLBs the coming-out process is never complete, and they withhold information about their sexual orientation to some degree throughout their lives. According to one recent longitudinal study, the coming-out process takes longer for African Americans and Latinos than for Whites, perhaps because of stronger antihomosexual views in these cultures (Rosario et al., 2004).

Given the **homophobia** (fear and hatred of homosexuals) that exists in many societies (Baker, 2002), coming to the realization of a GLB identity can be traumatic for many adolescents. Studies indicate that about one third of GLB adolescents have attempted suicide, a much higher rate than among straight adolescents (Bobrow, 2002; D'Augelli, 2002). Rates of substance abuse, school difficulties, and running away from home are also higher among GLB adolescents (D'Augel-

li & Patterson, 2002). All these problems tend to increase after the adolescent comes out to parents, because parents' responses are often highly negative (Hetherington & Lavner, 2008).

Adolescents and emerging adults who are GLB also face potential mistreatment from their peers, including harassment, verbal abuse, and even physical abuse (Horn, 2006). In one study, more than three fourths of GLB adolescents reported that they had been verbally abused because of their sexual orientation, and 15% reported physical attacks (D'Augelli, 2002). More than one third said they had lost friends because of their sexual orientation. Given the unpleasant reception that often awaits them if they come out, it is not surprising that many GLB adolescents hide their homosexual feelings and behavior (Davis & Stewart, 1997; D'Augelli et al., 2005).

Nevertheless, in recent years there has been a noticeable change in American attitudes toward GLBs, constituting "a dramatic cultural shift" toward more favorable and tolerant perceptions, according to Ritch Savin-Williams (2005), a prominent researcher on GLB adolescents. Savin-Williams notes changes in popular culture, such as the TV show *Queer Eye for the Straight Guy,* in which straight men seek fashion and decorating advice from gay men, and movies such as *Kissing Jessica Stein,* in which two young women test out a lesbian relationship. (The recent pop music hit "I Kissed a Girl," by Katie Perry, could be added here.) He also cites a national survey of 13 to 19 year-olds in the U.S. showing that the percentage who "don't have any problem" with homosexuality tripled over the past decade, to 54%. Of course, 54% is barely half and leaves plenty of room for continued homophobia and abuse, but it does show that public attitudes toward GLBs are becoming less hostile.

As for GLB adolescents and emerging adults themselves, Savin-Williams and others are finding in current research that young people who engage in homosexual behavior are increasingly resistant to being labeled with a stable sexual identity as gay, lesbian, or bisexual. Lisa Diamond interviewed "nonheterosexual" young women at ages 18–25, then every 2 years for the next 10 years (Diamond, 2008). She found that over this time the young women who engaged in same-sex sexual behavior became increasingly reluctant to categorize themselves as lesbian or even bisexual, "because they are still engaged in the process of sexual questioning or because they find the existing range of sexual identity categories, and the process of categorization altogether, to be limiting and restrictive" (p. 7). Savin-Williams has found similar results in his research on adolescents and emerging adults, and provides this example of a young man's sexual fluidity upon entering college:

> "I dated females and realized that I was attracted to females and so I thought of myself as straight . . . Then in the early months of my sophomore year I realized that my feelings for guys must mean something, and it must mean that I'm bisexual. Or maybe what I was, was just sexual . . . I want to find emotional attractiveness with males like I have with females. Now I know that I prefer males, though I'm probably more bi than most gays" (Savin-Williams, 2005, p. 206).

In sum, homophobia is still pervasive, and the problems faced by GLB adolescents and emerging adults are formid-

---

homophobia Fear and hatred of homosexuals.

able, but young people today seem to be developing a more flexible and tolerant view of sexual variability than their parents or grandparents did.

THINKING CRITICALLY •••

What do you think explains the homophobia that exists in many cultures? Why does homosexuality make many people uncomfortable and even angry?

Contraceptive Use and Nonuse

Just as cultures have a variety of ways of viewing adolescent sexuality, from encouraging it to strictly prohibiting it, adolescent pregnancy is viewed by different cultures in a variety of ways. In most of the 186 traditional cultures described by Schlegel and Barry (1991), girls marry by the time they reach age 18. Thus, they tend to marry within 2 years of reaching menarche because menarche tends to take place later in most traditional cultures—age 15 or 16—than in industrialized societies. Furthermore, as discussed in Chapter 2, in the first 2 years after menarche girls tend to ovulate irregularly and are less likely to become pregnant during this time than later, after their cycle of ovulation has been established (Finkelstein, 2001a). This means that for most adolescent girls in traditional cultures, even if they begin having sexual intercourse before marriage, their first child is likely to be born in the context of marriage. And in some traditional cultures, even if a girl has a child before marriage it may be viewed positively, as an indication that she is fertile and will be able to have more children once she has married (Schlegel & Barry, 1991; Whiting, Burbank, & Ratner, 1986).

Clearly, the situation is quite different for adolescent girls in Western countries. They reach menarche much earlier, usually around age 12 or 13, and they tend to marry much later, usually in their mid- to late 20s. Because the majority of adolescent girls in Western countries begin having sexual intercourse at some time in their mid- to late teens, this leaves a period of a decade or more for many girls between the time they begin having intercourse and the time they enter marriage. Furthermore, for adolescent girls in the West, having a child while unmarried and in their teens has serious detrimental effects on their future prospects. Unlike in traditional cultures, the late teens and early 20s are crucial years in the West for educational and occupational preparation. For Western girls who have a child outside of marriage during those years, their educational and occupational prospects are often severely impeded, as we will see in the next section.

Of course, unlike girls in most traditional cultures, adolescents in industrialized societies also have various methods of contraception to prevent pregnancy. It is at least theoretically possible that adolescents who have begun having sexual intercourse and do not yet want to produce a child could use one of the highly effective methods of contraception available to them.

However, this theoretical possibility does not always match reality, especially in the United States. The reality is that many American adolescents who are having sex do not use contraception responsibly and consistently. Over 1 mil-

Girls in traditional cultures often marry by age 18, about 2 or 3 years after reaching menarche. Here, a young bride in Nepal.

lion teenage American girls become pregnant each year, and over one third of sexually active girls become pregnant at some time during their teen years (Boyle, 2000; CDCP, 1998). Although condom use among adolescents increased substantially during the 1980s and early 1990s, in a national study only 60% of sexually active adolescents reported using contraception "always" in their most recent sexual relationship, whereas 20% responded "sometimes" and 20% "never" (Manlove et al., 2006). Contraceptive use is slightly higher among European adolescents, with rates over 80% at most recent intercourse in most countries (Avery & Lazdane, 2008).

Among American adolescents, contraceptive use is often inconsistent (Ford, Sohn, & Lepowski, 2001; Manlove et al., 2006). If they know how to obtain and use contraception , why do they so often fail to use it consistently? One of the best analyses of this question is a classic article by Diane Morrison (1985), in which she reviewed dozens of articles on this topic. She concluded that the core of the answer is that most adolescent sexual activity is *unplanned* and *infrequent*. Adolescents typically do not anticipate that they will have sex on a given occasion. The opportunity is there—they start necking, they start taking their clothes off—and "it just happens." If contraception is available at that moment, they may use it, but if it is not, they sometimes simply take their chances. Also, the fact that adolescent sex tends to be infrequent—only once or twice a month, much less often than for adults—means that they may never get into the habit of preparing for sex as something they take part in on a regular basis.

Some scholars have suggested that cognitive development in adolescence may play a role in contraceptive use. Planning for and anticipating the future is enhanced by formal operations, and the ability for this kind of thinking is only just developing when many adolescents become sexually active. One study of 300 sexually active adolescents aged 14 to 19 found that the adolescents who had higher scores on a measure of formal operations were more likely to report using contraception (Holmbeck et al., 1994). Also, the personal fable of adolescence makes it easy for adolescents to believe that getting pregnant "won't happen to me" (Kershaw et al., 2003), especially when they are caught up in the heat of the moment.

Other scholars have identified a variety of other factors related to the likelihood that adolescents will use contraception. Both male and female adolescents are more likely to use contraception if they are in their late rather than early teens, involved in an ongoing relationship with their partner, and doing well in school (Alan Guttmacher Institute [AGI], 1994; Civic, 1999; Cooper et al., 1999). Embarrassment over purchasing and using contraception is often stated as a reason for not using it (Helweg-Larsen & Collins, 1994; MacDonald et al., 1990). Also, some young people resist using contraception because they believe it interferes with the sexual mood and with romantic feelings (Helweg-Larsen & Collins, 1994; Sheer & Cline, 1994), and some males resist using condoms because they believe condoms reduce sexual pleasure (MacDonald et al., 1990).

Cultural factors are also involved in contraceptive use. The United States has a higher rate of teenage pregnancy than any other industrialized country (AGI, 1994, 2001; Teitler, 2002), as Figure 9.4 shows. This is not because adolescents in the United States have more sex than those in other countries. The pregnancy rate among adolescents in Canada, for example, is only half the rate in the United States, even though the percentages of adolescents in the two countries who are sexually active are nearly identical (AGI), 2001. Adolescents in European countries such as Sweden and Denmark are as likely as adolescents in the United States to be sexually active but much less likely to become pregnant (Avery & Lazdane, 2008; Teitler, 2002).

What explains this difference? In part, higher American rates of adolescent pregnancy are due to higher rates of poverty, compared with European countries. Numerous studies have found that adolescents who are from low-income families are less likely than other adolescents to use contraception (e.g., AGI, 1994; Boyle, 2000; Chilman, 1986). However, even when analyses are restricted to White middle-class adolescents, Americans have higher rates of premarital pregnancy than adolescents in any other Western country (Avery & Lazdane, 2008; Jones et al., 1987; Manlove, 1998).

Most analyses of these cross-national differences have concluded that the core of the problem of inconsistent contraceptive use is the mixed messages that American adolescents receive about sexuality (Alan Guttmacher Institute, 2002). Earlier we stated that American society has a semi-restrictive approach to adolescent sex. What this means, in practice, is that American adolescents are not strongly prohibited from having sex, but neither is adolescent sex widely accepted (Graber et al., 1999). Adolescents receive different messages from different socialization sources, and few clear messages from any source, about the morality and desirability of premarital sex.

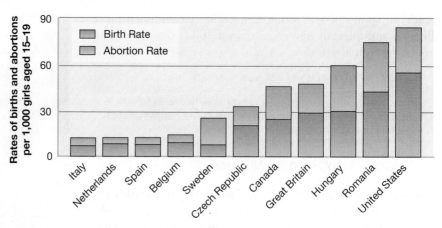

FIGURE 9.4 Rates of adolescent births and abortions in Western countries.

Source: Singh & Darroch (2000).

The media are often blamed for stoking adolescent sexual desires in a simplistic and irresponsible way (Brown et al., 2002). A recent analysis of sexual content in four media (television, magazine, music, and movies) found that sexual health information was found to be frequently inaccurate and to promote gender stereotypes that "boys will be boys and girls better be prepared"(Hust, Brown, & Engle, 2008). In school, most adolescents receive sex education, but this "education" rarely includes an explicit discussion of contraceptive use, as we will discuss in more detail later in this chapter. Communication between parents and adolescents about sexual issues tends to be low, in part because of the discomfort both feel about discussing such issues (Crockett, Raffaelli, & Moilanen, 2003; Hutchinson & Cooney, 1998). Religion plays a role, too. Americans are more religious than people in other Western countries, and religions tend to discourage premarital sex. Nevertheless, American adolescents who are highly religious are no less likely than nonreligious adolescents to have sex, but they are more likely to feel guilty about it (Regnerus, 2007). This guilt can make them avoid using contraception because using contraception would mean acknowledging that they are sexually active.

As a consequence of the influences from these different socialization sources, many American adolescents end up somewhere in the middle—having sex occasionally but feeling guilty or at least ambivalent about it, and not really acknowledging that they are sexually active. Using contraception would mean acknowledging their sexual activity and planning ahead for the next time, and many of them are reluctant to do so (Tschann & Adler, 1997).

Two types of countries have low rates of teenage pregnancy: those that are permissive about adolescent sex and those that adamantly forbid it. Countries such as Denmark, Sweden, and the Netherlands have low rates of adolescent pregnancy because they are permissive about adolescent sex (Avery & Lazdane, 2008; Boyle, 2001; Jones et al., 1987). There are explicit safe-sex campaigns in the media. Adolescents have easy access to all types of contraception. Parents accept that their children will become sexually active by their late teens. It is not uncommon for adolescents in these countries to have a boyfriend or girlfriend spend the

Countries with permissive views of adolescent sex, such as the Scandinavian countries, have low rates of adolescent pregnancy. Here, two adolescents in Norway.

night—in their bedroom in their parents' home, a practice barely imaginable to most Americans (Arnett & Balle-Jensen, 1993).

At the other end of the spectrum, restrictive countries such as Japan, South Korea, and Morocco strictly forbid adolescent sex (Davis & Davis, 1989; Hatfield & Rapson, 2005; Stevenson & Zusho, 2002). Adolescents in these countries are even strongly discouraged from dating until they are well into emerging adulthood and are seriously looking for a marriage partner. It is rare for an adolescent boy and girl even to spend time alone together, much less have sex. Some adolescents follow the call of nature anyway and violate the taboo, but violations are rare because the taboo is so strong and the shame of being exposed for breaking it is so great.

Pregnancy, Parenthood, and Abortion in Adolescence

When adolescents fail to use contraceptives effectively and pregnancy takes place, what are the consequences for the adolescent parents and their child? About 30% of teen pregnancies in America end in abortion, and another 14% end in miscarriage (AGI, 1999). Of the children who are born, only about 5% are put up for adoption. The others are raised by their adolescent mothers, sometimes with the help of the father of the child, more often with the help of the adolescent mother's own mother.

About half a million children are born to teenage mothers in the United States every year. This may seem like a large number—and it is—but in fact the birth rate among teenage girls has declined steadily from the mid-1950s to the present, not just in the United States but in every Western country (Teitler, 2002). Why, then, is there so much more concern about adolescent pregnancy in American society today than there was in the 1950s? The reason is that in the 1950s only about 15% of births to teenage mothers took place outside of marriage, whereas today about two thirds of teenage births are to unmarried mothers. In the 1950s and 1960s, the medi-

an age of marriage for females was just 20 (Arnett & Taber, 1994). This means that many girls at that time married in their teens and had their first child soon after. Today, with the median marriage age for females about 26, it is very rare for young people to marry while still in their teens. If a teenage girl has a child, it is quite likely that she will be unmarried.

Birth rates among American teens rose sharply in the late 1980s but declined substantially (by about 20%) from the early 1990s to the present (Lewin, 1998; Santelli et al., 2007). The decline appears to be a result of a variety of factors, including a slight decline in sexual activity, the effects of HIV/AIDS prevention programs, and—especially—a sharp increase in the use of condoms (CDCP, 2002, 2005; Santelli et al., 2004; Santelli et al., 2007). According to a yearly national American survey, among 9th–12th graders condom use at last intercourse increased from 46% in 1991 to 61% in 2007 (CDCP, 2009).

In recent years, birth rates have become highest of all among Latina adolescents, as Figure 9.5 shows. According to two studies (Erickson, 2003; O'Sullivan & Meyer-Bahlberg, 2003), the sexual scripts in Latino culture, specifically the greater power of males in male-female relationships and the belief that love often overpowers reason, make it unlikely that Latino adolescent partners will use contraception. However, Latina adolescent birth rates have also fallen since the early 1990s, though not as fast as the rates among Whites and Blacks.

White adolescent girls are far more likely than Black or Latino adolescents to abort their pregnancy. Also, about two thirds of White and Latino adolescents who become mothers are unmarried, but nearly all Black adolescent mothers are unmarried (Santelli et al., 2004). Whether White, Black, or Latino, girls are more likely to become unmarried teenage mothers if they are from poor families and if they live in a single-parent household (Boyle, 2000; Manlove, 1998).

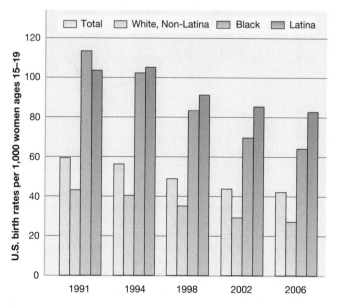

FIGURE 9.5 Teen birth rates in different ethnic groups.
Source: National Vital Statistics Report (2007).

Before recent decades, adolescent pregnancy was often followed by a hasty "shotgun wedding" to avoid scandal and make certain the baby would be born to a married couple (Graber, Britto, & Brooks-Gunn, 1999). According to one estimate, about half of the teenage American girls who married in the late 1950s were pregnant on their wedding day (Furstenberg et al., 1987). Today, the stigma of unmarried motherhood has receded (although certainly not disappeared), and adolescent girls who become pregnant are considerably more likely to have the child even while remaining unmarried. Figure 9.6 shows the pattern over the past half century.

The Consequences of Early Parenthood The concern over adolescent pregnancy is not only moral, based on the view of many Americans that adolescents should not be having sex. The concern is also based on the practical consequences for the adolescent mother and her child. For the unmarried adolescent mother, having a child means that she will be twice as likely as her peers to drop out of school and less likely to become employed or to go on to college after high school, even compared to peers who come from a similar economic background (Miller et al., 2003). Furthermore, adolescent mothers are less likely than their peers to get married and more likely to get divorced if they do marry (Moore & Brooks-Gunn, 2002). In addition, many adolescent mothers are still a long way from maturity in their emotional and social development, and they feel overwhelmed by the responsibilities of motherhood (Leadbeater, & Way, 2001). Adolescent mothers often had problems even before becoming pregnant, such as

poor school performance, conduct problems, and psychological problems, and becoming a parent only deepens their difficulties (Miller-Johnson et al., 1999; Stouthamer-Loeber & Wei, 1998; Woodward & Fergusson, 1998).

Do adolescent mothers eventually get back on track and catch up with their peers? A classic study by Furstenberg, Brooks-Gunn, and Morgan (1987) began with a sample of 300 urban, mostly Black, low-SES teenage mothers in 1966 when they first had their children, and followed both mothers and children every few years until 1984, when the children were 18 years old. Five years after giving birth, the mothers lagged behind their peers in their educational, occupational, and economic progress. By the final follow-up, however, 18 years after the study began, the life situations of the mothers were striking in their diversity. One fourth of the mothers were still on welfare and had remained there for most of the 18-year period. In contrast, another one fourth had succeeded in making it into the middle class, gaining enough education and occupational experience to make substantial progress economically. A majority of the mothers had eventually completed high school, and one third had completed at least some college education. Obtaining education and getting married eventually were related to the most favorable economic outcomes.

In a more recent study, Leadbeater & Way (2001) followed over 100 mostly Puerto Rican and African American teenage mothers in New York City for 6 years. At the 6-year follow-up, 63% of the mothers were still on welfare and 61% had had at least one more child, but 78% had moved out of their mothers' household to live independently or with a partner. Of special interest in the study were the 15 mothers who showed exceptional resilience; that is, in spite of early motherhood they were functioning well after 6 years in their educational attainment, employment, and mental and physical health. There were a variety of reasons for their resilience, including having family members who supported them emotionally but demanded responsible behavior from them, having family members or boyfriends who highly valued education, and having a strong will to succeed. Overall, studies show both the perils of adolescent motherhood and—for some—the possibilities of eventual success.

Not nearly as many studies have been conducted on adolescent fatherhood as on adolescent motherhood, but the available studies indicate that becoming a father as a teen is also related to a variety of negative outcomes. Adolescent fathers are more likely than their male peers to become divorced, to have a lower level of education, and to have a lower-paying job (Nock, 1998; Resnick, Wattenberg, & Brewer, 1992). They are also more prone to a variety of problems, including use of drugs and alcohol, violations of the law, and feelings of anxiety and depression (Buchanan & Robbins, 1990; Miller-Johnson et al., 2004). Like adolescent mothers, the problems of adolescent fathers often began before parenthood (Fagot et al., 1998; Nock, 1998; Thornberry et al., 1997). In one longitudinal study (Miller-Johnson et al., 2004), aggressive behavior as early as age 8 predicted becoming a father in adolescence. For the most part, adolescent fathers are unlikely to be heavily involved in the life of their

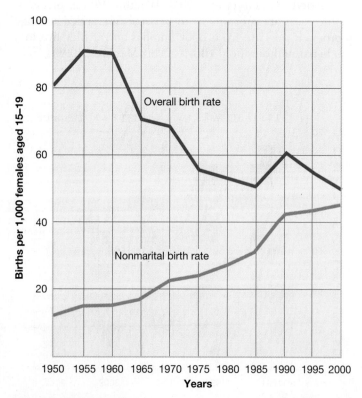

FIGURE 9.6 Total teen birth rate and nonmarital rate, 1950–2000.
Source: www.childstats.gov (2000).

Having a baby in adolescence puts both mother and baby at risk for a variety of difficulties.

majority of adolescent mothers do—face an environmer. which it will be difficult for them to thrive.

Abortion If having a child in adolescence often results in dire consequences for adolescent mothers and their babies, what about adolescent girls who have an abortion? Studies have consistently found little evidence of serious physical or psychological harm for adolescents who abort an unwanted pregnancy (Adler, Ozer, & Tschann, 2003; Russo, 2008). Nevertheless, many experience guilt and emotional stress and feel highly ambivalent about their decision to abort (Franz & Reardon, 1992; Miracle et al., 2003). Abortion remains tremendously controversial in American society, especially with respect to adolescents. By the year 2000, 29 states required either **parental notification** (adolescents were required to notify their parents before having the abortion) or **parental consent** (adolescents were required to obtain their parents' permission to have an abortion) (Adler et al., 2003).

Sexuality in Emerging Adulthood

"Sex is just a normal part of life and no one flips about you having it."

—19-year-old female (quoted in Lefkowitz, 2006, p. 251)

child. One study found that only one fourth of adolescent fathers were viewed by the adolescent mother as having a "close" relationship with the child by the time the child was 3 years old (Leadbeater et al., 1994).

What are the consequences for the children born to adolescent mothers? These children face a higher likelihood of difficulties in life, beginning even before they are born (Miller et al., 2003). Only one in five adolescent mothers receives any prenatal care during the first 3 months of pregnancy. Partly for this reason, babies born to adolescent mothers are more likely to be born prematurely and to have a low birth weight; prematurity and low birth weight in turn predict a variety of physical and cognitive problems in infancy and childhood. Children of adolescent mothers also face a greater likelihood of behavioral problems throughout childhood, including school misbehavior, delinquency, and early sexual activity (Brooks-Gunn & Chase-Lansdale, 1995; Moore & Brooks-Gunn, 2002).

However, scholars have stressed that the children's problems are due not just to the young age of their mothers but also to the fact that most adolescent mothers are poor as well (Boyle, 2000; Levine, Emery, & Pollack, 2007). Having a mother who is young, unmarried, or poor puts children at greater risk for a variety of developmental problems. Children whose mothers have all three characteristics—as the

Adults often view sexual activity (especially intercourse) among adolescents as a problem to be prohibited or at least minimized. This is true both among the general public and among researchers, who tend to include sex as a type of "problem behavior" among adolescents (Jessor, 1999; Jessor & Jessor, 1977). This is partly because of the high rates of unintended pregnancy and sexually transmitted diseases that accompany adolescent sex and partly because adults often believe that adolescents are not emotionally mature enough for sex (Michael et al., 1995).

With respect to emerging adults, however, sex is viewed more as "a normal part of life," by adults generally and by emerging adults themselves (Lefkowitz, 2005, 2006). This does not mean that adults entirely accept or approve of sex among emerging adults. In fact, many American parents do not allow their emerging adult children to have a romantic partner spend the night in their household (Arnett, 2004a). However, parents are at least less opposed to sex among emerging adults than among adolescents. As for the emerging adults themselves, most of them have had sex at least once as adolescents and few of them expect to get married before at least their mid-20s, so they tend to see sex as a normal part of their lives during emerging adulthood.

In their sexual behavior as in other aspects of their lives, there is a great deal of diversity among emerging adults. The

---

parental notification A legal requirement, in some states, that minors must notify their parents before having the abortion.

parental consent A legal requirement, in some states, that minors must obtain their parents' permission to have an abortion.

most common pattern among American 18- to 24-year-olds is to have had one partner in the past year (Lefkowitz, 2006; Michael et al., 1995). However, emerging adults are more likely than adults in any older age group to have had either more or fewer sexual partners. About one third of 18- to- 24-year-olds report having had two or more partners in the past year (Civic, 1999), but about one third also report having had sex only a few times or not at all in the past year (Michael et al., 1995). At the beginning of emerging adulthood, age 18, about half of Americans have had intercourse at least once, and by age 25 nearly all emerging adults have had intercourse at least once, but those who have their first episode of intercourse relatively late tend to be "active abstainers" rather than "accidental abstainers" (Lefkowitz, 2006). That is, they remain virgins longer because they have chosen to wait rather than because they had no opportunity for sex. Common reasons for abstaining are fear of pregnancy, fear of STDs, religious or moral beliefs, and the feeling one has not yet met the right person (Lefkowitz, Gillen, Shearer, & Boone, 2004; Sprecher & Regan, 1996).

Sexual behavior in emerging adulthood most commonly takes place in the context of a close romantic relationship (Lefkowitz, 2006). However, emerging adults are more likely adults in older age groups to engage in recreational sex or "hooking up." In one study, 30% of emerging adult college students reported having at least one episode of hooking up that included intercourse, and an additional 48% reported at least one episode of hooking up that did not involve intercourse (Paul, McManus, & Hayes, 2000). Male emerging adults are more likely than females to have sexual attitudes that favor recreational sex. They tend to be more likely than females to be willing to have intercourse with someone they have known for only a few hours, to have sex with two different partners in the same day, and to have sex with someone they do not love (Knox, Sturdivant, & Zusman, 2001).

Frequently, episodes of hooking up are lubricated by alcohol. In various studies, from one fourth to one half of emerging adults report having consumed alcohol before their most recent sexual encounter (Lefkowitz, 2006), and emerging adults who drink often are more likely than others to have had multiple sexual partners (Santelli et al., 1998). The college environment is especially conducive to hooking up since it brings together so many emerging adults in a common setting that includes frequent social events involving alcohol use (Sperber, 2001).

Most emerging adults are quite responsible about contraceptive use. Only 6% of sexually active emerging adults report never using contraception, although an additional one fourth report inconsistent or ineffective contraceptive use (Civic, 1999; Hogben & Williams, 2001). Over 80% report using condoms during a hookup (Corbin & Fromme, 2002; Paul et al., 2000). As a romantic relationship develops between emerging adults, they often move from condom use to oral contraceptives because they believe sex feels better without a condom or because switching to oral contraceptives signifies a deeper level of trust and commitment (Hammer et al., 1996; Lefkowitz, 2006).

Sex in emerging adulthood may be fun and may be viewed by most of them as a normal and enjoyable part of life, but that does not mean it is without problems. The long period between the initiation of sexual activity in adolescence and the entry to marriage in young adulthood typically includes a series of romantic partners as well as occasional episodes of hooking up, and in the course of these years unintended pregnancies are not unusual. Although responsible contraceptive use is the norm among emerging adults, inconsistent and ineffective use of contraception is common enough to make emerging adulthood the age period when both abortion and nonmarital childbirth are most common (Jones, Darroch, & Henshaw, 2002; Singh, Darroch, & Frost, 2001). Emerging adulthood is also the peak period for sexually transmitted diseases, as we will see in detail in the next section.

Sexually Transmitted Diseases

"Today, you basically want the blood test before you go to bed with somebody. I don't think I would ever have unprotected sex, meaning without a condom. I've always known a lot about AIDS. I certainly wouldn't want to put my life in jeopardy for something like that."

—Gabriela, age 22 (in Arnett, 2004a, p. 91)

"I slept with this one guy one time—one guy, one time—and we actually didn't use anything, and I don't know why. We were both being stupid. . . . [After my next ob/gyn exam] they called me and said I was positive for chlamydia. That just shook me up because I couldn't believe that would happen to me."

—Holly, age 23 (in Arnett, 2004a, p. 93)

"[When I first found out I had herpes] it affected me a lot. A lot. It just really threw me for a loop. I was just like, 'Okay, scarred for life.' I feel really cheated somehow, but at the same I'm going to have to live with it. That's just the way it is."

—Freda, age 22 (in Arnett, 2004a, p. 93)

In addition to the problem of unwanted pregnancy, sex in adolescence and emerging adulthood carries a relatively high risk of sexually transmitted diseases (STDs). Few young people have sex with numerous partners, but as we have seen, "hooking up" occasionally with a temporary partner is quite common among adolescents and emerging adults. Even where sex takes place in a committed relationship, most youthful love relationships do not endure for long. Young people typically get involved in a relationship, it lasts for a few months, sometimes sexual intercourse is part of it, and then they break up and move on. In this way, young people gain experience with love and sex. Unfortunately, having sex with a variety of people, even if only one at a time, carries with it a substantial risk for STDs, as Table 9.6 shows. Consequently, many adolescents and emerging adults experience STDs. By age 24, one in three sexually active Americans have contracted an STD

(Boyer et al., 1999). One half of STDs in the United States occur in people who are aged 15–24 (Weinstock et al., 2004).

TABLE 9.6 Estimated Prevalence of Selected STDs Among 15–25 Year-Olds in the United States

STD	Prevalence
Chlamydia	1.0 million
Genital herpes	4.2 million
HPV	9.2 million

Source: Weinstock & Cates (2004).

The symptoms and consequences of STDs vary widely, from the merely annoying (pubic lice or "crabs") to the deadly (HIV/AIDS). In between these extremes, many other STDs leave young women at higher risk for later infertility because the female reproductive system is much more vulnerable than the male reproductive system to most STDs and their consequences (King, 2005). Another cause for concern about STDs is that rates of STDs are especially high among Black and Latino young people living in America's urban areas (CDCP, 2002; DiClemente & Crosby, 2003), in part because rates of STD-promoting behaviors such as intravenous drug use and unsafe sex are higher in these populations.

Two other general characteristics of STDs bear mentioning before we discuss specific STDs. One is that many people who have STDs are **asymptomatic**, meaning that they show no symptoms of the disease. Under these circumstances, they are especially likely to infect others because neither they nor others realize that they are infected. Second, some STDs (such as herpes and HIV) have a **latency period** that can last for years. This means that there may be years between the time people are infected and the time they begin to show symptoms, and during this time they may be infecting others without either themselves or their partners being aware of it.

Now we will consider briefly some of the major STDs: chlamydia, human papillomavirus (HPV), herpes, and HIV/AIDS.

THINKING CRITICALLY •••

Do you think adolescents and emerging adults would be more likely to use condoms if they knew that many people who have STDs are asymptomatic? Why or why not?

Chlamydia Chlamydia is one of the most common STDs, and the highest rates are among adolescents and emerging adults. Of reported cases in the United States, 74% occur in persons aged 15–24 (Weinstock et al., 2004). It is estimated to infect 1 in 7 adolescent females and 1 in 10 adolescent males,

with rates of up to 20% found on college campuses. Chlamydia is the leading cause of female infertility, in part because if left untreated it can develop into pelvic inflammatory disease (PID), which in turn causes infertility. Twenty to 40 percent of women with chlamydia develop PID (King, 2005).

Chlamydia is highly infectious, with 70% of women and 25% of men contracting the disease during a single sexual episode with an infected partner. Seventy-five percent of women and 25% of men with the disease are asymptomatic (Cates, 1999). When symptoms occur, they include pain during urination, pain during intercourse, and pain in the lower abdomen. Chlamydia can usually be treated effectively with antibiotics, but in recent years antibiotics have become less effective because widespread use has led to evolutionary adaptations in chlamydia that make it more resistant (King, 2005).

Human Papillomavirus (HPV) HPV infects cells on the surface of the body, especially on the penis and anus in men and the cervix, vagina, vulva, and anus in women. There are a wide variety of HPV infections, but they can be divided into two general categories: asymptomatic infections and genital warts. HPV is the most common STD, with one third of American women infected by age 24 (Brown, 2007). However, over 9 of 10 of HPV cases are asymptomatic, and at least 80% of asymptomatic cases disappear on their own within several months. For people who develop genital warts as a consequence of HPV, the first symptoms appear from three weeks to eight months after sexual contact with an infected partner. The warts result in itching, irritation, and bleeding.

Various treatments are available for genital warts, from medicines that cause the warts to dry up to laser surgery. However, none of the treatments attacks the underlying virus, so recurrences are common. Worse yet, women who carry the virus have a greatly increased risk of developing cervical cancer, even though it may take 5 to 25 years to develop. For these women, it is especially important to have regular pelvic exams so that if cervical cancer appears it can be detected early enough to be treated effectively.

Recently, a vaccine has been developed that prevents HPV. The vaccine is highly effective, but it is just beginning to be distributed. Public health advocates in many Western countries are vigorously advocating vaccination of girls in early adolescence, before they become sexually active (Kahn, 2007; Woodhall et al., 2007). The vaccine holds the potential for eliminating HPV, if it becomes universal.

Herpes Simplex Herpes simplex is an STD caused by a virus. It has two variations. Herpes simplex I (HSV-1) is characterized by sores on the mouth and face. Herpes simplex II (HSV-2) is characterized by sores on the genitals. The disease is highly infectious, and it is estimated that 75% of persons exposed to an infected partner become infected themselves

---

asymptomatic A condition common with STDs in which an infected person shows no symptoms of the disease but may potentially infect others.

latency period A period, common with STDs, between the time a person is infected with a disease and the time symptoms appear.

(Carroll & Wolpe, 1996). About 10% of 14- to 19-year-old Americans have HSV-2, but rates have decreased over the past decade (Xu, 2006).

Symptoms appear anywhere from 1 day to 1 month after infection. First, there is a tingling or burning sensation in the infected area, followed by the appearance of sores. The sores last 3 to 6 weeks and can be painful. Blisters may appear along with the sores, and they eventually burst and emit a yellowish liquid. Other symptoms include fever, headaches, itching, and fatigue. These other symptoms peak within 4 days of the appearance of the blisters.

After the sores and blisters heal, the majority of people with herpes have at least one recurrent episode, with the symptoms for women being especially intense and enduring. Treatment within 4 days of initial symptoms reduces the chance of recurrent episodes (Carroll & Wolpe, 1996). Various drugs have been developed to relieve the symptoms and speed up the healing process during an episode (King, 2005). However, currently there is no cure for herpes. Once people are infected, the chance of a recurrent episode is ever present, and women with herpes are at risk for cervical cancer and for transmitting the virus to their babies during childbirth. For this reason, psychological distress, including anxiety, guilt, anger, and depression, frequently results when herpes is diagnosed (Aral, Vanderplate, & Madger, 1988). Nevertheless, because herpes is infectious mainly when an episode is occurring, the disease can be managed if the person has an understanding and supportive partner (Longo et al., 1988).

HIV/AIDS

"It's a really scary thing right now. If for some reason you're not careful or you forget to use protection, you're like paranoid for a long time, until you get tested. Nobody that I know has [HIV] right now, but everybody's scared about it. You never know for sure."

—Holly, age 18 (in Bell, 1998, p. 119)

The STDs discussed so far have been around for a long time, but HIV/AIDS appeared only recently, first diagnosed in 1981 (King, 2005). In this STD, the human immunodeficiency virus (HIV) causes acquired immune deficiency syndrome (AIDS), which strips the body of its ability to fend off infections. Without this ability, the body is highly vulnerable to a wide variety of illnesses and diseases.

HIV is transmitted through bodily fluids, including semen, vaginal fluid, and blood. The virus typically enters the body through the rectum, vagina, or penis, during anal or vaginal intercourse. Another common form of transmission is through shared needles among intravenous drug users. Ninety percent of cases of HIV infection in the United States result from intercourse between homosexual or bisexual partners (CDCP, 1999), but outside the West HIV/AIDS is spread mainly between heterosexual partners (Ashford, 2002). The reasons for this difference are not clear. As with most other STDs, women are more vulnerable than men to the transmission of HIV/AIDS.

HIV/AIDS has an unusually long latency period. After the HIV virus is acquired, people who contract it tend to be asymptomatic for at least 5 years before the symptoms of AIDS appear, and in some cases as long as 10 years (King, 2005). Thus, few adolescents have AIDS, but the incidence of AIDS rises sharply in the early 20s, and cases of AIDS that appear in these years occur mostly in people who contracted the HIV virus in their teens. The incidence of AIDS has risen dramatically since it was first diagnosed in 1981, and by the mid-1990s it was the leading cause of death among Americans aged 25 to 44 (CDCP, 1999). Rates of HIV/AIDS are especially high among homeless adolescents (Rosenthal & Rotheram-Borus, 2005; Whitbeck & Hoyt, 1999) and among minority adolescents living in America's urban areas (Smith et al., 1993). AIDS has been most devastating in southern Africa, where 10 of every 11 new HIV infections worldwide take place and where more than one fourth of young people are infected in some countries, as Figure 9.7 shows (Bankole et al., 2004). Prevalence of AIDS is also rising dramatically in Russia, India, and China, especially among the young (United Nations Programme on HIV/AIDS, 2003).

No symptoms are evident when a person first contracts HIV, but evidence of HIV can be identified in a blood test about 6 weeks after infection. Later during the HIV latency period, a person may experience flu-like symptoms including fever, sore throat, fatigue, and swollen lymph nodes in the neck and armpits. After this initial outbreak of symptoms, no further evidence of the disease may appear until years later. Once AIDS does appear, it is usually in the form of symptoms of unusual diseases that people rarely get unless there is something seriously wrong with their immune system. AIDS-specific symptoms include wasting syndrome, in which the person loses a great deal of body weight and becomes extremely emaciated.

AIDS has proven to be extremely difficult to treat because the virus has the ability to change itself and thus render medications ineffective. However, in recent years effective drug treatments for prolonging the lives of AIDS sufferers have begun to be developed. Nevertheless, the mortality rate

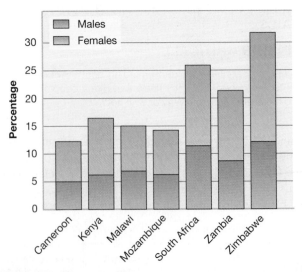

FIGURE 9.7 Estimated percentage of 15- to 25-year-olds with AIDS in selected African countries.

Source: Bankole et al. (2004).

for people who have AIDS remains extremely high. In Africa, where the prevalence of AIDS is greatest, the most effective drugs are rarely available. Intervention programs to reduce HIV risk among adolescents have now been conducted in many developing countries but with limited effectiveness (Bankole et al., 2004; Magnussen et al., 2004).

HIV/AIDS is having a devastating effect on life in Africa, especially for young people. Already 10 million African children under age 15 have lost their mother or both parents to AIDS, and 90% of the world's total of AIDS orphans are in Africa (Bankole et al., 2004). The AIDS epidemic will affect young Africans mainly in three ways (Bartholet, 2000; Nsamenang, 2002). First, many of them will be required to assume the leadership of their families due to their parents' deaths. Second, many of them will be forced into even deeper poverty by their parents' deaths and may end up joining the millions of AIDS orphans who have already become street children in African cities, where they are vulnerable to illness, malnutrition, and sexual exploitation. Third, many young Africans will become AIDS victims themselves in the 21st century if vast changes are not made soon in the prevalence of safe sex practices.

After this long litany of STDs and their consequences, are you feeling concerned? Well, if you are a sexually active emerging adult, you should be. Emerging adulthood is by far the age period when the risks of contracting STDs are greatest because emerging adults are so much more likely than persons in other age groups to have sex with a variety of partners (King, 2005). Hopefully, the information presented here will be enough to inspire you to have regular medical exams if you are sexually active. Young women in particular should receive regular pelvic exams and Pap smears because they are at higher risk than young men for virtually all STDs.

Sex Education

One might think that with such high rates of pregnancy and STDs in adolescence and emerging adulthood there would be a broad consensus in the United States to do a better job at educating young people to avoid these problems. However, the issues are never so simple and clear when it comes to Americans and sexuality. Nowhere is the American ambivalence about adolescent sex so evident as on the topic of sex education (Crockett et al., 2002).

True, a broad consensus exists in American society that high rates of premarital pregnancy and STDs in adolescence are serious problems that must be reduced. However, there is vehement disagreement about what the solution to these problems might be. On one side are the proponents of **comprehensive sexuality education**, who advocate sex education programs beginning at an early age that include detailed information on sexual development and sexual behavior, with easy access to contraception for adolescents who choose to become sexually active. On the other side are the opponents of sexuality education, who advocate programs that promote abstinence until marriage and who believe that sex education programs encourage promiscuity and are a symptom of the moral breakdown of American society. In between

Some studies have found school-based health clinics to be effective in lowering rates of adolescent pregnancy.

are America's adolescents, growing up in a socialization environment that includes both messages, and often choosing the "middle ground" of having premarital sex but not acknowledging their sexuality, thus failing to plan ahead for it and to use contraception responsibly.

School-based sex education programs must deal with this ambivalence and with the sharply divided opinions that may exist among the parents of the children they teach. Most schools do have some type of sex education program. As of the year 2000, 70% of American adolescents attending public schools received some type of sex education course (Landry, Singh, & Darroch, 2000).

Individual school systems in the United States usually choose the content of their sex education programs, resulting in a great deal of variability in the length and content of what children and adolescents are taught. Most often, such programs simply include information about the anatomy and physiology of sexual development, often as part of a biology or physical education course, perhaps along with a little information about STDs (DiClemente & Crosby, 2003). Most of the programs avoid topics such as abortion and sexual orientation, and only one third of sex education programs discuss sexual behavior at all (SIECUS, 2003). Less than 10% of American adolescents receive comprehensive sexuality education by the time they leave high school (SIECUS, 2003).

Analyses of the effectiveness of sex education programs in the United States have generally found that the programs often increase adolescents' knowledge of their anatomy, their physiology, and (where included) contraception. Unfortunately, overall the programs often have little effect on (1) communication with partners or parents about sex or contraception, (2) frequency of sexual intercourse, or (3) use of contraception (Kirby, 2000; Kohler, Manhart, & Lafferty, 2008). However, because the programs vary so much across

comprehensive sexuality education Sex education programs that begin at an early age and include detailed information on sexual development and sexual behavior, with easy access to contraception for adolescents who choose to become sexually active.

the United States, talking about the "overall" effects of sex education is misleading. Programs that focus on knowledge have little influence on adolescents' sexual behavior, but more extensive programs have often been found to be effective.

One report reviewed dozens of sex education programs and concluded that 10 characteristics make such programs work (Kirby, 2001):

1. Focus narrowly on reducing one or more sexual behaviors that lead to unintended pregnancy or HIV/AIDS infection.

2. Base the program on theoretical approaches developed to treat other risky behavior, such as cognitive behavioral theory, which rewards changes in thought and behavior.

3. Give a clear message about sexual activity and condom or contraceptive use and continually reinforce that message.

4. Provide basic, accurate information about risks and methods to avoid pregnancy and STDs.

5. Include activities that teach how to deal with social pressures, such as information that helps them refute frequently used lines like "everybody does it" or activities that generate peer support for withstanding social pressures.

6. Model and provide practice in negotiation and refusal skills, such as how to say no, how to insist on condoms or other contraception, and how to make sure body language supports the verbal message.

7. Use a variety of teaching methods to involve participants and personalize the information.

8. Incorporate behavioral goals, teaching methods, and materials that are specific to the age, culture, and sexual experience of the students.

9. Run the program over a sufficient period of time (at least 14 hours spread over several weeks).

10. Train teachers, youth workers, or peer leaders (generally for at least 6 hours) who believe in the program.

In recent years in the United States, much attention and money have been devoted to sex education programs that promote abstinence, encouraging adolescents to wait until marriage before having sexual intercourse. For the most part, programs that include only abstinence education have been found to be ineffective in decreasing rates of intercourse among adolescents (Kohler et al., 2008). A recent review of 56 studies compared abstinence-only programs and comprehensive sexuality education (CSE) programs (Kirby, 2008). Most abstinence programs did not delay initiation of sexual intercourse, and only three of nine had a significant positive effect on any sexual behavior. In contrast, about two thirds of comprehensive programs showed strong evidence that they positively affected young people's sexual behavior, including both delaying initiation of sexual intercourse and increasing condom and contraceptive use.

---

abstinence-plus programs Sex education programs that encourage adolescents to delay intercourse while also providing contraceptive information for adolescents who nevertheless choose to have intercourse.

Although abstinence-only sex education programs are usually ineffective, some of the most effective sex education programs have been **abstinence-plus programs** that encourage adolescents to delay intercourse while also providing contraceptive information for adolescents who nevertheless choose to have intercourse (Dionne, 1999; Haffner, 1998). Critics of these programs argue that this is a mixed message and that providing information about contraception undermines the message of abstinence. Nevertheless, the success of these programs suggests that adolescents are able to choose the message that appeals most to them personally. This is the approach most Americans support. In a national survey, 69% of adults and 67% of teens stated a preference for sex education programs that encourage teens to abstain from sex but also provide contraceptive information (National Campaign to Prevent Teen Pregnancy, 2002). It appears that, in a society with such mixed messages about adolescent sexuality, a mixed-message sex education program may work best.

SUMMING UP

In this chapter we have covered a variety of topics related to dating, love, and sexuality. Here are the main points we have discussed:

- Romantic relationships tend to begin with mixed-sex groups in early adolescence and develop into romantic partnerships by late adolescence. Most American adolescents have their first romantic relationships in their early teens. In Western countries, dating has been replaced in recent years by more informal ways of meeting potential romantic partners and establishing a relationship. Young people in Eastern countries tend to be discouraged from dating until they are looking seriously for a marriage partner.

- Sternberg's theory of love describes a variety of types of love derived from combinations of passion, commitment, and intimacy. Adolescent love usually lacks long-term commitment, so it is most often characterized by infatuation or romantic love. Adolescents in non-Western cultures also experience passion, but many cultures restrict adolescents' expressions of passionate love because they believe that marriage should be based on family interests rather than individual choice.

- With respect to their views on adolescent sexuality, cultures can be generally classified as restrictive, semirestrictive, or permissive. The United States today is probably best classified as semirestrictive, with a great deal of ambivalence and divided opinions about adolescent sexuality.

- Adolescent sexual activity tends to follow a progression that begins with masturbation, followed by kissing and necking, sexual intercourse, and oral sex. Having first intercourse at age 15 or younger tends to be associated with problems such as higher rates of drug and alcohol use. American adolescents tend to use contraceptives inconsistently, owing to deep ambivalence about adolescent sexuality.

- Gay, lesbian, and bisexual (GLB) adolescents often have difficulty coping with their sexual orientation in a culture that stigmatizes homosexuality. Consequently, they are more likely than other adolescents to have problems of suicide, substance abuse, school difficulties, and running away from home. However, acceptance of homosexuality has risen substantially in recent years, especially among young people.
- Most American emerging adults have had sexual intercourse at least once in the past year, but they are more likely than other adults to have had either two or more partners or no partner. Most sex in emerging adulthood takes place between romantic partners, but recreational sex or "hooking up" is also common, frequently involving alcohol use.
- Sexually transmitted diseases contracted by adolescents and emerging adults include chlamydia, HPV, herpes simplex, and HIV/AIDS. Rates of all these STDs are especially high in emerging adulthood.
- Sex education is controversial in American society. Most sex education programs are ineffective, but comprehensive sexuality programs and "abstinence-plus" programs are effective in delaying initiation of sexual intercourse and increasing contraceptive use.

One striking characteristic of research on sexuality in adolescence and emerging adulthood is that it is so heavily weighted toward the problems that can arise from premarital sexual contact, such as unwanted pregnancies and STDs. This emphasis is understandable, given the profound effects that these problems can have on young people's lives. Still, such an emphasis can leave a distorted impression of how young people experience sexuality. If you knew nothing about sex except what you read in academic studies of adolescents, you would never guess that sex can be pleasurable. It is true that young people's sexuality can be a source of difficulties and problems, but what about sexuality as a source of enjoyment? What positive feelings and thoughts do adolescents and emerging adults have as they experience kissing, necking, petting, and intercourse? How are love and sex related in young people's relationships? In what ways does sexual contact enhance emotional intimacy between young people in love? We need to learn much more about these questions in order to have a complete picture of love and sexuality among adolescents and emerging adults.

KEY TERMS

INTERNET RESOURCES

http://alanguttmacher.org
Web site for the Alan Guttmacher Institute, a research and public policy organization focused on issues related to sexuality. Includes a special link on adolescents, with information on STDs, pregnancy rates, access to contraception, sex education, and many other topics. Also contains a great deal of international information on adolescent sexuality.

http://www.siecus.org
Web site for the Sexuality Information and Education Council of the United States (SIECUS). This group conducts research and disseminates information on sexuality, especially related to adolescents. It especially focuses on promoting comprehensive sexuality education for adolescents. The site contains many useful SIECUS reports.

http://marriage.rutgers.edu
Web site of the National Marriage Project at Rutgers University, directed by David Popenoe and Barbara Whitehead. Contains a wealth of information about love in emerging adulthood, including many research publications that can be downloaded free.

FOR FURTHER READING

Hatfield, E., & Rapson, R. L. (2005). *Love & sex: Cross-cultural perspectives*. Boston: Allyn & Bacon. A lively, fascinating account of beliefs and behavior on love and sex around the world, including material related to adolescents and emerging adults.

For more review plus practice tests, videos, flashcards, and more, log on to MyDevelopmentLab.

10 CHAPTER School

14-year-old Mike is slouching his way through another day of earth science. Around him, other students sit listening to the teacher and leafing through their textbooks, the thin white pages rustling softly through the room. He makes no pretense of following the lesson, however. He has not even bothered to take a book off the shelf. The teacher's trying to get him to join the rest of the class, but he's ignoring her. . . .

In a room at the end of B wing, an English teacher with short gray hair and a sly smile sits perched on a stool in front of one of her senior advanced placement classes. By tomorrow, she says, she wants the class to have read the final act of Henrik Ibsen's *A Doll's House.*

A collective moan rises from the desks.

"Is that so much?" says [the teacher]. "One lousy act?"

Down the aisles, the kids mimic her in high-pitched, singsongy voices usually reserved for imitating parents.

"Is that so much? One lousy act?"

[The teacher] fights back a smirk, trying her best to look stern. This is a game that she and her seniors play. She assigns a reading, they pretend to pitch a fit, she pretends to be shocked. But tomorrow, when the bell rings and they take their seats, she knows—and they know she knows—that most if not all of them will have read the one lousy act and will be prepared to dissect it with ruthless efficiency. These are advanced placement kids. This year they will read, among other things, *Hamlet, Macbeth, Othello, Antigone, Medea, Lord of the Flies, Wuthering Heights, Lord Jim,* and Albert Camus's *The Stranger.* Furthermore, some of them will like it. (French, 1993, pp. 21, 151)

THESE SCENES, TAKEN FROM A BOOK BY JOURNALIST Thomas French (1993), provide an illustration of what occurs in a typical American **secondary school** (including middle school, junior high school, and high school). It is a place that contains all sorts of students, with a vast range of interests and abilities. With nearly all of them, teachers wage a daily struggle to keep them engaged in learning, with only intermittent success. School competes for adolescents' attention with family problems, part-time work, media stimulation, and the many allurements of leisure with friends. Schools also struggle against the ambivalence of Americans' beliefs about adolescence. Most Americans want adolescents to succeed in school and learn what they need to prepare themselves for work (or at least for further education), but most Americans also want adolescence to be a time when young people are free to enjoy life to the fullest before the responsibilities of adulthood arrive.

In other industrialized countries, secondary education tends to be more demanding than it is in the United States,

in part because performance in secondary school is much more significant in determining what kind of job an adolescent will be able to obtain in adulthood. However, in countries that are not yet industrialized, many adolescents do not go to secondary school at all or drop out before finishing, because their families need their labor and because the long-term economic benefits of attending secondary school are uncertain.

In this chapter we examine young people's school experiences in the past and present in secondary schools and in colleges and universities in the United States and other countries. The chapter begins with a historical account of the rise of secondary schooling. This history is important because secondary schooling is relatively recent as a standard part of adolescence and because it would be difficult to understand secondary schools today without knowing how they developed. Following this history, we look at secondary education around the world, including international comparisons of academic performance.

An American high school.

and adolescents who drop out of high school. At the end of the chapter we turn our attention to emerging adulthood and examine the characteristics of today's college students, the factors related to success and failure in college, and college students' accounts of their educational experiences.

The Rise of Schooling for Adolescents

Compulsory secondary school education is relatively recent. Until about a hundred years ago, most American states did not have any laws requiring children to attend school beyond the primary grades. It was during the Age of Adolescence (1890 to 1920) that this changed dramatically. During this time, states began to pass laws requiring school attendance through the early teens, and the proportion of 14- to 17-year-olds in school rose from just 5% in 1890 to 30% by 1920 (Arnett & Taber, 1994). The trend did not stop there. By 1970, the proportion of 14- to 17-year-olds in school had risen to 90%, and it has remained over 90% since that time (see Figure 10.1).

In other Western countries, a similar trend occurred during these decades. Schooling became the normative experience for adolescents, and an increasing proportion of emerging adults also remained in school. For example, in Norway, as recently as 1950 only 20% of adolescents continued school past age 15; today education is compulsory until age 16, and 90% of 16- to 18-year-olds are still in school (Hansen & Wold, 2006).

American schools are extremely diverse, in part because the United States has no national educational policy as other industrialized countries do. Although the overall quality of American secondary education is troubling in many ways, many schools do succeed, and we spend part of this chapter looking at the characteristics of effective schools. We also examine adolescents' school achievement in the context of the rest of their lives. Scholars have concluded that adolescents' academic performance is related in crucial ways to their family relationships, friendships, and work and leisure patterns. We also consider the role of cultural beliefs in what is required from adolescents academically.

Just as schools vary in their effectiveness, adolescents vary in their academic achievement. We focus especially on ethnic differences and gender differences in achievement, two areas that have been the focus of much research. We also consider the characteristics of adolescents who are at the extremes of achievement: gifted adolescents, adolescents with disabilities, adolescents who are in lower academic tracks,

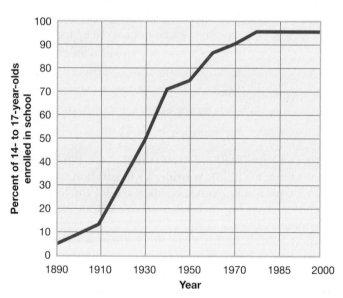

FIGURE 10.1 Increasing enrollment in high school, 1890 to the present, United States.

Sources: Tanner (1972); Arnett & Taber (1994); NCES (2002).

---

secondary school The schools attended by adolescents, usually including a lower secondary school and an upper secondary school.

comprehensive high school The form of the American high school that arose in the 1920s and is still the main form today, which encompasses a wide range of functions and includes classes in general education, college preparation, and vocational training.

TABLE 10.1	Changes in Secondary School Enrollment in Selected Countries, 1980–2000			
	% Enrolled 1980		% Enrolled Latest Year	
	Males	Females	Males	Females
United States	91	92	98	97
Germany	93	87	99	99
Italy	73	70	94	95
Poland	75	80	98	97
Argentina	53	62	73	81
Egypt	66	41	83	73
China	54	37	74	67
Turkey	44	24	68	48
Mexico	51	46	64	64
India	39	20	59	39
Nigeria	25	13	36	30

Note: Percentages reflect the proportion of students enrolled in secondary school in the applicable age group in each country.

Source: Population Reference Bureau (2000).

In contrast, even now adolescents often do not attend school in societies that are not industrialized. In those societies, education beyond childhood is only for the elite (just as it was in the West a century ago). Adolescents are usually engaged in productive work rather than attending school. Their labor is needed by their families, and they can best learn the skills needed for adult work by working alongside adults rather than by attending school. However, these patterns are changing in many countries due to growing economic development. Virtually everywhere in the world, countries and cultures that were not industrialized 50 or more years ago are now becoming industrialized and entering the global economy. One consequence of economic development in these countries is that adolescents are increasingly likely to remain in school. Table 10.1 shows the changes in secondary school enrollment that have taken place over the past 20 years in various countries. Economic development introduces agricultural technologies that make children's and adolescents' labor less necessary to the family, while staying in school brings increasing economic benefits because more jobs become available that require educational skills.

The effects of economic development on adolescents' education in developing countries also are evident in the literacy of today's adolescents compared with their parents and grandparents (Bloom & Brender, 1993). For example, in Egypt, 74% of males aged 15 to 19 can read and write, compared with just 30% of males aged 65 and older; among females, 59% of girls aged 15 to 19 can read and write, compared with just 9% of women aged 65 and older. In Thailand, 97% of males aged 15 to 19 can read and write, compared with 58% of males aged 65 and older; among females,

95% of girls aged 15 to 19 can read and write, compared with just 22% of women aged 65 and older. This suggests that as economic development continues in developing countries, the proportion of adolescents receiving education will continue to rise.

Changes in Schooling for Adolescents

Not only has the proportion of adolescents attending secondary school in the United States changed dramatically in the past century, but the kinds of things adolescents learn in school have changed as well. An examination of these changes is useful for understanding the requirements that exist for adolescents today.

In the 19th century, when few adolescents attended school, secondary education was mainly for the wealthy. The curriculum was constructed to provide young people (mainly males) with a broad liberal arts education—history, art, literature, science, philosophy, Latin, and Greek—with no specific economic purpose (Church, 1976). By 1920, following the steep rise in the proportion of young people attending secondary school, there was a widespread consensus that educational reform was needed. The composition of the student population in secondary schools had changed from the privileged few to a broad cross section of the American population, many of whom were recent immigrants, and it was necessary to adapt the content of secondary education to respond to this change. Thus, the central goal of American secondary education shifted from education for its own sake to more practical goals focusing on training for work and citizenship. It was in the 1920s that the framework for the American high school as we know it today was established, designed to educate a diverse population of adolescents for life in American society. Rather than being restricted to the liberal arts, education in the **comprehensive high school** (as it came to be known) includes classes in general education, college preparation, and vocational training.

Between the 1920s and the middle of the 20th century, the proportion of young people attending secondary school continued to expand, and the diversity of the high school curriculum continued to expand as well. Now the curriculum was enlarged to include preparation for family life and leisure, with courses available on music, art, health, and physical education.

Since the 1950s, periodic cries of alarm have been sounded over the ineffectiveness of American schools, with much of the alarm focusing on the education of adolescents in secondary schools. In the late 1950s and early 1960s, concern focused on the perceived deficiencies of science education in the schools. In the early 1970s, the social upheaval of the previous decade led various committees of educational experts to heap blame on American high schools for the alienation and disillusionment of American young people. The problem, according to these committees, was that the education provided by high schools was too far removed from real life (Church, 1976; Coleman, 1974; Martin, 1976). *Relevance* became the new buzzword, and in pursuit of relevance high

For the most part, today's colleges and universities in Western countries extol independent thinking and intellectual exploration. Although it may be tempting to think that these values are inherently part of the educational mission of higher education, a look at the colleges and universities of a hundred years ago demonstrates that these are values based in cultural beliefs of individualism. A comparison of universities then and now shows how much has changed in American higher education as well as in American cultural beliefs. This comparison was the subject of an essay by Dennis O'Brien (1997).

A century ago, the mission of most colleges and universities was grounded explicitly in religious beliefs. Courses in religious instruction were not only required but considered central to the curriculum. For example, the 1896–1897 catalog of Lafayette College stated, "It is intended that the Bible shall be the central object of study throughout the [student's education]. It is dealt with reverently as the Word of God and as the inspired and infallible rule which God gives to His people."

Colleges and universities required not only religious study, but also religious practice—and not only at private colleges but at public universities as well. For example, at the University of North Dakota, every day began with a brief service in the chapel—with all students required to attend—featuring the singing of hymns, readings from the Bible, and recitation of the Lord's Prayer. The University of Maine required all students to attend daily morning prayer in the chapel. Missing 15% or more of these prayer sessions would lead to admonition by the president; if attendance did not improve, the student would be censured by the faculty.

Over the course of the 20th century, as the power of religious institutions waned and individualism became stronger as the basis of the cultural beliefs of the American majority culture, colleges and universities gradually ceased to promote religious beliefs. Instead, individualism became the basis of universities' educational mission. For example, according to Gettysburg College's mission statement for 1997, the goal of the college is to help students learn to "appreciate our common humanity in terms of such positive values as open-mindedness, personal responsibility, [and] mutual respect. . . . Students may develop greater freedom of choice among attitudes." The values stated are predominantly individualistic ones. Similarly, the University of North Dakota's 1997 catalog states that "education concerning values is important in general education—not seeking one right way to behave, but recognizing that choices cannot be avoided. Students should be aware of how many choices they make, how these choices are based on values, and how to make informed choices." Again, the individualistic values behind the university's mission are evident. The goal of most higher education today is not to communicate a specific way of looking at the world, but to teach students how to make "informed choices" as individuals, by themselves.

schools were encouraged to develop programs that would involve less time in the traditional classroom and more time learning skills in the workplace, obtaining direct occupational training and experience.

In the 1980s, a new alarm was sounded. Evidence began accumulating that students' educational achievement scores had declined since the 1960s. New committees of educational experts were formed, and they arrived at a new diagnosis. The problem? All this relevance had reduced the rigor of American education, according to the experts (National Commission on Excellence in Education, 1983). Relevance became the problem rather than the solution, and "back to basics" became the popular new battle cry. The critics advocated more stringent requirements for high school students to take courses in math, science, and English, along with more homework, tighter discipline, and a longer school year. The back-to-basics movement continued through the 1990s with calls for more rigorous and demanding high school curriculums (National Education Commission on Time and Learning, 1994). The amount of time per year that American adolescents spend in school has increased, and 20 states now have "exit exams" to ensure that adolescents who graduate from high school have obtained at least a minimal level of basic academic skills (NCES, 2005).

THINKING CRITICALLY ●●●

In your view, should high school courses be offered only on academic subjects such as math and English, or should courses in music, art, and physical education also be available? Justify your view.

The Diversity of American Education Something to keep in mind as you read about all of these educational reform movements over the past 50 years is that none of them has had much direct power to implement their proposed solutions in American schools. Unlike every other industrialized country in the world, most decisions about education in the United States are controlled on the local and state levels, not on the national level. This has always been true in the United States, and local control of schools remains an issue of great importance to many people.

Because schools are funded and controlled by states and cities rather than nationally, a great deal of variability exists across the different U.S. school districts in the curriculums they use and in school rules and requirements. School quality varies depending on the financial resources available in the school district and on what the people in the state and the district decide is the best way for children to learn.

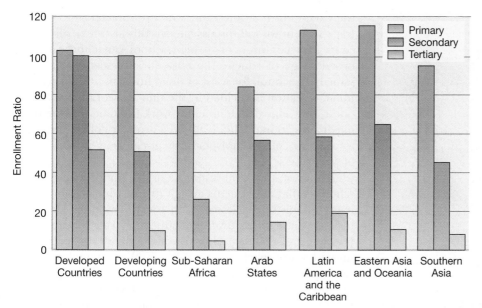

FIGURE 10.2 Educational enrollment in various world regions. (Number of students at level of schooling divided by number of people of appropriate age for that level of schooling, times 100.)

Source: Fussell & Greene (2002), p. 32.

Experts and critics can form all the committees they like and make recommendations until they turn blue, but no state or school district is obliged to comply.

Recently, however, definite steps have been taken toward establishing a national educational policy. In 1994, the federal government took a major step by establishing a national program of educational standards, through a program called "Goals 2000" (Cooper, 1999). More recently, the No Child Left Behind Act of 2001 provided billions of federal tax dollars toward a number of objectives, including national testing, new standards of teacher training, and evaluations of teaching effectiveness (Mathews, 2002a). This is the most ambitious federal educational program yet attempted, but it is only one step toward an effective national educational policy. Even with the No Child Left Behind Act of 2001, the federal government provides only about 5% of school funding, and control of schools is held mainly by local and state governments.

Secondary Education Around the World

There is a great deal of diversity worldwide in the kinds of secondary schools adolescents attend, and world regions also vary in how likely adolescents are to attend secondary school at all. There is an especially sharp contrast between industrialized countries and economically developing countries. Virtually all adolescents are enrolled in secondary school in industrialized countries. In contrast, only about 50% of adolescents in economically developing countries attend secondary school (Figure 10.2). Furthermore, tertiary education (college and university) is obtained by about half of emerging adults in industrialized countries but is only for the elite (and wealthy) 10% in developing countries. In this section

we look at secondary education first in industrialized countries and then in developing countries.

Secondary Education in Industrialized Countries The United States is unusual in having only one institution—the comprehensive high school—as the source of secondary education. Canada and Japan also have comprehensive high schools as the norm, but most other industrialized countries have several different kinds of schools that adolescents may attend. Most European countries have three types of secondary schools (Arnett, 2002b). One type is a *college-preparatory school* that is similar in many ways to the American high school in that it offers a variety of academic courses and the goal is general education rather than education for any specific profession. However, in Europe these schools do not include classes in recreational subjects such as music and physical education. In most European countries, about one half of adolescents attend this type of school. A second type of secondary school is the *vocational school*, where adolescents learn the skills involved in a specific occupation such as plumbing or auto mechanics. Usually, about one fourth of adolescents in European countries attend this type of school. Some European countries also have a third type of secondary school, a *professional school* devoted to teacher training, the arts, or some other specific purpose (Flammer & Alsaker, 2001). About one fourth of European adolescents usually attend this type of school. Some European countries, such as Germany and Switzerland, also have extensive apprenticeship systems, in which adolescents can attend a vocational or professional school part of the time and also spend time learning a profession in the workplace under the supervision of adults. We will discuss apprenticeships in more detail in the next chapter.

One consequence of the European system is that adolescents must decide at a relatively early age what direction to pursue for their education and occupation. At age 15 or 16 adolescents must decide which type of secondary school they will enter, and this decision is likely to have an enormous impact on the rest of their lives. Usually, the decision is made by adolescents in conference with their parents and teachers, based on the adolescents' interests as well as on their school performance (e.g., Motola, Sinisalo, & Guichard, 1998). Although adolescents sometimes change schools after a year or two, and adolescents who attend a vocational school sometimes attend university, these switches are rare. However, in recent years most countries have begun to offer professional colleges that students can attend after pursuing a vocational education in secondary school (Flammer & Alsaker, 2001). In addition to providing professional training, graduation from professional colleges also allows entrance to university. This has added flexibility to the system by providing young

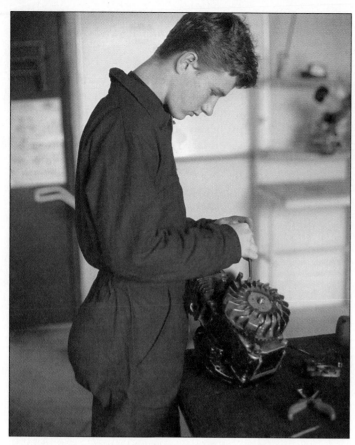

About one third of adolescents in Europe attend a vocational school. Here, a French student learns to repair engines.

people with an alternative route to university even if they did not attend the college-preparatory high school.

Nevertheless, in general the European system tends to require earlier decision making about career directions. A study by Motola et al. (1998) demonstrated how the timing of tracking (or "streaming" in European terminology) into different types of schools influences the timing of adolescents' decisions about which occupational path to pursue. They compared 11th-grade adolescents in France and Finland. French adolescents are tracked beginning at age 13, and at age 16 they must choose a stream from 5 academic and 16 technical programs, or enter a vocational high school or apprenticeship. In contrast, Finnish adolescents are in one comprehensive school until age 16, then tracked into either an upper secondary school or a vocational school. However, they are not required to make a decision about a specific occupation until they enter university or leave vocational school. In the study by Motola et al. (1998), French adolescents were three times as likely as Finnish adolescents (58% to 19%) to have a clear idea of their chosen occupation. Although no comparable data exist for Canadian and American adolescents, one might expect that they would make such choices even later than Finns, given that they typically do not have to decide on a major until the end of their second year of college or university (usually about age 20), whereas Finns must decide upon entering university.

Compared with the European system, the system of the comprehensive high school allows for greater flexibility. With the exception of adolescents who are directed into a lower track (whom we will discuss later in this chapter), all adolescents in a comprehensive high school can choose from a broad range of courses. Because all adolescents attend the same high school, for most of them little about their occupational direction is decided by the time they graduate. At that point, they may decide to enter work full-time, pursue training at a vocational school, attend a two-year college, enroll in a four-year college/university, or pursue some combination of work and school.

However, the great drawback of the comprehensive high school is that adolescents are all in the same school and in many of the same classes, even though by their mid-teens they may have widely divergent educational and occupational interests and abilities. This makes it difficult for teachers to find a level of teaching that will appeal to all adolescents. It can also be frustrating for adolescents who would prefer to be obtaining job-specific skills but are forced instead to take further years of general education (Steinberg, 1996).

Secondary Education in Developing Countries In contrast to industrialized countries, where attending secondary school is virtually universal for adolescents and the schools are well funded, in developing countries secondary education is often difficult to obtain and relatively few adolescents stay in school until graduation, as Figure 10.2 shows. In addition, the quality of the schools is often low (except for elite private schools) because they are poorly funded. Here we look at secondary education in the Arab countries of North Africa, sub-Saharan Africa, India, China, and Latin America.

In the Arab countries of North Africa (Booth, 2002), there are high rates of illiteracy among parents and grandparents—over 50% in most countries—but adolescents are much more likely than their parents or grandparents to be literate. Until recent decades, most education was oriented around the study of the Koran, the Muslim holy book, but now virtually all countries in the region have a secular educational system. Nevertheless, the influence of Islam remains very strong, and most of the secondary schools are segregated by sex, in the belief that this conforms to Islamic values. Girls are considerably less likely than boys to attend secondary school or to go on to college because their household labor is needed and because they are often subject to an early marriage arranged by their parents. Education for girls is rising as the marriage age rises and cultural values change in response to globalization (Arnett, 2002a). Still, it remains true that the long-term benefits of education go mainly to men, as few women continue to work after marriage (Booth, 2002).

Sub-Saharan Africa has the lowest rates of secondary school enrollment of any world region. However, rates of secondary school enrollment vary widely among countries, from 94% in Zimbabwe to just 3% in Rwanda and Tanzania (Population Reference Bureau, 2000). Reasons for low rates include poverty and civil war. Furthermore, the economy is not industrialized in many areas, and consequently school-based knowledge is of limited use, whereas the labor of adolescents is needed for agricultural work, animal care, household work, and child care. Rates of secondary school enrollment are especially low among girls because girls are generally not expected to enter the workplace and they have more responsibility than boys do for household work and for younger siblings.

Critics of the African educational system such as Bame Nsamenang (2002) of Cameroon argue that it is based on a model developed when European powers ruled Africa. The textbooks used are usually foreign and include little about African cultures. Rote learning is the main method of teaching. This method is not grounded in African cultures and fails to take into account their strengths. In Nsamenang's view, African educational systems should be remodeled so that they are based on indigenous African cultural practices. Adolescents should be taught not mainly in school but by working alongside adults in their daily economic activities. He believes this method would be truer to African traditions and values and would also be better suited to the current state of Africa's mostly rural and agricultural economy.

In India (Verma & Saraswathi, 2002), the educational system is similar to Africa's in that it was devised by a colonial government, in this case the British. The schools were designed on the British model—textbooks, rote learning, and exams—and English remains the main language of government and higher education. Secondary educational enrollment has grown in recent decades (see Table 10.1), but even now only about half of Indian adolescents receive secondary education. There are sharp differences in enrollment by gender, social class, and rural/urban residence. Poor girls in rural areas are the most disadvantaged. They rarely attend secondary school, and nearly 40% of them cannot even read and write (Verma & Saraswathi, 2002). However, India has a high-quality and growing system of higher education that is producing graduates with growing influence in the world economy, especially in computers and information technology (Arnett, 2002a).

The Chinese and Japanese secondary education systems are similar in many ways, although China is a developing country and Japan has one of the most advanced economies in the world (Stevenson & Zusho, 2002). In both countries, admission to university is restricted to the very highest-performing students, and consequently there is intense pressure at the high school level as students compete to prepare for the university entrance exam. Both countries also emphasize rote learning and memorization in the classroom. Both have long school days that include extensive after-school activities such as martial arts, calligraphy, and team sports. However, there are distinct differences between the two countries in educational attainment. In Japan virtually all adolescents graduate from high school, but in China less than three fourths of adolescents even attend high school (Population Reference Bureau, 2000; Stevenson & Zusho, 2002). Nevertheless, in China as in much of the rest of the world, enrollment in secondary school is rising.

Latin America, like the other developing regions we have discussed, has experienced a rise in enrollment rates in secondary education in recent decades (Welti, 2002). However, the gender gap that exists in most regions outside the West does not exist in most countries in Latin America; in fact, in

In most developing countries, boys are more likely than girls to attend secondary school, but the gap is shrinking. Here, girls in Johannesburg, South Africa.

countries such as Argentina, enrollment in secondary school is higher among girls, as Table 10.1 shows. Despite the impressive gender equality in access to secondary school, there are stark differences by social class in many Latin American countries. Public secondary schools are often overcrowded and underfunded. Consequently, most wealthy families send their adolescents to private secondary schools, which are much higher in quality. Among adolescents who attend public secondary schools there is a high dropout rate, 50% in urban areas and 75% in rural areas.

A number of common themes recur in accounts of secondary education in developing countries (Lloyd, 2005; Lloyd, Grant, & Ritchie, 2008). Most have gender differences (favoring boys) in secondary education enrollment, but the gender gap is decreasing, and all have rising rates of enrollment for both genders. That's about where the good news ends. Many of the schools are poorly funded and overcrowded. Many countries have too few teachers, and the teachers they have are insufficiently trained. Often families have to pay for secondary education, a cost they find difficult to afford, and it is typical for families to have to pay for books and other educational supplies. There tends to be one education for the elite—in exclusive private schools and well-funded universities—and a much inferior education for everyone else.

Comparing secondary education in industrialized countries and developing countries, what is most striking is how unequal educational opportunities are between the two. If you happen to be born in a developing country, you are likely to get an education through primary school but unlikely to have the resources to finish secondary school, and your chances of attending college are very small—especially if you are a girl. In contrast, if you happen to be born in an industrialized country, it is extremely likely that you will finish secondary school, and it is quite likely that you will have the opportunity to attend college if you wish—especially if you are a girl. In all parts of the world, education is the basis of many of the good things in life, from income level to physical and mental health (Lloyd, 2005; Lloyd et al., 2008; Stromquist, 2007). Yet for the majority of

TABLE 10.2 International Rankings in Reading, Math, and Science, Eighth Grade

Reading		Math		Science	
Country	Reading Score	Country	Math Score	Country	Science Score
Finland	546	South Korea	589	South Korea	558
Canada	534	Japan	570	Japan	552
New Zealand	529	Belgium	537	Hungary	543
South Korea	523	Netherlands	536	United Kingdom	538
United Kingdom	523	Canada	531	Netherlands	536
Japan	522	Hungary	529	Canada	533
Austria	507	Russian Federation	508	United States	527
France	505	United States	504	Belgium	516
United States	504	United Kingdom	496	Russian Federation	514
INTERNATIONAL AVERAGE	500	INTERNATIONAL AVERAGE	466	Italy	491
Denmark	497	Italy	484	INTERNATIONAL AVERAGE	473
Italy	487	Iran	411	Iran	453
Poland	479	Indonesia	411	Egypt	421
Russian Federation	462	Egypt	406	Indonesia	420
Mexico	422	Chile	387	Chile	413
Brazil	396	Morocco	387	Morocco	396
		South Africa	264	South Africa	244

Source: NCES (2006).

the world's adolescents and emerging adults, their educational fate was already largely determined at birth, simply on the basis of where they were born.

International Comparisons

For about 30 years, international studies have been published comparing adolescents on academic performance. Table 10.2 shows the most recent performance of adolescents in various countries around the world on 8th-grade achievement tests. The pattern of results is similar across reading, math, and science. In all three areas, the countries that tend to perform best are the industrialized countries of the West, along with Japan and South Korea. The United States tends to be around the international average, higher than developing countries but lower than most other industrialized countries. The countries below the international average are mostly developing countries in Africa, Latin America, and Asia.

The academic performance of American adolescents declined in the 1970s and 1980s but rose from the early 1990s to the present. The National Assessment of Educational Progress (NAEP), widely considered the most valid national assessment of American adolescents' academic performance, has examined students' performance since 1970 in four areas: math, science, reading, and writing. Throughout the 1970s and 1980s, the NAEP found declines in 8th grade

math, science, and reading, especially with respect to "higher-order thinking" (Newmann, 1992)—that is, thinking that requires students to interpret, analyze, and evaluate information rather than just memorize it. Students' performance on the NAEP rose during the 1990s in all areas (NCES, 2005). In the past decade, reading and science scores have changed little, but math scores have continued to rise, reaching their highest level ever in 2007 (NCES, 2008).

THINKING CRITICALLY •••

Based on what you have read so far about American and European secondary schools, what do you think explains the mixed performance of American adolescents in international comparisons?

What Works? The Characteristics of Effective Schools

Schools vary enormously, and some work better than others. Let's take a look at what educational research tells us about the characteristics of effective schools.

Does Size Matter?

What is the optimal size of schools and classes for adolescents? A considerable amount of educational research has been expended on this question. During the 20th century, as the overall population and the proportion of adolescents attending school steadily grew, the tendency was to build ever-larger schools to accommodate them. But what size school is best for the students?

Increased school size has both positives and negatives. Large schools can be alienating. In general, the larger the school, the less attachment students feel to their teachers and to the school as a whole (Crosnoe, Johnson, & Elder, 2004). However, large schools also provide advantages. Large schools have the advantage of being able to offer a more diverse range of classes than smaller schools. For example, students might benefit from having classes available on medieval literature, 19th-century novels, and 20th-century poets rather than simply one course on English literature. With respect to academic achievement, no definite relationship to school size has been found (Rutter et al., 1979; Steinberg, 1996).

Although smaller schools offer less diversity in extracurricular activities, students in smaller schools are actually *more* likely to participate in them (Crosnoe et al., 2004). At larger schools, most students end up being observers rather than participants. At smaller schools, fewer students compete for the available positions, and students are more likely to be recruited because a team or club needs somebody to fill a spot. Consequently, students at smaller schools are more likely to be placed in positions of leadership and responsibility—vice president of the drama club, treasurer of the girls' chorus, and so on. These students typically report that their participation makes them feel more confident in their abilities and more needed and important (Boyer, 1983).

All things considered, scholars have reached a consensus that the best school size for adolescents is between 500 and 1,000 students (Crosnoe et al., 2004; Entwisle, 1990)—not too small, not too large, perhaps a size that combines the best of both.

With respect to class size, however, scholars disagree. Some claim that a direct and negative relationship exists between class size and students' academic performance (Boyesen & Bru, 1999). In contrast, other scholars find that variation within the typical range—20 to 40 students—has little effect on students' achievement (McGee, 2004; Rutter, 1983). They agree that for students with academic difficulties, small classes are preferable because each student is likely to need more individual attention. However, in this view it would not benefit most students to have the size of their classes reduced from 40 to 20, and it would cost schools a great deal of money to do so.

Junior High, Middle School, or Neither?

Another issue of importance in the quality of adolescents' education is how their secondary school careers should be divided. Is it best for adolescents to attend junior high school from 7th through 9th grade, followed by high school from 10th through 12th grade? This is the 6-3-3 plan: 6 years of primary school, 3 years of junior high, and 3 years of high school. Or is it preferable for adolescents to attend middle school (rather than junior high) beginning in 6th grade, followed by a four-year high school—the 5-3-4 plan? Or would it be best to dispense with junior high and middle school altogether and have adolescents proceed directly from primary school to high school—the 8-4 plan?

A number of studies have found that in both the 6-3-3 plan and the 5-3-4 plan, the first year of middle school or junior high school is a difficult time for many young adolescents (Seidman, Aber, & French, 2004; Simmons & Blyth, 1987; Way, Reddy, & Rhodes, 2007). The main reason is that school transitions taking place in early adolescence are likely to coincide with a variety of other changes. Any of the physical changes of puberty may coincide with the school transition, such as the growth spurt, changes in body shape, and increased acne. Peer relations change, too. As we noted in Chapter 9, early adolescence often marks the beginning of romantic and sexual experimentation.

The transition to middle school or junior high school also typically involves changes in school experience. It means moving from a small, personalized classroom setting to a larger setting where a student has not one teacher but five or six or more. It also usually means moving into a setting where the academic work is at a higher level and grades are suddenly viewed as a more serious measure of academic attainment than they may have been in primary school. These changes in school experience can add to the early adolescents' anxieties and school-related stress. One recent longitudinal study of over 1,500 adolescents found a steady decline from the beginning of 6th grade to the end of 8th grade in students' perceptions of teacher support, autonomy in the classroom, and clarity of school rules and regulations (Way et al., 2007). These declines were in turn related to declines in psychological well-being and increases in behavior problems.

Because school transitions in early adolescence tend to be difficult, might it not be better to dispense with the junior high–middle school transition altogether, as in the 8-4 plan? This question was addressed in a classic study conducted by two sociologists, Roberta Simmons and Dale Blyth (1987). They studied adolescents in the Milwaukee, Wisconsin, school system over a five-year period, from 6th through 10th grade. About half of the students attended schools in districts with a 6-3-3 plan, and the other half attended schools in districts with an 8-4 plan. Simmons and Blyth focused on four aspects of adolescents' functioning: self-esteem, grade point average, extracurricular activities, and perceived anonymity (feelings of being unknown and insignificant). The results showed significant differences among students in the two types of school plans for every measure except grade point average, with the differences favoring students in the 8-4 plan.

Other studies have reported similar advantages of the 8-4 plan for outcomes such as self-esteem, school attendance, and student engagement in the classroom (Eccles et al., 1997; Seidman et al., 2004). However, the 8-4 plan remains relatively rare in American schools. It is much more common

Japan has been a frequent focus of international educational comparisons for Americans in recent decades, partly because Japan is a major economic competitor to the United States and partly because Japan is often at or near the top in international comparisons of academic achievement. Especially in math and science, Japanese children and adolescents consistently outperform Americans, and the gap grows larger with age from childhood through adolescence (McKnight et al., 1987; NCES, 2005). Furthermore, 98% of Japanese adolescents graduate from high school, a percentage higher than in any Western country, and levels of college attendance and graduation are similar to levels in the United States (Stevenson & Zusho, 2002; Takahashi & Takeuchi, 2006).

What are the characteristics of the Japanese educational system with regard to adolescents and emerging adults? One notable feature of the Japanese system is the length of the school year. Japanese adolescents attend their high schools for 243 days a year, more than American adolescents (typically about 180 days), Canadian adolescents, or adolescents in any Western European country. Japanese secondary education is also notable for how smoothly the parts of the curriculum fit together. Japanese adolescents have fewer courses to choose from than American students do (Armstrong & Savage, 1997), and a more structured ordering of courses from one level to the next. The curriculum and the textbooks for each course are chosen on a national basis by the Ministry of Education, so that all Japanese students in a particular grade are learning the same things at the same time (Rohlen, 1983; Stevenson & Zusho, 2002). The curriculums are connected. For example, in math courses, students who have completed Math I have learned what they will need to know at the beginning of Math II. As a result, Japanese teachers spend much less time than American teachers reviewing material from previous courses before presenting fresh material for the current course. However, Japanese high schools focus almost exclusively on rote learning and memorization, with little time or encouragement for critical thinking.

Cultural beliefs are also important to the practices of Japanese schools. Teachers, adolescents, and parents believe that all children are capable of learning the material that teachers present (Stevenson & Zusho, 2002). The Japanese (as well as people in other Asian countries) generally believe that success or failure in school depends on effort, in contrast to the American belief that ability is what matters most. When students do poorly in school, these beliefs result in intense socialization pressure to try harder, pressure that comes from teachers, parents, peers, and the struggling students themselves.

The major underlying source of pressure on Japanese adolescents is the national system of entrance exams to high school and college, which the anthropologist Thomas Rohlen (1983), in his classic ethnography of Japanese high schools, called Japan's "national obsession." These two exams essentially determine young people's occupational fate for the rest of their lives because in Japanese society obtaining a job is based primarily on the status of the schools a person has attended.

To prepare for the entrance exams, the majority of Japanese students not only apply themselves seriously at school and in their homework but also from middle childhood through adolescence they attend "cram schools" after school or receive instruction from private tutors (Takahashi & Takeuchi, 2006). This system goes a long way toward explaining the high level of performance of Japanese children and adolescents. They work intensely on their schoolwork because the stakes are so high, much higher than in the United States where both the higher education system and the job market are much more open and much less about people's occupational future is determined by the time they leave high school.

Is there a cost for the high performance of Japanese adolescents? Surprisingly, most evidence indicates that the intense academic pressure does not make Japanese children and adolescents unhappy and psychologically disturbed. Japanese adolescents do not show higher rates of stress, depression, or psychosomatic ailments than American adolescents do, and rates of suicide are lower for Japanese than for American adolescents (Stevenson & Zusho, 2002). Asian American adolescents also report less stress, less anxiety, and fewer psychosomatic problems such as headaches, compared with White students, despite the pressure to achieve high academic performance (Steinberg, 1996).

in Europe, where primary school typically lasts from grade 1 through 8, often with the same teacher moving along with the class each year.

Improving the School Experience of Adolescents

So should we try to persuade all American school districts to adopt the 8-4 plan on the basis of this research? Some scholars have taken this position (Seidman et al., 2004), but keep in mind that most studies comparing different school plans have focused on a limited range of variables such as self-esteem and extracurricular activities. Although most of the results favor the 8-4 plan, other characteristics not included in these studies may favor the 6-3-3 plan. One study found that 7th-grade adolescents made more positive than negative comments about the transition to junior high school, with positive comments about topics such as peer relationships (more people to "hang around" with), academics (greater diversity of classes available), and independence (Berndt & Mekos, 1995).

In Japan, pressure for academic achievement is much greater in high school than in college.

For the Japanese, their time of leisure and fun comes during their college years. Once they enter college, grades matter little, and standards for performance are relaxed. Instead, they have "four years of university-sanctioned leisure to think and explore" (Rohlen, 1983, p. 168). This tradition continues today, more than 2 decades after Rohlen's observations (Fackler, 2007). Japanese college students spend a great deal of time in unstructured socializing, walking around the city and hanging out together. Average homework time for Japanese college students is half the homework time of junior high or high school students (Takahashi & Takeuchi, 2006). For most Japanese, this brief period in emerging adulthood is the only time in their lives, from childhood until retirement, that will be relatively free of pressure. Until they enter college the exam pressures are intense, and once they leave college they enter a work environment in which the hours are notoriously long. Only during their college years are they relatively free from responsibilities and free to enjoy extensive hours of leisure.

However, Asian cultures, including Japanese culture, have a general taboo against disclosing personal information, so Japanese adolescents may be underreporting their distress for reasons of social desirability. Many Japanese view the exam system as a problem for young people. There is a constant debate in Japanese society about the exam system, with many people objecting that it places too much pressure on young people and takes virtually all the fun out of childhood. With longer school days, a longer school year, cram schools, and private tutors, Japanese adolescents have far less time for after-school leisure and informal socializing with friends than American adolescents do (Rohlen, 1983; Stevenson & Zusho, 2002). Reforms in the 1990s reduced the length of the school day and cut the number of school days per week from 6 to 5, but the average school day remains long and cram schools remain the norm (Takahashi & Takeuchi, 2006). Also, because Japan has one of the lowest birth rates in the world (1.2 children per woman), competition for spots in colleges is steadily decreasing as the number of 18-year-olds in the population decreases, although it is still intense with respect to the top colleges (Fackler, 2007).

It should be noted that Japanese society is in the process of dramatic change, and the schools are changing as part of this process (French, 2002; Matsumoto, 2002; Takahashi & Takeuchi, 2006). Nearly 2 decades of economic stagnation have led many Japanese to begin to doubt whether their educational system is well suited to today's economy. Critics hold up the American system in favorable contrast for encouraging independent and creative thinking, even though the American system is less successful than the Japanese system at teaching facts. Globalization has made Japan more individualistic than in the past, and students in Japanese classrooms are no longer as orderly and obedient as they once were. The prospect of a lifelong job with a stable, well-paying company is no longer as certain as it was in the days when the Japanese economy was booming. Nor is that prospect as attractive to today's more individualistic adolescents and emerging adults. Nevertheless, Japanese adolescents continue to be near the top of international rankings of academic performance, indicating that the educational system remains one of the chief assets of Japanese society.

Furthermore, considerable evidence suggests that the reason for difficulties with school transitions in early adolescence lies not so much in the timing of the transition as in the nature of adolescents' school experiences in most junior high and middle schools (Barber & Olsen, 2004). Jacquelynne Eccles, a scholar who has conducted several studies on early adolescents' school experiences, attributes the difficulties of these transitions to the fact that many adolescents find the environment of middle schools and junior high schools alienating and oppressive (Eccles et al., 1997; Eccles & Roeser, 2003). Compared with primary schools, middle schools and junior high schools tend to have less individual contact between students and teachers and less opportunity for close relationships with teachers, in part because students have many teachers rather than just one. Also, there is a greater emphasis on teacher control. According to Eccles and her colleagues, this increased emphasis on control is especially mismatched with early adolescents' increased abilities and desires for autonomy, and consequently undermines their motivation and self-esteem.

Early adolescents' difficulties with school transitions are also due to junior high teachers' beliefs about adolescents (Eccles et al., 1993, Eccles & Roeser, 2003). Although why these teachers would differ from teachers in the 8-4 plan is not clear, Eccles and her colleagues have found that junior high teachers are considerably more negative in their views of adolescents. They are less likely to trust their students and more likely to see adolescents as inherently troublesome and unruly. When compared with primary school teachers, junior high teachers report less confidence in their abilities, perhaps because the majority of them have not had any specialized training on adolescence (Eccles et al., 1993; Scales & McEwin, 1994). If the findings from Eccles's studies are widely true of middle school and junior high school teachers, it would go a long way toward explaining the difficulties adolescents have with school transitions in early adolescence.

Fortunately, other studies indicate that schools and parents can take steps to make school transitions more enjoyable and successful for early adolescents. One study compared two different junior high schools—one that grouped students into smaller teams of 100 students and four teachers, and one that was a more typical junior high school—and found that students in the team-organized school adjusted better to the transition, primarily because of the support they felt from their teachers (Hawkins & Berndt, 1985). In another study, some parents of adolescents in low-income families in Vermont participated in an 11-week program to provide parents with information about adolescence and promote their effectiveness as parents (Bronstein et al., 1994). The program took place just prior to the adolescents' transition to middle school. Adolescents whose parents participated in the program did not show the typical decline in functioning after their transition to middle school and were better off following the transition than adolescents in a control group whose parents did not participate in the program. This finding is consistent with another study, which found that when parents are aware of and sensitive to adolescents' needs and developmental characteristics, their adolescents are more likely to make the transition to junior high school without experiencing a decline in their self-esteem (Lord, Eccles, & McCarthy, 1994).

School Climate

Although many studies indicate that school size and the timing of school transitions can be important influences on adolescents' school experience, most scholars in education would agree that these factors are important only insofar as they influence the kinds of interactions that students and teachers have in the classroom. **School climate** is the term for the quality of these interactions (Brand et al., 2003; Rutter, 1983; Way et al., 2007). It refers to how teachers interact with students, what sort of expectations and standards they have for students, and what kinds of methods are used in the classroom.

The term *school climate* was coined by Michael Rutter (1983; Rutter et al., 1979), a British psychiatrist who has done extensive research on adolescents and schools. Rutter and his colleagues studied several thousand young adolescents in British secondary schools. Their study included observations in the classrooms as well as students' attendance records, achievement test scores, and self-reports of participation in delinquent behavior.

The results indicated that the most important differences among the schools were related to school climate. Students were better off in schools where teachers tended to be supportive and involved with students but also applied firm discipline when necessary and held high expectations for students' conduct and academic performance. Specifically, students in schools with this kind of school climate had higher attendance and achievement test scores and lower rates of delinquency compared with students in the schools where the school climate was not as favorable.

This was true even after taking into account statistically the differences in the students' IQ and socioeconomic background. So, it was not simply that the students in the better

School climate is an important indicator of adolescents' school experiences.

---

school climate The quality of interactions between teachers and students, including how teachers interact with students, what sort of expectations and standards they have for students, and what kinds of methods are used in the classroom.

engagement The quality of being psychologically committed to learning, including being alert and attentive in the classroom and making a diligent effort to learn.

schools also came from more advantaged backgrounds. The schools themselves made a substantial difference in students' performance, based on differences in school climate.

Another large study compared public and private (mostly Catholic) schools in the United States, and reached conclusions similar to those of Rutter and his colleagues (Coleman & Hoffer, 1987; Coleman, Hoffer, & Kilgore, 1982). This study was led by James Coleman, a prominent scholar on adolescents and education, and focused on high school (in contrast to the Rutter study, which had focused on younger adolescents). Like Rutter and his colleagues (1979), Coleman and his colleagues found that students had higher levels of achievement and lower levels of delinquency in schools that maintained high expectations for students along with a spirit of involvement and dedication on the part of teachers. This was true regardless of whether the school was public or private, although private schools generally rated more favorably than public schools on various aspects of school climate. The findings remained true (as in the Rutter study) even after controlling statistically for differences in students' abilities and social class background.

More recent research has confirmed and expanded the findings of the Rutter and Coleman studies, showing that a favorable school climate is related to lower levels of depression and behavior problems (Loukas & Robinson, 2004) as well as higher levels of motivation and participation (Anderson, Hamilton, & Hattie, 2004). One study of over 100,000 students in over one hundred American middle schools found that school climate was favorably related to academic, behavioral, and socioemotional outcomes (Brand et al., 2003).

THINKING CRITICALLY •••

Imagine that you have just become the principal of an American secondary school. What could you do to assess the school climate in your school? How would you go about improving it if it were less than satisfactory?

We can conclude from these studies that successful teaching looks a lot like successful parenting in that both combine demandingness and responsiveness. A combination of warmth, clear communication, high standards for behavior, and a moderate level of control seems to work as well in the classroom as it does in the home (Haynes et al., 1997; Zedd, Brooks, & McGarvey, 2002). However, as with parenting, the practices that take place in schools are often rooted in a particular set of cultural beliefs. Coleman and his colleagues (1982) concluded that one of the key reasons for the success of the private schools was that a common set of Catholic religious beliefs was held by parents, teachers, and students. These beliefs included respect for authority (including teachers), consideration for and cooperation with others, and the importance of striving to make the most of one's abilities. Schools did not have to introduce these beliefs to students and persuade them to accept them. The beliefs were taught to the children from an early age, at home and in church, and school simply reinforced the attitudes shaped in those settings.

Engagement and Achievement in School: Beyond the Classroom

The studies by Rutter and Coleman show that a favorable school climate succeeds in promoting adolescents' engagement while they are in school. **Engagement** is the quality of being psychologically committed to learning (Guthrie, 2008; Newmann, 1992; Sirin & Rogers-Sirin, 2005). It means being alert and attentive in the classroom, and approaching educational assignments with the aim of truly learning the material, not just scraping by with minimal effort.

Unfortunately, engagement is the exception rather than the norm in the school experience of American adolescents. Research indicates that a remarkably high proportion of adolescents not only fall short of an ideal of engagement, but are strikingly disengaged during their time in school, "physically present but psychologically absent" (Steinberg, 1996, p. 67). In a comprehensive study of American high schools by Steinberg and colleagues (Steinberg, 1996; see the Research Focus box), more than one third of the students in the study indicated that they rarely try hard, and a similar proportion indicated that they rarely pay attention in class. Over two thirds admitted they had cheated on a test at least once in the past year, and *9 out of 10* said they had copied someone else's homework within the past year. Furthermore, as Figure 10.3 shows, national data indicate that the trend in recent decades is for the worse, and currently only a small proportion of 12th-grade students find their schoolwork meaningful and interesting. These findings make a persuasive case that the majority of American adolescents are seriously disengaged from school. For many of them, their commitment seems to be not to learning but to getting by with the least effort possible.

It seems clear that school climate makes a difference. A favorable school climate enhances students' engagement, which in turn results in higher levels of achievement (Zedd et al., 2002). The structure of the classroom environment matters, too, with students more engaged when they are working on individual or group tasks rather than listening to a lecture or watching a video (Shernoff et al., 2003). Nevertheless, there is substantial evidence that the main problems with American secondary education lie "beyond the classroom" (Steinberg, 1996), in the family environments, peer relations, work and leisure patterns, and cultural beliefs experienced by American adolescents. The following sections address each of these in turn.

Family Environments and School

We saw in Chapter 7 that parenting styles are related to a variety of important aspects of adolescent development. Parenting affects not only the quality of the relationship between parents and adolescents but also a variety of other aspects of adolescents' lives, including their attitudes toward and performance in school.

Two of the most important studies of adolescents' school experiences published in the past decade provide a striking contrast in research methods. The study by Laurence Steinberg (1996) is a classic of quantitative, questionnaire-focused research. Consider some of the features of this study:

- 20,000 students participated in the study.
- The students were from nine different schools in two states (Wisconsin and California). The schools were in urban, rural, and suburban communities.
- Forty percent of the sample was African American, Asian American, or Latino.
- Data were collected from the adolescents each year for 4 years, so that patterns of change over time could be investigated.
- Before any data were collected, planning and **pilot testing** of the measures took 2 years. (Pilot testing means trying out the measures on a small number of potential participants before the larger study begins to make sure the measures have adequate reliability and validity.)
- Questionnaire measures were included on adolescents' academic attitudes and beliefs, academic performance, psychological functioning, and problem behavior, among other topics. Questionnaires were also included on adolescents' views of their parents' parenting practices, on their views of their peers' attitudes and behavior with regard to education and other areas, and on adolescents' work and leisure attitudes and behavior.

The study has yielded an enormous amount of useful and interesting information on school engagement, academic performance, and many other topics, summarized in the book by Steinberg (1996) and in numerous articles in academic journals. I have cited the book and the articles often in this chapter.

In contrast, Niobe Way (1998) interviewed 24 adolescents of various ethnic backgrounds at one urban school over a 3-year period. Although her study was much smaller in scale than the Steinberg (1996) study, she got to know the adolescents and their school extremely well. Her interviews yielded many insights into their experiences in school and the intersection between school and the rest of their lives. For example, take this comment from Chantel:

"I was coming to school for a while and doing no work. I just sat there and was like I didn't want to deal with nothing. When I was having problems with my father, and then I had broke up with my boyfriend. . . . I just didn't care any more." (p. 192)

Or this comment from Sonia:

"It gets boring sometimes. . . . I fall asleep sometimes. . . . I was working every night 'til 10 o'clock [at a local pharmacy]. So I would come home so tired that I wouldn't even think about homework." (p. 195)

In addition, Way's (1998) own ethnographic experience within the school gave her vivid and disturbing insights into the quality of education the adolescents received:

"During my time working and conducting research at this school, I have repeatedly seen teachers spend entire class periods having their students fill out worksheets rather than actively engaging with them about class materials. I have heard about and seen teachers arrive fifteen or twenty minutes late to their fifty-minute classes. . . . I have watched teachers reading a book or a newspaper during class while the students slept, threw notes, or chatted among themselves. I have heard students and teachers yelling at each other, calling one another "animals," "fat slob," "slut," or "bitch" in the classroom or in the stairwells. . . . I have witnessed some teachers—especially the new ones—put tremendous efforts into trying to create cohesive and supportive environments for their colleagues and students only to be met with hostile and resentful responses from the school administrators, teaching staff, and the students themselves." (pp. 201–202)

Steinberg's information is of the kind that can only be obtained with a large-scale study; Way's insights can be obtained only through the kind of qualitative, ethnographic research she conducts. Both kinds of research are valuable, and the combination is essential for a complete understanding of adolescent development.

One way parents influence adolescents' academic performance is through their expectations for achievement. Adolescents whose parents expect them to do well tend to live up to those expectations, as reflected in their grades in high school; adolescents whose parents have lower expectations for their school performance tend to perform less well (Juang & Silbereisen, 2002; Roeser, Lord, & Eccles, 1994; Schneider & Stevenson, 1999). Parents who have high expectations also tend to be more involved in their adolescents' education, assisting with course selection, attending school programs, and keeping track of their adolescents' performance. This involvement contributes to adolescents' school success (Bogenschneider, 1997; Grolnick & Slowiaczek, 1994; Steinberg, Dornbusch, & Brown, 1992).

However, it is useful to keep in mind the possibility of passive genotype environment interactions here. That is, it is

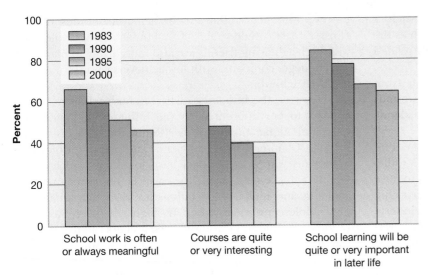

FIGURE 10.3 American high school students' school engagement, 1983–2000.

Source: NCES (2002), p. 72.

likely to be true that parents with higher intellectual abilities not only have high expectations for their adolescents' educations but also provide their children with a genetic contribution to high intelligence and high academic performance. Studies on parents' expectations in relation to adolescents' academic performance do not control for this possibility.

Parents' involvement in their adolescents' education tends to reflect their overall parenting style (Juang & Silbereisen, 2002; Steinberg, 1996). For school as for other areas, authoritative parenting has the most favorable associations with adolescents' development. Adolescents whose parents combine high demandingness with high responsiveness have the highest levels of engagement in school and the highest levels of school success (Bronstein et al., 1996; Dornbusch et al., 1987; Steinberg, 1996). Authoritative parents contribute to adolescents' school success directly by being more involved than other parents in their adolescents' education (Paulson, 1994). Such parents also have a variety of favorable indirect effects on their adolescents' school performance. Adolescents with authoritative parents are more likely than other adolescents to develop personal qualities such as self-reliance, persistence, and responsibility, which in turn lead to favorable school performance (Steinberg, 1996).

Adolescents with authoritarian, permissive, or neglectful parents all tend to perform worse in school than adolescents with authoritative parents (DeBaryshe, Patterson, & Capaldi, 1993; Melby & Conger, 1996). Adolescents' academic achievement tends to be worst when they have neglectful parents (low levels of both demandingness and responsiveness; Dornbusch et al., 1987; Steinberg, 1996). These are adolescents whose parents know little about how they are doing in school and who also know little or nothing about how the adolescent's time is spent outside of school. Adolescents with such parents have the lowest estimation of their abilities, the weakest engagement to school, and the poorest grades (Steinberg, 1996).

Of course, here as with other parenting research, the direction of effects is not clear and the results should be interpreted carefully. It could be that authoritative parenting helps adolescents do well in school, or it could be that adolescents who do well in school are easier to parent with an admirable combination of demandingness and responsiveness. Nevertheless, research shows some disturbing findings regarding American parents' involvement in their adolescents' education. In one large multistate study, one third of adolescents indicated that their parents did not know how they were doing in school (Steinberg, 1996). Over half reported that their parents would not mind if they got Cs on their report card. Forty percent of the parents indicated that they never attend school programs.

However, other studies have shown that schools can design effective programs to increase parents' involvement in their adolescents' education (Comer, 1993; Epstein & Dunbar, 1995). When parents become engaged, their adolescents' engagement and academic achievement also tend to improve. Such programs are especially important in the light of studies showing that, in general, parents tend to be less involved in their adolescents' education than they were when their children were younger (Eccles & Harold, 1993).

Family Social Class and School Another aspect of adolescents' families that has been found to be strongly related to academic achievement is the family's social class or socioeconomic status (SES). Numerous studies have found a positive association between family SES and adolescents' grades and achievement test scores, as well as between family SES and the highest level of education that adolescents or emerging adults ultimately attain (Featherman, 1980; Gutman & Eccles, 1999; Kelly, 2004; Sewell & Hauser, 1972; Zedd et al., 2002). These social class differences appear long before adolescence. Even before entering school, middle-class children score higher than working-class and lower-class children on tests of basic academic skills. By middle childhood, these class differences are clearly established, and class differences in academic achievement remain strong through high school (Kelly, 2004). Middle-class emerging adults are also more likely than emerging adults from lower social classes to attend college following high school (Hanson, 1994).

What makes social class so important in predicting academic achievement? Social class represents many other family characteristics that contribute to achievement. Middle-class parents tend to have higher IQs than lower-class parents, and they pass this advantage on to their children through both genes and environment; in turn, IQ is related to academic achievement (Snow & Yalow, 1988). Middle-class children also tend to receive better nutrition and health care than lower-class children, beginning prenatally and continuing through adolescence; for lower-class children, health problems may interfere with their ability to perform academically (Children's Defense Fund, 1994; Teachman, 1996). Lower-class families tend to be subject to more stresses than middle-class families, with respect to major stresses (such as losing a job) as well as day-to-day minor stresses (such as the car breaking down), and these stresses are negatively related to adolescents' school performance (Gutman & Eccles, 1999). One recent longitudinal study of adolescents from Mexican, Chinese, and European American backgrounds found that across groups, family stressors predicted academic problems (Flook & Fuligni, 2008).

Parents' behavior also varies by social class in ways that are related to adolescents' academic achievement. Middle-class parents are more likely than lower-class parents to have an authoritative parenting style that contributes to their children's school success (Dornbusch et al., 1987; Steinberg, 1996). Middle-class parents are also more likely than lower-class parents to be actively involved in their adolescents' education, through behavior such as guiding adolescents' selection of classes and attending parent-teacher conferences (Gutman & Eccles, 1999; Lee & Croninger, 1994). However, social classes are large categories, and substantial variability exists within each social class. In the lower class as well as the middle class, adolescents' academic performance benefits from authoritative parents and from parents who are involved in their education and have high expectations for their academic achievement (Annunziata et al., 2006).

Peers, Friends, and School

"With my crowd, if you cut school and got away with it, that meant you were all right. You had a scam on those teachers. Everyone thought that was great. You'd be stoned in class and sit back and make a fool of yourself and everybody would laugh and you'd be considered fun. Like you'd be entertaining everyone. And if you didn't get caught, you were cool."

—Annie, age 17 (in Bell, 1998, p. 76)

Although the influence of friends tends to be strongest in relatively less important areas such as dress, hairstyle, and music, school is one important area in which the influence of friends is in some respects greater than the influence of parents. Several studies have found that in high school, friends' influence is greater than the influence of parenting practices in a variety of school-related ways: how consistently adolescents attend class, how much time they spend on homework, how hard they try in school, and the grades they achieve (Midgely & Urdan, 1995; Steinberg, 1996).

Of course, as we have seen in Chapter 8, the influence of peers is not necessarily negative and may in fact be quite positive. Adolescent friends with high educational achievements and aspirations tend to give each other support and encouragement for doing well in school (Steinberg, 1996). This is true even taking into account selective association (the fact that adolescents tend to choose friends who are similar to themselves). When low-achieving adolescents have high-achieving friends, over time the high achievers tend to have a positive influence, so that the low achievers' grades improve (Epstein, 1983; Zedd et al., 2002). Low-achieving adolescents with high-achieving friends are also more likely to plan to attend college, compared with low achievers whose friends are not high achievers.

However, the influence of having high-achieving *friends* appears to be different from the influence of being in a school of high-achieving *peers*. (Remember the distinction made in Chapter 8 between friends and peers.) Adolescents in schools where their peers have lower average levels of school achievement tend to have better academic self-concepts and higher expectations for academic attainment than adolescents surrounded by high-achieving classmates (Zedd et al., 2002). Educational researchers call this the "big fish in a little pond effect" (Marsh, Chessor, Craven, & Roche, 1995; Marsh & Hau, 2004). Adolescents naturally compare themselves to their classmates. If classmates mostly seem to be doing fair or poor in their schoolwork, the slightly above-average adolescent is likely to feel pretty good about how school is going—like a "big fish," in other words. However, in a school of high achievers, the same adolescent may well feel inferior to others in academic abilities and prospects. One study of over 100,000 adolescents in 26 countries found that the "big fish" effect existed in all 26 countries: adolescents in less selective schools had a significantly higher academic self-concept than adolescents in more selective schools (Marsh & Hau, 2004).

Studies suggest other reasons for concern about the influence of friends and peers on adolescents' school performance. By the time they reach middle school, many adolescents become concerned with concealing a high-achievement orientation from their peers. For example, in one study 8th-grade students indicated that they wanted their teachers to know that they worked hard in school—but not their peers, because they feared that their peers would disapprove (Juvonen & Murdock, 1995). Also, adolescents who are more concerned than other adolescents about what their friends think of them tend to perform worse in school (Fuligni & Eccles, 1992).

In school as in other areas, the influences of parents and peers are often intertwined. On the one hand, parents influence adolescents' choices of friends, which can in turn influence school performance (Brown et al., 1993; Gonzales et al., 1996). On the other hand, having friends who denigrate school tends to be related to lower school success, even for adolescents with authoritative parents (Brown et al., 1993; Steinberg, 1996).

Work, Leisure, and School

Part-time work in high school tends to be damaging to school performance in a variety of ways, especially for adolescents who work more than 10 hours per week (Steinberg, 1996). Beyond 10 hours a week the more adolescents work, the lower their grades, the less time they spend on homework, the more they cut class, the more they cheat on their schoolwork, the less committed they are to school, and the lower their educational aspirations (Marsh & Kleit-

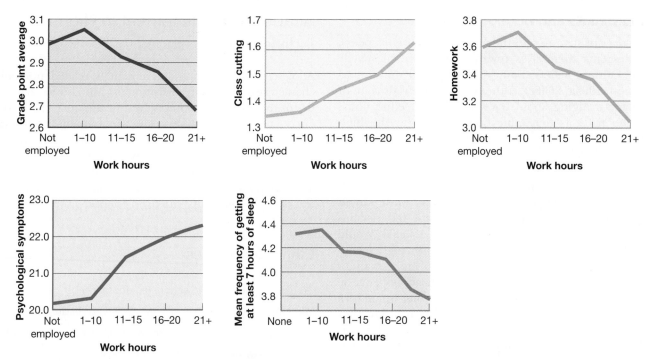

FIGURE 10.4 Relation between work hours and school performance. Beyond about 10 hours per week, the more adolescents work, the poorer their school performance.

Sources: Steinberg & Dornbusch (1991); Bachman & Schulenberg (1993).

man, 2005). Figure 10.4 illustrates some of these patterns. Of course, some degree of self-selection is involved here—students may decide to work more because they do not care about school (Zierold et al., 2005). Nevertheless, evidence indicates that working more than 10 hours has effects beyond self-selection. In Steinberg's (1996) study, one third of adolescents said they took easier courses because of their jobs, and the same proportion said they were frequently too tired from their jobs to do their homework. In the course of the 3-year study, students who increased the number of hours they worked also reported declines in school commitment, whereas those who decreased the number of hours they worked reported increased school commitment.

Abundant leisure also interferes with adolescents' attention to school and schoolwork. Steinberg (1996) found that socializing with friends was adolescents' most common daily activity. Adolescents reported socializing—activities such as "hanging out with friends" and "partying"—an average of 20 to 25 hours per week, more than the average time they worked and more than the amount of time they spent in school. In turn, amount of time spent socializing was negatively associated with grades in school. However, it should be noted that adolescents who participate in extracurricular activities (such as sports and music) have better academic performance and are less likely to drop out of high school (Zedd et al., 2002). So unstructured socializing is negatively related to academic performance, but structured leisure in extracurricular activities appears to have positive effects.

For both work and leisure, the ethnic comparisons are striking, especially with respect to Asian Americans. Accord-

ing to Steinberg (1996), Asian American adolescents are less likely than other adolescents to have a part-time job and less likely to work 20 or more hours per week if they are employed. On average, Asian Americans spend only half as much time socializing, compared with adolescents in other ethnic groups. Because they spend less time on part-time employment, less time on socializing, and more nonschool time on academics, Asian Americans have the highest levels of academic achievement of any ethnic group, including Whites (Qin, Way, & Mukherjee, 2008).

Asian American adolescents tend to have high levels of academic achievement.

Cultural Beliefs and School

The practices of schools and the attitudes of parents, peers, and adolescents themselves toward school are ultimately rooted in cultural beliefs about what is valuable and important (Arnett, 1995a, 2006c). Although Americans do a lot of public hand-wringing about the state of their educational system, the truth is that education—at least at the high school level—is not as highly valued by Americans as it is by people of many other industrialized countries (Stevenson & Stigler, 1992). Sure, Americans would like to see their adolescents perform better in international comparisons with adolescents from other countries. But would most Americans support a law restricting employment for persons under age 18 to no more than 10 hours a week? Would Americans support restricting participation in high school athletics to a similar time commitment, no more than 10 hours a week? Would parents of American adolescents be pleased if high school teachers began assigning homework that routinely required three or four hours per day after school and began handing out failing grades to adolescents who did not measure up to a high and inflexible standard of performance?

All the evidence indicates that the answer to these questions is a resounding no (Stevenson & Stigler, 1992; Steinberg, 1996). For example, the majority of American adults are opposed to lengthening the school day or the school year. Although Americans value education and would like to see their adolescents perform well, for most Americans it is more important that their adolescents have time for fun in addition to schoolwork, and also have time for a variety of nonacademic interests so that they can be "well-rounded."

THINKING CRITICALLY •••

Steinberg (1996) asserts that to change American adolescents' school performance, Americans would have to change their beliefs about what should be required of adolescents. Do you think more should be required of adolescents in high school in your country? Why or why not?

The contrast between American and Asian cultural beliefs regarding education is striking and informative. Asian cultures have a long tradition of valuing education. In India and China, for example, the high value on education is a tradition thousands of years old. Today's educational systems for adolescents in Asian countries are built on this tradition. The value placed on education is so high that the focus on school performance often comes first in adolescents' lives, and other aspects of life are expected to be given a much lower priority, including time with friends, romantic involvements, and extracurricular activities (Asakawa & Csikszentmihalyi, 1999; Lee & Larson, 2000). We will discuss this tradition further in the next section, specifically with respect to Asian American adolescents.

Academic Achievement in High School: Individual Differences

Adolescents' academic achievement is related not only to characteristics of their environments but also to characteristics of the adolescents themselves. In this area, ethnic differences and gender differences in achievement are two issues that have been of particular interest to scholars. We will examine these two issues first, then examine the characteristics of students at the extremes of achievement: gifted adolescents, adolescents with disabilities, adolescents in lower academic tracks, and adolescents who drop out of high school.

Ethnic Differences

"You don't have to go to school to necessarily become successful. You can go about it another way. . . . If you do drop out, you can still make it in life, because I know people who dropped out at an early age like 14 and they're still making it."

—Tony, urban African American adolescent (in Figueira-McDonough, 1998)

Although looking at the overall academic performance of American adolescents provides interesting insights and information, the overall patterns obscure the sharp differences that exist between different ethnic groups. It is well established that Asian American adolescents have the best academic performance of any ethnic group in American society, followed by Whites, with the performance of African American and Latino adolescents below Whites (Qin et al., 2008; Steinberg, 1996; Warren, 1996). These differences exist even in early primary school, but they become more pronounced in adolescence.

What explains these differences? To some extent, the explanation lies in ethnic group differences in the factors we have already discussed as important in school success, such as social class, parenting practices, and friends' influences. With regard to social class, African Americans and Latinos are more likely than Asian Americans or Whites to live in poverty, and living in poverty is negatively associated with academic performance regardless of ethnicity (Gillock & Reyes, 1999; Gutman & Eccles, 1999; NCES, 1998).

We have seen the importance of parental expectations in adolescents' educational achievement, and ethnic differences exist here as well. As noted previously, although the majority of parents in all ethnic groups say they value education highly, the emphasis on education is especially strong in Asian cultures (Asakawa & Csikszentmihalyi, 1999; Lee & Larson, 2000), and Asian American parents tend to have higher educational expectations than parents in other ethnic groups (Chen & Stevenson, 1995; Fuligni & Tseng, 1999; Steinberg, 1996). Furthermore, Asian American parents and adolescents tend to believe that academic success is due mainly to *effort*; in contrast, parents and adolescents in other ethnic

Educational performance among Black adolescents has improved in recent years but remains well below that of Whites.

groups are more likely to believe that academic success is due mainly to *ability* (Holloway, 1988). Consequently, Asian American parents are less likely than parents in the other ethnic groups to accept mediocre or poor academic performance as due to fixed limitations in their adolescents' academic abilities, and are more likely to insist that their adolescents address academic difficulties by trying harder and spending more time on their schoolwork.

One ethnic difference that does not correspond to other findings on adolescents' academic performance concerns parenting styles. Asian American parents are less likely than White parents to be classified by researchers as authoritative, and more likely to be classified as authoritarian (Steinberg, 1996); Asian American adolescents excel even though authoritative parenting is more likely than authoritarian parenting to be associated with academic success in adolescence. However, as we discussed in the chapter on families, it makes more sense to view most Asian American parents as "traditional" rather than authoritarian because they tend to combine a high level of demandingness with strong attachments to their adolescents and intense involvements in their lives (Chao, 2001; Chao & Tseng, 2002; Lim & Lim, 2004).

Ethnic differences can also be seen in friends' attitudes toward education. The differences correspond to ethnic differences in academic achievement—Asian Americans are most likely to have academically oriented friends, African Americans and Latinos least likely, with Whites somewhere in between (Steinberg, 1996). Specifically, Asian American adolescents are most likely to study with friends, most likely to say their friends think it is important to do well in school,

and most likely to say they work harder on schoolwork to keep up with their friends. Although the influence of friends on school performance is usually positive for Asian Americans, for adolescents in other ethnic groups the influence is more likely to be negative (Steinberg, 1996; Way, 1998).

Although ethnic groups differ in social class, parenting, and friends' influence in ways that explain ethnic differences in adolescents' academic achievement, many scholars have argued that other forces are at work as well, forces related specifically to prejudice and discrimination against ethnic groups in American society. In particular, some scholars have argued that the relatively low achievement of African American and Latino adolescents is due substantially to these adolescents' perception that even if they excel educationally, their prospects for occupational success will be limited due to prejudice against them (Taylor et al., 1994). Some scholars have asserted that such prejudice leads many Black adolescents to view striving for educational achievement as "acting White" (Fordham & Ogbu, 1986; Ogbu, 2003; Price 1999). Studies have found that minority adolescents who believe that their opportunities are unfairly limited by ethnic discrimination have lower achievement than their minority peers who do not believe this (Taylor et al., 1994; Wood & Clay, 1996). Educational expectations decline from 8th grade through high school for many Black adolescents, especially those from lower SES families, perhaps reflecting a growing perception of their limited opportunities after high school (Trusty, Harris, & Morag, 1999).

However, in a contradictory finding, Steinberg (1996) reported that African American and Latino students were equal to White and Asian students in their perceptions of the potential value of academic achievement for promoting future career success. Where the adolescents in the Steinberg study differed was in their perceptions of the consequences of *not* succeeding academically. African American and Latino students generally agreed that doing well in school helps in finding later employment, but they also tended to believe that they could succeed in a career even if they did not obtain a high level of academic achievement, whereas White and Asian American students—especially Asian American students—tended to believe that failing to succeed academically would have more serious negative consequences. Thus, contrary to the view that African American and Latino adolescents are inhibited from academic achievement by a pessimistic view of the value of academic success, this study indicates that these adolescents may have less motivation to strive academically because they are optimistic about their chances of succeeding in the future even without excelling academically. Similar findings were reported by Figueira-McDonough (1998) in a qualitative study of urban African American and Latino adolescents.

Is it true that achieving well in school will not help African Americans in the workplace due to discrimination against them? For the most part, the answer is no. In fact, the most recent figures show that African American women who obtain a four-year college degree earn about 20% more than White women with the same education (Chronicle of Higher

Education, 2005). Black men with a college degree earn slightly less than White men with the same education, but they still earn 35% more than the average White high school graduate (NCES, 2005).

For adolescents whose families have immigrated to the United States in recent generations, one consistent finding is that their school performance is related to how long their families have been in the United States. One would reasonably expect that the longer an adolescent's family has been in the United States, the better the adolescent would do in school, because English would more likely be the language spoken at home, the adolescent would be more familiar with the expectations of American schools, the parents would be more comfortable communicating with teachers and other school personnel, and so on.

However, research shows *just the opposite*. The more generations an Asian American or Latino adolescent's family has been in the United States, the *worse* the adolescent tends to do in school (Fuligni, 1997; Kao & Tienda, 1995; Steinberg, 1996). The main reason seems to be that the longer the family has been in the United States, the more "Americanized" the adolescent is likely to become—that is, the more likely the adolescent is to value part-time work and socializing with friends over striving for academic excellence. For example, in one recent study, first-generation Chinese immigrant adolescents were highly motivated to work hard in school and valued demanding teachers, whereas those who were second-generation—that is, born in the United States, not in China—valued more entertaining teachers and did not want to work as hard for school success (Kaufman, 2004). Becoming American means becoming more likely to have adopted the American cultural value of placing good times before academic achievement in adolescence (Steinberg, 1996).

Nevertheless, every ethnic group has a substantial amount of individual differences. Not all Asian American adolescents do well in school; many African American and Latino adolescents excel. The kinds of parenting practices that we have discussed as important to academic achievement—high expectations, high involvement, and so on—make a difference within every ethnic group (Steinberg, 1996).

Gender Differences

As we discussed in Chapter 5, few differences in intellectual abilities exist between males and females. However, gender differences do exist in academic achievement. For the most part, these differences favor females. From the first grade of primary school to the last grade of high school, girls tend to achieve higher grades than boys and have higher educational aspirations (Sommers, 2000). Girls are also less likely to have learning disabilities, less likely to be held back a grade, and less likely to drop out of high school. The gender differences in favor of girls are especially strong among African American adolescents (Hacker, 2002b; Zedd et al., 2002). The female advantage continues into emerging adulthood. Young women are more likely to attend college and

Girls generally perform better academically than boys at all levels.

more likely to graduate (NCES, 2005). From grade school through college, the female advantage in academic achievement exists not only in the United States but also across all Western countries (Arnett, 2002b; Chisholm & Hurrelmann, 1995).

What explains girls' superior performance in school and the relatively poor performance of boys? One reason is that girls tend to enjoy the school environment more. Adolescent girls report more positive experiences and interactions in the classroom than adolescent boys and have more favorable relationships with their teachers (Sommers, 2000). For example, in one national (American) survey, nearly one third of boys in grades 7 through 12 stated that they feel that teachers do not listen to what they have to say, compared with one fifth of girls (Public Education Network, 1997). In another survey, adolescent girls had more contact with teachers and were more likely to feel that teachers and administrators cared about them (Horatio Alger Association, 1998). A second reason lies "beyond the classroom." Adolescent girls are more likely than adolescent boys to feel supported by their parents, academically as well as in other areas, and are more likely to have supportive relationships with adults outside the family as well (Sommers, 2000). Boys also do less homework, watch more TV, and read fewer books on their own (Hacker, 2002b).

Even in the area of math and science, where males once had greater levels of achievement in adolescence and beyond, the most recent evidence indicates that gender differences in math and science orientation have nearly disappeared (Zedd et al., 2002). By the year 2000, girls were as likely as boys to take math courses in high school, and they performed as well as boys in those courses (NCES, 2005). Although women continue to be less likely than males to choose college majors such as engineering and the physical sciences, female representation has grown in all traditionally male-dominated fields in the past 2 decades, as we will see in more detail later in the chapter. These trends indicate that progress is being made in eroding the gender biases that have kept females out of traditionally male fields emphasizing math and science skills.

Gender differences in academic performance have been the subject of heated debates among scholars and in the public arena (Sommers, 2000). However, for this topic as for others, it is important to keep in mind that gender comparisons involve comparing one half of the population to the other half, and there is a great deal of variability within each group. Girls generally do better academically than boys, but many boys excel and many girls struggle. Although the group differences are genuine, we should avoid stereotypes that might lead us to prejudge the abilities and performance of any individual boy or girl.

THINKING CRITICALLY •••

Much more research has been conducted on why adolescent girls do less well than adolescent boys in math and science than on why boys generally do worse than girls on virtually every other measure of academic achievement. What hypotheses would you propose to explain why boys generally do worse than girls academically, from grade school through emerging adulthood?

Extremes of Achievement

Because American secondary schools place all students in the same school regardless of their abilities and interests, schools often have policies for addressing variations in students' learning abilities and particular talents or problems that students may have. Here we examine the characteristics of adolescents at the high end of achievement—gifted students—as well as students who have disabilities that interfere with their academic achievement. We also look at the controversial issue of tracking, specifically at students who are tracked into a less rigorous secondary school curriculum. Then we examine the characteristics of adolescents who drop out of school, including a look at programs for preventing dropping out.

Gifted Adolescents In recent decades, programs for **gifted students** have become more common. Traditionally, the criterion for considering students gifted was an IQ of at least 130 (Winner, 1996). Today, however, partly in response to Gardner's (2000) theory of multiple intelligences (presented in Chapter 3), many schools have gifted programs that recognize special talents that students may have, for example, in art or music (Castellano & Diaz, 2002; Sarouphim, 2004). Other qualities, such as creativity, leadership, and wisdom, are increasingly being touted as aspects of giftedness (Davidson, 2000; Oades-Sese et al., 2007; Strauss, 2002).

Four characteristics distinguish children and adolescents who are gifted (Winner, 1996, 2000, 2003, 2005; Sternberg & Clinkenbeard, 1995):

- *Precocity.* Adolescents who are gifted usually showed signs of precocity, meaning that their gifts were evident at an early age. Typically, they could read, write, and do simple math at an earlier age than normal. Giftedness in music, art, and athletics also tends to be evident in childhood. It is unusual for a person suddenly to show signs of exceptional intelligence or other abilities in adolescence if they have not before that time.

- *Independence.* Gifted children and adolescents tend to prefer to work independently. They need less instruction and support than other children and adolescents do. They prefer to work at their own pace and solve problems on their own.

- *Drive for mastery.* Children and adolescents who are gifted display an intense drive to master the area of their gifts. They are capable of focusing for long periods on the topic or challenge before them.

- *Excellence in information processing.* Gifted children and adolescents excel at information processing (discussed in Chapter 3). This means that they process information faster, learn more quickly, make fewer reasoning errors, and use more effective learning strategies, some of which they may develop themselves.

Many American high schools have **Advanced Placement (AP) classes** for gifted students, in specific subjects such as math or English. These classes have higher-level material than normal classes to provide a challenging curriculum for gifted students (Zeidner & Schleyer, 1999). Students who

Many American high school students have Advanced Placement classes for gifted students. Here, adolescents in a Los Angeles AP class.

---

gifted students Students who have unusually high abilities in academics, art, or music.

Advanced Placement (AP) classes Classes for gifted students in high schools that have higher-level material than normal classes in order to provide a challenging curriculum.

take AP classes often like these classes better than their other classes because they find the more challenging material more engaging (Bleske-Rechek et al., 2004). By performing well on national AP exams at the end of their AP classes, gifted high school students can earn college credits. Participation in the AP program has grown rapidly in recent years. In 2004, the number of AP tests taken by high school students was up by 65% from 5 years earlier (NCES, 2005).

A problem with keeping gifted children and adolescents in regular classrooms is that they may become bored and alienated from school. According to scholars on giftedness, children and adolescents who are gifted often become socially isolated in regular classrooms (Winner, 1996). High-achieving adults often recall their school experiences negatively, as a time of being bored and frustrated because there was so little for them to learn (Howe, 1999). Other students may resent their abilities, and their detachment and disinterest in what other students are learning may be evident to both students and teachers. It has become rare now for gifted children to skip a grade in school in order to be in a grade that would match their abilities, because such children often had difficulty with the social adjustment of being surrounded by children who were older. Experts on giftedness such as Ellen Winner (1996, 2000, 2003, 2005) now recommend that gifted adolescents be allowed to take college courses so that they will be intellectually challenged.

Although children and adolescents who are gifted have a legitimate need for programs that suit their abilities, the definition of "gifted" has become so elastic that in some schools it is applied to one half of children (Strauss, 2002). At this level, the situation begins to approach Garrison Keillor's fictional "Lake Wobegon," where "all the children are above average." More seriously, if half the children are considered gifted, it becomes more difficult to implement programs that will address the needs of those who truly have exceptional abilities. Furthermore, as developmental psychologist Howard Gardner observes, "Labeling half the kids gifted is disastrous for those who are *not* so labeled" (quoted in Strauss, 2002). For this reason, some researchers have proposed that no more than 5% of any school population be considered gifted (Strauss, 2002). However, at this point there is no generally accepted definition of "gifted" among educators and no way of definitely determining who is gifted and who is not.

Adolescents With Disabilities

At the other extreme of achievement are adolescents who have disabilities of various kinds that make it difficult for them to succeed in school. Some of the common disabilities related to school difficulties are speech handicaps, mental retardation, emotional disorders, and learning disabilities (Hallahan & Kauffman, 2003). In this section we will discuss **learning disabilities** in detail, as they are the most common category of disability.

About 10% of adolescents in American schools have been diagnosed as having some kind of disability, and of these about half have a learning disability (Hallahan & Kauffman, 2003). The diagnosis of learning disability is made when a child or an adolescent has normal intelligence but has difficulty in one or more academic areas and the difficulty cannot be attributed to any other diagnosed disorder. Recent research indicates that learning disabilities may indicate deficits in brain development and brain functioning (Brown et al., 2008). However, currently the diagnosis of a learning disability is based not on a neurological test but on a gap between intelligence test scores and academic achievement test scores.

Boys are twice as likely as girls to have a learning disability (NCES, 2005). The reasons for this are not well understood, but it contributes to the pattern we discussed earlier, of girls generally having more success than boys in school. African Americans and Latinos are more likely to have learning disabilities than Whites and Asian Americans are (NCES, 2005). Again, this is part of a larger pattern of more academic difficulties among African Americans and Latinos.

Reading is the academic area that is the most common source of difficulty for adolescents with a learning disability (Lipka & Siegel, 2006), but learning disabilities also exist for written language and math (Hallahan & Kauffman, 2003). Adolescents with learning disabilities often have social and emotional difficulties that compound their difficulties in school, and they are at high risk for dropping out of school (Deshler, 2005; Hutchinson et al., 2004; Martínez & Semrud-Clikeman, 2004). Interventions to address learning disabilities have been shown to be most effective if introduced as soon as children enter school (Kamphaus, 2000). By adolescence, the learning problems resulting from learning disabilities are firmly entrenched and are difficult to ameliorate. However, interventions with adolescents who have learning disabilities can be effective if they are delivered by teachers who are highly committed and involved (Deshler, 2005; Swanson & Deshler, 2003).

Attention-deficit hyperactivity disorder (ADHD) is a disability that includes problems of inattention, hyperactivity, and impulsiveness. ADHD is classified as a learning disability, and about one half of learning-disabled adolescents have been diagnosed specifically with ADHD (Hallahan & Kauffman, 2003). Most adolescents who have ADHD also have an additional learning disability. Because so much of school requires sitting quietly in a classroom, adolescents with ADHD often find school to be a stressful, unpleasant experience (Brook & Boaz, 2005).

Boys are four times more likely than girls to be diagnosed with ADHD (Guyer, 2000). ADHD is usually diagnosed in childhood, but the majority of children with ADHD still have the disorder in adolescence (Barkley, 2002; Whalen, 2000). The causes of ADHD are unclear, but it appears to be at least

---

learning disability In schools, a diagnosis made when a child or adolescent has normal intelligence but has difficulty in one or more academic areas and the difficulty cannot be attributed to any other disorder.

attention-deficit hyperactivity disorder (ADHD) Disorder characterized by difficulty in maintaining attention on a task along with a high activity level that makes self-control problematic.

partly inherited, as nearly 50% of children and adolescents with ADHD also have a sibling or parent with the disorder (Guyer, 2000).

Nearly 9 of 10 children and adolescents diagnosed with ADHD receive Ritalin or other medications to suppress their hyperactivity and help them concentrate better (Whalen, 2001). Medication is often effective in controlling the symptoms of ADHD, but studies find that the combination of medication and behavioral therapy is more effective than either one alone (Brown & La Rosa, 2002; Evans et al., 2001). Effective behavioral therapies include parent training, classroom interventions, and summer programs (Hoza et al., 2008).

Although most research on ADHD has taken place in the United States, recently a large study of ADHD was completed in Europe, involving over 1,500 children and adolescents (ages 6–18) in 10 countries (Rotheberger et al., 2006). In this Attention-deficit/hyperactivity Disorder Observational Research in Europe (ADORE) study, pediatricians and child psychiatrists across Europe collected observational data on the children and adolescents at seven time points over 2 years, with data including diagnosis, treatment, and outcomes. Parents also participated, and their assessments showed high agreement with the pediatricians and child psychiatrists.

Like the American studies, ADORE found higher rates of ADHD among boys than among girls, but the ratios varied widely among countries, from 3:1 to 16:1 (Novik et al., 2006). Symptoms of ADHD were similar among boys and girls, but girls with ADHD were more likely than boys to have additional emotional problems and to be bullied by their peers, whereas boys were more likely than girls to have additional conduct problems. For both boys and girls, having ADHD resulted in frequent problems in their relations with peers, teachers, and parents (Coghill et al., 2006). Parents reported frequent stresses and strains due to children's and adolescents' ADHD behavior, including frequent disruptions of family activities and worries about the future (Riley et al., 2006). In contrast to the American approach of relying heavily on Ritalin and other medications, the European approaches to treatment were diverse: medications (25%), psychotherapy (19%), combination of medications and psychotherapy (25%), other therapy (10%), and no treatment (21%) (Preuss et al., 2006).

Tracking Another way that American secondary schools address the diversity in interests and abilities among their students is through placing students into different groups, or "tracks." Not all secondary schools use tracking, and schools that do vary in the number and types of tracks. However, typically a tracking system includes an upper-level, college preparatory track; a general education track for average students; and a remedial or special education track for students who are academically behind their peers. Some schools also have a vocational education track in which students learn skills such as welding or auto mechanics. Students in different tracks attend some classes together—physical education,

Alternative schools have been found to be effective with adolescents who would otherwise drop out of school. Here, a biology class in an alternative school in Hartford, Connecticut.

music, some general education classes—but take most classes only with students in the same track.

Tracking has been a target of fierce debate among educators for many years (Eccles & Roeser, 2003). Advocates argue that tracking is the best way to ensure that all students are engaged in the schoolwork that is best suited to their varying levels of ability and achievement (Hallinan, 1992). According to this perspective, placing all high school students in the same classes makes no sense. The brightest and most advanced ones will be bored to death, and the slowest will be not only bored but humiliated that all the other students seem to be more advanced than they are. Also, not all students plan to attend college. As we have noted, even today nearly 40% of Americans begin working full time after high school instead of going to college. Advocates of tracking argue that it would be better to give these students some useful vocational preparation as part of their high school education, instead of alienating them by forcing them to sit through courses on topics that do not interest them.

However, critics of tracking argue that it dooms students in lower tracks to a second-rate education. The critics point to research indicating that students in the highest tracks often have the most skilled and most experienced teachers, and that the teaching in high-track classes is more likely to require critical thinking rather than simple memorization (Gamoran, 1993). Meanwhile, students in the lower tracks are often labeled as slow or stupid by their peers, and often come to see themselves that way as well (Eccles & Roeser, 2003).

Furthermore, students in the lower tracks tend to fall further and further behind their classmates with each year of school. Once students are placed in a low track, they receive a lower level of academic materials and a lower level of requirements compared with students in the higher tracks, making it difficult for students ever to get out of a low track once they are placed in one (Akos et al., 2007; Dornbusch, 1994; Hallinan, 1992). Over time, tracking increases the gap in learning between high-track and low-track students; ultimately, tracking influences students' achievement in high school and how much education they go on to obtain after high school (Akos et la., 2007; Gamoran, 1992). Finally, research has shown that Black and Latino students are more likely to be placed in a low track than White students of similar abilities, raising the question of whether tracking decisions may be made in a way that is unfair and discriminatory (Eccles & Roeser, 2003).

High School Dropouts

"I didn't like school. I just didn't like it. There was nothing I liked about it. Having to do all this reading and writing, and all that stuff. I had better things to do. I didn't want to be tied down with some schoolwork that I wasn't even going to remember in six weeks, or six days. I just found it all pointless. I'd rather go out in real life and learn real-life things than sit in a classroom and read a book, and answer questions from a teacher."

—Rich, age 17, high school dropout (in Arnett, 1996, p. 120)

Fifty years ago in American society, leaving high school before graduation was not unusual and did not severely affect a young person's occupational prospects. Many well-paying manufacturing jobs were available in automobile factories, steel mills, and the like, which made it possible for a young person to earn an adequate income without obtaining a high school degree. Today, however, with the economy having changed from a manufacturing base to a services and information base, the consequences of having low education are much more harsh. Young people who fail to obtain a high school degree are at high risk for unemployment (Barton, 2005). Dropouts who do obtain employment often find themselves in low-paying service jobs.

As the importance of obtaining education has increased over the past half century, the proportion of young people who fail to obtain a high school degree has steadily declined. By the year 2002, only 10% of young Americans had not obtained a high school diploma by age 24 (NCES, 2005). A higher percentage, about 30%, actually leave high school before graduating, but many of them obtain a General Education Development (GED) certificate afterward—which is considered to be equivalent to a high school diploma—to lower the overall "dropout rate" to 10% by age 24.

Distinct ethnic differences exist in dropout rates (NCES, 2008). As Figure 10.5 shows, dropout rates in all ethnic groups have declined over the past 30 years. Latinos have a relatively high dropout rate, 23%, but the dropout rate in this group is three times as high for Latino immigrant adolescents as for Latino adolescents who were born in the United States. African Americans have experienced the steepest decline in dropout rates over the past 30 years, and currently their dropout rate is just 12%. Dropout rates are lowest among Whites (7%) and Asian Americans (10%). In all ethnic groups except Asian Americans, males are more likely than females to drop out.

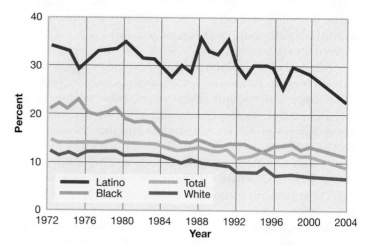

FIGURE 10.5 Ethnic differences in high school dropout rates.
Source: NCES (2007), p. 73.

What leads adolescents to drop out of school? For most, dropping out is not a sudden event but the culmination of many years of school problems (Barton, 2005). Adolescents who drop out are more likely than other adolescents to have repeated a grade (Connell et al., 1995). They are also more likely to have had a history of other school difficulties, including low grades, behavior problems, and low scores on achievement and intelligence tests (Connell et al., 1995; Jordan, Lara, & McPartland, 1996). Given the difficulties they have in school, it is not surprising that dropouts often report that they disliked school and found it boring and alienating (Janosz et al., 2008; Reyes & Jason, 1993).

Personal characteristics and problems are also related to adolescents' risk of dropping out. Dropouts sometimes have aggressive, active, high-sensation-seeking personalities that make it difficult for them to endure the typical classroom environment, which often involves working alone quietly or listening to someone else talk (Cairns et al., 1989). Adolescents who have learning disabilities of various kinds are more likely than other adolescents to drop out, in part because their difficulties in learning may have left them hopelessly behind their peers by the time they reach high school. For girls, having a child puts them at high risk for dropping out, although such girls often report lower school engagement even before becoming pregnant (Leadbeater & Way, 2001; McGaha-Garnett, 2008).

A variety of family factors also predict adolescents' risk for dropping out of school. Parents' education and income are strong predictors. Adolescents with parents who have dropped out of school are at high risk of dropping out themselves, as are adolescents whose families are in poverty (Barton, 2005). The two often go together, of course—parents who have dropped out often have low incomes. Parents who have dropped out provide a model of dropping out to their adolescents and often have lower educational expectations for their children (Rumberger, 1995). Also, families with low incomes often live in low-income neighborhoods where the quality of the schools is poor (Wilson, 1996). In addition, the stresses of living in a low-income family make it more difficult for parents to support their children's education, for example, by helping them with their homework or attending school conferences. Rates of dropping out are higher for adolescents in single-parent families, largely because of the lower incomes and higher stresses experienced in such families (Barton, 2005; Buchanan, 2000). Among Latinos, difficulty using English is an important contributor to dropping out (NCES, 2008; Singh & Hernandez-Gantes, 1996).

School characteristics also predict adolescents' risk of dropping out. Here as in other areas we have discussed, school climate is of primary importance. Dropout rates are lower in schools where teachers are supportive of students and dedicated to teaching and where the classroom environment is orderly (Connell et al., 1995; Salmelo-Aro et al., 2008). Dropout rates are higher in larger schools, at least partly because it is more difficult to sustain a healthy school climate in large schools (Bryk & Thum, 1989; Pittman & Haughwout, 1987).

Dropping out of high school is related to a variety of present and future problems. Rates of substance use are considerably higher among dropouts than among adolescents who stay in school (Wu et al., 2003). Dropouts are also at high risk for depression and other psychological problems. Job prospects for dropouts are limited, both in the short term and the long term. Only 40% are employed at age 16–19, and only 60% at age 20–24 (Barton, 2005). Even for those who do obtain a job, it is likely to be a low-paying one. Dropouts earn less in adolescence, emerging adulthood, and beyond than their peers who obtain more education. High-paying manufacturing jobs are no longer widely available, and as a result, wages for dropouts have actually *declined* by 35% over the past 30 years, adjusted for inflation (Hamilton & Hamilton, 2006; NCES, 2005).

Because dropping out predicts a variety of future problems, intervention programs have been designed to assist adolescents who drop out or who are at risk for dropping out because of poor school performance or because of attending a school where the dropout rate is high. In general, these programs have concluded that because the problems that lead to dropping out are diverse, programs to prevent dropping out need to be adapted to adolescents' individual needs and problems (Prevatt & Kelly, 2003). One promising approach is the establishment of alternative schools for students who are at risk for dropping out (Barton, 2005; Franklin et al., 2007). Evaluations of these programs have shown that students in the alternative schools are half as likely to drop out as students in control groups who were similarly at risk but did not participate in the programs.

The key to the success of the alternative school programs appears to lie in three factors: attention from caring adult staff members who serve as counselors and social workers; low student-teacher ratios, so that each student receives a substantial amount of attention from teachers; and starting the program in middle school, because by high school students may have fallen too far behind for the interventions to succeed. As one administrator of these programs observed, "If you get kids into a controlled environment where the

expectations are high and there is a lot of adult contact and a lot of adult supervision, guess what: They do pretty well" (Boyle & Lutton, 1999, p. 19).

Privately sponsored dropout prevention programs have also achieved success by identifying at a young age children who are at risk for dropping out and offering them extra assistance and incentives long before they reach high school. Perhaps the best known of these programs is the I Have a Dream (IHAD) program founded in 1986 by philanthropist Eugene Lang (Kahne, 1999; Rhodes et al., 2005). The program began when Lang, speaking to a class of 6th graders in inner-city New York about their educational prospects, spontaneously offered them this incentive: For any of them who graduated from high school with at least a B average, he would pay all of their expenses through college. The dropout rate in that area of New York was 75%, but among Lang's "adopted" class only 10% dropped out and 60% attended college!

Since that time, IHAD has established over 160 projects in 28 states involving over 12,000 children (Kahne, 1999; Rhodes et al., 2005). Local project administrators "adopt" a 3rd- or 4th-grade class in an area where the high school dropout rate is high. The children in these classes are provided with special academic, cultural, and recreational activities through high school, and those who graduate from high school and enter college or vocational school are supported during the time they receive higher education. A key part of the program is the personal involvement of the project staff in the lives of the children, just as Lang became deeply involved with the lives of the children in the New York City class he first adopted. The success of the program has attracted national attention, and it has been suggested that some form of this program should be instituted as a federal program. Some states (e.g., Georgia) now provide financial support throughout college to any student who attains a B average by the end of high school and then attends a state college.

Education in Emerging Adulthood: College and University

The proportion of Americans attending college has risen dramatically in recent decades, as Figure 10.6 shows. Furthermore, about one third of people who obtain an undergraduate degree enter graduate studies within 1 year (Mogolensky, 1996). The extension of education has been an important influence in creating a distinct period of emerging adulthood (Arnett, 2000a, 2004a). Emerging adulthood is characterized by exploration in a variety of aspects of life, and attending college allows young people to explore various possible educational directions that offer different occupational futures. Colleges in the United States and Canada also allow for the exploration of ideas that may be unrelated to any occupational future. You may be a business major and nevertheless enjoy courses on literature or art or philosophy that lead you to explore a variety of ideas about what it means to be

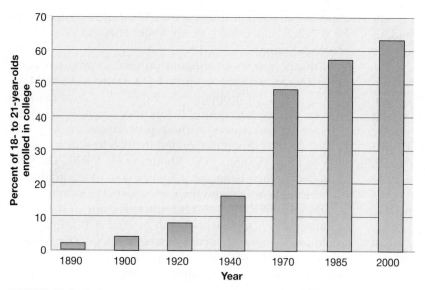

FIGURE 10.6 College attendance over the past century. Bars indicate percentage of 18- to 21-year-olds in the United States attending college during the year indicated.

Sources: Adapted from Arnett & Taber (1994); Bianchi & Spain (1996); NCES (2002).

human. You may be a psychology major and yet find it engaging to explore ideas in astronomy or chemistry courses. In contrast, students in European universities must decide on a specific field of study before they arrive, and they study only that subject (Lipmann, 2002).

In this section we will first examine current characteristics of American college undergraduates. This will be followed by a discussion of what leads to educational success in college—or the lack of it. We will also examine college students' perspectives on the quality of their educational experiences.

Characteristics of College Students

In the United States, although over 60% of recent high school graduates enter college, rates of college attendance are not equal in all groups in American society. Females are more likely than males to enter college; currently, the undergraduate population is 56% female (NCES, 2005). In European countries as well, more females than males obtain higher education (United Nations Economic Commission for Europe, 2005). As of 2007, according to a worldwide survey there were more young women than young men in higher education in 83 of 141 countries, including many developing countries (Economist, 2007).

In the United States, Asian Americans are the ethnic group most likely to attend college. About 70% of Asian Americans have obtained at least some college education by age 25–29, compared with 60% of Whites, 55% of Blacks, and one third of Latinos (NCES, 2005). In the past 2 decades, these percentages have increased for all ethnic groups.

Most undergraduates are in their late teens or early 20s. However, it is increasingly common for people to enter college or return to college in their later 20s or beyond. In 1974, only 22% of entering students were "nontraditional" students

(older than 23); by 2000, this proportion had risen to 43% (Dey & Hurtado, 1999; NCES, 2002). In this section we will discuss traditional students because our focus is on the emerging adulthood age period of the late teens and early 20s.

The areas of study chosen by college students have changed over the decades. Business has consistently been among the top preferred majors, but the proportion of entering students preferring business has fluctuated from 14% in 1966 to 27% in 1987 to 16% in 2007 (Dey & Hurtado, 1999; Higher Education Research Institute (HERI), 2008). Education and engineering have also ranked consistently among the top preferred majors, at about 10% each. The major area that has increased most in preference over the past 3 decades is health professions, which rose from 5% in 1966 to 16%—tied for first with business—in 2000 (NCES, 2002).

There are distinct gender differences in the major preferences stated by college students, and the extent of some of these gender differences has changed substantially over recent decades (Dey & Hurtado, 1999; NCES, 2008). Females are about four times as likely as males to major in education and about three times as likely to major in psychology. Males and females are about equally represented in biological sciences, business, premed, and prelaw; in all of these areas, female representation has increased since 1972. In 1972 females were only one fourth as likely as males to major in the physical sciences, but now they are nearly equal to males. Males continue to be about four times as likely as females to major in computer science and engineering.

Gender differences have also changed dramatically in attainment of postgraduate degrees (Bianchi & Spain, 1996; Smallwood, 2003; NCES, 2008). Women earn 34% of dentistry degrees, up from just 1% in 1970. They also earn half of medical doctor degrees (8% in 1970), half of law degrees (5% in 1970), and nearly half of master of business administration (MBA) degrees (4% in 1970). Across fields, women earn 57% of postgraduate degrees, up from just 10% in 1960.

For most young people, it takes longer now to obtain a 4-year undergraduate degree than it did 2 or 3 decades ago. Currently, it takes an average of 6 years for students to obtain a "4-year" degree (Roonly, 2003). A number of factors explain why it now takes students longer to graduate (Dey & Hurtado, 1999). Financial concerns are at the top of the list. Tuition rates have increased to a shocking extent and were over *four times higher* (even taking into account inflation) in 2007 than they were in 1982 in both public and private colleges and universities (Lewin, 2008). Financial aid has also shifted markedly from grants to loans, which has led many students to work long hours while attending college in order to avoid accruing excessive debt before they graduate (Dey & Hurtado, 1999; HERI, 2005). In 2006, 46% of full-time college students were employed (compared to 32% in 1970), and 81% of part-time students (NCES, 2008). Also, some students prefer to extend their college years to switch majors,

The proportion of women in fields such as medicine and law has increased dramatically since 1970.

TABLE 10.3	Ethnic Differences in Financial Support for College

"In high school, I knew that if I wanted to go to college, it would be possible for me to find financial support either from my family or from scholarships, loans, or other programs."

Whites: 86% strongly agree (0% strongly disagree)

Blacks: 9% strongly agree (42% strongly disagree)

Latinos: 9% strongly agree (33% strongly disagree)

"For as long as I wished to continue my education, it would be possible for me to find financial support either from my family or from scholarships, loans, or other programs."

Whites: 59% strongly agree

Blacks: 19% strongly agree

Latinos: 12% strongly agree

Asian Americans: 63% strongly agree

"It has been difficult for me to find the financial support to get the kind of education I really want."

Whites: 5% strongly agree

Blacks: 61% strongly agree

Latinos: 36% strongly agree

Asian Americans: 0% strongly agree

Based on a sample of 304 emerging adults aged 20–29.

Source: Arnett (2004a).

add a minor field of study, or take advantage of internship programs or study-abroad programs.

In Europe, university education traditionally lasted even longer than in the United States, often 6, 7, 8 years, or more. Most European systems offered a university degree that was like the American bachelor, master's, and doctoral degrees rolled into one, so naturally it took longer than the American bachelor degree. However, just recently the European system has changed to match the American system, with separate bachelor's, master's, and doctoral degrees (Economist, 2008). This was done to shorten the time European emerging adults spend in university, and to promote the development of coordinated programs between European and American universities. It also reflects the growing globalization of education.

Educational Success in College

Although college students take an average of 6 years now to graduate with a 4-year degree, even at 6 years or more graduation is by no means inevitable. In fact, about one half of college students drop out before obtaining a degree (Hamilton & Hamilton, 2006). For years, researchers have been studying factors that contribute to individual decisions to stay in or leave higher education. **Retention** is the term for maintaining students in college until they graduate. Some factors related to retention are students' previous academic performance, ethnic background, and family SES. A variety of studies have found that retention is higher among students of higher academic ability and better precollege academic performance (Arnold, Mares, & Calkins, 1986; DeBerard et al., 2004; Tinto, 1993). Retention is higher among White students than among African American or Latino students, in part because minority students often come

from high schools where they received poor academic preparation for college (Hamilton & Hamilton, 2006; Tinto, 1993).

Retention is also positively related to students' family SES (Hamilton & Hamilton, 2006; Tinto, 1993)—the higher the students' family SES, the more likely they are to stay in college until they graduate. As tuition rates have increased substantially over the past 2 decades, college costs as a percentage of family income have grown, especially for low-income families (HERI, 2005). Furthermore, surveys indicate that families that need financial aid the most often know the least about what aid is available (Shea, 2003). Consequently, it is not surprising that lack of adequate financial support often causes students' premature departure. As Table 10.3 shows, this is especially a problem for African American and Latino students because they tend to come from families with less money than White and Asian American students do (NCES, 2008). Students who receive financial aid are more likely to get a bachelor's degree than students who do not get any aid, regardless of whether the aid is a loan or grant (Hamilton & Hamilton, 2006). Finally, personal concerns may also contribute to students' decisions to leave before graduating. Some of these personal concerns are marriage, family responsibilities, health problems, and accepting a new job (Tinto, 1993).

retention The degree of success in maintaining students in college until they graduate.

In an effort to enhance retention rates, many colleges and universities have instituted programs for this purpose (Braxton et al., 2007). Programs have also been developed specifically for students from ethnic minorities who have the lowest retention rates, including African Americans, Latinos, and Native Americans. Successful programs have used a variety of approaches, such as peer mentoring and special programs to support first-year student (Braunstein et al., 2008; Shotton et al., 2007). Scholars in this area recommend emphasizing the strengths of minority students and not just their problems (Maton et al., 2008).

THINKING CRITICALLY •••

Do you think that by the end of the 21st century nearly all emerging adults will attend college, just as high school education became nearly universal for adolescents in the 20th century? Why or why not?

Students' College Learning Experiences

What kind of experiences do emerging adults have at college? What kind of an education do they get? What sorts of things do they learn and fail to learn? How do they change during the course of their college years? These questions have been the target of considerable research and growing concern over the past 25 years.

At the outset, it should be noted that the college experience is many different things to many different people. The colleges emerging adults attend vary widely, from enormous research-oriented universities with tens of thousands of students to small liberal arts colleges with a few hundred students, to community colleges whose students are mostly people who work as well as go to school. The nature of the college experience also depends on the goals and attitudes of the students themselves, as we will see in the next section.

Four Student Subcultures One useful way of characterizing young people's college experiences was developed in the early 1960s by the sociologists Burton Clark and Martin Trow (1966), who described four student "subcultures": the collegiate, the vocational, the academic, and the rebel. The *collegiate* subculture centers around fraternities, sororities, dating, drinking, big sports events, and campus fun. Professors, courses, and grades are a secondary priority. Students in this subculture do enough school work to get by, but they resist or ignore any encouragement from faculty to become seriously involved with ideas. Their main purpose during their college years is fellowship and partying. This subculture thrives especially at big universities.

Students in the *vocational* subculture have a practical view of their college education. To them, the purpose of college is to gain skills and a degree that will enable them to get a better job than they would have otherwise. Like collegiates, students in the vocational subculture resist professors' demands

for engagement in ideas, beyond the requirements of the course work. But vocationals have neither the time nor the money for the frivolous fun of the collegiate subculture. Typically, they work 20 to 40 hours a week to support themselves and help pay their college tuition. Students who attend community colleges are mostly in this category.

The *academic* subculture is the one that identifies most strongly with the educational mission of college. Students in this subculture are drawn to the world of ideas and knowledge. They study hard, do their assignments, and get to know their professors. These are the students professors like best because they are excited about and engaged with the materials their professors present.

Students in the *rebel* subculture are also deeply engaged with the ideas presented in their courses. However, unlike academics, rebels are aggressively nonconformist. Rather than liking and admiring their professors, they tend to be critically detached from them and skeptical of their expertise. Rebels enjoy learning when they feel the material is interesting and relevant to their lives, but they are selectively studious. If they like a course and respect the professor, they do the work required and often receive a top grade, but if they dislike a course and find it irrelevant to their personal interests they may slack off and receive a low grade.

Clark and Trow (1966) described these student subcultures in the early 1960s, four decades ago. Do the same subcultures still apply to today's emerging adults attending college? Observers of higher education think so (Sperber, 2000), and from my experience as a professor I would agree their description still rings true. All of these subcultures are likely to be familiar to anyone who teaches college students. But it is important to emphasize that these are types of subcultures, not types of students. Most students are blends of the four subcultural types, to different degrees, although most identify with one subculture more than the others.

To put it another way, the four subcultural types represent different kinds of goals that emerging adults have for their college experience. As collegiates they pursue fun, as vocationals they pursue a degree, as academics they pursue knowledge, and as rebels they pursue an identity. Most students hope to make all of these things a part of their college years (American Council on Education, 2003). For example, in one recent study of American college freshmen, 77% responded that it was "very important" for them during college "to learn more about the things that interest me," an academic goal, and nearly as many, 75%, intended "to get training for a specific profession," a vocational goal, but 52% also intended "to find my purpose in life," a rebel/identity goal (HERI, 2005).

THINKING CRITICALLY •••

Do you think the four student subcultures described here exist at your college or university? What subcultures might you delete or add? Which subculture do you identify with most, personally?

The Classroom Experience Critics of American higher education have long deplored the way undergraduate courses are taught at most large universities (Sperber, 2000). Especially in their first 2 years, students often find themselves in classes of several hundred students. The professor is merely a speck on a stage who knows few if any of the students by name and who is far more devoted to research than to teaching. Class periods are devoted almost entirely to lectures, and students sit there passively (if they come to class at all), scribbling occasional notes, struggling to stay awake. Research confirms that students learn much better in smaller classes that require active involvement, and that they enjoy those classes much more (Magolda, 1997; Sperber, 2000). But most students experience few small classes in their first 2 years of college, especially at large universities.

Given these criticisms, and given the research indicating that students generally dislike the large classes that are often their only option, it is surprising that a large majority of students respond favorably to survey questions about the education they are receiving. In a national survey of over 9,000 students, Arthur Levine and Jean Cureton (1998) found that 81% indicated that they were "Satisfied with the teaching at your college." Also, 65% indicated that there were faculty at their college who took a special interest in students' academic progress, and more than half had professors who had "greatly influenced" their academic career. More than half also had professors whom they felt they could turn to for advice on personal matters. In all respects, students' satisfaction with their academic experience at college had increased compared to earlier surveys Levine and Cureton (1998) conducted in 1969 and 1976. Other studies have reported similar findings that most college students believe that the education they receive at college is of high quality and that student satisfaction has increased in recent decades (Dey & Hurtado, 1999; Hoover, 2004; Mathews, 2002b).

Do the results of these studies mean that the educational critics are wrong and that everything is fine with American higher education? Not exactly. Although students are generally satisfied with the education they receive, they tend to be more satisfied at small colleges with small classes than at large universities where the classes are often enormous (Pascarella et al., 2004). In the *Princeton Review*'s annual survey of students at 300 American colleges of various sizes (Sperber, 2000), small colleges consistently rank highest on almost all positive measures, such as "professors make themselves accessible," "professors bring material to life," and "best overall academic experience for undergraduates." In contrast, big research universities dominate the top rankings for all the negative items, such as "professors suck all life from material," "professors make themselves scarce," and "class discussion rare." Table 10.4 illustrates the differences. Of course, the diversity of each category should be kept in mind. Not all professors at small colleges are capable teachers, and many professors at big universities are dedicated and excellent teachers.

The responses of my students to questions about their satisfaction with their college experience illustrate how students can be satisfied overall even as they are dissatisfied with

TABLE 10.4	Students at Small Colleges Tend to Rate Their Professors Higher than Students at Large Universities

"Professors Bring Material to Life"			
Teachers Rated by Students on a Scale of 60 to 100			
High Scores		**Low Scores**	
Reed	99	UCLA	61
Carleton	99	Texas	65
Wabash	99	Michigan	68
Middlebury	98	Harvard	69
Kenyon	98	Penn	69
Amherst	98	Berkeley	70
Kalamazoo	97	Columbia	70
Grinnell	96	NYU	73

Source: *Princeton Review* (2005).

some aspects of the education they have received (Arnett, 2004a). Most have had some professors they found impressive and inspiring, even if others were disappointing. Kim complained about having professors who were "not challenging, engaging, or even remotely human," but she also said she'd had "some wonderful, memorable, and influential professors." Some students have goals that are primarily vocational, so their satisfaction is based on the prospect of getting a degree. Tom said, "I don't feel I have learned as much as I anticipated," but nevertheless he is pleased that he is "achieving a college degree, which is very satisfying," and he expects his degree to be "a great deal of help when I am looking for a job."

But the most common theme that emerges when I ask my students to write about whether they are satisfied or dissatisfied overall with their college experience is that their satisfaction is based mainly on what they have experienced in terms of *personal growth*. This theme could be seen as a combination of the collegiate's search for fun and the rebel's search for identity, with an additional element of becoming more organized and responsible in learning how to be a self-sufficient emerging adult. For example, Mike said he was satisfied with his college experience, but his satisfaction "has nothing to do with school. I have experienced so many different things, become much more responsible for myself and have become more grounded in my views and beliefs." Juggling classes, homework, and a part-time job "has made me manage my time better and work harder." He also feels he has "become more reflective on my life as a result of having a certain amount of freedom and privacy in college." Laurie feels that "most of my classes have been relatively enlightening and beneficial," but what she has learned in them has consisted mostly of "useless, easily forgotten knowledge." Far more important, "college has forced me to think, to question, and sometimes just to accept." Her college experience has been "full of revelations and growth. Because of college,

I am closer to possessing the knowledge I need to be who and what I want to be."

A large body of research supports these students' accounts that college has multiple benefits. Ernest Pascarella and Patrick Terenzini (1991; Pascarella, 2005, 2006) have conducted research on this topic for many years. They find a variety of intellectual benefits from attending college, in areas such as general verbal and quantitative skills, oral and written communication skills, and critical thinking. These benefits hold up even after taking into account factors such as age, gender, precollege abilities, and family social class background. Pascarella and Terenzini also find that in the course of the college years students become less "vocational" in their college goals—that is, they place less emphasis on college as a way to a better job—and more "academic"—that is, they place more emphasis on learning for its own sake and for the sake of enhancing their intellectual and personal growth.

In addition to intellectual, academic benefits, Pascarella and Terenzini describe a long list of nonacademic benefits. In the course of the college years, students develop clearer aesthetic and intellectual values. They gain a more distinct identity and become more confident socially. They become less dogmatic, less authoritarian, and less ethnocentric in their political and social views. Their self-concepts and psychological well-being improve. As with the intellectual benefits, these nonacademic benefits hold up even after taking into account characteristics such as age, gender, and family social class background.

The long-term benefits of going to college are also well established, according to research by Pascarella and Terenzini as well as many others (e.g., NCES, 2002; Schneider & Stevenson, 1999). Emerging adults who attend college tend to have considerably higher earnings, occupational status, and career attainment over the long run, compared to those who do not attend college.

It seems clear, then, that going to college yields a variety of rewards for emerging adults, both personally and professionally. Is college in the United States too expensive? Yes. Is attending college at a big university often frustrating and alienating? Yes. Could the college experience offered to emerging adults be improved? Certainly. But despite these limitations, going to college pays off in multiple ways for emerging adults.

SUMMING UP

In this chapter, we have discussed a variety of topics related to adolescents' and emerging adults' school experiences and performance. Here is a summary of the main points:

- Over the past century, the secondary school curriculum in the United States has changed from a focus on liberal arts to a curriculum intended to prepare students for work and citizenship, to a curriculum that includes a wide range of courses from math and English to music and physical education. These changes have taken place partly in response to the changing characteristics of the young people attending secondary school, and partly in response to changes in cultural beliefs about what adolescents need to learn.

- Secondary education around the world varies greatly in terms of availability and quality. Industrialized countries tend to provide relatively high-quality secondary education for most adolescents. Adolescents in developing countries are less likely to complete secondary school and the quality of secondary education available to them is often poor, but the proportion of adolescents enrolled in secondary school is increasing.

- In international comparisons, industrialized countries rank higher than developing countries in academic performance, and the academic performance of American high school students tends to be toward the lower end compared with the performance of students in most other industrialized countries.

- School climate—the quality of the classroom interactions between teachers and students—affects students' academic performance and their participation in delinquency. The same qualities of warmth and moderate control that are effective in parenting are also effective in schools.

- Adolescents' school performance is influenced not only by factors within the school but also by many influences beyond the classroom, including family, friends, work and leisure, and cultural beliefs.

- Ethnic differences in adolescents' academic performance are explained in part by social class differences and in part by different influences from family and friends.

- Girls perform better than boys on nearly all measures of academic performance, and in recent years they have become increasingly likely to pursue math and science.

- Gifted adolescents are distinguished by precocity, independence, a drive for mastery, and exceptional information-processing skills. About 10% of adolescents have a learning disability, with half of these diagnosed as ADHD.

- Tracking is a controversial practice in the United States, with advocates arguing that it results in a better fit between students' abilities and interests and their curriculum, and critics maintaining that it relegates students in lower tracks to a second-rate education in which they fall steadily further behind other students.

- Dropping out of high school is predicted by a variety of factors, including previous problems in school, personality characteristics, and family difficulties. Successful programs to prevent dropping out have focused on providing alternative schools or on promising adolescents long-term financial help for their education if they perform well in school.

- Most college students are satisfied with the education they receive, and abundant research indicates that college has multiple benefits. College students who obtain a bachelor's degree now take an average of 6 years to do so, but about half of students drop out of college before obtaining a degree. Factors related to dropping out of college include previous academic performance, ethnic background, and socioeconomic status.

The practice of having adolescents spend many hours each day in school is fairly recent historically and has developed in response to economic changes that require young people to have academic skills in order to fulfill the requirements of jobs in an increasingly information-based economy. As the material in this chapter shows, to some extent industrialized societies are still struggling with how best to teach their young people. European societies allow young people to begin specialized education by the time they are just 14 or 15 years old. This may make young people more engaged in their education because they will be studying topics in areas they have chosen themselves, but such a system makes it difficult for them to change directions in their later teens or early 20s. In the United States, no such early decision is required, and young people often postpone a decision about occupational choice until after a year or two of college or even until deciding on graduate school. Such a system allows for a substantial amount of individual choice, but during adolescence it means that all students are together in the same schools despite their widely varying abilities and interests. This system seems inadequate and unstimulating to many of them. Perhaps the European and American systems involve different but inevitable trade-offs, or perhaps both systems will eventually be seen as early experiments on the way to other educational forms that will prove to be more effective.

For adolescents in economically developing countries, secondary school and higher education are currently restricted mainly to the elite, just as they were in industrialized countries a century ago. The proportion of young people in secondary school and beyond in developing countries is growing and is likely to continue to grow as a consequence of globalization and the requirements of the global economy. Currently, however, the focus of daily activity for adolescents in developing countries is not school but work. In the next chapter, we will explore in depth the nature of their work experiences and discuss the work experiences of young people in industrialized countries as well.

KEY TERMS

INTERNET RESOURCES

http://nces.ed.gov
Web site for the National Center for Education Statistics, a government agency. The site contains useful information on education from grade school through grad school, including a great deal of information that pertains to adolescents and emerging adults. Their immensely valuable yearly report, *The Condition of Education*, can be downloaded free from the site.

FOR FURTHER READING

Barton, P. E. (2005). *One-third of a nation: Rising dropout rates and declining opportunities*. Princeton, NJ: Educational Testing Service. Barton presents an insightful analysis of why adolescents drop out of school and the consequences of doing so.

Hamilton, S., & Hamilton, M. A. (2006). School, work, and emerging adulthood. In J. J. Arnett & J. L. Tanner (Eds.), *Coming of age in the 21st Century: The lives and contexts of emerging adults*. Washington, DC: American Psychological Association. In this chapter the Hamiltons provide a complete analysis of the educational paths that emerging adults take after high school. They do an especially good job of describing the diversity of those paths, including attaining the GED credential, attending community college, and attending university.

Lloyd, C. (Ed.) (2005). *Growing up global: The changing transitions to adulthood in developing countries*. Washington, DC: National Research Council and Institute of Medicine. This book contains excellent chapters on a variety of topics, including the diversity of adolescents' school experiences worldwide and how schooling for adolescents is becoming more widespread due to globalization.

PEARSON
mydevelopmentlab

For more review plus practice tests, videos, flashcards, and more, log on to MyDevelopmentLab.

11 Work

OUTLINE

" I like working. I mean, you work in school, but you don't get money for it. You just get a paper that says you completed your courses in high school. You work and you get money for it, so I like that. But working at Burger Barn did interfere with school a little bit. My grades went down some. My mom was, 'If you don't bring your grades up you have to quit.' Then I brought my grades up real quick. Work do interfere if you don't know how to level with it."

        —Tawana, African American adolescent, New York City (in Newman, 1999)

"I always knew I wanted to be a doctor. But premed took up too much time and I didn't have a life, and I figured that once I became a doctor I still wouldn't be able to spend time with kids. And I want to have kids and be around them. So I figure the next best thing is to be a nurse."

        —Chalantra, age 20 (in Arnett, 2004a, p. 149)

"I average about $16 an hour [as a server in a restaurant], so I mean, where else can I go right now and make that much money? I'm just kind of lazy right now. I'm just taking it easy. I'll probably end up being an engineer. I'm really good at math and I know I could pick up on it real easy. I could also own or manage a restaurant, because I've been in the restaurant business for eight years so I know a lot about it. I cook, I've waited tables, I've bartended. But right now, I'm just kind of 'treading water,' as my mom says."

        —Scott, age 23 (Arnett, unpublished data)

"This is my fourth year teaching. It's very fulfilling. I love it! I mean, I enjoy everything that I do. I went into English teaching because I love literature and I love writing and I wanted to talk about books, and I get to do that. It's great. I mean, I always tell people 'I can't believe that someone's going to pay me to read books and to talk about them with other people.' "

        —Simon, 25-year-old Asian American (Arnett, unpublished data)

"LOVE AND WORK" WAS SIGMUND FREUD'S TERSE response when he was asked what a person should be able to do well in order to be considered psychologically healthy. Work is, in all cultures and in all historical times, one of the fundamental areas of human activity. Earlier, we discussed preparation for adult roles as one of the three principal goals of socialization. All cultures expect their members to contribute some kind of work, whether it be paid employment; cooperative hunting, fishing, or farming; or taking care of children and running a household. Adolescence is often a key time of preparation for adult work roles. Whatever work young people may have contributed as children, adolescence is the time when work expectations grow more serious, as adolescents prepare to take their place as full members—which always means working members—of their culture.

In this chapter, we begin by discussing adolescent work in traditional cultures. This is a good place to start because work has a special prominence for adolescents in traditional cultures. Unlike adolescents in industrialized societies, most adolescents in traditional cultures are no longer in school, and most of their day is devoted to work. As noted in earlier chapters, in traditional cultures adolescents typically work alongside adults, doing the kind of work that adults do. Thus we begin this chapter by taking a look at the types of work that occupy adolescents and adults in most traditional cultures: hunting, fishing, and gathering; farming; and child care. Then we look at how the economies of traditional cultures are changing with globalization and how adolescents in these cultures increasingly work in new industries that offer them economic opportunities but often exploit them.

Adolescents in traditional cultures are now in a position, with regard to work, that is similar to what was experienced by adolescents in industrialized societies a century ago. In both cases, prolonged schooling was rarely available or useful to adolescents, given the jobs available in their economy. In both cases, industrialization left adolescents vulnerable to exploitation in unhealthy and unsafe working conditions. Both cases involve an economy rapidly becoming industrialized. In the second part of this chapter, we examine these issues in the history of adolescent work in industrialized societies.

Following this discussion, we take a look at various issues related to adolescent work as it currently takes place in industrialized societies. This will include a look at what adolescents typically do in their jobs and at how work influences various aspects of their development. We will also look at the transition from school to work, both for emerging adults who attend college and for those who do not. This will include an examination of the occupational choices that young people make and of how emerging adults view work. At the end of the chapter we will examine the characteristics and experiences of young people who perform volunteer work.

Adolescent Work in Traditional Cultures

For many millennia of human history before industrialization, most human work involved the same basic activities: hunting, fishing, and gathering edible fruits and vegetables; farming and caring for domestic animals; and caring for children while doing household work. These kinds of work are still common in many traditional cultures, and we will first look at adolescents' participation in such work. However, because virtually all traditional cultures are in the process of industrializing, it will be important to look at adolescents' experiences in industrial settings as well.

Hunting, Fishing, and Gathering

Hunting and fishing in traditional cultures are typically undertaken by men, and adolescent boys learn how it is done by accompanying their fathers and other men on hunting or fishing expeditions (Gilmore, 1990). Females are rarely the principal hunters, but they sometimes assist in the hunting enterprise by holding nets, setting traps, or beating the bushes to flush out game.

Hunting often provides not only food but also materials for tools, clothing, and other purposes. As such, it serves many important functions in cultures that rely on it, and success at hunting may be required of adolescent boys as a way of showing that they are ready for manhood. For example, among the nomadic Bushmen of the Kalahari Desert in southwest Africa, an adolescent boy is not considered a man—and is not allowed to marry—until he has successfully killed his first antelope. Doing so is a way of demonstrating

Adolescent boys in traditional cultures learn the work of adult men. Here, a boy in the Abouri tribe of West Africa learns to carve a dugout canoe.

that he will be able to provide for a family as part of his adult work role.

Fishing is another form of work that adolescent boys learn through observing and assisting their fathers and other men. The skills required for success at fishing include not only fishing itself but boating and navigation. For example, adolescents in the South Sea Islands in the Pacific Ocean traditionally learned complex systems of nighttime navigation from their fathers, using a "star compass" through which they set their course according to the positions of the constellations (Gladwin, 1970; Hutchins, 1983).

Often in cultures where males have the responsibility for hunting or fishing, women have a complementary responsibility for gathering. This means that they find edible wild fruits and vegetables growing in the surrounding area and collect them to contribute to their families' food supply. This can be a substantial contribution. Anthropologists have observed that in cultures that rely on a combination of hunting and gathering, women contribute as much or more to the family food supply through gathering as men do through hunting (Dahlberg, 1981).

Hunting and gathering cultures have rapidly changed in the past half century in response to globalization, and only a few such cultures exist in the present (Schlegel & Barry, 1991; Schlegel, 2003, 2009). The nomadic way of life typical of hunting and gathering cultures—moving from place to place, following the food supply—is not well suited to the global economy, with its stable communities and its property boundaries. Fishing, too, has largely disappeared as a central basis for a culture's economy. Even in cultures that have a long tradition of fishing, such as in Norway and Japan, modern fishing techniques are so advanced that a very small proportion of people engaged in fishing can provide more than enough fish to feed the entire population.

Farming and Care of Domestic Animals

Farming and care of domestic animals often go together in the same way that hunting and gathering tend to go together—one for providing meat, the other for providing grains, vegetables, and fruit. Adolescents in cultures with economies based on farming and care of domestic animals often provide useful work to their families. Care of domestic animals is a frequent responsibility of adolescents and even preadolescents all over the world—cattle in southern Africa, sheep and goats in northern Africa and southern Europe, small livestock in Asia and Eastern Europe— perhaps because such work requires little in the way of skill or experience (Schlegel & Barry, 1991). Farming often requires a higher level of training and skill, particularly if the amount of land to be farmed is large. This enterprise is typically carried out by fathers and sons working together, with the sons not only contributing to their families in the present but also learning how to manage the land they will eventually inherit.

Even today, farming remains the main occupation of a substantial proportion of the world's population. In developing countries such as Brazil, India, and the Philippines, over half of the adult males are employed in agricultural work (Lloyd, 2005; UNDP, 2006). However, in all developing countries, the proportion of people in farming is declining in the course of industrialization. Just as with fishing, advanced technology and equipment make it possible for a few people to do work that once required hundreds.

Child Care and Household Work

When it comes to child care, women and girls have the main responsibility in most traditional cultures, with men and boys occasionally providing support. The work of child care usually begins quite early in life for girls. If they have younger siblings, girls often become at least partly responsible for taking care of them as early as age 6 or 7 (Whiting & Edwards, 1988). By the time she reaches adolescence, the oldest girl in a family may have several younger siblings to help care for, and perhaps cousins as well.

Along with child care, working alongside her mother often means household work for an adolescent girl living in a traditional culture. A great deal of household work needs to be done in a traditional culture that has no access to electricity and the many conveniences that go along with it. Chores such as collecting firewood, starting and tending the fire, and fetching water must be done on a daily basis. Preparing food is also heavily labor intensive in such cultures. Want a chicken for dinner? You have to do more than defrost it and zap it in the microwave oven (or stop by the drive-through window at Chuck-Full-O-Chicks)—you have to kill it, trim it, and pluck it before you can cook it.

With so much work to be done, women in these cultures often enlist the help of their daughters from an early age,

Adolescent girls in traditional cultures typically have responsibility for household work such as food preparation. Here, a girl of the Sahelian culture of northern Africa prepares a meal.

and by adolescence, daughters typically work alongside their mothers and other women of the family as near-equal partners (Lloyd, 2005). By doing this kind of work, the adolescent daughter prepares herself for her adult work role and also demonstrates to others, including potential marriage partners, that she is capable of fulfilling the expectations for running a household that are typically required of women in traditional cultures.

Globalization and Adolescent Work in Traditional Cultures

Adolescents and adults in traditional cultures have been doing the kinds of work described above for thousands of years. However, as we have seen in previous chapters, all traditional cultures today are being influenced by globalization. An important aspect of globalization is economic integration, including increasing trade between countries and increasingly large-scale agriculture and manufacturing in many cultures and countries that have known only small, local, family-based economic activity until very recently. Globalization has certainly conferred some economic benefits on the people in these cultures. Preindustrial economic life can be hard. Simply providing the everyday necessities of life is a lot of work without industrialization, as the chicken example above illustrates. Entry into the global economy is usually accompanied by increased access to electricity, which often makes food preparation, clothes washing, heating, and other tasks considerably easier. Entry into the global economy is also usually accompanied by increased access to education and medical care.

The globalization of economic life thus holds the promise of making life better for people in the many cultures around the world that are just now being introduced to it. Adolescents and their families derive several benefits when adolescents work (Larson et al., 2010). Poor families in developing countries often depend on adolescents' contributions to the family income for basic necessities like food and clothing. Adolescents gain status and respect within the family by being able to bring money into the family. Although jobs in industrial settings are often difficult and may even be hazardous, the alternative of agricultural work is just as hard, and working in an industrial setting is often seen as a way for adolescents to gain skills and contacts that will eventually lead to a better job and a higher income.

However, the transition from a preindustrial economy to the global economy is proving to be problematic in many places. Currently, many people are experiencing not increased comfort and opportunity but brutal work in terrible conditions for miserable pay. And the burden of much of this work is falling on the shoulders of adolescents, mainly those between 10 and 15 years of age, who are more capable than children of doing useful industrial work and less capable than adults of asserting their rights and resisting maltreatment.

The **International Labor Organization (ILO)** has estimated that about *200 million* children and adolescents are employed worldwide and that 95% of them are in developing countries (ILO, 2002, 2004, 2006, 2008). They are numerous in Latin America and Africa, but the greatest number of adolescent workers and the worst working conditions are found in Asia (including countries such as India, Bangladesh, Thailand, Indonesia, the Philippines, and Vietnam). Agricultural work is the most common form of employment for adolescents, usually on commercial farms or plantations, often working alongside their parents but for only one third to one half the pay (ILO, 2002).

In addition, many adolescents in these countries work in factories and workshops where they perform labor such as weaving carpets, sewing clothes, gluing shoes, curing leather, and polishing gems. The working conditions are often horrific—crowded garment factories where the doors are locked and the adolescents (and adults) work 14-hour shifts, small poorly lit huts where they sit at a loom weaving carpets for hours on end, glass factories where the temperatures are unbearably hot and adolescents carry hot rods of molten glass from one station to another (ILO, 2004). Other adolescents work in cities in a wide variety of jobs, including domestic service, grocery shops, tea stalls, road construction, and prostitution.

In India, a common and particularly brutal system for exploiting adolescent labor is called **debt bondage** (Basu & Chau, 2007). Debt bondage begins when a person needs a loan and has no money to offer for security, so instead pledges his labor or that of his children. The poor of India are most often the ones desperate enough to accept this kind of loan. Because many of them are illiterate, they are easily exploited by lenders who manipulate the interest and the payments in such a way that the loan becomes virtually impossible to pay back. In desperation, parents sometimes offer the labor of their children in an effort to pay off the debt.

Adolescents are especially valuable for bonded labor because they are more productive than children. According to the ILO, adolescents most often end up as bonded laborers in agriculture, domestic service, prostitution, and industries such as the manufacture of hand-knitted carpets. Once adolescents have been committed by their parents to debt bondage, it is extremely difficult for them to free themselves of it; in fact, the United Nations has condemned debt bondage as a modern form of slavery (ILO, 2004).

Perhaps the worst form of exploitation of adolescents' work is prostitution. Estimates of the number of adolescent prostitutes in developing countries vary, but it is widely agreed that adolescent prostitution is a pervasive and growing problem, especially in Asia, and within Asia especially in Thailand (Basu & Chau, 2007; ILO, 2002). Of course, there are adolescent prostitutes in industrialized countries as well, but the problem is much more widespread in developing countries.

Adolescent girls in these countries become prostitutes in several ways. Some are kidnapped and taken to a separate country. Isolated in a country where they are not citizens and where they do not know the language, they are highly vulnerable and dependent on their kidnappers. Some are rural adolescent girls who are promised jobs in restaurants or domestic service, then forced to become prostitutes once the recruiter takes them to their urban destination. Sometimes parents sell the girls into prostitution, out of desperate poverty or simply out of the desire for more consumer goods (ILO, 2004). A large proportion of the customers in Asian brothels are Western tourists. The proportion is large enough that the United States and several European countries now have laws permitting prosecution of their citizens for sexually exploiting young adolescent girls in other countries. The demand is increasingly for younger adolescent girls because they are perceived to be less likely than older girls to be carrying the HIV virus.

Although the exploitation of adolescents in developing countries is widespread and often brutal, signs of positive changes can be seen. According to the ILO, from 2002 to 2006 the number of child and adolescent laborers fell 11% worldwide, and the number engaged in hazardous work fell even more, by 26% (ILO, 2006). This decline has taken place because the issue of child and adolescent labor has received in-

---

International Labor Organization (ILO) An organization that seeks to prevent children and adolescents from being exploited in the workplace.

debt bondage Arrangement in which a person who is in debt pledges his labor or the labor of his children as payment.

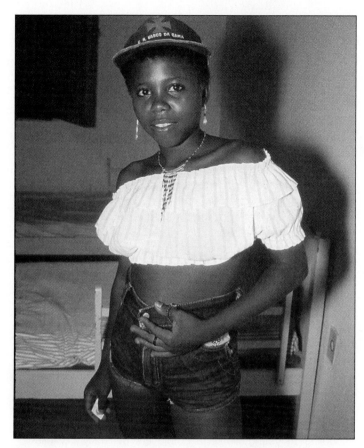
Many adolescent girls in developing countries have been forced into prostitution. Here, a young prostitute at a rehabilitation center in Brazil.

involvement in farming and other family economic activities became exploitation in the factories and other early settings of industrialization. In response to this exploitation, governments in industrialized countries restricted adolescent work early in the 20th century. By mid-century most adolescents attended high school, and few high school students held part-time jobs. Since 1950, adolescents have increasingly combined school with part-time work, especially in the United States.

Adolescent Work Before 1900

Before industrialization began in the 17th and 18th centuries, adolescent work in the West was much like adolescent work today in traditional cultures whose economies center on farming and care of domestic animals. Boys helped their fathers on the farm from middle childhood onward, and in adolescence they gradually learned to take over the responsibilities for running the farm they would eventually inherit. Girls helped with the care of the domestic animals and worked alongside their mothers to turn the harvests and the animals into meals on the table, with adolescent girls becoming near-equal partners to their mothers in running the household.

As industrialization proceeded in the 18th and 19th centuries, it became increasingly common for adolescents to work in factories. Over the course of the 19th century, the proportion of the labor force working in farming in the United States declined from over 70% to under 40% (Hernandez, 1997). (Today it is about 2%.) For many adolescents, this meant a transition from working alongside their parents on the family farm to working in a city, often in a factory setting. Industrialization created a huge demand for cheap labor, and adolescents were often recruited to fill this demand. By the 1870s, young men aged 16 to 20 comprised nearly half the male workforce in New England textile mills and about one third of the workers in rubber factories and agricultural tool factories. In boot and shoe factories, over 40% of the female workers were aged 16 to 20 (Kett, 1977). Adolescents also worked in large numbers in coal mines, food canneries, and seafood-processing plants (Freedman, 1994).

Working in factories, mines, and processing plants often meant working long hours under dangerous and unhealthy conditions. A typical work schedule was 10 to 14 hours a day, six days a week. Of course, adults were subject to the same conditions, but children and adolescents were more vulnerable to accident and injury. It is estimated that the accident rate for children and adolescents in factories was twice as

creased attention from the world media, governments, and international organizations such as the ILO and the United Nations Children's Fund (UNICEF). Furthermore, many countries have taken legislative action to raise the number of years children and adolescents are legally required to attend school and to enforce the often-ignored laws in many countries against employing children younger than their mid-teens (ILO, 2008). For example, India now has a program, monitored by UNICEF, to mark carpets that have not involved child labor with a RUGMARK label—a logo of a smiling child superimposed on a drawing of a carpet. Amid such signs of progress, it remains true that millions of adolescents work in miserable conditions all around the world (ILO, 2002, 2004, 2006, 2008).

THINKING CRITICALLY •••

Do you think people living in the West have any responsibility for the conditions of adolescent work in developing countries? Why or why not? Do they have more responsibility if they buy the items that such adolescents produce through their labor?

The History of Adolescent Work in the West

As noted at the outset of the chapter, adolescents' work in the West has followed a historical path similar to the one now being experienced by adolescents in traditional cultures. Traditional

As we have seen in this chapter, the working conditions currently experienced by adolescents in developing countries are in many ways dangerous, unhealthy, underpaid, and exploitative. Adolescents in industrialized countries generally work in conditions that are much more favorable, but this is a relatively recent development. In fact, the working conditions of adolescents in the 19th century in industrialized countries were remarkably similar to the conditions experienced today by adolescents in developing countries.

Information on child and adolescent labor in the 19th century is especially abundant in Great Britain, where government statistics were kept much more systematically and accurately than in the United States. The history of child and adolescent labor in Great Britain is described in a book by Pamela Horn (1994), *Children's Work and Welfare, 1780–1890.*

Because Britain was the first country in which industrialization took place, it was also the first country in which child and adolescent labor was widely used. Textile manufacturing (the making of cloth and clothing) was the first area, beginning in the 1770s when for the first time textiles were mass produced in factories rather than made one at a time in homes. Children and adolescents were especially attractive to employers, partly because there was a shortage of adult workers and partly because younger workers could be paid lower wages. Moreover, with their nimble fingers they could perform much of the work even better than adults.

Many of these children and adolescents had no parents and were sent to the textile mills by officials in city orphanages and institutions for the poor, who were glad to be relieved of the cost of caring for them. Young people had no choice but to go and were not free to leave until they reached age 21. For those who did have parents, their parents usually did not object to them working in textile mills but encouraged it in order to increase the family's income.

Working conditions varied in the mills, but 12- to 14-hour workdays were common, with an hour break for lunch. The work was monotonous, exhausting, and dangerous. A momentary lapse of attention could lead to serious injury, and crushed hands and fingers were common. Dust and residue from the spinning process damaged their lungs and caused stomach illnesses and eye infections.

The first attempts at government regulation of the mills were tentative, to say the least. Because the British economy depended so heavily on the young millworkers, even reformers were reluctant to advocate an end to their labor. There was also little public support for abolishing child and adolescent labor, and labor restrictions were fiercely resisted by parents who depended on their income. Thus, the first law, the Health and Morals of Apprentices Act of 1802, simply limited young workers to 12 hours of labor a day! The act also mandated minimum standards of ventilation and sanitation in the mills, but mill owners widely ignored these provisions.

In addition, the act required employers to provide daily schooling to young workers. Employers generally complied with this requirement because they believed that educated children would be more compliant and more valuable as workers. The result was a significant increase in literacy among young workers. The schooling requirement spread to other industries over the following decades and became the basis of the *half-time system*, in which young workers in factories received schooling for a half day and worked for a half day. This system survived in British society until the end of the 19th century.

high as for adults (Freedman, 1994). Their developing bodies also made them more vulnerable than adults to illness from unhealthy working conditions. For example, young millworkers often developed tuberculosis, bronchitis, and other respiratory diseases. Children and adolescents who worked in cotton mills were only half as likely to live past age 20 as those outside the mills.

THINKING CRITICALLY ●●●

Compare the history of adolescent work in the West to the recent history of adolescent work in developing countries. What are the similarities and differences?

Adolescent Work in the 20th Century

As we have seen in Chapter 1, this pattern of adolescents being typically engaged in full-time work began to change during the Age of Adolescence, 1890 to 1920. Concern developed over the

Before industrialization, most adolescents in the West grew up on a family farm.

In the 1830s, regulatory attention turned to mining. Just as changes in textile production had created a boom in jobs in the late 1700s, an increase in the need for coal in the early 1800s created a mining boom. Once again, children and adolescents were sought as workers because they were cheap, manageable, and could do some jobs better than adults. Once again, parents urged their children to become laborers as early as possible to contribute to the family income, even though the work in the mines was especially hazardous.

A workday of 12 to 14 hours per day six days a week was common for young miners. Many of them descended into the mine before sunrise and came up again after sunset, so that they never saw daylight for weeks at a time except on Sundays. Accidents were common, and coal dust damaged young miners' lungs. The first reforms, in the 1842 Mines Act, prohibited boys under age 10 from working in mines and required boys over age 10 to be provided with schooling by the mine owners, but did nothing about the working conditions in the mines. As this law and others restricted the employment of children, employment among adolescents became even more widespread.

Over the second half of the 19th century, legal regulations on child and adolescent labor slowly and gradually reduced the exploitation of young workers in British industrial settings. Regulations increased concerning the work young workers could be required to do. The half-time system, once celebrated as a way of protecting young workers from exploitation, became viewed as an obstacle to their educational opportunities. Public schools were established, and attendance at school became legally required for all children in the 1880s. This essentially marked the end of child labor in

In the 19th century, adolescents often worked in dangerous and unhealthy conditions. Here, young mine workers.

Great Britain, and in the following decades more and more adolescents attended secondary school rather than working, just as in the United States.

exploitation of children and adolescents—a striking parallel to what is going on currently in developing countries—and laws were passed that restricted the times and places children and adolescents could work and that required children to attend school. Nevertheless, the changes in patterns of child and adolescent labor took place slowly. Even as recently as 1925 the majority of American adolescents left school by age 15 to become full-time workers (Horan & Hargis, 1991; Modell, Furstenberg, & Hershberg, 1976). Most families viewed the labor of their adolescents as an important contributor to the family income, and only relatively affluent families could afford the luxury of keeping their adolescents in school past their early teens.

However, the trend toward increasing time in school that had begun early in the century continued steadily, and in the 1930s the proportion of adolescents staying in school through their mid-teens continued to grow. Furthermore, increasingly adolescents were either in school or working, but not both. By 1940, fewer than 5% of the 16- to 17-year-olds attending high school were also employed (U.S. Department of Commerce, 1940). American adolescents lived in two sep-

arate worlds, with 70% of 14- to 17-year-olds in high school and most of the other 30% in the full-time labor force.

This pattern changed dramatically in the decades following World War II, toward combining school with part-time work. One reason for this new trend was the shift in the American economy. From 1950 through the 1990s, the fastest-growing sectors of the American economy were retail trade and service (Aronson et al., 1996; Ginzberg, 1977). In the late 20th century, jobs became numerous for young people who were willing to work part time for relatively low wages in jobs such as cook, restaurant server, or clerk in a department store.

And American adolescents proved to be willing. By 1980, one half of high school sophomores and two thirds of high school seniors were working in part-time jobs (Lewin-Epstein, 1981), and by the late 1990s, over 80% of seniors had held at least one part-time job by the time they left high school (Barling & Kelloway, 1999). By the end of the 20th century, part-time employment during high school had changed from the rare exception to the typical experience.

The current rate of adolescent employment in the United States is higher than in any other industrialized country. In Japan, adolescent employment is almost nonexistent. In Canada, the proportion of adolescents who work by their late teens (45%) is higher than in Japan, but still substantially lower than in the United States (Sears et al., 2006). In Western Europe, rates of work in late adolescence vary among countries from about 30% to 50% (Bonino, Cattelino, & Ciarino, 2006; Meeus, 2006). In many of these countries, adolescents have a longer school day and more homework on a typical evening, leaving less time for part-time jobs. American adolescents are not only willing to work but able to do so because their schools make relatively low demands on them. In turn, pervasive employment among adolescents makes it difficult for high schools to require more academic work from them because many adolescents have little time or energy left over for homework after school and work (Steinberg, 1996).

By 1980, part-time work had become typical for American high school students.

The Adolescent Workplace

We have seen what kind of work adolescents do in traditional cultures, and what kinds of work they did in Western countries in the 19th century and most of the 20th century. What kinds of jobs are held by today's American adolescents?

You won't find many American adolescents these days whose work involves hunting, fishing, farming, or factory work. Interestingly enough, however, American girls in early adolescence have something in common with girls in traditional cultures in that their first kind of work involves child care. Baby-sitting is the most common first job for American girls (Mortimer, 2003). For boys, the most common first job is yard work—mowing lawns, trimming bushes, and so on. But the work done in these kinds of jobs is more or less informal and does not require a substantial commitment of time. An adolescent girl may baby-sit for Mr. and Mrs. Jones on Saturday night every couple of weeks, and for Mr. and Mrs. Peabody on the occasional afternoon until they get home from work. An adolescent boy may mow a couple of neighbors' lawns once a week from early spring to late fall. Typically, these jobs are unlikely to interfere much with the rest of an adolescent's life.

For older adolescents, the work is different, and the amount of time involved tends to be greater. The majority of jobs held by American and Canadian adolescents in high school involve restaurant work (server, cook, busboy/girl, hostess, etc.) or retail sales (Loughlin & Barling, 1999; Staff et al., 2004). These jobs involve a more formal commitment. You are assigned a certain number of hours a week, and you are expected to be there at the times you are assigned. Typically, this does not mean simply a few hours one week and a few the next. On average, employed high school sophomores work 15 hours per week, and employed high school seniors work 20 hours per week (Barling & Kelloway, 1999).

That is a substantial amount of weekly hours. What are adolescents typically doing during that time? One important source of information on this topic comes from a classic book by Ellen Greenberger and Laurence Steinberg (1986), who studied over 200 adolescent 10th and 11th graders in Orange County, California. Rather than relying only on adolescents' reports of what goes on in the places they work, the research team observed adolescents directly in their work settings, recording the behavior of the adolescents, the things they said, and the people with whom the adolescents interacted. The researchers also interviewed the adolescents and had them fill out questionnaires about their work experiences.

The kinds of work performed by the adolescents fell into five general categories: restaurant work, retail, clerical (e.g., secretarial work), manual labor (e.g., working for a moving company), and skilled labor (e.g., carpenter's apprentice). With the exception of the jobs involving skilled labor, the work performed by the adolescents tended to be repetitive and monotonous, involving little that would challenge them or help them develop new skills. Twenty-five percent of their time on the job was spent cleaning or carrying things—not exactly work that entails much of a cognitive challenge. Furthermore, the work was almost never connected to anything the adolescents were learning or had previously learned in school. Again, if you think about the work—cooking burgers, taking food orders, answering the phone, helping people find their size in clothes—this is hardly surprising.

With respect to the people they interacted with at work, adolescents spent about an equal proportion of their time interacting with other adolescents and with adults. However, their relationships with adult bosses and coworkers were rarely close. For the most part they did not see these adults except at work, they were reluctant to speak to them about personal issues, and they felt less close to them than they felt to the other people in their lives, such as parents and friends.

You can see how different the work experience of American adolescents is, compared with adolescents in traditional cultures (before industrialization) or adolescents in European countries who work in apprenticeships. Unlike

© 1990 Universal Press Syndicate

Adolescents often work in low-status service jobs.

these other adolescents, American adolescents rarely do work that involves a close partnership with an adult who teaches them and provides a model. Unlike these other adolescents the work done by American adolescents does little to prepare them for the kind of work they are likely to be doing as adults. Consequently, few adolescents see their high school jobs as the basis for a future career (Mortimer et al., 2008).

Work and Adolescent Development

You might expect that, given the dreary work they do and lack of connection between this work and their futures, the work done by American adolescents does little to promote their development in favorable ways. There is some evidence that this is true, as we will see in this section, although the connection between cause and effect is not always clear. In the previous chapter, we discussed the relationship between part-time work and school performance. Now let's look at the relationships between work and two other aspects of development, psychological functioning and problem behavior.

Work and Psychological Functioning

"I need to work because I need the money for car insurance and the prom. I like being involved in everything, but sometimes I feel really overloaded with my job and schoolwork and baseball and committees, and I need to take time to just chill out."

—Brian, a 17-year-old high school senior working 20 to 40 hours per week as a busboy for a catering company (in Salzman, 1993)

Both for psychological functioning and for problem behavior, the amount of time worked per week is an important variable. Most studies find that working up to 10 hours a week at a part-time job has little effect on adolescents' devel-

opment. However, beyond 10 hours a week problems arise, and beyond 20 hours a week the problems become considerably worse.

Working up to 10 hours a week is not related to increased psychological symptoms such as anxiety and depression (Frone, 1999; Lee & Staff, 2007). However, reports of psychological symptoms jump sharply for adolescents working more than 10 hours a week and continue to rise among adolescents working 20 hours a week or more (see Figure 10.4 on p. 293).

Up to 10 hours a week, working has little effect on the amount of sleep adolescents get. However, beyond 10 hours a week, amount of sleep per night declines steadily as work hours increase (see Figure 10.4). Studies also show that working more than 10 hours a week is disruptive to eating and exercise habits (Bachman & Schulenberg, 1993). Recent Canadian research reports that when adolescents take on demanding jobs they reduce their sleep by an hour per night and eliminate nearly all sports activities (Sears et al., 2006).

Some studies report positive findings concerning work and psychological functioning. Working at a job that involves learning new skills is positively related to psychological well-being and self-esteem (Mortimer, 2003; Mortimer et al., 1992). Also, learning new skills on the job is related to higher life satisfaction (Schulenberg & Bachman, 1993). We will consider the case in favor of adolescent work in more detail shortly.

Work and Problem Behavior

"Last week I cut off a pair of jeans to make shorts and my father got angry. He said I was wasting money. But I don't care, because I have a job now and can buy my own clothes. I feel more like an adult."

—Chonita, age 16 (in Salzman, 1993, p. 72)

One of the most ambitious studies of adolescents and work has been conducted by Jeylan Mortimer of the University of Minnesota and her colleagues (Mortimer, 2003; Mortimer & Finch, 1996; Mortimer et al., 1996, 1999; Mortimer & Johnson, 1998; Mortimer & Staff, 2004; Mortimer et al., 2008). The focus of the study was on work in relation to mental health and post–high school education and employment. The study began in 1987 with a sample of 1,000 adolescents who were randomly selected from a list of ninth graders attending public schools in St. Paul, Minnesota. The adolescents completed questionnaires each year of high school and each year after high school—every year from age 14 to 30. Their parents also completed questionnaires when the adolescents were in 9th grade and again when they were in 12th grade.

One of the impressive features of this study is the **retention rate**, which means the percentage of participants who continued to take part in the study after the first year. Retention rates are sometimes a problem in longitudinal studies because people move, change phone numbers, or fail to return the questionnaire mailed to them. This would especially be likely to be a problem in a study like this one, in which young people are being followed through emerging adulthood, a time that involves frequent changes of residence for many people. In Mortimer's study, the retention rate was 93% after four years of high school and 78% over eight years (Mortimer et al., 1999). Normally, 50% would be considered adequate after eight years. They were able to keep the retention rate so high in this study by maintaining regular contact with the participants to see whether they had moved or were planning to move.

The longitudinal design of the study enabled Mortimer and her colleagues to provide insights into important aspects of the influences of work on adolescent development. One of the key questions in this area is, does working influence adolescents' problem behavior, especially substance use? It is well established that adolescents who work report higher rates of problem behavior, especially if they work more than 20 hours a week, but this leaves open the question: does working long hours cause adolescents to engage in problem behavior, or do adolescents who engage in problem behavior also choose to work more? Mortimer and her colleagues (1999), focusing on alcohol use, found that adolescents who work long hours in high school already have higher rates of alcohol use in 9th grade, before they start working long hours. However, they also found that working long hours contributed to even greater alcohol use.

A second, related question is, does the higher rate of alcohol use among adolescents working long hours in high school establish a pattern that continues beyond high school? Again, the answer to this question could only be determined through a longitudinal study that follows adolescents from high school to several years beyond. Mortimer and Johnson (1997) found that four years after high school, the emerging adults who had worked long hours in high school had rates of alcohol use in their early 20s that were no higher than for emerging adults who had worked less in high school. It was not that the high-working adolescents had decreased their use of alcohol as emerging adults, but that the other adolescents had "caught up," reporting higher rates of alcohol use by the time they reached their early 20s.

Longitudinal studies like this one require a great deal of effort and patience (not to mention a considerable amount of money), but they often provide results that help unravel complex questions of cause and effect with respect to development among adolescents and emerging adults.

One strong and consistent finding in research on adolescents and work is that adolescents who work are more likely to use alcohol, cigarettes, and other drugs, especially if they work more than 10 hours a week (Bachman et al., 2003; Brame et al., 2004; Frone, 1999; Longest & Shanahan, 2007; Mortimer et al., 1999; Steinberg, 1996; Wu, Schlenger, & Galvin, 2003). However, scholars disagree on whether this means that working leads to greater substance use or whether adolescents who work already have a tendency toward substance use. Some scholars have argued that the relationship is merely correlational. In this view, adolescents who work more than 10 hours a week also have a tendency toward substance use, but this tendency was evident even before they began working long hours (Bachman et al., 2003; Bachman & Schulenberg, 1993). In contrast, other scholars report that increases in work hours *precede* increases in drug and alcohol use, suggesting that working long hours causes an increase in substance use. But these explanations are not incompatible, and both may be valid. Adolescents who work relatively long hours may already have a tendency toward substance use, and that tendency may be further amplified by working long hours. (For further information on this topic, see the Research Focus box above.)

The United States is not the only country where part-time work is associated with problem behavior. In a Finnish study (Kuovonen & Kivivuori, 2001) on a nationally representative sample of 15- to 16-year-olds, working more than 20 hours a week was associated with a variety of types of problem behavior, including vandalism, driving while intoxicated, and beating up someone. Adolescents who worked more than

---

retention rate In a longitudinal study, the percentage of participants who continued to take part in the study after the first year.

occupational deviance Deviant acts committed in relation to the workplace, such as stealing supplies.

20 hours a week were two to three times as likely as other adolescents to commit these acts. However, because the study was cross-sectional rather than longitudinal, this does not necessarily show that working intensively caused them to engage in problem behavior. They may have had a propensity for problem behavior even before they became employed.

Not only is working related to problem behavior outside of work, but there is also a considerable amount of on-the-job deviance among adolescents who work. Greenberger and Steinberg investigated a variety of behaviors they called **occupational deviance** as part of their research on adolescents and work (Ruggiero, Greenberger, & Steinberg, 1982). They had first-time adolescent workers indicate on a confidential questionnaire how often they had engaged in each of nine behaviors that involved some kind of occupational deviance, such as falsely calling in sick and stealing things at work. Altogether, over 60% of the working adolescents had engaged in at least one type of occupational deviance after being employed for nine months.

That may seem like a lot, and it is, but keep in mind that the study included only adolescents. Adults have also been known to call in sick when they were not, take things from work that did not belong to them, and so on. We have no way of knowing, from this study alone, whether adolescents tend to do these things more than adults do.

Nevertheless, the combination of studies clearly indicates a relationship between work and problem behavior in adolescence. Why would this be the case? The answer seems to be different for occupational deviance than it is for other types of problem behavior. For occupational deviance, the characteristics of the typical adolescent workplace offer likely explanations (Steinberg et al., 1993). The work is often boring and tedious, and adolescents do not see the jobs as leading to anything they plan to be doing in the future, so they rarely have much of a feeling of personal investment in the job. If you get caught doing something wrong, you might get fired, but who cares? There are plenty of other jobs of the same type (i.e., low skilled and low paying) easily available. Also, the adolescent workplace has little adult supervision, and adolescents do not feel close to the adults they work with, so they may feel they have little obligation or responsibility to behave ethically.

With regard to higher rates of substance use among adolescents who work, as we have noted, some scholars believe that this tendency exists among adolescents who work even before they start working. However, other scholars have found that adolescents who work in jobs with a high level of stress are more likely to use drugs and alcohol than adolescents who work in lower-stress jobs (Greenberger, Steinberg, & Vaux, 1981; Mortimer & Staff, 2004). This suggests that substance use may be serving as a stress reliever, and provides further evidence that the role of work in problem behavior is causal, not just correlational.

Also important is that having a part-time job gives adolescents more money to spend on leisure. Very little of the money they make goes to their family's living expenses or saving for their future education (Mortimer, 2003; Thomas, 1998). Instead, it goes toward purchases for themselves, here and now: snazzy clothes, CDs, car payments, gas and insurance for a car, concert tickets, movies, eating out—and alcohol, cigarettes, and other drugs (Bachman, 1983; Greenberger & Steinberg, 1986; Mortimer et al., 2004). Adolescents tend to spend the money they make at their jobs in pursuit of good times, and for some of them the pursuit of good times includes substance use.

The Case in Favor of Adolescent Work

Jeylan Mortimer (2003) and her colleagues at the University of Minnesota argue that the case against adolescent work has been overstated and that in fact a strong case can be made in favor of adolescent work. Although some of Mortimer's own research has revealed certain problems associated with adolescent work, she argues that on the whole, the benefits outweigh the problems.

According to her research, adolescents see many benefits from their work. As Table 11.1 shows, far more of them see benefits in their work than see problems. They believe they gain a sense of responsibility from working, improve their abilities to manage money, develop better social skills, and learn to manage their time better. Over 40% believe that their jobs have helped them develop new occupational skills, in contrast to the portrayal of adolescent work as involving nothing but dreary tasks (although we might note that 40%, while substantial, is still a minority). Mortimer (2003) also argues that good relationships with the adults they meet in the workplace can be a protective factor for adolescents from difficult and stressful family situations.

Mortimer and her colleagues (1999) concede that nearly half of adolescents report that working gives them less time for homework, and over one fourth believe that working has negatively affected their grades, as you can see in Table 11.1. However, Mortimer argues that the main activity that working adolescents spend less time on is watching television. According to her argument, American adolescents simply spend too little time on homework for working to make much difference in their school performance. She claims that no consistent relationship exists across studies between

Adolescents who work are more likely to use substances, including tobacco.

	Girls	Boys
TABLE 11.1 Percentages of Adolescents Indicating Benefits and Costs of Employment		
Benefits		
Responsibility	90	80
Money management	66	57
Learned social skills	88	78
Work experience/skill development	43	42
Work ethics	73	68
Independence	75	78
Time management	79	75
Learned about life/shaped future	26	29
Problems		
Less leisure time	49	49
Lower grades	28	25
Less time for homework	48	49
Think about work during class	78	11
Fatigue	51	45

Source: Aronson et al. (1996), Table 2.10.

working and school performance in adolescence, even among adolescents who work 20 or more hours per week.

My own judgment is that the case against adolescent work at over 20 hours or even 10 hours per week is strong. Look at Figure 10.4 again, on page 293 in the previous chapter. Problems consistently develop across a wide range of areas beyond 10 hours a week of work. Even Mortimer's data indicate that adolescents perceive negative effects of working on their school performance, and enough studies find a relationship between working long hours and poor grades to make this case convincingly (e.g., Committee on Child Labor, 1998; Greenberger & Steinberg, 1986; Marsh, 1991). Also, there is little dispute that working over 20 hours per week leads to higher substance use. However, Mortimer's research is a useful reminder that the effects of work on adolescent development are complex and that work does offer certain benefits to many adolescents.

THINKING CRITICALLY •••

American adolescents clearly prefer to work, even though the work is often boring and is frequently related to negative outcomes (although to some positive outcomes as well). Given this situation, would you be for or against national legislation to limit adolescents' work (under age 18) to 10 hours a week? Justify your answer in terms of development in adolescence and in emerging adulthood.

From School and Part-Time Work to a "Real Job"

As we have observed, few American adolescents see their part-time jobs as the beginning of the kind of work they expect to be doing as adults. Waiting tables, washing dishes, mowing lawns, sales clerking, and the like are fine for bringing in enough money to finance an active leisure life, but generally these are jobs that adolescents view as temporary and transient, not as forming the basis of a long-term career. Full-time work in a "real job" comes only after adolescents have completed their education—the end of high school for some, the end of college or graduate school for others. Let's take a look at the transition to work, first for those who take on full-time work immediately after high school, then for those who make the transition to full-time work following college or graduate school.

The Post–High School Transition to Work

Although the proportion of American adolescents attending college after high school rose steadily in the 20th century and now exceeds 60% (NCES, 2009), that still leaves nearly 40% of adolescents who begin full-time work after high school instead of attending college. In most European countries, the proportion of young people entering work immediately after secondary school is even higher (Arnett, 2006b). What are the work prospects like for these adolescents, and how successfully are they able to make the transition from school to the workplace?

In 1987, a distinguished panel of scholars, and public policy officials was assembled by the William T. Grant Foundation and asked to address this question with respect to young Americans. They produced an influential and widely read report entitled *The Forgotten Half: Non-College Youth in America* (William T. Grant Commission on Work, Family, and Citizenship, 1988), which contained an analysis of **the forgotten half** of young Americans who do not attend college and a set of policy suggestions for promoting a successful transition from high school to work.

The report begins by describing the changes in the American economy in previous decades, with a special focus on the loss of manufacturing jobs (for example, working in a steel mill or automobile factory) that used to provide well-paying jobs for unskilled workers. "A fast-changing economy has produced millions of new jobs in the service and retail sectors, but with wages at only half the level of a typical manufacturing job," the report states. "Stable, high-wage employment in manufacturing, communications, transportation, utilities, and forestry that was once open to young people leaving high school is rapidly declining. For male high school

the forgotten half The nearly half of young Americans who enter the workplace following high school rather than attending college.

the new basic skills Skills identified by Murnane and Levy that are required for high school graduates who wish to be able to obtain the best jobs available in the new information-based economy.

graduates, employment in these high-wage sectors fell remarkably, from 57 percent in 1968 to 36 percent in 1986" (pp. 1, 19). Largely because of the decline in the number of these high-wage jobs available, the average income of male high school graduates aged 20 to 24 actually *declined* by 28% (adjusted for inflation) between 1973 and 1986. The decline for dropouts was even steeper: 42%. The Commission's recommendations for addressing this problem were of two kinds: better occupational preparation in high school and government job-training programs.

The Commission's report was published in 1988. How has the situation changed since that time? In 1998, a follow-up report was published, entitled *The Forgotten Half Revisited* (Halpern, 1998). This report concluded that in the decade since the Commission's original report, prospects for the "forgotten half" have become worse, not better. Young people who do not attend college are "still in a free-fall of declining earnings and diminished expectations" (p. xii).

Also in the late 1990s, Richard Murnane (an economist) and Frank Levy (a scholar on education) published a book looking at changes in the job skills needed by members of the "forgotten half" (Murnane & Levy, 1997). The book is entitled *Teaching the New Basic Skills: Principles for Educating Children to Thrive in a Changing Economy.*

Murnane and Levy conducted observations in a variety of factories and offices to gain information about the kinds of jobs now available to high school graduates and the skills those jobs require. They focused not on routine jobs that require little skill and pay low wages but on the most promising new jobs available to high school graduates in the changing economy, jobs that offer the promise of career development and middle-class wages. They concluded that six basic skills are necessary for success at these new jobs:

- Reading at a 9th-grade level or higher
- Doing math at a 9th-grade level or higher
- Solving semistructured problems
- Communicating orally and in writing

Teaching skills to adolescents directly in the workplace tends to be effective.

- Using a computer for word processing and other tasks
- Collaborating in diverse groups

The good news is that all of what Murnane and Levy (1997) call **the new basic skills** could be taught to adolescents by the time they leave high school. The bad news is that many American adolescents currently graduate from high school without learning them adequately. Murnane and Levy focused on reading and math skills because those are the skills on which the most data are available. They concluded that the data reveal "a sobering picture: close to half of all seventeen-year-olds cannot read or do math at the level needed" to succeed at the new jobs. The half who do have these skills are also the half who are most likely to go to college rather than seeking full-time work after high school. The result of this shortfall in skills is a vicious circle. Employers are wary of hiring high school graduates for the new jobs because they are unimpressed with the skills typical of these graduates; for adolescents the awareness that a high school diploma will be of little help to them in securing a good job gives them little incentive to apply themselves in school; their inadequate skills reinforce employers' perceptions that it is not wise to hire high school graduates. In a more recent book, Murnane and Levy (2004) focus on the growing importance of computer skills, again concluding that high schools are failing to provide adolescents with the knowledge they need to succeed in the new economy.

Of course, this does not mean that the current situation cannot be changed. There is certainly no reason that schools could not be expected to require that high school students can read and do math at a 9th-grade level or higher by the time they graduate. Ensuring that students are capable of "solving semistructured problems" and "communicating effectively orally and in writing" is also quite reasonably part of any high school's objectives and responsibility. Learning to use computer skills is a growing part of the school curriculum, not just at the high school level but from grade school on up. The ability to work in diverse groups is also a teachable skill, and certainly practice in such situations in the school setting would help promote the development of this skill. All together, the results of Murnane and Levy's research suggest that it may be wise for administrators of high schools and job-training programs to revise their curricula to fit the requirements of the new information- and technology-based economy.

School-to-Work Programs in the United States

Although there is great concern over the lack of sufficient job skills in high school graduates, no system currently exists that coordinates the requirements of the workplace—for example, as in the "new basic skills" just described—with the educational efforts of the schools. Small-scale apprenticeship programs have shown promise. For example, Stephen and Mary Agnes Hamilton (Hamilton & Hamilton, 2000; 2006) of Cornell University have developed a program that provides apprenticeships for high school sophomores in three areas: administration and office technology, health care, and manufacturing and engineering technology. The program has demonstrated favorable effects on work-based learning and academic achievement. However, few adolescents in the United States have access to such programs.

There are also job-training programs for emerging adults in the United States. The largest government job-training program is the Job Corps, which began in 1964 and currently serves 62,000 new participants aged 16 to 24 each year at 122 centers in low-income areas all over the United States (U.S. Department of Labor, 2008). An extensive evaluation found that the Job Corps program is highly effective in improving the occupational prospects of noncollege emerging adults (Mathematica Policy Research, 2001). Job Corps participants were compared to a control group of nonparticipants who had applied for the program but were not accepted due to funding limitations. (Thus, they had job-training motivations similar to the program participants.) The results indicated numerous benefits of participation in the Job Corps 4 years later, compared to the control group, including:

- Employed more hours per week
- Earned $22 more per week
- Improved literacy and numeracy skills
- More likely to earn a GED (42% of participants, 27% control group)
- Less likely to be arrested (29% participants, 33% control group)

The Job Corps is an expensive program, in part because participants actually live on site as they receive educational and occupational training. However, the study described here found that every dollar spent on Job Corps produced $2.02 in returns through higher earnings, taxes paid on the higher earnings, and savings in public expenditures in areas such as criminal justice and welfare. Nevertheless, some critics argue that the goals of Job Corps can be met with less ex-

apprenticeship An arrangement, common in Europe, in which an adolescent "novice" serves under contract to a "master" who has substantial experience in a profession, and through working under the master, learns the skills required to enter the profession.

pensive programs. One new program called YouthBuild, which involves having adolescents participate in building and renovating houses while receiving assistance in obtaining a high school diploma or GED, has claimed results similar to those of Job Corps but with less expense per participant (Boyle, 2001, 2004). However, YouthBuild has not yet been tested with a longitudinal control-group study as Job Corps has.

It should be noted, too, that even the 60,000 per year participation in Job Corps, large as it may seem, serves only a small proportion of the 20 million Americans aged 16 to 24, millions of whom are low-income members of the "forgotten half." Job Corps—and all other American job-training programs put together—do not begin to approach a national school-to-work program of the kind found in many European countries.

Unlike in European countries, where school-to-work programs are a basic part of the national government, in the United States there is no political consensus on the value of such programs. Many educators and business leaders believe that American secondary schools are having enough trouble ensuring that graduates have mastered basic skills and should focus on teaching those skills rather than spending students' time in vocational internships that may not teach them anything. As the head of IBM, Louis Gerstner, observed, "We are not interested in public schools teaching work-related skills. What's killing us is having to teach new hires to read, compute, communicate, and think" (Mathews, 2001, p. A13). Furthermore, the American tradition of state autonomy makes many people wary of a federal school-to-work program that would apply nationwide. Taken together, these factors make it unlikely that a national school-to-work program will be instituted in the United States in the foreseeable future.

Apprenticeships in Western Europe

All of the school-to-work programs tried thus far in the United States have been limited in scale. What would it be like to have a coherent national program available to all adolescents, coordinating the curriculum of the schools with the needs of employers and focused on training in the workplace that would lead directly to long-term employment? We don't need to use our imaginations to find out. Western European countries have had such programs for a long time.

The focus of work preparation programs in Western Europe is on apprenticeships (Hamilton, 1994; Hamilton & Hamilton, 2000, 2006; Vazsonyi & Snider, 2008). In an **apprenticeship**, an adolescent "novice" serves under contract to a "master" who has substantial experience in a profession, and through working under the master the novice learns the skills required to enter the profession successfully. Although apprenticeships originally began centuries ago in craft professions such as carpentry and blacksmithing, today they are undertaken to prepare for a wide range of professions, from auto mechanics and carpenters to police officers, computer technicians, and child-care workers (Fuller, Beck, & Unwin, 2005; Hamilton, 1990, 1994; Hamilton &

Hamilton, 2000; Hamilton & Hurrelman, 1994). Apprenticeships are common in Western Europe, especially in central and northern Europe. For example, Germany's apprenticeship program includes over 60% of all 16- to 18-year-olds (Hamilton, 1990; Heckhausen & Tomasik, 2002), and Switzerland's includes about one third of the adolescents who do not attend college after secondary school (Vazsonyi & Snider, 2008). The Cultural Focus box in this chapter provides more detail about Germany's apprenticeship program.

Common features of apprenticeship programs are (Hamilton, 1994; Hamilton & Hamilton, 2000, 2006; Hamilton & Hurrelman, 1994):

- Entry at age 16, with the apprenticeship lasting 2 to 3 years;
- Continued part-time schooling while in the apprenticeship, with the school curriculum closely connected to the training received in the apprenticeship;
- Training that takes place in the workplace, under real working conditions; and
- Preparation for a career in a respected profession that provides an adequate income.

This kind of program requires close coordination between schools and employers, so that what adolescents learn at school during their apprenticeships will complement and reinforce what is being learned in the workplace. This means that schools consult employers with respect to the skills required in the workplace, and employers make opportunities available for adolescent apprentices and provide masters for them to work under. In Europe, the employers see this effort as worth their trouble because apprenticeships provide them with a reliable supply of well-qualified entry-level employees (Dustmann & Schoenberg, 2008).

THINKING CRITICALLY •••

Apprenticeships in Europe appear to work quite well, but they require that adolescents make career decisions by their mid-teens, much earlier than is typical in American society. Do you think the benefits of apprenticeships outweigh the fact that they require these early decisions, or do you prefer the American system of allowing for a longer period of exploration—well into emerging adulthood—before such decisions are made? Is it a question of what is best developmentally, or is it just a question of different values?

Although the European school-to-work system has some advantages over the American system, it has some disadvantages as well. Educational psychologist Stephen Hamilton, in comparing the American and European systems, makes a useful distinction between *transparency* and *permeability* (Hamilton, 1994; Hamilton & Hamilton, 2006). Transparency is Hamilton's term for how clearly the path is marked through the educational system leading to the labor market. In a transparent system, the educational and training requirements for various occupations are clearly laid out and young people are well informed about them from an early

Apprenticeships are common in some European countries. Here, an apprentice in Poissy, France, learns to become a chef.

age. Permeability refers to how easy it is to change directions within the educational system. A permeable system makes it easy to drop one educational/career path and move to another.

The American system is low in transparency and high in permeability. Even in emerging adulthood, most Americans have only a limited understanding of how to obtain the education or training that will lead to the job they want, but it is easy to enter college and easy to switch paths once they get there. In contrast, the European system is high in transparency but low in permeability. European adolescents know which education and training path leads to which job, but once they choose a path—as they are required to do at the age of just 14 or 15—the system makes it difficult for them to change their minds. Currently, the European system is becoming more permeable because emerging adults are pushing for more choices and because the traditional system is increasingly viewed as too inflexible to respond to today's rapidly changing information-based economy (Hamilton & Hamilton, 2006).

Occupational Choice

"In talking to my peers, I realize increasingly that there is no one place to find your passion. For myself, like many others, my career decisions included a mix of all these reasons: a lifelong interest in working with people, a need for a sustainable career that will pay the bills, and a feeling of accomplishment at the end of the day. A friend, paraphrasing the words of novelist Frederick Buechner, once said to me, 'Your place is where the world's greatest need meets your greatest love.' While the needs of the world are infinite, and how we find our interests takes a number of different paths, this formula is the best and most universal advice I've heard for making career decisions."

—Emily, 3rd-year university student
(in Spengler, 2002, p. C10)

As we saw at the outset of the chapter, adolescents in preindustrial traditional cultures (and in Western cultures historically) work alongside their parents—boys with their fathers and other men, girls with their mothers and other women—doing the kind of work adults do. Because the economies in such cultures are usually not diverse, there are few "occupations" to choose from. Boys learn to do what men do, whether it is hunting or farming or something else, and girls learn to do what women do, which is usually child care and running the household, and perhaps some gathering or gardening or other work. There is a certain security in this arrangement—you grow up knowing that you will have useful and important work to do as an adult, and you grow up gradually learning the skills required for it. On the other hand, there is a certain narrowness and limitation to it as well—if you are a boy, you must do the work that men do whether you care for it or not; and if you are a girl, your role is to learn child care and running a household regardless of what your individual preferences or talents might be.

Adolescents in cultures with industrialized economies face a different kind of trade-off. Industrialized economies are astonishingly complex and diverse. This means that, as an adolescent or emerging adult, you can choose from a tremendous range of possible occupations. Figure 11.1 shows predicted job growth in a variety of fields in the early years of the 21st century, and it also gives you some idea of the range of occupations that now exists. However, every adolescent has to find a place among all of that fabulous diversity of choice. And even once you make your choice, you have to hope that the occupation you decide you want will be achievable for you. More young people would like to be medical doctors, veterinarians, musicians, and professional athletes than is possible (Sandberg et al., 1991; Schneider & Stevenson, 1999).

Let us take a look now at the developmental pattern in how American adolescents make occupational choices and at the various influences that play a part in their choices.

The Development of Occupational Goals

Although children and adolescents may have occupational dreams—fantasies of being a famous basketball player, singer, or movie star—adolescence and especially emerging adulthood are times when more serious reflection on occupational goals often begins (Arnett, 2004a). For emerging adults, decisions must be made about educational and occupational preparation that will have potential long-term effects on their adult lives.

One influential theory of the development of occupational goals, by Donald Super (1967, 1976, 1980, 1992; Tracey et al., 2005), begins with adolescence and continues through five stages into adulthood, as follows:

- *Crystallization*, ages 14 to 18. In this initial stage, adolescents begin to move beyond fantasizing and start to con-

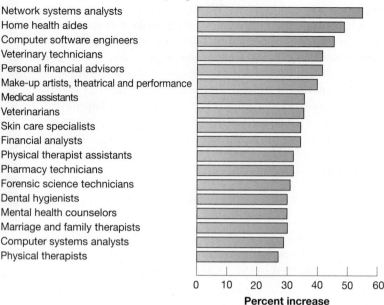

Fastest predicted job growth, 2006–2016

Network systems analysts
Home health aides
Computer software engineers
Veterinary technicians
Personal financial advisors
Make-up artists, theatrical and performance
Medical assistants
Veterinarians
Skin care specialists
Financial analysts
Physical therapist assistants
Pharmacy technicians
Forensic science technicians
Dental hygienists
Mental health counselors
Marriage and family therapists
Computer systems analysts
Physical therapists

Percent increase

FIGURE 11.1 Predicted job growth, 2006–2016.
Source: U.S. Bureau of the Census (2009).

sider how their talents and interests match up with the occupational possibilities available to them. During this time, they may begin to seek out information about careers that are of interest to them, perhaps by talking over various possibilities with family and friends. Also, as adolescents begin to decide on their own beliefs and values, this helps to guide their occupational explorations as they consider how various job possibilities may confirm or contradict those values.

- *Specification*, ages 18 to 21. During this stage, occupational choices become more focused. For example, a young person who decided during the crystallization stage to seek an occupation that involves working with children may now decide whether that means being a child psychologist, a teacher, a daycare worker, or a pediatrician. Making this choice usually involves seeking information about what is involved in these occupations, as in the crystallization stage, but with more of a focus on specific occupations rather than a general field. It also usually involves beginning to pursue the education or training required to obtain the desired occupation.

- *Implementation*, ages 21 to 24. This stage involves completing the education or training that began in the specification stage and entering the job itself. This may mean that young people must reconcile any discrepancy between what they would like to do and what is available in the work world. For example, you may have been educated to be a teacher but find out after graduation that there are more teachers than available jobs, so that you end up working in a social service agency or a business.

- *Stabilization*, ages 25 to 35. This is the stage in which young adults establish themselves in their careers. The initial period of getting their feet wet in a job comes to an

"Anna is only a few months away from the completion of her apprenticeship in a large [German] manufacturing firm. At age 17, Anna has worked in the firm's accounting, purchasing, inventory, production, personnel, marketing, sales, and finance departments, and studied those functions in school. She is very enthusiastic about the recent news that the company will give her an additional 18 months of training in electronic data processing before hiring her as a regular employee. She is already skilled and reliable enough to have substituted for two weeks in cost accounting during her supervisor's vacation."

This case example is taken from a book by the developmental psychologist Stephen Hamilton (1990) of Cornell University about Germany's apprenticeship system. Hamilton describes Germany's system and suggests how a similar system might be established in the United States.

Germany's apprenticeship system has existed in various forms for several hundred years (Dustmann & Schoenberg, 2008). In the present, more than 60% of all 16- to 18-year-olds are apprentices, making apprenticeships the most common form of education in the final years of secondary school and the primary passage from school to work (Hamilton & Hamilton, 2000). As Anna's example illustrates, the apprenticeships train young people not just for trades or skilled labor, but for professional and managerial positions as well. Young people are usually in the program for three years, and during that time they spend one day a week in a vocational school and the other four in their apprenticeship placement. More than half of apprentices remain with the company that trained them for at least two years after they complete the apprenticeship.

Employers pay all the costs of training their apprentices and in addition pay them a modest salary during the apprenticeship. About 10% of industrial and commercial businesses (e.g., insurance or banking) and 40% of craft businesses take part in the apprenticeship program. What is the incentive for employers? They participate partly out of German cultural traditions and partly because, once an apprentice learns to do useful work, the employer will have relatively cheap labor during the rest of the apprenticeship and a well-trained employee after the apprenticeship is completed (Dustmann & Schoenberg, 2008).

Hamilton's ethnographic research demonstrates the effectiveness of the German apprenticeship system. Apprentices have numerous opportunities for learning on the job, and what they learn on the job is coordinated with and reinforced by what they learn in school. Motivation for learning in school is enhanced by the awareness that the knowledge they gain in school will have a direct and immediate application in the workplace. Adolescents work closely with adults who are in charge of instructing them and providing them with learning opportunities, and typically they have a variety of different positions during the apprenticeship so that they learn a variety of skills. Furthermore, Hamilton notes, "Germany's apprenticeship system is more than a training program intended to teach the knowledge and skills related to a specific job. In addition to fulfilling that function, it is a form of general education and an institution for socializing youth to adulthood" (1990, p. 63).

Could a system like this work in the United States? In some places it already does, but it is very rare—less than 5% of adolescents have participated by the time they leave high school (Hamilton, 1990, 1994; Hamilton & Hamilton, 2000). A vast government-sponsored system would be required to coordinate schools with employers. It would also require earlier decisions about what road to take occupationally; this decision would have to be made by age 15 or 16, rather than putting it off until well after high school.

However, the benefits would be great. Young people would leave their teens much better prepared for the workplace than they are now. School would be less boring to them and more clearly related to their futures. Hamilton and others are currently conducting small-scale apprenticeship programs in the United States (Hamilton & Hamilton, 2000), and if the benefit of these programs can be demonstrated, increased enthusiasm may be seen for a national apprenticeship system.

---

end, and they become more stable and experienced in their work.

- *Consolidation*, age 35 and up. From this point onward, occupational development means continuing to gain expertise and experience and seeking advancement into higher-status positions as expertise and experience grow.

Although this theory remains important in shaping the way scholars think about occupational development and career counselors provide advice to young people, not everyone fits the pattern prescribed by the theory, and certainly not according to these precise ages. Because education is stretching out further and further into the 20s for more and more people, it is not unusual for the implementation stage to begin in the mid-20s rather than the early 20s. Perhaps more important, it is less and less common for occupational development to follow the kind of linear path through the life course that is described in Super's theory. Increasingly, people have not just one career or occupation, but two or more in the course of their working lives. Most of today's adolescents and emerging adults will change career directions at least once (Donahue, 2007). Also, for women and increasingly for men, balancing work and family goals may mean taking time off or at least working fewer hours during the years when they have to care for young children.

The occupational development theories of Super and others do not take into account the kinds of considerations often faced by women. Traditional theories assume that occupational development follows a single path. However, this assumption ignores the fact that most women in Western societies lead a dual-career life, with their role as homemaker and mother as a "second career" in addition to the out-of-home occupation they hold (Cinamon, 2006; Hochschild, 1990, 1998). Most women have a period of their lives, during the time they have one or more young children, when they spend as much or more time in the homemaker-mother role as they do in the role of their paid occupation. And throughout the years their children are growing up, women face the challenge of integrating these two roles, more so than men because even now in Western cultures (as in Eastern and traditional cultures), women have the main responsibility for child care (van der Lippe et al., 2006). For this reason, theories of career development that neglect the challenge of this integration do not fit the career paths that today's emerging adult women are likely to follow.

Influences on Occupational Goals

Theories of occupational development provide a general outline of how adolescents and emerging adults may progress through their working lives. But how do adolescents and emerging adults make choices among the great variety of occupations available to them? What influences enter into their decisions? A great deal of research has been conducted on these questions, especially focusing on the influence of personality characteristics and gender.

Personality Characteristics One influence on occupational choice in cultures where people are allowed to choose from a wide range of possible occupations is the individual's judgment of how various occupations would be suited to his or her personality. People seek occupations that they judge to be consistent with their interests and talents. One influential theorist, John Holland (1985, 1987, 1996; Gottfredson, Jones, & Holland, 1993), investigated the personality characteristics typical of people who hold various jobs and of adolescents who aspire to those jobs. Holland's theory describes six personality categories to consider when matching a person with a prospective occupation:

- *Realistic.* High physical strength, practical approach to problem solving, and low social understanding. Best occupations: those that involve physical activity and practical application of knowledge, such as farming, truck driving, and construction.
- *Intellectual.* High on conceptual and theoretical thinking. Prefer thinking problems through rather than applying knowledge. Low on social skills. Best occupations: scholarly fields such as math and science.
- *Social.* High in verbal skills and social skills. Best professions: those that involve working with people, such as teaching, social work, and counseling.

- *Conventional.* High on following directions carefully, dislike of unstructured activities. Best occupations: those that involve clear responsibilities but require little leadership, such as bank teller or secretary.
- *Enterprising.* High in verbal abilities, social skills, and leadership skills. Best occupations: sales, politics, management, running a business.
- *Artistic.* Introspective, imaginative, sensitive, unconventional. Best occupations: artistic occupations such as painting or writing fiction.

You can probably see the potential for overlap in some of these categories. Obviously, they are not mutually exclusive. A person could have some Artistic qualities as well as some Social qualities, or some Intellectual qualities as well as some Enterprising qualities. Holland (1987) does not claim that all people fall neatly into clear types. However, he and other researchers believe that most people will be happiest and most successful in their careers if they are able to find a match between their personality qualities and an occupation that allows them to express and develop those qualities (Vondracek & Porfelli, 2003). Career counselors use Holland's ideas to help adolescents gain insights into the fields that might be best for them to pursue. The widely used Strong-Campbell Vocational Interest Inventory is based on Holland's ideas.

Keep in mind the limitations of this approach to understanding occupational choice. Within any particular profession, you are likely to find persons with a considerable variety of personality traits. If you think of teachers you have known, for example, you will probably find that they varied considerably in their personalities, even if they may have had some characteristics in common. Their different personalities may have allowed each of them to bring a different combination of strengths and weaknesses to the job. So, there probably is not just one personality type that is potentially well suited to a particular type of job.

In the same way, any one person's personality could probably fit well with many of the jobs available in a diverse economy. Because most people's personalities are too complex to fall neatly into one type or another, different occupations may bring out different combinations of strengths and weaknesses in a particular person. For this reason, assessing your personality traits may narrow somewhat the range of fields that you think are suitable for you, but for most people in industrialized countries that would still leave a considerable number of possible occupations to choose from.

Gender Gender has a substantial influence on job choice. In Chapter 10 we observed the relation between gender and choice of major in college. This relation holds in the workplace as well. Although the proportion of young women who are employed rose steeply in the 20th century, and although women aged 18 to 25 are now as likely as young men to be employed (U.S. Bureau of the Census, 2009), it remains true that some jobs are held mainly by men and some jobs are held mainly by women (Porfelli et al., 2008; Vondracek & Porfeli, 2003). Jobs held mainly by women are concentrated

in the service sector—for example, teacher, nurse, secretary, and child-care worker. Jobs held mainly by men include engineer, chemist, surgeon, and computer software designer. In general, "women's jobs" tend to be low paying and low status, whereas "men's jobs" tend to be high paying and high status. These patterns have changed somewhat in recent years; for example, women are now nearly as likely as men to become lawyers and medical doctors. However, for many jobs the gender differences have proven to be remarkably stable. Even within high-status professions, women tend to have the lower status and lower-paying positions; for example, women who are physicians are more likely to be family practice doctors than surgeons.

Why do these gender differences in job choice persist, despite the fact that women now exceed men in terms of overall educational attainment? Gender socialization is certainly part of it. Children learn early on that some jobs are appropriate for either males or females, in the same way that

they learn other aspects of gender roles (Maccoby, 2002; Porfelli et al., 2008). By the time young people reach the age when it is time for them to choose an occupational direction, their gender identities are well established and constitute a powerful influence on their job selection (Desmairis & Curtis, 1999). One recent study of emerging adult women found that even mathematically talented young women often avoid information technology (IT) fields because they view IT as male-dominated, a perception that in turn perpetuates the male domination of IT (Messersmith et al., 2008). Similarly, a study in the Netherlands found that adolescent girls avoid going into computer science because they believe that others view women in computer science as sexually unattractive (Rommes et al., 2007).

Another important influence is that, already in emerging adulthood, young women anticipate the difficulties they are likely to face in balancing their work and family roles, and this too influences their job selection. It has long been true that wives spend considerably more time on family tasks than husbands do, especially when the couple has young children. Although men now handle more of the child care than in previous generations, wives still do more housework than their husbands, even when both of them work full time (Gershury, Bittman, & Brice, 2005; Strandh & Nordenmark, 2006; van der Lippe et al., 2006). Sociologists have called this the **second shift** (Hochschild, 1990, 1998), referring to the domestic work shift that women must perform after they complete their shift in the workplace.

THINKING CRITICALLY •••

How would you explain the fact that wives usually end up doing most of the household work and child care even when they work as many hours as their husbands? Do you think this is likely to change in the current generation of emerging adults?

Occupations such as nursing continue to be highly gender segregated.

second shift The domestic work shift performed in the household by women after they complete their first shift in the workplace.

While they are still emerging adults, young women often anticipate the crunch they are likely to face with their roles as worker, spouse, and mother (Arnett, 2004a; Cinamon, 2006). This realization affects their occupational choices, making them less likely to choose jobs that will be highly demanding and time consuming, even if the job is high paying and is in an area they enjoy and for which they have talent (Hochschild, 1990, 1998). They anticipate, too, that they will leave the workplace at some point to focus on caring for their young children. For example, one study asked college seniors majoring in business about their future work and family plans (Dey & Hurtado, 1999). The young women expected to work a total of 29 years full time, nearly 8 years less than their male classmates. Even though these young women were majoring in business, an area that is traditionally "male," they, too, expected to take time away from the workplace to care for their young children.

In contrast, it is extremely rare for young men to take time away from the workplace to raise young children. Even in European countries where the government pays up to 100% of a person's salary for up to a year for those who wish to leave the workplace temporarily while they have infant children, few young men take advantage of these policies (Douglass, 2005; Plantin, 2007). However, this does not mean these patterns will never change. The period of women's entry into the workplace is still relatively brief in historical terms—less than 50 years. Many dramatic changes in gender roles have already taken place that could not have been anticipated a half century ago. The changes appear to be continuing. Young men now say they give time with family a higher priority than prestigious or high-paying work, more than older men and similar to young women (Grimsley, 2000). Furthermore, technologically driven changes in work that are likely to allow an increasing proportion of work to be done at home or in flexible shifts may make it easier for both men and women to balance successfully—and equally—the demands of work and family.

Work in Emerging Adulthood

"I didn't really choose my job [as a bank teller]. It chose me. I needed the money. I was so broke! And they pay well. But I hate my job! There's no opportunity for growth there. I want to do something in maybe the health care field or fashion industry."

—Wendy, age 25 (in Arnett, 2004a, p. 151)

"At first I majored in journalism. Then I got a part-time job at a preschool. They asked me to teach a three-year-old classroom and I did it and I loved it and I thought 'You know, this is what I need to do.' So I changed my major to education. I love teaching. I can't imagine doing anything else."

—Kim, age 23 (in Arnett, 2004a, p. 147)

Because most Americans hold jobs beginning in their mid-teens, work is nothing new to them when they reach emerging adulthood. They are used to applying for a job, learning the ropes of a new job, and receiving a check at the end of each pay period. What changes in emerging adulthood is that it is no longer enough to have just any job. Most high school students do not expect their jobs to provide them with skills that will be the basis for the kinds of work they will be doing as adults. They simply want to find a job that will bring in enough cash to allow them to pursue an active leisure life. In contrast, most emerging adults are looking for a job that will turn into a career, a long-term occupation, something that will not only bring in a paycheck but provide personal fulfillment (Arnett, 2004a; Taylor, 2005).

Work in emerging adulthood focuses on identity questions: What do I really want to *do*? What am I best at? What do I enjoy the most? How do my abilities and desires fit in with the kinds of opportunities that are available to me? In asking themselves what kind of work they want to do, emerging adults are also asking themselves what kind of person they are. In the course of emerging adulthood, as they try out various jobs they begin to answer their identity questions, and they develop a better sense of who they are and what work suits them best.

Many adolescents have an idea, in high school, of what kind of career they want to go into (Schneider & Stevenson, 1999). Often that idea dissolves in the course of emerging adulthood, as they develop a clearer identity and discover that their high school aspiration does not align with it. In place of their high school notions, many seek another career that does fit their identity, something they really enjoy and really want to do (Vaughan, 2005).

For most American emerging adults, the process of finding the right job takes several years at least. Usually the road to a stable, long-term job is a long and winding one, with many brief, low-paying, dreary jobs along the way. The average American holds seven to eight different jobs between the ages of 18 and 30, and 1 in 4 young workers has over 10 different jobs during this period (U.S. Department of Labor, 2005).

Some emerging adults engage in systematic exploration as they go about looking for a career path that they wish to settle into for the long term. They think about what they want to do, they try a job or a college major in that area to see if the fit is right, and if it is not they try another path until they find something they like better. But for many others, "exploration" is a bit too lofty a word to describe their work history during their late teens and early 20s (Arnett, 2004a; Mortimer et al., 2002). Often it is not nearly as systematic, organized, and focused as "exploration" implies. "Meandering" might be a more accurate word, or maybe "drifting" or even "floundering" (Hamilton & Hamilton, 2006). Their eventual goal is to find a job they love and that fits their interests and abilities, but virtually all of them have many jobs in their late teens and early 20s that have little or nothing to do with this goal. For many emerging adults, working in emerging adulthood simply means finding a job, any job, that will pay the bills until something better comes along. In Canada and

Western Europe, too, job changes and periods of unemployment and part-time employment are common during emerging adulthood (Sneeding & Phillips, 2002).

Many emerging adults express a sense that they did not really choose their current job; one day they just found themselves in it, like a ball that rolls randomly on a pocked surface until it lands in one of the holes. In my interviews with emerging adults, "I just fell into it" is a frequently used phrase when they describe how they found their current job (Arnett, 2004a). For the most part, emerging adults who got their jobs in this random fashion are looking for something else. Falling into a job rarely results in the kind of fit with one's identity that makes a job fully satisfying. Most emerging adults want to find that kind of fit, and any job that does not provide it is viewed as a way station on the road to that goal.

Even for emerging adults who meander or drift through various jobs in their early 20s rather than exploring their options in a systematic way, the process of trying various jobs often serves the function of helping them sort out what kind of work they want to do. When you are in a dead-end job, at least you find out what you do *not* want to do. You may also find out that a job has to be more than a paycheck, that you are not willing to do something boring and pointless in the long run even if it pays the bills, that you are willing to keep looking until you find something interesting and enjoyable. And there is also the possibility that as you drift through various jobs you may happen to drift into one you enjoy, one that unexpectedly clicks.

Unemployment

"I feel trapped. When you work hard and you're motivated, they should give you a chance. They don't."

—Stephanie, age 25, unemployed emerging adult in Paris (in Swardson, 1999)

Although most young people in industrialized countries are able to find a job once they leave high school or college, this is not true for all of them. In both Europe and the United States, the unemployment rate for emerging adults is consistently at least twice as high as for adults beyond age 25 (Wolbers, 2007). Most European countries have much higher unemployment rates than the United States does, especially for young people (Hämäläinen et al., 2005; Sneeding & Phillips, 2002). In both Europe and the United States, unemployment has been found to be associated with higher risk for depression, especially for emerging adults who lack strong parental support (Axelsson & Ejlertsson, 2002; Bjarnason & Sigurdardottir, 2003; Dooley, Prause, & Ham-Rowbottom, 2000; Hämäläinen et al., 2005). The relation between unemployment and depression has also been found in longitudinal studies (Dooley et al., 2000), which indicates that unemployment leads to depression more often than being depressed makes it hard to find a job.

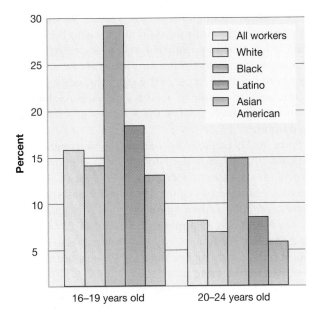

FIGURE 11.2 Youth unemployment by ethnicity.
Source: U.S. Bureau of the Census (2009).

Unemployed does not just mean that the person does not have a job. A large proportion of young people in their late teens and early 20s are attending high school or college, but they are not classified as unemployed because school is considered to be the focus of their efforts, not work. People whose time is devoted mainly to caring for their own children also would not be classified as unemployed. *Unemployment* refers only to people who are not in school, are not working, and are looking for a job.

This status applies to a substantial proportion of young people in the United States. Figure 11.2 shows the unemployment rates for young people in their late teens and early 20s. As you can see from the figure, unemployment is especially concentrated among Black and Latino adolescents. Also, unemployment is extremely high among young people who drop out of high school. *Over half* of high school dropouts aged 18 to 21 are unemployed (NCES, 2009).

What explains the high rates of unemployment among minority groups? This was not always the case. Consider that in 1954, the teenage unemployment rate for Blacks was only slightly higher than for Whites—16.5% for Blacks, lower than it is today, and 12% for Whites (Quillian, 2003). To a large extent, the explanation for the change lies in shifting employment patterns in the American economy. As noted earlier in the chapter, over the past several decades, as the economy has become more strongly focused on information and technology rather than manufacturing, the number of jobs available to unskilled workers has diminished sharply (Murnane & Levy, 1997; Quillian, 2003). The days are gone in the United States when stable, high-paying jobs were plentiful in

unemployed The status of persons who are not in school, not working, and who are looking for a job.

settings such as automobile factories and steel mills. Today, young people with few or no skills are likely to have difficulty finding a job that pays well enough to support themselves and may have difficulty finding any job at all. As we have seen earlier in this chapter, most of the new jobs, and certainly the best jobs, require people to have at least a minimal level of information skills such as basic math knowledge and ability to use a computer.

Those skills come from education, and young African Americans and Latinos tend to obtain less education than young Whites or Asian Americans. This is especially true for Latinos. As noted in Chapter 10, educational attainment is lower among Latinos than among Whites, African Americans, or Asian Americans (Hamilton & Hamilton, 2006). Among African American adolescents, the dropout rate from high school is only slightly higher than for Whites, but the proportion of Blacks obtaining a college degree is still only half as high as for Whites (NCES, 2008). Without educational credentials, gaining access to jobs in the new economy is difficult.

However, there is more to the problem of minority unemployment than a lack of education. Changes that have taken place in urban areas in recent decades have resulted in a combination of dire conditions that are proving difficult to reverse. The changes began with the decline in high-paying, low-skilled manufacturing jobs (Quillian, 2003; Wilson, 1996, 2006). As economic activity in the inner cities declined, many people followed the movement of jobs out of the cities into the suburbs. The people who took the initiative to move were often the most able, the most educated, and the most ambitious, including community leaders who had been important in building and sustaining institutions such as churches, businesses, social clubs, and political organizations.

With the departure of these community leaders, the downward spiral of life in the cities accelerated. Neighborhoods eroded and crime increased, giving the businesses that had remained in the cities more incentive to join the exodus (Wilson, 1996, 2006). As the tax base of the cities declined with the departure of businesses and the more affluent citizens, the quality of schools also declined from lack of adequate funding. By the early 1980s, many young people living in the cities lacked the basic skills of reading and arithmetic necessary even for low-paying, entry-level jobs. With few jobs available and with many of the young people lacking the skills to qualify for the available jobs, rates of crime, drug use, and gang violence among young people in urban areas climbed steadily higher.

What can be done about this complex and so far intractable situation? Most scholars and policy makers now agree that, given the number and seriousness of the problems in the cities, simply offering job-training programs will not be enough. William Julius Wilson (1996, 2006), one of the most prominent sociologists on this topic, has proposed an approach with the following elements:

community service Volunteer work provided as a contribution to the community, without monetary compensation.

- *Upgrade education.* The current system of local funding of schools perpetuates inequality because poor areas such as the inner cities have a smaller tax base to draw from than wealthy areas do. Financial support for schools should be more centralized and more equal. Also, the quality of teachers in the inner cities should be enhanced through scholarships to attract promising young people to teach in city schools and through reforms in teacher licensing and certification that require teachers to demonstrate competence in the subjects they teach.

- *Improve school-to-work programs.* Young people in urban areas are especially harmed by the lack of effective school-to-work programs in the United States, as shown in their high rates of unemployment. The programs currently available (such as those described earlier in this chapter) are a good start but should be expanded.

- *Improve access to employment.* Because most new jobs are opening up in suburban rather than urban locations, young people in the inner cities are at a disadvantage because few of them own automobiles and public transportation between cities and suburbs is inadequate in many American urban areas. Organized car pool and van pool networks to carry urban young people to jobs in suburban areas would improve their access to employment. Also, because newly available jobs are most often filled not through want ads but through personal contacts, young people in urban areas with high concentrations of unemployment have less information about available jobs. Creating job information and placement centers in urban areas would address this problem.

- *Provide government-funded public service jobs.* Urban areas have many needs that less skilled workers could help to address in public service jobs. Having young people serve in jobs such as nurse's aides, playground supervisors, bridge painters, pothole fillers, and library staffers would not only give them useful work experience—and provide a substitute for unemployment payments—but would also enhance the quality of life in the areas where they live, both for themselves and for others.

Volunteer Work—Community Service

In addition to the paid work that adolescents and emerging adults do, a substantial proportion of them also do volunteer work for little or no pay. Scholars refer to such work as **community service** because it involves volunteering to serve members of the young person's community without monetary compensation (McIntosh, Metz, & Youniss, 2005; McLellan & Youniss, 2003; Yates & Youniss, 1996; Youniss & Yates, 1997, 2000).

Americans are more than twice as likely as people in any other Western country to take part in volunteer work ("Helping Hands," 2001), and this includes a strikingly high proportion of American adolescents. According to national surveys, consistently from the mid-1970s through the present about 22% of high school seniors have reported taking part in volunteer work on a weekly or monthly basis, and an additional 45% have reported yearly participation (McIntosh et al., 2005; Yates & Youniss, 1996; Youniss & Yates, 2000). Taking these two figures together, then, two thirds of American adolescents report community service at least once per year. This service encompasses a wide variety of activities, such as serving meals to the homeless, cleaning up parks and playgrounds, and collecting money, food, and clothing for the poor. Often, the service takes place under the guidance of a community organization, such as religious organizations, 4-H, Boy and Girl Scouts, and Boys and Girls Clubs. Also, local, state, and federal governments have made numerous efforts to promote community service among adolescents. Nearly 30% of American high schools require some type of community service before graduation (HERI, 2005; Metz & Youniss, 2005)—involuntary volunteer work, you might call it.

Community Service and Adolescent Development

Research on adolescents and community service has focused on two main questions: What are the distinctive characteristics of adolescents who do volunteer work? And what effects does volunteer work have on adolescents who take part in it?

Adolescents who volunteer tend to have a high sense of personal competence, and they tend to have higher educational goals and performance than other adolescents (Bloom, 2000; Johnson et al., 1998; Pancer et al., 2007). They tend to have high ideals and to perceive a higher degree of similarity between their "actual selves" and their "ideal selves" than other adolescents do (Hart & Fegley, 1995; McIntosh et al., 2005). Adolescents who participate in community service often report that one or both parents do so as well (Pancer et al., 2007). By their participation, parents provide both a model for community service and concrete opportunities for adolescents to participate (Yates & Youniss, 1996).

For most adolescents, their community service is motivated by both individualistic and collectivistic values. Often, of course, they are motivated by collectivistic values such as wanting to help others or a concern for those who have been less fortunate than themselves. However, perhaps less obviously, studies have found that individualistic values are equal to collectivistic values as a motivation for adolescents' community service. In addition to wanting to help others, adolescents also volunteer because it gives them a sense of personal satisfaction and they enjoy doing the work. As Yates and Youniss (1996) suggest, it may be that performing community service "requires a personal investment in which the action of helping others becomes part of one's identity and, thus, is understood and articulated in terms of what makes one feel good" (p. 91).

With regard to the effects of community service, scholars have observed that such service is often part of adolescents' political socialization. Through their participation, adolescents become more concerned about social issues and develop an understanding of themselves as members of their society (McIntosh et al., 2005; Metz, McLellan, & Youniss, 2003; Pancer et al., 2007; Reinders & Youniss, 2006). In one example of this effect, Youniss and Yates (1997, 2000) studied adolescents who were volunteering in a soup kitchen for homeless people. Through the course of the year of their service, the adolescents began to reassess themselves, not only reflecting on their fortunate lives in comparison to the people they were working with but also seeing themselves as potential actors in working for the reforms needed to address the problem of homelessness. Furthermore, the adolescents began to raise questions about characteristics of the American political system in relation to homelessness, such as policies regarding affordable housing and job training. Thus, their participation made them more conscious of themselves as American citizens but also led them to be more critical of political policies and also more aware of their own responsibility in addressing social problems in American society.

Studies have also examined the long-term effects of taking part in volunteer work in adolescence. In general, these studies indicate that people who take part in volunteer work in adolescence are also more likely to be active in political activities and volunteer organizations as adults (Hart et al., 2007; Sherrod, Flanagan, & Youniss, 2002; Yates & Youniss, 1996). Of course, these studies do not show that community service in adolescence causes people to volunteer in adulthood as well. As we have seen, adolescent volunteers already differ from their peers in ways that explain their greater participation in community service in adolescence and beyond.

Nevertheless, the study by Youniss and Yates (1997, 2000) and other studies (e.g., Flanagan et al., 1998; Johnson et al., 1998; McIntosh et al., 2005; Metz et al., 2003) indicate that community service does have a variety of favorable effects on the young people who take part in it. One longitudinal study found that among adolescents who were required to perform community service in high school, those who indicated that they would have served voluntarily showed no changes from their participation (Metz & Youniss, 2005). However, those who would not have volunteered to serve without the requirement showed an increase on measures of civic attitudes and behaviors, such as interest in political and social issues and interest in participating in civic organizations. This indicates positive effects of community service even on—in fact, especially on—adolescents who might not have been inclined to serve.

THINKING CRITICALLY •••

Does the prevalence of community service indicate that American adolescents and emerging adults have stronger collectivistic values than scholars may have realized—or not, since only a relatively small proportion of young people take part in community service on a frequent basis?

Community Service in Emerging Adulthood

Like many adolescents, many emerging adults do volunteer work, such as working with children and collecting and distributing food, clothing, and other resources to the poor. However, in emerging adulthood, volunteer work in American society has taken the distinctive form of two major, government-sponsored institutions: the Peace Corps and AmeriCorps.

The **Peace Corps** is an organization that sends American volunteers all around the world to assist people in other nations by providing knowledge and skills in areas such as medical care, housing, sanitation, and food production. The organization began in 1961, when President John F. Kennedy exhorted young college graduates to give 2 years of their time in service to those in other nations who lacked the basic necessities of life. The Peace Corps is open to adults (age 18 and older) of any age, but the main participants have been emerging adults. Over half of current Peace Corps volunteers are ages 18 to 25 (Peace Corps, 2009).

From its beginnings, the size of the Peace Corps grew rapidly, to a peak of 15,000 volunteers in 1966. All together, over 195,000 people have served as of 2009. Currently, nearly 8,000 volunteers are in the field in 76 countries. They are a highly educated group: 95% have undergraduate degrees. Volunteers serve in a variety of areas, including education, environment, business, agriculture, and health. During their service they receive a monthly living allowance only high enough to enable them to live at the level of others in their community—not much, in other words. However, after the completion of their two years of service, they receive a bonus of about $6,000 to assist them in making the transition back to American society.

As benefits of serving in the Peace Corps, the organization points to the enhancement of career prospects from obtaining overseas experience, gaining cross-cultural knowledge, and learning the language of the host country (Peace Corps, 2000b, 2009). Although returning Peace Corps volunteers have written numerous personal accounts, few systematic studies have been conducted on the volunteers' experience and how it affects them. However, in 2000 the first comprehensive survey of returning volunteers was published (Peace Corps, 2000c). Among the findings were that 94% of them indicated they would make the same decision to join if they had it to do again. Also, 78% of returning volunteers had been involved in community service once they returned home.

In contrast to the Peace Corps, the **AmeriCorps** program is relatively recent, with the first group of volunteers serving in 1994. However, AmeriCorps has been larger than the Peace Corps from its inception. Over 20,000 volunteers served in 1994, and by 2009 over 75,000 AmeriCorps volun-

Volunteers in the Peace Corps and AmeriCorps tend to be emerging adults. Here, a volunteer and friends in Togo, West Africa.

teers were serving each year (AmeriCorps, 2009). About half the volunteers are White, 25% are African American, and 13% Latino (Aguirre International, 1999).

The AmeriCorps agency does not administer a volunteer program but instead sponsors volunteers to work in local community organizations, doing such work as tutoring children and adults, rehabilitating housing for low-income families, immunizing children against diseases, and helping persons with disabilities and elderly persons to maintain independent living. Although AmeriCorps is open to any person aged 18 or older, nearly all volunteers in the program are emerging adults aged 18 to 25. In return for their service they receive a small living allowance, health insurance, and an education award of $4,725 for each year served (1 or 2 years) to be applied toward college expenses, existing student loans, or an approved vocational training program (AmeriCorps, 2009).

Evaluations of the AmeriCorps program have shown the benefits that it provides both to emerging adults and to their communities (Simon & Wang, 2002). An assessment of a random sample of volunteers before and after their participation in the program showed that 76% gained significantly in all five "life skills areas" examined: Communication, Interpersonal, Analytical Problem Solving, Understanding Organizations, and Using Information Technology (Aguirre International, 1999). One independent study showed that each tax dollar spent on the AmeriCorps program results in a direct and demonstrable benefit of $1.60 to $2.60 for the community in which the volunteer serves (AmeriCorps, 2000). A recent longitudinal study reported that 8 years after their service in the program, Americorps volunteers were higher than the comparison group (who expressed interest in Americorps but did not enroll) on understanding of

---

Peace Corps An international service program in which Americans provide service to a community in a foreign country for 2 years.

AmeriCorps The national service program in the United States in which young people serve in a community organization for up to 2 years for minimal pay.

community problems, engagement in civic activity such as attending meetings of community organizations, and overall life satisfaction (Corporation for National and Community Service, 2008).

Military service is another type of service experienced by many emerging adults. Several times during the 20th century—World Wars I and II, the Korean War, and most of the Vietnam War—all young men in the United States were required to serve in the military, but since the early 1970s the military has been staffed by volunteers. Emerging adults who volunteer for military service tend to be different from other emerging adults in a variety of ways (Bachman, Segal, Freedman-Doan, & O'Malley, 2000). They are more likely than other emerging adults to come from low-SES family backgrounds. They tend to have mediocre grades in high school—neither above average nor well below average—and low college aspirations. African Americans and Latinos are more likely than Whites to enlist. Motivations for enlistment include patriotism, of course, but also the prospect of receiving money, educational support, and job training, as well as the belief that military service would promote the development of personal qualities such as maturity, responsibility, and discipline (Griffith & Perry, 1993).

How does serving in the military influence the development of emerging adults? The answer to this question is mixed. Most veterans of World War II and the Vietnam War believed that military service broadened them intellectually and made them more self-reliant, but many of them had difficulty making the transition to civilian employment after their service, and Vietnam veterans were more likely than nonveterans to have problems with alcohol abuse, especially if they had witnessed intense combat (Bookwala, Frieze, & Grote, 1994). For more recent veterans, since the establishment of the all-volunteer military, the effects of military service have been found to be largely positive (Gade et al., 1991). Veterans report that their service benefited them in multiple ways, including self-confidence, self-discipline, leadership skills, and ability to work with others. Benefits have been found to be especially strong for African Americans and Latinos, who often receive educational and job-training opportunities in the military that would not be readily available to them in the civilian world. However, the death of over 4,000 American soldiers in the Iraq War—mostly emerging adults—is a sobering reminder that for emerging adults who join the military, their expanded educational and occupational opportunities come with serious risks attached.

SUMMING UP

In this chapter we have discussed work in traditional cultures, the history of young people's work in the West, and current patterns of work among adolescents and emerging adults in the West. The main points we have discussed are as follows:

- Adolescents in traditional cultures have typically worked alongside their parents, the boys in work such as hunting, fishing, and farming, the girls in work such as gathering, child care, and household work. However, because of globalization, virtually all traditional cultures are moving toward industrialization. The result in many countries is that people in traditional cultures, especially adolescents, are being subjected to hard work in terrible conditions for very low pay, such as on commercial farms and plantations, in factories, and in prostitution.

- Before industrialization, adolescents in the West typically worked alongside their parents, boys with their fathers mostly in farming, girls with their mothers mostly in child care and household work. During the 19th century, adolescents made up a substantial proportion of the workforce in factories.

- Since World War II, the proportion of American adolescents in part-time work has risen steeply, so that by now over three fourths of high school seniors have had a part-time job. Research results on the effects of working part-time during high school are complex, but evidence is quite strong that working more than 10 hours per week has a variety of negative effects.

- For the "forgotten half" of American emerging adults who move to full-time work after high school rather than going to college, prospects have dimmed over the past 30 years as high-paying jobs for low-skilled workers have become more scarce in the American economy and high schools have failed to provide young people with the skills necessary for obtaining the best jobs available in the new technological economy.

- Most European countries have a national school-to-work program that coordinates secondary education with the need of employers, for example through apprenticeships. In the United States, school-to-work programs have been shown to be effective on a relatively small scale, but currently there is little political support for a national school-to-work program.

- Super's widely used theory of occupational development focuses on adolescence and emerging adulthood as an important period containing stages of crystallization, specification, and implementation.

- Holland's theory describes six personality types and the jobs to which they are likely to be best suited. However, most people have personality characteristics that fit into more than one type, and most occupations can be performed with success and satisfaction by persons with a variety of personality characteristics.

- Most emerging adults spend several years changing jobs frequently as they seek work that will not only pay well but will also fit their identity and provide personal fulfillment. Their work explorations often are haphazard and unsystematic.

- Unemployment is highly prevalent among African American and Latino emerging adults living in American cities, due to the decline in low-skilled but high-paying manufacturing jobs over the past 30 years.

- Volunteer work (community service) is common among American adolescents and emerging adults. Three prominent types of volunteering for emerging adults are the Peace Corps, AmeriCorps, and military service.

Because school extends for so many years for most adolescents in industrialized countries, work plays less of a role in their lives than it does for young people in developing countries. The work that most American adolescents do in their jobs is not work that many of them expect or want to be doing beyond adolescence. Still, it is striking how many adolescents spend 20 hours or more per week in employment, especially since their employment as adolescents does little to help them develop skills for adult work. They work in adolescence to finance an active leisure life, and their leisure is important enough to them that they are willing to spend a considerable number of hours a week in employment to be able to pay for it. It is a paradox—they give up leisure hours for employment, in order to be able to spend more money on their remaining leisure. In doing so, they often sacrifice their school performance, which can have real effects on the success they are likely to have in their future occupations.

Emerging adults face different kinds of work challenges. Work becomes more serious for emerging adults as a foundation for their occupations as adults. The central challenge for emerging adults in industrialized countries is to sort through the sometimes daunting range of possible occupations available to them and choose one occupational path they will find reasonably fulfilling and well-paying. They have to hope, too, that the path they choose will be open to them and that they will succeed in the pursuit of the work they want.

For young people in developing countries, work is especially a problem. The economy of their parents' and grandparents' generations is disappearing under the influence of globalization, so they may feel that learning the skills that were central to work in their culture in the past is now pointless. However, the alternatives open to them right now in their industrializing economies are grim for the most part and often involve arduous work under dangerous, unhealthy, exploitative conditions. The history of the work experience of adolescents in the West suggests that for young people in developing countries, changes in the 21st century will be in the direction of better work conditions, higher pay, and an increasing number of years in adolescence and emerging adulthood devoted to education and preparation for meaningful work that they choose for themselves. However, this will not happen through some inevitable mechanism of history—if it happens at all—but through the activism of committed people in their own countries as well as in industrialized countries.

KEY TERMS

International Labor Organization (ILO) 312

debt bondage 312

retention rate 318

occupational deviance 319

the forgotten half 320

the new basic skills 321

apprenticeship 322

second shift 327

unemployed 329

community service 330

Peace Corps 332

AmeriCorps 332

INTERNET RESOURCES

http://www.ilo.org
Website for the International Labor Organization, a United Nations agency dedicated to collecting information about work conditions around the world and working to improve them. Among their top priorities are eliminating child labor and improving labor conditions for adolescents.

http://www.peacecorps.gov and http://www.americorps.gov
These sites contain information about the Peace Corps and Americorps, including research on the programs as well as information about how to join.

FOR FURTHER READING

Barling, J., & Kelloway, E. K. (1999). *Young workers: Varieties of experience.* Washington, DC: American Psychological Association. The authors of the chapters in this edited book emphasize that employment is not necessarily good or bad for adolescents but can have different effects depending on the characteristics of the work and the characteristics of the adolescent.

Greenberger, E., & Steinberg, L. (1986). *When teenagers work: The psychological and social costs of adolescent employment.* New York: Basic Books. A classic study of the effects of work on adolescents by two prominent psychologists. The emphasis is on the negative effects of work, especially for adolescents who work over 15 hours per week.

Murnane, R. J., & Levy, F. (1997). *Teaching the new basic skills: Principles for educating children to thrive in a changing economy.* New York: Free Press. The authors examine the

employmen
attend college.
portunities exist,
have not learned e
tage of those opportu
suggestions for rectifying

PEARSON
mydevelopment

For more review plus practice tests, videos, flashcards, and more, log on to MyDevelopmentLab.

prospects of emerging adults who do not
They conclude that many promising op-
but noncollege emerging adults often
ough in high school to take advan-
ities. The authors supply specific
this problem.

In 1774, the great German writer Johann Wolfgang von Goethe (pronounced gur'-tuh) published *The Sorrows of Young Werther*, about a young man who kills himself in despair over his unrequited love for a married woman. The novel immediately became immensely popular all over Europe, inspiring poems, plays, operas, songs, even jewelry and an "Eau de Werther" scent for ladies. At the same time, the novel inspired immense controversy. It was banned in some parts of Germany for fear that impressionable young readers might interpret it as recommending suicide, and in Denmark a proposed translation was prohibited for the same reason. Although claims that Werther caused an epidemic of suicide in Europe are now regarded as unfounded (Hulse, 1989), in one verified case a young woman who had been deserted by her lover drowned herself in the river behind Goethe's house in Weimar, Germany, a copy of *Werther* in her pocket. Goethe was sufficiently disturbed by the controversy over the book to add an epigraph to the 1775 edition of the novel urging his readers not to follow Werther's example.

IN GOETHE'S TIME AS WELL AS OUR OWN, THE QUESTION of media effects has been a source of public debate and concern, often with a particular focus on the lives of adolescents. One more recent example took place in the autumn of 1993, concerning a movie called *The Program* released by the Walt Disney Company. The movie, about the players and coach of a college football program, quickly became controversial because of a scene in which one of the players demonstrates his manly toughness by lying down in the middle of a busy highway at night as cars and trucks whoosh by him. Some adolescents who had seen the movie proceeded to try the stunt for themselves. An 18-year-old Pennsylvania boy was killed and two other boys were critically injured, one of them paralyzed. In response to the resulting outcry, Disney hastily recalled the film and deleted the scene in question, while strenuously denying responsibility for the boys' reckless acts.

This is about as definite an example of media effects as it is possible to find. There can be little doubt that the boys were imitating the behavior they had witnessed in the movie. They had seen the movie just days before, and friends who accompanied them the night of the accidents testified later that they were imitating the stunt they had seen in the film.

At the same time, this example illustrates why drawing a simple cause-and-effect relationship between the media consumed by adolescents and their subsequent behavior is problematic. Literally hundreds of thousands of people (mostly adolescents) saw the movie with the controversial scene. It was playing in 1,220 theaters at the time, and even estimating modestly at 100 persons per theater would put the total number of viewers over 100,000. Yet the total number of reported incidents that resulted from adolescents imitating the scene was *three*. Even if it were generously estimated that 100 times as many adolescents imitated the scene as were injured in the process, the total proportion of adolescents who were affected by the scene to the point of imitating it would amount to one fourth of 1% of the people who watched it. Evidently, then, the adolescents who imitated the scene had traits or circumstances that led them to imitate it, even though the vast majority of the people who watched it did not.

This incident illustrates both the potentially profound effects of the media on adolescents and the complexity involved in tracing those effects. Debates over media effects are often polarized, with those at one extreme glibly blaming media for every social ill and those at the other extreme dismissing (just as glibly) all claims of media effects as unverifiable. I believe both extremes are mistaken, and in this chapter I will present you with a more complex (and, I hope, more true-to-life) approach to understanding young people's uses of media.

THINKING CRITICALLY •••

If one or two people out of a million who watch a particular movie or listen to a particular song are negatively affected by it, is that reason enough to ban or withdraw the movie or song? Or should people—even adolescents—be responsible for how they respond to media?

Media and Young People's Development

No account of young people's development would be complete without a description of the media they use. Recorded music, television, movies, magazines, and the Internet are part of the daily environment for nearly all young people currently growing up in industrialized countries (and increasingly, as we will see, in developing countries as well). The typical American adolescent listens to music for about 2 hours a day and watches television for another 2 hours (Roberts, Foehr, & Rideout, 2005). Forty percent of American secondary schools now begin their day with news *and advertisements* transmitted by Channel One, an in-school TV news program for teens (Palmer, 2006). Adolescents in Europe and Japan also watch TV for an average of about two hours a day (Flammer, Alsaker, & Noack, 1999; Stevenson & Zusho, 2002). Adolescents in the United States watch more movies than any other segment of the population; over 50% of adolescents aged 12 to 17 go to at least one movie per month (Brown, Steele, & Walsh-Childers, 2002). Seventy percent of adolescent girls report regular magazine reading (Walsh-Childers, Gotthoffer, & Lepre, 2002). About 90% of American adolescents have access to computers both at home and at school, and they use them for school work as well as for Internet access and e-mail (Roberts et al., 2005).

American adolescents listen to music for an average of 2 hours a day.

Add videos, books, and newspapers, and the total amounts to a large proportion of the daily experience of adolescents. All together, American adolescents typically spend about $6\frac{1}{2}$ hours per day using media. About one fourth of their media use involves multiple media—listening to music while doing e-mail, for example, or reading a magazine while watching TV. A substantial amount of adolescents' media use takes place alone—in their own bedroom over half have a DVD player, two thirds have their own TV, and nearly all have a radio and a CD player. There are few statistics on media use among emerging adults, but there is no reason to expect media use to decline between adolescence and emerging adulthood. In fact, emerging adults might be hypothesized to use media even more than adolescents do because they spend more of their time alone (Arnett, 2004a; Brown, 2006).

Another reason for looking at media in relation to young people's development is that a great deal of concern exists about the potential effects of media on this age group. These effects are generally viewed as negative (Brown & Witherspoon, 2002; Villani, 2001). Television is blamed for inspiring young people to drink alcohol, have unsafe sex, behave aggressively, and hold stereotyped beliefs about gender roles. Music is blamed for motivating young people to commit violent acts toward others or themselves. Movies and computer games, too, are blamed for violence. Magazines are held responsible for promoting an emaciated female form as the ideal so relentlessly that many girls become emaciated themselves in their attempts to emulate it. The Internet is accused of promoting social isolation and making adolescents vulnerable to adult sexual predators. Given all this controversy over young people and media, it is important for us to consider what the research evidence tells us about the merit of the accusations. And it is important to consider the possibility of positive media effects, as well.

In this chapter, then, we will look first at theories of media influence and then at some of the uses of media that are typical among young people and how those uses reflect certain developmental needs. This will include a discussion of how socialization through the media is related to socialization from other sources, such as parents, peers, and school. In the second half of the chapter we will examine the research concerning various controversial media, from violent television and computer games to sex in music to cigarette advertising to the Internet. Last we will consider two types of new media, the Internet and mobile phones, and the role media play in the globalization of adolescence.

Theories of Media Influence

Two theories have been especially prominent in guiding scholars' understanding of how media influence young people. *Cultivation Theory* argues that watching television gradually shapes or "cultivates" a person's worldview, so that over time it comes to resemble the worldview most frequently depicted on TV (Appel, 2008; Gerbner, Gross, Morgan, & Signorelli, 1994; Tan, Tan, & Gibson, 2003). For example, adolescent girls who are frequent viewers of soap operas have been found to be more likely than other girls to believe that single mothers have relatively easy lives because this is how single mothers are often depicted on soap operas (Larson, 1996).

One aspect of Cultivation Theory is known as Mean World Syndrome (Gerbner et al., 1994). In Mean World Syndrome, the more people watch TV, the more they are likely to believe that the world is a dangerous place, that crime rates are high and rising, and that they themselves are at risk for being a victim of a crime (Romer, Jamieson, & Aday, 2003). According to Cultivation Theory, they believe this because television often depicts crime and violence on dramas and news shows, which leads viewers to cultivate a view of the world as mean, violent, and dangerous.

The second prominent theory of media influence is *Social Learning Theory* (Bandura, 1994; Tan et al., 2003). According to this theory, people will be more likely to imitate behaviors they see frequently performed by models who are rewarded or at least not punished. In a famous experiment known as the "Bobo doll" study, children watched an adult kicking and punching a clownlike doll ("Bobo"). Later, the children imitated the adult's behavior almost exactly.

Over the past 40 years, hundreds of media studies have been conducted using Social Learning Theory as the guiding framework (Wade & Tavris, 2003). For example, studies have found that heavier exposure to sexual content on TV is related to earlier initiation of sexual intercourse, and this has been interpreted as indicating that the adolescents modeled their sexual behavior after the TV characters (Brown et al., 2002). Many of the studies using Social Learning Theory have concerned the relationship between television and aggression, as we will see in more detail later in this chapter.

Both Cultivation Theory and Social Learning Theory are presented mainly in terms of media effects, with the media consumer depicted as relatively passive and easily manipulated. In research using these theories, correlations between media use and attitudes or behavior are routinely interpreted as causation, because it is assumed that media have effects and the consumer is a relatively passive recipient of those effects. However, an alternative approach has developed that recognizes that the role media play in the lives of adolescents and others is usually more complex than a simple cause-and-effect relationship. This approach is known as the **uses and gratifications approach**, and the emphasis is on viewing people as active media consumers (Paik et al., 2001; Pierce, 2006; Rubin, 1993; von Salisch, Oppl, & Kristen, 2006). This approach will serve as the framework for this chapter.

The uses and gratifications approach is based on two key principles. The first is that people differ in numerous ways that lead them to make different choices about which media to consume. For example, not all adolescents like violent TV shows; the uses and gratifications approach assumes that adolescents who like such shows differ from adolescents who do not, prior to any effect that watching violent shows may have (Haridakis & Rubin, 2003). The second principle is that people consuming the same media product will respond to it in a

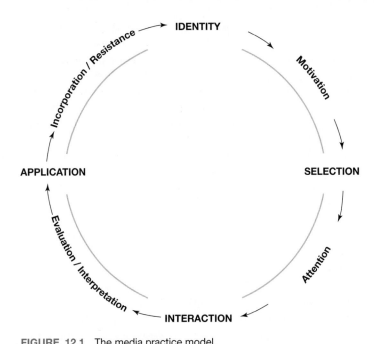

FIGURE 12.1 The media practice model.
Source: Brown et al. (2002), p. 9.

variety of ways, depending on their individual characteristics. For example, some adolescent girls may read teen magazines and respond by feeling extremely insecure about the way they look compared with the models in the magazine, whereas other girls may read the same magazines and be relatively unaffected (Brown et al., 2002).

Recently, Jane Brown and her colleagues presented a model of how the uses and gratifications theory works in the lives of adolescents (Brown, 2006; Brown et al., 2002; Steele, 2006). Their model, called the *Media Practice Model*, is illustrated in Figure 12.1. As the figure shows, the model proposes that adolescents' media use is active in a number of ways. Adolescents do not all have the same media preferences. Rather, each adolescent's identity motivates the *selection* of media products. Paying attention to certain media products leads to *interaction* with those products, meaning that the products are evaluated and interpreted. Then adolescents engage in *application* of the media content they have chosen. They may incorporate this content into their identities—for example, girls who respond to thin models by seeking to be thin themselves—or they may resist the content—for example, girls who respond to thin models by rejecting them as a false ideal. Their developing identity then motivates new media selections, and so on.

uses and gratifications approach Approach to understanding media that emphasizes that people differ in numerous ways that lead them to make different choices about which media to consume and that even people consuming the same media product will respond to it in a variety of ways, depending on their individual characteristics.

Rather than viewing young people as the passive, easily manipulated targets of media influences, the uses and gratifications approach asks, "What sort of *uses* or purposes motivate young people to watch a television show, or go to a movie, or listen to a CD, or read a magazine, or use the Internet? And what sort of *gratifications* or satisfactions do they receive from the media they choose?" Similarly, the Media Practice Model asks how adolescents select, interact with, and apply media products in the course of developing an identity. We will keep these questions at the forefront as we discuss media in this chapter. Let's start out by taking a look at five of the principal uses that young people make of media.

Five Uses

Five uses of media by adolescents can be specified (Arnett, 1995b): entertainment, identity formation, high sensation, coping, and youth culture identification. All of the uses described except entertainment are *developmental* in the sense that they are more likely to be uses of media for adolescents and emerging adults than for children or adults (Arnett, 1995b).

Entertainment

Adolescents and emerging adults, like children and adults, often make use of media simply for entertainment, as an enjoyable part of their leisure lives (Brake, 1985; Nabi & Krcmar, 2004). Music often accompanies young people's leisure, from driving around in a car to hanging out with friends to secluding themselves in the privacy of their bedrooms for contemplation (Larson, 1995). The most common motivation stated by adolescents for listening to music is "to have fun" (Tarrant, North, & Hargreaves, 2000). Television is used by many adolescents as a way of diverting themselves from personal concerns with entertainment that is passive, distracting, and undemanding (Larson, 1995; Roberts & Foehr, 2004). Entertainment is clearly one of the uses young people seek in movies and magazines as well. Young people generally use media for the entertainment purposes of fun, amusement, and recreation.

Identity Formation

"[I'd like to be like] Cher, Madonna, and Tina Turner all rolled together, because they all have attitude and they know what they want."

—Stephanie, age 13 (in Currie, 1999, p. 262)

"I like it in YM and Seventeen magazines how they have like your horoscope and what you're like—your color and if you're an 'earth person' or a 'water person,' something like that. They tell you what you are."

—Lauren, age 14 (in Currie, 1999, p. 154)

As we have seen in previous chapters, one of the most important challenges of adolescence and emerging adulthood is identity formation—the development of a conception of one's values, abilities, and hopes for the future. In cultures where media are available, media can provide materials that young people use toward the construction of an identity (Boehke, Muench, & Hoffman, 2002). Part of identity formation is thinking about the kind of person you would like to become, and in media adolescents find ideal selves to emulate and feared selves to avoid. The use of media for this purpose is reflected in the pictures and posters adolescents put up in their rooms, which are often of media stars from entertainment and sports (see the Research Focus box).

Media can also provide adolescents with information that would otherwise be unavailable to them, and some of this information may be used to help construct an identity. For example, adolescents may learn about different possible occupations by watching television or reading magazines (Clifford, Gunter, & McAleer, 1995). In my research on adolescent heavy metal fans (discussed in more detail later in the chapter), over one third of them, inspired by their heavy metal heroes, stated their intention to go into music as a career, preferably as heavy metal heroes themselves (Arnett, 1996).

An important aspect of identity formation, and one for which adolescents may especially make use of media, is gender role identity (Hust, 2006; Steele & Brown, 1995). Adolescents take ideals of what it means to be a man or a woman partly from the media. Adolescents use the information provided in media to learn sexual and romantic scripts (Brown et al., 2002)—for example, how to approach a potential romantic partner for the first time, what to do on a date, and even how to kiss. One study of adolescents' messages in Internet chat rooms found that the exchange of identity information allowed participants to "pair off" with partners of their choice, despite the disembodied nature of chat participants (Subramanyam, Greenfield, & Tynes, 2004). The authors concluded that the virtual world of teen chat may offer a safer environment for exploring emerging sexuality than the real world. For both girls and boys, gender, sexuality, and relationships are central to the kind of identity exploration and identity formation for which adolescents use media (Ward, 1995).

Magazines are a medium where gender roles are an especially common theme, particularly in magazines for adolescent girls. As noted in Chapter 5, the most popular magazines for teenage girls devote most of their space to advertisements and articles that focus on physical appearance, heterosexual relationships, and sexuality (Currie, 1999; Kim, 2006; Walsh-Childers, Gotthoffer, & Lepre, 2002). In contrast, the magazines most popular among adolescent boys are devoted to sports, computer games, humor, and cars—with little or no mention of how to improve physical appearance or how to form relationships with girls or any topic related to sexuality (Kantrowitz & Wingert, 1999; Taylor, 2006).

This gender difference in magazines changes in emerging adulthood. Magazines for young women, like the magazines for adolescent girls, continue to emphasize physical appearance, sexuality, and heterosexual relationships, but magazines for young men such as *Maxim* and *GQ* also contain

Adolescents take gender ideals in part from media icons. Here, the singer-songwriter Taylor Swift.

substantial content on these topics, unlike the magazines popular among adolescent boys.

THINKING CRITICALLY •••

Why is it that physical appearance and relationships are virtually the only topics in magazines read by adolescent girls, but these topics scarcely exist in magazines read by adolescent boys?

High Sensation

Sensation seeking is a personality characteristic defined by the extent to which a person enjoys *novelty* and *intensity* of sensation. Adolescents and emerging adults tend to be higher in sensation seeking than adults (Arnett, 1994b; Zuckerman, 2007), and certain media provide the intense and novel sensations that appeal to many young people. Overall, sensation seeking is related to higher media consumption in adolescence, especially TV, music, and computer games (Lachlan, 2006; Roberts et al., 2005; Zuckerman, 2006).

Many media products appeal to adults as well as young people, but some appeal almost exclusively to young people, at least partly because of the high-sensation quality of the stimulation. The audience for "action" films is composed mostly of males in adolescence and emerging adulthood, because this is the segment of the population that is highest in sensation seeking and consequently most likely to be drawn to films that portray scenes involving explosions, car chases (and car crashes), gunfire, and suspense (Hoffner & Levine, 2005; Slater, 2003). Adolescent boys also dominate the audiences for the high-sensation musical forms of rap, heavy metal, and hard rock (Arnett, 1996; Rawlings, Barrantes, & Furnham, 2000).

Music is a media form that may especially lend itself to high-sensation intensity. Most popular music is created by people who are adolescents and emerging adults or just be-

yond (with geriatric exceptions such as the Rolling Stones), and the sensory stimulation of most popular music is much higher than for television (think of the volume level of the last rock concert you attended). Adolescents' emotional arousal when listening to music tends to be high, at least partly because of the high sensory and emotional intensity of music (Larson, 1995).

Coping

Young people use media to relieve and dispel negative emotions. Several studies indicate that "Listen to music" and "Watch TV" are the coping strategies adolescents most commonly use when they are angry, anxious, or unhappy (Kurdek, 1987; Oliver, 2006). Music may be particularly important in this respect (Saarikallio & Erkkilä, 2007). Larson (1995) reports that adolescents often listen to music in the privacy of their bedrooms while pondering the themes of the songs in relation to their own lives, as part of the process of emotional self-regulation. In early adolescence, when the number of problems at home, at school, and with friends increases, time spent listening to music also increases (Roberts et al., 2005).

Certain types of music, such as hip-hop or heavy metal, may appeal especially to young people who use music for coping. Adolescent fans of heavy metal report that they listen to heavy metal especially when they are angry, and that the music typically has the effect of purging their anger and calming them down (Arnett, 1991, 1996; Scheel & Westefeld, 1999; we will discuss this in more detail later in the chapter).

Young people also sometimes use television for coping purposes. Larson (1995) reports that adolescents use television as a way of turning off the stressful emotions that have accumulated during the day. Similarly, Kurdek (1987) found that adolescents use watching TV as a deliberate coping strategy when experiencing negative emotions. Adolescents also may choose media materials for specific coping purposes. A study of Israeli adolescents, in the aftermath of the 1991 Persian Gulf War, indicated that the media were an important source of information during the war and that adolescents used the information obtained through the media to help them cope with the stress of the war (Zeidner, 1993).

THINKING CRITICALLY •••

Why do you think watching television and listening to music have calming effects on adolescents' emotions? Do you think emerging adults would experience the same effects?

Youth Culture Identification

Media consumption can give adolescents a sense of being connected to a youth culture or subculture that is united by certain youth-specific values and interests. In cultures where

sensation seeking A personality characteristic defined by the extent to which a person enjoys novelty and intensity of sensation.

Jane Brown and her colleagues have used a number of creative methods to study adolescents' uses of media (Brown et al., 2002). In one study (Brown, White, & Nikopolou, 1993), adolescent girls were asked to keep a daily journal about whatever they saw in the media about sex and relationships. In another study (Steele & Brown, 1995), high school seniors were asked to interview each other about how they used media in their bedrooms at home, including television, magazines, and stereos as well as room decorations that reflected media use (posters of rock musicians, sports stars, etc.). Another method they have used in their research is what they call "room touring," where the researchers actually "tour" adolescents' bedrooms and have the adolescents describe everything that holds special meaning or significance for them, usually including numerous media artifacts (posters, pictures from magazines, CDs and cassette tapes, etc.).

The bedroom is often the location of adolescent's media use.

All of these research methods are qualitative. The focus is not on quantifying experience into patterns that can be reflected in numbers and analyzed in statistical tests, but on the experience of individuals and how they interpret and articulate their experiences.

Qualitative methods can result in rich data about the lives of individual adolescents, as in these two descriptions:

In [14-year-old] Rachel's room the bed is covered with clothes, cassette tapes and magazines, a red phone, and the cassette player. The walls are plastered with posters of the Beatles, the B52s, and a leering rock musician with his hand stuck down in his pants. The posters cover over an Impressionist art print of a little girl with flowers. One wall is full of advertisements torn from magazines featuring muscular men and thin women modeling the latest fashions. . . .

Sixteen years old and a sophomore in high school, Jack safeguards an eclectic mix of childhood artifacts and teenage fantasies and aspirations in his bedroom. On one wall a wooden box displays a fleet of multihued model cars, painstakingly crafted during grade school. A shelf is piled high with the audiotaped "mixes" that now occupy his time. Perched on top is a teddy bear dressed in a white sailor suit. . . . On the wall next to his bed are more current concerns: a Ferrari Testarossa poster, and pictures of girls clipped from magazines. "If they look good," Jack explains, "I just put them up on the wall." (Steele & Brown, 1995, pp. 551–552)

In addition to individual examples, qualitative research such as the research conducted by Brown and her colleagues allows scholars to describe general patterns of development. However, for qualitative researchers, these general patterns are usually ascertained through the researcher's insights and judgment rather than on the basis of statistical analyses. For example, in the study in which adolescent girls kept journals of their responses to sexual media content, the researchers concluded that the girls' responses fell into three general patterns (Brown et al., 1993). Those they termed "Disinterested" tended to ignore sexual content in media, and preferred not to talk or think about it even when prodded to do so. Their rooms tended to be filled with stuffed animals and dolls rather than media items. In contrast, a second group labeled "Intrigued" had rooms filled with magazines, musical recordings, and television, and their walls were filled with images of popular media stars, including media items with sexual content. A third group, "Resisters," also had rooms with evidence of high media use, but they tended to select images from less mainstream media—political leaders and female sports stars rather than popular music performers. They were termed "Resisters" because they were often critical of sexual media content, particularly the media depiction of women as sexual objects. In the journal of Audrey, age 14, was this critique of cosmetic ads:

I think that they use these beautiful people to sell their products because they want fat old ladies sitting at home with curlers in their hair watching the soaps to think that if they buy Loreal's [sic] 10 day formula they'll end up looking that beautiful. I think that's really stupid because for one, I know perfectly well I don't look like Cybil Shepard [sic] and Loreal's [sic] 10 day formula's not going to change that. (Steele & Brown, 1995, p. 564)

In this and many other examples, Brown and her colleagues show that adolescents are not just passive targets of media but active consumers who use media for a variety of purposes. At the same time, the qualitative focus on the experience of individuals also allows for revealing examples suggesting media effects. Audrey, seemingly so adept at deflecting the lure of media images, reported in her journal a couple of days after the entry above that she had spent the afternoon buying "basically cosmetics!"

Adolescents often use music to cope with strong emotions.

people change residence frequently (such as the United States), the media provide common ground for all adolescents. No matter where they move within the United States, adolescents will find peers in their new area who have watched the same television programs and movies, listened to the same music, and are familiar with the same advertising slogans and symbols. Music, especially, is a medium for expressing adolescent-specific values (Gregson, 2006; Roe, 1985). Worldwide, media are a driving force behind the globalization of youth culture, as we will see in more detail later in the chapter.

Adolescents' identification may be not to youth culture as a whole but to a youth subculture. For example, youth subcultures in recent decades have been defined by punk, heavy metal, and hip-hop. Adolescents who participate in these subcultures often feel alienated from the mainstream of their societies (Arnett, 1996, 2007b).

Media and Adolescent Socialization

We have seen that media use is a big part of the lives of most adolescents in the West. This prominence is even more striking when we think about it in historical perspective. At the beginning of the 20th century, adolescents' exposure to media would have been limited to print media such as books, magazines, and newspapers. Television, radio, CD players, DVDs, computer games, and the Internet did not even exist. In less than a century, all these media have become a central part of the cultural environment of industrialized societies.

What does this transformation in the cultural environment imply for young people's development? Essentially it amounts to the creation of a new source of socialization (Arnett, 1995b; 2006c). Of course, the media have become part of the social environment of people of all ages, but the potential role of media in the socialization of young people is perhaps especially strong. Adolescence and emerging adulthood are times when important aspects of socialization are

taking place, especially with regard to identity-related issues such as beginning occupational preparation, learning gender roles, and developing a set of values and beliefs. It is also a time when the presence and influence of the family have diminished relative to childhood, as we discussed in Chapter 7. At the same time that parents' influence on socialization recedes during adolescence, the role of the media in socialization grows. In one national American survey of 10- to 15-year-olds, 49% said they "learn a lot from" television and movies, a higher percentage than learned a lot from their mothers (38%) or their fathers (31%; Kantrowitz & Wingert, 1999).

As a socialization influence, the media tend toward broad socialization in societies that have freedom of speech and where the media are relatively uncontrolled and uncensored by government agencies. In such societies, there is tremendous diversity in the media offerings available, providing adolescents a diverse array of potential models and influences. This is likely to promote a broad range of individual differences in values, beliefs, interests, and personality characteristics because adolescents can choose from diverse media offerings the ones that resonate most strongly with their own particular inclinations.

Most Western societies value free speech highly, so a diverse range of media content is allowed. However, the United States takes this principle further than European countries do. For example, Germany has a legal prohibition against music lyrics that express hatred or advocate violence toward minorities. In Norway, one person in the government reviews all movies before they are allowed to be shown in theaters and prohibits the showing of movies judged to be too violent. Neither of these prohibitions would be likely to survive a legal challenge in the United States because of the protection of free speech in the First Amendment of the Constitution.

Nevertheless, the principle of free speech does not mean that all media must be accessible to all persons regardless of age. Age restrictions on access to media are allowable under the First Amendment, and the United States has rating systems for movies, music, television, and computer games that are designed to indicate to children, adolescents, and their parents which media may be unsuitable for persons under a certain age (Funk et al., 1999; Lambe, 2006). However, the enforcement of these guidelines and restrictions requires substantial parental involvement (for the most part they are guidelines, not legal requirements). Because parents are often either unaware of the media their adolescents are using or hesitant to place restrictions, most American adolescents easily gain access to whatever media they like (Funk et al., 1999; Roberts et al., 2005).

Media and Other Sources of Socialization

An important difference exists between media and other socialization agents in the adolescent's environment, such as family members, teachers, community members, law enforcement agents, and religious authorities. Typically, these other socializers have an interest in encouraging the adolescent to accept the attitudes, beliefs, and values of adults in order to preserve social order and pass the culture on from one generation to the next. In contrast, media are typically presented by people whose primary concern is the economic success of the media enterprise. As a result, the content of media consumed by adolescents is driven not by a desire to promote successful socialization but by the uses adolescents themselves can make of media. Because the media are largely market-driven, media providers are likely to provide adolescents with whatever it is they believe adolescents want—within the limits imposed on media providers by other adult socializers such as parents and legal authorities.

This means that adolescents have greater control over their socialization from the media than they do over socialization from family or school. This has two important consequences (Arnett, 2006c). First, it results in a great deal of diversity in the media available to adolescents, from classical music to heavy metal, from public television to MTV, from *Seventeen* to *Mad* magazine, as media providers try to cover every potential niche of the market for media products. Adolescents can choose from among this diversity whatever media materials best suit their personalities and preferences, and on any given occasion adolescents can choose the media materials that best suit the circumstances and their emotional state.

Second, to some extent this socialization goes *over the heads* of the other socializing adults in the adolescent's environment (Strasburger, 2006; Taillon, 2004). Parents may try to impose restrictions on the music, television shows, movies, and electronic games their adolescents consume, but these restrictions are unlikely to be successful if an adolescent is determined to avoid them. The limited time parents and adolescents spend in each other's company makes it difficult for parents to enforce such restrictions (Larson & Richards, 1994). In any case, few parents even attempt to impose restrictions. For example, in one national American study, fewer than 20% of adolescents reported that their parents had rules about the amount of time they spent watching television or about the content of the TV programs they watched (Roberts et al., 2005). The percentages concerning computer and Internet use were similarly low.

As a source of adolescent socialization, media bear the greatest similarity to peers. With media as with peers, adolescents have substantial control over their own socialization, as they make choices with only limited influence from their

parents and other adult socializers. With media as with peers, adolescents sometimes make choices that adults find troublesome. Indeed, media scholars have proposed that the media function as a **super peer** for adolescents, meaning that adolescents often look to media for information (especially concerning sexuality) that their parents may be unwilling to provide, in the same way they might look to a friend (Brown, Halpern, & L'Engles, 2005; Strasburger, 2006).

Examples of how adolescents may use media in ways disturbing to their parents and other adults in their immediate social environment can be seen in relation to each of the five uses of media described earlier. They may find *entertainment* in media that many adults consider disturbingly violent. In assembling materials toward *identity formation* they may develop admiration for media stars who seem to reject the values of the adult world, stars who may in fact reject the very idea of "growing up" to a responsible adulthood (Steele & Brown, 1995). Adolescents also may be attracted to *high-sensation* media that adults find disagreeable for precisely the reason it is so appealing to adolescents—the extraordinary high-sensation intensity of it (Arnett, 1996; Lachlan, 2006). Adolescents may seclude themselves in their rooms and use media in *coping* with their problems in a way that seems to shut out their parents (Larson, 1995). Finally, adolescents may become involved in a media-based *youth subculture* that actively and explicitly rejects the future that adult society holds out to them. In all of these ways, socialization from the media may be subversive to the socialization promoted by other adult socializers.

However, this portrayal of adolescents' media use as oppositional should be modified in several respects. First, it bears repeating that media are diverse, and not all of the media used by adolescents are contrary to the aims and principles of adult society. Much of it is, in fact, quite conservative. Many media providers, especially in television, shrink from controversy and tend to avoid topics that could subject them to public attack (and advertisers' boycotts). In most cases, adolescents perceive television programs as reinforcing conventional values such as "honesty is the best policy," "good wins over evil," and "hard work yields rewards" (Brown et al., 2002). Second, adolescents do not come to media as blank slates, but as members of a family, community, and culture that have socialized them from birth and from whom they have learned ideals and principles that are likely to influence their media choices and how they interpret the media they consume.

Third, the range of media available to adolescents, though vast, is not unlimited. Parents can place restrictions on how adolescents may use media at least when the parents are present; schools often restrict adolescents' media use during and between classes; and many countries have guidelines for the content of television programs (at least on the major networks) and for the magazines and movies that may be sold to adolescents under age 18 (Roberts et al., 2005).

The portrait of media socialization presented here applies to the contemporary West, and media socialization may be quite different in traditional cultures. Legal and parental

super peer One of the functions of media for adolescents, meaning that adolescents often look to media for information (especially concerning sexuality) that their parents may be unwilling to provide, in the same way they might look to a friend.

Adolescents often make media choices their parents find unsettling.

controls over adolescents' access to media are tighter in traditional cultures with narrow socialization, so that adolescents are unlikely to be able to use media as freely. However, today even in many traditional cultures the introduction of Western media is opening up new possibilities to adolescents, loosening the extent of parental control and increasing the extent to which adolescents choose the materials of their own socialization. Later in this chapter, we will look at examples of Western media influencing adolescents in traditional cultures.

THINKING CRITICALLY •••

Suppose you had an adolescent who liked to listen to a kind of music you believed was potentially harmful because of the level of violence in it. How would you handle it—would you forbid it, ignore it, discuss it—and why?

Controversial Media

Because adolescents spend a lot of time daily consuming media, and because media play an important role in adolescent socialization, parents and other adults express concern when they perceive the media as containing material that may have damaging effects on adolescents. In this section, we consider criticisms of controversial media and examine the available research evidence in relation to those criticisms. The areas of controversy discussed here are television and aggressiveness; computer games and aggressiveness; television and movies and adolescent sex; hip-hop and heavy metal music; and cigarette advertising.

Television and Aggressiveness

A great deal of research attention has focused on the extent to which media promote and provoke violence in young people. Most of this research has concerned television, and the majority of it has involved preadolescent chil-

dren (Anderson et al., 2003; Cantor, 1998, 2000; Finney, 2006). However, this an issue of particular importance with regard to adolescents and emerging adults because the overwhelming majority of violent crimes all over the world are committed by young males aged 15 to 25 (Eisner, 2002).

Unfortunately, most of the studies on adolescents and television violence are correlational studies, which ask adolescents about the television programs they watch and about their aggressive behavior. As we have often noted in this book, correlational studies do not show causality, and these studies merely indicate the unremarkable finding that aggressive adolescents prefer aggressive television programs (Selah-Shayovits, 2006). They cannot answer the crucial question "Does watching violence on TV cause adolescents to become more aggressive, or are adolescents who are more aggressive simply more likely to enjoy watching violence on TV?" In an effort to address this question, numerous **field studies** have been conducted on the effects of television on adolescent aggression. Typically, adolescents (usually boys) in a setting such as a residential school or summer camp are separated into two groups, and one group is shown TV or movies with violent themes whereas the other views TV or movies with nonviolent themes. Then the behavior of the boys in the two groups is recorded and compared. However, the findings of these studies are weak and inconsistent, and overall they do not support the claim that viewing violent media causes adolescents to be more aggressive (Freedman, 1988; Strasburger, 1995).

The study most often cited to support claims that violent television causes aggressiveness is a longitudinal study by Eron and Huesmann (Bushman & Huesmann, 2002; Coyne, 2006; Huesmann, Eron, Lefkowitz, & Walder, 1984). They

---

field studies Studies in which people's behavior is observed in a natural setting.

Does watching violent television programs cause adolescents to become more aggressive?

began their study when the participants were 8 years old and continued it until the participants reached age 30. Television-viewing patterns and aggressive behavior were assessed at ages 8, 19, and 30. A correlation was found between aggressiveness and watching violent TV at age 8, not surprisingly. But watching violent TV at age 8 also predicted aggressive behavior in boys at age 19, and by age 30 the men who had been aggressive at age 8 were more likely to be arrested, more likely to have traffic violations, and more likely to abuse their children. This relation was found even controlling for boys' initial levels of aggressiveness at age 8. So, it was not simply that aggressive persons especially liked to watch violent television at all three ages, but that aggressive 8 year-olds who watched high levels of TV violence were more likely to be aggressive at later ages than similarly aggressive 8 year-olds who watched lower levels of TV violence. The relation between watching violent TV and later aggressive behavior was not found for girls.

A study using a natural experiment provides perhaps the most compelling support for the argument that watching violent television causes aggressive behavior, at least in children (MacBeth, 2006). In this study a Canadian community (called "Notel" by the researchers) was studied before and after the introduction of television into the community. Aggressive behavior among children in Notel was compared with the behavior of children in two comparable communities, one with only one television channel ("Unitel") and one with multiple TV channels ("Multitel"). In each community several ratings of aggressiveness were obtained, including teachers' ratings, self-reports, and observers' ratings of children's verbal and physical aggressiveness. At the beginning of the study, aggressive behavior was lower among children in Notel than among children in Unitel or Multitel, but aggressive behavior increased significantly among children in Notel after TV was introduced, so that Notel children were equal to their Unitel and Multitel peers 2 years after the introduction of TV. However, the study involved children in middle childhood rather than adolescents, and there is no information on how the adolescents of the community reacted.

Although the findings of this study are intriguing, overall the research provides only mixed support for the claim that watching violent television causes adolescents to behave aggressively. The evidence is more persuasive that violent television causes aggression in *children* (Browne & Hamilton-Giachritsis, 2005; Cantor, 2000; Paradise, 2006). As the father of 9-year-old twins who have spent a substantial proportion of their childhood pretending to be characters from *Scooby-Doo*, I can attest to the power of television to inspire imitative behavior in children. However, adolescents are not children. Their cognitive abilities usually enable them to reflect on what they are watching and to recognize it as fantasy rather than as a model to be imitated. Even Rowell Huesmann, one of the most prominent proponents of the claim that televised violence causes aggression in children, states that "we do not need to be as concerned about adults' or even teenagers' exposure to media violence as much as we do with children's exposure. Media violence may have short-term effects on adults, but the real long-term effects seem to occur only with children" (Huesmann, Moise-Titus, Podolski, & Eron, 2003, p. 219).

This is not to dismiss the potential of televised violence for provoking violence in some adolescents under some circumstances, especially for adolescents who are already at risk for violence due to factors in their personalities and social environments (Browne & Hamilton-Giachritsis, 2005; Huesmann et al., 2003; Kronenberger et al., 2005). It is probably true that, for some adolescents, watching television violence acts as a model for their own aggressiveness. However, if watching violent television were a substantial contributor to aggressive behavior among adolescents in general, the relationship would be stronger than it has been in the many field studies and longitudinal studies that have been conducted.

The evidence is stronger that television violence influences *attitudes* toward violence among adolescents, making them more accepting of violent behavior and less empathic toward the victims of violence (Paradise, 2006). Also, recently two scholars have begun to look at the relation between television watching and what they term "indirect aggression," which is like the relational aggression we discussed in Chapter 8. In one of their studies (Coyne & Archer, 2005), over 300 adolescents aged 11–14 were asked to list their five favorite television programs. These programs were analyzed for the amount and type (direct or indirect) of aggression they contained. Peer-nominated indirect aggression was higher among adolescents who watched programs containing indirect aggression. In particular, indirectly aggressive girls viewed more indirect aggression on television than any other group. This study suffers from the common correlation-causation problem in media studies, but nevertheless this is a new concept and a new line of research worth following.

THINKING CRITICALLY •••

Even if violent television does not have clear effects on adolescents' aggressive behavior, is it possible that it has other effects, such as on their moral development? What other effects should be considered, and how would you design a study to test your hypotheses?

Computer Games and Aggressiveness

"The whole thug thing seems kind of cool [in computer games], but in real life, I wouldn't really want to have that life. In the game, you don't mind just getting out of your car and killing somebody, because you're not going to get in trouble for it. You can just turn off the game system and you're done."

—13-year-old boy (in Olson et al., 2008, p. 64)

"Last week, I missed one homework and my teacher yelled at me. . . . When I went home, I started playing *Vice City* and I got a tank and I ran over everybody. And I smashed a lot of cars and blew them up. . . . I was mad, and I turned happy afterwards."

—14-year-old boy (in Olson et al., 2008, p. 66)

A relatively new type of media that has become popular among adolescents is computer games. It used to be that you had to go to a video arcade to play video games, but now these games are played mostly at home on personal computers. This form of media use has quickly become popular among adolescents, especially boys (Olson et al., 2008). In a recent study of middle school students in the United States (Olson et al., 2007), 94% reported having played computer games during the preceding six months. Of those who played computer games, one third of boys and 11% of girls said they played nearly every day. A study in 10 European countries and Israel found that children ages 6 to 16 averaged more than a half hour per day playing computer games (Beentjes, Koolstra, Marseille, & van der Voort, 2001).

Some of these computer games are in the category of harmless entertainment. A substantial proportion of the games simply involve having a computerized character jump from one platform to the next; or sports simulations of baseball, tennis, soccer, or hockey; or fantasies in which the player can escape to other worlds and take on new identities (Klimmt, 2006). However, the majority of adolescents' favorite computer games involve violence. A content analysis of nearly 400 of the most popular computer games found that 94% contained violence (Haninger & Thompson, 2004). Because violent games have proven to be so popular, manufacturers have steadily increased the levels of violence in computer games over the past decade (Sherry, 2006). Here are a few examples of violent games:

- *Quake*. A Marine lands on an alien planet to seek and destroy a huge weapon known as "the big gun." Players, controlling the Marine, blast away at aliens called Scroggs using an arsenal of weapons such as rocket launchers and "rail guns" that can pierce several aliens in a row.
- *Mortal Kombat*. Two opponents engage in a three-round martial arts contest. In the "gory" version, the winner finishes off the loser by either cutting his head off or tearing his heart out of his chest.

Many of the computer games most popular with adolescent boys have violent themes. Here, a scene from the game "Hitman."

- *Night Trap*. Vampires attack attractive young women while the player tries to save them. If they are not defeated, the vampires end the game by drilling the young women through the neck with a power tool.
- *Doom*. Player has been assigned to a research station on Mars, which turns out to be populated by evil aliens. Player must use a variety of weapons to kill all the aliens and stop them from reaching the earth.
- *Postal*. Players try to slaughter an entire high school marching band using various weapons such as flame throwers.

This all sounds potentially unhealthy, on the face of it, and there have been some notorious cases of the games appearing to inspire violence. For example, one of the two boys who murdered 12 students and a teacher in the massacre at Columbine High School in 1999 named the gun he used in the murders "Arlene," after a character in the gory Doom computer game. And in a video the boys made before the murders, the same boy said of the murders they would commit, "It's going to be like fucking Doom. Tick, tick, tick, tick . . . Haaa! That fucking shotgun is straight out of Doom!" (Gibbs & Roche, 1999).

A number of studies have examined the relation between computer games and aggressiveness (Anderson et al., 2007; Brake, 2006; Funk et al., 1999, 2002, 2005). One early study found that aggressiveness and hostility were heightened after playing arcade video games (Mehrabian & Wixen, 1986). Another found that the content of computer video games was related to adolescents' emotional responses, with levels of hostility and anxiety increasing in correlation with the level of violence in the computer game they were playing (Anderson & Ford, 1987). A more recent study of adolescents aged 11 to 15 found that a preference for violent computer games was related to anxiety and depression but unrelated to aggression (Funk et al., 2002). One study in which college undergraduates played computer games with varying levels of violence found that the students reported decreased feelings of aggressiveness after playing a moderately violent game, but increased feelings of aggressiveness after playing a highly violent game (Scott, 1995).

Some experimental studies seem to show that violent computer games actually cause aggressive behavior. In one study (Anderson & Dill, 2000), college students were assigned randomly to two groups. One group played a nonviolent computer game, while the other played a violent game, Wolfenstein 3D, in which the player chooses from an array of weapons to kill Nazi guards, with the ultimate goal of killing Adolf Hitler. Students were "tested" against each other on three different days, supposedly to see how well they played the game. On the third day, they were told to punish their opponent with an unpleasant blast of noise when the opponent lost. Students who played the violent game blasted their opponents for a longer time than students who played the nonviolent game.

The authors' interpretation of the results was that violent computer games cause aggressive behavior. But do you see the problem in the research design? It does not take into account the uses and gratifications insight that people make choices about what media to use. It may sound good to assign students randomly into two different groups, playing either violent or noviolent games, but in fact this means that you do not know which students would actually have chosen to play the violent games themselves. Although some of the students in the "violent game" condition behaved more aggressively than students who played the nonviolent game, without knowing their game-playing preferences we cannot say if the ones who behaved more aggressively are also the ones who would choose to play the more violent games. So, this design does not really prove causality after all. This is a very common research design problem, not just for computer games studies but for other media studies as well.

One recent study asked boys themselves about the effects of playing violent computer games (Olson et al., 2008). The interviews showed that the boys (ages 12–14) used computer games to experience fantasies of power and fame, and to explore what they perceived to be exciting new situations. The boys enjoyed the social aspect of computer games, in playing with friends and talking about the games with friends. The boys also said they used computer games to work through feelings of anger or stress, and that playing the games had a cathartic effect on these negative feelings. They did not believe that playing violent computer games affected them negatively.

It seems likely that with computer games, as with other violent media, there is a wide range of individual differences in responses, with young people who are already at risk for violent behavior—such as the Columbine murderers—being most likely to be affected by the games, as well as most likely to be attracted to them (Funk, 2003; Funk et al., 1999; Slater et al., 2003; Unsworth et al., 2007). With computer games as with television, effects may be less definite for violent behavior than for more common characteristics, such as empathy and attitudes toward violence (Anderson, 2004; Funk, 2005; Funk et al., 2005).

Television and Movies and Sex

Sex is second only to violence as a topic of public concern with respect to the possible effects of media on adolescents.

The movies and television shows most popular among adolescents often contain sexual content. Here, a scene from the movie *American Pie*.

A high proportion of prime-time television shows contain sexual themes. What sort of information about sexuality does television present to adolescents?

In one study, Cope-Farrar and Kunkel (2002) analyzed the top 15 shows watched by American adolescents. Eighty-two percent of the programs they analyzed contained sexual content (sexual talk or sexual behavior). Sexual behavior was more frequent than sexual talk and tended to take place between partners who were not married but had an established relationship. Usually, the sexual behavior was limited to kisses and hugs—intercourse was depicted or strongly implied in only 7% of the programs—and nudity was also infrequent. Discussions of sexual risks or responsibilities rarely took place. Another recent content analysis, a study of the 20 TV programs most popular among adolescents in the U.S., found similar results (Eyal et al., 2007).

What uses do adolescents make of the portrayals of sexuality on television? With sexuality as with aggressiveness, it is difficult to establish causality, but most scholars in this area agree that through TV programs adolescents learn cultural beliefs about how male and female roles differ in sexual interactions and what is considered physically attractive in males and females (Pardun, L'Engle, & Brown, 2005; Rivadeneyra, 2005). Television also informs adolescents about appropriate sexual scripts (Gagnon, 1973; Rivadeneyra, 2005; Ward & Rivadeneyra, 1999), that is, the expected patterns of sexual interactions based on cultural norms of what is acceptable and desirable. For adolescents, who are just beginning to date, this information may be eagerly received, especially if their culture provides little in the way of explicit instruction in male and female sexual roles.

Of course, the "information" adolescents receive about sexual scripts from TV may not be the kind most adults would consider desirable. Television shows portray strong gender stereotypes, with the message that "boys will be boys and girls better be prepared," that is, that boys seek sex actively and aggressively and girls act as "sexual gatekeepers" who are supposed to attract boys' sexual interest but also resist their advances (Hust et al., 2008; Kim et al., 2007; Tolman et al., 2007). Often, the sexual scripts in TV shows portray a "sniggering attitude" (Smith, 1991) and a "recreational orientation" toward sex (Ward, 1995). However, this may be mainly because most of the TV shows popular among adolescents are situation comedies (Cope-Farrar & Kunkel, 2002), and they rely on standard comedic devices such as sexual innuendo, double entendre (that is, words or phrases that have two meanings), irony, and exaggeration. Most adolescents are cognitively capable of separating what is intended to be humorous from what is intended to be a true portrayal of sexuality (Ward, 1995; Ward, Gorvine, & Cytron, 2002). Nevertheless, watching TV depictions of sexual interactions may affect adolescents' own sexual scripts (Tolman et al., 2007).

THINKING CRITICALLY •••

To what extent is the portrayal of sexuality in television shows watched by adolescents similar to and different from the way adolescents regard sexuality in real life?

Movies are another medium in which adolescents witness portrayals of sexual behavior. Like TV shows, movies provide adolescents with sexual scripts, but in a more explicit way than TV does (Freeman, 2006; Pardun, 2002; Steele, 2002). As one prominent researcher in this area has observed, "What television suggests, movies and videos do" (Greenberg, 1994, p. 180). Now that pornographic movies are easily accessible on the Internet, more adolescents may be exposed to them and have their sexuality shaped by them. One recent study of Dutch adolescents concluded that boys who watched sexually explicit on-line movies were more likely than other boys to view women as sex objects (Peter & Valkenburg, 2007). There was no effect for exposure to pornographic magazines, only movies.

Sex and Violence on Music Television

Today's adolescents have grown up with a new medium that combines television and music: music television, often referred to by the initials of the most popular music television network, MTV. MTV began in 1981 and was instantly popular among adolescents (Hansen, 2006). Although MTV began in the United States, by now MTV is broadcast to more than one billion people in 164 countries worldwide, making it a significant force toward globalization (Roberts, 2005). There are also many other music television stations around the world today. Studies indicate that most American adolescents watch music videos for about 15 to 30 minutes per day (Roberts et al., 2005).

What uses are made of music videos by adolescents? Music videos can be divided into two general categories (Strasburger, 1995): **performance videos**, which show an individual performer or a group singing a song in a concert setting or a studio, and **concept videos**, which enact a story to go along

with the lyrics of the song. For the most part, performance videos simply convey the songs and have generated no more (or less) controversy than the songs themselves. Most research attention has been directed at the concept videos and the stories they depict. The targets of concern among critics are the same as for television more generally: violence and sex.

Only about 15% of music videos show violence (Smith & Boyson, 2002), and the violence tends to be relatively mild (e.g., pushing rather than stabbing or shooting). Sexual themes appear in more than three fourths of music videos (Arnett, 2002c; Sherman & Dominick, 1986), but for the most part the sexuality is implied rather than shown—that is, the videos are more likely to contain provocatively dressed women than actually to show people kissing, fondling, and so forth. Rap videos have been found to be especially high in sexual content, compared to other videos (Jones, 1997; Peterson et al., 2007). Content analyses indicate that the characters in music videos tend to be highly gender stereotyped, with the men aggressive and the women sexual and subservient (Arnett, 2002c; Gow, 1996; Sommers-Flanagan, Sommers-Flanagan, & Davis, 1993).

Do these gender stereotypes influence adolescents' own views of gender? A study of African American adolescents by Monique Ward and her colleagues (2005) found that more frequent music video viewing was associated with more stereotyped views of gender roles among adolescents. There is the usual correlation-causation problem of media research here. Does watching music videos make their views of gender more stereotyped, or are adolescents with stronger gender stereotypes more attracted to music videos, or both? But the authors also included an experimental component to the study, dividing the sample in half and showing one half of the adolescents four gender-stereotyped music videos and the other half four non–gender-stereotyped music videos. Afterward, the adolescents who viewed the gender-stereotyped music videos were more likely than the other adolescents to endorse gender stereotypes, providing at least a slightly stronger case for causality.

Nevertheless, it should be noted that studies show considerable diversity in how adolescents interpret the content of concept videos (Hansen, 2006). This is consistent with the uses and gratifications theme we have emphasized in this chapter. Adolescents may watch the same music video, yet the messages they perceive in it and the uses they make of it may be quite variable.

Controversial Music: Rap and Heavy Metal

Television is not the only medium that has been criticized for promoting unhealthy and morally questionable tendencies in adolescents. Music has been criticized just as much, and the criticism goes back even further. Jazz was criticized in the 1920s for promoting promiscuity and alcohol use. Rock and

---

performance videos Music videos that show an individual performer or a group singing a song in a concert setting or a studio.

concept videos Music videos that enact a story to go along with the lyrics of the song.

In the spring of 1953, an 18-year-old delivery truck driver named Elvis Presley walked into a recording studio in Memphis, Tennessee, and paid $4 for the opportunity to record two songs as a birthday present for his mother. Three years later, Elvis Presley was 21 years old, a multimillionaire entertainer, and the most famous person on the planet.

How did this happen? Part of the explanation, of course, lies in Elvis's extraordinary talents. He had a uniquely rich, expressive, and versatile singing voice, and he sang with an extraordinary sensual intensity. He had grown up in the South listening to rhythm-and-blues songs performed by Black musicians, and he incorporated the sensuality and power of their styles into his own. Many people recognized the Black influence in his singing, and Elvis himself acknowledged it.

Not only his singing but his performing was influenced by Black musicians he had seen, as he developed a performance style of bracing himself against the microphone stand and thrusting his pelvis back and forth in a distinctly sexual way (leading to the nickname "Elvis the Pelvis"), his legs pumping rhythmically, his body shaking all over. He made Black rock-and-roll music and styles popular to White audiences at a time in American history when racist beliefs about Black people possessing an uncontrolled sexuality would have made it difficult for a Black person to be accepted by the American majority culture singing in that style.

However, in addition to Elvis's talents, four media forms interacted to fuel his fame: radio, newspapers, television, and movies. His career got its initial burst through radio, when a Memphis radio station played a recording of him singing "That's All Right (Mama)" and within days thousands of adolescents were storming Memphis record stores seeking copies of the record (which had not actually been released yet). Soon, radio stations all over the South were playing "That's All Right" and every other Elvis song as he recorded more of them.

Next, newspapers came into the mix. A Memphis newspaper printed a front-page story with the title "He's Sex!" and it was reprinted in newspapers all over the South. This, along with increasingly widespread exposure on radio stations, gave Elvis a hot reputation as he and his band began to tour and perform in cities throughout the South. Everywhere he performed, newspapers covered his concerts, mostly with rave reviews, further enhancing his popularity.

But it was television that made Elvis a world-famous star. Following his first television appearance on *The Ed Sullivan Show* early in 1956, when he was still relatively unknown outside the South, CBS was flooded with phone calls and letters from aroused adolescent fans. He appeared several more times on television in 1956, each time to an enormous national audience.

As he became increasingly popular, his critics grew louder and more numerous, calling his performances "lewd" and "obscene." Jackie Gleason, a popular TV performer of the day, sneered, "The kid has no right behaving like a sex maniac on a national show" (Lichter, 1978, p. 22). A newspaper critic was one of many to express concern about the potential effects on young people: "When Presley executes his bumps and grinds, it must be remembered by [CBS] that even the twelve-year-old's curiosity may be overstimulated" (Lichter, 1978, p. 34). By the time Elvis appeared on *The Ed Sullivan Show* again in September 1956, CBS executives decided he would be shown only from the waist up, so as not

roll was criticized throughout the 1950s and 1960s for promoting rebellion and sexual license (see the Historical Focus box). In recent decades, the criticism has focused on two particular genres of popular music: rap and heavy metal.

Rap Rap music (also called hip-hop) began in the late 1970s as street music in urban New York City (Berry, 1995; Decker, 1994). It started out with disc jockeys "rapping" (speaking or shouting rhythmically) spontaneous lyrics to a background of a lively beat and perhaps a repeated line of music. Only gradually did it develop into "songs" that were recorded. It was not until the late 1980s that rap attained widespread popularity. MTV had no program devoted to rap until 1988, but when MTV added *Yo! MTV Raps* it quickly became one of the station's most popular programs and helped to spread the influence of rap. By the 1990s, a wide range of rap groups were appearing on lists of the highest-selling albums. Rap is now by far the most popular music genre among American adolescents. Two thirds of 12- to 18-year-olds report listening to rap/hip-hop within the past 24 hours, a percentage over twice as high as any other genre (Roberts et al., 2005). Although rap is especially popular among Black and Latino adolescents, it is also the most popular music genre among Whites. Rap is highly popular not only in the United States but in Europe and many other places around the world (Motley & Henderson, 2008).

Not all rap is controversial. Queen Latifah and other female rap performers often stress themes of self-esteem and self-reliance for young Black women (Emerson, 2002). Other rap performers also enjoy a wide mainstream audience for their themes of love, romance, and celebration. The controversy over rap has focused on "gangsta rap" performers such as Jay-Z and 50 Cent. The criticism has concerned three themes (Berry, 1995; Ward, 2006a): sexual exploitation of women, violence, and racism.

Controversial rap has been criticized for presenting images of women as objects of contempt, deserving sexual exploitation and even sexual assault. Women in controversial rap songs are often referred to as "hos" (whores) and "bitches," and sexuality is frequently portrayed as a man's success-to provoke any unruly sexual impulses among America's youth.

Elvis's first performance on *The Ed Sullivan Show* still ranks as the highest rated television show ever broadcast in the United States, with an astonishing 83% of the television sets in the country tuned in. It is worth noting that the rise of Elvis coincided fortuitously with the rise of TV. In 1950, just 9% of American households owned a television; by the time of Elvis's first TV performance over half of American households had one, and by 1960 the figure would rise to nearly 90% (Lichty, 1989). Television propelled Elvis into unprecedented national fame. His fame became international as his performances and stories of his performances were distributed in newspapers, radio stations, and television networks all over the world.

Soon Elvis added movies to his media machine. His first film, *Love Me Tender*, was released near the end of 1956. Neither this film nor any of his 32 other films was highly regarded by movie critics, but Elvis's adolescent fans worldwide had a different opinion. They made this film and many of the others huge box office hits. Even in the mid-1960s, after Elvis's musical career had been eclipsed by the Beatles and other new performers, his movies continued to bring in millions of dollars (Lichter, 1978).

These four interacting media contributed substantially to Elvis's fame, but from the beginning the explosion of his fame was driven by the responses of his adolescent fans—their calls to radio stations demanding to hear his songs again and again, the raucous screaming crowds at the concerts covered by newspaper reporters, the rapt and enormous television audiences, and a devoted moviegoing audience even for Elvis movies that were (to put it mildly) less than memorable.

Elvis was wildly popular among adolescents.

Although corporate businesspeople have tried hard ever since Elvis to control the highly lucrative business of popular music, the enthusiasms of adolescents have usually proven difficult to predict (Brake, 1985), and ultimately it is adolescents who drive the direction of popular music.

ful assertion of power over a woman (Berry, 1995; Emerson, 2002; Stephens & Few, 2007; Ward, 2006a).

Violence is another common theme in the lyrics of controversial rap performers (Watkins, 2006). Their songs depict scenes such as drive-by shootings, gang violence, and violent confrontations with the police. The violence spouted by gangsta rap performers is not just a pose but is part of the world many of them live in. In the late 1990s rappers Tupac Shakur and Notorious B.I.G. were shot to death, and other gangsta rap performers have been arrested for offenses from illegal possession of firearms to sexual assault to attempted murder.

With regard to racism, critics of rap have denounced the views toward Whites and Asians that rap performers have expressed in both songs and interviews. Also, research has found that rap songs reinforce racial stereotypes in listeners because the songs frequently depict Black men as violent, misogynist, and sex-obsessed (Johnson, Trawalter, & Dovidio, 2000; Rudman & Lee, 2002; Ward, 2006b; Watkins, 2006). Rap has also been accused of promoting homophobia, for ex-

ample, in some of the songs of Eminem, one of the most popular rap performers.

What effect—if any—does listening to rap lyrics with themes of sexism, violence, and racism have on the development of adolescents? Unfortunately, although many academics have speculated about the uses of rap by adolescents, thus far few studies have provided research evidence on the topic. Rap has been found to be most popular among adolescents who have high rates of risk behavior (Miranda & Claes, 2004; Rubin, West, & Mitchell, 2001; Wingood et al., 2003), but this finding shows only correlation, not causation. One study found that rap was the favorite type of music of juvenile offenders (Gardstrom, 1999). However, only 4% of them believed that music contributed to their deviant behavior, whereas 72% believed the lyrics of the songs reflected the grim conditions of their lives. Some research indicates an association between rap listening and negative stereotypes of women among adolescents, although here, too, it is difficult to identify causality with any precision (Squires et al., 2006; Stephens & Few, 2007).

Two studies that asked adolescent rap fans about their views on the effects of rap in their lives found that many of them perceived positive, life-affirming messages in rap (Mahiri & Conner, 2003; Sullivan, 2003). However, these studies did not report whether adolescents found these messages in "gangsta rap" as well as in other types of rap.

From the uses and gratifications perspective, it may be expected that some adolescents—especially Black adolescents in urban America—use rap as an expression of their frustration and rage in the face of the difficult conditions in which they live. Other adolescents may use rap simply as entertainment, and some may find positive messages in types other than gangsta rap. Rap has even been used in therapy with adolescents (Ciardiello, 2003) because its themes help them express feelings of loss, rejection, and abandonment.

Heavy Metal

"Sometimes I'm upset and I like to put on heavy metal. It kind of releases the aggression I feel. I can just drive along, put a tape in, and turn it up. It puts me in a better mood. It's a way to release some of your pressures, instead of going out and starting a fight with somebody, or taking it out on your parents or your cat or something like that."

—Ben, age 21 (in Arnett, 1996, p. 82)

The history of heavy metal goes back to the late 1960s and early 1970s and groups such as Led Zeppelin, Iron Maiden, and Black Sabbath. The peak of heavy metal's popularity—and controversy—came during the 1980s, with performers such as Metallica, Ozzy Ozbourne, Megadeth, Judas Priest, and Slayer selling millions of albums and performing in large arenas all over the world. Heavy metal's popularity has waned since the 1990s, but the most popular "metal" groups still sell millions of albums and play to concert halls of fervently devoted fans. Hard rock/heavy metal is the third most popular music genre among adolescents, after rap/hip-hop and alternative rock (Roberts et al., 2005).

As with rap, not all heavy metal is controversial. Metal is quite diverse, from "lite metal" groups such as Kiss that sing mostly about partying and sex, to groups such as Metallica and Creed that address serious social issues such as war and environmental destruction, to groups such as Slayer and Cannibal Corpse whose themes are relentlessly violent. Controversy and criticism have focused not on the "lite metal"

cathartic effect Effect sometimes attributed to media experiences, in which media experience has the effect of relieving unpleasant emotions.

Rap has become one of the most popular types of music among adolescents. Here, the rap performer 50 Cent.

groups but on the other heavy metal groups, especially concerning issues of suicide and violence.

Is there any credible evidence that heavy metal promotes suicide or violence? It is true that violence is a common theme in heavy metal songs; in fact, it is the most common theme (Arnett, 1996). However, this alone is not evidence that heavy metal causes violent behavior in those who listen to it. What the listeners hear in it, how they use it, is the crucial question.

Some of my own early research concerned the heavy metal subculture, and the effect of the music is one of the topics I investigated in a study of over 100 heavy metal fans (Arnett, 1991, 1996, 2007c). I found that it is true that heavy metal fans ("metalheads" or "headbangers" as they call themselves) tend to have a dark view of the world. They are alienated from mainstream society; cynical about teachers, politicians, and religious leaders; and highly pessimistic about the future of the human race. They also tend to be more reckless than other adolescents, reporting higher rates of behavior such as high-speed driving, drug use, and vandalism (Selfout et al., 2008).

However, I do not believe that their alienation or their risk behavior can accurately be blamed on the music. I asked them if they listen to the music when they are in any particular mood, and if the music *puts* them in any particular mood. Consistently, they said they listen to the music especially when they are angry; this is not surprising, in view of the violent, angry quality of the music and lyrics. However, they also consistently reported that the music has the effect of *calming them down*. Heavy metal songs have a **cathartic effect** on their

Heavy metal fans often report that the music has a cathartic effect on their anger.

anger; in other words, they *use* the music as a way of purging their anger harmlessly (also see Scheel & Westefeld, 1999). The songs express their alienated view of the world and help them cope with the anger and frustration of living in a world they see as hopelessly corrupt (Rafalovich, 2006). Because it has this cathartic effect on their anger and frustration, if anything the music makes them *less* likely to commit suicide or violence than they would be if they did not have the music available to use for this purpose. This cathartic effect of heavy metal music has also been demonstrated experimentally (Wooten, 1992).

We cannot and should not rule out the possibility that the despair and violence of the songs could spur the listener to suicide or violence in some extreme cases. As noted, adolescents can respond to the same media stimulus in widely different ways. However, for the great majority of the millions of adolescent metalheads around the world, heavy metal appears to act as a useful outlet for difficult youthful emotions.

THINKING CRITICALLY •••

Thus far the cathartic effect has been studied mainly for heavy metal music. Do you think this effect would be found for other types of music as well? What about for television? Movies?

Controversial Advertising: The Marlboro Man and Friends

Most media used by adolescents contain advertising in some form. Television, of course, has commercials punctuating every program every few minutes. Radio is similar—ads every few minutes, interspersed among the talk and music. Almost all magazines and newspapers have numerous advertisements, and as we have seen this is especially true of the magazines most popular among adolescent girls. Even movies have advertisements in a subtle form called "product placements," which means that companies pay to have their products used by actors in movies.

In recent years, the most controversial form of advertising with respect to adolescents has been cigarette advertising. Advertising cigarettes on television or radio has been illegal in the United States since 1971, but since that time cigarette companies have simply poured more money into other forms of advertising and promotion, such as billboards, magazines, newspapers, movie product placements, and sponsorship of sporting events and concerts. In fact, cigarettes are the second most heavily promoted consumer product in the United States, with cigarette advertising and promotion totaling over *six billion dollars* per year (Cummings, 2002).

Critics of cigarette advertising claim that it is targeted especially toward adolescents (Biener & Siegel, 2000; Cummings, 2002; Ling & Glantz, 2002; Pollay, 1997, 2006). The tobacco companies claim that their advertising is intended only to persuade adult smokers to switch brands, but critics note that only a small percentage of adults switch brands in a given year, a percentage far too small to justify the tobacco companies' massive advertising budgets. Where the real market lies is among adolescents. Ninety percent of smokers begin smoking by age 18 (Cummings, 2002), and brand loyalty is very strong once established, which makes adolescents a ripe target for cigarette companies seeking to expand their share of the market. Furthermore, because so few people begin smoking after age 18, critics argue that tobacco companies try to persuade adolescents to smoke so that they will become addicted to nicotine before they are mature enough to realize fully the potential risks of smoking (Arnett, 2000b; Romer & Jamieson, 2001; Slovic, 1998). Thus, according to the critics, cigarette companies present images of independence (the Marlboro Man), youthful fun and vigor (Newport, Kool), and "coolness" (Camel, Kool) in order to appeal to adolescents (Arnett, 2006d).

Several studies have established a relationship between cigarette advertising campaigns and adolescent smoking. Pollay et al. (1996) traced tobacco companies' advertising expenditures in relation to rates of smoking among adolescents (aged 12 to 18) and adults over the period 1979 to 1993. They concluded that the effect of advertising on brand choice was *three times as strong* for adolescents as for adults.

Marlboro is both the most heavily advertised cigarette brand and the brand by far the most popular among adolescents.

The "Joe Camel" campaign provides an example of this effect. Between 1988, when the "Joe" character was introduced, and 1993, Camel's market share among 12- to 17-year-olds rose from less than 1% to 13%, and the proportion of adolescents who smoke increased. Under criticism, RJR Nabisco canceled the Joe Camel ad campaign in 1998.

Pierce and his colleagues (1994) examined trends in smoking initiation from 1944 to 1988. They found that for girls aged 14 to 17, a sharp rise in smoking initiation coincided with the introduction of three brands targeted at females—Virginia Slims, Silva Thins, and Eve—between 1967 and 1973. No such increase occurred during this period for girls aged 18 to 20 or 10 to 13, or for males. The ad campaigns were evidently particularly effective among—and targeted to?—adolescent girls in the age range when smoking initiation is most likely to take place, ages 14 to 17.

Also, in a study I published with a colleague (Arnett & Terhanian, 1998), adolescents were shown ads for five different brands of cigarettes (Camel, Marlboro, Lucky Strike, Benson & Hedges, and Kool) and asked various questions about their responses. The ads for Camel and Marlboro were the ads the adolescents had seen the most, the ads they liked the best, and the ads they were most likely to see as making smoking appealing (Figure 12.2). In a number of respects, smokers' responses to the ads were more favorable than the responses of nonsmokers. For all brands, smokers were significantly more likely to indicate that they liked the ad. For the Camel and Marlboro ads (but not for the other brands), smokers were more likely than nonsmokers to indicate that the ad made smoking more appealing. A second study yielded similar results (Arnett, 2001b).

Marlboro and Camel are two of the brands most popular among adolescents. Marlboro is by far the most popular, smoked by about half of 12- to 17-year-old smokers, with Newport second (25%) and Camel third at about 13% (Pollay, 2006). These are also the three most heavily promoted brands, indicating the influence of advertising and promotion in adolescent smoking (Arnett, 2001b). The fact that the ads for the most popular brands are so attractive to adolescents, especially to adolescent smokers, suggests that cigarette advertising is one of the influences that lead them to smoke (Arnett & Terhanian, 1998).

Of course, findings of a relationship between the appeal of cigarette advertisements and rates of adolescent smoking or brand preferences do not prove that the cigarette companies *intended* to appeal to adolescents. However, in lawsuits against the tobacco companies, the companies have been forced to release literally tons of internal documents, many of which provide stark evidence that for decades these companies have discussed the psychological characteristics of adolescents and have been acutely aware of the importance of adolescents as the perpetually new market for cigarettes (Cummings, 2002; Ling & Glantz, 2002). The documents contain such statements as "Today's teenager is tomorrow's potential regular customer," "The base of our business is the high school student," and "Realistically, if our Company is to survive and prosper over the long term, we must get our share of the youth market" (Pollay, 1997). This evidence has strengthened the claim that tobacco companies have directly attempted to market their cigarettes to adolescents.

In recent years, as a consequence of lawsuits and government policies, tobacco advertising in industrialized countries has decreased dramatically and cigarette smoking among young people has also declined (Krugman et al., 2006). Anti–tobacco advertising has also proven to be effective in decreasing the likelihood that adolescents will begin smoking (Terry-McElrath, 2007). However, the tobacco companies are now targeting developing countries, where smoking is increasing as wealth increases (Ho et al., 2007).

THINKING CRITICALLY •••

Given the research showing that cigarette advertisements appeal strongly to adolescents and make smoking more appealing to them, do you believe there should be a total ban on cigarette advertising (except perhaps in adult-only magazines)? Or would you defend the tobacco companies' right to advertise on the grounds of "freedom of speech"?

New Media

Most of the media we have discussed so far have been around for a long time in one form or another. Even television has been around for over half a century. However, new media forms have appeared in recent years. In fact, the newest media forms have become so important in the lives of today's adolescents and emerging adults that Jane Brown, a prominent scholar in media research, calls them the "new media generation."

> They are the first cohort to have grown up learning their ABCs on a keyboard in front of a computer screen, playing games in virtual environments rather than their backyards or neighborhood streets, making friends with people they have never and may never meet through internet chat rooms, and creating custom CDs for themselves and their friends. This new media environment is dramatically different from the one in which their parents grew up because it is more accessible, more interactive and more under their control than any other ever known before. (Brown, 2006, p. 279)

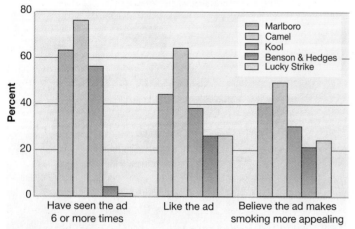

FIGURE 12.2 Adolescents' responses to cigarette ads.
Source: Arnett & Terhanian (1998).

In this section, we will consider two of the new media that have become most important in the lives of young people: the Internet and mobile phones. The section on the Internet will include a subsection on two recently developed Internet formats: social-networking websites (such as Facebook and MySpace) and blogs.

The Internet

The Internet has burgeoned in popularity and pervasiveness in industrialized countries over the past decade. In one national American survey, over 90% of adolescents aged 11 to 18 said they have access to the Internet at school, and one third said they use it at school "almost every day" (Roberts et al., 2005). Nearly 90% said they have a computer at home, nearly 80% with an Internet connection, and nearly half used the computer at home "almost every day." The average amount of time per day on the Internet for 14- to 18-year-olds is 50 minutes (Hellenga, 2002). Adolescents are more likely than older age groups to use the Internet (Anderson, 2002). Furthermore, as Figure 12.3 shows, it is the medium they prefer the most, even more than music or TV. Findings on adolescent Internet use in other industrialized countries are similar (Anderson, 2002).

Internet use is also high worldwide among emerging adults. In the World Internet Project, a survey of Internet use among persons ages 18 and over in 13 countries in Europe, Asia, and the Americas, Internet use was over 80% among 18-24 year-olds in all countries but one (World Internet Project, 2008). Furthermore, in all countries Internet use was higher among emerging adults than in any other age group.

Ten years ago there was a "digital divide" among different segments of the population in their Internet access and use, but that gap has rapidly diminished (Roberts et al., 2005). Ninety percent of adolescents from high-SES families have a computer at home, but so do over 80% of low-SES families, and nearly all of these computers have an Internet connec-

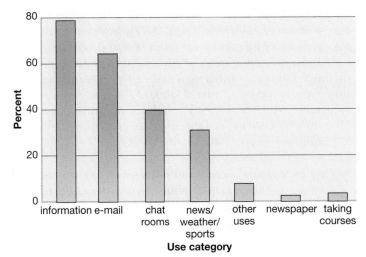

FIGURE 12.4 Internet uses by 12- to 17-year-olds.
Source: Hellenga (2002), p. 214.

tion. Ninety percent of adolescents in White families have a computer at home, but so do 78% of Blacks and 80% of Latinos, again, with nearly all having an Internet connection. Girls were initially less likely than boys to use the Internet, but this gap has also closed in recent years (Hellenga, 2002; Reese & Noyes, 2007). With remarkable speed, computers and the Internet have become a standard part of the households of families in industrialized societies (Anderson, 2002).

Adolescents use the Internet for a variety of purposes. As you can see from Figure 12.4, the most common use is searching for information (often for school projects), but e-mail and chat rooms are also common uses. Adolescents are more likely than younger or older persons to use chat rooms. Nearly 40% of 11- to 20-year-olds say they access chat rooms daily or weekly (Hellenga, 2002). They especially favor chat rooms on "relationships and lifestyles," followed by "entertainment" and "hobbies or groups" (Roberts & Foehr, 2004). However, a substantial amount of their "chatting" is done with their own friends in "Instant Messaging" (IM) formats that allow multiple friends to carry on a simultaneous Internet conversation. About one third of American adolescents use e-mail and IM on a daily basis (Roberts et al., 2005). Girls are more likely than boys to use the Internet for social purposes such as e-mail and visiting chat rooms, whereas boys are more likely to use it to play computer games and download music (Anderson, 2002; Hellenga, 2002), but the gender differences are not large (Roberts et al., 2005).

The Internet is perhaps the greatest invention in human history for providing access to information. With a few clicks, people are able to find a staggering array of information sources on virtually any topic. The Internet has tremendous potential to enhance education in childhood and adolescence, which is why schools have been so zealous about becoming connected to it.

As with other types of media, however, research on Internet use in adolescence has focused less on the positive uses than on the potential perils it holds (Livingstone, 2003; Tynes, 2007). Numerous dangers have been claimed to be associated with adolescents' Internet use. The chat rooms that

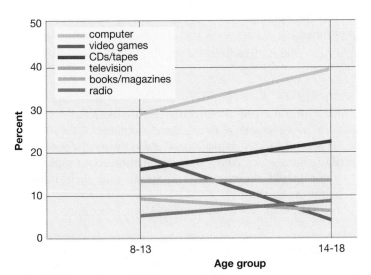

FIGURE 12.3 Media preferences by age group.
Source: Hellenga (2002), p. 212.

adolescents enjoy so much may give them a free arena to practice their social skills (Hellenga, 2002), but chat rooms are also sometimes frequented by adult sexual predators. There have been horrifying cases of adolescent girls developing an on-line relationship with a man that ended in sexual exploitation, rape, and even murder. A study of "on-line victimization" (Finkelhor, Mitchell, & Wolak, 2000) among adolescents aged 10 to 17 who were regular Internet users reported the following findings:

- One in four adolescents had been subjected to unwanted sexual exposure on-line (defined as pictures of naked people or people having sex), usually through surfing the Web.

- One in five adolescents had received a sexual solicitation, defined as a request for sex or sexual information.

- 3% reported an "aggressive solicitation," defined as a suggestion for sexual contact by mail, phone, or in person.

Of course, not all of adolescents' cybersexual experiences are involuntary. As noted in Chapter 9, pornography is among the most commonly viewed content on the Internet, for adolescents, emerging adults, and other adults (Carroll et al., 2008).

Another concern related to adolescents and the Internet involves academic cheating. Although the Internet can be a great information resource for school projects, it also allows adolescents to find and purchase prewritten papers that they can use for school assignments (Anderson, 2002). This is a concern with respect to emerging adult college students as well.

For both adolescents and emerging adults, the concern has been raised that use of the Internet may promote social isolation (Nie & Erbring, 2000). However, research has shown that for most adolescents and emerging adults the Internet is more likely to relieve social isolation and promote social connections (Sundar, 2000). For example, one study that followed adolescents for 3 years after high school found that e-mail and Instant Messaging helped them maintain their high school friendships even after they had moved away in emerging adulthood (Theil, 2006). Of course, some people do become dependent on the Internet to an extent that reduces their direct social contacts (Griffiths, 2006), but for most adolescents and emerging adults the social effects of the Internet are positive.

Another positive use of the Internet is that it provides adolescents with an opportunity to practice social communication and engage in "identity play," in which they actively choose how to represent themselves in terms of gender, personality, and conversational style (Theil, 2006). Adolescents who have particular interests or problems not shared by their peers may be able to find like-minded adolescents on-line. For example, the website <http://www.outproud.org> developed by the National Coalition for Gay, Lesbian, and Trans-

Social networking websites such as Facebook and MySpace have become highly popular among adolescents and emerging adults.

gender Youth offers an archive of coming-out stories, publications on sexual orientation, and a "high school forum" chat room with various discussion topics. The Internet, like other media, holds both positive and negative potentials for adolescent development depending on what the content is and how it is used.

New Internet Forms

The Internet is highly flexible to different uses, and new uses are constantly being invented for it. Two of the most important innovations pertaining to adolescents and emerging adults in recent years are social-networking websites and blogs.

Social-Networking Websites The use of **social-networking websites** such as Facebook and MySpace has become increasingly popular among adolescents and emerging adults. Facebook and MySpace were originally developed by and for college students, and college students and other emerging adults are still the main users, but the sites have rapidly become widely used by adolescents and adults as well (Baker & Moore, 2008; Raacke & Bonds-Raacke, 2008).

Users of social-networking websites construct a profile describing themselves, containing information about topics such as their family, their romantic partner, and their interests (Magnuson & Dundes, 2008). Most profiles also include a photo (Hinduja & Patchin, 2008). Many users have a "blog"

social-networking websites Internet websites such as Facebook and MySpace that allow users a forum for identity presentation and for making and maintaining social contacts.

blog A public Internet journal of a person's thoughts, feelings, and activities.

text messaging Communication through cell phones that involves typing a message on the cell phone screen and sending it like an e-mail message.

linked to their profile (more on this below). Profiles are an arena for identity presentation (Mazur, 2009). Users can individualize the site's template by changing the template's layout, design, and colors, or by adding photos, poems, videos, and links to other websites. Page design, images, and links are expressions of self that enable users to communicate a style and personality (Stern, 2002; Zhao, Grasmuck, & Martin, 2008).

Having a profile also allows users to maintain and expand their social networks. Adolescents and emerging adults use the sites mainly to keep in touch with old friends and current friends and make new ones (Ellison, Steinfield, & Lampe, 2007; Raacke & Bonds-Raacke, 2008). This function is especially important in emerging adulthood because emerging adults frequently change educational settings, jobs, and residences (Arnett, 2004). Social-networking websites allow them to keep in contact with the friends they leave behind as they move through emerging adulthood and to make new friends in each new place.

Blogs

"Zack just came and delivered us pizza. He's so cute."

—16-year-old female blogger

"All of a sudden she crossed my mind today. Reminding me of all the good times we spent together. We didn't have any problems, we didn't have any crises. That explains why it hurt so bad when she stopped loving me."

—19-year-old male blogger

"I really don't like myself, but that is starting to change. I am learning that there are good things about me and that I am an ok person."

—19-year-old female blogger

"My mom is drunk the day she said we could spend time together. I know it sounds childish but I really did want to spend time with her."

—16-year-old female blogger
(All quotes are from Mazur, 2009)

As part of their social-networking profile, many adolescents keep a **blog**, which is a public Internet journal of a person's thoughts, feelings, and activities (Mazur, 2009). National surveys in the United States have found that about one in four adolescents ages 12–17 (27%) have created their own blog, and half (49%) read others' blogs (Lenhart, Arafeh, Smith, & Macgill, 2008; Lenhart, Madden, Macgill, & Smith, 2007). Adolescents are more likely than adults to create and read blogs (Lenhart & Madden, 2005).

The most common kind of blog content is simply daily activities—what I ate, read, watched, or bought today (Mazur, 2009). Interactions or conversations with friends or family members are frequently described. Discussion of past, present, and potential romantic relationships is another common topic. Research also indicates that blogs can be an arena for identity explorations, as adolescents and emerging adults reflect on their experiences and their feelings about themselves (Schmitt et al., 2008). In one study of adolescents' and emerging adults' blogs, over three fourths of blog content focused on the author (Mazur, 2009).

What makes blogs a fascinating and unique media form is that they are at once private and public, personal and social. Bloggers often record a highly personal account of their lives, as a person might in a journal only he or she would read, yet blogs are posted publicly so that anyone else can read them. Analyses of blog content report that many adolescent and emerging adult bloggers freely express their previously private ideas and concerns and discuss their sexual behavior, drug use, and other sensitive topics (Mazur, 2009). One study found that half of all teenage bloggers discussed sexual identity, love relationships, and real or desired boyfriends and girlfriends (Huffaker and Calvert, 2005).

Another way that blogs are both personal and social is that they often contain links to other blogs, and anyone reading a blog can post a comment on a blog entry. One analysis of randomly selected teenage blogs found that half offered links to other blogs and 67% contained a comment section (Huffaker, 2006). A national U.S. survey indicated that three of four on-line adolescent social network users have posted at least one comment to a friend's blog (Lenhart and Madden, 2007). Because blogs are often interconnected, they may facilitate the fulfillment of adolescents' and emerging adults' needs for conversation, social bonding, and relationship building and maintenance, with both their close friends and a larger group of acquaintances they are unlikely ever to meet (Bortree, 2005; Lenhart & Madden, 2005).

Mobile Phones and Text Messaging

Like the Internet, the pervasiveness and popularity of mobile phones (also called cell phones) have skyrocketed in the past decade, and like the Internet, mobile phones are most popular of all among adolescents and emerging adults (Madell & Muncer, 2004). For example, mobile phones are used by 77% of 15- to 19-year-olds in Finland (Oksman & Rautainen, 2003) and by 80% of 13- to 20-year-olds in Norway (Ling, 2003). In the United States, rates are lower but rising; about half of late adolescents and emerging adults own a mobile phone (Roberts et al., 2005; Weiss, 2003). Young people use mobile phones not only for calling someone and talking the way other phones have long been used but also for **text messaging**, which involves typing a message on the mobile phone screen and sending it the way an e-mail message is sent. A study of Japanese adolescents found that they used their mobile phones much more often for text messaging than for talking (Kamibeppu & Hitomi, 2005). More than half of those who owned a mobile phone sent at least 10 text messages a day to their friends.

Mobile phones, like e-mail and social-networking websites, allow adolescents and emerging adults to remain in contact with each other when they are apart, virtually all day long. The social worlds of young people are no longer neatly divided into time with family and time with friends or at school. Rather, the new media allow the world of friends to be a nearly constant presence in their lives. The limited evidence so far indicates that young people enjoy the way the new media allow them to keep in touch with their friends. In one ESM study in Italy, adolescents reported that many of their happiest moments took place while communicating with friends on the Internet or using their mobile phones (Bassi & Antonella, 2004).

Media and Globalization

There are interesting similarities and differences in the media uses of adolescents across cultures. Some of the similarities reflect the globalization of adolescence. All over the world, on every continent, adolescents are increasingly familiar with the same television shows, the same movies, and the same musical recordings and performers (Taillon, 2004). (Magazines are the only exception; they still tend to be locally produced.) For example, in a study of adolescents in Botswana (southern Africa), two thirds reported watching American television programs on a weekly basis (Lloyd & Mendez, 2001). Adolescents and emerging adults with access to the Internet can use it to make contacts with young people in other parts of the world (although there is also a "digital divide" between countries, with adolescents in industrialized countries being much more likely than those in developing countries to have Internet access; Anderson, 2002).

Adolescents are not the only ones who enjoy Western—especially American—media. However, Western media tend to be especially appealing to adolescents for several reasons. First, in developing countries around the world, social and economic change has been extremely rapid in the past 50 years. Today's adolescents in these countries often have parents and grandparents who grew up in a time when their country had less economic and technological contact with the West, so that these adults are more familiar with and more attached to their native traditions, such as their native musical forms and songs. In contrast, the adolescents have grown up with Western media, which compete for their attention even if they also learn the songs and arts of their own culture. Second, adolescents are more capable than younger children of exploring the environment outside of the family, so they are better able than younger children to obtain media products that their parents would not have provided for them. Third, adolescence is a time when young people are forming an identity, a sense of themselves and their place in the world. When social and economic change is rapid and they sense that the world of their future is going to be different from the world that has been familiar to their parents and grandparents, they look outside the family for information and instruction on the world they will inhabit and how they might find a place in it (Goode, 1999; Mead, 1970; see the Cultural Focus box for an example).

Several of the ethnographies from the Harvard Adolescence Project provide examples of the role of the media in promoting globalization in the lives of adolescents. Among the Moroccan adolescents studied by Davis and Davis (1989, 1995, 2007), this influence is especially notable with respect to gender roles. In the past, Moroccan culture, like many traditional cultures, had strictly defined gender roles. Marriages were arranged by parents and were made on the basis of practical family considerations rather than romantic love. Female

Mobile phones have quickly become popular with adolescents worldwide. Here, an adolescent girl in China.

(but not male) virginity at marriage was considered essential, and adolescent girls were forbidden to spend time in the company of adolescent boys.

These gender differences and the narrower socialization for girls continue to be part of Moroccan culture today, particularly in rural areas, and they are reflected in different standards for adolescent boys and girls with respect to their access to media (Davis & Davis, 2007). Adolescent boys attend movies frequently (in Davis and Davis's [1995] data, 80% attended movies occasionally or more), whereas for adolescent girls attendance at movies—*any* movie—is considered shameful (only 20% had *ever* been to see a movie in a theater). Adolescent boys are also allowed freer access to cassette tapes and players, as well as to videocassettes. However, for both adolescent boys and adolescent girls, their exposure to television, music, and (for boys) movies is changing the way they think about gender relations and gender roles. The TV programs, songs, and movies they are exposed to are produced not only in Morocco and other Islamic countries but also include many from France (Morocco was once a French colony) and the United States.

From these various sources, Moroccan adolescents are seeing portrayals of gender roles quite different from what they see among their parents, grandparents, and other adults around them. In the media the adolescents use, romance and passion are central to male-female relationships. Love is the central basis for entering marriage, and the idea of accepting a marriage arranged by parents is either ignored or portrayed as something to be resisted. Young women are usually portrayed not in traditional roles but in professional occupations and as being in control of their lives and unashamed of their sexuality.

Young people are using all this new information to construct a conception of gender roles quite different from the traditional conceptions in their culture (Obermeyer, 2000).

Few places in the world have been more remote and more isolated from the West historically than Nepal, which is located between southwest China and northeast India. Not only is Nepal thousands of miles from the nearest Western country, but until 1951 the government made a special effort to isolate its citizens, banning all communications (travel, trade, books, movies, etc.) between Nepal and "the outside." Since then, Nepal, and especially its largest city, Kathmandu, has been undergoing a rapid transition into the world of global trade, Western tourism, and electronic mass media. Ethnographic research by the anthropologist Mark Liechty (1995) provides a vivid look at how adolescents and emerging adults in Kathmandu are responding to Western media, and at how media are a potent force toward globalization.

According to Liechty and his colleagues, a variety of imported media are highly popular with young people in Kathmandu. Movies and videos from both India and the United States find a broad audience of young people. American and Indian television shows are also popular, and televisions and VCRs are a standard feature of middle-class homes. There is an avid audience among the young for Western music, including rock, heavy metal, and rap. Sometimes young people combine local culture with imported Western styles; Liechty gives the example of a local rock band that had recorded an original Nepali-language album in the style of the Beatles. However, many urban young people reject older traditions such as Nepali folk songs.

A locally produced magazine called *Teens* embodies the appeal of Western media to young people in Kathmandu. In addition to features such as comic strips, Nepali folk tales, puzzles, and games, each issue contains pages of profiles devoted to Western pop music heroes, including biographical data and lyrics to popular songs. Each issue also includes a list of the top 10 English-language albums of the month and a list of recent English video releases. A substantial proportion of the magazine is devoted to fashion, much as in American teen magazines, and the fashions shown are Western.

Nepalese people use the terms *teen* and *teenager* in English, even when speaking Nepali, to refer to young people who are oriented toward Western tastes, especially Western media. Not all Nepalese young people are "teenagers," even if they are in their teen years—the term is not an age category but a social category that refers to young people who are pursuing a Western identity and style based on what they have learned through media. To many young people in Kathmandu, being a "teenager" is something they covet and strive for. They associate it with leisure, affluence, and expanded opportunities. However, many adults use *teenager* with less favorable connotations to refer to young people who are disobedient, antisocial, and potentially violent. Their use of the term in this way reflects their view that Western media have had corrupting effects on many of their young people.

Even to "teenagers" themselves, the availability of Western media is a mixed blessing. They enjoy it, and it provides them with information about the wider world beyond the borders of Nepal. Many of them use media to help them make sense of their own lives, growing up as they are in a rapidly changing society, and as material for imagining a broad range of possible selves. However, Western media also tend to disconnect them from their own culture and from their cultural traditions, leaving many of them confused and alienated. The media ideals of Western life raise their expectations for their own lives to unattainable levels, and they eventually collide with the incompatibility between their expectations and their real lives. As 21-year-old Ramesh told Liechty:

> You know, now I know sooooo much [from films, books, and magazines about the West]. Being a frog in a pond isn't a bad life, but being a frog in an ocean is like hell. Look at this. Out here in Kathmandu there is nothing. We have nothing (p. 187).

Altogether it amounts to an influence toward globalization and toward the broad socialization of the West, as media are "used by adolescents in a period of rapid social change to reimagine many aspects of their lives, including a desire for more autonomy, for more variety in heterosexual interactions, and for more choice of a job and of a mate" (Davis & Davis, 1995, p. 578). Here we see an example of socialization from the media going "over the heads" of parents and other adult socializers, as discussed earlier in the chapter.

Another example of media and globalization comes from Richard Condon's (1988, 1995) study of the Inuit (Eskimos) of the Canadian Arctic. Condon's ethnography is of particular interest with respect to media because he first observed Inuit adolescents in 1978, just before television first became available (in 1980), and he subsequently returned there for further observations several times during the 1980s. Between his first visit and his subsequent visits he observed striking changes in adolescents' behavior with respect to romantic relationships and competition in sports. Condon and many of the Inuit he interviewed attributed the changes to the introduction of television.

With respect to sports, before TV arrived Inuit adolescents rarely played sports, and when they did they were reluctant to appear that they were trying hard to win and establish superior skills over other players because of Inuit cultural traditions that discourage competition and encourage cooperation. All of this changed after the introduction of television. Baseball, football, and hockey games quickly became among the most popular TV programs, especially among adolescents, and participation in these sports (especially hockey) became a central part of the recreational activities of adolescent boys, with adolescent girls often coming to watch. Furthermore, adolescent boys became intensely competitive in the games they played, no longer shy about trying hard to win and talking loudly about their superior talent when they did win—clearly emulating the players they watched on TV. It is rare to see such an unambiguous example of the *effects* of media on adolescents.

The other area in which the influence of television was observed by Condon was male-female relationships. Before the introduction of television, adolescents' dating and sexual behavior was furtive and secretive. Couples rarely displayed affection for one another in public; in fact, couples rarely even acknowledged any special relationship when they were around others. Condon described one adolescent boy whom he had known closely for a year before the boy confided that he had a girlfriend he had been dating for the past 4 years—and even then, the boy refused to reveal her name!

However, all this changed after a couple of years of exposure to TV. Teenage couples were frequently seen together in public, holding hands or hugging. At community dances, young couples no longer ignored each other at opposite ends of the dance hall but sat together as couples and danced as couples. When Condon inquired about the reason for the change, many of the adolescents told him they thought it was due to the introduction of television. *Happy Days*, a program about American teens in the 1950s, was a particular favorite.

A recent study of adolescent girls in Fiji was also able to observe them before and after the introduction of television (Becker, 2004). The study found positive effects: the girls indicated their explicit imitation of the perceived positive attributes of television characters. However, there were also negative effects. Specifically, from observing the slim Western women on TV, girls became preoccupied with their weight and body shape, and there was a disturbing increase in purging behavior to control weight. The girls also began to perceive the slimmest among them as having the highest status.

Does all of this mean that, eventually, Western (especially American) media will obliterate all the other media of the world and establish a homogeneous global culture dominated by the United States? It is difficult to say. In some countries, locally produced media are having difficulty competing with the popularity of American media. However, what seems to be happening in most places, at least so far, is that local media

are coexisting with American media. Young people watch American television shows, but they also view shows in their own language produced in their own country, and perhaps shows from other countries as well. They go to American movies, but they also attend movies that are locally produced. They listen to American and British music, but also to the music of their own culture and their own artistic traditions. As we discussed in Chapter 6, globalization appears to promote a bicultural identity, with one rooted in the local culture and one attached to the global culture (Arnett, 2002a), and this appears to be true for media use as in other areas.

In some places, new blends of music are resulting from increasing globalization. For example, in Britain, immigrant musicians from India have developed a musical style dubbed "Indipop," a combination of traditional Indian musical forms and instruments with British and American popular music forms and technology. Whether creative and original new forms will continue to develop from globalization or whether globalization will lead to a relentless homogenization into one global media culture will be substantially determined by what appeals most to the adolescents and emerging adults of the world.

SUMMING UP

In this chapter we have discussed a wide range of media and how they are used by young people. The main points we have covered are as follows:

- Media use is an important part of young people's daily experience in industrialized countries and increasingly in traditional cultures as well.
- The uses and gratifications approach depicts young people as active media users rather than as the passive recipients of media stimulation. This approach recognizes that young people vary in the media choices they make and in their responses to the same media experience. The Media Practice Model applies this approach to adolescents. Uses of media among young people include entertainment, identity formation, high sensation, coping, and youth culture identification.
- Although hundreds of studies have been conducted on television and aggression, mostly on children, the evidence that television is a motivator of aggressive behavior in adolescents is mixed. Computer games have also been said to promote aggressive behavior, but this effect has not been persuasively demonstrated.
- The television shows most popular among adolescents contain a high proportion of sexual interactions. Generally, these interactions emphasize the importance of physical appearance in male-female relationships and display a "recreational" attitude toward sex.
- Criticisms of "gangsta" rap target themes of sexual exploitation of women, violence, and racism in rap songs. Little is known about the responses of adolescents who like rap music.
- Heavy metal music has been accused of promoting suicidal and violent tendencies. However, adolescent heavy metal fans generally report that the music has a cathartic effect on their anger.

Media are a potent and pervasive force in globalization. Here, young Muslim women in Malaysia.

- Studies find that cigarette advertisements for Marlboro, Camel, and Newport are highly attractive to adolescents, especially adolescent smokers, and that these brands are also the ones adolescents are most likely to smoke. Internal tobacco company documents provide evidence that tobacco companies have explicitly sought to appeal to adolescents.

- Internet use is becoming increasingly popular among adolescents. There are concerns that Internet use puts adolescents at risk for sexual exploitation and social isolation, but Internet use has positive functions as well, especially for providing access to educational information and for allowing adolescents to practice social skills. Two new Internet forms popular among adolescents and emerging adults are social-networking websites and blogs.

- Mobile phone use has spread quickly over the past decade, and now most adolescents in industrialized countries own one. Research indicates that mobile phones allow adolescents to keep in perpetual contact with their friends through phoning and (especially) texting.

- Media are a powerful force in the globalization of adolescence, but in most traditional cultures young people use local media as well as Western media.

Perhaps the most striking characteristic of young people's immersion in media today is that it marks such a dramatic change from the environment they experienced just a century ago. Six and a half hours a day is a lot of time to spend on anything, and it is remarkable that today's young people in industrialized countries spend this much time with media. Young people in developing countries are headed in the same direction. In fact, current trends in these countries represent a research opportunity to study them before and after their immersion in a media environment. Effects—rather than correlations—of media use are much easier to discern under these circumstances.

Many people find adolescents' uses of media alarming in both amount and content. Some of this concern is undoubtedly legitimate. It is important to keep a close eye on what is being produced in the media and how adolescents are using it because media producers usually are motivated more by profit than by a desire to promote the general good. At the same time, however, it is wise to be skeptical when claims of media effects are made without definite evidence. Young people use media in many different ways, and their media uses may have positive as well as negative implications for their development.

KEY TERMS

uses and gratifications approach 339
sensation seeking 341
super peer 344
field studies 345

performance videos 349
concept videos 349
cathartic effect 352
social-networking websites 356

blog 357
text messaging 357

INTERNET RESOURCES

http://www.kff.org
Website for the Henry J. Kaiser Family Foundation. The Kaiser Foundation does research and public policy advocacy on a range of topics, especially related to health issues, but it has also sponsored some of the most important research on adolescents and media. The 2005 Kaiser Foundation study *Generation M: Media in the Lives of 8–18 Year-olds*, examined media use among a nationally representative sample of more than 2,000 3rd through 12th graders who completed detailed questionnaires, including nearly 700 self-selected participants who also maintained 7-day media diaries. The report can be downloaded free from this site.

FOR FURTHER READING

Arnett, J. J. (Ed.) (2007). *Encyclopedia of children, adolescents, and the media*. Thousand Oaks, CA. Two volumes containing nearly 500 entries on virtually every imaginable topic related to adolescents and the media.

Brown, J. D., Steele, J. R., & Walsh-Childers, K. (2002). *Sexual teens, sexual media: Investigating media's influence on adolescent sexuality*. Mahwah, NJ: Erlbaum. An excellent book on media and adolescent sexuality, edited by three of the top scholars in this area. They take the uses and gratifications approach, and present the Media Practice Model discussed in this chapter.

13 CHAPTER

Problems and Resilience

Y ou do not have to look very far to find evidence of young people's problems in most societies. Your local newspaper is likely to provide plenty of examples on a daily basis. A typical story appeared recently in my local newspaper. Four young men ages 17–22 were killed when the driver, a 17-year-old boy, lost control of his car while rounding a curve. The car veered off the road and slammed into a telephone pole. The driver and his three passengers died at the scene after being thrown from the car. None of them had been wearing seat belts, and the car had been traveling an estimated 75 miles per hour in a 40-miles-per-hour zone. "Speed was definitely a factor," said the police officer who was called to the scene. "They could have had seat belts on. This crash was so horrific there was no chance of survival."

TERRIBLE STORIES LIKE THIS ARE PROBABLY FAMILIAR to you, and you may have noticed that these stories frequently involve young people in their teens and early 20s. Scholars sometimes complain that such stories promote stereotypes about young people, especially the stereotype that adolescence is inherently a time of "storm and stress" and that adolescents are disproportionately the cause of social problems such as crime (e.g., Steinberg & Levine, 1997). To the extent that such a stereotype exists, applying it to all adolescents and emerging adults would be unfair. In examining many aspects of development in the various chapters of this book, we have seen that the teens and early 20s are years of many changes, some of them profound and dramatic. However, for most young people these changes are manageable, and they develop through adolescence and emerging adulthood without suffering any serious or enduring problems.

Nevertheless, the teens and 20s remain the period of life when various problems are *more likely* to occur than at other times (Arnett, 1999a). Most adolescents and emerging adults do not develop serious problems, but the risk of a wide range of problems is higher for them than it is for children or adults. These problems range from automobile accidents to criminal behavior to eating disorders to depressed mood. We will explore all of these problems in this chapter.

Before we examine specific problems, you should be introduced to some of the ideas that provide a context for understanding the problems. These ideas will be the topic of the next section.

Two Types of Problems

Scholars studying young people's problems often make a distinction between **internalizing problems** and **externalizing problems** (Ollendick, Shortt, & Sander, 2008). Internalizing problems are problems that primarily affect a person's internal world. This includes problems such as depression, anxi-ety, and eating disorders. Internalizing problems tend to go together. For example, adolescents who have an eating disorder are more likely than other adolescents to be depressed. Adolescents who are depressed are more likely than other adolescents to have an anxiety disorder. Young people who have internalizing problems are sometimes called **overcontrolled** (Asendorpf & van Aken, 1999; Van Leeuwen et al., 2004). They tend to come from families in which parents exercise tight psychological control (Barber, 2002). As a result, their own personalities are often overly controlled and self-punishing. Internalizing problems are more common among females than among males (Ollendick et al., 2008).

Externalizing problems create difficulties in a person's external world. Types of externalizing problems include delinquency, fighting, substance use, risky driving, and unprotected sex. Like internalizing problems, externalizing problems tend to go together (Frick & Kimonis, 2008). For example, adolescents who fight are more likely than other adolescents to commit crimes; adolescents who have unprotected sex are more likely than other adolescents to use substances such as alcohol and marijuana. Young people with externalizing problems are sometimes called **undercontrolled** (Asendorpf & van Aken, 1999; Van Leeuwen et al., 2004). They tend to come from families where parental monitoring and control is lacking (Barber, Olsen, & Shagle, 1994). As a result, they tend to lack self-control themselves, which then leads to their externalizing problems. Externalizing problems are more common among males than among females (Bongers et al., 2004; Frick & Kimonis, 2008).

Another key difference between internalizing and externalizing problems is that young people with internalizing problems usually experience distress, whereas young people with externalizing problems often do not (Maggs, 1999). The majority of young people in Western societies take part in externalizing behaviors from time to time (Arnett, 2002b). Although externalizing behaviors may be a manifestation of problems with family, friends, or school, many young people who take part in externalizing behaviors have no such problems.

Externalizing behaviors are often motivated not by underlying unhappiness or psychopathology but by the desire for excitement and intense experiences (Arnett, 1992a, 1994b; Zuckerman, 2003), and can also be one way of having fun with friends (Maggs, 1999). Externalizing behaviors are almost always viewed as problems by adults, but young people themselves may not see it that way.

The distinction between internalizing and externalizing problems is useful, but it should not be taken to be absolute. In general, the problems within each category occur together, but some young people have both kinds of problems. For example, delinquent adolescents are sometimes depressed as well (Beyers & Loeber, 2003; Loeber et al., 1998), and depressed adolescents sometimes abuse drugs and alcohol (Henry et al., 1993; Saluja, Iachan, & Scheidt, 2004). Some studies have found that adolescents with both externalizing and internalizing problems have had especially difficult family backgrounds (Capaldi & Stoolmiller, 1992).

We will examine externalizing problems first, then internalizing problems.

Externalizing Problems

Externalizing problems in adolescence have been intensively studied by social scientists, especially in the past 30 years. Scholars have used various terms in studying this topic, including not only externalizing problems but also **risk behavior** and **problem behavior**. Regardless of the terms used, these behaviors generally include risky sexual behavior, risky driving behavior, substance use, and crime. We will discuss each of these types of behavior (except for risky sexual behavior, which was discussed in Chapter 9), and for each type we will discuss interventions designed to prevent the problem. Then we will discuss the various factors that have been found to be related to these behaviors.

Risky Automobile Driving

"I love to drive fast, but after awhile driving fast just wasn't doing it any more. So I started driving without the lights on [at night], going about ninety on country roads. I even got a friend to do it. We'd go cruising down country roads, turn off the lights, and just fly. It was incredible. We'd go as fast as we could, [and] at night, with no lights it feels like you're just flying."

—Nick, age 23 (in Arnett, 1996, p. 79)

Across industrialized countries, the most serious threat to the lives and health of adolescents and emerging adults is automobile driving (Heuveline, 2002). As Figure 13.1 shows, in the United States young people aged 16 to 24 have the highest rates of automobile accidents, injuries, and fatalities of any age group (National Highway Traffic Safety Administration [NHTSA], 2009). In other Western countries, a higher minimum driving age (usually 18) and less access to automobiles have made rates of accidents and fatalities among young people substantially lower than in the United States. Nevertheless, motor vehicle injuries are the leading cause of death in those countries as well during adolescence and emerging adulthood (Pan et al., 2007; Twisk & Stacey, 2007).

What is responsible for these grim statistics? Is it young drivers' inexperience or their risky driving behavior? Inexperience certainly plays a large role. Rates of accidents and fatalities are extremely high in the early months of driving but fall dramatically by one year after licensure (McNight & Peck, 2002; Williams, 1998). Studies that have attempted to disentangle experience and age in young drivers have generally concluded that inexperience is partly responsible for young drivers' accidents and fatalities.

However, these studies and others have also concluded that inexperience is not the only factor involved. Equally important is the way young people drive and the kinds of risks they take (Arnett, 2002d; Ferguson, 2003). Compared to older drivers, young drivers (especially males) are more likely to drive at excessive speeds, follow other vehicles too closely, violate traffic signs and signals, take more risks in lane changing and passing other vehicles, allow too little time to merge, and fail to yield to pedestrians (Bina et al., 2006; Williams & Ferguson, 2002). They are also more likely than older drivers to report driving under the influence of alcohol. Drivers aged 21 to 24 involved in fatal accidents are more likely to have been intoxicated at the time of the accident than persons in any other age group (NHTSA, 2009). Nearly half of American college students report driving while intoxicated within the past year (Finken, Jacobs, & Laguna, 1998). Young people are also less likely than older drivers to wear seat belts (Williams & Ferguson, 2002), and in serious car crashes persons not wearing seat belts are twice as likely to be killed and three times as likely to be injured, compared with those wearing seat belts (NHTSA, 2009).

In addition to inexperience and specific driving behaviors, a variety of other factors are involved in young drivers' crash risks. Jean Shope (2002) of the University of Michigan has proposed a useful model, presented in Figure 13.2. The model shows the importance of various aspects of the socialization environment, from parental involvement to cultural

---

internalizing problems Problems such as depression and anxiety that affect a person's internal world, for example depression, anxiety, and eating disorders.

externalizing problems Problems that affect a person's external world, such as delinquency and fighting.

overcontrolled Personality characterized by inhibition, anxiety, and self-punishment, sometimes ascribed to adolescents who have internalizing problems.

undercontrolled Personality characterized by a lack of self-control, sometimes ascribed to adolescents who have externalizing problems.

risk behavior Problems that involve the risk of negative outcomes, such as risky driving and substance use.

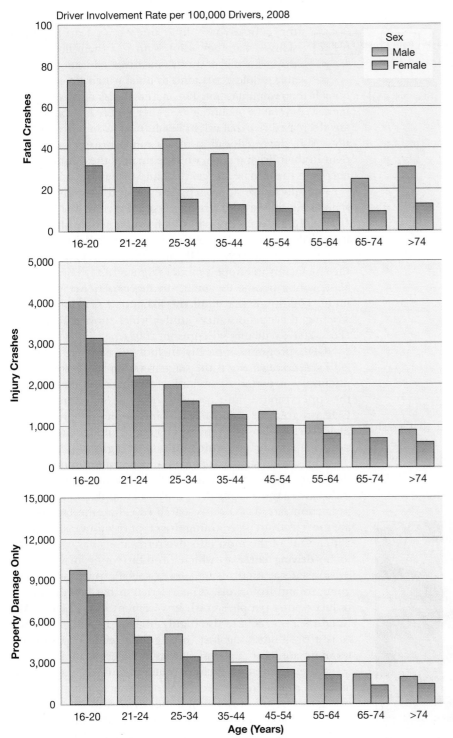

Driver Involvement Rate per 100,000 Drivers, 2008

FIGURE 13.1 Driver crash involvement rates per 100,000 drivers by age and gender, 2007.

Source: NHTSA (2009).

norms to media that glamorize high-speed driving. Parental involvement and monitoring of adolescents' driving behavior has been shown to be especially important in the early months of driving, and interventions to increase parental involvement have been shown to be effective (Simons-Morton, 2007; Simons-Morton, Hartos, & Leaf, 2002; Simons-Morton, Hartos, Leaf, & Preusser, 2006). Friends' influence has been found to promote risky driving. Young drivers are more likely than older drivers to believe their friends would approve of risky driving behavior such as speeding, closely following another vehicle, and passing another car in risky circumstances (Chen et al., 2007; U.S. Department of Transportation, 1995).

Driver characteristics matter, too. Personality characteristics such as sensation seeking and aggressiveness promote risky driving and subsequent crashes, and these characteristics tend to be highest in young male drivers (Arnett, 2002f). The optimistic bias leads people to believe that they are less likely than others to be in a crash, and this bias is especially strong in younger drivers (Mayhew & Simpson, 2002). Driver characteristics and the driving environment interact with the socialization environment to result in driving behavior that leads to crashes, and seat belt use plays a large part in determining whether a crash results in injuries or fatalities.

Preventing Automobile Accidents and Fatalities What can be done to reduce the rates of automobile accidents and fatalities among young drivers? The two approaches that have been tried most often in the United States are **driver education**, which generally has not worked very well, and a program of restricted driving privileges called **graduated driver licensing (GDL)**, which has been much more effective.

On the face of it, driver education would seem promising as a way to improve adolescents' driving practices. It seems logical that if beginning drivers were taught by professional educators, they would become more proficient more quickly and therefore be safer drivers. However, studies that have compared adolescents who have taken driver education

---

problem behavior Behavior that young people engage in that is viewed by adults as a source of problems, such as unprotected premarital sex and substance use.

driver education Programs designed to teach young drivers safe driving skills before they receive their driver's license.

graduated driver licensing (GDL) A program that allows young people restricted driving privileges when they first receive their license, gradually increasing the privileges if the restrictions are not violated.

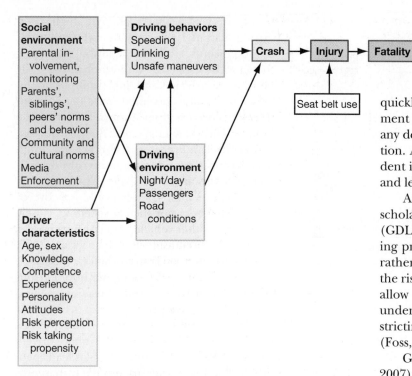

FIGURE 13.2 Shope's model of young driver crash risks.

Source: Shope (2002), p. 15.

courses to adolescents who have not have found that crash involvement tends to be as high or *higher* for the adolescents who have taken driver education (Hirsch, 2003; Mayhew & Simpson, 2002; Mayhew, 2007). Driver education programs generally fail to teach the knowledge and skills necessary for

Young drivers tend to take more risks than older drivers, with sometimes fatal consequences.

safe driving, in part because the adolescents who take the courses have little interest in learning those skills—what they want is to get their license and drive. Furthermore, when driver education is available, adolescents tend to obtain their licenses more quickly than when it is not. The increased risk of crash involvement as a result of obtaining an earlier license is stronger than any decreased risk that might result from taking driver education. Also, driver education makes young drivers more confident in their driving skills, which enhances the optimistic bias and leads them to be less cautious and take more risks.

An alternative approach, one favored strongly by most scholars on adolescent driving, is graduated driver licensing (GDL). GDL is a program in which young people obtain driving privileges gradually, contingent on a safe driving record, rather than all at once. GDL programs address a variety of the risk factors in Shope's model (Figure 13.2). The goal is to allow young people to obtain driving experience gradually, under conditions that limit the likelihood of crashes by restricting the circumstances under which novices can drive (Foss, 2007; Williams & Ferguson, 2002).

GDL programs typically include three stages (Shope, 2007). *Learning license* is the stage in which the young person undergoes a period of obtaining driving experience under the supervision of an experienced driver. For example, the GDL program in California requires young people to complete learning license training of 50 hours under the supervision of a parent, 10 of which must be at night.

The second stage is a period of *restricted license* driving. In this stage adolescents are allowed to drive unsupervised, but with tighter restrictions than those that apply to adults. The restrictions are based on research revealing the factors that are most likely to place young drivers at risk for crashes (Foss, 2007). One of the most effective restrictions has been found to be **driving curfews**, which prohibit young drivers from driving late at night except for a specific purpose such as going to and from work. This restriction has been found to reduce young people's crash involvement dramatically (McKnight & Peck, 2002). Also highly effective in reducing crashes is a prohibition against driving with teenage passengers when no adults are present (Williams & Ferguson, 2002).

Other restrictions include requirements for seat belt use and a "zero tolerance" rule for alcohol use, which means that young drivers are in violation if they drive with any alcohol at all in their blood. In the restricted license stage, any violations of these restrictions may result in a suspended license. It is only after the restricted license period has passed—usually no more than 1 year—that a young person obtains a *full license* and has the same driving privileges as adults.

driving curfews In graduated licensing programs, a feature of the restricted license stage in which young drivers are prohibited from driving late at night except for a specific purpose such as going back and forth to work.

substance use Use of substances that have cognitive and mood-altering effects, including alcohol, cigarettes, and illegal drugs such as marijuana, LSD, and cocaine.

binge drinking Drinking a large number of alcoholic drinks in one episode, usually defined as drinking five or more alcoholic drinks in a row.

Numerous studies in the past decade have shown the effectiveness of GDL programs (Foss, 2007; Hedlund & Compton, 2005; Shope, 2007). One recent analysis of 21 studies concluded that GDL programs consistently reduce young drivers' crash risk by 20% to 40% (Shope, 2007). Fatal crashes among 16-year-old drivers in the United States decreased by 40% in the past decade, and this improvement is attributed mainly to GDL programs (Ferguson et al., 2007). Legislators in many states have responded to this evidence by passing more of these programs. About two thirds of American states now have some kind of GDL program, a dramatic rise over the past 10 years (Hedlund & Compton, 2005; Preusser & Tison, 2007). GDL programs have also been instituted in Canada and are becoming more common in European countries (Pan et al., 2007; Twisk & Stacey, 2007).

THINKING CRITICALLY •••

Are you in favor of a graduated licensing program for your state? If so, what provisions would you include? Are such programs unfair to young people who drive safely and nevertheless have their driving privileges restricted?

Substance Use

Another common form of risk behavior in adolescence and emerging adulthood is the use of alcohol and other drugs. Scholars often use the term **substance use** to refer to this topic, with "substances" including alcohol, cigarettes, and illegal drugs such as marijuana, LSD, Ecstasy, and cocaine.

Current and Past Rates of Substance Use Rates of substance use vary across Western countries. A recent study by the World Health Organization (WHO) investigated rates of

Marijuana is one of the most common types of substances used by young people.

using alcohol, cigarettes, and marijuana among 15 year-olds in 41 Western countries (WHO, 2008). A summary of the results is shown in Figures 13.3, 13.4, and 13.5. As you can see, rates of substance use depended on the substance. For example, American and Canadian adolescents were relatively high in marijuana use but relatively low in alcohol use and cigarette smoking. More details on the reasons for these cross-national differences will be presented later in the chapter.

Research on American adolescents shows that substance use rates continue to rise past age 15, through the end of high school. According to national Monitoring the Future

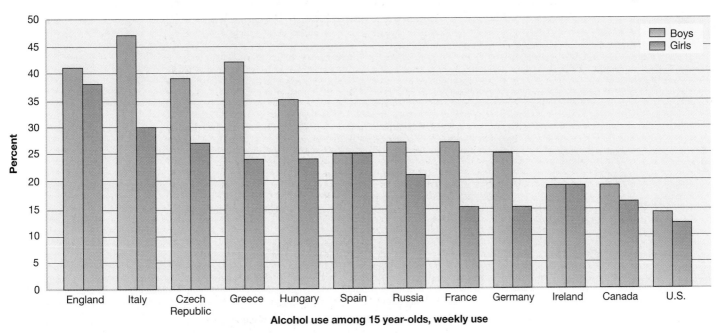

FIGURE 13.3 Alcohol use among 15 years-old, weekly use.

Source: WHO (2008).

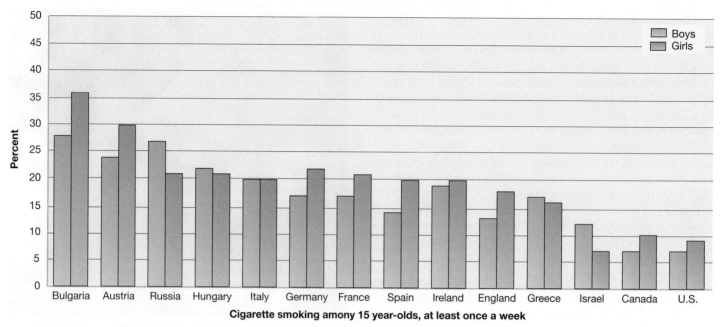

FIGURE 13.4 Cigarette smoking among 15 years-olds, at least once a week.

Source: WHO (2008).

(MTF) data, in 2008, 43% of American high school seniors used alcohol and 28% reported **binge drinking**—consuming five or more alcoholic drinks in a row—at least once in the past month. Cigarette use (at least once in the past 30 days) was reported by 20% of high school seniors in 2008. Rates of marijuana use were similar: 19% of high school seniors reported using marijuana in the past month in the 2008 MTF survey. In general, substance use in adolescence is highest among Native Americans, followed by White and Latino adolescents, with African American and Asian American adolescents lowest (Gil, Vega, & Biafora, 1998; Grunbaum, 2004).

Other than alcohol, cigarettes, and marijuana, substance use is uncommon among American adolescents. A small proportion of adolescents experiment with other substances. For example, according to the MTF survey, in 2008 11% of high school seniors had tried amphetamines, 10% had tried inhalants (e.g., glue, gasoline), 9% had tried hallucinogens (e.g., LSD), 9% had tried sedatives, 7% had tried cocaine, and 6% had tried Ecstasy. However, frequent use of these substances was very rare. None of them had been used by more than 3% of high school seniors in the past 30 days.

The peak of substance use actually comes not in adolescence but in emerging adulthood (Schulenberg & Maggs,

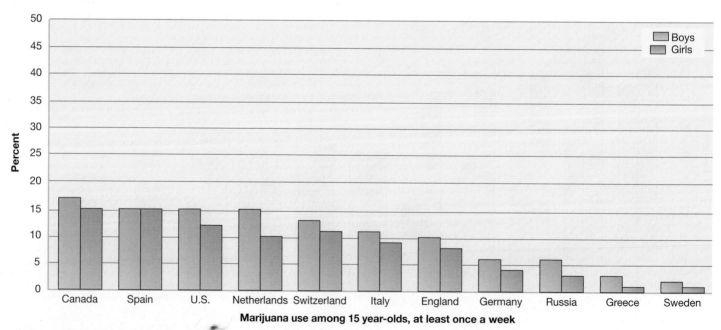

FIGURE 13.5 Marijuana use among 15 years-old, at least once a week.

Source: WHO (2008).

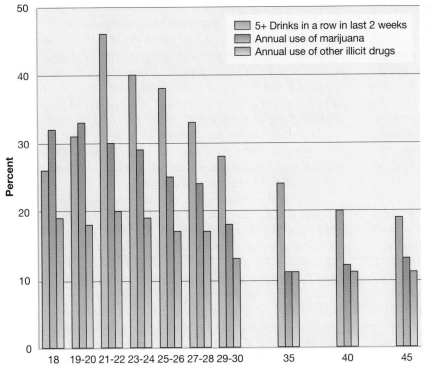

FIGURE 13.6 Substance abuse by age.

Source: Johnston et al. (2008).

Legend:
- 5+ Drinks in a row in last 2 weeks
- Annual use of marijuana
- Annual use of other illicit drugs

2000). The MTF studies have followed up several cohorts after high school through their 20s, and now provide excellent data on substance use in emerging adulthood as well. These data show that substance use of all kinds continues to rise through the late teens and peaks in the early 20s before declining in the late 20s. Figure 13.6 shows the pattern from age 18 through 45 (Johnston et al., 2008). Substance use, especially alcohol use, is highest among emerging adults who are college students (Kalb & McCormick, 1998; Okie, 2002; Schulenberg, 2000; Wechsler & Nelson, 2001).

Some evidence shows that substance use is also high among emerging adults in other Western countries. A study of Spanish adults reported that among 18- to 24-year-olds, rates of binge drinking in the past 30 days were 31% for men and 18% for women, far higher than in any other age group (Valencia-Martín et al., 2007). A peak in binge drinking in emerging adulthood has been found in other European countries as well (Kuntsche, Rehm, & Gmel, 2004). Among female college students in Scotland, most regarded binge drinking as "harmless fun" (Guise & Gill, 2007).

What explains the higher rates of substance use among emerging adults? Wayne Osgood has proposed a useful answer to this question. Osgood (Osgood, Anderson, & Schaffer, 2005; Osgood et al., 1996) borrows from a sociological theory that explains all deviance on the basis of *propensity* and *opportunity* (see Gottfredson & Hirschi, 1990). People behave deviantly when they have a combination of sufficient propensity (that is, sufficient motivation for behaving deviantly) along with sufficient opportunity. In his explanation, Osgood especially focuses on the high degree of opportunity that

emerging adults have for engaging in substance use and other deviant behavior, as a result of spending a high proportion of their time in unstructured socializing.

Osgood uses the term **unstructured socializing** to include behavior such as riding around in a car for fun, going to parties, going shopping, and going out with friends. Using MTF data, he shows that unstructured socializing is highest in the late teens and early 20s, and that within this age period, emerging adults who are highest in unstructured socializing are also highest in the use of alcohol and marijuana (Osgood et al., 1996, 2005). Rates of most types of substance use are especially high among emerging adults who are college students because they have so many opportunities for unstructured socializing. Substance use declines in the mid- to late 20s, as role transitions such as marriage, parenthood, and full-time work cause a sharp decline in unstructured socializing (Monitoring the Future, 2003; Schulenberg et al., 1996).

How do the current rates of substance use in adolescence and emerging adulthood compare with previous decades? Because the MTF studies go back to 1975, there are excellent data on this question for American adolescents over more than three decades (Johnston et al., 2008). Rates of most types of substance use (past month) declined from the late 1970s to the early 1990s, rose through the rest of the 1990s, then declined further over the past decade. Alcohol use declined from about 70% in 1975 to 43% in 2008. Cigarette smoking declined from nearly 40% in 1975 to 20% in 2008. Marijuana use declined from a peak of 37% in 1978 to 19% in 2008. Use of amphetamines peaked at 15% in 1981 and declined to under 3% by 2008. During this period, an increasing proportion of young people defined themselves as "straight-edge," meaning that they abstain from all substance use (Kalb & McCormick, 1998). The reasons for this shift away from substance use are not clear, but it is likely that an intensive government-funded public campaign against teenage substance use during this period contributed to the decline.

The Sequence of Substance Use Substance use in adolescence and emerging adulthood has been found to follow a typical sequence of four stages: (1) drinking beer and wine; (2) smoking cigarettes and drinking hard liquor; (3) smoking marijuana; and (4) using "hard" drugs (e.g., cocaine, LSD). Almost all adolescents who begin to smoke cigarettes or use hard liquor have already tried beer and wine; almost all adolescents who try marijuana have already tried cigarettes and hard liquor; and almost all adolescents who use hard drugs have already tried marijuana (Kandel, 1975, 2002; Van Kammen, Loeber, & Stouthamer-Loeber, 1991). Beer, wine,

unstructured socializing The term for young people spending time together with no specific event as the center of their activity.

cigarettes, and marijuana have been called **gateway drugs** because most adolescents who try hard drugs have already passed through the "gates" of these substances (Kandel, 2002).

Of course, this does not mean that all or even most of the people who try one type of substance will go on to try the next substance in the sequence. It simply means that young people who try one type of substance are *more likely* than young people who have not tried it to move along the sequence to the next substance. So, for example, most young people who try marijuana will never try hard drugs, but among young people who try hard drugs almost all of them have used marijuana first.

A good example of the sequence of substance use comes from the classic study by Kandel and Faust (1975) that originally inspired the "gateway drug" theory. The study assessed high school students' substance use on two occasions 6 months apart. At the 6-month follow-up, 27% of the students who had smoked or used alcohol at the time of the original study had subsequently tried marijuana, compared with only 2% of the students who had not smoked or used alcohol. Similarly, 26% of the students who had used marijuana at the time of the original study had subsequently tried hard drugs, compared with only 1% of the students who had never used marijuana. From these statistics we can see both that young people who use one substance in the sequence are more likely to use the next one and that most young people who use one substance do not proceed right away to use the next one in the sequence. Recent longitudinal studies continue to support the gateway drug theory, showing that use of cigarettes and alcohol predicts entry to marijuana use and that use of marijuana predicts use of hard drugs (Fergusson, Boden, & Harwood, 2006; Tarter et al., 2006). In a book summarizing research on the "gateway drug" theory, Denise Kandel (2002), author of the theory, concluded that it accurately describes the sequence of substance use, but using earlier drugs in the sequence does not necessarily cause young people to use the later drugs.

THINKING CRITICALLY •••

Some people have interpreted the "gateway drug" theory as indicating that if adolescents could be prevented from using alcohol and cigarettes, they would also be less likely to use marijuana and hard drugs. Do you think this is true, or would they be more likely to use other drugs if their access to alcohol and cigarettes were curtailed?

Substance Use and Abuse Young people use substances for a variety of purposes, which can be classified as experimental,

social, medicinal, and addictive (Weiner, 1992). Young people who take part in **experimental substance use** try a substance once or perhaps a few times out of curiosity and then do not use it again. A substantial proportion of substance use in adolescence and emerging adulthood is experimental. "To see what it was like" has been found to be the most common motivation given by young people when asked why they used an illicit drug (Arnett, 1992).

Social substance use involves the use of substances during social activities with one or more friends. Parties and nightclubs are common settings for social substance use in adolescence and emerging adulthood.

Medicinal substance use is undertaken to relieve an unpleasant emotional state such as sadness, anxiety, stress, or loneliness (Woodward & Fergusson, 2001). Using substances for these purposes has been described as a kind of **self-medication** (Miranda, Meyerson, Long, Marx, & Simpson, 2002). Young people who use substances for this purpose tend to use them more frequently than those whose purposes are mainly social or experimental. Frequent substance users are three times as likely as other adolescents to be depressed, which suggests the role of self-medication as a motivation for frequent substance use (Repetto et al., 2004; Saluja et al., 2004).

Finally, **addictive substance use** takes place when a person has come to depend on regular use of substances to feel good physically or psychologically. Addictive substance users experience **withdrawal symptoms** such as high anxiety and tremors when they stop taking the substance to which they are addicted. Addictive substance use involves the most regular and frequent substance use of the four categories described here.

All substance use in adolescence and emerging adulthood is considered "problem behavior" in the sense that it is something that adults generally view as a problem if young people engage in it. However, the four categories described here indicate that young people may use substances in very different ways, with very different implications for their development. Research has found that young people who engage in experimental or social substance use are healthier psychologically compared with adolescents who are frequent substance users (the "medicinal" and "addictive" users; Brook et al., 1989; Kandel, 1998; Shedler & Block, 1990). Frequent substance users are also more likely than other adolescents to have problems in school, to be withdrawn from peers, to have problems in their relationships with their parents, and to engage in delinquent behavior (Brook et al., 1989; Tubman, Gil, & Wagner, 2004).

---

gateway drugs Term sometimes applied to alcohol, cigarettes, and marijuana because young people who use harder drugs usually use these drugs first.

experimental substance use Trying a substance once or perhaps a few times out of curiosity.

social substance use The use of substances in the course of social activities with one or more friends.

medicinal substance use Substance use undertaken for the purpose of relieving an unpleasant emotional state such as sadness, anxiety, stress, or loneliness.

self-medication The use of substances for relieving unpleasant states such as sadness or stress.

addictive substance use Pattern of substance use in which a person has come to depend on regular use of substances to feel good physically and/or psychologically.

withdrawal symptoms States such as high anxiety and tremors experienced by persons who stop taking the substance to which they are addicted.

parental monitoring The degree to which parents keep track of where their adolescents are and what they are doing.

Preventing Substance Use Efforts to prevent or reduce substance use among young people have generally been delivered through schools (Dryfoos, 1998). A variety of approaches have been tried. Some programs attempt to raise students' self-esteem, in the belief that the main cause of substance use is low self-esteem. Some programs present information about the health dangers of substance use in the hope that becoming more knowledgeable about the effects of substance use will make students less likely to use them. Other programs, including the most widely used program, Project DARE, have focused on teaching students to resist "peer pressure," in the belief that peer pressure is the main reason young people use drugs. None of these approaches has worked very well (Triplett & Payne, 2004).

More successful programs have focused on family functioning, addressing family problems that may be motivating adolescents' substance use (Austin, Mcgowan, & Wagner, 2005) or teaching parents how to enhance skills such as **parental monitoring**, the extent to which parents know where their adolescents are and what they are doing at any given time (Mason et al., 2003). For example, in one study high-risk 7th-grade adolescents and their families were videotaped at home and in a laboratory task assessing parental monitoring. Parents were then given instructions on how to improve their monitoring skills and provided with additional feedback at annual follow-ups for 4 years (Dishion et al., 2003). Adolescents in the intervention group reported lower rates of substance use 4 years later than adolescents in the control group, and their parents reported higher levels of monitoring than control group parents did. Other successful programs have combined a variety of strategies and have been implemented not only in school but through families, peers, and neighborhoods as well (Horn et al., 2005; Swenson et al., 2005). We will discuss this **multisystemic approach** in more detail below. The most successful programs also start young, in early adolescence, and continue on a yearly basis through high school (Perry et al., 1996; Stockwell et al., 2004).

With regard to emerging adults, prevention of substance use has focused especially on college students and on binge drinking in particular. Approaches include providing freshman orientation workshops on alcohol use and abuse, handing out alcohol awareness pamphlets, sponsoring alcohol-free events, and pressuring local bars to limit offers of cheap drinks (Kalb & McCormick, 1998). Overall, these programs have had little effect on college students' drinking behavior (Okie, 2002).

One recent approach is to increase students' awareness of how many of their peers *do not* binge drink. Students often believe the percentage is higher than it is, and this can create a social norm that encourages binge drinking. Social norms programs are based on the premise that students will drink less if they realize that many of their peers do not binge drink. However, although some social norms programs have shown favorable results (Kalb & McCormick, 1998), a 5-year study of over 100 social norms programs found that not only did they have no effect on the behavior of frequent binge drinkers, but they appeared to increase alcohol consumption among low to moderate drinkers (Wechsler et al., 2003). Binge drinking is so much a part of the culture of American college campuses that it is difficult for an intervention program to fight it.

Delinquency and Crime

Because criminal acts are so disruptive to societies, and because crime became increasingly pervasive with the development of modern cities, crime is one of the oldest and most intensively studied topics in the social sciences. In more than 150 years of research on crime, one finding stands out prominently with remarkable consistency: The great majority of crimes are committed by young people—mostly males—who are between the ages of 12 and 25 (Eisner, 2002).

Before proceeding further, some definitions are necessary. Crimes, of course, are acts that violate the law. When violations of the law are committed by persons defined by the legal system as **juveniles**, these violations are considered acts of **delinquency**. Legal systems in most countries define juveniles as persons under 18 years of age.

There are three kinds of criminal acts. **Status offenses** are offenses that are defined as violations of the law only because they are committed by juveniles. For example, adults can leave home any time they wish, but juveniles who leave home without their parents' consent may be found guilty of running away from home. Other examples of status offenses include truancy (failure to attend school), consensual sex, and purchasing alcohol.

Index crimes are serious crimes, and they are offenses that would be considered violations of the law if committed by a person of any age, juvenile or adult. Index offenses include two subcategories, **violent crimes**, such as rape, assault, and murder, and **property crimes**, such as robbery, motor vehicle theft, and arson. **Nonindex crimes** are less serious offenses such as illegal gambling and disorderly conduct. Like

---

multisystemic approach Delinquency prevention strategy that addresses risk factors at several levels, including the home, the school, and the neighborhood.

juveniles Persons defined by the legal system as being younger than adult status.

delinquency Violations of the law committed by juveniles.

status offenses Offenses such as running away from home that are defined as violations of the law only because they are committed by juveniles.

index crimes Serious crimes divided into two categories: violent crimes such as rape, assault, and murder, and property crimes such as robbery, motor vehicle theft, and arson.

violent crimes Crimes that involve physical harm to others, for example, assault and murder.

property crimes Crimes that involve taking or damaging others' property, for example, robbery and arson.

nonindex crimes Crimes such as illegal gambling, prostitution, and disorderly conduct, considered less serious offenses than index crimes.

index crimes, nonindex crimes would be considered violations of the law no matter what the age of the person committing them.

By definition, status offenses are committed entirely by adolescents—they are acts that would not be criminal if performed by someone who is legally an adult. However, the dramatic relationship between age and crime—the finding that criminal acts are committed mostly by males aged 12 to 25—is true for index and nonindex offenses as well. In the West, this finding is remarkably consistent over a period of greater than 150 years. Figure 13.7 shows the age–crime relationship at two points, one in the 1840s and one relatively recent year. At any point before, after, or in between these times, in most countries, the pattern would look very similar (Eisner, 2002; Gottfredson & Hirschi, 1990; Wilson & Herrnstein, 1985). Adolescent and emerging adult males are not only more likely than children or adults to commit crimes but also more

likely to be the victims of crimes (Cohen & Potter, 1999; Eisner, 2002).

Although young men aged 12 to 25 have committed most of the crimes in every historical period of the past 2 centuries, there have also been quite substantial historical fluctuations in the rates of crimes. Of particular interest is that crime rates rose sharply from the mid-1960s to the mid-1970s (Wilson & Herrnstein, 1985), and sharply again from the mid-1980s to the early 1990s (Federal Bureau of Investigation, 1999), before declining steadily from the mid- to late 1990s to the present. The reasons for these changes are not clear.

What explains the strong and consistent relationship between age and crime? One theory suggests that the key to explaining the age-crime relationship is that adolescents and emerging adults combine increased independence from parents and other adult authorities with increased time with peers and increased orientation toward peers (Wilson & Herrnstein, 1985). A consistent finding of research on crime is that crimes committed by young men in their teens and early 20s usually take place in a group, much more so than among adult offenders (Dishion & Dodge, 2005). Crime is an activity that in some adolescent cliques is encouraged and admired (Dishion, McCord, & Poulin, 1999).

Of course, as we noted in Chapter 8, peers and friends can influence each other in a variety of ways, including toward conformity to adult standards, not just toward deviance and norm-breaking. However, adolescence and emerging adulthood

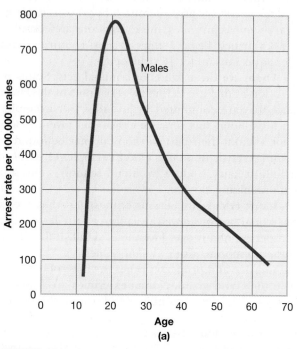
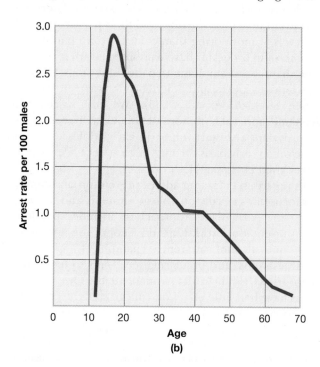

FIGURE 13.7 Age and crime for males in (a) 1842 and (b) 1977.
Source: Gottfredson & Hirschi (1990), p. 125.

life-course-persistent delinquents (LCPDs) In Moffitt's theory, adolescents who show a history of related problems both prior to and following adolescence.

adolescence-limited delinquents (ALDs) In Moffitt's theory, delinquents who engage in criminal acts in adolescence and/or emerging adulthood but show no evidence of problems before or after these periods.

appear to be the times of life when peer groups that value and reinforce norm-breaking are most likely to form (Dishion & Dodge, 2005; Gifford-Smith et al., 2005). In their search for excitement and sensation-seeking adventure, young men in these peer groups may engage in activities that violate the law. Their motives are rarely economic—even when their activities involve theft, the thefts tend to be for small amounts. When they reach their mid-20s, these antisocial peer groups break up as emerging adults enter the various roles of young adulthood, and participation in crime subsequently declines (Moffitt, 2003; Sampson & Laub, 1994).

Two Kinds of Delinquency Breaking laws of various kinds is quite common in the teens and early 20s, especially for males. Most surveys find that over three fourths of adolescents commit at least one criminal act some time before the age of 20 (Moffitt, 2003; Wilson & Herrnstein, 1985). However, there are obvious differences between committing one or two acts of minor crime—vandalism or small theft, for example—and committing crimes frequently over a long period, including more serious crimes such as rape and assault. It has been found that 10% of young people commit over two thirds of all offenses (Yoshikawa, 1994). What are the differences between adolescents who commit an occasional minor violation of the law and adolescents who are at risk for more serious, long-term criminal behavior?

Terrie Moffitt (1993, 2003, 2007) has proposed a provocative theory in which she distinguishes between "adolescence-limited" delinquency and "life-course-persistent" delinquency. In Moffitt's view, these are two distinct types of delinquency, each with different motivations and different sources. However, the two types may be hard to distinguish from one another in adolescence, when criminal offenses are more common than in childhood or adulthood. The way to tell them apart, according to Moffitt, is to look at behavior before adolescence.

Life-course-persistent delinquents (LCPDs) show a pattern of problems from birth onward. Moffitt believes their problems originate in neuropsychological deficits that are evident in a difficult temperament in infancy and a high likelihood of attention-deficit hyperactivity disorder (ADHD) and learning

Participation in delinquency is common during adolescence, especially for boys.

disabilities in childhood. Children with these problems are also more likely than other children to grow up in a high-risk environment (e.g., low-income family, single parent), with parents who have a variety of problems of their own. Consequently, their neurological deficits tend to be made worse rather than better by their environments. When they reach adolescence, children with the combination of neurological deficits and a high-risk environment are highly prone to engage in criminal activity. Furthermore, they tend to continue their criminal activity long after adolescence has ended, well into adulthood.

Adolescence-limited delinquents (ALDs) follow a much different pattern. They show no signs of problems in infancy or childhood, and few of them engage in any criminal activity after their mid-20s. It is just during adolescence—actually, adolescence and emerging adulthood, from about age 12 to about age 25—that they have a period of occasional criminal activity, breaking the law with behavior such as vandalism, theft, and use of illegal drugs.

Moffitt's theory is supported by her research on young people in New Zealand (Moffitt, 2003, 2007; Moffitt & Caspi, 2001, 2005; Moffitt, Caspi, Harrington, & Milne, 2002; Moffitt, Caspi, Michael, & Phil, 2002; also see Piquero & Brezina, 2001). Known as the Dunedin longitudinal study, it began when the participants were in infancy and has followed them through age 26 (so far). The results show that, as predicted by the theory, LCPDs exhibited problems of neurological functioning, temperament, and behavior from an early age, whereas ALDs did not. In emerging adulthood, LCPDs continued to have difficulties such as mental health problems, financial problems, work problems, substance use, and criminal behavior. The risk behavior of ALDs mostly diminished by age 26, although they continued to have more substance use and financial problems than emerging adults who did not engage in delinquent behavior in adolescence.

THINKING CRITICALLY •••

LCPDs' problems have deep roots in early development, but what explains delinquency among ALDs?

Life-course-persistent delinquents have problems from an early age.

Externalizing problems such as fighting, stealing, and substance use are far more common among males than among females, everywhere in the world and in every era of the historical record. The reasons for this may be partly biological, but they are also clearly connected to gender role socialization. In a wide range of cultures, what we have been calling "externalizing problems" are in fact part of the requirements for demonstrating an adolescent male's readiness for manhood (Gilmore, 1990).

One vivid example of this interaction between externalizing problems and manhood requirements can be found among the people of Truk Island, an island that is part of a string of small islands in the South Pacific known as Micronesia. The culture of Truk Island has been vividly described by the anthropologist Mac Marshall (1979) and summarized by David Gilmore (1990). Their accounts provide an excellent demonstration not only of the importance of gender role socialization in the externalizing behavior of young males but also of the effect of globalization on young people even in cultures in the remotest parts of the world.

The globalization of the Trukese culture goes back more than a hundred years. Even long before that, the Trukese were known far and wide as fierce warriors who fought frequently among themselves and made short work of any Western sailors unlucky enough to drift nearby. However, in the late 1800s, German colonists arrived and took control of the islands and of the Trukese people. They stamped out local warfare, introduced Christianity, and also brought in alcohol, which soon became widely and excessively used by young men. After World War II, the Americans replaced the Germans on Truk Island and introduced television, baseball, and other features of Western life. Today, Truk Island remains an American territory.

Much has changed on Truk Island during the century of Western influence, but the emphasis on strictly defined gender roles remains strong. When they reach puberty, girls learn the traditional female role of cooking, sewing, and performing other household duties. Meanwhile, boys are expected to demonstrate their manhood principally in three ways: fighting, drinking large quantities of alcohol, and taking daredevil risks.

Fighting among young Trukese men is a group activity. It takes place in the context of rivalries between clans (extended family networks). Young men fight not just for their own prestige but for the honor and prestige of their clan. On weekend evenings, they roam the streets in clan groups looking for other groups to challenge and taking part in brawls when they find them.

Drinking alcohol is also part of the weekend group activities of young males. By the time they are 13, getting drunk with their clan pals is a regular part of weekend evenings for adolescent boys. The drinking contributes to the fighting because it diminishes any trepidation a boy might have over becoming injured. Also, on weekend days groups of young men sometimes take risky trips in motorboats (see the opening of Chapter 3). They take long trips with limited fuel, a small motor, and nothing for sustenance except beer, risking the open sea in order to demonstrate their bravery and thereby prove their readiness for manhood.

Although nearly all Trukese males in their teens and 20s engage in these activities, their externalizing escapades are limited to the weekends, and they rarely drink or fight during the week. In fact, Marshall's (1979) book on them is entitled *Weekend Warriors*. Also, when they reach about age 30, the expectations for manhood change. At that point, they are expected to marry and settle down. They rarely fight after reaching that age, and most stop drinking alcohol entirely. The externalizing behavior of males in adolescence and emerging adulthood is not viewed as a social problem but, rather, as an accepted behavior during a limited period of their lives, when their culture demands it as part of fulfilling the expectations for becoming a man.

Preventing Crime and Delinquency The seriousness of crime as a social problem has drawn a great deal of attention to preventing young people from committing crimes and trying to rehabilitate young offenders so that they will not commit further crimes. For most young people, as we have discussed, criminal acts are limited to adolescence and emerging adulthood, and once they grow beyond their early 20s they no longer have any inclination to commit such acts. The real focus of concern is the life-course-persistent offenders, who have problems from early childhood onward, become chronic delinquents in adolescence, and are at high risk for a life of continued crime in adulthood.

peer contagion Term for the increase in delinquent behavior that often takes place as an unintended consequence of bringing adolescents with problems together for an intervention, because in the intervention setting they reinforce each other's delinquent tendencies and find new partners for delinquent acts.

Prevention programs to help children who show signs of being headed for trouble in adolescence or to help adolescents who have become involved in serious delinquency are enormously varied. They include individual therapy, group therapy, vocational training, "Outward Bound" kinds of programs that involve group activities in the outdoors, "Scared Straight" programs that take young offenders into a prison to show them the grim conditions of prison life, and many, many, many others. Unfortunately, few of these types of programs have worked very well (Dishion & Dodge, 2005; Greenwood, 2006). The overall record of delinquency prevention and intervention programs is frustratingly poor, despite the best intentions of the many dedicated and highly skilled people who have undertaken them. Some interventions have even been found to increase delinquency because they bring together high-risk adolescents who then form a delinquent clique, a phenomenon known as **peer contagion** (Dishion & Dodge, 2005; Dishion et al., 1999, 2006).

Two problems seem to be at the heart of the failure of these programs. One is that delinquents rarely welcome the opportunity to participate in them (Heilbrun et al., 2005; Stone, 1993). Typically, they are required to participate in the programs against their will, often because the legal system commands them to participate or face incarceration. They do not see themselves as having a problem that needs to be "cured," and their resistance makes progress extremely difficult.

A second problem is that prevention programs typically take place in adolescence, after a pattern of delinquency has already been clearly established, rather than earlier in childhood when signs of problems first appear (Moffitt, 2007). This is due partly to the limited resources for addressing these problems. The money tends to go to where the problems are most obvious and serious—current offenders rather than possible future offenders. Furthermore, the problems of children frequently originate at least partly in the family, and in Western societies, especially in the United States, the state has limited authority to intervene in family life until a clear and serious problem is established.

Nevertheless, some programs do show definite success (Greenwood, 2006). One successful approach has been to intervene at several levels, including the home, the school, and the neighborhood. This is known as the *multisystemic approach* (Borduin et al., 2003; Henggler et al., 2007; Saldana & Henggler, 2006; Swenson et al., 2005). Programs based on this approach include parent training, job training and vocational counseling, and the development of neighborhood institutions such as youth centers and athletic leagues. The goal is to direct the energy of delinquents into more socially constructive directions.

The multisystemic approach has now been adopted by youth agencies in a number of states, including South Carolina, Tennessee, and Washington (Alexander, 2001). As Figure 13.8 illustrates, programs using this approach have been shown to be effective in reducing arrests and out-of-home placements among delinquents (Alexander, 2001; Henggler et al., 2007; Ogden & Amlund, 2006). Furthermore, multisystemic programs have been found to be cheaper than other programs, primarily because they reduce the amount of time that delinquent adolescents spend in foster homes and detention centers (Alexander, 2001). Because of this combination of proven effectiveness and low cost per person, the use of multisystemic approaches is likely to grow in the future.

Factors Involved in Risk Behavior

As mentioned earlier, the various types of risk behavior tend to be correlated. Adolescents who have one kind of externalizing problem tend to have others as well. For this reason it makes sense to look at the factors involved in risk behaviors as a group of behaviors rather than separately. At the same time, it will be important to mention factors that are distinctive to one type of risk behavior but not others. We will focus on various sources of socialization, including family,

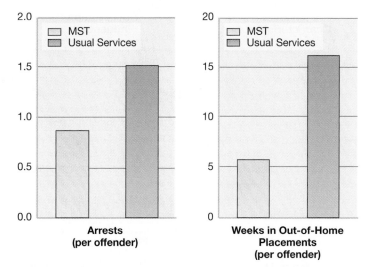

FIGURE 13.8 Multisystemic therapy versus usual juvenile justice services for serious adolescent offenders.

Source: Alexander (2001), p. 42.

friends/peers, school, neighborhood/community, and religious beliefs. Then we will consider individual characteristics such as sensation seeking and aggressiveness that are related to participation in risk behavior. A summary model is presented in Figure 13.9. We will focus mostly on substance use and crime/delinquency because the sources of risky driving were discussed earlier in the chapter.

As we discuss the factors involved in risk behavior, keep in mind that the *majority* of American adolescents and emerging adults take occasional risks of the kind that have been described in this chapter. Many of them have no evidence of problems in their socialization environment. Thus, although problems in the environment tend to be *related* to degree of participation in risk behavior, this does not mean that such problems necessarily exist among all or even most young people who engage in risk behavior. In general, the more serious a young person's involvement in risk behavior, the more likely these problems are to exist in the socialization environment. Keep in mind, too, that adolescents are active participants in their socialization environment, as Figure 13.9 shows. They are influenced by socialization agents, but they make choices about their environment (e.g., with respect to friends, media, and religious participation) and they respond to their socialization environments in different ways, depending on their individual characteristics.

Family A great deal of research has focused on the ways that family characteristics are related to risk behavior. This research is mainly on adolescents rather than emerging adults because most emerging adults leave home by their late teens, so parents' control and influence over them diminishes. Consistently, this research supports a relationship between parenting styles and risk behavior. Specifically, adolescents who have authoritative parents—parents who combine warmth and control in their relationships with their adolescents—take part in risk behavior to a lesser extent

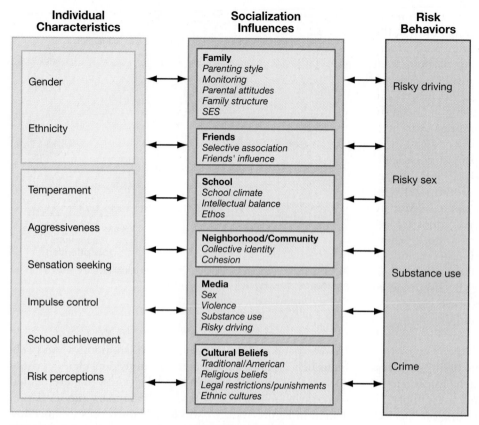

Individual Characteristics	Socialization Influences	Risk Behaviors

Individual Characteristics

Gender

Ethnicity

Temperament

Aggressiveness

Sensation seeking

Impulse control

School achievement

Risk perceptions

Socialization Influences

Family
Parenting style
Monitoring
Parental attitudes
Family structure
SES

Friends
Selective association
Friends' influence

School
School climate
Intellectual balance
Ethos

Neighborhood/Community
Collective identity
Cohesion

Media
Sex
Violence
Substance use
Risky driving

Cultural Beliefs
Traditional/American
Religious beliefs
Legal restrictions/punishments
Ethnic cultures

Risk Behaviors

Risky driving

Risky sex

Substance use

Crime

FIGURE 13.9 Summary model of factors related to risk behaviors.

than other adolescents. In contrast, adolescents whose parents are authoritarian (harshly controlling but not warm), permissive (high warmth, low control), or disengaged (low in both warmth and control) tend to have higher rates of participation in risk behavior.

Thus, adolescents with substance abuse problems are more likely than other adolescents to have parents who are permissive, disengaged, or hostile (Barrera, Biglan, Ari, & Li, 2001). In contrast, adolescents in families where closeness and warmth are high are less likely to have substance abuse problems (Bogenschneider et al., 1998; Keisner & Kerr, 2004). Other family factors related to adolescent substance abuse are high levels of family conflict and family disorganization (Austin et al., 2005). As noted in Chapter 7, adolescents in divorced families are more likely to use substances, due in part to the high family conflict that often precedes and accompanies divorce (Peris & Emery, 2005).

Adolescents are also more likely to use substances when one or more other family members use substances or have a lenient attitude toward substance use (Bogenschneider et al., 1998; Peterson et al., 1994). One reason for the low rates of substance use among African American adolescents is that many African American parents are vehemently opposed to substance use and make their position clear to their adolescents (Peterson et al., 1994). A good relationship with a parent or an adult outside the family can act as a protective factor, making substance use and other risk behavior less likely (Beam, Gil-Rivas, Greenberger, & Chen, 2002).

A similar pattern of family factors has been found in studies of delinquency. Nearly a half century ago, McCord

and McCord (1959) found that delinquents were about twice as likely as nondelinquents to come from homes where discipline was inconsistent or lenient, and this finding has been confirmed numerous times since then. An especially important concept in research on delinquency has been parental monitoring (Kerr & Stattin, 2000), which was mentioned earlier in the chapter. Parental monitoring is one reflection of the control dimension of parenting, and when parental monitoring is lacking adolescents are considerably more likely to engage in delinquent acts (Dishion et al., 2003; Jacobson & Crockett, 2000). Adolescents in divorced families have higher rates of delinquency (Buchanan, 2000) partly because monitoring is more difficult when there is only one parent.

Parental monitoring tends to weaken as adolescents get older, so parents are often unaware of their older adolescents' involvement in risk behavior. In one study of high school students, over 50% of the adolescents reported engaging in sexual intercourse and alcohol use, even though over 98% of their parents thought they had not (Strasburger & Wilson, 2002). Parental monitoring is especially likely to be low once adolescents move out of their parents' household and enter emerging adulthood. This helps explain why emerging adults consistently have higher rates of risk behavior than adolescents (Arnett, 1998b; Bachman et al., 1996; Schulenberg & Zarrett, 2006). Emerging adults have neither parents nor spouses to provide social control (Arnett, 2006c; Gottfredson & Hirschi, 1990; Sampson & Laub, 1994), and this relative freedom makes risk behavior more likely.

THINKING CRITICALLY •••

Is it possible that passive genotype-environment interactions are involved in crime and delinquency? Explain how you would test this possibility.

Friends' Influence Because of the widespread belief that peers play a strong role in risk behavior, risk behavior has been the most common focus of research on the influence of peers and friends in adolescence. However, as we saw in Chapter 8, this research has shown that the role of friends' influence in adolescents' risk behavior is considerably more complicated than originally supposed. In particular, studies have shown that similarity between friends in their risk behavior is due both to selective association and to friends' influence. That is, young people tend to seek out friends who are like themselves—in their tendencies for risk behavior as

Most adolescent risk behavior takes place in the company of friends.

well as in other respects—but if they remain friends, they tend to influence each other; that is, they become more alike in their levels of risk behavior (Brown, 2004; Jaccard et al., 2005; Rose, 2002).

In studies of delinquency, friends' influence has been argued to play an especially strong role in "socialized delinquency" (Dishion & Dodge, 2005; Quay, 1987), which involves committing acts of delinquency as part of a group or gang. **Socialized delinquents** rarely commit crimes alone, and other than their criminal activity they are very similar to nondelinquent adolescents in their psychological functioning and family relationships. In contrast, **unsocialized delinquents** usually have few friends and commit their crimes alone.

Socialized delinquents commit offenses, despite being similar in many ways to adolescents who do not, because their friendship group or gang both supports and rewards illegal behavior (Dishion et al., 1999; Dishion & Dodge, 2005). Although they may be alienated from school and other adult institutions, they tend to form close interpersonal relationships within their delinquent friendship group. They see their delinquent behavior not as immoral or deviant but as a way of finding excitement, proving their manly bravery, and demonstrating their support and loyalty to one another. Adolescents who are gang members often fit this profile of socialized delinquents (Taylor et al., 2003).

A number of studies have explored the connections between family factors and peer factors in relation to risk behavior. Judith Brook and her colleagues (Brook et al., 1990; Brook, Brook, & Pahl, 2006; Kasen, Cohen, & Brook, 1998) have argued that the path to drug abuse in adolescence begins in early childhood with a lack of warmth from parents and a high level of conflict in the family. Children who experience this kind of family environment develop alienation and low self-control, which are expressed in adolescence through drug use and affiliation with drug-using peers. In contrast, experiencing close and supportive relationships with parents in childhood makes substance use less likely even in a peer environment where drug use is common. Other studies have also found that close relationships to parents in adolescence tend to be related to lower orientation to peers, which is in turn related to lower substance use (Bogenschneider et al., 1998; Kiesner & Kerr, 2004).

Gerald Patterson and his colleagues have developed a similar model to explain delinquency (Patterson, 1986; Dishion & Patterson, 2006; Granic & Patterson, 2006; Snyder, Reid, & Patterson, 2003). In their extensive longitudinal research, Patterson and colleagues have found that the first risk factors for delinquency begin in infancy, with an infant temperament that is aggressive and difficult. This kind of temperament is especially challenging for parents, and some respond not with the extra measure of love and patience that would be required to ameliorate it but with harsh, inconsistent, or permissive parenting. This family environment leads by middle childhood to the development of personality characteristics such as impulsiveness and low self-control, which makes friendships with most other children problematic. Children with these characteristics are often left with no one to have as friends but each other, and associations in friendship groups of aggressive and rejected children lead in turn to delinquency in adolescence.

Other Socialization Influences Family and peer factors have been the areas studied most in relation to risk behavior in adolescence, but some research also exists on the ways that other aspects of socialization are related to risk behavior, including school, neighborhood/community, and religious beliefs. School has been of interest because of the consistent finding that poor school performance is associated with a variety of types of risk behavior, especially substance use and delinquency (Bryant et al., 2003; Wilson & Herrnstein, 1985). However, problems in school have fared poorly as an explanation for risk behavior because tendencies toward the most serious and enduring involvement in risk behavior begin before children enter school (Moffitt, 1993, 2003, 2007).

socialized delinquents Delinquents who commit crimes in groups and are similar to non-delinquents in psychological functioning and family relationships.

unsocialized delinquents Delinquent adolescents who have few friends and commit their crimes alone.

Nevertheless, some studies have found that the overall school environment can have an influence on adolescents' risk behavior (Kasen et al., 1998). The classic study of British schools described in Chapter 10, by Michael Rutter and his colleagues (Rutter, 1983; Rutter et al., 1979), showed the influence of the school environment on delinquency. They studied early adolescents in 12 schools in London, beginning at age 10 and following them for 4 years. The results indicated that school climate had a significant effect on rates of delinquency, even after controlling for such influences as social class and family environment.

In addition to school climate, two other qualities of the school environments stood out as having the most positive effects. One was having an intellectual balance in the school that included a substantial proportion of bright and achievement-oriented students who identified with the aims and rules of school. These students tended to be leaders and discouraged misbehavior by setting norms for behavior that other students followed. The other important quality was what Rutter and his colleagues called the **ethos** of the school, meaning the school's prevailing belief system. A favorable ethos—one that emphasized the value of schoolwork, rewarded good performance, and established fair but firm discipline—was related to lower rates of delinquency through early adolescence.

Neighborhood and community factors have also been studied in relation to risk behavior in adolescence, particularly in relation to delinquency (Swenson et al., 2005). A number of classic studies in sociology focused on the ways that neighborhood factors promote or discourage delinquency (e.g., Whyte, 1943). These studies described how a sense of neighborhood identity and cohesion has the effect of discouraging delinquency. More recent studies on neighborhood and community factors have noted that high rates of residential mobility tend to be related to high rates of crime and delinquency, perhaps because when people move in and out of a neighborhood frequently, residents tend to have weaker attachments to their neighbors and less regard for neighborhood opinion (e.g., Sampson, Castellano, & Laub, 1981; Wilson, 1996). Also, neighborhood and community norms regarding drug use and the availability of drugs in a community have been found to be related to substance use in adolescence (Petraitis, Flay, & Miller, 1995).

Finally, in recent years religious beliefs have become a topic of interest in relation to risk behavior. Numerous studies have found that religiosity is inversely related to participation in risk behavior in adolescence and emerging adulthood (Nonnemaker, McNeely, & Blum, 2003; Smith and Denton, 2005; Steinman & Zimmerman, 2004). It may be that religious beliefs and religious participation, like good schools and authoritative parents, act as a **protective factor** that makes participation in risk behavior less likely. However, unlike with schools or family, with religious beliefs self-selection

Community norms regarding substance use influence adolescents' substance use.

has to be considered as a possible explanation. That is, it may be that it is not so much that religious involvement causes adolescents and emerging adults to be less likely to take part in risk behavior, but rather that young people who strive for a high standard of moral behavior are both less likely to be interested in risk behavior and more likely to be interested in religious involvement.

What Matters Most in Preventing Risk Behavior? The Add Health Study Among all the factors involved in adolescent risk behavior, which are most important? This question has been addressed by the most comprehensive study of adolescent risk behavior yet conducted, the National Longitudinal Survey of Adolescent Health (known for short as "Add Health"; Blum, Beuring, & Mann-Rinehart, 2000; Blum et al., 2000; Roche, Ahmed, & Blum, 2008). The study has included more than 12,000 adolescents from 7th to 12th grade in schools across the United States. Questions were asked not only about a wide range of risk behaviors—substance use, violence, sex, and suicidal behavior—but also about numerous aspects of adolescents' socialization environment, from family and friends to school and religious beliefs.

Like other studies, the Add Health study found that risk behavior was significantly related to family structure, SES, and ethnic background. Adolescents from single-parent families were more likely than other adolescents to engage in risk behavior. Adolescents from high-SES families were less likely to smoke but more likely to use alcohol. African American adolescents were less likely to use substances or consider suicide but more likely to have sexual intercourse and more likely to be involved in violent behavior.

However, the Add Health study found that these factors were only weakly related to risk behavior and explained only

---

ethos The beliefs about education that characterize a school as a whole.

protective factor Characteristics of young people that are related to lower likelihood of participation in risk behavior.

a small part of the variance. This means that simply knowing an adolescent's family structure, SES, or ethnic background would be of little use in predicting the adolescent's risk behavior. Far more important, and far more influential in predicting risk behavior, were socialization variables involving family, friends, school, and religious beliefs. Parental monitoring was an especially strong predictor of risk behavior; adolescents who spent more time "just hanging out with friends" without parental supervision were more likely to take part in risk behavior. As Robert Blum, the lead researcher in the study, noted, "the strong message to parents is that you need to be in your kid's life: know their friends, what their friends do, who their friends' parents are" (Zuckerman, 2001, p. 15).

Individual Factors in Risk Behavior

"I was good at [theft]. The intensity of being in someone else's room when they're sleeping, taking their jewelry, their money, and their car keys, right there while they're sleeping in the bed, and you're looking right over them. . . . It was real intense, it was a rush. You know, 'What can you get away with? How far can you push your limit?' I found out."

—Jack, age 18 (in Arnett, 1996, p. 4)

We have examined various aspects of socialization that have been found to promote or discourage risk behavior. Within any particular socialization context, what makes some young people more likely than others to participate in risk behavior? Given the same or similar types of family, peer, school, and community environments, some adolescents take part in risk behavior and others do not. Thus, in addition to socialization influences, a variety of individual factors need to be considered in relation to various types of risk behavior in adolescence and emerging adulthood.

One individual factor related to a variety of risk behaviors is aggressiveness. Aggressiveness is obviously related to delinquency and crime because many delinquent and criminal acts—destroying property, assault, rape—inherently involve aggressiveness (Wilson & Herrnstein, 1985). However, aggressiveness is also related to reckless driving behavior in the teens and 20s. Risky driving is often an expression of anger and hostility (Begg & Langley, 2004; Donovan, 1993; Donovan, Umlauf, & Salzberg, 1988). Aggressiveness also has been found to be related to substance use, for reasons that are not clear (Brook et al., 1986; Hayatbakhsh et al., 2008). Perhaps some adolescents use substances as a self-medication for aggressiveness, just as they do for anxiety and depression.

Another characteristic consistently related to risk behavior is sensation seeking. As discussed in Chapter 12, sensation seeking is a personality trait characterized by the degree to which a person seeks out *novelty* and *intensity* of experience (Arnett, 1994b; Zuckerman, 1995, 2003). Many types of risk behavior provide novelty and intensity of experience—for example, substance use leads to novel mental states, and breaking the law in delinquent and criminal acts

is often described in terms of the intensity of the experience (Lyng, 1991). For this reason, young people who are high in sensation seeking also are more likely to engage in a variety of risk behaviors, including substance use, risky driving, delinquency, and risky sexual behavior (Comeau, Stewart, & Loba, 2001; Hansen & Breivik, 2001; Hartos, Eitel, & Simons-Morton, 2002; van Beurden et al., 2005). Sensation seeking rises at puberty (Martin et al., 2002) and tends to be higher in the teens and early 20s than in adulthood, which helps explain why risk behavior is most common among the young (Arnett, 1994b; Romer & Hennessy, 2007; Zuckerman, 1995, 2003).

A third individual factor often related to risk behavior is *poor school achievement.* Although we have noted that future delinquents often exhibit problems even before they begin school, it has been a long-standing and consistent finding that poor school achievement is a predictor of delinquency (Moffitt, 1993, 2003, 2007; Wilson & Herrnstein, 1985). Poor school achievement has also been found in numerous studies to be related to substance use (Bryant et al., 2003; Kasen et al., 1998). To some extent, poor school achievement is a reflection of other characteristics. Sensation seeking (Zuckerman, 1995, 2003) and aggressiveness (Farrington & West, 1991; Moffitt, 2003) are related to poor school achievement, as well as to risk behavior. ADHD is related to poor school achievement and to delinquency (Farrington, 1989; Loeber et al., 2001; Moffitt, 1993). Low performance on intelligence tests is also related both to poor school achievement and to delinquency (Farrington, 1989; Moffitt & Silva, 1988). Although poor school achievement may not directly cause risk behavior, the fact that poor school achievement represents such a wide range of other problems makes it an especially strong predictor of risk behavior in adolescence.

Low impulse control, which means difficulty in exercising self-control, is another characteristic related to risk behaviors in adolescence such as substance use and delinquency (Cooper et al., 2003; De Li, 2004; Loeber et al., 2001). Low impulse control is often a reflection of a family environment that is either too harsh or too permissive (Dishion et al., 1991; Moffitt, 1993, 2003). Finally, the *optimistic bias* also contributes to a variety of risk behaviors. As discussed in Chapter 3, adolescents have a tendency to assume that accidents, diseases, and other misfortunes are more likely to happen to other people than to themselves (Weinstein, 1998). Thus, young people who participate in risk behavior tend to be more likely than others to believe that nothing bad will happen to them as a result of such behavior (Reyna & Farley, 2006).

For every one of the individual factors described here, males are more at risk than females. Males tend to be higher in aggressiveness (Bongers et al., 2004), higher in sensation seeking (Arnett, 1994b; Zuckerman, 2003), lower in school

low impulse control Difficulty in exercising self-control, often found to be related to risk behavior in adolescence.

achievement (Bryant et al., 2003), lower in impulse control (De Li, 2004), and higher in optimistic bias (Weinstein, 1989). Together, these gender differences in individual risk factors largely explain why males are more likely than females to engage in risk behavior during adolescence and emerging adulthood.

Culture and Risk Behavior So far we have been focusing on the American majority culture because that is the population that has been the focus of most research on risk behavior among young people. To what extent is young people's risk behavior a problem in cultures worldwide, and to what extent is it peculiar to American society? Schlegel and Barry (1991), in their analysis of 186 traditional cultures, concluded that "for boys but not for girls, adolescence tends to be the stage during which antisocial behavior most often occurs, if it occurs at all" (p. 39). (By "antisocial behavior" they meant behavior such as fighting and stealing.) However, they found notable evidence of adolescent antisocial behavior in *less than half* of the traditional cultures they studied. Thus, traditional cultures have less of a problem with antisocial behavior than cultures in the West, and antisocial behavior is especially rare among adolescent girls in traditional cultures, in part because they are usually monitored closely by adults.

American adolescents have higher rates of most types of risk behavior than adolescents in other Western countries. This is true for risky driving behavior, delinquency, and use of illegal drugs (Eisner, 2002; Heuveline, 2002). With regard to automobile driving, the main reason young people in other Western countries engage in less risky driving behavior is simply that they are much less likely to have access to automobiles. As noted earlier in the chapter, other Western countries typically have a minimum legal driving age of 18, rather than 16 as in the United States. Even after age 18, in most Western countries automobiles are heavily taxed and therefore extremely expensive, whereas public transportation is inexpensive, safe, and widely available. For these reasons, rates of automobile accidents and fatalities among young people in their teens and early 20s are considerably lower in other Western countries than they are in the United States (Eisner, 2002).

With regard to delinquency and crime, rates are substantially higher in the United States than in other Western countries for a wide variety of offenses, but especially for violent crimes (Heuveline, 2002). As shown in Figure 13.10, among young men aged 15 to 24 the homicide rate in the United States is 5 times as high as in France; 8 times as high as in Canada, Germany, or Italy; and 20 times as high as in Japan (PRB, 2002). High rates of violent crime in the United States appear to be due in part to higher rates of poverty. In poor urban areas of the United States, homicide rates among the young are appallingly high; homicide is the leading cause of death among young Blacks and Latinos (Baffour, 2007).

Another important reason for the high homicide rate among young people in the United States is the easy availability of firearms. Because of the widespread availability of

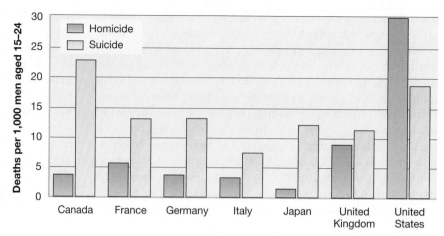

FIGURE 13.10 Deaths from homicide and suicide among men ages 15 to 24.

Source: PRB (2002), p. 15.

firearms in American society—an estimated 200 million—what might be a fistfight between young men in London or Tokyo easily becomes murder in Chicago or Washington, D.C.

As described earlier in the chapter, rates of alcohol and cigarette use are higher among adolescents and emerging adults in Europe than in the Canada and the United States, whereas for marijuana use the United States and Canada are higher (WHO, 2008). The higher European rates of alcohol use are partly attributable to the legal drinking age in European countries, which is 18 or younger, compared to 21 in the United States, but even more important are the cultural differences in how alcohol use is viewed. Alcohol use among adolescents and emerging adults in the United States is not strongly prohibited—the penalties for underage drinking are light and rarely enforced—but it is discouraged, and many high schools and colleges have programs to prevent alcohol use. In contrast, Europeans are less ambivalent about alcohol use, and drinking is an accepted part of social occasions for both young people and adults. This cultural difference is due partly to the conservative religious strain in American society, but also to the fact that in the United States the combination of alcohol use and driving is a greater problem. Because American adolescents usually begin driving at age 16 and most have regular access to a car, driving while intoxicated is more of a problem among adolescents and emerging adults in the United States than in Europe. Strict European laws also discourage driving while intoxicated, whereas in the United States the laws are more lenient and are less likely to be enforced.

Rates of cigarette smoking are lower among adolescents in the United States and Canada than in Europe, most likely because the governments in these two countries have waged large-scale public health campaigns against smoking, whereas European countries have not. Cigarette smoking among young people is of particular concern because in the long run it is the source of more illness and mortality than all illegal drugs combined and because the majority of persons who smoke begin in their early teens (Cummings, 2002). As for the higher rates of marijuana use among adolescents in the United States and Canada, the reasons for this difference are not clear.

Longitudinal studies of crime and delinquency go back far enough into the early part of the 20th century that the boys who originally took part in them have long since become men, and we have information on what became of their lives in adulthood. One of the most influential and informative of these studies was conducted by Sheldon and Eleanor Glueck, a husband-and-wife team of scholars who followed delinquent and nondelinquent boys in the Boston area from their teens until their early 30s. The study provides rich information on the factors involved in delinquency as well as the implications of delinquency for adult development.

The Gluecks' study began in the early 1940s with 1,000 Boston boys aged 10 to 17, including 500 delinquents and 500 nondelinquents (Glueck & Glueck, 1950). The delinquent boys were residents at correctional schools for delinquents. The nondelinquent boys were recruited from public schools, and they were not randomly selected but were matched case by case with the delinquent boys for age, ethnic group, IQ, and neighborhood socioeconomic status. The Gluecks chose this method because they wanted to be able to show that any differences between the two groups were not due to these preexisting characteristics. Boys in both groups grew up in family and neighborhood environments that were characterized by poverty and high exposure to delinquency and crime.

The Gluecks' study lasted 18 years, and their research team collected data on the boys at three times: adolescence (ages 10 to 17), emerging adulthood (ages 21 to 28), and young adulthood (ages 28 to 35). At each time, an abundance of information was collected. In adolescence, information was collected from the boys themselves as well as from parents, teachers, social workers, and local police. In the two follow-ups, information was collected from the young men and their families as well as from employers, neighbors, and officials in criminal justice and social welfare agencies. Ninety-two percent of the participants remained in the study through all three times of data collection, an exceptionally high rate across an 18-year period.

An enormous amount of information was collected in the study, and only the outlines of the results can be described here (see Glueck & Glueck, 1950, 1968; Sampson & Laub, 1994). Briefly, the Gluecks found that the key to delinquency lay in an interaction between constitutional factors and family environments. By "constitutional factors" they meant biological predispositions. The constitutional factors they found to be related to delinquency were body type and temperament. Delinquent adolescent boys were more likely than nondelinquents to have a "mesomorphic" body type, that is, a body that was stocky and muscular rather than rounded (endomorphic) or tall and slim (ectomorphic). Also, delinquents were more likely than nondelinquents to have had a difficult temperament as children. That is, their parents more often reported that as infants and children they cried often, were difficult to soothe when upset, and had irregular patterns of eating and sleeping.

With regard to family environment, delinquent boys were more likely to be from families in which one or both parents were neglectful or hostile toward them. Parents' discipline in the families of delinquents tended to be either permissive or inconsistent, alternating periods of neglect with outbursts of punishment. This is now a familiar pattern to scholars, but the Gluecks were among the first to establish systematically the relationship between parenting and outcomes in adolescence.

And how did the boys "turn out" once they reached their 20s and early 30s? For the most part, their behavior in adolescence was highly predictive of their later development. By age 25, the 500 boys in the delinquent group had been arrested for 7 homicides, 100 robberies, 172 burglaries, 225 larcenies, and numerous other offenses (Wilson & Herrnstein, 1985). These rates were more than five times as high as for the nondelinquent group. However, it was not just crime that was predicted by delinquent status in adolescence. In young adulthood, those who had been adolescent delinquents were four times as likely as nondelinquents to abuse alcohol, seven times as likely to have a pattern of unstable employment, three times as likely to be divorced, and far less likely to have finished high school (Sampson & Laub, 1990).

In sum, delinquent status in adolescence was a strong predictor of a wide range of serious future problems. However, not all of the adolescent delinquents went on to have difficulties in adulthood. For those who did not, job stability and attachment to spouse were the best predictors of staying out of trouble in adulthood (Sampson & Laub, 1990). Income itself was a poor predictor, but job stability made a difference. Similarly, simply getting married was a poor predictor by itself, but a close emotional attachment to a spouse made a positive difference.

The Gluecks' study has been criticized on methodological grounds. The most serious criticism is that the persons collecting data on the boys and their environments were not blind to the boys' status as delinquent or nondelinquent. This means that researchers who interviewed the boys' parents or conducted psychological interviews with the boys knew in advance whether a boy was part of the delinquent or the nondelinquent group. Because the conclusions for much of the study were based on interpretations from interviews rather than questionnaires or objective tests, the interpretations may have been biased by what the researchers knew about the boys in advance. However, the Gluecks' conclusions have stood the test of time quite well, and their study continues to be regarded as a classic of social science research.

Within the United States, substantial cultural/ethnic differences exist in rates of risk behavior. As noted earlier, Whites and Latinos have higher rates of substance use in adolescence than African Americans or Asian Americans (Gil et al., 1998; Grunbaum, 2004). African American and Latino adolescents are considerably more likely than White adolescents to be arrested for index crimes (Baffour, 2007). However, the higher crime rates among Blacks and Latinos are more a reflection of social class than of ethnicity or culture. Growing up in a family that has a low socioeconomic status (SES) is associated with a greater likelihood of delinquency for adolescents of all ethnic backgrounds, but African American and Latino adolescents are more likely than White adolescents to come from a low-SES family. In addition, African American adolescents are more likely than White adolescents to be arrested for similar crimes and tend to receive more severe penalties if found guilty (Fletcher, 2000).

Internalizing Problems

So far we have been discussing externalizing problems. Now we turn to the class of problems known as internalizing problems. We will focus on two of the most common types of these problems in adolescence and emerging adulthood: depression and eating disorders.

Depression

Depression, as a general term, means an enduring period of sadness. However, psychologists make distinctions between different levels of depression (Compas et al., 1998). **Depressed mood** is a term for an enduring period of sadness by itself, without any related symptoms. **Depressive syndrome** means an enduring period of sadness along with other symptoms such as frequent crying, feelings of worthlessness, and feeling guilty, lonely, or worried. The most serious form of depression is **major depressive disorder**. An episode of major depressive disorder includes the following specific symptoms (American Psychiatric Association, 1994):

1. Depressed or irritable mood for most of the day, nearly every day.
2. Reduced interest or pleasure in all or almost all activities, nearly every day.
3. Significant weight loss or gain, or decrease in appetite.
4. Insomnia or oversleeping.
5. Psychomotor agitation or retardation, observable by others.
6. Low energy or fatigue.
7. Feelings of worthlessness or inappropriate guilt.
8. Diminished ability to think or concentrate.
9. Recurrent thoughts of death, recurrent suicidal thoughts.

For a diagnosis of a major depressive episode, five or more of these symptoms must be present during a 2-week period and must represent a change from previous functioning. At least one of the symptoms must be depressed mood or reduced interest/pleasure.

Depressed mood is the most common kind of internalizing problem in adolescence. Several studies find that adolescents have higher rates of depressed mood than adults or children (Compas et al., 1998; Petersen et al., 1993; Saluja et al., 2004). Episodes of depressed mood before adolescence are relatively rare (Curry & Reinecke, 2003), although they do sometimes occur. The beginning of adolescence marks a steep increase in the pervasiveness of depressed mood. Studies of rates of depressed mood at different ages have concluded that there is a "midadolescence peak" in depressed mood (Petersen et al., 1993). Rates of depressed mood rise steeply from age 10 to about ages 15 to 17, then decline in the late teens and 20s.

A variety of studies have shown that the proportion of adolescents who report experiencing depressed mood within the past 6 months is about 35% (Petersen et al., 1993; Saluja et al., 2004). In contrast, rates of depressive syndrome and major depressive disorder among adolescents range in various studies from 3% to 7% (Achenbach et al., 1991; Cheung et al., 2005; Compas et al., 1993), which is about the same rate found in studies of adults.

Causes of Depression The causes of depression in adolescence and emerging adulthood differ somewhat depending on whether the diagnosis is depressed mood or the more serious forms of depression (depressive syndrome and depressive disorder). The most common causes of depressed mood tend to be common experiences among young people—conflict with friends or family members, disappointment or rejection in love, and poor performance in school (Costello et al., 2008; Larson & Richards, 1994).

THINKING CRITICALLY •••

Few studies have been conducted on depressed mood among emerging adults. How would you expect the sources of depressed mood in emerging adulthood to be similar to or different from the sources of depressed mood in adolescence?

depression An enduring period of sadness.

depressed mood An enduring period of sadness, without any other related symptoms of depression.

depressive syndrome An enduring period of sadness along with other symptoms such as frequent crying, feelings of worthlessness, and feeling guilty, lonely, or worried.

major depressive disorder Psychological diagnosis that entails depressed mood or reduced interest or pleasure in all or almost all activities, plus at least four other specific symptoms. Symptoms must be present over at least a 2-week period and must involve a change from previous functioning.

The causes of the more serious forms of depression are more complicated and less common. Studies have found that both genetic and environmental factors are involved (Glowinski et al., 2003; Petersen et al., 1993). Of course, both genetic and environmental influences are involved in most aspects of development, but the interaction of genes and environment is especially well established with respect to depression. One useful model of this interaction that has been applied to depression as well as to other mental disorders is the **diathesis-stress model** (Ingram & Smith, 2008). The theory behind this model is that mental disorders such as depression often begin with a *diathesis*, meaning a *preexisting vulnerability*. Often, this diathesis will have a genetic basis, but not necessarily. For example, being born prematurely is a diathesis for many physical and psychological problems in development, but it is not genetic. However, a diathesis is only a vulnerability, a potential for problems. Expression of that vulnerability requires the existence of a stress as well, meaning *environmental conditions* that interact with the diathesis to produce the disorder.

The role of a genetic diathesis in depression has been established in twin studies and in adoption studies. Identical twins have a much higher *concordance rate* for depression—meaning the probability that if one gets the disorder, the other gets it as well—than fraternal twins do (Glowinski et al., 2003; Nurnberger & Gershon, 1992). This is true even for identical twins who are raised in different homes and who thus have different family environments. Also, adopted children whose biological mothers have experienced depression are more likely than other adopted children to develop depression themselves (Wender et al., 1986).

There is also evidence that the diathesis for depression may be stronger when the onset of depressive disorder occurs in childhood or adolescence rather than adulthood (Zalsman et al., 2006). In Moffitt's Dunedin study, described earlier in the chapter, people who were diagnosed with depressive disorder in adolescence (ages 11 to 15) were more likely than those diagnosed in emerging adulthood (ages 18 to 26) to have experienced prenatal difficulties and early deficits in the development of motor skills (Jaffee, Moffitt, Caspi, Fombonne, Poulton, & Martin, 2002). Such early difficulties suggest that they had a neurological diathesis for depression that was expressed when the stresses of adolescence arrived.

What sort of stresses bring out the diathesis for depression in adolescence? A variety of family and peer factors have been found to be involved. In the family, factors contributing to depression in adolescence include emotional unavailability of parents, high family conflict, economic difficulties, and parental divorce (Forkel & Silbereisen, 2001; Hammack et al., 2004). With respect to peers, less contact with friends and more experiences of rejection contribute to depression over time (Vernberg, 1990). Unfortunately, poor peer relationships tend to be self-perpetuating for depressed adolescents because other adolescents tend to avoid being around adolescents who are depressed (Petersen et al., 1993). Studies on depression in adolescence have also taken the approach of calculating an overall stress score, which usually includes stress in the family and in peer relationships as well as stresses such as changing schools and experiencing pubertal changes. These studies find that overall stress is related to depression in adolescence (Allgood-Merton et al., 1990; Compas & Grant, 1993; Rubin et al., 1992).

Gender Differences in Depression One of the factors that constitutes the highest risk for depression in adolescence is simply being female. In childhood, when depression is relatively rare, rates are actually higher among boys. However, in adolescence the rates become substantially higher among females, and they remain higher among females throughout adulthood, for depressed mood as well as major depressive disorder (Curry & Reinecke, 2003; Hammack et al., 2004; Hoffman et al., 2003). What explains the gender difference in adolescent depression?

A variety of explanations have been proposed. There is little evidence that biological differences (such as the earlier entry of females into puberty) can explain it (Petersen, 2000). Some scholars have suggested that the female gender role itself leads to depression in adolescence. As we have discussed in earlier chapters, because of the gender intensification that takes place in adolescence (Hill & Lynch, 1983), concerns about physical attractiveness become a primary concern, especially for girls. There is evidence that adolescent girls who have a poor body image are more likely than other girls to be depressed (Allgood-Merton et al., 1990; Marcotte, Forton, Potrin, & Papillon, 2002).

A study of adolescents and emerging adults in Norway is especially enlightening on this issue (Wichstrom, 1999). The study was on a representative national sample of young people aged 12 to 20. At age 12 no gender difference in depressed

Depressed mood peaks in midadolescence.

diathesis-stress model A theory that mental disorders result from the combination of a diathesis (biological vulnerability) and environmental stresses.

mood was found. However, by age 14 girls were more likely to report depressed mood, and this gender difference remained stable through age 20. Statistical analyses showed that the gender difference could be explained by girls' responses to the physical changes of puberty. As their bodies changed, they became increasingly dissatisfied with their weight and their body shape, and that dissatisfaction was linked to depressed mood. Depressed mood in girls was also related to an increase in describing themselves in terms of feminine gender role traits of the kind we discussed in Chapter 5: shy, soft-spoken, tender, and so on. In contrast, depressed mood was not related to masculine gender role identification in boys. A recent American study reported similar findings, indicating that girls' body shame in early adolescence preceded an increase in the prevalence of depressed mood (Grabe, Hyde, & Lindberg, 2007). Just as in the Norwegian study, there was no gender difference in depressed mood in early adolescence, but girls' greater body shame led to greater prevalence of depressed mood by mid-adolescence.

Other explanations have also been offered. Stress is related to depression in adolescence, and adolescent girls generally report experiencing more stress than adolescent boys do (Cyranowski et al., 2003; Petersen, Kennedy, & Sullivan, 1991). Also, when faced with the beginning of a depressed mood, males are more likely to distract themselves (and forget about it), whereas females have a greater tendency to ruminate on their depressed feelings and thereby amplify them (Grant et al., 2004; Jose & Brown, 2008; Nolen-Hoeksema, Wisco, & Lyubomirsky, 2008). Adolescent girls are more likely than adolescent boys to devote their thoughts and feelings to their personal relationships, and these relationships can be a source of distress and sadness (Gore, Aseltine, & Colten, 1993; Larson & Richards, 1994).

Males and females generally differ in their responses to stress and conflict, which helps explain both the greater tendency toward externalizing problems in boys and the greater tendency toward internalizing problems in girls (Gjerde & Westenberg, 1998). In adolescence as well as in childhood and adulthood, males tend to respond to stress and conflict by directing their feelings *outward*—in the form of externalizing behavior (Gjerde, Block, & Block, 1988; Nolen-Hoeksma & Girgus, 1994). Females, in contrast, tend to respond to these problems by turning their distress *inward,* in the form of critical thoughts *toward themselves* (Calvete & Cardeñoso, 2005). Thus, studies have found that *even when exposed to the same amount of stress* as adolescent boys, adolescent girls are more likely to respond by becoming depressed (Ge et al., 1996). Furthermore, depression in adolescence is often accompanied for boys (but not for girls) by externalizing problems such as fighting and disobedience (Block, Gjerde, & Block, 1991; Gjerde et al., 1988; Loeber et al., 1998).

Treatments for Depression Just because depression in adolescence is common does not mean that it should be ignored or viewed as something that will go away eventually, especially when it persists over an extended period or reaches the level of depressive syndrome or major depressive disorder. Depressed adolescents are at risk for a variety of other problems, including school failure, delinquency, and suicide (Compas et al., 1998; Fleming, Boyle, & Offord, 1993). For many adolescents, symptoms of depression that begin in adolescence persist into emerging adulthood (Gjerde & Westenberg, 1998). Symptoms of depression in adolescence should be taken seriously, and treatment provided when necessary.

For adolescents as for adults, the two main types of treatment for depression are antidepressant medications and psychotherapy. Studies of the effectiveness of antidepressant medications typically use a **placebo design**, meaning that all of the depressed adolescents take pills but only the pills taken by adolescents in the treatment group contain the drug. Adolescents in the control group take a *placebo*, that is, a pill that does not contain any medication, although the adolescents do not know this.

Recent studies indicate that newly developed antidepressants such as Prozac are often effective in treating adolescent depression (Bostic et al., 2005; Brent, 2004; Cohen et al., 2004; Michael & Crowley, 2002). For example, in one study, adolescents diagnosed with major depressive disorder were randomly assigned to take either Prozac or a placebo for 8 weeks (Emslie, Heiligenstein, & Wagner, 2002). At the end of this period, symptoms of depression were significantly improved in 41% of the treatment group but only 20% of the control (placebo) group.

However, there is also disturbing evidence that antidepressant medications, including Prozac, may increase suicidal thinking and behavior among some depressed adolescents (Cheung et al., 2004). Researchers in this area agree that when antidepressants are used with depressed adolescents, parents and adolescents should be fully informed of the possible risks, and the adolescents should be monitored closely for evidence of adverse effects (Brent, 2004; Bostic et al., 2005; Cheung et al., 2004). Suicidal thinking and behavior are lower among depressed adolescents when antidepressants are combined with psychotherapy than when they are used alone (Treatment for Adolescents with Depression Study Team, 2007).

Psychotherapy for adolescent depression takes a variety of forms, including individual therapy, group therapy, and skills training (Bostic et al., 2005; Petersen et al., 1993). Studies that have randomly assigned depressed adolescents to either a treatment group (which received psychotherapy) or a control group (which did not) have found that therapy tends to be effective in reducing the symptoms of depres-

---

placebo design Research design in which some persons in a study receive medication and others receive placebos, which are pills that contain no medication.

cognitive-behavior therapy (CBT) An approach to treating psychological disorders that focuses on changing negative ways of thinking and practicing new ways of interacting with others.

negative attributions Beliefs that one's current unhappiness is permanent and uncontrollable.

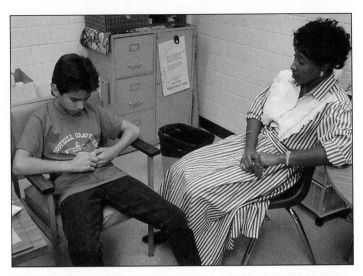

Psychotherapy is often effective in treating young people's depression.

sion (Bostic et al., 2005; Kahn et al., 1990; Lewinsohn et al., 1990).

One especially effective type of therapy for depression is **cognitive-behavior therapy (CBT)** (Gaynor et al., 2003; Treatment for Adolescents with Depression Study Team, 2007). This approach describes depression as characterized by **negative attributions**, that is, negative ways of explaining what happens in one's life. Typically, young people who are depressed believe their situation is *permanent* ("It's never going to get better") and *uncontrollable* ("My life is awful and there's nothing I can do about it"). Depressed people also have a tendency for *rumination*, which means they dwell on the things that are wrong with their lives and brood about how worthless they feel and how pointless life seems. As noted earlier, one of the explanations for the gender difference in depression is that girls and women tend to ruminate more than boys and men.

The goal of CBT, then, is to help the young person recognize the cognitive habits that are promoting depression and work to change those habits (Kaufman et al., 2005; Persons, Davidson, & Tompkins, 2001). The therapist actively challenges the negative attributions, so that the client will examine them critically and begin to see them as distortions of reality. In addition to changing cognitive habits, CBT works on changing behavior. For example, the therapist and client might engage in role playing, where the therapist pretends to be the client's parent, or spouse, or colleague at work. Through role playing the client is able to practice new ways of interacting. People who have received CBT are less likely than those who have received antidepressant drugs to relapse when the treatment is over, indicating that the new ways of thinking and interacting endure beyond the therapeutic period (Persons et al., 2001; Rohde et al., 2005).

The combination of the newest medications and CBT appear to be the most effective approach to treating adolescent depression. In one recent major study of 12- to 17-year-olds at 13 sites across the United States who had been diagnosed with major depression, 71% of the adolescents who received both Prozac and CBT experienced an improvement in their symptoms (Treatment for Adolescents with Depression Study Team, 2004, 2007). Improvement rates for the other groups were 61% for Prozac alone, 43% for CBT alone, and 35% for the placebo group.

Suicide

"When Sandy told me she wanted to break up, I thought there was no point in going on. I loved her so much. I wanted to spend the rest of my life with her. So I started thinking about killing myself. I imagined how I could do it and what kind of note I'd leave my parents. Then I started thinking about my parents and my little sister, and I thought of them at the funeral crying and being so sad, and I knew I couldn't go through with it. I realized I didn't really want to die; I just wanted everything to be okay again."

— Donnie, age 16 (in Bell, 1998, p. 176)

One reason for taking young people's depression seriously is that it is a risk factor for suicide. Suicide attempts are usually preceded by symptoms of depression (Pfeffer, 2006; Spirito & Overholser, 2003). However, often young people's suicide attempts take place as the symptoms of depression appear to be abating. At the depths of depression, young people are often too dispirited to engage in the planning required to commit suicide. As they improve slightly, they remain depressed but now have enough energy and motivation to make a suicide attempt. Making a plan to commit suicide may also raise the mood of deeply depressed young people because they may believe that the suicide will mean an end to all the problems they feel are plaguing them.

Among American adolescents in grades 9–12, 24% report that they have seriously considered suicide and 3% have actually made an attempt (Waldrop et al., 2007). Suicide is the third most common cause of death among young people aged 15 to 19, after automobile accidents and homicide (Grunbaum, 2004; Mazza, 2007). The current suicide rate among American teens is *four times* the suicide rate among teens in the 1950s (Oltmanns & Emery, 2006). The reason for this increase is not well understood. The suicide rate among emerging adults aged 20 to 24 also increased during this time and is nearly twice as high as among 15- to 19-year-olds (CDC, 2007). Rates of suicide among young people are substantially higher in Canada and the United States than in most other industrialized countries, as Figure 13.10 illustrates (p. 380). Even though suicide rates among American adolescents have declined substantially since 1990 (CDC, 2007), they remain higher than a half century ago and higher than those in other industrialized countries.

There are substantial ethnic differences in adolescent suicide rates. Rates of suicide in adolescence and emerging adulthood are higher among Whites than among Blacks, and highest of all among Native Americans (Colucci & Martin, 2007). However, suicide rates rose alarmingly among young Black males in the 1990s and now nearly equal the rates for young White males (Joe & Marcus, 2003). The reasons for this increase are not known.

Suicide rates among young people are highest in countries where guns are easy to obtain.

Sharp gender differences also exist in rates of suicide and suicide attempts. Females are about four times as likely as males to attempt suicide in adolescence and emerging adulthood, but males are about four times as likely as females actually to kill themselves (Oltmanns & Emery, 2006). These gender differences exist in adulthood as well. The higher rate of attempts among females is probably a consequence of their higher rates of depression (Wichstrom & Rossow, 2002). The reason for the higher rate of completed suicides among males seems to be due mainly to gender differences in the methods used. Males are more likely to use guns or hang themselves, and these methods are more deadly than the method of taking poison or pills that is more commonly used by females in their suicide attempts (CDC, 2007). In a study comparing suicide rates among young people in 34 countries (Johnson, Krug, & Potter, 2000), rates were highest in countries where guns were most easily available.

Other than depression, what are the risk factors for suicide? One major factor for adolescents is *family disruption*. Attempted and completed suicide has frequently been found to be related to a family life that is chaotic, disorganized, high in conflict, and low in warmth (Brent & Mann, 2003; Breton, Tousignant, Bergeron, & Berthiaume, 2002; Wagner & Cohen, 1997). Furthermore, an adolescent's suicide is often preceded by a period of months in which family problems have worsened (Brent et al., 1993; de Wilde et al., 1992). Adoption and twin studies indicate that families also contribute genetic vulnerability to suicide, via susceptibility to major depression and other mental illnesses (Brent & Melhem, 2007).

In addition to family risk factors, suicidal adolescents often have substance abuse problems (Wolpers et al., 2007), perhaps as an attempt at self-medication for distress over their family problems and their depression. Also, suicidal adolescents have usually experienced problems in their relationships outside the family. Because they often come from families where they receive little in the way of emotional nurturance, suicidal adolescents may be more vulnerable to the effects of experiences such as school failure, loss of a boyfriend or girlfriend, or feelings of being rejected by their peers (Maris, Silverman, & Canetto, 1997).

Nevertheless, most adolescents who experience family disruption or substance use problems never attempt or commit suicide (Brent & Mann, 2006). How can the adolescents at most serious risk be identified? One group of researchers used interviews with family members and friends to identify three different pathways among adolescents who had committed suicide (Fortune et al., 2007). The largest group had experienced years of difficulty in relations with family, friends, and teachers. They had attempted suicide previously and had communicated their suicidal intentions and plans to friends and family. A second, midsized, group had struggled with severe mental illness such as major depression or bipolar disorder. The third and smallest group consisted of young people who had previously been functioning well but experienced an acute crisis that led to the suicide, without apparent mental illness or previous suicidal intention. However, even in this group two out of five communicated specific suicidal intent in the weeks before their death.

Other studies concur that in almost all cases, adolescent suicide takes place not in response to a single stressful or painful event but only after a series of difficulties extending over months or even years (Spirito & Overholser, 2003). It is rare for suicidal adolescents to show no warning signs of emotional or behavioral problems prior to attempting suicide (see Table 13.1). Often, they have made efforts to address the problems in their lives, and the failure of these efforts has sent them on a downward spiral that deepened their hopelessness and led them to suicide.

TABLE 13.1 Early Warning Signs of Adolescent Suicide

1. Direct suicide threats or comments such as "I wish I were dead"; "My family would be better off without me"; "I have nothing to live for."

2. A previous suicide attempt, no matter how minor. Four out of five people who commit suicide have made at least one previous attempt.

3. Preoccupation with death in music, art, and personal writing.

4. Loss of a family member, pet, or boy/girlfriend through death, abandonment, or breakup.

5. Family disruptions such as unemployment, serious illness, relocation, or divorce.

6. Disturbances in sleeping and eating habits and in personal hygiene.

7. Declining grades and lack of interest in school or hobbies that had previously been important.

8. Drastic changes in behavior patterns, such as a quiet, shy person becoming extremely gregarious.

9. Pervasive sense of gloom, helplessness, and hopelessness.

10. Withdrawal from family members and friends and feelings of alienation from significant others.

11. Giving away prized possessions and otherwise "getting their affairs in order."

12. Series of "accidents" or impulsive, risk-taking behaviors. Drug or alcohol abuse, disregard for personal safety, taking dangerous dares.

Sources: Brent & Melhem (2007); Pfeffer (2006).

Adolescents who attempt suicide are at high risk for future attempts and for completed suicide (Pfeffer, 2006). In one study of attempters, at a 3-month follow-up assessment 45% reported continued suicidal thoughts and 12% reported a repeat attempt (Spirito et al., 2003). As with depression, the most effective treatments for suicidal adolescents combine CBT with antidepressants (Donaldson, Spirito, & Overholser, 2003).

Eating Disorders

"At 102 pounds I thought I would be happy. But when I lost another two pounds, I was even happier. By the time I was down to 98 pounds, I stopped getting my period. . . . Also, my hair, which was normally healthy and shiny, became very brittle and dull, and it started falling out. . . . [My skin] took on a yellowish tone that on me looked sick, but I didn't care. I thought I looked better than I ever had in my whole life."

—Alicia (in Bell, 1998, p. 191)

Even when they are so thin they risk starving to death, anorexic girls see themselves as "too fat."

Adolescents find that people in their environment, such as peers and parents, respond differently to them as they show outward signs of reaching sexual maturity. These responses from others, along with their own self-reflection, lead to changes in the way adolescents think about their bodies.

For many adolescents, changes in the way they think about their bodies are accompanied by changes in the way they think about food. Girls, in particular, pay more attention to the food they eat once they reach adolescence, and worry more about eating too much and getting "fat" (Nichter, 2001). Presented with a cultural ideal that portrays the ideal female body as slim, at a time when their bodies are biologically tending to become less slim and more rounded, many of them feel distressed at the changes taking place in their body shape, and they attempt to resist or at least modify those changes. Sixty percent of American adolescent girls and 30% of boys believe they weigh too much, even though 15% of girls and 16% of boys are actually overweight by medical standards (CDC, 2008).

This dissatisfaction exists far more often among girls than among boys (Vincent & McCabe, 2000). Boys are much less likely to believe they are overweight and much more likely to be satisfied with their bodies (Walcott et al., 2003). Even long before adolescence, girls are more likely to worry about becoming overweight and to desire to be thinner than they are (McKnight Investigators, 2003). Body dissatisfaction among girls increases during the teens and continues through emerging adulthood and beyond (Rosenblum & Lewis, 1999). In fact, extreme weight-loss behaviors among adolescent girls, such as fasting, "crash dieting," and skipping meals, are related to their mothers' own extreme weight-loss behavior (Benedikt, Wertheim, & Love, 1998; Nichter, 2001). Exposed to this cultural emphasis on slimness as part of social and sexual attractiveness for women, some girls go to extremes in controlling their food intake and develop eating disorders. About 90% of eating disorders occur among females (Reijonen et al., 2003).

The two most common eating disorders are **anorexia nervosa** (intentional self-starvation) and **bulimia** (binge eating combined with purging [intentional vomiting]). About 1 of every 200 American adolescents has anorexia nervosa and about 3% have bulimia (McKnight Investigators, 2003). About half of anorexics are also bulimic, meaning that they avoid food except for episodes of bingeing and purging (Polivy et al., 2003). Most cases of eating disorders have their onset among females in their teens and early 20s (Reijonen et al., 2003). Eating disorders are more prevalent among White American girls than in other American ethnic groups (Hoek, 2006).

Far more prevalent than full-fledged eating disorders are eating disordered symptoms (including fasting for 24 hours or more, use of diet products, purging, and use of laxatives). According to a national U.S. study, about 20% of American adolescent girls and 10% of boys in grades 9–12 report engaging in eating disordered behavior in the past 30 days (CDC, 2008). Similar findings have been reported in other Western countries. In a national study of German 11- to 17-year-olds, one third of girls and 15% of boys reported

---

anorexia nervosa Eating disorder characterized by intentional self-starvation.

bulimia An eating disorder characterized by episodes of binge eating followed by purging (self-induced vomiting).

Scholars generally view anorexia nervosa as a modern disorder, resulting primarily from current cultural pressures for young women to be thin. However, the phenomenon of young women voluntarily, willfully reducing their food intake, even to the point of self-starvation, has a surprisingly long history in the West, extending back many centuries. An examination of that history, with its illuminating similarities to and differences from present-day anorexia, is provided by Dutch scholars Walter Vandereycken and Ron Van Deth (1994) in their book *From Fasting Saints to Anorexic Girls: A History of Self-Starvation*.

Fasting, involving partial or total abstinence from food, has long been a part of both Eastern and Western religions. It has been undertaken for a variety of purposes—to purify the body while engaging in prayer, to demonstrate the person's elevation of spiritual concerns over bodily needs, or as a sign of penance and remorse for sins. Fasting has been a part of the religious ideal in the Eastern religions of Hinduism and Buddhism for millennia. In ancient Egypt, Pharaohs fasted for days before important decisions and religious celebrations. In the Bible, Moses and Jesus undertake periods of fasting. Fasting was required for all believers during the first millennium of the Christian Church, at various times of the year including the period prior to Christmas. It remains a requirement of Islam, during the yearly holy period of Ramadan.

It was only from the 12th century onward that religious fasting in the West became associated mainly with young women. Why this happened when it did is not entirely clear, but it appears to be linked to females' being allowed greater participation in church life. For both males and females during the medieval period, religious faith was demonstrated in ways that seem extreme from the modern perspective. Men would often demonstrate their piety by such practices as self-flagellation; piercing their tongues, cheeks, or other body parts with iron pins; or sleeping on beds of thorns or iron points. For women, in contrast, extreme fasting became the characteristic path to holiness.

Young women who engaged in extreme fasting often gained great fame and were regarded by their contemporaries with reverence and awe. For example, in the 13th century an English girl became known far and wide as "Joan the Meatless" for reputedly abstaining from all food and drink except on Sundays, when she fed only on the morsel of bread distributed as part of the communion ritual. Many of these young women became anointed as saints by the Church, although official Church policy discouraged extreme fasting as detrimental to physical and mental well-being. In the 16th and 17th centuries, Catholic officials sharply tightened the rules for proving fasting "miracles," in response to exposed cases of fraud as well as concern over the health of girls seeking sainthood, and extreme fasting lost its religious allure.

Extreme fasting as a commercial spectacle now arose in place of extreme religious fasting. From the 16th through the 19th century, young women who had supposedly fasted for months or even years were exhibited at fairs. Their renown now came not from the piety their fasting demonstrated but from the way their fasting supposedly enabled them to transcend the requirements of nature. When these "miraculous maidens" were

---

eating disorder symptoms (Herpetz-Dahlmann et al., 2008). In Finland, a large study of 14- to 15-year-olds found eating disordered behavior among 24% of girls and 16% of boys (Hautala et al., 2008).

For a diagnosis of anorexia nervosa, food intake is reduced so much that the person loses at least 15% of body weight (Roberto et al., 2008). As weight loss continues, it eventually results in **amenorrhea**, which means that menstruation ceases. Hair becomes brittle and may begin to fall out, and the skin develops an unhealthy, yellowish pallor. As anorexics become increasingly thin, they frequently develop physical problems that are symptoms of their starvation, such as constipation, high sensitivity to cold, and low blood pressure.

One of the most striking symptoms of anorexia is the cognitive distortion of body image (Bowers et al., 2003; Striegel-Moore & Franko, 2006). The reduction in food intake is accompanied by an intense fear of gaining weight, a fear that persists even when the person has lost so much weight as to be in danger of literally starving to death. Young women with anorexia sincerely believe themselves to be too fat, even when they have become so thin that their lives are threatened. Standing in front of a mirror with them and pointing out how emaciated they look does no good—the anorexic looks in the mirror and sees a fat person, no matter how thin she is.

Bulimia is an eating disorder characterized by *binge eating* and *purging* (Striegel-Moore & Franko, 2006). Like anorexics, bulimics have strong fears that their bodies will become big and fat (Bowers et al., 2003). Bulimics engage in binge eating, which means eating a large amount of food in a short time. Then they purge themselves; that is, they use laxatives or induce vomiting to get rid of the food they have just eaten during a binge episode. Bulimics often suffer damage to their teeth from repeated vomiting. Unlike anorexics, bulimics typically maintain a normal weight because they have more or less normal eating patterns in between their episodes of bingeing and purging. Another

amenorrhea Cessation of menstruation, sometimes experienced by girls whose body weight falls extremely low.

put to the test in conditions where they could be monitored closely, some starved to death trying to prove their legitimacy, whereas others were exposed as frauds—one such young woman was found to have sewn a substantial quantity of gingerbread into the hem of her dress!

During this same period, cases of self-starvation received increasing attention from physicians. The first medical description of anorexia nervosa was made by the British physician Richard Morton in 1689. All of the characteristics of Morton's clinical description of the disorder remain part of the clinical diagnosis of anorexia nervosa in the present, over 3 centuries later:

1. Occurs primarily in females in their teens and 20s;
2. Characterized by striking emaciation as a consequence of markedly decreased intake of food;
3. Often accompanied by constipation and amenorrhea (absence of menstruation);
4. Affected persons usually lack insight into the illness (that is, they do not believe anything is wrong with them); consequently, treatment is resisted;
5. No physical cause is responsible for the symptoms; they are psychological in origin.

Although these symptoms still characterize anorexia nervosa, it was only from the early 19th century onward that the disorder became motivated by a desire to conform to cultural standards of female attractiveness. In the early 19th century, the standard of beauty for young women in the West became the "hourglass figure," characterized by a substantial bosom and hips and the slimmest waist possible. In pursuit of this figure young women had themselves laced tightly into corsets (often made of whalebone or some other unforgiving material), ignoring the physicians who warned against the unhealthiness of the fashion. By the early 20th century, corsets had gone out of fashion, but in their place came an ideal of the female form as slim all over, not just the waist but the bosom and hips as well—not unlike the ideal that exists today.

That this thin ideal motivated self-starvation among girls is evident from clinical reports of the time, for example, by this late-19th-century physician who, while examining an anorexic patient, "found that she wore on her skin, fashioned very tight around her waist, a rose-colored ribbon. He obtained the following confidence: the ribbon was a measure which the waist was not to exceed. 'I prefer dying of hunger to becoming as big as mamma'" (Vandereycken & Deth, 1994, p. 171).

Although fasting saints may seem a long way from anorexic girls, Vandereycken and Deth (1994) point out the striking similarities. In both cases the self-starvers were striving for an elusive perfection—the fasting girls for sainthood and the anorexic girls for the feminine ideal, a kind of secular sainthood—and typically their perfectionism extended into all aspects of their lives, not just their eating habits. In both cases, their abnormal eating patterns were often evident in childhood before developing into a fixed pattern in adolescence. And in both cases, the phenomenon reached its peak in the late teens and early twenties, sometimes with fatal consequences.

difference from anorexics is that bulimics do not regard their eating patterns as normal. Bulimics view themselves as having a problem and often hate themselves in the aftermath of their binge episodes.

Studies of anorexics and bulimics provide evidence that these eating disorders have cultural roots. First, eating disorders are more common in cultures that emphasize slimness as part of the female physical ideal, especially Western countries (Gowen et al., 1999; Walcott, Pratt, & Patel, 2003). Second, eating disorders are most common among females who are part of the middle to upper socioeconomic classes, which place more emphasis on female slimness than lower classes do. Third, most eating disorders occur among females in their teens and early 20s, which is arguably when gender intensification and cultural pressures to comply with a slim female physical ideal are at their strongest. Fourth, girls who read magazines such as *Seventeen*, which contain numerous ads and articles featuring thin models, are especially likely to strive to be thin themselves and to engage in eating disordered behavior (Utter, Neumark-Sztainer, Wall, & Story, 2003).

Although many girls in cultures that emphasize a thin female ideal strive for thinness themselves, only a small percentage actually have an eating disorder. What factors lead some young females but not others to develop an eating disorder? In general, the same factors are involved for both anorexia and bulimia (Shisslak & Crago, 2001). One factor appears to be a general susceptibility to internalizing disorders. Females who have an eating disorder are also more likely than other females to have other internalizing disorders, such as depression and anxiety disorders (Johnson, Cohen, Kasen, & Brook, 2002; Striegel-Moore et al., 2003; Swinbourne & Touyz, 2007). Eating disordered behavior is also related to substance use, especially cigarette smoking, binge drinking, and use of inhalants (Pisetsky et al., 2008).

THINKING CRITICALLY •••

What other causes of eating disorders would you hypothesize, besides the ones stated here?

Eating disorders are highest in cultures that prize thinness as attractive in females.

spite being emaciated, and on changing patterns of eating behavior (Bowers et al., 2003; Gore, Vander Wal, & Thelen, 2001). However, these same cognitive distortions lead many adolescents with eating disorders to deny they have a problem and resist attempts to help them (Fisher, Schneider, Burns, Symons, & Mandel, 2001). Perhaps for this reason, CBT has been found to be no more effective than other types of individual therapy in treating eating disorders (Bulik et al., 2007). Many adolescents get no treatment at all; in one study, only 22% of the adolescents with eating disorders had received treatment within the past year (Johnson et al., 2002).

Even for adolescents who do receive treatment, the success of treating anorexia and bulimia is often limited. About two thirds of anorexics treated in hospital programs improve, but one third remain chronically ill despite treatment and remain at high risk for chronic health problems or even death from the disorder (Steinhausen et al., 2003). Similarly, although treatments for bulimia are successful in about 50% of cases, there are repeated relapses in the other 50% of cases, and recovery is often slow (Garner & Garfinkel, 1997; Oltmanns & Emery, 2006). Emerging adult women with a history of adolescent eating disorders often continue to show significant impairments in mental and physical health, self-image, and social functioning even after their eating disorder has faded (Berkman, Lohr, & Bulik, 2007; Striegel-Moore, Seeley, & Lewinsohn, 2003). About 10% of anorexics eventually die from starvation or from physical problems caused by their weight loss, the highest mortality rate of any psychiatric disorder (Polivy et al., 2003; Striegel-Moore & Franko, 2006).

Resilience

"Hopefully with what I've got behind me and the experiences I've had, I'm equipped to make better judgments to push my life in a better direction. . . . There's a lot of bad things that have happened in my life, and I just kind of feel like, anymore, they kind of roll off."
—Jeremy, age 25 (in Arnett, 2004, p. 193)

"Mom was good at verbal abuse, and Dad was good at the physical. . . . It's always been bad, and now that I've moved out it's just not there, which I guess is good. I don't have to deal with it on a daily basis. . . . There's been a lot of pain and a lot of hurt, but I've really grown from it. It's made me the person who I am today."
—Bridget, age 23 (in Arnett, 2004, pp. 198, 200)

This chapter has covered a wide range of problems that adolescents and emerging adults may have, together with the risk factors related to their problems, such as poverty, poor family relationships, and inadequate schools. However, there are also many adolescents and emerging adults who face dire

Treatments for Eating Disorders Because anorexia is eventually life threatening, a hospital-based program is usually recommended as a first step to begin to restore the person's physical functioning (Cleaves & Latner, 2008). In addition to physical treatment, a variety of treatment approaches have been found to be effective for anorexia and bulimia, including family therapy (to address family issues that may contribute to or be caused by the problem) and individual therapy (Polivy et al., 2003). There is some evidence that, for adolescents, family therapy is more effective than individual treatment (Le Grange, Lock, & Dymek, 2003; Paulson-Karlsson et al., 2009). A variety of drug therapies have been tried but have been mostly ineffective (Crow et al., 2009).

Cognitive-behavior therapy (CBT) might seem to be an especially appropriate treatment because cognitive distortions often accompany eating disorders (Lock, 2002). CBT focuses on changing beliefs that the person is "too fat" de-conditions and yet manage to adapt and function well. Resilience is the term for this phenomenon, defined as "good outcomes in spite of serious threats to adaptation and development" (Masten, 2001, p. 228). Sometimes "good outcomes" are measured as notable academic or social achievements, sometimes as internal conditions such as well-being or self-esteem, and sometimes as the absence of notable problems. Young people who are resilient are not necessarily high achievers who have some kind of extraordinary ability. More often they display what resilience researcher Ann Masten calls the "ordinary magic" of being able to function reasonably well despite being faced with unusually difficult circumstances (Masten, 2001, p. 227).

Resilience is promoted by protective factors that enable adolescents and emerging adults to overcome the risk factors in their lives. Some of the most important protective factors identified in resilience research are high intelligence, parenting that provides an effective balance of warmth and control, and a caring adult "mentor" outside the family. For example, high intelligence may allow an adolescent to perform well academically despite going to a low-quality school and living in a disorderly household (Masten, Obradovic, & Burt, 2006). Effective parenting may help an adolescent have a positive self-image and avoid antisocial behavior despite growing up in poverty and living in a rough neighborhood (Brody & Flor, 1998). A mentor may foster high academic goals and good future planning in an adolescent whose family life is characterized by abuse or neglect (Rhodes & DuBois, 2008).

One classic study of resilience followed a group of infants from birth through adolescence (Werner & Smith, 1982, 1992, 2001). It is known as the Kauai (kow' ee) study, after the Hawaiian island where the study took place. The Kauai study focused on a high-risk group of children who had four or more risk factors by age 2, such as problems in physical development, parents' marital conflict, parental drug abuse, low maternal education, and poverty. Out of this group, there was a resilient subgroup that showed good social and academic functioning and few behavior problems by ages 10–18. Compared with their less resilient peers, adolescents in the resilient group were found to benefit from several protective factors, including one well-functioning parent, higher intelligence, and higher physical attractiveness.

More recent studies have supported the Kauai findings but also broadened the range of protective factors (Masten, 2007; Gardner, Dishion, & Connell, 2008). A study of Native American adolescents found high levels of family adversity, such as poverty and parental alcohol abuse—only 38% of the adolescents were classified as living in low-adversity households—but adolescents with a relatively strong ethnic identity were higher in prosocial behavior and lower in risk behaviors (LaFromboise et al., 2006). Religiosity has become recognized as an especially important protective factor. Adolescents who have a strong religious faith are less likely to have problems such as substance abuse, even when they have grown up in a high-risk environment (Howard et al., 2007; Wallace et al., 2007).

Emerging adulthood has been proposed as a key period for the expression of resilience (Arnett, 2004). Unlike children and adolescents, emerging adults have the ability to leave an unhealthy, high-risk family environment. Unlike older adults, emerging adults have not yet made the commitments that structure adult life for most people. Consequently, emerging adulthood is a period when there is an unusually high scope for making decisions that could turn life in a new and better direction. Experiences such as military service, romantic relationships, higher education, development of religious faith, and work opportunities may provide turning point opportunities for changing the course of life during emerging adulthood (Masten, et al., 2006). In the Kauai study, a surprise finding was that many of the participants who had been placed in the nonresilient category in adolescence turned out to be resilient after all in emerging adulthood (Werner & Smith, 2001). The experiences that helped them change their lives for the better included participation in higher education, learning new occupational skills through military service, and conversion to a religious faith that provided a community of support.

But the question remains, why do some people take advantage of and benefit from turning point opportunities in emerging adulthood, whereas others do not? One researcher examining resilience in emerging adulthood suggested the key may lie in "planful competence," which includes realistic goal setting, dependability, and self-control (Clausen, 1991). However, this begs the question of why some emerging adults exhibit planful competence in response to adverse conditions whereas others do not. The stories of resilient emerging adults are fascinating and inspiring, and there is much more to be learned from them.

SUMMING UP

In this chapter we have discussed a wide range of problems in adolescence and emerging adulthood, including both externalizing and internalizing problems. The main points we have discussed are as follows:

- The two main classes of adolescent problems are externalizing problems (such as delinquency and risky driving) and internalizing problems (such as depression and eating disorders).

- Automobile accidents are the leading cause of death among young people in their late teens and early 20s in industrialized societies, and young people at these ages have the highest rates of automobile accidents and fatalities of any age group. These high rates appear to be due to the risks they take while driving as well as inexperience. Graduated driver licensing programs have been shown to be highly effective in reducing accidents and fatalities among young people.

- With regard to substance use, young people in the United States and Canada are more likely to use marijuana than young people in other Western countries, but young people in Europe use alcohol and cigarettes more than Americans and Canadians do. Across countries, emerging adults have higher rates of substance use than adolescents do, partly because they spend more time in unstructured socializing.

- Alcohol and cigarettes have been called "gateway drugs" because they typically precede use of illegal drugs. Patterns of substance use can be classified as experimental, social, medicinal, and addictive.

- Studies over the past 150 years have found consistently that crime rates peak in the late teens and that crimes are committed mainly by males. Crime is highest in adolescence and emerging adulthood because these periods combine independence from parents with a high amount of time spent with peers, and peer groups sometimes seek out crime as a source of excitement. Among programs to deter delinquents from committing further crimes, the most promise has been shown in multisystemic programs that intervene in a variety of contexts, including family, peer group, and neighborhood.

- Family factors that contribute to adolescent risk behavior include high conflict and parents who are neglectful, harsh, or inconsistent. Parental monitoring has been found to be an especially important predictor of adolescent delinquency. Other factors involved in risk behavior include friends' influence, school qualities, neighborhood cohesion, and religious beliefs. Individual factors that predict involvement in risk behavior include aggressiveness, sensation seeking, poor school achievement, low impulse control, and optimistic bias.

- Depressed mood is more common in adolescence than in adulthood. Rates of depression in adolescence are considerably higher among girls than among boys. Explanations for this difference include gender differences in coping with problems, girls' greater concern with body image, and an internalizing response to stress among girls. Major depression is most effectively treated with a combination of cognitive-behavior therapy and antidepressant medications.

- Female adolescents attempt suicide four times as often as males, but males are about four times as likely to kill themselves. Family disruptions and substance abuse are among the strongest predictors of suicide among adolescents.

- Anorexia nervosa and bulimia are most common among females in their teens and early 20s. Factors proposed to explain eating disorders include a tendency toward internalizing disorders and a cultural emphasis on slimness. Treatment for anorexia generally requires hospitalization. Relapse rates are high for both anorexia and bulimia.

- Many adolescents exhibit resilience despite growing up in high-risk conditions. Some of the key protective factors that promote resilience are high intelligence, high religiosity, and a supportive relationship with one person within or outside of the family. Emerging adulthood may be an especially important period for the expression of resilience, as it is a time when people are most likely to have the scope of individual choice that may enable them to make decisions that change their lives for the better.

We have focused on young people's tendencies for risk behavior as a source of problems in this chapter. In most societies, it is adolescents and emerging adults who are most likely to break the rules and violate social norms for behavior. This tendency can be disruptive and threatening to others, whether it be expressed in fighting, stealing, substance use, risky driving, or many other behaviors. Adolescence and (especially) emerging adulthood are times that are relatively free from the constraints of social roles. In childhood, behavior is restrained by parental control; in adulthood, obligations and expectations as spouse, parent, and employer/employee include restraints. It is in between, during adolescence and emerging adulthood, that social control is most lenient, and increased risk behavior is one consequence.

However, not all risky or norm-breaking behavior is negative. Young people have often been the ones willing to take risks for political and social changes by defying oppressive authorities. As we have seen in Chapter 4, young people are often at the forefront of the political changes. Their relative freedom from role obligations provides the opportunity not just for socially disruptive behavior but for socially constructive risks as well. They are often the explorers, the creative thinkers, the innovators, in part because they have fewer roles that structure and constrict their daily thoughts and behavior.

In the course of many years of studying young people, conducting hundreds of interviews and spending countless hours in informal conversations with them, I have been struck again and again by how adolescence and emerging adulthood are times of life when hopes for the future tend to be high. There are exceptions, of course, but for the most part even if their lives have so far been difficult and filled with problems, young people tend to see their futures as bright and filled with promise. Adolescents and emerging adults are setting the foundation for their adult lives and making decisions that will affect their futures. But for now, while they remain adolescents and emerging adults, the fate of their dreams has yet to be determined, the possible lives lying before them have yet to harden into accomplished facts. For the most part, they still believe their dreams will be fulfilled and they will ultimately achieve the kind of life they envision.

Given the formidable problems that lie before today's young people, should we conclude that their high hopes are misplaced, that such hopes constitute a distortion of the realities they face? Perhaps it is rather that their hopes provide them with the motivation and energy to proceed with confidence in a world that is fraught with peril.

KEY TERMS

INTERNET RESOURCES

http://nhtsa.gov

Website for the National Highway Traffic Safety Administration, a U.S. government agency whose mission it is to work to lower rates of automobile accidents and fatalities. Their yearly report *Traffic Safety Facts*, a comprehensive summary of automobile crash statistics, can be downloaded from this site. It contains information on rates of crashes in relation to a variety of variables, including age, and provides details about the variables related to high crash rates in adolescence and emerging adulthood.

http://www.cdc.gov/HealthyYouth

This part of the Centers for Disease Control website contains statistics and reports from their annual research on risk behavior among adolescents, including substance use, injury and violence, nutrition/obesity, and sexual behavior.

http://www.monitoringthefuture.org

This website contains statistics, reports, and research papers from the Monitoring the Future project that surveys a representative sample of American 8th-, 10th-, and 12th-grade students every year. The focus of the project is on rates of substance use.

FOR FURTHER READING

Hedlund, J., & Compton, R. (2005). Graduated driver licensing research in 2004 and 2005. *Journal of Safety Research, 32,* 109–119. A recent update of research on graduated driver licensing programs, demonstrating that the programs have been highly effective in reducing accidents and fatalities among young drivers.

Moffitt, T. E. (2003). Life-course-persistent and adolescence-limited antisocial behavior: A 10-year research review and a research agenda. In B. B. Lahey & T. E. Moffitt (Eds.), *Causes of conduct disorder and juvenile delinquency* (pp. 49–75). New York: Guilford. An update of Moffitt's influential theory of antisocial behavior.

Swenson, C. C., Henggeler, S. W., Taylor, I. S., & Addison, O. W. (2005). *Multisystemic therapy and neighborhood partnerships: Reducing adolescent violence and substance abuse.* New York: Guilford. A comprehensive description of the multisystemic approach to interventions for adolescent problem behavior.

Treatment for Adolescents with Depression Study (TADS) Team (2004). Fluoxetine, cognitive-behavioral therapy, and their combination for adolescents with depression: Treatment for Adolescents with Depression Study (TADS) randomized controlled trial. *JAMA, 292,* 807–820. The definitive study to date of the effectiveness of treatments for adolescent depression, conducted among adolescents ages 12–17 at 13 sites in the United States. Results show that both antidepressants and cognitive-behavior therapy are effective treatments, but they are most effective when used together.

PEARSON
mydevelopmentlab™

For more review plus practice tests, videos, flashcards, and more, log on to MyDevelopmentLab.

Glossary

absolute performance In IQ tests, performance results compared to other persons, regardless of age.

abstinence-plus programs Sex education programs that encourage adolescents to delay intercourse while also providing contraceptive information for adolescents who nevertheless choose to have intercourse.

abstract thinking Thinking in terms of symbols, ideas, and concepts.

accommodation The cognitive process that occurs when a scheme is changed to adapt to new information.

active genotype–environment interactions Occur when people seek out environments that correspond to their genotypic characteristics.

actual self A person's perception of the self as it is, contrasted with the possible self.

addictive substance use Pattern of substance use in which a person has come to depend on regular use of substances to feel good physically and/or psychologically.

adolescence A period of the life course between the time puberty begins and the time adult status is approached, when young people are in the process of preparing to take on the roles and responsibilities of adulthood in their culture.

adolescence-limited delinquents (ALDs) In Moffitt's theory, delinquents who engage in criminal acts in adolescence and/or emerging adulthood but show no evidence of problems before or after these periods.

adolescent egocentrism Type of egocentrism in which adolescents have difficulty distinguishing their thinking about their own thoughts from their thinking about the thoughts of others.

adolescent growth spurt The rapid increase in height that takes place at the beginning of puberty.

adrenocorticotropic hormone (ACTH) The hormone that causes the adrenal glands to increase androgen production.

Advanced Placement (AP) classes Classes for gifted students in high schools that have higher-level material than normal classes in order to provide a challenging curriculum.

affection phase In Brown's developmental model of adolescent love, the third phase, in which adolescents come to know each other better and express deeper feelings for each other, as well as engaging in more extensive sexual activity.

affective functions Emotional functions of the family, pertaining to love, nurturance, and attachment.

age norms Technique for developing a psychological test, in which a typical score for each age is established by testing a large random sample of people from a variety of geographical areas and social class backgrounds.

age-graded Organized by age, for example in schools.

Alfred Binet French psychologist who developed the first intelligence test in the early 20th century, which later became known as the Stanford-Binet.

amenorrhea Cessation of menstruation, sometimes experienced by girls whose body weight falls extremely low.

AmeriCorps The national service program in the United States in which young people serve in a community organization for up to 2 years for minimal pay.

androgens The sex hormones that have especially high levels in males from puberty onward and are mostly responsible for male primary and secondary sex characteristics.

androgyny A combination of "male" and "female" personality traits.

anorexia nervosa Eating disorder characterized by intentional self-starvation.

apprenticeship An arrangement, common in Europe, in which an adolescent "novice" serves under contract to a "master" who has substantial experience in a profession, and through working under the master, learns the skills required to enter the profession.

areola Area surrounding the nipple on the breast; enlarges at puberty.

argot (pronounced *ar-go'*) In youth culture, a certain vocabulary and a certain way of speaking.

arranged marriage A marriage in which the marriage partners are determined not by the partners themselves but by others, usually the parents or other family elders.

assimilation In the formation of an ethnic identity, the approach that involves leaving the ethnic culture behind and adopting the ways of the majority culture.

assimilation The cognitive process that occurs when new information is altered to fit an existing scheme.

asymptomatic A condition common with STDs in which an infected person shows no symptoms of the disease but may potentially infect others.

asynchronicity Uneven growth of different parts of the body during puberty.

attachment theory Theory originally developed by British psychiatrist John Bowlby, asserting that among humans as among other primates, attachments between parents and children have an evolutionary basis in the need for vulnerable young members of the species to stay in close proximity to adults who will care for and protect them.

attention-deficit hyperactivity disorder (ADHD) Disorder characterized by difficulty in maintaining attention on a task along with a high activity level that makes self-control problematic.

authoritarian parents Parenting style in which parents are high in demandingness but low in responsiveness, i.e., they require obedience from their children and punish disobedience without compromise, but show little warmth or affection toward them.

authoritative parents A parenting style in which parents are high in demandingness and high in responsiveness, i.e., they love their children but also set clear standards for behavior and explain to their children the reasons for those standards.

automaticity Degree of cognitive effort a person needs to devote to processing a given set of information.

autonomous morality Piaget's term for the period of moral development from about age 10 to age 12, involving a growing realization that moral rules are social conventions that can be changed if people decide they should be changed.

autonomy The quality of being independent and self-sufficient, capable of thinking for one's self.

Bar Mitzvah Jewish religious ritual for boys at age 13 that signifies the adolescents' new responsibilities with respect to Jewish beliefs.

barometric self-esteem The fluctuating sense of worth and well-being people have as they respond to different thoughts, experiences, and interactions in the course of a day.

baseline self-esteem A person's stable, enduring sense of worth and well-being.

Bat Mitzvah Jewish religious ritual for girls at age 13 that signifies the adolescents' new responsibilities with respect to Jewish beliefs.

behavioral decision theory Theory of decision making that describes the decision-making process as including (1) identifying the range of possible choices; (2) identifying the consequences that would result from each choice; (3) evaluating the desirability of each consequence; (4) assessing the likelihood of each consequence; and (5) integrating this information.

bicultural Having an identity that includes aspects of two different cultures.

biculturalism In the formation of ethnic identity, the approach that involves developing a dual identity, one based in the ethnic group of origin and one based in the majority culture.

bidirectional effects In relations between parents and children, the concept that children not only are affected by their parents but affect their parents in return. Also called reciprocal effects.

binge drinking Drinking a large number of alcoholic drinks in one episode, usually defined as drinking five or more alcoholic drinks in a row.

blog A public Internet journal of a person's thoughts, feelings, and activities.

bonding phase In Brown's developmental model of adolescent love, the final phase, in which the romantic relationship becomes more enduring and serious and partners begin to discuss the possibility of a lifelong commitment to each other.

breast buds The first slight enlargement of the breast in girls at puberty.

broad socialization The process by which persons in an individualistic culture come to learn individualism, including values of individual uniqueness, independence, and self-expression.

buddy relationship Between siblings, a relationship in which they treat each other as friends.

bulimia An eating disorder characterized by episodes of binge eating followed by purging (self-induced vomiting).

bullying In peer relations, the aggressive assertion of power by one person over another.

cardiac output A measure of the quantity of blood pumped by the heart.

care orientation Gilligan's term for the type of moral orientation that involves focusing on relationships with others as the basis for moral reasoning.

caregiver relationship Between siblings, a relationship in which one sibling serves parental functions for the other.

caste system Hindu belief that people are born into a particular caste based on their moral and spiritual conduct in their previous life. A person's caste then determines their status in Indian society.

casual relationship Between siblings, a relationship that is not emotionally intense, in which they have little to do with one another.

cathartic effect Effect sometimes attributed to media experiences, in which media experience has the effect of relieving unpleasant emotions.

cerebellum A structure in the lower brain, well beneath the cortex long thought to be involved only in basic functions such as movement, now known to be important for many higher functions as well, such as mathematics, music, decision making, and social skills.

chador or **burka** A garment that covers the hair and most of the face, worn by many girls and women in Muslim societies.

child study movement Late 19th century group, led by G. Stanley Hall, that advocated research on child and adolescent development and the improvement of conditions for children and adolescents in the family, school, and workplace.

chronosystem In Bronfenbrenner's ecological theory, changes that occur in developmental circumstances over time, both with respect to individual development and to historical changes.

cliques Small groups of friends who know each other well, do things together, and form a regular social group.

clitoris Part of vulva in which females' sexual sensations are concentrated.

closed question Questionnaire format that entails choosing from specific responses provided for each question.

cofigurative cultures Cultures in which young people learn what they need to know not only from adults but also from other young people.

cognitive development Changes over time in how people think, how they solve problems, and how their capacities for memory and attention change.

cognitive-behavior therapy (CBT) An approach to treating psychological disorders that focuses on changing negative ways of thinking and practicing new ways of interacting with others.

cognitive-developmental approach Approach to understanding cognition that emphasizes the changes that take place at different ages.

cognitive-developmental theory of gender Kohlberg's theory, based on Piaget's ideas about cognitive development, asserting that gender is a fundamental way of organizing ideas about the world and that children develop through a predictable series of stages in their understanding of gender.

cohabitation Living with a romantic partner outside of marriage.

collectivism A set of beliefs asserting that it is important for persons to mute their individual desires in order to contribute to the well-being and success of the group.

coming out For homosexuals, the process of acknowledging their homosexuality and then disclosing the truth to their friends, family, and others.

commitment Cognitive status in which persons commit themselves to certain points of view they believe to be the most valid while at the same time being open to reevaluating their views if new evidence is presented to them.

communal manhood Anthony Rotundo's term for the norm of manhood in 17th- and 18th-century colonial America, in which the focus of gender expectations for adolescent boys was on preparing to assume adult male role responsibilities in work and marriage.

community service Volunteer work provided as a contribution to the community, without monetary compensation.

companionate love In Sternberg's theory of love, the type of love that combines intimacy and commitment, but without passion.

companionship support Between friends, reliance on each other as companions in social activities.

complex thinking Thinking that takes into account multiple connections and interpretations, such as in the use of metaphor, satire, and sarcasm.

componential approach Description of the information-processing approach to cognition, indicating that it involves breaking down the thinking process into its various components.

comprehensive high school The form of the American high school that arose in the 1920s and is still the main form today, which encompasses a wide range of functions and includes classes in general education, college preparation, and vocational training.

comprehensive sexuality education Sex education programs that begin at an early age and include detailed information on sexual development and sexual behavior, with easy access to contraception for adolescents who choose to become sexually active.

concept videos Music videos that enact a story to go along with the lyrics of the song.

concrete operations Cognitive stage from age 7 to 11 in which children learn to use mental operations but are limited to applying them to concrete, observable situations rather than hypothetical situations.

consensual validation In social science studies of interpersonal attraction, the principle that people like to find in others an agreement or consensus with their own characteristics and view of life.

consent form Written statement provided by a researcher to potential participants in a study, informing them of who is conducting the study, the purposes of the study, and what their participation would involve, including potential risks.

consummate love In Sternberg's theory of love, the form of love that integrates passion, intimacy, and commitment.

context The environmental settings in which development takes place.

continuous A view of development as a gradual, steady process rather than as taking place in distinct stages.

control group In experimental research, the group that does not receive the treatment.

controversial adolescents Adolescents who are aggressive but who also possess social skills, so that they evoke strong emotions both positive and negative from their peers.

conventional reasoning In Kohlberg's theory of moral development, the level of moral reasoning in which the person advocates the value of conforming to the moral expectations of others. What is right is whatever agrees with the rules established by tradition and by authorities.

correlation versus causation A correlation is a predictable relationship between two variables, such that knowing one of the variables makes it possible to predict the other. However, just because two variables are correlated does not mean that one causes the other.

critical relationship Between siblings, a relationship characterized by a high level of conflict and teasing.

critical thinking Thinking that involves not merely memorizing information but analyzing it, making judgments about what it means, relating it to other information, and considering ways in which it might be valid or invalid.

cross-sectional study Study that examines individuals at one point in time.

crowds Large, reputation-based groups of adolescents.

crystallized intelligence Accumulated knowledge and enhanced judgment based on experience.

cultural beliefs The predominant beliefs in a culture about right and wrong, what is most important in life, and how life should be lived. May also include beliefs about where and how life originated and what happens after death.

cultural psychology Approach to human psychology emphasizing that psychological functioning cannot be separated from the culture in which it takes place.

custodial parent The parent who lives in the same household as the children following a divorce.

custom complex A customary practice and the beliefs, values, sanctions, rules, motives, and satisfactions associated with it; that is, a normative practice in a culture and the cultural beliefs that provide the basis for that practice.

cyberbullying Bullying via electronic means, mainly through the Internet.

date rape An act of sexual aggression in which a person, usually a woman, is forced by a romantic partner, date, or acquaintance to have sexual relations against her will.

dating scripts The cognitive models that guide dating interactions.

debt bondage Arrangement in which a person who is in debt pledges his labor or the labor of his children as payment.

delinquency Violations of the law committed by juveniles.

demandingness The degree to which parents set down rules and expectations for behavior and require their children to comply with them.

demeanor In Brake's description of youth cultures, refers to distinctive forms of gesture, gait, and posture.

depressed mood An enduring period of sadness, without any other related symptoms of depression.

depression An enduring period of sadness.

depressive syndrome An enduring period of sadness along with other symptoms such as frequent crying, feelings of worthlessness, and feeling guilty, lonely, or worried.

dialectical thought Type of thinking that develops in emerging adulthood, involving a growing awareness that most problems do not have a single solution and that problems must often be addressed with crucial pieces of information missing.

diathesis-stress model A theory that mental disorders result from the combination of a diathesis (biological vulnerability) and environmental stresses.

differential gender socialization The term for socializing males and females according to different expectations about what attitudes and behavior are appropriate to each gender.

differential parenting When parents' behavior differs toward siblings within the same family.

discontinuous A view of development as taking place in stages that are distinct from one another rather than as one gradual, continuous process.

disengaged parents Parenting style in which parents are low in both demandingness and responsiveness and relatively uninvolved in their children's development.

disequilibrium In the family systems approach, this term is used in reference to a change that requires adjustments from family members.

divided attention The ability to focus on more than one task at a time.

divorce mediation An arrangement in which a professional mediator helps divorcing parents negotiate an agreement that both will find acceptable.

dizygotic (DZ) twins Twins with about half their genotype in common, the same as for other siblings. Also known as fraternal twins.

dormitory In some traditional cultures, a dwelling in which the community's adolescents sleep and spend their leisure time.

double standard Two different sets of rules for sexual behavior, one applying to males and the other females, with rules for females usually being more restrictive.

driver education Programs designed to teach young drivers safe driving skills before they receive their driver's license.

driving curfews In graduated licensing programs, a feature of the restricted license stage in which young drivers are prohibited from driving late at night except for a specific purpose such as going back and forth to work.

dual-earner family A family in which both parents are employed.

dualistic thinking Cognitive tendency to see situations and issues in polarized, absolute, black-and-white terms.

dyadic relationship A relationship between two persons.

early adolescence Period of human development lasting from about age 10 to about age 14.

ecological theory Urie Bronfenbrenner's sociocultural theory of human development, with five interrelated systems: the microsystem (the immediate environment), the mesosystem (connections between microsystems), the exosystem (institutions such as schools and community organizations), the macrosystem (the overarching system of cultural beliefs and values), and the chronosystem (the changes in the individual and the cultural environment over time).

effect size The difference between two groups in a meta-analysis, represented by the letter *d*.

emerging adulthood Period from roughly ages 18 to 25 in industrialized countries during which young people become more independent from parents and explore various life possibilities before making enduring commitments.

emotional loneliness Condition that occurs when people feel that the relationships they have lack sufficient closeness and intimacy.

empty love In Sternberg's theory of love, the type of love that is based on commitment alone, without passion or intimacy.

endocrine system A network of glands in the body. Through hormones, the glands coordinate their functioning and affect the development and functioning of the body.

engagement The quality of being psychologically committed to learning, including being alert and attentive in the classroom and making a diligent effort to learn.

esteem support The support friends provide each other by providing congratulations for success and encouragement or consolation for failure.

estradiol The estrogen most important in pubertal development among girls.

estrogens The sex hormones that have especially high levels in females from puberty onward and are mostly responsible for female primary and secondary sex characteristics.

ethnographic research Research in which scholars spend a considerable amount of time among the people they wish to study, usually living among them.

ethnography A book that presents an anthropologist's observations of what life is like in a particular culture.

ethos The beliefs about education that characterize a school as a whole.

evocative genotype–environment interactions Occur when a person's inherited characteristics evoke responses from others in their environment.

exosystem In Bronfenbrenner's ecological theory, societal institutions such as schools, religious institutions, systems of government, and media.

experimental group In experimental research, the group that receives the treatment.

experimental research method A research method that entails assigning participants randomly to an experimental group that received a treatment and a control group that does not receive the treatment, then comparing the two groups in a posttest.

experimental substance use Trying a substance once or perhaps a few times out of curiosity.

expressive traits Personality characteristics such as gentle and yielding, more often ascribed to females, emphasizing emotions and relationships.

externalizing problems Problems that affect a person's external world, such as delinquency and fighting.

extremities The feet, hands, and head.

exuberance See overproduction.

false self The self a person may present to others while realizing that it does not represent what he or she is actually thinking and feeling.

familismo Concept of family life characteristic of Latino cultures that emphasizes the love, closeness, and mutual obligations of family life.

family process The quality of relationships among family members.

family structure The outward characteristics of a family, such as whether or not the parents are married.

family systems approach An approach to understanding family functioning that emphasizes how each relationship within the family influences the family as a whole.

fatuous love In Sternberg's theory of love, the type of love that involves passion and commitment without intimacy.

feared self The self a person imagines it is possible to become but dreads becoming.

feedback loop System of hormones involving the hypothalamus, the pituitary gland, and the gonads, which monitors and adjusts the levels of the sex hormones.

field studies Studies in which people's behavior is observed in a natural setting.

filial piety Confucian belief, common in many Asian societies, that children are obligated to respect, obey, and revere their parents, especially the father.

first-generation families The status of persons who were born in one country and then immigrated to another.

fluid intelligence Mental abilities that involve speed of analyzing, processing, and reacting to information.

fMRI A technique for measuring brain functioning during an ongoing activity.

follicle-stimulating hormone (FSH) Along with LH, stimulates the development of gametes and sex hormones in the ovaries and testicles.

formal operations Cognitive stage from age 11 on up in which people learn to think systematically about possibilities and hypotheses.

friends Persons with whom an individual has a valued, mutual relationship.

frontal lobes The part of the brain immediately behind the forehead. Known to be involved in higher brain functions such as planning ahead and analyzing complex problems.

gametes Cells, distinctive to each sex, that are involved in reproduction (egg cells in the ovaries of the female and sperm in the testes of the male).

gateway drugs Term sometimes applied to alcohol, cigarettes, and marijuana because young people who use harder drugs usually use these drugs first.

gender The social categories of male and female, established according to cultural beliefs and practices rather than being due to biology.

gender identity Children's understanding of themselves as being either male or female, reached at about age 3.

gender intensification hypothesis Hypothesis that psychological and behavioral differences between males and females become more pronounced at adolescence because of intensified socialization pressures to conform to culturally prescribed gender roles.

gender roles Cultural beliefs about the kinds of work, appearance, and other aspects of behavior that distinguish women from men.

gender schema theory Theory in which gender is viewed as one of the fundamental ways that people organize information about the world.

generalizable Characteristic of a sample that refers to the degree to which findings based on the sample can be used to make accurate statements about the population of interest.

gifted students Students who have unusually high abilities in academics, art, or music.

globalization Increasing worldwide technological and economic integration, which is making different parts of the world increasingly connected and increasingly similar culturally.

gonadotropin-releasing hormone (GnRH) Hormone released by the hypothalamus that causes gonadotropins to be released by the pituitary.

gonadotropins Hormones (FSH and LH) that stimulate the development of gametes.

gonads The ovaries and testicles. Also known as the sex glands.

graduated driver licensing (GDL) A program that allows young people restricted driving privileges when they first receive their license, gradually increasing the privileges if the restrictions are not violated.

gray matter The outer layer of the brain, where most of the growth in brain cells occurs.

guided participation The teaching interaction between two people (often an adult and a child or adolescent) as they participate in a culturally valued activity.

Harvard Adolescence Project Project initiated by Beatrice and John Whiting of Harvard University in the 1980s, in which they sent young scholars to do ethnographic research in seven different cultures in various parts of the world.

health promotion Efforts to reduce health problems in young people through encouraging changes in the behaviors that put young people at risk.

heteronomous morality Piaget's term for the period of moral development from about age 4 to about age 7, in which moral rules are viewed as having a sacred, fixed quality, handed down from figures of authority and alterable only by them.

homophobia Fear and hatred of homosexuals.

hormones Chemicals, released by the glands of the endocrine system, that affect the development and functioning of the body, including development during puberty.

hybrid identity An identity that integrates elements of various cultures.

hymen The thin membrane inside a girl's vagina that is usually broken during her first experience of sexual intercourse. Tested in some cultures before marriage to verify the girl's virginity.

hypothalamus The "master gland," located in the lower part of the brain beneath the cortex, that affects a wide range of physiological and psychological functioning and stimulates and regulates the production of hormones by other glands, including the ones involved in the initiation of puberty.

hypotheses Ideas, based on theory or previous research, that a scholar wishes to test in a scientific study.

hypothetical-deductive reasoning Piaget's term for the process by which the formal operational thinker systematically tests possible solutions to a problem and arrives at an answer that can be defended and explained.

ideal self The person an adolescent would like to be.

identifications Relationships formed with others, especially in childhood, in which love for another person leads one to want to be like that person.

identity Individuals' perceptions of their characteristics and abilities, their beliefs and values, their relations with others, and how their lives fit into the world around them.

identity achievement The identity status of young people who have made definite personal, occupational, and ideological choices following a period of exploring possible alternatives.

identity crisis Erikson's term for the intense period of struggle that adolescents may experience in the course of forming an identity.

identity diffusion An identity status that combines no exploration with no commitment. No commitments have been made among the available paths of identity formation, and the person is not seriously attempting to sort through potential choices and make enduring commitments.

identity foreclosure An identity status in which young people have not experimented with a range of possibilities but have nevertheless committed themselves to certain choices—commitment, but no exploration.

identity moratorium An identity status that involves exploration but no commitment, in which young people are trying out different personal, occupational, and ideological possibilities.

identity status model An approach to conceptualizing and researching identity development that classifies people into one of four identity categories: foreclosure, diffusion, moratorium, or achievement.

identity versus identity confusion Erikson's term for the crisis typical of the adolescent stage of life, in which individuals may follow the healthy path of establishing a clear and definite sense of who they are and how they fit into the world around them, or follow the unhealthy alternative of failing to form a stable and secure identity.

image In Brake's description of the characteristics of youth culture, refers to dress, hair style, jewelry, and other aspects of appearance.

imaginary audience Belief that others are acutely aware of and attentive to one's appearance and behavior.

incest taboo The prohibition on sexual relations between family members. Believed to be biologically based, as children born to closely related parents are at higher risk for genetic disorders.

independent self A conception of the self typically found in individualistic cultures, in which the self is seen as existing independently of relations with others, with an emphasis on independence, individual freedoms, and individual achievements.

index crimes Serious crimes divided into two categories: violent crimes such as rape, assault, and murder, and property crimes such as robbery, motor vehicle theft, and arson.

individual differences Approach to research that focuses on how individuals differ within a group, for example, in performance on IQ tests.

individualism Cultural belief system that emphasizes the desirability of independence, self-sufficiency, and self-expression.

individuating-reflective faith Fowler's term for the stage of faith most typical of late adolescence and emerging adulthood, in which people rely less on what their parents believed and develop a more individualized faith based on questioning their beliefs and incorporating their personal experience into their beliefs.

infatuation In Sternberg's theory of love, the type of love that is based on passion alone, without intimacy or commitment.

informational support Between friends, advice and guidance in solving personal problems.

information-processing approach An approach to understanding cognition that seeks to delineate the steps involved in the thinking process and how each step is connected to the next.

informed consent Standard procedure in social scientific studies that entails informing potential participants of what their participation would involve, including any possible risks.

initiation phase In Brown's developmental model of adolescent love, the first phase, usually in early adolescence, when the first tentative explorations of romantic interests begin, usually superficial and brief, often fraught with anxiety, fear, and excitement.

insecure attachment Type of attachment to caregiver in which infants are timid about exploring the environment and resist or avoid the caregiver when she attempts to offer comfort or consolation.

instrumental support Between friends, help with tasks of various kind.

instrumental traits Personality characteristics such as self-reliant and forceful, more often ascribed to males, emphasizing action and accomplishment.

intelligence quotient A measure of a person's intellectual abilities based on a standardized test.

interdependence The web of commitments, attachments, and obligations that exist in some human groups.

interdependent self A conception of the self typically found in collectivistic cultures, in which the self is seen as defined by roles and relationships within the group.

internal consistency A statistical calculation that indicates the extent to which the differ-

ent items in a scale or subscale are answered in a similar way.

internal working model In attachment theory, the term for the cognitive framework, based on interactions in infancy with the primary caregiver, that shapes expectations and interactions in relationships to others throughout life.

internalizing problems Problems such as depression and anxiety that affect a person's internal world, for example depression, anxiety, and eating disorders.

International Labor Organization (ILO) An organization that seeks to prevent children and adolescents from being exploited in the workplace.

interventions Programs intended to change the attitudes and/or behavior of the participants.

interview Research method that involves asking people questions in a conversational format, such that people's answers are in their own words.

intimacy The degree to which two people share personal knowledge, thoughts, and feelings.

intimacy versus isolation Erikson's term for the central issue of young adulthood, in which persons face alternatives between committing themselves to another person in an intimate relationship or becoming isolated as a consequence of an inability to form an enduring intimate relationship.

Jean Piaget Influential Swiss developmental psychologist, best known for his theories of cognitive and moral development.

justice orientation A type of moral orientation that places a premium on abstract principles of justice, equality, and fairness.

juveniles Persons defined by the legal system as being younger than adult status.

Koran The holy book of the religion of Islam, believed by Muslims to have been communicated to Muhammad from God through the angel Gabriel.

labia majora Part of vulva; Latin for "large lips."

labia minora Part of vulva; Latin for "small lips."

Lamarckian Reference to Lamarck's ideas, popular in the late 19th and early 20th centuries, that evolution takes place as a result of accumulated experience such that organisms pass on their characteristics from one generation to the next in the form of memories and acquired characteristics.

late adolescence Period of human development lasting from about age 15 to about age 18.

latency period A period, common with STDs, between the time a person is infected with a disease and the time symptoms appear.

learning disability In schools, a diagnosis made when a child or adolescent has normal intelligence but has difficulty in one or more academic areas and the difficulty cannot be attributed to any other disorder.

leptin A protein, produced by fat cells, that signals the hypothalamus to initiate the hormonal changes of puberty.

life-course-persistent delinquents (LCPDs) In Moffitt's theory, adolescents who show a history of related problems both prior to and following adolescence.

life-cycle service A period in their late teens and 20s in which young people from the 16th to the 19th century engaged in domestic service, farm service, or apprenticeships in various trades and crafts.

liking In Sternberg's theory of love, the type of love that is based on intimacy alone, without passion or commitment.

longitudinal study A study in which data is collected from the participants on more than one occasion.

long-term memory Memory for information that is committed to longer-term storage, so that it can be drawn upon after a period when attention has not been focused on it.

low impulse control Difficulty in exercising self-control, often found to be related to risk behavior in adolescence.

luteinizing hormone (LH) Along with FSH, stimulates the development of gametes and sex hormones in the ovaries and testicles.

machismo Ideology of manhood, common in Latino cultures, which emphasizes males' dominance over females.

macrosystem In Bronfenbrenner's ecological theory, the broad system of cultural beliefs and values, and the economic and governmental systems that are built on those beliefs and values.

major depressive disorder Psychological diagnosis that entails depressed mood or re-

duced interest or pleasure in all or almost all activities, plus at least four other specific symptoms. Symptoms must be present over at least a 2-week period and must involve a change from previous functioning.

marginality In the formation of ethnic identity, the option that involves rejecting one's culture of origin but also feeling rejected by the majority culture.

maturation Process by which abilities develop through genetically based development with limited influence from the environment.

maximum oxygen uptake (VO₂ max) A measure of the ability of the body to take in oxygen and transport it to various organs; peaks in the early 20s.

median In a distribution of scores, the point at which half of the population scores above and half below.

medicinal substance use Substance use undertaken for the purpose of relieving an unpleasant emotional state such as sadness, anxiety, stress, or loneliness.

men's house In some traditional cultures, a dormitory where adolescent boys sleep and hang out along with adult men who are widowed or divorced.

menarche A girl's first menstrual period.

mental operations Cognitive activity involving manipulating and reasoning about objects.

mental structure The organization of cognitive abilities into a single pattern, such that thinking in all aspects of life is a reflection of that structure.

mesosystem In Bronfenbrenner's ecological theory, the network of interconnections between the microsystems.

meta-analysis A statistical technique that integrates the data from many studies into one comprehensive statistical analysis.

metacognition The capacity for "thinking about thinking" that allows adolescents and adults to monitor and reason about their thought processes.

method A scientific strategy for collecting data.

microsystem Bronfenbrenner's term for the settings where people experience their daily lives, including relationships with parents, siblings, peers/friends, teachers, and employers.

midlife crisis The popular belief, largely unfounded according to research, that most

people experience a crisis when they reach about age 40, involving intensive reexamination of their lives and perhaps sudden and dramatic changes if they are dissatisfied.

mikveh Among Orthodox Jews, the traditional ritual bath taken by a woman 7 days after her menstrual period was finished, as a way of ridding herself of the uncleanness believed to be associated with menstruation.

mnemonic devices Memory strategies.

monozygotic (MZ) twins Twins with exactly the same genotype. Also known as identical twins.

multiple thinking Cognitive approach entailing recognition that there is more than one legitimate view of things and that it can be difficult to justify one position as the true or accurate one.

multisystemic approach Delinquency prevention strategy that addresses risk factors at several levels, including the home, the school, and the neighborhood.

mutual perspective taking Stage of perspective taking, often found in early adolescence, in which persons understand that their perspective-taking interactions with others are mutual, in the sense that each side realizes that the other can take their perspective.

myelination Process by which myelin, a blanket of fat wrapped around the main part of the neuron, grows. Myelin serves the function of keeping the brain's electrical signals on one path and increasing their speed.

narrow socialization The process by which persons in a collectivistic culture come to learn collectivism, including values of obedience and conformity.

national survey Questionnaire study that involves asking a sample of persons in a country to respond to questions about their opinions, beliefs, or behavior.

natural experiment A situation that occurs naturally but that provides interesting scientific information to the perceptive observer.

nature–nurture debate Debate over the relative importance of biology and the environment in human development.

negative attributions Beliefs that one's current unhappiness is permanent and uncontrollable.

negative identity Erikson's term for an identity based on what a person has seen portrayed as most undesirable or dangerous.

neglected adolescents Adolescents who have few or no friends and are largely unnoticed by their peers.

neurons Cells of the nervous system, including the brain.

nonindex crimes Crimes such as illegal gambling, prostitution, and disorderly conduct, considered less serious offenses than index crimes.

nonshared environmental influences Influences experienced differently among siblings within the same family, e.g., when parents behave differently with their different children.

normal distribution or **bell curve** The bell-shaped curve that represents many human characteristics, with most people around the average and a gradually decreasing proportion toward the extremes.

occupational deviance Deviant acts committed in relation to the workplace, such as stealing supplies.

ontogenetic Something that occurs naturally in the course of development as part of normal maturation; that is, it is driven by innate processes rather than by environmental stimulation or a specific cultural practice.

open-ended question Questionnaire format that involves writing in responses to each question.

optimistic bias The tendency to assume that accidents, diseases, and other misfortunes are more likely to happen to other people than to one's self.

organizational core Term applied especially to cognitive development, meaning that cognitive development affects all areas of thinking, no matter what the topic.

overcontrolled Personality characterized by inhibition, anxiety, and self-punishment, sometimes ascribed to adolescents who have internalizing problems.

overevaluation Evaluating persons favorably because they violate gender norms.

overproduction or **exuberance** A rapid increase in the production of synaptic connections in the brain.

ovum Mature egg that develops from follicle in ovaries about every 28 days.

parental consent A legal requirement, in some states, that minors must obtain their parents' permission to have an abortion.

parental monitoring The degree to which parents keep track of where their adolescents are and what they are doing.

parental notification A legal requirement, in some states, that minors must notify their parents before having the abortion.

parenting styles The patterns of practices that parents exhibit in relation to their children.

participant observation A research method that involves taking part in various activities with the people being studied, and learning about them through participating in the activities with them.

passionate manhood Anthony Rotundo's term for the norm of manhood in the 20th-century United States, in which self-expression and self-enjoyment replaced self-control and self-denial as the paramount virtues young males should learn in the course of becoming a man.

passive genotype–environment interactions Situation in biological families that parents provide both genes and environment for their children, making genes and environment difficult to separate in their effects on children's development.

patriarchal authority Cultural belief in the absolute authority of the father over his wife and children.

Peace Corps An international service program in which Americans provide service to a community in a foreign country for 2 years.

peak height velocity The point at which the adolescent growth spurt is at its maximum rate.

peer contagion Term for the increase in delinquent behavior that often takes place as an unintended consequence of bringing adolescents with problems together for an intervention, because in the intervention setting they reinforce each other's delinquent tendencies and find new partners for delinquent acts.

peer-reviewed When a scholarly article or book is evaluated by a scholar's peers (i.e., other scholars) for scientific credibility and importance.

peers People who share some aspect of their status, such as being the same age.

pendulum problem Piaget's classic test of formal operations, in which persons are asked to figure out what determines the speed at which a pendulum sways from side to side.

Performance subtests In the Wechsler IQ tests, subtests that examine abilities for attention, spatial perception, and speed of processing.

performance videos Music videos that show an individual performer or a group singing a song in a concert setting or a studio.

permissive cultures Cultures that encourage and expect sexual activity from their adolescents.

permissive parents Parenting style in which parents are low in demandingness and high in responsiveness. They show love and affection toward their children but are permissive with regard to standards for behavior.

personal fable A belief in one's personal uniqueness, often including a sense of invulnerability to the consequences of taking risks.

perspective taking The ability to understand the thoughts and feelings of others.

PET scans A technique for assessing ongoing brain functioning, in which a chemical that emits positrons is injected into the body and detectors measure their activity levels in various parts of the brain.

pheromones Airborne chemicals, secreted by the sweat glands, that have effects on other mammals of the same species.

pituitary gland A gland about half an inch long located at the base of the brain that releases gonadotropins as part of the body's preparation for reproduction.

placebo design Research design in which some persons in a study receive medication and others receive placebos, which are pills that contain no medication.

poetic-conventional faith Fowler's term for the stage of faith development most typical of early adolescence, in which people become more aware of the symbolism used in their faith and religious understanding becomes more complex in the sense that early adolescents increasingly believe that there is more than one way of knowing the truth.

population The entire group of people of interest in a study.

possible selves A person's conception of the self as it potentially may be. May include both an ideal self and a feared self.

postconventional reasoning In Kohlberg's theory of moral development, the level in which moral reasoning is based on the individual's own independent judgments rather than on egocentric considerations or considerations of what others view as wrong or right.

postfigurative cultures Cultures in which what children and adolescents need to learn to function as adults changes little from one generation to the next, and therefore children and adolescents can learn all they need to know from their elders.

postformal thinking Type of thinking beyond formal operations, involving greater awareness of the complexity of real-life situations, such as in the use of pragmatism and reflective judgment.

postmodern identity A conception of identity as complex and as highly variable across contexts and across time.

pragmatism Type of thinking that involves adapting logical thinking to the practical constraints of real-life situations.

preconventional reasoning In Kohlberg's theory of moral development, the level in which moral reasoning is based on perceptions of the likelihood of external rewards and punishments.

predictive validity In longitudinal research, the ability of a variable at Time 1 to predict the outcome of a variable at Time 2.

prefigurative cultures Cultures in which young people teach knowledge to adults.

premenstrual syndrome (PMS) The combination of behavioral, emotional, and physical symptoms that occur in some females the week before menstruation.

preoperational stage Cognitive stage from age 2 to 7 during which the child becomes capable of representing the world symbolically—for example, through the use of language—but is still very limited in ability to use mental operations.

primary caregiver The person mainly responsible for caring for an infant or young child.

primary sex characteristics The production of eggs and sperm and the development of the sex organs.

proactive script A dating script, more common for males than for females, that includes initiating the date, deciding where they will go, controlling the public domain (e.g., driving the car and opening the doors), and initiating sexual contact.

problem behavior Behavior that young people engage in that is viewed by adults as a source of problems, such as unprotected premarital sex and substance use.

procedure Standards for the way a study is conducted. Includes informed consent and certain rules for avoiding biases in the data collection.

procreate In the manhood requirements of traditional cultures, the requirement of being able to function sexually well enough to produce children.

property crimes Crimes that involve taking or damaging others' property, for example, robbery and arson.

prosocial Promoting the well-being of others.

protect In the manhood requirements of traditional cultures, the requirement of being able to assist in protecting one's family and community from human and animal attackers.

protective factor Characteristics of young people that are related to lower likelihood of participation in risk behavior.

provide In the manhood requirements of traditional cultures, the requirement of being able to provide economically for one's self as well as a wife and children.

psychohistory The psychological analysis of important historical figures.

psychometric approach Attempt to understand human cognition by evaluating cognitive abilities using intelligence tests.

psychosocial moratorium Erikson's term for a period during adolescence when adult responsibilities are postponed as young people try on various possible selves.

puberty The changes in physiology, anatomy, and physical functioning that develop a person into a mature adult biologically and prepare the body for sexual reproduction.

qualitative Data that is collected in verbal rather than numerical form, usually in interviews.

quantitative Data that is collected in numerical form, usually on questionnaires.

Ramadan A month in the Muslim year that commemorates the revelation of the Koran from God to the prophet Muhammad, requiring fasting from sunrise to sunset each day and refraining from all sensual indulgences.

random sample Sampling technique in which the people selected for participation in a study are chosen randomly, meaning that no one in the population has a better or worse chance of being selected than anyone else.

reaction range Term meaning that genes establish a range of possible development and environment determines where development takes place within that range.

reactive script A dating script, more common for females than males, that focuses on the private domain (e.g., spending considerable time on dress and grooming prior to the date), responding to the date's gestures in the public domain (e.g., being picked up, waiting for him to open the doors), and responding to his sexual initiatives.

recapitulation Now-discredited theory that held that the development of each individual recapitulates the evolutionary development of the human species as a whole.

reciprocal effects In relations between parents and children, the concept that children not only are affected by their parents but affect their parents in return. Also called bidirectional effects.

reductionism Breaking up a phenomenon into separate parts to such an extent that the meaning and coherence of the phenomenon as a whole becomes lost.

reflective judgment The capacity to evaluate the accuracy and logical coherence of evidence and arguments.

rejected adolescents Adolescents who are actively disliked by their peers.

relatedness The quality of being emotionally close to another person.

relational aggression A form of nonphysical aggression that harms others by damaging their relationships, for example by excluding them socially or spreading rumors about them.

relative performance In IQ tests, performance results compared to other persons of the same age.

relativism Cognitive ability to recognize the legitimacy of competing points of view but also compare the relative merits of competing views.

reliability Characteristic of a measure that refers to the extent to which results of the measure on one occasion are similar to results of the measure on a separate occasion.

representative Characteristic of a sample that refers to the degree to which it accurately represents the population of interest.

resilience Overcoming adverse environmental circumstances to achieve healthy development.

response bias On a questionnaire, the tendency to choose the same response for all items.

responsiveness The degree to which parents are sensitive to their children's needs and express love, warmth, and concern for them.

restrictive cultures Cultures that place strong prohibitions on adolescent sexual activity before marriage.

retention The degree of success in maintaining students in college until they graduate.

retention rate In a longitudinal study, the percentage of participants who continued to take part in the study after the first year.

risk behavior Problems that involve the risk of negative outcomes, such as risky driving and substance use.

rival relationship Between siblings, a relationship in which they compete against each other and measure their success against one another.

role preparation An outcome of socialization that includes preparation for occupational roles, gender roles, and roles in institutions such as marriage and parenthood.

roles Defined social positions in a culture, containing specifications of behavior, status, and relations with others. Examples include gender, age, and social class.

romantic love In Sternberg's theory of love, the type of love that combines passion and intimacy, but without commitment.

sample The people included in a given study, who are intended to represent the population of interest.

sampling Collecting data on a subset of the members of a group.

scaffolding The degree of assistance provided to the learner in the zone of proximal development, gradually decreasing as the learner's skills develop.

schema A mental structure for organizing and interpreting information.

scheme A mental structure for organizing and interpreting information.

school climate The quality of interactions between teachers and students, including how teachers interact with students, what sort of expectations and standards they have for students, and what kinds of methods are used in the classroom.

scientific method A systematic way of finding the answers to questions or problems that includes standards of sampling, procedure, and measures.

second shift The domestic work shift performed in the household by women after they complete their first shift in the workplace.

secondary school The schools attended by adolescents, usually including a lower secondary school and an upper secondary school.

secondary sex characteristics Bodily changes of puberty not directly related to reproduction.

second-generation families The status of persons who were born in the country they currently reside in but whose parents were born in a different country.

secular Based on nonreligious beliefs and values.

secular trend A change in the characteristics of a population over time.

secure attachment Type of attachment to caregiver in which infants use the caregiver as a "secure base from which to explore" when all is well, but seek physical comfort and consolation from her if frightened or threatened.

selective association The principle that most people tend to choose friends who are similar to themselves.

selective attention The ability to focus on relevant information while screening out information that is irrelevant.

self-concept Persons' views of themselves, usually including concrete characteristics (such as height and age) as well as roles, relationships, and personality characteristics.

self-esteem A person's overall sense of worth and well-being.

self-image A person's evaluation of his or her qualities and relations with others. Closely related to self-esteem.

self-made manhood Anthony Rotundo's term for the norm of manhood in 19th-century America, in which males were increasingly expected to become independent from their families in adolescence and emerging adulthood as part of becoming a man.

self-medication The use of substances for relieving unpleasant states such as sadness or stress.

self-perception A person's view of his or her characteristics and abilities. Closely related to self-esteem.

self-regulation The capacity for exercising self-control in order to restrain one's impulses and comply with social norms.

self-socialization In gender socialization, refers to the way that children seek to maintain consistency between the norms they have learned about gender and their behavior.

semenarche A male's first ejaculation.

semirestrictive cultures Cultures that have prohibitions on premarital adolescent sex, but the prohibitions are not strongly enforced and are easily evaded.

sensation seeking A personality characteristic defined by the extent to which a person enjoys novelty and intensity of sensation.

sensorimotor stage Cognitive stage in first 2 years of life that involves learning how to coordinate the activities of the senses with motor activities.

separation In the formation of ethnic identity, the approach that involves associating only with members of one's own ethnic group and rejecting the ways of the majority culture.

set point Optimal level of sex hormones in the body. When this point is reached, responses in the glands of the feedback loop cause the production of sex hormones to be reduced.

sex The biological status of being male or female.

sex hormones Androgens and estrogens that cause the development of primary and secondary sex characteristics.

sexual harassment A wide range of threatening or aggressive behaviors related to sexuality, from mild harassment such as name-calling, jokes, and leering looks to severe harassment involving unwanted touching or sexual contact.

sexual scripts Cognitive frameworks, often different for males and females, for understanding how a sexual experience is supposed to proceed and how sexual experiences are to be interpreted.

sexuality Biological sexual development as well as sexual values, beliefs, thoughts, feelings, relationships, and behavior.

short-term memory Memory for information that is the current focus of attention.

social and conventional system perspective taking Realizing that the social perspectives of self and others are influenced not just by their interaction with each other but by their roles in the larger society.

social cognition How people think about other people, social relationships, and social institutions.

social desirability The tendency for people participating in social science studies to report their behavior as they believe it would be approved by others rather than as it actually occurred.

social information processing The interpretation of others' behavior and intentions in a social interaction.

social loneliness Condition that occurs when people feel that they lack a sufficient number of social contacts and relationships.

social-networking websites Internet websites such as Facebook and MySpace that allow users a forum for identity presentation and for making and maintaining social contacts.

social roles theory Theory that social roles for males and females enhance or suppress different capabilities, so that males and females tend to develop different skills and attitudes, which leads to gender-specific behaviors.

social skills Skills for successfully handling social relations and getting along well with others.

social substance use The use of substances in the course of social activities with one or more friends.

socialization The process by which people acquire the behaviors and beliefs of the culture in which they live.

socialized delinquents Delinquents who commit crimes in groups and are similar to

non-delinquents in psychological functioning and family relationships.

sociometry A method for assessing popularity and unpopularity that involves having students rate the social status of other students.

sources of meaning The ideas and beliefs that people learn as part of socialization, indicating what is important, what is to be valued, what is to be lived for, and how to explain and offer consolation for the individual's mortality.

spermarche Beginning of development of sperm in boys' testicles at puberty.

stage A period in which abilities are organized in a coherent, interrelated way.

Stanford-Binet Widely used IQ test developed by Alfred Binet and revised by scholars at Stanford University.

status offenses Offenses such as running away from home that are defined as violations of the law only because they are committed by juveniles.

status phase In Brown's developmental model of adolescent love, the second phase, in which adolescents begin to gain confidence in their skills at interacting with potential romantic partners and begin to form their first romantic relationships, assessing not just how much they like and are attracted to the person, but also how their status with friends and peers would be influenced.

stereotype A belief that others possess certain characteristics simply as a result of being a member of a particular group.

storm and stress Theory promoted by G. Stanley Hall asserting that adolescence is inevitably a time of mood disruptions, conflict with parents, and antisocial behavior.

stratified sampling Sampling technique in which researchers select participants so that various categories of people are represented in proportions equal to their presence in the population.

style The distinguishing features of youth culture, including image, demeanor, and argot.

substance use Use of substances that have cognitive and mood-altering effects, including alcohol, cigarettes, and illegal drugs such as marijuana, LSD, and cocaine.

subterranean values Values such as hedonism, excitement, and adventure, asserted

by sociologists to be the basis of youth culture.

super peer One of the functions of media for adolescents, meaning that adolescents often look to media for information (especially concerning sexuality) that their parents may be unwilling to provide, in the same way they might look to a friend.

survey A questionnaire study that involves asking a large number of people questions about their opinions, beliefs, or behavior.

symbolic inheritance The set of ideas and understandings, both implicit and explicit, about persons, society, nature, and divinity that serve as a guide to life in a particular culture. Expressed symbolically through stories, songs, rituals, sacred objects, and sacred places.

synapse The point of transmission between two nerve cells.

synaptic pruning Following **overproduction**, the process by which the number of synapses in the brain are reduced, making brain functioning faster and more efficient but less flexible.

testosterone The androgen most important in pubertal development among boys.

test-retest reliability Type of reliability that examines whether or not persons' scores on one occasion are similar to their scores on another occasion.

text messaging Communication through cell phones that involves typing a message on the cell phone screen and sending it like an e-mail message.

the forgotten half The nearly half of young Americans who enter the workplace following high school rather than attending college.

the new basic skills Skills identified by Murnane and Levy that are required for high school graduates who wish to be able to obtain the best jobs available in the new information-based economy.

theory of genotype–environment interactions Theory that both genetics and environment make essential contributions to human development but are difficult to unravel because our genes actually influence the kind of environment we experience.

theory of mind The ability to attribute mental states to one's self and others, including beliefs, thoughts, and feelings.

theory of multiple intelligences Howard Gardner's theory that there are eight separate types of intelligence.

traditional parenting style The kind of parenting typical in traditional cultures, high in responsiveness and high in a kind of demandingness that does not encourage discussion and debate but rather expects compliance by virtue of cultural beliefs supporting the inherent authority of the parental role.

transracial adoption The adoption of children of one race by parents of a different race.

undercontrolled Personality characterized by a lack of self-control, sometimes ascribed to adolescents who have externalizing problems.

unemployed The status of persons who are not in school, not working, and who are looking for a job.

unsocialized delinquents Delinquent adolescents who have few friends and commit their crimes alone.

unstructured socializing The term for young people spending time together with no specific event as the center of their activity.

uses and gratifications approach Approach to understanding media that emphasizes that people differ in numerous ways that lead them to make different choices about which media to consume and that even people consuming the same media product will respond to it in a variety of ways, depending on their individual characteristics.

validity The truthfulness of a measure, that is, the extent to which it measures what it claims to measure.

verbal subtests In the Wechsler IQ tests, subtests that examine verbal abilities.

violent crimes Crimes that involve physical harm to others, for example, assault and murder.

vital capacity The amount of air that can be exhaled after a deep breath, which increases rapidly during puberty, especially for boys.

vulva External female sex organs, including the labia majora, the labia minora, and the clitoris.

Vygotsky Russian psychologist who emphasized the cultural basis of cognitive development.

Wechsler Adult Intelligence Scale (WAIS-IV) Intelligence test for persons aged 16 and up, with six Verbal and five Performance subtests.

Wechsler Intelligence Scale for Children (WISC-IV) Intelligence test for children aged 6 to 16, with six Verbal and five Performance subtests.

withdrawal symptoms States such as high anxiety and tremors experienced by persons who stop taking the substance to which they are addicted.

women's movement Organized effort in the 20th century to obtain greater rights and opportunities for women.

working memory An aspect of short-term memory that refers to where information is stored as it is comprehended and analyzed.

worldview A set of cultural beliefs that explain what it means to be human, how human relations should be conducted, and how human problems should be addressed.

youth Prior to the late 19th century, the term used to refer to persons in their teens and early twenties.

youth culture The culture of young people as a whole, separate from children and separate from adult society, characterized by values of hedonism and irresponsibility.

zone of proximal development The gap between how competently a person performs a task alone and when guided by an adult or more competent peer.

References

AAUW. (1993). *Hostile hallways: The AAUW survey on sexual harassment in America's schools.* Washington, DC: American Association of University Women Educational Foundation.

Abma, J., Driscoll, A., & Moore, K. (1998). Young women's degree of control over intercourse: An exploratory analysis. *Family Planning Perspectives, 30,* 12–18.

Aboud, F. E., & Mendelson, M. J. (1998). Determinants of friendship selection and quality: Developmental perspectives. In W. M. Bukowski, W. H. Hartup, & A. F. Newcomb (Eds.), *The company they keep: Friendship in childhood and adolescence* (pp. 87–112). New York: Cambridge University Press.

Abreu, J. M., Goodyear, R. K., Campos, A., & Newcomb, M. D. (2000). Ethnic belonging and traditional masculine ideology among African Americans, European Americans, and Latinos. *Psychology of Men & Masculinity, 1,* 75–86.

Abu-Rayya, H. M. Ethnic identity, ego identity, and psychological well-being among mixed-ethnic Arab-European adolescents in Israel. *British Journal of Developmental Psychology, 24*(4) 669–679.

Achenbach, T. M., & Edelbrock, C. (1986). *Manual for the teacher's report form and teacher version of the child behavior profile.* Burlington: University of Vermont, Department of Psychiatry.

Achenbach, T. M., Howell, C. T., Quay, H. C., & Conners, C. K. (1991). National survey of problems and competencies among four- to sixteen-year-olds. *Monographs of the Society for Research in Child Development, 56* (3, Serial No. 225).

Adams, G. R. (1999). *The objective measure of ego identity status: A manual on test theory and construction.* Guelph, Canada: Author.

Adams, G. R., Gullotta, T. P., & Montemayor, R. (Eds.). (1992). *Adolescent identity formation.* Newbury Park, CA: Sage.

Adams, G. R., Openshaw, D. K., Bennion, L., Mills, T., & Noble, S. (1988). Loneliness in late adolescence: A social skills training study. *Journal of Adolescent Research, 3,* 81–96.

Adegoke, A. (1993). The experience of spermarche (the age of onset of sperm emission) among selected adolescent boys in Nigeria. *Journal of Youth and Adolescence, 22,* 201–209.

Adelson, J. (1971). The political imagination of the young adolescent. *Daedalus, 100,* 1013–1050.

Adelson, J. (1991). Political development. In R. M. Lerner, A. C. Petersen, & J. Brooks-Gunn (Eds.), *Encyclopedia of adolescence* (Vol. 2, pp. 792–793). New York: Garland.

Adler, N. E., Ozer, E. J., & Tschann, J. (2003). Abortion among adolescents. *American Psychologist, 58,* 211–217.

Adler, P., & Adler, P. (1998). *Peer power.* New Brunswick, NJ: Rutgers University Press.

Afifi, T. D., McManus, T., Hutchinson, S., & Baker, B. (2007) Inappropriate parental divorce disclosures, the factors that prompt them, and their impact on parents' and adolescents' well-being. *Communication Monographs, 74*(1), 78–102.

Aguirre International. (1999). *Making a difference: Impact of AmeriCorps state/national direct on members and communities, 1994–95 and 1995–96.* San Mateo, CA: Author.

Ahmed, L. (1992). *Women and gender in Islam.* New Haven, CT: Yale University Press.

Ainsworth, M. D. S. (1967). *Infancy in Uganda: Infant care and the growth of love.* Baltimore, MD: Johns Hopkins University Press.

Ainsworth, M. D. S. (1982). Attachment: Retrospect and prospect. In C. M. Parkes & J. Stevenson-Hinde (Eds.), *The place of attachment in human behavior.* New York: Basic Books.

Akos, P., Lambie, G. W., Milsom, A., Gilbert, K. Early adolescents' aspirations and academic tracking: An exploratory investigation. *Professional School Counseling 11*(1), 57–64.

Al-Mateen, C. S., & Afzal, A. (2004). The Muslim child, adolescent, and family. *Child and Adolescent Psychiatric Clinics of North America, 13,* 183–200.

Alan Guttmacher Institute (1999). *Teen sex and pregnancy: Facts in brief.* New York: Author. Available: www.agi-usa.org

Alan Guttmacher Institute (AGI) (2001). *Teenage sexual and reproductive behavior in developed countries: Can more progress be made?* New York: Author. Available: www.agi-usa.org.

Alan Guttmacher Institute (2002). *Policy analysis: Issues in brief.* New York: Author.

Alberts, A., Elkind, D., & Ginsberg, S. (2007) The personal fable and risk-taking in early adolescence. *Journal of Youth and Adolescence, 36*(1), 71–76.

Alexander, B. (2001, June). Radical idea serves youth, saves money. *Youth Today,* pp. 1, 42–44.

Alexander, K., & Eckland, B. (1975). School experience and status attainment. In S. Dragastin & G. Elder, Jr. (Eds.), *Adolescence in the life cycle.* Washington, DC: Hemisphere.

Alexander, P. C., Moore, S., & Alexander, E. R., III (1991). What is transmitted in the intergenerational transmission of violence? *Journal of Marriage and the Family, 53,* 657–668.

Alfieri, T., Ruble, D. N., & Higgins, E. T. (1996). Gender stereotypes during adolescence: Developmental changes and the transition to junior high school. *Developmental Psychology, 32,* 1129–1137.

Allen, F. L. (1964). *Only yesterday: An informal history of the 1920s.* New York: Harper & Row.

Allen, J. P., & Bell, K. L. (1995, March). *Attachment and communication with parents and peers in adolescence.* Paper presented at the meeting of the Society for Research in Child Development, Indianapolis.

Allen, J. P., & Kuperminc, G. P. (1995, March). *Adolescent attachment, social competence, and problematic behavior.* Paper presented at the meeting of the Society for Research in Child Development, Indianapolis.

Allen, J. P., Moore, C., Kuperminc, G., & Bell, K. (1998). Attachment and adolescent psychosocial functioning. *Child Development, 69,* 1406–1419.

Allen, J. P., Porter, M. R., & McFarland, F. C. (2006). Leaders and followers in adolescent close friendships: Susceptibility to peer influence as a predictor of risky behavior, friendship instability and depression. *Development and Psychopathology, 18*(1), 155–172.

Allen, J., Hauser, S., Bell, K., & O'Connor, T. (1994). Longitudinal assessment of autonomy and relatedness in adolescent-family interactions as predictors of adolescent ego development and self-esteem. *Child Development, 65,* 179–194.

Allen, J., & Land, P. (1999). Attachment in adolescence. In J. Cassidy & P. R. Shaver (Eds.), *Handbook of attachment: Theory, research, and clinical applications.* New York: Guilford.

Allen, L. S., & Gorski, R. A. (1992). Sexual orientation and the size of the anterior commissure in the human brain. *Proceedings of the National Academy of Sciences, USA, 89,* 7199–7202.

Allgood-Merten, B., Lewinsohn, P. M., Hops, H. Sex differences and adolescent depression. *Journal of Abnormal Psychology. 99*(1), 55–63.

Allison, R., & Furstenberg, F., Jr. (1989). How marital dissolution affects children: Variations by age and sex. *Developmental Psychology, 25,* 540–549,

Alpha Phi Alpha (2009). Project Alpha. Retrieved on January 13, 2009, from http://www.alpha-phi-alpha.com/Page.php?id=165&key=mentor

Alsaker, F. D., & Flammer, A. (1999). Cross-national research in adolescent psychology: The Euronet project. In F. D. Alsaker & A. Flammer (Eds.), *The adolescent experience: European and American adolescents in the 1990s* (pp. 1–14). Mahwah, NJ: Erlbaum.

Alsaker, F. D., & Flammer, A. (1999a). *The adolescent experience: European and American adolescents in the 1990s.* Mahwah, NJ: Erlbaum.

Alsaker, F. D., & Flammer, A. (1999b). Cross-national research in adolescent psychology: The Euronet project. In F. D. Alsaker & A. Flammer (Eds.), *The adolescent experience: European and American adolescents in the 1990s* (pp. 1–14). Mahwah, NJ: Erlbaum.

Alsaker, F. D., & Flammer, A. (2006) Pubertal maturation. In S. Jackson & LucGoossens (Eds.), *Handbook of adolescent development* (pp. 30–50). New York: Psychology Press.

Altermatt, E. R., & Pomerantz, E. M. (2005). The implications of having high-achieving versus low-achieving friends: A longitudinal analysis. *Social Development, 14,* 61–81.

Alwin, D. F. (1988). From obedience to autonomy: Changes in traits desired in children, 1928–1978. *Public Opinion Quarterly, 52,* 33–52.

Alwin, D. F., Xu, X., & Carson, T. (1994, October). *Childrearing goals and child discipline.* Paper presented at the Public World of Childhood Project workshop on Children Harmed and Harmful, Chicago.

Amato, P. (2000). The consequences of divorce for children and adults. *Journal of Marriage and the Family, 62,* 1269–1287.

Amato, P. R. (1993). Children's adjustment to divorce: Theories, hypotheses, and empirical support. *Journal of Marriage and the Family, 55,* 23–38.

Amato, P. R., & Keith, B. (1991). Parental divorce and the well-being of children: A meta-analysis. *Psychological Bulletin, 100,* 26–46.

Amato, P. R., Loomis, L. S., & Booth, A. (1995). Parental divorce, marital conflict, and offspring well-being during early adulthood. *Social Forces, 73,* 895–915.

American Association of University Women (1991). *The AAUW Report: How schools shortchange girls.* Washington, DC: Author.

American Association of University Women. (1993). *Hostile hallways*. Washington, DC: Author.

American Council on Education (2003). *The American freshman: National norms for fall 2002*. UCLA Higher Education Research Institute. Los Angeles, CA: Author.

American Psychiatric Association. (1994). *Diagnostic and statistical manual of mental disorders* (4th ed.). Washington, DC: Author.

AmeriCorps. (2000a). Research: The history of AmeriCorps. Available: www.cns.gov/americorps/research/history.html

AmeriCorps. (2000b). Joining AmeriCorps: Check out the benefits. Available: www.cns.gov/americorps/joining/step2.html

AmeriCorps. (2000c). Partners in service: About partnerships: How partnerships deliver. Available: www.cns.gov/partners/summary/deliver.html

AmeriCorps. (2009). About Americorps. Available: http://www.americorps.gov/about/overview/index.asp. Retrieved on March 5, 2009.

Ammerman, R. T., & Hersen, M. (1992). Current issues in the assessment of family violence. In R. T. Ammerman & M. Hersen (Eds.), *Assessment of family violence* (pp. 3–11). New York: Wiley.

Anastasi, A. (1988). *Psychological testing*, 6th ed. New York: Macmillan.

Anderson, A., Hamilton, R. J., & Hattie, J. (2004). Classroom climate and motivated behavior in secondary schools. *Learning Environments Research, 7*, 211–225.

Anderson, C., & Ford, C. M. (1987). Affect of the game player: Short-term effects of highly and mildly aggressive video games. *Personality and Social Psychology Bulletin, 12*, 390–402.

Anderson, C. A. (2004). An update on the effects of playing violent video games. *Journal of Adolescence, 27*, 113–122.

Anderson, C. A., & Dill, K. E. (2000). Violent video games can increase aggression. *Journal of Personality and Social Psychology, 78*, 772–790.

Anderson, C. A., Duffy, D. L., Martin, N. G., & Visscher, P. M. (2007). Estimation of variance components for age of menarche in twin families. *Behavior Genetics, 37*, 668–677.

Anderson, C. A., Gentile, D. A., & Buckley, K. E. (2007). *Violent video game effects on children and adolescents: Theory, research, and public policy*. New York: Oxford University Press.

Anderson, E. R., Hetherington, E. M., & Clingempeel, W. G. (1989). Transformations in family relations at puberty: Effects of family context. *Journal of Early Adolescence, 9*, 310–334.

Anderson, R. E. (2000). *Youth and information technology*. Unpublished manuscript, University of Minnesota.

Anderson, R. E. (2002). Youth and information technology. In J. T. Mortimer & R. W. Larson (Eds.), *The changing adolescent experience: Societal trends and the transition to adulthood* (pp. 175–207). New York: Cambridge University Press.

Andersson, T., & Magnusson, D. (1990). Biological maturation in adolescence and the development of drinking habits and alcohol abuse among young males: A prospective longitudinal study. *Journal of Youth and Adolescence, 19*, 33–42.

Ando, M., Asakura, T., Simons-Morton, B. (2005). Psychosocial influences in physical, verbal and indirect bullying among Japanese early adolescents. *Journal of Early Adolescence, 25*(3), 268–297.

Annunziata, D., Hogue, A., Faw, L., Liddle, & H. A. Family functioning and school Success in at-risk, inner-city adolescents. *Journal of Youth and Adolescence, 35*(1), 105–113

Appel, M. (2008) Fictional narratives cultivate just-world beliefs. *Journal of Communication, 58*(1), 62–83.

Applebome, P. (1997, September 3). Students' test scores show slow but steady gains at nation's schools. *New York Times*, p. A-17.

Aptekar, L., & Ciano-Federoff, L. M. (1999). Street children in Nairobi: Gender differences in mental health. In M. Raffaelli & R. Larson (Eds.), *Homeless and Working Youth Around the World: Exploring Developmental Issues* (pp. 35–46). New Directions in Child and Adolescent Development, Number 85. San Francisco: Jossey-Bass.

Apter, T. (1990). *Altered loves: Mothers and daughters during adolescence*. New York: St. Martin's.

Aquilino, W. S. (2006). Family relationships and support systems in emerging adulthood. In J. J. Arnett and J. Tanner (Eds.), *Coming of age in the 21st century: The lives and contexts of emerging adults* (pp. 193–218). Washington, DC: American Psychological Association.

Aral, S., Vanderplate, C., & Madger, L. (1988). Recurrent genital herpes: What helps adjustment? *Sexually Transmitted Diseases, 15*, 164–166.

Archer, S. L. (1989). Gender differences in identity development: Issues of process, domain, and timing. *Journal of Adolescence, 12*, 117–138.

Archer, S. L. (1992). A feminist's approach to identity research. In G. R. Adams, T. P. Gullotta, & R. Montemayor (Eds.), *Adolescent identity formation: Advances in adolescent development* (pp. 25–49). Newbury Park, CA: Sage.

Archer, S. L. (2002). Commentary on "Feminist perspectives on Erikson's theory: Their relevance for contemporary identity development research." *Identity, 2*, 267–270.

Archibald, A. B., Graber, J. A., & Brooks-Gunn, J. (2003). Pubertal processes and physiological growth in adolescence. In G. Adams & M. Berzonsky (Eds.), *Blackwell handbook of adolescence*. Malden, MA: Blackwell.

Arciniega, G. M., Anderson, T. C., Tovar-Blank, Z. G., & Tracey, T. J. G. (2008). Toward a fuller conception of machismo: Development of a traditional machismo and caballerismo Scale. *Journal of Counseling Psychology, 55*(1), 19–33.

Arehart, D. M., & Smith, P. H. (1990). Identity in adolescence: Influences on dysfunction and psychosocial task issues. *Journal of Youth and Adolescence, 19*, 63–72.

Arlin, P. K. (1989). Problem solving and problem finding in young artists and young scientists. In M. L. Commons, J. D. Sinnott, F. A. Richards, & C. Armon (Eds.), *Adult development, Vol. 1: Comparisons and applications of developmental models* (pp. 197–216). New York: Praeger.

Arlin, P. K. (1990). Wisdom: The art of problem finding. In R. J. Sternberg (Ed.), *Wisdom: Its nature, origins, and development* (pp. 230–243). New York: Cambridge University Press.

Arnett, J. (1990). Contraceptive use, sensation seeking, and adolescent egocentrism. *Journal of Youth and Adolescence, 19*, 171–180. Reprinted in M. L. Patten (Ed.), *Educational and psychological research* (pp. 73–78). Los Angeles: Pyrczak Publishing.

Arnett, J. (1991). Adolescents and heavy metal music: From the mouths of metalheads. *Youth and Society, 23*, 76–98.

Arnett, J. (1992). Reckless behavior in adolescence: A developmental perspective. *Developmental Review, 12*, 339–373.

Arnett, J. (1994a). Are college students adults? Their conceptions of the transition to adulthood. *Journal of Adult Development, 1*, 154–168.

Arnett, J. (1994b). Sensation seeking: A new conceptualization and a new scale. *Personality and Individual Differences, 16*, 289–296.

Arnett, J. J. (1995a). Broad and narrow socialization: The family in the context of a cultural theory. *Journal of Marriage and the Family, 57*, 617–628.

Arnett, J. J. (1995b). Adolescents' uses of media for self-socialization. *Journal of Youth & Adolescence, 24*, 519–533.

Arnett, J. J. (1996). *Metalheads: Heavy metal music and adolescent alienation*. Boulder, CO: Westview Press.

Arnett, J. J. (1997). Young people's conceptions of the transition to adulthood. *Youth & Society, 29*, 1–23.

Arnett, J. J. (1998a). Learning to stand alone: The contemporary American transition to adulthood in cultural and historical context. *Human Development, 41*, 295–315.

Arnett, J. J. (1998b). Risk behavior and family role transitions during the twenties. *Journal of Youth & Adolescence, 27*, 301–320.

Arnett, J. J. (1999a). Adolescent storm and stress, reconsidered. *American Psychologist, 54*, 317–326.

Arnett, J. J. (2000a). Emerging adulthood: A theory of development from the late teens through the twenties. *American Psychologist, 55*, 469–480.

Arnett, J. J. (2000b). Optimistic bias in adolescent and adult smokers and nonsmokers. *Addictive Behaviors, 25*, 625–632.

Arnett, J. J. (2000c). High hopes in a grim world: Emerging adults' views of their futures and of "Generation X." *Youth & Society, 31*, 267–286.

Arnett, J. J. (2001a). Conceptions of the transition to adulthood: Perspectives from adolescence to midlife. *Journal of Adult Development, 8*, 133–143.

Arnett, J. J. (2001b). Adolescents' responses to cigarette advertisements for five "youth brands" and one "adult brand." *Journal of Research on Adolescence, 11*, 425–443.

Arnett, J. J. (2001c, April). *Adolescents' views of the transition to adulthood in Korea and the United States*. Paper presented at the biennial meeting of the Society for Research in Child Development, Minneapolis, Minnesota.

Arnett, J. J. (2002a). The psychology of globalization. *American Psychologist, 57*, 774–783.

Arnett, J. J. (2002b). Adolescents in Western countries in the 21st century: Vast opportunities—for all? In B. B. Brown, R. W. Larson, & T. S. Saraswathi (Eds.), *The World's Youth: Adolescence in Eight Regions of the Globe* (pp. 307–343). New York: Cambridge University Press.

Arnett, J. J. (2002c). The sounds of sex: Sex in teens' music and music videos. In J. D. Brown, J. R Steele, & K. Walsh-Childers (Eds.), *Sexual teens, sexual media: Investigating media's influence on adolescent sexuality* (pp. 253–264). Mahwah, NJ: Erlbaum.

Arnett, J. J. (2002d). Developmental sources of crash risk in young drivers. *Injury Prevention, 8*(Suppl. 2), ii17–ii21.

Arnett, J. J. (2003a). Conceptions of the transition to adulthood among emerging adults in American ethnic groups. *New Directions in Child and Adolescent Development, 100*, 63–75.

Arnett, J. J. (2003b). Music at the edge: Popular music and adolescents' pursuit of the transgressive. In D. Ravich & J. Viteritti (Eds.), *Kid stuff: Marketing sex and violence to America's youth* (pp. 125–142). Baltimore, Maryland: Johns Hopkins University Press.

Arnett, J. J. (2004a). *Emerging adulthood: The winding road from the late teens through the twenties*. New York: Oxford University Press.

Arnett, J. J. (2004b). Adolescence in the 21st century: A worldwide survey. In U. P. Gielen & J. L. Roopnarine (Eds.), *Childhood and adolescence in cross-cultural perspective* (pp. 277–294). New York: Guilford.

Arnett, J. J. (2005a). The Vitality Criterion: A new standard of publication for Journal of Adolescent Research. *Journal of Adolescent Research, 20*, 3–7.

Arnett, J. J. (2005b). The developmental context of substance use in emerging adulthood. *Journal of Drug Issues, 35*, 235–253.

Arnett, J. J. (2005c). The myth of peer influence in adolescent smoking initiation. *Health Education & Behavior.*

Arnett, J. J. (2005d). Talk is cheap: The tobacco companies' violations of their own Cigarette Advertising Code. *Journal of Health Communication, 10*, 419–431.

Arnett, J. J. (2006a). G. Stanley Hall's *Adolescence: Brilliance and nonsense*. *History of Psychology, 9*, 186–197.

Arnett, J. J. (2006b). Emerging adulthood: Understanding the new way of coming of age. In J. J. Arnett and J. L. Tanner (Eds.), *Emerging adults in America: Coming of age in the 21st century*, (pp. 3–20). Washington, DC: American Psychological Association Press.

Arnett, J. J. (2006c). The case for emerging adulthood in Europe. *Journal of Youth Studies, 9,* 111–123.

Arnett, J. J. (2006d). Socialization in emerging adulthood: From the family to the wider world, from socialization to self-socialization. In J. Grusec and P. Hastings (Eds.), *Handbook of socialization.* New York: Guilford.

Arnett, J. J. (2007a). Emerging adulthood: What is it, and what is it good for? *Child Development Perspectives, 1,* 68–73.

Arnett, J. J. (2007a). The myth of peer influence in adolescent smoking initiation. *Health Education & Behavior, 34*(4), 594–607.

Arnett, J. J. (2007b). Music, transgressive, history of. In J. J. Arnett (Ed.), *Encyclopedia of children, adolescents and the media* (Vol. 2, pp. 571–573). Thousand Oaks, CA: Sage.

Arnett, J. J. (2007c). Music genres, heavy metal. In J. J. Arnett (Ed.), *Encyclopedia of children, adolescents, and the media* (Vol. 2, pp. 575–577). Thousand Oaks, CA: Sage.

Arnett, J. J. (2008a). The neglected 95%: Why American psychology needs to become less American. *American Psychologist.*

Arnett, J. J., & Balle-Jensen, L. (1993). Cultural bases of risk behavior: Danish adolescents. *Child Development, 64,* 1842–1855.

Arnett, J. J., & Galambos, N. (2003). Culture and conceptions of the transition to adulthood. *New Directions in Child and Adolescent Development, 100,* 91–98.

Arnett, J. J., Hendry, L., Kloep, M., & Tanner, J. L. (2009). *Diverging perspectives on emerging adulthood: Stage or process?* London: Psychology Press.

Arnett, J. J., & Jensen, L. A. (2002). A congregation of one: Individualized religious beliefs among emerging adults. *Journal of Adolescent Research, 17,* 451–467.

Arnett, J. J., Ramos, K. D., & Jensen, L. A. (2001). Ideologies in emerging adulthood: Balancing the ethics of autonomy and community. *Journal of Adult Development, 8,* 69–79.

Arnett, J. J., & Taber, S. (1994). Adolescence terminable and interminable: When does adolescence end? *Journal of Youth & Adolescence, 23,* 517–537.

Arnett, J. J., & Terhanian, G. (1998). Adolescents' responses to cigarette advertising: Exposure, liking, and the appeal of smoking. *Tobacco Control, 7,* 129–133.

Aronson, P. J., Mortimer, J. T., Zierman, C., & Hacker, M. (1996). Generational differences in early work experiences and evaluations. In T. J. Mortimer & D. M. Finch (Eds.), *Adolescents, work, and family: An intergenerational developmental analysis.* Thousand Oaks, CA: Sage.

Artar, M. (2007). Adolescent egocentrism and theory of mind: In the context of family relations. *Behavior and Personality, 35*(9), 1211–1220.

Asakawa, K., & Csikszentmihalyi, M. (1999). The quality of experience of Asian American adolescents in activities related to future goals. *Journal of Youth & Adolescence, 27,* 141–163.

Asendorpf, J. B., & van Aken, M. A. (1999). Resilient, overcontrolled, and undercontrolled personality prototypes in childhood: Replicability, predictive power, and the trait-type issue. *Journal of Personality and Social Psychology, 77,* 815–832.

Ashcraft, M. H. (2002). *Cognition.* Upper Saddle River, NJ: Prentice Hall.

Asher, S., & Coie, J. (Eds.). (1990). *Peer rejection in childhood.* New York: Cambridge University Press.

Asher, S. R., Parkhurst, J. E., Hymel, S., & Williams, G. A. (1990). Peer rejection and loneliness in childhood. In S. R. Asher & J. D. Coie (Eds.), *Peer rejection in childhood* (pp. 253–273). New York: Cambridge University Press.

Ashford, L. (2002, February/March). Young women in sub-Saharan Africa face a high risk of HIV infection. *Population Today,* pp. 3, 6. Washington, DC: Population Reference Bureau.

Astone, N. M., & McLanahan, S. S. (1995). Family structure, residential mobility, and school dropout: A research note. *Demography, 9,* 375–388.

Austin, A. M., Macgowan, M. J., & Wagner, E. F. (2005). Effective family-based interventions for adolescents with substance use problems: A systematic review. *Research on Social Work Practice, 15,* 67–83.

Avery, L., & Lazdane, G. (2008). What do we know about sexual and reproductive health among adolescents in Europe? *European Journal of Contraception and Reproductive Health, 13,* 58–70.

Axelsson, L., & Ejlertsson, G. (2002). Self-reported health, self-esteem and social support among young unemployed people: A population-based study. *International Journal of Social Welfare, 11,* 111–119.

Bachman, J. (1983, Summer). Premature affluence: Do high school students earn too much? *Economic Outlook USA,* 64–67.

Bachman, J. G., Johnston, L. D., & O'Malley, P. M. (1995). *Monitoring the future: Questionnaire responses from the nation's high school seniors.* Ann Arbor: Institute for Social Research, University of Michigan.

Bachman, J. G., Johnston, L. D., O'Malley, P., & Schulenberg, J. (1996). Transitions in drug use during late adolescence and young adulthood. In J. A. Graber, J. Brooks-Gunn, & A. C. Petersen (Eds.), *Transitions through adolescence: Interpersonal domains and context* (pp. 111–140). Mahwah, NJ: Erlbaum.

Bachman, J. G., & O'Malley, P. M. (1986). Self-concepts, self-esteem, and educational experiences: The frog pond revisited (again). *Journal of Personality and Social Psychology, 50,* 35–46.

Bachman, J. G., Safron, D. J., Sy, S. R., & Schulenberg, J. E. (2003). Wishing to work: New perspectives on how adolescents' part-time work intensity is linked to educational engagement, substance use, and other problem behaviours. *International Journal of Behavioral Development.*

Bachman, J. G., & Schulenberg, J. How part-time work intensity relates to drug use, problem behavior, time use, and satisfaction among high school seniors: Are these consequences or just correlates? *Developmental Psychology, 29,* 220–235.

Bachman, J. G., Segal, D. R., Freedman-Doan, P., & O'Malley, P. M. (2000). Who chooses military service? Correlates of propensity and enlistment in the U.S. Armed Forces. *Military Psychology, 12,* 1–30.

Bachman, J. G., Wadsworth, K. N., O'Malley, P. M., Johnston, L. D., & Schulenberg, J. E. (1997). *Smoking, drinking, and drug use in young adulthood: The impacts of new freedoms and new responsibilities.* Mahwah, NJ: Erlbaum.

Bachman, J. G., Wadsworth, K. N., O'Malley, P. M., Schulenberg, J., & Johnston, L. D. (1999). Marriage, divorce, and parenthood during the transition to adulthood: Impacts on drug use and abuse. In J. Schulenberg, J. L. Maggs & K. Hurrelmann (Eds.), *Health risks and developmental transitions during adolescence* (pp. 246–282). New York: Cambridge University Press.

Bachrach, C. A., Clogg, C. C., & Carver, K. (1993). Outcomes of early childbearing: Summary of a conference. *Journal of Research on Adolescence, 3,* 337–348.

Baddeley, A. (2000). Short-term and working memory. In E. Tulving & F. I. M. Craik (Eds.), *The Oxford handbook of memory.* New York: Oxford University Press.

Baffour, T. D. (2007). Prevalence and incidence of black-on-black crime among youth. In L. A. See (Ed.), *Human behavior in the social environment from an African-American perspective* (2nd ed., pp. 293–308). New York: Haworth Press.

Bailey, B. L. (1989). *From front porch to back seat: Courtship in twentieth-century America.* Baltimore, MD: Johns Hopkins University Press.

Bailey, J. M., Pillard, R. C., Neale, M. C., & Agyei, Y. (1993). Heritable factors influence sexual orientation in women. *Archives of General Psychiatry, 50,* 217–223.

Baillargeon, R. H., Zoccolillo, M., Keenan, K., Côté, S., Pérusse, D., Wu, H., Boivin, M., & Tremblay, R. E. (2007). Gender differences in physical aggression: A prospective population-based survey of children before and after 2 years of age. *Developmental Psychology, 43*(1), 13–26.

Bain, S. K., & Allin, J. D. (2005). Stanford-Binet intelligence scales, fifth edition. *Journal of Psychoeducational Assessment, 23,* 87–95.

Baird, A. A., Gruber, S. A., Cohen, B. M., Renshaw, R. J., & Yureglun-Todd, D. A. (1999). FMRI of the amygdala in children and adolescents. *American Academy of Child and Adolescent Psychiatry, 38,* 195–199.

Baker, D. P., & Perkins-Jones, D. (1993). Creating gender equality: Cross-national gender stratification and mathematical performance. *Sociology of Education, 66,* 91–103.

Baker, J. M. (2002). *How homophobia hurts children: Nurturing diversity at home, at school, and in the community.* New York: Haworth Press.

Baker, J. R., & Moore, S. M. (2008). Distress, coping and blogging: Comparing new MySpace users by their intention to blog. *CyberPsychology & Behavior, 11*(1), 81–85.

Balikci, A. (1970). *The Netsilik Eskimo.* Prospect Heights, IL: Waveland Press.

Ballentine, L. W., Ogle, J. P. (2005). The making and unmaking of body problems in *Seventeen* magazine 1992–2003. *Family & Consumer Sciences Research Journal, 33,* 281–307.

Bamberger, M. (2004). *Wonderland: A year in the life of an American high school.* New York: Atlantic Monthly Press.

Bandura, A. (1994). Social cognitive theory of mass communication. In J. Bryant & D. Zillman (Eds.), *Media effects: Advances in theory and research* (pp. 61–90). Hillsdale, NJ: Erlbaum.

Bankole, A., Singh, S., Woog, V., & Wulf, D. (2004). *Risk and protection: Youth and HIV/AIDS in sub-Saharan Africa.* Washington, DC: Alan Guttmacher Institute.

Banks, R. (1995). *The rule of the bone.* New York: HarperCollins.

Barbarin, O., & Soler, R. (1993). Behavioral, emotional, and academic adjustment in a national probability sample of African-American children. *Journal of Black Psychology, 19,* 423–446.

Barber, B., & Eccles, J. (1992). Long-term influence of divorce and single parenting on adolescent family- and work-related values, behaviors, and aspirations. *Psychological Bulletin, 111,* 108–126.

Barber, B., Olsen, J., & Shagle, S. (1994). Associations between parental psychological and behavioral control and youth internalized and externalized behaviors. *Child Development, 65,* 1120–1136.

Barber, B. K. (2002). *Intrusive parenting: How psychological control affects children and adolescents.* Washington, DC: American Psychological Association.

Barber, B. K., & Olsen, J. A. (2004). Assessing the transitions to middle and high school. *Journal of Adolescent Research, 19,* 3–30.

Barenboim, C. (1981). The development of person perception in childhood and adolescence: From behavioral comparisons to psychological construction to psychological comparisons. *Child Development, 52,* 129–144.

Barkley, R. A. (2002). Major life activity and health outcomes associated with attention-deficit/hyperactivity disorder. *Journal of Clinical Psychiatry, 63,* 10–15.

Barling, J., & Kelloway, E. K. (1999). *Young workers: Varieties of experience.* Washington, DC: American Psychological Association.

Barnes, J. (2002, November 11). The SAT revolution. *U.S. News & World Report*, 50–60.

Barrera, M., Biglan, A., Ary, D., & Li, F. (2001). Replication of a problem behavior model with American Indian, Hispanic, and Caucasion youth. *Journal of Early Adolescence, 21*, 133–157.

Barrett, M. E., Simpson, D. D., & Lehman, W. E. (1988). Behavioral changes of adolescents in drug abuse prevention programs. *Journal of Clinical Psychology, 44*, 461–473.

Barrio, C., Morena, A., & Linaza, J. L. (2007). Spain. In J. J. Arnett, R. Ahmed, B. Nsamenang, T. S. Saraswathi, & R. Silbereisen (Eds.), *International encyclopedia of adolescence*. New York: Routledge.

Barry, D. (1995). *Dave Barry's complete guide to guys*. New York: Fawcett Columbine.

Barsalou, L. W. (1992). *Cognitive psychology: An overview for cognitive scientists*. Hillsdale, NJ: Erlbaum.

Bartholet, J. (2000, January 17). The plague years. *Newsweek*, 32–37.

Barton, P. E. (2005). *One-third of a nation: Rising dropout rates and declining opportunities*. Princeton, NJ: Educational Testing Service.

Basow, S. (2004). The hidden curriculum: Gender in the classroom. In M. A. Paludi, (Ed.), *Praeger guide to the psychology of gender* (pp. 117–131). Westport, CT: Praeger/Greenwood Publishing Group.

Basow, S. A., & Rubin, L. R. (1999). Gender influences on adolescent development. In N. B. Johnson, M. C. Roberts, & J. Worell (Eds.), *Beyond appearance: A new look at adolescent girls* (pp. 25–52). Washington, DC: American Psychological Association.

Bass, E., & Kaufman, K. (1996). *Free your mind: The book for lesbian, gay, and bisexual youth and their allies*. New York: HarperTrade.

Basseches, M. (1984). *Dialectical thinking and adult development*. Norwood, NJ: Ablex.

Basseches, M. (1989). Dialectical thinking as an organized whole: Comments on Irwin and Kramer. In M. L. Commons, J. D. Sinnott, F. A. Richards, & C. Armon (Eds.), *Adult development, Vol. 1: Comparisons and applications of developmental models* (pp. 161–178). New York: Praeger.

Bassi, M., & Fave, A. D. (2004). Adolescence and the changing context of optimal experience in time: Italy 1986–2000. *Journal of Happiness Studies, 5*, 155–179.

Bassi, M., Fave, & Antonella, D. Adolescence and the changing context of optimal experience in time: Italy 1986–2000. *Journal of Happiness Studies, 5*(2), 155–179.

Basu, A. K., & Chau, N. H. (2007). An exploration of the worst forms of child labor: Is redemption a viable option? In K. A. Appiah & M. Bunzl (Eds.), *Buying freedom: The ethics of economics of slave redemption* (pp. 37–76). Princeton, NJ: Princeton University Press.

Battaglia, D. M., Richard, F. D., Datteri, D. L., & Lord, C. G. (1998). Breaking up is (relatively) easy to do: A script for the dissolution of close relationships. *Journal of Social and Personal Relationships, 15*, 829–845.

Bauman, K. E., & Fisher, L. A. (1986). On the measurement of friend behavior in research on friend influence and selection: Findings from longitudinal studies of adolescent smoking and drinking. *Journal of Youth & Adolescence, 15*, 345–353.

Baumeister, R. F. (1987). How the self became a problem: A psychological review of historical research. *Journal of Personality and Social Psychology, 52*, 163–176.

Bauminger, N., Finzi-Dottan, R., Chason, S., & Har-Even, D. (2008). Intimacy in adolescent friendship: The roles of attachment, coherence and self-disclosure. *Journal of Social and Personal Relationships, 25*(3), 409–428.

Baumrind, D. (1968). Authoritative vs. authoritarian parental control. *Adolescence, 3*, 255–272.

Baumrind, D. (1971). Current patterns of parental authority. *Developmental Psychology Monographs, 4*(1, Pt.2).

Baumrind, D. (1987). A developmental perspective on adolescent risk taking in contemporary America. In C. E. Irwin, Jr. (Ed.), Adolescent social behavior and health. *New Directions for Child Development, 37*, 93–125.

Baumrind, D. (1991a). Effective parenting during the early adolescent transition. In P. A. Cowan & E. M. Hetherington (Ed.), *Advances in family research* (Vol. 2, pp. 111–163). Hillsdale, NJ: Erlbaum.

Baumrind, D. (1991b). The influence of parenting style on adolescent competence and substance use. *Journal of Early Adolescence, 11*, 56–95.

Baumrind, D. (1993). The average expectable environment is not enough: A response to Scarr. *Child Development, 64*, 1299–1317.

Baxter, B. L., De Riemer, C., Landini, A., Leslie, L., & Singletary, M. W. (1985). A content analysis of music videos. *Journal of Broadcasting and Electronic Media, 29*, 333–340.

Bayley, N. (1968). Behavioral correlates of mental growth: Birth to thirty-six years. *American Psychologist, 23*, 1–17.

Beam, M. R., Gil-Rivas, V., Greenberger, E., & Chen, C. (2002). Adolescent problem behavior and depressed mood: Risk and protection within and across social contexts. *Journal of Youth & Adolescence, 31*, 343–357.

Beasow, S. (2004). The hidden curriculum: Gender in the classroom. In A. M. Paludi (Ed.), *Praeger guide to the psychology of gender* (pp. 117–131). Westport, CT: Praeger.

Becker, A. E. (2004). Television, disordered eating, and young women in Fiji: Negotiating body image and identity during rapid social change. *Culture, Medicine & Psychiatry, 28*, 533–559.

Becker, B. E., & Luthar, S. S. (2007). Peer-perceived admiration and social preference: Contextual correlates of positive peer regard among suburban and urban adolescents. *Journal of Research on Adolescence, 17*(1), 117–144.

Becker, E. (1973). *The denial of death*. New York: Free Press.

Bednar, R. L., Wells, M. G., & Peterson, S. R. (1995). *Self-esteem* (2nd ed.). Washington, DC: American Psychological Association.

Beentjes, J. W. J., Koolstra, C. M., Marseille, N., & van der Voort, T. H. A. (2001). Children's use of different media: For how long and why? In S. M. Livingstone & M. Bovill (Eds.), *Children and their changing media environment: A European comparative study* (pp. 85–112). Hillsdale, NJ: Lawrence Erlbaum.

Beger, R. R. (2003). The "worst of both worlds": School security and the disappearing fourth amendment rights of students. *Criminal justice review, 28*, 336–354.

Begg, D. J., & Langley, J. D. (2004). Identifying predictors of persistent non-alcohol or drug-related risky driving behaviors among a cohort of young adults. *Accident Analysis & Prevention, 36*, 1067–1071.

Begley, S. (2000, May 8). A world of their own. *Newsweek*, 52–56.

Beirness, D. J., & Simpson, H. M. (1988). Lifestyle correlates of risky driving and accident involvement among youth. *Alcohol, Drugs and Driving, 4*, 193–204.

Bell, A., Weinberg, M., & Hammersmith, S. (1981). *Sexual preference: Its development in men and women*. Bloomington: Indiana University Press.

Bell, R. (1998). *Changing bodies, changing lives* (3rd ed.). New York: Times Books.

Bellah, R. N., Madsen, R., Sullivan, W. M., Swidler, A., & Tipton, S. M. (1985). *Habits of the heart: Individualism and commitment in American life*. New York: Harper & Row.

Belsky, J., Steinberg, L.D., Houts, R.M., Friedman, S.L., DeHart, G., Cauffman, E., Roisman, G.I, Halpern-Felsher, B., & Susman, E. (2007). Family rearing antecedents of pubertal timing. *Child Development, 78*, 1302–1321.

Bem, S. L. (1974). The measurement of psychological androgyny. *Journal of Consulting and Clinical Psychology, 42*, 155–162.

Bem, S. L. (1975). Sex role adaptability: One consequence of psychological androgyny. *Journal of Personality and Social Psychology, 31*, 634–643.

Bem, S. L. (1977). On the utility of alternative procedures for assessing psychological androgyny. *Journal of Consulting and Clinical Psychology, 45*, 196–205.

Bem, S. L. (1981). Gender schema theory: A cognitive account of sex-typing. *Psychological Review, 88*, 354–364.

Bem, S. L. (1993). *The lenses of gender: Transforming the debate on sexual inequality*. New Haven: Connecticut University Press.

Ben-Amos, I. K. (1994). *Adolescence and youth in early modern England*. New Haven, CT: Yale University Press.

Benbow, C. P., & Stanley, J. C. (1980). Sex differences in mathematical ability: Fact or artifact? *Science, 210*, 1262–1264.

Benedict, R. (1934/1989). *Patterns of culture*. New York: Houghton Mifflin.

Benedikt, R., Wertheim, E. H., & Love, A. (1998). Eating attitudes and weight-loss attempts in female adolescents and their mothers. *Journal of Youth & Adolescence, 27*, 43–57.

Bennett, N., Blanc, A., & Bloom, D. E. (1988). Commitment and the modern union: Assessing the link between premarital cohabitation and subsequent marital stability. *American Sociological Review, 53*, 127–138.

Bennett, S. (1987). *New dimensions in research on class size and academic achievement*. Madison, WI: National Center on Effective Secondary Schools.

Bensley, L. S., Van Eeenwyk, J., Spieker, S. J., & Schoder, J. (1999). Self-reported abuse history and adolescent problem behaviors. I: Antisocial and suicidal behaviors. *Journal of Adolescent Health, 24*, 163–172.

Benson, M., Harris, P., & Rogers, C. (1992). Identity consequences of attachment to mothers and fathers among late adolescents. *Journal of Research on Adolescence, 2*, 187–204.

Benson, P., Donahue, M., & Erickson, J. (1989). Adolescence and religion: Review of the literature from 1970–1986. *Research in the Social Scientific Study of Religion, 1*, 153–181.

Berenson, K. R., Crawford, T. N., Cohen, P., & Brook, J. (2005). Implications of identification with parents and parents' acceptance for adolescent and young adult self-esteem. *Self & Identity, 4*, 289–301.

Bergen, H. A., Martin, G, Richardson, A. S., Allison, S., & Roeger, L. (2003). Sexual abuse and suicidal behavior: A model constructed from a larger community sample of adolescents. *Jounal of the American Academy of Child & Adolescent Psychiatry, 42*, 1301–1309.

Berkman, N. D., Lohr, K. N., & Bulik, C. M. (2007). Outcomes of eating disorders: A systematic review of the literature. *International Journal of Eating Disorders, 40*(4), 293–309.

Berndt, T. J. (1989). Obtaining support from friends during childhood and adolescence. In D. Belle (Ed.), *Children's social networks and social supports* (pp. 308–331). New York: Wiley.

Berndt, T. J. (1992). Friendship and friends' influence in adolescence. *Current Directions in Psychological Science, 1*, 156–159.

Berndt, T. J. (1996). Transitions in friendship and friends' influence. In J. A. Graber, J. Brooks-Gunn, & A. C. Petersen (Eds.), *Transitions through adolescence: Interpersonal domains and context* (pp. 57–84). Mahwah, NJ: Erlbaum.

Berndt, T. J. (2004). Children's friendships: Shifts over a half-century in perspectives on their development and their effects. *Merrill-Palmer Quarterly, 50*, 206–223.

Berndt, T. J., & Das, R. (1987). Effects of popularity and friendship on perceptions of the personality and social behavior of peers. *Journal of Early Adolescence, 7*, 429–439.

Berndt, T. J., & Mekos, D. (1995). Adolescents' perceptions of the stressful and desirable aspects of the transition to junior high school. *Journal of Research on Adolescence, 5*, 123–142.

Berndt, T. J., & Perry, T. B. (1990). Distinctive features and effects of early adolescent friendships. In R. Montemayor (Ed.), *Advances in adolescent research.* Greenwich, CT: JAI Press.

Berndt, T. J., & Savin-Williams, R. C. (1993). Variations in friendships and peer-group relationships in adolescence. In P. Tolan & B. Cohler (Eds.), *Handbook of clinical research and practice with adolescents* (pp. 203–219). New York: Wiley.

Berry, J. W. (2007). Acculturation. In J. E. Grusec & P. D. Hastings (Eds.), *Handbook of socialization: Theory and research* (pp. 543–558). New York: Guilford.

Berry, J. W., Phinney, J. S., Sam, D. L., & Vedder, P. (Eds.). (2006). *Immigrant youth in cultural transition: Acculturation, identity, and adaptation across national contexts.* Mahwah, NJ: Lawrence Erlbaum.

Berry, V. (1995). Redeeming the rap music experience. In J. S. Epstein (Ed.), *Adolescents and their music* (pp. 165–188). New York: Garland.

Berzonsky, M. D. (1992). A process perspective on identity and stress management. In G. R. Adams, T. P. Gullotta, & R. Montemayor (Eds.), *Adolescent identity formation* (pp. 193–215). Newbury Park, CA: Sage.

Berzonsky, M. D. (2005). Ego identity: A personal standpoint in a postmodern world. *Identity, 5*, 125–136.

Berzonsky, M. D., & Adams, G. R. (1999). Reevaluating the identity status paradigm: Still useful after 35 years. *Developmental Review, 20*, 557–590.

Bettes, B. A., Dusenbury, L., Kerner, J., James-Ortiz, S., & Botvin, G. J. (1990). Ethnicity and psychosocial factors in alcohol and tobacco use in adolescence. *Child Development, 61*, 557–565.

Beyers, J. M., & Loeber, R. Untangling developmental relations between depressed mood and delinquency in male adolescents. *Journal of Abnormal Child Psychology, 31*(3), 247–266.

Beyth-Marom, R., Austin, L., Fischoff, B., Palmgren, C., & Jacobs-Quadrel, M. (1993). Perceived consequences of risky behaviors: Adults and adolescents. *Developmental Psychology, 29*, 549–563.

Beyth-Marom, R., & Fischoff, B. (1997). Adolescents' decisions about risks: A cognitive perspective. In J. Schulenberg & J. L. Maggs (Eds.), *Health risks and developmental transitions during adolescence* (pp. 110–135). New York: Cambridge University Press.

Bianchi, S. M., & Casper, L. M. (2000). American families. *Population Bulletin, 45*(4), 1–44.

Bianchi, S. M., & Spain, D. (1996). Women, work, and family in America. *Population Bulletin, 51*, 1–48.

Bibby, R. W., & Posterski, D. C. (1992). *Teen trends: A nation in motion.* Toronto, Canada: Stoddart.

Biblarz, T. J., Bengtson, V. L., & Bucur, A. (1996). Social mobility across three generations. *Journal of Marriage and the Family, 58*, 188–200.

Biehl, M. C., Natsuaki, M. N., & Ge, X. (2007). The influence of pubertal timing on alcohol use and heavy drinking trajectories. *Journal of Youth and Adolescence, 36*(2), 153–167.

Biener, L., & Siegel, M. (2000). Tobacco marketing and adolescent smoking: More support for a causal inference. *American Journal of Public Health, 90*, 407–411.

Bierman, K. L., & Montminy, H. P. (2001). Developmental issues in social skills assessment and intervention with children and adolescents. *Behavior Modification, 17*, 229–254.

Billy, J., Landale, N., Grady, W., & Zimmerle, D. (1988). Effects of sexual activity on adolescent social and psychological development. *Social Psychology Quarterly, 51*, 190–212.

Bina, M., Graziano F., & Bonino, S. (2006). Risky driving and lifestyles in adolescence. *Accident Analysis & Prevention, 38*(3), 472–481.

Bjarnason, T., & Sigurdardottir, T. J. (2003). Psychological distress during unemployment and beyond: Social support and material deprivation among youth in six Northern European countries. *Social Science & Medicine, 56*, 973–985.

Blain, M. D., Thompson, J. M., & Whiffen, V. E. (1993). Attachment and perceived social support in late adolescence. *Journal of Adolescent Research, 8*, 226–241.

Blair, S. L., & Johnson, M. P. (1992). Wives' perceptions of the fairness of the division of household labor: The intersection of housework and ideology. *Journal of Marriage and the Family, 54*, 570–581.

Blanchard-Fields, F. (1986). Reasoning on social dilemmas varying in emotional saliency: An adult development perspective. *Psychology and aging, 1*, 325–332.

Bleske-Rechek, A., Lubinski, D., & Benbow, C. P. (2004). Meeting the education needs of special populations: Advanced placement's role in developing exceptional human capital. *Psychological Science, 15*, 217–224.

Bloch, D. P. (1989). Using career information with dropouts and at-risk youth. *Career Development Quarterly, 38*, 160–171.

Block, J., & Block, J. H. (1980). *The California child Q-set.* Palo Alto, CA: Consulting Psychologists Press.

Block, J., Block, J., & Keyes, S. (1988). Longitudinally foretelling drug usage in adolescence: Early childhood personality and environmental precursors. *Child Development, 59*, 336–355.

Block, J., Gjerde, P. F., & Block, J. H. (1991). Personality antecedents of depressive tendencies in 18-year-olds: A prospective study. *Journal of Personality and Social Psychology, 60*, 726–738.

Block, J., & Robins, R. (1993). A longitudinal study of consistency and change in self-esteem from early adolescence to early adulthood. *Child Development, 64*, 909–923.

Bloom, D. E., & Brender, A. (1993). Labor and the emerging world economy. *Population Bulletin, 48*, 1–39. Washington, DC: Population Reference Bureau.

Bloom, M. (2000). The uses of theory in primary prevention practice: Evolving thoughts on sports and other after-school activities as influences on social competency. In S. J. Danish & T. P. Gullotta (Eds.), *Developing competent youth and strong communities through after-school programming* (pp. 17–66). New York: Child Welfare League of America.

Blosser, B. J. (1988). Ethnic differences in children's media use. *Journal of Broadcasting & Electronic Media, 32*, 453–470.

Blum, H. M., Boyle, M. H., & Offord, D. R. (1988). Single-parent families: Child psychiatric disorder and school performance. *Journal of the American Academy of Child and Adolescent Psychiatry, 27*, 214–219.

Blum, R., et al. (2000). The effects of race/ethnicity, income, and family structure on adolescent risk behaviors. *American Journal of Public Health, 90*, 1879–1884.

Blum, R. W. (2002). *Mothers' influence on teen sex: Connections that promote postponing sexual intercourse.* University of Minnesota: Center for Adolescent Health and Development.

Blum, R., Beuring, T., & Mann-Rinehart, P. (2000). *Protecting Teens: Beyond Race, Income, and Family Structure.* Center for Adolescent Health, University of Minnesota, Minneapolis, MN: Author.

Blum, R., & Rinehart, P. (2000). *Reducing the risk: Connections that make a difference in the lives of youth.* University of Minnesota, Division of General Pediatrics and Adolescent Health.

Blume, J. (1970). *Are you there, God? It's me, Margaret.* New York: Yearling.

Blumler, J. G. (1979). The role of theory in uses and gratifications studies. *Communication Research, 6*, 9–36.

Blyth, D., Hill, J., & Thiel, K. (1982). Early adolescents' significant others: Grade and gender differences in perceived relationships with familial and non-familial adults and young people. *Journal of Youth and Adolescence, 11*, 425–450.

Blyth, D., Simmons, R., & Zakin, D. (1985). Satisfaction with body image for early adolescent females: The impact of pubertal timing within different school environments. *Journal of Youth and Adolescence, 14*, 227–236.

Bobrow, R. S. (2002). Sexual orientation and suicide risk among teenagers. *JAMA: Journal of the American Medical Association, 287*, 1265–1266.

Bockting, W. O., & Coleman, E. (2003). *Masturbation as a means of achieving sexual health.* New York: Haworth.

Boehke, K., Muench, T., & Hoffman, D. (2002). Development through media use? A German study on the use of radio in adolescence. *International Journal of Behavioral Development, 26*, 193–201.

Bogenschneider, K. (1997). Parental involvement in adolescent schooling: A proximal process with transcontextual validity. *Journal of Marriage and the Family, 59*, 1–16.

Bogenschneider, K., & Steinberg, L. (1994). Maternal employment and adolescent academic achievement: A developmental analysis. *Sociology of Education, 67*, 60–77.

Bogenschneider, K., Wu, M., Raffaelli, M., & Tsay, J. C. (1998). Parent influences on adolescent peer orientation and substance use: The interface of parenting practices and values. *Child Development, 69*, 1672–1688.

Bohnert, A. M., Richards, M. H., Kolmodin, K. E., & Lakin, B. L. Young urban African American adolescents' experience of discretionary time activities. *Journal of Research on Adolescence, 18*(3), 517–539.

Bois-Reymond, M., & Ravesloot, J. (1996). The roles of parents and peers in the sexual and relational socialization of adolescents. In K. Hurrelmann & S. Hamilton (Eds.), *Social problems and social contexts in adolescence: Perspectives across boundaries* (pp. 175–197). Hawthorne, NY: Aldine de Gruyter.

Bois-Reymond, M., & van der Zande, I. (1994). The Netherlands. In K. Hurrelmann (Ed.), *International handbook of adolescence* (pp. 270–286). Westport, CT: Greenwood Press.

Bolger, N., Downey, G., Walker, E., & Steininger, P. (1989). The onset of suicidal ideation in childhood and adolescence. *Journal of Youth and Adolescence, 18*, 175–190.

Bond, L., Carlin, J. B., Thomas, L., Rubin, K., & Patton, G. (2001). Does bullying cause emotional problems? A prospective study of young teenagers. *British Medical Journal, 323*, 480–484.

Bond, L., Toumbourou, J. W., Thomas, L., Catalano, R. F., & Patton, G. (2005). Individual, family, school, and community risk and protective factors for depressive symptoms in adolescents: A comparison of risk profiles for substance use and depressive symptoms. *Prevention Science, 6*(2), 73–88.

Bond, S., & Cash, T. F. (1992). Black beauty: Skin color and body images among African American college women. *Journal of Applied Social Psychology, 22*, 874–888.

Bongers, I. L., Koot, H. M., van der Ende, J., & Verhulst, F. C. (2004). Developmental trajectories of externalizing behaviors in childhood and adolescence. *Child Development, 75*, 1523–1537.

Bonino, S., Cattelino, E., & Ciairano, S. (2007). Italy. In J. J. Arnett, R. Ahmed, B. Nsamenang, T. S. Saraswathi, & R. Silbereisen (Eds.), *International encyclopedia of adolescence.* New York: Routledge.

Bonkowski, S. E. (1989). Lingering sadness: Young adults' responses to parental divorce. *The Journal of Contemporary Social Work, 70*, 219–223.

Bookwala, J., Frieze, I. H., & Grote, N. (1994). The long-term effects of military service on quality of life: The Vietnam experience. *Journal of Applied Social Psychology, 24*, 529–545.

Booth, A., Crouter, A. C., & Shanahan, M. (Eds.). (1999). *Transitions to adulthood in a changing economy: No work, no family, no future?* Westport, CT: Praeger.

Booth, M. (2002). Arab adolescents facing the future: Enduring ideals and pressures for change. In B. B. Brown, R. Larson, & T. S. Saraswathi (Eds.), *The World's Youth: Adolescence in Eight Regions of the Globe* (pp. 207–242). NY: Cambridge University Press.

Borduin, C. M., Mann, B. J., Cone, L. T., Henggler, S. W., Fucci, B. R., Blaske, D. M., & Williams, R. A. (1995). Multisystemic treatment of serious juvenile offenders: Long-term prevention of criminality and violence. *Journal of Consulting and Clinical Psychology, 63*, 569–578.

Borduin, C. M., Schaeffer, C. M., Ronis, S. T. (2003). Multisystemic treatment of serious antisocial behavior in adolescents. In C. A. Essau (Ed.), *Conduct and oppositional defiant disorders: Epidemiology, risk factors, and treatment.* (pp. 299–318). Mahwah, NJ: Lawrence Erlbaum.

Bornholdt, L., Goodnow, J., & Cooney, G. (1994). Influences of gender stereotypes on adolescents' perceptions of their own achievement. *American Educational Research Journal, 31*, 675–692.

Bortree, D. S. (2005). Presentation of self on the web: An ethnographic study of teenage girls' weblogs. *Education, Communication and Information Journal, 5*, 25–39.

Bostic, J. Q., Rubin, D. H., Prince, J., & Schlozman, S. (2005). Treatment of depression in children and adolescents. *Journal of Psychiatric Practice, 11*, 141–154.

Bosworth, K., Espelage, D. L., & Simon, T. R. (1999). Factors associated with bullying behavior in middle school students. *Journal of Early Adolescence, 19*, 341–362.

Botcheva, L., Kalchev, P., & Leiderman, P. H. (2007). Bulgaria. In J. J. Arnett, R. Ahmed, B. Nsamenang, T. S. Saraswathi, & R. Silbereisen (Eds.), *International encyclopedia of adolescence.* New York: Routledge.

Botvin, M., & Vitaro, F. (1995). The impact of peer relationships on aggression in childhood: Inhibition through coercion or promotion through peer support. In J. McCord (Ed.), *Coercion and punishment in long-term perspective* (pp. 183–197). New York: Cambridge University Press.

Bowers, W. A., Evans, K., LeGrange, D., & Andersen, A. E. (2003). Treatment of adolescent eating disorders. In M. A. Reinecke & F. M. Dattilio (Eds.), *Cognitive therapy with children and adolescents: A casebook for clinical practice* (2nd ed., pp. 247–280). New York: Guilford Press.

Bowlby, J. (1969). *Attachment and loss, Vol. 1: Attachment.* New York: Basic Books.

Bowlby, J. (1973). *Attachment and loss, Vol. 2: Separation, anxiety, and anger.* New York: Basic Books.

Bowlby, J. (1980). *Attachment and loss, Vol. 3: Loss, sadness, and depression.* New York: Basic Books.

Bowman, S. (2004). Effects of fast-food consumption on energy intake and diet quality among children in a national household survey. *Pediatrics.*

Boy Scouts of America (2008). BSA at a glance. Retrieved August 7, 2008, from: www.scouting.org/Media/FactSheets/02-501.aspx

Boyer, C. B., Shafer, M. A., Teitle, E., Wibbelsman, C. J., Seeberg, F., & Schacter, J. (1999). Sexually-transitted diseases in a health maintenance organization teen clinic. *Archives of Pediatrics and Adolescent Medicine, 153*, 838–844.

Boyer, E. (1983). *High school.* New York: Harper & Row.

Boyesen, M., & Bru, E. (1999). Small school classes, small problems? A study of peer harassment, emotional problems and student perception of social support at school in small and large classes. *School Psychology International, 20*, 338–351.

Boyle, P. (2000, December/January). Latinas' perplexing lead in teen births. *Youth Today, 9,* 1, 47–49.

Boyle, P. (2001). Why are Dutch teens so sexually safe? *Youth Today, 10,* 1, 34.

Boyle, P. (2001, July/August). Job Corps delivers, study says. *Youth Today,* p. 7.

Boyle, P. (2004a). Snack attacks. *Youth Today, 13*(4), 1, 31–33.

Boyle, P. (2004b). Virginity pledges: Broken, but effective? *Youth Today,* April, 30–31.

Boyle, P. (2004c). YouthBuild tracks down alumni to assess itself. *Youth Today, 13*(7), 5, 11.

Boyle, P., & Lutton, L. (1999, November). Hard lessons in dropout prevention. *Youth Today, 8,* pp. 1, 17–20.

Bracey, J. R., Bámaca, M. Y., & Umaña-Taylor, A. J. (2004). Examining ethnic identity and self-esteem among biracial and monoracial adolescents. *Journal of Youth & Adolescence, 33,* 123–132.

Bradford, K., Barber, B. K., Olsen, J. A., Maughan, S. L., Erickson, L. D., Ward, D., & Stolz, H. E (2004). A multi-national study of interparental conflict, parenting, and adolescent functioning: South Africa, Bangladesh, China, India, Bosnia, Germany, Palestine, Columbia, and the United States. *Marriage & Family Review, 35,* 107–137.

Brady, B., & Kendall, P. (1992). Comorbidity of anxiety and depression in children and adolescents. *Psychological Bulletin, 111*, 244–255.

Brake, D. (2006). Electronic games, effects. In J. J. Arnett (Ed.), *Encyclopedia of children, adolescents, and the media.* Thousand Oaks, CA: Sage.

Brake, M. (1985). Comparative youth culture: *The sociology of youth cultures and youth subcultures in America, Britain, and Canada.* London: Routledge and Kegan Paul.

Brame, R., Bushway, S. D., Paternoster, R., & Apel, R. (2004). Assessing the effect of adolescent employment on involvement in criminal activity. *Journal of Contemporary Criminal Justice, 20,* 236–256.

Brand, S., Felner, R., Shim, M., Seitsinger, A., & Dumas, T. (2003). Middle school improvement and reform: Development and validation of a school level assessment of climate, culture pluralism, and school safety. *Journal of Educational Psychology, 95,* 570–588.

Brandt, P. (2002). European sex ed model: The rest of the story. *Youth Today, 11,* 48.

Brandtstadter, J., & Baltes-Gotz, B. (1990). Personal control over development and quality of perspectives in adulthood. In P. Baltes & M. M. Baltes (Eds.), *Successful aging* (pp. 197–224). Cambridge, England: Cambridge University Press.

Brandtstadter, J., & Greve, W. (1994). The aging self: Stabilizing and protective processes. *Developmental Review, 14,* 52–80.

Brandtstädter, J. (2006). Adaptive resources in later life: Tenacious goal pursuit and flexible goal adjustment. In M. Csikszentmihalyi & I. S. Csikszentmihalyi, (Eds.), *A life worth living: Contributions to positive psychology.* (pp. 143–164). New York: Oxford University Press.

Braunstein, A. W., Lesser, M. H., & Pescatrice, D. R. The impact of a program for the disadvantaged on student retention. *College Student Journal, 42*(1), 36–40.

Braxton, J. M., Brier, E. M.; Steele, S. L. Shaping retention from research to practice. *Journal of College Student Retention: Research, Theory and Practice, 9*(3), 377–399.

Bray, J., & Kelly, J. (1998). *Stepfamilies.* New York: Broadway.

Breivik, K., & Olweus, D. Adolescents' adjustment in four post-divorce family structures: Single mother, stepfather, joint physical custody and single father families. *Journal of Divorce & Remarriage. 44*(3–4), 99–124.

Brendgen, M., Vitaro, F., & Bukowski, W. M. Affiliation with delinquent friends: Contributions of parents, self-esteem, delinquent behavior, and rejection by peers. *The Journal of Early Adolescence. 18*(3), 244–265.

Brener, N., Lowry, R., Barrior, L., Simon, T., & Eaton, D. (2004). Violence related behaviors among high school students United States, 1991–2003. *JAMA: Journal of the American Medical Association, 292*, 1168–1169.

Brent, D. A. (2004). Antidepressants and pediatric depression: The risk of doing nothing. *New England Journal of Medicine, 35*, 1598–1601.

Brent, D. A., Kolko, A., Wartella, M. E., Boylan, M. B., Moritz, G., Baugher, M., & Zelenak, J. P. (1993). Adolescent psychiatric inpatients' risk of suicide attempts at 6-month follow-up. *Journal of the American Academy of Child and Adolescent Psychiatry, 32*, 95–105.

Brent, D. A., & Mann, J. J. (2003). Familial factors in adolescent suicidal behavior. In R. A. King & A. Apter (Eds.), *Suicide in children and adolescents* (pp. 86–117). New York, NY: Cambridge University Press.

Brent, D. A., & Mann, J. J. (2006). Familial pathways to suicidal behavior: Understanding and preventing suicide among adolescents. *New England Journal of Medicine, 355*(26), 2719–2721.

Brent, D. A., & Melhem, N. (2008). Familial transmission of suicidal behavior. *Psychiatric Clinics of North America, 31*(2), 157–177.

Breton, J. J., Tousignant, M., Bergeron, L., & Berthiaume, C. (2002). Informant-specific correlates of suicidal behavior in a community survey of 12–14 yearolds. *Journal of the American Academy of Child & Adolescent Psychiatry, 41*, 723–730.

Brewer, M. B., & Chen, Y-R. (2007). Where (who) are collectives in collectivism? Toward conceptual clarification of individualism and collectivism. *Psychological Review, 114*(1), 133–151.

Brewster, K., Billy, J., & Grady, W. (1993). Social context and adolescent behavior: The impact of community on the transition to sexual activity. *Social Forces, 71*, 713–740.

Bridges, L., & Moore, K. (2002). Religious involvement and children's well-being: What research tells us (and what it doesn't). *Child Trends Research Brief.* Washington, DC: Author. Available: www.childtrends.org

Briere, J., & Runtz, M. (1989). Symptomatology associated with childhood sexual victimization in a nonclinical adult sample. *Child Abuse and Neglect, 12*, 51–59.

Briere, J., & Runtz, M. (1991). The long-term effects of sexual abuse: A review and synthesis. In J. Briere (Ed.), *Treating victims of child sexual abuse* (pp. 3–13). *New Directions for Mental Health Services, 51.* San Francisco: Jossey-Bass.

Briere, J. N. (1992). *Child abuse trauma.* Newbury Park, CA: Sage.

Briggs, C. L. (1989). *Learning how to ask: A sociolinguistic appraisal of the role of the interview in social science research.* New York: Cambridge University Press.

Brim, O. G., Ryff, C. D., & Kessler, R.C. (Eds.). (2004). How healthy are we?: A national study of well-being at midlife. Chicago: University of Chicago Press. (2004).

Brody, G. H. (2004). Siblings' direct and indirect contributions to child development. *Current Directions in Psychological Science. 13*(3), 124–126.

Brody, G. H., & Flor, D. L. (1998). Maternal resources, parenting practices, and child competence in rural, single-parent African American families. *Child Development, 69*(3), 803–816.

Brody, G. H., Kim, S., Murry, V. M., & Brown, A. C. (2003). Longitudinal direct and indirect pathways linking older sibling competence to the development of young sibling competence. *Developmental Psychology, 39*, 618–628.

Brody, N. (1992). Intelligence (2nd ed.). San Diego, CA: Academic Press.

Bronfenbrenner, U. (2000). Ecological theory. In A. Kazdin (Ed.), *Encyclopedia of psychology*. Washington, DC: American Psychological Association.

Bronfenbrenner, U. (Ed.) (2005). *Making human beings human: Bioecological perspectives on human development*. Thousand Oaks, CA: Sage.

Bronfenbrenner, U., & Morris, P. A. (1998). The ecology of developmental processes. In W. Damon (Series Ed.) and R. Lerner (Vol. Ed.), *Handbook of child psychology, Vol. 1: Theoretical models of human development* (pp. 993–1028). New York: Wiley.

Bronstein, P., Duncan, P., D'Ari, A., Pieniadz, J., Fitzgerald, M., Abrams, C., Frankowski, B., Franco, O., Hunt, C., & Cha, S. (1996). Family and parenting behaviors predicting middle school adjustment: A longitudinal study. *Family Relations, 45*, 110–121.

Bronstein, P., Duncan, R., Clauson, J., Abrams, C., Yannett, N., Ginsburg, G., & Milne, M. (1994). *Enhancing middle school adjustment for children from lower-income families: A parenting intervention*. Unpublished manuscript, University of Vermont.

Brook, J. S., Brook, D. W., Gordon, A. S., & Whiteman, M. (1990). The psychosocial etiology of adolescent drug use: A family interactional approach. *Genetic, Social, and General Psychology Monographs, 116*, 111–267.

Brook, J. S., Brook, D. W., & Pahl, K. (2006). The developmental context for adolescent substance abuse intervention. In H. A. Liddie, & C. L. Rowe (Eds.), *Adolescent substance abuse: Research and clinical advances* (pp. 25–51). New York: Cambridge University Press.

Brook, J. S., Gordon, A. S., Brook, A., & Brook, D. W. (1989). The consequences of marijuana use on intrapersonal and interpersonal functioning in black and white adolescents. *Genetic, Social, and General Psychology Monographs, 111*, 317–330.

Brook, U., & Boaz, M. (2005). Attention deficit hyperactivity disorder (ADHD) and learning disabilities (LD): Adolescents' perspective. *Patient Education and Counseling, 58*(2), 187–191.

Brooks-Gunn, J., & Chase-Lansdale, P. L. (1995). Adolescent parenthood. In M. H. Bornstein (Ed.), *Children and parenting* (Vol. 3). Hillsdale, NJ: Erlbaum.

Brooks-Gunn, J., Duncan, G., Klebanov, P., & Sealand, N. (1993). Do neighborhoods influence child and adolescent development? *American Journal of Sociology, 99*, 353–395.

Brooks-Gunn, J., & Paikoff, R. (1993). 'Sex is a gamble, kissing is a game': Adolescent sexuality and health promotion. In S. Millstein, A. Petersen, & E. Nightingale (Eds.), *Promoting the health of adolescents: New directions for the twenty-first century* (pp. 180–208). New York: Oxford University Press.

Brooks-Gunn, J., & Paikoff, R. (1997). Sexuality and developmental transitions during adolescence. In J. Schulenberg, J. L. Maggs, & K. Hurrelmann (Eds.), *Health risks and developmental transitions during adolescence* (pp. 190–219). New York: Cambridge University Press.

Brooks-Gunn, J., Reiter, E. O. (1990). The role of pubertal processes. In E. O. Feldman, S. Shirley, & Elliott, G. R. (Eds.), *At the threshold: The developing adolescent* (pp. 16–53). Cambridge, MA: Harvard University Press.

Brooks-Gunn, J., & Ruble, D. (1982). The development of menstrual-related beliefs and behaviors during early adolescence. *Child Development, 53*, 1567–1577.

Brown, A., & Finkelhor, D. (1986). The impact of child sexual abuse: A review of the research. *Psychological Bulletin, 99*, 66–77.

Brown, B., & Lohr, M. J. (1987). Peer group affiliation and adolescent self-esteem: An integration of ego-identity and symbolic interaction theories. *Journal of Personality and Social Psychology, 52*, 47–55.

Brown, B., & Mounts, N. (1989, April). *Peer group structures in single versus multiethnic high schools.* Paper presented at the biennial meeting of the Society for Research in Child Development, Kansas City.

Brown, B., Mounts, N., Lamborn, S., & Steinberg, L. (1993). Parenting practices and peer group affiliation in adolescence. *Child Development, 64*, 467–482.

Brown, B. B. (1989). The role of peer groups in adolescents' adjustment to secondary school. In T. J. Berndt & G. W. Ladd (Eds.), *Peer relationships in child development* (pp. 188–215). New York: Wiley.

Brown, B. B. (2004). Adolescent relationships with peers. In R. Lerner & L. Steinberg (Eds.), *Handbook of adolescent psychology*. New York: Wiley.

Brown, B. B., Bakken, J. P. Ameringer, S. W., & Mahon, S. D. (2008). A comprehensive conceptualization of peer influence process in adolescence. In M. J. Prinstein & K. A. Dodge (Eds.), *Understanding peer influence in children and adolescents: Duke series in child development and public policy* (pp. 72–93). New York: Guilford Press.

Brown, B. B., Feiring, C., & Furman, W. (1999). Missing the love boat: Why researchers have shied away from adolescent romance. In W. Furman, B. B. Brown, & C. Feiring (Eds.), *The development of romantic relationships in adolescence* (pp. 1–18). New York: Cambridge University Press.

Brown, B. B., Herman, M., Hamm, J. V., & Heck, D. K. (2008). Ethnicity and image: Correlates of crowd affiliation among ethnic minority youth. *Child Development, 79*(3), 529–546.

Brown, B. B., & Klute, C. (2003). Friendships, cliques, and crowds. In R. G, Adams., & D. M, Berzonsky (Eds.), *Blackwell handbook of adolescence* (pp. 330–348). Malden, MA: Blackwell.

Brown, B. B., & Lohr, M. J. (1987). Peer group affiliation and adolescent self-esteem: An integration of ego-identity and symbolic interaction theories. *Journal of Personality and Social Psychology, 52*, 47–55.

Brown, B. B., Mory, M., & Kinney, D. A. (1994). Casting adolescent crowds in relational perspective: Caricature, channel, and context. In R. Montemayor, G. R. Adams, & T. P. Gullotta (Eds.), *Advances in adolescent development: Vol. 6. Personal relationships during adolescence*. Newbury Park, CA: Sage.

Brown, D. (2007, February 27). More American women have HPV than previously thought. *Washington Post*, p. A1.

Brown, E. F., & Hendee, W. R. (1989). Adolescents and their music. *JAMA: Journal of the American Medical Association, 262*, 1659–1663.

Brown, F. (1973). *The reform of secondary education: Report of the national commission on the reform of secondary education*. New York: McGraw-Hill.

Brown, F. T., Daly, B. P., & Stefanatos, G. A. (2008). Learning disabilities: Complementary views from neuroscience, neuropsychology, and public health. In E. Fletcher-Janzen & C. R. Reynolds (Eds.), *Neuropsychological perspectives on learning disabilities in the era of RTI: Recommendations for diagnosis and intervention* (pp. 159–178). Hoboken, NJ: John Wiley & Sons.

Brown, J. D. (2006). Emerging adults in a media-saturated world. In J. J. Arnett and J. Tanner (Eds.), *Coming of age in the 21st century: The lives and contexts of emerging adults* (pp. 279–299). Washington, DC: American Psychological Association.

Brown, J. D., Childers, K. M., & Waszak, C. S. (1990). Television and adolescent sexuality. *Journal of Adolescent Health Care, 11*, 62–70.

Brown, J. D., Halpern, C. T., & L'Engle, K. L. (2005). Mass media as a sexual super peer for early maturing girls. *Journal of Adolescent Health, 36*, 420–427.

Brown, J. D., Steele, J. R., & Walsh-Childers, K. (2002). Introduction and overview. In J. D. Brown, J. R Steele, & K. Walsh-Childers (Eds.), *Sexual teens, sexual media: Investigating media's influence on adolescent sexuality* (pp. 1–24). Mahwah, NJ: Erlbaum.

Brown, J. D., Steele, J., & Walsh-Childers, K. (Eds.) (2002). *Sexual teens, sexual media*. Mahwah, NJ: Erlbaum.

Brown, J. D., White, A. B., & Nikopolou, L. (1993). Disinterest, intrigue, and resistance: Early adolescent girls' use of sexual media content. In B. Greenberg, J. D. Brown, & N. Buerkel-Rothfuss (Eds.), *Media, sex, and the adolescent*. Cresskill, NJ: Hampton Press.

Brown, J. D., & Witherspoon, E. M. (2002). The mass media and American adolescents' health. *Journal of Adolescent Health, 31*, 153–170.

Brown, L. M., & Gilligan, C. (1992). *Meeting at the crossroads: Women's psychology and girls' development*. Cambridge, MA: Harvard University Press.

Brown, R. T., & La Rosa, A. (2002). Recent developments in the pharmacotherapy of attention-deficit/hyperactivity disorder (ADHD). *Professional Psychology: Research and Practice, 33*(6), 591–595.

Browne, K. D., & Hamilton-Giachritsis, C. (2005). The influence of violent media on children and adolescents: A public health approach. *Lancet, 356*, 702–710.

Brownstein, P. (2006). The family environment: Where gender role socialization begins. In J. Worell & C. D. Goodheart. (Eds.), *Handbook of girls' and women's psychological health: Gender and well-being across the lifespan* (pp. 262–271). Oxford series in clinical psychology. New York: Oxford University Press.

Bruer, J. T. (1993). The mind's journey from novice to expert. *American Educator, 17*, 6–15, 38–46.

Brumberg, J.J. (1997). *The body project: An intimate history of American girls*. New York: Random House.

Bryant, A. L., Schulenberg, J. E., O'Malley, P. M., Bachman, J. G., & Johnston, L. D. (2003). How academic achievement, attitudes, and behaviors relate to the course of substance use during adolescence: A 6 year, multiwave national longitudinal study. *Journal of Research on Adolescence, 13*, 361–397.

Bryant, B. K. (1992). Conflict resolution strategies in relation to children's peer relations. *Developmental Psychology, 13*, 35–50.

Bryk, A. S., & Thum, Y. M. (1989). The effects of high school organization on dropping out: An exploratory investigation. *American Educational Research Journal, 26*, 353–383.

Buchanan, C. M. (2000). The impact of divorce on adjustment during adolescence. In R. D. Taylor & M. Weng (Eds.), *Resilience across contexts: Family, work, culture, and community*. Mahwah, NJ: Erlbaum.

Buchanan, C. M., Eccles, J. S., Flanagan, C., Midgley, C., Feldlaufer, H., & Harold, R. D. (1990). Parents' and teachers' beliefs about adolescents: Effects of sex and experience. *Journal of Youth & Adolescence, 19*, 363–394.

Buchanan, C. M., & Holmbeck, G. N. (1998). Measuring beliefs about adolescent personality and behavior. *Journal of Youth & Adolescence, 27*, 609–629.

Buchanan, C. M., Maccoby, E. E., & Dornbusch, S. M. (1996). *Adolescents after divorce*. Cambridge, MA: Harvard University Press.

Buchanan, C., Maccoby, E., & Dornbusch, S. (1991). Caught between parents: Adolescents' experience in divorced homes. *Child Development, 62*, 1008–1029.

Buchanan, M., & Robbins, C. (1990). Early adult psychological consequences for males of adolescent pregnancy and its resolution. *Journal of Youth and Adolescence, 19*, 413–424.

Buckley, T., & Gottlieb, A. (1988). *Blood magic: The anthropology of menstruation.* Berkeley: University of California Press.

Bugental, D. B., & Grusec, J. E. (2006). Socialization processes. In N. Eisenberg, W. Damon, & R. M. Lerner (Eds.), *Handbook of child psychology: Vol. 3. Social, emotional, and personality development* (6th ed., pp. 366–428, xxiv, 1128). Hoboken, NJ: John Wiley & Sons.

Bugental, D. B, & Grusec, J. E. (2008). *Relational perspectives book series. Socialization Processes.* New York: Analytic Press/Taylor & Francis Group.

Buhrmester, D., & Carbery, J. (1992, March). *Daily patterns of self-disclosure and adolescent adjustment.* Paper presented at the biennial meeting of the Society for Research on Adolescence, Washington, DC.

Buhrmester, D., & Furman, W. (1987). The development of companionship and intimacy. *Child Development, 58,* 1101–1113.

Buhrmester, D., & Furman, W. (1990). Perceptions of sibling relationships during middle childhood and adolescence. *Child Development, 61,* 1387–1396.

Bukowski, W. M., Newcomb, A. F., & Hoza, B. (1987). Friendship conceptions among early adolescents: A longitudinal study of stability and change. *Journal of Early Adolescence, 7,* 143–152.

Bulik, C. M., Berkman, N. D., Brownley, K. A., Sedway, J. A., & Lohr, K. N. (2007). Anorexia nervosa treatment: A systematic review of randomized controlled trials. *International Journal of Eating Disorders, 40*(4), 310–320.

Bullough, V. L. Comments on Mosher's "Three dimensions of depth of involvement in human sexual response." *Journal of Sex Research, 17*(2), 177–178.

Bumpass, L., & Liu, H. H. (2000, March). Trends in cohabitation and implications for children's family contexts in the United States. *Population Studies.*

Burbank, V. (1994). Australian Aborigines: An adolescent mother and her family. In M. Ember, C. Ember, & D. Levinson (Eds.), *Portraits of culture: Ethnographic originals* (pp. 103–126). Upper Saddle River, NJ: Prentice Hall.

Burbank, V. (1995). Gender hierarchy and adolescent sexuality: The control of female reproduction in an Australian Aboriginal community. *Ethos, 23,* 33–46.

Burbank, V. K. (1988). *Aboriginal adolescence: Maidenhood in an Australian community.* New Brunswick, NJ: Rutgers University Press.

Burn, S. M. (1996). *The social psychology of gender.* New York: McGraw-Hill.

Burnett, R. (1990). From a whisper to a scream: Music video and cultural form. In K. Roe & U. Carlsson (Eds.), *Popular music research* (pp. 21–27). Goteborg, Sweden: Nordicom-Sweden.

Burns, A. (1992). Mother-headed families in Australia: An international perspective and the case of Australia. Social Policy Report, *Society for Research in Child Development, 6,* 1–22.

Burns, G. L., & Farina, A. (1992). The role of physical attractiveness in adjustment. *Genetic, Social, and General Psychology Monographs, 118,* 159–194.

Burra, N. B. (1997). *Born to work: Child labor in India.* New Delhi: Oxford University Press.

Burrow, A. L., & Finley, G. E. (2004). Transracial, same-race adoptions, and the need for multiple measures of adolescent adjustment. *American Journal of Orthopsychiatry, 74,* 577–583.

Busch-Rossnagel, N. A., & Zayas, L. H. (1991). Hispanic adolescents. In R. M. Lerner, A. C. Petersen, & J. Brooks-Gunn (Eds.), *Encyclopedia of adolescence* (pp. 492–498). New York: Garland.

Bush, J. E., & Ehrenberg, M. F. (2003). *Journal of Divorce & Remarriage, 39,* 1–35.

Bushman, B. J., & Huesmann, L. R. (2002). Effects of televised violence on aggression. In D. G. Singer & J. L. Singer (Eds.), *Handbook of children and media.* Thousand Oaks, CA: Sage.

Buss, D. M. (1989). Sex differences in human mate preferences: Evolutionary hypothesis tested in 37 cultures. *Behavioral and Brain Sciences, 12,* 1–49.

Buss, D. M. (1995). *The evolution of desire: Strategies of human mating.* New York: Basic Books.

Buss, D. M. (2001). The strategies of human mating. In P. W. Sherman & J. Alcock (Eds.), *Exploring animal behavior: Readings from American Scientist* (3rd ed., pp. 240–251).

Bussey, K., & Bandura, A. (1992). Self-regulatory mechanisms governing gender development. *Child Development, 63,* 1236–1250.

Buunk, A. P., Park, J. H., & Dubbs, S. L. (2008). Parent-offspring conflict in mate preferences. *Review of General Psychology, 12*(1), 47–62.

By Carroll, J. S., Padilla-Walker, L. M., Nelson, L. J., Olson, C. D., Barry, C. M., & Madsen, S. D. Generation XXX: Pornography acceptance and use among emerging adults. *Journal of Adolescent Research. 23*(1), 6–30.

By Laursen, B., Collins, W. A. (2004). Parent-child communication during adolescence. In A. L. Vangelisti (Ed.), *Handbook of family communication, LEA's communication series* (pp. 333–348). Mahwah, NJ: Lawrence Erlbaum.

Bynner, J. (2005). Rethinking the youth phase of the life course: The case for emerging adulthood. *Journal of Youth Studies,* 367–384.

Byrnes, J. P., Miller, D. C., & Reynolds, M. (1999). Learning to make good decisions: A self-regulation perspective. *Child Development, 70,* 1121–1140.

Cairns, R., Cairns, B., Neckerman, H., Gest, S., & Gariepy, J. L. (1988). Social networks and aggressive behavior: Peer support or peer rejection? *Developmental Psychology, 24,* 815–823.

Cairns, R. B., Cairns, B. D., Neckerman, H. J., Ferguson, L. L., & Gariepy, J. (1989). Growth and aggression: 1. Childhood to early adolescence. *Developmental Psychology, 25,* 320–330.

Calvete, E., & Cardeñoso, O. (2005). Gender differences in cognitive vulnerability to depression and behavior problems in adolescents. *Journal of Abnormal Child Psychology, 33,* 179–192.

Campbell, E. R., Devries, H. M., Fikkert, L., Kraay, & M., Ruiz, J. N. (2007). *Trajectory of marital satisfaction through the empty-nest transition.* Paper presented at the annual meeting of the American Psychological Association, Washington, DC.

Cantor, J. (1998). *Mommy, I'm scared: How TV and movies frighten children and what we can do to protect them.* New York: Harcourt.

Cantor, J. (2000). Violence in films and television. In R. Lee (Ed.), *Encyclopedia of international media and communications.* New York: Academic Press.

Capaldi, D., & Patterson, G. (1991). Relation of parental transitions to boys' adjustment problems, I: A linear hypothesis; II: Mothers at risk for transitions and unskilled parenting. *Developmental Psychology, 27,* 489–504.

Capaldi, D. M., & Stoolmiller, M. (1999). Co-occurrence of conduct problems and depressive symptoms in early adolescent boys, III: Prediction to young adult adjustment. *Development and Psychopathology, 11,* 59–84.

Caplow, T., Bahr, H. D. M., & Chadwick, B. E. A. (1982). *Middletown families: Fifty years of change and continuity.* Minneapolis: University of Minnesota Press.

Caplow, T., Bahr, H. M., & Call, Vaughn R. A. (2004). The Middletown replications: 75 years of change in adolescent attitudes, 1924–1999. *Public Opinion Quarterly, 68,* 287–313.

Cappell, C., & Heiner, R. B. (1990). The intergenerational transmission of family aggression. *Journal of Family Violence, 5,* 135–152.

Carnegie Council on Adolescent Development. (1992). *A matter of time: Risk and opportunity in the after-school hours.* Washington, DC: Author.

Carroll, J. L., & Wolpe, P. R. (1996). *Sexuality and gender in society.* Addison-Wesley.

Carroll, J. L., & Wolpe, P. R. (2005). *Sexuality now: Embracing diversity.* Wadsworth.

Carson, D. K., Chowdhury, A., Perry, C. K., & Pati, C. (1999). Family characteristics and adolescent competence in India: Investigation of youth in southern Orissa. *Journal of Youth & Adolescence, 28,* 211–233.

Cartwright, Claire (2006). You Want to Know How It Affected Me? Young Adults' Perceptions of the Impact of Parental Divorce. *Journal of of Divorce & Remarriage.* Vol. 44(3–4), 125–143.

Carvalho, A., & Dias, M. (1994). Portugal. In K. Hurrelmann (Ed.), *International handbook of adolescence* (pp. 322–331). Westport, CT: Greenwood Press.

Carver, K., Joyner, K., & Udry, J. R. (2003). National estimates of adolescent romantic relationships. In P. Florsheim (Ed.), *Adolescent romantic relations and sexual behavior: Theory, research, and practical implications* (pp. 23–56). Mahwah, NJ: Lawrence Erlbaum.

Case, R. (1985). *Intellectual development: Birth to adulthood.* New York: Academic Press.

Case, R. (1997). The development of conceptual structures. In D. Kuhn & R. S. Siegler (Eds.), *Handbook of child psychology* (5th ed., Vol. 2). New York: Wiley.

Casey, B. J., Getz, S., & Galvan, A. (2008). The adolescent brain. *Developmental Review, 28*(1), 62–77.

Cash, T. F. (1995). Developmental teasing about physical appearance: Retrospective descriptions and relationships with body image. *Social Behavior and Personality, 23,* 123–129.

Cash, T. F., & Henry, P. E. (1995). Women's body images: The results of a national survey in the USA. *Sex Roles, 33,* 19–28.

Cashmore, J., & Goodnow, J. (1987). Influences of Australian parents' values: Ethnicity versus socioeconomic status. *Journal of Cross-Cultural Psychology, 17,* 441–454.

Caspi, A., & Moffitt, T. (1991). Individual differences and personal transitions: The sample case of girls at puberty. *Journal of Personality and Social Psychology, 61,* 157–168.

Cass, V. C. (1979). Homosexual identity formation: A theoretical model. *Journal of Homosexuality, 4,* 219–235.

Casteel, M. (1993). Effects of inference necessity and reading goal on children's inferential generation. *Developmental Psychology, 29,* 346–357.

Castellano, J. A., & Diaz, E. (Eds.). (2002). *Reaching new horizons: Gifted and talented education for culturally and linguistically diverse students.* Boston: Allyn & Bacon.

Cates, W. (1999). Chlamydial infections and the risk of ectopic pregnancy. *JAMA: Journal of the American Medical Assotiaton, 281,* 117–118.

Catsambis, S. (1994). The path to math: Gender and racial-ethnic differences in mathematics participation from middle school to high school. *Sociology of Education, 67,* 199–215.

Cauce, A. M., Paradise, M., Ginzler, J. A., Embry, L., Morgan, C. J., Lohr, Y., & Theofelis, J. (2000). The characteristics and mental health of homeless adolescents: Age and gender differences. *Journal of Emotional and Behavioral Disorders, 8,* 230–239.

Cauffman, E., & Woolard, J. (2005). Crime, competence, and culpability: Adolescent judgment in the justice system. In E. J. Jacobs & P. A. Klaczynski (Eds.), *The development of judgment and decision making in children and adolescents* (pp. 279–302). Mahwah, NJ: Erlbaum.

Cejka, M. A., & Eagly, A. H. (1999). Gender-stereotypic images of occupations correspond to the sex segregation of employment. *Personality and Social Psychology Bulletin, 25,* 413–423.

Centers for Disease Control and Prevention (CDCP). (1999). *1996 Youth Risk Behavior Surveillance System (YRBSS).* Available: www.cdc.gov/nccdphp/dash/yrbs/suse.htm

Centers for Disease Control and Prevention (CDCP). (2000). Tobacco use among middle and high school students: National Youth Tobacco Survey, 1999. *MMWR, 51* (19), 409–412.

Centers for Disease Control (CDC). (2001). *Adolescent and school health—Programs that work.* Atlanta, GA: Author. Available: www.cdc.gov

Centers for Disease Control (CDC). (2002). Trends in sexual risk behaviors among high school students—United States, 1991–2001. *MMWR, 51* (38), 856–859.

Centers for Disease Control and Prevention (CDCP). (2005). *National Youth Risk Behavior Survey, 1991–2003: Trends in the prevalence of sexual behaviors.* Available: www.cdc.gov

Centers for Disease Control and Prevention (CDCP). (2007). Suicide trends among youths and young adults ages 10–24 years—United States, 1990–2004. *Morbidity and Mortality Weekly Report, 56*(35).

Chadwick, B. A., & Heaton, T. B. (1996). *Statistical handbook on adolescents in America.* New York: Oryx Press.

Chandler, M. J., Lalonde, C. E., Sokol, B. W., & Hallett, D. (2003). Personal persistence, identity development, and suicide: A study of Native and non-Native North American adolescents. *Monographs of the Society for Research in Child Development, 68,* vii–130.

Chanes, C. W. (2000, February). *Adolescents in Latin America toward the 21st century.* Paper prepared for the meeting of the Study Group on Adolescence in the 21st Century, Washington, DC.

Chang, L.T. (2008). *Factory girls: From village to factory in changing China.* New York: Spiegel & Grau.

Chao, R. (1994). Beyond parental control and authoritarian parenting style: Understanding Chinese parenting through the cultural notion of training. *Child Development, 65,* 1111–1119.

Chao, R. (2001). Extending research on the consequences of parenting style for Chinese Americans and European Americans. *Child Development, 72,* 1832–1843.

Chao, R., & Tseng, V. (2002). Parenting of Asians. In M. H. Bornstein (Ed.), *Handbook of parenting, Vol. 4: Social conditions and applied parenting* (pp. 59–93). Mahwah, NJ: Erlbaum.

Chase, W. G., & Simon, H. A. (1973). Perception in chess. *Cognitive Psychology, 4,* 55–81.

Chase-Lansdale, P. L., Cherlin, A. J., & Kiernan, K. E. (1995). The long-term effects of parental divorce on the mental health of young adults: A developmental perspective. *Child Development, 66,* 1614–1634.

Chaudhary, N., & Sharma, N. (2007). India. In J. J. Arnett (Ed.), *International encyclopedia of adolescence* (pp. 442–459). New York: Routledge.

Chen, C., & Stevenson, H. W. (1995). Motivation and mathematics achievement: A comparative study of Asian American, Caucasian American, and East Asian high school students. *Child Development, 66,* 1215–1234.

Chen, X., & Chang, L. (2007). China. In J. J. Arnett (Ed.), *International encyclopedia of adolescence.* New York: Routledge.

Chen, X., Tyler, K A., Whitbeck, L. B., & Hoyt, D. R. (2004). Early sexual abuse, street adversity, and drug use among female homeless and runaway adolescents in the Midwest. *Journal of Drug Issues, 34,* 1–21.

Cherlin, A. J. (1992). *Marriage, divorce, and remarriage.* Cambridge, MA: Harvard University Press.

Cherlin, A. J. (1999). Going to extremes: Family structure, children's well-being, and social science. *Demography, 36,* 421–428.

Cherlin, A. J., Burton, L. M., Tera, R., & Purvin, D. M. (2004). The influence of physical and sexual abuse on marriage and cohabitation. *American Sociological Review, 69,* 768–789.

Cherlin, A. J., Chase-Lansdale, P. L., & McCrae, C. (1998). Effects of parental divorce on mental health throughout the life course. *American Sociological Review, 63,* 239–249.

Cherlin, A. J., Furstenberg, F. F., Jr., Chase-Lansdale, P. L., Kiernan, K. E., Robins, P. K., Morrison, D. R., & Teitler, J. O. (1991). Longitudinal studies of effects of divorce on children in Great Britain and the United States. *Science, 252,* 1386–1388.

Cheung, A. H., Emslie, G. J., & Mayes, T. (2005). Review of the efficacy and safety of antidepressants in youth depression. *Journal of Child Psychology & Psychiatry, 46,* 735–754.

Cheung, A., Emslie, G. J., & Maynes, T. L. (2004). Efficacy and safety of antidepressants in youth depression. *Canadian Child & Adolescent Psychiatry Review, 13,* 98–104.

Chi, M. T. H., Glaser, R., & Rees, E. (1982). Expertise in problem solving. In R. J. Sternberg (Ed.), *Advances in the psychology of human intelligence.* Hillsdale, NJ: Erlbaum.

Children's Defense Fund (CDF). (1994). *The state of America's children, 1994.* Washington, DC: Author.

Children's Defense Fund (CDF). (1995). *The state of America's children, 1995.* Washington, DC: Author.

Chilman, C. (1986). Some psychosocial aspects of adolescent sexual and contraceptive behaviors in a changing American society. In J. Lancaster & B. Hamburg (Eds.), *School-age pregnancy and parenthood: Biosocial dimensions.* New York: Aldine de Gruyter.

Chilman, C. S. (1983). *Adolescent sexuality in a changing American society* (2nd ed.). New York: Wiley.

Chinas, L. (1992). *The Isthmus Zapotecs: A matrifocal culture of Mexico.* New York: Harcourt Brace Jovanovich College Publishers.

Chisholm, L., & Hurrelmann, K. (1995). Adolescence in modern Europe: Pluralized transition patterns and their implications for personal and social risks. *Journal of Adolescence, 18,* 129–158.

Cho, B. E., & Shin, H. Y. (1996). State of family research and theory in Korea. In M. B. Sussman & R. S. Hanks (Eds.), *Intercultural variation in family research and theory: Implications for cross-national studies* (pp. 101–135). New York: Haworth Press.

Choi, J. W., & Lee, Y. H. (1998). The effects of actual self, ideal self, and self-discrepancy on depression. *Korean Journal of Clinical Psychology, 17,* 69–87.

Christenson, P. G., & Roberts, D. F. (1998). *It's not only rock & roll: Popular music in the lives of adolescents.* Cresskill, NJ: Hampton Press.

Christopherson, B. B., Jones, R. M., & Sales, A. P. (1988). Diversity in reported motivations for substance use as a function of ego-identity development. *Journal of Adolescent Research, 3,* 141–152.

Chronicle of Higher Education (2005). Census data show value of a college education. Retrieved on April 14, 2005, from http://chronicle.com/daily/2005/03/2005032903n.htm

Chu, G. C., & Ju, Y. (1993). *The Great Wall in ruins.* New York: State University of New York Press.

Church, R. (1976). *Education in the United States.* New York: Free Press.

Ciardiello, S. (2003). Meet them in the lab: Using hip-hop music therapy groups with adolescents in residential settings. In E. N. Sullivan., S. E. Mesbur., & et al. (Eds.), *Social work with groups: Social justice through personal, community and societal change* (pp. 103–117). New York, NY: Haworth Press Inc.

Cicchetti, D., & Carlson, V. (Eds.). (1989). *Child maltreatment: Theory and research on the causes and consequences of child abuse and neglect.* New York: Cambridge University Press.

Cillessen, A. H. N., & Bukowski, W. M. (Eds.). (2000). *Recent advances in the measurement of acceptance and rejection in the peer system.* New Directions for Child & Adolescent Development. San Francisco: Jossey-Bass.

Cillessen, A. H. N., & Rose, A. J. (2005). Understanding popularity in the peer system. *Current Directions in Psychological Science, 14,* 102–105.

Cinamon, R. H. (2006). Anticipated work-family conflict: Effects of gender, self-efficacy, and family background. *Career Development Quarterly, 54*(3), 202–215.

Civic, D. (1999). The association between characteristics of dating relationships and condom use among heterosexual young adults. *AIDS Education and Prevention, 11,* 343–352.

Claes, M. (1998). Adolescents' closeness with parents, siblings, and friends in three countries: Canada, Belgium, and Italy. *Journal of Youth & Adolescence, 27,* 165–184.

Claes, M., Lacourse, E., Ercolani, A. P., Pierro, A., Leone, L., & Presaghi, F. (2005). Parenting, peer orientation, drug use, and antisocial behavior in late adolescence: A cross-national study. *Journal of Youth and Adolescence, 34*(5), 401–411.

Clark, B., & Trow, M. (1966). The organizational context. In T. M. Newcomb & E. K. Wilson (Eds.), *College peer groups: Problems and prospects for research* (pp. 17–70). Chicago: University of Chicago Press.

Clark, C. A., & Worthington, E. V., Jr. (1987). Family variables affecting the transition of religious values from parents to adolescents: A review. *Family Perspectives, 21,* 1–21.

Clasen, D., & Brown, B. (1985). The multidimensionality of peer pressure in adolescence. *Journal of Youth and Adolescence, 14,* 451–468.

Clausen, C. (1996, Summer). Welcome to post-culturalism. *American Scholar, 65*(3), 379–388.

Clausen, J. A. (1966). *Socialization and society.* Boston: Little, Brown.

Clausen, J. S. Adolescent competence and the shaping of the life course. *American Journal of Sociology, 96*(4), 805–842.

Clay, A. (2003). Keepin' it real: Black youth, hip-hop culture, and black identity. *American Behavioral Scientist, 46,* 1346–1358.

Clay, R. A. (1997, December). Are children being overmedicated? *APA Monitor,* pp. 1, 27.

Cleaves, D. H., & Latner, J. D. (2008). Evidence-based therapies for children and adolescents with eating disorders. In R. G. Steele, T. D. Elkin, & M. C. Roberts (Eds.), *Handbook of evidence-based therapies for children and adolescents: Bridging science and practice: Issues in clinical child psychology* (pp. 335–353). New York: Springer Science + Business Media.

Clifford, B. R., Gunter, B., & McAleer, J. L. (1995). *Television and children.* Hillsdale, NJ: Erlbaum.

Clingempeel, W., Colyar, J., Brand, E., & Hetherington, E. (1992). Children's relationships with maternal grandparents: A longitudinal study of family structure and pubertal status effects. *Child Development, 63,* 1404–1422.

Coghill, D., Spiel, G., Baldursson, G., Döpfner, M., Lorenzo, M. J., Ralston, S. J., & Rothenberger, A. [ADORE Study Group]. (2006). Which factors impact on clinician-rated impairment in children with ADHD? *European Child & Adolescent Psychiatry. 15*(Suppl. 1), 30–37.

Cohan, C. L., & Kleinbaum, S. (2002). Toward a greater understanding of the cohabitation effect: Premarital cohabitation and marital communication. *Journal of Marriage & the Family, 64,* 180–192.

Cohen, D., Gerardin, P., Mazet, P., Purper-Ouakil, D., & Flament, M. F. Pharmacological treatment of adolescent major depression. *Journal of Child and Adolescent Psychopharmacology. 14*(1) 19–31.

Cohen, J. (1969). *Statistical power analysis for the behavioral sciences.* New York: Academic Press.

Cohen, L. R., & Potter, L. B. (1999). Injuries and violence: Risk factors and opportunities. *Adolescent Medicine: State of the Art Reviews, 10,* 125–135.

Cohen, P., Kasen, S., Chen, H., Hartmark, C., & Gordon, K. (2003). Variations in patterns of developmental transitions in the emerging adulthood period. *Developmental Psychology, 39*(4), 657–669.

Cohn, D. (1999, November 24). Parents prize less a child's obedience. *Washington Post*, p. A8.

Coie, J., Terry, R., Lenox, K., Lochman, J., & Hyman, C. (1995). Childhood peer rejection and aggression as predictors of stable patterns of adolescent disorder. *Development and Psychopathology, 7*, 697–713.

Coie, J. D., & Dodge, K. A. (1997). Aggression and antisocial behavior. In N. Eisenberg (Ed.), *Handbook of child psychology* (5th ed., Vol. 3). York: Wiley.

Coie, J. D., Dodge, K. A., & Kupersmidt, J. B. (1990). Peer group behavior and social status. In S. R. Asher & J. D. Coie (Eds.), *Peer rejection in childhood* (pp. 17–59). New York: Cambridge University Press.

Colby, A., & Kohlberg, L. (1987). *The measurement of moral judgment.* New York: Cambridge University Press.

Colby, A., Kohlberg, L., Gibbs, J., & Lieberman, M. (1983). A longitudinal study of moral judgment. *Monographs of the Society for Research in Child Development, 48.*

Cole, M. (1996). *Cultural psychology: A once and future discipline.* Cambridge, MA: Harvard University Press.

Coleman, J. (1961). *The adolescent society.* Glencoe, IL: Free Press.

Coleman, J., & Hoffer, T. (1987). *Public and private high schools: The impact of communities.* New York: Basic Books.

Coleman, J., Hoffer, T., & Kilgore, S. (1982). *High school achievement: Public, Catholic and other private schools compared.* New York: Basic Books.

Coleman, J. S. (1974). *Youth: Transition to adulthood. Report of the Panel on Youth of the President's Science Advisory Committee.* Chicago: University of Chicago Press.

Coleman, M., & Ganong, L. H. (1990). Remarriage and stepfamily research in the 1980s: Increased interest in an old form. *Journal of Marriage and the Family, 52*, 925–939.

Coleman, M. C., & Webber, J. (2002). *Emotional and behavioral disorders* (4th ed.). Boston: Allyn & Bacon.

Coles, R., & Stokes, G. (1985). *Sex and the American teenager.* New York: Harper & Row.

Collins, W. A. (1990). Parent-child relationships in the transition to adolescence: Continuity and change in interaction, affect, and cognition. In R. Montemayor, G. Adams, & T. Gullotta (Eds.), *Advances in adolescent development, Vol. 2: The transition from childhood to adolescence* (pp. 85–106). Beverly Hills, CA: Sage.

Collins, W. A., Laursen, B., Mortenson, N., & Ferreira, M. (1997). Conflict processes and transitions in parent and peer relationships: Implications for autonomy and regulation. *Journal of Adolescent Research, 12*, 178–198.

Collins, W. A., Maccoby, E. E., Steinberg, L., Hetherington, E. M., & Bornstein, M. H. (2000). Contemporary research on parenting: The case for nature and nurture. *American Psychologist, 55*, 218–232.

Collins, W. A., & Sroufe, L. A. (1999). Capacity for intimate relationships: A developmental construction. In W. Furman, B. B. Brown, & C. Feiring (Eds.), *The development of romantic relationships in adolescence* (pp. 125–147). New York: Cambridge University Press.

Colom, R., Flores-Mendoza, C., & Rebollo, I. (2003). Working memory and intelligence. *Personality & Individual Differences, 34*, 33–39.

Colucci, E., & Martin, G. (2007). Ethnocultural aspects of suicide in young people: A systematic literature review. Part 1: Rates and methods of youth suicide. *Suicide and Life-Threatening Behavior, 37*(2), 197–221.

Comeau, N., Stewart, S. H., & Loba, P. (2001). The relations between trait anxiety, anxiety sensitivity, and sensation seeking to adolescents' motivations for alcohol, cigarette, and marijuana use. *Addictive Behaviors, 26*, 803–825.

Comer, J. P. (1993). *African American parents and child development: An agenda for school success.* Paper presented at the biennial meeting of the Society for Research in Child Development, New Orleans, LA.

Committee on Child Labor. (1998). Protecting youth at work. Washington, DC: National Academy of Sciences.

Compas, B. E., Connor, J. K., & Hinden, B. R. (1998). New perspectives on depression during adolescence. In R. Jessor, (Ed.), *New perspectives on adolescent risk behavior* (pp. 319–362). New York: Cambridge University Press.

Compas, B. E., Ey, S., & Grant, K. E. *Taxonomy, assessment, and diagnosis of depression during adolescence. Psychological Bulletin, 114*(2), 323–344.

Condon, R. G. (1987). Inuit youth: Growth and change in the Canadian Arctic. New Brunswick, NJ: Rutgers University Press.

Condon, R. G. (1995). The rise of the leisure class: Adolescence and recreational acculturation in the Canadian Arctic. *Ethos, 23*, 47–68.

Conklin, H. M., Luciana, M., Hooper, C. J., & Yarger, R. S. (2007). Working memory performance in typically developing children and adolescents: Behavioral evidence of protracted frontal lobe development. *Developmental Neuropsychology, 31*(1), 103–128.

Connell, J., Halpern-Flesher, B., Clifford, E., Crichlow, W., & Usinger, P. (1995). Hanging in there: Behavioral, psychological, and contextual factors affecting whether African American adolescents stay in high school. *Journal of Adolescent Research, 10*, 41–63.

Connolly, J., Craig, W., Goldberg, A., & Pepler, D. (2004). Mixed-gender groups, dating, and romantic relationships in early adolescence. *Journal of Research on Adolescence, 14*, 185–207.

Connolly, J., Furman, W., & Konarski, R. (2000). The role of peers in the emergence of heterosexual romantic relationships in adolescence. *Child Development, 71*, 1395–1408.

Connolly, J., & Goldberg, A. (1999). Romantic relationships in adolescence: The role of friends and peers in their emergence and development. In W. Furman, B. B. Brown, & C. Feiring (Eds.), *The development of romantic relationships in adolescence* (pp. 266–290). New York: Cambridge University Press.

Connolly, J., & Konarski, R. (1994). Peer self-concept in adolescence: Analysis of factor structure and of associations with peer experience. *Journal of Research on Adolescence, 4*, 385–403.

Connolly, J., McMaster, L., Craig, W., & Pepler, P. (1998, February). *Romantic relationships of bullies in early adolescence.* Paper presented at the biennial meeting of the Society for Research on Adolescence, San Diego, CA.

Constable, P. (2000, May 8). In Pakistan, women pay the price of "honor." *Washington Post*, pp. A1–A14.

Cooney, T. M. (1994). Young adults' relations with parents: The influence of recent parental divorce. *Journal of Marriage and the Family, 56*, 45–56.

Cooney, T. M., Smyer, M. A., Hagestad, G. O., & Klock, R. (1986). Parental divorce in young adulthood: Some preliminary findings. *American Journal of Orthopsychiatry, 56*, 470–477.

Cooper, C., & Grotevant, H. (1987). Gender issues in the interface of family experience and adolescents' friendship and dating identity. *Journal of Youth and Adolescence, 16*, 247–264.

Cooper, C. R., & Ayers-Lopez, S. (1985). Family and peer systems in early adolescence: New models of the role of relationships in development. *Journal of Early Adolescence, 5*, 9–22.

Cooper, K. J. (1999, October 1). Clinton, governors assess efforts to improve education. *Washington Post*, p. A13.

Cooper, M. L., Albino, A. W., Orcutt, H. K., & Williams, N. (2004). Attachment styles and intrapersonal adjustment: A longitudinal study from adolescence into young adulthood. In S. W. Rholes & J. A. Simpson (Eds.), *Adult attachment: Theory, research, and clinical implications* (pp. 438–466). New York: Guilford.

Cooper, M. L., Bede, A. V., & Powers, A. M. (1999). Motivations for condom use: Do pregnancy prevention goals undermine disease prevention among heterosexual young adults? *Health Psychology, 18*, 464–474.

Cooper, M. L., Wood, P. K., Orcutt, H. K., & Albino, A. (2003). Personality and the predisposition to engage in risky or problem behaviors during adolescence. *Journal of Personality & Social Psychology, 84*, 390–410.

Cope-Farrar, K., & Kunkel, D. (2002). Sexual messages in teens' favorite prime-time television programs. In J. D. Brown, J. R. Steele, & K. Walsh-Childers (Eds.), *Sexual teens, sexual media: Investigating media's influence on adolescent sexuality* (pp. 59–78). Mahwah, NJ: Erlbaum.

Corby, B. (1993). Child abuse: *Toward a knowledge base.* Buckingham, PA: Open University Press.

Corey, L., Adams, H. G., & Brown, Z. A. (1983). Genital herpes simplex virus infections. *Annals of Internal Medicine, 98*, 958–972.

Corrado, S. P., Patashnick, B. S., & Rich, M. (2004). Factors affecting change among obese adolescents. *Journal of Adolescent Health, 23*, 112–120.

Costello, D. M., Swendsen, J., Rose, J. S., & Dierker, L. C. (2008). Risk and protective factors associated with trajectories of depressed mood from adolescence to early adulthood. *Journal of Consulting and Clinical Psychology, 76*(2), 173–183.

Cota-Robles, S., Neiss, M., & Hunt, C. B. (2000, April). *Future selves, future scholars: A longitudinal study of adolescent "possible selves" and adult outcomes.* Poster presented at the biennial meeting of the Society for Research on Adolescence, Chicago.

Coté, J. (1994). *Adolescent storm and stress: An evaluation of the Mead-Freeman controversy.* Hillsdale, NJ: Erlbaum.

Coté, J. (2000). *Arrested adulthood: The changing nature of maturity and identity in the late modern world.* New York: New York University Press.

Côté, J. (2006). Emerging adulthood as an institutionalized moratorium: Risks and benefits to identity formation. In J. J. Arnett and J. L. Tanner (Eds.), *Emerging adults in America: Coming of age in the 21st century* (pp. 85–116). Washington, DC: American Psychological Association Press.

Coté, J. E., & Allahar, A. L. (1996). *Generation on hold: Coming of age in the late twentieth century.* New York: New York University Press.

Cotter, D. A., Hermsen, J. M., Kendig, S. M., & Vanneman, R. (2006, August). *The end of the U.S. gender revolution: Changing attitudes from 1974 to 2004.* Paper presented at the annual meeting of the American Sociological Association, Montreal, Quebec, Canada. Retrieved August 21, 2008, from http://www.allacademic.com/meta/p103486_index.html

Cowan, N., Saults, J. S., & Elliot, E. M. (2002). The search for what is fundamental in the development of working memory. In R. V. Kail & H. W. Reese, (Eds.), *Advances in child development and behavior* (Vol. 29, pp. 1–49). San Diego, CA: Academic Press.

Cowan, N., Saults, J., Scott, E., & Emily, M. (2002). The search for what is fundamental in the development of working memory. In V. R. Kail & W. H. Reese (Eds.), *Advances in child development and behavior, Vol. 29* (pp. 1–49). San Diego, CA: Academic Press.

Coyne, S. (2006). Violence, longitudinal studies. In J. J. Arnett (Ed.), *Encyclopedia* of children, adolescents, and the media. Thousand Oaks, CA: Sage.

Coyne, S. M., & Archer, J. (2005). The relationship between indirect and physical aggression on television and in real life. *Social Development, 14,* 324–338.

Coyne, S. M., Archer, J., & Eslea, M. (2006). "We're not friends anymore! Unless...": The frequency and harmfulness of indirect, relational and social aggression. *Aggressive Behavior, 32*(4), 294–307.

Cozby, P. C., Worden, P. E., & Kee, D. W. (1989). Research methods in human development. Mountain View, CA: Mayfield.

Craig, W. M. (2001). Developmental context of peer harassment in early adolescence: The role of puberty and the peer group. In J. Juvonen & S. Graham (Eds.), *Peer harassment in school: the plight of the vulnerable and victimized* (pp. 242–261). New York.

Cravatta, M. (1997). Online adolescents. *American Demographics, 19,* 29.

Crawford, M., & Popp, D. (2003). Sexual double standards: A review and methodological critique of two decades of research. *Journal of Sex Research, 40,* 13–26.

Crawford, M., & Unger, R. (2004). *Women and gender: A feminist psychology* (4th ed.). New York: McGraw-Hill.

Creasey, G., & Hesson-McInnis, M. (2001). Affective responses, cognitive appraisals, and conflict tactics in late adolescent romantic relationships: Associations with attachment orientations. *Journal of Counseling Psychology, 48,* 85–96.

Crick, N. R., & Rose, A. J. (2000). Toward a gender-balanced approach to the study of social-emotional development: A look at relational aggression. In P. H. Miller & E. K. Scholnick (Eds.), *Toward a feminist developmental psychology* (pp. 153–168). New York: Routledge.

Crisp, A. (1983). Some aspects of the psychopathology of anorexia nervosa. In P. Darby, P. Garfinkel, D. Garner, & D. Cosina (Eds.), *Anorexia nervosa: Recent developments in research* (pp. 15–28). New York: Alan R. Liss.

Crockett, L. J., Raffaelli, M., & Moilanen, K. (2002). Adolescent sexuality: Behavior and meaning. In G. R. Adams & M. Berzonsky (Eds.), *Blackwell handbook of adolescence.* Malden, MA: Blackwell.

Crockett, L. J., Rafaelli, M., & Moilanen, K. L. (2003). Adolescent sexuality: Behavior and meaning. In G. Adams & M. Berzonsky (Eds.), *Blackwell handbook of adolescence* (pp. 371–392). Malden, MA: Blackwell.

Crosnoe, R., Cavanagh, S., & Elder G. H., Jr. (2003). Adolescent friendships as academic resources: The intersection of friendship, race, and school disadvantage. *Sociological Perspectives, 46,* 331–352.

Crosnoe, R., Johnson, M. K., & Elder, G. H., Jr. (2004). School size and the interpersonal side of education: An examination of race/ethnicity and organizational context. *Social Science Quarterly, 85,* 1259–1274.

Cross, S. E., & Gore, J. S. (2003). Cultural models of the self. In E. S. Cross., S. J. Gore., & R. M. Leary (Eds.), *Handbook of self and identity* (pp. 536–564). New York: Guilford Press.

Crouter, A. C., & Booth, A. (Eds.). (2003). Children's influence on family dynamics: The neglected side of family relationships. Mahwah, NJ: Lawrence Erlbaum.

Crouter, A. C., Manke, B. A., & McHale, S. M. (1995). The family context of gender intensification in early adolescence. *Child Development, 66,* 317–329.

Crouter, A. C.; McHale, S. M. (2005). The long arm of the job revisited: Parenting in dual-earner families. In T. Luster & L. Okagaki (Eds.). *Parenting: An ecological perspective* (2nd ed., pp. 275–296). *Monographs in parenting.* Mahwah, NJ: Lawrence Erlbaum.

Crow, S. J., Mitchell, J. E., Roerig, J. D., & Steffen, K. (2009). What potential role is there for medication treatment in anorexia nervosa? *International Journal of Eating Disorders, 42*(1), 1–8.

Crump, A. D., Haynie, D. L., Aarons, S. J., Adair, E., Woodward, K., & Simons-Morton, B. G. (1999). Pregnancy among urban African-American teens: Ambivalence about prevention. *American Journal of Health Behavior, 23,* 32–42.

Csikszentmihalyi, M., & Larson, R. W. (1984). *Being adolescent: Conflict and growth in the teenage years.* New York: Basic Books.

Cummings, K. M. (2002). Marketing to America's youth: Evidence from corporate documents. *Tobacco Control, 11*(Suppl. 1), i5–i17.

Cunliffe, T. (1992). Arresting youth crime: A review of social skills training with young offenders. *Adolescence, 27,* 891–900.

Cunningham, M., & Thornton, A. (2007). Direct and indirect influences of parents' marital instability on children's attitudes toward cohabitation in young adulthood. *Journal of Divorce & Remarriage, 46*(3–4), 125–143.

Curran, P., Stice, E., & Chassin, L. (1997). The relation between adolescent alcohol and peer alcohol use: A longitudinal random coefficients model. *Journal of Consulting and Clinical Psychology, 65,* 130–140.

Currie, D. (1999). Girl talk: Adolescent magazines and their readers. Toronto, Canada: University of Toronto Press.

Curry, J. F., & Reinecke, M. A. (2003). Modular therapy with adolescents with major depression. In A. M. Reinecke., M. F. Dattilio., et al. (Eds.), *Cognitive therapy with children and adolescents: A casebook for clinical practice* (2nd ed., pp. 95–128). New York: Guilford Press.

Cutrona, C. E. (1982). Transition to college: Loneliness and the process of social adjustment. In L. A. Peplau & D. Perlman (Eds.), *Loneliness: A sourcebook of theory, research, and therapy* (pp. 291–309). New York: Wiley.

Cyr, M., Wright, J., McDuff, P., & Perron, A. (2002). Intrafamilial sexual abuse: Brother-sister incest does not differ from father-daughter and stepfather-stepdaughter incest. *Child Abuse & Neglect, 26,* 957–973.

Cyranowski, J. M., Frank, E., Young, E., & Shear, M. K. (2003). Adolescent onset of the gender difference in lifetime rates of major depression: A theoretical model. In E. M. Hertzig & A. E. Farber (Eds.), *Annual progress in child psychiatry and child development: 2000–2001* (pp. 383–398). New York: Brunner-Routledge.

D'Augelli, A. R. (2002). Mental health problems among lesbian, gay, and bisexual youths ages 14 to 21. *Clinical Child Psychology & Psychiatry, 7,* 433–456.

D'Augelli, A. R., Grossman, A. H., & Starks, M. T. (2005). Parents' awareness of lesbian, gay, and bisexual youths' sexual orientation. *Journal of Marriage & the Family, 67,* 474–482.

D'Augelli, A. R., & Patterson, C. J. (2002). *Lesbian, gay, and bisexual identities in youth: Psychological perspectives* (pp. 126–152).

Dahlberg, F. (1981). *Woman the gatherer.* New Haven, CT: Yale University Press.

Dailard, C. (2001). *The Guttmacher report on public policy.* New York: Alan Guttmacher Institute. Available: www.agi-usa.org

Damico, S., & Sparks, C. (1986). Cross-group contact opportunities: Impact on interpersonal relationships in desegregated middle schools. *Sociology of Education, 59,* 113–123.

Daniels, D., Dunn, J., Furstenberg, F., Jr., & Plomin, R. (1985). Environmental differences within the family and adjustment differences within pairs of adolescent siblings. *Child Development, 56,* 764–774.

Daniels, H., Cole, M., & Wertsch, J. V. (Eds.). (2007). *The Cambridge companion to Vygotsky.* New York: Cambridge University Press.

Darlington, Y. (2001). "When all is said and done": The impact of parental divorce and contested custody on young adults' relationships with their parents and their attitudes to relationships and marriage. *Journal of Divorce & Remarriage, 35,* 23–42.

Darroch, J. E., Landry, D. J., & Oslak, S. (1999). Age differences between sexual partners in the United States. *Family Planning Perspectives, 31,* 160–167.

Dasen, P. (1998). Rapid social change and the turmoil of adolescence: A cross-cultural perspective. *World Psychology.*

Davidson, J. (2000). Giftedness. In A. Kazdin (Ed.), Encyclopedia of psychology. Washington, DC: American Psychological Association.

Davies, E., & Furnham, A. (1986). The dieting and body shape concerns of adolescent females. *Journal of Child Psychology & Psychiatry, 27,* 417–428.

Davies, H. D., & Fitzgerald, H. E. (Eds.) (2008). *Obesity in childhood and adolescence, Vol. 1: Medical, biological, and social issues.* New York: Praeger.

Davies, M., & Kandel, D. B. (1981). Parental and peer influences on adolescents' educational plans: Some further evidence. *American Journal of Sociology, 87,* 363–387.

Davies-Netzley, S. A. (2002). Gender-stereotypic images of occupations correspond to the sex-segregation of employment. In A. E. Hunter & C. Forden (Eds.), *Readings in the psychology of gender: Exploring our differences and commonalities* (pp. 281–299). Needham Heights, MA: Allyn & Bacon.

Davis, D., Shaver, P. R., & Vernon, M. L. (2003). Physical, emotional, and behavioral reactions to breaking up: The roles of gender, age, emotional involvement, and attachment style. *Personality & Social Psychology Bulletin, 29,* 871–884.

Davis, J. (1988). Mazel tov: The bar mitzvah as a multigenerational ritual of change and continuity. In E. Imber-Black & J. Roberts (Eds.), *Rituals in families and family therapy.* New York: Norton.

Davis, J. A., & Smith, T. W. (1991, July). *General social surveys, 1972–1991.* Chicago: National Opinion Research Center, University of Chicago.

Davis, K., & Kirkpatrick, L. (1998). Attachment style, gender, and relationship stability: A longitudinal analysis. *Journal of personality and Social Psychology, 66,* 505–512.

Davis, L., & Stewart, R. (1997, July). *Building capacity for working with lesbian, gay, bisexual, and transgender youth.* Paper presented at the conference on Working with America's Youth, Pittsburgh, PA.

Davis, S. S., & Davis, D. A. (1989). *Adolescence in a Moroccan town.* New Brunswick, NJ: Rutgers.

Davis, S. S., & Davis, D. A. (1995). "The mosque and the satellite": Media and adolescence in a Moroccan town. *Journal of Youth & Adolescence, 24,* 577–594.

Davis, S.S., & Davis, D.A. (2007). Morocco. In J. J. Arnett, R. Ahmed, B. Nsamenang, T. S. Saraswathi, & R. Silbereisen (Eds.), *International encyclopedia of adolescence.* New York: Routledge.

de Bruyn, E. H., & Cillessen, A. H. N. (2006). Popularity in early adolescence: Prosocial and antisocial subtypes. *Journal of Adolescent Research, 21*(6), 607–627.

De Li, S. (2004). The impacts of self-control and social bonds on juvenile delinquency in a national sample of midadolescents. *Deviant Behavior, 25,* 351–373.

De Lisi, R. (2005). A lifetime of work using a developmental theory to enhance the lives of children and adolescents. *Journal of Applied Developmental Psychology, 26,* 107–110.

De Mey, L., Baartman, H. M., & Schultze, H. J. (1999). Ethnic variation and the development of moral judgment of youth in Dutch society. *Youth & Society, 31,* 54–75.

de Wilde, E. J., Kienhorts, I., Diekstra, R., & Wolters, W. (1992). The relationship between adolescent suicidal behavior and life events in childhood and adolescence. *American Journal of Psychiatry, 149,* 45–51.

Dean, B. B., Borenstein, J. E., Knight, K., & Yonkers, K. (2006). Evaluating the criteria used for identification of PMS. *Journal of Women's Health, 15*(5), 546–555.

Deaux, K., & Lewis, L. L. (1984). Structure of gender stereotypes: Interrelationships among components and gender label. *Journal of Personality and Social Psychology, 46,* 991–1004.

DeBaryshe, K., Patterson, G., & Capaldi, D. (1993). A performance model for academic achievement in early adolescent boys. *Developmental Psychology, 29,* 795–804.

DeBerard, M. S., Spielmans, G. L., & Julka, D. L. (2004). Predictors of academic achievement and retention among college freshmen: A longitudinal study. *College Student Journal, 38,* 66–80.

Deihl, L. M., Vicary, J. R., & Deike, R. C. (1997). Longitudinal trajectories of self-esteem from early to middle adolescence and related psychosocial variables among rural adolescents. *Journal of Research on Adolescence, 7,* 393–411.

Dekel, R., Peled, E., & Spiro, S. E. (2003). Shelters for houseless youth: A follow-up evaluation. *Journal of Adolescence, 26,* 201–212.

DeLoache, J., & Gottlieb, A. (2000). *A world of babies: Imagined childcare guides for seven societies.* New York: Cambridge University Press.

Delsing, M. J. M. H., ter Bogt, T. F. M., Engels, R. C. M. E., & Meeus, W. H. J. (2007). Adolescents' peer crowd identification in the Netherlands: Structure and associations with problem behaviors. *Journal of Research on Adolescence, 17*(2), 467–480.

Demir, A., & Tarhan, N. (2001). Loneliness and social dissatisfaction in Turkish adolescents. *Journal of Psychology, 135,* 113–123.

Demir, M., Urberg, K. A. (2004). Friendship and adjustment among adolescents. *Journal of Experimental Child Psychology, 88,* 68–82.

Demorest, A., Meyer, C., Phelps, E., Gardner, H., & Winner, E. (1984). Words speak louder than actions: Understanding deliberately false remarks. *Child Development, 55,* 1527–1534.

Dempster, N. W. (1984). Model of cognitive development across the lifespan. *Developmental Review, 4,* 171–191.

Denner, J., & Dunbar, N. (2004). Negotiating femininity: Power and strategies of Mexican American girls. *Sex Roles, 50,* 301–314.

Denner, J., & Guzman, B. L. (Eds.). (2006). *Latina girls: Voices of adolescent strength in the United States.* New York: New York University Press.

DeRose, L. M., & Brooks-Gunn, J. (2006). Transition into adolescence: The role of pubertal processes. In L. Balter & C. S. Tamis-LeMonda (Eds.), *Child psychology: A handbook of contemporary issues* (2nd ed., pp. 385–414). New York: Psychology Press.

Deshler, D. D. (2005). Adolescents with learning disabilities: Unique challenges and reasons for hope. *Learning Disability Quarterly, 28,* 122–124.

Desmairis, S., & Curtis, J. (1999). Gender differences in employment and income experiences among young people. In J. Barling & E. K. Kelloway (Eds.), *Youth workers: Varieties of experience* (pp. 59–88). Washington, DC: American Psychological Association.

Dey, E. L., & Hurtado, S. (1999). Students, colleges, and society: Considering the interconnections. In P. G. Altbach, R. O. Berndahl, & P. J. Gumport (Eds.), *American higher education in the twenty-first century: Social, political, and economic challenges* (pp. 298–322). Baltimore: Johns Hopkins University Press.

Deyhle, D. (1995). Navajo youth and Anglo racism: Cultural integrity and resistance. *Harvard Educational Review, 65,* 403–444.

Deyhle, D. (1998). From break dancing to heavy metal: Navajo youth, resistance, and identity. *Youth & Society, 30,* 3–31.

Diaz, R., & Berndt, T. (1982). Children's knowledge of a best friend: Fact or fancy? *Developmental Psychology, 18,* 787–794.

DiClemente, R. J., & Crosby, R. A. (2003). Sexually transmitted diseases among adolescents: Risk factors, antecedents, and prevention strategies. In R. G. Adams & D. M. Berzonsky (Eds.), *Blackwell handbook of adolescence* (pp. 573–605). Malden, MA: Blackwell Publishers.

Dijkstra, J. K., Lindenberg, S., & Veenstra, R. (2008). Beyond the class norm: Bullying behavior of popular adolescents and its relation to peer acceptance and rejection. *Journal of Abnormal Child Psychology, 36*(8), 1289–1299.

Dinges, N. G., Trimble, J. E., & Hollenbeck, A. R. (1979). American Indian adolescent socialization: A review of the literature. *Journal of Adolescence, 2,* 259–296.

Dionne, E. J., Jr. (1999, July 16). Abstinence-plus. *Washington Post,* p. A-23.

Dishion, T. J., & Dodge, K. A. (2005). Peer contagion in interventions for children and adolescents: Moving towards an understanding of the ecology and dynamics of change. *Journal of Abnormal Child Psychology, 33,* 395–400.

Dishion, T. J., Dodge, K. A., & Lansford, J. E. (2006). Findings and recommendations: A blueprint to minimize deviant peer influence in youth interventions and programs. In K. A. Dodge, T. J. Dishion, & J. E. Lansford (Eds.), *Deviant peer influences in programs for youth: Problems and solutions* (pp. 366–394). New York: Guilford Press.

Dishion, T. J., & Spracklen, K. M. (1996, March). *Childhood peer rejection in the development of adolescent substance abuse.* Paper presented at the meeting of the Society for Research on Adolescence, Boston.

Dishion, T. J., McCord, J., & Poulin, F. (1999). When interventions harm: Groups and problem behavior. *American Psychologist, 54,* 755–764.

Dishion, T. J., Nelson, S. E., & Kavanagh, K. (2003). The family check-up with high-risk young adolescents: Preventing early-onset substance use by parent monitoring. *Behavior Therapy, 34,* 553–571.

Dishion, T. J., & Patterson, G. R. (2006). The development and ecology of antisocial behavior in children and adolescents. In D. Cicchetti & D. J. Cohen (Eds.), *Developmental psychopathology, Vol. 3: Risk, disorder, and adaptation* (2nd ed., pp. 503–541). Hoboken, NJ: John Wiley & Sons.

Dishion, T. J., Piehler, T. F., & Myers, M. W. (2008). Dynamics and ecology of adolescent peer influence. In M. J. Prinstein & K. A. Dodge (Eds.), *Understanding peer influence in children and adolescence: Duke series in child development and public policy* (pp. 72–93). New York: Guilford Press.

DiTommaso, E., & Spinner, B. (1997). Social and emotional loneliness: A re-examination of Weiss' typology of loneliness. *Personality and Individual Differences, 22,* 417–427.

Dittus, P., & Jaccard, J. (2000). Adolescents' perceptions of maternal disapproval of sex: Relationship to sexual outcomes. *Journal of Adolescent Health, 26,* 268–278.

Diversi, M., Moraes filho, N., & Morelli, M. (1999). Daily reality on the streets of Campinas, Brazil. In M. Raffaelli & R. Larson (Eds.), *Homeless and working youth around the world: Exploring developmental issues* (pp. 19–34). New Directions in Child and Adolescent Development, Number 85. San Francisco: Jossey-Bass.

Dobkin, P., Tremblay, R., Masse, L., & Vitaro, F. (1995). Individual and peer characteristics in predicting boys' early onset of substance abuse: A seven-year longitudinal study. *Child Development, 66,* 1198–1214.

Dodd, J. M., Nelson, J. R., & Hofland, B. H. (1994). Minority identity and self-concept: The American Indian experience. In T. M. Brinthaupt & R. P. Lipka (Eds.), *Changing the self: Philosophies, techniques, and experiences* (pp. 307–336). Albany, NY: State University of New York Press.

Dodge, K. A. (1983). Behavioral antecedents of peer social status. *Child Development, 54,* 1386–1399.

Dodge, K. A., & Feldman, E. (1990). Issues in social cognition and sociometric status. In S. R. Asher & J. D. Coie (Eds.), *Peer rejection in childhood. Cambridge studies in social and emotional development* (pp. 119–155). New York: Cambridge University Press.

Dodge, K. A. (1993, March). *Social information processing and peer rejection factors in the development of behavior problems in children.* Paper presented at the biennial meeting of the Society for Research in Child Development, New Orleans, LA.

Dodge, K. A., Lansford, J. E., Burks, V. S., Bates, J. E., Pettit, G. S., Fontaine, R. P., & Joseph M. (2003). Peer rejection and social information-processing factors in the development of aggressive behavior problems in children. *Child Development, 74,* 374–393.

Donaldson, D., Spirito, A., & Overholser, J. (2003). In A. Spirito & J. C. Overholser (Eds.), *Evaluating and treating adolescent suicide attempters: From research to practice.* (pp. 295–321). San Diego, CA: Academic Press.

Donnellan, M. B., Trzesniewski, K. H., Robins, R. W., Moffitt, T. E., & Caspi, A. (2005). Low self-esteem is related to aggression, antisocial behavior, and delinquency. *Psychological Science, 16,* 328–335.

Donohue, R. (2007). Examining career persistence and career change intent using the career attitudes and strategies inventory. *Journal of Vocational Behavior, 70*(2), 259–276.

Donovan, D. M., Marlatt, G. A., & Salzberg, P. M. (1983). Drinking behavior, personality factors, and high-risk driving: A review and theoretical formulation. *Journal of Studies on Alcohol, 44,* 395–428.

Donovan, D. M., Queisser, H. R., Salzberg, P. M., & Umlauf, R. L. (1985). Intoxicated and bad drivers: Subgroups within the same population of high-risk men drivers. *Journal of Studies on Alcohol, 46,* 375–382.

Donovan, D. M., Umlauf, R. L., & Salzberg, P. M. (1988). Derivation of personality subtypes among high-risk drivers. *Alcohol, Drugs and Driving, 4,* 233–244.

Donovan, J. E. (1993). Young adult drinking-driving: Behavioral and psychosocial correlates. *Journal of Studies on Alcohol, 54,* 600–613.

Donovan, J., & Jessor, R. (1985). Structure of problem behavior in adolescence and young adulthood. *Journal of Consulting and Clinical Psychology, 53,* 890–904.

Dooley, D., Prause, J., & Ham-Rowbottom, K. A. (2000). Underemployment and depression: Longitudinal relationships. *Journal of Health and Social Behavior, 41,* 421–436.

Dorn, L. D., Dahl, R., Williamson, D. E., Birmaher, B., Axelson, D., Perel, J., Stull, S. D., & Ryan, N. D. (2003). Developmental markers in adolescence: Implications for studies of pubertal development. *Journal of Youth & Adolescence, 32,* 315–324.

Dornbusch, S. (1994, February). *Off the track.* Presidential address to the Society for Research on Adolescence, San Diego, CA.

Dornbusch, S., Carlsmith, J., Bushwall, S., Ritter, P., Leiderman, P., Hastorf, A., & Gross, R. (1985). Single parents, extended households, and the control of adolescents. *Child Development, S6,* 326–341.

Dornbusch, S. M., Carlsmith, J. M., Gross, R. T., Martin, J. A., Jennings, D., Rosenberg, A., & Duke, P. (1981). Sexual development, age, and dating: A comparison of biological and social influences upon one set of behaviors. *Child Development, 52,* 179–185.

Dornbusch, S., M. Ritter, R., Liederman, P., Roberts, D., & Fraleigh, M. (1987). The relation of parenting style to adolescent school performance. *Child Development, 58,* 1244–1257.

Dornbusch, S. M., Ritter, P. L., Mont-Reynaud, R., & Chien, Z. (1990). Family decision making and academic performance in a diverse high school population. *Journal of Adolescent Research, 5,* 143–160.

Douglass, C. B. (2005). *Barren states: The population "implosion" in Europe.* New York: Berg.

Douglass, C. B. (2007). From duty to desire: Emerging adulthood in Europe and its consequences. *Child Development Perspectives, 1,* 101–108.

Douvan, E., & Adelson, J. (1966). *The adolescent experience.* New York: Wiley.

Dowda, M., Ainsworth, B. E., Addy, C. L., Saunders, R., & Riner, W. (2001). Environmental influences, physical activity, and weight status in 8 to 16 year-olds. *Archives of Pediatric and Adolescent Medicine, 155,* 711–717.

Dreyer, P. (1982). Sexuality during adolescence. In B. Wolman (Ed.), *Handbook of developmental psychology.* Englewood Cliffs, NJ: Prentice-Hall.

Dryfoos, J. G. (1998). *Full-service schools: A revolution in health and social services for children, youth, and families.* San Francisco: Jossey-Bass.

du Bois-Reymond, M., & van der Zande, I. (1994). The Netherlands. In K. Hurrelmann (Ed.), *International handbook of adolescence* (pp. 270–286). Westport, CT: Greenwood Press.

Dubas, J., Graber, J., & Petersen, A. (1991). A longitudinal investigation of adolescents' changing perceptions of pubertal timing. *Developmental Psychology, 27,* 580–586.

Dubas, J. S., & Petersen, A. C. (1996). Geographical distance from parents and adjustment during adolescence and young adulthood. In J. A. Graber & J. S. Dubas (Eds.), *New Directions for Child Development, 71,* 3–19.

Duben, A., & Behar, C. (1991). *Istanbul households.* Cambridge, England: Cambridge University Press.

DuBois, D. L. (2003). Self-esteem, adolescence. In T. P. Gullotta & M. Bloom (Eds.) and T. P. Gullotta & G. Adams (Section Eds.), *Encyclopedia of primary prevention and health promotion* (pp. 953–961). New York: Kluwer Academic/Plenum.

DuBois, D. L., Bull, C. A., Sherman, M. D., & Roberts, M. (1998). Self-esteem and adjustment in early adolescence: A social-contextual perspective. *Journal of Youth & Adolescence, 27,* 557–584.

DuBois, D. L., & Hirsch, B. J. (1990). School and neighborhood friendship patterns of blacks and whites in early adolescence. *Child Development, 61,* 524–536.

DuBois, D. L., & Hirsch, B. J. (1993). School/nonschool friendship patterns in early adolescence. *Journal of Early Adolescence, 13,* 102–122.

DuBois, D. L., & Silverthorn, N. (2004). Do deviant peer associations mediate the contributions of self-esteem to problem behavior during early adolescence? A 2-year longitudinal study. *Journal of Clinical Child & Adolescent Psychology, 33,* 382–388.

DuBois, D. L., & Tevendale, H. D. (1999). Self-esteem in childhood and adolescence: Vaccine or epiphenomenon? *Applied & Preventive Psychology, 8,* 103–117.

DuBois, D., Felner, R., Brand, S., Adan, A., & Evans, E. (1992). A prospective study of life stress, social support, and adaptation in early adolescence. *Child Development, 63,* 542–557.

DuBois, D., Felner, R., Brand, S., Phillip, R., & Lease, A. (1996). Early adolescent self-esteem: A developmental-ecological framework and assessment strategy. *Journal of Research on Adolescence, 6,* 543–579.

Dubow, E. F., Huesmann, L. R., & Greenwood, D. (2007). Media and youth socialization: Underlying processes and moderators of effects. In J. E. Grusec & P. D. Hastings (Eds.), *Handbook of socialization: Theory and research* (pp. 404–430). New York: Guilford Press.

Ducharme, J., Doyle, A. B., & Markiewicz, D. (2002). Attachment security with mother and father: Associations with adolescents' reports of interpersonal behavior with parents and peers. *Journal of Social and Personal Relationships, 19,* 203–231.

Dudley, J. R. (1991). Increasing our understanding of divorced fathers who have infrequent contact with their children. *Family Relations, 40,* 279–285.

Due, P., Holstein, B. E., Lunch, J., Diderichsen, F., Gabhain, S. N., Scheidt, P., & Currie, C. (2005). The health behavior in school-aged children bullying working group. *European Journal of Public Health, 15*(2), 128–132.

Duemmler, S. L., & Kobak, R. (2001). The development of commitment and attachment in dating relationships: Attachment security as relationship construct. *Journal of Adolescence, 24,* 401–415.

Duffy, M., & Gotcher, J. M. (1996). Crucial advice on how to get the guy: The rhetorical vision of power and seduction in the teen magazine YM. *Journal of Communication Inquiry, 20,* 32–48.

Duke, L. (2002). Get real! Cultural relevance and resistance to the mediated feminine ideal. *Psychology & Marketing, 19,* 211–233.

Duncan, P., Ritter, P., Dornbusch, S., Gross, R., & Carlsmith, J. (1985). The effects of pubertal timing on body image, school behavior, and deviance. *Journal of Youth and Adolescence, 14,* 227–236.

Dunphy, D. (1963). The social structure of urban adolescent peer groups. *Sociometry, 26,* 230–246.

Dunphy, D. (1969). *Cliques, crowds, and gangs.* Melbourne: Ghesire.

Durham, M. G. (1998). Dilemmas of desire: Representations of sexuality in two teen magazines. *Youth & Society, 29,* 369–389.

Dustmann, C., & Schoenberg, U. (2008). Why does the German apprenticeship system work? In K. U. Mayer & H. Solga (Eds.), *Skill information: Interdisciplinary and cross-national perspective* (p. 85–108). New York: Cambridge University Press.

Duthie, J .K., Nippold, M. A., Billow, J. L., & Mansfield, T. C. (2008). Mental imagery of concrete proverbs: A developmental study of children, adolescents and adults. *Applied Psycholinguistics, 29*(1), 151–173.

Duvander, A. E. (1999). The transition from cohabitation to marriage: A longitudinal study of the propensity to marry in Sweden in the early 1990s. *Journal of Family Issues, 20,* 698–717.

Dworkin, J. B., & Larson, R. (2001). Age trends in the experience of family discord in single-mother families across adolescence. *Journal of Adolescence, 24,* 529–534.

Dyk, P., & Adams, G. (1990). Identity and intimacy: An initial investigation of three theoretical models using crosslag panel correlations. *Journal of Youth and Adolescence, 19,* 91–110.

Eagly, A. H. (1987). *Sex differences in social behavior: A social-role interpretation.* Hillsdale, NJ: Erlbaum.

Eagly, A. H., Wood, W., & Johannesen-Schmidt, M. C. (2004). Social role theory of sex differences and similarities: Implications for the partner preferences of women and men. In A. H. Eagly, A. E. Beall, & R. A. Sternberg (Eds.), *The psychology of gender* (2nd ed., pp. 269–295). New York: Guilford Press.

Eccles, J., Midgley, C., Wigfield, A., Buchanan, C., Reuman, D., Flanagan, C., & Mac Iver, D. (1993). Development during adolescence: The impact of stage-environment fit on young adolescents' experiences in schools and families. *American Psychologist, 48,* 90–101.

Eccles, J. S., & Harold, R. D. (1993). Parent-school involvement during the adolescent years. In R.

Takanishi (Ed.), *Adolescence in the 1990s.* New York: Columbia University Press.

Eccles, J. S., Lord, S. E., Roeser, R. W., Barber, B. L., & Hernandez Jozefowicz, D. M. (1997). The association of school transitions in early adolescence with developmental trajectories through high school. In J. Schulenberg, J. L. Maggs, & K. Hurrelmann (Eds.), *Health risks and developmental transitions during adolescence* (pp. 283–320). New York: Cambridge University Press.

Eccles, J. S., & Roeser, R. W. (2003). Schools as developmental contexts. In G. Adams & M. Berzonsky (Eds.), *Blackwell handbook of adolescence* (pp. 129–148). Malden, MA: Blackwell.

Eckenrode, J., Laird, M., & Doris, J. (1993). School performance and disciplinary problems among abused and neglected children. *Developmental Psychology, 29,* 53–62.

Eckert, P. (1995). Trajectory and forms of institutional participation. In L. J. Crockett & A. C. Crouter (Eds.), *Pathways through adolescence* (pp. 175–195). Mahwah, NJ: Erlbaum.

Economist (2007). A man's world? Good news. The education gap between men and women is narrowing. *Economist, 75,* November 3.

Economist (2008). Under threat of change, slowly but surely, universities in France—and all across Europe—are reforming. *Economist, 62,* June 7.

Eder, D. (1993). "Go get ya a French!" Romantic and sexual teasing among adolescent girls. In D. Tannen (Ed.), *Gender and conversational interaction* (pp. 17–31). New York: Oxford University Press.

Eder, D. (1995). *School talk: Gender and adolescent culture.* New Brunswick, NJ: Rutgers University Press.

Education Trust. (1996). *Education watch: The 1996 Education Trust state and national data book.* Washington, DC: Author.

Educational Testing Service. (1992). *Cross-national comparisons of 9–13 year olds' science and math achievement.* Princeton, NJ: Author.

Egeland, B., & Carlston, E. A. (2004). Attachment and psychopathology. In L. Atkinson & S. Goldberg (Eds.), *Attachment issues in psychopathology and intervention* (pp. 27–48). Mahwah, NJ: Erlbaum.

Eichorn, D. H. (1970). Physiological development. In P. H. Mussen (Ed.), *Carmichael's manual of child psychology* (Vol. 2, 3rd ed., pp. 152–183). New York: Wiley.

Eichorn, D. H. (1975). Asynchronizations in adolescent development. In S. Dragastin & G. H. Elder, Jr. (Eds.), *Adolescence in the life cycle: Psychological change and the social context* (pp. 81–96). New York: Halsted.

Eisenberg, N., Zhou, Q., & Koller, S. (2001). Brazilian adolescents' prosocial moral judgment and behavior: Relations to sympathy, perspective taking, gender-role orientation, and demographic characteristics. *Child Development, 72,* 518–534.

Eisner, M. (2002). Crime, problem drinking, and drug use: Patterns of problem behavior in cross-national perspective. *Annals of the American Academy of Political and Social Science, 580,* 201–225.

El-Bakri, Z. B., & Kameir, E. M. (1983). Aspects of women's political participation in Sudan. *International Social Science Journal, 35,* 605–623.

Elder, G. H., Jr. (1974/1999). *Children of the Great Depression: Social change in life experience.* Boulder, CO: Westview Press.

Elder, G. H., Jr., Caspi, A., & van Nguyen, T. (1986). Resourceful and vulnerable children: Family influences in stressful times. In R. Silbereisen, K. Eyferth, & G. Rudinger (Eds.), *Development as action in context.* Heidelberg, Germany: Springer.

Elder, G. H., Jr., van Nguyen, T., & Caspi, A. (1985). Linking family hardship to children's lives. *Child Development, 56,* 361–375.

Elkind, D. (1967). Egocentrism in adolescence. *Child Development, 38,* 1025–1034.

Elkind, D. (1978). Understanding the young adolescent. *Adolescence, 13,* 127–134.

Elkind, D. (1985). Egocentrism redux. *Developmental Review, 5,* 218–226.

Elkind, D. (2001). Cognitive development. In J. V. Lerner & R. M. Lerner (Eds.), *Adolescence in America: An encyclopedia,* (pp. 127–134). Santa Barbara, CA: ABC-CLIO.

Elliott, D. S., Huizinga, D., & Menard, S. (1989). *Multiple problem youth: Delinquency, substance abuse, and mental health problems.* New York: Springer.

Ellis, B. J., & Garber, J. (2000). Psychosocial antecedents of variation in girls' pubertal timing: Maternal depression, stepfather presence, and marital and family stress. *Child Development, 71,* 485–501.

Ellis, N. (1991). An extension of the Steinberg accelerating hypothesis. *Journal of Early Adolescence, 11,* 221–235.

Ellison, N. C., Steinfield, C., & Lampe, C. (2007). The benefits of Facebook "friends": Social capital and college students' use of online social network sites. *Journal of Computer-Mediated Communication, 12*(4), 1143–1168.

Elster, A., Lamb, M., Peters, L., Kahn, J., & Tavare, J. (1987). Judicial involvement and conduct problems of fathers of infants born to adolescent mothers. *Pediatrics, 79,* 230–234.

Emerson, R. A. (2002). "Where my girls at?" Negotiating Black womanhood in music videos. *Gender & Society, 16,* 115–135.

Emery, R. E. (1999). *Marriage, divorce, and children's adjustment* (2nd ed.). Newbury Park, CA: Sage.

Emery, R. E., Sbarra, D., & Grover, T. (2005). Divorce mediation: Research and reflections. *Family Court Review, 43,* 22–37.

Emery, R. E., & Tuer, M. (1993). Parenting and the marital relationship. In T. Luster & L. Okagaki (Eds.), *Parenting: An ecological perspective.* Hillsdale, NJ: Erlbaum.

Emslie, G. J., Heiligenstein, J. H., & Wagner, K. D. (2002). Fluoxetine for acute treatment of depression in children and adolescents: A placebo-controlled randomized clinical trial. *Journal of the American Academy of Child & Adolescent Psychiatry, 41,* 1205–1214.

Engeland, A., Bjorge, T., Tverdal, A., & Sogaard, A. J. (2004). Obesity in adolescence and adulthood and the risk of adult mortality. *Epidemiology, 15,* 79–85.

Engels, R. C. M. E., & ter Bogt, T. (2004). Outcome expectancies and ecstasy use in visitors of rave parties in the Netherlands. *European Addiction Research, 10,* 156–162.

Engels, R. C. M. E., Dekovic, M., & Meeus, W. (2002). Parenting practices, social skills, and peer relationships in adolescence. *Social Behavior and Personality, 30,* 3–18.

Engels, R. C. M. E., Finkenauer, C., Meeus, W., & Dekovic, M. (2001). Parental attachment and adolescents' emotional adjustment: The associations with social skills and relational competence. *Journal of Counseling Psychology, 48,* 428–439.

Engles, R. C. M. E., Knibbe, R. A., de Vries, H., Drop, M. J., & van Breukelen, G. J. P. (1999). Influences of parental and best friends' smoking and drinking on adolescent use: A longitudinal study. *Journal of Applied Social Psychology, 29,* 337–361.

Ennett, S., Tobler, N., Ringwalt, C., & Flewelling, R. (1994). How effective is drug abuse resistance education? A meta-analysis of Project DARE outcome evaluations. *American Journal of Public Health, 84,* 1394–1401.

Entwisle, D. R. (1990). Schools and the adolescent. In S. S. Feldman & G. R. Elliott (Eds.), *At the threshold: The developing adolescent* (pp. 197–224). Cambridge, MA: Harvard University Press.

Ephron, N. (2000). *Crazy salad: Some things about women.* New York: Random House.

Epstein, J. (1983). Selecting friends in contrasting secondary school environments. In J. Epstein & N. Karweit (Eds.), *Friends in school.* New York: Academic Press.

Epstein, J. L., & Dunbar, S. L. (1995). Effects on students of an interdisciplinary program linking social studies, art, and family volunteers in the middle grades. *Journal of Early Adolescence, 15,* 114–144.

Epstein, J. S., Pratto, D. J., & Skipper, J. K. (1990). Teenagers, behavioral problems, and preferences for heavy metal and rap music: A case study of a Southern middle school. *Deviant Behavior, 11,* 381–394.

Ericsson, K. A. (1990). Peak performance and age: An examination of peak performance in sports. In P. Baltes & M. M. Baltes (Eds.), *Successful aging* (pp. 164–196). Cambridge, MA: Cambridge University Press.

Erikson, E. H. (1950). *Childhood and society.* New York: Norton.

Erikson, E. H. (1958). *Young man Luther.* New York: Norton.

Erikson, E. H. (1959). Identity and the life cycle. *Psychological Issues, 1,* 1–171.

Erikson, E. H. (1968). *Identity: Youth and crisis.* New York: Norton.

Erickson, P. I. (2003). Cultural factors affecting the negotiation of first sexual intercourse among Latina adolescent mothers. In I. M. Torres & P. G. Cernada (Eds.), *Sexual and reproductive health promotion in Latino populations: Parteras, promotoras y poetas: Case studies across the Americas* (pp. 63–79). Amityville, NY: Baywood.

Etaugh, C. A., & Bridges, J. S. (2006). Midlife transitions. In J. Worell, J. & C. D. Goodheart (Eds.), *Handbook of girls' and women's psychological health: Gender and well-being across the lifespan. Oxford series in clinical psychology* (pp. 359–367). New York: Oxford University Press.

Evans, E. D., Rutberg, J., Sather, C., & Turner, C. (1991). Content analysis of contemporary teen magazines for adolescent females. *Youth & Society, 23,* 99–120.

Evans, M. E. (1992, March). *Achievement and achievement-related beliefs in Asian and Western contexts: Cultural and gender differences.* Paper presented at the biennial meeting of the Society for Research on Adolescence, Washington, DC.

Evans, J. St. B. T. (2008). Dual-processing accounts of reasoning, judgment, and social cognition. *Annual Review of Psychology, 59,* 255–278.

Evans, S. W., Pelham, W. E., Smith, B. H., et al. (2001). Dose-response effects of methylphenidate on ecologically valid measures of academic performance and classroom behavior in adolescents with ADHD. *Experimental and Clinical Psychopharmacology, 9,* 163–175.

Eveleth, P. B., & Tanner, J. M. (1990). *Worldwide variation in human growth.* Cambridge, MA: Cambridge University Press.

Eyal, K., Kunkel, D., Biely, E. N., & Finnerty, K. L. (2007). Sexual socialization messages on television programs most popular among teens. *Journal of Broadcasting & Electronic Media, 51*(2), 316–336.

Eyre, S. L., & Millstein, S. G. (1999). What leads to sex? Adolescent preferred partners and reasons for sex. *Journal of Research on Adolescence, 9,* 277–307.

Facio, A., & Micocci, F. (2003). Emerging adulthood in Argentina. In J. J. Arnett & N. Galambos (Eds.), *New Directions in Child and Adolescent Development, Vol. 100,* 21–31.

Fackler, M. (2007, June 22). As Japan ages, universities struggle to fill classrooms. *New York Times,* p. A3.

Fagan, P. J., & Anderson, A. E. (1990). Sexuality and eating disorders in adolescence. In M. Sugar (Ed.), *Atypical adolescence and sexuality* (pp. 108–126). New York: Norton.

Fagot, B. I., Pears, K. C., Capaldi, D. M., Crosby, L., & Leve, C. S. (1998). Becoming an adolescent father: Precursors and parenting. *Developmental Psychology, 34,* 1209–1219.

Farrell, A. D., & Danish, S. J. (1993). Peer drug association and emotional restraint: Causes or consequences of adolescent drug use? *Journal of Consulting and Clinical Psychology, 61,* 327–334.

Farrington, D. (1989). Early predictors of adolescent aggression and adult violence. *Violence and Victims, 4,* 79–100.

Farrington, D., & West, D. (1991). The Cambridge Study in Delinquent Development: A long-term follow-up of 411 London males. In H. Kerner & G. Kaiser (Eds.), *Criminality: Personality, behavior, and life history* (pp. 115–138). New York: Springer-Verlag.

Farruggia, S. P., Chen, C., Greenberger, E., Dmitrieva, J., Macek, P. (2004). Adolescent self-esteem in cross-cultural perspective: Testing measurement equivalence and a mediation model. *Journal of Cross-Cultural Psychology, 35,* 719–733.

Farver, J. A., Bhadha, B. R., & Narang, S. K. (2002). Acculturation and psychological functioning in Asian Indian adolescents. *Social Development, 11,* 11–29.

Farver, J. A. M., Narang, S. K., & Bhadha, B. R. (2002). East meets West: Ethnic identity, acculturation, and conflict in Asian Indian families. *Journal of Family Psychology, 16,* 338–350.

Featherman, D. (1980). Schooling and occupational careers: Constancy and change in worldly success. In O. Brim, Jr., & J. Kagan (Eds.), *Constancy and change in human development.* Cambridge, MA: Harvard University Press.

Federal Bureau of Investigation. (1999). *Uniform crime reports for the United States.* Washington, DC: U.S. Government Printing Office.

Federal Interagency Forum on Child and Family Statistics. (1999). *America's children: Key national indicators of well-being, 1999.* Washington, DC: U.S. Government Printing Office.

Fehr, B. (1993). How do I love thee? Let me consult my prototype. In S. Duck (Ed.), Individuals in relationships: *Understanding relationship process series* (Vol. 1, pp. 87–120). Newbury Park, CA: Sage.

Feinberg, M., & Hetherington, E. M. (2001). Differential parenting as a within-family variable. *Journal of Family Psychology, 15,* 22–37.

Feinberg, M., Howe, G. W., Reiss, D., & Hetherington, E. M. (2000). Relationship between perceptual differences of parenting and adolescent antisocial behavior and depressive symptoms. *Journal of Family Psychology, 14,* 531–555.

Feinberg, M., Neiderhiser, J., Howe, G., & Hetherington, E. M. (2001). Adolescent, parent, and observer perceptions of parenting: Genetic and environmental influences on shared and distinct perceptions. *Child Development, 72,* 1266–1284.

Feiring, C. (1996). Concepts of romance in 15-year-old adolescents. *Journal of Research on Adolescence, 6,* 181–200.

Feiring, C., & Lewis, M. (1991). The transition from middle childhood to early adolescence: Sex differences in the social network and perceived self-competence. *Sex Roles, 24,* 289–310.

Feldman, R. S. (2003). *Development across the lifespan* (3rd ed.). Upper Saddle River, NJ: Prentice Hall.

Feldman, S. S., & Cauffman, E. (1999). Sexual betrayal among late adolescents: Perspectives of the perpetrator and the aggrieved. *Journal of Youth & Adolescence, 28,* 235–258.

Feldman, S. S., Feldman, D., Brown, N., & Canning, R. (1995). Predicting sexual experience in adolescent boys from peer acceptance and rejection during childhood. *Journal of Research on Adolescence, 5,* 387–411.

Feldman, S. S., Mont-Reynaud, R., & Rosenthal, D. A. (1992). When East meets West: The acculturation of values of Chinese adolescents in the U.S. and Australia. *Journal of Research on Adolescence, 2,* 147–173.

Feldman, S. S., Rosenthal, D. A., Mont-Reynaud, R., Leung, K., & Lau, S. (1991). Ain't misbehavin': Adolescent values and family environments as correlates of misconduct in Australia, Hong Kong, and the United States. *Journal of Research on Adolescence, 1*, 109–134.

Feldman, S. S., Turner, R. A., & Araujo, K. (1999). Interpersonal context as an influence on the sexual timetables of youths: Gender and ethnic effects. *Journal of Research on Adolescence, 9*, 25–52.

Felix, R. (2004). Understanding youth culture: Techno music consumption at live events in Spanish speaking countries. *Journal of international consumer marketing, 16*, 7–37.

Felmlee, D. H. (2001). From appealing to appalling: Disenchantment with a romantic partner. *Sociological Perspectives, 44*, 263–280.

Female genital mutilation: Is it crime or culture? (1999, February 13). *Economist*, p. 45.

Ferguson, S. A. (2003). Other high-risk factors for young drivers—how graduated licensing does, doesn't, or could address them. *Journal of Safety Research, 34*, 71–77.

Ferguson, S. A., Teoh, E. R., & McCartt, A. T. (2007). Progress in teenage crash risk during the last decade. *Journal of Safety Research, 38*(2), 137–145.

Fergusson, D. M., Boden, J. M., & Horwood, L. J. *Addiction, 101*(4), 556–569.

Ferrier, M. B. (1996, July/August). Alphas apply "each one, teach one" rule to help turn boys to men. *Youth Today*, pp. 46, 48.

Fife-Schaw, C., & Barnett, J. (2004). Measuring optimistic bias. In G. M. Breakwell (Ed.),. *Doing social psychology research* (pp. 54–74). Leicester, England: British Psychological Society; Blackwell Publishing.

Figueira-McDonough, J. (1998). Environment and interpretation: Voices of young people in poor innercity neighborhoods. *Youth & Society, 30*, 123–163.

Fine, M. (1988). Sexuality, schooling, and adolescent females: The missing discourse of desire. *Harvard Educational Review, 58*, 29–53.

Finkelhor, D. (1990). Early and long-term effects of child sexual abuse: An update. *Professional Psychology, 21*, 325–330.

Finkelhor, D., Mitchell, K. J., & Wolak, J. (2000). Online victimization: *A report on the nation's youth*. Durham, NH: Crimes Against Children Research Center. Available: http://www.unh.edu/ccrc/VictimizationOnlineSurvey.pdf

Finkelstein, J. W. (2001a). Menstrual cycle. In J. V. Lerner & R. M. Lerner (Eds.), *Adolescence in America: An encyclopedia*, pp. 432–433. Santa Barbara, CA: ABCCLIO.

Finkelstein, J. W. (2001b). Health promotion. In J. V. Lerner & R. M. Lerner (Eds.), *Adolescence in America: An encyclopedia*, (pp. 333–337). Santa Barbara, CA: ABC-CLIO.

Finkelstein, J. W. (2001c). Puberty: Physical changes. In J. V. Lerner & R. M. Lerner (eds.), A*dolescence in America: An encyclopedia*, pp. 555–558. Santa Barbara, CA: ABC-CLIO.

Finkelstein, J. W. (2001d). Menstruation. In J. V. Lerner & R. M. Lerner (Eds.), *Adolescence in America: An encyclopedia*, (pp. 434–436). Santa Barbara, CA: ABCCLIO.

Finken, L. L., Jacobs, J. E., & Laguna, K. D. (1998). Risky driving and driving/riding decisions: The role of previous experience. *Journal of Youth & Adolescence, 27*, 493–511.

Finney, M. (2006). Television violence. In J.J. Arnett (Ed.), *Encyclopedia of Children, Adolescents, and the Media*. Thousand Oaks, CA: Sage.

Fischer, J. L. (1981). Transitions in relationship styles from adolescence to young adulthood. *Journal of Youth and Adolescence, 10*, 11–24.

Fischer, K. W., & Pruyne, E. (2003). Reflective thinking in adulthood: Emergence, development, & variation. In J. Demick & C. Andreotti (Eds.), *Handbook of adult psychology* (pp. 169–198). New York: Kluwer.

Fischoff, B. (1992). Risk taking: A developmental perspective. In J. Yates (Ed.), *Risk taking behavior* (pp. 133–162). New York: Wiley.

Fischoff, B. (2005). Afterword: Development of and in behavioral decision research. In E. J. Jacobs & P. A. Klaczynski (Eds.), *The development of judgment and decision making in children and adolescents* (pp. 335–346). Mahwah, NJ: Erlbaum.

Fisher, B. S., Cullen, F. T., & Turner, M. G. (2000). *The sexual victimization of women*. Washington, DC: National Institute of Justice.

Fisher, L. A., & Bauman, K. E. (1988). Influence and selection in the friend-adolescent relationship: Findings from studies of adolescent smoking and drinking. *Journal of Applied Social Psychology, 18*, 289–314.

Fisher, M., Schneider, M., Burns, J., Symons, H., & Mandel, F. S. (2001). Differences between adolescents and young adults at presentation to an eating disorders program. *Journal of Adolescent Health, 28*, 222–227.

Fisher, M., Trieller, K., & Napolitano, B. (1989). Premenstrual symptoms in adolescence. *Journal of Adolescent Health Care, 10*, 369–375.

Fitness, J., & Fletcher, G. J. O. (1993). Love, hate, anger, and jealousy in close relationships: A prototype and cognitive appraisal analysis. *Journal of Personality and Social Psychology, 65*, 942–958.

Fitzgerald, F. S. (1920/1995). *This side of paradise*. New York: Barnes and Noble Books.

Flammer, A., & Alsaker, F. D. (1999). Time use by adolescents in international perspective: The case of necessary activities. In F. D. Alsaker & A. Flammer (Eds.), *The adolescent experience: European and American adolescents in the 1990s* (pp. 61–84). Mahwah, NJ: Erlbaum.

Flammer, A., & Alsaker, F. D. (2001). Adolescents in school. In L. Goossens & S. Jackson (Eds.), *Handbook of adolescent development: European perspectives*. Hove, UK: Psychology Press.

Flammer, A., Alsaker, F. D., & Noack, P. (1999). Time use by adolescents in international perspective: The case of leisure activities. In F. D. Alsaker & A. Flammer (Eds.), *The Adolescent experience: European and American adolescents in the 1990s* (pp. 33–60). Mahwah, NJ: Erlbaum.

Flanagan, C., & Botcheva, L. (1999). Adolescents' preference for their homeland and other countries. In F. D. Alsaker & A. Flammer (Eds.), *The adolescent experience: European and American adolescents in the 1990s* (pp. 131–144). Mahwah, NJ: Erlbaum.

Flanagan, C., Jonsson, B., Botcheva, L., Csapo, B., Bowes, J., Macek, P., Averina, I., & Sheblanova, E. (1999). Adolescents and the "social contract": Developmental roots of citizenship in seven countries. In M. Yates, & J. Youniss, *Roots of civic identity: International perspectives on community service and activism in youth*, (pp. 135–155). New York: Cambridge University Press.

Flanagan, T. J., & Maguire, K. (Eds.). (1992). *Sourcebook of criminal justice statistics—1991*. Washington, DC: U.S. Department of Justice.

Flavell, J. H. (1985). *Cognitive development* (2nd ed.). Englewood Cliffs, NJ: Prentice-Hall.

Flavell, J. H., Miller, P. A., & Miller, S. A. (1993). *Cognitive development* (3rd ed.). Englewood Cliffs, NJ: Prentice-Hall.

Flavell, J. H., Miller, P. A., & Miller, S. A. (2002). *Cognitive development* (4th ed.). Upper Saddle River, NJ: Prentice-Hall.

Fleming, J. E., Boyle, M. H., & Offord, D. R. (1993). The outcome of adolescent depression in the Ontario Child Health Study follow-up. *Journal of the American Academy of Child and Adolescent Psychiatry, 32*, 28–83.

Fleming, M., & Towey, K. (Eds.). *Educational forum on adolescent health: Obesity, nutrition, and physical activity*. Chicago: American Medical Association.

Fletcher, M. A. (2000, February 3). California minority youth treated more harshly, study says. *Washington Post*, p. A-16.

Flook, L., & Fuligni, A. J. Family and school spillover in adolescents' daily lives. *Child Development. 79*(3), 776–787.

Flowers, P., & Buston, K. (2001). "I was terrified of being different": Exploring gay men's accounts of growing up in a heterosexist society. *Journal of Adolescence, 24*, 51–66.

Floyd, F., & Bakeman, R. (2006). Coming-out across the life course: Implications of age and historical context. *Archives of Sexual Behavior, 35*(3), 287–297.

Ford, C., & Beach, F. (1951). *Patterns of sexual behavior*. New York: Harper & Row.

Ford, K., Sohn, W., & Lepowski, J. (2001). Characteristics of adolescents' sexual partners and their association with use of condoms and other contraceptive methods. *Family Planning Perspectives, 33*, 100–105.

Fordham, S., & Ogbu, J. U. (1986). Black students' school success: The "burden of 'acting white.' " *The Urban Review, 18*, 176–206.

Forkel, I., & Silbereisen, R. K. (2001). Family economic hardship and depressed mood among young adolescents in the former East and West Germany. *American Behavioral Scientist, 44*, 1955–1971.

Fortune, S., Stewart, A., Yadav, V., & Hawton, K. (2007). Suicide in adolescents: Using life charts to understand the suicidal process. *Journal of Affective Disorders, 100*(1–3), 199–210.

Forum on Child and Family Statistics. (1999). *America's children, 1999* [On-line]. Available: www.childstats.gov

Foss, R. D. (2007). Improving graduated driver licensing systems: A conceptual approach and its implications. *Journal of Safety Research, 38*(2), 185–192.

Fowler, J. W. (1981). *Stages of faith: The psychology of human development and the quest for meaning*. San Francisco: Harper & Row.

Fowler, J. W. (1991). Stages in faith consciousness. In F. K. Oser & W. O. Scarlett (Eds.), *New directions for child development: Special issue on religious development in childhood and adolescence* (Vol. 52, pp. 27–45). San Francisco: Jossey-Bass.

Fowler, J. W., & Dell, M. L. (2004). Stages of faith and identity: Birth to teens. *Child & adolescent psychiatric clinics of North American, 13*, 17–33.

Fowler, J. W., Dell, M. L. (2006). Stages of faith from infancy through adolescence: Reflections on three decades of faith development theory. In E. C. Roehlkepartain, P. King, L. Wagener, & P. L. Benson (Eds.), *The handbook of spiritual development in childhood and adolescence* (pp. 34–45, xvi, 543). Thousand Oaks, CA: Sage.

Frank, A. (1942/1997). *The diary of Anne Frank*. New York: Bantam.

Frankel, L. (2002). "I've never thought about it": Contradictions and taboos surrounding American males' experiences of their first ejaculation (semenarche). *Journal of Men's Studies, 11*, 37–54.

Franklin, C., Streeter, C. L., Kim, J. S., Tripodi, S. J. The effectiveness of a solution-focused, public alternative school for dropout prevention and retrieval. *Children & Schools. 29*(3), 133–144.

Frayser, S. G. (1985). *Varieties of sexual experience: An anthropological perspective on human sexuality*. New Haven, CT: Human Relations Area Files Press.

Franz, W., & Reardon, D. (1992). Differential impact of abortion on adolescents and adults. *Adolescence, 27*, 161–172.

Franzoni, S. L., Davis, M. H., & Vasquez-Suson, K. A. (1994). Two social worlds: Social correlates and stability of adolescent status groups. *Journal of Personality and Social Psychology, 67*, 462–473.

Fraser, S. (1995). *The bell curve wars: Race, intelligence, and the future of America*. New York: Basic Books.

Freedle, R. O. (2003). Correcting the SAT's ethnic and social-class bias: A method for reestimating SAT scores. *Harvard Educational Review, 73*, 1–43.

Freedman, J. L. (1984). Effects of television violence on aggressiveness. *Psychological Bulletin, 96*, 227–246.

Freedman, J. L. (1988). Television violence and aggression: What the evidence shows. *Applied Social Psychology Annual, 8*, 144–162.

Freedman, R. (1994). *Kids at work: Lewis Hine and the crusade against child labor*. New York: Clarion.

Freeman, H. S. (1993, March). *Parental control of adolescents through family transitions*. Paper presented at the biennial meeting of the Society for Research in Child Development, New Orleans, LA.

Freeman, S. K. (2006). Facts of life and more: Adolescent sex and sexuality education. In C. Cocca (Ed.), *Adolescent sexuality: A historical handbook and guide. Children and youth: History and culture* (pp. 45–63). Westport, CT: Praeger Publishers/Greenwood Publishing Group.

French, D., Conrad, J., & Turner, T. (1995). Adjustment of antisocial and nonantisocial rejected adolescents. *Development and Psychopathology, 7*, 857–874.

French, D. C., Eisenberg, N., Vaughan, J., Purwono, U., & Suryanti, T. A. (2008). Religious involvement and the social competence and adjustment of Indonesian Muslim adolescents. *Developmental Psychology, 44*(2), 597–611.

French, D. C., Jansen, E. A., & Pidada, S. (2002). United States and Indonesian children's and adolescents' reports of relational aggression by disliked peers. *Child Development, 73*, 1143–1150.

French, D. C., Rianasari, J. M., Pidada, S., Nelwan, P., & Buhrmester, D. (2001). Social support of Indonesian and U. S. children and adolescents by family members and friends. *Merrill-Palmer Quarterly, 47*, 377–394.

French, H. W. (2002, September 23). Educators try to tame Japan's blackboard jungles. *New York Times*, p. A6.

French, M. (1992). *The war against women*. New York: Summit Books.

French, S., Story, M., Downes, B., Resnick, M., & Blum, R. (1995). Frequent dieting among adolescents: Psychosocial and health behavior correlates. *American Journal of Public Health, 85*, 695–701.

French, T. (1993). *South of heaven: Welcome to the American high school at the end of the twentieth century*. New York: Pocket Books.

Freud, A. (1946). *The ego and the mechanisms of defense*. New York: International Universities Press.

Freud, A. (1958). Adolescence. *Psychoanalytic Study of the Child, 15*, 255–278. New York: International Universities Press, Inc.

Freud, A. (1968). Adolescence. In A. E. Winder & D. Angus (Eds.), *Adolescence: Contemporary studies* (pp. 13–24). New York: American Book.

Freud, A. (1969). Adolescence as a developmental disturbance. In G. Caplan & S. Lebovici (Eds.), *Adolescence: Psychosocial perspectives* (pp. 5–10). New York: Basic Books.

Freud, S. (1940/64). *An outline of psychoanalysis*. Standard edition of the works of Sigmund Freud. London: Hogarth Press.

Frick, P. J., & Kimonis, E. R. (2008). Externalizing disorders of childhood. In J. E. Maddux & B. A. Winstead (Eds.), *Psychopathology: Foundations for a contemporary understanding* (2nd ed., pp. 349–374). New York: Routledge/Taylor & Francis Group.

Friedman, L. (1989). Mathematics and the gender gap: A meta-analysis of recent studies on sex differences in mathematical tasks. *Review of Educational Research, 59*, 185–213.

Friedman-Klein, A. E., & Farthing, C. (1990). Human immunodeficiency virus infection: A survey with special emphasis on mucocutaneous manifestations. *Seminars in Dermatology, 9*, 167–177.

Friend, M., & Bursuck, W. D. (2002). *Including students with special needs* (3rd ed.). Boston: Allyn & Bacon.

Frith, H., & Kitzinger, C. (2001). Reformulating sexual script theory: Developing a discursive psychology of sexual negotiation. *Theory and Psychology, 11*, 209–232.

Frith, S. (1983). *Sound effects*. London: Constable.

Frone, M. R. (1999). Developmental consequences of youth employment. In J. Barling & E. K. Kelloway (Eds.), *Youth workers: Varieties of experience* (pp. 89–128). Washington, DC: American Psychological Association.

Frost, J., & McKelvie, S. (2004). Self-esteem and body satisfaction in male and female elementary school, high school, and university students. *Sex Roles, 51*, 45–54.

Fry, A. F., & Hole, S. (1996). Processing speed, working memory, and fluid intelligence: Evidence for a developmental cascade. *Psychological Science, 7*, 237–241.

Fuentes, C. D. L., & Vasquez, M. J. T. (1999). Immigrant adolescent girls of color: Facing American challenges. In N. B. Johnson, M. C. Roberts, & J. Worell (Eds.), *Beyond appearance: A new look at adolescent girls* (pp. 131–150). Washington, DC: American Psychological Association.

Fukuyama, F. (1993). *The end of history and the last man*. New York: Free Press.

Fuligni, A. (1994, February). *Academic achievement and motivation among Asian-American and European-American early adolescents*. Paper presented at the biennial meetings of the Society for Research on Adolescence, San Diego, CA.

Fuligni, A. (1997). The academic achievement of adolescents from immigrant families: The roles of family background, attitudes and behavior. *Child Development, 68*, 351–363.

Fuligni, A., & Eccles, J. (1992, March). *The effects of early adolescent peer orientation on academic achievement and deviant behavior in high school*. Paper presented at the biennial meeting of the Society for Research on Adolescence, Washington.

Fuligni, A., & Eccles, J. (1993). Perceived parent-child relationships and early adolescents' orientation toward peers. *Developmental Psychology, 29*, 622–632.

Fuligni, A. J., & Tseng, V. (1999). Family obligation and the academic motivation of adolescents from immigrant and American-born families. *Advances in Motivation and Achievement, 11*, 159–183.

Fuligni, A. J., Tseng, V., & Lam, M. (1999). Attitudes toward family obligations among American adolescents with Asian, Latin American, and European backgrounds. *Child Development, 70*, 1030–1044.

Fuligni, A. J., & Witkow, M. (2004). The postsecondary educational progress of youth from immigrant families. *Journal of Research on Adolescence, 14*, 159–183.

Fuller, A., Beck, V., & Unwin, L. (2005). The gendered nature of apprenticeship: Employers' and young peoples' perspectives. *Education & Training, 47*(4–5), 298–311.

Funk, J. (2003). Violent video games: Who's at risk? In D. Ravitch & J. P. Viteritti (Eds.), *Kid stuff: Marketing sex and violence to America's children* (pp. 168–192). Baltimore, MD: Johns Hopkins University Press.

Funk, J. B. (2005). Children's exposure to violent video games and desensitization to violence. *Child & Adolescent Psychiatric Clinics of North America, 14*, 387–404.

Funk, J. B., Baldacci, H. B., Pasold, T., & Baumgardner, J. (2004). Violence exposure in real life, video games, television, movies, and the internet: Is there desensitization? *Journal of adolescence, 27*, 23–39.

Funk, J. B., Flores, B., Buchman, D. D., & Germann, J. N. (1999). Rating electronic video games: Violence is in the eye of the beholder. *Youth & Society, 30*, 283–312.

Funk, J. B., Hagan, J., Schimming, J., Bullock, W. A., Buchman, D. D., & Myers, M. (2002). Aggression and psychopathology in adolescents with a preference for violent electronic games. *Aggressive Behavior, 28*, 134–144.

Furby, M., & Beyth-Marom, R. (1992). Risk-taking in adolescence: A decision-making perspective. *Developmental Review, 12*, 1–44.

Furman, W. (2002). The emerging field of adolescent romantic relationships. *Current Directions in Psychological Science, 11*, 177–180.

Furman, W., Brown, B. B., & Feiring, C. (Eds.). (1999). *The development of romantic relationships in adolescence*. New York: Cambridge University Press.

Furman, W., & Buhrmester, D. (1985). Children's perceptions of the personal relationships in their social networks. *Developmental Psychology, 21*, 1016–1024.

Furman, W., & Buhrmester, D. (1992). Age and sex differences in perceptions of networks of personal relationships. *Child Development, 63*, 103–115.

Furman, W., & Hand, L. S. (2006). The slippery nature of romantic relationships: Issues in definition and differentiation. In A. C. Crouter & A. Booth (Eds.), *Romance and sex in adolescence and emerging adulthood: Risks and opportunities* (pp. 171–178). The Penn State University family issues symposia series. NJ: Lawrence Erlbaum.

Furman, W., Ho, M. J., & Low, S. M. (2007). The rocky road of adolescent romantic experience: Dating and adjustment. In R. C. M. E. Engels, M. Kerr, & H. Stattin (Eds.), *Friends, lovers and groups: Key relationships in adolescence. Hot topics in developmental research* (pp. 61–80). New York: John Wiley & Sons Ltd.

Furman, W., Low, S., & Ho, M. J. (2009). Romantic experience and psychosocial adjustment in early adolescence. *Journal of Consulting and Clinical Psychology*.

Furman, W., & Simon, V. A. (1999). Cognitive representations of adolescent romantic relationships. In W. Furman, B. B. Brown, & C. Feiring (Eds.), *The development of romantic relationships in adolescence* (pp. 75–98). New York: Cambridge University Press.

Furman, W., & Simon, V. A. (2008). Homophily in adolescent romantic relationships. In M. J. Prinstein & K. A. Dodge (Eds.), *Understanding peer influence in children and adolescents. Duke series in child development and public policy* (pp. 203–224). New York: Guilford Press.

Furman, W., Simon, V. A., Shaffer, L., & Bouchey, H. A. (2002). Adolescents' working models and styles for relationships with parents, friends, and romantic partners. *Child Development, 73*, 241–255.

Furman, W., & Wehner, E. A. (1994). Romantic views: Toward a theory of adolescent romantic relationships. In R. Montemayor, G. R. Adams, & G. P. Gullotta (Eds.), *Advances in adolescent development: Vol. 6, Relationships during adolescence: Developmental perspectives* (pp. 21–36). Thousand Oaks, CA: Sage.

Furman, W., & Wehner, E. A. (1997). Adolescent romantic relationships: A developmental perspective. In S. Shulman & W. A. Collins (Eds.), *Romantic relationships in adolescence: Developmental perspectives* (pp. 21–36). San Francisco: Jossey-Bass.

Furnham, A., & Singh, A. (1986). Memory for information about sex differences. *Sex Roles, 15*, 479–486.

Furstenberg, E. F., Jr., Brooks-Gunn, J., & Morgan, S. P. (1987). *Adolescent mothers in later life*. New York: Cambridge University Press.

Furstenberg, F. (1991). Is teenage sexual behavior rational? *Journal Applied Social Psychology, 21*, 957–986.

Furstenberg, F. F., Jr., & Cherlin, A. J. (1991). Divided families: *What happens to children when parents part.* Cambridge, MA: Harvard University Press.

Furstenberg, F., Jr., Brooks-Gunn, J., & Chase-Lansdale, L. (1989). Teenaged pregnancy and child-bearing *American Psychologist 44,* 313–320.

Fussell, E., & Greene, M. (2002). Demographic trends affecting adolescents around the world. In B. B. Brown, R. Larson, & T. S. Saraswathi (Eds.), *The world's youth: Adolescence in eight regions of the globe* (pp. 21–60). New York: Cambridge University Press.

Gaddis, A., & Brooks-Gunn, J. (1985). The male experience of pubertal change. *Journal of Youth and Adolescence, 14,* 61–69.

Gade, P. A., Lakhani, H., & Kimmel, M. (1991). Military service: A good place to start? *Military Psychology, 3,* 251–267.

Gagnon, J. H. (1973). Scripts and the coordination of sexual conduct. *Nebraska Symposium on Motivation, 21,* 27–59.

Galambos, N. L. (2004). Gender and gender role development in adolescence. In R. Lerner & L. Steinberg (Eds.), *Handbook of adolescent psychology.* New York: Wiley.

Galambos, N. L., Barker, E. T., & Krahn, H. J. (2006). Depression, anger, and self-esteem in emerging adulthood: Seven-year trajectories. *Developmental Psychology.*

Galambos, N. L. & Ehrenberg, M. F. (1997). The family as health risk and opportunity: A focus on divorce and working families. In J. Schulenberg, J. L. Maggs, & K. Hurrelmann, Klaus (Eds.), Health risks and developmental transitions during adolescence. (pp. 139–160). New York: Cambridge University Press.

Galambos, N. L., & Tilton-Weaver, L. C. (1998). Multiple-risk behavior in adolescents and young adults. *Statistics Canada, Health Reports, 10,* 9–20.

Galambos, N., Almeida, D., & Petersen, A. (1990). Masculinity, femininity, and sex role attitudes in early adolescence: Exploring gender intensification. *Child Development, 61,* 1905–1914.

Galambos, N., & Maggs, J. (1991). Out-of-school care of young adolescents and self-reported behavior. *Developmental Psychology, 27,* 644–655.

Galambos, N., & Martinez, M. (2007). Poised for emerging adulthood in Latin America: A pleasure for the privileged. *Child Development Perspectives, 1,* 109–114.

Gallagher, W. (1993, May). Midlife myths. *Atlantic Monthly,* pp. 51–68.

Gallup, G., Jr. (1990). *America's youth in the 1990s.* Princeton, NJ: Author.

Gallup, G., Jr., & Castelli, J. (1989). *The people's religion: American faith in the '90s.* New York: Macmillan.

Gallup, G., Jr., & Lindsay, D. M. (1999). *Surveying the religious landscape: Trends in U.S. beliefs.* Harrisburg, PA: Morehouse.

Gallup, G. W., & Bezilla, R. (1992). *The religious life of young Americans.* Princeton, NJ: Gallup Institute.

Galotti, K. (1989). Gender differences in self-reported moral reasoning: A review and new evidence. *Journal of Youth and Adolescence, 18,* 475–488.

Galotti, K., Kozberg, S., & Farmer, M. (1991). Gender and developmental differences in adolescents' conceptions of moral reasoning. *Journal of Youth and Adolescence, 20,* 13–30.

Gamoran, A. (1992). The variable effects of high school tracking. *American Sociological Review, 57,* 812–828.

Gamoran, A. (1993). Alternative uses of ability grouping in secondary schools: Can we bring high-quality instruction to low-ability classes? *American Journal of Education, 69,* 1–21.

Ganong, L. H., & Coleman, M. (1994). *Remarried family relationships.* Thousand Oaks, CA: Sage.

Gans, J. (1990). *America's adolescents: How healthy are they?* Chicago: American Medical Association.

Gao, G. (1991). Stability of romantic relationships in China and the United States. In S. T. Toomey &

F. Korzenny (Eds.), *Cross-cultural interpersonal communication* (Vol. 15, pp. 99–115). London: Sage Publications.

Garbarino, J. (1989). Troubled youth, troubled families: The dynamics of adolescent maltreatment. In D. Cicchetti & V. Carlson (Eds.), Child maltreatment: *Theory and research on causes and consequences of child abuse and neglect* (pp. 685–706). New York: Cambridge University Press.

Garbarino, J., & Asp, C. (1981). *Successful schools and competent students.* Lexington, MA: Lexington Books.

Garbarino, J., Schellenbach, C. J., & Sebes, J. M. (1986). *Troubled youth, troubled families: Understanding families at risk for adolescent maltreatment.* New York: Aldine de Gruyter.

Gardiner, H. W. (2001). Child and adolescent development: Cross-cultural perspectives. In L. L. Adler & U. P. Gielen (Eds.), *Cross-cultural topics in psychology* (pp. 63–79). Westport, CT: Praeger Publishers.

Gardner, H. (1983). *Frames of mind.* New York: Basic Books.

Gardner, H. (1989). Beyond a modular view of mind. In W. Damon (Ed.), *Child development today and tomorrow.* San Francisco: Jossey-Bass.

Gardner, H. (1999, February). Who owns intelligence? *Atlantic Monthly,* 67–76.

Gardner, T. W., Dishion, T. J., & Connell, A. M. (2008). Adolescent self-regulation as resilience: Resistance to antisocial behavior within the deviant peer context. *Journal of Abnormal Child Psychology, 36*(2), 273–284.

Gardstrom, S. C. (1999). Music exposure and criminal behavior: Perceptions of juvenile offenders. *Journal of Music Therapy, 36,* 207–221.

Garner, D. M., & Garfinkel, P. E. (Eds.) *Handbook of treatment for eating disorders* (2nd ed.). New York: Guilford Press.

Garwick, A. W., Rhodes, K. L., Peterson-Hickey, M., & Hellerstedt, W. L. (2008). Native teen voices: Adolescent pregnancy prevention recommendations. *Journal of Adolescent Health, 42*(1), 81–88.

Gaughan, M. (2006). The gender structure of adolescent peer influence on drinking. *Journal of Health and Social Behavior, 47*(1), 47–61.

Gavin, L., & Furman, W. (1989). Age differences in adolescents' perceptions of their peer groups. *Developmental Psychology, 25,* 827–834.

Gaylord-Harden, N. K.; Ragsdale, B. L.; Mandara, J., Richards, M. H., Petersen, A. C. (2007). Perceived support and internalizing symptoms in African American adolescents: Self-esteem and ethnic identity as mediators. *Journal of Youth and Adolescence, 36*(1), 77–88.

Gaynor, S. T., Weersing, V. R., Kolko, D. J., Birmaher, B., Heo, J., & Brent, D. A. (2003). The prevalence and impact of large sudden improvements during adolescent therapy for depression: A comparison across cognitive-behavioral, family, and supportive therapy. *Journal of Consulting & Clinical Psychology, 71,* 386–393.

Ge, X., Best, K., Conger, R., & Simons, R. (1996). Parenting behaviors and the occurrence and co-occurrence of adolescent depressive symptoms and conduct problems. *Developmental Psychology, 32,* 717–731.

Ge, X., Conger, R. D., & Elder, G. H., Jr. (1996). Coming of age too early: Pubertal influences on girls' vulnerability to psychological distress. *Child Development, 67,* 3386–3400.

Ge, X., Conger, R. D., & Elder, G. H., Jr. (2001). The relation between puberty and psychological distress in adolescent boys. *Journal of Research on Adolescence, 11,* 49–70.

Ge, X., Elder, G. H., Jr., Regnerus, M., & Cox, C. (2001). Pubertal transitions, perceptions of being overweight, and adolescents' psychological maladjustment: Gender and Ethnic Differences. *Social Psychology Quarterly, 64,* 363–375.

Ge, X., Natsuaki, M. N., Neiderhiser, J. M., & Reiss, D. (2007). Genetic and environmental influences

on pubertal timing: Results from two national sibling studies. *Journal of Research on Adolescence, 17*(4), 767–788.

Gearheart, B., Gearheart, C., & Mullen, R. (1993). *Exceptional individuals: An introduction.* New York: Brooks/Cole.

Gecas, V., & Seff, M. (1990). Families and adolescents: A review of the 1980s. *Journal of Marriage and the Family, 52,* 941–958.

Gelbard, A., Haub, C., & Kent, M. M. (1999). World population beyond six billion. *Population Bulletin, 54,* (1) 1–40.

Gentile, D. A. (1993). Just what are sex and gender, anyway? A call for a new terminological standard. *Psychological Science, 4,* 120–122.

Gerbner, G., Gross, L., Morgan, M., & Signorelli, N. (1994). Growing up with television: The cultivation perspective. In J. Bryant & D. Zillman (Eds.), *Media effects: Advances in theory and research* (pp. 17–41). Hillsdale, NJ: Erlbaum.

Gerrard, M., Gibbons, F. X., Benthin, A. C., & Hessling, R. M. (1996). A longitudinal study of the reciprocal nature of risk behaviors and cognitions in adolescents: What you do shapes what you think, and vice versa. *Health Psychology, 15,* 344–354.

Gershuny, J. B. (2004). Exit, voice, and suffering: Do couples adapt to changing employment patterns? *Journal of Marriage and Family. 67*(3), 656–665.

Gershuny, J., Bittman, M., & Brice, J. Exit, voice, and suffering: Do couples adapt to changing employment patterns? *Journal of Marriage and Family. 67*(3), 656–665.

Ghuman, P. A. S. (1998). Ethnic identity and acculturation of South Asian adolescents: A British perspective. *International Journal of Adolescence & Youth, 7,* 227–247.

Giang, M. T., & Wittig, M. A. (2006). Implications of adolescents' acculturation strategies for personal and collective self-esteem. *Cultural Diversity and Ethnic Minority Psychology, 12*(4), 725–739.

Gibbons, F. X., Gerrard, M., & Lane, D. J. (2003). A social reaction model of adolescent health risk. In J. Suls & K. A. Wallston (Eds.), *Social psychological foundations of health and illness* (pp. 107–136). Malden, MA: Blackwell.

Gibbons, J. L., & Stiles, D. A. (2004). *The thoughts of youth: An international perspective on adolescents' ideal persons.* Greenwich, CT: IAP Information Age Publishing.

Gibbs, J. C., Basinger, K. S., Grime, R. L., & Snarey, J. R. (2007). Moral judgment development across cultures: Revisiting Kohlberg's universality claims. *Developmental Review, 27*(4), 443–500.

Gibbs, N., & Roche, T. (1999, December 20). *The Columbine tapes. Time,* 40–51.

Gibbs, R., Jr., Leggitt, J., & Turner, E. (2002). What's special about figurative language in emotional communication? In S. R. Fussell (Ed.), *The verbal communication of emotion* (pp. 125–149). Mahwah, NJ: Erlbaum.

Giddens, A. (2000). *Runaway world: How globalization is reshaping our lives.* New York: Routledge.

Giedd, J. (2002, October 15). *The teen brain.* Paper presented at the Medicine for the Public Lecture Series, NIH Clinical Center, Bethesda, MD. Available: www.cc.nih.gov/ccc/mfp/series.html

Giedd, J. N. (2008). The teen brain: Insights from neuroimaging. *Journal of Adolescent Health, 42*(4), 335–343.

Giedd, J. N., Blumenthal, J., & Jeffries, N. O. (1999). Brain development during childhood and adolescence: A longitudinal MRI study. *Nature Neuroscience, 2,* 861–863.

Gifford-Smith, M., Dodge, K. A., Dishion, T. J., & McCord, J. (2005). Peer influence in children and adolescents: Crossing the bridge from developmental to intervention Science. *Journal of Abnormal Child Psychology, 33,* 255–265.

Gil, A. G., Vega, W. A., & Biafora, F. (1998). Temporal influences of family structure and family risk factors on drug use initiation in a multiethnic sample of adolescent boys. *Journal of Youth & Adolescence, 27,* 373–394.

Gilbert, L. A., Lee, R. N., & Chiddix, S. (1981). Influence of presenter's gender on students' evaluations of presenters discussing sex fairness in counseling: An analogue study. *Journal of Counseling Psychology, 28,* 258–264.

Gilligan, C. (1982). *In a different voice.* Cambridge, MA: Harvard University Press.

Gilligan, C. (2008). Exit-voice dilemmas in adolescent development. In D. L. Browning (Ed.), *Adolescent identities: A collection of readings* (pp. 141–156). Relational perspectives book series. New York: Analytic Press/Taylor & Francis Group.

Gilligan, C., Lyons, N. P., & Hanmer, T. J. (1990). *Making connections.* Cambridge, MA: Harvard University Press.

Gilligan, C., Lyons, N., & Hanmer, T. (Eds.). (1990). *Making connections: The relational worlds of adolescent girls at Emma Willard School.* Cambridge, MA: Harvard University Press.

Gillis, J. R. (1974). *Youth and history.* New York: Academic Press.

Gillock, K. L., & Reyes, O. (1999). Stress, support, and academic performance of urban, low-income Mexican-American adolescents. *Journal of Youth & Adolescence, 28,* 259–282.

Gilmore, D. (1990). *Manhood in the making: Cultural concepts of masculinity.* New Haven: Yale University Press.

Gilpin, E. A., & Pierce, J. P. (1997). Trends in adolescent smoking initiation in the United States: Is tobacco marketing an influence? *Tobacco Control, 6,* 122–127.

Gini, G., Albierto, P., Benelli, B., & Altoe, G. (2008). Determinants of adolescents' active defending and passive bystanding behavior in bullying. *Journal of Adolescence, 31*(1), 93–105.

Ginsburg, H. P., & Opper, S. (1988). *Piaget's theory of intellectual development* (3rd ed.). Englewood Cliffs, NJ: Prentice-Hall.

Ginzberg, E. (1977). The job problem *Scientific American, 237,* 43–51.

Giordano, P. C., Manning, W. D., & Longmore, M. A. (2006). Adolescent romantic relationships: *An emerging portrait of their nature and developmental significance.* In A. C. Crouter & A. Booth (Eds.), *Romance and sex in adolescence and emerging adulthood: Risks and opportunities* (pp. 127–150). The Penn State University family issues symposia series. NJ: Lawrence Erlbaum.

Girl Scouts USA (2008). *Program.* Retrieved August 7, 2008, from: www.gsusa.org/organization/program.htm

Gitchel, S., & Foster, L. (1985). *Let's talk about sex.* Fresno, CA: Planned Parenthood of Central California.

Gjerde, P. F., Block, J., & Block, J. H. (1988). Depressive symptoms and personality during late adolescence: Gender differences in the externalization-internationalization of symptom expression. *Journal of Abnormal Psychology, 97,* 475–486.

Gjerde, P. F., & Westenberg, P. M. (1998). Dysphoric adolescents as young adults: A prospective study of the psychological sequelae of depressed mood in adolescence. *Journal of Research on Adolescence, 8,* 377–402.

Gladding, S. T. (2002). *Family therapy: History, theory, and practice.* Upper Saddle River, NJ: Prentice Hall.

Gladue, B. (1990, November). Adolescents' sexual practices: Have they changed? *Medical Aspects of Human Sexuality,* 53–54.

Gladwin, E. T. (1970). *East is a big bird.* Cambridge, MA: Harvard University Press.

Glass, G. V., & Smith, M. L. (1978, September). *Meta-analysis of research on the relationship of class size and achievement.* San Francisco: Far West Educational Laboratory.

Glick, P. (1989). Remarried families, stepfamilies, and stepchildren: A brief demographic review. *Family Relations, 38,* 24–27.

Glowinski, A. L., Madden, P. A. F., Bucholz, K. K., Lynskey, M. T., Heath, A. C. (2003). Genetic epidemiology of self-reported lifetime *DSM-IV* major depressive disorder in a population-based twin sample of female adolescents. *Journal of Child Psychology & Psychiatry, 44,* 988–996.

Glueck, S., & Glueck, E. (1950). *Unraveling juvenile delinquency.* New York: Commonwealth Fund.

Glueck, S., & Glueck, E. (1968). *Delinquents and non-delinquents in perspective.* Cambridge, MA: Harvard University Press.

Gold, D. P., Andres, D., Etezadi, J., Arbuckle, T., Schwartzman, A., & Chaikelson, J. (1995). Structural equation model of intellectual change and continuity and predictors of intelligence in older men. *Psychology and Aging, 10,* 294–303.

Gold, M., & Yanof, D. (1985). Mothers, daughters, and girlfriends. *Journal of Personality and Social Psychology, 49,* 654–659.

Goldberg, A. P., Dengel, D. R., & Hagberg, J. M. (1996). Exercise physiology and aging. In E. L. Schneider & J. W. Rowe (Eds.), *Handbook of the biology of aging* (4th ed., pp. 331–354). San Diego, CA: Academic Press.

Goldberg, P. H. (1968). Are women prejudiced against women? *Transaction, 5,* 28–30.

Goldenberg, H., & Goldenberg, I. (2005). Family therapy. In R. J. Corsini & D. Wedding (Eds.), *Current psychotherapies* (7th ed., instr. ed., pp. 372–404). Belmont, CA: Thomson Brooks/Cole Publishing.

Goldscheider, F., & Goldscheider, C. (1994). Leaving and returning home in 20th century America. *Population Bulletin, 48*(4).

Goldscheider, F., & Goldscheider, C. (1999). *The changing transition to adulthood: Leaving and returning home.* Thousand Oaks, CA: Sage.

Goldstein, B. (1976). *Introduction to human sexuality.* Belmont, CA: Star.

Goldstein, S. E., Davis-Kean, P. E., & Eccles, J. S. (2005). Parents, peers, and problem behavior: A longitudinal investigation of the impact of relationship perceptions and characteristics on the development of adolescent problem behavior. *Developmental Psychology, 41,* 401–413.

Goldstein, S. E., Malanchuk, O., Davis-Kean, P. E., & Eccles, J. S. (2007). Risk factors of sexual harassment by peers: A longitudinal investigation of African American and European American adolescents. *Journal of Research on Adolescence, 17*(2), 285–300.

Goldston, D. B. Molock, S. D., Davis; Whitbeck, L. B., Murakami, J. L.; Zayas, L. H., Hall, G. C. N. Cultural considerations in adolescent suicide prevention and psychosocial treatment. *American Psychologist, 63*(1) 14–31.

Goleman, D. (1997). *Emotional intelligence.* New York: Bantam.

Gonzales, N., Cauce, A., Friedman, R., & Mason, C. (1996). Family, peer, and neighborhood influences on achievement among African American adolescents: One-year prospective effects. *American Journal of Community Psychology, 24,* 365–387.

Goode, E. (1999, May 20). *Study finds TV trims Fiji girls' body image and eating habits. New York Times,* p. A1.

Goodlad, J. A. (1984). *A place called school.* New York: McGraw-Hill.

Goodwin, C. J. (1995). *Research in psychology: Methods and design.* New York: Wiley.

Goodwin, M. P., & Roscoe, B. (1990). Sibling violence and agonistic interactions among middle adolescents. *Adolescence, 25,* 451–467.

Goossens, L. (1994). Belgium. In K. Hurrelmann (Ed.), *International handbook of adolescence* (pp. 51–64). Westport, CT: Greenwood Press.

Goossens, L., Beyers, W., Emmen, M., & van Aken, M. (2002). The imaginary audience and the personal fable: Factor analysis and concurrent validity of the "New Look" measures. *Journal of Research on Adolescence, 12,* 193–215.

Goossens, L., & Luyckx, K. (2007). Belgium. In J. J. Arnett, U. Gielen, R. Ahmed, B. Nsamenang, T. S. Saraswathi, & R. Silbereisen (Eds.), *International encyclopedia of adolescence.* New York: Routledge.

Goossens, L., Seiffge-Krenke, L., & Marcoen, A. (1992). The many faces of adolescent egocentrism: Two European replications. *Journal of Adolescent Research, 7,* 43–48.

Gore, S., Aseltine, R. H., & Colten, M. E. (1993). Gender, social-relational involvement, and depression. *Journal of Research on Adolescence, 3,* 101–125.

Gore, S. A., Vander Wal, J. S., & Thelen, M. H. (2001). Treatment of eating disorders in children and adolescents. In J. K. Thompson & L. Smolak (Eds.), *Body image, eating disorders, and obesity in youth: Assessment,* treatment, and prevention (pp. 293–311).

Gottfredson, G. D., Jones, E. M., & Holland, J. L. (1993). Personality and vocational interests: The relation of Holland's six interest dimensions to five robust dimensions of personality. *Journal of Counseling Psychology, 40,* 518–524.

Gottfredson, M., & Hirschi, T. (1990). *A general theory of crime.* Stanford, CA: Stanford University Press.

Gould, S. J. (1981). *The mismeasure of man.* New York: Norton.

Gow, J. (1996). Reconsidering gender roles on MTV: Depictions in the most popular music videos of the early 1990s. *Communication Reports, 9,* 151–161.

Gowen, L. K., Feldman, S. S., Diaz, R., Yisrael, D. S. (2002). A comparison of the sexual behaviors and attitudes of adolescent girls with older vs. similar-aged boyfriends. *Journal of Youth and Adolescence, 33*(2), 167–175.

Gowen, L. K., Hayward, C., Killen, J. D., Robinson, T. N., & Taylor, C. B. (1999). Acculturation and eating disorder symptoms in adolescent girls. *Journal of Research on Adolescence, 9,* 67–83.

Grabe, S., Hyde, J. S., & Lindberg, S. M. (2007). Body objectification and depression in adolescents: The role of gender, shame, and rumination. *Psychology of Women Quarterly, 31*(2), 164–175.

Grabe, S., Ward, L. M., & Hyde, J. S. (2008). The role of the media in body image concerns among women: A meta-analysis of experimental and correlational studies. *Psychological Bulletin, 134*(3), 460–476.

Graber, J. A., Britto, P. R., & Brooks-Gunn, J. (1999). What's love got to do with it? Adolescent and young adult's beliefs about sexual and romantic relationships. In W. Furman, B. B. Brown, & C. Feiring (Eds.), *The development of romantic relationships in adolescence* (pp. 364–395). New York: Cambridge University Press.

Graber, J. A., Brooks-Gunn, J., & Galen, B. R. (1999). Betwixt and between: Sexuality in the context of adolescent transitions. In R. Jessor (Ed.), *New perspectives on adolescent risk behavior* (pp. 270–318). New York: Cambridge University Press.

Graber, J. A., Brooks-Gunn, J., Paikoff, R. L., & Warren, M. P. (1994). Prediction of eating problems: An 8-year study of adolescent girls. *Developmental Psychology, 30,* 823–834.

Graber, J., Brooks-Gunn, J., & Warren, M. (1995). The antecedents of menarcheal age: Heredity, family environment, and stressful life events. *Child Development, 66,* 346–359.

Graber, J. A., & Dubas, J. S. (1996). Leaving home: Understanding the transition to adulthood. *New Directions for Child Development, 71.*

Graber, J. A., Lewinsohn, P. M., Seeley, J. R., & Brooks-Gunn, J. (1997). Is psychopathology associated with the timing of pubertal development? *Journal of the American Academy of Child and Adolescent Psychiatry, 36,* 1768–1776.

Graber, J. A., Seeley, J. R., Brooks-Gunn, J., & Lewinsohn, P. M. (2004). Is pubertal timing associated with psychopathology in young adulthood? *Journal of the American Academy of Child & Adolescent Psychiatry, 43,* 718–726.

Graham, J. W., Marks, G., & Hansen, W. B. (1991). Social influence processes affecting adolescent substance abuse. *Journal of Applied Developmental Psychology, 76,* 291–298.

Graham, M. J., Larsen, U., & Xu, X. (1999). Secular trend in age of menarche in China: A case study of two rural counties in Anhui province. *Journal of Biosocial Science, 31,* 257–267.

Granic, I., Dishion, T. J., & Hollenstein, T. (2003). The family ecology of adolescence: A dynamic systems perspective on normative development. In G. R. Adams & M. D. Berzonsky (Eds.), *Blackwell handbook of adolescence* (pp. 60–91). Malden, MA: Blackwell.

Granic, I., & Patterson, G. R. (2006). Toward a comprehensive model of antisocial development: A dynamic systems approach. *Psychological Review, 113*(1), 101–131.

Grant, K. E., Lyons, A. L., Finkelstein, J. S., Conway, K. M., Reynolds, L. K., O'Koon, J. H., Waitkoff, G. R., & Hicks, K. J. (2004). Gender differences in rates of depressive symptoms among low-income, urban, African American Youth: A test of two mediational hypotheses. *Journal of Youth & Adolescence, 33,* 523–533.

Gray, M. R., & Steinberg, L. (1999). Adolescent romance and the parent-child relationship. In W. Furman, B. B. Brown, & C. Feiring (Eds.), *The development of romantic relationships in adolescence* (pp. 235–265). New York: Cambridge University Press.

Gray, W. M. (1990). Formal operational thought. In W. F. Overton (Ed.), *Reasoning, necessity, and logic: Developmental perspectives* (pp. 227–253). Hillsdale, NJ: Erlbaum.

Green, A. H. (1991). Child sexual abuse and incest. In M. Lewis (Ed.), *Child and adolescent psychiatry* (pp. 1019–1029). Baltimore, MD: Williams & Wilkins.

Green, E. G. T., Deschamps, Jean-Claude., & Páez, D. (2005). Variation of individualism and collectivism within and between 20 countries: A typological analysis. *Journal of cross-cultural psychology, 36,* 321–339.

Greenberg, B. S. (1994). Content trends in media sex. In D. Zillman, J. Bryant, & A. C. Huston (Eds.), *Media, children and the family: Social scientific, psychodynamic, and clinical perspectives* (pp. 165–182). Hillsdale, NJ: Erlbaum.

Greenberg, B. S., Siemicki, M., & Dorfman, S. (1986). *Sex content in R-rated films viewed by adolescents.* Project CAST Report #3. East Lansing: Michigan State University.

Greenberger, E., & Steinberg, L. (1986). *When teenagers work: The psychological social costs of adolescent employment.* New York: Basic Books.

Greenberger, E., Steinberg, L., & Vaux, A. (1981). Adolescents who work: Health and behavioral consequences of job stress. *Developmental Psychology, 17,* 691–703.

Greenberger, E., Steinberg, L., Vaux, A., & McAuliffe, S. (1980). Adolescents who work: Effects of part-time employment on family and peer relations. *Journal of Youth and Adolescence, 9,* 189–202.

Greene, A. L., Wheatley, S. M., & Aldava J. F., IV. (1992). Stages on life's way: Adolescents' implicit theories of the life course. *Journal of Adolescent Research, 7,* 364–381.

Greene, C. G., & Maccoby, E. E. (1986). How different is the "different voice"? *Signs, 11,* 310–316.

Greene, M. L., & Way, N. (2005). Self-esteem trajectories among ethnic minority adolescents: A growth curve analysis of the patterns and predictors of change. *Journal of Research on Adolescence, 15,* 151–178.

Greenwood, P. W. (2006). *Changing lives: Delinquency prevention as crime-control policy.* Chicago: University of Chicago Press.

Gregson, K. (2006). Youth cultures. In J. J. Arnett (Ed.), *Encyclopedia of children, adolescents, and the media.* Thousand Oaks, CA: Sage.

Griffin, C. (2001). Imagining new narratives of youth: Youth research, the "new Europe," and global youth culture. Childhood: *A Global Journal of Child Research, 8,* 147–166.

Griffith, J., & Perry, S. (1993). Wanting to soldier: Enlistment motivations of Army Reserve recruits before and after Operation Desert Storm. *Military Psychology, 5,* 127–139.

Griffiths, M. (1997). Computer game playing in early adolescence. *Youth & Society, 29,* 223–237.

Griffiths, M. (2006). Internet use, addiction. In J. J. Arnett (Ed.), *Encyclopedia of children, adolescents, and the media.* Thousand Oaks, CA: Sage.

Grimsley, K. D. (2000, April 3). Family a priority for young workers: Survey finds change in men's thinking. *Washington Post,* pp. E1–2.

Grissman, D. W. (2000). The continuing use and misuse of SAT scores. *Psychology, Public Policy, & Law, 6,* 223–232.

Grisso, T., Steinberg, L., Woolard, J., Cauffman, E., Scott, E., Graham, S., Lexcen, F., Reppucci, N. D., & Schwartz, R. (2003). Juvenile's competence to stand trial: A comparison of adolescents' and adults' capacities as trial defendants. *Law & Human Behavior, 27,* 333–363.

Grolnick, W., & Slowiaczek, M. (1994). Parents' involvement in children's schooling: A multidimensional conceptualization and motivational model. *Child Development, 65,* 230–252.

Grossman, D., Milligan, C., & Deyo, R. (1991). Risk factors for suicide attempts among Navajo adolescents. *American Journal of Public Health, 81,* 870–874.

Grossman, K. E., Grossman, K., and Waters, E. (Eds.) (2005). Presents the results of several attachment studies beginning in infancy and extending into adolescence and emerging adulthood. *Attachment from infancy to adulthood: The major longitudinal studies.* New York: Guilford.

Grotevant, H. D. (1987). Toward a process model of identity formation. *Journal of Adolescent Research, 2,* 202–222.

Grotevant, H., & Cooper, C. (1988). The role of family experience in career exploration during adolescence. In R. Baltes, D. Featherman, & R. Lerner (Eds.), *Life-span development and behavior* (Vol. 8). Hillsdale, NJ: Erlbaum.

Grotevant, H. D., & Adams, G. R. (1984). Development of an objective measure to assess ego identity in adolescence: Validation and replication. *Journal of Youth and Adolescence, 13,* 419–438.

Grover, R. L., Nangle, D. W., Serwik, A., & Zeff, K. R. (2007). Girl friend, boy friend, girlfriend, boyfriend: Broadening our understanding of heterosocial competence. *Journal of Clinical Child and Adolescent Psychology, 36*(4), 491–502.

Gruber, S., & Boreen, J. (2003). Teaching critical thinking: Using experience to promote learning in middle school and college students. *Teachers & Teaching: Theory & Practice, 9,* 5–19.

Gruber, J. E., & Fineran, S. (2008). Comparing the impact of bullying and sexual harassment victimization on the mental and physical health of adolescents. *Sex Roles, 59*(1–2), 1–13.

Grumbach, M., Roth, J., Kaplan, S., & Kelch, R. (1974). Hypothalamic-pituitary regulation of puberty in man: Evidence and concepts derived from clinical research. In M. Grumbach, G. Grave, & F. Mayer (Eds.), *Control of the onset of puberty.* New York: Wiley.

Grunbaum, J. A. (2004). Youth Risk Behavior Surveillance—United States, 2003. *Morbidity and Mortality Weekly Report, 53,* SS-2.

Grusec, J. (2002). Parental socialization and children's acquisition of values. In M. Bornstein (Ed.), *Handbook of parenting* (Vol. 5, pp. 245–281). Mahwah, NJ: Erlbaum.

Gruskin, E. (1994, February). *A review of research on self-identified gay, lesbian, and bisexual youth from 1970–1993.* Paper presented at the meeting of the Society for Research on Adolescence, San Diego, CA.

Guastello, D. D., & Guastello, S. J. (2003). Androgyny, gender role behavior, and emotional intelligence among college students and their parents. *Sex Roles, 49,* 663–673.

Guise, J. M. F., & Gill, J. S. (2007). "Binge drinking? It's good, it's harmless fun": A discourse analysis of accounts of female undergraduate drinking in Scotland. *Health Education Research, 22*(6), 895–906.

Gullota, T. P. (2003). Leaving home: The runaway and the forgotten throwaway. In R. G. Adams & D. M. Berzonsky (Eds.), *Blackwell handbook of adolescence* (pp. 494–501). Malden, MA: Blackwell.

Gupta, A. K. (1987). *Parental influences on adolescents.* New Delhi, India: Ariana.

Güre, A., Uçanok, Z., & Sayil, M. (2006). The associations among perceived pubertal timing, parental relations, and self-perceptions in Turkish adolescents. *Journal of Youth and Adolescence, 35*(4), 541–550.

Guthrie, J. T. (2008). Reading motivation and engagement in middle and high school: Appraisal and intervention. In J. T. Guthrie (Ed.), *Engaging adolescents in reading* (pp. 1–16). Thousand Oaks, CA: Corwin Press.

Gutman, L. M., & Eccles, J. S. (1999). Financial strain, parenting behaviors, and adolescents' achievement: Testing model equivalence between African American and European American single- and two-parent families. *Child Development, 70,* 1464–1476.

Gutmann, D. (1987). *Reclaimed powers: Toward a new psychology of men and women in later life.* New York: Basic Books.

Guyer, B. (2000). *ADHD.* Boston: Allyn & Bacon.

Haberland, N., Chong, E. L., & Bracken, H. J. (2004). *A world apart: The disadvantage and social isolation of married adolescent girls.* Brief based on background paper prepared for the WHO/UNFPA/Population Council Technical Consultation on Married Adolescents. New York: Population Council.

Hacker, A. (2002a, December 5). Gore family values. *New York Review of Books,* 20–25.

Hacker, A. (2002b, April 11). How are women doing? *New York Review of Books,* pp. 63–66.

Haffner, D. (1998, March/April). Realism in sex ed. *Youth Today,* 7.

Häggström-Nordin, E., Hanson, U., & Tydén, T. (2005). Associations between pornography and consumption and sexual practices among adolescents in Sweden. *International Journal of STD & AIDS, 16*(2), 102–107.

Häggström-Nordin, E., Hanson, U., & Tydén, T. Associations between pornography consumption and sexual practices among adolescents in Sweden. *International Journal of STD & AIDS. 16*(2), 102–107.

Haidt, J., Koller, S. H., & Dias, M. G. (1993). Affect, culture, and morality, or is it wrong to eat your dog? *Journal of Personality and Social Psychology, 65,* 613–628.

Hale, S. (1990). A global developmental trend in cognitive processing speed. *Child Development, 61,* 653–663.

Halgunseth, L. C.; Ispa, J. M., & Rudy, D. Parental control in Latino families: An integrated review of the literature. *Child Development, 77*(5), 1282–1297.

Hall, G. S. (1904). *Adolescence: Its psychology and its relation to physiology, anthropology, sociology, sex, crime, religion, and education* (Vols. 1 & 2). Englewood Cliffs, NJ: Prentice-Hall.

Hallahan, D. P., & Kauffman, J. M. (1998). *Introduction to learning disabilities.* New York: Simon & Schuster Trade.

Hallahan, D. P., & Kauffman, J. M. (2003). *Exceptional learners*. Boston: Allyn & Bacon.

Hallinan, M. (1992). The organization of students for instruction in the middle school. *Sociology of Education, 65*.

Hallinan, M., & Sorensen, A. (1987). Ability grouping and sex differences in mathematics achievement. *Sociology of education, 60*, 63–72.

Halpern, C. J. T., Udry, J. R., Suchindran, C., & Campbell, B. (2000). Adolescent males' willingness to report masturbation. *Journal of Sex Research, 37*, 327–332.

Halpern, S. (1998). *The forgotten half revisited: American youth and young families, 1988–2008*. Washington, DC: American Youth Policy Forum.

Halvor, N., Hanne-Trine, E., & Bjorkheim, J. O. (2000). Who would you most like to be like? Adolescents' ideals at the beginning and the end of the century. *Scandinavian Journal of Educational Research, 44*, 5–26.

Hamalainen, J., Poikolainen, K., Isometsa, E., Kaprio, J., Heikkinen, M., Lindermman, S., & Aro, H. (2005). Major depressive episode related to long unemployment and frequent alcohol intoxication. *Nordic Journal of Psychiatry, 59*(6), 486–491.

Hamer, D. H., Hu, S., Magnuson, V. L., Hu, N., & Pattatucci, A. M. L. (1993). A linkage between DNA markers on the X chromosome and male sexual orientation. *Science, 261*, 321–327.

Hamilton, H. A. (2005). Extended families and adolescent well-being. *Journal of Adolescent Health, 36*, 260–266.

Hamilton, S. F. (1990). *Apprenticeship for adulthood: Preparing youth for the future*. New York: Free Press.

Hamilton, S. F. (1994). Employment prospects as motivation for school achievement: Links and gaps between school and work in seven countries. In R. K. Silbereisen & E. Todt (Eds.), *Adolescence in context: The interplay of family, school, peers, and work in adjustment* (pp. 267–284). New York: Springer-Verlag.

Hamilton, S. F., & Hamilton, M. A. (2000). Research, intervention, and social change: Improving adolescents' career opportunities. In L. J. Crockett & R. K. Silbereisen (Eds.), *Negotiating adolescence in times of social change* (pp. 267–283). New York: Cambridge University Press.

Hamilton, S., & Hamilton, M. A. (2006). School, work, and emerging adulthood. In J. J. Arnett & J. L. Tanner (Eds.), *Coming of age in the 21st century: The lives and contexts of emerging adults* (pp. 257–277). Washington, DC: American Psychological Association.

Hamm, J. V. (2000). Do birds of a feather flock together? The variable bases for African American, Asian American, and European American adolescents' selection of similar friends. *Developmental Psychology, 36*, 209–219.

Hammack, P. L., Robinson, W. LaVome., Crawford, I., & Li, S. T. (2004). Poverty and depressed mood among urban African-American adolescents: A family stress perspective. *Journal of Child & Family Studies, 13*, 309–323.

Hammer, J. C., Fisher, J. D., Fitzgerald, P., & Fisher, W. A. (1996). When two heads aren't better than one: AIDS risk behavior in college-age couples. *Journal of Applied Social Psychology, 26*, 375–397.

Handsfield, H. (1992). Recent developments in STDs: Viral and other syndromes. *Hospital Practice, 14*, 175–200.

Haninger, K., & Thompson, K. M. (2004). Content and ratings of teen rated video games. *JAMA: Journal of the American Medical Association, 291*, 856–865.

Hannah, J. S., & Kohn, S. E. (1989). The relationship of socioeconomic status and gender to the occupational choices of grade 12 students. *Journal of Vocational Behavior, 34*, 161–178.

Hansen, C. (2006). Music videos, effects. In J. J. Arnett (Ed.), *Encyclopedia of children, adolescents, and the media*. Thousand Oaks, CA: Sage. York: Wiley.

Hansen, D. J., Conaway, L. P., & Christopher, J. S. (1990). Victims of child physical abuse. In R. T. Ammerman & M. Hersen (Eds.), *Treatment of family violence* (pp. 17–49). New York: Wiley.

Hansen, D. J., & Warner, J. E. (1992). Child physical abuse and neglect. In R. T. Ammerman & M. Hersen (Eds.), *Assessment of family violence* (pp. 123–147).

Hansen, E. B., & Breivik, G. (2001). Sensation seeking as a predictor of positive and negative risk behavior among adolescents. *Personality and Individual Differences, 30*, 627–640.

Hansen, F., & Wold, B. (2007). Norway. In J. J. Arnett, R. Ahmed, B. Nsamenang, T. S. Saraswathi, & R. Silbereisen (Eds.), *International encyclopedia of adolescence*. New York: Routledge.

Hanson, S. (1994). Lost talent: Unrealized educational aspirations and expectations among U.S. youths. *Sociology of Education, 67*, 159–183.

Hardaway, C. K., Marler, P. L., & Chaves, M. (1993). What the polls don't show: A closer look at U.S. church attendance. *American Sociological Review, 58*, 741–752.

Hardway, C., & Fuligni, A. J. Dimensions of family connectedness among adolescents with Mexican, Chinese, and European backgrounds. *Developmental Psychology, 42*(6), 1246–1258.

Harevan, T. K. (1984). Themes in the historical development of the family. In R. D. Parke (Ed.), *Review of child development research* (Vol. 7, pp. 137–178). Chicago: University of Chicago Press.

Haridakis, P. M., & Rubin, A. M. (2003). Motivation for watching television violence and viewer aggression. *Mass Communication & Society, 6*, 29–56.

Harkness, S., & Super, C. M. (1995). *Parents' cultural belief systems: Their origins, expressions, and consequences*. New York: Guilford.

Harkness, S., Super, C. M. & van Tijen, N. (2000). Individualism and the "Western mind" reconsidered: American and Dutch parents' ethnotheories of the child. In S. Harkness & C. Raeff (Eds.), *Variability in the social construction of the child* (pp. 23–39). San Francisco: Jossey-Bass.

Harlan, W. R., Harlan, E. A., & Grillo, G. R. (1980). Secondary sex characteristics of girls 12–17 years of age: The U.S. Health Examination Survey. *Journal of Pediatrics, 96*, 1074–1087.

Harmon, A. (1998, May 8). Underreporting found on male teen-age sex. *New York Times*, p. A-14.

Harris & Associates (1987). *Attitudes about television, sex and contraceptive advertising*. New York: Planned Parenthood Federation of America.

Harris, J. R. (1999). *The nurture assumption: Why children turn out the way they do*. New York: Free Press.

Harris, R. L., Ellicott, A. M., & Holmes, D. S. (1986). The timing of psychosocial transitions and changes in women's lives: An examination of women aged 45 to 60. *Journal of Personality and Social Psychology, 51*, 409–416.

Hart, D., & Atkins, R. (2004). Religious participation and the development of moral identity in adolescence. In T. A. Thorkildsen & H. J. Walberg (Eds.), *Nurturing morality* (pp. 157–172). New York: Kluwer.

Hart, D., Burock, D., London, B., & Atkins, R. (2003). Prosocial tendencies, antisocial behavior, and moral development. In A. Slater & G. Bremner (Eds.), *An introduction to developmental psychology* (pp. 334–356). Malden, MA: Blackwell.

Hart, D., Donnelly, T. M., Touniss, J., & Atkins, R. (2007). High school community service as a predictor of adult voting and volunteering. *American Educational Research Journal, 44*(1), 197–219.

Hart, D., & Fegley, S. (1995). Prosocial behavior and caring in adolescence: Relations to self-understanding and social judgment. *Child Development, 66*, 1346–1359.

Harter, S. (1986). Processes underlying the enhancement of the self-concept of children. In J. Suis & A. Greenald (Eds.), *Psychological perspective on the self* (Vol. 3). Hillsdale, NJ: Erlbaum.

Harter, S. (1988). *Self-perception profile for adolescents*. Denver, CO: University of Denver.

Harter, S. (1989). Causes, correlates, and the functional role of global self-worth: A life-span perspective. In J. Kolligian & R. Sternberg (Eds.), *Perceptions of competence and incompetence across the life-span*. New Haven, CT: Yale University Press.

Harter, S. (1990a). Processes underlying adolescent self-concept formation. In R. Montemayor, G. R. Adams, & T. P. Gullotta (Eds.), *From childhood to adolescence: A transitional period?* Newbury Park, CA: Sage.

Harter, S. (1990b). Self and identity development. In S. S. Feldman & G. R. Elliott (Eds.), *At the threshold: The developing adolescent* (pp. 352–387). Cambridge, MA: Harvard University Press.

Harter, S. (1993). Causes and consequences of low self-esteem in children and adolescents. In R. F. Baumeister (Ed.), *Self esteem: The puzzle of low self-regard* (pp. 87–116). New York: Plenum.

Harter, S. (1997). The development of self-representations. In N. Eisenberg (Ed.), *Handbook of child psychology* (5th ed., Vol. 3). New York: Wiley.

Harter, S. (1999). *The construction of the self: A developmental perspective*. New York: Guilford.

Harter, S. (2001). On the importance of importance ratings in understanding adolescents' self-esteem: Beyond statistical parsimony. In R. J. Riding & S. G. Rayner (Eds.), *Self perception: International perspectives on individual differences* (Vol. 2, pp. 3–23). Westport, CT: Ablex.

Harter, S. (2002). Authenticity. In R. C. Snyder & J. S. Lopez (Eds.), *Handbook of positive psychology* (pp. 382–394). London: Oxford University Press.

Harter, S. (2003). The development of self-representations during childhood and adolescence. In M. R. Leary & J. P. Tagney (Eds.), *Handbook of self and identity* (pp. 610–642). New York: Guilford Press.

Harter, S. (2006). The development of self-esteem. In M. H. Kernis (Ed.), *Self-esteem issues And answers: A sourcebook of current perspectives* (pp. 144–150). New York: Psychology Press.

Harter, S., Bresnick, S., Bouchey, H. A., & Whitesell, N. R. (1997). The development of multiple role-related selves during adolescence. *Development and Psychopathology, 9*, 835–853.

Harter, S., & Lee, L. (1989). *Manifestations of true and false selves in adolescence*. Paper presented at the meeting of the Society for Research in Child Development, Kansas City.

Harter, S., Marold, D. B., Whitesell, N. R., & Cobbs, G. (1996). A model of the effects of perceived parent and peer support on adolescent false self behavior. *Child Development, 67*, 360–374.

Harter, S., Waters, P., & Whitesell, N. (1996, March). *False self behavior and lack of voice among adolescent males and females*. Paper presented at the meeting of the Society for Research on Adolescence, Boston.

Harter, S., Waters, P. L., & Whitesell, N. R. (1997). Lack of voice as a manifestation of false-self behavior among adolescents: The school setting as a stage upon which the drama of authenticity is enacted. *Educational Psychologist, 32*, 153–173.

Harter, S., Waters, P., Whitesell, N. R., & Kastelic, D. (1998). Predictors of level of voice among high school females and males: Relational context, support, and gender orientation. *Developmental Psychology, 34*, 1–10.

Harter, S., & Whitesell, N. R. (2003). Beyond the debate: Why some adolescents report stable self-worth over time and situation, whereas others report changes in self-worth. *Journal of Personality, 71*, 1027–1058.

Hartos, J., Eitel, P., & Simons-Morton, B. (2002). Parenting practices and adolescent risky driving: A three-month prospective study. *Health Education and Behavior, 29*, 194–206.

Hartos, J. L., Simons-Morton, B. G., Beck, K. H., & Leaf, W. A. (2005). Parent-imposed limits on high-risk adolescent driving: Are they stricter with graduated driver licensing? *Accident Analysis & Prevention, 37*, 557–562.

Hartup, W. W. (1993). Adolescents and their friends. In B. Laursen (Ed.), *New directions for child development: Close friendships in adolescence* (pp. 3–22). San Francisco: Jossey-Bass.

Hartup, W. W. (1996). The company they keep: Friendships and their developmental significance. *Child Development, 67*, 1–13.

Hartup, W. W., & Overhauser, S. (1991). Friendships. In R. M. Lerner, A. C. Petersen, & J. Brooks-Gunn (Eds.), *Encyclopedia of adolescence* (pp. 378–384). New York: Garland.

Hartup, W. W., & Stevens, N. (1999). Friendship and adaptation across the life span. *Current Directions in Psychological Science, 8*, 76–79.

Harwood, R., Leyendecker, B., Carlson, V., Asencio, M., & Miller, A. (2002). Parenting among Latino families in the U.S. In M. H. Bornstein (Ed.), *Handbook of parenting, Vol. 4: Social conditions and applied parenting* (2nd ed., pp. 21–46). Mahwah, NJ: Erlbaum.

Hass, A. (1979). *Teenage sexuality: A survey of teenage sexual behavior.* New York: Macmillan.

Hatcher, J. L., & Scarpa, J. (2001). *Background for community-level work on physical health and safety in adolescence: Reviewing the literature on contributing factors.* Washington, D. C.: Child Trends. Available: www.childtrends.org

Hatfield, E., & Rapson, R. L. (1996). *Love and sex: Cross-cultural perspectives.* Boston: Allyn & Bacon.

Hatfield, E., & Rapson, R. L. (2006). *Love and sex: Cross-cultural perspectives.* New York: University Press of America.

Haugaard, J. J. (1992). Epidemiology and family violence involving children. In R. I. Ammerman & M. Hersen (Eds.), *Assessment of family violence* (pp. 89–120). New York: Wiley.

Haugaard, J. J., & Reppucci, N. D. (1988). *The sexual abuse of children.* San Francisco: Jossey-Bass.

Hauser, S. L., Borman, R., Jacobson, A. M., & Powers, S. L. (1991). Understanding family contexts of adolescent coping: A study of parental ego development and adolescent coping strategies. *Journal of Early Adolescence, 11*, 96–124.

Hautala, L. A., Junnila, J., Helenius, H., Vaananen, A-M., Liuksila, P-R., Raiha, H., Valimaki, M., & Saarijarvi, S. (2008). Towards understanding gender differences in disordered eating among adolescents. *Journal of Clinical Nursing, 17*(13), 1803–1813.

Hawkins, J. A., & Berndt, T. J. (1985, April). *Adjustment following the transition to junior high school.* Paper presented at the biennial meeting of the Society for Research in Child Development, Toronto, Canada.

Hawley, P. H., Little, T. D., & Card, N. A. (2007). The allure of a mean friend: Relationship quality and processes of aggressive adolescents with prosocial skills. *International Journal of Behavioral Development, 31*(2), 170–180.

Hayatbakhsh, M. R., Najman, J. M., Jamrozik, K., Al Mamun, A., Bor, W., & Alati, R. (2008). Adolescent problem behaviors predicting *DSM-IV* diagnoses of multiple substance use disorder: Findings of a prospective birth cohort study. *Social Psychiatry and Psychiatric Epidemiology, 43*(5), 356–363.

Hayford, S. R. (2005). Conformity and change: Community effects on female genital cutting in Kenya. *Journal of Health and Social Behavior, 46*(2), 121–140.

Haynes, N. M., Emmons, C., & Ben-Avie, M. (1997). School climate as a factor in student adjustment and achievement. *Journal of Educational & Psychological Consultation, 8*, 321–329.

Hayward, C., Killen, J. D., Wilson, D. M., & Hammer, L. D. (1997). Psychiatric risk associated with early puberty in adolescent girls. *Journal of the American Academy of Child and Adolescent Psychiatry, 36*, 255–262.

Haywood, C., Gotlib, I. H., Schraedley, P. K., & Litt, I. F. (1999). Ethnic differences in the association between pubertal status and symptoms of depression in adolescent girls. *Journal of Adolescent Health, 25*, 143–149.

Hazan, C., & Zeifman, D. (1994). Sex and the psychological tether. In K. Bartholomew & D. Perlman (Eds.), *Advances in personal relationships, Vol. 5: Attachment processes in adulthood* (pp. 151–180). London: Jessica Kingsley.

Heatherington, L., & Lavner, J. A. (2008). Coming to terms with coming out: Review and recommendations for family systems-focused research. *Journal of Family Psychology, 22*(3), 329–343.

Hecht, D. B., Inderbitzen, H. M., & Bukowski, A. L. (1998). The relationship between peers status and depressive symptoms in children and adolescents. *Journal of Abnormal Child Psychology, 26*, 153–160.

Hecker, D. E. (1992, July). Reconciling conflicting data on jobs for college graduates. *Monthly Labor Review*, 3–12.

Heckhausen, J., & Tomasik, M. J. (2002). Get an apprenticeship before school is out: How German adolescents adjust vocational aspirations when getting close to a developmental deadline. *Journal of Vocational Behavior, 60*, 199–219.

Hedges, L. V., & Stock, W. (1983, Spring). The effects of class size: An examination of rival hypotheses. *American Educational Research Journal*, 63–85.

Hedlund, J, Compton, R. Graduated driver licensing research in 2004 and 2005. *Journal of Safety Research. 36*(2), 109–119.

Heilbrun K., Goldstein, N. E. S., & Redding, R. E. (2005). *Juvenile delinquency: Prevention, assessment and intervention.* New York: Oxford University Press.

Heilman, M. E., Martell, R. F., & Simon, M. C. (1988). The vagaries of sex bias: Conditions regulating the undervaluation, equivaluation, and overvaluation of female job applicants. *Organizational Behavior and Human Decision Processes, 41*, 98–110.

Hein, K. (1988). *Issues in adolescent health: An overview.* Washington, DC: Carnegie Council on Adolescent Development.

Heine, S. H. Lehman, D. R., Markus, H. R., & Kitayama, S. (1999). Is there a universal need for positive self-regard? *Psychological Review, 106*, 766–794.

Helgeson, V. (2002). *The psychology of gender.* Upper Saddle River, NJ: Prentice Hall.

Hellenga, K. (2002). Social space, the final frontier: Adolescents on the internet. In J. T. Mortimer & R. W. Larson (Eds.), *The changing adolescent experience: Societal trends and the transition to adulthood* (pp. 208–249). New York: Cambridge University Press.

Helping hands (2003). *Washington Post*, p. A12.

Helson, R., & Kwan, V. S. Y. (2000). Personality development in adulthood: The broad picture and processes in one longitudinal sample. In S. Hampton (Ed.), *Advances in personality psychology*, (Vol. 1, pp. 77–106). London: Routledge.

Helweg-Larsen, M., & Collins, B. E. (1994). The UCLA multidimensional condom attitudes scale: Documenting the complex determinants of condom use in college students. *Health Psychology, 13*, 224–237.

Hemmer, J. D., & Kleiber, D. A. (1981). Tomboy and sissies: Androgynous children? *Sex Roles, 7*, 1205–1211.

Hemmings, A. (1998). The self-transformations of African American achievers. *Youth & Society, 29*, 330–368.

Henderson, V. L., & Dweck, C. S. (1990). Motivation and achievement. In S. S. Feldman & G. R. Elliott (Eds.), *At the threshold: The developing adolescent* (pp. 308–329). Cambridge, MA: Harvard University Press.

Hendry, L. B., & Shucksmith, J. (1994). The United Kingdom. In K. Hurrelmann (Ed.), *International handbook of adolescence* (pp. 400–413). Westport, CT: Greenwood Press.

Henerey, A. (2004). Evolution of male circumcision as normative control. *Journal of Men's Studies, 12*(3), 265–276.

Henggeler, S. W., Sheidow, A. J., & Lee, T. (2007). Multisystemic treatment of serious clinical problems in youths and their families. In D. W. Springer & A. R. Roberts (Eds.), *Handbook of forensic mental health with victims and offenders: Assessment, treatments, and research* (pp. 3315–345). Springer series on social work. New York: Springer Publishing Co.

Henry, B., Feehan, M., McGee, R., Stanton, W., Moffitt, T., & Silva, R. (1993). The importance of conduct problems and depressive symptoms in predicting adolescent substance use. *Journal of Abnormal Child Psychology, 21*, 469–480.

Herdt, G. (1987). The Sambia: *Ritual and gender in New Guinea.* New York: Holt, Rinehart & Winston.

Herdt, G. (1989). *Gay and lesbian youth.* New York: Harrington Park Press.

Herdt, G., & Leavitt, S. C. (1998). *Adolescence in Pacific island societies.* Pittsburgh, PA: University of Pittsburgh Press.

Herek, G. M. (1986). The social psychology of homophobia: Toward a practical theory. *New York University Review of Law and Social Changes, 14*, 923–935.

Herman-Giddens, M., Slora, E., Wasserman, R., Bourdony, C., Bhapkar, M., Koch, G., & Hasemeier, C. (1997). Secondary sexual characteristics and menses in young girls seen in office practice: A study from the Pediatric Research in Office Settings Network. *Pediatrics, 88*, 505–512.

Herman-Giddens, M., Wang, L., & Koch, G. (2001). Secondary sexual characteristics in boys. *Archives of Pediatrics and Adolescent Medicine, 155*, 1022–1028.

Hermans, H. J. M.; Dimaggio, G. Self, identity, and globalization in times of uncertainty: A dialogical analysis. *Review of General Psychology, 11*(1) 31–61.

Hermans, H. J. M., & Kempen, H. J. G. (1998). Moving cultures: The perilous problems of cultural dichotomies in a globalizing society. *American Psychologist, 53*, 1111–1120.

Hernandez, D. J. (1994). Children's changing access to resources: A historical perspective. *SRCD Social Policy Report*, VIII(1).

Hernandez, D. J. (1997). Child development and the social demography of childhood. *Child Development, 68*, 149–169.

Heron, A. (1995). *Two teenagers in twenty: Writings by gay and lesbian youth.* New York: Alyson Press.

Herpertz-Dahlmann, B., Wille, N., Holling, J., Vloet, T. D., Ravens-Sieberer, U. [BELLA study group (Germany)]. (2008). Disordered eating behavior and attitudes, associated psychopathology and health-related quality of life: Results of the BELLA study. *European Child & Adolescent Psychiatry, 17*(Suppl. 1), 82–91.

Herrnstein, R. J., & Murry, C. (1995). *The bell curve: Intelligence and class structure in American life.* New York: Simon & Schuster.

Hertzog, C., & Schaie, K. W. (1986). Stability and change in adult intelligence: 1. Analysis of longitudinal covariance structures. *Psychology and Aging, 1*, 159–171.

Hertzog, N. B. (1998, January/February). Gifted education specialist. *Teaching Exceptional Children*, 39–43.

Herzog, D. B., Keller, M. B., Lavori, P. W., & Bradbum, L. S. (1991). Bulimia nervosa in adolescence.

Journal of Development and Behavioral Pediatrics, 12, 191–195.

Herzog, M. J., & Cooney, T. M. (2002). Parental divorce and perceptions of past interparental conflict: Influences on the communication of young adults. *Journal of Divorce and Remarriage, 36,* 89–109.

Hetherington, E. M. (1991). Presidential address: Families, lies, and videotapes. *Journal of Research on Adolescence, 1,* 323–348.

Hetherington, E. M. (1993). An overview of the Virginia longitudinal study of divorce and remarriage with a focus on early adolescence. *Journal of Family Psychology, 7,* 39–56.

Hetherington, E. M., Arnett, J., & Hollier, E. A. (1986). Adjustments of parents and children to remarriage. In S. Wolchik & P. Karoly (Eds.), *Children of divorce: Perspectives on adjustment* (pp. 132–151). New York: Gardner Press.

Hetherington, E. M., Bridges, M., & Insabella, G. M. (1998). What matters? What does not? Five perspectives on the association between marital transitions and children's adjustment. *American Psychologist, 53,* 167–184.

Hetherington, E. M., & Clingempeel, W. G. (1992). Coping with marital transition: A family systems perspective. *Monographs of the Society for Research in Child Development* (Vol. 57, No. 2–3, Serial No. 227).

Hetherington, E. M., Henderson, S., & Reiss, D. (1999). Adolescent siblings in stepfamilies: Family functioning and adolescent adjustment. *Monographs of the Society for Research in Child Development, 64.*

Hetherington, E. M., & Kelly, J. (2002) *For better or worse: Divorce reconsidered.* New York: Norton.

Hetherington, E. M., & Stanley-Hagan, M. (2000). Diversity among stepfamilies. In D. H. Demo & K. R. Allen (Eds.), *Handbook of family diversity* (pp. 173–196). New York: Oxford University Press.

Hetherington, E. M., & Stanley-Hagan, M. (2002). Parenting in divorced and remarried families. In M. H. Bornstein (Ed.), *Handbook of parenting: Vol. 3: Being and becoming a parent* (2nd ed., pp. 287–315). Mahwah, NJ: Erlbaum.

Hetherington, E. M., Stanley-Hagan, M., & Anderson, E. (1989). Marital transitions: A child's perspective. *American Psychologist, 44,* 303–312.

Heuveline, P. (2002). An international comparison of adolescent and young adult mortality. *Annals of the American Academy of Political Social Science, 580,* 172–200.

Higher Education Research Institute (HERI) (2005). *The American freshman: National norms for Fall 2004.* Los Angeles, CA: Author.

Hill, C., Rubin, Z., & Peplau, L. (1979). Breakups before marriage: The end of 103 affairs. In G. Levinger & O. Moles (Eds.), *Divorce and separation.* New York: Basic Books.

Hill, J. P. (1987). Research on adolescents and their families: Past and prospect. In C. E. Irwin (Ed.), *Adolescent social behavior and health* (pp. 13–31). San Francisco: Jossey-Bass.

Hill, J., & Holmbeck, G. (1986). Attachment and autonomy during adolescence. In G. Whitehurst (Ed.), *Annals of child development.* Greenwich, CT: JAI Press.

Hill, J., & Holmbeck, G. (1987). Disagreements about rules in families with seventh-grade girls and boys. *Journal of Youth & Adolescence, 16,* 221–246.

Hill, J., & Lynch, M. (1983). The intensification of gender-related role expectations during early adolescence. In J. Brooks-Gunn & A. Petersen (Eds.), *Female puberty.* New York: Plenum.

Hill, J., & Palmquist, W. (1978). Social cognition and social relations in early adolescence. *International Journal of Behavioral Development, 1,* 1–36.

Hinduja, S., & Patchin, J. W. (2008). Personal information of adolescents on the internet: A quantitative content analysis of MySpace. *Journal of Adolescence, 31*(1), 125–146.

Hingson, R., & Howland, J. (1993). Promoting safety in adolescents. In S. Millstein, A. Petersen, & E. Nightingale (Eds.), *Promoting the health of adolescents: New directions for the twenty-first century.* (pp. 305–327). New York: Oxford University Press.

Hird, M. J., & Jackson, S. (2001). Where "angels" and "wusses" fear to tread: Sexual coercion in adolescent dating relationships. *Journal of Sociology, 37,* 27–43.

Hirsch, B., & DuBois, D. (1991). Self-esteem in early adolescence: The identification and prediction of contrasting longitudinal trajectories. *Journal of Youth and Adolescence, 20,* 53–72.

Hirsch, B. J., & DuBois, D. L. (1989). The school-nonschool ecology of early adolescent friendships. In D. Belle (Ed.), *Children's social networks and social supports* (pp. 260–274). New York: Wiley.

Hirsch, P. (2003). Adolescent driver risk taking and driver education: Evidence of a mobility bias in public policymaking. *Journal of Safety Research, 34,* 289–298.

Ho, D. Y. F., & Chiu, C-Y. (1994). Component ideas of individualism, collectivism and social organization: An application in the study of Chinese culture. In U. Kim, H. C. Triandis, C. Kagitcibasi, S-C. Choi, & G. Yoon (Eds.), *Individualism and collectivism: Theory, method, and application.* Newbury Park, CA: Sage.

Ho, M. G., Shi, Y., Ma, S., & Novotny, T. R. (2007). Perceptions of tobacco advertising and marketing that might lead to smoking initiation among Chinese high school girls. *Tobacco Control: An International Journal, 16*(5), 359–360.

Hochschild, A. R. (1990). *The second shift.* New York: William Morrow.

Hochschild, A. R. (1998). *The time bind: When work becomes home and home becomes work.* New York: Henry Holt.

Hochschild, A. R. (2001). Emotion work, feeling rules, and social structure. In A. Branaman (Ed.), *Self and society. Blackwell readers in sociology* (pp. 138–155). Malden, MA: Blackwell.

Hodkinson, P. (2005). "Insider research" in the study of youth cultures. *Journal of Youth Studies, 8,* 131–149.

Hoek, H. W. (2006). Incidence, prevalence and mortality of anorexia nervosa and other eating disorders. *Current Opinion in Psychiatry, 19*(4), 389–394.

Hoem, B. (1992). Early phases of family formation in contemporary Sweden. In M. K. Rosenheim & M. F. Testa (Eds.), *Early parenthood and coming of age in the 1990s* (pp. 183–199). New Brunswick, NJ: Rutgers University Press.

Hofferth, S. (1992). The demand for and supply of child care in the 1990s. In A. Booth (Ed.), *Child care in the 1990s: Means, ends and consequences* (pp. 3–25). Hillsdale, NJ: Erlbaum.

Hoffman, B. R., Monge, P. R., Chou, C-P., & Valente, T. W. (2007). Perceived peer influence and peer selection on adolescent smoking. *Addictive Behaviors, 32*(8), 1546–1554.

Hoffman, B. R., Monge, P. R., Chou, C-P., & Valente, T. W. Perceived peer influence and peer selection on adolescent smoking. *Addictive Behaviors, 32*(8), 1546–1554.

Hoffman, L. (1991). The influence of the family environment on personality: Accounting for sibling differences. *Psychological Bulletin, 110,* 187–203.

Hoffmann, J. P., Baldwin, S. A. & Cerbone, F. G. (2003). Onset of major depressive disorder among adolescents. *Journal of the American Academy of Child & Adolescent Psychiatry, 42,* 217–224.

Hoffman, L. W. (1984). Work, family, and the socialization of the child. In R. D. Parke (Ed.), *Review of child development research* (Vol. 7, pp. 223–281). Chicago: University of Chicago Press.

Hoffman, L. W. Cross-cultural differences in childrearing goals. *New Directions for Child Development. 40,* 99–122.

Hoffner, C. A., & Levine, K. J. (2005). Enjoyment of mediated fright and violence: A meta analysis. *Media Psychology, 7*(2), 207–237.

Hofstede, G. (1980). *Culture's consequences.* Newbury Park, CA: Sage.

Hogan, D. P., & Astone, N. M. (1986). The transition to adulthood. *Annual Review of Sociology, 12,* 109–130.

Hogben, M. & Williams, S. P. (2001). Exploring the context of women's relationship perceptions, sexual behavior, and contraceptive strategies. *Journal of Psychology and Human Sexuality, 13,* 1–19.

Hoge, D. R., Johnson, B., & Luidens, D. A. (1993). Determinants of church involvement of young adults who grew up in Presbyterian churches. *Journal for the Scientific Study of Religion, 32,* 242–255.

Hokoda, A., Lu, H-H. A., & Angeles, M. (2006). School bullying in Taiwanese adolescents. *Journal of Emotional Abuse, 6*(4), 69–90.

Holahan, Carole K., Sears, R. R., Cronbach, L. J. (1995). *The gifted group in later maturity.* Stanford University Press.

Holland, J. (1985). *Making vocational choice: A theory of careers* (2nd ed.). Englewood Cliffs, NJ: Prentice-Hall.

Holland, J. L. (1987). *Current status of Holland's theory of careers: Another perspective. Career Development Quarterly, 36,* 24–30.

Holland, J. L. (1996). Exploring careers with a typology: What we have learned and some new directions. *American Psychologist, 51,* 397–406.

Hollinger, D. (Ed.). (1993). *Single-sex schooling: Perspectives from practice and research.* Washington, DC: U.S. Department of Education, Office of Educational Research and Improvement.

Hollinger, P. C., & Lester, D. (1991). Suicide, homicide, and demographic shifts: An epidemiologic study of regional and national trends. *Journal of Nervous and Mental Disease, 179,* 574–575.

Hollos, M., & Leis, P. E. (1989). *Becoming Nigerian in Ijo society.* New Brunswick, NJ: Rutgers University Press.

Hollos, M., & Richards, F. A. (1993). Gender-associated development of formal operations in Nigerian adolescents. *Ethos, 21,* 24–52.

Holloway, S. (1988). Concepts of ability and effort in Japan and the United States. *Review of Educational Research, 58,* 327–345.

Holmbeck, G. N., Crossmaii, R. E., Wandrei, M. L., & Gasiewski, E. (1994). Cognitive development, egocentrism, self-esteem, and adolescent contraceptive knowledge, attitudes, and behavior. *Journal of Youth and Adolescence, 23,* 169–193.

Holmbeck, G., & Hill, J. (1991). Conflictive engagement, positive affect, and menarche in families with seventh-grade girls. *Child Development, 62,* 1030–1048.

Holmes, J., & Silverman, E. L. (1992). *We're here, listen to us: A survey of young women in Canada.* Ottawa: Canadian Advisory Council on the Status of Women.

Holms, V. L., & Esses, L. M. (1988). Factors influencing Canadian high school girls' career motivation. *Psychology of Women Quarterly, 12,* 313–328.

Hong, T.K., Dibley, M.J., Sibbritt, D., Phan, N.T., Trang, N.H.H.D., & Tran, T. M. (2007). Overweight and obesity are rapidly emerging among adolescents in Ho Chi Minh City, Vietnam, 2002-04. *International Journal of Pediatric Obesity, 2,* 194–201.

Hoof, A. van (1999). The Identity Status field re-viewed: An update of unresolved and neglected issues with a view on some alternative approaches. *Developmental Review, 19,* 497–556.

Hooghe, M., & Wilkenfeld, B. (2008). The stability of political attitudes and behaviors cross adolescence and early adulthood: A comparison of survey data on adolescents and young adults in eight countries. *Journal of Youth and Adolescence, 37*(2), 155–167.

Hoover, E. (2005, November 26). Students study less than expected, survey finds. *Chronicle of Higher Education*, pp. A1, A31.

Hopkinson, N., & Martinez, B. E. (2002, September 21). *Rave off: "Buzz" canceled after drug sting*. *Washington Post*, pp. C1, C3.

Hops, H., Davis, B., Alpert, A., & Longoria, N. (1997, April). *Adolescent peer relations and depressive symptomatology*. Paper presented at the meeting of the Society for Research in Child Development, Washington, DC.

Horan, P., & Hargis, P. (1991). Children's work and schooling in the late nineteenth-century family economy. *American Sociological Review, 56*, 583–596.

Horatio Alger Association. (1998). *Back-to-school survey, 1998*. New York: Author.

Horgan, C. (2001). *Substance abuse: The nation's number one health problem*. Robert Wood Johnson Foundation. Princeton, NJ: Author. Available: www.rwjfliterature.org/chartbook/chartbook.htm

Horn, J. L. (1982). The aging of human abilities. In B. B. Wolman (Ed.), *Handbook of developmental psychology* (pp. 847–870). Englewood Cliffs, NJ: Prentice-Hall.

Horn, K., Dino, G., Kalsekar, I., & Mody, R. (2005). The impact of *Not On Tobacco* on teen smoking cessation: End-of-program evaluation results, 1998–2003. *Journal of Adolescent Research, 20*.

Horn, P. (1994). *Children's work and welfare, 1780–1890*. New York: Cambridge University Press.

Horn, S. (2003). Adolescents' reasoning about exclusion from social groups. *Developmental Psychology*.

Horn, S. (2006). Heterosexual adolescents' and young adults' beliefs and attitudes about homosexuality and gay and lesbian peers. *Cognitive Development, 21*(4), 420–440.

Horn, S. S., Killen, M., & Stangor, C. S. (1999). The influence of group stereotypes on adolescents' moral reasoning. *Journal of Early Adolescence, 19*, 98–113.

Hornblower, M. (1997, June 9). Great Xpectations. *Time*, 58–68.

Horowitz, A. D., & Bromnick, R. D. (2007). Contestable adulthood: Variability and disparity in markers for negotiating the transition to adulthood. *Youth and Society, 39*, 209–231.

Horowitz, F. D., & O'Brien, M. (1985). *The gifted and talented: Developmental perspectives*. Washington, DC: American Psychological Association.

Horowitz, A. D., & Bromnick, R. D. "Contestable adulthood": Variability and disparity in markers for negotiating the transition to adulthood. *Youth & Society. 39*(2), 209–231.

Howard, A. (1998). Youth in Rotuma, then and now. In G. Herdt & S. C. Leavitt (Eds.) *Adolescence in Pacific island societies* (pp. 148–172). Pittsburgh, PA: University of Pittsburgh Press.

Howard, K. S., Carothers, S. S., Smith, L. E., & Akai, C. E. (2007). Overcoming the odds: Protective factors in the lives of children. In J. G. Borkowski, J. R. Farris, T. L. Whitman, S. S. Carothers, K. Weed, et al. (Eds.), *Risk and Resilience: Adolescent mothers and their children grow up*. (pp. 205–232). NJ: Lawrence Erlbaum.

Howe, M. J. A. (1999). *Genius explained*. New York: Cambridge University Press.

Howell, M. R., Kassler, W. J., & Haddix, A. (1997). Partner notification to prevent pelvic inflammatory disease in women: Cost effectiveness of two strategies. *Sexually Transmitted Diseases, 24*, 287–292.

Howie, G. & Shail, A. (Eds.). (2005). *Menstruation: A Cultural History*. New York: Palgrave MacMillan.

Hoza, B., Kaiser, N., & Hurt, E. (2008). Evidence-based treatments for attention deficit/hyperactivity disorder (ADHD). In R. G. Steele, D. T. Elkin, & M. C. Roberts (Eds.), *Handbook of evidence-based therapies for children and adolescents: Bridging science and practice. Issues in clinical child psychology* (pp. 197–219). New York: Springer.

Hsu, F. L. K. (1983). *Rugged individualism reconsidered*. Knoxville: University of Tennessee Press.

Hsu, F. L. K. (1985). The self in cross-cultural perspective. In A. J. Marsella, G. DeVos, & F. L. K. Hsu (Eds.), *Culture and self: Asian and Western perspectives* (pp. 24–55). London: Tavistock.

Huang-Pollock, C. L., Carr, T. H., & Nigg, J. T. (2002). Development of selective attention: Perceptual load influences early versus late attentional selection in children and adults. *Developmental Psychology, 38*, 363–375.

Huesmann, L. R., Eron, L. D., Lefkowitz, M. M., & Walder, L. O. (1984). Stability of aggression over time and generations. *Developmental Psychology, 20*, 1120–1134.

Huesmann, L. R., Moise-Titus, J., Podolski, C., & Eron, L. D. (2003). Longitudinal relations between children's exposure to TV violence and their aggressiveness in young adulthood, 1977–1992. *Developmental Psychology, 39*, 201–221.

Huffaker, D. (2006). *Teen blogs exposed: The private lives of teens made public*. Paper presented at the meeting of the American Association for the Advancement of Science, St. Louis, MO.

Huffaker, D. A., & Calbert, S. L. (2005). Gender, identity, and language use in teenage blogs. *Journal of Computer-Mediated Communication, 10*(2). Retrieved January 22, 2008, from http://www.jcmc.indiana.edu/vol10/issue2/huffaker.html.

Hulse, M. (1989). *The sorrows of young Werther, by Johann Wolfgang von Goethe, translated with an Introduction and Notes*. London: Penguin.

Hunt, E. (1989). Cognitive science: Definition, status, and questions. *Annual Review of Psychology, 40*, 603–629.

Hurrelmann, K. (1996). The social world of adolescents: A sociological perspective. In K. Hurrelmann & S. Hamilton (Eds.), *Social problems and social contexts in adolescence: Perspectives across boundaries* (pp. 39–62). Hawthorne, New York: Aldine de Gruyter.

Hurrelmann, K., & Settertobulte, W. (1994). Germany. In K. Hurrelmann (Ed.), *International handbook of adolescence* (pp. 160–176). Westport, CT: Greenwood Press.

Hust, S. (2006). Gender identity development. In J. J. Arnett (Ed.), *Encyclopedia of children, adolescents, and the media*. Thousand Oaks, CA: Sage.

Hust, S. J. T., Brown, J. D., & L'Engle, K. L. (2008). Boys will be boys and girls better be prepared: An analysis of the rare sexual health messages in young adolescents' media. *Mass Communication and Society, 11*(1), 3–23.

Hutchins, E. (1983). Understanding Micronesian navigation. In D. Gentner & A. Stevens (Eds.), *Mental models*. Hillsdale, NJ: Erlbaum.

Hutchinson, M. K., & Cooney, T. M. (1998). Patterns of parent-teen sexual risk communication: Implications for intervention. *Family Relations, 47*, 185–194.

Hutchinson, N. L., Freeman, J. G., & Berg, D. H. (2004). Social competence of adolescents with learning disabilities: Interventions and issues. In L. Y. Wong (Ed.), *Learning about learning disabilities* (3rd ed., pp. 415–448). San Diego, CA: Elsevier Academic Press.

Huynh, V. W.; Fuligni, A. J. Ethnic socialization and the academic adjustment of adolescents from Mexican, Chinese, and European backgrounds. *Developmental Psychology, 44*(4), 1202–1208.

Hyde, J. S. (1985). *Half the human experience: The psychology of women* (3rd ed.). Lexington, KY: D. C. Heath.

Hyde, J. S. (1992). Gender and sex: So what has meta-analysis done for me? *Psychology Teacher Network Newsletter, 2*, 2–6.

Iacovou, M. (2002). Regional differences in the transition to adulthood. *Annals of the American Academy of Political Science Studies, 580*, 40–69.

Iannotti, R. J., & Bush, P. J. (1992). Perceived vs. actual friends' use of alcohol, cigarettes, marijuana, and cocaine: Which has the most influence? *Journal of Youth & Adolescence, 21*, 375–389.

ILO (2002). *A future without child labour*. New York: Author.

ILO (2004). *Investing in every child. An economic study of the costs and benefits of eliminating child labour*. New York: Author.

Inclan, J. E., & Herron, D. G. (1990). Puerto Rican adolescents. In J. T. Gibbs & L. N. Huang (Eds.), *Children of color: Psychological interventions with minority youth* (pp. 251–277). San Francisco: Jossey-Bass.

Inderbitzen, H. M., Walters, K. S., & Bukowski, A. L. (1997). The role of social anxiety in adolescent peer relations: Differences among sociometric status groups and rejected subgroups. *Journal of Clinical Child Psychology, 26*, 338–348.

Ingram, R., & Smith, L. T. (2008). Mood disorders. In J. E. Maddux & B. A. Winstead, *Psychopathology: Foundations for a contemporary understanding* (2nd ed., pp. 171–197). New York: Routledge/Taylor & Francis Group.

Inhelder, B., & Piaget, J. (1958). *The growth of logical thinking from childhood to adolescence*. New York: Basic Books.

Irwin, C. E., Jr., Igra, V., Eyre, S., & Millstein, S. (1997). Risk-taking behavior in adolescents: The paradigm. In M. S. Jacobson, J. M. Rees, N. H. Golden, & C. E. Irwin (Eds.), *Adolescent nutritional disorders: Prevention and treatment* (pp. 1–35). New York: New York Academy of Sciences.

Irwin, C., Jr. (1993). Topical areas of interest for promoting health: From the perspective of the physician. In S. Millstein, A. Petersen, & E. Nightingale (Eds.), *Promoting the health of adolescents: New directions for the twenty-first century.* (pp. 328–332). New York: Oxford University Press.

Jaccard, J., Blanton, H., & Dodge, T. (2005). Peer influences on risk behavior: An analysis of the effects of a close friend. *Developmental Psychology, 41*, 135–147.

Jaccard, J., Dittus, P. J., & Gordon, V. V. (1998). Parent-adolescent congruency in reports of adolescent sexual behavior and in communications about sexual behavior. *Child Development, 69*, 247–261.

Jack, D. J. (1991). *Silencing the self: Women and depression*. Cambridge, MA: Harvard University Press.

Jackson, L. M., Pratt, M. W., Hunsberger, B., & Pancer, S. M. (2005). Optimism as a mediator of the relation between perceived parental authoritativeness and adjustment among adolescents: Finding the sunny side of the street. *Social Development, 14*, 273–304.

Jackson, S. M., & Cram, F. (2003). Disrupting the sexual double standard: Young women's talk about heterosexuality. *British Journal of Social Psychology, 42*, 113–127.

Jacobs, J. E., & Klaczynski, P. A. (2002). The development of judgment and decision making during childhood and adolescence. *Current directions in psychological science, 11*, 145–149.

Jacobs, J. E., & Klaczynski, P. A. (2005). *The development of judgment and decision making in children and adolescents*. Mahwah, NJ: Erlbaum.

Jacobs, J. W. (1983). Treatment of divorcing fathers: Social and psychotherapeutic considerations. *American Journal of Psychiatry, 140*, 1294–1299.

Jacobs, J. W. (1988). *Islam in transition: Religion and identity among British Pakistani youth*. New York: Routledge.

Jacobson, K. C., & Crockett, L. J. (2000). Parental monitoring and adolescent adjustment: An ecological perspective. *Journal of Research on Adolescence, 10*, 65–98.

Jaffee, S. R., Moffitt, T. E., Caspi, A., Fombonne, E., Poulton, R., & Martin, J. (2002). Differences in early childhood risk factors for juvenile-onset and adult-onset depression. *Archives of General Psychiatry, 59*, 215–222.

Jankowiak, W. R., & Fischer, E. F. (1992). A cross-cultural perspective on romantic love. *Ethology, 31*, 149–155.

Janosz, M., Archambault, I., Morizot, J., & Pagani, L. S. (2008). School engagement trajectories and their differential predictive relations to dropout. *Journal of Social Issues, 64*(1), 21–40.

Jarvinen, D., & Nicholls, J. (1996). Adolescents' social goals, beliefs about the causes of social success, and satisfaction in peer relations. *Developmental Psychology, 32*, 435–441.

Jason, L. A., Reichler, A., Easton, J., Neal, A., & Wilson, M. (1984). Female harassment after ending a relationship: A preliminary study. *Alternative Lifestyles, 6*, 259–269.

Jeffries, E. D. (2004). Experiences of trust with parents: A qualitative investigation of African American, Latino, and Asian American boys from low income families. In N. Way., Y. Judy, Chu (Eds.), *Adolescent boys: Exploring diverse cultures of boyhood* (pp. 107–128). New York: New York University Press.

Jensen, J. M., & Howard, M. O. (1990). Skill deficits, skills training, and delinquency. *Children and Youth Services Review, 12*, 213–228.

Jensen, L. A. (1995). Habits of the heart revisited: Autonomy, community and divinity in adults' moral language. *Qualitative Sociology, 18*, 71–86.

Jensen, L. A. (1997a). Culture wars: American moral divisions across the adult life span. *Journal of Adult Development, 4*, 107–121.

Jensen, L. A. (1997b). Different worldviews, different morals: America's culture war divide. *Human Development, 40*, 325–344.

Jensen, L. A. (1998). Moral divisions within countries between orthodoxy and progressivism: India and the United States. *Journal of the Scientific Study of Religion, 37*, 90–107.

Jensen, L. A. (2003). *A cultural-developmental approach to moral psychology.* Manuscript submitted for publication.

Jensen, L. A. (2008). Coming of age in a multicultural world: Globalization and adolescent cultural identity formation. In D. L. Browning (Ed.), *Adolescent identities: A collection of readings* (pp. 3–17). Relational perspectives book series. New York: Analytic Press/Taylor & Francis Group.

Jensen, L. A., & Williams, E. (2001, March). *The everyday moral life of American emerging adults: A diary study.* Paper presented at the biennial meeting of the Society for Research on Adolescence, New Orleans, LA.

Jessor, R. (1987). Risky driving and adolescent problem behavior: An extension of problem-behavior theory. *Alcohol, Drugs, and Driving, 3*, 1–11.

Jessor, R. (1999). New perspectives on adolescent risk behavior. In R. Jessor (Ed.), *New perspectives on adolescent risk behavior* (pp. 1–10). New York: Cambridge University Press.

Jessor, R., Colby, A., & Shweder, R. A. (1996). *Ethnography and human development: Context and meaning in social inquiry.* Chicago: University of Chicago Press.

Jessor, R., Costa, F., Jessor, L., & Donovan, J. (1983). Time of first intercourse: A prospective study. *Journal of Personality and Social Psychology, 44*, 608–626.

Jessor, R., Donovan, J. E., & Costa, F. M. (1991). *Beyond adolescence: Problem behavior and young adult development.* New York: Cambridge University Press.

Jessor, R., & Jessor, S. (1977). *Problem behavior and psychosocial development: A longitudinal study of youth.* New York: Academic Press.

Jessor, R., Turbin, M. S., Costa, F. M., Dong, Qi, Zhang, H., & Wang, C. (2003). Adolescent problem behavior in China and the United States: A cross-national study of psychosocial protective factors. *Journal of Research on Adolescence, 13*, 329–360.

Jeynes, W. (2002). *Divorce, family structure, and the academic success of children.* New York: Haworth Press.

Jeynes, W. H. (1999). Effects of remarriage following divorce on the academic achievement of children. *Journal of Youth & Adolescence, 28*, 385–393.

Jeynes, W. H. The impact of parental remarriage on children: A meta-analysis. *Marriage & Family Review, 40*(4), 75–102.

Joe, S., & Marcus, S. C. (2003). Datapoints: Trends by race and gender in suicide attempts among U.S. adolescents, 1991–2001. *Psychiatric Services, 54*, 454.

John, R. (1998). Native American families. In C. H. Mindel, R. W. Habenstein, & R. Wright, Jr. (Eds.), *Ethnic families in America: Patterns and variations* (pp. 382–421). Upper Saddle River, NJ: Prentice-Hall.

Johnson, B. M., Shulman, S., & Collins, W. A. (1991). Systemic patterns of parenting as reported by adolescents: Developmental differences and implications for psychosocial outcomes. *Journal of Adolescent Research, 6*, 235–252.

Johnson, G. R., Krug, E. G., & Potter, L. B. (2000). Suicide among adolescents and young adults: A cross-national comparison of 34 countries. *Suicide & Life-Threatening Behavior, 30*, 74–82.

Johnson, J. D., Adams, M. S., Ashburn, L., & Reed, W. (1995). Differential gender effects of exposure to rap music on African American adolescents' acceptance of teen dating violence. *Sex Roles, 33*, 597–605.

Johnson, J. D., Trawalter, S., & Dovidio, J. F. (2000). Converging interracial consequences of exposure to violent rap music on stereotypical attributions of blacks. *Journal of Experimental Social Psychology, 36*, 233–251.

Johnson, J. G., Cohen, P., Kasen, S., & Brook, J. S. (2002). Eating disorders during adolescence and the risk for physical and mental disorders during early adulthood. *Archives of General Psychiatry, 59*, 545–552.

Johnson, M. K., Beebe, T., Mortimer, J. T., & Snyder, M. Volunteerism in adolescence: A process perspective. *Journal of Research on Adolescence, 8*(3), 309–332.

Johnson, N. G., Roberts, M. C., & Worrell, J. (1999). *Beyond appearance: A new look at adolescent girls.* Washington, DC: American Psychological Association.

Johnson, P. (1992). *Modern times: The world from the twenties to the nineties.* New York: HarperCollins.

Johnson, S. K., Murphy, S. R., Zewdie, S., & Reichard, R. J. (2008). The strong, sensitive type: Effects of gender stereotypes and leadership prototypes on the evaluation of male and female leaders. *Organizational Behavior and Human Decision Processes, 106*(1), 39–60.

Johnston, L. D., O'Malley, P. M., & Bachman, J. G. (1995). *National survey results on drug use from the Monitoring the Future Study, Vol. I: Secondary school students.* Ann Arbor, MI: Institute for Social Research.

Johnston, L., Bachman, J., & O'Malley, P. (1996). *Monitoring the future.* Ann Arbor, MI: Institute for Social Research.

Jonah, B. A. (1986). Accident risk and risk-taking behaviour among young drivers. *Accident Analysis and Prevention, 18*, 255–271.

Jones, E. F., Forrest, J. D., Goldman, N., Henshaw, S., Lincoln, R., Rosoff, J. I., Westoff, C. F., & Wulf, D. (1986). *Teenage pregnancy in industrialized countries.* New Haven: Yale University Press.

Jones, E. F., Forrest, J. D., Goldman, N., Henshaw, S., Lincoln, R., Rosoff, J. I., Westoff, C. F., & Wulf, D. (1987). *Teenage pregnancy in industrialized countries.* New Haven: Yale University Press.

Jones, E. F., Forrest, J. D., Henshaw, S. K., Silverman, J., & Torres, A. (1988). Unintended pregnancy, contraceptive practice and family planning services in developed countries. *Family Planning Perspectives, 20*, 53–67.

Jones, K. (1997). Are rap videos more violent? Style differences and the prevalence of sex and violence in the age of MTV. *Howard Journal of Communications, 8*, 343–356.

Jones, R. K., Darroch, J. E., & Henshaw, S. K. (2002). Contraceptive use among U.S. women having abortions in 2000–2001. *Perspectives on Sexual and Reproductive Health, 34*, 294–303.

Jordan, W., Lara, J., & McPartland, J. (1996). Exploring the causes of early dropout among race-ethnic and gender groups. *Youth & Society, 28*, 62–94.

Jose, P. E., & Brown, I. (2008). When does the gender difference in rumination begin? Gender and age differences in the use of rumination by adolescents. *Journal of Youth and Adolescence, 37*(2), 180–192.

Josselson, R. (1988). *Finding herself: Pathways to identity development in women.* San Francisco: Jossey-Bass.

Josselson, R. (1989). Identity formation in adolescence: Implications for young adulthood. In S. C. Feinstein (Ed.), *Adolescent psychiatry* (Vol. 16, pp. 142–154). Chicago: University of Chicago Press.

Josselson, R. L. (1992). *The space between us.* San Francisco: Jossey-Bass.

Juang, L. P., & Nguyen, H. H. (1997, April). *Autonomy and connectedness: Predictors of adjustment in Vietnamese adolescents.* Paper presented at the meeting of the Society for Research in Child Development, Washington, DC.

Juang, L. P., & Silbereisen, R. K. (2002). The relationship between adolescent academic capability beliefs, parenting and school grades. *Journal of Adolescence, 25*, 3–18.

Juang, L. P., Silbereisen, R. K., & Wiesner, M. (1999). Predictors of leaving home in young adults raised in Germany: A replication of a 1991 study. *Journal of Marriage and the Family, 61*, 505–515.

Juvonen, J., & Galván, A. (2008). In M. J. Prinstein & K. A. Dodge (Eds.), *Understanding peer influence in children and adolescents. Duke series in child development and public policy* (pp. 225–244). New York: Guilford Press.

Juvonen, J., & Murdock, T. (1995). Grade-level differences in the social value of effort: Implications for self-presentation tactics of early adolescents. *Child Development, 66*, 1694–1705.

Kahn, J. A. (2007). Maximizing the potential public health impact of HPV vaccines: A focus on parents. *Journal of Adolescent Health, 40*(2), 101–103.

Kahn, J. S., Kehle, T. J., Jensen, W. R., & Clark, E. (1990). Comparison of cognitive-behavioral, relaxation, and self-modeling interventions for depression among middle-school students. *School Psychology Review, 19*, 196–211.

Kahne, J. (1999). Personalized philanthropy: Can it support youth and build civic commitments? *Youth & Society, 30*, 367–387.

Kail, R. (1991a). Processing time declines exponentially during childhood and adolescence. *Developmental Psychology, 27*, 259–266.

Kail, R. (1991b). Developmental change in speed of processing during childhood and adolescence. *Psychological Bulletin, 109*, 490–501.

Kail, R., & Hall, L. K. (2001). Distinguishing short-term memory from working memory. *Memory and Cognition, 29*, 1–9.

Kail, R., & Pellegrino, J. W. (1985). *Human intelligence.* New York: Freeman.

Kakar, S. (1998). Asian Indian families. In R. L. Taylor (Ed.), *Minority families in the United States: A multicultural perspective* (pp. 208–223). Upper Saddle River, NJ: Prentice Hall.

Kalb, C., & McCormick, J. (1998, September 21). Bellying up to the bar. *Newsweek*, 89.

Kalev, H. D. (2004). Cultural rights or human rights: The case of female genital mutilation. *Sex Roles, 51*(5–6), 339–348.

Kalin, R., & Tilby R. (1978). Development and validation of a sex-role ideology scale. *Psychological Reports, 42*, 731–738.

Kallman, D. A., Plato, C. C., & Tobin, J. D. (1990). The role of muscle loss in the age-related decline of grip strength: Cross-sectional and longitudinal perspectives. *Journals of Gerontology: Medical Sciences, 45*, M82–88.

Kaltiala-Heino, R., Kosunen, E., & Rimpelä, M. (2003). Pubertal timing, sexual behaviour and self-reported depression in middle adolescence. *Journal of Adolescence, 26*, 531–545.

Kamagai, F. (1984). The life cycle of the Japanese family. *Journal of Marriage and the Family, 46*, 191–204.

Kamibeppu, K., & Sugiura, H. (2005). Impact of the mobile phone on *junior-high school* students' friendships in the Tokyo *metropolitan* area. *CyberPsychology & Behavior, 8*, 121–130.

Kamphaus, R. W. (2000). Learning disabilities. In A. Kazdin (Ed.), *Encyclopedia of psychology*. Washington, DC: American Psychological Association.

Kandel, D. B. (1975). Stages in adolescent involvement in drug use. *Science, 190*, 912–914.

Kandel, D. B. (1978). Homophily, selection, and socialization in adolescent friendships. *American Journal of Sociology, 84*, 426–437.

Kandel, D. B. (1998). Persistent themes and new perspectives on adolescent substance use: A lifespan perspective. In R. Jessor (Ed.), *New perspectives on adolescent risk behavior* (pp. 43–89). New York: Cambridge University Press.

Kandel, D. B. (Ed.) (2002). *Stages and pathways of drug involvement: Examining the gateway hypothesis*. New York: Cambridge University Press.

Kandel, D. B., & Faust, R. (1975). Sequence and stages in patterns of adolescent drug use. *Archives of General Psychiatry, 32*, 923–932.

Kandel, D. B., & Jessor, R. (2002). The gateway hypothesis revisited. In D. B. Kandel (Ed.), *Stages and pathways of drug involvement: Examining the gateway hypothesis* (pp. 365–372). New York: Cambridge University Press.

Kantrowitz, B., & Wingert, P. (1999, October 18). The truth about teens. *Newsweek*, 62–72.

Kao, G., & Joyner, K. (2004). Do race and ethnicity matter among friends? Activites among interracial, interethnic, and intraethnic, adolescent friends. *Sociological Quarterly, 45*, 557–573.

Kao, G., & Tienda, M. (1995). Optimism and achievement: The educational performance of immigrant youth. *Social Science Quarterly, 76*, 1–19.

Kaplan, S. J. (1991). Physical abuse and neglect. In M. Lewis (Ed.), *Child and adolescent psychiatry* (pp. 1010–1018). Baltimore, MD: Williams & Wilkins.

Kasen, S., Cohen, P., & Brook, J. S. (1998). Adolescent school experiences, and dropout, adolescent pregnancy, and young adult deviant behavior. *Journal of Adolescent Research, 13*, 49–72.

Kasen, S., Cohen, P., Brook, J. S., & Hartmark, C. (1996). A multiple-risk interaction model: Effects of temperament and divorce on psychiatric disorder in children. *Journal of Abnormal Child Psychology, 24*, 121–150.

Kashani, J. H., Daniel, A. E., Dandoy, A. C., & Holcomb, W. R. (1992). Family violence: Impact on children. *Journal of the American Academy of Child and Adolescent Psychiatry, 31*, 181–189.

Kassam, A. (2006). Encounters with the north: Psychiatric consultation with Inuit youth. Journal of the Canadian Academy of Child and Adolescent Psychiatry. *Journal de l'Académie Canadienne de Psychiatrie de l'Enfant et de l'Adolescent, 15*(4), 174–178.

Kassler, W. J., & Cates, W. (1992). The epidemiology and prevention of sexually transmitted diseases. *Urology Clinics of North America, 19*, 1–12.

Katchadourian, H., & Boli, J. (1985). *Careerism and intellectualism among college students*. San Francisco: Jossey-Bass.

Katz, A. N., Blasko, D. G., & Kazmerski, V. A. (2004). Saying what you don't mean: Social influences on sarcastic language processing. *Current Directions in Psychological Science, 13*, 186–189.

Katz, J. (Ed.). (1995). *Messengers of the wind: Native American women tell their life stories*. New York: Ballantine.

Kaufman, A. S., & Lichtenberger, E. O. (2006). *Assessing adolescent and adult intelligence* (3rd ed.). Hoboken, NJ: John Wiley & Sons.

Kaufman, D. R. (1991). *Rachel's daughters: Newly orthodox Jewish women*. New Brunswick, NJ: Rutgers University Press.

Kaufman, J. (2004). The interplay between social and cultural determinants of school effort and success: An investigation of Chinese immigrant and second generation Chinese students' perceptions toward school. *Social Science Quarterly, 85*, 1275–1298.

Kaufman, N. K., Rohde, P., Seeley, J. R., Clarke, G. N., & Stice, E. (2005). Potential mediators of cognitive-behavioral therapy for adolescents with comorbid major depression and conduct disorder. *Journal of Consulting & Clinical Psychology, 73*, 38–46.

Keage, H. A. D, Clark, C. R., Hermens, D. F., Williams, L. M., Kohn, M. R., Clarke, S., Lamb, C., Crewther, D., & Gordon, E. (2008). Putative biomarker of working memory systems development during childhood and adolescence. *Neuroreport: For Rapid Communication of Neuroscience Research, 19*(2), 197–201.

Keating, D. (1990). Adolescent thinking. In S. Feldman & G. Elliott (Eds.), *At the threshold: The developing adolescent* (pp. 54–89). Cambridge, MA: Harvard University Press.

Keating, D. (2004). Cognitive and brain development. In L. Steinberg & R. M. Lerner (Eds.), *Handbook of adolescent psychology* (2nd edition). New York: Wiley.

Keating, D. P., & Sasse, D. K. (1996). Cognitive socialization in adolescence: Critical period for a critical habit of mind. In G. R. Adams, R. Montemayer, & T. Gullotta (Eds.), *Psychosocial development during adolescence* (pp. 232–258). Thousand Oaks, CA: Sage.

Keefe, K. (1994). Perceptions of normative social pressure and attitudes toward alcohol use: Changes during adolescence. *Journal of Studies on Alcohol, 55*, 46–54.

Keefe, K., & Berndt, T. (1996). Relations of friendship quality to self-esteem in early adolescence. *Journal of Early Adolescence, 16*, 110–129.

Keel, P. K., Fulkerson, J. A., & Leon, G. R. (1997). Disordered eating precursors in pre- and early-adolescent girls and boys. *Journal of Youth & Adolescence, 26*, 203–216.

Kellogg, A. (2001, January). Looking inward, freshman care less about politics and more about money. *Chronicle of Higher Education*, A47–A49.

Kelly, J. A., O'Brien, G. G., & Hosford, R. (1981). Sex roles and social skills: Considerations for interpersonal judgment. *Psychology of Women Quarterly, 5*, 758–766.

Kelly, J. B. (2000). Children's adjustment in conflicted marriage and divorce: A decade review of research. *Journal of the American Academy of Child & Adolescent Psychiatry, 39*, 963–973.

Kelly, J. B. (2003). Changing perspectives on children's adjustment following divorce: A view from the United States. Childhood: *A Global Journal of Child Research, 10*, 237–254.

Kelly, S. (2004). Do increased levels of parental involvement account for social class differences in track placements? *Social Science Research, 33*, 626–659.

Kendall-Tackett, K. A., Williams, L. M., & Finkelhor, D. (1993). Impact of sexual abuse on children: A review and synthesis of recent empirical studies. *Psychological Bulletin, 113*, 164–180.

Kendall-Tackett, K. A., Williams, L. M., & Finkelhor, D. (2001). Impact of sexual abuse on children: A review and synthesis of recent empirical studies. In R. Bull (Ed.), *Children and the law: The essential readings* (pp. 31–76). Malden, MA: Blackwell.

Kennedy, J. H. (1990). Determinants of peer social status: Contributions of physical appearance, reputation, and behavior. *Journal of Youth and Adolescence, 19*, 233–244.

Kenny, M. E., & Hart, K. (1992). Relationship between parental attachment and eating disorders in an inpatient and a college sample. *Journal of Counseling Psychology, 39*, 521–526.

Kerber, L. K. (1997). *Toward an intellectual history of women*. Chapel Hill: University of North Carolina Press.

Kerestes, M., Youniss, J., & Metz, E. (2004). Longitudinal patterns of religious perspective and civic integration. *Applied Developmental Science, 8*, 39–46.

Kerns, K. (1994). Individual differences in friendship quality: Links to child-mother attachment. In W. Bukowski, A. Newcomb, & W. Hartup (Eds.), *The company they keep: Friendship in childhood and adolescence*. New York: Cambridge University Press.

Kerr, M., & Stattin, H. Parenting of adolescents: Action or reaction? In A. C. Crouter & A. Booth (Eds.). *Children's influence on family dynamics: The neglected side of family relationships* (pp. 121–151). Mahwah, NJ: Erlbaum.

Kerr, M., & Stattin, H. (2000). What parents know, how they know it, and several forms of adolescent adjustment: Further support for a reinterpretation of parental monitoring. *Developmental Psychology, 36*, 366–380.

Kershae, T. S., Ethier, K. A., Niccolai, L. M., Lewis, J. B., & Lckovics, J. R. (2003). Misperceived risk among female adolescents: Social and psychological factors associated with sexual risk accuracy. *Health Psychology, 22*, 523–532.

Kett, J. (1977). *Rites of passage: Adolescence in America, 1790 to the present*. New York: Basic Books.

Kieran, K. (2002). Cohabitation in Western Europe: Trends, issues, and implications. In A. Booth & A. C. Crouter (Eds.), *Just living together: Implications of cohabitation on families, children, and social policy* (pp. 3–31). Mahwah, NJ: Erlbaum.

Kiernan, K. (2004). Cohabitation and divorce across nations and generations. In P. L. Chase-Lansdale, K. Kiernan, R. J. Friedman (Eds.), *Human development across lives and generations: The potential for change* (pp. 139–170). New York: Cambridge University Press.

Kiesner, J., & Kerr, M. (2004). Families, peers, and contexts as multiple determinants of adolescent problem behavior. *Journal of Adolescence, 27*, 493–495.

Killen, M. (2002). Early deliberations: A developmental psychologist investigates how children think about fairness and exclusion. *Teaching Tolerance, 22*, 44–49.

Killen, M., Crystal, D. S., & Watanabe, H. (2002). Japanese and American children's evaluations of peer exclusion, tolerance of differences, and prescriptions of conformity. *Child Development, 73*, 1788–1802.

Killen, M., & Hart, D. (1999). *Morality in everyday life*. New York: Cambridge University Press.

Killen, M., & Stangor, C. (2001). Children's social reasoning about inclusion and exclusion in gender and race peer group contexts. *Child Development, 72*, 174–186.

Killen, M., & Wainryb, C. (1998). Independence and interdependence in diverse cultural contexts. *New Directions for Child Development*.

Killen, M., & Wainryb, C. (2000). Independence and interdependence in diverse cultural contexts. In S. Harkness & C. Raeff (Eds.), *Variability in the social construction of the child* (pp. 5–21). New

Larson, R. (1990). The solitary side of life: An examination of the time people spend alone from childhood to old age. *Developmental Review, 10*, 155–183.

Larson, R. (1995). Secrets in the bedroom: Adolescents' private use of media. *Journal of Youth & Adolescence, 24*, 535–550.

Larson, R. (2002). Globalization, societal change, and new technologies: What they mean for the future of adolescence. *Journal of Research on Adolescence, 12*, 1–30.

Larson, R., Clore, G. L., & Wood, G. A. (1999). The emotions of romantic relationships: Do they wreak havoc on adolescents? In W. Furman, B. B. Brown, & C. Feiring (Eds.), *The development of romantic relationships in adolescence* (pp. 19–49). New York: Cambridge University Press.

Larson, R., Csikszentmihalyi, M., & Graef, R. (1982). Time alone in daily experience: Loneliness or renewal? In L. A. Peplau & D. Perlman (Eds.), *Loneliness: A sourcebook of theory, research, and therapy* (pp. 40–53). New York: Wiley.

Larson, R., & Ham, M. (1993). Stress and "storm and stress" in early adolescence: The relationship of negative life events with dysphoric affect. *Developmental Psychology, 29*, 130–140.

Larson, R., Moneta, G., Richards, M. H., & Wilson, S. (2002). Continuity, stability, and change in daily emotional experience across adolescence. *Child Development, 73*, 1151–1165.

Larson, R., & Richards, M. H. (1994). *Divergent realities: The emotional lives of mothers, fathers, and adolescents.* New York: Basic Books.

Larson, R., & Richards, M. (1998). Waiting for the weekend: Friday and Saturday nights as the emotional climax of the week. *New Directions for Child and Adolescent Development, 82*, 37–52.

Larson, R., Verman, S., & Dworkin, J. (2000, March). Adolescence without family disengagement: The daily family lives of Indian middle-class teenagers. Paper presented at the biennial meeting of the Society for Research on Adolescence, Chicago.

Larson, R. W., Csikszentmihalyi, M., & Graef, R. (1980). Mood variability and the psycho-social adjustment of adolescents. *Journal of Youth & Adolescence, 9*, 469–490.

Larson, R. W., Moneta, G., Richards, M. H., & Wilson, S. (2002). Continuity, stability, and change in daily emotional experience across adolescence. *Child Development, 73*, 1151–1165.

Larson, R. W., Richards, M. H., Moneta, G., Holmbeck, G., & Duckett, E. (1996). Changes in adolescents' daily interactions with their families from ages 10 to 18: Disengagement and transformation. *Developmental Psychology, 32*, 744–754.

Larson, R. W, Wilson, S., & Rickman, A. (2010). Globalization, societal change, and adolescence across the world. In R. Lerner & L. Steinberg (Eds.), *Handbook of Adolescent Psychology.*

Lasch, C. (1979). *Haven in a heartless world.* New York: Basic Books.

Lau, S. (1988). The value orientations of Chinese university students in Hong Kong. *International Journal of Psychology, 23*, 583–596.

Laumann-Billings, L., & Emery, R. E. (2000). Distress among young adults from divorced families. *Journal of Family Psychology, 14*, 671–687.

Lauritsen, J. (1994). Explaining race and gender differences in adolescent sexual behavior. *Social Forces, 72*, 859–884.

Laursen, B., & Collins, W. (1994). Interpersonal conflict during adolescence. *Psychological Bulletin, 115*, 197–209.

Laursen, B., & Collins, W. Andrew. (2004). Parent-child communication during adolescence. In L. Anita, Vangelisti (Ed.), *Handbook of family communication* (pp. 333–348). Mahwah, NJ: Lawrence Erlbaum.

Laursen, B., & Jensen-Campbell, L. A. (1999). The nature and functions of social exchange in adoles-

cent romantic relationships. In W. Furman, B. B. Brown, & C. Feiring (Eds.), *The development of romantic relationships in adolescence* (pp. 50–74). New York: Cambridge University Press.

Laursen, B., Coy, K. C., & Collins, W. A. (1998). Reconsidering changes in parent-child conflict across adolescence: A meta-analysis. *Child Development, 69*, 817–832.

Laursen, B., & Williams, Vickie. (2002). The role of ethnic identity in personality development. In Lea, Pulkkinen & Avshalom, Caspi (Eds.), *Paths to successful development: Personality in the life course* (pp. 203–226). New York: Cambridge University Press.

Lave, J. (1988). *Cognition in practice: Mind, mathematics, and culture in everyday life.* Cambridge: Cambridge University Press.

Lawson, A. E., & Wollman, W. T. (2003). Encouraging the transition from concrete to formal operations: An experiment. *Journal of Research in Science Teaching, 40*(Suppl.), S33–S50.

Le Grange, D., Lock, J., & Dymek, M. (2003). Family-based therapy for adolescents with bulimia nervosa. *American Journal of Psychotherapy, 57*, 237–251.

Leadbeater, B. J. (1994, February). *Reconceptualizing social supports for adolescent mothers: Grandmothers, babies, fathers, and beyond.* Paper presented at the meeting of the Society for Research on Adolescence, San Diego, CA.

Leadbeater, B. J. R., & Way, N. (2001). *Growing up fast: Transitions to early adulthood of inner-city adolescent mothers.* Mahwah, NJ: Erlbaum.

Leavitt, S. C. (1998). The Bikhet mystique: Masculine identity and patterns of rebellion among Bumbita adolescent males. In G. Herdt & S. C. Leavitt (Eds.), *Adolescence in Pacific island societies* (pp. 173–194). Pittsburgh, PA: University of Pittsburgh Press.

Lee, B. (1998). *The changes of Korean adolescents' lives.* Unpublished manuscript, Department of Human Development and Family Studies, University of Missouri.

Lee, J. C., & Staff, J. (2007). When work matters: The varying impact of work intensity on high school dropouts. *Sociology of Education, 80*(2), 158–178.

Lee, K., & Freire, A. (2003). Cognitive development. In A. Slater & G. Bremner (Eds.), *An introduction to developmental psychology* (pp. 359–387). Malden, MA: Blackwell.

Lee, M., & Larson, R. (2000). The Korean "examination hell": Long hours of studying, distress, and depression. *Journal of Youth & Adolescence, 29*, 249–271.

Lee, M. M. C., Chang, K. S. F., & Chan, M. M. C. (1963). Sexual maturation of Chinese girls in Hong Kong. *Pediatrics, 32*, 389–398.

Lee, P. A. (1980). Normal ages of pubertal events among American males and females. *Journal of Adolescent Health Care, 1*, 26–29.

Lee, S. J., & Vaught, S. (2003). "You can never be too rich or too thin": Popular and consumer culture and the Americanization of Asian American girls and young women. *Journal of Negro Education, 72*, 457–466.

Lee, V., & Bryk, A. (1986). Effects of single-sex secondary schools on achievement and attitudes. *Journal of Educational Psychology, 78*, 381–395.

Lee, V., & Croninger, R. (1994). The relative importance of home and school in the development of literacy skills for middle-grade students. *American Journal of Education, 102*, 286–329.

Lee, V., Croninger, R., Linn, E., & Chen, X. (1996). The culture of harassment in secondary schools. *American Educational Research Journal, 33*, 383–417.

Lee, V., Marks, H., & Byrd, T. (1994). Sexism in single-sex and co-educational independent secondary school classrooms. *Sociology of Education, 67*, 92–120.

Lee, V. E., Burkam, D. T., Zimiles, H., & Ladewski, B. (1994). Family structure and its effect on behav-

ioral and emotional problems in young adolescents. *Journal of Research on Adolescence, 4*, 405–437.

Lefkowitz, E. S. (2005). "Things have gotten better": Developmental changes among emerging adults after the transition to university. *Journal of Adolescent Research, 20*, 40–63.

Lefkowitz, E. S., & Gillen, M. M. (2006). "Sex is just a normal part of life": Sexuality in emerging adulthood. In J. J. Arnett & J. L. Tanner (Eds.), *Coming of age in the 21st century: The lives and contexts of emerging adults* (pp. 235–256) Washington, DC: American Psychological Association.

Lefkowitz, E. S., Gillen, M. M., Shearer, C. L., & Boone, T. L. (2004). Religiosity, sexual behaviors, and sexual attitudes during emerging adulthood. *Journal of Sex Research, 41*, 150–159.

Lefley, H. P. (1976). Acculturation, childrearing, and self-esteem in two North American Indian tribes. *Ethos, 4*, 385–401.

Leineweber, M., & Arensman, E. (2003). Culture change and mental health: The epidemiology of suicide in Greenland. *Archives of Suicide Research, 7*, 41–50.

Leitenberg, H., Detzer, M. J., & Srebnik, D. (1993). Gender differences in masturbation and the relation of masturbation experience in preadolescence and/or early adolescence to sexual behavior and sexual adjustment in young adulthood. *Archives of Sexual Behavior, 22*, 87–98.

Lemann, N. (2000). The Big Test: *The secret history of the American meritocracy.* New York: Farrar, Straus, & Giroux.

Lempers, J. D., & Clark-Lempers, D. S. (1993). A functional comparison of same-sex and opposite-sex friendships during adolescence. *Journal of Adolescent Research, 8*, 89–108.

Lenhart, A., Arafeh, S., Smith, A., & Macgill, A. R. (2008). *Writing, technology, and teens.* Retrieved July 18, 2008, from http://www.pewinternet.org/pdfs/PIP_Writing_Report_FINAL3.pdf

Lenhart, A., & Fox, S. (2006). *Bloggers: A portrait of the internet's new storytellers.* Retrieved January 11, 2008, from http://www.pewinternet.org/PPF/r/186/report_display.asp

Lenhart, A., & Madden, M. (2005). *Teen content creators and consumers.* Retrieved June 1, 2008, from http://www.pewinternet.org/pdfs/PIP_Teens_Content_Creation.pdf

Lenhart, A., & Madden, M. (2007). *Social networking websites & teens: An overview.* Retrieved January 2, 2008, from http://www.pewinternet.org/PPf/R/198/report_display.asp

Lenhart, A., & Madden, M. (2007, January 7). *Social networking websites and teens: An overview.* Retrieved January 3, 2008, from http://www.pewinternet.org/PPF/R/198/report_display.asp

Lepper, M. R., & Gurtner, J. (1989). Children and computers: Approaching the 21st century. *American Psychologist, 44*, 170–178.

Lerner, R. M (2006) Developmental science, developmental systems, and contemporary theories of human development. In R. M. Lerner & W. Damon (Eds.), *Handbook of child psychology (6th ed.): Vol 1, Theoretical models of human development* (pp. 1–17). Hoboken, NJ: John Wiley & Sons.

Leszczynski, J. P., & Strough, J. (2008) The contextual specificity of masculinity and femininity in early adolescence. *Social Development, 17*(3), 719–736.

LeVay, S. (1991). A difference in hypothalamic structure between heterosexual and homosexual men. *Science, 253*, 1034–1037.

Levesque, R. J. (1993). The romantic experience of adolescents in satisfying love relationships. *Journal of Youth & Adolescence, 22*, 219–251.

Levin, T. (2008, December 3). Higher education may soon be unaffordable for most Americans, report says. *New York Times*, p. A17.

Levine, A., & Cureton, J. S. (1998). When hope and fear collide: *A portrait of today's college student.* San Franciso: Jossey–Bass.

LeVine, D. N. (1966). The concept of masculinity in Ethiopian culture. *International Journal of Social Psychiatry, 12,* 17–23.

Levine, J. A., Emery, C. R., & Pollack, H. (2007). The well-being of children born to teen mothers. *Journal of Marriage and Family, 69*(1), 105–122.

Levine, M., Smolak, L., & Hayden, H. (1994). The relation of sociocultural factors to eating attitudes and behaviors among middle school girls. *Journal of Early Adolescence, 14,* 471–490.

Levinson, D. J. (1978). *The seasons of a man's life.* New York: Knopf.

Levitt, M. J., Guacci-Franco, N., & Levitt, J. L. (1993). Convoys of social support in childhood and early adolescence: Structure and function. *Developmental Psychology, 29,* 811–818.

Lewin, T. (1998, May 1). Birth rates for teen-agers declined sharply in the 90's. *New York Times,* p. A-17.

Lewin, T. (2008, December 3). Higher education may soon be unaffordable for most Americans, report says. *New York Times,* p. A-17.

Lewin-Epstein, N. (1981). *Youth employment during high school.* Washington, DC: National Center for Education Statistics.

Lewinsohn, P. M., Clarke, G. N., Hops, H., & Andrews, J. (1990). Cognitive, behavioral treatment for depressed adolescents. *Behavior Therapy, 21,* 385–401.

Lewis, C. G. (1981). How adolescents approach decisions: Changes over grades seven to twelve and policy implications. *Child Development, 52,* 538–554.

Lewis, D. O., Mallouh, C., & Webb, V. (1989). Child abuse, delinquency, and violent criminality. In D. Cicchetti & V. Carlson (Eds.), *Child maltreatment: Theory and research in the causes and consequences of child abuse and neglect* (pp. 707–721). New York: Cambridge University Press.

Lewis, M., Feiring, C., & Rosenthal, S. (2000). Attachment over time. *Child Development, 71,* 707–720.

Lewis, T., Stone, J., Shipley, W., & Madzar, S. (1998). The transition from school to work: An examination of the literature. *Youth & Society, 29,* 259–292.

Lichter, P. (1978). *The boy who dared to rock: The definitive Elvis.* New York: Dolphin Books.

Lichty, L. W. (1989). Television in America: Success story. In P. S. Cook, D. Gomery, & L. W. Lichty (Eds.), *American media* (pp. 159–176). Los Angeles: Wilson Center Press.

Licitra-Klecker, D. M., & Waas, G. A. (1993). Perceived social support among high-stress adolescents. The role of peers and family. *Journal of Adolescent Research, 8,* 381–402.

Lieber, E., Nihira, K., & Mink, I. T. (2004). Filial piety, modernization, and the challenges of raising children for Chinese immigrants: Quantitative and qualitative evidence. *Ethos, 32,* 324–347.

Liebkind, K., & Kosonen, L. (1998). Acculturation and adaptation: A case of Vietnamese children and youths in Finland. In J. Nurmi (Ed.), *Adolescents, cultures, and conflicts* (pp. 199–224). New York: Garland.

Liechty, M. (1995). Media, markets, and modernization: Youth identities and the experience of modernity in Kathmandu, Nepal. In V. Amit-Talai & H. Wulff (Eds.), *Youth cultures: A cross-cultural perspective* (pp. 166–201). New York: Routledge.

Lien, L., Dalgard, F., Heyerdahl, S., Thoresen, M., & Bjertness, E. (2006). The relationship between age of menarche and mental distress in Norwegian adolescent girls and girls from different immigrant groups in Norway: Results from urban city cross-sectional survey. *Social Science & Medicine, 63*(2), 285–295.

Lillard, A. (2007). Pretend play in toddlers. In C. A. Brownell & C. B. Kopp (Eds.), *Socioemotional development in the toddler years* (pp. 149–176). New York: Guilford.

Lim, S-L., & Lim, B. K. (2004). Parenting style and child outcomes in Chinese and immigrant Chinese families-current findings and cross-cultural considerations in conceptualization and research. *Marriage & Family Review, 35,* 21–43.

Lin, C. C., & Fu, V. R. (1990). A comparison of child-rearing practices among Chinese, immigrant Chinese, and Caucasian-American parents. *Child Development, 61,* 429–433.

Linares, L. O., Leadbeater, B. J., Kato, P. M., & Jaffe, L. (1991). Predicting school outcomes for minority group mothers: Can subgroups be identified? *Journal of Research on Adolescence, 1,* 379–400.

Lindberg, L. D., Jones, R., & Santelli, J. S. (2008). Noncoital sexual activities among adolescents. *Journal of Adolescent Health, 43*(3), 231–238.

Linden-Ward, B., & Green, C. H. (1993). *American women in the 1960s: Changing the future.* New York: Twayne.

Ling, P. M., & Glantz, S. A. (2002). Why and how the tobacco industry sells cigarettes to young adults: Evidence from industry documents. *American Journal of Public Health, 92,* 908–916.

Ling, R. (2003). Fashion and vulgarity in the adoption of the mobile telephone among teens in Norway. In L. Fortunati & J. Katz (Eds.), *Mediating the human body: Technology, communication, and fashion* (pp. 93–102). Mahwah, NJ: Lawrence Erlbaum.

Linn, M., & Songer, N. (1991). Cognitive and conceptual change in adolescence. *American Journal of Education, 99,* 379–417.

Linn, M., & Songer, N. (1993). How do students make sense of science? *Merrill-Palmer Quarterly, 39,* 47–73.

Linn, M. C., De Benedictus, T., & Delucchi, K. (1982). Adolescent reasoning about advertising: Preliminary investigations. *Child Development, 53,* 1599–1613.

Lipka, O., & Siegel, L. S. (2006). Learning disabilities. In D. A. Wolfe & E. J. Mash (Eds.), *Behavioral and emotional disorders in adolescents: Nature assessment and treatment* (pp. 410–443). New York: Guilford Publications.

Lips, H. M. (1993). *Sex and gender: An introduction.* Mountain View, CA: Mayfield.

Lips, H. M. (2004). The gender gap in possible selves: Divergence of academic self-views among high school and university students. *Sex Roles, 50,* 357–371.

Lissau, I. (2004). Body mass index and overweight in adolescents in 13 European countries, Israel, and the United States. *Archives of Pediatric and Adolescent Medicine.*

Litt, I. F., & Vaughan, V. C., III (1987). Growth and development during adolescence. In R. E. Behrman, V. C. Vaughan, & W. E. Nelson (Eds.), *Textbook of pediatrics* (13th ed., pp. 20–24). Philadelphia: Saunders.

Liu, L. L., Slap, G. B., Kinsman, S. B., & Khalid, N. (1994). Pregnancy among American Indian adolescents: Reactions and prenatal care. *Journal of Adolescent Health, 15,* 336–341.

Liu, X., Kaplan, H. B., & Risser, W. (1992). Decomposing the reciprocal relationships between academic achievement and general self-esteem. *Youth & Society, 24,* 124–148.

Liu, Y-L. (2008). An examination of three models of the relationships between parental attachments and adolescents' social functioning and depressive symptoms. *Journal of Youth and Adolescence, 37*(8), 941–952.

Livesley, W. J., & Bromley, D. B. (1973). *Person perception in childhood and adolescence.* New York: Wiley.

Livingstone, S. (2003). Children's use of the internet: Reflections on the emerging research agenda. *New Media & Society, 5,* 147–166.

Livson, N., & Peskin, H. (1980). Perspectives on adolescence from longitudinal research. In J. Adel-

son (Ed.), *Handbook of adolescent psychology* (pp. 47–98). New York: Wiley.

Lloyd, B. T., & Mendez, J. L. (2001). Botswana adolescents' interpretation of American music videos: So that's what that means! *Journal of Black Psychology, 27,* 464–476.

Lloyd, C. (Ed.). (2005). *Growing up global: The changing transitions to adulthood in developing countries.* Washington, DC: National Research Council and Institute of Medicine.

Lloyd, C. B., Grant, M., & Ritchie, A. Gender differences in time use among adolescents in developing countries: Implications of rising school enrollment rates. *Journal of Research on Adolescence, 18*(1), 99–120.

Lo, V., & Wei, R. (2005). Exposure to internet pornography and Taiwanese adolescents' sexual attitudes and behavior. *Journal of Broadcasting & Electronic Media, 49*(2), 221–237.

Lobel, T. E., Nov-Krispin, N., Schiller, D., Lobel, O., & Feldman, A. (2004). Perceptions of social status, sexual orientation, and value dissimilarity. Gender discriminatory behavior during adolescence and young adulthood: A developmental analysis. *Journal of Youth & Adolescence, 33,* 535–546.

Lock, J. (2002). Treating adolescents with eating disorders in the family context: Empirical and theoretical considerations. *Child & Adolescent Psychiatric Clinics of North America, 11,* 331–342.

Loeber, R., Farrington, D. P., Stouthamer-Loeber, M., Moffitt, T. E., & Caspi, A. (2001). The development of male offending: Key findings from the first decade of the Pittsburgh Youth Study. In R. Bull (Ed.), *Children and the law: The essential readings* (pp. 336–378). Malden, MA: Blackwell.

Loeber, R., Farrington, D. P., Stouthamer-Loeber, M., & Van Kammen, W. B. (1998). Multiple risk factors for multiproblem boys: Co-occurrence of delinquency, substance use, attention deficit, conduct problems, physical aggression, covert behavior, depressed mood, and shy/withdrawn behavior. In R. Jessor, (Ed.), *New perspectives on adolescent risk behavior* (pp. 90–149). New York: Cambridge University Press.

Long, B. (1989). Heterosexual involvement of unmarried undergraduate females in relation to self-evaluations. *Journal of Youth and Adolescence, 18,* 489–500.

Long, N., Slater, E., Forehand, R., & Fauber, R. (1988). Continued high or reduced interparental conflict following divorce: Relation to young adolescent adjustment. *Journal of Consulting and Clinical Psychology, 56,* 467–469.

Longest, K. C., & Shanahan, M. J. (2007). Adolescent work intensity and substance use: The mediational and moderational roles of parenting. *Journal of Marriage & Family, 69*(3), 703–720.

Longmore, M. A., Manning, W. D., & Giordano, P. C. (2001). Preadolescent parenting strategies and teens' dating and sexual initiation: A longitudinal analysis. *Journal of Marriage and the Family, 63,* 322–335.

Longo, D. J., Clum, G. A., & Yaeger, N. J. (1988). Psychosocial treatment for recurrent genital herpes. *Journal of Consulting and Clinical Psychology, 56,* 61–66.

Lord, S., Eccles, J. S., & McCarthy, K. (1994). Risk and protective factors in the transition to junior high school. *Journal of Early Adolescence, 14,* 162–199.

Loughlin, C., & Barling, J. (1999). The nature of youth employment. In J. Barling & E. K. Kelloway (Eds.), *Youth workers: Varieties of experience* (pp. 17–36). Washington, DC: American Psychological Association.

Loukas, A., & Robinson, S. (2004). Examining the moderating role of perceived school climate in early adolescent adjustment. *Journal of Research on Adolescence, 14,* 209–233.

Lucas, A. R. (1991). Eating disorders. In M. Lewis (Ed.), *Child and adolescent psychiatry* (pp. 573–583). Baltimore, MD: Williams & Wilkins.

Lucas, S. (1996). Selective attrition in a newly hostile regime: The case of 1980 sophomores. *Social Forces, 75*, 511–533.

Luciana, M., Conklin, H. M., Hooper, C. J., & Yarger, R. S. (2005). The development of nonverbal working memory and executive control processes in adolescents. *Child Development, 76*, 697–712.

Lull, J. (1980). The social uses of television. *Human Communication Research, 6*, 197–209.

Luna, B., Graver, K. E., Urban, T. A., Lazar, N. A., & Sweeney, J. A. (2004). Maturation of cognitive processes from late childhood to adulthood. *Child Development, 75*, 1357–1372.

Luo, Q., Fang, X., & Aro, P. (1995, March). *Selection of best friends by Chinese adolescents.* Paper presented at the meeting of the Society for Research in Child Development, Indianapolis, IN.

Luo, S., Klohnen, E. C. (2005). Assortative mating and marital quality in newlyweds: A couple-centered approach. *Journal of Personality & Social Psychology, 88*, 304–326.

Lupia, A., & Philpot, T. S. (2005). Views from inside the net: How websites affect young adults' political interest. *Journal of Politics, 67*(4), 1122–1142.

Luria, Z., Friedman, S., & Rose, M. D. (1987). *Human sexuality.* New York: Wiley.

Lykken, D. T., & Tellegen, A. (1993). Is human mating advantageous or the result of lawful choice? A twin study of mate selection. *Journal of Personality and Social Psychology, 65*, 56–68.

Lynch, M. E. (1991). Gender intensification. In R. M. Lerner, A. C. Petersen, & J. Brooks-Gunn (Eds.), *Encyclopedia of adolescence* (Vol. 1). New York: Garland.

Lynd, R. S., & Lynd, H. M. (1927/1957). Middletown: *A study of modern American culture.* New York: Harvest.

Lynd, R. S., & Lynd, H. M. (1929). Middletown: *A study in modern American culture.* New York: Harvest Books.

Lyng, S. (1991). Dysfunctional risk taking: Criminal behavior as edgework. In N. J. Bell & R. W. Bell (Eds.), *Adolescent risk taking* (pp. 107–130). Newbury Park, CA: Sage.

Lynne, S. D., Graber, J. A., Nichols, T. R., Brooks-Gunn, J., & Botvin, G. J. (2007). Links between pubertal timing, peer influences, and externalizing behaviors among urban students followed through middle school. *Journal of Adolescent Health, 40*(2).

Lytle, L. J., Bakken, L., & Romig, C. (1997). Adolescent female identity development. *Sex Roles, 37*, 175–185.

Lytton, H., & Romney, D. M. (1991). Parents' differential socialization of boys and girls: A meta-analysis. *Psychological Bulletin, 109*, 267–296.

Ma, H. K. (2005). The relation of gender-role classifications to the prosocial and antisocial behavior of Chinese adolescents. *Journal of Genetic Psychology, 166*, 189–201.

Ma, J., Betts, N. M., Horacek, T., Georgiou, C., White, A., & Nitzke, S. (2002). The importance of decisional balance and self-efficacy in relation to stages of change for fruit and vegetable intakes by young adults. *American Journal of Health Promotion, 16*, 157–166.

MacBeth, T. (2006). Notel, Unitel, Multitel study. In J. J. Arnett (Ed.), *Encyclopedia of children, adolescents, and the media.* Thousand Oaks, CA: Sage.

Maccoby, E. (1990). Gender and relationships: A developmental account. *American Psychologist, 45*, 755–775.

Maccoby, E., & Martin, J. (1983). Socialization in the context of the family: Parent-child interaction. In E. M. Hetherington (Ed.), *Handbook of child psychology: Socialization, personality, and social development* (Vol. 4). New York: Wiley.

Maccoby, E. E. (2002). Gender and group process: A developmental perspective. *Current Directions in Psychological Science, 11*, 54–57.

Maccoby, E. E., Depner, C. E., & Mnookin, R. H. (1988). Custody of children following divorce. In E. M. Hetherington & J. D. Aresteh (Eds.), *Impact of divorce, single parenting, and stepparenting* (pp. 91–114). Hillsdale, NJ: Erlbaum.

Maccoby, E. E., & Jacklin, C. N. (1974). *The psychology of sex differences.* Stanford, CA: Stanford University Press.

MacDonald, N. E., Wells, G. A., Fisher, W. A., Warren, W. K., King, M. A., Doherty, J. A., & Bowie, W. R. (1990). High-risk STD/HIV behavior among college students. *JAMA: Journal of the American Medical Association, 263*, 3155–3159.

Macek, P. (2007). Czech Republic. In J. J. Arnett, R. Ahmed, B. Nsamenang, T. S. Saraswathi, & R. Silbereisen (Eds.), *International encyclopedia of adolescence.* New York: Routledge.

Macek, P. Bejček, J., & Vaníčková, J. (2007). Contemporary Czech emerging adults: Generation growing up in the period of social changes. *Journal of Adolescent Research, 22*, 444–475.

MacFarquhar, R., & Schoenhals, J. (2006). *Mao's last revolution.* Cambridge, MA: Harvard University Press.

Madaras, L., & Madaras, A. (2002). *My body, myself for girls/boys.* New York: Newmarket.

Maddell, D., & Muncer, S. (2004). Back from the beach but hanging on the telephone? English adolescents' attitudes and experiences of mobile phones and the internet. *CyberPsychology & Behavior, 73*, 359–367.

Maggs, J. L. (1999). Alcohol use and binge drinking as goal-directed action during the transition to post-secondary education. In J. Schulenberg, J. L. Maggs, & K. Hurrelmann (Eds.), *Health risks and developmental transitions during adolescence* (pp. 345–371). New York: Cambridge University Press.

Magnuson, M. J., & Dundes, L. (2008). Gender differences in "social portraits" reflected in MySpace profiles. *CyberPsychology & Behavior, 11*(2), 239–241.

Magnussen, L., Ehiri, J. E., Ejere, H. O. D., & Jolly, P. E. (2004). Interventions to prevent HIV/AIDS among adolescents in less developed countries: Are they effective? *International Journal of Adolescent Medicine & Health, 16*, 303–323.

Magnusson, D., Stattin, H., & Allen, V. (1986). Differential maturation among girls and its relation to social adjustment in a longitudinal perspective. In P. Baltes, D. Featherman, & R. Lerner (Eds.), *Life span development and behavior* (Vol. 7). Hillsdale, NJ: Erlbaum.

Magolda, M. B. B. (1997). Students' epistemologies and academic experiences: Implications for pedagogy. In K. Arnold & I. C. King (Eds.), *Contemporary higher education: International issues for the 21st century* (pp. 117–140). New York: Garland.

Mahiri, J., & Conner, E. (2003). Black youth violence has a bad rap. *Journal of Social Issues, 59*, 121–140.

Mahn, H. (2003). Periods in child development: Vygotsky's perspective. In A. Kozulin, & B. Gindis (Eds.), *Vygotsky's educational theory in cultural context* (pp. 119–137). New York: Cambridge University Press.

Maira, S. (2004). Imperial feelings: Youth culture, citizenship, and globalization. In M. M. Suárez-Oroszco & B. D. Hilliard-Qin (Eds.), *Globalization: Culture and education in the new millennium* (pp. 203–234). Berkeley: University of California Press.

Majors, R. (1989). Cool pose: The proud signature of black survival. In M. S. Kimmel & M. A. Messner (Eds.), *Men's lives* (pp. 83–87). New York: Macmillan.

Majors, R., & Billson, J. M. (1992). *Cool pose.* New York: Lexington.

Makhlouf, H., & Abdelkader, M. (1997). *The current status of research and training in population and health in the Arab region and the future needs.* Cairo, Egypt: Cairo Demographic Center.

Males, M. (2002). Is Joseph Califano a gateway drug? *Youth Today, 11*, 51.

Malik, S. (2000, February). *Arab adolescents facing the 3rd millennium.* Paper prepared for the meeting of the Study Group on Adolescence in the 21st Century, Washington, DC.

Mallett, S., Rosenthal, D., & Keys, D. (2005). Young people, drug use and family conflict: Pathways into homelessness. *Journal of Adolescence, 28*, 185–199.

Malyon, A. K. (1981). The homosexual adolescent: Developmental issues and social bias. *Child Welfare, 60*, 321–330.

Manchester, W. (1973). *The glory and the dream: A narrative history of America, 1932–1972.* New York: Bantam.

Manis, F. R., Keating, D. P., & Morrison, F. J. (1980). Developmental differences in the allocation of processing capacity. *Journal of Experimental Child Psychology, 29*, 156–169.

Manlove, J., Franzetta, K., Ryan, S., & Moore, K. (2006). Adolescent sexual relationships, contraceptive consistency, and pregnancy prevention approaches. In A. C. Crouter & A. Booth (Eds.), *Romance and sex in adolescence and emerging adulthood: Risks and opportunities* (pp. 181–212). The Penn State University family issues symposia series. Mahwah, NJ: Lawrence Erlbaum.

Manlove, J. The influence of high school dropout and school disengagement on the risk of school-age pregnancy. *Journal of Research on Adolescence. 8*(2), 187–220.

Mantzoros, C. S. (2000). The role of leptin in reproduction. *Annals of the New York Academy of Sciences, 900*, 174–83.

Marcia, J. (1966). Development and validation of ego identity status. *Journal of Personality and Social Psychology, 3*, 551–558.

Marcia, J. (1980). Identity in adolescence. In J. Adelson (Ed.), *Handbook of adolescent psychology.* New York: Wiley.

Marcia, J. (1989). Identity and intervention. *Journal of Adolescence, 12*, 401–410.

Marcia, J. E. (1993). The relational roots of identity. In J. Kroger (Ed.), *Discussions on ego identity* (pp. 101–120). Hillsdale, NJ: Erlbaum.

Marcia, J. E. (1994). The empirical study of ego identity. In H. A. Bosma & L. G. Tobi (Ed.), *Identity and development: An interdisciplinary approach* (pp. 67–80). Thousand Oaks, CA: Sage.

Marcia, J. E. (1999). Representational thought in ego identity, psychotherapy, and psychosocial developmental theory. In I. E. Siegel (Ed.), *Development of mental representation: Theories and applications* (pp. 391–414). Mahwah, NJ: Erlbaum.

Marcia, J. E. (2002). Identity and psychosocial development in adulthood. *Identity, 2*, 7–28.

Marcia, J. E., & Carpendale, J. (2004). Identity: Does thinking make it so? In C. Lightfoot & M. Chandler (Eds.), *Changing conceptions of psychological life.* Mahwah, NJ: Erlbaum.

Marcotte, D., Fortin, L., Potvin, P., & Papillon, M. (2002). Gender differences in depressive symptoms during adolescence: Role of gender-typed charateristics, self-esteem, body image, stressful life events, and pubertal status. *Journal of Emotional and Behavioral Disorders, 10*, 29–42.

Margolin, G. (1988). Marital conflict is not marital conflict is not marital conflict. In R. D. Peters & R. J. McMahon (Eds.), *Social learning and systems approaches to marriage and the family* (pp. 193–216). New York: Brunner/Mazel.

Maris, R. W., Silverman, M., & Canetto, S. S. (1997). *Review of suicidology, 1997.* New York: Guilford.

Markstrom-Adams, C. (1989). Androgyny and its relation to adolescent psychological well-being: A review of the literature. *Sex Roles, 21*, 469–473.

Markstrom-Adams, C. (1992). A consideration of intervening factors in adolescent identity formation. In G. R. Adams, T. P. Gullotta, & R. Montemayor (Eds.), *Adolescent identity formation* (pp. 173–192). Newbury Park, CA: Sage.

Markstrom, C. A. (2008). *Empowerment of North American Indian girls: Ritual expressions at puberty.* Lincoln, NE: University of Nebraska Press.

Markus, H., & Kitayama, S. (1991). Culture and the self: Implications for cognition, emotion, and motivation. *Psychological Review, 98,* 224–253.

Markus, H., & Nurius, R. (1986). Possible selves. *American Psychologist, 41,* 954–969.

Markus, H. R., & Kitayama, S. (2003). Culture, self, and the reality of the social. *Psychological Inquiry, 14,* 277–283.

Marohn, R. C. (1993). Residential services. In P. H. Tolan & B. J. Cohler (Eds.), *Handbook of clinical research and practice with adolescents* (pp. 453–466). New York: Wiley.

Marsh, H. W. (1991). Employment during high school: Character building or subversion of academic goals? *Sociology of Education, 64,* 172–189.

Marsh, H. W., Chessor, D., Craven, R., & Roche, L. (1995). The effects of gifted and talented programs on academic self-concept: The big fish strikes again. *American Educational Research Journal, 32,* 285–319.

Marsh, H. W., & Hau, K. T. (2003). Big fish little pond effect on academic self-concept: A cross-cultural (26-country) test of the negative effects of academically selective schools. *American Psychologist, 58,* 364–376.

Marsh, H. W., & Kleitman, S. (2005). Consequences of employment during High School: Character building, subversion of academic goals, or a threshold? *American Educational Research Journal, 42,* 331–369.

Marshall, M. (1979). *Weekend warriors.* Palo Alto, CA: Mayfield.

Marshall, R. (1994). *School to work processes in the United States.* Paper presented at the Carnegie Council/Johann Jacobs Foundation, November 3–5, Marbach Castle, Germany.

Marshall, T. C. Cultural differences in intimacy: The influence of gender-role ideology and individualism-collectivism. *Journal of Social and Personal Relationships. 25*(1), 143–168.

Marshall, W. (1978). *Puberty.* In F. Falkner & J. Tanner (Eds.), *Human growth* (Vol. 2). New York: Plenum.

Marshall, W. A., & Tanner, J. M. (1970). Variations in the pattern of pubertal changes in boys. *Archives of Disease in Childhood, 45,* 13–23.

Marston, P. J., Hecht, M. L., & Robers, T. (1987). "True love ways": The subjective experience and communication of romantic love. *Journal of Social and Personal Relationships, 4,* 387–407.

Martin, C. A., Kelly, T. H., Rayens, M. K., et al. (2002). Sensation seeking, puberty and nicotine, alcohol, and marijuana use in adolescence. *Journal of the American Academy of Child & Adolescent Psychiatry, 41,* 1495–1502.

Martin, C. L. (1987). A ratio measure of sex stereotyping. *Journal of Personality and Social Psychology, 52,* 489–499.

Martin, J. (1976). The education of adolescents. Washington, DC: U.S. Office of Education.

Martin, N. C. (1997, April). *Adolescents' possible selves and the transition to adulthood.* Paper presented at the meeting of the Society for Research in Child Development, Washington, DC.

Martinez, R. S., & Semrud-Clikeman, M. (2004). Emotional adjustment and school functioning of young adolescents with multiple versus single learning disabilities. *Journal of Learning Disabilities, 37,* 411–420.

Marván, M. L., Vacio, A., García-Yáñez, G., & Espinosa-Hernández, G. (2007). Attitudes toward menarche among Mexican preadolescents. *Women & Health, 46*(1), 7–23.

Mason, M. G., & Gibbs, J. C. (1993). Social perspective taking and moral judgment among college students. *Journal of Adolescent Research, 8,* 109–123.

Mason, W. A., Kosterman, R., Hawkins, J. D., Haggerty, K. P., & Spoth, R. L. (2003). Reducing adolescents' growth in substance use and delinquency: Randomized trial effects of a parent-training prevention intervention. *Prevention Science, 4*(3), 203–213.

Mason, W. A., & Windle, M. (2002). A longitudinal study of the effects of religiosity on adolescent alcohol use and alcohol-related problems. *Journal of Adolescent Research, 17,* 346–363.

Massad, C. (1981). Sex role identity and adjustment during adolescence. *Child Development, 52,* 1290–1298.

Massoni, K. (2004). Modeling work: Occupational messages in seventeen magazines. *Gender & Society, 18,* 47–65.

Masten, A. S. (2001). Ordinary magic: Resilience processes in development. *American Psychologist, 56*(3), 227–238.

Masten, A. S. (2007). Competence, resilience, and development in adolescence: Clues for prevention science. In D. Romer & E. F. Walker (Eds.), *Adolescent psychopathology and the developing brain: Integrating brain and prevention science* (pp. 31–52). New York: Oxford University Press.

Masten, A. S., Obradovic, J., & Burt, K.B. (2006). Resilience in emerging adulthood: Developmental perspectives on continuity and transformation. In J. J. Arnett and J. L. Tanner (Eds.), *Emerging adults in America: Coming of age in the 21st century* (pp. 173–190). Washington, DC: American Psychological Association Press.

Masters, W. H., Johnson, V. E., & Kolodny, R. C. (1994). *Heterosexuality.* New York: HarperCollins.

Mathematica Policy Research (2001). *Evaluation of the Job Corps program: A longitudinal study.* Washington, DC: Author.

Mathews, J. (2001, April 24). Value of teens' work questioned. *Washington Post,* p. A13.

Mathews, J. (2002a, December 14). Teaching schools forced to rethink approach. *Washington Post,* p. A12.

Mathews, J. (2002b, November 26). Rating a college's intellectual intangibles. *Washington Post,* p. A12.

Mathur, R., & Berndt, T. J. (2006). Relations of friends' activities to friendship quality. *Journal of Early Adolescence, 26*(3), 365–388.

Maton, K. I., Hrabowski, F. A., Özdemir, M., & Wimms, H. (2008). Enhancing representation, retention, and achievement of minority students in higher education: A social transformation theory of change. In Shinn, M. & Yoshikawa, H. (Eds.), *Toward positive youth development: Transforming schools and community programs* (pp. 115–132). New York: Oxford University Press.

Matsumoto, D. (2002). *The new Japan: Debunking seven cultural stereotypes of Japan.* New York: Intercultural Press.

Matyas, M. L. (1987). Keeping undergraduate women in science and engineering: Contributing factors and recommendations for action. In J. Z. Daniels & J. B. Kahle (Eds.), *Contributions to the fourth GASAT conference* (Vol. 3, pp. 112–122). Washington, DC: National Science Foundation.

Matza, D., & Sykes, G. (1961). Juvenile delinquency and subterranean values. *American Sociological Review, 26,* 712–719.

Maxwell, K. A. (2002). Friends: The role of peer influence across adolescent risk behaviors. *Journal of Youth & Adolescence, 31,* 267–277.

Mayhew, D. R. (2007). Driver education licensing in North America: Past, present, and future. *Journal of Safety Research, 38*(2), 229–235.

Mayhew, D. R., & Simpson, H. M. (2002). The safety value of driver education and training. *Injury Prevention, 8(Suppl 2),* ii3–ii8.

Maynard, A. E., & Martini, M. I. (Eds.) (2005). *Learning in cultural context: Family, peers, and school.* New York: Kluwer.

Mayseless, O., & Scharf, M. (2003). What does it mean to be an adult? The Israeli experience. In J. J. Arnett & N. Galambos (Eds.), *New Directions in Child and Adolescent Development* (Vol. 100, pp. 5–20). San Francisco: Jossey-Bass.

Mazur, E. Self-presentation and interaction in blogs of adolescents and young emerging adults. *Journal of Adolescent Research.*

Mazza, J. J. (2006). Youth suicidal behavior: A crisis in need of attention. In F. A. Villarruel & T. Luster (Eds.), *The crisis in youth mental health: Critical issues and effective programs, Vol. 2: Disorders in adolescence. Child psychology and mental health* (pp. 155–177). Westport, CT: Praeger Publishers/Greenwood Publishing Group.

McAdoo, H. P. (1996). *Black families* (3rd ed.). Newbury Park, CA: Sage.

McAdoo, H. P. (Ed.). (1993). *Family ethnicity.* Newbury Park, CA: Sage.

McAdoo, H. P. (1998). African American families. In C. H. Mindel, R. W. Haberstein, & R. Wright, Jr. (Eds.), *Ethnic families in America: Patterns and variations* (pp. 361–381). Upper Saddle River, NJ: Prentice-Hall.

McBurnett, K., Raine, A. Stouthamer-Loeber, M., Loeber, R., Kumar, A. M., Kumar, M., & Lahey, B. B. (2005). Mood and hormone responses to psychological challenge in adolescent males with conduct problems. *Biological Psychiatry. 57.*

McCarthy, B. (1994). Youth on the street: Violent offenders and victims. In H. Coward (Ed.), *Anger in our city: Youth seeking meaning* (pp. 69–107). Victoria, B.C., Canada: Centre for Studies in Religion and Society.

McCarthy, B., & Hagan, J. (1992). Surviving on the street: The experiences of homeless youth. *Journal of Adolescent Research, 7,* 412–430.

McCarthy, D. M., Tomlinson, K. L., Anderson, K. G., Marlatt, G. A., & Brown, S. A. (2005). Relapse in alcohol- and drug-disordered adolescents with comorbid psychopathology: Changes in psychiatric symptoms. *Psychology of Addictive Behaviors, 19,* 28–34.

McCord, J. (1990). Problem behaviors. In S. Feldman & G. Elliott (Eds.), *At the threshold: The developing adolescent* (pp. 414–430). Cambridge, MA: Harvard University Press.

McCord, W., & McCord, J. (1959). *Origins of crime: A new evaluation of the Cambridge-Somerville study.* New York: Columbia University Press.

McDade, T. W., & Worthman, C. M. (2004). Socialization ambiguity in Samoan adolescents: A model for human development and stress in the context of culture change. *Journal of Research on Adolescence, 14,* 49–72.

McDaniel, A. K., & Coleman, M. (2003). Women's experiences of midlife divorce following long-term marriage. *Journal of Divorce & Remarriage, 38,* 103–128.

McDowell, M. A., Brody, D. J., & Hughes, J. P. Has age at menarche changed? Results from the National Health and Nutrition Examination Survey (NHANES) 1999–2004. *Journal of Adolescent Health, 40*(3) 227–231.

McElhaney, K. B., Antonishak, J., & Allen, J. P. "They like me, they like me not": Popularity and adolescents' perceptions of acceptance predicting social functioning over time. *Child Development, 79*(3), 720–731.

McFalls, J. A., Jr. (1990). The risks of reproductive impairment in the later years of childbearing. *Annual Review of Sociology, 16,* 491–519.

McGaha-Garnett, V. (2008) Needs assessment for adolescent mothers: Building resiliency and student success towards high school completion. In G.

R. Walz, J. C. Bleuer, & R. K Yep (Eds.), *Compelling counseling interventions: Celebrating VIS-TAS' fifth anniversary* (pp. 11–20). Alexandria, VA: American Counseling Association.

McGee, G. W. (2004). Closing the achievement gap: Lessons from Illinois' golden spike high poverty high performing schools. *Journal of Education for Students Placed at Risk, 9,* 97–125.

McHale, S. M, Crouter, A. C., & Whiteman, S. D. (2003). The family contexts of gender development in childhood and adolescence. *Social Development, 12*(1), 125–148.

McIntosh, H., Metz, E., & Youniss, J. (2005). Community service and identity formation in adolescents. In J. L. Mahoney, R. W., Larson, & J. S., Eccles (Eds.), *Organized activities as contexts of development: Extracurricular activities, after-school and community programs* (pp. 331–351). Mahwah, NJ: Lawrence Erlbaum.

McKenry, P. C., & Price, S. J. (1995). Divorce: A comparative perspective. In B. B. Ingoldsby & S. Smith (Eds.), *Families in multicultural perspective* (pp. 187–212). New York: Guilford.

McKnight, A. J., & Peck, R. C. (2002). Graduated licensing: What works? *Injury Prevention, 8*(Suppl 2), ii32–ii38.

McKnight, C. C., Crosswhite, F. J., Dossey, J. A., Kifer, E., Swafford, J. O., Travers, K. J., & Cooney, T. J. (1987). *The underachieving curriculum: Assessing U.S. school mathematics from an international perspective.* Champaign, IL: Stipes.

McKnight Investigators. (2003). Risk factors for the onset of eating disorders in adolescent girls: Results on the McKnight longitudinal risk factor study. *American Journal of Psychiatry, 160,* 248–254.

McLanahan, S., & Bumpass, L. (1988). Intergenerational consequences of family disruption. *American Journal of Sociology, 94,* 130–152.

McLanahan, S., & Sandefur, G. (1994). *Growing up in a single-parent family: What hurts, what helps.* Cambridge, MA: Harvard University Press.

McLaughlin, C. S., Chen, C., Greenberger, E., & Biermeier, C. (1997). Family, peer, and individual correlates of sexual experience among Caucasian and Asian American late adolescents. *Journal of Research on Adolescence, 7,* 33–54.

McLean Taylor, J., Carmen N. V., & Martina C. V. (2007) Latina girls: "We're like sisters—most times!" In B. J. R. Leadbeater & N. Way (Eds.), *Urban girls revisited: Building strengths* (pp. 157–174). New York: New York University Press.

McLeer, S. V., Deblinger, E., Henry, D., & Orvaschel, H. (1992). Sexually abused children at high risk for posttraumatic stress disorder. *Journal of the American Academy of Child and Adolescent Psychiatry, 31,* 875–879.

McLellan, J. A. & Youniss, J. (1999). A representational system for peer crowds. In I. E. Sigel (Ed.), *Development of mental representation: Theories and applications* (pp. 437–449). Mahwah, NJ: Erlbaum.

McLellan, J. A., & Youniss, J. (2003). Two systems of youth service: Determinants of voluntary and required youth community service. *Journal of Youth & Adolescence, 32,* 47–58.

McMahon, S. D., & Watts, R. J. (2002). Ethnic identity in urban African American youth: Exploring links with self-worth, aggression, and other psychosocial variables. *Journal of Community Psychology, 30,* 411–432.

McMaster, L., Connolly, J., Pepler, D., & Craig, W. (1997, June). Peer to peer sexual harassment in early adolescence: A developmental perspective. Paper presented at the annual meeting of the Canadian Psychological Association, Toronto, Canada.

McNamara, J. R., & Grossman, K. (1991). Initiation of dates and anxiety among college men and women. *Psychological Reports, 69,* 252–254.

McNelles, L. R., & Connolly, J. A. (1999). Intimacy between adolescent friends: Age and gender differences in intimate affect and intimate behaviors. *Journal of Research on Adolescence, 9,* 143–159.

McRobbie, A. (1994). Shut up and dance: Youth culture and changing modes of femininity. In A. McRobbie (Ed.), *Postmodernism and popular culture* (pp. 177–197). London: Routledge.

Mead, M. (1928). *Coming of age in Samoa.* New York: Morrow.

Mead, M. (1928/1978). *Culture and commitment.* Garden City, NY: Anchor.

Mead, M. (1970). *Culture and commitment: A study of the generation gap.* Garden City, NY: Doubleday.

Meaden, P. M., Hartlage, S. A., & Cook-Karr, J. (2005). Timing and severity of symptoms associated with the menstrual cycle in a community-based sample in the midwestern United States. *Psychiatry Research, 134,* 27–36.

Means, J. (1991). Coping with a breakup: Negative mood regulation expectancies and depression following the end of a romantic relationship. *Journal of Personality and Social Psychology, 60,* 327–334.

Mechanic, D., & Hansell, S. (1989). Divorce, conflict, and adolescent well-being. *Journal of Health and Social Behavior, 30,* 105–116.

Meeus, W. (2007). Netherlands. In J. J. Arnett, R. Ahmed, B. Nsamenang, T. S. Saraswathi, & R. Silbereisen (Eds.), *International encyclopedia of adolescence.* New York: Routledge.

Meeus, W., Iedema, J., Helsen, M., & Vollebergh, W. (1999). Patterns of adolescent identity development: Review of literature and longitudinal analysis. *Developmental Review, 19,* 419–461.

Mehrabian, A., & Wixen, W. J. (1986). Preferences for individual video games as a function of their emotional effects on players. *Journal of Applied Social Psychology, 16,* 3–15.

Melby, J., & Conger, R. (1996). Parental behaviors and adolescent academic performance: A longitudinal analysis. *Journal of Research on Adolescence, 6,* 113–137.

Mendelson, M. J., Mendelson, B. K., & Andrews, J. (2000). Self-esteem, body esteem, and body mass in late adolescence: Is a competence * importance model needed? *Journal of Applied Developmental Psychology, 21,* 249–266.

Mendle, J., Turkheimer, E., & Emery, R. E. (2007). Detrimental psychological outcomes associated with early pubertal timing in adolescent girls. *Developmental Review, 27,* 151–171.

Mensch, B. S., Bruce, J., & Greene, M. E. (1998). *The uncharted passage: Girls' adolescence in the developing world.* New York: Population Council.

Messersmith, E. E., Garrett, J. L., Davis-Kean, P. E., Malanchuk, O., & Eccles, J. S. (2008). Career development from adolescence through emerging adulthood: Insights from information technology occupations. *Journal of Adolescent Research, 23*(2), 206–227.

Metz, E., McLellan, J., & Youniss, J. (2003). Types of voluntary service and adolescents' civic development. *Journal of Adolescent Research, 18,* 188–203.

Metz, E. C., & Youniss, J. (2005). Longitudinal gains in civic development through school-based required services. *Political Psychology, 26,* 413–437.

Michael, K. D., & Crowley, S. L. (2002). How effective are treatments for child and adolescent depression? A meta-analytic review. *Clinical Psychology Review, 22,* 247–269.

Michael, R. T., Gagnon, J. H., Laumann, E. O., & Kolata, G. (1994). *Sex in America.* Boston: Little, Brown.

Michael, R. T., Gagnon, J. H., Laumann, E. O., & Kolata, G. (1995). *Sex in America: A definitive survey.* New York: Warner Books.

Midgely, C., & Urdan, T. (1995). Predictors of middle school students' use of self-handicapping strategies. *Journal of Early Adolescence, 15,* 389–411.

Migliazzo, A. C. (1993, Winter). Korean leadership in the 21st century: A profile of the coming generation. *Korea Journal,* pp. 60–67.

Miller, B. (1998). *Families matter: A research synthesis of family influences on adolescent pregnancy.* Washington, DC: National Campaign to Prevent Teen Pregnancy.

Miller, B. C., Bayley, B. K., Christensen, M., Leavitt, S. C., & Coyl, D. D. (2003). Adolescent pregnancy and childbearing. In R. G. Adams & D. M. Berzonsky (Eds.), *Blackwell handbook of adolescence* (pp. 415–449). Malden, MA: Blackwell.

Miller, B. C., & Benson, B. (1999). Romantic and sexual relationship development during adolescence. In W. Furman, B. B. Brown, & C. Feiring (Eds.), *The development of romantic relationships in adolescence. Cambridge studies in social and emotional development* (pp. 99–121). New York: Cambridge University Press.

Miller, B. D. (1995). Precepts and practices: Researching identity formation among India Hindu adolescents in the United States. *New Directions for Child Development, 67,* 71–85.

Miller, B., & Moore, K. (1990). Adolescent sexual behavior, pregnancy, and parenting: Research through the 1980s. *Journal of Marriage and the Family, 52,* 1025–1044.

Miller, J. B. (1976). *Toward a new psychology of women.* New York: Routledge & Kegan Paul.

Miller, J. B. (1991). The development of women's sense of self. In J. V. Jordan, A. G. Kaplan, J. B. Miller, I. P. Stiver, & J. L. Surrey (Eds.), *Women and growth in connection* (pp. 11–26). New York: Guilford.

Miller, K. S., Forehand, R., & Kotchick, B. A. (1999). Adolescent sexual behavior in two ethnic minority samples: The role of family variables. *Journal of Marriage & the Family, 61*(1), 85–98.

Miller, P., & Simon, W. (1980). The development of sexuality in adolescence. In J. Adelson (Ed.), *Handbook of adolescent psychology* New York: Wiley.

Miller, P. H., & Weiss, M. G. (1981). Children's attention allocation, understanding of attention, and performance on the incidental learning task. *Child Development, 52,* 1183–1190.

Miller-Johnson, S., & Costanzo, P. (2004). If you can't beat 'em ... induce them to join you: Peer-based interventions during adolescence. In J. G. Kupersmidt & K. A. Dodge (Eds.), *Children's peer relations: From development to intervention* (pp. 209–222). Washington, DC: American Psychological Association.

Miller-Johnson, S., Costanzo, P. R., Cole, J. D., Rose, M. R., & Browne, D. C. (2003). Peer social structure and risk-taking behaviors among African American early adolescents. *Journal of Youth & Adolescence, 32,* 375–384.

Miller-Johnson, S., Winn, D. M., Coie, J., Maumary-Gremaud, A., Hyman, C., Terry, R., & Lochman, J. (1999). Motherhood during the teen years: A developmental perspective on risk factors for childbearing. *Development and Psychopathology, 11,* 85–100.

Miller-Johnson, S., Winn, D. M. C., Coie, J. D., Malone, P. S., & Lochman, J. (2004). Risk factors for adolescent pregnancy reports among African American males. *Journal of Research on Adolescence, 14,* 471–495.

Miller-Jones, D. (1989). Culture and testing. *American Psychologist, 44,* 360–366.

Millett, K. (1970/2000). *Sexual politics.* Urbana-Champaign: University of Illinois Press.

Mills, C. J., & Noyes, H. L. (1984). Patterns and correlates of initial and subsequent drug use among adolescents. *Journal of Consulting and Clinical Psychology, 52,* 231–243.

Millstein, S. (1989). Adolescent health: Challenges for behavioral scientists. *American Psychologist, 44,* 837–842.

Millstein, S., Petersen, A., & Nightingale, E. (Eds.) (1993). *Promoting the health of adolescents: New directions for the twenty-first century.* New York: Oxford University Press.

Min, A. (1995). *Katherine.* New York: Berkley.

Mines, M. (1988). Conceptualizing the person: Hierarchical society and individual autonomy in India. *American Anthropologist, 90,* 568–579.

Minuchin, P. (2002). Looking toward the horizon: Present and future in the study of family systems. In J. P. McHale & W. S. Grolinick (Eds.), *Retrospect and prospect in the study of families.* Mahwah, NJ: Erlbaum.

Minuchin, S. (1974). Families and family therapy. Cambridge, MA: Harvard University Press.

Minuchin, S., Rosman, B., & Baker, L. (1978). *Psychosomatic families: Anorexia nervosa in context.* Cambridge, MA: Harvard University Press.

Miracle, T. S., Miracle, A. W., & Baumeister, R. F. (2003). *Human sexuality: Meeting your basic needs.* Upper Saddle River, NJ: Prentice Hall.

Miranda, D., & Claes, M. (2004). Rap music genres and deviant behaviors in French-Canadian adolescents. *Journal of Youth & Adolescence, 33,* 113–122.

Miranda, R., Meyerson, L. A., Long, P. J., Marx, B. P., & Simpson, S. M. (2002). Sexual assault and alcohol use: Exploring the self-medication hypothesis. *Violence & Victims, 17,* 205–217.

Mirchev, M. (1994). Bulgaria. In K. Hurrelman (Ed.), *International handbook of adolescence* (pp. 77–91). Westport, CT: Greenwood.

Modell, J. (1989). *Into one's own: From youth to adulthood in the United States,* 1920–1975. Berkeley: University of California Press.

Modell, J., Furstenberg, E., Jr., & Hershberg, T. (1976). Social change and transitions to adulthood in historical perspective. *Journal of Family History, 1,* 7–32.

Modell, J., & Goodman, M. (1990). Historical perspectives. In S. S. Feldman & G. Elliott (Eds.), *At the threshold: The developing adolescent.* Cambridge, MA: Harvard University Press.

Moffitt, T. (1993). Adolescence-limited and life-course persistent antisocial behavior: A developmental taxonomy. *Psychological Review, 100,* 674–701.

Moffitt, T. E. (2003). Life-course-persistent and adolescence-limited antisocial behavior: A 10-year research review and a research agenda. In B. B. Lahey & T. E. Moffitt (Eds.), *Causes of conduct disorder and juvenile delinquency* (pp. 49–75). New York: Guilford.

Moffitt, T. E. (2007). A review of research on the taxonomy of life-course persistent versus adolescence-limited antisocial behavior. In D. J. Flannery, A. T. Vazsonyi, & I. D. Waldman (Eds.), *The Cambridge handbook of violent behavior and aggression* (pp. 49–74). New York: Cambridge University Press.

Moffitt, T. E., Caspi, A. (2001). Childhood predictors differentiate life-course persistent and adolescence-limited antisocial pathways among males and females. *Development & Psychopathology, 13,* 355–375.

Moffitt, T. E., & Caspi, A. (2005). Life-course persistent and adolescent-limited antisocial males: Longitudinal follow-up to adulthood. In D. M. Stoff & E. J. Susman (Eds.), *Developmental psychobiology of aggression* (pp. 161–186). New York: Cambridge University Press.

Moffitt, T. E., Caspi, A., Belsky, J., & Silva, P. A. (1992). Childhood experience and onset of menarche: A test of a sociobiological model. *Child Development, 63,* 47–58.

Moffitt, T., Caspi, A., Harkness, A., & Silva P. (1993). The natural history of change in intellectual performance: Who changes? How much? Is it meaningful? *Journal of Child Psychology and Psychiatry, 34,* 455–506.

Moffitt, T. E., Caspi, A., Harrington, H., & Milne, B. J. (2002). Males on the life-course persistent and adolescence-limited antisocial pathways: Follow-up at 26 years. *Development and Psychopathology, 14,* 179–207.

Moffitt, T. E., Caspi, A., Rutter, M., & Phil, S. (2002). Sex differences in antisocial behavior: Conduct disorder, delinquency, and violence in the Dunedin longitudinal study. New York: Cambridge University Press.

Moffitt, T., & Silva, P. (1988). IQ and delinquency: A direct test of the differential detection hypothesis. *Journal of Abnormal Psychology, 97,* 330–333.

Moffitt, T. E., Caspi, A., Rutter, M., & Silva, P. A. Sex differences in antisocial behaviour: Conduct disorder, delinquency and violence in the Dunedin longitudinal study: Book review. *European Journal of Psychiatry, 16*(3).

Mogelonsky, M. (1996, May). The rocky road to adulthood. *American Demographics, 26–36,* 56.

Molina, B., & Chassin, L. (1996). The parent-adolescent relationship at puberty: Hispanic ethnicity and parent alcoholism as moderators. *Developmental Psychology, 32,* 675–686.

Moline, A. E. (1987). Financial aid and student persistence: An application of causal modeling. *Research in Higher Education, 26*(2), 130–147.

Money, J. (1980). Love and love sickness: *The science of sex, gender difference, and pair-bonding.* Baltimore, MD: Johns Hopkins University Press.

Money, J. (1988). Gay, straight, and in-between: *The sexology of erotic orientation.* New York: Oxford University Press.

Monitoring the Future. (2000). Available: www.monitoringthefuture.org

Monitoring the Future. (2002). *ISR study finds drinking and drug use decline after college.* Ann Arbor, MI: Author. Available: www.umich.edu/newsinfo/releases/2002/Jan02/r013002a.html.

Monitoring the Future. (2005). Data tables and figures. Retrieved on September 30, 2005, from http://www.monitoringthefuture.org

Montemayor, R. (1982). The relationship between parent–adolescent conflict and the amount of time adolescents spend alone and with parents and peers. *Child Development, 53,* 1512–1519.

Montemayor, R. (1984). Maternal employment and adolescents' relations with parents, siblings, and peers. *Journal of Youth and Adolescence, 13,* 543–557.

Montemayor, R., & Flannery, D. J. (1989). A naturalistic study of the involvement of children and adolescents with their mothers and friends: Developmental differences in expressive behavior. *Journal of Adolescent Research, 4,* 3–14.

Montgomery, D. (1999, May 14). No rant. Just rave: Peaceful protesters defend party scene. *Washington Post,* pp. C-1, C-6.

Montgomery, M. J. (2005). Psychosocial intimacy and identity: From early adolescence to emerging adulthood. *Journal of Adolescent Research, 20,* 346–374.

Moore, K., Myers, D., Morrison, D., Nord, C., Brown, B., & Edmonston, B. (1993). Age at first childbirth and later poverty. *Journal of Research on Adolescence, 3,* 393–422.

Moore, K., Peterson, J., & Furstenberg, E., Jr. (1986). Parental attitudes and the occurrence of early sexual activity. *Journal of Marriage and the Family, 48,* 777–782.

Moore, K. A., Chalk, R., Scarpa, J., & Vandivere, S. (2002, August). Family strengths: Often overlooked, but real. *Child Trends Research Brief,* 1–8.

Moore, K. A., & Stief, T. M. (1991). Changes in marriage and fertility behavior: Behavior versus attitudes of young adults. *Youth & Society, 22,* 362–386.

Moore, M., & Brooks-Gunn, J. (2002). Adolescent parenthood. In M. H. Bornstein (Ed.), *Handbook of parenting, Vol. 3: Being and becoming a parent* (2nd ed., pp. 173–214). Mahwah, NJ: Erlbaum.

Moore, R. (2005) Alternative to what? Subcultural capital and the commercialization of a music scene. *Deviant Behavior, 26,* 229–252.

Moore, S., & Cartwright, C. Adolescents' and young adults' expectations of parental responsibilities in stepfamilies. *Journal of Divorce & Remarriage, 43*(1–2), 109–127.

Moore, S., & Rosenthal, D. (2006). *Sexuality in adolescence: Current trends.* New York: Routledge/Taylor & Francis Group.

Moretti, M. M., & Wiebe, V. J. (1999). Self-discrepancy in adolescence: Own and parental standpoints on the self. *Merrill-Palmer Quarterly, 45,* 624–649.

Moriguchi, Y., Ohnishi, T., Mori, T., Matsuda, H., & Komaki, G. Changes of brain activity in the neural substrates for theory of mind during childhood and adolescence. *Psychiatry and Clinical Neurosciences. 61*(4), 355–363.

Morris, B. R. (1999, February 25). You want fries with that website? For some young techies, after-school tinkering turns into work and wealth. *New York Times,* pp. E-1, E-7.

Morrison, D. M. (1985). Adolescent contraceptive behavior: A review. *Psychological Bulletin, 98,* 538–568.

Mortimer, J., & Finch, M. (1996). *Adolescents, work, and family: An intergenerational developmental analysis.* Newbury Park, CA: Sage.

Mortimer, J., Finch, M., Ryu, S., Shanahan, M., & Call, K. (1993, March). *The effects of work intensity on adolescent mental health, achievement and behavioral adjustment: New evidence from a prospective study.* Paper presented at the biennial meeting of the Society for Research in Child Development, New Orleans, LA.

Mortimer, J., Finch, M., Ryu, S., Shanahan, M. J., & Call, K. (1996). The effects of work intensity on adolescent mental health, achievement, and behavioral adjustment: New evidence from a prospective study. *Child Development, 67,* 1243–1261.

Mortimer, J. T.; Finch, M., Shanahan, M., & Ryu, S. Adolescent work history and behavioral adjustment. *Journal of Research on Adolescence, 2*(1), 59–80.

Mortimer, J. T. (2003). *Working and growing up in America.* Cambridge, MA: Harvard University Press.

Mortimer, J. T., Harley, C., & Aronson, P. J. (1999). How do prior experiences in the workplace set the stage for transitions to adulthood? In A. Booth, A. C. Crouter, & M. J. Shanahan (Eds.), *Transitions to adulthood in a changing economy: No work, no family, no future?* (pp. 131–159). Westport, CT: Praeger.

Mortimer, J. T., & Johnson, M. K. (1998). New perspectives on adolescent work and the transition to adulthood. In R. Jessor (Ed.), *New perspectives on adolescent risk behavior* (pp. 425–496). New York: Cambridge University Press.

Mortimer, J. T., & Staff, J. (2004). Early work as a source of developmental discontinuity during the transition to adulthood. *Development & Psychopathology, 16,* 1047–1070.

Mortimer, J. T., Vuolo, M., Staff, J., Wakefield, S., & Xie, W. (2008). Tracing the timing of "career" acquisition in a contemporary youth cohort. *Work and Occupations, 35*(1), 44–84.

Mortimer, J. T., Zimmer-Gembeck, M. J., Holmes, M., & Shanahan, M. J. (2002). The process of occupational decision making: Patterns during the transition to adulthood. *Journal of Vocational Behavior, 61,* 439–465.

Motley, C. M., & Henderson, G. R. (2008). The global hip-hop diaspora: Understanding the culture. *Journal of Business Research, 61*(3), 243–253.

Motola, M., Sinisalo, P., & Guichard, J. (1998). Social habitus and future plans. In J. Nurmi (Ed.), *Adolescents, cultures, and conflicts* (pp. 43–73). New York: Garland.

Mounts, N. S. (2004). Adolescents' perceptions of parental management of peer relationships in an ethnically diverse sample. *Journal of Adolescent Research, 19,* 446–467.

Mouw, T., & Entwisle, B. Residential segregation and interracial friendship in schools. *American Journal of Sociology, 112*(2), 394–441.

Mullatti, L. (1995). Families in India: Beliefs and realities. *Journal of Comparative Family Studies, 26,* 11–26.

Mullis, I., & Jenkins, L. B. (1988). *The science report card: Elements of risk and recovery: Trends and achievement based on the 1986 national assessment.* Princeton, NJ: Educational Testing Service.

Mullis, I., Owen, E., & Phillips, G. (1990). *America's challenge: Accelerating academic achievement.* A summary of findings from 20 years of NAEP. Washington, DC: U.S. Department of Education.

Mum's Not the Word. (1999, September). *Population Today,* p. 3.

Mundy, L. (1999, May 16). Teen angels. *Washington Post Magazine,* p. 6.

Munoz, R. A., & Amado, H. (1986). Anorexia nervosa: An affective disorder. *New Directions for Mental Health Services, 31,* 13–19.

Munsch, J., & Wampler, R. (1993). Ethnic differences in early adolescents' coping with school stress. *American Journal of Orthopsychiatry, 63,* 633–646.

Murnane, R. J., & Levy, F. (1997). *Teaching the new basic skills: Principles for educating children to thrive in a changing economy.* New York: Free Press.

Murnan, R. J., & Levy, F. (2004). *The new division of labor: How computers are creating the next job market.* Princeton, NJ: Princeton University Press.

Murnen, S. K., & Levine, M. P. (2007). *Do fashion magazines promote body dissatisfaction in girls and women?* Paper presented at the annual meeting of the American Psychological Association, San Francisco, CA.

Murphy, K., & Schneider, B. (1994). Coaching socially rejected early adolescents regarding behaviors used by peers to infer liking: A dyad-specific intervention. *Journal of Early Adolescence, 14,* 83–95.

Mussen, P. H., Conger, J. J., Kagan, J., & Huston, A. (1990). *Child development and personality* (7th ed.). New York: Harper & Row.

Myers, D. G. (1990). *Social psychology* (3rd ed.). New York: McGraw Hill.

Myers, J. (2000, December/January). Columbine's shadow shades U.S. budget. *Youth Today,* 9.

Mytton, J., DiGuiseppi, C., & Gough, D. (2002). School-based violence prevention programs. *Archives of Pediatric and Adolescent Medicine, 156,* 752–762.

Naar-King, S., Silvern, V., Ryan, V., & Sebring, D. (2002). Type and severity of abuse as predictors of psychiatric symptoms in adolescence. *Journal of Family Violence, 17,* 133–149.

Nabi, R. L., & Krcmar, M. (2004). Conceptualizing media enjoyment as attitude: Implications for mass media effects research. *Communication Theory, 14,* 288–310.

Nader, P. R., Bradley, R. H., Houts, R. M., McRitchie, S. L., & O'Brien, M. (2008). Moderate-to-vigorous physical activity from ages 9 to 15 years. *JAMA: Journal of the American Medical Association, 300*(3), 295–305.

Naito, T., & Gielen, U. P. (2003). The changing Japanese family: A psychological portrait. In J. L. Roopnarine & U. P. Gielen (Eds.), *Families in global perspective.* Boston: Allyn & Bacon.

Nangle, D. W., Erdley, C. A., Carpenter, E. M., & Newman, J. E. (2002). Social skills training as a treatment for aggressive children and adolescents: A developmental-clinical integration. *Aggression and Violent Behavior, 7,* 169–199.

Nanji, A. (1993). The Muslim family in North America: Continuity and change. In H. P. McAdoo (Ed.), *Family ethnicity: Strength in diversity* (pp. 229–242). Mahwah, NJ: Erlbaum.

Nash, S. C., & Feldman, S. S. (1981). Sex role and sex-related attributes: Continuity and change across the family life cycle. In M. E. Lamb & A. L. Brown (Eds.), *Advances in developmental psychology* (pp. 1–36). Hillsdale, NJ: Erlbaum.

National Campaign to Prevent Teen Pregnancy (2002). *With one voice: America's adults and teens sound off about teen pregnancy.* Washington, DC: Author. Available: www.teenpregnancy.org

National Center for Education Statistics (1999). *The condition of education, 1999.* Washington, DC: U.S. Department of Education.

National Center for Education Statistics (2002). *The condition of education 2002.* Washington, DC: U.S. Department of Education. Available: www.nces.gov

National Center for Education Statistics (2005). *The condition of education, 2005.* Washington, DC: U.S. Department of Education. Available: www.nces.gov

National Center for Health Statistics (2000). *Healthy United States, 2000, with adolescent health chartbook.* Bethesda, MD: *U.S. Department of Health and Human Services.*

National Commission on Excellence in Education. (1983). *A nation at risk: The imperative for educational reform.* Washington, DC: U.S. Department of Education.

National Education Commission on Time and Learning. (1994). *Prisoners of time.* Washington, DC: U.S. Government Printing Office.

National Highway Traffic Safety Administration (NHTSA). (1996). *Graduated driver licensing system for novice drivers.* Washington, DC: U.S. Department of Transportation.

National Highway Traffic Safety Administration (NHTSA). (1999). Traffic safety facts, 1998. Washington, DC: Author.

National Highway Traffic Safety Administration (NHTSA). (2002). *Traffic safety facts.* Washington, DC: U.S. Department of Transportation.

National Math, Reading Tests Fail in House (1997, September 17). *St. Louis Post-Dispatch,* p. A-1.

National Study of Youth & Religion (2002a). *Religion and American adolescent delinquency, risk behaviors, and constructive social activities.* Chapel Hill, NC: Author. Available www.youthandreligion.org

National Study of Youth & Religion (2002b). Religious youth are more likely to have positive relationships with their fathers. Available: http://www.youthandreligion.org

Needle, R., Su, S., & Doherty, W. (1990). Divorce, remarriage, and adolescent substance use: A prospective longitudinal study. *Journal of Marriage and the Family, 52,* 157–169.

Neiderhiser, J. M.; Reiss, D., & Hetherington, E. M. The Nonshared Environment in Adolescent Development (NEAD) Project: A longitudinal family study of twins and siblings from adolescence to young adulthood. *Twin Research and Human Genetics. 10*(1), 74–83.

Neisser, U., Boodoo, G., Bouchard, T. J., Boykin, A. W., Brody, N., Ceci, S. J., Halpern, D. F., Loehlin, J. C., Perloff, R., Sternberg, R. J., & Urbina, S. (1996). Intelligence: Knowns and unknowns. *American Psychologist, 51,* 77–101.

Nelson, L. J. (2003). Rites of passage in emerging adulthood: Perspectives of young Mormons. *New Directions in Child and Adolescent Development.*

Nelson, L. J., Badger, S., & Wu, B. (2004). The influence of culture in emerging adulthood: Perspectives of Chinese college students. *International Journal of Behavioral Development, 28,* 26–36.

Nelson, L. J., & Chen, X. (2007). Emerging adulthood in China: The role of social and cultural factors. *Child Development Perspectives, 1,* 86–91.

Nelson, L. (2008). Perceived status of adulthood, adult roles, and culture: An examination of emerging adulthood in Romania. *International Journal of Behavioral Development.*

Neto, F. (2002). Acculturation strategies among adolescents from immigrant families in Portugal. *International Journal of Intercultural Relations, 26,* 17–38.

Nevid, J. S., Rathus, S. A., & Greene, B. (2003). *Abnormal psychology in a changing world.* Upper Saddle River, NJ: Prentice Hall.

Newcomb, A. F., Bukowski, W. M., & Pattee, L. (1993). Children's peer relations: A meta-analytic review of popular, rejected, neglected, controversial, and average sociometric status. *Psychological Bulletin, 113,* 99–128.

Newcomer, S., & Udry, J. R. (1985). Oral sex in an adolescent population. *Archives of Sexual Behavior, 14,* 41–56.

Newcomer, S., & Udry, J. R. (1987). Parental marital status effects on adolescent sexual behavior. *Journal of Marriage and the Family, 49,* 235–240.

Newman, K. S. (1999). *No shame in my game: The working poor in the inner city.* New York: Knopf.

Newmann, F. (1992). Higher-order thinking and prospects for classroom thoughtfulness. In F. Newmann (Ed.), *Student engagement and achievement in American high schools.* New York: Teachers College Press.

NIAID (2000). *Fact sheet: Chlamydial infection.* Bethesda, MD: Author.

Nichter, M. (2001). *Fat talk: What girls and their parents say about dieting.* Cambridge, MA: Harvard University Press.

Nickerson, A. B., & Nagle, R. J. (2005). Parent and peer attachment in late childhood and early adolescence. *Journal of Early Adolescence, 25,* 223–249.

Nie, N. H., & Erbring, L. (2000). *Internet and society: A preliminary report.* Palo Alto, CA: Stanford Institute for the Quantitative Study of Society. Available: http://www.stanford.edu/group/siqss/Press_Release/Preliminary_Report.pdf

Nishikawa, S., Norlander, T., Fransson, P., & Sundbom, E. (2007). A cross-cultural validation of adolescent self-concept in two cultures: Japan and Sweden. *Social Behavior and Personality, 35*(2), 269–286.

Noble, J., Cover, J., & Yanagishita, M. (1996). *The world's youth.* Washington, DC: Population Reference Bureau.

Nock, S. L. (1998). The consequences of premarital fatherhood. *American Sociological Review, 63,* 250–263.

Noell, J. W., & Ochs, L. M. (2001). Relationship of sexual orientation to substance use, suicidal ideation, suicide attempts, and other factors in a population of homeless adolescents. *Journal of Adolescent Health, 29,* 31–36.

Noguchi, K. (2007). Examination of the content of individualism/collectivism scales in cultural comparisons of the USA and Japan. *Asian Journal of Social Psychology, 10*(3), 131–144.

Nolan, S. A., Flynn, C., & Garber, J. (2003). Prospective relations between rejection and depression in young adolescents. *Journal of Personality & Social Psychology, 85,* 745–755.

Nolen-Hoeksma, S. (1987). Sex differences in unipolar depression: Evidence and theory. *Psychological Bulletin, 101,* 259–282.

Nolen-Hoeksma, S., & Girgus, J. (1994). The emergence of gender differences in depression during adolescence. *Psychological Bulletin, 115,* 424–443.

Nolen-Hoeksema, S., Wisco, B. E., & Lyubomirsky, S. (2008). Rethinking rumination. *Perspectives on Psychological Science, 3*(5), 400–424.

Noller, P. (2005). Sibling relationships in adolescence: Learning and growing together. *Personal Relationships, 12,* 1–22.

Noller, P., Feeney, J. A., & Ward, C. M. (1997). Determinants of marital quality: A partial test of Lewis & Spanier's model. *Journal of Family Studies, 3,* 226–251.

Nonnemaker, J. M., McNeely, C. A., & Blum, R. W. M. (2003). Public and private domains of religiosity and adolescent health risk behaviors: Evidence from the national longitudinal study of adolescent health. *Social Science & Medicine, 57,* 2049–2054.

Nora, A. (1987). Determinants of retention among Chicano college students: A structural model. *Research in Higher Education, 26 (1)*, 31–59.

Nottelmann, E. D., Susman, E. J., Blue, J. H., Inoff-Germain, G., Dorn, L. D., Loriaux, D. L., Cutler, G. B., & Chrousos, G. P. (1987). Gonadal and adrenal hormone correlates of adjustment in early adolescence. In R. M. Lerner & T. T. Foch (Eds.), *Biological-psychological interactions in early adolescence.* Hillsdale, NJ: Erlbaum.

Novik, T. S., Hervas, A., Ralston, S. J., Dalsgaard, S., Pereira, R. R., & Lorenzo, M. J. (2006). ADORE Study Group. *European Child & Adolescent Psychiatry, 15*(Suppl. 1), 5–24.

Nsamenang, A. B. (1998). Work organization and economic management in sub-Saharan Africa: From a Eurocentric orientation toward an Afrocentric perspective. *Psychology and Developing Societies, 10*, 75–97.

Nsamenang, A. B. (2000, February). *Adolescence in sub-Saharan Africa.* Paper prepared for the meeting of the Study Group on Adolescence in the 21st Century, Washington, DC.

Nsamenang, A. B. (2002). Adolescence in sub-Saharan Africa: An image constructed from Africa's triple inheritance. In B. B. Brown, R. Larson, & T. S. Saraswathi (Eds.), *The World's Youth: Adolescence in Eight Regions of the Globe* (pp. 61–104). New York: Cambridge University Press.

Nurmi, J., & Siurala, L. (1994). Finland. In K. Hurrelmann (Ed.), *International handbook of adolescence* (pp. 131–145). Westport, CT: Greenwood Press.

Nurnberger, J. I., Jr., & Gershon, E. S. (1992). Genetics. In E. S. Paykell (Ed.), *Handbook of affective disorders* (2nd ed., pp. 131–148). New York: Guilford.

Nussbaum, M. (1992). Human functioning and social justice: In defense of Aristotelian essentialism. *Political Theory, 20*, 202–246.

O'Brien, D. (1997). The disappearing moral curriculum. *The Key Reporter, 62 (4)*, 1–4.

O'Brien, S., & Bierman, K. (1988). Conceptions and perceived influence of peer groups: Interviews with preadolescents and adolescents. *Child Development, 59*, 1360–1365.

O'Connor, T. G., Allen, J. P., Bell, K. L., & Hauser, S. T. (1996). Adolescent–parent relationships and leaving home in young adulthood. *New Directions in Child Development, 71*, 39–52.

O'Connell, J. M., Novins, D. K., Beals, J., Whitesell, N., Libby, A. M., Orton, H. D., & Croy, C. D [AI-SUPERPFP Team, US]. (2007). Childhood characteristics associated with stage of substance use of American Indians: Family background, traumatic experiences, and childhood. *Addictive Behaviors, 32*(12), 3142–3152.

O'Hare, W. P. (1992). America's minorities: The demographics of diversity. *Population Bulletin, 47 (4)*, 1–47. (Washington, DC: Population Reference Bureau).

O'Hare, W. P., Pollard, K. M., Mann, T. L., & Kent, M. M. (1991). African Americans in the 1990s. *Population Bulletin, 46 (1)*, 1–40. (Washington, DC: Population Reference Bureau).

O'Leary, K. D., Malone, J., & Tyree, A. (1994). Physical aggression in early marriage: Prerelationship and relationship effects. *Journal of Consulting and Clinical Psychology, 62*, 594–602.

O'Malley, P., & Bachman, J. (1983). Self-esteem: Change and stability between ages 13 and 23. *Developmental Psychology, 19*, 257–268.

O'Malley, P. M., Bachman, J. G., & Johnston, L. D. (1988). Period, age, and cohort effects on substance use among young Americans: A decade of change, 1976–1986. *American Journal of Public Health, 78*, 1315–1321.

O'Sullivan, L. F., & Meyer-Bahlberg, H. F. L. (2003). African American and Latina inner-city girls' reports of romantic and sexual development. *Journal of Social & Personal Relationships, 20*, 221–238.

Oades-Sese, G. V.; Esquivel, G. B.; & Añon, C. (2007). Identifying gifted and talented culturally and linguistically diverse children and adolescents. In G. B. Esquivel, E. C. Lopez, & Nahari, S. G. (Eds.), *Handbook of multicultural school psychology: An interdisciplinary perspective* (pp. 453–477). Mahwah, NJ: Lawrence Erlbaum.

Obeidallah, D., Brennan, R. T., Brooks-Gunn, J., & Earls, F. (2004). Links between pubertal timing and neighborhood contexts: Implications for girls' violent behavior. *Journal of the American Academy of Child & Adolescent Psychiatry, 43*, 1460–1468.

Oberlander, S. E., Black, M. M., Starr, R. H., Jr. African American adolescent mothers and grandmothers: A multigenerational approach to parenting. *American Journal of Community Psychology, 39*(1–2), 37–46.

Obermeyer, C. M. (2000). Sexuality in Morocco: Changing context and contested domain. *Culture, Health and Sexuality, 2*, 239–254.

Offer, D. (1969). *The psychological world of the teenager.* New York: Basic Books.

Offer, D., Ostrov, E., & Howard, K. L. (1981). *The adolescent: A psychological self-portrait.* New York: Basic Books.

Offer, D., & Schonert-Reichl, K. A. Debunking the myths of adolescence: Findings from recent research. *Journal of the American Academy of Child & Adolescent Psychiatry. 31*(6), 1003–1014.

Ogbu, J. (1989, April). *Academic socialization of black children: An inoculation against future failure?* Paper presented at the biennial meeting of the Society for Research in Child Development, Kansas City.

Ogbu, J. (1990a). Minority status and literacy in comparative perspective. *Daedalus, 119*, 141–168.

Ogbu, J. (1990b). Minority education in comparative perspective. *Journal of Negro Education, 59*, 45–57.

Ogbu, J. U. (2003). *Black American students in an affluent suburb: A study of academic disengagement.* Mahwah, NJ: Lawrence Erlbaum.

Ogden, T., & Haden, K. A. (2006). Multisystemic treatment of serious behavior problems in youth: Sustainability of effectiveness two years after intake. *Child and Adolescent Mental Health, 11*(3), 142–149.

Okie, S. (2002, April 10). Study cites alcohol link in campus deaths. *Washington Post*, p. A2.

Oksman, V., & Rautainen, P. (2003). Extension of the hand: Children's and teenagers' relationship with the mobile phone in Finland. In L. Fortunati & J. E. Katz (Eds.), *Mediating the human body: Technology, communication and fashion* (pp. 103–111). Mahwah, NJ: Erlbaum.

Oliver, J. E., & Ha, S. E. (2008). The segregation paradox: Neighborhoods and interracial contact in multiethnic America. In B. A. Sullivan, M. Snyder, & J. Sullivan (Eds.), *Cooperation: The political psychology of effective human interaction* (p. 161–180). Malden, MA: Blackwell Publishing.

Oliver, M. B. (2006). Mood management theory. In J. J. Arnett (Ed.), *Encyclopedia of children, adolescents, and the media* (pp. 539–540). Thousand Oaks, CA: Sage.

Ollendick, T. H., Shortt, A. L., & Sander, J. B. (2008). Internalizing disorders in children and adolescents. In J. E. Maddux & B. A. Winstead (Eds.), *Psychopathology: Foundations for a contemporary understanding* (2nd ed., pp. 375–399). New York: Routledge/Taylor & Francis Group.

Olson, C. K., Kutner, L. A., & Warner, D. E. (2008). The role of violent video game content in adolescent development: Boys' perspectives. *Journal of Adolescent Research, 23*, 55–75.

Olson, C. K., Kutner, L. A., Warner, D. E., Almerigi, J., Naer, L., Nicholi, A. M., et al. (2007). Factors correlated with violent video game use by adolescent boys and girls. *Journal of Adolescent Health, 41*, 77–83.

Olson, E. (2007, May 28). OMG! Cute boys, kissing tips and lots of pics, as magazines find a niche. *New York Times*, 156.

Olthof, T., & Goossens, F. A. (2008). Bullying and the need to belong: Early adolescents' bullying-related behavior and the acceptance they desire and receive from particular classmates. *Social Development, 17*(1), 24–46.

Oltmanns, T. F., & Emery, R. E. (2001). *Abnormal psychology (3rd ed.).* Upper Saddle River, NJ: Prentice Hall.

Olweus, D. (2000). Bullying. In A. E. Kazdin (Ed.), *Encyclopedia of psychology, Vol. 1* (pp. 487–489). Washington, DC: American Psychological Association, Oxford University Press.

Oritz, V. (1995). The diversity of Latino families. In R. E. Zambrana (Ed.), *Understanding Latino families: Scholarship, policy and practice.* Thousand Oaks, CA: Sage.

Orr, E., & Ben-Eliahu, E. (1993). Gender differences in idiosyncratic sex-typed self-images and self-esteem. *Sex Roles, 29*, 271–296.

Osgood, D. W. (2008, November). *Illegal behavior.* Presented to the National Research Council Committee on the Science of Adolescence workshop on Individual Processes and Adolescent Risk Behavior, Washington, DC.

Osgood, D. W., Anderson, A. L., & Shaffer, J. N. (2005). Unstructured leisure in the after-school hours. In L. J. Mahoney, W. R. Larson et al. (Eds.), *Organized activities as contexts of development: Extracurricular activities, after-school and community programs* (pp. 45–64). Mahwah, NJ: Lawrence Erlbaum.

Osgood, D. W., Johnston, L., O'Malley, P., & Bachman, J. (1988). The generality of deviance in late adolescence and early adulthood. *American Sociological Review, 53*, 81–93.

Osgood, D. W., & Lee, H. (1993). Leisure activities, age, and adult roles across the life span. *Society and Leisure, 16*, 181–208.

Osgood, D. W., Wilson, J. K., Bachman, J. G., O'Malley, P. M., & Johnston, L. D. (1996). Routine activities and individual deviant behavior. *American Sociological Review, 61*, 635–655.

Osofsky, J. D. (1990, Winter). Risk and protective factors for teenage mothers and their infants. *SRCD Newsletter*, 1–2.

Oswald, H., Bahne, J., & Feder, M. (1994, February). *Love and sexuality in adolescence: Gender-specific differences in East and West Berlin.* Paper presented at the biennial meeting of the Society for Research on Adolescence, San Diego, CA.

Overton, W. F., & Byrnes, J. P. (1991). Cognitive development. In R. M. Lerner, A. C. Petersen, & J. Brooks-Gunn (Eds.) *Encyclopedia of adolescence* (Vol. 1, pp. 151–156). New York: Garland.

Oyserman, D., Bybee, D., & Terry, K. (2006). Possible selves and academic outcomes: How and when possible selves impel action. *Journal of Personality and Social Psychology, 91*(1), 188–204.

Oyserman, D., & Fryberg, S. (2006). The possible selves of diverse adolescents: Content and function across gender, race and national origin. In C. Dunkel & J. Kerpelman (Eds.), *Possible selves: Theory, research and applications* (pp. 17–39). Hauppauge: Nova Science Publishers.

Oyserman, D., & Lee, S. W. S. (2008). Does culture influence what and how we think? Effects of priming individualism and collectivism. *Psychological Bulletin, 134*(2), 311–342.

Oyserman, D., & Markus, H. (1990). Possible selves and delinquency. *Journal of Personality and Social Psychology, 59*, 112–125.

Padgham, J. J., & Blyth, D. A. (1991). Dating during adolescence. In R. M. Lerner, A. C. Petersen, & J. Brooks-Gunn (Eds.), *Encyclopedia of adolescence* (pp. 196–198). New York: Garland.

Page, K. (1999, May 16). The graduate. *Washington Post Magazine*, pp. 18, 20.

Pahl, K., Greene, M., & Way, N. (2000, April). *Self-esteem trajectories among urban, low-income, ethnic minority high school students*. Poster presented at the biennial meeting of the Society for Research on Adolescence, Chicago.

Pahl, K., & Way, N. Longitudinal trajectories of ethnic identity among urban black and Latino adolescents. *Child Development, 77*(5), 1403–1415.

Paik, H., Desmond, R., Comstock, G., Sharrer, E., Subrahmanyan, K., Kraut, R., Greenfield, P., & Gross, E. (2001). Children's uses and gratifications. In D. G. Singer & J. L. Singer (Eds.), *Handbook of children and the media* (pp. 7–99). Thousand Oaks, CA: Sage.

Paikoff, R. L., & Brooks-Gunn, J. (1991). Do parent–child relationships change during puberty? *Psychological Bulletin, 110*, 47–66.

Pakaslahti, L., Karjalainen, A., & Keltikangas-Jaervinen, L. (2002). Relationships between adolescent prosocial problem-solving strategies, prosocial behavior, and social acceptance. *International Journal of Behavioral Development, 26*, 137–144.

Palmer, E. (2006). Schools, advertising/marketing. In J. J. Arnett (Ed.), *Encyclopedia of children, adolescents, and the media*. Thousand Oaks, CA: Sage.

Paludi, M. A., & Strayer, L. A. (1985). What's in an author's name? Differential evaluations of performance as a function of author's name. *Sex Roles, 12*, 353–362.

Pan, S. Y., Desmueles, M., Morrison, H., Semenciw, R., Ugnat, A-M., Thompson, W., & Mao, Y. (2007). Adolescent injury deaths and hospitalization in Canada: Magnitude and temporal trends (1979–2003). *Journal of Adolescent Health, 41*(1), 84–92.

Pancer, S. M., Pratt, M., Hunsberger, B., & Alisat, S. (2007). Community and political involvement in adolescent: What distinguishes the activists from the uninvolved? *Journal of Community Psychology, 35*(6), 741–759.

Papini, D. R., Micka, J. C., & Barnett, J. K. Perceptions of intrapsychic and extrapsychic functioning as bases of adolescent ego identity statuses. *Journal of Adolescent Research, 4*(4), 462–482.

Paradise, A. (2006). Television violence, susceptibility. In J. J. Arnett (Ed.), *Encyclopedia of children, adolescents, and the media*. Thousand Oaks, CA: Sage.

Pardun, C. J. (2002). Romancing the script: Identifying the romantic agenda in top-grossing movies. In J. D. Brown, J. R. Steele, & K. Walsh-Childers (Eds.), *Sexual teens, sexual media: Investigating media's influence on adolescent sexuality* (pp. 211–225). Mahwah, NJ: Erlbaum.

Pardun, C. J., L'Engle, K. L., & Brown, J. D. (2005). Linking exposure to outcomes: Early adolescents' consumption of sexual content in six media. *Mass Communication & Society, 8*, 75–91.

Pareles, J. (1992, February 2). Fear and loathing along pop's outlaw trail. *New York Times*, pp. 1, 23.

Park, I. H., & Cho, L. J. (1995). Confucianism and the Korean family. *Journal of Comparative Family Studies, 26*, 1134–1170.

Park, S. H., Shim, Y. K., Kim, H. S., & Eun, B. L. (1999). Age and seasonal distribution of menarche in Korean girls. *Journal of Adolescent Health, 25*, 97.

Parker, H., & Parker, S. (1986). Father-daughter sexual abuse: An emerging perspective. *American Journal of Orthopsychiatry, 56*, 531–549.

Parker, J., & Asher, S. (1987). Peer acceptance and later personal adjustment. Are low accepted children at risk? *Psychological Bulletin, 102*, 357–389.

Parker, J., & Seal, J. (1996). Forming, losing, renewing, and replacing friendships: Applying temporal parameters to the assessment of children's friendship experiences. *Child Development, 67*, 2248–2268.

Parker, S., Nichter, M., Vuckovic, N., Sims, C., & Ritenbaugh, C. (1995). Body image and weight concerns among African American and White adolescent females: Differences which make a difference. *Human Organization, 54*, 103–114.

Parsons, J., Eccles, J., Adler, T., & Kaczala, C. (1982). Socialization of achievement attitudes and beliefs: Parental influences. *Child Development, 53*, 310–321.

Parsons, T. (1964). *Essays in sociological theory*. Chicago: Free Press.

Pascarella, E., & Terenzini, P. (1991). *How college affects students: Findings and insights from twenty years of research*. San Francisco: Jossey-Bass.

Pascarella, E. T. (2005). Cognitive impacts of the first year of college. In R. S. Feldman (Ed.), *Improving the first year of college: Research and practice* (pp. 111–140). NJ: Lawrence Erlbaum.

Pascarella, E. T. (2006). How college affects students: Ten directions for future research. *Journal of College Student Development, 47*(5), 508–520.

Pascarella, E. T., Wolniak, G. C., Cruce, T. M., & Blaich, C. F. (2004). Do liberal arts college really foster good practices in undergraduate education? *Journal of College Student Development, 45*, 57–74.

Pascoe, C. J. (2003). Multiple masculinities? Teenage boys talk about jocks and gender. *American Behavioral Scientist, 46*, 1423–1438.

Pascoe, C. J. (2007). *Dude, you're a fag: Masculinity and sexuality in high school*. Berkeley: University of California Press.

Pasley, K., & Gecas, V. (1984). Stresses and satisfactions of the parental role. *Personnel and Guidance Journal, 2*, 400–404.

Patel-Amin, N., & Power, T. G. (2002). Modernity and childrearing in families of Gujarati Indian adolescents. *International Journal of Psychology, 37*, 239–245.

Pathak, R. (1994, January 31). The new generation. *India Today*, 72–87.

Patrikakou, E. (1996). Investigating the academic achievement of adolescents with learning disabilities: A structural modeling approach. *Journal of Educational Psychology, 88*, 435–450.

Patterson, G. (1986). Performance models for antisocial boys. *American Psychologist, 41*, 432–444.

Patterson, G., & Stoolmiller, M. (1991). Replications of a dual failure model for boys' depressed mood. *Journal of Consulting and Clinical Psychology, 59*, 491–498.

Patterson, G., & Stouthamer-Loeber, M. (1984). The correlation of family management practices and delinquency. *Child Development, 55*, 1299–1307.

Patterson, G. R., & Fisher, P. A. (2002). Recent developments in our understanding of parenting: Bidirectional effects, causal models, and the search for parsimony. In M. H. Bornstein (Ed.), Handbook of parenting, Vol. 5: *Practical issues in parenting* (pp. 59–88). Mahwah, NJ: Erlbaum.

Patterson, S. J., Sochting, I., & Marcia, J. E. (1992). The inner space and beyond: Women and identity. In G. R. Adams, T. P. Gullotta, & R. Montemayor (Eds.), *Adolescent identity formation* (pp. 9–24). Newbury Park, CA: Sage.

Paul, E. L., & White, K. M. (1990). The development of intimate relationships in late adolescence. *Adolescence, 25*, 375–400.

Paul, E. L., McManus, B., & Hayes, A. (2000). "Hookups": Characteristics and correlates of college students' spontaneous and anonymous sexual experiences. *The Journal of Sex Research, 37*, 76–88.

Paulson, S. E. (1994, February). *Parenting style or parental involvement: Which is more important for adolescent achievement?* Paper presented at the meeting of the Society for Research on Adolescence, San Diego.

Paulson-Karlsson, G., Engstrom, I., & Nevonen, L. (2009). A pilot study of a family-based treatment for adolescent anorexia nervosa: 18- and 36-month follow-ups. *Eating Disorders: The Journal of Treatment & Prevention, 17*(1), 72–88.

Paus, T., Gächter, S., Starmer, C., & Wilkinson, R. (In press). Cooperative behavior, conflict resolution and positive youth development. In R. M. Lerner, R. W. Roeser, & E. Phelps (Eds.), *Positive youth development and spirituality: From theory to research*. West Conshohocken, PA: Templeton Foundation Press.

Paus, T., Zijdenbos, A., Worsley, K., et al. (1999). Structural maturation of neural pathways in children and adolescents: In vivo study. *Science, 283*, 1908–1911.

Paykel, E. (1996). Tertiary prevention: Longer-term drug treatment in depression. In T. Kendrick & A. Tylee (Eds.), *The prevention of mental illness in primary care* (pp. 281–293). Cambridge, England: Cambridge University Press.

Peace Corps. (2000a). Peace Corps facts. Retrieved on March 24, 2003, from www.peacecorps.gov/about/facts/index.html

Peace Corps. (2000b). Two years of service, a lifetime of benefits. Retrieved on March 24, 2003, from www.peacecorps.gov/volunteer/benefits.html

Peace Corps. (2000c). Peace Corps history. Retrieved on March 24, 2003, from www.peacecorps.gov/about/history/chronology.html

Peace Corps. (2009). About the Peace Corps. Available: http://www.peacecorps.gov/index.cfm?shell=learn.whyvol. Retrieved on January 15, 2009

Pellegrini, A. D., & Long, J. D. (2002). A longitudinal study of bullying, dominance, and victimization during the transition from primary school through secondary school. *British Journal of Developmental Psychology, 20*, 259–280.

Peng, K., & Nisbett, R. E. (1999). Culture, dialectics, and reasoning about contradiction. *American Psychologist, 54*, 741–754.

Pepler, D. J., Craig, W. M., Connolly, J.A., Yuile, A., McMaster, L., & Jiang, D. (2006). A developmental perspective on bullying. *Aggressive Behavior, 32*(4), 376–384.

Pepler, D. J., Jiang, D., Craig, W. M., & Connolly, J. A. (2008). Developmental trajectories of bullying and associated factors. *Child Development, 79*(2), 325–338.

Peris, T. S., & Emery, R. E. (2004). A prospective study of the consequences of marital disruption for adolescents: Predisruption family dynamics and postdisruption adolescent adjustment. *Journal of Clinical Child & Adolescent Psychology, 33*, 694–704.

Perren, S., & Hornung, R. (2005). Bullying and delinquency in adolescence: Victims' and perpetrators' family and peer relations. *Swiss Journal of Psychology, 64*(1), 51–64.

Perry, C., Williams, C., Veblen-Mortenson, S., Toomey, T., Komro, K., Anstine, P., et al. (1996). Project Northland: Outcomes of a community-wide alcohol use prevention program during early adolescence. *American Journal of Public Health, 86*, 956–965.

Perry, W. G. (1970/1999). *Forms of ethical and intellectual development in the college years: A scheme*. San Francisco: Jossey-Bass.

Persons, J., Davidson, J., & Tompkins, M. A. (2001). *Essential components of cognitive behavior therapy for depression*. Washington, DC: American Psychological Association.

Peskin, H. (1967). Pubertal onset and ego functioning: A psychoanalytic approach. *Journal of Abnormal Psychology, 72*, 1–15.

Peter, J., & Valkenburg, P. M. (2007). Adolescents' exposure to a sexualized media environment and their notions of women as sex objects. *Sex Roles, 56*(5–6), 381–395.

Petersen, A. (1985). Pubertal development as a cause of disturbance: Myths, realities, and unanswered questions. *Genetic, Social, and General Psychology Monographs, 111*, 205–232.

Petersen, A. C. (1987, September). Those gangly years. *Psychology Today*, 28–34.

Petersen, A. C. (1993). Creating adolescents: The role of context and process in developmental trajectories. *Journal of Research on Adolescence, 3,* 1–18.

Petersen, A. C. (2000, March). *Biology, culture, and behavior: What makes young adolescent boys and girls behave differently?* Paper presented at the biennial meeting of the Society for Research on Adolescence, Chicago.

Petersen, A. C., Compas, B. E., Brooks-Gunn, J., Stemmler, M., Ey, S., & Grant, K. E. (1993). Depression in adolescence. *American Psychologist, 48,* 155–168.

Petersen, A. C., Kennedy, R. E., & Sullivan, P. (1991). Coping with adolescence. In M. E. Colten & S. Gore (Eds.), *Adolescent stress: Causes and consequences* (pp. 93–110). New York: Aldine de Gruyter.

Peterson, J. L., & Zill, N. (1986). Marital disruption, parent–child relationships, and behavior problems in children. *Journal of Marriage and the Family, 48,* 295–307.

Peterson, P., Hawkins, J., Abbott, R., & Catalano, R. (1994). Disentangling the effects of parental drinking, family management, and parental alcohol norms on current drinking by Black and White adolescents. *Journal of Research on Adolescence, 4,* 203–227.

Peterson, S. H., Wingood, G. M., DiClemente, R. J., Harrington, K., & Davis, S. (2007). Images of sexual stereotypes in rap videos and the health of African American female adolescents. *Journal of Women's Health, 16*(8), 1157–1164.

Petraitis, J., Flay, B., & Miller, T. (1995). Reviewing theories of adolescent substance use: Organizing pieces in the puzzle. *Psychological Bulletin, 117,* 67–86.

Pettit, G. S., Bates, J. E., Dodge, K. A., & Meece, D. W. The impact of after-school peer contact on early adolescent externalizing problems is moderated by parental monitoring, perceived neighborhood safety, and prior adjustment. *Child Development, 70*(3), 768–778.

Pfeffer, C. R. (2002). Suicide in mood disordered children and adolescents. *Child & Adolescent Psychiatric Clinics of North America, 11,* 639–648.

Pfeffer, C. R. (2006). Suicide in children and adolescents. In D. J. Stein, D. J. Kupfer, & A. F. Schatzberg (Eds.), *The American Psychiatric Publishing textbook of mood disorders* (pp. 497–507). Arlington, VA: American Psychiatric Publishing.

Phinney, J. S. (1990). Ethnic identity in adolescents and adults: A review of research. *Psychological Bulletin, 108,* 499–514.

Phinney, J. S. (2000, March). *Identity formation among U.S. ethnic adolescents from collectivist cultures.* Paper presented at the biennial meeting of the Society for Research on Adolescence, Chicago.

Phinney, J. S. (2006). Ethnic identity in emerging adulthood. In J. J. Arnett and J. L. Tanner (Eds.), *Emerging adults in America: Coming of age in the 21st century,* (pp. 117–134). Washington, DC: American Psychological Association Press.

Phinney, J. S. (2008). Ethnic identity exploration in emerging adulthood. In D. L. Browning (Ed.), *Adolescent identities: A collection of readings* (pp. 47–66). Relational perspectives book series. New York: Analytic Press/Taylor & Francis Group.

Phinney, J. S., & Alipuria, L. (1987). *Ethnic identity in older adolescents from four ethnic groups.* Paper presented at the biennial meeting of the Society for Research in Child Development, Baltimore, MD.

Phinney, J. S., & Devich-Navarro, M. (1997). Variation in bicultural identification among African American and Mexican American adolescents. *Journal of Research on Adolescence, 7,* 3–32.

Phinney, J. S., Devich-Navarro, M., DuPont, S., Estrada, A., & Onwughala, M. (1994, February). *Bicultural identity orientations of African American and Mexican American Adolescents.*

Paper presented at the biennial meetings of the Society for Research on Adolescence, San Diego, CA.

Phinney, J. S., DuPont, S., Espinosa, A., Revill, J., & Sanders, K. (1994). Ethnic identity and American identification among ethnic minority adolescents. In E. van de Vijver (Ed.), *Proceedings of 1992 conference of the International Association for Cross-cultural Psychology.* Tilburg, The Netherlands: Tilburg University Press.

Phinney, J. S., Kim-Jo, T., Osorio, S., & Vilhjalmsdottir, P. (2003). *Cultural and developmental factors in responses to hypothetical adolescent-parent disagreements across four ethnic groups.* Manuscript submitted for publication.

Phinney, J. S., & Ong, A. D. (2002). Adolescent-parent disagreement and life satisfaction in families from Vietnamese and European American backgrounds. *International Journal of Behavioral Development.*

Phinney, J. S., Ong, A., & Madden, T. (2000). Cultural values and intergenerational value discrepancies in immigrant and nonimmigrant families. *Child Development, 71,* 528–539.

Phinney, J. S., & Rosenthal, D. A. (1992). Ethnic identity in adolescence: Process, context, and outcome. In G. R. Adams, T. P. Gullotta, & R. Montemayor (Eds.), *Adolescent identity formation* (pp. 145–172). Newbury Park, CA: Sage.

Phinney, J. S. Kim-Jo, T., Osorio, S.,& Vilhjalmsdottir, P. Autonomy and relatedness in adolescent-parent disagreements: Ethnic and developmental factors. *Journal of Adolescent Research, 20*(1), 8–39.

Piaget, J. (1932). *The moral judgment of the child.* New York: Harcourt Brace Jovanovich.

Piaget, J. (1967). *Six psychological studies.* New York: Random House.

Piaget, J. (1972). Intellectual evolution from adolescence to adulthood. *Human Development, 15,* 1–12.

Piaget, J., & Inhelder, B. (1969). *The psychology of the child.* New York: Basic Books.

Picard, C. L. (1999). The level of competition as a factor for the development of eating disorders in female collegiate athletes. *Journal of Youth & Adolescence, 28,* 583–594.

Pierce, J. P., Lee, L., & Gilpin, E. A. (1994). Smoking initiation by adolescent girls, 1944 through 1988: An association with targeted advertising. *JAMA: Journal of the American Medical Association, 271,* 608–611.

Pierce, K. (1993). Socialization of teenage girls through teenage magazine fiction: The making of a new woman or an old lady. *Sex Roles, 29,* 59–68.

Pierce, K. (2006). Uses and gratifications theory. In J. J. Arnett (Ed.), *Encyclopedia of children, adolescents, and the media.* Thousand Oaks, CA: Sage.

Pipher, M. (1994). *Reviving Ophelia: Saving the selves of adolescent girls.* New York: Ballantine.

Piquero, A. R., & Brezina, T. (2001). Testing Moffitt's account of adolescence-limited delinquency. *Criminology, 39,* 901–919.

Pirttilae-Backman, A. M., & Kajanne, A. (2001). The development of implicit epistemologies during early adulthood. *Journal of Adult Development, 8,* 81–97.

Pisetsky, E. M., Chao, Y. M., Dierker, L. C., May, A. M., & Striegel-Moore, R. H. Disordered eating and substance use in high school students: Results from the Youth Risk Behavior Surveillance System. *International Journal of Eating Disorders 41*(5), 464–470.

Pittman, R. B., & Haughwout, P. (1987). Influence of high school size on dropout rate. *Educational Evaluation and Policy Analysis, 9,* 337–343.

Plantin, L. (2007). Different classes, different fathers?: On fatherhood, economic conditions and class in Sweden. *Community, Work & Family, 10*(1), 93–110.

Pleck, J. H. (1983). The theory of male sex role identity: Its rise and fall, 1936–present. In M. Lewin (Ed.), *In the shadow of the past: Psychology portrays the sexes.* New York: Columbia University Press.

Pleck, J. H., Sonnenstein, F., & Ku, L. (1998). Problem behaviors and masculine ideology in adolescent males. In R. Ketterlinus & M. E. Lamb (Eds.), *Adolescent problem behaviors* (pp. 165–186). Hillsdale, NJ: Erlbaum.

Plomin, R., & Daniels, D. (1987). Why are children in the same family so different from one another? *Behavioral and Brain Sciences, 10,* 1–60.

Plomin, R., & Rende, R. (1991). Human behavioral genetics. *Annual Review of Psychology, 42,* 161–190.

Plowman, S. A., Drinkwater, B. L., & Horvath, S. M. (1979). Age and aerobic power in women: A longitudinal study. *Journal of Gerontology, 34,* 512–520.

Podolskij, A. I. (1994). Russia. In K. Hurrelman (Ed.), *International handbook of adolescence* (pp. 332–345). Westport, CT: Greenwood.

Polivy, J., Herman, C. P., Mills, J. S., & Wheeler, H. B. (2003). Eating disorders in adolescence. In R. G. Adams & D. M. Berzonsky (Eds.), *Blackwell handbook of adolescence* (pp. 523–549). Malden, MA: Blackwell.

Pollack, W. (1998). *Real boys: Rescuing our sons from the myths of boyhood.* New York: Henry Holt.

Pollard, K. M., & O'Hare, W. P. (1999). America's racial and ethnic minorities. *Population Bulletin, 54,* 1–48.

Pollay, R. (2006). Cigarette advertising, history. In J. J. Arnett (Ed.), *Encyclopedia of children, adolescents, and the media.* Thousand Oaks, CA: Sage.

Pollay, R. W. (1997). Hacks, flacks, and counterattacks: Cigarette advertising, sponsored research, and controversies. *Journal of Social Issues, 53,* 53–74.

Pollay, R. W., Siddarth, S., Siegel, M., Haddix, A., Merritt, R. K., Giovino, G. A., et al. (1996). The last straw? Cigarette advertising and realized market shares among youths and adults, 1979–1993. *Journal of Marketing, 60,* 1–16.

Pool, M. M., Koolstra, C. M., van der Voort, T. H. A. (2003). The impact of background radio and television on high school students' homework performance. *Journal of Communication, 53,* 74–87.

Popenoe, D., & Whitehead, B. D. (2001). *The state of our unions, 2001: The social health of marriage in America.* Report of the National Marriage Project, Rutgers, New Brunswick, NJ. Available: http://marriage. rutgers.edu

Popenoe, D. (2007). What is happening to the family in developed nations? In A. S. Loveless & T. B. Holman (Eds.), *The family in the new millennium: World voices supporting the "natural" clan, Vol 1: The place of family in human society* (pp. 186–190). Westport, CT: Praeger

Popp, D., Lauren, B., Kerr, M., Stattin, H., & Burk, W. K. (2008). Modeling homophily over time with an actor-partner independence model. *Developmental Psychology, 44*(4), 1028–1039.

Population Reference Bureau (2000). *The world's youth 2000.* Washington, DC: Author.

Population Reference Bureau (2002). *Kids Count international data sheet.* Washington, DC: Author.

Population Reference Bureau (PRB) (2002). What drives U.S. population growth? *Population Bulletin, 57,* 1–40.

Population Reference Bureau (2009). *World population data sheet.* Washington, DC: Author.

Porfeli, E. J., Hartung, P. J., & Vondracek, F. W. (2008). Children's vocational development: A research rationale. *Career Development Quarterly, 57*(1), 25–37.

Portes, P. R., Dunham, R., & Castillo, K. D. (2000). Identity formation and status across cultures: Exploring the cultural validity of Eriksonian theory. In A. Comunian & U. P. Gielen (Eds.), *International perspectives on human development* (pp. 449–459). Lengerich, Germany: Pabst Science Publishers.

Posner, R. B. (2006). Early menarche: A review of research on trends in timing, racial differences, etiology and psychosocial consequences. *Sex Roles, 54*(5–6), 315–322.

Posterski, D., & Bibby, R. (1988). *Canada's youth, ready for today: A comprehensive survey of 15- to 24-year-olds.* Ottawa: Canadian Youth Foundation.

Postman, N. (1985). *Amusing ourselves to death: Public discourse in the age of show business.* New York: Penguin.

Potvin, L., Champagne, F., & Laberge-Nadeau, C. (1988). Mandatory driver training and road safety: The Quebec experience. *American Journal of Public Health, 78,* 1206–1209.

Powell, A., Farrar, E., & Cohen, D. (1985). *The shopping mall high school.* Boston: Houghton Mifflin.

Prakasa, V. V., & Rao, V. N. (1979). Arranged marriages: An assessment of the attitudes of college students in India. In G. Kurian (Ed.), *Cross-cultural perspectives on mate selection and marriage* (pp. 11–31). Westport, CT: Greenwood Press.

Pratt, M. W., Skoe, E. E., & Arnold, M. L. (2004). Care reasoning development and family socialisation patterns in later adolescence: A longitudinal analysis. *International Journal of Behavioral Development, 28,* 139–147.

Presser, S., & Stinson, L. (1998). Data collection mode and social desirability bias in self-reported religious attendance. *American Sociological Review, 63,* 137–146.

Pressley, M., & Schneider, W. (1997). *Introduction to memory development during childhood and adolescence.* Mahwah, NJ: Erlbaum.

Preuss, U., Ralston, S. J., Baldursson, G., Falissard, B., Lorenzo, M. J.; Rodrigues Pereira, R. [ADORE Study Group]. *European Child & Adolescent Psychiatry, 15*(Suppl. 1), 4–19.

Preusser, D. F., & Tison, J. (2007). GDL then and now. *Journal of Safety Research, 38*(2), 159–163.

Preusser, D. F., Williams, A. F., Lund, A. K., & Zador, P. L. (1990). City curfew ordinances and motor vehicle injury. *Accident Analysis and Prevention, 22,* 391–397.

Preusser, D. F., Zador, P. L., & Williams, A. F. (1993). City curfew ordinances and teenage motor vehicle fatalities. *Accident Analysis and Prevention, 25,* 641–645.

Prevatt, F., & Kelly, F. D. (2003). Dropping out of school: A review of intervention programs. *Journal of School Psychology, 41,* 377–395.

Price, J. N. (1999). Racialized masculinities: The diploma, teachers, and peers in the lives of young, African American men. *Youth & Society, 31,* 224–263.

Princeton Review (2005). *Complete book of colleges, 2006.* Princeton, NJ: Princeton Review.

Prinstein, M. J., Boergers, J., & Spirito, A. (2001). Adolescents' and their friends' health-risk behavior: Factors that alter or add to peer influence. *Journal of Pediatric Psychology, 26,* 287–298.

Prinstein, M. J., Boergers, J., & Vernberg, E. M. (2001). Overt and relational aggression in adolescents: Social-psychological adjustment of aggressors and victims. *Journal of Clinical Child & Adolescent Psychology, 30,* 479–491.

Prinstein, M. J., & Dodge, J. A. (Eds.). (2008). *Understanding peer influence in children and adolescence.* New York: Guilford Press.

Prinstein, M. J., & La Greca, A. M. (2002). Peer crowd affiliation and internalizing distress in childhood and adolescence: A longitudinal followback study. *Journal of Research on Adolescence, 12,* 325–351.

Prinstein, M. J., & La Greca, A. M. (2004). Childhood peer rejection and aggression as predictors of adolescent girls' externalizing and health risk behaviors: A 6-year longitudinal study. *Journal of Consulting & Clinical Psychology, 72,* 103–112.

Prinstein, M. J., & Wang, S. S. (2005). False consensus and adolescent peer contagion: Examining discrepancies between perceptions and actual reported levels of friends' deviant and health risk behaviors. *Journal of Abnormal Psychology, 33,* 293–306.

PROBE. (1999). *Peoples' report on basic education.* New Delhi: Oxford University Press.

Promoting abstinence among teens. (2001, February/
March). *Population Today,* p. 7. Washington, DC: Population Reference Bureau.

Provenzo, E. F., Jr. (1991). *Video kids: Making sense of Nintendo.* Cambridge, MA: Harvard University Press.

Pruitt, J. A., Kappius, R. E., & Gorman, P. W. (1992). Bulimia and fear of intimacy. *Journal of Clinical Psychology, 48,* 472–476.

Pryke, S. (2001). The Boy Scouts and the "girl question." *Sexualities, 4*(2), 191–210.

Psychological Corporation. (2000). Technical/product information [On-line]. Available: www.psychcorp.com

Public Education Network (PEN). (1997). *The American teacher 1997: Examining gender issues in public schools.* New York: Author.

Purdie, N., Carroll, A., & Roche, L. (2004). Parenting and adolescent self-regulation. *Journal of Adolescence, 27,* 663–676.

Putnam, R. D. (2000). *Bowling alone: The collapse and revival of American community.* New York: Touchstone Books/Simon & Schuster.

Qin, D. B. Being "good" or being "popular": Gender and ethnic identity negotiations of Chinese immigrant adolescents. *Journal of Adolescent Research. 24*(1), 37–66.

Qin, D. B., Way, N., & Mukherjee, P. (2008). The other side of the model minority story: The familial and peer challenges faced by Chinese American adolescents. *Youth and Society, 39*(4), 480–506.

Quadrel, M., Fischoff, B., & Davis, W. (1993). Adolescent(in)vulnerability. *American Psychologist, 48,* 102–116.

Quay, H. C. (1987). Patterns of delinquent behavior. In H. C. Quay (Ed.), *Handbook of juvenile delinquency* (pp. 118–138). New York: Wiley.

Quillian, L. (2003). The decline of male employment in low income black neighborhoods, 1950–1990. *Social Science Research, 32,* 220–250.

Raacke, J., & Bonds-Raacke, J. (2008). MySpace and Facebook: Applying the uses and gratifications theory to exploring friend-networking sites. *CyberPsychology & Behavior, 11*(2), 169–174.

Rabow, J., Choi, H., & Purdy, D. (1998). The GPA perspective: Influences, significance, and sacrifices of students. *Youth & Society, 29,* 451–470.

Racism rock. (1992, April 27). *Chicago Tribune,* p. 2.

Radmacher, K., & Azmitia, M. (2006). Are there gendered pathways to intimacy in early adolescents' and emerging adults' friendships? *Journal of Adolescent Research, 21*(4), 415–448.

Rafalovich, A. (2006). Broken and becoming god-sized: Contemporary metal music and masculine individualism. *Symbolic Interaction, 29*(1), 19–32.

Raffaelli, M., & Duckett, E. (1989). "We were just talking": Conversations in early adolescence. *Journal of Youth and Adolescence, 18,* 567–582.

Raffaelli, M., & Larson, R. (1999). Editor's notes. In M. Raffaelli & R. Larson (Eds.), *Homeless and Working Youth Around the World: Exploring Developmental Issues* (pp. 1–4). New Directions in Child and Adolescent Development, No. 85. San Francisco: Jossey-Bass.

Raffaelli, M., & Larson, R. W. (1999). *Homeless and working youth around the world: Exploring developmental issues.* San Francisco: Jossey-Bass.

Raja, S. N., McGee, R., & Stanton, W. R. (1992). Perceived attachment to parents and peers and psychological well-being in adolescence. *Journal of Youth and Adolescence, 21,* 471–485.

Rapoport J., & J. Giedd. (2006). Intellectual ability and cortical development in children and adolescents. *Nature, 440,* 676–679.

Ratzan, S. C., Filerman, G. L., & LeSar, J. W. (2000). Attaining global health: Challenges and opportunities. *Population Bulletin, 55*(1), 1–48.

Ravi, S., Forsberg, S., Fitzpatrick, K., & Lock, J. (2009). Is there a relationship between parental self-reported psychopathology and symptom severity in adolescents in anorexia nervosa? *Eating Disorders: The Journal of Treatment & Prevention, 17*(1), 63–71.

Ravn, M. N. (2005). A matter of free choice? Some structural and cultural influences on the decision to have or not to have children in Norway. In C. B. Douglas (Ed.), *Barren states: The population "implosion" in Europe* (pp. 29–47) New York: Berg.

Rawlings, D., Barrantes, V. N., & Furnham, A. (2000). Personality and aesthetic preference in Spain and England: Two studies relating sensation seeking and openness to experience to liking for paintings and music. *European Journal of Personality, 14,* 553–576.

Ream, G. L., & Savin-Williams, R. C. (2003). Religious development in adolescence. In G. R. Adams & M. D. Berzonsky (Eds.), *Blackwell handbook of adolescence* (pp. 51–59). Malden, MA: Blackwell.

Rebok, G. W. (1987). *Life-span cognitive development.* New York: Holt, Reinhart and Winston.

Reddy, R., & Gibbons, J. L. (1999). School socioeconomic contexts and self-descriptions in India. *Journal of Youth & Adolescence, 28,* 619–631.

Rees, H., & Noyes, J. M. (2007). Mobile telephones, computers, and the internet: Sex differences in adolescents' use and attitudes. *CyberPsychology & Behavior, 10*(3), 482–484.

Regan, P. C., Durvasula, R., Howell, L., Ureño, O., & Rea, M. (2004). Gender, ethnicity, and the developmental timing of first sexual and romantic experiences. *Social Behavior & Personality, 32,* 667–676.

Regnerus, M. D. (2007). *Forbidden fruit: Sex and religion in the lives of American teenagers.* New York: Oxford University Press.

Reid, T. R. (2001, July 10). Little to bar British students from bellying up: Universities unconcerned over undergraduate drinking. *Washington Post,* p. A14.

Reifman, A., Arnett, J. J., & Colwell, M. J. (2007). Emerging adulthood: Theory, assessment, and application. *Journal of Youth Development, 1,* 1–12.

Reijonen, J. H., Pratt, H. D., Patel, D. R., & Greydanus, D. E. (2003). Eating disorders in the adolescent population: An overview. *Journal of Adolescent Research, 18,* 209–222.

Reinders, H., & Youniss, J. (2006). School-based required community service and civic development in adolescents. *Applied Developmental Science, 10*(1), 2–12.

Reiss, D., Neiderhiser, J., Hetherington, E. M., & Plomin, R. (2000). *The relationship code: Deciphering genetic and social influences on adolescent development.* Cambridge, MA: Harvard University Press.

Renk, K., Donelly, R., McKinney, C., & Agliata, A. K. (2006) The development of gender identity: Timetables and influences. In K. S. Yip (Ed.), *Psychology of gender identity: An international perspective* (pp. 49–68). New York: Nova Science Publishers.

Repetto, P. B., Zimmerman, M. A., & Caldwell, C. H. (2004). A longitudinal study of the relationship between depressive symptoms and alcohol use in a sample of inner-city black youth. *Journal of Studies on Alcohol, 65,* 169–178.

Repinski, D., & Leffert, N. (1994, February). *Adolescents' relations with friends: The effects of a psychoeducational intervention.* Paper presented at the biennial meeting of the Society for Research on Adolescence, San Diego.

Reskin, B. (1993). Sex segregation in the workplace. *Annual Review of Sociology, 19,* 241–270.

Resnick, M. D., Wattenberg, E., & Brewer, R. (1992, March). *Paternity avowal/disavowal among partners of low income mothers.* Paper presented at the meeting of the Society for Research on Adolescence, Washington, DC.

Rest, J. (1983). Morality. In J. Flavell & E. Markman (Eds.), *Handbook of child psychology, Vol. III: Cognitive development.* New York: Wiley.

Rest, J. R. (1986). *Moral development: Advances in theory and research.* New York: Praeger.

Retschitzki, J. (1989). Evidence of formal thinking in Baoule aierle players. In D. M. Keats, D. Munro, & L. Mann (Eds.), *Heterogeneity in cross-cultural psychology.* Amsterdam: Swets & Zeitlinger.

Reyes, O., & Jason, L. A. (1993). Pilot study examining factors associated with academic success for Hispanic high school students. *Journal of Youth and Adolescence, 22,* 57–72.

Reyna, V. F., & Farley, F. (2006). Risk and rationality in adolescent decision making: Implications for theory, practice, and public policy. *Psychological Science in the Public Interest, 7*(1), 1–44.

Reynolds, S. (1998). *Generation ecstasy: Into the world of techno and rave culture.* New York: Little, Brown.

Rhodes, J. E. (2002). *Stand by me: The risks and rewards of mentoring today's youth.* Cambridge, MA: Harvard University Press.

Rhodes, J. E., Reddy, R., & Grossman, J. B. The protective influence of mentoring on adolescents' substance use: Direct and indirect pathways. *Applied Developmental Science. 9*(1), 31–47.

Rhodes, J. R., & DuBois, D. L. (2008). Mentoring relationships and programs for youths. *Current Directions in Psychological Science, 17*(4), 254–258.

Richards, M. H., Crowe, P. A., Larson, R., & Swarr, A. (2002). Developmental patterns and gender differences in the experience of peer companionship in adolescence. *Child Development, 69,* 154–163.

Richards, M., & Duckett, E. (1994). The relationship of maternal employment to early adolescent daily experience with and without parents. *Child Development, 65,* 225–236.

Richardson, J., Dwyer, K., McGuigan, K., Hansen, W., Dent, C., Johnson, C., et al. (1989). Substance use among eighth-grade students who take care of themselves after school. *Pediatrics, 84,* 556–566.

Riggs, D. S., O'Leary, K. D., & Breslin, F. C. (1990). Multiple correlates of physical aggression in courting couples. *Journal of Interpersonal Violence, 5,* 61–73.

Riley, A. W., Lyman, L. M., Spiel, G., Döpfner, M., Lorenzo, M. J., Ralston, S. J. [ADORE Study Group]. *European Child & Adolescent Psychiatry. 15*(Suppl. 1), 72–78.

Riley, S. C. E., James, C., Gregory, D., Dingle, H., & Cadger, M. (2001). Patterns of recreational drug use at dance events in Edinburgh, Scotland. *Addiction, 96,* 1035–1047.

Rivadeneyra, R., & Ward, L. M. (2005). From Ally McBeal to Sábado Gigante: Contributions of television viewing to the gender role attitudes of Latino adolescents. *Journal of Adolescent Research, 20,* 453–475.

Roberto, C. A., Steinglass, J., Mayer, L. E. S., Attia, E., & Walsh, B. T. (2008). The clinical significance of amenorrhea as a diagnostic criterion for anorexia nervosa. *International Journal of Eating Disorders, 41*(6), 559–563.

Roberts, B. W., Caspi, A., & Moffitt, T. E. (2001). The kids are alright: Growth and stability in personality development from adolescence to adulthood. *Journal of Personality and Social Psychology, 81,* 670–683.

Roberts, B. W., & Chapman, C. (2000). Change in dispositional well-being and its relation to role quality: A 30-year longitudinal study. *Journal of Research in Personality, 34,* 26–41.

Roberts, D. F. & Foehr, U. G. (2004). *Kids and media in America.* Cambridge: Cambridge University Press.

Roberts, D. F., Foehr, U. G., & Rideout, V. (2005). *Generation M: Media in the lives of 8–18 year-olds.* Washington, DC: The Henry J. Kaiser Family Foundation.

Roberts, D. F., Foehr, U. G., Rideout, V. J., & Brodie, M. (1999). *Kids & media @ the new millennium: A comprehensive national analysis of children's media use.* New York: Henry J. Kaiser Family Foundation.

Roberts, J. L. (2005, June 6). World tour: MTV has mastered a nifty trick. *Newsweek,* 34–35.

Roberts, K. A. (2005). Associated characteristics of stalking following termination of romantic relationships. *Applied Psychology in Criminal Justice, 1*(1), 15–35.

Robins, R. W., Trzesniewski, K. H., Tracy, J. L., Gosling, S. D., & Potter, J. (2002). Global self-esteem across the life span. *Psychology & Aging, 17,* 423–434.

Robinson, D. C., Buck, E. B., & Cuthbert, M. (1991). *Music at the margins: Popular music and global cultural diversity.* Newbury Park, CA: Sage.

Robinson, G. (1997). Families, generations and self: Conflict, loyalty and recognition in an Australian aboriginal society. *Ethos, 25*(3), 303–332.

Roche, K. M., Ahmed, S., & Blum, R. W. (2008). Enduring consequences of parenting for risk behaviors from adolescence into early adulthood. *Social Science & Medicine, 66*(9), 2023–2034.

Rodgers, J., & Rowe, D. (1993). Social contagion and adolescent sexual behavior: A developmental EMOSA model. *Psychological Review, 100,* 479–510.

Roe, K. (1985). Swedish youth and music: Listening patterns and motivations. *Communication Research, 12,* 353–362.

Roe, K. (1987). The school and music in adolescent socialization. In J. Lull (Ed.), *Popular music and communication* (pp. 212–230). Beverly Hills, CA: Sage.

Roe, K. (1992). Different destinies, different melodies: School achievement, anticipated status and adolescents' tastes in music. *European Journal of Communication, 7,* 335–337.

Roe, K. (1995). Adolescents' use of socially disvalued media: Toward a theory of media delinquency. *Journal of Youth & Adolescence, 24,* 595–616.

Roeschl-Heils, A., Schneider, W., & van Kraayenoord, C. E. (2003). Reading, metacognition, and motivation: A follow up study of German students in grades 7 and 8. *European Journal of Psychology of Education, 18,* 75–86.

Roeser, R., Lord, S., & Eccles, J. (1994, February). *A portrait of academic alienation in adolescence: Motivation, mental health, and family experience.* Paper presented at the biennial meeting of the Society for Research on Adolescence, San Diego, CA.

Rogoff, B. (1990). *Apprenticeship in thinking: Cognitive development in social context.* New York: Oxford University Press.

Rogoff, B. (1993). Children's guided participation and participatory appropriation in sociocultural activity. In R. Wozniak & K. Fischer (Eds.), *Development in context: Acting and thinking in specific environments.* Hillsdale, NJ: Erlbaum.

Rogoff, B. (1995). Observing sociocultural activities on three planes: Participatory appropriation, guided participation, and apprenticeship. In J. V. Wertsch, P. del Rio, & A. Alvarez (Eds.), *Sociocultural studies of mind* (pp. 273–294). New York: Cambridge University Press.

Rogoff, B. (1997). Cognition as a collaborative process. In D. Kuhn & R. S. Siegler (Eds.), *Handbook of child psychology* (5th ed., Vol. 2). New York: Wiley.

Rogoff, B. (1998). Cognition as a collaborative process. In W. Damon (Ed.), *Handbook of child psychology* (5th ed., Vol. 2). New York: Wiley.

Rogoff, B. (2003). *The cultural nature of human development.* New York: Oxford University Press.

Rogoff, B., Baker-Sennett, J., Lacasa, P., & Goldsmith, D. (1995). Development through participation in sociocultural activity. In J. Goodnow, P. Miller, & F. Kessen (Eds.), *Cultural practices as contexts for development* (pp. 45–65). San Francisco: Jossey-Bass.

Rohde, P., Lewinsohn, P. M., Clarke, G. N., Hops, H., & Seeley, J. R. (2005). The adolescent coping with depression course: A cognitive behavioral approach to the treatment of adolescent depression. In E. D. Hibbs & P. S. Jensen (Eds.), *Psychosocial treatments for child and adolescent disorders: Empirically based strategies for clinical practice* (pp. 219–237). Washington, DC: American Psychological Association.

Rohde, P., Noell, J., Ochs, L., & Seeley, J. R. (2001). Depression, suicidal ideation, and STD-related risk in homeless older adolescents. *Journal of Adolescence, 24,* 447–460.

Rohlen, T. P. (1983). *Japan's high schools.* Berkeley: University of California Press.

Roisman, G. I., Madsen, S. D., Hennighausen, K. H., Sroufe, L. A., & Collins, W. A. (2001). The coherence of dyadic behavior across parent-child and romantic relationships as mediated by internalized representations of experience. *Attachment & Human Development, 3,* 156–172.

Rokach, A. (2000). Perceived causes of loneliness in adulthood. *Journal of Social Behavior and Personality, 15,* 67–84.

Romer, D., & Hennessy, M. (2007). A biosocial-affect model of adolescent sensation seeking: The role of affect evaluation and peer-group influence in adolescent drug use. *Prevention Science, 8*(2), 89–101.

Romer, D., & Jamieson, P. (2001). Do adolescents appreciate the risks of smoking? Evidence from a national survey. *Journal of Adolescent Health, 29,* 12–21.

Romer, D., Jamieson, K. H., & Anday, S. (2003). Television news and the cultivation of fear of crime. *Journal of Communication, 53,* 88–104.

Romm, T. (1980–81). Interaction of vocational and family factors in the career planning of teenage girls. *Interchange, 11,* 13–24.

Rommes, E., Overbeek, G., Scholte, R., Engels, R., & de Kamp, R. (2007). "I'm not interested in computers.": Gender-biased occupational choices of adolescents. *Information, Communication & Society, 10*(3), 299–319.

Roof, W. C. (1993). *A generation of seekers.* New York: HarperCollins.

Rook, A. (1999, September). High school violence down, but does anybody notice? *Youth Today,* p. 58.

Rooney, M. (2003, March 19). Fewer college students graduate in 4 years, survey finds. *Chronicle of Higher Education: Today's News,* pp. 1–2. Available: http://chronicle.com/daily/2003/03/2003031901n.htm

Rosario, M., Schrimshaw, E. W., & Hunter, J. (2004). Ethnic/racial differences in the coming-out process of lesbian, gay, and bisexual youths: A comparisons of sexual indentity development over time. *Cultural Diversity & Ethnic Minorities, 10,* 215–228.

Roscoe, B., Dian, M. S., & Brooks, R. H. (1987). Early, middle, and late adolescents' views on dating and factors influencing partner selection. *Adolescence, 22,* 59–68.

Rose, A. J., Swenson, L. P., & Waller, E. M. (2004). Overt and relational aggression and perceived popularity: Developmental differences in concurrent and prospective relations. *Developmental Psychology, 40,* 378–387.

Rose, R. J. (2002). How do adolescents select their friends? A behavior-genetic perspective. In L. Pulkinnen & A. Caspi (Eds.), *Paths to successful development: Personality in the life course* (pp. 106–125). New York: Cambridge University Press.

Rose, S., & Frieze, L. R. (1993). Young singles' contemporary dating scripts. *Sex Roles, 28,* 499–509.

Rosen, R. (2000). *The world split open: How the modern women's movement changed America.* New York: Viking.

Rosenbaum, J. (1976). *Making inequality: The hidden curriculum of high school tracking.* New York: Wiley.

Rosenberg, M. (1986). Self concept from middle childhood through adolescence. In J. Suls & A. Greenwald (Eds.), *Psychological perspectives on the self (Vol. 3).* Hillsdale, NJ: Erlbaum.

Rosenberg, M., Schooler, C., & Schoenbach, C. (1989). Self-esteem and adolescent problems: Modeling reciprocal effects. *American Sociological Review, 54,* 1004–1018.

Rosenblatt, P. C., & Anderson, R. M. (1981). Human sexuality in cross-cultural perspective. In M. Cook (Ed.), *The bases of human sexual attraction* (pp. 215–250). London: Academic Press.

Rosenbloom, S. R., & Way, N. (2004). Experiences of discrimination among African American, Asian American, and Latino adolescents in an urban high school. *Youth & Society, 35,* 420–451.

Rosenblum, G. D., & Lewis, M. (1999). The relations between body image, physical attractiveness, and body mass in adolescence. *Child Development, 70,* 50–64.

Rosenthal, D. (1984). Intergenerational conflict and culture: A study of immigrant and non-immigrant adolescents and their parents. *Genetic Psychology Monographs, 109,* 53–79.

Rosenthal, D. (1987). *Child-rearing and cultural values: A study of Greek and Australian mothers.* Paper presented at the biennial meeting of the International Society for the Study of Behavioral Development, Tours, France.

Rosenthal, D., & Rotheram-Borus, M. J. (2005). Young people and homelessness. *Journal of Adolescence, 28,* 167–169.

Rosenthal, M. (1986). *The character factory: Baden-Powell and the origins of the Boy Scout movement.* New York: Pantheon.

Rothe, P. (1992). Traffic sociology: Social patterns of risk. *International Journal of Adolescent Medicine and Health, 5,* 187–197.

Rothenberger, A., Coghill, D., Dopfner, M., Falissard, B., & Stenhausen, H. C. (2006). Naturalistic observational studies in the framework of ADHD health care. *European Child and Adolescent Psychiatry, 15*(Suppl. 1), 1–3.

Rotheram-Borus, M. J. (1990). Adolescents' reference group choices, self-esteem, and adjustment. *Journal of Personality and Social Psychology, 59,* 1075–1081.

Rotundo, E. A. (1993). *American manhood: Transformations in masculinity from the revolution to the modern era.* New York: Basic Books.

Rowe, D. C. (1995). *The limits of family influence.* New York: Guilford.

Rowley, S. J., Kurtz-Costes, B., Mistry, R., & Feagans, L. (2007). Social status as a predictor of race and gender stereotypes in late childhood and early adolescence. *Social Development, 16*(1), 150–168.

Roy, R., Benenson, J. F., & Lilly, F. (2000). Beyond intimacy: Conceptualizing sex differences in same-sex relationships. *Journal of Psychology, 134,* 93–101.

Rozencwajg, P. (2003). Metacognitive factors in scientific problem-solving strategies. *European Journal of Psychology of Education, 18,* 281–294.

Rubin, A. M. (1979). Television use by children and adolescents. *Human Communication Research, 5,* 109–120.

Rubin, A. M. (1993). Uses, gratifications, and media effects research. In J. Bryant & D. Zillman (Eds.), *Perspectives on media effects.* Hillsdale, NJ: Erlbaum.

Rubin, A. M., West, D. V., & Mitchell, W. S. (2001). Differences in aggression, attitudes toward women, and distrust as reflected in popular music preferences. *Media Psychology, 3,* 25–42.

Rubin, C., Rubenstein, J. L., Stechler, G., & Heeren, T. (1992). Depressive affect in "normal" adolescents: A relationship to life stress, family, and friends. *American Journal of Orthopsychiatry, 62,* 430–441.

Rubin, K., Fredstrom, B., & Bowker, J. (2008). Future directions in friendship in childhood and early adolescence. *Social Development, 17*(4), 1085–1096.

Rubin, K., LeMare, L., & Lollis, S. (1990). Social withdrawal in childhood: Developmental pathways to peer rejection. In S. Asher & J. Coie (Eds.), *Peer rejection in childhood* (pp. 217–249). New York: Cambridge University Press.

Rubinstein, D. H. (1995). Love and suffering: Adolescent socialization and suicide in Micronesia. *The Contemporary Pacific, 7,* 21–53.

Rudman, L. A., & Lee, M. R. (2002). Implicit and explicit consequences of exposure to violent and misogynous rap music. *Group Processes and Intergroup Relations, 5,* 133–150.

Ruggiero, M., Greenberger, E., & Steinberg, L. (1982). Occupational deviance among first-time workers. *Youth and Society, 13,* 423–448.

Ruiz, S. A., & Silverstein, M. Relationships with grandparents and the emotional well-being of late adolescent and young adult grandchildren. *Journal of Social Issues. 63*(4), 793–808.

Rumberger, R. W. Dropping out of middle school: A multilevel analysis of students and schools. *American Educational Research Journal. 32*(3), 583–625.

Rushkoff, D. (2001). Ecstasy: Prescription for cultural renaissance. In J. Holland (Ed.), *Ecstasy: The complete guide: A comprehensive look at the risks and benefits* (pp. 350–357). London: Inner Traditions International.

Russell, D., Cutrona, C. E., Rose, J., & Yurko, K. (1984). Social and emotional loneliness: An examination of Weiss's typology of loneliness. *Journal of Personality and Social Psychology, 46,* 1313–1321.

Russo, N. F. (2008). Understanding emotional responses after abortion. In J. C. Chrisler, C. Golden, & P. D. Rozee (Eds.), *Lectures on the psychology of women* (4th ed., pp. 173 189). New York: McGraw-Hill.

Rust, J. O., & Troupe, P. A. (1991). Relationships of treatment of child sexual abuse with school achievement and self-concept. *Journal of Early Adolescence, 11,* 420–429.

Rutter, M. (1983). School effects on pupil progress: Research findings and policy implications. *Child Development, 54,* 1–29.

Rutter, M., Maughan, B., Mortimore, P., & Ouston, J. (1979). *Fifteen thousand hours: Secondary schools and their effects on children.* Cambridge, MA: Harvard University Press.

Ryan, J. J., & Lopez, S. J. (2001). Wechsler adult intelligence scale-III. In I. W. Dorfman & M. Hersen (Eds.) *Understanding psychological assessment* (pp. 19–42). Dordrecht, Netherlands: Kluwer.

Ryan, R. M., & Lynch, J. H. (1989). Emotional autonomy versus attachment: Revisiting the vicissitudes of adolescence and young adulthood. *Child Development, 60,* 340–356.

Ryu, S., & Mortimer, J. T. (1996). The 'occupational linkage hypothesis' applied to occupational value formation in adolescence. In J. T. Mortimer & M. D. Finch (Eds.), *Adolescents, work, and family: An intergenerational developmental analysis* (pp. 167–190). Thousand Oaks, CA: Sage.

Saadawi, N. (1980). *The hidden face of Eve: Women in the Arab world.* London: Zed Press.

Saarikallio, S., & Erkkila, J. (2007). The role of music in adolescents' mood regulation. *Psychology of Music, 35*(1), 88–109.

Sadker, M., & Sadker, D. (1982). *Sex equity handbook for schools.* New York: Longman.

Sadker, M., & Sadker, D. (1994). *Failing at fairness: How America's schools cheat girls.* New York: Scribner.

Sagestrano, L. M., McCormick, S. H., Paikoff, R. L., & Holmbeck, G. N. (1999). Pubertal development and parent–child conflict in low-income, urban, African American adolescents. *Journal of Research on Adolescence, 9,* 85–107.

Sahay, S., & Piran, N. (1997). Skin-color preferences and body satisfaction among South Asian-Canadian and European-Canadian female university students. *Journal of Social Psychology, 137,* 161–172.

Saldana, L., & Henggeler, S. W. (2006). Multisystemic therapy in the treatment of adolescent conduct disorder. In W. M. Nelson, III, A. J., Finch, Jr., & K. L. Hart (Eds.), *Conduct disorders: A practioner's guide to comparative treatments.* (pp. 217–258). New York: Springer.

Salinger, J. D. ([1951] 1964). *The catcher in the rye.* New York: Bantam.

Salkind, N. J. (2003). *Exploring research.* Upper Saddle River, NJ: Prentice Hall.

Salmela-Aro, Katariina; Kiuru, Noona; Pietikäinen, Minna; Jokela, Jukka (2008). Does school matter? The role of school context in adolescents' school-related burnout. *European Psychologist.* Vol. 13(1), 12–23.

Saluja, G., Iachan, R., & Scheidt, P. (2004). Prevalence and risk factors for depressive symptoms among young adolescents. *Archives of Pediatrics and Adolescent Medicine, 158,* 760–765.

Salzinger, S., Feldman, R. S., Manner, M., & Rosario, M. (1993). The effects of physical abuse on children's social relationships. *Child Development, 64,* 169–187.

Salzman, A. (1993, May 17). Mom, Dad, I want a job. *U.S. News & World Report,* 68–72.

Sampson, R. J., Castellano, T. C., & Laub, J. H. (1981). *Juvenile criminal behavior and its relation to neighborhood characteristics.* Washington, DC: Office of Juvenile Justice and Delinquency Prevention.

Sampson, R. J., & Laub, J. H. (1990). Crime and deviance over the life course: The salience of adult social bonds. *American Sociological Review, 55,* 609–627.

Sampson, R. J., & Laub, J. H. (1994). Urban poverty and the family context of delinquency: A new look at structure and process in a classic study. *Child Development, 65,* 523–540.

Samter, W. (2003). Friendship interaction skills across the lifespan. In O. J. Greene & R. B. Burleson (Eds.), *Handbook of communication and social interaction skills* (pp. 637–684). Mahwah, NJ: Lawrence Erlbaum.

Samuels, D. (1991, November 11). The rap on rap. *The New Republic,* 24–29.

Sandberg, D. E., Ehrhardt, A. A., Ince, S. E., & Meyer-Bahlburg, H. (1991). Gender differences in children's and adolescents' career aspirations: A follow-up study. *Journal of Adolescent Research, 6,* 371–386.

Sandler, D. P., Wilcox, A. J., & Horney, L. F. (1984). Age at menarche and subsequent reproductive events. *American Journal of Epidemiology, 119,* 765–774.

Sansone, L. (1995). The making of a black youth culture: Lower-class young men of Surinamese origin in Amsterdam. In V. Amit-Talai & H. Wulff (Eds.), *Youth cultures: A cross-cultural perspective* (pp. 114–143). New York: Rutledge.

Santelli, J. S., Abma, J., Ventura, S., Lindberg, L., Morrow, B., Anderson, J. E., Lyss, S., & Hamilton, B. E. (2004). Can changes in sexual behaviors among high school students explain the decline in teen pregnancy rates in the 1990s? *Journal of Adolescent Health, 35,* 80–90.

Santelli, J. S., Brener, N. D., Lowry, R., Bhatt, A., & Zabin, L. S. (1998). Multiple sexual partners among US adolescents and young adults. *Family Planning Perspectives, 30,* 271–275.

Santelli, J. S., Lindberg, L. D., Finer, L. B., & Singh, S. (2007). Explaining recent declines in adolescent pregnancy in the United States: The contribution of abstinence and improved contraceptive use. *American Journal of Public Health, 97*(1), 150–156.

Saraswathi, T. S. (1999). Adult–child continuity in India: Is adolescence a myth or an emerging reality? In T. S. Saraswathi (Ed.), *Culture, socialization, and human development: Theory, research, and applications in India* (pp. 213–232). Thousand Oaks, CA: Sage.

Saraswathi, T. S., & Larson, R. (2002). Adolescence in global perspective: An agenda for social policy. In B. B. Brown, R. Larson, & T. S. Saraswathi, (Eds.), *The world's youth: Adolescence in eight regions of the globe* (344–362). New York: Cambridge University Press.

Sarigiani, P. A. & Petersen, A. C. (2000). Adolescence: Puberty and biological maturation. In A. E. Kazdin (Ed.), *Encyclopedia of psychology* (Vol. 1, pp. 39–46). Washington, DC: American Psychological Association.

Sarouphim, K. M. (2004). Discover in middle school: Identifying gifted minority students. *Journal of Secondary Gifted Education, 15*, 61–69.

Sasinska-Klas, T. (1988). *Turbulence of the masses: The sociological phenomenon of rock music in Poland.* Paper presented at the ICYC conference, Geltow, German Democratic Republic.

Savin-Williams, R. (1994). Verbal and physical abuse as stressors in the lives of lesbian, gay male, and bisexual youths: Associations with school problems, running away, substance abuse, prostitution, and suicide. *Journal of Consulting and Clinical Psychology, 62*, 261–269.

Savin-Williams, R. (2001). *Mom, Dad, I'm gay.* Washington, DC: American Psychological Association.

Savin-Williams, R., & Berndt, T. (1990). Friendship and peer relations. In S. Feldman & G. Elliott (Eds.), *At the threshold: The developing adolescent* (pp. 277–307). Cambridge, MA: Harvard University Press.

Savin-Williams, R. C. (1998). The disclosure to families of same-sex attractions by lesbian, gay, and bisexual youth. *Journal of Research on Adolescence, 8*, 49–68.

Savin-Williams, R. C. (2006). *The new gay teenager.* New York: Trilateral.

Savin-Williams, R. C., & Diamond, L. (2004). Sex. In R. Lerner & L. Steinberg (Eds.), *Handbook of Adolescent Psychology.* New York: Wiley.

Savin-Williams, R. C., & Ream, G. L. (2007). Prevalence and stability of sexual orientation components during adolescence and young adulthood. *Archives of Sexual Behavior, 36*(3), 385–394.

Saxe, G. B. (1994). Studying cognitive development in sociocultural context: The development of a practice-based approach. *Mind, culture, & activity, 1*, 135–157.

Sbarra, D. A., & Emery, R. E. Deeper into divorce: Using actor-partner analyses to explore systemic differences in coparenting conflict following custody dispute resolution. *Journal of Family Psychology, 22*(1), 144–152.

Scales, E., & McEwin, C. (1994). *Growing pains: The making of America's middle schoolteachers.* Columbus, OH: National Middle School Association.

Scales, P. C., & Leffert, N. (1998). *Development assets: A synthesis of scientific research on adolescent development.* Minneapolis, MN: Search Institute.

Scarr, D., Phillips, D., & McCartney, K. (1989). Working mothers and their families. *American Psychologist, 44*, 1402–1409.

Scarr, S. (1992). Developmental theories for the 1990s: Development and individual differences. *Child Development, 63*, 1–19.

Scarr, S. (1993). Biological and cultural diversity: The legacy of Darwin for development. *Child Development, 64*, 1333–1353.

Scarr, S., & McCartney, K. (1983). How people make their own environments: A theory of genotype environment effects. *Child Development, 54*, 424–435.

Schachter, E. P. (2005). Context and identity formation: A theoretical analysis and a case study. *Journal of Adolescent Research, 20*, 375–395.

Schachter, E. P. (2005). Erikson meets the postmodern: Can classic identity theory rise to the challenge? *Identity, 5*, 137–160.

Scharf, M., Shulman, S., & Avigad-Spitz, L. (2005). Sibling relationships in emerging adulthood and in adolescence. *Journal of Adolescent Research, 20*, 64–90.

Scheel, K. R., & Westefeld, J. S. Heavy metal music and adolescent suicidality: An empirical investigation. *Adolescence, 34*(134), 253–273.

Scheer, S. D., Unger, D. G., & Brown, M. (1994, February). Adolescents becoming adults: Attributes for adulthood. Poster presented at the biennial meeting of the Society for Research on Adolescence, San Diego, CA.

Scheidel, D. G., & Marcia, J. E. (1985). Ego identity, intimacy, sex role orientation, and gender. *Developmental Psychology, 21*, 149–160.

Schlegel, A. (1973). The adolescent socialization of the Hopi girl. *Ethnology, 4*, 449–462.

Schlegel, A. (2000). The global spread of adolescent culture. In L. Crockett & R. K. Silbereisen (Eds.), *Negotiating adolescence in a time of social change.* Cambridge: Cambridge University Press.

Schlegel, A. (2008). A cross-cultural approach to adolescence. In D. L. Browning (Ed.), *Adolescent identities: A collection of readings. Relational perspectives book series* (pp. 31–44). New York: Analytic Press/Taylor & Francis Group.

Schlegel, A. (2009). Societal communities. In L. A. Jensen (Ed.), *Bridging cultural and developmental psychology: New syntheses for theory, research, and practice.* New York: Oxford University Press.

Schlegel, A., & Barry, H. (1991). *Adolescence: An anthropological inquiry.* New York: Free Press.

Schmidt, J. R., & Thompson, V. A. (2008) At least one problem with some formal reasoning paradigms. *Memory & Cognition, 36*(1), 217–229.

Schmitt, K. L., Dayanim, S., & Matthais, S. (2008). Personal homepage construction as an expression of social development. *Developmental Psychology, 44*(2), 496–506.

Schneider, B., & Stevenson, D. (1999). *The ambitious generation: America's teenagers, motivated but directionless.* New Haven, CT: Yale University Press.

Schneider, B., & Waite, L. J. (Eds.). (2005). *Being together, working apart: Dual-career families and the work-life balance.* New York: Cambridge University Press.

Schulenberg, J. (2000, April). *College students get drunk, so what? National panel data on binge drinking trajectories before, during and after college.* Paper presented at the biennial meeting of the Society for Research on Adolescence, Chicago.

Schulenberg, J., & Bachman, J. (1993, March). *Long hours on the job? Not so bad for some adolescents in some types of jobs: The quality of work and substance use, affect, and stress.* Paper presented at the biennial meeting of the Society for Research in Child Development, New Orleans, LA.

Schulenberg, J., Bachman, J. G., Johnston, L. D., & O'Malley, P. M. (1995). American adolescents' views on family and work: Historical trends from 1976–1992. In P. Noack, M. Hofer, & J. Youniss (Eds.), *Psychological responses to social change: Human development in changing environments* (pp. 37–64). New York: Walter De Gruyter.

Schulenberg, J., & Maggs, J. L. (2000). *A developmental perspective on alcohol use and heavy drinking during adolescence and the transition to adulthood.* Washington, DC: National Institute on Alcohol Abuse and Alcoholism.

Schulenberg, J., O'Malley, P. M., Bachman, J. G., Wadsworth, K. N., & Johnston, L. D. (1996). Getting drunk and growing up: Trajectories of frequent binge drinking during the transition to adulthood. *Journal of Studies on Alcohol, 57*, 1–15.

Schulenberg, J. E., & Zarrett, N. R. (2006). Mental health during emerging adulthood: Continuity and discontinuity in courses, causes, and functions. In J. J. Arnett & J. L. Tanner (Eds.), *Emerging adults in America: Coming of age in the 21st century* (pp. 135–172). Washington, DC: American Psychological Association.

Schultz, R., & Curnow, C. (1988). Peak performance and age among superathletes: Track and field, swimming, baseball, tennis, and golf. *Journal of Gerontology: Psychological Sciences, 43*, P113–P120.

Schwartz, S. J. (2005). A new identity for identity research: Recommendations for expanding and refocusing the identity literature. *Journal of Adolescent Research, 20*, 293–308.

Schwartz, S.J., Cote, J.E., and Arnett, J.J. (2005). Identity and agency in emerging adulthood: Two evelopmental routes in the individualization process. *Youth & Society, 37*, 201-229.

Scott, D. (1995). The effect of video games on feelings of aggression. *Journal of Psychology, 129*, 121–132.

Scouller, K. M., & Smith, D. I. (2002). Prevention of youth suicide: How well-informed are the potential gatekeepers of adolescents in distress? *Suicide & Life-Threatening Behavior, 32*, 67–79.

Sears, H. A., Simmering, M. G., & MacNeil, B. A. (2007). Canada. In J. J. Arnett (Ed.), *International encyclopedia of adolescence.* New York: Routledge.

Sears, H. (2006). Canada. In J. J. Arnett (Ed.), *International encyclopedia of adolescence.* New York: Routledge.

Sedgh, G., Jackson, E., & Ibrahim, B. (2005). Toward the abandonment of female genital cutting: Advancing research, communication and collaboration. *Culture, Health & Sexuality, 7*(5), 425–427.

Segal, D. (2000, January 12). *The pied piper of racism: William Pierce wants young people to march to his hate records. Washington Post,* pp. C-1, C-8.

Segal, U. A. (1998). The Asian Indian-American family. In C. H. Mindel, R. W. Habenstein, & R. Wright, Jr. (Eds.), *Ethnic families in America* (4th ed.; pp. 331–360). Upper Saddle River, NJ: Prentice Hall.

Segall, M. H., Dasen, P. R., Berry, J. W., & Poortinga, Y. H. (1999). *Human behavior in global perspective: An introduction to cross-cultural psychology.* Boston: Allyn & Bacon.

Seginer, R. (1998). Adolescents' perceptions of relationships with older siblings in the context of other close relationships. *Journal of Research on Adolescence, 8*, 287–308.

Seidman, E., Aber, J. L. & French, S. E. (2004). The organization of schooling and adolescent development. In K. I. Maton, C. J. Schellenbach, B. J. Leadbeater, & A. L. Solarz (Eds.), *Investing in children, youth, families, and communities: strengthsbased research and policy* (pp. 233–250). Washington, DC: American Psychological Association.

Seidman, E., Allen, L., Aber, J., Mitchell, C., & Feinman, J. (1994). The impact of school transitions in early adolescence on the self-system and perceived social context of poor urban youth. *Child Development, 6S*, 507–522.

Seiffge-Krenke, I. (2003). Testing theories of romantic development from adolescence to young adulthood: Evidence of a developmental sequence. *International Journal of Behavioral Development, 27*, 519–531.

Selah-Shayovits, R. (2006). Adolescent preferences for violence in television shows and music video clips. *International Journal of Adolescence and Youth, 13*(1), 99–112.

Selfhout, M. H. W., Delsing, M. J. M. H., ter Bogt, T. F. M., & Meeus, W. H. J. (2008). Heavy metal and hip-hop style preferences and externalizing problem behavior: A two-wave longitudinal study. *Youth & Society, 39*(4), 435–452.

Seligman, M. E. P. (1993). *What you can change and what you can't: The complete guide to successful self-improvement.* New York: Fawcett.

Sells, C. W., & Blum, R. W. (1996). Morbidity and mortality among U.S. adolescents: An overview of data and trends. *American Journal of Public Health, 86*, 513–519.

Selman, R. (1976). Social-cognitive understanding. In T. Lickona (Ed.), *Moral development and behavior.* New York: Holt, Rinehart & Winston.

Selman, R. (1980). *The growth of interpersonal understanding: Developmental and clinical analyses.* New York: Academic Press.

Selman, R., & Byrne, D. (1974). A structural developmental analysis of levels of role-taking in middle childhood. *Child Development, 45*, 803–806.

Sen, K., & Samad, A. Y. (Eds.). (2007). *Islam in the European Union: Transnationalism, youth and the war on terror.* New York: Oxford University Press.

Sentse, M., Scholte, R., Salmivalli, C., & Voeten, M. (2007). Person-group dissimilarity in involvement in bullying and its relation with social status. *Journal of Abnormal Child Psychology, 35*(6), 1009–1019.

Serbin, L. A., Powlishta, K. K., & Gulko, J. (1993). The development of sex typing in middle childhood. *Monographs of the Society for Research in Child Development, 58*, 1–74.

Sercombe, H. (2009). The "teen brain" research: An introduction and implications for practitioners. *Youth & Policy.*

Serow, R. C., Ciechalski, J., & Daye, C. (1990). Students as volunteers: Personal competence, social diversity, and participation in community service. *Urban Education, 25*, 157–168.

Sewell, W. H., & Hauser, R. M. (1975). *Education, occupation, and earnings: Achievement in the early career.* New York: Academic Press.

Sewell, W., & Hauser, R. (1972). Causes and consequences of higher education: Models of the status attainment process. American *Journal of Agricultural Economics, 54*, 851–861.

Sexton, M. A., & Geffen, G. (1979). Development of three strategies of attention in dichotic monitoring. *Developmental Psychology, 15*, 299–310.

Shaaban, B. (1991). *Both right and left handed: Arab women talk about their lives.* Bloomington: Indiana University Press.

Shakin, M., Shakin, D., & Sternglanz, S. H. (1985). Infant clothing: Sex labeling for strangers. *Sex Roles, 12*, 955–964.

Shalatin, S., & Phillip, M. (2003). The role of obesity and leptin in the pubertal process and pubertal growth: A review. *International Journal of Obesity and Related Metabolic Disorders, 27*, 869–874.

Shanahan, L., McHale, S. M., Crouter, A. C., & Osgood, D. W. (2007) Warmth with mothers and fathers from middle childhood to late adolescence: Within- and between-families comparisons. *Developmental Psychology, 43*(3), 551–563.

Shantz, C. U. (1983). Social cognition. In P. H. Mussen (Ed.), *Handbook of child psychology* (Vol. 3, pp. 495–555). New York: Wiley.

Shapka, J. D., & Keating, D. P. (2005). Structure and change in self-concept during adolescence. *Canadian Journal of Behavioural Science, 37*, 83–96.

Shaughnessy, J. J., & Zechmeister, E. B. (1985). *Research methods in psychology.* New York: Knopf.

Shaver, P. R., & Hazan, C. (1993). Adult romantic attachment: Theory and evidence. In D. Perlman & W. Jones (Eds.), *Advances in personal relationships* (Vol. 4, pp. 29–70). London: Jessica Kingsley.

Shaver, P., Furman, W., & Buhrmester, D. (1985). Transition to college: Network changes, social skills, and loneliness. In S. Duck & D. Perlman (Eds.), *Understanding personal relationships: An interdisciplinary approach.* Newbury Park, CA: Sage.

Shaw, P., Greenstein, D., Lerch, J., Clasen, L., Lenroot, R., Gogtay, N., Evans, A. (2006). Intellectual ability and cortical development in children and adolescents. *Nature, 440*, 676–679.

Shea, R. H. (2003, February 3). The college aid gap: A new survey finds that the neediest families have the least information about financial help. *U.S. News & World Report*, p. 42.

Shedler, J., & Block, J. (1990). Adolescent drug use and psychological health. *American Psychologist, 45*, 612–630.

Sheehan, G., Darlington, Y., Noller, P., & Feeney, J. (2004). Children's perceptions of their sibling relationships during parental separation and divorce. *Journal of Divorce & Remarriage, 41*, 69–94.

Sheehan, G., Darlington, Y., Noller, P., & Feeney, J. Children's perceptions of their sibling relationships during parental separation and divorce. *Journal of Divorce & Remarriage, 41*(1–2), 69–94.

Sheel, K. R., & Westefeld, J. S. (1999). Heavy metal music and adolescent suicidality: An empirical validation. *Adolescence, 34*, 253–273.

Sheer, V. C., & Cline, R. J. (1994). The development and validation of a model explaining sexual behavior among college students: Implications for AIDS communication campaigns. *Health Communication Research, 21*, 280–304.

Sherman, B. L., & Dominick, J. R. (1986). Violence and sex in music videos: TV and rock 'n' roll. *Journal of Communication, 36*, 79–93.

Shernoff, D. J., & Csikszentmihalyi, M. (2003). Student engagement in high school classrooms from the perspective of flow theory. *School Psychology Quarterly, 18*, 158–176.

Sherrod, L. R., Flanagan, C., & Youniss, J. (2002). Dimensions of citizenship and opportunities for youth development: The what, why, when, where, and who of citizenship development. *Applied Developmental Science, 6*, 264–272.

Sherry, J. (2006). Electronic games, violence. In J. J. Arnett (Ed.), *Encyclopedia of children, adolescents, and the media.* Thousand Oaks, CA: Sage.

Shisslak, C. M., & Crago, M. (2001). Risk and protective factors in the development of eating disorders. In J. K. Thompson & L. Smolak (Eds.), *Body image, eating disorders, and obesity in youth: Assessment, treatment, and prevention* (pp. 103–125). Washington, DC: American Psychological Association.

Shonk, S. M., & Cicchetti, D. (2001). Maltreatment, competency deficits, and risk for academic and behavioral maladjustment. *Developmental Psychology, 37*, 3–17.

Shope, J. T. (2002). Discussion paper. *Injury Prevention, 8*(Suppl. 2), ii14–ii16.

Shope, J. T. (2007). Graduated driver licensing: Review of evaluation results since 2002. *Journal of Safety Research, 38*(2), 165–175.

Shotton, H. J., Oosahwe, E. S. L., Cintrón, R. Stories of success: Experiences of American Indian students in a peer-mentoring retention program. *Review of Higher Education: Journal of the Association for the Study of Higher Education, 31*(1), 81–107.

Shukla, M. (1994). India. In K. Hurrelmann (Ed.), *International handbook of adolescence* (pp. 191–206). Westport, CT: Greenwood.

Shulman, S., & Scharf, M. (2000). Adolescent romantic behaviors and perceptions: Age-and gender-related differences, and links with family and peer relationships. *Journal of Research on Adolescence, 10*, 99–118.

Shulman, S., Laursen, B., Kalman, Z., & Karpovsky, S. (1997). Adolescent intimacy revisited. *Journal of Youth & Adolescence, 26*, 597–617.

Shweder, R. (2003). *Why do men barbecue? Recipes for cultural psychology.* Cambridge, MA: Harvard University Press.

Shweder, R. A. "What about female genital mutilation?" And why understanding culture matters in the first place. In R. A. Shweder & M. Minow (Eds.), *Engaging cultural differences: The multicultural challenge in liberal democracies* (pp. 216–251). New York: Russell Sage Foundation.

Shweder, R. A. (Ed.). (1998). *Welcome to middle age! (And other cultural fictions).* Chicago: University of Chicago Press.

Shweder, R. A. (1999). Why cultural psychology? *Ethos, 27*, 62–73.

Shweder, R. A., Goodnow, J., Hatano, G., Levine, R. A., Markus, H., & Miller, P. (2006). The cultural psychology of development: One mind, many mentalities. In W. Damon (Ed.), *Handbook of child development* (5th ed., Vol. 1, pp. 865–937) New York: Wiley.

Shweder, R. A., Mahapatra, M., & Miller, J. G. (1990). Culture and moral development. In J. W. Stigler, R. A. Shweder, & G. Herdt (Eds.), *Cultural psy-chology* (pp. 130–204). New York: Cambridge University Press.

Shweder, R. A., Much, N. C., Mahapatra, M., & Park, L. (1997). The "big three" of morality (autonomy, community, divinity), and the "big three" explanations of suffering. In A. Brandt & D. Rozin (Eds.), *Morality and health* New York: Routledge.

Sidorowicz, L. S., & Lunney, G. S. (1980). Baby X revisited. *Sex Roles, 6*, 67–73.

SIECUS (2003). Sexuality education. Available: www.siecus.org/school/sex_ed

Siegel, B. (1997, April). *Developmental and social policy issues and the practice of educational mainstreaming and full inclusion.* Paper presented at the biennial meeting of the Society for Research on Child Development, Washington, DC.

Siegel, D. L. (1992). *Sexual harassment: Research and resources.* Washington, DC: National Council for Research on Women.

Siegel, J. M. (2002). Body image change and adolescent depressive symptoms. *Journal of Adolescent Research, 17*, 27–41.

Siegler, R. (1988). Individual differences in strategy choices: Good students, not-so-good students, and perfectionists. *Child Development, 59*, 833–851.

Sieving, R. E., Perry, C. L., & Williams, C. L. (2000). Do friendships change behaviors, or do behaviors change friendships? Examining paths of influence in young adolescents' alcohol use. *Journal of Adolescent Health, 26*, 27–35.

Sigelman, C., & Toebben, J. (1992). Tolerant reactions to advocates of disagreeable ideas in childhood and adolescence. *Merrill-Palmer Quarterly, 38*, 542–557.

Silbereisen, R. K., & Kracke, B. (1997). Self-reported maturational timing and adaptation in adolescence. In J. Schulenberg, J. L. Maggs, & K. Hurrelman (Eds.), *Health risks and developmental transitions during adolescence* (pp. 85–109). New York: Cambridge University Press.

Silbereisen, R. K., Meschke, L. L., & Schwarz, B. (1996). Leaving the parental home: Predictors for young adults raised in the former East and West Germany. *New Directions in Child Development, 71*, 71–86.

Silbereisen, R., Petersen, A., Albrecht, H., & Kracke, B. (1989). Maturational timing and the development of problem behavior: Longitudinal studies in adolescence. *Journal of Early Adolescence, 9*, 247–268.

Silverberg, S., & Steinberg, L. (1990). Psychological well-being of parents at midlife: The impact of early adolescent children. *Developental Psychology, 26*, 658–666.

Silverberg K. S., Wallace. S., Jacobs Lehman, S., Lee, Sun-A., & Escalante, K. A. (2004). Sensitivity mother-to-adolescent disclosures after divorce: Is the experience of sons different from that of daughters? *Journal of Family Psychology, 18*, 46–57.

Silverberg Koerner, S., Wallace, S., Jacobs, L., S., Lee, S-A., & Escalante, K. A. Sensitive mother-to-adolescent disclosures after divorce: Is the experience of wons different from that of daughters? *Journal of Family Psychology, 18*(1), 6–57.

Simmons, R. (2002). *Odd girl out: The hidden culture of aggression in girls.* New York: Harcourt.

Simmons, R. (2004). *Odd girl speaks out: Girls write about bullies, cliques, popularity, and jealousy.* New York: Harvest.

Simmons, R. G., & Blyth, D. A. (1987). *Moving into adolescence.* New York: Aldine de Gruyter.

Simmons, R., Blyth, D., & McKinney, K. (1983). The social and psychological effects of puberty on white females. In J. Brooks-Gunn & A. Petersen (Eds.), *Girls at puberty.* New York: Plenum.

Simon, C. A., & Wang, C. (2002). The impact of Americorps on volunteer participants. *Administration & Society, 34*, 522–540.

Simons, R., Whitbeck, L., Conger, R., & Chyi-In, W. (1991). Intergenerational transmission of harsh parenting. *Developmental Psychology, 27*, 159–171.

Simons-Morton, B. (2007). Parent involvement in novice teen driving: Rationale, evidence of effects, and potential for enhancing graduated driver licensing effectiveness. *Journal of Safety Research, 38*(2), 192–202.

Simons-Morton, B. G. (2002). Reducing young driver crash risk. *Injury Prevention, 8(Suppl 2),* ii1–ii2.

Simons-Morton, B. G., Hartos, J. L. , & Leaf, W. A. (2002). Promoting parental management of teen driving. *Injury Prevention, 8(Suppl 2),* ii24–ii31.

Simons-Morton, B. G., Hartos, J. L., Leaf, W. A., & Preusser, D. F. Increasing parent limits on novice young drivers: Cognitive mediation of the effect of persuasive messages. *Journal of Adolescent Research, 21*(1), 83–105.

Singh, G., & Hernandez-Gantes, V. (1996). The relation of English language proficiency to educational aspirations of Mexican-American eighth graders. *Journal of Early Adolescence, 16,* 154–167.

Singh, G., & Yu, S. (1996). U.S. childhood mortality, 1950 through 1993: Trends and socioeconomic differentials. *American Journal of Public Health, 86,* 505–512.

Singh, S., Darroch, J. E., & Frost, J. J. (2001). Socioeconomic disadvantage and adolescent women's sexual and reproductive behavior: the case of five developed countries. *Perspectives on Sexual and Reproductive Health, 33,* 251–258, & 289.

Sinnott, J. D. (1998). *The development of logic in adulthood: Postformal thoughts and its applications.* New York: Plenum.

Sinnott, J. D. (2003). Postformal thought and adult development: Living in balance. In J. Demick & C. Andreotti (Eds.), *Handbook of adult development* (pp. 221–238). New York: Kluwer.

Sirin, S. R., & Rogers-Sirin, L. (2005). Components of school engagement among African American adolescents. *Applied Developmental Science, 9,* 5–13.

Sirin, S. R., McCreary, D. R., & Mahalik, J. R. (2004). Differential reactions to men and women's gender role transgressions. *Journal of Men's Studies, 12,* 119–132.

Skoe, E. E., & Gooden, A. (1993). Ethic of care and real-life moral dilemma content in male and female early adolescents. *Journal of Early Adolescence, 13,* 154–167.

Slater, M. D. (2003). Alienation, aggression, and sensation seeking as predictors of adolescent use of violent film, computer, and website content. *Journal of Communication, 53,* 105–121.

Slater, M. D., Henry, K. L., Swaim, R. C., & Anderson, L. L. (2003). Violent media content and aggressiveness in adolescents: A downward spiral model. *Communication Research, 30,* 713–736.

Slavin, L. A., & Rainer, K. L. (1990). Gender differences in emotional support and depressive symptoms among adolescents: A prospective analysis. *American Journal of Community Psychology, 18,* 407–421.

Slavkin, M. L. (2001). Gender schematization in adolescents: Differences based on rearing in single-parent and intact families. *Journal of Divorce and Remarriage, 34,* 137–149.

Sligh, A. C., Conners, F. A, & Roskos-Ewoldsen, B. (2005). Relation of creativity to fluid and crystallized intelligence. *Journal of Creative Behavior, 39*(2), 123–136.

Slonje, R., & Smith, P. K. (2008). Cyberbullying: Another main type of bullying? *Scandinavian Journal of Psychology, 49*(2), 147–154.

Slovak, K., & Singer, M. (2001). Gun violence exposure and trauma among rural youth. *Violence and Victims, 16,* 389–400.

Slovic, P. (1998). Do adolescent smokers know the risks? *Duke Law Journal, 47,* 1133–1141.

Smallwood, S. (2003). Women take lead in number of U.S. doctorates awarded, as total falls again. *Chronicle of Higher Education, Daily News.* Retrieved on December 12, 2003, from http://chronicle.com/prm/daily/2003/12/2003120502n.htm

Smart, T., Stoughton, S., & Behr, P. (1999, September 12). Working their way up: Economy's expansion has lifted those on the bottom rung, but will gains last? *Washington Post,* p. H-1.

Smetana, J. (1988). Concepts of self and social convention: Adolescents' and parents' reasoning about hypothetical and actual family conflicts. In M. Gunnar & W. A. Collins (Eds.), *Minnesota Symposium on Child Psychology* (Vol. 21, pp. 79–122). Hillsdale, NJ: Erlbaum.

Smetana, J. (1989). Adolescents' and parents' reasoning about actual family conflict. *Child Development, 59,* 1052–1067.

Smetana, J., & Asquith, R. (1994). Adolescents' and parents' conceptions of parental authority and personal autonomy. *Child Development, 65,* 1147–1162.

Smetana, J., & Gaines, C. (1999). Adolescent-parent conflict in middle-class African American families. *Child Development, 70,* 1447–1463.

Smetana, J. G. (1993). Morality in context: Abstractions, ambiguities, and applications. *Annals of Child Development, 10,* 83–130.

Smetana, J. G. (2005). Adolescent-parent conflict: Resistance and subversion as developmental process. In L. Nucci (Ed.), *Conflict, contradiction, and contrarian elements in moral development and education* (pp. 69–91). Mahwah, NJ: Erlbaum.

Smetana, J. G., Daddis, C., & Chuang, S. S. (2003). "Clean your room!" A longitudinal investigation of adolescent-parent conflict and conflict resolution in middle-class African American families. *Journal of Adolescent Research, 18,* 631–650.

Smetana, J. G., Metzger, A., & Campione-Barr, N. (2004). African American late adolescents' relationships with parents: Developmental transitions and longitudinal patterns. *Child Development, 75,* 932–947.

Smetana, J., Yau, J., Restrepo, A., & Braeges, J. (1991). Adolescent–parent conflict in married and divorced families. *Developmental Psychology, 27,* 1000–1010.

Smith, C. (1991). Sex and gender on prime time. *Journal of Homosexuality, 12,* 119–138.

Smith, C., & Denton, M. L. (2005). *Soul searching: The religious and spiritual lives of American teenagers.* New York: Oxford University Press.

Smith, D. (2000, May 6). *Jocks and couch potatoes Washington Post .* p. A13.

Smith, E., & Udry, J. (1985). Coital and non-coital sexual behaviors of white and black adolescents. *American Journal of Public Health, 75,* 1200–1203.

Smith, K., McGraw, S., Crawford, S., Costa, L., & McKinlay, J. (1993). HIV risk among Latino adolescents in two New England cities. *American Journal of Public Health, 83,* 1395–1399.

Smith, P. K., Shu, S., & Madsen, K. (2001). Characteristics of victims of school bullying: Developmental changes in coping strategies and skills. In J. Juvonen & S. Graham (Eds.), *Peer harassment in school: The plight of the vulnerable and victimized* (pp. 332–351). New York: Guilford.

Smith, S. L., & Boyson, A. R. (2002). Violence in music videos: Examining the prevalence and context of physical aggression. *Journal of Communication, 52,* 61–83.

Smith, T. (1992). Gender differences in the scientific achievement of adolescents: Effects of age and parental separation. *Social Forces, 71,* 469–484.

Smith, T. (1993, March). *Federal employment training programs for youth: Failings and opportunities.* Paper presented at the biennial meeting of the Society for Research in Child Development, New Orleans, LA.

Smock, P. J. (1993). The economic costs of marital disruption for young women over the past two decades. *Demography, 30,* 353–371.

Smoll, F., & Schutz, R. (1990). Quantifying gender differences in physical performance: A developmental perspective. *Developmental Psychology, 26,* 360–369.

Snarey, J. R. (1985). Cross-cultural universality of social moral development: A review of Kohlbergian research. *Psychological Bulletin, 97,* 202–232.

Sneeding, T. M., & Phillips, K. R. (2002). Cross-national differences in employment and economic sufficiency. *Annals of the American Academy of Political Social Science, 580,* 103–133.

Snow, R. E., & Yalow, E. (1988). Education and intelligence. In R. J. Sternberg (Ed.), *Handbook of human intelligence* (pp. 493–585). New York: Cambridge University Press.

Snyder, J., Reid, J., & Patterson, G. (2003). A social learning model of child and adolescent antisocial behavior. In B. B. Lahey & T. E. Moffitt (Eds.), *Causes of conduct disorder and juvenile delinquency* (pp. 27–48). New York: Guilford.

Solarzano, D. G. (1992). An exploratory analysis of the effects of race, class, and gender on student and parent mobility aspirations. *Journal of Negro Education, 61,* 30–44.

Solarzano, L. (1984, August 27). Students think schools are making the grade. *U.S. News & World Report,* pp. 49–51.

Solberg, M. E., Olweus, D., & Endresen, I. M. (2007). Bullies and victims at school: Are they the same pupils? *British Journal of Educational Psychology, 77*(2), 441–464.

Sommers, C. H. (2000, May). The war against boys. *Atlantic Monthly,* pp. 59–74.

Sommers-Flanagan, R., Sommers-Flanagan, J., & Davis, B. (1993). What's happening on music television? A gender role content analysis. *Sex Roles, 28,* 745–753.

Sommerville, J. (1982). *The rise and fall of childhood.* Beverly Hills, CA: Sage.

Sonenstein, E. L., Pleck, J. H., & Ku, L. C. (1991). Levels of sexual activity among adolescent males in the United States. *Family Planning Perspectives, 23,* 162–167.

Sorell, G. T., & Montgomery, M. J. (2001). Feminist perspectives on Erikson's theory: Their relevance for contemporary identity development research. *Identity, 1,* 97–128.

Sorell, G. T., & Montgomery, M. J. (2002). The ubiquity of gendered cultural contexts: A rejoinder to Kroger, Archer, Levine, and Côté. *Identity, 2,* 281–285.

Sourander, A., Helstelae, L., Helenius, H., & Piha, J. (2000). Persistence of bullying from childhood to adolescence: A longitudinal 8-year follow-up study. *Child Abuse & Neglect, 24,* 873–881.

Sowell, E., Trauner, D., Ganst, A. & Jernigan, T. (2002). Development of cortical and subcortical brain structures in childhood and adolescence: A structural MRI study. *Developmental Medicine and Child Neurology, 44,* 4–16.

Sowell, E. R., Thompson, P. M., Holmes, C. J., Jernigan, T. I., & Toga, A. W. (1999). In vivo evidence for post-adolescence brain maturation in frontal and striatal regions. *Nature Neuroscience, 2,* 859–861.

Sparrow, P. R., & Davies, D. R. (1988). Effects of age, tenure, training, and job complexity on technical performance. *Psychology and Aging, 3,* 307–314.

Spear, P. (2000). The adolescent brain and age-related behavioral manifestations. *Neuroscience and Biobehavioral Review, 24,* 417–463.

Spence, J., & Helmreich, R. (1978). *Masculinity and femininity: Their psychological dimensions, correlates, and antecedents.* Austin: University of Texas Press.

Spencer, M., & Dornbusch, S. (1990). Challenges in studying minority youth. In S. Feldman & G. Elliott (Eds.), *At the threshold: The developing adolescent* (pp. 123–146). Cambridge, MA: Harvard University Press.

Spencer, M., & Markstrom-Adams, C. (1990). Identity processes among racial and ethnic minority children in America. *Child Development, 61,* 290–310.

Spencer, P. (1965). *The Samburu: A study of gerontocracy in a nomadic tribe.* Berkeley: University of California Press.

Spencer, R., Porche, M. V., & Tolman, D. L. (2003). We've come a long way – Maybe: New challenges for gender equity in education. *Teachers College Record, 105,* 1774–1807.

Spengler, E. A. (2002, April 29). Career choice: It's a tough job. *Washington Post,* p. C10.

Spera, C. (2005). A review of the relationship among parenting practices, parenting styles, and adolescent school achievement. *Educational Psychology Review, 17,* 125–146.

Sperber, M. (2000). *Beer and circus: How big-time college sports is crippling undergraduate education.* New York: Henry Holt.

Spirito, A., Overholser, J. C. (2003). *Evaluating and treating adolescent suicide attempters: From research to practice.* San Diego, CA: Academic Press.

Spirito, A., Valeri, S., & Boergers, J. (2003). Predictors of continued suicidal behavior in adolescents following a suicide attempt. *Journal of Clinical Child & Adolescent Psychology, 32,* 284–289.

Sprecher, S. (1994). Two sides to the breakup of dating relationships. *Personal Relationships, 1,* 199–222.

Sprecher, S., & Chandak, R. (1992). Attitudes about arranged marriages and dating among men and women from India. *Journal of Sex Research, 32,* 3–15.

Sprecher, S., Barbee, A., & Schwartz, P. (1995). "Was it good for you, too?" Gender differences in first sexual intercourse experiences. *Journal of Sex Research, 32,* 3–15.

Sprecher, S., & Regan, P. C. (1996). College virgins: How men and women perceive their sexual status. *Journal of Sex Research, 33,* 3–15.

Squires, C. R., Kohn-Wood, L. P., Chavous, T., & Carter, P. L. (2006). Evaluating agency and responsibility in gendered violence: African American youth talk about violence and hip hop. *Sex Roles, 55*(11–12), 725–737.

Sroufe, L. A., Carlson, E., & Schulman, S. (1993). Individuals in relationships: Development from infancy through adolescence. In D. C. Funder, R. D. Parke, C. Tomlinson-Keasey, & K. Widaman (Eds.), *Studying lives through time: Personality and development* (pp. 51–60). Norwood, NJ: Ablex.

Sroufe, L. A., Egeland, B., Carlson, E. A., & Collins, W. A. (2005). The development of the person: The Minnesota study of risk and adaptation from birth to adulthood. New York: Guilford.

St. Louis, G. R., & Liem, J. H. (2005). Ego identity, ethnic identity, and the psychosocial well-being of ethnic minority and majority college students. *Identity, 5,* 227–246.

Staff, J., Mortimer, J. T., & Uggen, C. (2004). Work and leisure in adolescence. In R. M. Lerner & L. Steinberg (Eds.), *Handbook of adolescent psychology* (2nd ed., pp. 429–450). Hoboken, NJ: John Wiley & Sons.

Stafseng, O. (1994). Norway. In K. Hurrelmann (Ed.), *International handbook of adolescence* (pp. 287–298). Westport, CT: Greenwood Press.

Stake, J. E., & Nickens, S. D. (2005). Adolescent girls' and boys' science peer relationships and perceptions of the possible self as scientist. *Sex Roles, 52,* 1–11.

Stanger, C., Achenbach, T., & McConaughy, S. (1993). Three-year course of behavioral/emotional problems in a national sample of 4- to 16-year-olds, 3: Predictors of signs of disturbance. *Journal of Consulting and Clinical Psychology, 61,* 839–848.

Stangor, C., & Ruble, D. N. (1987). Development of gender role knowledge and gender constancy. In L. Liben & M. Signorella (Eds.), *Children's gender schemata* (pp. 5–22). San Francisco: Jossey Bass.

Stangor, C., & Ruble, D. N. (1989). Differential influences of gender schemata and gender constancy on children's information processing and behavior. *Social Cognition, 7,* 353–372.

Stanley, S. M., Rhoades, G. K., & Markman, H. J. (2006) Sliding versus deciding: Inertia and the premarital cohabitation effect. *Family Relations, 55*(4), 499–509.

Stanley, S. M., Whitton, S. W., & Markman, H. J. (2004). Maybe I do: Interpersonal commitment and premarital or nonmarital cohabitation. *Journal of Family Issues, 25,* 496–519.

Stanton-Salazar, R. D., & Spina, S. U. (2005). Adolescent peer networks and a context for social and emotional support. *Youth & Society, 36*(4), 379–417.

Stattin, H., & Magnusson, D. (1990). *Pubertal maturation in female development.* Hillsdale, NJ: Erlbaum.

Stedman, L., & Smith, M. (1983). Recent reform proposals for American education. *Contemporary Education Review, 2,* 85–104.

Steele, J. (2006). Media practice model. In J. J. Arnett (Ed.), *Encyclopedia of children, adolescents, and the media.* Thousand Oaks, CA: Sage.

Steele, J. R. (2002). Teens and movies: Something to do, plenty to learn. In J. D. Brown, J. R. Steele, & K. Walsh-Childers (Eds.), *Sexual teens, sexual media: Investigating media's influence on adolescent sexuality* (pp. 227–252). Mahwah, NJ: Erlbaum.

Steele, J. R., & Brown, J. D. (1995). Adolescent room culture: Studying media in the context of everyday life. *Journal of Youth & Adolescence, 24,* 551–576.

Stein, J., Newcomb, M., & Bentler, P. (1987). An 8-year study of the multiple influences on drug use and drug use consequences. *Journal of Personality and Social Psychology, 53,* 1094–1105.

Stein, J., & Reiser, L. (1994). A study of white middle-class adolescent boys' responses to "semenarche" (the first ejaculation). *Journal of Youth & Adolescence, 23,* 373–384.

Stein, J. A., Newcomb, M. D., & Bentler, P. M. (1994). Psychosocial correlates and predictors of AIDS risk behaviors, abortion, and drug use among a community sample of young adult women. *Health Psychology, 13,* 308–318.

Stein, J. H., & Reiser, L. W. (1993). A study of White middle-class adolescent boys' responses to "semenarche" (the first ejaculation). *Journal of Youth & Adolescence, 23,* 373–383.

Stein, N. (1995). Sexual harassment in school: The public performance of gendered violence. *Harvard Educational Review, 65,* 145–162.

Steinberg, L. (1986). Latchkey children and susceptibility to peer pressure: An ecological analysis. *Developmental Psychology, 22,* 433–439.

Steinberg, L. (1987a). The impact of puberty on family relations: Effects of pubertal status and pubertal timing. *Developmental Psychology, 23,* 451–460.

Steinberg, L. (1987b, September). Bound to bicker: Pubescent primates leave home for good reasons. Our teens stay with us and squabble. *Psychology Today,* 36–39.

Steinberg, L. (1987c). Single parents, stepparents, and the susceptibility of adolescents to antisocial peer pressure. *Child Development, 58,* 269–275.

Steinberg, L. (1988). Reciprocal relation between parent–child distance and pubertal maturation. *Developmental Psychology, 24,* 122–128.

Steinberg, L. (1989). Pubertal maturation and parent–adolescent distance: An evolutionary perspective. In G. Adams, R. Montemayor, & T. Gullotta (Eds.), *Advances in adolescent development* (Vol. 1, pp. 71–97). Beverly Hills, CA: Sage.

Steinberg, L. (1990). Autonomy, conflict, and harmony in the family relationship. In S. Feldman & G. Elliott (Eds.), *At the threshold: The developing adolescent* (pp. 255–276). Cambridge, MA: Harvard University Press.

Steinberg, L. (1996). *Beyond the classroom: Why school reform has failed and what parents need to do.* New York: Simon & Schuster.

Steinberg, L. (2000, April). *We know some things: Parent–adolescent relations in retrospect and prospect.* Presidential Address: presented at the biennial meeting of the Society for Research on Adolescence, Chicago.

Steinberg, L. (2001). Presidential Address: We know some things ... *Journal of Research on Adolescence, 11,* 1–19.

Steinberg, L. (2008). A social neuroscience perspective on adolescent risk-taking. *Developmental Review, 28,* 78–106.

Steinberg, L., & Cauffman, E. (1995). The impact of employment on adolescent development. In R. Vasta (Ed.), *Annals of Child Development* (Vol. 11, pp. 131–166). London: Jessica Kingsley.

Steinberg, L., & Cauffman, E. (1996). Maturity of judgment in adolescence: Psychosocial factors in adolescent decision making. *Law and Human Behavior, 20,* 249–272.

Steinberg, L., & Cauffman, E. (2001). Adolescents as adults in court: A developmental perspective on the transfer of juveniles to criminal court. *SRCD Social Policy Report, 15*(4), 9–13.

Steinberg, L., Dornbusch, S. M., & Brown, B. B. (1992). Ethnic differences in adolescent achievement: An ecological perspective. *American Psychologist, 47,* 723–729.

Steinberg, L., Greenberger, E., Garduque, L., Ruggiero, M., & Vaux, A. (1982). Effects of working on adolescent development. *Developmental Psychology, 18,* 385–395.

Steinberg, L., Lamborn, S., Darling, N., Mounts, N., & Dornbusch, S. (1994). Over-time changes in adjustment and competence among adolescents from authoritative, authoritarian, indulgent, and neglectful families. *Child Development, 65,* 754–770.

Steinberg, L., & Levine, A. (1997). *You and your adolescent: A parents' guide for ages 10 to 20* (rev. ed.). New York: HarperCollins.

Steinberg, L., Mounts, N., Lamborn, S., & Dornbusch, S. (1991). Authoritative parenting and adolescent adjustment across various ecological niches. *Journal of Research on Adolescence, 1,* 19–36.

Steinberg, L., & Silk, J. S. (2002). Parenting adolescents. In M. H. Bornstein (Ed.), *Handbook of Parenting, Vol. 1: Children and parenting* (2nd ed., pp. 103–133). Mahwah, NJ: Erlbaum.

Steinberg, L., & Steinberg, W. (1994). *Crossing paths: How your child's adolescence triggers your own crisis.* New York: Simon & Schuster.

Steinhauer, J. (1995, January 4). Teen-age girls talk back on exercise. *New York Times,* pp. B1, B4.

Steinhausen, H. (1995). The course and outcome of anorexia nervosa. In K. D. Brownell & C. G. Fairburn (Eds.), *Eating disorders and obesity: A comprehensive handbook* (pp. 234–237). New York: Guilford.

Steinhausen, H. -C., Boyadjieva, S., Griogoroiu-Serbanescue, M., & Neumärker, K. -J. (2003). The outcome of adolescent eating disorders: Findings from an international collaborative study. *European Child & Adolescent Psychiatry, 12,* i91–i98.

Steinman, K. J., & Zimmerman, M. A. (2004). Religious activity and risk behavior among Africa American adolescents: Concurrent and developmental effects. *American Journal of Community Psychology, 33,* 151–161.

Stephens, D. P., & Few, A. L. (2007). Hip hop honey or video ho: African American preadolescents' understanding of female sexual scripts in hip hop culture. *Sexuality & Culture: An Interdisciplinary Quarterly, 11*(4), 48–69.

Steptoe, A., & Wardle, J. (2001). Health behavior, risk awareness, and emotional well-being in students from Eastern and Western Europe. *Social Science and Medicine, 53,* 1621–1630.

Stern, D., Rahn, M. L., & Chung, Y. (1998). Design of work-based learning for students in the United States. *Youth & Society, 29,* 471–502.

Stern, P. (2003). Upside-Down and backwards: Time discipline in a Canadian inuit town. *Anthropologica, 45,* 147–161.

Stern, S. (2002). Sexual selves on the World Wide Web: Adolescent girls' home pages as sites for sexual self-expression. In J. D. Brown, J. R. Steele, & K. Walsh-Childers (Eds.), *Sexual teens, sexual media: Investigating media's influence on adolescent sexuality* (pp. 265–285). Mahwah, NJ: Erlbaum.

Stern, S. R. (2002). Virtually speaking: Girls' self-disclosure on the WWW. *Women's Studies in Communications, 25,* 223–253.

Sternberg, R. (1977). *Intelligence, information processing, and analogical reasoning: The componential analysis of human abilities.* Hillsdale, NJ: Erlbaum.

Sternberg, R. (1983). Components of human intelligence. *Cognition, 15,* 1–48.

Sternberg, R. (1988). *The triarchic mind: A new theory of human intelligence.* New York: Viking Penguin.

Sternberg, R. J. (1986). A triangular theory of love. *Psychological Review, 93,* 119–135.

Sternberg, R. J. (1986). *Intelligence applied.* San Diego, CA: Harcourt Brace Jovanovich.

Sternberg, R. J. (1987). Liking versus loving: A comparative evaluation of theories. *Psychological Bulletin, 102,* 331–345.

Sternberg, R. J. (1988). Triangulating love. In R. J. Sternberg & M. L. Barnes (Eds.), *The psychology of love* (pp. 119–138). New Haven, CT: Yale University Press.

Sternberg, R. J. (1990). *Metaphors of mind: Conceptions of the nature of intelligence.* New York: Cambridge University Press.

Sternberg, R. J. (1997, April). *Practical intelligence differs from academic intelligence.* Paper presented at the meeting of the Society for Research in Child Development, Washington, DC.

Sternberg, R. J., (2005). Augmenting the SAT through assessments of analytical, practical, and creative skills. In W. J. Camara & E. W. Kimmel (Eds.), *Choosing students: Higher education admissions tools for the 21st century* (pp. 159–176). Mahwah, NJ: Erlbaum.

Sternberg, R. J., & Clinkenbeard, P. R. (1995, May/June). The triarchic model applied to identifying, teaching, and assessing gifted children. *Roeper Review,* pp. 255–260.

Sternberg, R. J., Conway, B. E., Ketron, J. L., & Berstein, M. (1981). People's conceptions of intelligence. *Journal of Personality and Social Psychology, 41,* 37–55.

Sternberg, R., & Rifkin, B. (1979). The development of analogical reasoning processes. *Journal of Experimental Child Psychology, 27,* 195–232.

Sternberg, R. J., & Nigro, C. (1980). Developmental patterns in the solution of verbal analogies. *Child Development, 51,* 27–38.

Stevens, J. H. (1984). Black grandmothers' and black adolescent mothers' knowledge about parenting. *Developmental Psychology, 20,* 1017–1025.

Stevenson, H., & Stigler, J. (1992). *The learning gap: Why our schools are failing and what we can learn from Japanese and Chinese education.* New York: Simon & Schuster.

Stevenson, H. C. (2004). Boys in the men's clothing: Racial socialization and neighborhood safety as buffers to hypervulnerability in Africa American adolescent males. In N. Way & J. Y. Chu (Eds.), *Adolescent boys: Exploring diverse cultures of boyhood* (pp. 59–77). New York: New York University Press.

Stevenson, H. W. (1992, December). Learning from Asian schools. *Scientific American* pp. 6, 70–76.

Stevenson, H. W., & Zusho, A. (2000, February). *Adolescence in China and Japan.* Paper prepared for the meeting of the Study Group on Adolescence in the 21st Century, Washington, DC.

Stevenson, H. W., & Zusho, A. (2002). Adolescence in China and Japan: Adapting to a changing environment. In B. B. Brown, R. Larson, & T. S. Saraswathi (Eds.), *The World's Youth: Adolescence in Eight Regions of the Globe* (pp. 141–170). New York: Cambridge University Press.

Stewart, R. B., Beilfuss, M. L., & Verbrugge, K. M. (1995, March). *That was then, this is now: An empirical typology of adult sibling relationships.* Paper presented at the biennial meeting of the Society for Research on Child Development, Indianapolis, IN.

Stice, E., Shaw, H., & Marti, C.N. (2006). A meta-analytic review of obesity programs for children and adolescents. *Psychological Bulletin, 132,* 667-691.

Stigler, J. W., Shweder, R. A., & Herdt, G. (Eds.) (1990). *Cultural psychology.* New York: Cambridge University Press.

Stiles, D. A., Gibbons, J. L., & Schnellman, J. (1990). The smiling sunbather and the chivalrous football player: Young adolescents' images of the ideal women and man. *Journal of Early Adolescence, 7,* 411–427.

Stockwell, T., Toumbourou, J. W., Letcher, P., Smart, D., Sanson, A., & Bond, L. (2004). Risk and protection factors for different intensities of adolescent substance use: When does the prevention paradox apply? *Drug & Alcohol Review, 23,* 67–77.

Stoll, B. M., Arnaut, G. L., Fromme, D. K., & Felker-Thayer, J. A. Adolescents in stepfamilies: A qualitative analysis. *Journal of Divorce & Remarriage, 44*(1–2), 177–189.

Stone, M. H. (1993). Long-term outcome in personality disorders. *British Journal of Psychiatry, 162,* 299–313.

Stone, M. R., Barber, B. L., & Eccles, J. S. (2000, April). *Adolescent "crowd" clusters: An adolescent perspective on persons and patterns.* Paper presented at the biennial meeting of the Society for Research on Adolescence, Chicago.

Stone, M. R., & Brown, B. B. (1998). In the eye of the beholder: Adolescents' perceptions of peer crowd stereotypes. In R. Muuss (Ed.), *Adolescent behavior and society: A book of readings* (5th ed., pp. 158–169). San Francisco: Jossey-Bass.

Stone, M. R., & Brown, B. B. (1999). Identity claims and projections: Descriptions of self and crowds in secondary schools. *New Directions for Child and Adolescent Development, 84,* 7–20.

Stones, M. J., & Kozma, A. (1996). Activity, exercise, and behavior. In J. E. Birren & K. W. Schaie (Eds.), *Handbook of psychology of aging* (4th ed., pp. 338–352). San Diego, CA: Academic Press.

Storch, E. A., Bagner, D. M., Geffken, G. R., & Baumeister, A. L. (2004). Association between overt and relational aggression and psychosocial adjustment in undergraduate college students. *Violence & Victims, 19,* 689–700.

Stouthamer-Loeber, M., & Wei, E. H. (1998). The precursors of young fatherhood and its effects on delinquency of teenage males. *Journal of Adolescent Health, 22,* 56–65.

Strachen, A., & Jones, D. (1982). Changes in identification during adolescence: A personal construct theory approach. *Journal of Personality Assessment, 46,* 139–148.

Strahan, D. B. (1983). The emergence of formal operations in adolescence. *Transcendence, 11,* 7–14.

Strandh, M., & Nordenmark, M. (2006). The interference of paid work with household demands in different social policy contests: Perceived work-household conflict in Sweden, the UK, the Netherlands, Hungary & the Czech Republic. *British Journal of Sociology, 57*(4), 597–617.

Strasburger, V. (2006). Super peer. In J. J. Arnett (Ed.), *Encyclopedia of children, adolescents, and the media.* Thousand Oaks, CA: Sage.

Strasburger, V. C. (1995). *Adolescents and the media: Medical and psychological impact.* Thousand Oaks, CA: Sage.

Strasburger, V., & Wilson, B. (2002). *Children, adolescents, and the media.* Thousand Oaks, CA: Sage.

Strauch, B. (2003). *The primal teen: What the new discoveries about the teenage brain tell us about our kids.* New York: Anchor.

Strauss, V. (2002, September 17). Looking for a few wise children: In the confused arena of the gifted and talented, research suggests a new basis for selecting students. *Washington Post,* p. A11.

Strickland, B. R. (1995). Research on sexual orientation and human development: A commentary. *Developmental Psychology, 31,* 137–140.

Striegel-Moore, R. H. (1997). Risk factors for eating disorders. In M. S. Jacobson & J. M. Rees (Eds.), *Adolescent nutritional disorders: Prevention and treatment* (pp. 98–109). New York: New York Academy of Sciences.

Striegel-Moore, R. H., & Cachelin, F. M. (1999). Body image concerns and disordered eating in adolescent girls: Risk and protective factors. In N. B. Johnson, M. C. Roberts, & J. Worell (Eds.), *Beyond appearance: A new look at adolescent girls* (pp. 85–108). Washington, DC: American Psychological Association.

Striegel-Moore, R. H., & Franko, D. L. (2006). Adolescent eating disorders. In C. A. Essau (Ed.), *Child and adolescent psychopathology: Theoretical and clinical implications.* (pp. 160–183). New York: Routledge/Taylor & Francis.

Striegel-Moore, R. H., Seeley, J. R., & Lewinsohn, P. M. (2003). Psychosocial adjustment in young adulthood of women who experienced an eating disorder during adolescence. *Journal of the American Academy of Child & Adolescent Psychiatry, 42,* 587–593.

Strommen, E. F. (1989). "You're a what?" Family member reactions to the disclosure of homosexuality. *Journal of Homosexuality, 19,* 37–58.

Stromquist, N. P. (2007). Gender equity education globally. In S. S. Klein, B. Richardson, D. A. Grayson, L. H. Fox, C. Kramarae, et al. (Eds.), *Handbook for achieving gender equity through education* (2nd ed., pp. 33–42). Mahwah, NJ: Lawrence Erlbaum.

Studer, J. (1993). A comparison of the self-concepts of adolescents from intact, maternal custodial, and paternal custodial families. *Journal of Divorce and Remarriage, 19,* 219–227.

Suárez-Orozco, C. (2004). Formulating identity in a globalized world. In M. Suárez-Orozco, D. Baolian, & M. Hilliard-Qin (Eds.), *Globalization: Culture and education in the new millennium* (pp. 173–202). Berkeley: University of California Press.

Suárez-Orozco, C., & Qin-Hilliard, D. B. (2004). Immigrant boys' experiences in U.S. schools. In N. Way & J. Y. Chu (Eds.), *Adolescent boys: Exploring the diverse cultures of boyhood* (pp. 295–316). New York: New York University Press.

Suárez-Orozco, C., & Suarez-Orozco, M. (1996). *Transformations: Migration, family life and achievement motivation among Latino adolescents.* Palo Alto, CA: Stanford University Press.

Subrahmanyam, K., Greenfield, P. M., & Tynes, B. (2004). Constructing sexuality and identity in an online. *Journal of Applied Developmental Psychology, 25,* 651–666.

Substance Abuse and Mental Health Services Administration. (1999). *1998 National survey on drug abuse.* Rockville, MD: Author.

Sudman, S., & Bradburn, N. M. (1989). *Asking questions: A practical guide to questionnaire design.* San Francisco: Jossey-Bass.

Sue, D. Asian American masculinity and therapy: The concept of masculinity in Asian American males. *Susan, David: Western Washington University, Center for Cross-Cultural Research.* Belllingham, WA.

Sullivan, H. S. (1953). *The interpersonal theory of psychiatry.* New York: Norton.

Sullivan, L. C., & Sullivan, A. (1980). Adolescent–parent separation. *Developmental Psychology, 16,* 93–99.

Sullivan, R. E. (2003). Rap and race: It's got a nice beat, but what about the message? *Journal of Black Studies, 33,* 605–622.

Sun, S., & Lull, J. (1986). The adolescent audience for music videos and why they watch. *Journal of Communication, 36,* 115–125.

Sun, S. S., Schubert, C. M., Liang, R., Roche, A. F., Kulin, H. E, Lee, P. A., Himes, J. H., & Chumlea, W. C. (2005). Is sexual maturity occurring earlier among U.S. children? *Journal of Adolescent Health, 37*(5), 345–355.

Sundar, S. (2006). Internet, positive uses. In J. J. Arnett (Ed.), *Encyclopedia of children, adolescents, and the media.* Thousand Oaks, CA: Sage.

Sung, B. L. (1979). *Transplanted Chinese children.* Washington, DC: Department of Health, Education, and Welfare. (ERIC Document Reproduction Service No. ED 182–040).

Sung, B. L. (1985). Bicultural conflicts in Chinese immigrant children. *Journal of Comparative Studies, 16,* 255–270.

Super, D. (1992). Toward a comprehensive study of career development. In D. H. Montross & C. J. Shinkman (Eds.), *Career development: Theory and practice* (pp. 35–64). Springfield, IL: Charles C. Thomas.

Super, D. E. (1967). *The psychology of careers.* New York: Harper & Row.

Super, D. E. (1976). *Career education and the meanings of work.* Washington, DC: U.S. Office of Education.

Super, D. E. (1980). A life-span life-space approach to career development. *Journal of Vocational Behavior, 16,* 282–298.

Supple, A. J., Aquilino, W. S., & Wright, D. L. (1999). Collecting sensitive self-report data with laptop computers: Impact on the response tendencies of adolescents in a home interview. *Journal of Research on Adolescence, 9,* 467–488.

Surbey, M. (1990). Family composition, stress, and human menarche. In F. Bercovitch & T. Zeigler (Eds.), *The socioendocrinology of primate reproduction.* New York: Alan R. Liss.

Surrey, J. L. (1991). The self-in-relation: A theory of women's development. In J. V. Jordan, A. G. Kaplan, J. B. Miller, L. R. Stiver, & J. L. Surrey (Eds.), *Women and growth in connection* (pp. 51–66). New York: Guilford.

Susman, E., Koch, R., Maney, D., & Finkelstein, J. (1993). Health promotion in adolescence: Developmental and theoretical considerations. In R. Lerner (Ed.), *Early adolescence: Perspectives on research, policy, and intervention.* (pp. 247–260). Hillsdale, NJ: Erlbaum.

Susman, E. J., & Rogol, A. (2004). Puberty and psychological development. In R. Lerner & L. Steinberg (Eds.), *Handbook of adolescent psychology.* New York: Wiley.

Susman, E. J. (1997). Modeling developmental complexity in adolescence: Hormones and behavior in context. *Journal of Research on Adolescence, 7,* 283–306.

Susman, E. J., Dorn, L. D., & Schiefelbein, V. L. (2003). Puberty, sexuality, and health. In R. M. Lerner & A. M. Easterbrooks (Eds.), *Handbook of psychology: Developmental psychology,* (Vol. 6, pp. 295–324). New York: Wiley.

Sussman, S., Pokhrel, P., Ashmore, R. D., & Brown, B. B. (2007). Adolescent peer group identification and characteristics: A review of the literature. *Addictive Behaviors, 32*(8), 1602–1627.

Swanson, D. P., Spencer, M. B., & Petersen, A. (1998). Identity formation in adolescence. In K. Borman & B. Schneider (Eds.), *The adolescent years: Social influences and educational challenges: Ninety-seventh yearbook of the National Society for the Study of Education, Part 1* (pp. 18–41). Chicago: National Society for the Study of Education.

Swanson, H. L., & Deshler, D. (2003). Instructing adolescents with learing disabilities: Converting a meta-analysis to practice. *Journal of Learning Disabilities, 36,* 124–135.

Swardson, A. (1999, September 28). In Europe's economic boom, finding work is a bust. *Washington Post,* pp. 1, 20.

Swensen, C. H., Eskew, R. W., & Kohlhepp, K. A. (1981). Stage of family life cycle, ego development, and the marriage relationship. *Journal of Marriage and the Family, 43,* 841–853.

Swenson, C. C., Henggeler, S. W., Taylor, I. S., & Addison, O. W. (2005). Multisystemic therapy and neighborhood partnerships: Reducing adolescent violence and substance abuse. New York: Guilford.

Swidler, A. (1986). Culture in action: Symbols and strategies. *American Sociological Review, 51,* 273–286.

Swinbourne, J. M., & Touyz, S. W. (2007). The co-morbidity of eating disorders and anxiety disorders: A review. *European Eating Disorders Review, 15*(4), 253–274.

Szeszulski, R., Martinez, A., & Reyes, B. (1994, February). *Patterns and predictors of self-satisfaction among culturally diverse high school students.* Paper presented at the biennial meeting of the Society for Research on Adolescence, San Diego.

TADS Team. (2007). The Treatment for Adolescents with Depression Study (TADS): Long term effectiveness and safety outcomes. *Archives of General Psychiatry, 64*(10), 1132–1144.

Taga, K. A., Markey, C. N, & Friedman, H. S. (2006). A longitudinal investigation of associations between boys' pubertal timing and adult behavioral health and well-being. *Journal of Youth and Adolescence, 35*(3), 401–411.

Taillon, G. (2004). *Remote control wars: The media battle for the hearts and minds of our youths.* Frederick, MD: Publish American Baltimore.

Takahashi, K., and Takeuchi, K. (2007). Japan. In J. J. Arnett, R. Ahmed, B. Nsamenang, T. S. Saraswathi, & R. Silbereisen (Eds.), *International encyclopedia of adolescence.* New York: Routledge.

Talbani, A., & Hasanali, P. (2000). Adolescent females between tradition and modernity: Gender role socialization in south Asian immigrant families. *Journal of Adolescence, 23,* 615–627.

Tamir, L. M. (1982). *Men in their forties: The transition to middle age.* New York: Springer.

Tamis-LeMonda, C. S., Way, N., Hughes, D., Yoshikawa, H., Kalman, R. K., & Niwa, E. Y. (2008). Parents' goals for children: The dynamic coexistence of individualism and collectivism in cultures and individuals. *Social Development, 17*(1), 183–209.

Tan, A. S., Tan, G., & Gibson, T. (2003). Socialization effects of American television on international audiences. In G. M. Elasmar (Ed.), *The impact of international television: A paradigm shift* (pp. 29–38). Mahwah, NJ: Lawrence Erlbaum.

Tang, C. S., Yeung, D. Y. L., & Lee, A. M. (2003). Psychosocial correlates of emotional responses to menarche among Chinese adolescent girls. *Journal of Adolescent Health, 33,* 193–201.

Tang, C. S., Yeung, D. Y. L., & Lee, A. M. (2004). A comparison of premenarcheal expectations and postmenarcheal experiences in Chinese early adolescents. *Journal of Early Adolescence, 24,* 180–195.

Tanner, D. (1972). *Secondary education.* New York: Macmillan.

Tanner, J. M. (1962). *Growth at adolescence (2nd ed.).* Springfield, IL: Thomas.

Tanner, J. M. (1970). Physical growth. In P. H. Mussen (Ed.), *Carmichael's manual of child psychology* (Vol. 2, 3rd ed., pp. 77–156). New York: Wiley.

Tanner, J. M. (1971). Sequence, tempo, and individual variation in the growth and development of boys and girls aged twelve to sixteen. *Daedalus, 100,* 907–930.

Tanner, J. M. (1991). Growth spurt, adolescent. In R. M. Lerner, A. C. Petersen, & J. Brooks-Gunn (Eds.), *Encyclopedia of adolescence* (Vol. 2, pp. 419–424). New York: Garland.

Tanon, F. (1994). *A cultural view on planning: The case of weaving in Ivory Coast.* Tilburg: Tilburg University Press.

Tarrant, M., North, A. C., & Hargreaves, D. J. (2000). English and American adolescents' reasons for listening to music. *Psychology of Music, 28,* 166–173.

Tarter, R. E., Vanyukov, M., Kirisci, L., Reynolds, M., & Clark, D. B. (2006). Predictors of marijuana use in adolescents before and after licit drug use: Examination of the gateway hypothesis. *American Journal of Psychiatry, 163*(12), 2134–2140.

Tavris, C. (1992). *The mismeasure of woman: Why women are not the better sex, the inferior sex, or the opposite sex.* New York: Touchstone.

Taylor, A. (2005). It's for the rest of your life: The pragmatics of youth career decision making. *Youth & Society, 36,* 471–503.

Taylor, C. S., Lerner, R. M., von Eye, A., Bobek, D. L., Balsano, A. B., Dowling, E. M., et. al. (2003). Positive individual and social behavior among gang and nongang Africa American male adolescents. *Journal of Adolescent Research, 18,* 548–574.

Taylor, J. M., Veloria, C. N., & Verba, M. C. (2007). Latina girls: "We're like sisters—most times!" In B. J. Leadbeater & N. Way (Eds.), *Urban girls revisited: Building strengths* (pp. 157–174). New York: New York University Press.

Taylor, L. (2006). Magazines for adolescent boys. In J. J. Arnett (Ed.), *Encyclopedia of children, adolescents, and the media.* Thousand Oaks, CA: Sage.

Taylor, R., Casten, R., & Flickinger, S. (1993). The influence of kinship social support on the parenting experiences and psychosocial adjustment of African American adolescents. *Developmental Psychology, 29,* 382–388.

Taylor, R., Casten, R., Flickinger, S., Roberts, D., & Fulmore, C. (1994). Explaining the school performance of African-American adolescents. *Journal of Research on Adolescence, 4,* 21–44.

Taylor, R. D. (1994, February). *Kinship support and family management in African-American families.* Paper presented at the biennial meeting of the Society for Research in Adolescence, San Diego, CA.

Taylor, R. D. (1996). Adolescents' and perceptions of kinship support family management practices: Association with adolescent adjustment in African American families. *Developmental Psychology, 32,* 687–695.

Taylor, R. D. (1997). The effects of economic and social stressors on parenting and adolescent adjustment in African-American families. In R. D. Taylor & M. C. Wang (Eds.), *Social and emotional adjustment and family relations in ethnic minority families.* Mahwah, NJ: Erlbaum.

Taylor, R. L. (1998). Minority families in America: An introduction. In R. L. Taylor (Ed.), *Minority families in the United States: A multicultural perspective* (pp. 1–16). Upper Saddle River, NJ: Prentice-Hall.

Teachman, J. (1996). Intellectual skill and academic performance: Do families bias the relationship? *Sociology of Education, 69,* 35–48.

Teen Birth Rate Continues to Drop. (January, 2000). *Population Today,* 3.

Teitelman, A. M. (2004). Adolescent girls' perspectives of family interactions related to menarche and sexual health. *Qualitative Health Research, 14,* 1292–1308.

Teitler, J. O. (2002). Trends in youth sexual initiation and fertility in developed countries: 1960–1995. *Annals of the American Academy of Political Science Studies, 580,* 134–152.

Terrelonge, P. (1989). Feminist consciousness and Black women. In J. Freeman (Ed.), *Women: A feminist perspective* (4th ed., pp. 556–566). Mountain View, CA: Mayfield.

Terry-McElrath, Y. M., Wakefield, M. A., Emery, S., Saffer, H., Szczypka, G., O'Malley, P. M., Johnston, L. D., & Chaloupka, F. J., et al. (2007). State anti-tobacco advertising and smoking outcomes by gender and race/ethnicity. *Ethnicity & Health, 12*(4), 339–362.

Teti, D., & Lamb, M. (1989). Socioeconomic and marital outcomes of adolescent marriage, adolescent childbirth, and their co-occurrence. *Journal of Marriage and the Family, 51,* 203–212.

Thapar, V. (1998, November). *Family life education in India: Emerging challenges.* Background paper for the National Convention on Family Life Education, New Delhi, India.

Tharinger, D. (1990). Impact of child sexual abuse on developing sexuality. *Professional Psychology, 21,* 331–337.

Theil, S. (2006). Internet use, HomeNet study. In J. J. Arnett (Ed.), *Encyclopedia of children, adolescents, and the media.* Thousand Oaks, CA: Sage.

Thelen, M. H., Powell, A. L., Lawrence, C., & Kuhnert, M. E. (1992). Eating and body image concerns among children. *Journal of Clinical Child Psychology, 21,* 41–46.

Thio, A. (1997). *Sociology: A brief introduction.* New York: Addison Wesley Longman.

Thomas, J. (1998, May 13). Experts take a second look at virtue of student jobs. *New York Times,* p. A-16.

Thompson, S. (1994). Changing lives, changing genres: Teenage girls' narratives about sex and romance, 1978–1986. In A. S. Rossi (Ed.), *Sexuality across the life course* (pp. 209–232). Chicago: University of Chicago Press.

Thomson, E., & Colella, U. (1992). Cohabitation and marital stability: Quality or commitment? *Journal of Marriage and the Family, 54,* 259–267.

Thornberry, T. P., Smith, C. A., & Howard, G. J. (1997). Risk factors for teenage fatherhood. *Journal of Marriage and the Family, 59,* 505–522.

Thornton, A. (1990). The courtship process and adolescent sexuality. *Journal of Family Issues, 11,* 239–273.

Tienda, M. & Wilson, W. J. (Eds.) (2002). *Youth in cities: A cross-national perspective.* New York: Cambridge University Press.

Tilton-Weaver., L. C., & Galambos, N. L. (2003). Adolescents' characteristics and parents' beliefs as predictors of parents' peer management behaviors. *Journal of Research on Adolescence, 13,* 269–300.

Ting-Toomey, S. (1991). Intimacy expressions in three cultures: France, Japan, and the United States. *International Journal of Intercultural Relations, 15,* 29–46.

Tinto, V. (1993). *Leaving college: Rethinking the causes and cures of student attrition research.* Chicago: University of Chicago.

Titzmann, P. F., Silbereisen, R. K., & Schmitt-Rodermund, E. (2007). Friendship homophily among diaspora migrant adolescents in Germany and Israel. *European Psychology, 12*(3), 181–195.

Tobach, E. (2004). Development of sex and gender: Biochesmistry, physiology, and experience. In A. M. Paludi (Ed.) *Praeger guide to the psychology of gender* (pp. 240–270) Westport, Ct: Praeger.

Tolman, D. L., Kim, J. L., Schooler, D., & Sorsoli, C. L. (2007). Rethinking the associations between television viewing and adolescent sexuality development: Bringing gender into focus. *Journal of Adolescent Health, 40*(1), e9–e16.

Tolman, D. L., Spencer, R., Harmon, T., Rosen-Reynoso, M., & Striepe, M. (2004). Getting close, staying cool: Early adolescent boys' experiences with romantic relationships. In N. Way & J. Chu (Eds.) *Adolescent boys: Exploring diverse cultures of boyhood* (pp. 235–255) New York: New York University Press.

Tomb, D. A. (1991). The runaway adolescent. In M. Lewis (Ed.), *Child and adolescent psychiatry* (pp. 1066–1071). Baltimore, MD: Williams & Wilkins.

Tomlinson-Keasey, C., & Eisert, D. C. (1981). From a structured "ensemble" to separate organizations for cognitive and affective development. In J. A. Meacham & R. Santilli (Eds.), *Social development*

in youth. Structure and content (pp. 1–19). Basel: S. Karger.

Top, T. J. (1991). Sex bias in the evaluation of performance in the scientific, artistic, and literary professions: A review. *Sex Roles, 24,* 73–106.

Torney-Purta, J. (1990). From attitudes and knowledge to schemata: Expanding the outcomes of political socialization research. In O. Ichilov (Ed.), *Political socialization, citizenship, education, and democracy* (pp. 98–115). New York: Columbia University Press.

Torney-Purta, J. (1992). Cognitive representations of the political system in adolescents: The continuum from pre-novice to expert. In H. Haste & J. Torney-Purta (Eds.), *New directions for child development: The development of political understanding* (Vol. 56, pp. 11–25). San Francisco: Jossey-Bass.

Torney-Purta, J. (2004). Adolescents' political socialization in changing contexts: An international study in the spirit of Nevitt Sanford. *Political Psychology, 25,* 465–478.

Tracey, T. J. G., Robbins, S. B., & Hofsess, C. D. (2005). Stability and change in interests: A longitudinal study of adolescents from grades 8 through 12. *Journal of Vocational Behavior, 66,* 1–25.

Travers, K. R., Lyvers, M. (2005). Mood and impulsivity of recreational ecstasy users in the week following a "rave". *Addiction Research & Theory, 13,* 43–52.

Treatment for Adolescents with Depression Study (TADS) team, US. (2004). Fluoxetine, cognitive-behavioral therapy, and their combination for adolescents with depression: Treatment for Adolescents With Depression Study (TADS) randomized controlled trial. *JAMA: Journal of the American Medical Association, 29,* 807–820.

Treiman, D. J., & Yip, K. (1989). Educational and occupational attainment in 21 countries. In M. L. Kohn (Ed.), *Cross-national research in sociology* (pp. 373–394). Newbury Park, CA: Sage.

Treise, D., & Gotthoffer, A. (2002). Stuff you couldn't ask your parents: Teens talking about using magazines for sex information. In J. D. Brown, J. R. Steele, & K. Walsh-Childers (Eds.), *Sexual teens, sexual media: Investigating media's influence on adolescent sexuality* (pp. 173–208). Mahwah, NJ: Erlbaum.

Trevethan, S. D., & Walker, L. J. (1989). Hypothetical versus real-life moral reasoning among psychopathic and delinquent youth. *Development and Psychopathology, 1,* 91–103.

Triandis, H. C. (1995). *Individualism and collectivism.* Boulder, CO: Westview Press.

Triplett, R., & Payne, B. Problem solving as reinforcement in adolescent drug use: Implications for theory and policy. *Journal of Criminal Justice. 32*(6), 617–630.

Trusty, J., Harris, C., & Morag, B. (1999). Lost talent: Predictors of the stability of educational expectation across adolescence. *Journal of Adolescent Research, 14,* 359–382.

Tschann, J. M., & Adler, N. E. (1997). Sexual self-acceptance, communication with partner, and contraceptive use among adolescent females: A longitudinal study. *Journal of Research on Adolescence, 7,* 413–430.

Tseng, V. (2004). Family interdependence and academic adjustments in college: Youth from immigrant and U.S.-born families. *Child Development, 75,* 966–983.

Tubman, J. G., Gil, A. G., & Wagner, E. F. (2004). Co-occurring substance use and delinquent behaviour during early adolescence: Emerging relations and implications for intervention strategies. *Criminal Justice & Behavior, 31,* 463–488.

Tudge, J. R. H., & Scrimsher, S. (2002). Lev S. Vygotsky on education. In B. J. Zimmerman & D. H. Schunk (Eds.), *Educational psychology.* Mahwah, NJ: Erlbaum.

Tveskov, M. A. (2007). Social identity and culture change on the southern northwest coast. *American Anthropologist, 109*(3), 431–441.

Twenge, J. M., & Crocker, J. (2002). Race and self-esteem: Meta-analyses comparing Whites, Blacks, Hispanics, Asians, American Indians and comment on Gray-Little and Hafdahl (2000). *Psychological Bulletin, 128,* 371–408.

Twisk, D. A. M., & Stacey, C. (2007). Trends in young driver risk and countermeasures in European countries. *Journal of Safety Research, 38*(2), 245–257.

Tyack, D. B. (1990). *The one best system: A history of American urban education.* Cambridge, MA: Harvard University Press.

Tyler, K. A., Hoyt, D. R., & Whitbeck, L. B. (2000). The effects of early sexual abuse on later sexual victimization among female homeless and runaway adolescents. *Journal of Interpersonal Violence, 15,* 235–250.

Tyler, K. A., Whitbeck, L. B., Hoyt, D. R., & Cauce, A. M. (2004). Risk factors for sexual victimization among male and female homeless and runaway youth. *Journal of Interpersonal Violence, 19,* 503–520.

Tynes, B. M. (2007). Internet safety gone wild?: Sacrificing the educational and psychosocial benefits of online social environments. *Journal of Adolescent Research, 22*(6), 575–584.

U.S. Bureau of the Census. (1991). *Current population reports, population characteristics series P-20, #433.* Washington, DC: U.S. Government Printing Office.

U.S. Bureau of the Census. (1996). *Statistical abstracts of the United States.* Washington, DC: Author.

U.S. Bureau of the Census. (1998). *Statistical abstracts of the United States. Washington,* DC: U.S. Government Printing Office.

U.S. Bureau of the Census. (1999). *Statistical abstracts of the United States.* Washington, DC: U.S. Government Printing Office.

U.S. Bureau of the Census. (2000). Geographic mobility: March 1997 to March 1998. *Current Population Reports* (Series P-20, No. 520). Washington, DC: U.S. Government Printing Office.

U.S. Bureau of the Census. (2000). *Statistical abstracts of the United States: 2000.* Washington, DC: U.S. Bureau of the Census.

U.S. Bureau of the Census. (2009). *Statistical abstracts of the United States.* Washington, DC: U.S. Government Printing Office.

U.S. Department of Commerce, Bureau of the Census. (1940). *Characteristics of the population.* Washington, DC: U.S. Government Printing Office.

U.S. Department of Health & Human Services. (1990). *Vital statistics of the United States, Volume III, Natality.* Washington, DC: U.S. Government Printing Office.

U.S. Department of Health and Human Services. (1994). *Preventing tobacco use among young people: A report of the surgeon general.* Atlanta, GA: Author.

U.S. Department of Labor (2008). *What is Job Corps?* Washington, DC: Author. Retrieved on October 31, 2008, from http://jobcorps.dol.gov/docs/jc_flier.pdf

U.S. public schools with access to the Internet, 1994, 1997, and 1998. (1999, April). *Population Today,* p. 6.

Uggen, C., & Blackstone, A. (2004). Sexual harassment as a gendered expression of power. *American Sociological Review, 69,* 64–92.

Umaña-Taylor, A. J. (2004). Ethnic identity and self-esteem: Examining the role of social context. *Journal of Adolescence, 27,* 139–146.

Underwood, L. E., & Van Wyk, J. J. (1981). Hormones in normal and aberrant growth. In R. H. Williams (Ed.), *Textbook of endocrinology* (6th ed., pp. 11–49). Philadelphia: Saunders.

Underwood, M. K. (2003). *Social aggression among girls.* New York: Guilford Press.

Underwood, M. K., Kupersmidt, J. B., & Coie, J. D. (1996). Childhood peer sociometric status and aggression as predictors of adolescent child-bearing. *Journal of Research on Adolescence, 6,* 201–223.

Unger, J. B. (2003). Peers, family, media, and adolescent smoking: Ethnic variation in risk factors in a national sample. *Adolescent & Family Health, 3,* 65–70.

Unger, S. (1977). *The destruction of American Indian families.* New York: Association on American Indian Affairs.

UNICEF (2003). *The state of the world's children.* Oxford, England: Oxford University Press.

United Nations Department of Economic and Social Affairs (UNDESA) (2005). *World youth report, 2005.* New York: Author.

United Nations Development Programme (2009). *Human development report.* New York: Oxford University Press.

United Nations Economic Commission for Europe (2005). *Gender statistics database.* Retrieved on September 30, 2005, from http://w3.unece.org/stat/scriptsdb/showResults.asp

Unsworth, G., Devilly, G. J., & Ward, T. (2007). The effect of playing violent video games on adolescents: Should parents be quaking in their boots? *Psychology, Crime & Law, 13*(4), 383–394.

Updegraff, K. A., McHale, S. M., & Crouter, A. (2002). Adolescents' sibling relationship and friendship experiences: Developmental patterns and relationship linkages. *Social Development, 11,* 182–204.

Updegraff, K. A., Thayer, S. M., Whiteman, S. D., Denning, D. J., & McHale, S. M. (2005). Relational aggression in adolescents' sibling relationships: Links to siblings and parent-adolescent relationship quality. *Family Relations, 54,* 373–385.

Urberg, K. A., Degirmencioglu, S. M., & Tolson, J. M. (1998). Adolescent friendship selection and termination: The role of similarity. *Journal of Social and Personal Relationships, 15,* 703–710.

Urberg, K. A., Degirmencioglu, S. M., Tolson, J. M., & Halliday-Sher, K. (2000). Adolescent social crowds: Measurement and relationship to friendships. *Journal of Adolescent Research, 15,* 427–445.

Urberg, K. A., Luo, Q., Pilgrim, C., & Degirmencioglu, S. M. A two-stage model of peer influence in adolescent substance use: Individual and relationship-specific differences in susceptibility to influence. *Addictive Behaviors, 28*(7), 1243–1256.

Urberg, K. A., Shyu, S., & Liang, J. (1990). Peer influence in adolescent cigarette smoking. *Addictive Behaviors, 15,* 247–255.

Utter, J., Neumark-Sztainer, D., Wall, M., & Story, M. (2003). Reading magazine articles about dieting and associated weight control behaviors among adolescents. *Journal of Adolescent Health, 32,* 78–82.

Valencia-Martín, J. L., Galán, I., & Rodríguez-Artalejo, F. Binge drinking in Madrid, Spain. *Alcoholism: Clinical and Experimental Research, 31*(10), 1723–1730.

Van Beurden, E., Zask, A., Brooks, L & Dight, R. (2005). Heavy episodic drinking and sensation seeking in adolescents as predictors of harmful driving and celebrating behaviors: Implications for prevention. *Journal of Adolescent Health, 37,* 37–43.

van den Berg, S. M., & Boomsma, D. J. (2007). The familial clustering of age at menarche in extended twin families. *Behavior Genetics, 37,* 661–667.

van der Lippe, T., Jager, A., & Kops, Y. (2006). Combination pressure: The paid work-family balance of men and women in European countries. *Acta Sociologica, 49*(3), 303–319.

Van Hoff, A., & Raaijmakers, Quinten Q. A. W. (2003). The search for the structure of identity formation. *Identity, 3,* 271–289.

van Hoof, A. The identity status approach: In need of fundamental revision and qualitative change. *Developmental Review, 19*(4), 622–647.

Van Hoorn, J. L., Komlosi, A., Suchar, E., & Samuelson, D. A. (2000). *Adolescent development and rapid social change: Perspectives from Eastern Europe.* Albany, New York: State University of New York Press.

Van Horn, K. R., & Cunegatto M. J. (2000). Interpersonal relationships in Brazilian adolescents. International *Journal of Behavioral Development, 24,* 199–203.

Van Kammen, W. B., Loeber, R., Stouthamer-Loeber, M. (1991). Substance use and its relationship to conduct problems and delinquency in young boys. *Journal of Youth and Adolescence, 20,* 399–414.

Van Leeuwen, K., De Fruyt, F., & Mervielde, I. (2004). A longitudinal study of the utility of the resilient, overcontrolled, and undercontrolled personality types as predictors of children's and adolescents' problem behaviour. *International Journal of Behavioral Development, 28,* 210–220.

Vandereycken, W., & Van Deth, R. (1994). *From fasting saints to anorexic girls: The history of self-starvation.* New York: New York University Press.

Vanfossen, B., Jones, J., & Spade, J. (1987). Curriculum tracking and status maintenance. *Sociology of Education, 60,* 104–122.

Varenne, H. (1982). Jocks and freaks: The symbolic structure of the expression of social interaction among American senior high school students. In G. Spindler (Ed.), *Doing the ethnography of schooling* (pp. 213–235). New York: Holt, Rinehart and Winston.

Vartanian, L. R. (2000). Revisiting the imaginary audience and the personal fable constructs of adolescent egocentrism: A conceptual review. *Adolescence, 35,* 639–661.

Vasquez, M. J. T., & Fuentes, C. D. L. (1999). American-born Asian, African, Latina, and American Indian adolescent girls: Challenges and strengths. In N. B. Johnson, M. C. Roberts, & J. Worell (Eds.), *Beyond appearance: A new look at adolescent girls* (pp. 151–173). Washington, DC: American Psychological Association.

Vaughan, K. (2005). The pathways framework meets consumer culture: Young people, careers, and commitment. *Journal of Youth Studies, 8,* 173–186.

Vazsonyi, A. T., & Snider, J. B. (2008). Mentoring, competencies, and adjustment in adolescents: American part-time employment and European apprenticeships. *International Journal of Behavioral Development, 32*(1), 46–55.

Veenstra, R., Lindenberg, S., Zijlstra, B. J. H., De Winter, A. F., Verhulst, F. C., & Ormel, J. (2007). The dyadic nature of bullying and victimization: Testing a dual-perspective theory. *Child Development, 78*(6), 1843–1854.

Verjooijen, K. T., de Vries, N. K., & Nielsen, G. A. (2007). Youth crowds and substance abuse: The impact of perceived group norm and multiple group identification. *Psychology of Addictive Behaviors, 21*(1), 55–61.

Verkuyten, M. (2002). Multiculturalism among minority and majority adolescents in the Netherlands. *International Journal of Intercultural Relations, 26,* 91–108.

Verma, S. (1999). Socialization for survival: Developmental issues among working street children in India. In M. Raffaelli & R. Larson (Eds.), *Homeless and working youth around the world: Exploring Developmental Issues* (pp. 5–18). New Directions in Child and Adolescent Development, Number 85. San Francisco: Jossey-Bass.

Verma, S., & Larson, R. (1999). Are adolescents more emotional? A study of the daily emotions of middle class Indian adolescents. *Psychology and Developing Societies, 11,* 179–194.

Verma, S., & Saraswathi, T. S. (2000, February). *The current state of adolescence in India: An agenda for the next millennium.* Paper prepared for the meeting of the Study Group on Adolescence in the 21st Century, Washington, DC.

Verma, S., & Saraswathi, T. S. (2002). Adolescents in India: Street urchins or Silicon Valley millionaires? In B. B. Brown, R. Larson, & T. S. Saraswathi (Eds.), *The world's youth: Adolescence in eight regions of the globe* (pp. 105–140). New York: Cambridge University Press.

Vernberg, E., Ewell, K., Beery, S., & Abwender, D. (1994). Sophistication of adolescents' interpersonal negotiation strategies and friendship formation after relocation: A naturally occurring experiment. *Journal of Research on Adolescence, 4,* 5–19.

Vernberg, E. M. (1990). Psychological adjustment and experience with peers during early adolescence: Reciprocal, incidental, or unidirectional relationships? *Journal of Abnormal Child Psychology, 18,* 187–198.

Vicary, J. R., Klingaman, L. R., & Harkness, W. L. (1995). Risk factors associated with date rape and sexual assault of adolescent girls. *Journal of Adolescence, 18,* 289–306.

Vigil, J. M., Geary, D. C., Byrd-Craven, J. (2005). A life history assessment of early childhood sexual abuse in women. *Developmental Psychology. 41*(3), 553–561.

Villani, S. (2001). Impact of media on children and adolescents: A 10-year review of the research. *Journal of the American Academy of Child & Adolescent Psychiatry, 40,* 392–401.

Vincent, M. A., & McCabe, M. P. (2000). Gender differences among adolescents in family and peer influences on body dissatisfaction, weight loss, and binge eating disorders. *Journal of Youth & Adolescence, 29,* 205–221.

Vincent, R. C., Davis, D. K., & Bronszkowski, L. A. (1987). Sexism in MTV: The portrayal of women in rock videos. *Journalism Quarterly, 64,* 750–755.

Visher, E., & Visher, J. (1988). *Old loyalties, new ties: Therapeutic strategies with stepfamilies.* New York: Brunner/Mazel.

Volk, A., Craif, W., Boyce, W., & King, M. (2006). Adolescent risk correlates of bullying and different types of victimization. *International Journal of Adolescent Medicine and Health, 18*(4), 575–586.

von Salisch, M., Oppl, C., & Kristen, A. (2006). What attracts children? In P. Vordere & J. Bryant (Eds.), *Playing video games: Motives, responses, and consequences* (pp. 147–163). Mahwah, NJ: Lawrence Erlbaum.

Vondracek, F. W., & Porfeli, E. J. (2003). The world of work and careers. In G. R. Adams & M. D. Berzonsky (Eds.), *Blackwell handbook of adolescence: Blackwell handbooks of developmental psychology* (pp. 109–128). Malden, MA: Blackwell Publishing.

Vondracek, F. W., & Porfeli, E. J. (2003). The world of work and careers. In G. Adams & M. Berzonsky (Eds.), *Blackwell handbook of adolescence* (pp. 109–128). Malden, MA: Blackwell.

Vossekkuil, B., Reddy, M., & Rein, R. (2000). *Safe school initiative: An interim report on the prevention of targeted violence in schools.* U.S. Secret Service National Threat Assessment Center. Washington, DC: Author. Available: www.usss.treas.gov

Votta, E., & Manion, I. (2004). Suicide, high-risk behaviors, and coping style in homeless adolescent males' adjustment. *Journal of Adolescent Health, 34,* 237–243.

Voydanoff, P. (1988). Work, community, and parenting resources and demands as predictors of adolescent roblems and grades. *Journal of Adolescent Research, 19,* 155–173.

Voyer, D. (1996). The relation between mathematical achievement and gender differences in spatial abilities: A suppression effect. *Journal of Educational Psychology, 88,* 563–571.

Vuchinich, S., Hetherington, E., Vuchinich, R., & Clingempeel, W. (1991). Parent–child interaction and gender differences in early adolescents' adaptation to stepfamilies. *Developmental Psychology, 27,* 618–626.

Vukman, K. B. (2005). Developmental differences in metacognition and their connections with cognitive development in adulthood. *Journal of Adult Development, 12*(4), 211–221.

Wade, C., & Tavris, C. (2003). *Psychology* (7th edition). Upper Saddle River, NJ: Prentice Hall.

Wagner, B., & Cohen, P. (1997). Adolescent sibling differences in suicidal symptoms: The role of parent-child relationships. *Journal of Abnormal Child Psychology, 22*, 321–337.

Waizenhofer, R. N., Buchanan, C. M., & Jackson-Newsom, J. (2004). Mothers' and fathers' daily activities: Its sources and its links with adolescent adjustment. *Journal of Family Psychology, 18*, 348–360.

Walcott, D. D., Pratt, H. D., & Patel, D. R. (2003). Adolescents and eating disorders: Gender, racial, ethnic, sociocultural and socioeconomic issues. *Journal of Adolescent Research, 18*, 223–243.

Waldrop, A. E., Hanson, R. F., Resnick, H. S., Kilpatrick, D. G., Naugle, A. E., & Saunders, B. E. Risk factors for suicidal behavior among a national sample of adolescents: Implications for prevention. *Journal of Traumatic Stress, 20*(5), 869–879.

Walker, A. (1992). *Possessing the secret of joy.* New York: Harcourt, Brace, Jovanovich.

Walker, L., de Vries, B., & Trevethan, S. (1987). Moral stages and moral orientations in real-life and hypothetical dilemmas. *Child Development, 58*, 842–858.

Walker, L. J. (1984). Sex differences in the development of moral reasoning. A critical review. *Child Development, 51*, 131–139.

Walker, L. J. (1989). A longitudinal study of moral reasoning. *Child Development, 60*, 157–166.

Walker, L. J. (2004). What does moral functioning entail? In T. A. Thorkildsen & H. J. Walberg (Eds.), *Nurturing morality* (pp. 3–17). New York: Kluwer.

Walker, L. J., & Moran, T. J. (1991). Moral reasoning in a communist Chinese society. *Journal of Moral Education, 20*, 139–155.

Walker, L. J., Pitts, R. C., Hennig, K. H., & Matsuba, M. K. (1999). Reasoning about morality and real-life moral problems. In M. Killen & D. Hart (Eds.), *Morality in everyday life* (pp. 371–407). New York: Cambridge University Press.

Wallace, J. M. Jr., Bachman, J. G., O'Malley, P. M., Schulenberg, J. E., Cooper, Shauna M., & Johnston, Lloyd D. (2003). *Addiction, 98*, 225–234.

Wallace, J. M., & Williams, D. R. (1997). Religion and adolescent health-compromising behavior. In J. Schulenberg, J. L. Maggs, & K. Hurrelmann (Eds.), *Health risks and developmental transitions during adolescence* (pp. 444–468). New York: Cambridge University Press.

Wallace, J. M., Yamaguchi, R., Bachman, J. G., O'Malley, P. M., Schulenberg, J. E., & Johnston, L. D. (2007). Religiosity and adolescent substance use: The role of individual and contextual influences. *Social Problems, 54*(2), 308–327.

Wallerstein, J. S., & Blakeslee, S. (1996). *Second chances: Men, women and children a decade after divorce.* New York: Houghton Mifflin.

Wallerstein, J. S., & Corbin, S. B. (1991). The child and the vicissitudes of divorce. In M. Lewis (Ed.), *Child and adolescent psychiatry* (pp. 1108–1118). Baltimore, MD: Williams & Wilkins.

Wallerstein, J. S., Lewis, J. M., & Blakeslee, S. (2000). *The unexpected legacy of divorce.* New York: Hyperion.

Walsh-Childers, K., Gotthoffer, A., & Lepre, C. R. (2002). From "just the facts" to "downright salacious": Teens' and womens' magazine coverage of sex and sexual health. In J. D. Brown, J. R. Steele, & K. Walsh-Childers (Eds.), *Sexual teens, sexual media: Investigating media's influence on adolescent sexuality* (pp. 153–171). Mahwah, NJ: Erlbaum.

Walthrop, A. E., Hanson, R. F., Resnick, H. S., Kilpatrick, D. G., Naugle, A. E., & Saunders, B. E.

(2007). Risk factors for suicidal behavior among a national sample of adolescents: Implications for prevention. *Journal of Traumatic Stress, 20*(5), 869–879.

Wang, Y., Monteiro, C., & Popkin, B. M. (2002). Trends in obesity and underweight in older children and adolescents in the United States, Brazil, China, & Russia. *American Journal of Clinical Nutrition, 75*, 971–977.

Ward, C. (2006a). Hip hop, masculinity. In J. J. Arnett (Ed.), *Encyclopedia of children, adolescents, and the media.* Thousand Oaks, CA: Sage.

Ward, C. (2006b). Hip hop, portrayals of women. In J. J. Arnett (Ed.), *Encyclopedia of children, adolescents, and the media.* Thousand Oaks, CA: Sage.

Ward, J. V. (1990). Racial identity formation and transformation. In C. Gilligan, N. P. Lyons, & T. J. Haruner (Eds.), *Making connections* (pp. 215–232). Cambridge, MA: Harvard University Press.

Ward, L. M. (1995). Talking about sex: Common themes about sexuality in the prime-time television programs children and adolescents view most. *Journal of Youth & Adolescence, 24*, 595–616.

Ward, L. M., Gorvine, B., & Cytron, A. (2002). Would that really happen? Adolescents' perceptions of sexual relationships according to prime-time television. In J. D. Brown, J. R. Steele, & K. Walsh-Childers (Eds.), *Sexual teens, sexual media: Investigating media's influence on adolescent sexuality* (pp. 95–123). Mahwah, NJ: Erlbaum.

Ward, L. M., Hansbrough, E., & Walker, E. (2005). Contributions of music video exposure to black adolescents' gender and sexual schemas. *Journal of Adolescent Research, 20*(2), 143–166.

Ward, L. M., & Rivadeneyra, R. (1999). Contributions of entertainment television to adolescents' sexual attitudes and expectations: The role of viewing amount versus viewer involvement. *Journal of Sex Research, 36*, 237–249.

Warren, J. (1996). Educational inequality among White and Mexican-origin adolescents in the American Southwest: 1990. *Sociology of Education, 69*, 142–158.

Waterman, A. S. (1992). Identity as an aspect of optimal functioning. In G. R. Adams, T. P. Gullotta, & R. Montemayor (Eds.), *Adolescent identity formation.* Newbury Park, CA: Sage.

Waterman, A. S. (1999). Issues of identity formation revisited: United States and the Netherlands. *Developmental Review, 19*, 462–479.

Waterman, A. S. Doing well: The relationship of identity status to three conceptions of well-being. *Identity, 7*(4) 289–307.

Waters, E., Weinfield, N. S., & Hamilton, C. E. (2000). The stability of attachment security from infancy to adolescence and early adulthood: General discussion. *Child Development, 71*, 703–706.

Watkins, S. C. (2006). Hip hop, violence. In J. J. Arnett (Ed.), *Encyclopedia of children, adolescents, and the media.* Thousand Oaks, CA: Sage.

Watkins, W. G., & Bentovim, A. (1992). The sexual abuse of male children and adolescents: A review of current research. *Journal of Child Psychology & Psychiatry, 33*, 197–248.

Way, N. (2004). Intimacy, desire, and distrust in the friendships of adolescent boys. In N. Way & J. Chu (Eds.), *Adolescent boys: Exploring diverse cultures of boyhood* (pp. 167–196). New York: New York University Press.

Way, N., & Chen, L. (2000). Close and general friendships among African American, Latino, and Asian American adolescents. *Journal of Adolescent Research, 15*, 274–301.

Way, N., Reddy, R., & Rhodes, J. Students' perceptions of school climate during the middle school years: Associations with trajectories of psychological and behavioral adjustment. *American Journal of Community Psychology, 40*(3–4), 194–213.

Weatherford, D. (1997). *Milestones: A chronology of American women's history.* New York: Facts on File.

Web envelopes young adults. (1999, August 9). *Washington Post,* p. 5.

Weber, R., & Crocker, J. (1983). Cognitive processes in the revision of stereotypical beliefs. *Journal of Personality and Social Psychology, 45*, 961–977.

Wechsler, H., Brener, N. D., Kuester, S., & Miller, C. (2001). Food service and foods and beverages available in school: Results from the School Health Policies and Programs study, 2000. *Journal of School Health, 71*, 313–324.

Wechsler, H., & Nelson, T. F. (2001). Binge drinking and the American college student: What's five drinks? *Psychology of Addictive Behaviors, 15*, 287–291.

Wechsler, H., Nelson, T. F., Lee, J. E., Seibring, M., Lewis, C., & Keeling, R. P. (2003). *Quarterly Journal of Studies on Alcohol, 64*, 484–494.

Weichold, K., Silbereisen, R. K., & Schmitt-Rodermund, E. (2003). Short-term and long-term consequences of early vs. late physical maturation in adolescents. In C. Haywood (Ed.), *Puberty and Psychopathology.* New York: Cambridge University Press.

Weinberg, R. A. (1989). Intelligence and IQ: Landmark issues and great debates. *American Psychologist, 44*, 98–104.

Weinberg, R. A., Scarr, S., & Waldman, I. D. (1992). The Minnesota transracial adoption study: A follow-up of IQ test performance. *Intelligence, 44*, 98–104.

Weiner, I. B. (1992). *Psychological disturbance in adolescence.* (2nd ed.) New York: Wiley.

Weinfield, N. S., Sroufe, L. A., & Egeland, B. (2000). Attachment from infancy to early adulthood in a high-risk sample: Continuity, discontinuity, and their correlates. *Child Development, 71*, 695–702.

Weinraub, M., & Wolf, B. M. (1983). Effects of stress and social supports on mother–child interactions in single and two-parent families. *Child Development, 54*, 1297–1311.

Weinreich, H. E. (1974). The structure of moral reasoning. *Journal of Youth and Adolescence, 3*, 135–143.

Weinstein, N. D. (1998). Accuracy of smokers' risk perceptions. *Annals of Behavioral Medicine, 20*, 135–140.

Weinstock, H., Berman, S., & Cates, W. (2004). Sexually transmitted diseases among American youth: Incidence and prevalence estimates, 2000. *Perspectives on Sexual and Reproductive Health, 36*, 6–10.

Weiss, B., Dodge, K. A., Bates, J. E., & Pettit, G. S. (1992). Some consequences of early harsh discipline: Child aggression and a maladaptive social information processing style. *Child Development, 63*, 1321–1335.

Weiss, M. J. (2003). To be about to be. *American Demographics.* Retrieved on September 30, 2005, from http://www.adage.com/news.cms?newsId=4405 2

Weiss, R. S. (1973). *Loneliness: The experience of emotional and social isolation.* Cambridge, MA: MIT Press.

Weissberg, R., Caplan, M., & Harwood, R. (1991). Promoting competent young people in competence-enhancing environments: A systems-based perspective on primary prevention. *Journal of Consulting and Clinical Psychology, 59*, 830–841.

Wells, Y. D., & Johnson, T. M. (2001). Impact of parental divorce on willingness of young adults to provide care for parents in the future. *Journal of Family Studies, 7*, 160–170.

Welti, C. (2002). Adolescents in Latin America: Facing the future with skepticism. In B. B. Brown, R. Larson, & T. S. Saraswathi (Eds.), *The world's youth: Adolescence in eight regions of the globe* (pp. 276–306). New York: Cambridge University Press.

Wender, P. H., Kety, S. S., Rosenthal, D., Schulsinger, E., Ortmann, J., & Lunde, L. (1986). Psychiatric disorders in the biological and adoptive families of adopted individuals with affective disorders. *Archives of General Psychiatry, 43,* 923–929.

Wentzel, K. R., & Asher, S. R. (1995). The academic lives of neglected, rejected, popular, and controversial children. *Child Development, 66,* 754–763.

Wentzel, K. R., & Feldman, S. S. (1993). Parental predictors of boys' self-restraint and motivation to achieve at school: A longitudinal study. *Journal of Early Adolescence, 13,* 183–203.

Werner, B., & Bodin, L. (2007). Obesity in Swedish school children is increasing in both prevalence and severity. *Journal of Adolescent Health, 41,* 536–543.

Werner, E. E., & Smith, R. S. (1982). *Vulnerable but invincible: A study of resilient children.* New York: McGraw-Hill.

Werner, E. E., & Smith, R. S. (2001). *Journeys from childhood to midlife: Risk, resilience, and recovery.* Ithaca, NY: Cornell University Press.

Werner, N. E., & Crick, N. R. (1999). Relational aggression and social-psychological adjustment in a college sample. *Journal of Abnormal Psychology, 108,* 615–623.

Westin, C. (1998). Immigration, xenophobia, and youthful opinion. In J. Nurmi (Ed.), *Adolescents, cultures, and conflicts* (pp. 225–241). New York: Garland.

Westling, E., Andrews, J.A., Hampson, S.E., & Peterson, M. (2008). Pubertal timing and substance use: The effects of gender, parental monitoring and deviant peers. *Journal of Adolescent Health, 42,* 555–563.

Westoff, C. (1988). Unintended pregnancy in America and abroad. *Family Planning Perspectives, 20,* 254–261.

Whalen, C. K. (2000). Attention deficit hyperactivity disorder. In A. Kazdin (Ed.), *Encyclopedia of psychology.* Washington, DC: American Psychological Association.

Whalen, C. K. (2001). ADHD treatment in the 21st century. *Journal of Clinical Child Psychology, 30,* 136–140.

Whipple, E. E., & Webster-Stratton, C. (1991). The role of parental stress in physically abusive families. *Child Abuse and Neglect, 15,* 279–291.

Whisman, M. A. (1993). Mediators and moderators of change in cognitive therapy of depression. *Psychological Bulletin, 114,* 248–265.

Whitbeck, L. B., & Hoyt, D. R. (1999). *Nowhere to grow: Homeless and runaway adolescents and their families.* New York: Aldine de Gruyter.

Whitbeck, L. B., Johnson, K. D., Hoyt, D. R., & Cauce, A. M. (2004). Mental disorder and comorbidity among runaway and homeless adolescents. *Journal of Adolescent Health, 35,* 132–140.

Whitbourne, S. K., & Willis, S. L. (Eds.). (2006). The baby boomers grow up: Contemporary perspectives on midlife. Mahwah, NJ: Lawrence Erlbaum.

White, L., & Edwards, J. N. (1990). Emptying the nest and parental well-being: An analysis of national panel data. *American Sociological Review, 55,* 235–242.

White, L. K., Brinkerhoff, D. B., & Booth, A. (1985). The effect of marital disruption on child's attachment to parents. *Journal of Family Issues, 6,* 5–22.

White, M. J., & White, G. B. (2006) Implicit and explicit occupational gender stereotypes. *Sex Roles, 55*(3–4), 259–266.

White, N. R. (2002). "Not under my roof!" Young people's experience of home. *Youth and Society, 34,* 214–231.

Whiting, B. B., & Edwards, C. P. (1988). *Children of different worlds: The formation of social behavior.* Cambridge, MA: Harvard University Press.

Whiting, J. W. M., & Child, I. (1953). *Child training and personality.* New Haven, CT: Yale University Press.

Whiting, J. W. M., Burbank, V. K., & Ratner, M. S. (1986). The duration of maidenhood across cultures. In J. B. Lancaster & B. A. Hamburg (Eds.), *School-age pregnancy and parenthood: Biosocial dimensions* (pp. 273–302). New York: Aldine de Gruyter.

Whitty, M. (2002). Possible selves: An exploration of the utility of a narrative approach. *Identity, 2,* 211–228.

Whyte, W. F. (1943). *Street corner society.* Chicago: University of Chicago Press.

Wichstrom, L. (1999). The emergence of gender difference in depressed mood during adolescence: The role of intensified gender socialization. *Developmental Psychology, 35,* 232–245.

Wichstrom, L. (2001). The impact of pubertal timing on adolescents' alcohol use. *Journal of Research on Adolescence, 11,* 131–150.

Wichstrom, L., & Rossow, I. (2002). Explaining the gender difference in self-reported suicide attempts: A nationally representative study of Norwegian adolescents. *Suicide and Life-Threatening Behavior, 32,* 101–116.

Wilcox, W. B. (2008). Focused on their families: Religion, parenting, and child well-being. In K. K. Kline, (Ed.), *Authoritative communities: The scientific case for nurturing the whole child* (pp. 227–244). The Search Institute series on developmentally attentive community and society. New York: Springer Science + Business Media.

Wild, L. G., Flisher, A. J., Bhana, A., & Lombard, Cl. (2004). Associations among adolescent risk behaviors and self-esteem in six domains. *Journal of Child Psychology & Psychiatry, 45,* 1454–1467.

Wildavsky, R. (1997, June). What teens really want. *Reader's Digest,* 50–57.

Will, G. (2000, January 10). AIDS crushes a continent. *Newsweek,* 64.

Will, G. (2002, November 11). Eurasia and the epidemic. *Newsweek,* 80.

William T. Grant Foundation Commission on Work, Family, and Citizenship. (1988). *The forgotten half: Noncollege-bound youth in America.* New York: William T. Grant Foundation.

Williams, A. F., & Ferguson, S. A. (2002). Rationale for graduated licensing and the risks it should address. *Injury Prevention, 8*(Suppl. 2), ii9–ii16.

Williams, A. F., Preusser, D. F., Ulmer, R. G., & Weinstein, H. B. (1995). Characteristics of fatal crashes of 16-year-old drivers: Implications for licensure policies. *Journal of Public Health Policy, 16,* 347–390.

Williams, A. F. (1998). Risky driving behavior among adolescents. In R. Jessor (Ed.), *New perspectives on adolescent risk behavior* (pp. 221–237). New York: Cambridge University Press.

Williams, J. E., & Best, D. L. (1990). *Measuring sex stereotypes: A multination study.* Newbury Park, CA: Sage.

Williams, J. M., & Dunlop, L. C. (1999). Pubertal timing and self-reported delinquency among male adolescents. *Journal of Adolescence, 22,* 157–171.

Williams, T. B. (Ed.). (1986). *The impact of television: A natural experiment in three communities.* New York: Academic Press.

Williamson, J., Borduin, C., & Howe, B. (1991). The ecology of adolescent maltreatment: A multilevel examination of adolescent physical abuse, sexual abuse, and neglect. *Journal of Consulting and Clinical Psychology, 59,* 449–457.

Willits, F. K., & Crider, D. M. (1989). Church attendance and traditional religious beliefs in adolescence and young adulthood: A panel study. *Review of Religious Research, 31,* 68–81.

Wills, T. A., Resko, J. A., Ainette, M. G., & Mendoza, D. (2004). Role of parent support and peer support in adolescent substance use: A test of mediated effects. *Psychology of Addictive Behaviors, 18,* 122–134.

Wilson, B., & Atkinson, M. (2005). Rave and straightedge, the virtual and the real: Exploring online and offline experiences in Canadian youth subcultures. *Youth & society, 36,* 276–311.

Wilson, B. J., & Gottman, J. M. (1995). Marital interaction and parenting. In M. H. Bornstein (Ed.), *Children and parenting* (Vol. 4). Hillsdale, NJ: Erlbaum.

Wilson, J. Q., & Herrnstein, R. J. (1985). *Crime and human nature.* New York: Simon and Schuster.

Wilson, M. N. (1989). Child development in the context of the black extended family. *American Psychologist, 44,* 380–383.

Wilson, S. M., Peterson, G. W., & Wilson, P. (1993). The process of educational and occupational attainment of adolescent females from low-income, rural families. *Journal of Marriage and the Family, 55,* 158–175.

Wilson, W. J. (1987). *The truly disadvantaged: The inner city, the underclass, and public policy.* Chicago: University of Chicago Press.

Wilson, W. J. (1996). *When work disappears: The world of the new urban poor.* New York: Knopf.

Wilson, W. J. (2006). Social theory and the concept "underclass." In D. B. Grusky, & R. Kanbur (Eds.), *Poverty and inequality: Studies in social inequality* (pp. 103–116). University Press.

Windle, M. (1989). Substance use and abuse among adolescent runaways: A four-year follow-up study. *Journal of Youth and Adolescence, 18,* 331–344.

Windle, M. (1992). A longitudinal study of stress buffering for adolescent problem behaviors. *Developmental Psychology, 28,* 522–530.

Wingood, G. M., Diclemente, R. J., Bernhardt, J. M., Harrington, K., Davies, S. L., Robillard, A., et. al. (2003). A prospective study of exposure to rap music videos and African American female adolescents' health. *American Journal of Public Health, 93,* 437–439.

Winner, E. (1988). *The point of words: Children's understanding of metaphor and irony.* Cambridge, MA: Harvard University Press.

Winner, E. (1996). *Gifted children: Myths and realities.* New York: Basic Books.

Winner, E. (2000). The origins and ends of giftedness. *American Psychologi, 55,* 159–169.

Winner, E. (2003). Creativity and talent. In M. H. Bornstein & L. Davison (Eds.), *Well-being: Positive development across the life course* (pp. 371–380). Mahwah, NJ: Lawrence Erlbaum.

Winner, E. (2005). Extreme giftedness. In R. J. Sternberg & J. E. Davidson (Eds.), *Conceptions of giftedness* (2nd ed., pp. 377–394). New York: Cambridge University Press.

Wiseman, H. (1995). The quest for connectedness: Loneliness as process in the narratives of lonely university students. In R. Josselson & A. Lieblich (Eds.), *Interpreting experience: The narrative study of lives* (pp. 116–152). Thousand Oaks, CA: Sage.

Withers, L. E., & Kaplan, D. W. (1987). Adolescents who attempt suicide: A retrospective clinical chart review of hospitalized patterns. *Professional Psychology, 18,* 391–393.

Wolak, J., Mitchell, K. J., & Finkelhor, D. (2007). Does online harassment constitute bullying? An exploration of online harassment by known peers and online-only contracts. *Journal of Adolescent Health, 41*(Suppl. 6), S51–S58.

Wolbers, M. H. J. (2007). Patterns of labor market entry: A comparative perspective on school-to-work transitions in 11 European countries. *Acta Sociologica, 50*(3), 189–210.

Wolfe, D. A. (1985). Child-abusive parents: An empirical review and analysis. *Psychological Bulletin, 97,* 462–483.

Wolfe, D. A., et al. (2001). Child maltreatment: Risk of adjustment problems and dating violence in adolescence. *Journal of the American Academy of Child & Adolescent Psychiatry, 40,* 282–289.

Wolff, T. (1989). *This boy's life.* New York: Harper-Trade.

Wong, C. A. (1997, April). *What does it mean to be African-American or European-American growing up in a multi-ethnic community?* Paper presented at the biennial meeting of the Society for Research in Child Development, Washington, DC.

Wood, P., & Clay, W. (1996). Perceived structural barriers and academic performance among American Indian high school students. *Youth & Society, 28,* 40–61.

Woodhall, S. C., Lehtinen, M., Verho, T., Huhtala, H., Hokkanen, M., & Kosunen, E. (2007). Anticipated acceptance of HPV vaccination at the baseline of implementation: A survey of parental and adolescent knowledge and attitudes in Finland. *Journal of Adolescent Health, 40*(5), 466–469.

Woods, P. D., Haskell, W. L., Stern, S. L., & Perry, C. (1977). Plasma lipoprotein distributions in male and female runners. *Annals of the New York Academy of Sciences, 301,* 748–763.

Woodward, K. L. (1993, November 29). The rites of Americans. *Newsweek,* 80–82.

Woodward, L., & Fergusson, D. (1999). Early conduct problems and later risk of teenage pregnancy in girls. *Development and Psychopathology, 11,* 127–142.

Woodward, L., Fergusson, D. M., & Belsky, J. (2000). Timing of parental separation and attachment to parents in adolescence: Results of a prospective study from birth to age 16. *Journal of Marriage & the Family, 62,* 162–174.

Woodward, L. J., & Fergusson, D. M. (2001). Life course outcomes of young people with anxiety disorders in adolescence. *Journal of the American Academy of Child and Adolescent Psychiatry, 40,* 1086–1093.

Wooten, M. A. (1992). The effects of heavy metal music on affect shifts of adolescents in an inpatient psychiatric setting. *Music Therapy Perspectives, 10,* 93–98.

World Health Organization (2008). *Inequalities in young people's health: Health behavior in school-aged children.* Retrieved on February 12, 2009, from http://www.hbsc.org/

World Internet Project (2008). Center for the digital future at USC Annenberg with 13 partner countries release the first World Internet Project report. Retrieved on April 24, 2009, from http://www.worldinternetproject.net

World Organization of the Scout Movement (2008). Facts and figures. Retrieved on August 7, 2008, from www.scout.org/en/about_scouting/facts_figures

Worthman, C. M. (1987). Interactions of physical maturation and cultural practice in ontogeny: Kikuyu adolescents. *Cultural Anthropology, 2,* 29–38.

Wright, M. J., Gillespie, N. A., Luciano, M., Zhu, G., & Martin, N. G. Genetics of personality and cognition in adolescents. (2008). In J. J. Hudziak (Ed.), *Developmental psychopathology and wellness: Genetic and environmental influences* (pp. 85–107). Arlington, VA: American Psychiatric Publishing.

Wrong, D. H. (1994). *The problem of order: What unites and divides society.* New York: Free Press.

Wu, L., Schlenger, W., & Galvin, D. (2003). The relationship between employment and substance abuse among students aged 12 to 17. *Journal of Adolescent Health, 32,* 5–15.

Wu, Z. (1999). Premarital cohabitation and the timing of first marriage. *Canadian Review of Sociology and Anthropology, 36,* 109–127.

Wulff, H. (1995a). Inter-racial friendship: Consuming youth styles, ethnicity and teenage femininity in south London. In V. Amit-Talai & H. Wulff (Eds.), *Youth cultures: A cross-cultural perspective* (pp. 63–80). New York: Routledge.

Wulff, H. (1995b). Introducing youth culture in its own right: The state of the art and new possibilities. In V. Amit-Talai & H. Wulff (Eds.), *Youth cultures: A cross-cultural perspective* (pp. 1–18). New York: Routledge.

www.bsa.scouting.org
www.norc.uchicago.edu/gss
www.psychorp.com/sub/featured/fpwwfaq.htm

Wyatt, G. E. (1990). Changing influences on adolescent sexuality over the past 40 years. In J. Bancroft & J. M. Reinisch (Eds.), *Adolescence and puberty* (pp. 182–206). New York: Oxford University Press.

Wyatt, J. M., & Carlo, G. (2002). What will my parents think? Relations among adolescents' expected parental reactions, prosocial moral reasoning, and prosocial and antisocial behaviors. *Journal of Adolescent Research, 17,* 646–666.

Xu, F., Sternberg, M. R., Kottiri, B. J., McQuillan, G. M., Lee, F. K., Nahmias, A. J.; Berman, S. M., & Markowitz, L. E. (2006). Trends in herpes simplex virus type 1 and type 2 seroprevalence in the United States. *JAMA: Journal of the American Medical Association, 296*(8), 964–973.

Xu, X., & Whyte, M. K. (1990). Love matches and arranged marriages: A Chinese replication. *Journal of Marriage and the Family, 52,* 709–722.

Yacoubian, G. S., Jr., & Deutsch, J. K. (2004). Estimating the prevalence of ecstasy use among club rave attendees. *Contemporary Drug Problems, 31,* 163–177.

Yang, K. S. (1986). Chinese personality and its change. In M. H. Bond (Ed.), *The psychology of the Chinese people* (pp. 106–170). Hong Kong: Oxford University Press.

Yasui, M., Dorham, Carole LaRue, & Dishion, T. J. (2004). Ethnic identity and psychological adjustment: A validity analysis for European American and African American adolescents. *Journal of Adolescent Research, 19,* 807–825.

Yates, M., & Youniss, J. (1996). A developmental perspective on community service in adolescence. *Social Development, 5,* 85–101.

Ybarra, M. L., & Mitchell, K. J. (2005). Exposure to internet pornography among children and adolescents: A national survey. *CyberPsychology & Behavior, 8*(5), 473–486.

Yelsma, P., & Athappilly, K. (1988). Marital satisfaction and communication practices: Comparisons among Indian and American couples. *Journal of Comparative Family Studies, 19,* 37–54.

Yeung, D. Y. L. (2005). Psychosocial and cultural factors influencing expectations of menarche: A study on Chinese premenarcheal teenage girls. *Journal of Adolescent Research, 20,* 118–135.

Yip, T., Fulgni, A. J. (2002). Daily variation in ethnic identity, ethnic behaviors, and psychological well-being among American adolescents of Chinese descent. *Child Development, 73,* 1557–1572.

Yip, Kam-Shing (Ed.). (2006). *Psychology of gender identity: An international perspective* (pp. 49–68). Hauppauge, NY: Nova Science Publishers.

Yoder, K. A., Hoyt, D. R., & Whitbeck, L. B. (1998). Suicidal behavior in homeless and runaway adolescents. *Journal of Youth & Adolescence, 27,* 753–772.

Yonkers, K. A., Holthausen, G. A., Poschman, K., & Howell, H. B. Symptom-onset treatment for women with premenstrual dysphoric disorder. *Journal of Clinical Psychopharmacology, 26*(2), 198–202.

Yonkers, K. A., O'Brien, P. M., & Shaughn; E. E. Premenstrual syndrome. *Lancet, 371,* 1200–1210.

Yoshikawa, H. Prevention as cumulative protection: Effects of early family support and education on chronic delinquency and its risks. *Psychological Bulletin, 115*(1), 28–54.

Youn, G. (1996). Sexual activities and attitudes of adolescent Koreans. *Archives of Sexual Behavior, 25,* 629–643.

Young, A. M., & D'Arcy, H. (2005). Older boyfriends of adolescent girls: The cause or a sign of the problem? *Journal of Adolescent Health, 36,* 410–419.

Youniss, J. (2006). G. Stanley Hall and his times: Too much so, yet not enough. *History of Psychology.*

Youniss, J., McLellan, J. A., & Yates, M. (1999). Religion, community service, and identity in American youth. *Journal of Adolescence, 22,* 243–253.

Youniss, J., & Smollar, J. (1985). *Adolescent relations with mothers, fathers, and friends.* Chicago: University of Chicago Press.

Youniss, J., & Yates, M. (1997). *Community service and social responsibility in youth: Theory and policy.* Chicago: University of Chicago Press.

Youniss, J., & Yates, M. (2000). Adolescents' public discussion and collective identity. In N. Budwig & I. C. Uzgiris (Eds.), *Communication: An arena of development* (pp. 215–233). New York: Greenwood.

Youth Indicators. (1996). *Trends in the well-being of American youth.* Washington, DC: U.S. Government Printing Office.

Yussen, S. R. (1977). Characteristics of moral dilemmas written by adolescents. *Developmental Psychology, 13,* 162–163.

Zabin, L. S. (1986, May/June). Evaluation of a pregnancy prevention program for urban teenagers. *Family Planning Perspectives, 119.*

Zabin, L., Hirsch, M., & Emerson, M. (1989). When urban adolescents choose abortion: Effects on education, psychological status and subsequent pregnancy. *Family Planning Perspectives, 21,* 248–255.

Zakaria, F. (2008). *The post-American world.* New York: Norton.

Zalsman, G., Oquendo, M. A., Greenhill, L., Goldberg, P. H., Pamali, M., Martin, A., & Mann, J. J. (2006). Neurobiology of depression in children and adolescents. *Child and Adolescent Psychiatric Clinics of North America, 15*(4), 843–868.

Zedd, Z., Brooks, J., & McGarvey, A. M. (2002, August). Educating America's youth: What makes a difference? *Child Trends Research Brief.* Washington, DC: Author.

Zeidner, M. (1993). Coping with disaster: The case of Israeli adolescents under threat of missile attack. *Journal of Youth & Adolescence, 22,* 89–108.

Zeidner, M., & Schleyer, E. J. (1999). The effects of educational context on individual difference variables, self-perceptions of giftedness, and school attitudes in gifted adolescents. *Journal of Youth & Adolescence, 28,* 687–703.

Zeijl, E., te Poel, Y., de Bois-Reymond, M., Ravesloot, J., & Meulman, J. (2000). The role of parents and peers in the leisure activities of young adolescents. *Journal of Leisure Research, 32,* 281–302.

Zettergren, P. (2003). School adjustment in adolescence for previously rejected, average and popular children. *British Journal of Educational Psychology, 73,* 207–221.

Zhang, W., & Fuligni, A. J. Authority, autonomy, and family relationships among adolescents in urban and rural China. *Journal of Research on Adolescence, 16*(4), 527–537.

Zhao, S., Grasmuck, S., & Martin, J. (2008). Identity construction on Facebook: Digital empowerment in anchored relationships. *Computers in Human Behavior, 24*(5), 1816–1836.

Zhou, M. (1997). Growing up American: The challenge confronting immigrant children and children of immigrants. *Annual Review of Sociology, 23,* 63–95.

Zierold, K. M., Garman, S., & Anderson, H. A. (2005). A comparison of school performance and behaviors among working and nonworking high school students. *Family & Community Health, 28,* 214–224.

Zigler, E., & Hall, N. W. (1989). Physical child abuse in America: Past, present, and future. In D. Cicchetti & V. Carlson (Eds.), *Child maltreatment: Theory and research on the causes and consequences of child abuse and neglect* (pp. 38–75). New York: Cambridge University Press.

Zill, N., & Nord, C. W. (1994). *Running in place: How American families are faring in a changing economy and an individualistic society.* Washington, DC: Child Trends.

Zill, N., Morrison, D. R., & Coiro, M. J. (1993). Long-term effects of parental divorce on parent–child relationships, adjustment, and achievement in young adulthood. *Journal of Family Psychology, 7,* 91–103.

Zimiles, H., & Lee, V. (1991). Adolescent family structure and educational progress. *Developmental Psychology, 27,* 314–320.

Zimmer-Gembeck, M. J., & Collins, W. A. (2003). Autonomy development during adolescence. In G. Adams & M. Berzonsky (Eds.), *Blackwell handbook of adolescence.* Malden, MA: Blackwell.

Zimmerman, M. A., Copeland, L. A., Shope, J. T., & Dielman, T. E. A longitudinal study of self-esteem: Implications for adolescent development. *Journal of Youth and Adolescence, 26*(2), 117–141.

Zimring, F. E. (2000). Penal proportionality for the young offender: Notes on immaturity, capacity, and diminished responsibility. In T. Grisso & R. Schwartz (Eds.), *Youth on trial: A developmental perspective on juvenile justice* (pp. 271–289). Chicago, IL: University of Chicago Press.

Zuckerman, D. (2001, February). *Controversy: What factors predict youth trouble? Youth Today,* pp. 14–15.

Zuckerman, M. (1995). *Behavioral expressions and psychobiological bases of sensation seeking.* New York: Cambridge University Press.

Zuckerman, M. (2006). Sensation seeking in entertainment. In J. Bryant & P. Vorderer (Eds.), *Psychology of entertainment* (pp. 367–387). Mahwah, NJ: Lawrence Erlbaum.

Zuckerman, M. (2007). *Sensation seeking and risky behavior.* Washington, DC: American Psychological Association.

Zukow-Goldring, P. (2002). Sibling caregiving. In M. H. Bornstein (Ed.), *Handbook of parenting, Vol. 3: Being and becoming a parent* (pp. 253–286). Mahwah, NJ: Erlbaum.

Zumwalt, M. (2008). Effects of the menstrual cycle on the acquisition of peak bone mass. In J. J. Robert-McComb, R. Norman, & M. Zumwalt (Eds.). *The active female: Health issues throughout the lifespan* (pp. 141–151). Totowa, NJ: Humana Press.

Zwick, R. (2002). Fair game? *The use of standardized admissions tests in higher education.* New York: Taylor & Francis.

Credits

Photos and Cartoons

FM p. xvii Courtesy of Jeffrey Arnett.

Chapter 1 Opener Robert Frerck/ Odyssey Productions, Inc.; p. 3 © Mary Evans Picture Library/Edwin Wallace/The Image Works; p. 4 (top) Lewis Hine/Corbis/Bettmann; p. 4 (bottom) Corbis/Bettmann; p. 6 (top) Corbis/Bettmann; p. 6 (bottom) Corbis/Bettmann; p. 11 Peter Reid/Stock Connection; p. 12 (left) David Young-Wolff/PhotoEdit Inc.; p. 12 (middle) David Young-Wolff/PhotoEdit Inc.; p. 12 (right) David Young-Wolff/PhotoEdit Inc.; p. 13 Dean Chapman/Panos Pictures; p. 15 © Kazuyoshi Nomachi/CORBIS All Rights Reserved; p. 17 Courtesy of the Library of Congress; p. 19 JOSEPH C. JUSTICE JR./istockphoto.com; p. 22 Alamy Images; p. 23 (left) © imagebroker/Alamy; p. 23 (right) DAVE BARTRUFF/DanitaDelimont.com; p. 24 (left) Ziyah Gafic/Getty Images, Inc.–Reportage; p. 24 (right) © Mitch Diamond/Alamy; p. 25 www.photos.com/Jupiter Images; p. 27 M. L. Corvetto/The Image Works.

Chapter 2 Opener Jay P. Morgan/Jupiter Images–Workbook Stock; p. 35 Justin Pumfrey Getty Images; p. 38 Ezra Shaw/Getty Images; p. 39 FOR BETTER OR FOR WORSE © Lynn Johnston Productions. Dist. By Universal Press Syndicate. Reprinted with permission. All rights reserved; p. 43 Sylvain Grandadam/Photo Researchers, Inc.; p. 45 Blackwell Science Ltd.; p. 46 The Image Works; p. 47 Bob Krist/Corbis/Bettmann; p. 51 Scott Swanson; p. 53 Chad Ehlers/Stock Connection; p. 55 Tony Freeman/PhotoEdit Inc.

Chapter 3 Opener EJS Photo.Com, Inc.; p. 60 Getty Images, Inc.; p. 62 Mimi Forsyth; p. 64 © FOR BETTER OR FOR WORSE © 2004 Lynn Johnston Productions. Dist. By Universal Press Syndicate. Reprinted with permission. All right reserved; p. 66 David R. Austen/Stock Boston; p. 67 Eastcott/Momatiuk/Woodfin Camp & Associates, Inc.; p. 68 J. Nordell/The Image Works; p. 70 J. Pickerell/The Image Works; p. 72 Odilon Dimier/Getty Images Royalty Free–PhotoAlto; p. 73 Getty Images, Inc.; p. 75 John Neubauer/PhotoEdit Inc.; p. 76 © Tom & Dee Ann McCarthy/CORBIS All Rights Reserved; p. 79 "© Zits Partnership. Reprinted with special permission of King Features Syndicate"; p. 84 The Chronicle, Gary J. Cichowski/AP Wide World Photos; p. 85 FRANCK FIFE/AFP/Getty Images; p. 88 Richard Lord/The Image Works.

Chapter 4 Opener Angelo Cavalli/Getty Images–Digital Vision; p. 95 Jonathan Nourok/PhotoEdit Inc.; p. 97 (top left) Jupiter Images–Comstock Images; p. 97 (top middle) Steven Rubin/The Image Works; p. 97 (top right) J. Holmes/Panos Pictures; p. 97 (bottom) D. Young Wolff/PhotoEdit Inc.; p. 100 Penny Tweedie/Panos Pictures; p. 101 © Kevin Dodge/Corbis; p. 103 (top) Joseph Sohm/Corbis/Bettmann; p. 103 (bottom) Lawrence Migdale/Photo Researchers, Inc.; p. 107 © Arlene Gottfried/The Image Works; p. 109 © CORBIS All Rights Reserved; p. 112 Richard Lord/The Image Works; p. 118 Stephen Chernin/Stringer/Getty Images, Inc.

Chapter 5 Opener Goodshoot RF/Jupiterimages/Jupiter Images–Thinkstock Images Royalty Free; p. 122 Jeff Greenberg/PhotoEdit Inc.; p. 126 Peter Johnson/Corbis/ Bettmann; p. 127 © Bettmann/CORBIS & 129 Courtesy of the Library of Congress; p. 131 (left) Stockbyte/ Getty Images, Inc.–Stockbyte Royalty Free; p. 131 (right) Lawrence Migdale/Pix; p. 133 Michael Newman/PhotoEdit Inc.; p. 134 KING FEATURES SYNDICATE; p. 136 Jennifer K. Berman; p. 137 Mary Ellen Mark; p. 138 Lucas/The Image Works; p. 143 Morris Carpenter/Panos Pictures.

Chapter 6 Opener Corbis Royalty Free; p. 150 David Young-Wolff/PhotoEdit Inc.; p. 155 SW Productions/Getty Images, Inc.–Photodisc./Royalty Free; p. 157 Katja Zimmermann/Getty Images; p. 158 The Bridgeman Art Library International; p. 160 Ted Streshinsky/Corbis/Bettmann; p. 164 David Schmidt/ Masterfile Stock Image Library; p. 165 © Sean Sprague/The Image Works; p. 167 Dennis MacDonald/PhotoEdit Inc.; p. 169 (top) Eastcott/The Image Works; p. 169 (bottom) © Amit Dave/CORBIS All Rights Reserved; p. 170 Elizabeth Crews/Elizabeth Crews Photography; p. 171 Universal Press Syndicate.

Chapter 7 Opener Nasi Sakura/SuperStock, Inc.; p. 177 M. Ferguson/PhotoEdit Inc.; p. 180 (top) Copyright © John Morrison/ PhotoEdit; p. 180 (bottom) Giacomo Pirozzi/Panos Pictures; p. 181 Dennis Lane/Jupiter Images–FoodPix–Creatas; p. 184 © Zits Partnership. Reprinted with special permission of King Features Syndicate; p. 185 Nancy Ney/Getty Images/Digital Vision; p. 186 © Jack Hollingsworth/Corbis; p. 187 Dinodia Picture Agency; p. 189 Charles Gupton/Stock Boston; p. 191 (top) Jim Whitmer/Stock Boston; p. 191 (bottom) Universal Press Syndicate; p. 194 © Danita Delimont/Alamy; p. 195 David Young-Wolff/PhotoEdit Inc.; p. 197 Culver Pictures, Inc.; p. 199 (top) © Bettmann/CORBIS All Rights Reserved; p. 200 Bananastock/Jupiter Images Royalty Free; p. 204 Bruce Ayres/Getty Images Inc.–Stone Allstock; p. 206 © Najlah Feanny/CORBIS All Rights Reserved.

Chapter 8 Opener HIRB/Photolibrary.com; p. 212 Andrey Shadrin/Shutterstock; p. 215 Megapress/Alamy Images; p. 216 (left) Bob Daemmrich/Stock Boston; p. 216 (right) Jeff Greenberg/Stock Boston; p. 217 "© Zits Partnership. Reprinted with special permission of King Features Syndicate"; p. 218 Jupiter Images; p. 219 Jacky Chapman/Janine Wiedel Photolibrary/Alamy Images; p. 220 Telegraph Colour Library/Dick Makin Imaging; p. 223 © Spencer Grant/ PhotoEdit; p. 224 "© Zits Partnership. Reprinted with special permission of King Features Syndicate"; p. 227 Don Smetzer/PhotoEdit Inc.; p. 231 Penny Tweedie/Getty Images Inc.–Stone Allstock; p. 233 © Martin Ruetschi/Keystone/Corbis; p. 235 © Underwood & Underwood/CORBIS All Rights Reserved; p. 236 (top left) Corbis/Bettmann; p. 236 (top right) Getty Images, Inc.; p. 236 (bottom left) Corbis/Bettmann; p. 236 (bottom right) Catherine Karnow/Woodfin Camp & Associates, Inc.; p. 237 Hunter Freeman/Getty Images Inc.–Stone Allstock.

Chapter 9 Opener Kaz Mori/Taxi/Getty Images; p. 242 Willinger/Getty Images, Inc.; p. 244 Culver Pictures, Inc.; p. 245 Jenny Acheson; p. 246 (bottom) KING FEATURES SYNDICATE; p. 247 Peter Correz, Getty ImagesInc.–Stone Allstock; p. 249 Copyright © Jeff Greenberg/PhotoEdit; p. 251 Universal Press Syndicate; p. 253 Hari Mahidhar/The Image Works; p. 256 Telegraph Colour Library/Getty Images, Inc.; p. 258 François Perri/Cosmos/Woodfin Camp & Associates, Inc.; p. 260 Steve Stanford/Alamy Images; p. 264 Bob Daemmrich/Stock Boston; p. 265 David Hanson/Getty Images Inc.–Stone Allstock; p. 267 Massimo Borchi/© Atlantide Phototravel/Corbis; p. 269 Bob Daemmrich/The Image Works; p. 273 Bob Daemmrich/The Image Works.

Chapter 10 Opener Photodisc/Getty Images; p. 278 (top) Bob Daemmrich/Bob Daemmrich Photography, Inc.; p. 282 Michael A. Dwyer/Stock Boston; p. 283 Shaun Harris/iAfrika Photos; p. 287 Charles Gupton/Stock Boston; p. 288 David Young-Wolff/PhotoEdit Inc.; p. 293 JIM CUMMINS/Getty Images, Inc.–Taxi; p. 295 Bob Daemmrich/Stock Boston; p. 296 Yellow Dog Productions/Image Bank/Getty Images; p. 297 Copyright © Michael Newman/PhotoEdit; p. 299 AP Wide World Photos; p. 303 Ron Sherman/Stock Boston.

Chapter 11 Opener Alan Becker/Image Bank/Getty Images; p. 310 M & E Bernheim/Woodfin Camp & Associates, Inc.; p. 311 © Wolfgang Kaehler/Alamy; p. 313 Sean Sprague/Panos Pictures; p. 314 Lewis W. Hine/Courtesy of the Library of Congress; p. 315 Getty Images Inc.; p. 316 Lawrence Migdale/Stock Boston; p. 317 Universal Press Syndicate; p. 319 © JUPITERIMAGES/ Creatas/Alamy; p. 321 © vario images GmbH & Co.KG/Alamy; p. 323 Nubar Alexanian/Stock Boston; p. 327 (top) © Zits Partnership. Reprinted with special permission of King Features Syndicate; p. 327 (bottom) Telegraph Colour Library/Getty Images, Inc.; p. 332 © DigitalVues/Alamy.

Chapter 12 Opener Goodshoot RF/jupiterimages/Jupiter Images–Thinkstock Images Royalty Free; p. 338 © JAUBERT BERNARD/Alamy; p. 341 IAN WEST/PA Photos/Landov; p. 342 David Young-Wolff/ PhotoEdit Inc.; p. 343 "© Rob Bartee/Alamy; p. 345 "© Zits Partnership. Reprinted with special permission of King Features Syndicate"; p. 346 Adam Taylor/© NBC/Courtesy everett collection; p. 347 Copyright © Raquel Ramirez/PhotoEdit; p. 348 Universal Pictures/Photofest; p. 351 Corbis/Bettmann; p. 352 Photo by Scott Gries/Getty Images; p. 353 (top) M. Benjamin/The Image Works; p. 353 (bottom) J. Griffin/The Image Works; p. 356 Copyright © Colin Young-Wolff/PhotoEdit; p. 358 Jack Hollingsworth/Photodisc/Getty Images; p. 360 Chris Brown/Stock Boston.

Chapter 13 Opener Bananastock/Photolibrary.com–Royalty Free; p. 366 (bottom) John C. Panella Jr./Shutterstock; p. 367 (top) Richard Hutchings/Photo Researchers, Inc.; p. 373 (bottom) © Pegaz/Alamy;

p. 373 (top) Topham/The Image Works; p. 377 BLONDIE–KING FEATUR- ERS SYNDICATE; p. 378 Joe Sohm/The Image Works; p. 383 Steve Weber/Stock Boston; p. 385 Bob Daemmrich/Stock Boston; p. 386 © Les Stone/Sygma/Corbis; p. 387 Tony Latham/Getty Images Inc.–Stone Allstock; p. 390 Karl Prouse Getty Images, Inc.

Figures, Tables, and Text

Chapter 1   Figure 1.1 Goldschneider/Goldschneider (1994): Leaving and Returning Home in the 20th Century America, *Population Bulletin 48 (4);* U.S Bureau of the Census (2003); **Table 1.2** United Nations Economic Commission for Europe (2005); Population Reference Bureau (2000); **Page 1** Chinas (1991); **Page 1** Hollos & Leis (1989); **Page 7** Page (1999, pp. 18, 20); **Page 8** From *Emerging Adulthood: The Winding Road from the Late Teens Through The Twenties,* Jeffrey Jensen Arnett. Copyright © 2004 Oxford University Press. Reprinted by permission of Oxford University Press; **Page 12** Arnett, 2004a, p. 14.

Chapter 2   Figure 2.2 Nottelman, Sussman, et.al (1987): Gonadal and Adrenal Hormone Correlates of Adjustment in Early Adolescence, in Lerner & Gochs (eds.) *Biological Psychological Interactions in Early Adolescence.* © 1987 Lawrence Erlbaum & Associates. Reprinted by permission; **Figure 2.3** Adapted from Grumback et al. (1974): *Control of the Onset of Puberty.* New York: John Wiley Sons, Inc. Reprinted by permission of Williams & Wilkins on behalf of the author; **Figure 2.4** From Human Growth, Vol.2, (1978), Falkner & Tanner (eds.) "Growth in Height of Average Males & Females" by Marshall. Copyright © 1978 Plenum Publishers. With kind permission from Springer Science and Business Media; **Figure 2.6** From "Effects of Fast Food Consumption on Energy Intake and Diet Quality Among Children in National Household Survey", S. Bowman, (2004), *Pediatrics;* **Figure 2.7** From "Variations in the Pattern of Pubertal Changes in Boys", W.A. Marshall, J.M Tanner, *Archives of Disease in Childhood, 45, 1970, p.22.* Used with permission; **Figure 2.8** From *World Wide Variation in Human Growth,* Phyllis Eveleth & James M. Tanner, Cambridge University Press © 1990. Reprinted with permission of the Cambridge University Press; **Figure 2.9** From "Variations in the Pattern of Pubertal Changes in Boys", W.A. Marshall, J.M. Tanner, *Archives of Disease in Childhood, 45, 1970, p. 22;* **Figure 2.10** From *World Wide Variation in Human Growth,* Phyllis Eveleth & James M. Tanner, Cambridge University Press © 1990. Reprinted with permission of the Cambridge University Press; **Figure 2.11** Montemayor & Flannery, A Naturalistic Study of the Involvement of Children and Adolescents with their Mothers & Friends. *Journal of Adolescent Research, (4)* 3–14. Copyright © 1989 Sage Publications. Reprinted by permission of the Copyright Clearance Center; **Page 40** From *Crazy Salad: Some Things About Women,* Nora Ephron, Random House 1975, pp. 2–4. Reprinted by permission of the International Creative Management, Inc. Copyright © 2000 by Nora Ephron; **Page 50** From *Diary of A Young Girl, The Definitive Edition* by Anne Frank. Otto M. Frank & Mirjam Pressler, editors, translated by Susan Massotty. Copyright © 1985 by Doubleday, a division of Random House, Inc. Used by permission of Doubleday, a division of Random House, Inc.; **Page 53** From *Crazy Salad: Some Things About Women,* Nora Ephron, Random House 1975, pp. 2–4. Reprinted by permission of the International Creative Management, Inc. Copyright © 2000 by Nora Ephron; **Page 54** Reprinted with permission of Antheneum Books for Young Readers, an imprint of Simon & Schuster Children's Publishing Division from *Are you There God, It's Me, Margaret* by Judy Blume. Copyright © 1970 Judy Blume.

Chapter 3   Figure 3.4 From *Adolescence, 10th edition,* by John W. Stanrock. Copyright © 2005 The McGraw-Hill Companies, Inc. Reprinted with permission; **Figure 3.5** From *Adolescence, 10th edition* by John W. Stanrock. Copyright © 2005 The McGraw-Hill Companies, Inc. Reprinted with permission; **Table 3.2** Simulated items similar to those in the Weschler Adult Intelligence Scale-Third edition. Copyright © 1997 NCS Pearson, Inc. Reproduced with permission. All rights reserved; **Page 63** Excerpt from *A Dedication to My Wife,* in Collected Poems of T.S. Elliott, 1909–1962. Copyright © 1936 by Harcourt, Inc. Copyright © 1964, 1964 by T. S. Eliot. Used with permission of Faber & Faber, Ltd.

Chapter 4   Table 4.4 From *Cultural Psychology: Essays in Comparative and Human Development,* J.W. Stigler, R.A. Schweder. G.S. Herdt. Copyright © 1990 Cambridge University Press.   Reprinted with permission of Cambridge University Press; **Page 102** Boy Scout Oath: Used with permission of The Boy Scouts of America.

Chapter 5   Figure 5.1 © The Economist Newspaper Limited, London (February 11, 1999). Reprinted with permission; **Figure 5.2** *General Social Survey, (GSS) 1977–2006.* Reprinted by permission of the National Opinion Research Center; **Figure 5.3** Evans et al., Teen Magazine Content, *Youth & Society,* Sept. 1991, Copyright © 1991 Sage Publications. Used with permission; **Table 5.2** "Creating Gender Equality: Cross-National Gender and Mathematical Performance", by David P. Baker & Deborah Jenkins-Jones from *Sociology of Education. Copyright © 1983 by American Sociological Association.* Reprinted by permission; **Page 138** Manhood Pledge: Reprinted with permission of Youth Today.

Chapter 6   Figure 6.1 From "A Longitudinal Study of Self Esteem: Implications of Adolescent Development", Marc A. Zimmerman, Journal of Youth & Adolescence, Vol. 26, No. 2, Apr. 1997, pp. 117–141. Copyright © Springer. With kind permission of Springer Science and Business Media; **Figure 6.2** From *Monitoring the Future,* Institute of Social Research. Used with permission; **Figure 6.3** From "Continuity, Stability, and Change in Daily Emotional Experience, Across Adolescence", R.W. Larson, Giovanni Monetta, Maryse H. Richards, Suzanne Wilson, *Child Development,* (73:4). Reprinted with permission of Blackwell Publishers; **Figure 6.4** From "Identity Formation Revisited", W. Meeus, J. Iedema, W. Vollebergh, *Development Review,* December 1999, Academic Press, 1999. Reprinted with permission; **Table 6.2** Adapted from Phinney & Devish-Navarro (1997); **Table 6.3** Based on Phinney & Devish-Navarro (1994): *Bicultural Identity Orientations of African American Adolescents.* Paper presented at the Society for Research on Adolescence, San Diego, CA.; **Page 148** Octavio Paz (1985, p.9) quoted in Herdt & Leavitt (1998); Page 159 Young Man Luther: From *Young Man Luther,* Erik Erickson, Copyright © 1958. Reprinted with permission.

Chapter 7   Figure 7.1 Larson, "Changes in Adolescent's Daily Interactions With Their Families Ages, 10–18", *Developmental Psychology,* 32, Copyright © 1996 by The American Psychology Association; **Figure 7.2** Adapted from Granic, Dishion, and Hollenstein (2003); **Figure 7.3** Adapted from Iacovov, M. (2002); **Figure 7.4** R.E. Emery, *Marriage, Divorce, & Children's Adjustment,* Sage Publications, Copyright © 1999. Used with permission.

Chapter 8   Figure 8.1 From *Adolescent Relations with Mothers, Fathers & Friends,* Youniss & Smollar, University of Chicago Press, 1985. Reprinted with permission; **Figure 8.2** Adapted from Larson & Richards (1998); **Figure 8.4** From Csikszenthmilalyi & Larson (1984): *Being Adolescent: Conflict & Growth in the Teenage Years,* p. 183. Copyright © 1983 by Basic Books, Inc., a member of Perseus Books, LLC.

Chapter 9   Figure 9.1 From "Sexual Development, Age, Dating: A Comparison of Biological Influences Upon One Set of Behaviors", Dornbusch, et al., *Child Development,* Copyright © 1981 Blackwell Publishers. Reprinted with permission; **Figure 9.2** From "Triangulating Love", R.J. Sternberg & M.L. Barnes, ed., *The Psychology of Love,* Yale University Press © 1988, p. 122. Used with permission; **Figure 9.7** Adapted from Bankole et al. (2004); **Table 9.1** From "Two Sides to Breakup of Dating Relationships", Sprecher, *Personal Relationships,* Vol. 10.il, Copyright © 1994 Blackwell Publishers. Used with permission; **Table 9.2** Based on Hartfield & Rapson, *Love & Crosscultural Perspectives,* 2005, p. 28; **Table 9.4** From *Love and Sex: Cross-Cultural Perspectives,* E. Hatfield & R.L. Rapson, Allyn & Bacon, 2005; **Table 9.5** Savin-Williams and Ream (2007). Used with permission; **Table 9.6** Based on "Sexually Transmitted Diseases Among American Youth: Incidence and Prevalence Estimates, 2000", H. Weinstock, S. Berman & W. Cates, *Perspectives on Sexual Reproductive Health,* 36, 2004, 6–10.

Chapter 10   Figure 10.1 From D. Tanner (1972): *Secondary Education.* New York: Macmillan; **Figure 10.2** Fussell & Greene (2002); **Figure 10.4** Steinberg/Dornbusch (1991): Negative Correlates of Part-time Employment During Adolescence. *Replication and Elaboration. Developmental Psychology* 27: 304–313, fig. 1. Copyright © 1991 The American Psychological Association. Reprinted by permission; **Table 10.4** "Professors Bring Material to Life" Teachers Rated by Students on a Scale of 60 to 100. Based on Princeton Review (2005); **Page 290** From   "Close & General Friendships Among African American, Latino, and Asian American Adolescents", N. Way & C. Chen, Journal of Adolescent Research, 15. Reprinted with permission.

Chapter 11   Page 321 From *Teaching New Basic Skills: Principles for Education Children to Thrive in a Changing Economy,* Richard J. Murnane, Frank Levy. The Free Press, a division of Simon & Schuster Adult Publishing Group. Copyright © 1996 by Richard J. Murnane and Frank Levy.

Chapter 12   Figure 12.2 *Adolescent Responses to Cigarette Advertising Exposure, Liking and The Appeal of Smoking* by J. Arnett & Terhanian. Copyright © 1998 by TOBACCO CONTROL, Vol 7, No 2. Reproduced with permisison of BMJ Publishing; **Figure 12.3** Kaiser Family Foundation (1999). Reprinted by permission; **Figure 12.4** U.S. Census Bureau 1999 (Corrected by the U.S. Census March 20th, 2000); **Page 342** From "Adolescent Room Culture: Studying Media in the Context of Everyday Live", Jeanne R. Steele, *Journal of Youth & Adolescence,* Springer Publishers. Reprinted with permission; **Page 355** World Internet Project (2008). Center for the Digital Future at USC Annenberg with 13 partner countries release the first World Internet Project report. Available: **http://www.worldinternetproject.net/**. Downloaded April 24, 2009.

Chapter 13   Figure 13.6 Johnston, L.D., O'Malley, P.M., Bachman, J.G., & Schulenberg, J.E. (2008). *Monitoring the Future: National survey results on drug use, 1975–2007. Volume 2: College students and adults ages 19–45.* Bethesda, Maryland: United States Department of Health and Human Services; **Figure 13.10** Based on data from the *Population Bulletin,* Vol. 57, No. 4; December 2002, p. 15. Population Reference Bureau; World Health Organization, 1997–1999 World Health Statistics Annual (**www3.who.int/whosis/whsa/whsa_table1.cfm**, accessed Sept. 23, 2002): table 1.

Name Index

Feder, M., 260
Federal Bureau of Investigation, 372
Feeney, J. A., 177
Fegley, S., 331
Fehr, B., 251
Feinberg, M., 185
Feiring, C., 243, 247
Feldlaufer, H., 201
Feldman, A., 140
Feldman, E., 231
Feldman, R. S., 177
Feldman, S. S., 104, 184, 188, 232, 242, 247, 255
Felmlee, D. H., 250
Ferguson, S. A., 364, 366, 367
Fergusson, D. M., 190, 268, 370
Ferrier, M. B., 138
Few, A. L., 351
Fife-Schaw, C., 80
Figueira-McDonough, J., 295
Finch, M., 318
Fine, M., 261
Fineran, S., 263
Finkelhor, D., 205, 356
Finkelstein, J. W., 33, 39, 40, 42, 50, 52
Finken, L. L., 364
Finkenauer, C., 231
Finley, G. E., 84
Fischer, E. F., 247, 248
Fischer, K. W., 63
Fischoff, B., 75, 76
Fisher, B. S., 263
Fisher, L. A., 220
Fisher, M., 50, 390
Fisher, P. A., 184
Fitness, J., 251
Fitzgerald, H. E., 37, 38
Flammer, A., 37, 101, 219, 242, 281, 338
Flanagan, C., 116, 117, 201, 331
Flannery, D. J., 48
Flavell, J. H., 61, 62, 65, 77
Flay, B., 378
Fleming, J. E., 384
Fleming, M., 37, 38
Fletcher, G. J. O., 251
Fletcher, M. A., 382
Flickinger, S., 203
Flisher, A. J., 154
Flook, L., 292
Flor, D. L., 391
Flores-Mendoza, C., 71
Flowers, P., 264
Flynn, C., 232
Foehr, U. G., 338, 340, 355
Fombonne, E., 383
Ford, C. M., 258, 259, 347
Ford, K., 265
Fordham, S., 227, 295
Forehand, R., 261
Forkel, I., 383
Fortin, L., 383
Fortune, S., 386
Foss, R. D., 366, 367
Fowler, J. W., 108
Frankel, L., 52
Franklin, C., 301
Franko, D. L., 388, 390
Franzoni, S. L., 245
Fraser, S., 84
Freedman, J. L., 345
Freedman, R., 313, 314
Freedman-Doan, P., 333
Freeman, S. K., 349
Freire, A., 63, 65
French, D. C., 107, 212, 215, 225, 232
French, H. W., 287
French, S. E., 132, 285
French, T., 277
Freud, A., 190
Freud, S., 189
Frick, P. J., 363

Frieze, I. H., 333
Frith, H., 260
Frith, S., 233
Frone, M. R., 317, 318
Frost, J. J., 152, 153, 154, 270
Fry, A. F., 70, 71, 72
Fryberg, S., 149
Fuentes, C. D. L., 138, 139
Fuligni, A. J., 103, 167, 181, 187, 188, 195, 292, 294, 296
Fuller, A., 322
Funk, J. B., 343, 347, 348
Furby, M., 76
Furman, W., 155, 180, 181, 194, 212, 213, 224, 229, 241, 242, 243, 245, 247, 248, 256
Furnham, A., 141, 341
Furrow, J. L., 106
Furstenberg, E., Jr., 315
Furstenberg, F. F., Jr., 202

G

Gaddis, A., 52
Gade, P. A., 333
Gagnon, J. H., 260, 348
Gaines, C., 192
Galambos, N. L., 9, 10, 24, 151, 154, 155, 156, 204, 213
Galen, B. R., 261
Gallagher, W., 177
Gallup, G., Jr., 106
Galotti, K., 112
Galvan, A., 85, 233
Galvin, D., 318
Gamoran, A., 299, 300
Ganong, L. H., 203
Gans, J., 38, 39
Garber, J., 49, 232
Gardiner, H. W., 87
Gardner, H., 84, 85
Gardner, T. W., 391
Gardstrom, S. C., 351
Garfinkel, P. E., 390
Garner, D. M., 390
Garwick, A. W., 168
Gaughan, M., 220
Gavin, L., 155, 224
Gaylord-Harden, N. K., 151
Gaynor, S. T., 385
Ge, X., 42, 43, 52, 53, 384
Geary, D. C., 8
Gecas, V., 191
Gerbner, G., 338, 339
Gerrard, M., 76
Gershon, E. S., 383
Gershuny, J., 327
Getz, S., 85
Ghuman, P. A. S., 109
Giang, M. T., 167
Gibbons, F. X., 76
Gibbons, J. L., 24, 106, 135, 186, 187, 251
Gibbs, J. C., 111, 112
Gibbs, N., 347
Gibbs, R., Jr., 63
Gibson, T., 338
Giddens, A., 163
Giedd, J. N., 85, 86, 156
Gielen, U. P., 13, 97, 98
Gifford-Smith, M., 373
Gil, A. G., 368, 370
Gill, J. S., 369
Gilbert, L. A., 140
Gillen, M. M., 270
Gilligan, C., 112, 113, 150, 157, 163, 164, 197
Gillis, J. R., 224
Gillock, K. L., 294
Gilmore, D., 48, 123, 125, 310, 374
Gil-Rivas, V., 376
Gini, G., 233
Ginsberg, S., 79, 80

Ginsburg, H. P., 63
Ginzberg, E., 315
Giordano, P. C., 243, 256
Girgus, J., 384
Gjerde, P. F., 384
Gladding, S. T., 191
Gladue, B., 256
Gladwin, E. T., 310
Glantz, S. A., 353, 354
Glaser, R., 65, 73
Glowinski, A. L., 383
Glueck, E., 381
Glueck, S., 381
Gmel, G., 369
Goldberg, A. P., 38, 262, 263
Goldberg, P. H., 140
Goldenberg, H., 176
Goldenberg, I., 176
Goldscheider, C., 8, 9, 171, 194, 195
Goldscheider, F., 8, 9, 171, 194, 195
Goldsmith, D., 88
Goldstein, S. E., 183
Goldston, D. B., 168
Goleman, D., 85
Gonzales, N., 292
Goode, E., 358
Gooden, A., 112
Goodman, M., 4, 6
Goodnow, J., 105
Goodwin, C. J., 7, 14, 16
Goodwin, M. P., 179
Goodyear, R. K., 139
Goossens, L., 106, 117, 233
Gore, J. S., 148
Gore, S. A., 384, 390
Gorvine, B., 349
Gotcher, J. M., 131
Gotlib, I. H., 53
Gottfredson, G. D., 326
Gottfredson, M., 369, 372, 376
Gotthoffer, A., 338, 340
Gottlieb, A., 46, 122
Gottman, J. M., 176
Gould, S. J., 72, 81, 84
Gow, J., 349
Gowen, L. K., 262, 389
Grabe, S., 132, 384
Graber, J. A., 53, 54, 154, 176, 245, 261, 266, 268
Graef, R., 156, 170
Graham, J. W., 220
Graham, M. J., 44
Granic, I., 191, 192, 377
Grant, K. E., 384
Grasmuck, S., 357
Gray, M. R., 249
Gray, W. M., 62, 65
Green, E. G. T., 148
Greenberg, B. S., 349
Greenberger, E., 180, 316, 319, 320, 376
Greene, A. L., 247
Greene, B., 204
Greene, C. G., 197
Greene, M. L., 151, 154
Greenfield, P. M., 340
Greenwood, P. W., 374, 375
Gregson, K., 343
Greve, W., 177
Griffin, C., 237
Griffith, J., 333
Griffiths, M., 356
Grimsley, K. D., 328
Grisso, T., 76
Grolnick, W., 290
Gross, L., 338
Grote, N., 333
Grotevant, H. D., 161, 164
Grover, R. L., 222
Grover, T., 202
Gruber, J. E., 263
Gruber, S., 75, 222

Minuchin, S., 176
Miracle, A. W., 49
Miracle, T. S., 49
Miranda, D., 351
Miranda, R., 370
Mitchell, K. J., 257, 356
Mitchell, W. S., 351
Modell, J., 4, 6, 315
Mody, R., 18
Moffitt, T. E., 49, 155, 231, 261, 373, 377, 379, 383
Mogelonsky, M., 301
Moilanen, K. L., 258, 266
Moise-Titus, J., 346
Molina, B., 49
Monitoring the Future, 369
Monteiro, C., 37
Montemayor, R., 48, 204
Montgomery, M. J., 163, 164, 165, 243, 247
Montminy, H. P., 232
Moore, K., 107
Moore, K. A., 175
Moore, M., 268
Moore, S., 203, 260, 261
Moore, S. M., 356
Moraes filho, N., 207
Morag, B., 295
Moran, T. J., 115
Morelli, M., 207
Morena, A., 117
Moretti, M. M., 149
Morgan, M., 338
Moriguchi, Y., 78
Morris, B. R., 238
Morrison, D. R., 201, 265
Morrison, F. J., 70
Mortimer, J. T., 316, 317, 318, 319, 328
Mory, M., 226
Motley, C. M., 350
Motola, M., 281, 282
Mounts, N. S., 213, 227
Mouw, T., 218
Muench, T., 340
Mukherjee, P., 293
Mullatti, L., 187
Muncer, S., 357
Murdock, T., 292
Murnane, R. J., 321, 329
Murnen, S. K., 132
Murphy, K., 232
Murry, C., 84
Mussen, P. H., 36

N

Naar-King, S., 205
Nabi, R. L., 340
Nader, P. R., 37
Nagle, R. J., 212
Naito, T., 13, 97, 98
Nangle, D. W., 230, 232
Nanji, A., 109
Napolitano, B., 50
Narang, S. K., 105, 167
Narasimham, G., 76
National Assessment of Educational Progress
   (NAEP), 284
National Center for Education Statistics (NCES),
   131, 294, 296, 298, 300, 302, 306, 320, 329, 330
National Center for Health Statistics, 37, 39
National Commission on Excellence in
   Education, 280
National Highway Traffic Safety Administration
   (NHTSA), 39, 364, 365
Neal, A., 251
Neiderhiser, J., 185
Neinstein, L. S., 36
Neiss, M., 149
Nelson, J. R., 168
Nelson, L. J., 9, 10, 12, 13, 23
Nelson, T. F., 369

Nelwan, P., 212
Neto, F., 166
Neumark-Sztainer, D., 389
Nevid, J. S., 204, 205
Newcomb, A. F., 216
Newcomb, M. D., 139
Newcomer, S., 261
Newman, J. E., 230
Newman, K. S., 309
Newmann, F., 284, 289
Nguyen, H. H., 189
Nicholls, J., 230
Nichter, M., 387
Nickens, S. D., 131
Nickerson, A. B., 212
Nie, N. H., 356
Nigg, J. T., 70
Nightingale, E., 39
Nigro, C., 63, 71
Nihira, K., 187
Nikopolou, L., 342
Nisbett, R. E., 68
Nishikawa, S., 148, 151, 153
Noack, P., 37
Noell, J. W., 206
Noguchi, K., 98
Nolan, S. A., 232
Nolen-Hoeksema, S., 384
Noller, P., 177, 179, 180
Nonnemaker, J. M., 378
Nord, C. W., 203
Nordenmark, M., 327
North, A. C., 340
Nottelmann, E. D., 33, 34
Novik, T. S., 299
Nov-Krispin, N., 140
Noyes, J. M., 355
Nsamenang, A. B., 22, 283
Nurius, R., 149
Nurnberger, J. I., Jr., 383

O

Oades-Sese, G. V., 297
Obeidallah, D., 53
Oberlander, S. E., 181, 203
Obermeyer, C. M., 358
Obradovic, J., 391
O'Brien, S., 225
Ochs, L. M., 206
O'Connell, J. M., 168
O'Connor, T. G., 155, 194, 196
Offer, D., 175, 190, 197
Offord, D. R., 202, 384
Ogbu, J. U., 227, 295
Ogden, T., 375
Ogle, J. P., 131
O'Hare, W. P., 104
Okie, S., 369, 371
Oksman, V., 357
Oliver, M. B., 341
Oliver, J. E., 218
Ollendick, T. H., 363
Olsen, J. A., 287, 363
Olson, C. K., 132, 347, 348
Oltmanns, T. F., 385, 386, 390
Oltof, T., 233
Olweus, D., 200, 232, 233
O'Malley, P. M., 154, 333
Ong, A. D., 103, 193
Opper, S., 63
Oppl, C., 339
Osgood, D. W., 218, 222, 223, 235, 369
Osorio, S., 193
Oswald, H., 260, 261
Overhauser, S., 216, 217
Overholser, J. C., 385, 386
Overton, W. F., 65
Oyserman, D., 96, 149
Ozer, E. J., 269

P

Padgham, J. J., 242
Páez, D., 148
Pahl, K., 151, 165, 377
Paik, H., 339
Paikoff, R. L., 44, 48, 49, 261
Pakaslahti, L., 231
Palmer, E., 338
Paludi, M. A., 140
Pan, S. Y., 364, 367
Pancer, S. M., 331
Papillon, M., 383
Papini, D. R., 162
Paradise, A., 346
Pardun, C. J., 348, 349
Park, J. H., 252
Park, S. H., 44
Parker, H., 205
Parker, J., 230, 232
Parker, S., 154, 205
Parsons, T., 234, 235, 236
Pascal, B., 220
Pascarella, E. T., 69, 305, 306
Pascoe, C. J., 130, 132, 133, 155
Patchin, J. W., 356
Patel, D. R., 389
Patel-Amin, N., 187
Patterson, G. R., 184, 203, 232, 291, 377
Patterson, S. J., 164
Paul, E. L., 270
Paulson, S. E., 291
Paulson-Karlsson, G., 390
Paus, T., 18, 86
Payne, B., 371
Peace Corps, 332
Peck, R. C., 364, 366
Pellegrino, J. W., 84
Peng, K., 68
Peplau, L., 250
Pepler, D. J., 233
Pepler, P., 262
Peris, T. S., 201, 376
Perren, S., 233
Perron, A., 205
Perry, C., 371
Perry, C. L., 220
Perry, S., 333
Perry, T. B., 216
Perry, W. G., 68
Perry, W. G., 69
Persons, J., 385
Peter, J., 349
Petersen, A. C., 39, 48, 53, 149, 154, 162, 194, 262,
   382, 383, 384
Peterson, P., 376
Peterson, S. H., 349
Peterson, S. R., 154
Petraitis, J., 378
Pettit, G. S., 204
Pfeffer, C. R., 385, 386, 387
Phillip, M., 33
Phillips, K. R., 25, 329
Philpot, T. S., 116
Phinney, J. S., 103, 162, 165, 166, 167, 193, 218
Piaget, J., 60, 61, 62, 63, 64, 65, 66, 73, 78, 109
Picard, C. L., 45
Pidada, S., 212, 225
Pierce, J. P., 354
Pierce, K., 131, 339
Pipher, M., 154, 157
Piquero, A. R., 373
Piran, N., 154
Pirttilae-Backman, A. M., 69
Pisetsky, E. M., 389
Pittman, R. B., 301
Pitts, R. C., 115
Plantin, L., 328
Plato, 2
Plato, C. C., 38
Pleck, J. H., 133

Subject Index

Note: Page numbers followed by *f* and *t* indicate figures and tables respectively.

A

Aborigines, the, 99–100
Abortion, 266*f*, 267, 269
Absolute performance, 80, 81
Abstinence education programs, 273, 274
Abstinence-plus programs, 274
Abstract thinking, 63
   intimacy in friendships and, 217
   political belief and, 116
   self-conception and, 148–49
Academic achievement
   of adolescents in stepfamilies, 203
   demand for more rigorous education and, 280
   ethnic differences in, 294–96
   extremes in, 297–301
   gender differences in, 131, 296–97
   international comparisons on, 284
   parental influence on, 290–91
   risk behavior and, 379
   social class and, 291–92
   in young people from divorced families, 200
Academic subculture, college, 304
Accommodation, 61
Active genotype-environment interactions, 54, 55, 84
Actual self, 149
Add Health study, 378–79
Addictive substance use, 370
Adolescence, 2
   age range of, 7
   formal operations in, 62–66
   terminology, 4
Adolescence: Its Psychology and Its Relations to Physiology, Anthropology, Sociology, Sex, Crime, Religion, and Education (Hall), 6
Adolescence-limited delinquents (ALDs), 372, 373
Adolescent development. *See also* Cognitive development
   community service and, 331
   intelligence tests and, 83–84
   work and, 317–20
Adolescent egocentrism, 78–79
Adolescent growth spurt, 34–35, 36
Adolescent love
   changing forms of, 241–42
   developmental course of, 242–45
   reasons for, 243
Adolescent work. *See also* Child/adolescent labor
   adolescent development and, 317–20
   benefits of, 319, 320*t*
   life-cycle service for, 2, 3–4
   longitudinal study on, 318
   problem behavior and, 317, 318–19
   problems with, 320*t*
   psychological functioning and, 317
   school performance and, 292–93
   volunteer, 330–33
   workplace for, 316–17
Adoption, 19, 267
Adoption studies, 54, 55, 83, 84, 383
Adrenal glands, 34
Adrenocorticotropic hormone (ACTH), 34
Adulthood
   beginning of, 11
   cultural differences on, 13

Advanced Placement (AP) classes, 297
Advertising, controversial, 353–54
Affection phase, 249–50
Affective functions, 197
Africa. *See also* North Africa
   age of menarche in, 44, 45
   AIDS in, 272, 273
   birth rate in, 22
   education system in, 282–83
   Mbuti Pygmies of, 224
   premarital sex in, 259
African Americans
   academic achievement of, 295
   average age of menarche among, 44–45
   college education among, 303, 304
   computers in the home among, 355
   early maturation and, 53
   emerging adults staying at home among, 195
   extended family relationships among, 181, 203
   gender roles of, 138–39
   high school dropout rate among, 300
   identity formation and, 166, 167
   individualism-collectivism dimension and, 103
   IQ scores and, 84
   obesity among, 37
   parenting styles among, 188
   perceived physical appearances by, 154
   reasons for early sexual activity among, 261
   religiosity among, 106, 107
   research on opportunities of, 17
   risk behavior by, 378, 382
   self-esteem among, 151
   substance use among, 368, 376
   suicide rates among, 385
   teen mothers, 268
   timing of first sexual intercourse among, 255
   unemployment among, 330
Age, crime and, 371, 372
Age-graded, 52
Age norms, 82
Age of adolescence (1890–1920), 4–7, 278
Age of feeling in-between, 9
Age of identity exploration, 8
Age of instability, 8
Age of possibilities, 9
Age-related roles, 94
Aggressiveness
   computer games and, 347–48
   emphasis on, problems with, 132–33
   popularity and, 231
   risk behaviors and, 379
   television and, 345–46
   unpopularity and, 231
AIDS. *See* HIV/AIDS
Alcohol use. *See also* Substance use
   automobile accidents and, 364, 366
   country comparison on, 380
   date rape and, 263
   rates of, 367*f*
   work and, 318, 319
Alfred Binet, 80, 81
Algeria, 258
Alpha Phi Alpha, 138
Alternative schools, 301
Alternative script, 236
Amenorrhea, 388
American majority culture
   defined, 5*t*

   extended family relationships among, 181
   minority culture exposed to gender roles of, 138–39
   minority culture versus, 102
   personal responses to menstruation in, 50
American Manhood (Rotundo), 128
American Psychological Association, 6
AmeriCorps, 332
Amhara, the, 48
Amphetamines, 368, 369
Analysis and interpretation, 19–20
Analytical reasoning, 76
Ancient Greece, 2–3
Ancient times, 2–3
Androgens, 33–34
Androgyny, 136
Anorexia nervosa, 387, 388, 389
Antagonistic interactions, 224
Anthropologists, 17
Antidepressant medications, 384
Antisocial behaviors, 380
Apprenticeships
   defined, 322
   in Europe, 281, 322–23
   in Germany, 325
   life-cycle service and, 3–4
   in United States, 321–22
Arab countries
   education system in, 282
   on premarital sex, 258
Areola, 40, 41
Argentina
   school enrollment changes in, 279*t*
   transition to adulthood viewed in, 12
Argot, of youth culture, 234, 235, 236
Arranged marriages, 252–53
Asante, the, 46–47
Asian Americans
   academic achievement of, 293
   college education among, 302
   conflict with parents among, 193
   cultural beliefs among, 103
   emerging adults staying at home among, 195
   gender role expectations of, 139
   grandparents and, 181
   identity formation and, 166
   parenting styles among, 188
   self-esteem among, 151
   sexual activity among, 255
Asian cultures. *See also* Eastern cultures
   arranged marriages in, 253
   context of adolescence in, 23
   dating in, 242
   opinion on premarital sex in, 257
   parenting in, 187
   premarital sex in, 257, 260
Assimilation, 61, 166
Asymptomatic, 271
Asynchronicity, 36
Athletic activity, 36–37, 38
Attachment
   to parents, 188–90
   to romantic partners, 248–49
   to stepparent, 203
Attachment theory, 188, 189–90
Attention, 69–70
Attention-deficit hyperactivity disorder (ADHD), 298–99, 373, 379

Communal manhood, 128
Communist countries, 117–18
Community service
    adolescent development and, 331
    defined, 330
    in emerging adulthood, 332–33
Companionate love, 246
Companionship support, 221–22
Complex thinking, 63–64, 217
Componential approach, 69
Comprehensive high school, 279
Comprehensive sexuality education, 273
Computer games, 338, 347–48
Computers, information-processing approach and, 69, 74
Concept videos, 349
Concrete operations stage, 61*t*, 62–63
Conflict, parent-adolescent. *See* Parent-adolescent conflict
Conflict, sibling, 179–80
Confucianism, 23
Consensual validation, 248
Consent form, 14, 15
Consummate love, 246, 247
Context, 21
Continuous, cognitive development as, 69
Contraception, 265–67
Control group, 18
Controversial adolescent, 231
Conventional reasoning, 111
"Cool Pose," 138
Coping, media use and, 341
Cornell University, 321
Correlation versus causation, 19, 220
Courtship. *See also* Dating
    "calling" and, 244
    in Mexico, 123
    during twenties, 234
Cramps, menstrual, 50, 52
Crime. *See* Delinquency and crime
Critical relationship, 178, 179
Critical thinking, 74–75
Cross-sectional studies, 44, 45, 222
Crowds
    across cultures, 227, 228
    in American minority cultures, 227
    changes in composition of, 229
    changes in role and importance of, 226
    defined, 222, 223
    developmental changes in, 225–28
    function of, 223
    participant observation of, 228
Crystallized intelligence, 82, 83
Cultural beliefs
    adolescent sexuality and, 257–60
    custom complex and, 101–2
    defined, 93, 94
    gender socialization and, 130
    higher education and, 280
    importance of examining, 93
    individualism versus collectivism and, 96–97
    moral development and, 109–15
    minority cultures living in the West and, 104
    in multicultural societies, 102–5
    political beliefs and, 116–18
    religious beliefs and, 105–9
    roles and, 94
    school and, 294
    socialization and, 95–101
    symbolic inheritance and, 93, 94
Cultural context of adolescence
    Asia, 23
    implications of, 25
    India, 23–24
    Latin America, 24
    Middle East, 22–23
    North Africa, 22–23
    sub-Saharan Africa, 22
    West, 24–25

Cultural differences, 2, 22. *See also* Traditional cultures
    desired traits in a marriage partner and, 251–52
    emerging adulthood and, 9–10
    examples, 1
    formal operations stage and, 65–66
    Moroccan conceptions of adolescence and, 15
    parent-adolescent distancing and, 49
    on risk behavior, 380, 382
    transition to adulthood and, 13
Cultural focus topics, 25
    apprenticeships in Germany, 325
    Bar and Bat Mitzvah, 94, 95
    externalizing problems, 374
    formal operations among the Inuit, 67
    interethnic friendships, 219
    Japanese education, 286, 287
    puberty rituals, 47
    Western media in Nepal, 359
Cultural psychology, 88–89
Culture/cultural influences. *See also* Youth culture
    biological changes of puberty and, 32
    cognitive development and, 87–89
    conflict with parents and, 193–94
    defined, 5*t*
    eating disorders and, 389
    identity formation and, 164–65
    moral development and, 113–14
    responses to puberty and, 46–48
    the self and, 148
    timing of puberty and, 43–46
Custodial parent, 198
Custom complex, 101–2
Cyberbullying, 233
Czechoslovakia, 117
Czech Republic
    adolescent births/abortions in, 266*f*
    transition to adulthood viewed in, 12

D

DARE program, 371
Data collection, 14
Date rape, 263
Dating, 101–2, 241, 242. *See also* Romantic relationships
    birth of, 244
    boys versus girls initiating, 243
    ethnic identity and, 165–66
    in European cultures, 242
    exhibiting a false self during, 150
    in non-Western cultures, 242
    reasons for, 243
Dating scripts, 243
Deaths
    homicide as leading cause of, 380
    leading causes of, 39
    suicide as third most common cause of, 385
Debt bondage, 312
Delinquency, 371
Delinquency and crime
    age and, 371, 372
    cultural comparisons on, 380
    family influence on, 376
    preventing, 374–75
    remarriage by parents and, 203
    research on, 381
    terminology, 371
    two kinds of, 373
Demandingness, 182, 184, 185
Demeanor, of youth culture, 234, 235
Denmark
    academic score in, 284*t*
    adolescent pregnancy in, 266
    emerging adults living at home in, 196*f*
Depressed mood, 382
Depression
    among runway adolescents, 206

causes of, 382–83
    defined, 382
    discrepancy between real and ideal self, 149
    gender difference in, 383–84
    high rates of, during adolescence, 382
    suicide and, 385–87
    terminology, 382
    treatments for, 384–85
Depressive syndrome, 382
Developing countries. *See also* Traditional cultures
    defined, 5*t*
    discrimination against girls in, 143
    schooling in, 279
    secondary education in, 282–84
    Western media and, 358–60
Dialectical thought, 68
Diathesis-stress model, 383
Differential gender socialization, 130–31
Differential parenting, 185
Dioula culture, 88
Disabilities, adolescents with, 298
Disengaged parents, 182–83
Disequilibrium, 176, 177
Discontinuous, cognitive development as, 69
Distancing hypothesis, 49
Divergent Realities: The Emotional Lives of Mothers, Fathers, and Adolescents (Larson/Richards), 178
Divided attention, 70
Divorce
    economic stress following, 202
    effects of, 200–202
    family process and, 201
    increased contact with grandparents and, 181
    parenting change after, 201
    rise in rates of, 197–98
    sibling relationships and, 180
Divorce meditation, 202
Dizygotic (DZ) twins, 19
Djibouti, 125*f*
Doom (computer game), 347
Dormitory, 227
Double standard, 258
Driver education, 365
Driving curfew, 366
Dropouts, high school, 300–301
Druggies, 223
Drugs use, 75, 76. *See also* Substance use
Dual-earner families, 199–200, 204
Dualistic thinking, 68
Dunedin longitudinal study, 373, 383
Dyadic relationship, 176

E

Early adolescence, 10
Eastern cultures. *See also* Asian cultures
    expectations of marriage in, 252
    Western cultures versus, 96–97, 104
Eastern European countries, 117–18
Eating disorders
    cultural emphasis on slimness and, 387
    factors contributing to, 389
    history of, 388
    treatments for, 390
    two most common, 387
Ecological theory, 20–22
Economic issues
    conflict with parents and, 193
    effect of, on education, 279
    employment for high school graduates and, 320–21
    Great Depression and, 198, 199
    impact of divorce and, 202
    perception of gender roles in, 143
Ecstasy, 367, 368
Education. *See also* Academic achievement
    ancient Greek on, 2
    cultural beliefs on higher, 280
    diversity in American, 280–81

history of higher, 72
Japanese higher, 286, 287
laws requiring longer period of, 5
parents involvement in adolescents, 289, 290–91
sex, 273–74
Effect size, 142, 143
Egg production, 39
Egocentrism, 78–81
Egypt
  academic score in, 284*t*
  female circumcision in, 125*f*
  median marriage age in, 11*t*
  personal response to menstruation in, 50
  school enrollment changes in, 279*t*
  schooling in, 279
Electric bullying. *See* Cyberbullying
Emerging adulthood, 2. *See also* College; College students
  characteristics of, 8–9
  cognitive development in, 66–69
  cohabitation during, 253
  commitment in love relationship during, 247
  community service in, 332–33
  cultural differences and, 9–10
  defined, 8
  during1920s, 234, 235
  Eastern European, political beliefs and, 117
  effects of parental divorce on, 200, 202
  emotionality in, 155–56
  ethic of autonomy during, 114–15
  friends and leisure activities in, 222–23
  gender stereotypes in, 139–40
  identity development in, 163
  impact of secure parental attachment on, 189
  in Japan, 287
  physical functioning in, 38–39
  political thinking in, 118–19
  reasons for dating during, 243
  relationships with parents in, 194–96
  relationships with stepparents in, 203
  religiosity in, 107–8
  romantic relationship in, 249
  self-esteem in, 155
  sexuality in, 269–70
  sibling relationship in, 180
  substance use prevention and, 371
  time spent alone in, 170–71
  transition to adulthood and, 12–13
  vision of a possible self in, 149
  work in, 328–29
Emerging adults
  leaving home, 194–95
  returning to live at home, 195
Emotional intelligence, 85
Emotional loneliness, 170
Emotional self, the, 155–58
Emotional understanding, 147
Emotions
  friends and, 214
  parent-adolescent relations and, 179
Employment. *See also* Adolescent work
  balancing demand between family and, 327, 328
  dual-earner families and, 199, 204
  in emerging adulthood, 328–29
  gender stereotypes on, 139
  occupational choices for, 323–28
  opportunities for, among African Americans, 17
  post-high school transition to, 320–21
  school-to-work programs for, 321–22
Empty love, 246
Empty-nest syndrome, 177
Endocrine system, 32–34
Engagement, in high school, 288, 289, 291
England, 104
Entertainment, media used for, 340
Environment
  biological development and, 54–56
  causes of depression and, 383

cognitive development and, 60–61
  parental influence and, 54–55
Erikson's theory on identity formation, 158–61
Eritrea, 125*f*
Eskimo children/adolescents, 67, 359
Esteem support, 222
Estradiol, 33
Estrogens, 33
Ethic of autonomy, 114
Ethic of community, 114
Ethic of divinity, 114
Ethiopia, 48, 125*f*
Ethnic differences
  academic achievement and, 294–96
  in college attendance, 302
  in financial support for college, 303*t*
  in perceived physical appearances, 154
  in risk behavior, 382
  in school dropout rates, 300
  in suicide rates, 385
  in teen birth rates, 267
  in timing of first sexual intercourse, 255
Ethnic identity, 165–67
Ethnicity, choosing friends and, 218
Ethnographic research, 17–18, 99, 228, 358, 359
Ethnography, 17
Ethos, 378
Europe
  adolescent culture in, 242
  adolescent pregnancies in, 266
  adolescent smoking in, 380
  adolescent work in, 316
  alcohol use in, 380
  apprenticeships in, 322–23
  cohabitation in, 253
  drug use in, 380
  emerging adults living at home in, 195, 196
  extended family relationships in, 181
  higher education in, 302, 303
  media use in, 338
  post-high-school work in, 320
  school-to-work programs in, 322
  secondary schools in, 281
  unemployment in, 329
Evaluations, gender-related, 140
Evocative genotype-environment interactions, 54, 55, 184–85
Exercise, 37
Exosystem, 21
Experience Sampling Method (ESM)
  on changes in time spent with family, 212
  on daily rhythms of family lives, 178
  on dual-earner families, 204
  on emotional states with friends, 214
  self-esteem and, 152, 155–56
  on time spent alone, 170
Experimental group, 18
Experimental research method, 18
Experimental substance use, 370
Exploration (identity), 159, 160
Expressive traits, 134, 135
Extended family relationships, 181, 203
Externalizing problems, 363, 364, 374. *See also* Risk behaviors
Extremities, 36
Exuberance, 86

F

Facial hair, 40, 42
False self, 150
Familismo, 188
Family. *See also* Parents
  balancing demands between work and, 327, 328
  closeness with extended, 181
  daily rhythms in lives of, 178, 179
  dual-earner, 199–200, 204
  friends and, 212–13, 215
  historical change and, 196–200

impact of divorce on, 200–202
  in India, 186, 187
  physical abuse in, 204, 205
  sexual abuse in, 204, 205
  sibling relationships within, 178, 179–81
  social class of, school and, 291–92
  sources of socialization in, 98
  substance use prevention and, 371
  subsystems within, 176
Family, influence of
  depression and, 383
  eating disorder and, 390
  on religious beliefs of adolescents, 106
  on risk behavior, 375–76
  risk factors for suicide and, 386
Family process, 201, 203
Family structure
  defined, 201
  with remarriage, 203
  single parenthood and, 203
Family systems approach, 176
Farming, 311
Fast-food meals, 37
Fathers
  adolescent, 268–69
  adolescent interactions with, 179
  relations with, divorce and, 201–2
  sexual abuse by, 205
Fatuous love, 246
Feared self, 149
Feedback loop, endocrine system, 34
Females. *See also* Gender differences; Gender roles; Gender socialization; Girls
  breast development in, 41
  child care and household work by, 311
  circumcision of, 124, 125
  hair growth in, 40
  history of higher education for, 72
  in hunting and gathering cultures, 310
  magazines for, 131–32
  occupational choices by, 327–28
  perceptions on traits of, 135–36, 137–38
  physical changes in, 41*t*
  portrayed in rap songs, 350, 351
  prostitution among, 206, 207, 312
  reaction to breaking up by, 250, 251
  reproductive anatomy in, 40
  sex hormones of, 33
Feminine traits, 135–36, 137–38
Fertility, 40
Field studies, 345
Fiji, 360
Filial piety, 23, 187
Financial aid, college, 302
Finland, 282, 284*t*
Firearms, 380
First-generation families, 104
Fishing cultures, 310–11
Fluid intelligence, 82, 83
fMRI (functional Magnetic Resonance Tomography), 85, 86
Follicle-stimulating hormone (FSH), 33, 34
The Forgotten Half: Non-College Youth in America, 320
Formal operations stage, 61*t*
  abstract thinking and, 63
  among the Inuit, 67
  assessing attainment of, 63
  autonomous morality, 110
  complex thinking and, 63–64
  culture and, 65–66
  gender socialization and, 134
  individual differences in, 65
  metacognition and, 63, 64
France
  academic score in, 284*t*
  education system in, 282
  emerging adults living at home in, 196*f*
  median marriage age in, 11*t*
  minority populations in, 104

Free speech, 343
Friends. *See also* Peers
  choosing, 218
  defined, 212
  in emerging adulthood, 222–23
  emotional states with, 214
  ethnic segregation and, 218
  family and, 212–13, 215
  gender socialization and, 129
  intimacy in friendships with, 215–18
  peer versus, 211–12
  relationship with family compared with, 212–13
  sources of socialization from, 98
  support and nurturance from, 221–22
  value and importance of, 211
Friends, influence of
  on academic achievement, 295
  peer pressure and, 219–20
  risk behavior and, 220–21, 365, 376–77
  romantic relationship and, 249, 250
  school and, 292
From Fasting Saints to Anorexic Girls: A History of Self-Starvation (Vandereycken/Van Deth), 388
From Front Porch to Back Seat: Courtship in Twentieth-Century America (Bailey), 244
Frontal lobes, 86
Full license, 366

G

Gambia, 125*f*
Gamepro (magazine), 131
Gametes, 33
Gangsta rap, 350, 351, 352
Gateway drugs, 369–70
Gay, lesbian, and bisexual adolescents, 263–64
GED certificate, 300
Geeks, 223, 230
Gender
  the emotional self and, 156–57
  influence, on occupational choices, 326–28
  sex versus, 121
Gender differences, 26
  academic achievement and, 296–97
  in attainment of postgraduate degree, 302
  in college major preferences, 302
  cognitive development and, 72, 73
  in dating scripts, 243
  education system and, 283
  in emotional development, 157
  emphasis on physical appearance and, 152
  expectations for physical activity and, 37
  in hormonal changes, 33*f*
  in identity formation, 163–64
  in Internet use, 355
  in intimacy in friendships and, 217–18
  meta-analysis of, 142
  in parent-adolescent relationships, 179
  in physical growth, 34–35
  relational aggression and, 225
  in relationship to peers and family, 214
  risk behavior and, 379–80
  in sexual scripts, 261
  suicide and, 386
  theory of moral development and, 112–13
Gender expectations
  in American history, 126–29
  in emerging adulthood, 139–40
  in traditional cultures, 122–23, 124, 125–26
Gender identity, 133
Gender intensification hypothesis, 129–30
Gender issues, 26
Gender roles
  in American minority groups, 138–39
  cultural beliefs and, 94, 95
  exposure to Western media and, 358
  globalization and, 141–43
  media and, 340
  on television, 348

in traditional cultures, 122–23, 124, 125–26
  on Truk Island, 374
Gender schemas, 134, 139–40, 141
Gender schema theory, 134
Gender socialization
  cognition and, 133–35
  cultural beliefs and, 130
  differential gender socialization and, 130–31
  gender intensification hypothesis on, 129–30
  masculine/feminine traits and, 135–36, 137–38
  from the media, 131–32
  parental influence and, 130, 131
  persistence of beliefs on gender differences and, 140–41
  school influence and, 130–31
  as a source of problems, 132–33
Gender stereotypes, 121
General Education Development (GED) certificate, 300
Generalizable, 14, 15
Genetics, 43
  causes of depression and, 383
  interaction with environment and, 54–56
Genotype-environment interactions, 55–56
Germany
  apprenticeships in, 325
  education in, 281
  freedom of expression in, 343
  median marriage age in, 11*t*
  minority populations in, 104
  premarital sex in, 260*t*
  school enrollment changes in, 279*t*
Ghana, 11*t*, 46
Gifted students, 297
Girls. *See also* Gender differences; Gender socialization; Menarche
  dating and, 245
  early and late maturation among, 52–53
  eating disorders among, 387, 388, 389
  egg production in, 39
  gender expectations of, 122–23, 126–28
  magazines for, 131–32
  masturbation by, 254
  muscle mass in, 36
  self-esteem of, 150, 152, 154
  sequence of pubertal events for, 42
  types of adolescent work by, 313, 316
Girl scouts, 51, 102, 103, 128
Globalization, 26–27
  adolescent work in traditional cultures and, 311–13
  arranged marriages and, 252–53
  gender roles and, 141–43
  identity and, 167, 168, 170
  media and, 358–60
  tattooing ritual and, 47
Goals 2000, 281
Gonadotropin-releasing hormone (GnRH), 32, 33, 34
Gonadotropins, 33
Gonads, 33, 34
Graduated driver licensing (GDL), 365–67
Grandfathers, 181
Grandparents, 181
Gray matter, 86
Great Britain. *See also* England
  adolescent births/abortions in, 266*f*
  adolescent labor in, 314, 315
  interethnic friendships in, 219
  magazines for girls in, 132
Great Depression, the, 198, 199
Greece
  ancient, 2–3
  emerging adults living at home in, 196*f*
Guided participation, 88

H

Half-time system, 315

Hall, Stanley
Harassment, romantic, 251
Harassment, sexual, 262–63
Harvard Adolescence Project, 15, 17–18, 99
Health and Morals of Apprentices Act (1802), 314
Health promotion, programs for, 38, 39
Health risks from obesity, 38
Heavy metal music, 352–53
Hedonism, 234, 235
Height, growth in, 34–35
Herpes simplex, 271–72
Heteronomous morality, 110
Heuristic reasoning, 76
High school
  dropouts from, 300–301
  engagement in, 288, 289, 291
  enrollment in, 8
  learning the new basic skills in, 321
  part-time employment during, 315–16
High self-esteem, 150, 154
Hip hop music (rap), 350, 351
History, of adolescence, 25
  from 1500 to 1890, 3–4
  from 1890 to 1920, 4–7
  ancient times and, 2–3
  changes in schooling and, 279–81
  cognitive development in emerging adulthood and, 72, 73
  dating and, 244
  early Christian times through the Middle Ages and, 3
  eating disorders and, 388, 389
  the family and, 196–200
  gender expectations and, 126–29
  menarche as a taboo topic and, 51
  work and, 313–16
  youth culture of the twenties and, 234, 235
HIV/AIDS, 272–73
Holistic perspective, 74
Home
  leaving, 194–95
  returning to live at home, 195
  running away from, 206
Homelessness, 206, 207
Homicide, 39, 380
Homophobia, 264
Homosexual experiences, sexual orientation versus, 264
Hong Kong, 46*f*, 260*t*
"Hooking up," 256
Hopi, the, 224
Hormonal levels, 18
Hormones, 32–34
Hot Rod (magazine), 131
Household work, 311
Human papillomavirus (HPV), 271
Hungary
  academic score in, 284*t*
  adolescent births/abortions in, 266*f*
  political ideas and, 117–18
Hunting and gathering cultures, 310–11
Hybrid identity, 166, 167, 168
Hymen, 127
Hypothalamus, 32–33, 34
Hypotheses, 14
Hypothetical-deductive reasoning, 62–63

I

Ideal self, 149
Identifications, 160
Identities/identity, 147
  defined, 158
  globalization, 167, 168, 170
Identity achievement, 162, 163
Identity crisis, 161
Identity diffusion, 161
Identity explorations, age of, 8
Identity foreclosure, 162

Identity formation
    culture and, 164–65
    in emerging adulthood, 163
    Erikson's theory on, 158–61
    gender differences in, 163–64
    identity status model and, 161, 162, 163
    of Martin Luther, 158, 159
    media use and, 340
    of Native Americans, 168, 169
Identity moratorium, 162
Identity status model, 161, 162, 163
Identity versus identity confusion, 158, 159
Ideology
    capacity to develop, 116
    ethnic identity and, 165
Idiots savants, 85
I Have a Dream (IHAD) program, 301
Image, of youth culture, 234, 235
Imaginary audience, 79, 151
Immigrant adolescents
    academic achievement and, 296
    Chinese, 104–5, 296
    high school dropout rates among, 300
Impotence, 126
Incest taboo, 49
Independence, in gifted students, 297
Independent self, 96, 97
Index crimes, 371
India
    AIDS in, 272
    arranged marriages in, 252–53
    child labor in, 312
    cultural context of adolescence in, 23–24
    education system in, 283
    family living arrangements in, 181
    identity formation and, 167
    median marriage age in, 11*t*
    moral adolescent development in, 113–14
    school enrollment changes in, 279*t*
    street children in, 206–7
    time spent with family versus friends in, 215
    young people and their families in, 186, 187
Indipop, 360
Individual differences, 65
Individualism
    conception of the self and, 148
    higher education and, 280
    religious beliefs and, 108, 109
    socialization beliefs and, 96–97, 100
    transition to adulthood and, 12
Individuating-reflective faith, 108
Indonesia
    academic score in, 284*t*
    child labor in, 312
    median marriage age in, 11*t*
Industrialization, 4–5, 313
Industrialized countries. *See also* West, the
    age of first childbirth in, 176–77
    conflict with parents in, 193
    defined, 5*t*
    emerging adulthood existing in, 10
    occupational choices in, 324
    pubertal timing in, 52
    religious beliefs and, 106
    secondary education in, 277, 281–82
    suicide rates in, 385
Industrial revolution, 4, 5
Infatuation, 245, 247
Informational support, by friends, 221
Information-processing approach
    attention, 69–70
    automaticity, 71, 72–73
    defined, 69
    developmental focus in, 69
    limitations to, 73–74
    memory, 70–71
    speed and, 71, 73
Informed consent, 14, 15
Inhalants, 368

Initiation phase, 248, 249
Insecure attachment, 189
Instability, age of, 8–9
Instant Messaging (IM), 355
Instrumental support, 221
Instrumental traits, 134, 135
Intelligence quotient (IQ), 80, 81. *See also*
    Intelligence testing
Intelligence testing
    adolescent development and, 83–84
    changes in scores on, 81*f*
    by Piaget, 60
    reliability of, 82
    Stanford-Binet, 80, 81
    theory of multiple intelligences and, 84–85
    Wechsler, 80, 81, 82
Interdependence, 12, 13
Interdependent self, 96
Interdisciplinary approach, 25–26
Interethnic friendships, 218, 219
Internal consistency, 152, 153
Internalizing problems, 363, 364, 382. *See also*
    Depression; Eating disorders; Suicide
Internal working model, 189
International Labor Organization (ILO), 312, 313
Internet pornography, 257
Internet, the, 355–57
Interpersonal intelligence, 85
Interventions, 18
Interviews, 16–17
Intimacy
    in adolescent friendships, 215–18
    in adolescent romantic relationship, 247
    defined, 215, 245
Intimacy versus isolation, 164
Intrapersonal intelligence, 85
Inuit, the, 67, 104, 359
Iran, 284*t*
Iraq, 46*f*
Irresponsibility, 234, 235
Islam, 109, 282
Israel
    media's coping function in, 341
    sibling relationship in, 180
    transition to adulthood viewed in, 12
Italy
    academic score in, 284*t*
    adolescent births/abortions in, 266*f*
    emerging adults living at home in, 196*f*
    median marriage age in, 11*t*
    school enrollment changes in, 279*t*
Ivory Coast, 88

J

Jackie (magazine), 132
Japan
    academic score in, 284*t*
    adolescent labor in, 316
    education system in, 283, 286, 287
    median marriage age in, 11*t*
    media use in, 338
    premarital sex in, 260*t*
    self-esteem and, 150
    sexual attitudes in, 267
Jewish traditions
    Bar/Bat mitzvah, 94, 95
    circumcision, 124
Job Corps, 322
Job-training programs, 322
Jocks, 223, 227
Joe Camel, 354
Journal of Adolescence, 20
Journal of Adolescent Research, 20
Journal of Research on Adolescence, 20
Journal of Youth & Adolescence, 20
Journal of Youth Studies, 20
Journals, peer reviews and, 20
Junior high school, 285, 287, 288

Junk food, 38
Justice orientation, 112
Juveniles, 371

K

Kathmandu, Nepal, 359
Kenya, 42, 207
Kikuyu, the, 42
Kissing, 255
Kissing Jessica Stein, 264
Koran, the, 108, 109

L

Labia majora, 40
Labia minora, 40
Labor. *See* Adolescent work; Child/adolescent labor;
    Employment
Lamarckian evolutionary ideas, 10
Late adolescence, 10
Latency period, 271
Latin America
    cultural context of adolescence in, 24
    education system in, 283
Latinos
    academic achievement of, 295
    college education among, 303
    computers in the home among, 355
    conflict with parents among, 193
    cultural beliefs of, 102, 103
    early maturation and, 53
    emerging adults staying at home among, 195
    gender roles among, 139
    high school dropout rate among, 300
    identity formation and, 167
    IQ scores and, 84
    obesity among, 37
    parenting styles among, 188
    risk behavior by, 382
    self-esteem among, 151
    sexually transmitted diseases among, 271
    substance use by, 368
    teen birth rates among, 267
    timing of first sexual intercourse among, 255
    unemployment among, 329, 330
Laws
    on child/adolescent labor, 4, 5, 313, 314, 315
    on schooling, 5
Learning disabilities, 298, 373
Learning license, 366
Leisure activities. *See also* Media
    academic achievement and, 293
    in emerging adulthood, 222–23
Leptin, 32, 33
Lesbian adolescents, 263–64
Liberia, premarital sex in, 260*t*
Life-course-persistent delinquents (LCPDs),
    372, 373
Life-cycle service, 2, 3–4
Life expectancy, 196–97
Liking, 245
Literacy, 279, 282
Logic
    formal operations stage and, 63
    pragmatism and, 66–68
    Western, versus dialectical thought, 68
Longitudinal studies, 19, 44, 45
    on adolescent crowds, 226
    on adolescents and work, 318
    on attachment, 190
    on delinquency, 373, 381
    on emotionality, 156
    on influence of television, 345–46
    on pubertal development, 44–45
    on substance abuse, 370
    on supportive friendships, 222
    on risk behavior, 221
Long-term memory, 70, 71, 74

Non-industrialized countries. *See* Developing countries
Nonshared environmental influences, 185
Normal distribution, 140
Normals, 223
North Africa. *See also* Egypt; Morocco
    cultural context of adolescence in, 22–23
    education system in, 282
Norway
    gender differences in depression in, 383–84
    media prohibitions in, 343
    premarital sex in, 260t
    schooling in, 278
Notel (Canadian study), 346
Nutrition, timing of menarche and, 43, 44

O

Oakland Growth Study, 198
Oberlin College, 72
Obesity, 37–38
Occupational choices, 323
    development of occupational goals, 324, 325–26
    influences on occupational goals, 326–28
Occupational deviance, 319
Ontogenetic, 101
Open-ended question, 16
Optimistic bias, 80–81, 379
Oral sex, 255, 256
Orthodox Jews, responses to puberty among, 47–48. *See also* Jewish traditions
Other-sex friends, 212, 229f
Overcontrolled, 363
Overevaluated, 140
Overproduction, 86
Ovulation, 40
Ovum, 38, 39, 40

P

Parent-adolescent conflict
    clash in cultural beliefs and, 105
    communicating about sexual issues with, 266
    culture and, 193–94
    degree of, 190
    sources of, 192–93
Parent-adolescent relations, puberty and, 48–49
Parental consent, 269
Parental influence, 175, 183–84
    academic achievement and, 290–91
    adolescent sexual activity and, 258, 261
    on choice of peer relationships, 213
    on driving behavior, 364–65
    gender socialization, 130–31
    intellectual development and, 84
    restrictions on media and, 343, 344–45
    on self-esteem, 154
    transition to junior high/middle school and, 288
Parental monitoring, 370, 371
Parental notification, 269
Parenting styles, 182
    in America, 183
    effect of, on adolescents, 183–84
    research on, 182
    in traditional cultures, 186, 187–88
    types of, 182, 183
Parents. *See also* Fathers; Mothers
    Asian American, on education, 294–95
    attachment to, 188–90
    changes in parenting after divorce, 201–2
    decline in importance of, 211, 212
    emerging adult's relationship with, 194–96
    filial piety and, 187
    genetic and environmental influences, 54–55
    midlife development of, 176–77
    perception of adolescence by, 191
    physical abuse by, 205
    time spent alone with adolescents, 178, 179

Participant observation, 228
Passion
    in adolescent romantic relationships, 247
    defined, 245
    in non-Western cultures, 247–48
Patterns of sexual behavior (Ford/Beach), 257, 258
Patriarchal authority, 23
Peace Corps, 332
Peak height velocity, 34, 35
Peer contagion, 374
Peer-reviewed, 20
Peers. *See also* Cliques; Crowds; Youth culture
    defined, 211
    friends versus, 211–12
    importance of, 211
    parental influence and, 213
    popularity/unpopularity, 230–33
    sources of socialization from, 98
Peers, influence of
    criminal behavior and, 372–73
    depression and, 383
    friend's influence and, 219–20
    romantic relationship and, 249–50
    school and, 292
    on self-esteem, 151
    sexual activity and, 262
Pendulum problem, 62
Penis, 40
Performance subtests, 81, 83t
Performance videos, 349
Permeable apprenticeship system, 323
Permissive cultures, 258, 266
Permissive parents, 182, 183, 376
Personal fable, 79–81
Perspective taking, 77–78
PET scans (Positron Emission Tomography), 85
Petting, 254–55
Petting parties, 234
Pheromones, 49
Philippines, child labor in, 312
Physical abuse, 204, 205, 206
Physical appearance
    cultural emphasis on slimness and, 389
    gender socialization on, 129
    girl's magazine and, 131–32, 340
    history of American expectations of, 127
    popularity and, 230
    problems from focus on, 132–33
    self-esteem and, 152, 154
Physical growth, during puberty, 34–39
Piaget's theory of cognitive development, 60–66, 110
Pituitary gland, 32, 33
Placebo design, 384
Poetic-conventional faith, 108
Poland, 279t, 284t
Political beliefs, 116–18
Popularity, 230, 231–32
Populars, 223
Popular Science (magazine), 131
Population, 14
Pornography, 257
Possibilities, age of, 9
Possible selves, 149
Postal (computer game), 347
Postconventional reasoning, 111, 113, 114
Postfigurative cultures, 237, 238
Postformal thinking, 66–69
Postgraduate degrees, 302
Postmodern identity, 162, 163
Practical cognition, 74–77
Pragmatism, 66–68
Preconventional reasoning, 110–11
Predictive validity, 83
Prefigurative cultures, 238
Pregnancy, teen, 266, 267, 268
Premarital sex
    cultural beliefs on, 257–58, 259–60

gender differences on attitudes toward, 261
    gender roles in traditional cultures, 123
    percentage of youth engaging in, 260t
Premenstrual syndrome (PMS), 50
Preoperational stage, 61t, 110
Preppies, 223
Prevention programs
    for crime and delinquency, 374–75
    substance use, 371
Primary caregiver, 189
Primary sex characteristics, 38, 39–40
Princeton Review, 305
Private schools, 289
Proactive script, 243
Problem behavior, 364, 365
Problems. *See also* Internalizing problems; Risk behaviors
    of adolescent mothers, 268
    divorce and, 200, 201
    for high school dropouts, 300, 301
    with identity confusions, 168
    related to gender socialization, 132–33
    from relational aggression, 225
    of runaway adolescents, 206
    two types of, 363–64
    of unpopular children, 232
    work and, 317, 318–19
Procedure, 14
Procreate, gender expectations of males and, 123, 124
Professional schools, 281
The Program (movie), 337
Property crimes, 371
Prosocial behavior, 78
Prostitution, 206, 207, 312
Protect, gender expectations of males and, 123, 124
Protective factor
    defined, 378
    of resilience, 391
Provide, gender expectations of males and, 122, 123, 124
Prozac, 384
Psychohistory, 158
Psychometric approach, 80, 81. *See also* Intelligence testing
Psychosocial moratorium, 160, 164–65
Psychotherapy, 384
Puberty. *See also* Biological development
    cultural responses to, 46–48
    culture and timing of, 43–46
    depression and, 383, 384
    early and late timing of, 52–54
    Latin translation of, 32
    order of events in, 42–43
    parent-adolescent relations and, 48–49, 192
    personal responses to, 49–52
    physical growth during, 34–39
    reasons for early, 49
    typical age of initiation of, 8
    universality of, 2
Puberty rites, 52
Pubic hair, 40, 42
Public schools, 289
Pueblo Indians, 48
Puerto Rican teen mothers, 268
Purging, 387, 388

Q

Quake (computer game), 347
Qualitative data, 16, 17
Quantitative data, 16, 17
Queer Eye for the Straight Guy, 264
Questionnaires, 16

R

Racial differences. *See also* Ethnic differences
    intelligence testing and, 84
    IQ scores and, 84

Racism, rap music and, 351
Ramadan, 108, 109
Random sample, 7
Rape, date, 263
Rap music, 350, 351
Rap videos, 349
Reaction range, 44, 45
Reactive script, 243
Reason(ing)
    ability to make decisions and, 76
    ancient Greek thought on, 3
    formal operations stage and, 61, 62
    moral, 110, 111, 112–14, 115
Rebel subculture, 304
Recapitulation, 6
Reciprocal effects, 184, 185
Reductionism, 74
Reflective judgment, 68–69
Rejected adolescents, 230
Relatedness, 189, 190
Relational aggression, 225
Relative performance, 81
Relativism, 68
Reliability, 16, 153
Religious beliefs
    American adolescents, 106–7
    cognitive development and, 108–9
    decline in, throughout the teens, 107–8
    protective value of, 107
    risk behavior and, 378
    social desirability and, 107
Religious fasting, 388
Remarriage, 202–3
Representative, of the population, 14
Reproductive anatomy, 40
Residential changes, 8
Resilience, 27, 390–91
Response bias, 152, 153
Responsiveness, 182, 184, 185, 188
Restricted license, 366
Restrictive cultures, 257–58, 267
Retention, 303
Retention rate, 318
Reviving Ophelia (Pipher), 154, 157
Ridicule, 224–25
Risk behaviors, 364
    automobile driving, 364–67
    choosing friends and, 218
    crime and delinquency, 371–75
    cultural differences on, 380, 382
    factors involved in, 375–78
    friend's influence and, 220–21
    individual factors in, 379–80, 382
    preventing, 378–79
    research on delinquency, 381
    substance use, 367–71
Rituals
    to prevent impotence, 126
    puberty, 46, 47–48, 52
Rival relationship, 178, 179
Roaring Twenties, the, 234, 235
Role preparation, 96
Roles, 94, 95
Romania
    adolescent births/abortions in, 266*f*
    transition to adulthood viewed in, 12
Romantic harassment, 251
Romantic love, 246, 247
Romantic partners, 211, 213
    adolescents expectations from, 243
    attachment to, 248–49
    choosing, 248
Romantic relationships
    breaking up from, 250–51
    commitment, passion and intimacy in, 245
    phases in forming, 249–50
    time spent with friends and, 229
Runaways, 206

Russia
    academic score in, 284*t*
    AIDS in, 272

S

Sambia, the, 48
Samburu, the, 48
Same-sex friends, 212, 229*f*
Samoans, the, 17, 51, 258
Sample, 14
Sampling, 14
Sarcasm, 64, 224–25
Sassy (magazine), 131, 132
Saudi Arabia, 21, 258
Scaffolding, 87–88
Schema, 134
Schemes, Piaget's theory of cognitive development
    and, 61
School climate, 288–89
Schools/schooling. *See also* Academic achievement;
    Education; Secondary education
    age at end of adolescence and, 8
    changes in, for adolescents, 279–81
    class size in, 284–85
    cultural beliefs and, 294
    improving experiences for adolescents in, 286,
        287–88
    influence of, on risk behavior, 377–78
    leisure and, 293
    for Mexican adolescents, 123
    for Native Americans, 168, 169
    peers and friends and, 292
    research on experiences in, 290
    rise of, for adolescents, 278–79
    self-esteem and, 154
    size of, 284–85
    socialization at, 98, 130–31
    soft-drinks sold in, 38
    teaching critical thinking skills in, 74–75
    work and, 292–93
School-to-work programs, 321–22, 330
Scientific method, 14, 16–19
Secondary education. *See also* High school
    changes in, 279
    in developing countries, 282–84
    in industrialized countries, 281–82
    Japanese, 286
Secondary school, 277, 278
Secondary sex characteristics, 38, 40–41
Second-generation families, 104
Second shift, 327
Secular, 43, 106
Secure attachment, 189
Selective association, 221
Selective attention, 70
Self-concept, 150
    capacity for abstractions and, 149
    increasing complexity of, 150
Self-conceptions, 147
Self-consciousness, 151
Self-esteem, 147
    American concern about, 150
    barometric, 152
    baseline, 150, 151
    causes and effects of, 154–55
    defined, 150
    different aspects of, 151–52
    eight domains of, 152
    in emerging adulthood, 155
    invention of term, 148
    of Native American adolescents, 168
    physical appearance and, 152, 154
    from preadolescence through adolescence, 151
Self-focused age, 9
Self-image, 150
Self-made manhood, 128
Self-medication, 370

Self-perception, 150
Self-Perception Profile for Adolescents (Harter), 152, 153
Self-regulation, 95–96
Self-socialization, 133
Self-sufficiency, 12
Self, the
    culture and, 148
    the emotional, 155–58
    Native American, 168, 169
    time spent alone and, 170–71
Semenarche, 52
Semiarranged marriages, 253
Semirestrictive cultures, 258
Sensation seeking, 341
Sensorimotor stage, 61*t*
Separation, 166, 167
Set point, 34
Seventeen (magazine), 131, 132
Sex
    gender versus, 121
    Internet use and, 355–56
    in the media, 348–51
Sex characteristics
    primary, 38, 39–40
    secondary, 38, 40–41
Sex differences. *See* Gender differences
Sex education, 273–74
Sex hormones, 33
Sexual abuse, 204, 205, 206
Sexual behavior
    in emerging adulthood, 269–70
    masturbation, 254
    necking and petting, 254–55
    oral sex and, 255–56
Sexual code, roaring twenties and, 234
Sexual experiences
    differences in virgin adolescents and adolescents
        with, 261
    gender role in traditional cultures and, 122
    manhood requirements in traditional cultures
        and, 124, 125
    sexual scripts for, 260–61
Sexual harassment, 262–63
Sexual intercourse. *See also* Premarital sex
    contraception and, 265–67
    menstruation and, 48
    sexual experiences before, 254
    timing of first episode of, 255, 261
Sexuality, adolescent, 254. *See also* Sexual intercourse
    American history of adolescent girls and, 127–28
    cultural beliefs and, 257–60
    mixed messages given to American adolescents
        on, 266
    in Netherlands, 259
    parent-adolescent conflict and, 192
    U.S. attitudes on, 258, 259
Sexually transmitted diseases (STDs), 39, 270–73
Sexual orientation, 264
Sexual Politics (Millett), 137
Sexual scripts, 260–61, 267, 348–49
Shelters, for runaways, 206
Short-term memory, 70–71, 81
Siblings
    relationships among, 178, 179–81
    research on parent-adolescent relations and, 185
This Side of Paradise (1920), 234
Sierra Leone, 125*f*
Single parenthood, 203
Single-parent households, rise in rate of, 198
Small colleges, 305
Smoking. *See* Cigarette smoking
Social and conventional system perspective taking,
    78
Social class. *See* Socioeconomic status (SES)
Social cognition, 77–81, 231
Social desirability, 106, 107
Social information processing, 231
Socialization, 95. *See also* Gender socialization

broad, 97, 98
  example of, for cultural beliefs, 98–100
  as factor in risk behavior, 375–78
  individualism and collectivism on, 96–97
  intimacy in friendships and, 217
  media and, 343–45
  narrow, 97, 98
  outcomes of, 95–96
  political, in Communist countries, 117
  risky automobile driving and, 364–65
  sources of, 98
  in the West, 100–101
Socialized delinquents, 377
Social learning theory, 339
Social loneliness, 170
Social-networking web sites, 356–57
Social roles theory, 140, 141
Social skills
  defined, 230
  importance of, 230
  social cognition and, 231
Social substance use, 370
Society, 5t
Socioeconomic status (SES)
  age at menarche and, 46f
  college retention and, 303
  defined, 5t
  Internet use and, 355
  risk behavior and, 382
  school and, 291
Sociometry, 230
Soft-drinks, 38
Somalia, 125f
The Sorrows of Young Werther (Goethe), 337
Sources of meaning, 96
South Africa, 46f, 284t
South America, 257, 259. *See also* Latinos
South Korea
  academic score in, 284t
  premarital sex in, 260t
  sexual attitudes in, 267
  transition to adulthood viewed in, 12
South Sea Islands, 310
Spain, 106, 196f, 266f
Spatial intelligence, 85
Spermarche, 38, 39–40, 42
Sperm production, 39–40
Sport (magazine), 131
Stages, Piaget's theory of cognitive development and, 60
Standard Cross-Cultural Sample, 247
Stanford-Binet intelligence test, 80, 81
Status offenses, 371
Status phase, 248, 249
Stepfathers, 203, 205
Stepparents, 203
Stereotype, 139
Storm and stress theory, 6, 10, 20
Stratified sampling, 7
"Street children," 206–7
Strong-Campbell Vocational Interest Inventory, 326
"Sturm und drang," 155
Style, of youth culture, 234, 235
Subcultures, youth, 237
  in college, 304
  media consumption and, 341, 343
Sub-Saharan Africa, cultural context of adolescence in, 22
Substance use
  abuse and, 370
  adolescent work and, 318, 319
  country comparison on, 380, 382
  current and past rates of, 367–69
  family influence on, 376
  preventing, 371
  sequence of, 369–70
Subterranean values, 234
Sudan, 125f

Suicide
  among gay, lesbian and bisexual adolescents, 264
  among Native Americans, 168
  among runaway adolescents, 206
  depression and, 385–87
  early warning signs of, 386t
  in Japan, 286
  rates of, 385
  risk factors of, 386
Super peer, media as a, 344
Survey, 7
Sweden, 266f
Switzerland, 281
Symbolic inheritance, 94, 95
Synapses, 85–86
Synaptic pruning, 86
Syria, 258

T

Tattooing, 47
Teachers, 130–31
Teaching the New Basic Skills: Principles for Educating Children to Thrive in a Changing Economy (Murname/Levy), 321
Technological change, 237–38
Teenager(s), 359
Teen births, 267, 268–69
Teen pregnancy, 266, 267, 268
Television
  aggressiveness and, 345–46
  amount of time spent viewing, 338
  coping function of, 341
  harmful effect of, 338
  influence of, in developing countries, 359–60
  obesity and, 37
  sex and violence on music, 349
  sexual content in, 348–49
  theory on influence of, 338–39
Testosterone, 33–34
Test-retest reliability, 82
Tewa people, the, 48
Text messaging, 357
Thailand, 279, 312
Theories
  ecological, 20–22
  research and, 20
Theory of genotype-environment interactions, 54
Theory of mind, 78
Theory of multiple intelligences, 84–85
Tracking, 299–300
Traditional cultures. *See also* Developing countries
  adolescent passion in, 247
  adolescent peer crowd in, 227
  adolescent work in, 310–13
  antisocial behavior in, 380
  beliefs about menstruation in, 50, 51
  conflicts with parents in, 193–94
  defined, 5t
  family and friends in, 214–15
  gender and, 122–23, 124, 125–26, 143
  identity confusions and, 168
  marriage/pregnancy in, 265
  occupational choices in, 324, 326
  parent-adolescent distancing in, 49
  parenting in, 186, 187–88
  postfigurative to cofigurative cultures in, 238
  sarcasm and ridicule in, 224
  sibling relationship in, 180–81
Traditional parenting style, 188
Transparent apprenticeship system, 323
Transracial adoption, 84, 85
Trobriand Islands, 258
Truk Island, 374
Trust versus mistrust, 159
Tuition rates, college, 302, 303
Tunisia, 46f

Turkey, 279t
Twin studies, 383

U

Undercontrolled, 363
Unemployment, 329–30
United Kingdom. *See also* Great Britain
  academic score in, 284t
  emerging adults living at home in, 196f
  premarital sex in, 260t
  transition to adulthood viewed in, 12
United Nations Children's Fund (UNICEF), 313
United States. *See also* American majority culture; West, the
  academic achievement in, 284
  academic score in, 284t
  adolescent births/abortions in, 266f
  attitudes toward adolescent sexuality in, 258, 259
  cohabitation in, 253
  concern about self-esteem in, 150
  contraceptive use in, 265, 266
  cultural beliefs among multicultural societies in, 104
  educational changes in, 279, 280–81
  education in, value of, 294
  emerging adults living at home in, 196f
  freedom of expression in, 343
  individualism promoted in, 148
  life-cycle service in, 4
  median age of first marriage in, 10, 11t
  moral adolescent development in, 113–14
  parenting style in, 183
  pornography in, 257
  premarital sex in, 260t
  rate of adolescent labor in, 316
  religious beliefs by adolescents in, 106
  residential changes during emerging adulthood in, 8–9
  risk behavior in, 380, 382
  school enrollment changes in, 279t
  school-to-work program in, 321–22
  sex education in, 273, 274
  smoking in, 380
  socialization in, 101
  taboo against menarche in, 51
  transition to adulthood viewed in, 12
  typical age of menarche in, 8, 44, 46f
  unemployment in, 329, 330
  women's movement in, 137
Unpopularity
  continuity, 231–32
  interventions for, 232
  social skills and, 230
Unsocialized delinquents, 377
Unstructured socializing, 369
Urbanization, 197
U.S. census (1900), 4–5
Uses and gratifications approach, 339–40

V

Validity, 16, 153
Velvet Revolution (Czechoslovakia), 117
Verbal subtests, 81, 83t
Vietnam, child labor in, 312
Violence
  media influence and, 345–48
  on music television, 349
  in rap music, 351
Violent crimes, 371
Virginity
  American history of gender expectations and, 127
  gender roles and, 26
  in Mexican culture, 123
Vital capacity, 36
Vocational schools, 281

Vocational subculture, 304
Voluntary organizations, 128, 129
Volunteer work, 330–33
Vulva, 40

W

Wechsler Adult Intelligence Scale (WAIS-IV), 81, 82
Wechsler Intelligence Scale for Children (WISC-IV), 80, 81, 82
Weight gain, 37
West Africa, 48
West, the, 5t. *See also* Europe
  broad socialization in, 98
  cultural context of adolescence in, 24–25
  early maturation in, 52–54
  Eastern cultures contrasted with, 96–97, 104–5
  emphasis on autonomy in, 193
  expectations of marriage in, 252
  gender-specific expectations in, 26
  globalization of the media and, 358–61
  having a child outside of marriage in, 265
  minority cultures in, 104

postconventional thinking in, 113
socialization and gender in, 129–41
socialization for cultural beliefs in, 100–101
youth culture in, 237
"Wet dreams," 52
William T. Grant Foundation, 320
Withdrawal symptoms, 370
Women's movement, 136, 137, 138
Work. *See also* Adolescent work; Child/adolescent labor
Working memory, 71
Worldview, 114
Worldviews approach to moral development, 114–15

Y

YMCA, 4, 128
Young men and women, 4
Young Men's Christian Association (YMCA), 4, 128
Young Miss (magazine), 131
Young people. *See also* Emerging adulthood
  defined, 5t
  transition to adulthood, 12

Young Women's Christian Association (YWCA), 4, 128
Youth, 4, 5
YouthBuild, 322
Youth culture, 233–38. *See also* Subcultures, youth
  components to style of, 235–36
  defined, 233
  media consumption providing identification with, 341, 343
  reasons for development of, 236, 237
  of the Roaring twenties, 234, 235
  technological change and, 237–38
  years available for participation in, 235
Youth organizations
  Communist, 117–18
  soft-drink sales in schools and, 38
Youth & Society, 20
YWCA, 4, 128

Z

Zapotecs, the, 214–15
Zone of proximal development, 87